Footprint Argentina

Christabelle Dilks

4th edition

There are moments when I think with profound longing of those wonderful areas in our south. Perhaps one day, tired of circling the world, I'll return to Argentina and settle in the Andean lakes, if not indefinitely then at least for a pause while I shift from one understanding of the world to another.

Che Guevara, *The Motorcycle Diaries*

Argentina Highlights

See colour maps at back of book

❶ Quebrada de Humahuaca
A rugged gorge of terracotta rock with ancient oasis villages

❷ Santa Rosa de Tastil
Ruins of a pre-Inca city in the breathtaking Quebrada de Toro

❸ Valles Calchaquíes
Unspoilt Andean villages and high-altitude wine at Colomé

❹ Ischigualasto
See 200 million years of strata and dinosaur fossils in a weird lunar landscape

❺ Acongagua, Mendoza Province
The highest peak in the Americas, with stunning trekking

❻ Bodegas, Mendoza
Tour the wineries and stay in style at Tapíz

❼ Villa Pehuenia, Lake District
Hide away at La Escondida on the tranquil lake shore

❽ Los Alerces National Park
Virgin forest, hanging glaciers and perfect hikes

❾ Mount Fitz Roy
Trekking heaven around this striking granite peak

❿ Estancia Cristina
Splendid isolation and endless ice fields

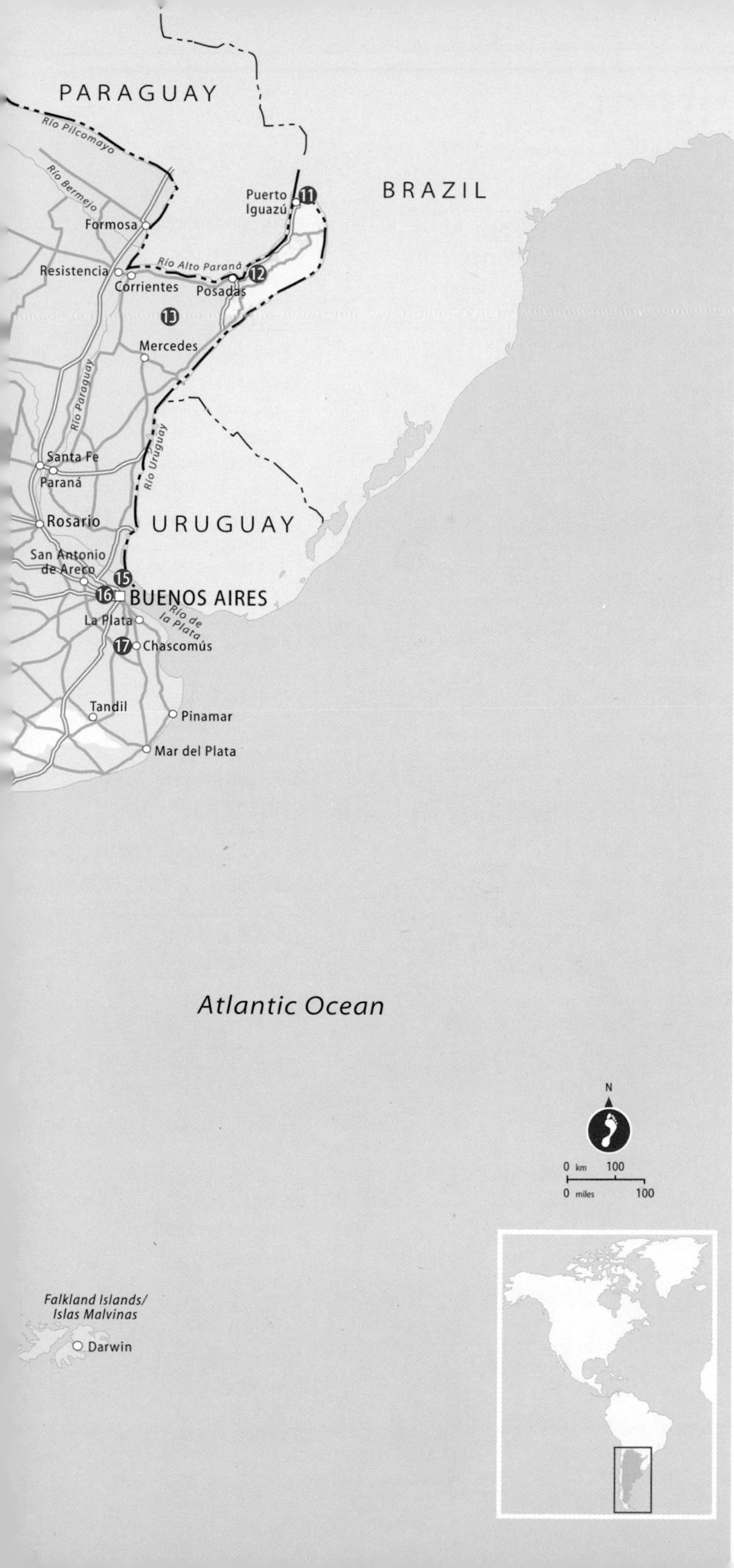

PARAGUAY

Río Pilcomayo

Río Bermejo

BRAZIL

Puerto Iguazú 11

Formosa

Resistencia

Corrientes

Río Alto Paraná

Posadas 12

13

Mercedes

Río Paraguay

Río Uruguay

Santa Fe

Paraná

Rosario

URUGUAY

San Antonio de Areco

15

16 BUENOS AIRES

Río de la Plata

La Plata

17 Chascomús

Tandil

Pinamar

Mar del Plata

Atlantic Ocean

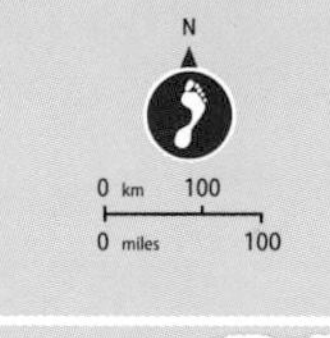

Falkland Islands/ Islands Malvinas

Darwin

11 Iguazú Falls
See the spectacular falls and then stay in rainforest lodge Yacutinga

12 San Ignacio Mini
Evocative Jesuit ruins reclaimed from the jungle

13 Esteros del Iberá
A birdwatchers' heaven and floating islands in paradise

14 Sierras Chicas, Córdoba
Marvel at Jesuit estancias, then ride the sierras at Estancia Los Potreros

15 Tigre Delta
Take a boat deep into the jungle

16 Palermo Viejo
Fine food and smart bars in the charming, fashionable district of Buenos Aires

17 Estancia Dos Talas, Chascomús
Ride like a gaucho, live like a king

18 Península Valdés
Basking whales, penguin colonies, and harems of sea lions on glorious beaches

19 Gaiman, Patagonia
Moving history and traditional teas

20 Estancia Harberton, Tierra del Fuego
Pioneer life on the serene Beagle Channel

Contents

Northwest

Northeast

Lake District

Patagonia

Chilean Patagonia

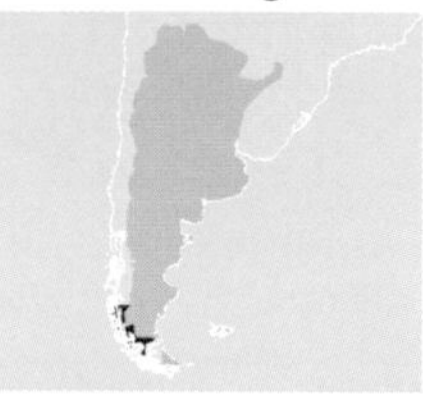

Tierra del Fuego

Escape from it all – as Butch and Sundance did – to the idyllic Parque Nacional Los Alerces in Patagonia.

Background

Footnotes

Inside back cover

Iguazú Falls
You've never seen so much water flowing with such force. Take a boat under the falls and get drenched by the spray. Not to be missed.

A foot in the door

Argentina is immense, intense and dramatic. Wherever you go, the contrasts are breathtaking. Buenos Aires seems like a modern European city: life races past grand baroque buildings, hip bars and chic shops. But step into a *milonga*, and the mysterious rituals of the tango belong to another world. Huge sizzling steaks are unmistakably Argentine. And just a *boleadora*'s throw from the sophistication of the city lies a complete wilderness, perfect for adventure.

At one end of the country the mighty Iguazú Falls thunder through jungle filled with electric blue butterflies. At the other, silent glaciers stretch out endlessly before you, then shatter with a roar into a milky turquoise lagoon. In between: infinite space. Drive the Ruta 40 through Patagonia and the only sign of life will be a couple of condors and a thousand prehistoric handprints on a cave wall. Surprises abound: cross the desert steppe with only the wind for company, and end up in a village full of Welsh tea rooms. Off Península Valdés, whales bask right by your boat and a thousand sea lions make a bronze velvet tideline on the shore. Nature here is utterly unspoilt. Along 5000 km of the Andes, you can hike, ride, raft and climb among steep forested mountains dropping into lakes of all hues from indigo to pea-green: all empty of people. Cross a dazzling white salt-flat in the high-altitude puna, and a traditional Pachamama ceremony takes you back in time to before the Incas. There are ancient ruined cities and cloudforest jungle, sumptuous colonial *fincas* and eco-lodges. Climb Aconcagua, and then sample fine wines at a boutique *bodega* in the foothills.

And at the end of your travels, the land of fire has a haven of calm in Ushuaia. As you look out over the Beagle Channel towards the end of the world, you may well ask yourself: do I have to go home?

10 Salvation by tourism?

With a population flung out over such a vast area, it's not surprising the Argentines say they lack a sense of identity. Four hundred years of colonialism left a culturally rich, but sadly undervalued, indigenous population in the north and west, struggling to integrate with Argentines of European descent. Then there's the legacy of the dark years of military rule: the 'disappearances' of 30,000 people eroded a generation and created a culture where obedience came more easily than dissent. Some Argentines say, 'We're a nation of teenagers!' their gaze firmly fixed on Europe. And indeed, after the economic crisis of 2002, many young professionals left Argentina to make money in Spain and Italy, rather than end up driving a taxi in Buenos Aires. But the Argentines have an extraordinary optimism and capacity for recovery. The financial situation is improving. Middle class Argentines are buying cars and foreign holidays again, and few of them complain about the rising inflation. Petty crime is under control, and the

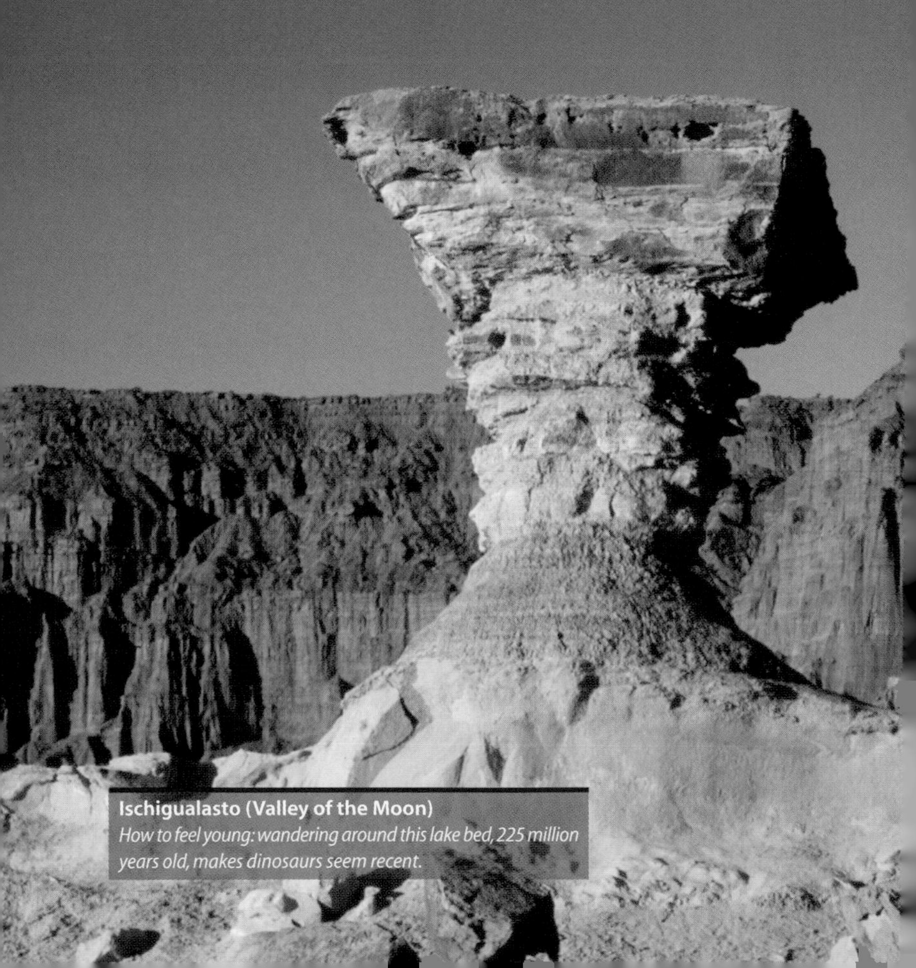

Ischigualasto (Valley of the Moon)
How to feel young: wandering around this lake bed, 225 million years old, makes dinosaurs seem recent.

piqueteros don't block the roads so much. President Kirchner has succeeded in getting poverty levels down, though a large percentage of the population is still dependent on his *plan trabajar* (handouts for the unemployed), causing some concern that the work ethic will be lost. Without developing industry, the future for the working classes looks bleak. But Argentines possess a resilient resourcefulness, and they're rapidly making the best of the devaluation of their *peso*. Where once Argentina was South America's most expensive country for tourists, it's now one of the cheapest. The infrastructure is excellent, services and accommodation are of the highest standards, it's safe to travel, and – best of all – the Argentines are the most naturally hospitable people you're likely to meet. Tourism is now Argentina's third largest source of income. Quite apart from the spectacular beauty of the country, the great steaks and the fine wines, Argentina's greatest asset is the incredible warmth of its people. Get off the beaten track, learn some Spanish, and you'll make friends wherever you go.

Parque Nacional Lanín

The grand extinct volcano Lanín watches over the Lake District, turning every snapshot into a picture postcard.

1
2
4
5
7
8
10
11

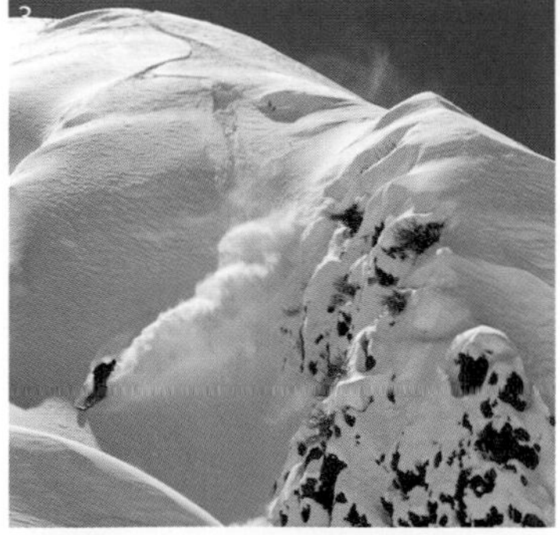

1 *Get a real taste of life on the land, rounding up the cattle with the gauchos, Estancia Los Potreros, Córdoba province.* ▸▸ *See page 177.*

2 *Buenos Aires boasts many fine galleries, besides some flamboyant public art, such as MALBA.* ▸▸ *See page 78.*

3 *World-class snowboarding in Argentina's most upmarket ski resort, Las Leñas.* ▸▸ *See page 232.*

4 *A southern right whale frolicking within stroking distance, off Península Valdés.* ▸▸ *See page 480.*

5 *A cousin of the llama, the guanaco is indigenous to South America and can typically be seen roaming wild in La Payunia.* ▸▸ *See page 233.*

6 *Guaraní carvings in the Jesuit mission of San Ignacio Mini: testimony to creative and spiritual harmony.* ▸▸ *See page 344.*

7 *Twice as many sheep as people. Visiting an estancia is the best way to experience traditional Argentine rural life.* ▸▸ *See page124.*

8 *Cachi's colonial church front is typical of all those in northwest Argentina.* ▸▸ *See page 273.*

9 *Take a trip across the high-altitude puna to be dazzled by the shimmering salt flats of Salinas Grandes.* ▸▸ *See page 296.*

10 *The mothers of the 'disappeared' still protest in the Plaza de Mayo, Buenos Aires, every Thursday.* ▸▸ *See page 70.*

11 *Peppers, laid out to dry, make a dramatic splash of red on arid hillsides in the Valles Calchaquíes.* ▸▸ *See page 271.*

12 *Plaza Dorrego's Sunday market in atmospheric San Telmo: pick up antique china and a few dance steps.* ▸▸ *See page 83.*

Infinite space

There is no experience like Patagonia. Whether escaping like Butch and Sundance, or seeking freedom like the Welsh pioneers, you'll find liberating expanses of nothing here. Head east to Puerto Madryn for amazing marine life: southern right whales cavorting right in front of your eyes. Travel the Ruta 40 in Che Guevara's tyre tracks and contemplate a revolutionary life. The welcome is warm but the wind's relentless. You'll be relieved when you spot Mount Fitz Roy's granite towers rising up from the steppe: heavenly trekking in grand mountain landscapes. From El Calafate, cross an iceberg-strewn lake to luxurious Estancia Cristina, for breathtaking views of the southern ice field. Tierra del Fuego is the ultimate wilderness and, as you take a boat trip along the Beagle Channel, you'll feel like the first pioneers.

Snow-capped peaks and chocolate

The Argentine Andes stretch along a wonderland of snow-capped mountains, dotted with lakes and lagoons of all shades of blue. Start at picturesque Bariloche: chalet-style hotels, chocolate shops and a backdrop of peaks, where you could hike for a week without getting bored. Head north, along the Seven Lakes Drive to upmarket San Martín de los Andes or south to laid-back El Bolsón, for superb hiking along crystalline rivers. Hide out in an *estancia* to ride the wild lands, or go whitewater rafting into Chile. Discover quiet Villa Pehuenia, set amidst forests of silent Monkey Puzzle trees, or fish giant trout at Junín de los Andes. South of El Bolsón, the *Old Patagonian Express* chugs into the hills: hike into the pristine forests of Los Alerces to camp by a jade green river.

Fine wines at high altitudes. Bodega Colomé in Salta province is a chic retreat hotel producing exquisite estate Malbecs from these improbably arid mountains.

Estancia Huechahue in the Lake District is the place for real riding. They won't make you break horses on your first day!

Water water everywhere

More than just the Iguazú Falls, the northeast's rare wonders include Jesuit missions: striking red stone ruins in the emerald green jungle. Once you've seen the Falls, immerse yourself in rainforest at a jungle lodge, and then head down through the lush rolling hills to one of the largest expanses of uncontaminated wetlands in the world. The Esteros del Iberá are a paradise for birds – and birdwatchers. After a day suspended between sky and water, find perfect peace in a typical Corrientes *estancia*.

Blast from the past

The northwest is another Argentina, of rich indigenous culture and ancient civilisations, with ruined cities at Quilmes, Las Pailas, El Shinkal and Tastil. Explore the Quebrada de Humahuaca, a vast red gorge dotted with quaint oasis villages, or the timeless Valles Calchaquíes, where high-altitude wine is grown in dramatic rugged landscapes. Salta's colonial splendour contrasts perfectly with the culture of the Puna, where Pachamama festivities are a glimpse of another time. But Talampaya and Ischigualasto make dinosaurs look positively young: sandstone canyons which make you feel impossibly small. Mendoza is the capital for wine lovers, with superb *bodegas* stretching out to a backdrop of the Andes, and excellent hiking for serious mountaineers.

Buenos Aires is a great first port of call, whether you want to watch opera, try tango, dine out, or shop. Chic Palermo Viejo is *the* place for cool restaurants and new design, and Tigre is a calm retreat of houses on stilts in the jungly river delta. Whatever you do, allow more time than you think: Argentina offers you a complete escape.

Glaciar Perito Moreno
Endless silent ice fields, created millions of years ago, rupture with a roar into the lake below.

Essentials

Footprint features

Planning your trip

Where to go

Argentina is immense. Unless you have unlimited time and budget, you probably have to accept form the start that you can't see it all. Distances are huge, and it's time consuming getting around. Tourists tend to flock to the best known sites of extraordinary natural beauty, such as the glaciers, the lakes, the Northwest, and the Iguazú Falls, but bear in mind that the distances between these places are huge. There are daily flights to all the major destinations, but most go via Buenos Aires, so that travelling between the glaciers and Iguazú for example will take a day out of your itinerary. There are few trains in Argentina, but an extensive network of long distance buses, although a two hour flight might take 15 hours by bus, and you may not feel like hiking the day you arrive. Inevitably, you'll want to allow more time in some places than others. While three days each are quite enough to see the glaciers or the Iguazú Falls, it really takes at least a week to enjoy exploring the Lake District or the Northwest. Part of the pleasure of travelling in Argentina is in adjusting to a slower pace of life, and in allowing things to be spontaneous. Argentines are very friendly and sociable, and may well invite you to join them for a day, particularly if you're travelling alone, so it's good to allow enough time to be flexible, and for following recommendations of people you meet on your travels. So rather than just ticking places off your list in a relentless itinerary leave at least couple of days free in each place if you can, and don't try to do too much. It's much more satisfying to explore one area in real depth than to dart about all over the country, which may leave you with the 'Rome was where we saw the yellow dog' sensation. One tip it's worth passing on is never to spend only one night in a place, if you can avoid it.

Preparing your itinerary depends on which areas of Argentina most inspire you in this book, how much time you have available, the time of year, and what kinds of activities you want to combine. Below is a quick summary of each area with the ideal times of year for a visit. Then a few suggested itineraries

When to go

The southern hemisphere summer is from December to March, spring from mid-September to November, autumn from March to May and winter from June to August. Argentina an appealing destination for warm, sunny holidays in the middle of the northern hemisphere winter, though since the country covers such a vast area, there is somewhere to visit at any time of year.

Holidays

School holiday are from Late December to the first week of March, during Easter week and mid July to mid-August. During these times, all Argentines tend to travel, and hotels and flights for all destinations book up very quickly.

Best time to visit

Buenos Aires City At its best in spring and autumn, when the weather is sunny and mild. But the city can be unbearably hot and humid in the height of summer, with temperatures over 40 degrees centigrade and humidity at 80%. If you come in summer, consider spending a night at Tigre or an estancia, to cool down. Winters are mild and very pleasant, with lots of clear bright days.

Buenos Aires province The beaches are packed during January and February, and much more pleasant in March, although not so hot. The interior of the province can be very hot in summer, though not as humid as the city, and so it's ideal for getting out to the estancias, where you can cool down in a pool. The whole province is ideal in spring and autumn. Winters can be bleak, with harsh winds further south. So for hiking in Sierra de la Ventana and Tandil, it's best to come in late summer or autumn.

Córdoba and the Central Sierras Great all year round, but there is snow in winter in the sierras, making riding and hiking more difficult. Cooler than Buenos Aires in the summer and a great time for riding.

Mendoza and the West The wine harvest in March gives a good focus to a late summer visit, although you can visit wineries all year round. The area is particularly beautiful in spring and autumn, when there are fresh clear days, and summers are great too, thanks to the higher altitude. For hiking in Aconcagua and the Andes to the west of Mendoza, it's essential to come from January to March, since snow may prevent access at other times. The skiing season at Las Leñas is June to October in theory, depending on the year, and this resort it impossibly booked up in July and August. Book ahead.

The Northwest Salta and Jujuy have three different zones: puna, valleys and yunga (cloudforest). The high-altitude puna and Valles Calchaquíes are wonderful all year round, with clear sunny days and cold nights. The rainy season in Salta and Jujuy cities, and in the yungas is January to March, when roads may be partly washed away. The wine harvest in the Cafayate vineyards is late February to early March. High mountain climbing is only possible January and February with inhospitable cold and winds at other times of the year. Easter and carnival are exceptional in the northwest, though you need to book ahead. Try to come in August for the Pachamama festivities.

The Northeast The Iguazú Falls are wonderful all year round, though rainfall is usually heaviest in April, making the falls more abundant. Global warming is having an effect on the climate here, so the rainy season can no longer be predicted. This is, of course, rainforest, so expect at least one downpour in your visit, whenever you travel.

Lake District Argentine tourists flock here in January and February, ruining the tranquillity. Come in March or April instead and have the beauty all to yourself. The lakes area is stunningly beautiful from November to April, and magnificent in autumn, when the trees turn. For hiking, you'd have to come from January to March, since snow fall on higher peaks makes trekking impossible. Skiing at all lakes ski resorts is from June to September, and Bariloche is particularly busy in July and August.

Patagonia Famous for its fierce winds, much of Patagonia is really only hospitable from October to May. El Calafate and El Chaltén can really only be visited in the summer, and most tourist services close down completely in the winter. There are plans to make El Calafate a year-round resort, but this is some way off yet. Trekking in El Chaltén is best January to March, when it's also very busy. Whale watching on the Atlantic coast is possible from September to December, but there is marine life for much of the year, though tourist services close down everywhere in winter.

Tierra del Fuego Ushuaia can become overwhelmed with visitors in January, and is much more pleasant in December, or February and March. Book flights and accommodation ahead whenever you plan to come. The southern part of the island is particularly ravishing in autumn, when the forested mountains turn yellow and scarlet. Winter is not as cold as you'd think there, and skiing is good from July to October with grand views and little breeze.

One week

With just one week in the country, your best bet is to head straight to one area of the country, such as the south or the northeast. Or combine Buenos Aires city with one other destination, such as Mendoza or Península Valdés.

Summer A week is enough time to see the glaciers at **El Calafate** and one other place in southern Patagonia: **El Chaltén** or **Ushuaia**, as flights and bus travel between these places is simple. You could also combine El Calafate with **Torres del Paine**, but bear in mind that for trekking in either Torres or **Fitz Roy** regions you really need an entire week, at least. In El Calafate, consider spending one day on a conventional trip to the glaciers, possibly including trekking on the ice, plus one day horse riding, or visiting **Estancia Cristina**. After three nights here, three nights in Ushuaia would be the perfect complement, with time for a boat trip along the **Beagle Channel**, a trip to **Harberton**, and a day's hiking in the national park.

Any time of year, a week would be ideal for visiting the **Iguazú Falls** plus the **Esteros del Iberá**. Two days is sufficient to see both the Argentine and Brazilian sides of the falls, or better still to have two days to explore the larger Argentine park. You could extend this to four days, by visiting nearby jungle lodge **Yacutinga**, for a deeper experience of the rain forest. On your way to the blissfully tranquil wetlands of Iberá, stop off at the **Jesuit missions** for a couple of hours, then plan to spend at least two days on the Esteros, spotting birds and other wildlife. From here, the overnight bus is the quickest way to return to Buenos Aires.

Buenos Aires city could entertain you for one hectic day, a week's shopping, or a lifetime's exploration, depending how much you like cities. If you really want to see the main sites, allow at least three days, with an afternoon's relaxing in **Tigre**. You could combine the city with a couple of nights at a nearby estancia in the pampas, hiking in the sierras of **Tandil** or **Sierra de la Ventana**, or a few days on a beach. Or to combine with another region, fly to the sierras of **Córdoba** to ride horses for a few days, or fly to **Puerto Madryn** (September to December) to see the whales. It's best to see Buenos Aires at the start, rather than the end of your trip, since after all the space and silence that you'll find in Argentina, the city's pace of life can be jarring. Consider spending your last night on an estancia such as **Dos Talas**, before flying home from Ezeiza Airport.

A week is not long enough to really explore the **Lake District** unless you focus on one area. You could chose to explore the area around **San Martín** and **Junín de los Andes**, for example, with some horse riding at Huechahue, or head straight to **El Bolsón** and **Esquel** for some hiking and a trip on the *Old Patagonian Express*. Don't try to see both ends of the Lake District in less than two weeks, as you'll spend more time on the road than up a mountain.

The Northwest really needs two weeks, if you're going to unwind enough to get into the slow paced Andean way of life, and this area is time consuming to travel around. However, a week would allow you to spend a couple of days in **Salta city**, and then south to the **Calchaquí Valley** for four days, before sampling the wine at **Cafayate**. Alternatively, head up to the puna and then down into the **Quebrada de Humahuaca**.

Winter A week in winter would be perfect for skiing at superb **Las Leñas**, and stopping at **Mendoza** to see a vineyard or two. There are also several good ski resorts in the lakes, near Villa La Angostura, Bariloche or Esquel, or Ushuaia where the cross-country skiing is superb.

Two weeks

Combine contrasts A week in the far south for glaciers and **Ushuaia** (if it's summer), would be perfectly complemented by a week in the warm northeast for **Iguazú** and the **Esteros del Iberá**, if your budget will stretch to five flights. You'll need to stop off in **Buenos Aires** in between.

Two weeks in **Patagonia** (summer) would give you a feel for the immensity of the place, with a week between **El Calafate** and **El Chaltén**, a few days in **Ushuaia**, and then heading north for whale-spotting at **Península Valdés**. Flights between towns in Patagonia can be arranged with the army airline **LADE**, but book ahead. If you're travelling by bus, add three days to this itinerary, and allow time for recovery.

Mendoza is a great base for a week in summer to visit the surrounding vineyards and the mountains to the west. You'd need two weeks alone to climb **Aconcagua**, however but there are many more peaks to the north near quiet villages in lush valleys. Combine this with the intriguing **Ishigualasto** and **Talampaya** parks, and you'd really feel you'd got off the beaten track. Alternatively, after a week around Mendoza, take the overnight bus north to **Salta**, and work your way up through the **Valles Calchaquíes**.

Another option would be to experience the remote landscapes and ancient culture in the **Northwest**. Two weeks would give you time to unwind in the pretty villages of **Cachi** and **Molinos**, with some hiking in the mountains, visits to ancient sites such as **Las Pailas** and **Quilmes**, or a trip to remote **Colomé** winery, and to visit the vineyards of **Cafayate**. Then spend a couple of nights in the colonial city of **Salta** to lap up the history and live music, before heading up the **Quebrada del Toro** into the remote puna, and into the **Quebrada de Humahuaca**. Make time to visit the remote hamlet of **Iruya**, or take the long trip to **Nazareno** – unforgettable experiences.

Two weeks is just about long enough for a quick tour of the **Lake District**. Most visitors to this stunning region wish they'd allowed more time. Away form the main tourist centres, there are wonderful places to hike, go rafting, or retreat to beautiful estancias, and it's important to give yourself enough time to unwind in the beauty of this area, as well as packing in adventures. In two weeks you could explore the mountains around **Bariloche**, based in the town and in *refugios* in the mountains, plus a trip either north to **San Martín** and onto **Pehuenia**, or to ride horses at **Huechachue**. Or head south to **El Bolsón** for hiking and *cerveza*, and **Esquel** for the *Old Patagonian Express* and **Los Alerces National Park.**

Three weeks/a month

A month is the ideal time to spend in Argentina, but three weeks is a good compromise, giving you enough time to get a feel for the country's extraordinary contrasts.

Heading south Start with three days in **Buenos Aires** for steak, art and tango, with a night at **Tigre** or an estancia nearby, before heading off for an adventure. In summer, you could travel through the entire **Lake District**, starting in **Pehuenia** and heading via **San Martín** and **Bariloche** to **Esquel** (two weeks), and from there, taking a bus down the legendary **Ruta 40**, like Che, to reach trekking heaven at **El Chaltén**. You could stop off at remote **Perito Moreno National Park**, or hike around **Mount Fitz Roy**, before seeing the glaciers, and then finishing your journey a the end of the world in **Ushuaia**. Alternatively, spend three weeks in the lakes alone to allow time for longer treks, horse riding into Chile, or longer stays at remote estancias. This trip would work in summer or autumn only.

Explore the north Fly to **Tucumán**, and hire a car to head up through **Tafí del Valle** over the mountain pass into the spectacular **Valles Calchaquíes**. Explore the ancient site at **Quilmes**, the wineries of **Cafayate**, and then meander along the valley, staying in oasis villages to completely relax before heading to the city of **Salta**. Take a couple of days to stay at a *finca*, ride horses into the cloudforest, or hike up a peak from the puna. Then head north into the **Quebrada de Humahuaca**, and cross the **Chaco** to **Resistencia** to spend three days at the **Esteros del Iberá**. From here, take a transfer up to **Iguazú**, a marvellous finale for any trip. This would work at any time of year, though rural roads may be impassable after heavy summer rains.

Complete Argentina With a month, you could start in **Buenos Aires**, fly south to **Ushuaia**, and **El Calafate**, taking the bus to **El Chaltén** for a day's hiking, then return to Buenos Aires (week one). Spend the next two weeks either in the **Lake District** (in which case you'd probably take the bus up the **Ruta 40** to **Esquel**), or the west and north: fly west to **Mendoza** for the wineries and a day's trip to the mountains, before heading north to **Ischigualasto National Park**, and from here take the bus via **San Juan** to **Salta city**. Relax here in a smart boutique hotel, or *finca*, and explore Salta's history and culture. Take time to explore the **Quebrada del Toro**, with the ruined city at **Santa Rosa de Tastil** and the puna, or the **Quebrada de Humahuaca** (weeks two and three). Finally, fly back to Buenos Aires from Salta, and rest in an estancia in the **Pampas**, before flying to the **Iguazú Falls** for your last three days.

Beware that this is a relentless schedule which might leave you in need of a holiday. It can be quite overwhelming seeing such dramatic contrasts, and it's far better to spend, say, two weeks in the lakes, and then two weeks in Salta, to really allow yourself to unwind and adapt to the rhythm of the new place. A good tip when planning your itinerary is to make sure that you are not travelling more than on every third day.

Tour operators

If the choices available in Argentina are overwhelming, and you have little time to spend, or if you're not keen on travelling alone, it's worth considering booking a package with a specialist tour operator. Whether you choose from an adventurous expedition, or a more sedate trip; a bespoke journey just for you, or a group holiday, these companies work with on the ground agents who will book all your transport and accommodation, so that you can just enjoy the experience. UK travellers should always choose a tour operator from LATA, the Latin American travel association. www.lata.org.

UK

Abercrombie and Kent, St George's House, Ambrose St, Cheltenham, Glos, GL50 3LG, UK, T0845-0700614, www.abercrombiekent.co.uk. Upmarket tailor-made travel.

Andean Trails, The Clockhouse, Bonnington Mill Business Centre, 72 Newhaven Rd, Edinburgh, EH6 5QG, T0131-467 7086, www.andeantrails.co.uk.

Audley Travel, The New Mill, New Mill Lane, Witney, Oxfordshire, OX29 9TF, T01869-276210, www.audleytravel.com. High-quality tailor-made travel, including the North west, the lakes and Patagonia. Good on the ground knowledge. Recommended.

Austral Tours, 20 Upper Tachbrook St, London SW1V 1SH, T020-7233 5384, www.latinamerica.co.uk. Good tailor made tours, combining Argentina and Chile, in the lake district and in the wine regions. Estancia stays, cultural trips and places off the beaten track.

Cazenove and Loyd, 9 Imperial Studios, 3-11 Imperial Rd, London, SW6 2AG, T020-7384 2332, www.cazloyd.com. Upmarket tailor made travel.

Cox and Kings, Gordon House, 10 Greencoat Place, London, SW1P 1PH, T020-7873 5000, www.coxandkings.co.uk.

Discover the World, 29 Norl Way, Banstead, Surrey, SM7 1PB, T01737-214250, www.discover-the-world.co.uk.

Dragoman, Camp Green, Debenham, Suffolk, IP14 6LA, T01728-861133, www.dragoman.co.uk.

Explore, Nelson House, 55 Victoria Rd, Farnborough, Hants, GU14 7PA, T0870-333 4002, www.explore.co.uk. Quality small-group trips, especially in Patagonia. Also offers family adventures, or with a focus on culture, wildlife or trekking.

Journey Latin America, 12-13 Heathfield Terrace, Chiswick, London, W4 4JE, T020-8747 8315, also 12 St Ann's Sq, Manchester, M2 7HW, T0161-832 1441, www.journeylatinamerica.co.uk. Deservedly well regarded, this excellent long-established company runs adventure tours, escorted groups and tailor-made tours to Argentina and other destinations in South America. Also cheap flights and expert advice. Well organized, and very professional. Recommended.

Last Frontiers, Fleet Marston Farm, Aylesbury, Bucks, HP18 0QT, T01296-653000, www.lastfrontiers.com. Excellent company offering top quality tailor made trips all over Argentina, including superb wine tours, trips combining Iguazú and Salta, trips to the Esteros del Iberá, and horse riding in Patagonia and Córdoba. By far the best company for estancia stays; a real in depth knowledge of Argentina. Highly recommended.

Select Latin America, 79 Maltings Place, 169 Tower Bridge Rd, London, SE1 3LJ, T020-7407 1478, www.selectlatinamerica.co.uk. Specializing in tailormade and small-group tours with a cultural or natural history emphasis, this is a friendly small company with some good itineraries, including bird watching in the Los Esteros del Iberá, Antarctica, Ruta 40 and their speciality: the Galápagos.

Trips Worldwide, 14 Frederick Place, Clifton, Bristol, BS8 1AS, T0117-311 4400, www.tripsworldwide.co.uk. Tailor-made itineraries and trips.

Essentials Planning your trip

Specialist tour operators

There are many more specialized tour operators, offering specialist trips for birdwatching and horse riding: below is just a selection.

Adventures Abroad, www.adventures-abroad.com. Impressive company running superb and imaginative tours for small groups to Patagonia, Iguazú and Puerto Madryn, the glaciers and Ushuaia. Great itineraries.

Encounter Overland, 267 Old Brompton Rd, London, SW5 9JA, T020-7370 6845, www.encounteroverland.co.uk. Adventurous expeditions in groups across wild terrain, eg Santiago to Ushuaia, taking in the lakes and the glaciers.

Exodus, Grange Mills, Weir Rd, London SW12 ONE, T020-8675 5550, www.exodus.co.uk. Excellent, well-run trekking and climbing tours of Patagonia, and Chile, including Torres del Paine, cycling in the lake district, Antarctica and a great tour following Shackleton's footsteps.

Naturetrek, www.naturetrek.co.uk. Bird-watching small group tours, fixed departure.
South American Explorers, T0800-274-0568, T607-277 0488, www.saexplorers.org. Volunteer programmes, languages courses and guided tours.
STA Travel, offices worldwide, www.statravel.co.uk. Cheap flights, and sell Dragoman's trip which includes Argentina.
Steppes Latin America, T01285-885333, www.steppeslatinamerica.co.uk. Tailor-made holidays including Patagonia escorted tours, riding trips and birdwatching.
Trailfinders, 194 Kensington High St, London, W8 7RG, T020-7938 3939, www.trailfinders.co.uk. Reliable for cheap flights and tours.

North America

4StarSouth America, 3003 Van Ness St NW, Ste, Washington DC 20008, T1-800-747 4540, www.4starsouthamerica.com (tours), www.4starsouthflights.com (flights).
Argentina For Less, 7201 Wood Hollow Dr, Austin, TX 78731, USA, T1-877-269 0309, T+44-203-002 0571 (UK), www.argentinaforless.com. Progressive tourism company with a focus solely on Latin America. US based but with local offices and operations.
Discover Latin America, 6205 Blue Lagoon Dr, Suite310, Miami, Florida 33126, T305-266 5827, www.discoverlatinamerica.com.
ExpeditionTrips.com, 6553 California Av SW, Seattle, WA 98136, T206-547-0700, www.expeditiontrips.com.
Worldwide Horseback Riding Adventures, PO Box 807, 10 Stalnaker St, Dubois, Wyoming 82513, toll free T0800-545.0019, T307-455 3363, www.ridingtours.com. US-based horse riding company. US-based horse riding company.

Argentina

Exprinter Viajes, San Martin 170, 1 of 101, Buenos Aires 1004, T0054-11-4341 6600, www.exprinterviajes.com.
Say Hueque Patagonia SRL, Viamonte 749, 6 p of 1, Buenos Aires, T0054-11-5199 2517/20, www.sayhueque.com. Travel agency for independent travellers.

Finding out more

There are tourist information offices in provincial capitals and in major tourist destinations and many bus terminals/airports in popular destinations also have a tourist desk. Infrastructure varies across the country, but they can usually give you a town map and sometimes also a list of accommodation, as well as the tours, sights and festivals in the area. Staff in more popular tourist areas usually speak at least some English (and sometimes French, German, Italian) and are usually helpful. Opening hours are long – typically 0800-2000 in summer but may close at weekends. All bus terminals have an office (often signed *Informes*) which provides bus information. Argentina's boom in tourism has happened only over the last four years, since financial collapse in 2002, and while more visited destinations are now very well set up for foreign visitors, you might have to be patient in some parts of the country, even when requesting the most basic information on buses and accommodation. Take comfort from the fact that you're exploring a part of the world that's little visited.

Tourist offices

Loads of information on Argentina is now available on the internet, much of it reasonably updated, and in English. Most provinces in Argentina have their own website and it's useful to have a look before you come for inspiration and information. Each province has a tourist office, **Casa de Provincia**, in Buenos Aires, Mon-Fri 1000-1630/1730. The following regional websites are recommended:
Buenos Aires Province, Av Callao 237, T011-4371 7046, www.casaprov.gba.gov.ar. Also www.bue.gov.ar. www.sanantoniodeareco.com/turismo
Catamarca, Av Córdoba 2080, T/F03833-4374 6891, www.catamarca.gov.ar.
Chaco, Av Callao 322, T03722-4372 5209, www.ecomchaco.com.ar.

Chubut, Sarmiento 1172, T02965-4382 2009, www.chubut.com.ar.
Córdoba, Av Callao 332, T0351-4373 4277, www.cba.gov.ar. Also www.cordobatrip.com and www.cordoba.net.
Corrientes, San Martín 333, p 4, T/F03783-4394 2808, www.corrientes.gov.ar.
Formosa, Hipólito Yrigoyen 1429, T03717-4381 2037, www.casadeformosa.gov.ar.
Jujuy, Av Santa Fe 967, T0388-4393 6096. www.casadejujuy.gov.ar. Also www.turismo.jujuy.gov.ar.
La Pampa, Suipacha 346, T011-4326 1145, www.turismolapampa.gov.ar.
La Rioja, Av Callao 745, T03822-4815 1929, www.larioja.gov.ar/turismo.
Mar del Plata, Av Corrientes 1660, local 16, T0223-4384 5658, www.mardelplata.gov.ar.
Mendoza, Av Callao 445, T0261-4374 1105, www.mendoza.gov.ar. Also www.turismo.mendoza.gov.ar, www.mendoza.com.ar and www.welcometomendoza.com.ar.
Misiones, Santa Fe 989, T 03752-4322 1097, www.misiones.gov.ar/turismo.
Municipalidad de la Costa, B Mitre 737, www.lacostaturismo.com.ar.
Neuquén, Maipú 48, T0299-4343 2324, www.neuquen.gov.ar.
Río Negro, Tucumán 1916, www.rionegrotur.com.ar.
Salta, Diagonal Norte 933, T0387-4326 2456, www.turismosalta.gov.ar.
San Juan, Sarmiento 1251, T02646-4382 9241, www.sanjuan.gov.ar.
San Luis, Azcuénaga 1083, T02652-5778 1621, www.sanluis.gov.ar.
Santa Cruz, 25 de Mayo 279, www.epatagonia.gov.ar.
Santa Fé, Montevideo 373, p 2, T0342-5811 4327.
Santiago del Estero, Florida 274, T0385-4326 9418, www.mercotur.com/santiagodelestero.
Tierra del Fuego, Sarmiento 745, www.tierradelfuego.org.ar.
Tucumán, Suipacha 140, T0381-4322 0010, www.tucumanturismo.gov.ar.

For tourist information on **Patagonia**, see www.patagonia.com.ar, www.patagonia-argentina.com or www.patagonia-chile.com. For Patagonia and bookings for cheap accommodation and youth hostels, contact Asatej, see Useful addresses on page 110.

Websites

www.liveargentina.com Information for the whole country. In several languages.
www.museosargentinos.org.ar/museos Argentina's museums.
http://ar.yahoo.com, www.grippo.com.ar, www.google.com.ar Search engines.
www.terra.com.ar News, entertainment, weather, tourism and Spanish phone directory.
www.mercotour.com Information on travel and other matters in Argentina, Uruguay, Chile and Brazil, in Spanish, English and Portuguese.
www.meteonet.com.ar Useful web site for forecasts and weather satellite images.
www.alojar.com.ar Accommodation search engine and tourist information in Spanish.
www.tageblatt.com.ar *Argentinisches Tageblatt*, German-language weekly, very informative.
www.buenosairesherald.com *Buenos Aires Herald*, English language daily.

Language

➔ *For useful words and phrases and a menu reader, see Footnotes, pages 614 and 620.*

Your experience in Argentina will be completely transformed if you can learn even a little of the language before you arrive. Spanish is the first language, with a few variations and a distinctive pronunciation. In areas popular with tourists, you'll find some people speak English and perhaps French or Italian, but since much of the pleasure of Argentina is in getting off the beaten track, you'll often find yourself in situations where only Spanish is spoken. Argentines are welcoming and curious, and they're very likely to strike up conversation on a bus, shop or in a queue for the cinema. They're also incredibly hospitable, and are quite inclined to invite you for dinner, or to travel with them, and your attempts to speak Spanish will be enormously appreciated.

If you have a few weeks before you arrive, try and learn a few basic phrases, useful verbs and numbers. If you're reading this on the plane, it's not too late to get a grasp of basic introductions, food and directions. See page 614 for a useful list of words and phrases, and page 620 for the food and drink glossary.

Argentine Spanish sounds like no other. The main difference is that in words with 'll' and 'y' , this sound is pronounced like a soft 'j' sound, as in 'beige '. The 'd' sound is usually omitted in words ending in 'd' or '-ado', and 's' sounds are often omitted altogether at the ends of words. And in the north and west of the country, you'll hear the normal rolled 'r' sound replaced by a hybrid 'r j' put together. Grammatically, the big change is that the Spanish '*tû*' is replaced by '*vos*' also used almost universally instead of '*usted*', unless you're speaking to someone much older or higher in status. I In the conjunction of verbs, the accent is on the last syllable eg *vos tenés podés*. In the north and northwest, though, the Spanish is more akin to that spoken in the rest of Latin America. In Buenos Aires, you might here the odd word of *lunfardo*, Italian-oriented slang.

Language classes are available at low cost in a number of centres in Argentina. See the travelling text, Language courses. Learn about Argentine wines with your Spanish at the **Spanish and Wine School**: http://cablemodem.fibertel.com.ar/aeav.

Language schools

Amerispan, PO Box 58129, Philadelphia, PA 19102, USA, T011-215-751 1100, www.amerispan.com. North American company offering Spanish immersion programmes, educational tours, volunteer and internship positions in Buenos Aires, Córdoba and Mendoza. Also programmes for younger people.

IBL, 165 Florida St, 8th Floor, Buenos Aires www.ibl.com.ar T-54-11-4331 4250. Complete immersion language teaching to a high standard. Group and private courses, beginning every Mon of the year.

Spanish Abroad, 5112 N, 40th St, Suite 103, Phoenix, AZ 85018, T1-888-722 7623, www.spanishabroad.com. Spanish classes in Buenos Aires and Córdoba.

Disabled travellers

Facilities for the disabled in Argentina are sorely lacking, since so far, there's a general absence of information and education. Wheelchair users won't find many ramps or even lowered curbs, although this is improving in Buenos Aires; pavements tend to be shoddy and broken even in big cities. Only a few upmarket hotels have

AmeriSpan
THE BRIDGE BETWEEN CULTURES

been fully-adapted for wheelchair use, although many more modern hotels are fine for those with limited mobility. The best way to assess this is to ring or email the hotel in advance and check. Argentines generally go out of their way to help you, making up for poor facilities with kindness and generosity. Tourist sights aren't generally well adapted for disabled visitors, with limited access for the physically disabled, particularly in archaeological sites. However, many museums have ramps or lifts, and some offer special guided tours for the visually-impaired, and signed tours for the hearing-impaired. The superb dinosaur museum in Trelew is setting the trend here. Iguazú Falls has good access for wheelchair users or those with walking difficulties, along sturdy modern walkways with no steps, right up to the Falls. Getting close to glacier Perito Moreno is not easy, since steps are involved in descending the walkways, but boat trips to the glacier should be possible with prior arrangement. Airlines can be helpful, but you must absolutely let them know your needs in advance. Some airports, incredibly, have only one or two wheelchairs, and there have been stories of passengers waiting for an hour on the plane for the one wheelchair to make its way to gate 5. Speaking Spanish is obviously a great help, and travelling with a companion is advisable.

Useful websites and contacts

Some travel companies specialize in holidays tailor made for the individual's level of disability. You might like to read *Nothing Ventured* by Alison Walsh, (Harper Collins) which gives personal accounts of worldwide journeys by disabled travellers, plus advice and listings. Other useful contacts include **Directions Unlimited**, New York, **Mobility International USA**, *Twin Peaks Press*, Vancouver, Canada.

Disability Action Group, www.drc.org.uk, for information on independent travel.

Global Access Disabled Network, www.geocities.com/Paris/1502.

Royal Association for Disability and Rehabilitation, www.radar.org.

Society for Accessible Travel and Hospitality, www.sath.org. Lots of advice on how to travel with specific disabilities.

Other useful sites include: www.access-able.com, www.justargentina.org/argentina/argentina-disabled-travellers.asp, www.globalaccessnews.com, www.disabledtravels.com, www.transitionsabroad.com/listings/travel/disability/disabilityorganizations.shtml.

Gay and lesbian travellers

Sad to say, in a country whose people are generally incredibly warm and welcoming, homosexuality has yet to be widely accepted in Argentina. In the interior of the country, away from Buenos Aires, it has to be said that you might encounter homophobia. Being openly demonstrative in public will certainly raise eyebrows everywhere apart from the hipper places in Buenos Aires. However Buenos Aires is fast becoming one of the top gay destinations in the world, with plenty of gay friendly bars, night clubs and hotels. The tourist office even produces a handy leaflet with a map showing gay bars, pubs, clothing (what do they mean?), saunas, health centres and wine bars. Look out for 'BSASgay'. A In 2007, gay hotel chain **Axel** will open its second gay hotel, Monserrat (their first one is in Barcelona) at Venezuela in the 600 block. Local Buenos Aires businesses, waking up the power of the gay peso have started to jump on the band wagon, competing to target the gay tourist . For instance, in Maipu 900 there's even a new gay wine store. You may wonder how different this could possibly be from a straight wine store, but it's got to be worth dropping in!

Change is gradually reaching government levels to. Discrimination on the grounds of sexual orientation was banned in 1996, and in 2002, the first same sex marriages were legally performed.

Useful websites and contacts

Pride Travel, Paraguay 523, 2nd floor, Buenos Aires, T011-5218 6556, www.pride-travel.com. The city's own gay travel agency, often recommended, which organizes tours and trips, nights out in Buenos Aires, and travel advice for the rest of the country.

A couple of other agencies worth trying: **Adia Turismo**, Av Córdoba 836, 9th floor, T011 4393 0531, www.adiatur.com; and **Calu Travel Service**, Paraguay 946, T011 4325 5477, www.calutravel.com.ar, lots of travel services, and access to the only gay beach in the country at Mar del Plata.

Useful websites include:

www.gaytravel.co.uk, good online travel agent offering good deals and gay hotels.

www.gaytravel.com, excellent site with information on gay travel.

www.nexo.org, a useful site for gay information within Argentina (Spanish only).

www.gay.com, directory for gay life in Argentina.

www.thegayguide.com.ar, for travel tips on bars in Buenos Aires, look at

Student travellers

If you're in full-time education, you're entitled to an International Student Identity Card (ISIC), available from student travel offices and agencies, which gives you special prices on transport, cultural events and a variety of other concessions and services. All student cards must carry a photograph. Youth hostels can be found in all tourist areas and big cities, and are a good way of meeting other travellers. The two big hostel chains are: **Argentina Hostels Club** (AHC), www.argetinahostels.com, with the excellent **V&S** hostel in Buenos Aires and great hostels all over the country; and **Hostelling International**, www.hihostels.com.

There's a good travel agency, **Asatej**, Paraguay 523, 2nd floor, Buenos Aires, To11-5218 6556, www.asatej.com, which sells flights, hire cars and accommodation, as well as group and individual tours to places in Argentina. They are cheap and a good way to make friends.

Travelling with children

Travelling with children in Argentina is potentially safe, easy and a great adventure. The country is so full of wonders that children can enjoy, travelling here is much more like travelling in Spain than Latin American, and Argentine people are extremely affectionate to children. There's a real feeling here that children are part of society, not to be sent to be bed at 2000, and often seen running around restaurants at 2300, or out with their parents walking along beaches or plazas in the evenings. This means that many family restaurants have play zones for kids with a climbing frame or soft play area, usually within sight of your table. And if you'd rather dine without your children, more expensive hotels provide a baby-sitter service. There are plenty of plazas or other green spaces in all towns for children to run around in, and lots of sports to join in too, football being the most ubiquitous. You'll find people everywhere particularly helpful and respectful to children and families.

Food

Food is easy in Argentina, since most dishes aren't strongly seasoned, and easy meals like pasta, pizza and salads are of a high standard and available everywhere. The meat is lean and portions are huge, so that if you order a steak in a restaurant there will generally be enough for you and a child (or two hungry children). However, children's meals are offered at most restaurants, and many establishments have high chairs. Try *milanesas*, thin cuts of chicken, beef or lamb cooked in breadcrumbs, and *ñoquis*, delicious pasta made with potato, good in tomato sauce. Argentine children tend to drink fizzy drinks, but freshly squeezed orange juice widely available, and although the water is drinkable from the tap in many areas of the country, it's best to order mineral water. The leading local brands, Villavicencio, and Eco are good and available everywhere. There will be lots of new treats for your kids to try: the most amazing ice creams in the world (Persicco, Jauja and Freddo particularly), and dulce de leche, a sweet soft toffee-like spread that's liberally applied to all cakes and pastries, and on *alfajores*, delicious soft biscuits made of corn flour. If your children have special dietary needs, it's worth learning the Spanish to explain and similarly if your child doesn't eat meat: 'no come carne' will be useful.

Transport

For most tourist attractions, there are cheaper prices for children. However, on all long-distance buses you pay a fare for each seat, and there are no half-fares if the children occupy a seat each. For shorter trips it is cheaper, if less comfortable, to seat small children on your knee. For long bus journeys, it's a good idea to bring water, fruit and biscuits, since the food provided may not be to your children's taste. There are toilets on all long-distance buses, and these are definitely improving, but they may not be clean or have water and toilet paper, so bring tissues. All bus stations have a *kiosko*, selling drinks, snacks and tissues. Bring games and books to keep children entertained; the videos shown on most buses are generally action movies, not suitable for under 12s. On sightseeing tours you could try and bargain for a family rate – often children can go free. All civil airlines charge half for children under 12 but some military services don't have half-fares, or have younger age limits.

Accommodation

Hotel accommodation in Argentina is good value for families; most places have rooms for three, four or even five people, or two rooms with a connecting door. And many quite modest hotels have a suite, with two rooms and a bathroom, for families. If you're happy to be self-catering, look out for *cabañas* all over rural areas, like the Lake District, these are attractive self-contained cottages or flats which you can rent by the day, and are extremely good value for three or more people. Prices start at around US$40 per night for a basic *cabaña* sleeping four, US$50 in tourist areas where they're usually spacious, and can be extremely luxurious.

Travel with children will most definitely bring you into closer contact with Argentine families and individuals, and you may find officials tend to be more amenable where children are concerned. Everyone will be delighted if your child knows a little Spanish.

Women travellers

Single women might attract surprise – *Estas sola?* You're travelling alone? – but this is rather because Argentines are such sociable people and love to travel in groups, rather than because it's dangerous. Argentine men can't seem to help paying women attention, and you may hear the traditional *piropo* as you walk past: a compliment, usually fairly unimaginative, and nothing to cause offence. Just ignore it and walk on. Men are generally respectful of a woman travelling alone, and won't make improper suggestions, but just in case here are some tips: It's a good idea to wear a ring on your wedding finger, and carry a photograph of '*mi marido*', your 'husband'. By saying that your 'husband' is close at hand, you may dissuade an aspiring suitor. Argentine men are famously charming and persistent chatters up, so firmly discourage any unwanted contact and be aware of any signals which might be interpreted as encouragement. If politeness fails, don't feel bad about showing offence and leaving. It's best not to go hiking alone, since hiking areas in Argentina are generally far less visited than those in Europe, and if you twist an ankle, it might be a long time before someone finds you. So try to join up with other people, and always register with *guardaparques* (rangers) before you set off. Do not walk alone around Buenos Aires in quiet areas or at night. When accepting a social invitation, make sure that someone knows the address you're going to and the time you left. And if you don't know your hosts well, a good ploy is to ask if you can bring a friend, even if you've no intention of doing so, to check the intentions of whoever's inviting you. Wherever you are, try to act with confidence, and walk as though you know where you are going, even if you don't. Someone who looks lost is more likely to attract unwanted attention. Do not disclose to strangers where you are staying. When you set out, err on the side of caution until your instincts have adjusted to the customs of a new culture.

Book accommodation ahead so that when you arrive in a new town you can take a taxi straight to your hotel or hostel and avoid looking lost and vulnerable at bus stations. Many hotels or hostels are open 24 hours, but if you arrive in the early morning, it's safest to wait in the bus station *confitería*, where there are usually people around, than to venture into the centre.

Women should be aware that tampons and towels must never be flushed, whether in a private home or hotel, since the water pressure is too low in Argentina to cope. Carry a supply of plastic bags in case bins aren't provided.

Working in Argentina

Foreigners can't work in Argentina without a work permit which you'll only get with an official job. At a time of high unemployment, it's hard to find work and you might consider it unfair to take work away from Argentines. The exception to this is teaching English, and it's possible to pick up work with a school, if you have the TEFL qualification and plenty of experience. Otherwise, private lessons are always an option, but pay very poorly, currently around US$5 per hour. Jobs in schools are advertised in the English-language newspaper, the *Buenos Aires Herald*.

Before you travel

Visas and immigration

➔ *Visit www.mrecic.gov.ar for a full list of embassies.*

Passports are not required by citizens of neighbouring countries who hold identity cards issued by their own governments. Visas are not necessary for US citizens, British citizens and nationals of other Western European countries, plus Canada, Bolivia, Brazil, Chile, Panama, Paraguay, Uruguay, Venezuela, Mexico, El Salvador, Guatemala, Nicaragua, Honduras, Costa Rica, Colombia, Ecuador, Peru, Dominican Republic, Haiti, Barbados, Jamaica, Malaysia, Israel, Czech Republic, Hungary, Poland, Turkey, Croatia, Slovenia, South Africa, Australia, New Zealand, Singapore and Japan. Visitors from these countries are given a tourist card on entry and may stay for three months

For visitors from all other countries, there are three forms of visa: a business 'temporary' visa (US$35, valid one year), a tourist visa (US$35 approximately, fees may change), and a transit visa. Tourist visas are usually valid for three months and are multiple entry. All visitors can renew their tourist visas for another three months by going in person to the **National Directorate of Migration** ⓘ *Antártida Argentina 1365, Buenos Aires, T011-4312 8663 (ring first to check opening times)*, and paying a fee of US$35: ask for 'Prorrogas de Permanencia'. No renewals are given after the expiry date. Alternatively, for a 90-day extension of your stay in Argentina, just leave the country at any land border, and you'll get another 3 month Tourist Visa stamped in your passport on return. Alternatively, you can forego all the paperwork by paying a US$50 fine at a border immigration post (queues are shorter than in Buenos Aires, but still allow 30 minutes).

All visitors are advised to carry their passports at all times, and it is illegal not to have identification handy. In practice, though, this is not advisable. Photocopy your passport twice, carry one copy, and leave another at home with someone who could fax a copy to you if yours gets stolen. You'll often be asked for the number of your passport, when checking into hotels and if paying by credit card, so learn it off by heart and there'll be no problem. The police like searching backpackers at border points: remain calm – this is normal procedure. If you are staying in the country for several weeks, it may be worth while registering at your embassy or consulate; if your passport is stolen, the process of replacing it is simplified and speeded up.

Customs

Unusually, you can buy duty-free goods on arrival at Ezeiza Airport, though the shops are small and pricey.

Duty-free allowance

No duties are charged on clothing, personal effects or toiletries. Cameras, typewriters, binoculars, radios and other things which a tourist normally carries are duty-free if they have been used and only one of each article is carried. This is also true of scientific and professional instruments for personal use. Travellers may only bring in new personal goods up to a value of US$300 (US$100 from neighbouring countries). The amount of duty and tax payable amounts to 50% of the item's cost. At airport customs, you press a button for the red or green channel. Make sure you have the baggage claim tag (usually stuck to your ticket or boarding card) as these are inspected at the exit from the customs inspection area. Two litres of alcoholic drinks, 400 cigarettes and 50 cigars are also allowed in duty-free. For tourists originating from neighbouring countries the quantities allowed are one litre of alcoholic drinks, 200 cigarettes and 20 cigars.

If you have packages sent to Argentina, the green customs label should not be used unless the contents are of real value and you expect to pay duty. For such things as books or samples use the white label if available. A heavy tax is imposed on packages sent to Argentina by courier.

Vaccinations

No vaccination certificates are required for entry. Take malaria pills if travelling to the humid north east in summer: there are very occasional cases. » *For further details, see Health page 54.*

What to take

You'll be able to buy most things you're likely to need once you're in Argentina, and at cheaper prices than in much of Europe, (except imported goods, which are prohibitively expensive). Photocopy all documents, your passport, and flight ticket, and leave a set at home to be faxed to you if there's an emergency. Carry a photocopy of your passport at all times. See page 57 for a list of trekking equipment.

Buy as big a memory card for your camera as you can afford. There are plenty of places in all towns who will download your photos onto CD and wipe the card, but you'll take many more photos than you think in any given day. Bring mini DV tapes for your video camera, as these can be very pricey. And a word of advice for long bus journeys: carry small packs of tissues (available at the *kiosko* in the terminal) for toilet roll, and water for teeth brushing, since toilets on buses can be quite an adventure.

Along with your usual clothes, camera and diary, consider bringing: a light waterproof jacket, comfortable walking shoes or boots, a lightweight fleece top, a smartish set of clothes (for the occasional night at a good hotel or restaurant, since Argentines tend to dress formally), a money pouch (worn under your clothes, particularly in Buenos Aires), a padlock (if you're planning to stay in youth hostels), sun protection cream (particularly in the south with the ozone hole), insect repellent, sunglasses, a torch or Maglite (useful for walking around remote, unlit villages at night), a folding knife (handy for picnics, but remember not to carry it in hand luggage).

Money

Currency

The unit of currency is the Argentine peso (Arg $), divided into 100 centavos. Peso notes in circulation are 2, 5, 10, 20, 50 and 100. Coins in circulation are 1, 5, 10, 25 and 50 centavos and 1 peso. Most major towns have exchange places (*casas de cambio*), and exchange rates are quoted in major newspapers daily.

Credit and debit cards

By far the easiest way to get cash while you're in Argentina is to use a credit card at an ATM (*cajero automatico*). These can be found in every town or city (with the notable exception of El Chaltén in the south) and most accept all major cards, with Visa and Mastercard being the most widely accepted in small places. The rate of exchange is that which applies at the moment the money is withdrawn and commission is usually around 2-3%, but check with your credit card company before leaving home. You may also be charged a cash handling fee by credit cards. Carry all your cards' emergency numbers in case your card is lost or stolen. And note that in Argentine ATMs, you'll be given your cash and receipt before the card is returned: don't walk away without the card, as many travellers are reported to have done. Credit cards are now accepted almost everywhere as payment, but it's a good idea to carry cash to pay in cheaper shops, restaurants and hotels. Mastercard emergency number is T0800-5550507 and Visa is T0800-32222.

Exchange rate as of November 2006: US dollar = Arg $3 UK pound = Arg $5.50.

Traveller's cheques

There's little point in carrying traveller's cheques in Argentina, since there are exchange facilities only in big towns, and commission is very high: usually 10%. A passport is essential and you may have to show proof of purchase; so transactions can take a long time. Traveller's cheques also attract thieves and though you can of course arrange a refund, the process will hold up your travel plans. Far better to bring your debit card and withdraw money from ATMs.

Transfers

These are almost impossible: Money can be transferred between banks but you'll need to find out which local bank is related to your own and give all the relevant information with the routing codes. Allow two to three days; cash is usually paid in pesos and is be subject to tax. For Western Union in Argentina, T011-4322-7774.

Cost of living

Argentina's economy has picked up since the 2002 economic crisis, but prices have risen steeply, particularly for hotels and tourist services. Nevertheless, you'll find Argentina a very economical country to travel around, compared with Europe and north America.

Cost of travelling

You can find comfortable accommodation with a private bathroom and breakfast for around US$50 for two people, while a good dinner in the average restaurant will be around US$7-10 per person. Prices are much cheaper away from the main touristy areas: El Calafate, Ushuaia and Buenos Aires can be particularly pricey. Single rooms (or single occupancy of double rooms) will usually cost two thirds that of a double room, but in high season, you may be charged the full price for a double room in an upmarket hotel. For travellers on a budget, hostels usually cost between US$10 per person in a shared dorm. Cheap breakfasts can be found in any ordinary café for around US$1.50, and there are cheap set meals for lunchtime at many restaurants, costing around US$5, US$7 in Buenos Aires. For cheap eats, most towns have *rotiserias* selling ready cooked chickens and meat, and tasty vegetable pies, all freshly prepared and reliable. Pasta is widely available to take away, whether cooked or uncooked, making a good cheap meal, and fruit and vegetables are cheap and abundant. Camping costs vary widely, but expect to pay no more than US$3 per tent, usually less. Long-distance bus travel on major routes is very cheap, and it's well worth splashing out an extra 20% for *coche cama* service on overnight journeys, where your seat fully reclines so you can sleep.

Getting there

Air

From Europe There are flights to Buenos Aires from London, Amsterdam, Barcelona, Madrid, Frankfurt, Paris, Milan, Rome, Zurich with **Aerolíneas Argentinas** ⓘ *1st floor, 22 Conduit St, London, W1S 2XR, T0800-0969 747, www.aerolineas.com*, and other European carriers. From Britain, only **British Airways** goes direct to Buenos Aires, and has been repeatedly recommended for comfort and service.

From North America and Canada **Aerolíneas Argentinas** and other South American and North American airlines fly from Miami, New York, Washington, Los Angeles, San Francisco, Atlanta, New Orleans, Dallas and Chicago. **Canadian Air International** and **Lan Chile** fly from Toronto and Montreal.

From Australasia and South Africa **Aerolíneas Argentinas** and **Qantas** fly from Sydney, Australia, via Auckland, New Zealand, two or three times a week. **Malaysia Airlines** fly twice a week from Kuala Lumpur to Buenos Aires, via Johannesburg, and **South African Airways** fly four times a week from Johannesburg, via Sao Paulo.

From Latin America **Aerolíneas Argentinas** and other carriers fly between Buenos Aires and all the South American capitals, plus Santa Cruz and Cochabamba in Bolivia and Guayaquil in Ecuador. Several flights between Buenos Aires and Rio de Janeiro and São Paulo stop over in Porto Alegre, Florianópolis and Curitiba. There are also flights from Belo Horizonte, Salvador, Recife and Fortaleza, Havana, Mexico City and Cancún.

General tips

Check your baggage allowance as airlines vary widely. The limit is usually between 20-32 kg per person for economy class; strictly enforced with extortionate charges for excess baggage. For internal flights in Argentina, the baggage limit with **Aerolineas Argentinas** is now 15 kg, and they are extremely inflexible, also charging wildly for excess. This means you will either have to leave some things in your hotel in Buenos Aires, or consider limiting your baggage to 15 kg when you leave home.

Prices and discounts

Fares vary considerably from airline to airline, so it's worth checking with an agency for the best deal for when you want to travel. The cheap-seat allocation in aircraft will sell out quickly in holiday periods. The busiest seasons for travelling to Argentina are 7 December to 15 January, Easter, and 1 July to 10 September, when you should book as far ahead as possible. There might be special offers available from February to May and September to November. Fares usually fall into one month, three month or yearly fare categories, and it's more expensive the longer you want to stay. Return dates must be booked when the ticket is bought, but most airlines will let you change the date for a penalty of around US$100. With student (or under 26) fares, some airlines are flexible on the age limit, others strict, and usually these tickets are the most flexible, though they're not always the cheapest available.

Discount flight agents

Using the web to book flights, hotels and other services directly is becoming increasingly popular and you can get some good deals. Be aware, though, that cutting out the travel agents is denying yourself the knowledge and experience that they can give, not just in terms of the best flights to suit your itinerary, but also advice on documents, insurance, safety, routes and lodging. A reputable agent will also be bonded to give you some protection if arrangements collapse while you are travelling.

UK and Ireland

Journey Latin America, 12-13 Heathfield Terrace, Chiswick, London W4 4JE, T020-8747 8315, www.journeylatinamerica.co.uk.

STA Travel, 86 Old Brompton Rd, London, SW7 3LH, T020-74376262, www.sta travel.co.uk. Branches throughout the UK and many university campuses. Specialists in low-cost student/youth flights and tours. Good for student IDs and insurance.

Trailfinders, 194 Kensington High St, London, W8 7RG, T020-7938 3939, www.trail finders.com. 18 branches in London and throughout the UK. Also one in Dublin and 5 travel centres in Australia.

North America

Air Brokers International, 323 Geary St, Suite 411, San Francisco, CA94102, T01-800-883 3273, www.airbrokers.com. Consolidator and specialist on RTW and Circle Pacific tickets.

Discount Airfares Worldwide On-Line, www.etn.nl/discount.htm. A hub of consolidator and discount agent links.

International Travel Network/Airlines of the Web, www.itn.net/airlines Online air travel information and reservations.

STA Travel, 5900 Wilshire Blvd, Suite 2110, Los Angeles, CA 90036, T1-800-777 0112, www.sta-travel.com. Also branches in New York, San Francisco, Boston, Miami, Chicago, Seattle and Washington DC.

Travel CUTS, 187 College St, Toronto, ON, M5T 1P7, T1-800-667 2887, www.travelcuts.com. Specialist in student discount fares, IDs and other travel services. Branches in other Canadian cities.

Travelocity, www.travelocity.com. Online consolidator.

Australia and New Zealand

Flight Centres, 82 Elizabeth St, Sydney, T13-1600; 205 Queen St, Auckland, T09-309 6171. Branches in other towns and cities.

STA Travel, T1300-360960, www.statravelaus.com.au 702 Harris St.

Travel.com.au, 80 Clarence St, Sydney, T02-929 01500, www.travel.com.au.

Ultimo, Sydney, and 256 Flinders St, Melbourne. In New Zealand: 10 High St, Auckland, T09-366 6673. Also in major towns and university campuses.

Road

There are many entry points from the neighbouring countries, and with good long-distance bus services, this is a convenient way of entering Argentina if you're travelling around South America.

The main route are as follows: in the west from Santiago (Chile) to Mendoza; in the northwest from Villazón (Bolivia) to Jujuy and Salta; in the northeast from Asunción (Paraguay) to Resistencia, from Encarnación (Paraguay) to Posadas and from Foz do Iguazú (Brazil) to Puerto Iguazú; in the Lake District by boat and bus from Puerto Montt (Chile) to Bariloche; in Patagonia by road from Puerto Natales (Chile) to El Calafate or by road and ferry crossings from Tierra del Fuego to Río Gallegos and El Calafate. There are also three road crossings from Uruguay via bridges over the Río Uruguay as well several ferry crossings, the most important of which are from Montevideo and Colonia de Sacramento to Buenos Aires.

Sea

It's possible to cruise to Argentina and there are some luxurious options available, as well as more basic freight travel options. Contact a specialist agency, such as Strand Travel in London, www.strandtravel.co.uk Or www.cruise-locators.com who have information on all cruise lines.

Touching down

Airport information

All flights from outside Argentina, apart from those from neighbouring countries, arrive at Ezeiza International Airport (officially known as Ministro Pistarini), situated 35 km southwest of Buenos Aires (for detailed information including transport to Buenos Aires, see page 119). All internal flights as well as some flights to/from neighbouring countries come to Jorge Newbery Airport, generally known as Aeroparque, situated 4 km north of the centre of Buenos Aires on the bank of the Río de la Plata (see page 119 for details). Most provincial airports have a desk offering tourist information, banking facilities and a confitería (cafeteria) as well as car hire. There are usually minibus services into the city and taxis are available.

Airport tax

Airport tax of US$28 to be paid on all international flights, except to Montevideo from Aeroparque Airport, which is subject to US$14 tax. Airport tax can be prepaid, and you should check if it's included in your ticket when you book. Internal flights are subject to US$12, included in your ticket everywhere but the airport at El Calafate, where you must pay in pesos. When in transit from one international flight to another, you may be obliged to pass through immigration and customs, have your passport stamped and be made to pay an airport tax on departure. There is a 5% tax on the purchase of air tickets.

Local customs and laws

Greetings Argentines are extremely courteous and friendly people, and start every interaction, no matter how small, with a greeting (unlike the practice in many big European and North American cities). You'll be welcomed in shops and ticket offices with *Hola!* (Hi), *Buen Dia* (good morning) or *Buenos Tardes* (good afternoon) and often *Que tal?* or *Como estas?* (how are you?) too. Take the time to respond with a smile and a *Buenos Dias* or *Hola* in return (or to *Que tal?* say *Bien, gracias*) before continuing. Argentines are social people, and haven't yet lost the art of passing the time of day, you'll be considered a bit abrupt if you don't too. As you leave, say *Chau* (bye) or *Hasta luego* (see you later). Strangers are generally treated with great kindness and generosity and your warmth in return will be greatly appreciated.

If you're introduced to new people or friends, you'll be kissed, once, on the right cheek as you say hello and goodbye. This sometimes goes for men to men too, if they're friends. It's more of a touching of cheeks than a kiss, but you should respond enthusiastically. In a business context, Argentines tend to be formal, and very polite, and this goes for officials too. It's wise not to show impatience, and to avoid criticizing in public. Always, always ask permission before taking photographs of people. For further information on responsible tourism, see box page 42.

The mate ritual Wherever you go in Argentina, you'll see groups of people sharing a mate (pronounced mattay). Whatever their class, or job, everyone, from students and upwards, drinks several mates a day. See box, page 53. It's an absolutely essential part of your trip to Argentina that you give it a go, at least. You might find it a little bitter at first, but the experience of sharing it includes you in the social group and your new Argentine friends will be enormously impressed.

Appearance Argentines of whatever class tend to dress neatly, and take care to be clean and tidy so it's much appreciated if you do the same. In the 'interior', outside Buenos Aires particularly, people are more conservative, and the way you dress is mostly how people will judge you. Buying clothing locally can help you to look less like a tourist, and clothes are cheap in Argentina in comparison with western Europe. Shorts are worn in Buenos Aires and residential suburbs in spring, summer and autumn, but they're not usually worn outside the capital, except on the beach.

Begging There's little begging in Argentina but you might be asked for *una moneda* (some change) outside big city supermarkets.

Safety

Argentina was one of the safest countries in South America, until the economic crisis of 2002, when petty crime increased, particularly in Buenos Aires, along with rather less petty crimes such kidnapping, which was reported in the media to be a daily occurrence for a while. However, as the economy has improved, crime is less prevalent, but security remains a concern in certain areas of Buenos Aires such as La Boca, and in bus stations and crowded markets in all big cities. The following tips are meant to forewarn but not alarm you. They apply to Buenos Aires and major cities. Everywhere else in Argentina is still extremely safe.

Protecting documents and valuables Keep all documents secure in a pouch worn under your clothes. Hide your main cash supply in different places or under your clothes: extra pockets sewn inside shirts and trousers, pockets closed with a zip or safety pin, or a moneybelt. Keep your camera in a bag, preferably with a chain or wire in the strap to defeat the slasher. Don't wear wrist-watches or jewellery. If you carry a shoulder-bag in a market, carry it in front of you. Backpacks are vulnerable to slashers – try not to stand still for too long. Use a pack which is lockable at its base. It is best, if you can trust your hotel, to leave any valuables you don't need in a safe-deposit there, when sightseeing locally. Always keep an inventory of what you have deposited. If you don't trust the hotel, lock everything in your pack and secure it in your room. Backpackers should bring a padlock which you can also use for lockers in hostels. If you lose valuables, or if you're mugged, always report to the police and get a copy of the report – for insurance purposes.

Touching down

Business hours Shops and services in Buenos Aires most are open 0900-1800. Elsewhere, everything closes for siesta 1300-1700. Big indoor shopping malls are open 1000-2200. Banks, government offices and businesses usually 0800-1300 in summer, 1000-1500 in winter, weekdays only. Some businesses open again in the evening, 1700- 2000. Post offices are often open *corrido* – don't close for lunch and siesta. Restaurants open for lunch 1230-1500, dinner 2100-2400. Most Argentines start eating at 2200 or 2300. Nightclubs open at 2400, but usually get busy around 0200. Cafés are usually busy after 2400.

In an emergency Police T101. If robbed or attacked, call the tourist police, Comisaría del Turista, Av Corrientes 436, Buenos Aires, T011-4346 5748 (24 hrs) or T0800-999 5000, English spoken, turista@ policia federal.gov.ar. Urgent medical service T107.

International phone code +54. Ringing: equal tones with long pauses. Engaged: equal tones with equal pauses.

Official time GMT -3.

Tipping 10% in restaurants and cafés. Porters and ushers are usually tipped.

VAT/IVA 21%; VAT is not levied on medicines, books and some foodstuffs.

Voltage 220 volts (and 110 too in some hotels), 50 cycles, AC, European Continental-type plugs in old buildings, Australian three-pin flat-type in the new. Adaptors can be purchased locally for either type (ie from new three-pin to old two-pin and vice-versa). Best to bring a universal adapter, not available for British 3 pin plugs in Argentina.

Weights and measures Metric.

When you have all your luggage with you at a bus or railway station, be especially careful: don't get into arguments with any locals if you can help it, and lock all the items together with a chain or cable if you are waiting for some time. Take a taxi between airport/bus station/railway station and hotel, if you can afford it. Keep your bags with you in the taxi and pay only when you and your luggage are safely out of the vehicle. Make sure the taxi has inner door handles, in case a quick exit is needed. Travelling on night buses is generally extremely safe in Argentina and they arrive in the early morning, which is much safer than late at night. Watch your belongings being stowed in the boot of the bus, and keep the ticket you'll be given since you'll need it to claim your luggage on arrival (a small tip, 50 centavos, is appreciated when you collect your luggage.

Tricksters In Buenos Aires and other major cities, beware of the common trick of spraying mustard, ketchup or some other substance on you and then getting an accomplice to clean you off (and remove your wallet). If you are sprayed, walk straight on. Ignore also strangers' remarks like 'what's that on your shoulder?' or 'have you seen that dirt on your shoe?'. Furthermore, don't bend over to pick up money or other items in the street. These are all ruses intended to distract your attention and make you easy for an accomplice to steal from. While you should take local advice about being out at night, do not assume that daytime is safer than night-time. If walking after dark in dangerous parts of big cities, walk in the road, not on the pavement.

Be wary if 'plainclothes policemen' ask to see your documents. Insist on seeing identification, and on going to the police station by main roads. Do not hand over your identification (or money – which he should not need to see anyway) until you are at the station. On no account take 'police' directly back to your lodgings. Be even more suspicious if a policeman seeks confirmation of his status from a passer-by. If someone tries to bribe you, insist on a receipt. If attacked, remember your assailants may well be armed, try not to resist. See the brilliant Argentine movie, Nine Queens: an accurate portrayal of slick petty crime on the streets of Buenos Aires.

Rape If you are the victim of a sexual assault, you are advised in the first instance to contact a doctor (this can be your home doctor if you prefer). You will need tests to determine whether you have contracted any sexually transmitted diseases; you may also need advice on post-coital contraception. You should also contact your embassy, where consular staff are very willing to help in cases of assault.

Drugs Users of drugs, even of soft ones, without medical prescription should be particularly careful, as Argentina imposes heavy penalties – up to 10 years' imprisonment – for even possession of such substances, and tends to make little distinction between marijuana and hard drugs. The planting of drugs on travellers, by traffickers or the police, is not unknown. If offered drugs on the street, make no response at all and keep walking. Note that people who roll their own cigarettes are often suspected of carrying drugs and can be subjected to intensive searches. It is advisable to stick to commercial brands of cigarettes.

Police Whereas in Europe and North America we are accustomed to law enforcement on a systematic basis, enforcement in Argentina is more of a sporadic affair. Many people feel that the police are corrupt and not reliable. In fact, they are usually courteous, and will be helpful to tourists.

Eco travel in Argentina

Argentina is an immense country, and you'll almost inevitably want to book at least a couple of internal flights in order to see one or more areas, especially if these are a far flung as the Iguazú Falls and the glaciers. But spare a thought for the environment: Richard Hammond, the *Guardian's* green travel correspondent reminds you that bus travel is far less damaging to the environment than plane travel: just one seat on a return flight from London to New York does the same damage as a whole year's use of a car with a 2.2 litre engine. (See www.seat61.com.) So consider linking two of your destinations within Argentina by long-distance bus: these can be pretty comfortable, if you book the most expensive ticket, *coche-cama* (car-bed), and often the service includes dinner and drinks as well as an on-board movie or two. And since almost all flights start in Buenos Aires, a bus connection can save you returning to the capital, and work out far cheaper. Buenos Aires to Bariloche is 15 hours, Mendoza to Salta 18 hours, and Puerto Madryn to Bariloche 15 hours.

Eco travel is not just about looking after the physical environment, but can involve a consideration of the impact of tourism on the local community. There are several estancias now committed to generating their own energy, organic farming, and in taking care of their community of employees so that the profits of tourism are fairly distributed: **Los Potreros,** Córdoba; **Colomé winery,** Valles Salchaquíes, Salta; **Estancia Santa Anita,** Salta; **Estancia Huechahue,** Junín de los Andes; **Portal Del Piedra** jungle lodge, Jujuy; **Estancia Peuma Hue,** Bariloche; **Yacutinga Jungle Lodge,** Iguazú.

In the north west of Argentina, where tourism has boomed in the last four years, the impact on local communities is particularly devastating. The provincial governments cheerfully exploit the colourful local culture while sharing little of the profit. So rather than taking a tour with those flashy companies based in Salta city, seek out local indigenous guides in the towns and village you visit, in places like Cachi and San Antonio de los Cobres, Tilcara and Santa Rosa de Tastil. You'll have a far richer experience, and make real contact with Andean and Puna culture, its histories and traditions.

How big is your footprint?

The Travel Foundation, www.thetravelfoundation.co.uk provides the following tips:

- Consider compensating for the environmental impact of your flight. See www.climatecare.org.uk, www.futureforests.com and www.foc-uk.com
- Try to avoid displaying overt wealth, such as expensive jewellery, or carrying your camera very obviously, as this will distance you from the culture you're come to visit.
- Minimize waste by re-using plastic bags, bringing your own water filter bottle, or purifier, and by taking your used batteries home with you.
- Always carry a bag to take waste away with you, and never litter. Patagonia may seem limitless, but your litter will have an effect.
- Use local taxis, and go with local guides when possible, rather than relying on big businesses, as this supports the local economy.
- Hire a car only when you need to. Use alternatives such as public transport, bicycles and walking – which means you're more likely to meet local people too.
- Always, always, ask permission before taking photographs of people or their homes. And don't be offended if they decline, or expect to be paid.
- Don't pick flowers and plants, or remove pebbles and sea shells.
- Buy locally made products. Shop, eat and drink in locally owned outlets, rather than international chains. This brings enormous benefits to local people. At bus stations all over Argentina, local people sell fruit, home made bread and *empanadas* at a fraction of the price of the shops, and often far more delicious.
- Always bargain with humour, and remember that a small cash saving to you could be a significant amount of money to the seller.
- In your hotel, turn off/down air conditioning when it's not required. Switch off lights when leaving the room, and turn the TV off, rather than leaving it on standby.
- Take quick showers instead of baths, and let staff know you're happy to reuse your towels rather than having them replaced daily.

Other useful websites for tips and inspiration: **Tourism Concern**, www.tourismconcern.org.uk, and **Responsible Tourism Awards**, www.responsibletourismawards.info.

Getting around

Air

There are plenty of internal flights from Buenos Aires to all over Argentina with two airlines: **Aerolíneas Argentinas**, and **Lan Chile**. There are some flights between cities without having to return to Buenos Aires, such as Córdoba and Salta, El Calafate and Ushuaia – more in high season. The army airline **LADE**, provides a weekly service connecting towns in Patagonia, useful to avoid going via Buenos Aires – but these are heavily booked ahead of time.

After the devaluation of the peso in 2002, **Aerolineas Argentinas** introduced two price categories: one for Argentines, who are eligible for discounted tickets booked in advance, and one for foreigners, who have to pay the standard fare. See below for information about airpasses (several internal flights prebooked).

All internal flights are fully booked way in advance for travel in December and January, at Easter and in July too. Flights to El Calafate, Ushuaia, Bariloche and Puerto Iguazú are particularly heavily booked, and if travelling during these periods, consider booking at least your first internal flight before you leave home. Outside busy periods, it's usually possible to book internal flights with just a few days' notice, though note that flights to Ushuaia are always heavily booked. It's wise to leave some flexibility in your schedule to allow for bad weather, which may delay flights in the south, at El Calafate and Ushuaia. Meals are rarely served on internal flights, though you'll get a hot drink and a cake. Don't lose your baggage ticket; you won't be able to collect your bags without it.

Airpasses

Airpasses allow you to pre-book between three to six internal flights at a discount as long as your transatlantic flight is also with that company. Airpasses are no longer the most cheapest way of getting around, and can be very restricting since you have to book all dates when you book your international ticket. You'll probably find it easier to book book internal flights separately. But check with the airlines directly, in case they have a promotion: **LAN**, from within Chile T+600-526 2000, from within Argentina T0810-999 9525, www.lan.com; **Aerolineas Argentinas**, T0845-6011915, from within Argentina T0800 222 86527, www.aerolineas.com.

The following are the current cheapest available fares, one way, from Buenos Aires to: Bariloche (two hours) US$140, Salta (two hours) US$125, El Calafate (3¼ hours) US$141, Iguazú (two hours) US$120, Ushuaia (four hours) US$155, Trelew (two hours) US$94, Chapelco ski resort, San Martín de los Andes, (two hours) US$140. Other useful routes for connecting popular destinations without having to return to Buenos Aires: Trelew to El Calafate US$167, Ushuaia to El Calafate US$159, El Calafate to Bariloche US$202.

Bus

This enormous country is connected by a network of efficient long-distance buses, which are by far the cheapest way of getting around, as well as being more environmentally friendly than plane travel. They are safe and comfortable, and long journeys are travelled overnight, which saves time, as long as you can sleep. There are three levels of service: *commún*, which offers little comfort for overnight buses, and with lots of stops (*intermedios*); *semi-cama*, with a slightly reclining seat; and *coche-cama*, where seats recline (some almost completely flat) and there are few stops. On *semi-cama* and *coche-cama* services videos will be shown (usually action movies, very loud, just as you're about to go to sleep), and meals will be provided. This might be anything from a *sandwich de miga* (very soft white bread with a slice of cheese and ham) to a full meal, with wine and a pudding. There will also be a toilet on board (of dubious cleanliness), and the bus will usually stop somewhere en route for toilets and food. The difference in price between the services is often small, and coche-cama is most definitely worth the extra for a good night's sleep. It's a good idea to bring with you on long bus journeys: water, both to drink and for brushing your teeth, as the water in the toilet usually runs out; tissues or toilet roll, fruit or snacks, and a sandwich if you'd vegetarian, since the food provided will inevitably be meaty.

Local buses are to be recommended too: since many Argentines reply o public transport, buses run to small villages and places in mountains, steppe or puna. Services are less frequent, but worth waiting for, to get off the beaten track, and completely away from other tourists. Information on frequency and prices is given in the text, where possible, but services may change, so it's worth ringing the bus terminal to check.

Bus companies may give a 20% student discount if you show an international student card, and to teachers and university professors, with proof of employment, though discounts aren't usually available December to March. You can usually request the seat you want from the computer screen; on old buses, seats at the back can be intolerably noisy with air conditioning (take a sweater in summer, since the air conditioning can be fierce). Make sure your seat number is on your ticket. Luggage is safely stored in a large hold at the back of the bus, and you'll be given a numbered ticket to reclaim it on arrival. *Maleteros* take the bags off the bus, and expect a small tip – 50 centavos or a peso is fine (many Argentines refuse to pay).

Bus company websites: www.andesmar.com.ar www.viabariloche.com.ar useful for route planning across Argentina. The website www.plataforma10.com has useful routes, timetables and prices near Buenos Aires.

Car

It's worth hiring a car if there are several of you, for more freedom in exploring the remoter reaches of the country, where buses and tours may not yet have been established. Go carefully though: distances are huge, and road surfaces in rural places are often earth (*tierra*) or gravel (*ripio*), so allow plenty of time – 60 kph is the maximum speed for cars on *ripio*. Apart from the unreliability of the gravel surface, there are unpredictable potholes and rocks in the road, and swerving at speed is inevitably dangerous. Check the vehicle carefully with the hire company for scratches and cracks in the windscreen before you set off, so that you won't be blamed for them on your return. Some main roads now have private tolls, charging around US$1-2 every 100 km, and generally main roads are in good condition. With the exception of roads around Buenos Aires, there's little traffic and roads are single lane in each direction. Service stations for fuel, toilets, water and food are much further apart than in Europe and the States; so always carry water and keep the tank full .

Car hire

Renting a car costs from US$40 to US$100 a day, depending how big a car you want, and how much mileage (kilometrage) is included: discounts might be offered for longer periods. Busy tourist places are more expensive than quieter towns, but small towns have fewer cars for hire. For most roads, even *ripio*, a conventional car will be fine, but if you're planning to head off into the puna, jungle, or remote parts of Patagonia, consider hiring a four wheel drive vehicle (referred to in the text as 4WD). These may be *camionetas* in Argentina – small trucks, high off the ground, and with space at the back, useful for storing luggage and bicycles. Diesel (*gasoil*) cars are much cheaper to run than petrol (*nafta*), and the fuel is easily available. Make sure that insurance is included, and note that the insurance excess (what you'll have to pay if there's an accident) is extremely high in Argentina, because tourists have a history of turning cars over on *ripio* roads.

You'll need a credit card to hire a car, since companies take a print of the card as their guarantee, instead of a deposit. But don't worry: they are honourable about not using it for extra charges. You'll be required to show a drivers' licence (just the plastic bit of a British licence) and minimum age for renting is 25 (private arrangements may be possible). You must ensure that the renting agency gives you ownership papers of the vehicle, which have to be shown at police and military checks, and if you plan to take the car over a border into Chile or Bolivia, for example, you must let the hire company know, as they'll need to arrange special papers for you to show, and the car must have the numberplate etched on its windows. The multinational car hire companies (**Hertz, Avis**) are represented all over Argentina, along with Brazilian company **Localiza,** who are very reliable. Local companies may be cheaper, but check the vehicles carefully.

Driving in Argentina

Roads Only 29% of Argentina's roads are paved and a further 17% improved. Most main roads are rather narrow but roadside services are good. To avoid flying stones on gravel and dirt roads, don't follow trucks too closely, overtake with plenty of room, and pull over and slow down for oncoming vehicles. Most main roads have private tolls about every 100 km, US$0.20-1.50. Unprivatized secondary roads are generally poor. Internal checkpoints prevent food, vegetable and meat products from entering Patagonia, Mendoza, San Juan, Catamarca, Tucumán, Salta and Jujuy provinces.

Road safety All motorists are required to carry two warning triangles, a fire extinguisher, a tow rope or chain, and a first aid kit. The handbrake must be fully operative and seat belts must be worn. Headlights must be on during the day in Buenos Aires province.

Documents Full car documentation must be carried (including an invoice for the most recently paid insurance premium) together with international driving licence (for non-residents).

Organizations Automóvil Club Argentino (ACA), Av Libertador Gen San Martín 1850, Buenos Aires, T011-4808 4000 or T0800-888 9888, www.aca.org.ar, has a travel documents service, car service facilities and road maps. Foreign automobile clubs with reciprocity with ACA are allowed to use facilities and discounts (with a membership card). ACA accommodation comprises: Motel, Hostería, Hotel, and Unidad Turística, and they also organize campsites. All have meal facilities of some kind.

Fuel

Fuel prices are a third lower in Patagonia than in the rest of the country as no tax is levied. Cars in Argentina are increasingly converting to gas GNC, *gas natural comprimido*, which costs about 25% of using nafta. GNC stations are further apart than petrol stations and there can be long queues, but it's incredibly economical.

Security

Car theft has become common in Buenos Aires, much less so in the rest of the country, but park the car in busy well-lit places, where possible throughout the country. Always remove all belongings and leave the empty glove compartment open when the car is unattended to reduce temptation. In tourist areas, street children will offer to guard your car, worth 50 centavos, or outside restaurant areas in cities, there may be a man guarding cars for a peso.

Cycling

If you have the time, cycling offers you one of the most rewarding ways to explore Argentina. You can get to all the out of the way places, and enjoy some exhilarating rides, especially in the Andes – anywhere between Salta to El Calafate, with some breathtaking and hair-raising rides in the lakes in between. Travelling by bike gives you the chance to travel at your own pace and meet people who are not normally in contact with tourists. There's little traffic on the roads in much of the country, which are wide enough to let trucks past with ease in most places. The challenges are the enormous distances, that there are few places for food and drink stops in much of the country, and there's almost no shade.

Main roads are paved, apart from the famous Route 40 in its southern half, and many roads into rural areas, which are ripio, gravel. For these, a mountain bike is advisable. Bring a comprehensive tool kit and spares. Bike shops are few and far between, although there are excellent shops in the lake district for example. Consider hiring bikes here if you just want some gentle riding for a few days or so. It goes without saying that you'll need tough waterproof panniers and clothing.

Useful tips

Wind, not hills, will be your biggest enemy cycling in Argentina. Try to make the best use of the mornings when wind is lowest. In parts of Patagonia there can be gusting winds of 80 kph around the clock at some times of year, whereas in other areas there can be none. Take care to avoid dehydration by drinking regularly, and carry the basic food staples (sugar, salt, dried milk, tea, coffee, porridge oats, raisins, dried soups, etc) and supplement these with whatever local foods can be found in the markets.

Always camp out of sight of a road. Remember that thieves are attracted to towns and cities, so when sight-seeing, try to leave your bicycle with someone such as a café owner. However, don't take unnecessary risks; always see that your bicycle is secure (most hotels will allow bikes to be kept in rooms). All over Argentina, the dogs are famous for barking at bikes, and some can be vicious; carry a stick or some small stones to frighten them off. There's little traffic on most roads, but make yourself conspicuous by wearing bright clothing and for protection wear a helmet.

Train

The British built a fine network of railways all over the country, which gradually fell into decline through the second half of the 20th century, and were dealt the final blow by handing over control to the provinces in 1994. Few provinces had the resources to run trains and now the few tracks operating run freight trains only.

The only passenger services are within the area of Gran Buenos Aires, to Tigre with **Tren de la Costa**, T011-4732 6343, and an efficient service from Buenos Aires Constitución station south through the Pampas to the coast: via Chascomús to Mar del Plata, Necochea and Tandil, run by **Ferrobaires**, T011-4304 0038. There are only two long-distance train lines: from Buenos Aires to Tucúman with **TUFESA**: long, uncomfortable, and not recommended. The other is from Viedma (on the east coast, south of Bahía Blanca) to Bariloche in the Lake District, a more comfortable overnight service which also takes cars. In Viedma, T02920-422130, in Bariloche, T02944-423172, www.trenpatagonico.com.ar. The only other train services are the tourist **Tren a las Nubes** which runs from Salta up to San Antonio de los Cobres in the puna, and the narrow gauge railway from Esquel in Patagonia, **La Trochita** (made famous by Paul Theroux as the *Old Patagonian Express*), www.latrochita.com.ar.

Maps

Several road maps are available including those of the **ACA** (the most up to date), the **Firestone** road atlas and the **Automapa**, www.automapa.com.ar (regional maps, Michelin-style, high quality). Topographical maps are issued by the **Instituto Geográfico Militar** ⓘ *Av Cabildo 381, Buenos Aires, T011-4576 5578 (one block from Subte Ministro Carranza, Line D, or take bus 152), Mon-Fri, 0800-1300, www.igm.gov.ar*. 1:500,000 sheets cost US$3 each; better coverage of 1:100,000 and 1:250,000, but no city plans. For walkers, the *Sendas y Bosques* (walks and forests) series, are 1:200,000, laminated and easy to read, with good books containing English summaries, www.guiasendasybosques.com.ar, are recommended.

Sleeping

Hotels, hosterías, residenciales and hospedajes

The standard of accommodation in Argentina is generally good, and although prices have risen in the last two years, good hotels are generally very good value for visitors from western countries. You'll find that most cities and tourist towns list hotels and *hosterías* as separate: this is no reflection on quality or comfort, but simply on size: a *hostería* has less than 20 rooms. Both hotels and *hosterías* will have rooms with private bathrooms, (usually showers rather than bath tubs, which you'll find only in the more expensive establishments). Prices often rise in high summer (January/February) at Easter and in July too. During public holidays or high season you should always book ahead. A few of the more expensive hotels in Buenos Aires and major tourist centres such as Puerto Madryn, Bariloche and El Calafate charge foreigners higher prices than Argentines: very frustrating, though there's little you can do about it, since a passport is required as proof of Argentine residency. If you're given a price in US$, ask if there's a reduction if you pay cash in pesos. Most places now accept credit cards, but check before you come. It's worth booking your first few nights' accommodation before you come, and most hotels have an email address on their websites (given throughout the book) so that you can make contact before you come.

Estancias

Estancias are the large farms and cattle ranches found all over the country, many of them now open to tourists, and offering a marvellous insight into Argentine life. Most are extremely comfortable places to stay, and offer wonderful horse riding and other activities such as birdwatching and walking, in addition to the authentic experience of life on the land. They can be pricey but meals, drinks, transfers and activities are included. It will certainly be the most memorable part of your stay.

Estancia tourism An estancia refers to an extensive area of farmed land with a substantial house at its centre, and includes cattle ranches, sheep farms, polo pony stables, tobacco plantations and country houses. These great homes belonging to some of the country's wealthiest landowners are now opening their doors to paying guests offering wonderful places to stay. There's a whole spectrum of estancias from a simple dwelling on the edge of a pristine lake in the Patagonian wilderness to a Loire-style chateau in the Pampas. They might offer incredible luxury and the chance to be completely pampered, or the rare opportunity to spend a few days in the middle of otherwise inaccessible natural beauty and enjoy activities such as walking, fishing, horse riding and birdwatching. Often there's the chance to learn about how the farm is run, watch sheep shearing or to join in with cattle mustering. You'll certainly be treated to the traditional *asado*, meat cooked over an open fire, and most impressively, *asado al palo*, where the animal is speared on a cross-shaped stick and roasted to perfection.

Gauchos still work the land on horseback in their traditional outfit of *bombachas* (baggy trousers, comfortable for spending hours on horseback), *trensa* (a wide leather belt with silver clasps), a *poncho* (in the northwest), a *pañuelo* (neckerchief), a *boyna* (beret) and on the feet *alpargatas* (simple cotton shoes). The best part about an estancia visit is the chance to get to know the *dueños* (owners) and gain an insight into the history and traditions of estancia life, which is so essential to understanding the country. Some estancia owners have turned to tourism as a means of earning

Sleeping price codes

LL	over US$200	C	US$31-45
L	US$151-200	D	US$21-30
AL	US$101-150	E	US$12-20
A	US$66-100	F	US$7-11
B	US$46-65	G	US$6 and under

Prices are for a double room in high season, including taxes.

extra income as farming fails to be profitable, and on some estancias it is fast becoming their main activity, with added facilities like a pool or tennis courts. Perhaps the most charming places simply offer the splendour of their land, and the genuine hospitality of the owners. Many speak English and are fascinating hosts.

Price Estancias can be pricier than hotels, but since devaluation, are now accessible even to travellers on a budget, at least for a day visit. *Día de campo* (day on the farm) is offered by lots of estancias, a full day of horse riding, or a ride in a horse-drawn carriage, an *asado* lunch, and then often other farm activities, or time to relax in the peaceful grounds. Overnight stays costs from US$50 for two in the most humble places, to US$150 per person for the most luxurious, with all meals, drinks, transfers and activities included.

Location Though estancias are found throughout rural Argentina, they vary enormously in style and activities. In the province of Buenos Aires you will find estancias covering thousands of hectares of flat grassland with large herds of cattle and windpumps to extract water; horse riding will certainly be offered and perhaps cattle-mustering, at La Luisa and Palantelén for example. Some of the finest buildings are in this area, such as Dos Talas and La Porteña. In Patagonia there are giant sheep estancias overlooking glaciers, mountains and lakes, such as estancias **Maipú**, **Helsingfors** or **Alma Gaucha**. There are estancias on Tierra del Fuego, full of the history of the early pioneers who built them: **Viamonte** and **Harberton**, while on the mainland nearby, **Estancia Monte Dinero**, has a colony of Magellanic penguins on its doorstep. There's more wildlife close at hand in the estancias on Península Valdés. And in Salta, there are colonial-style *fincas* whose land includes jungly cloudforest with marvellous horse riding.

Further information The most distinctive or representative estancias are mentioned in the text, but for more information see the national tourist website: www.turismo.gov.ar, in English, with all estancias listed, www.vivalaspampas.com.ar for estancias in the province of Buenos Aires, and www.caminodelgaucho.com.ar, an excellent organization which can arrange stays in the Pampas estancias. www.estanciasdesantacruz.com is a helpful agency which arranges estancia stays Santa Cruz and the south, including transport, and www.raturstancias.com.ar, which covers estancias over the whole country. A useful book *Tursimo en Estancias y Hosterías* is produced by **Tierra Buena**, www.tierrabuena.com.ar, who arranges visits through www.southtrip.com. You can of course contact estancias directly, and reserve, ideally with a couple of weeks warning.

Cabañas

Cabañas are a great option if you have transport and there are at least two of you. These are self-catering cottages, cabins, or apartments, usually in rural areas, and often in superb locations. They're tremendously popular among Argentine holiday makers, who tend to travel in large groups of friends, or of several families together, and as a result, the best *cabañas* are well-equipped and comfortable. They can be very economical, too, especially for groups of four or more, but are feasible even for two, with considerable reductions off season. If you're travelling by public transport, cabañas are generally more difficult to get to, but ask the tourist office if there are any within walking or taxi distance. Throughout the Lake District, *cabañas* are plentiful and competitively priced with hotels for two or more.

Camping

Organized campsites are referred to in the text immediately below hotel lists, under each town. Camping is very popular in Argentina (except in Buenos Aires) and there are many superbly situated sites, most have good services, whether municipal, or private. There are many quieter, family orientated places, but if you want a livelier time, look for a campsite (often by the beaches) with younger people, where there's likely to be partying until the small hours. Camping is allowed at the side of major highways and in all national parks (except at Iguazú Falls), but in Patagonia strong winds can make camping very difficult. Wherever you camp, pack out your rubbish, and put out fires with earth and water. Fires are not allowed in many national parks because of the serious risk of forest fires. It's a good idea to carry insect repellent.

Equipment If taking a cooker, the most frequent recommendation is a multi-fuel stove which will burn unleaded petrol or, if that is not available, kerosene or white fuel. Alcohol-burning stoves are simple reliable, but slow and you have to carry a lot of fuel. Fuel can usually be found in chemists/pharmacies. Gas cylinders and bottles are usually exchangeable, but if not can be recharged; specify whether you use butane or propane. Gas canisters are not always available. White gas (*bencina blanca*) is readily available in hardware shops (*ferreterías*).

Eating and drinking

Food

Asado and parrillas

The great classic meal throughout the country is the *asado* – beef or lamb cooked expertly over an open fire. This ritual is far more than a barbecue, and with luck you'll be invited to sample an asado at a friend's home or estancia, to see how it's done traditionally. *Al asador* is the way meat is cooked in the country, with a whole cow splayed out on a cross shaped stick, stuck into the ground at an angle over the fire beneath. And in the *parrilla* restaurants, found all over Argentina, cuts of meat are grilled over an open fire in much the same way. You can order any cuts from the range as individual meals, but if you order *parrillada* (usually for two or more people), you'll be brought a selection from the following cuts: *achuras* – offal, *chorizos* – sausages including *morcilla* – British black pudding or blood sausage, *tira de asado* – ribs, *vacío* – flank, *bife ancho – entrecote*, *lomito* – sirloin, *bife de chorizo* – rump steak, *bife de lomo* – fillet steak. You can ask for '*cocido*' to have your meat well-done, a '*punto*' for medium, and '*jugoso*' for rare. Typical accompaniments are *papas fritas* (chips), salad, and the spicy *chimichurri* sauce made from oil, chilli pepper, salt, garlic and vinegar.

Other typically Argentine meals → *See also language glossary page 620.*

Other Argentine dishes to try include the *puchero*, a meat stew; *bife a caballo*, steak topped with a fried egg; *achoripán*, a roll with a chorizo inside (hot dog). *Puchero de gallina* is chicken, sausage, maize, potatoes and squash cooked together. *Milanesas*, breaded, boneless chicken or veal, are found everywhere and good value. Good snacks are *lomitos*, a juicy slice of steak in a sandwich; and *tostados*, delicate toasted cheese and tomato sandwiches, often made from the soft crustless *pan de miga*.

Italian influences

It might seem that when Argentines aren't eating meat, they're eating pizza. Italian immigration has left a fine legacy in thin crispy pizzas available from even the humblest pizza joint, adapted to the Argentine palate with some unusual toppings. *Palmitos* are tasty, slightly crunchy hearts of palm, usually tinned, and a popular Argentine delicacy, though they're in short supply, and the whole plant has to be sacrificed for one heart. They're often accompanied on a pizza with the truly unspeakable *salsa golf*, a lurid mixture of tomato ketchup and mayonnaise. You'll probably prefer excellent *provolone* or roquefort on your pizza – both Argentine and delicious. Fresh pasta is widely available, bought ready to cook from dedicated shops. Raviolis are filled with ricotta, *verduras* (spinach), or *cuatro quesos* (four cheeses), and with a variety of sauces. These are a good option for vegetarians, who need not go hungry in this land of meat. Most restaurants have *pasta casero* – homemade pasta – and sauces without meat, such as *fileto* (tomato sauce) or pesto. *Ñoquis* (gnocchi), potato dumplings normally served with tomato sauce, are cheap and delicious (traditionally eaten on the 29th of the month). But vegetarians must specify: '*No como carne, ni jamón, ni pollo*', (I don't eat meat, or ham, or chicken) since many Argentines think that vegetarians will eat chicken or ham, and will certainly not take it seriously that you want to avoid all meat products.

Eating price codes

ΨΨΨ over US$15
ΨΨ US$7-15
Ψ under US$7

Prices refer to the cost of a two-course meal for one person, excluding drinks or service charge.

Vegetarian

Vegetables in Argentina are cheap, of excellent quality, many of them organic, and available fresh in *verdulerías* (vegetable shops) all over towns. Look out for *acelga*, a large leafed chard with a strong flavour, often used to fill pasta, or *tarta de verduras*, vegetable pies, which you can buy everywhere, fresh and very good. Butternut squash, *zapallo*, is used to good effect in *tartas* and in filled pasta. Salads are quite safe to eat in restaurants, and fresh, although not wildly imaginative. The basic salad is *ensalada mixtaFor a two-course meal for one person, excluding drinks or service charge*, which can involve nothing more exotic than lettuce, tomato, carrot and onion, but often there will be *remolacha* (fresh beetroot), *choclo* (sweet corn) and boiled egg too. Only in remote areas in the north west of the country should you be wary of salads, since the water here is not reliable.

Regional specialities

Throughout Argentina The Argentine speciality *empanadas* are tasty small semicircular pies traditionally filled with meat, but now widely available filled with cheese, *acelga* (chard) or corn. They originate in Salta and Tucumán, where you'll still find the best examples, but can be found all over the country as a starter in a *parrilla*, or ordered by the dozen to be delivered at home with drinks among friends.

Northwest Around Salta and Jujuy you'll find *humitas*, parcels of sweet corn and onions, steamed in the corn husk, superb, and *tamales*: balls of corn flour filled with beef and onion, and similarly wrapped in corn husk leaves to be steamed. The other speciality of the region is *locro* – a thick stew made of maize, white beans, beef, sausages, pumpkin and herbs. Good fish is serves in many areas of the country. Along the east coast, you'll always be offered *merluza* (hake), *lenguado*, (sole), and often salmon too.

Atlantic Coast If you go to Puerto Madryn or the Atlantic coast near Mar del Plata, the seafood is a must: *arroz con mariscos* is similar to paella and absolutely delicious. There will often be *ostras* (oysters) and *centolla* (king crab) on the menu too.

Lake District In the lakes, trout are very good, best served grilled, but like all Argentine fish, you'll be offered a bewildering range of sauces, such as roquefort, which drowns the flavour rather. Also try smoked trout and the wild boar. Berries are very good here in summer, with raspberries and strawberries abundant and flavoursome, particularly around El Bolsón. And in Puehuenia, you must try the pine nuts of the monkey puzzle trees: sacred food to the Mapuche people.

Northeast In the northeast, there are some superb river fish to try: *pacú* is a large, firm fleshed fish with lots of bones, but very tasty. The other great speciality is *surubí*, a kind of catfish, particularly good cooked delicately in banana leaves.

Desserts

Argentines have a sweet tooth, and are passionate about *dulce de leche* – milk and sugar evaporated to a pale, soft fudge, and found on all cakes, pastries, and even for breakfast. If you like this, you'll be delighted by *facturas* and other pastries, stuffed with *dulce de leche*, jams of various kinds, and sweet cream fillings. *Helados* (ice cream) is really excellent in Argentina, and for US$1.50 in any *heladeria*, you'll get 2 flavours, from a huge range, piled up high on a tiny cone; an unmissable treat. Jauja (El Bolsón) and Persicco (Buenos Aires) are the best makes. Other popular desserts are *dulce de batata*, a hard, dense sweet potato jam, so thick you can carve it, *dulce de membrillo* (quince preserve), *dulce de zapallo* (pumpkin in syrup); all eaten with cheese. The most loved of all is flan, not a flan at all, but crème caramel, often served on a pool of caramelized sugar, and pretty good. Every Argentine loves *alfajores*, soft maize-flour biscuits filled with *dulce de leche* or apricot jam, and then coated with chocolate, especially the brand Havanna. Croissants (*media lunas*) come in two varieties: *de grasa* (savoury, made with beef fat) and *dulce* (sweet and fluffy). These will often be your only breakfast since Argentines are not keen on eating first thing in the morning (because they've only just had dinner), and only supply the huge buffet style 'American breakfast' in international hotels to please tourists.

Drink

The great Argentine drink, which you must try if invited, is **mate** (pronounced mattay). A kind of tea made from dried yerba leaves, drunk from a cup or seasoned gourd through a silver perforated straw, it is shared by a group of friends or work colleagues as a daily social ritual. The local **beers**, mainly lager-type, are fine: Quilmes is the best seller, but look out for homemade beers from microbreweries in the lakes, especially around El Bolsón. **Spirits** are relatively cheap, other than those that are imported; there are cheap drinkable Argentine gins and whiskeys. Clericó is a white-wine **sangría** drunk in summer. It is best not to drink the **tap water**; in the main cities it's safe, but often heavily chlorinated. Never drink tap water in the northwest, where it is notoriously poor. Many Argentines mix soda water with their wine (even red wine) as a refreshing drink.

Wines

Argentine wines are excellent and drinkable throughout the price range. Red grape varieties of Merlot, Syrah, Cabernet Sauvignon, and the white Torrontes are particularly recommended; try brands Lurton, Norton, Bianchi, Trapiche or Etchart in any restaurant. Good champagnes include the brut nature of Navarro Correas, whose Los Arboles cabernet sauvignon is an excellent red wine, and Norton's Cosecha Especial. See Mendoza and Salta chapters for more details.

Eating out

Restaurants rarely open before 2100 and most people turn up at around 2230, often later. If you're invited to someone's house for dinner, don't expect to eat before 2300, and have a few *facturas* at 1700, the Argentine *merienda*, to keep you going. The siesta is strictly observed everywhere but Buenos Aires city. Offices usually close between 1300 and 1630. At around 1700, many people go to a *confitería* for *merienda* – tea, sandwiches and cakes. Dinner usually begins at 2200 or 2230; Argentines like to eat out, and usually bring babies and children along, however late it is.

If you're on a tight budget, ask for the *menu fixo* (set price menu), usually good value, also try *tenedor libre* restaurants – eat all you want for a fixed price. Markets usually have cheap food. Food in supermarkets is cheap and good quality.

The *mate* ritual

Mate (pronounced *mattay*) is the essential Argentine drink. All over the country, whenever groups of Argentines get together, they share a *mate*. Try it, at least once. It's a stimulating green tea made from the leaves of the yerba mate plant, *ilex paraguaiensis*, encouraged by the Jesuits as an alternative to alcohol, and grown in their plantations in the northeast of Argentina. The *mate* container is traditionally made of a hollowed gourd, but can also be wood or tin, and there are ornate varieties made to traditional gaucho patterns by the best silversmiths.

Dried yerba leaves are placed in the *mate* to just over half full, and hot water is added to create the infusion, which is then sipped through a *bombilla*, a perforated metal straw. One person in the group acts as *cebador*, trickling fresh hot water into the mate and passing it to each person in turn to sip. The water must be at 80-82°c (just as the kettle starts to 'sing') and generally *mate* is drunk *amargo* – without sugar. But add a little if it's your first time, as the drink is slightly bitter. The drink is mildly stimulating, less so than caffeine, and effective at ridding the body of toxins as well as being mildly laxative and diuretic. When you've had enough, simply say *gracias* as you hand the mate back to the *cebador*, and you'll be missed out on the next round.

If you're invited to drink *mate* on your visit to Argentina, always accept, and then keep trying it: it might take a few attempts before you actually like the stuff. And don't worry – you won't catch any diseases from the *bombilla*. To share a *mate* is to be part of a very special Argentine custom, and you'll delight your hosts by giving it a go.

Entertainment

Argentines, of whatever age, are extremely sociable and love to party. This means that even small towns have a selection of bars catering for varied tastes, plenty of live music and somewhere to dance, even if they are not the chic clubs you might be used to in western urban cities. The point of going out here is to meet and chat rather than drink yourself under the table, and alcohol is consumed in moderation. Argentines are amazed at the quantities of alcohol that northern Europeans put away. If invited to an Argentine house party, a cake or *masitas* (a box of little pastries) will be just as much appreciated as a bottle of wine.

Dancing → *For further information, see Background page 602.*

Argentines eat dinner at 2200, and then go for a drink at around 2400, so the dancing usually starts at around 0200, and goes on till 0600 or 0700. *Boliches* can mean anything from a bar with dancing, found in most country towns, to a disco on the outskirts, a taxi ride away from the centre. In Buenos Aires, there's a good range of clubs, playing the whole range from tango, salsa, and other Latin American dance music, to electronic music. Elsewhere in Argentina nightclubs play a more conventional mixture of North American and Latin American pop with a bit of Argentine *rock nacional* thrown in, though you'll find a more varied scene in bigger cities like Córdoba, Rosario and Mendoza. **Tango** classes are popular all over the country, and especially in Buenos Aires, where *milongas* are incredibly trendy: a class followed by a few hours of dancing. Even if you're a complete novice, it's worth trying at least one class to get a feel for the steps; being whisked around the floor by an experienced dancer is quite a thrill even if you haven't a clue what to do with your legs.

Music

Live music is everywhere in Argentina, with bands playing Latin American pop or jazz in bars even in small cities. The indigenous music is *folclore* (pronounced foke-LAW-ray) which varies widely over the country. Traditional gaucho music around the pampas includes *payadores*: witty duels with guitars for two singers, much loved by Argentines, but bewildering if your Spanish is limited to menus and directions. The northwest has the country's most stirring folclore, where you should seek out *peñas* to see live bands playing fabulous *zambas* and *chacareras*. The rhythms are infectious, the singing passionate, and Argentine audiences can't resist joining in. Even tourist oriented peñas can be atmospheric, but try to find out where the locals go, like **La Casona del Molino** in Salta. Most cities have *peñas*, and you'll often see some great bands at the gaucho **Day of Tradition** festivals (mid-November) throughout Argentina and at local town fiestas (dates given in the relevant town's sections).

Festivals and events

The main holiday period is January to March when all Argentine schoolchildren are on holiday and most families go away for a few weeks, or even two months. All popular tourist destinations become extremely busy at this time, with foreign visitors adding to the crowds, particularly in Bariloche, El Calafate and Ushuaia. You should book transport and accommodation ahead at these times. During Easter week, and the winter school holidays throughout July, hotels may also fill fast, particularly in ski resorts. No one works on the national holidays, and these are often long weekends, with a resulting surge of people to popular holiday places.

Public holidays and festivals

1 Jan, **Good Fri**, **2 Apr**, **1 May**, **25 May**, **10 Jun**, **20 Jun**, **9 Jul**, **17 Aug**, **12 Oct** and **25 Dec**. Banks are closed and there are limited bus services on 25 and 31 Dec.

There are gaucho parades throughout Argentina on the days leading up to the Día de la Tradición, **10 Nov**, with fabulous displays of horsemanship, gaucho games, enormous *asados* and traditional music. It's worth seeing the festivities in any small town.

On **30 Dec** (not 31 because so many offices in centre are closed) there is a ticker-tape tradition in downtown Buenos Aires: it snows paper and the crowds stuff passing cars and buses with long streamers.

The northwest particularly, has a rich culture, and many colourful festivals, such as Pachamama, which you can join in some places; see page 293.

Shopping

Best buys

Shopping in Argentina is relatively cheap for visitors from western Europe and USA since the devaluation of the peso in 2002. Argentine fashion and leather goods are particularly good value; shoes, sunspecs and outdoor gear too, are very reasonably priced, and if you have a free afternoon in Buenos Aires, it might be worth considering buying your holiday clothes here when you arrive: head straight for Palermo Viejo.

Tax free shopping is relatively easy and worth following this simple procedure, to get the IVA (shopping tax) returned to you at the airport as you leave the country; Shop at places displaying the Global Refund TAX FREE sign. Before you pay, ask for the TAX FREE refund form. The shop must fill this out for you as you pay. Keep this form, in the envelope they'll give you, together with your receipt. At the airport, once you've passed through security, and before going through passport control, look out for the Tax Free kiosk. Hand them all your Tax Free envelopes, with the receipts, and they will give them the customs stamp. Then once you've gone through passport control, look for the Tax Free Refund desk, also called Assist Card, where your stamped forms will be taken, and the tax will be refunded either in cash or to your credit card. See www.globalrefund.com for more information, or call in Argentina T011-4342 2413.

Argentine specialities

In Buenos Aires, leather is the best buy, with many shops selling fine leather jackets, coats and trousers, as well as beautifully made bags and shoes. With a mixture of Italian influenced design, and a flavour of the old gaucho leather-working traditions, there's a strong emerging Argentine style.

Handicrafts, *artesanía*, are available all over the country, and are distinctly region to region. Traditional gaucho handicrafts, available across most of the country, include woven or plaited leather belts of excellent quality, as well as key rings and other pieces made of silver. These are small and distinctive and make excellent gifts. Look out, too, for the traditional baggy gaucho trousers, *bombachas*, comfortable for days in the saddle, and ranging from cheap sturdy cotton to smart versions with elaborate tucks.

Take home a *mate*, the hollowed gourd, often decorated, and the silver *bombilla* that goes with it, for drinking the national drink. In the northwest there are beautifully made woven items: brightly coloured rugs, or saddle mats, and the country's best ponchos. Look out for the hand-dyed and woven ponchos, instead of the mass-produced variety, available in smaller rural areas, or in the fine handicrafts market at Salta or Catamarca. There are the deep red Güemes versions or soft fine ponchos made of *vicuña* (a local cousin of the llama), usually in natural colours. In markets all over the northwest, you'll find llama wool jumpers, hats and socks, and brightly coloured woven bags, Bolivian influenced, but typical of the puna region. There are also fine carved wooden pieces. In the lakes too, there's lots of woodwork, and weavings of a different kind, from the Mapuche peoples, with distinctive black and white patterns. Smoked fish and meat, and delicious homemade jams from *sauco* (elderberry) or *frambuesa* (raspberry) are among the local delicacies. In the northeast, there are Guaraní handicrafts such as bows and arrows. Argentina's national stone, the fleshy pink and marbled rhodochrosite, is mined in the northwest, but available all over Buenos Aires too, worked into fine jewellery, and less subtle paperweights and ashtrays.

Sport and activities

Argentina's spectacular geography offers a huge range of adventure tourism from white water rafting to skiing, and some of the finest trekking and horse riding anywhere in the world. The variety of climates and terrain means that there's enormously varied wildlife and birdlife, particularly in the extensive network of national parks, and some of the finest fishing on the planet in many places. Spectator sports are heavily biased towards football, but there's polo and basketball too.

If you're looking for culture and history, there are good museums of Buenos Aires, but perhaps even more fascinating are the ancient cultures of the northwest. And you can delve further into the past at several pre-historic sites and along the dinosaur belt. You could base a whole trip around the picturesque wine producing areas of Argentina, and to get to the heart of the country's great rural tradition, seek out the estancias.

Climbing

The Andes offer great climbing opportunities. Among the most popular peaks are Aconcagua, in Mendoza province, Pissis in Catamarca, and Lanín and Tronador, reached from the Lake District. The northern part of Los Glaciares National Park, around El Chaltén, has some spectacular peaks with very difficult mountaineering. Climbing clubs (**Club Andino**) can be found in Mendoza, Bariloche, Esquel, Junín de los Andes, Ushuaia and other cities and in some places equipment can be hired.

Fishing

Argentina offers some of the world's finest fishing, in beautiful virgin landscape, and with good accommodation. In the Lake District, there's world renowned fly fishing for trout (rainbow, brown and brook); and for chinook or landlocked salmon. The epicentre is around Junín de los Andes and Bariloche, in rivers Quilquihue, Chimehuín, Collón-Curá, Meliquina and Caleufú, and Lagos Traful, Gutiérrez, Mascardi, Cholila, Futalaufquen (in Los Alerces National Park), Falkner, Villarino; Huechulafquen, Paimún, Epulafquen, Tromen (all in Lanín National Park), and, in the far north, Quillén. Throughout the lakes, the season lasts usually from November to Easter.

In Tierra del Fuego, huge brown trout can be fished from Río Grande, and Lago Fagnano, while over the border in Chilean Tierra del Fuego, Lago Blanco is fast becoming popular. In the northeast, sorubim and giant pacu can be fished at the confluence of rivers Paraná and Paraguay, as well as dorado, known for its challenging fight. The closed season in this area is November to January. On the Atlantic Coast, San Blas is famous for shark fishing, for bacota shark and bull shark weighing up to 130kg, while all along the coast, there's good sea fishing. Fishing can also be found in other parts of the country and is offered by many estancias. Pejerrey, corvina and pescadilla can be found in large quantities along the coast of Buenos Aires province, and many of the reservoirs of the Central Sierras, the West and Northwest are well stocked.

All rivers are 'catch and release', and to fish anywhere in Argentina you need a permit costing US$5 per day, US$15 per week, US$50 per year. It certainly makes sense to do some research before you arrive, to find the right area for the kind of fishing you want to do. The national tourism website has a helpful section: www.turismo.gov.ar/pesca; fishing queries to fishing@turismo.gov.ar will be answered in 48 hours, and they produce a helpful booklet *Pesca Deportiva en la Patagonia Argentina*, which you can request. www.flyfishingtravel.com is a good site in English with descriptions of places you can fish and where to stay, and if you're looking for fishing guides, contact the following in Chubut, rsm@teletel.com.ar in Neuquén, patout@smandes.com.ar and www.guiaspatagonicos.com.ar for northern Patagonia. For fishing licences, contact the **Fly Fishing Association of Argentina**, T011-4773 0821, and for Patagonia, there's assistance from the **National Parks Administration**, T011-4311 8853/0303. More details are provided in the travelling text for the appropriate area.

Birdwatching

It's no surprise in a country so rich in untouched natural habitats that the bird life is extraordinary, and extremely varied. From the wealth of seabirds at Península Valdés to the colourful species in the subtropical rainforest near the Iguazú Falls from the marshlands of Esteros del Iberá or the Chaco savannah to the Lake District and the mountainous interior of Tierra del Fuego there marvellous opportunities to spot birds. At least 980 of the 2926 species of birds registered in South America exist in Argentina, and in many places, with easy access. There are specialist tours led by expert guides in most areas: see the travelling text for details.

All Patagonia, www.allpatagonia.com/Eng, runs birdwatching trips in Patagonia and Tierra del Fuego. In the northeast, contact the excellent Daniel Samay of **Explorador Expediciones**, www.rainforestevt.com.ar, and in the Lake District, **Angel Fernandez**, T02944-524609, T15609799, is warmly recommended, along with **Daniel Feinstein**, T/F02944-442259, both extremely knowledgeable. An excellent British-based tour operator who can arrange bird watching trips is **Select Latin America**, T020-7407 1478, www.selectlatinamerica.co.uk.

Skiing

The skiing season runs from mid-June to mid-October, but dates vary between resorts. The country's best, and deservedly famous is Las Leñas, south of Mendoza, due to its long, varied and challenging pistes, its spectacular setting, superb accommodation, and also for being a dedicated snowboarding area. It's also the most expensive resort, and if you're looking for a cheaper option in the same area, consider Los Penitentes, a more modest but friendly resort. There's good skiing all along the Lake District, with the biggest centre at Cerro Catedral, near Bariloche. This is a huge resort with scope for cross country skiing and snowboarding, and the advantages of major town with excellent hotels and services. Nearby, the smaller but upmarket resorts of Cerro Bayo at Villa la Angostura and Cerro Chapelco at San Martín de los Andes have even more beautiful settings and cater for families. La Hoya, near Esquel, is much cheaper with a laid-back family feel. And at the end of the world, in Ushuaia, there's great cross-country skiing at Cerro Castor, as well as downhill. Details of all of these resorts are given in the text, together with their websites.

Trekking

The whole of the west of the country, along the mountains of the Andes, offers superb opportunities for trekking. The Lake District in summer is the most rewarding because there are so many spectacular landscapes to explore within easy reach of the centres of Bariloche, El Bolsón and San Martín de los Andes. The national parks here are well set-up for walkers, with good information and basic maps available, and *refugios* and campsites convenient for accommodation in longer hikes. However, it's worth exploring the lesser known extremes of the lakes, at Pehuenia in the north, with wonderful walks among the araucaria trees, and at Los Alerces National Park with trekking into the virgin forest. All these walks are described in detail in the relevant areas. The season for walking is December to April.

The mountainous region to the west of Mendoza, around Aconcagua, offers good and challenging trekking, as well as further north in the Cordon del Plata in San Juan, where oasis villages in the valley are good bases for several peaks around Mercedario. Altitude sickness (see Health, page 58) can be a problem in these areas, and you should allow time in your schedule for adjustment. Further north, in Salta and Jujuy, there's a complete contrast of landscape. The puna to the west is dramatic desert, dropping to the arid and rocky mountainous landscape in the Quebrada de Humahuaca, and continuing east, there are cloudforests. It's possible to walk through all three zones in a single extended expedition, though you'd need to go with a guide. Throughout the area there are attractive villages to use as bases for day walks. In the northeast, there are a few good walks in the national park of the Iguazú Falls, and many more good places to walk in the provinces to the south. The centre of the country, in the sierras around Córdoba are good for day walks, especially in the Traslasierra. In Patagonia, there are petrified forests and caves with pre-historic handprints to walk to, as well as the remoter reaches of Parque Nacional Perito Moreno. The most dramatic trekking is in the south of Patagonia, whether in the mountains around Mount Fitz Roy or ice trekking on the glaciers themselves in Parque Nacional los Glaciares. And near Ushuaia, there are unforgettable views from peaks in the Parque Nacional Tierra del Fuego, along the shores of the Beagle Channel and from wilder peaks in mountains behind the town.

These are the highlights, but wherever you go in Argentina, you can find somewhere to trek . The spaces are wide open and there really are no limits. Try checking out www.parquesnacionales.gov.ar for more detailed information.

What to take You could consider taking the following equipment: many of the clothes and camping supplies are available in large towns. **Clothing**: a warm hat (wool or man-made fibre), wicking thermal underwear, T-shirts/shirts, trousers (quick-drying and preferably windproof, never jeans), warm (wool or fleece) jumper/jacket (preferably two), gloves, waterproof jacket and over trousers (preferably Gore-Tex), shorts, walking boots and socks, change of footwear or flip-flops. **Camping gear**: tent (capable of withstanding high winds), sleeping mat (closed cell, Karrimat, or inflatable, Thermarest), sleeping bag (three-season minimum), sleeping bag liner, stove and spare parts, fuel, matches and lighter, cooking and eating utensils, pan scrubber, survival bag. **Food**: take supplies for at least two days more than you plan to use; tea, coffee, sugar, dried milk; porridge, dried fruit, honey; soup, pasta, rice, soya (TVP); fresh fruit and vegetables; bread, cheese, crackers; biscuits, chocolate; salt, pepper, other herbs and spices, cooking oil. **Miscellaneous**: map and compass, torch and spare batteries, pen and notebook, Swiss army knife, sunglasses, sun cream, lip salve and insect repellent, first aid kit, water bottle, toiletries and towel.

Safety Hikers have little to fear from the animal kingdom apart from insects, and robbery and assault are very rare. You are much more of a threat to the environment than vice versa. Leave no evidence of your passing and carry out your litter.

Whitewater rafting

There are some good whitewater rafting runs in Mendoza province, near the provincial capital and near San Rafael and Malargüe. In the Lake District there are possibilities in the Lanín, Nahuel Huapi and Los Alerces national parks.

Health

Before you go

Ideally, you should see your GP/practice nurse or travel clinic at least six weeks before your departure for general advice on travel risks and recommended vaccinations. Your local pharmacist can also be a good source of readily accessible advice. Make sure you have travel insurance, get a dental check (especially if you are going to be away for more than a month), know your own blood group and if you suffer a long-term condition such as diabetes or epilepsy make sure someone knows or that you have a Medic Alert bracelet/necklace with this information on it.

Recommended vaccinations

Vaccinations for rabies, hepatitis B and tuberculosis are commonly recommended for Argentina. The final decision, however, should be based on a consultation with your GP or travel clinic. You should also confirm your primary courses and boosters are up to date (diphtheria, tetanus, poliomyelitis, hepatitis A, typhoid). A yellow fever certificate is recommended if travelling to other parts of South America.

A-Z of health risks

Altitude sickness

Acute mountain sickness can strike from about 3000 m upwards and in general is more likely to affect those who ascend rapidly (for example by plane) and those who over-exert themselves. Acute mountain sickness takes a few hours or days to come on and presents with heachache, lassitude, dizziness, loss of appetite, nausea and vomiting. Insomnia is common and often associated with a suffocating feeling when lying down in bed. You may notice that your breathing tends to wax and wane at night and your face is puffy in the mornings – this is all part of the syndrome. If the symptoms are mild, the treatment is rest and painkillers (preferably not aspirin-based) for the headaches. Should the symptoms be severe and prolonged it is best to descend to a lower altitude immediately and reascend, if necessary, slowly and in stages. The symptoms disappear very quickly – even after a few hundred metres of descent.

The best way of preventing acute mountain sickness is a relatively slow ascent. When trekking to high altitude, some time spent walking at medium altitude, getting fit and acclimatising is beneficial. When flying to places over 3000 m a few hours' rest and the avoidance of alcohol, cigarettes and heavy food will go a long way towards preventing acute mountain sickness.

Bites and stings

This is a very rare event indeed for travellers, but if you are unlucky (or careless) enough to be bitten by a venomous snake, spider, scorpion or sea creature, try to identify the culprit, without putting yourself in further danger (do not try to catch a live snake).

Snake bites in particular are very frightening, but in fact rarely poisonous – even venomous snakes bite without injecting venom. Victims should be taken to a hospital or a doctor without delay. It is not advised for travellers to carry snake bite antivenom as it can do more harm than good in inexperienced hands. Reassure and comfort the victim frequently. Immobilize the limb with a bandage or a splint and get the patient to lie still. Do not slash the bite area and try to suck out the poison. This also does more harm than good. You should apply a tourniquet in these circumstances, but only if you know how to. Do not attempt this if you are not experienced.

Certain tropical fish inject venom into bathers' feet when trodden on, which can be exceptionally painful. Wear plastic shoes if such creatures are reported. The pain can be relieved by immersing the foot in hot water (as hot as you can bear) for as long as the pain persists.

Diarrhoea and intestinal upset

Diarrhoea can refer either to loose stools or an increased frequency of bowel movement, both of which can be a nuisance. Symptoms should be relatively short-lived but if they persist beyond two weeks specialist medical attention should be sought. Also seek medical help if there is blood in the stools and/or fever.

Adults can use an antidiarrhoeal medication such as loperamide to control the symptoms but only for up to 24 hours. In addition keep well hydrated by drinking plenty of fluids and eat bland foods. Oral rehydration sachets taken after each loose stool are a useful way to keep well hydrated. These should always be used when treating children and the elderly.

Bacterial traveller's diarrhoea is the most common form. Ciproxin (Ciprofloxacin) is a useful antibiotic and can be obtained by private prescription in the UK. You need to take one 500 mg tablet when the diarrhoea starts. If there are so signs of improvement after 24 hours the diarrhoea is likely to be viral and not bacterial. If it is due to other organisms such as those causing giardia or amoebic dysentery, different antibiotics will be required.

The standard advice to prevent problems is to be careful with water and ice for drinking. Ask yourself where the water came from. If you have any doubts then boil it or filter and treat it. There are many filter/treatment devices now available on the market. Food can also transmit disease. Be wary of salads (what were they washed in, who handled them), re-heated foods or food that has been left out in the sun having been cooked earlier in the day. There is a simple adage that says wash it, peel it, boil it or forget it. Unpasteurised dairy products can also transmit a range of diseases.

Hepatitis

Hepatitis means inflammation of the liver. Viral causes of the disease can be acquired anywhere in the world. The most obvious symptom is a yellowing of your skin or the whites of your eyes. However, prior to this all that you may notice is itching and tiredness. Pre-travel hepatitis A vaccine is the best bet. Hepatitis B (for which there is a vaccine) is spread through blood and unprotected sexual intercourse, both of which can be avoided.

Malaria

Malaria can cause death within 24 hours and can start as something just resembling an attack of flu. You may feel tired, lethargic, headachy, feverish; or more seriously, develop fits, followed by coma and then death. Have a low index of suspicion because it is very easy to write off vague symptoms, which may actually be malaria. If you have a temperature, visit a doctor as soon as you can and ask for a malaria test. On your return home, if you suffer any of these symptoms, have a test as soon as possible. Even if a previous test proved negative, this could save your life.

Treatment is with drugs and may be oral or into a vein depending on the seriousness of the infection. Remember ABCD: Awareness (of whether the disease is present in the area you are travelling in), Bite avoidance, Chemoprohylaxis, Diagnosis.

To prevent mosquito bites wear clothes that cover arms and legs, use effective insect repellents in areas with known risks of insect-spread disease and use a mosquito net treated with an insecticide. Repellents containing 30-50% DEET (Di-ethyltoluamide) are recommended when visiting malaria endemic areas; lemon eucalyptus (Mosiguard) is a reasonable alternative. The key advice is to guard against contracting malaria by taking the correct anti-malarials and finishing the recommended course. If you are popular target for insect bites or develop lumps quite soon after being bitten use antihistamine tablets and apply a cream such as hydrocortisone.

Remember that it is risky to buy medicine, and in particular anti-malarials, in some developing countries. These may be sub-standard or part of a trade in counterfeit drugs.

Rabies

Rabies is endemic throughout certain parts of South America so be aware of the dangers of the bite from any animal. Rabies vaccination before travel can be considered but if bitten always seek urgent medical attention (regardless of whether you have been vaccinated), after first cleaning the wound and treating with an iodine base disinfectant.

Sun

Take good heed of advice regarding protecting yourself against the sun. Overexposure can lead to sunburn and, in the longer term, skin cancers and premature skin aging. The best advice is simply to avoid exposure to the sun by covering exposed skin, wearing a hat and staying out of the sun if possible, particularly between late morning and early afternoon. Apply a high factor sunscreen (greater than SPF15) and also make sure it screens against UVB. A further danger in tropical climates is heat exhaustion or more seriously heatstroke. This can be avoided by good hydration, which means drinking water past the point of simply quenching thirst. Also when first exposed to tropical heat take time to acclimatize by avoiding strenuous activity in the middle of the day. If you cannot avoid heavy exercise it is also a good idea to increase salt intake.

Underwater health

If you plan to dive make sure that you are fit do so. The **British Sub-Aqua Club (BSAC)** ⓘ *Telford's Quay, South Pier Rd, Ellesmere Port, Cheshire CH65 4FL, UK, T01513-506200, www.bsac.com*, can put you in touch with doctors who will carry out medical examinations. Check that any dive company you use are reputable and has appropriate certification from **BSAC** or **PADI** ⓘ *Unit 7, St Philips Central, Albert Rd, St Philips, Bristol, BS2 OTD, T0117-3007234, www.padi.com.*

Water

There are a number of ways of purifying water. Dirty water should first be strained through a filter bag and then boiled or treated. Bring water to a rolling boil for several minutes. There are sterilizing methods that can be used and products generally contain chlorine (eg Puritabs) or iodine (eg Pota Aqua) compounds. There are a number of water sterilizers now on the market available in personal and expedition size. Make sure you take the spare parts or spare chemicals with you and do not believe everything the manufacturers say.

Other diseases and risks

There are a range of other insect borne diseases that are quite rare in travellers, but worth finding out about if going to particular destinations. Examples are sleeping sickness, river blindness and leishmaniasis. Fresh water can also be a source of diseases such as bilharzia and leptospirosis and it is worth investigating if these are a danger before bathing in lakes and streams. Also take heed of advice regarding protecting yourself against the sun (see above) and remember that unprotected sex always carries a risk and extra care is required when visiting some parts of the world.

Further information

Books

Dawood R (editor). *Travellers' health*, 3rd Ed. Oxford University Press, 2002.

Warrell, David and Sarah Anderson (editors) *Expedition Medicine*, The Royal Geographic Society, ISBN 1 86197 040-4.

Websites

Foreign and Commonwealth Office (FCO) (UK), www.fco.gov.uk.

The National Travel Health Network and Centre (NaTHNaC) www.nathnac.org.

World Health Organisation, www.who.int.

Fit for Travel (UK), www.fitfortravel.scot.nhs.uk. This site from Scotland provides a quick A-Z of vaccine and travel health advice requirements for each country.

Keeping in touch

Communications

Internet

The best way to keep in touch is undoubtedly by email. Telephone is expensive in Argentina, and so all Argentines have adapted rapidly to Internet, with broadband widely available even in small towns, many of them also offering Skype. Most *locutorios* (phone centres) also have internet, and there are dedicated centres on almost every block in town. Prices vary, the more expensive in more remote towns from around US$0.80 to US$2 per hour.

Post

Letters from Argentina take 10-14 days to get to Europe and the USA. Rates for letters up to 20 g to Europe and USA: US$1.40, up to 150g, US$8. Post can be sent from the Correo (post office) or from private postal service Oca, through any shop displaying the purple sign. The post service is reliable, but for assured delivery, register everything.

Small parcels of up to 2kg can be sent from all post offices. Larger parcels must be sent from the town's main post office, where your parcel will be examined by customs to make sure that the contents are as stated on your customs form, and taken to *Encomiendas Internacionales* for posting. Any local *correo* (post office) can tell you where to go. Customs usually open in the morning only. Having parcels sent to Argentina incurs a customs tax, which depends on the value of the package, and all incoming packages are opened by customs. Poste restante is available in every town's main post office, fee US$1.

Telephone

Phoning in Argentina is made very easy by the abundance of *locutorios* – phone centres with private booths where you can talk for as long as you like, and pay afterwards, the price appearing on a small screen in your booth. There's no need for change or phone cards, and locutorios often have Internet, photocopying and fax services. The system works as follows: walk in and ask '*Una cabina, por favor*' and you'll be given a number corresponding to one of the booths in the shop. Simply dial from the comfort of the booth, as many calls as you like. They're added up and you pay at the counter at the end. All *locutorios* have phone directories, and staff are usually helpful sources of information. For local calls, if you can't find a *locutorio*, use a public payphone with coins, often next to *kioskos*, minimum 25 centavos.

Using the phone is relatively expensive in Argentina, and even the friendly and helpful Argentines will rarely offer you their phone to make a call. One solution is to carry a ready supply of plastic phone cards, which are much cheaper for long-distance national and international calls. Two good brands are Argentina Global and Hable Mas, available from kioskos and locutorios for 5 or 10 pesos. Dial the free, 0800, number on the card, and a code (which you scratch the card to reveal), and you can phone anywhere in the world. These can sometimes be used in locutorios too, though the rates are more expensive, and sometimes from your hotel room too: ask reception.

Media

Newspapers

The national daily papers are *La Nación*, a broadsheet, intelligent and well-written (www.lanacion.com.ar), *Clarín* more accessible, also a broadsheet (www.clarin.com.ar). Both these papers have good websites and excellent Sunday papers with informative travel sections. Other daily national papers are *La Prensa*, *La Razón*, and the left wing *Página-12*, always refreshing for a different perspective. There's a daily paper in English, the *Buenos Aires Herald*, www.buenosaires herald.com, which gives a brief digest of world news, as well as Argentine news. Magazines you might like to look at include: *Noticias* news and culture, *Gente* a kind of *Hello!* for Argentina, *El Gráfico*, a good sports magazine, and particularly *Lugares*. This glossy monthly travel magazine has superb photography and is a very useful resource for travel tips and ideas of where to go, often with English translation at the back. Issues are themed; the Northwest, the lakes, etc, and previous issues are often available from *kioskos* too.

Few foreign language newspapers are available outside Buenos Aires, but to keep in touch with world news, websites of your own favourite newspaper are invaluable. Many hotels have cable TV in the rooms, but rarely have any English news channels.

Buenos Aires

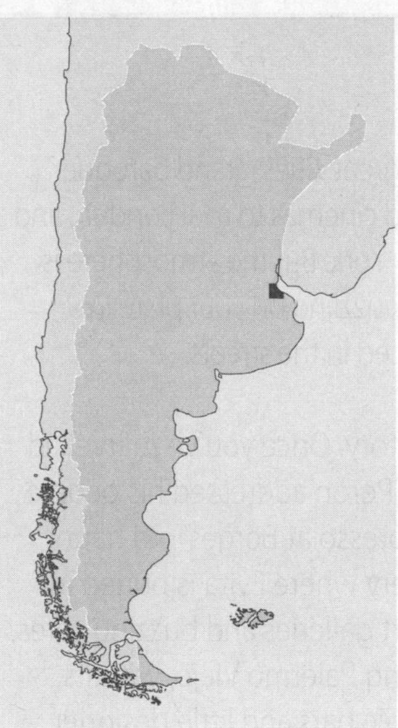

Footprint features

Introduction

Buenos Aires is one of the world's great cities: grand baroque buildings to rival Paris, theatres and cinemas to rival London, and restaurants and shops to rival New York. But the atmosphere is uniquely Argentine, from the steak sizzling on your plate in a crowded *parrilla* to the tango danced in the streets.

The city seethes with life and history. Once you've marvelled at the grand Casa Rosada where Perón addressed his people in Plaza de Mayo, and sipped espresso at Borges' old haunt, Café Tortoni, head to the cemetery where Evita is buried in swish Recoleta, amid stunning art galleries and buzzing cafés. Take a long stroll around charming Palermo Viejo, with its enticing cobbled streets full of chic bars and little designer shops. Or explore beautifully crumbling San Telmo, the oldest part of the city, for its Sunday antique market where tango dancers passionately entwine among the fading crystal and 1920s' tea sets.

Buenos Aires' nightlife is legendary and starts late. You'll have time for world class opera at opulent Teatro Colón, or your first tango class at a *milonga*, before tucking into piquant empanadas, a huge steak and a glass of fine Argentina Malbec at around 2300. Superb restaurants abound; wander around the renovated docks at Puerto Madero, try the trendy eateries of Las Cañitas or the hip hangouts of Palermo Viejo. Or combine the pleasures of fine food and a dazzling tango show. Nothing better crystallizes the Argentine psyche than this sensuous dance.

But if the city's thrills become too intense, take a train up the coast to the pretty 1900's suburb of San Isidro or take a boat through the lush jungly Tigre Delta, where you can hide away in a cabin, or retreat to a luxury lodge until you're ready for your next round of shopping, eating and dancing.

Don't miss...

1 **Teatro Colón** Take in a concert of world-class opera in Buenos Aires' most opulent building, page 76.

2 **MALBA** If you only have time for one museum, make it this one. Sizzling hot Latin American art in a cool building, page 78.

3 **Palermo Viejo** Stroll by the chic shops before sitting down to eat at one of the smart new restaurants overlooking the plaza, page 82.

4 **San Telmo** Wander through the Sunday market and soak up the free tango, great food and live music in crumbling splendour, page 83.

5 **Boca Juniors** Worship at the shrine of Argentina's real religion: football, page 85, and see a match in La Boca, page 102.

6 **Tigre** Take a boat trip along overgrown rivers and stay the night in chic isolation at La Pascuala, page 116.

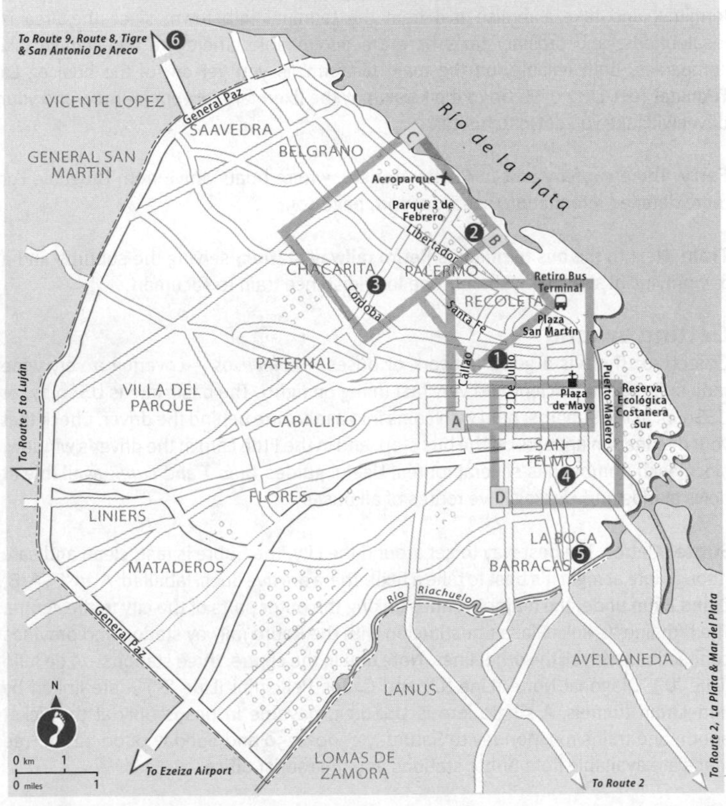

Ins and outs

Getting there

→ *Phone code: 011. Population: 2,776,138 (Greater Buenos Aires: 12,046,799)*

Air Buenos Aires has two airports: **Ezeiza**, for international flights, 35 km southwest of the centre, T011-5480 6111, and **Aeroparque** for domestic flights, just to the north of Palermo, T011-4576 5111. To get from **Ezeiza**, there's an efficient bus service run by **Manuel Tienda León** linking Ezeiza with the centre, (every 30 minutes, charging US$8.50 for the 40-minute journey). Alternatively, take a reliable radio taxi (such as Onda Verde – T011-4867 0000) US$15, or a *remise* taxi – these have a fixed fare, and can be from a desk at the airport, and charge US$18. Manuel Tienda León is the most reliable company, and has a clearly visible desk by Arrivals. **Aeroparque** is 4 km north of the city centre, right on the riverside, just 15 minutes drive from anywhere in the centre of town. Manuel Tienda León buses charge US$5 for the 20-minute journey to the centre, *remises* US$6 and ordinary taxis US$4. Again, Manuel Tienda León is the most reliable company. Their office in town is near Retiro bus station and from here you can order a radio taxi. But ask them about their free transfer service to hotels in the centre of town. There's a left luggage office here, phone and banks with ATMs a block away.

Bus Buses connect Buenos Aires with towns all over Argentina and from neighbouring countries, arriving at Retiro bus terminal at Ramos Mejía y Antártida Argentina, about five blocks north of Plaza San Martín, T011-4310 0700. Always take a radio taxi to the terminal, and take a remise taxi from the terminal into town, since the area is insalubrious, and ordinary taxis here are not reliable. There are two *remise* taxi companies, both reliable, on the main platform as you get out of the bus: eg **La Terminal** T011-4312 0711. Go to the kiosk, pay the fixed fare for your journey, and your driver will take you down to his car.

Ferry There's a ferry port at Puerto Madero, where boats arrive from Uruguay. For more detailed information, see Transport, page 105.

Train Next to the bus terminal is **Retiro railway station**, serving the suburbs and a few provincial stations, with only one long-distance train to Tucumán.

Getting around

Colectivo There is a good network of buses – *colectivos* – covering a very wide radius; frequent, efficient and very fast (hang on tight). The basic fare is US$0.27, or US$0.45 to the suburbs, paid with coins into a machine behind the driver. Check that your destination appears on the bus stop, and in the little card in the driver's window, since each number has several routes. Useful guides *Guía T* and *Lumi*, available at news stands and *kioskos*, give routes of all buses.

Subte (Metro) The best way to get around the city, the Subte is fast, clean and safe (though late at night it's best to take a taxi). There are five lines, labelled 'A' to 'E'. A, B, D and E run under the major avenues linking the outer parts of the city to the centre. The fifth line 'C' links Plaza Constitución with the Retiro railway station and provides connections with all the other lines. Note that in the centre, three stations – 9 de Julio (Line 'D'), Diagonal Norte (Line 'C') and Carlos Pellegrini (Line 'B') – are linked by pedestrian tunnels. A single fare is US$0.25, payable in pesos only at the ticket booth, and trains run Monday to Saturday 0500-2250 and Sunday 0800-2200. Free maps are available from Subte stations and the tourist office.

Taxi Taxis are painted yellow and black, and carry 'Taxi' flags, but for security they should never be hailed on the street. Taxis are the notorious weak link in the city's security, and you should always phone a **Radio Taxi**, since you're guaranteed that they're with a registered company; some 'Radio Taxis' you see on the street are false. Call one of these numbers: **Onda Verde**: T011-4867 0000; **Radio Taxi Sur**, T011-4638 2000, **Radio Taxi 5 Minutos**, T011-4523 1200, **Radio Taxi Diez**, T011-4585 5007, give your address and a taxi will pick you up in five minutes. You may need to give a phone number for reference – use your hotel number, and be ready to describe what you're wearing for identification. Ask your hotel before you leave for the day which taxi company they use, as these will be reliable, and then you can always call that company when you're out, giving the hotel name as a reference. Fares are shown in pesos. The meter starts at US$0.35 when the flag goes down; make sure it isn't running when you get in. A fixed rate of US$0.04 for every 200 m or one-minute wait is charged thereafter. A charge is sometimes made for each piece of hand baggage (ask first). Alternatively, *remise* taxis charge a fixed rate to anywhere in town, and are very reliable, though can work out more expensive for short journeys. **La Terminal**, T011-4312 0711 is recommended, particularly from Retiro bus station. *Remise* taxis operate all over the city; they are run from an office, have no meter but charge fixed prices, which can be cheaper than regular taxis. About 10% tip is expected. For more detailed transport information, see page 105.

Metro (Subte)

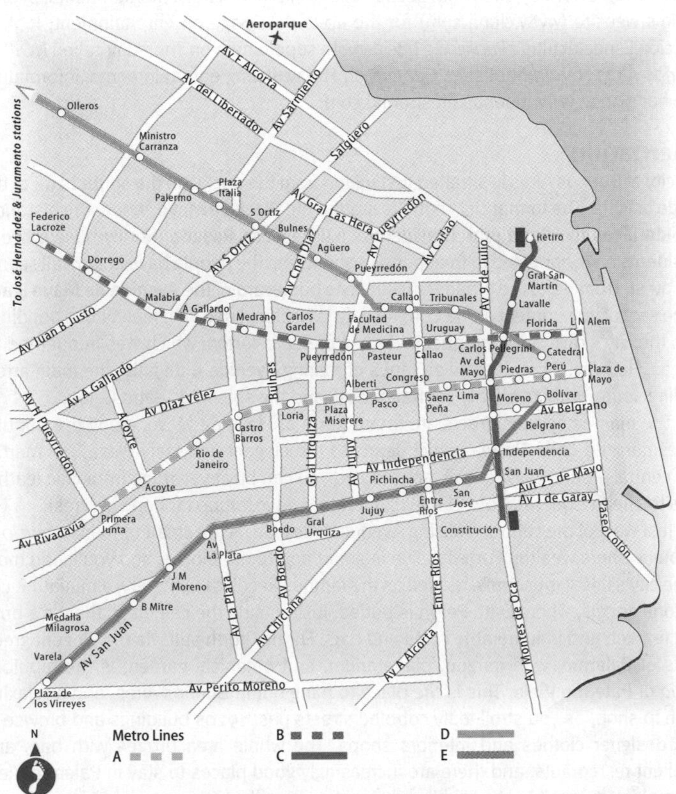

Tourist information

Tourist offices The **national office** ⓘ *Av Santa Fe 883, T011-4312 2232/5550, info@turismo.gov.ar, Mon-Fri 0900-1700*, provides maps and literature covering the whole country. There are kiosks at both **airports** (in the Aerolíneas Argentinas section of Aeroparque), daily 0800-2000. There are **city-run tourist kiosks** at ⓘ *Florida 100, junction with Roque Sáenz Peña*, in **Recoleta** ⓘ *Av Quintana 596, junction with Ortiz*, in **Puerto Madero** ⓘ *Dock 4*, in **San Telmo** ⓘ *Defensa 1250*, and at **Retiro bus station** (ground floor). For free tourist information anywhere in the country T0800-555 0016.

For **city information** ⓘ *T011-4313 0187, Mon-Fri 0730-1800, Sat, Sun 1000-1800, www.bue.gov.ar, in Spanish, English and Portuguese.* Free guided tours are usually organized by the city authorities: free leaflet from city-run offices. Audio guided tours in several languages are available for 12 different itineraries by downloading mp3 files and maps from www.bue.gov.ar. **Tango Information Centre** ⓘ *1st floor at Galerías Pacífico, Sarmiento 1551*, is a privately run tourist office, very helpful.

Information Good guides to bus and subway routes are *Guía T*, *Lumi*, *Peuser* and *Filcar* (usually covering the city and Greater Buenos Aires in two separate editions), US$1- 9 available at news stands. Also handy is Auto Mapa's pocket-size *Plano* of the federal capital, or the more detailed *City Map* covering La Boca to Palermo, both available at news stands, US$4.30; otherwise it is easy to get free maps of the city centre from most hotels. *Buenos Aires Day & Night* is a free bi-monthly tourist magazine with useful information and a downtown map available together with similar publications at tourist kiosks and hotels. *La Nación* has a Sunday tourism section (very informative). On Friday, the youth section of *Clarín* (*Sí*) lists free entertainments. Search Clarín's website (www.clarin.com) for the up-to-date page on entertainment; look at 'Sección Espectáculos'. *Página 12* has a youth supplement on Thursday called *NO*. The *Buenos Aires Herald* publishes *Get Out* on Friday, listing entertainments. Information on what's on at www.buenosairesherald.com.

Orientation

The city of Buenos Aires is situated just inland from the docks on the south bank of the Río de la Plata. The formal city centre is around the **Plaza de Mayo**, where the historical **Cabildo** faces the florid pink presidential palace **Casa Rosada**, from whose balcony presidents have appealed to their people, and where the people have historically come to protest. From here, the broad Parisian-style boulevard of the **Avenida de Mayo** leads to the seat of government at the Congreso de la Nación, lined with marvellous buildings from the city's own belle époque, including the *Café Tortoni* which was frequented by Borges. Halfway, it crosses the 22 lanes of roaring **Avenida 9 de Julio**, the main artery leading south, with its mighty central obelisk and the splendid Teatro Colón.

The main shopping streets are found north of Plaza de Mayo, along the popular pedestrianized **Calle Florida**, which leads to the elegant and leafy Plaza San Martín. This central area is easy to walk around and you can buy everything from chic leather bags to cheap CDs, with lots of banks, internet and *locutorios* (phone centres).

Just west of the centre, crossing Avenida 9 de Julio, is the smart upmarket *barrio* of **Recoleta** where wealthy *Porteños* live in smart apartment blocks, and you'll find most of the city's finest museums, as well as the famous Recoleta Cemetery, a miniature city of stone angels, where Evita Perón is buried. Just outside the cemetery, there's a busy craft market, and innumerable cafés and bars. Further north still, via the elegant green parks of **Palermo**, with its zoo, planetarium, and botanical garden, is the fabulous *barrio* of **Palermo Viejo**. This is *the* place to hang out in Buenos Aires, and a relaxing place to shop, as you stroll leafy cobbled streets past 1920s buildings and browse in cool designer clothes and interiors shops. The whole area buzzes with bars and excellent restaurants, and there are increasingly good places to stay in Palermo Viejo too, making it possible to avoid the city centre altogether if you want a quieter stay.

Puerto Madero has become the most popular place to eat close to the centre, with busy restaurants filling the handsome brick warehouses on the stylishly renovated docks area. This is a good place to go for an early evening drink, and stroll past old sailing ships and painted cranes. Further south, the green spaces of the **Costanera Sur** are busy in summer with Porteños relaxing, groups of friends sipping *mate* or barbecuing steak. Here there's a Reserva Ecológica where you could retreat for some inner city wildlife, and walk or cycle for a couple of hours. Just inland, the city's most atmospheric *barrio* is irresistible **San Telmo**, once the city's centre, with narrow streets where cafés and antique markets are tucked away in the attractively crumbling 1900's buildings. Now the area is a lively and bohemian artistic centre with a popular market in the quaint Plaza Dorrego on Sundays, where tango is danced for tourists among stalls selling silver, plates and bric-a-brac. Nightlife is lively here, but the city's best restaurants can be found in Recoleta, Palermo Viejo, or the Las Cañitas area in between the two.

Street layout

Streets are organized on a regular grid pattern, with blocks numbered in groups of one hundred. It's easy to find an address, since street numbers start from the dock side rising from east to west, and north/south streets are numbered starting from Avenida Rivadavia, one block north of Avenida de Mayo, and rise in both directions. Calle Juan D Perón used to be called Cangallo, and Scalabrini Ortiz used to be Canning (the old names are still referred to). Avenida Roque Sáenz Peña and Avenida Julio A Roca are commonly referred to as Diagonal Norte and Diagonal Sur respectively.

Background

Although Buenos Aires was founded in 1580, nothing remains of this early settlement, which didn't take off as a city for some 200 years. It has none of the colonial splendour of Salta (in the northwest of Argentina), because while Salta was by then a busy administrative centre on the main trade route for silver and mules from the main Spanish colony of Alto Perú, Santa María del Buen Aire, the city of the 'good winds', was left to fester, her port used only for a roaring trade in contraband. Some say that this is the source of the typically '*vivo*' attitude of the Porteños today – always looking to take advantage of someone – perfectly depicted in the recent movie *Nine Queens* – a convincing theory! But Jesuits came and built schools, churches and the country's first university in what is now San Telmo, a legacy left in the Manzana de las Luces, which you can still explore today.

In 1776 Buenos Aires became Viceroyalty of the Río de la Plata area, putting it firmly on the map for trade, and the city's strategic position on this estuary brought wealth and progress. A British invasion in 1806 was quickly quelled, but sparked a surge for independence in the burgeoning Argentine nation. After separating from Spain in 1816, Buenos Aires became its new capital, giving the Porteños a further sense of pride.

By 1914, Buenos Aires was rightfully regarded as the most important city in South America. The wealth generated from the vast fertile pampas manifested in the flamboyant architecture you see in Teatro Colón, Avenida de Mayo and the palaces of Recoleta. Massive waves of immigration from Italy and Spain had arrived in Buenos Aires in the late 19th-century, creating the characteristic Argentine identity, and the language described most accurately as Spanish spoken by Italians. The tango was born, music filled with nostalgia for the places left behind, and currently enjoying a revival among 20-somethings, who fill the *milongas*, breathing new passion into old steps. Now, nearly a third of the country's 36 million inhabitants live in Gran Buenos Aires, in the sprawling conurbation which stretches west from the smart areas of Palermo, San Isidro and Martinez, to the poorer Avellanda and La Matanza. It's one of the world's great cities, and a fine start to your trip to Argentina.

City centre

Plaza de Mayo

This broad open plaza is both the historic heart of the city, and its centre of power, since it's surrounded by some of the city's most important public buildings. Just behind the Plaza de Mayo were the city's original docks, where Argentina's wealth was built on exporting meat and leather from the Pampas. All the country's powers are gathered nearby, and the Plaza remains the symbolic political centre of the city. Most famously, there's pink Casa de Gobierno or **Casa Rosada** ⓘ *T011-4344 3804, tours Mon-Fri 1600 (Spanish and English on Fri only), book 2 hrs earlier at Hipólito Yrigoyen 219, passport required, free*, which lies on the east side, looking out towards the Río Plata, and contains the offices of the president of the Argentine Republic. The **Museo de los Presidentes** ⓘ *in the basement of the same building, T011-4344 3804, www.museo.gov.ar, Mon-Fri 1000-1800, Sun 1400-1800, guided visits in Spanish, Sun 1500 and 1630, free*, has historical memorabilia. The changing of the guards takes place every two hours from 0700-1900.

The decision to paint the seat of government pink resulted from President Sarmiento's desire to symbolize national unity by blending the colours of the rival factions which had fought each other for much of the 19th century: the Federalists (red) and the Unitarians (white). The colour itself was originally derived from a mixture of lime and ox blood and fat, to render the surface impermeable. The Plaza has been the site of many historic events: Perón and Evita frequently appeared on its balcony before the masses gathered in the plaza, and when the economy crumbled in December 2001, angry crowds of *cacerolazas* (including middle-class ladies banging their *cazerolas*, or saucepans) demonstrated outside, together with angry mobs. Since 1970, the Mothers and now, Grandmothers, of the Plaza de Mayo (*Madres de los Desaparecidos*) have marched in silent remembrance of their children who disappeared during the 'dirty war'. Every Thursday at 1530, they march anti-clockwise around the central monument with photos of their disappeared loved-ones pinned to their chests. In the plaza, there are statues of General Belgrano in front of the Casa Rosada and of Columbus, behind the Casa Rosada in the Parque Colón. The guided tours of the Casa de Gobierno allow you to see its statuary and the rich furnishing of its halls and its libraries.

Opposite the Casa Rosada, on the west side of the plaza, is the white-columned **Cabildo**, which has been rebuilt several times since the original structure was erected in the 18th century; most recently the façade in 1940. Inside, where the movement for independence from Spain was first planned, is the **Museo del Cabildo y la Revolución** ⓘ *T011-4334 1782, Tue-Fri 1030-1700, Sun 1130-1800, US$0.35; guided visits Tue, Thu 1200, 1400; Fri 1500; Sun 1630, US$0.70*, which is worth a visit, especially for the paintings of old Buenos Aires, the documents and maps recording the May 1810 revolution, and memorabilia of the 1806 British attack, as well as Jesuit art. In the patio is a café and stalls selling handicrafts (Thursday-Friday 1100-1800).

Many of the centre's most important buildings date from after 1776 when Buenos Aires underwent a big change, now the capital of the new viceroyalty and the official port. The **Cathedral Metropolitana** ⓘ *Rivadavia 437, T011-4331 2845, Mon-Fri 0800-1900, Sat-Sun 0900-1930; guided visits Mon-Fri at 1130 (San Martín's mausoleum and crypt) and 1315 (religious art), and daily at 1530 (temple and crypt); Jan-Feb Mon-Sat at 1100, both temple and crypt; Mass is held daily, check for times*, on the north side of the plaza, lies on the site of the first church in Buenos Aires, built in 1580. The current structure was built in French neoclassical style between 1758 and 1807, and inside, in the right-hand aisle, guarded by soldiers in fancy uniforms, is the imposing tomb of General José de San Martín (1880) Argentina's greatest hero who liberated the country from the Spanish.

Just east of the cathedral, the **Banco de la Nación** is regarded as one of the great works of the famous architect Alejandro Bustillo (who designed **Hotel Llao Llao** in Bariloche). Built 1940-1955, its central hall is topped by a marble dome 50 m in diameter. Take in all these buildings, and you become aware that the banks, political and religious institutions, together with the military headquarters opposite, are all gathered in one potent place. No wonder then that people always come here to demonstrate.

La City

Just north of the Plaza de Mayo, between 25 de Mayo and the pedestrianized Calle Florida, lies the main banking district known as La City, with some handsome buildings to admire. The **Banco de Boston**, Florida 99 and Avenida RS Peña, dates from 1924, and while there are no guided visits, you can walk inside during banking hours to appreciate its lavish ceiling and marble interior. There's the marvellous art-deco **Banco de la Provincia de Buenos Aires**, at San Martín 137, built in 1940, and the **Bolsa de Comercio**, at 25 de Mayo y Sarmiento, which dates from 1916 and houses the stock exchange, though visits aren't permitted. The **Banco Hipotecario** (formerly the Bank of London and South America), Reconquista y B Mitre, was designed by SEPRA (Santiago Sánchez Elia, Federico Peralta Ramos, and Alfredo Agostini). It was completed in 1963, in bold 'brutalist' design. You can visit during banking hours.

The **Basílica Nuesta Señora de La Merced** ⓘ *J D Perón y Reconquista 207, Mon-Fri 0800-1800*, founded in 1604 and rebuilt 1760-1769, was used as a command post in 1807 by Argentine troops resisting the British invasion. Its highly decorated interior has an altar with an 18th-century wooden figure of Christ, the work of indigenous carvers from Misiones, and it has one of the few fine carillons of bells in Buenos Aires. A craft fair is held on Thursday and Friday 1100-1900. Next door, at Reconquista 269, is the **Convento de la Merced** originally built in 1601, but reconstructed in the 18th and 19th centuries with a peaceful courtyard in its cloisters.

There are a few rather dry museums here, purely for historians: **Museo Numismático Dr José Evaristo Uriburu** , in the Banco Central library, tells the history of the country through its currency; **Museo y Biblioteca Mitre**, ⓘ *San Martín 336, T011-4394 8240, Mon-Fri 1300-1830, US$0.30*, preserves intact the colonial-style home of President Bartolomé Mitre. More interesting and accessible is the bizarre **Museo de la Policía Federal** ⓘ *San Martín 353, piso 8 y 9, T011-4394 6857, Tue-Fri 1400-1800*, which portrays the fascinating history of crime in the city, and includes an absolutely gruesome forensic section, definitely not for the squeamish.

South of Plaza de Mayo

To the south west of the Plaza de Mayo, towards San Telmo, there is an entire block of buildings built by the Jesuits between 1622 and 1767, called the **Manzana de las Luces** (Enlightenment Square) – bounded by streets Moreno, Alsina, Perú and Bolívar. The former Jesuit church of **San Ignacio de Loyola**, (see below for tours), begun in 1664, is the oldest colonial building in Buenos Aires and the best example of the baroque architecture introduced by the Jesuits (renovated in the 18th and 19th centuries), with splendid golden naves dating from 1710-1734. Also in this block are the **Colegio Nacional de Buenos Aires** ⓘ *Bolivar 263, T011-4331 0734*, formerly the Jesuits' Colegio Máximo in the 18th century, and now the city's most prestigious secondary school. Below these buildings are **18th-century tunnels** ⓘ *T011-4342 4655*. These are thought to have been used by the Jesuits for escape or for smuggling contraband from the port. For centuries the whole block was the centre of intellectual activity, and although little remains to see today, the history is fascinating.

All **guided tours** ⓘ *from Perú 272, Mon-Fri 1500, Sat-Sun 1500, 1630, 1800 (Mon 1300 free tour) in Spanish (in English by prior arrangement), arrive 15 mins before tour, US$1.40*, explore the tunnels; only weekend tours include San Ignacio and Colegio Nacional.

Buenos Aires centre

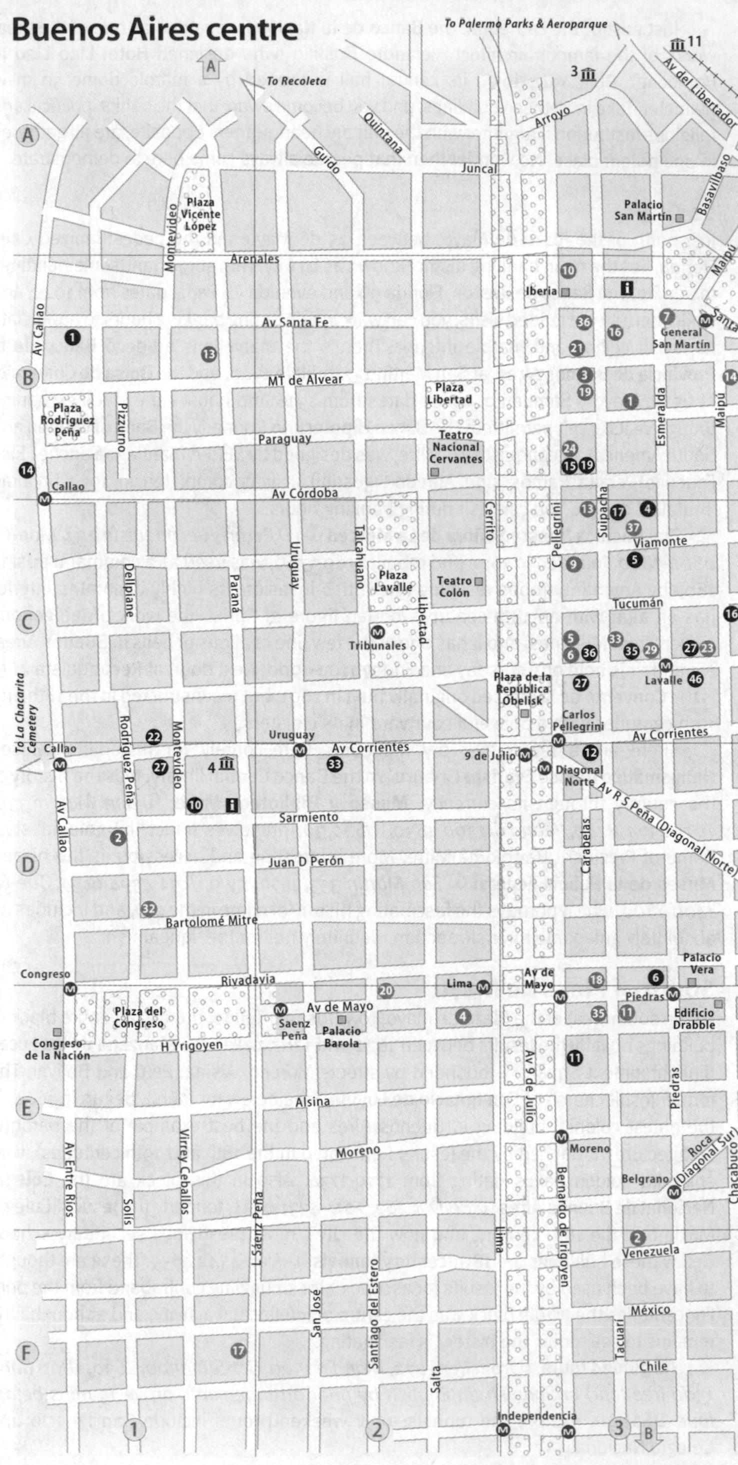

Sleeping
Aspen Towers 1 *B3*
Bisonte Palace 3 *B3*
Castelar 4 *E2*
Che Lagarto 2 *F3*
Colón 6 *C3*
Crillón 7 *B3*
Dolmen 16 *B3*
Dorá 14 *B3*
El Cachafaz 9 *C3*
El Conquistador 19 *B3*
El Hostal de Granados 8 *F4*
Embajador 10 *B3*
España 11 *E3*
Frossard 12 *C4*
Goya 13 *C3*
La Casa de Etty 17 *F1*
La Giralda 18 *D3*
Marbella 20 *E2*
Marriott Plaza 21 *B4*
NH City 26 *E4*
O'Rei 23 *C3*
Orly 25 *B4*
Panamericano 5 *C3*
Pestana 24 *B3*
Plaza San Martín Suites 36 *B3*
Regis 29 *C3*
St Nicholas 32 *D1*
Suipacha Inn 33 *C3*
Uruguay 35 *E3*
V&S 37 *C3*
Waldorf 38 *B4*
Gran Victoria 17 *C3*
Güerrín 33 *D2*
La Casona del Nonno 35 *C3*
La Chacra 19 *B3*
La Estancia 36 *C3*
La Madeleine 1 *B1*
La Trastienda 8 *E5*
La Ventana 45 *E4*
Los Inmortales 46 *C3*
Morizono 48 *B4*
Richmond 54 *C4*
Sorrento 25 *C4*
Tancat 20 *B4*

Eating
Aroma 3 *B4*
Brasserie Petanque 9 *F4*
Broccolino 4 *C3*
Café Tortoni 6 *D3*
Chiquilín 10 *D1*
Clásica y Moderna 14 *B1*
Club Español 11 *E3*
Confitería Ideal 12 *D3*
El Gato Negro 22 *C1*
El Palacio de la Papa
Frita 27 *C3/D1*
El Querandí 28 *E4*
Empire Bar 30 *B4*
Exedra 15 *B3*
Florida Garden 31 *B4*
Fratello 16 *C3*
Gianni's 5 *C3*

Bars & clubs
Celta 2 *D1*
Druid In 7 *A4*
Kilkenny 18 *B4*
La Cigale 23 *B4*
Milion 13 *B1*
Porto Pirata 24 *B4*
Temple 21 *B3*

Museums
Casa de Gobierno (Casa Rosada) & Museo de los Presidentes 1 *D5*
Centro Cultural San Martín, Museo de Arte Moderno & Teatro Municipal San Martín 4 *D1*
Museo de Arte Hispanoamericano Isaac Fernández Blanco 3 *A3*
Museo de la Ciudad 5 *E4*
Museo de la Policía Federal 13 *D4*
Museo del Cabildo y la Revolución 6 *E4*
Museo Etnográfico JB Ambrosetti 8 *E4*
Museo Nacional Ferroviario 11 *A3*
Museo Numismático Dr José Evaristo Uriburu 12 *D4*
Museo y Biblioteca Mitre 10 *D4*

Jorge Luis Borges 1899-1986

More than any writer, Borges has most vividly captured the spirit of Buenos Aires. Born in the city in 1899, he was obsessed with the myths and realities of Argentina and its culture, and by the wealth of literature from world classics. His entirely original blend of these two different worlds has made him the most influential figure in Argentine literary culture, with a world-wide reputation. In 1914, Borges travelled with his family to live in Switzerland and Spain, where he added Latin, French and German to his fluent English. He started to write, and became involved with the *Ultraísmo* literary movement, which scorned the mannerism and opulence of *Modernismo* for a style which embraced shocking imagery and free verse, and which Borges described as 'avoiding ornamental artefacts'. Borges became an active member of the literary avant garde when he returned to Buenos Aires in 1921, and in the following few years, he contributed regularly to literary magazines, publishing seven books of poetry and essays which established his lifelong obsessions: a view of life from the margins, and a fascination with authorship and individual consciousness.

From 1933, Borges was Literary Editor of the Newspaper *Crítica*, where he published his *Historia Universal de la Infamia* (A Universal History of Infamy) in 1935, establishing a style somewhere between the non-fictional essay and the fictional short story. In the late 1930's he published a series of significant essays and short stories collections, including *El Jardín de Senderos* (the Garden of Forking Paths), in 1931, with one of his most famous stories, *El Sur* (The South). In 1944 Borges published arguably the most important series of stories in the history of Latin American literature, the great *Ficciones* (Fictions), which overturned conventions of realism while exploring the nature of literature itself, together with philosophy and metaphysics. *El Aleph* followed in 1949, and his most important essays, *Otras Inquisiciones* (Other Inquisitions) in 1952. A masterful story teller, Borges never wrote more than a few pages, and was never tempted by the novel form, insisting that more could be explored in a few elliptical highly suggestive and poetic lines than in hundred of pages of dull realist prose.

The late forties brought almost total blindness due to glaucoma, and a running dispute with the Perón regime. Borges' work was overlooked in Europe and the US until the late 1960s, by which time he was completely blind, and wrote mainly poetry, a form which he could compose in his head. The worldwide popularity of his fiction led him to publish two further books of short stories later in life, *El Informe de Brodie* (Dr Brodie's Report, 1970), and *El Libro de Arena* (The Book of Sand, 1975), which makes a good introduction to his work. In his final years, he travelled the world with his companion María Kodama, whom he married. He died in Geneva, of liver cancer, in June 1986.

Museo de la Ciudad ⓘ *Alsina 412, T011-4343 2123, Mon-Fri, 1100-1900, Sat- Sun, 1500-1900, US$0.35 (US$1 for non-residents), free on Wed,* is worth visiting for an insight into 19th-century Buenos Aires life. The historical house includes a 1900s chemist's shop, Farmacia La Estrella, and has a permanent exhibition covering social history and popular culture, with special exhibitions on daily life in Buenos Aires. The **Church of San Francisco** ⓘ *Alsina y Defensa, Mon-Fri 0700-1300, 1500-1900, guided visits Tue 1530 and 1630, Sat 1630 and 1730,* was built by the Franciscan Order

1730-1754 and given a new façade in 1911 in German baroque style. There's a fine baroque pulpit and the chapel of San Roque.

Argentina has a rich heritage from numerous indigenous groups who inhabited the country before the Spanish arrived, and their history is well-charted in the anthropological museum **Museo Etnográfico J B Ambrosetti** ⓘ *1 block south of the San Francisco church at Moreno 350, T011-4345 8196, www.museoetnografico.filo.uba.ar, Wed-Sun 1500-1900 (closed Jan), US$0.70, guided visits Sat-Sun 1600.* Displays are limited, but very well laid out, and include some fascinating treasures, such as Inca textiles and ceramics, Bolivian and Mapuche silverwork, all in an attractive building dating from 1880.

One block further south at Defensa y Belgrano, the **Church of Santo Domingo**, ⓘ *Mon-Fri 0900-1300, Sun 1000-1200, no tours offered,* was founded in 1751. During the British attack on Buenos Aires in 1806 some of Whitelocke's soldiers took refuge in the church and it was bombarded by local forces. Look out for the huge wooden canon balls embedded in the towers on the outside: fakes, sadly. The British flags inside are worth seeing, and General Belgrano, a major figure in Argentine independence, is buried here.

Avenida de Mayo to Congreso

From the Plaza de Mayo, take a stroll down this broad leafy avenue which links the Casa Rosada to the Congress building to the west. The avenue was built between 1889 and 1894, inspired by the grand design of Paris, and filled with elaborate French Baroque and art nouveau buildings. At Perú and Avenida de Mayo is the **subte station Perú**, furnished by the Museo de la Ciudad to resemble its original state, with posters and furniture of the time. You'll need to buy a US$0.25 ticket to have a look, or take a train.

Along the avenue west from here, you'll see the splendid French-style **Casa de la Cultura** at number 575, home of the newspaper *La Prensa* and topped with bronze statues. At number 702 is the fine Parisian-style **Edificio Drabble**, and at number 769, the elegant **Palacio Vera**, from 1910. Argentina's most celebrated writer, Jorge Luis Borges, was fond of the many cafés which once filled Avenida de Mayo, of which **Café Tortoni**, at no 825, is the most famous in Buenos Aires and the haunt of illustrious writers, artists and poets since 1858. Its high ceilings with ornate plaster work and art nouveau stained glass, tall columns and elegant mirrors plunge you straight back into another era. It's an atmospheric place for coffee, but particularly wonderful for the poetry recitals, tango and live music, which are still performed here in the evenings. There are also plenty of places around for a quick lunch, and lots of cheap hotels.

Continuing west over Avenida 9 de Julio, there's the superb 1928 **Hotel Castelar** at number 1152, still open (see Sleeping page 86), and retaining its former glory, and the beautiful art nouveau **Hotel Chile** at number 1297. At the western end of the avenue, is the astounding **Palacio Barola** ⓘ *No 1370, Mon-Fri 0700-2200, Sat 0700-1200*, built by a textile magnate in 1923 with architectural details inspired by the Italian poet Dante. Avenida de Mayo culminates in the **Plaza del Congreso**, with the **congress building** ⓘ *T011-4953 3081, ext 3885 for guided visits, Mon, Tue Thu, Fri 1100, 1700, 1900,* in Italian academic style, housing the country's government.

Plaza San Martín and Retiro

Ten blocks north of the Plaza de Mayo, and just south of **Retiro station**, is the splendid Plaza San Martín, on a hill originally marking the northern limit of the city. It has since been designed by Argentina's famous landscape architect Charles Thays, and is filled with luxuriant mature palms and plane trees, and popular with runners in the early morning and office workers at lunchtimes. At the western corner is an equestrian **statue**

Buenos Aires was strategically located on the Río de la Plata, a broad brown estuary that is neither silver nor a river, but was named for the explorers' hopes of treasure.

 of San Martín, 1862, and at the northern end of the plaza is the **Malvinas memorial** with an eternal flame to those who fell in the Falklands/Malvinas War, 1982.

Around the plaza are several elegant mansions, among them the **Palacio San Martín**, designed in 1909 in French academic style for the wealthy Anchorena family, and now occupied by the Ministry of Foreign Affairs. Most striking is the elegant art deco **Edificio Kavanagh**, east of the plaza, which was the tallest building in South America when completed in 1936. Behind it is the **Basilica del Santísimo Sacramento** (1916), the church favoured by wealthy *Porteños*.

The **Plaza de la Fuerza Aérea**, northeast of Plaza San Martín, was until 1982 called the Plaza Británica; in the centre is a clock tower presented by British and Anglo-Argentine residents in 1916, still known as the Torre de los Ingleses.

Three blocks northwest of Plaza San Martín is one of the city's most delightful museums, the **Museo de Arte Hispanoamericano Isaac Fernández Blanco**, ⓘ *Suipacha 1422, Tue-Sun, 1400-1900, US$0.30; Thu free, closed Jan. For guided visits in English or French T011-4327 0228; guided tours in Spanish Sat, Sun 1600.* Housed in a beautiful 1920s neo-colonial mansion with tiled Spanish-style gardens, it contains a fascinating collection of colonial art, with fine Cuzqueño school paintings, and dazzling ornate silverware from Alto Perú and Río de la Plata. There are also temporary exhibitions of Latin American art. Highly recommended.

North of Plaza San Martín is **Retiro railway station**, really three separate termini. The area is not safe to walk around, but if you're catching a train, drop in to see the oldest and finest of these, the **Mitre**, dating from 1908, a classical construction with an atmospheric interior, and a *confitería*. Behind the station is the **Museo Nacional Ferroviario** ⓘ *accessed from Av del Libertador 405, Mon-Fri 1000-1600*, which contains locomotives, machinery and documents on the history of Argentine railways.

Avenida 9 de Julio is one of the world's widest thoroughfares, with eleven lanes of traffic in each direction, leading south to Plaza de la Constitución and routes south of the city. It's crossed by the major streets of Avenida de Mayo and Córdoba, and at the junction with Corrientes is the city's famous landmark, a 67m-tall **obelisk** commemorating the 400th anniversary of the city's founding, where football fans traditionally congregate in crowds to celebrate a victory. It's only possible to walk on the streets parallel to the roaring traffic: Cerrito (west) and Carlos Pellegrini (east). The city's main shopping street Avenida Santa Fé starts at Plaza San Martín, and crosses Avenida 9 de Julio, before heading through Retiro and Recoleta to Palermo. It's a huge stretch of shops, but the most well known brands are to be found between Talcahuano and Avenida Pueyrredon.

Four blocks west of the Obelisk, you can see art and theatre, and learn tango at the **Centro Cultural San Martín** ⓘ *Av Corrientes 1530, www.ccgsh.gov.ar, museum US$0.50, Wed free.* It's a rather austere 1970s concrete building, but it houses good photography exhibitions, the Teatro Municipal San Martín and a salon of the Museo Municipal de Arte Moderno. There's also a tango information desk at the entrance.

Teatro Colón

ⓘ *Main entrance on Libertad, between Tucumán and Viamonte, T011-4378 7132/33, www.teatrocolon.org.ar. Guided tours Mon-Sat hourly 1100-1600, Sun 1100, 1300, 1500 (Jan-Feb, Mon-Fri only, starting at 1100); in Spanish and English (at 1100, 1300, 1500). US$4, children or ISIC card US$0.70; tickets from the entrance at Toscanini 1168 (on C Viamonte side) or from Tucumán 1171.*

On Avenida 9 de Julio, a block north of the obelisk, is Teatro Colón, one of the world's greatest opera houses and one of the city's finest buildings. It opened in 1908 and is an extraordinary testimony to the country's former wealth. Behind the classical façade, the opulent foyer is decorated with three kinds of marble brought from Europe, a Parisian stained glass dome in the roof, and Venetian tiled mosaic floor. The perfectly preserved auditorium is French Baroque style, from the chandelier in the ceiling (which conceals a chamber where singers or musicians can be hidden to produce music from the heavens) to the French gilded lights and red velvet curtains. It has an almost perfect acoustic, due to the horseshoe shape and the mix of marble and soft fabrics, and an immense stage, 35 m deep. Workshops and rehearsal spaces lie underneath the Avenida 9 de Julio itself, and there are stores of costumes, including 22,000 pairs of shoes. A guided tour is highly recommended to appreciate the history and the splendour of the design.

The theatre is home to three orchestras, as well as the city's ballet and opera companies; world class performances can be seen in their season from April to early December. The opera season runs from April to November and there are concert performances most days. Tickets are sold five days before performance, from the Calle Tucumán side of the theatre, T011-4378 7344, Monday-Saturday 0900- 2000, Sunday 1000-1700.The cheapest seat is US$2.70 (available even on the same day) and 'El Paraíso' tickets are available for standing room or seats in 'The Gods' – queue for a good spot. Check for free concerts at Salón Dorado.

Puerto Madero

East of the city centre at Puerto Madero, the 19th-century docks have been successfully transformed into an attractive area with lots of good restaurants, among the modern developments of offices, shops, housing and even a university campus. It's a good place for a walk, among the tall brick buildings, with their cranes and winches now freshly painted. Restaurants are mostly found along the waterside of the old warehouses lining Avenida Alicia M de Justo from the northern end of Dique No 4, where you'll find a helpful **tourist information** kiosk in a glass construction under one of the cranes.

Walking south, there are a couple of interesting ships to look at. By Dique no 3, there's the **Fragata Presidente Sarmiento** ⓘ *Av Dávila y Perón, T011-4334 9386, Mon-Fri 0900-2000, Sat/Sun 0900-2200, US$0.70, free for children under 5*, which was the Argentine flagship from 1899 to 1938, and is now a museum. Walking further south, in Dique 1, Av Garay, is the **Corbeta Uruguay**, the sailing ship which rescued Otto Nordenskjold's Antarctic expedition in 1903. Also over Dique 3 is the striking harp-like bridge, the **Puente de la Mujer** (Bridge of Women), suspended by cables from a single arm. It's open daily 0800-2100.

Costanera Sur

Buenos Aires has an extraordinary green space right at the heart of the city and on the waterfront. At the southernmost end of Dique No 1, cross the pivoting bridge (level with Calle Brazil) to the broad avenue of the Costanera Sur. This pleasant wide avenue used to run east of the docks, a fashionable promenade by the waterside in the early 20th century. Now it's separated from the River Plata by the wide splay of land created in a 1970s landfill project, now enjoying a revival, with many restaurants open along the boulevard at night, and it's a pleasant place to walk by day. There's a wonderfully sensuous marble fountain designed by famous Tucumán sculptress Lola Mora, **Las Nereidas**, at the southernmost entrance to the **Reserva Ecológica** ⓘ *entrances at Av Tristán Achával Rodríguez 1550 (take Estados Unidos east from San Telmo) or next to the Buquebús ferry terminal (take Av Córdoba east), T011-4315 1320; for pedestrians and bikers only, Tue-Sun 0800-1800, in summer closes at 1900, free, bus No 2 passes next to the southern entrance*, where there are more than 200 species of birds, including the curve-billed reed hunter. Free guided tours are available at weekends 1030, 1530 (daily in summer), from the administration next to the southern entrance, but much can be seen from the road before then (binoculars useful). Also free nocturnal visits every month on the Friday closest to the full moon (book Monday before, T011-4893 1588). It is 30-minute walk from the entrance to the river shore, taking about three hours to walk the whole perimeter. In summer it is very hot with little shade. For details (birdwatching, in particular) contact **Aves Argentinas/AOP** (see Useful addresses, page 110).

Recoleta

The area of Recoleta is known as Barrio Norte, the chic place to live in the centre of the capital. Stretching west from Plaza San Martín, beyond Avenida 9 de Julio, Recoleta became a fashionable residential area when wealthy families started to move here from the crowded city centre after a yellow fever outbreak in 1871. Many of its French-style mansions date from the turn of the 20th century, and there are smart apartment blocks with marble entrances in leafy streets, making for a pleasant stroll around the many cafés, art galleries and museums. At its heart is the **Plaza de la Recoleta** by the **Recoleta Cemetery**. Running down its southeastern side is Calle Ortiz, lined with cafés and *confiterías* ranging from the refined and traditional to touristy eateries, most with tables outside. Overhead are the branches of the **gran gomero**, a rubber tree, whose limbs are supported on crutches. At weekends, the **Plaza Francia** is filled with an art and craft market from 1100 until 1800, when the whole place is lively, with street artists and performers.

Recoleta is famous for its cemetery, where Eva Perón is buried, among other illustrious figures from Argentina's history. **Cementerio de la Recoleta** ⓘ *entrance at Junín 1790, not far from Museo de Bellas Artes (see below), T011-4804 7040, 0700-1800, free tours in Spanish 1100, 1500 (on Tue and Thu 1100 in English), check times as they may change*, is like a miniature city, its narrow streets weaving between imposing family mausoleums built in every imaginable architectural style, a vast congregation of stone angels on their roofs. To negotiate this enormous labyrinth, a guided tour is recommended, but at the very least, you'll want to see Evita Perón's tomb, lying in the Duarte family mausoleum. To find it from the entrance, walk straight ahead to the first tree-filled plaza; turn left, and where this avenue meets a main avenue (go just beyond the Turriata tomb), turn right and then take the third passage on the left.

The former Jesuit church of **El Pilar**, next to the cemetery, is a beautiful example of colonial architecture dating from 1732, restored in 1930. There are stunning 18th-century gold altarpieces made in Alto Peru, and a fine wooden image of San Pedro de Alcántara, attributed to the famous 17th-century Spanish sculptor Alonso Cano, preserved in a side chapel on the left. Downstairs is an interesting small museum of religious art, from whose windows you have a good view of the cemetery next door.

The **Centro Cultural Recoleta** ⓘ *Tue-Fri 1400-2100, Sat, Sun, holidays 1000-2100, T011-4803 0358*, alongside the Recoleta cemetery, occupying the cloisters of a former monastery, has constantly changing exhibitions of contemporary local art by young artists. Next door, the **Buenos Aires Design Centre**, has stylish homewares by contemporary Argentine designers. There are also lots of good restaurants here, some with views over the nearby plazas from their open terraces, recommended for an evening drink at sunset. In **Plaza San Martín de Tours** next door, there are more huge gomera trees with their extraordinary sinuous roots, and here you're likely to spot one of Buenos Aires' legendary dog walkers, managing an unfeasible 20 or so dogs without tangling their leads. There's a **tourist information booth** at Ayacuco 1958, T011-4804 5667. **Village Recoleta**, on Vicente López y Junin, T011-4805 2220, houses a multiplex cinema, with bookshops and cafés at its entrance.

Recoleta museums

Most of the city's great museums are collected together in Recoleta, where the wide and fast avenue **Avenida del Libertador** runs north from Recoleta towards Palermo, past further parks and squares as well as several major museums. Of these the undoubted star is **Museo de Arte Latinoamericano (MALBA)** ⓘ *Av Figueroa Alcorta 3415, T011-4808 6500, daily 1200-2000 (Wed free till 2100; Tue closed), US$1.30, free for ISIC holders, cinema tickets US$1.30, book in advance*, opened in 2001 to house a permanent collection of Latin American art, and temporary exhibitions. The minimalist building may strike you as rather stark, but the works inside are full of passion – powerful, humorous and moving pieces, very accessible and highly recommended. There's also an elegant café serving delicious food and cakes, and a cinema showing well-chosen art house films as well as Argentine classics. If you've time for only one museum, make it this one.

For a taste of older Argentine art, visit the **Museo de Bellas Artes** ⓘ *Av del Libertador 1473, T011-4803 0802, www.mnba.org.ar, Tue-Fri 1230-1930, Sat-Sun 0930-1930, guided tours Tue-Sun 1600, 1700, 1800, tours for children in summer Tue-Fri 1100, 1700, Sat-Sun 1700, free.* There's a fairly ordinary survey of European works, but some particularly good post-Impressionist paintings and fine Rodin sculptures. Best of all though, there is a varied collection of Argentine 19th and 20th century paintings, sculpture and wooden carvings.

The **Biblioteca Nacional**, or National Library, ⓘ *Av del Libertador 1600 y Agüero 2502, T011-4806 6155, www.bibnal.edu.ar, Mon-Fri 0900-2100, Sat and Sun 1200-1900, closed Jan, excellent guided tours (Spanish) daily 1600 from main entrance, for tours in other languages contact in advance*, is a huge cube standing on four sturdy legs in an attractive garden with a bust of Eva Perón. Only a fraction of its stock of about 1.8 million volumes and 10,000 manuscripts is available, but it's open to visitors, and worth a look to enjoy one of the frequent exhibitions and recitals.

The **Museo Nacional de Arte Decorativo** ⓘ *Av del Libertador 1902, daily 1400-1900, T011-4802 6606, US$0.60, half-price to ISIC holders, guided tours Wed, Thu, Fri 1630*, contains collections of painting, furniture, porcelain, crystal, sculpture. It also hosts classical music concerts on Wednesdays and Thursdays. In the same building, but temporarily closed, is the **Museo Nacional de Arte Oriental**, containing a permanent exhibition of Chinese, Japanese, Hindu and Islamic art.

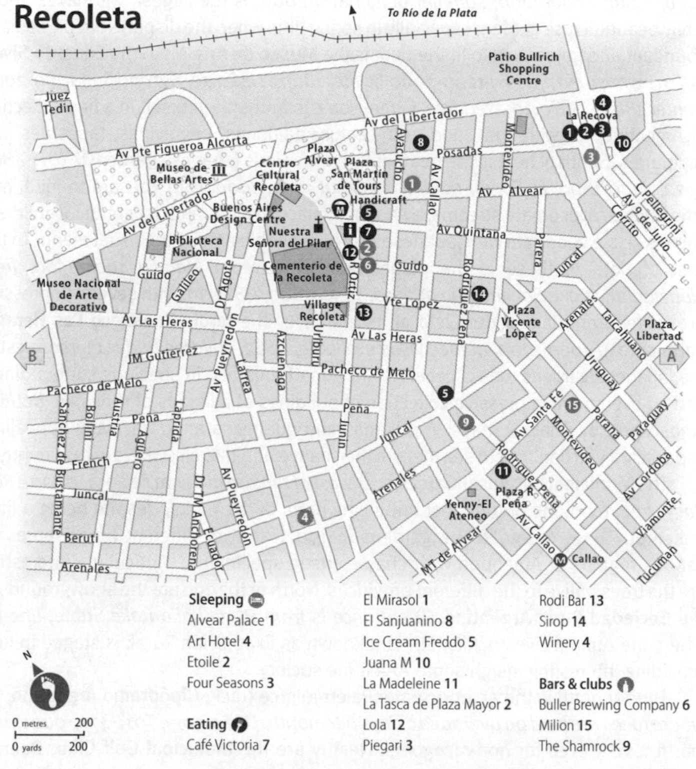

Much more entertaining, offering a real insight into the Argentine soul, the **Museo de Motivos Populares Argentinos José Hernández** ⓘ *Av Libertador 2373, T011-4802 7294, www.mujose.org.ar, Wed-Sun 1300-1900, US$0.30, free Sun, closed in Feb*, is named after the writer of Argentina's famous epic poem *Martín Fierro*, and contains one of the most complete collections of folkloric art in the country. There are plenty of gaucho artefacts: ornate silver *mates*, wonderful plaited leather *talebartería* and decorated silver stirrups, together with pre-Hispanic artefacts, and paintings from the Cuzco school. There is also a handicrafts shop and library.

Palermo

Palermo is Buenos Aires' most appealing area, growing in recent years from a peaceful residential *barrio* to a seriously hip and chic place to eat and shop. This part of Palermo is really known as Palermo Viejo, lying further southwest of the famous parks of Palermo.

Palermo parks

Palermo was originally named after Giovanni Domenico Palermo who transformed these lands into productive orchards and vineyards in the 17th century. President De Rosas built a sumptuous mansion, **La Quinta**, here in the early 19th century, and Palermo's great parks were established by Sarmiento and designed by Argentina's most famous landscape designer, Charles Thays, in the early 20th century. It remains a sought-after residential area for middle-class Porteños, and the wonderful parks are the most popular inner-city green space at weekends.

Of this series of parks, the **Parque Tres de Febrero** ⓘ *winter Mon-Fri 0800-1800, Sat and Sun 0800-2000; summer daily 0800-2000*, is the largest, with lakes and a really beautiful rose garden, especially in spring time when the displays are particularly abundant and fragrant. Also in the park is the **Museo de Arte Moderno Eduardo Sivori** ⓘ *T011-4774 9452, Tue-Fri 1200-2000 (winter 1800), US$0.70, Sat and Sun 1000-2000 (winter 1800), US$0.30, Wed free*, where you can immerse yourself in a fine collection of Argentine art, with 19th- and 20th-century paintings, engravings, tapestries and sculptures. South of here is the beautifully harmonious **Japanese garden** ⓘ *T011-4804 4922, 1000-1800, US$0.70, guided visits Sat 1500, 1600*, with koi carp to feed, and little bridges over ornate streams, a charming place to walk, and delightful for children. There's also a good café with Japanese dishes available among the usual menu. To the east of both of these is the **planetarium** ⓘ *museum Mon-Fri 1000-1500, free, planetarium shows Sat and Sun at 1500, 1630, 1800, US$1.30*, with several impressive meteorites from Campo del Cielo at its entrance. The **Jardín Zoológico Las Heras y Sarmiento** ⓘ *1000-1900, guided visits available, US$2, children under 13 free*, west of the Japanese gardens, has a decent collection of animals, in spacious surroundings, and an even more impressive collection of buildings of all kinds of styles, in grounds landscaped by Charles Thays. The llamas and guanacos are particularly appealing, especially if you don't get to see them in their native habitats elsewhere in the country.

The **Municipal Botanical Gardens,** ⓘ *west of the zoo at Santa Fe 2951, 0800-1800 daily, free*, form one of the most appealing parts of the parks, despite being a little unkempt. Thays designed the gardens in 1902, and its different areas represent various regions of Argentina with characteristic specimens; particularly interesting are the trees native to the different provinces. North of the zoo are the showgrounds of the **Sociedad Rural Argentina,** ⓘ *entrance is from Plaza Italia (take Subte, line D)*, where the Annual Livestock Exhibition, known as Exposición Rural, is staged in July, providing interesting insights into Argentine society.

Further north is the 45,000 seater Palermo race track, **Hipódromo Argentino,** ⓘ *where races are held on average 10 days per month, US$0.30-3, T011-4777 9001*, well worth a visit even for non-racegoers. Nearby are the **Municipal Golf Club, Buenos**

Aires Lawn Tennis Club, riding clubs and polo field, and the **Club de Gimnasia y Esgrima** (Athletic and Fencing Club). The parks are bordered to the north by Aeroparque (Jorge Newbery Airport), the city's domestic airport.

Carlos Gardel

Gardel, the legendary singer whose name is virtually synonymous with tango, was born in 1890 in Toulouse, France, to Berthe Gardés and an unknown father. To avoid social stigma, his mother emigrated to the Abasto market area of Buenos Aires when her son was just two years old, and it was partly these humble beginnings that helped him to become an icon for poor *Porteños*.

Just as the exact origin of tango itself is something of a mystery, Gardel's formative years around the city are obscure, until around 1912 when he began his artistic career in earnest, performing as one half of the duo Gardel-Razzano. He began his recording career with Columbia with a recording of 15 traditional songs, but with it was with his rendition of *Mi Noche Triste* (My Sorrowful Night) in 1917, that his mellifluous voice became known. As *tango-canción* became popular – the song rather than just a musical accompaniment to the dance – Gardel's career took off, and by the early 1920s he was singing entirely within this new genre, and achieving success as far afield as Madrid.

Gardel became a solo artist in 1925, and with his charm and natural machismo, was the very epitome of tango both in Argentina and, following his tours to Europe, around the world. Between 1933 and 1935, he was based in New York, starring in numerous Spanish speaking films, and the English language The *Tango on Broadway* in 1934. On 24 June 1935, while on a tour of South America, his plane from Bogota to Cali crashed into another on the ground while taking off. Gardel was killed instantly, to the immense grief of his public. Gardel had recorded some 900 songs during his career, and the brilliance of his voice, the way he represented the spirit of the Río de la Plata to his fans at home, and the untimely nature of his dramatic death ensured the endurance of his popularity.

Palermo Viejo

The most atmospheric, and oldest, part of Palermo can be found in the quadrant between the avenidas Córdoba and Santa Fe, south of Juan B Justo and north of Avenida Scalabrini Ortiz. This area is also known as **Palermo Soho** (the two names are interchangeable), supposedly because of similarities with SoHo in New York, rather than London. You'll also hear people mention **Palermo Hollywood**, which is on the other side of the railway tracks and Avenida Juan B Justo which bisects the area. There are fewer shops in this part, and it's so called because of the number of TV and film companies based here, but there are lots of restaurants, so it's worth exploring. The whole of Palermo is a very seductive place, with cobbled streets of tall bohemian houses bedecked with flowers and plants, lined with trees, and with leafy plazas. It's become a very fashionable place to live, but even more popular among young Porteños shopping for contemporary designs in clothing and interiors, and drinking in chic bars in the evenings. There's no Subte station right in the middle of Palermo, but there are three stations within five blocks or so, along Avenida Santa Fé.

To start exploring, take the Subte along Line D to either Scalabrini Ortiz, Plaza Italia or Palermo stations (depending on where you want to start). Walk up towards **Plaza Palermo Viejo** or to **Plaza Cortázar**, named after Argentina's famous novelist and writer, whose novel *Rayuela* ('Hopscotch') is set around here. These two plazas are both surrounded by cafés and bars, and in the four blocks between are all the clothing and accessories shops you could ever need. (See Shopping, page 99, for more details). Meander up **Calle Malabia**, and then around **Calles Costa Rica**, **El Salvador** and

Honduras, with detours along Armenia and Guruchaga when some boutique catches your eye. Even if you loathe the shopping, Palermo Viejo will appeal, since the whole area is wide open and relaxed and retains the quiet atmosphere of a residential district.

For bars and restaurants, you could wander the streets further afield, and stray onto the other side of Juan B Justo, though note that you can only cross the railway tracks at Calles Honduras, Paraguay and Santa Fé. Alternatively, take a radio taxi from the centre of town straight to one of the restaurants recommended in this guide, and wander the nearby blocks to lap up the atmosphere and satisfy yourself there's nowhere you fancy more. So many new restaurants have opened up in the last few years that you'll be spoilt for choice. Palermo is a great place for meeting in the evenings, with bars and restaurants attracting lively crowds of trendy locals as well as increasing numbers of tourists who'd rather be somewhere other than downtown. On the northwestern edge of Palermo, separated from the main area by yet another railway line, is **Las Cañitas**, a hugely popular area of restaurants centred around **Calle Báez**. For a list of recommended clothes shops, see page 99.

South of the centre

San Telmo

The city's most atmospheric barrio is also its oldest. San Telmo starts south of the Plaza de Mayo, and is built along a slope which was once the old beach of the Río de la Plata. Formerly one of the wealthiest areas of the city, it was abandoned by the rich during a serious outbreak of yellow fever in 1871, and so was never modernized or destroyed for rebuilding like much of the rest of the city. San Telmo is one of the few areas where buildings have survived from the mid-19th century, crumbling and largely unchanged, so it's a delightful place to stroll and explore the artists' studios and small museums hidden away in its narrow streets, with plenty of cafés and shops selling antiques, records, handmade shoes, secondhand books, and crafts of all kinds. In the last couple of years, new boutiques, design shops and chic bars have been opening up in newly renovated old houses in San Telmo and moving out towards Montserrat too, similar to those in Palermo Viejo. Montserrat is also getting the city's first gay hotel, from the chain Axel in 2007 (the first one is in Barcelona) somewhere in Calle Venezuela, around 600. Buenos Aires is, after all, one of the top gay destinations in the world.

A quiet place to meander during the week, the *barrio* comes alive on Sundays when there's an antiques and bric-a-brac market held in the central **Plaza Dorrego**, a small square enclosed by charming old houses. This is a good place to start exploring, after enjoying the free tango demonstrations which take place in the plaza on Sundays 1000-1800. Behind the plaza, on Carlos Calvo, there's a wonderful indoor fruit market – **Mercado de San Telmo** built in 1897. Walk south along Calle Defensa, filled with street musicians on Sundays, many of them excellent, and pop into the artists' studios, antique shops and cafés which line the street. Just a block from the plaza is the white stuccoed church of **San Pedro González Telmo** ⓘ *Humerto Primero, T011-4361 1168, guided tours Sun at 1500, 1600, free.* Begun by the Jesuits in 1734, but only finished in 1931, it's a wonderful confection of styles with ornate baroque columns and Spanish-style tiles.

One block further south, in an old tobacco warehouse, the **Museo de Arte Moderno de Buenos Aires** ⓘ *San Juan 350, T011-4361 1121, Tue-Fri 1000-2000, Sat, Sun and holidays 1100-2000, guided tours Tue-Sun 1700, US$0.30, Wed free*, houses good visiting exhibitions of contemporary international and Argentine art. There is also a small fine art bookshop.

At the end of Defensa, is the **Parque Lezama** ⓘ *Defensa y Brasil, Sat and Sun 1000-2000*, originally one of the most beautiful parks in the city, but now a little run down, and not a safe place to wander in at night. According to tradition, Pedro de Mendoza founded the city on this spot in 1535, and there's an imposing statue to him in the centre of the park. On the west side of the park is the **Museo Histórico Nacional** ⓘ *Defensa 1600, T011-4307 1182, Tue-Sun 1300-1800, US$0.30, guided tours Sat-Sun 1530*, which presents the history of the city and of Argentina through the key historical figures and events, with some impressive artefacts, portraits and war paintings, particularly of San Martín. Sadly, there's currently little information available in English.

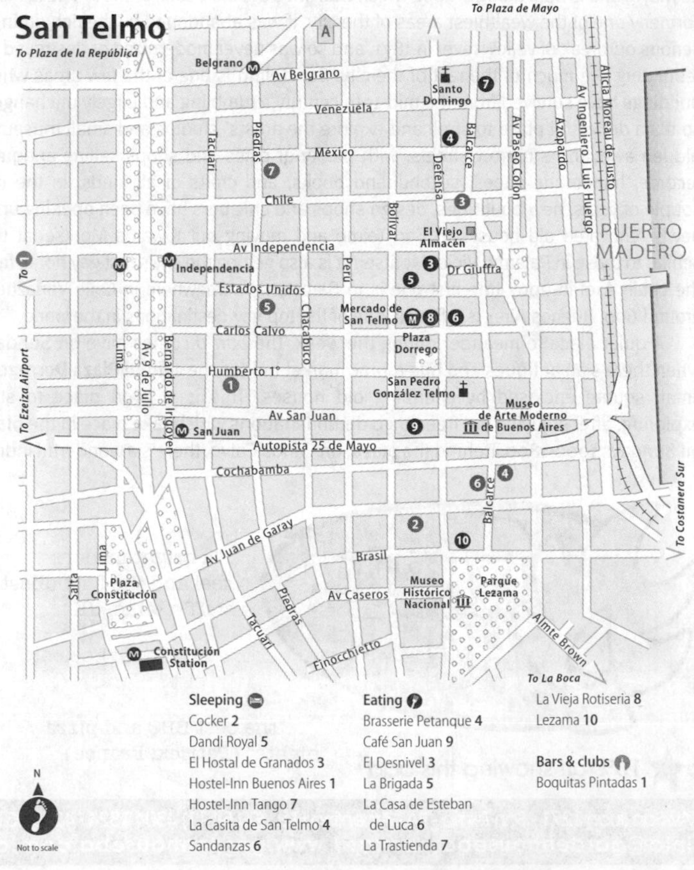

There is an ever-growing number of restaurants along Defensa, many of them cheap and lively places to eat, and several venues offering tango shows. The best is the historical **El Viejo Almacén** ⓘ *Independencia y Balcarce, T011-4307 7388, www.viejo almacen.com, daily, dinner from 2000, show 2200, US$67 with all drinks, dinner and show, show only, US$47*, started by celebrated tango singer Edmundo Rivero in the late 1960s. Here the city's finest tango dancers demonstrate their extraordinary skills in a small, atmospheric theatre, with excellent live music and singing from some the great names of tango. Highly recommended. There are plenty of good restaurants sprinkled through San Telmo, and most of the city's youth hostels are here too.

La Boca

East of the Plaza de Mayo, behind the Casa Rosada, a broad avenue, Paseo Colón, runs south towards the old port district of La Boca, where the putrid Riachuelo river flows into the Plata. An area of heavy Italian immigration in the early 1900s, La Boca was known for the brightly-painted blue, yellow and lime green zinc façades of its houses, a tradition brought over by Genoese immigrants who painted their homes with the leftover paint from ships. It's a much-touted tourist destination, but very disappointing in reality. There is nothing authentic left of the area, and just one block of brightly painted houses to see on pedestrianized **Calle El Caminito**, put there, somewhat cynically, by the Buenos Aires tourist board. Calle El Caminito, leads west from the little triangular plaza **La Vuelta de Rocha**, and this street is in fact the only place you're allowed to visit in La Boca, since policemen are permanently stationed there to stop tourists from straying further. This is because the area is rife with petty crime and tourist muggings are a daily occurrence. There's a small arcade of artists' workshops and a couple of cafés in the **Centro Cultural de los Artistas**, with tango dancers, street entertainers and touristy souvenir shops. You might be tempted to stray from this touristy area and find the 'real' La Boca: don't. The surrounding streets are notorious for violent crime, you will almost certainly be a very obvious target, and in any case, the Riachuelo river is far from picturesque, with its distinctive rotting smell. To reach La Boca from the centre, do not risk taking the bus. Phone instead for a Radio taxi, US$4 (see Ins and outs, page 119) and call from the *locutorio* in Centro Cultural for a taxi to take you home. Police are on hand in the Vuelta de Rocha to help and advise tourists who have been assaulted. There is a freephone number to contact the **tourist police office**, T0800-999 5000. Staff speak English and other European languages.

The real attractions here are two fine museums: La Boca really owes its fame to the artist Benito Quinquela Martín (1890-1977) who painted its ships, docks and workers all his life, and whose vivid and colourful paintings can be seen in the **Museo de Bellas Artes 'Benito Quinquela'** ⓘ *Pedro de Mendoza 1835, T011-4301 1080, Tue-Fri 1000-1730, Sat-Sun 1100-1730, closed Jan, US$0.35*. The artist lived here for many years, and you can also see his own extensive collection of paintings by Argentine artists, and sculpture on a roof terrace with wonderful views over the whole port, revealing the marginalised poverty behind the coloured zinc façades. There's more contemporary art a block away in the **Fundacíon Proa** ⓘ *Av Pedro de Mendoza 1929, T011-4303 0909, Tue-Sun, 1100-1900, US$1*, a modern space behind the ornate Italianate façade of a 1908 warehouse, showing temporary exhibitions of Argentine, Latin American and international contemporary art. Check the press for details. The roof terrace here is also great, and a nightclub venue for electronic music at times.

La Boca is home to one of the country's great football teams, **Boca Juniors**, and the area is especially rowdy when they're playing at home: do not attend a match alone. Football is one of the great Argentine experiences, and the easiest way to go to a match is as part of a group arranged with a company such as **Tangol** (see Tour operators below). Aficionados of the beautiful game will be entertained by the **Museo de la Pasión Boquense** ⓘ *Brandsen 805, T011-4362 1100, Tue-Sun 1000-1800*. Tickets are for the museum together with a stadium seat for a match on the same day; US$5.

Sleeping

Hotels in the upper ranges can often be booked more cheaply through Buenos Aires travel agencies. Hotels and guesthouses may display a star rating, but this doesn't necessarily match international standards. Many more expensive hotels charge different prices for *extranjeros* (non-Argentines) in US$, which is unavoidable since a passport is required as proof of residency. If you pay in cash (pesos) you may get a reduction. Room tax (VAT) is 21% and is not always included in the price. Many of the cheaper hotels in the central area give large reductions for long stays. All hotels will store luggage for a day, and most have English- speaking staff. For upmarket chain hotels throughout Argentina contact N/A Town & Country Hotels, www.newage- hotels.com. For hostels see Hostelling International Argenina, Florida 835 PB, T011-4511 8723/4312 0089, www.hostels.org.ar, which offers 20% discounts to card-holders and 10% off long-distance bus journeys.

City centre *p70, map p72*

LL Alvear Palace, Av Alvear 1891, T/F011-4808 2100, www.alvearpalace.com. The height of elegance, an impeccably preserved 1930s Recoleta palace, taking you back in time to Buenos Aires' wealthy heyday. A sumptuous marble foyer, with Louis XV-style chairs, and a charming orangery where you can take tea with superb patisseries (US$12). Antique-filled bedrooms. Recommended.
LL Four Seasons, Posadas 1086, T011-4321 1200, www.fourseasons.com/buenosaires. An entirely modern palace in traditional style, offering sumptuous luxury in an exclusive atmosphere. Spacious public areas, adorned with paintings and flowers, chic lavishly decorated rooms, and 7 suites in La Mansión residence, pool and health club.
LL Hilton, Av Macacha Güemes 351, Puerto Madero, T011-4891 0000, reservationsba@hilton.com. A modern business hotel built on the revamped docks area with views of the Costanera Sur, and with plenty of restaurants nearby, this has neat functional rooms, the El Faro restaurant, a health club and pool.
LL Marriott Plaza, Florida 1005, T011-4318 3000, www.marriott.com. With a superb location overlooking Plaza San Martín, this is the city's most historic hotel, built in Parisian style in 1909, and retaining period elegance in the public rooms and bedrooms, which are charming and luxurious. A pool and fitness centre, excellent restaurant, the **Plaza Grill**, and very good service throughout.
L-AL NH City Hotel, Bolivar 160, T011-4121 6464, www.nh-hoteles.com. Very chic indeed, with perfect minimalist design for a discerning younger clientele, this is one of 3 in the Spanish-owned chain in central Buenos Aires, with beautifully designed modern interiors in a 1930's building off Plaza de Mayo, and luxurious rooms. Small rooftop pool, good restaurant.
L-AL Panamericano, Carlos Pellegrini 551, T011-4348 5000, www.panamericanonews.com. Extremely smart and modern city hotel, with luxurious and tasteful rooms, a lovely covered rooftop pool, and superb restaurant, Tomo 1. Excellent service too.
AL Art Hotel, Azcuénaga 1268, T011-4821 4744, www.arthotel.com.ar. Great location on a quiet street in Recoleta and handy for the Subte and shopping in Santa Fé, this is a reliable and comfortable little hotel with small, neat, well-equipped rooms, good breakfasts – though ask for tea pots. It's a pricey option but made worthwhile by the great service from all the multi-lingual staff who go out of their way to make your stay comfortable. Free internet. Recommended.
AL Aspen Towers, Paraguay 857, T011-4313 1919, www.aspentowers.com.ar. A modern minimalist foyer in this small hotel belies the traditional 1900 French-style bedrooms, all with jacuzzi baths, and all facilities, including a good breakfast and a pool.
AL Bisonte Palace, MT de Alvear 910, T011-328 4751, www.hotelesbisonte.com. A rather charming place, with calm entrance foyer, which remains gracious thanks to charming courteous staff. The rooms are

For an explanation of the Sleeping and Eating price codes used in this guide, and other relevant information, see Essentials, pages 48 and 51.

plain, but spacious, breakfast is ample, and this is in a good location. Very good value.

AL Colón, Carlos Pellegrini 507, T011-4320 3500, www.colon-hotel.com.ar. With a splendid location overlooking Av 9 de Julio and Teatro Colón, in the heart of the city, extremely good value. Charming comfortable bedrooms, pool, gym, great breakfasts, and great service. Recommended.

AL Crillón, Av Santa Fe 796, T011-4310 2000, www.nh-hoteles.com. Centrally located on Plaza San Martín, this traditional place is now owned by the NH chain and being renovated in 2006 as a modern business hotel with every possible comfort.

AL Dolmen, Suipacha 1079, T011-4315 7117, www.hoteldolmen.com.ar. In a good location, this has a smart spacious entrance lobby, with a calm relaxing atmosphere, good professional service, comfortable modern well-designed rooms, and a little pool.

AL El Conquistador, Suipacha 948, T011-4328 3012, www.elconquistador.com.ar. A stylishly modernized 1970s boutique hotel, which retains the wood and chrome foyer, but has bright modern rooms, and a lovely light restaurant on the 10th floor with great views. Well situated and good value.

AL Etoile, R Ortiz 1835 in Recoleta, T011-805 2626, www.etoile.com.ar. Outstanding location, rooftop pool, rooms with kitchenette.

AL Pestana, Carlos Pellegrini 877, T011-5239 1000, www.pestana.com. A smart modern hotel overlooking Av 9 de Julio, a light entrance lounge and spacious comfortable bedrooms, sauna and gym. Not luxurious, but welcoming, with good service.

AL Plaza San Martín Suites, Suipacha 1092, T011-4328 4740, www.plazasanmartin.com.ar. Neat modern self-contained apartments, comfortable and attractively decorated, with lounge and little kitchen, so that you can relax in privacy, right in the city centre, with all the services of an hotel. Sauna, gym, room service. Good value.

A Castelar, Av de Mayo 1152, T011-4383 5000, www.castelarhotel.com.ar. A wonderfully elegant 1920s hotel which retains all the original features in the grand entrance and bar. Cosy bedrooms (some a bit too cosy), helpful staff, and excellent value. Ask if there's going to be a party, though, as it can be very noisy. Also a spa with Turkish baths and massage. Recommended.

A Embajador, Carlos Pellegrini 1181, T011-4326 5302, www.embajadorhotel.com.ar. Nothing fancy, but good value for such a central location, this has comfortable plain rooms, some overlooking Av 9 de Julio, good service, and a small breakfast is included.

A Waldorf, Paraguay 450, T011-312 2071, www.waldorf-hotel.com.ar. Welcoming staff and a comfortable mixture of traditional and modern in this centrally-located hotel. Good value, with a buffet breakfast, English spoken. Recommended.

B Dorá, Maipú 963, T011-4312 7391, www.dorahotel.com.ar. Charming old-fashioned place with comfortable rooms, good service, an attractive lounge decorated with paintings. Warmly recommended.

B Frossard, Tucumán 686, T011-4322 1811, www.hotelfrossard.com.ar. A lovely old 1940's building with high ceilings and the original doors, attractively modernized, and though the rooms are small, the staff are welcoming. This is good value and near C Florida.

B Orly, Paraguay 474, T/F011-312 5344, www.orly.com.ar. Good location, and smartened-up comfortable rooms in an old hotel, with helpful service.

B Regis, Lavalle 813, T011-4327 2605, www.orho-hoteles.com.ar. Good value in this old-fashioned but modernized place, with good breakfast and friendly staff. Good beds and spacious bathrooms. Full breakfast.

C Goya, Suipacha 748, T011-4322 9269, www.goyahotel.com.ar. A range of rooms offered in this friendly welcoming and central place, worth paying **B** for the superior rooms, though all are comfortable and well maintained. Good breakfast, English spoken.

C Marbella, Av de Mayo 1261, T/F011-4383 3573, www.hotelmarbella.com.ar. Modernized and central, though quiet, breakfast included, English, French, Italian, Portuguese and German spoken. Highly recommended.

C Suipacha Inn, Suipacha 515, T011-4322 0099, www.hotelsuipacha.com.ar. Good value, neat small rooms with a/c, basic breakfast.

D La Giralda, Tacuarí 17, T011-4345 3917. Nicely maintained and good value. Popular with budget travellers, with discounts for students and for long stays.

E España, Tacuarí 80, T011-4343 5541. Delightful, old-fashioned, very basic, but full

of character, run by a charmingly eccentric old couple. No breakfast. Recommended.
E O'Rei, Lavalle 733, T011-4393 7186. Slightly cheaper without bath, central, simple but comfortable, spotless, laundry facilities, helpful staff.
D Uruguay, Tacuarí 83, T011-4334 3456. A central and traditional old hotel, very clean and welcoming, good value.

Youth hostels

E pp **St Nicholas**, B Mitre 1691 (y Rodríguez Peña), T011-4373 5920, www.snhostel.com. Beautifully restored old house, spotless rooms, cooking facilities, large roof terrace, luggage store; also **D** double rooms. Discounts for HI members. Recommended.
E pp **V&S**, Viamonte 887, T011-4322 0994, www.hostelclub.com. **D** in attractive double rooms with bath. This is one of the city's best loved hostels, central and beautifully run by friendly English speaking staff, there's a welcoming little café and place to sit, a tiny kitchen, internet access, and lots of tours arranged, plus tango nights, etc. Good place to meet people. Highly recommended.
F pp **Che Lagarto**, Venezuela 857, T011-4343 4845, www.chelagarto.com. New location between Montserrat and San Telmo, large light dorms and **D** doubles (each with bath), attractive tango hall. The whole ground floor is a pub and restaurant open to all.
F pp **El Cachafaz**, Viamonte 982, T011-4328 1445, www.elcachafaz.com. A renovated central house, with dorms and **D** doubles, breakfast, free internet access, laundry.

Palermo *p80, map p81*

AL Five Cool Rooms, Honduras 4742, T011-5235 5555, www.fivebuenosaires.com. Too cool for its own good, perhaps, the style here is brutalist concrete with lots of black wood in the spacious rooms, all with king size beds and bathrooms. There's a living room with DVDs to watch and internet. There's a terrace upstairs too. It's a bit overpriced, but the staff are efficient and speak fluent English.
AL Home, Honduras 5860, T011-4778 1008, www.homebuenosaires.com. Another trendy boutique hotel, this one in Palermo Hollywood, with bold 1950's inspired textiles and minimalist concrete floors, creating a funky vibrant urban chic feel. Just a handful of minimalist rooms around a bar serving light snacks, (soup, salads and tapas). Small pool and space to sunbathe at the back. A cool place to hang out in the evenings.
AL Krista , Bonpland 1665, T011-4771 4697, www.kristahotel.com.ar. A delightful surprise: this intimate boutique hotel is hidden behind the plain façade of an elegant townhouse, once owned by Perón's doctor, in Palermo Hollywood, well placed for restaurants. It's a very appealing place to stay, and good value, with its comfortable, calm, individually designed spacious rooms, all with simple bathrooms, and smart bed linen. A lovely lounge is exquisitely designed by owner Cristina, who makes guests very welcome. Wi-fi, wheelchair access. A real gem. Recommended.
AL Malabia House, Malabia 1555, Palermo Viejo,T011-4833 2410, www.malabiahouse.com.ar. An elegant bed and breakfast in a tastefully converted old house, with 15 light and airy individually designed bedrooms in white and pale green, and lovely calm sitting rooms. Great breakfast. This was the original Palermo boutique hotel, and while it's not the cheapest of the options available, and always booked ahead, it's recommended as a reliable and welcoming option.
AL-A Bo Bo, Guatemala 4882, Palermo Viejo, T011-4774 0505, www.bobohotel.com. Very chic, and one of the most welcoming places to stay in Palermo. Bo Bo has just 7 rooms, designed around different themes, though all are warm, elegant and minimalist, with stylish bathrooms (some with disabled access). There's also an excellent restaurant (🍴) and bar, relaxing places in the evening, with lots of dark wood and smart tables, serving very classy food. Great service from friendly staff, who all speak English. Recommended.
A-B Como en Casa, Gurruchaga 2155, T011-4831 0517, www.bandb.com.ar. Homely rustic style in this converted old house, with exposed brick walls, red stone floors, and lots of woven rugs. A variety of rooms, for 2-4, some with bathrooms, and quieter rooms at the back, where there's a lovely little garden. The whole place is clean and neat, and the welcoming owner speaks English.
B Cypress In, Costa Rica 4828, Palermo Viejo, T011-4833 5834, www.cypressin.com. This cosy compact bed and breakfast offers 8 neat rooms on 2 floors, decorated in pleasing stark

modern style, in a centrally located house, where the staff are very friendly. Stylish small sitting and dining area, and outside patio. Charming. Very good value. Recommended.

B Solar Soler, Soler 5676, T011-4776 3065, www.solarsoler.com.ar. Very homely and extremely welcoming bed and breakfast in a great location in an old town house in Palermo Hollywood and recommended for its excellent service from the manager Victoria, and the charming multi-lingual staff. All rooms have bathrooms, ask for the quiet ones at the back, there's free internet and the breakfasts are good. Recommended.

C Che Lulu, Emilio Zola 5185, T011-4772 0289, www.chelulu.com. Some double rooms and more hostel-style accommodation in this friendly, rambling, laid-back house along a quaint quiet street just a few blocks from Palermo subte. Not luxurious, but great value and very welcoming. Often recommended.

Youth hostels

F pp **Casa Esmeralda**, Honduras 5765, T011-4772 2446, www.casaesmeralda.com.ar. Laid-back, dorms and **D** doubles, neat garden with hammocks and fishpond. Sebastián, owner of trendy bars **La Cigale** and **Zanzibar**, offers basic comfort with great charm.

F pp **Tango Backpackers Hostel**, Thames 2212, T011-4776 6871, www.tangobp.com. Well situated to enjoy Palermo's nightlife, this is a friendly hostel with shared rooms, and **D** doubles, all the usual facilities plus its own restaurant, HI discount.

San Telmo *p83, map p84*

A The Cocker, Av Garay 458, T011-4362 8451, www.thecocker.com. In the heart of the antiques district, this art nouveau house has been cleverly and tastefully restored by its English owners who now offer a perfect urban retreat with stylish suites, a cosy, light living room and delightful roof terraces and gardens. Recommended.

A Dandi Royal, Piedras 922, T011-4307 7623, www.hotelmansiondandiroyal.com. Perfectly restored 1900's house with stunningly elegant entrance hall and some beautiful rooms all decorated in the original style, with luxurious bathrooms. Interesting location between San

Telmo and Congreso, and the added benefit of tango classes downstairs. Charming welcome from English speaking staff, small pool, and much better value than most of the boutique hotels. Recommended.
C La Casita de San Telmo, Cochabamba 286 T/F011-4307 5073, www.lacasitadesantelmo.com. A restored 1840's house, 7 rooms, most of which open onto a garden with a beautiful fig tree. The owners are tango fans; rooms are rented by the day, week or month.

Youth hostels

D-F pp **Garden House Hostel**, San Juan 1271, T011-4305 0517, www.gardenhouseba.com.ar. Dorms or private rooms. Friendly, fun and relaxed hostel with a terrace, living room and kitchen. Rooms are light and have heater and fan. Breakfast included.
F pp **El Hostal de Granados**, Chile 374, T011-4362 5600, www.hostaldegranados.com.ar. Small well-equipped rooms in an interesting building on a popular street with bars and restaurants, lots of light, for 2 (**D**) to 4, with bath, breakfast included, kitchen, free internet, laundry service, reductions for longer stays.
F pp **Hostel-Inn Tango**, Piedras 680, T011-4300 5764, and **Hostel-Inn Buenos Aires**, Humberto Primero 820, T011-4300 7992. Both well-organized hostels in old renovated houses, popular, lively, lots of activities and facilities such as internet, transfers, Spanish lessons. Breakfast included. 20% discount for HI card holders and 10% off long-distance buses. **Hostel-Inn** is a chain of hostels in Argentina, T0800-666 4678, www.hostel-inn.com.
F Hostel Suites Obelisco, Av Correintes 830, T011-4328 4040, www.hostelsuites.com. Same owners as above. 20% discount to cardholders in HI hostels and 10% off long-distance buses.
F pp **Sandanzas**, Balcarce 1351, T011-4300 7375, www.sandanzas.com.ar. Arty hostel run by a group of friends who've created an original and welcoming space, small but with a nice light airy feel, lounge and patio, internet, kitchen, breakfast included. Also (**D**) double rooms with own bath.

Student residences

Accommodation for students and tourists with host families is arranged by **Argentina B&B**, run by Silvia Demetilla, with reliable and cheap accommodation in Buenos Aires and in other towns; recommended. Many hosts speak English, others will give you a chance to practise your Spanish; www.argentinabandb.com.ar. Rooms cost from US$40.
La Casa de Etty, Luis Sáenz Peña 617, T011-4384 6378, coret@ciudad.com.ar. Run by Esther Corcias, manager of **Organización Coret**, www.angelfire.com/pq/coret. For accommodation with host families and also furnished flats.
B&T Argentina, T011-4821 6057, www.bytargentina.com. Accommodation in residences and host families; also furnished flats.

Apartments/self catering

Apartments cost from US$40 per night.
Bahouse, T011-4815 7602, www.bahouse.com.ar. Very good flats, all furnished and well-located in Retiro, Recoleta, Belgrano, Palermo and the centre.
Tu Casa Argentina, Esmeralda 980 p 2 B, T011-4312 4127, www.tucasargentina.com. Furnished flats by the day, week or month; from about US$400 per month.

Eating

Eating out in Buenos Aires is one of the city's great pleasures, with a huge variety of restaurants from the chic to the cheap, and lots of eclectic and exotic choices alongside the inevitable *parrilla* restaurant where you can eat the legendary huge Argentine steak, cooked to perfection grilled over a wood fire. Argentines are very sociable and love to eat out, so if a restaurant is full, it's usually a good sign. Remember, though, that they'll usually start eating between 2130 and 2230. If in doubt, head for Puerto Madero, where there are lots of good mid-range places serving international as well as local cuisine. There are good deals at lunchtime in many restaurants where the *Menú del día* costs US$4-7 for 2 courses and coffee. The following list gives only those restaurants easily accessible for people staying in the city centre. Wherever you're staying, take a taxi to Palermo or Las Cañitas for a wide range of excellent restaurants all within strolling distance.

City centre *p70, map p72*

YYY La Chacra, Av Córdoba 941 (just off 9 de Julio). A superb traditional *parrilla* with excellent steaks brought sizzling to your table (US$16 for complete parrilla and salads for 2), impeccable old-fashioned service, and a lively buzzing atmosphere.

YYY Morizono, Reconquista 899. Japanese sushi and sashami, as well as other dishes.

YYY Sorrento Corrientes 668, (just off Florida). Intimate, elegant atmosphere, with dark wood, nicely lit tables, serving traditional menu with good fish dishes and steak.

YYY Tomo 1, Hotel Panamericano, Carlos Pellegrini 521, T011-4326 6695. Argentine regional dishes and international cuisine of a high standard in a sophisticated atmosphere.

YY Broccolino, Esmeralda 776. Good Italian food, very popular, try *pechuguitas*.

YY Chiquilín, Sarmiento 1599. *Parrilla* and pasta, good value.

YY Club Español, Bernardo de Irigoyen 180 (on Av 9 de Julio, near Av de Mayo). Faded splendour in this fine old Spanish social club serving excellent seafood.

YY El Palacio de la Papa Frita, Lavalle 735 and 954, Av Corrientes 1620. Great place for a filling feed, with a large menu, and quite atmospheric, despite the bright lighting.

YY El Querandí, Perú 302 y Moreno. Good food in an intimate atmosphere in this historical place that was opened in the 1920s. Also a popular café, good atmosphere, well known for its Gin Fizz, and a tango venue.

YY Empire Bar, Tres Sargentos 427. Serves Thai food in a tasteful atmosphere.

YY Fratello, Tucumán 688. Cheap pastas and other Italian dishes in attractive Italian-style surroundings.

YY La Estancia, Lavalle 941. A slightly touristy but reliable *parrilla* with frieze of *estancia* life on the wall, popular with business people for lunch, and serving good grills, US$14 for 2.

YY Los Inmortales, Lavalle 746. Specializes in pizza, all tasty and good value to share.

YY Tancat, Paraguay 645 . Really authentic Basque food and from other Spanish regions, delicious dishes: recommended.

Y Exedra, Carlos Pellegrini and Córdoba. A welcoming traditional-style café right on Av 9 de Julio, serving cheap set-price menu for US$5-8, including a glass of wine.

Y Gianni´s, Viamonte 834 and 25 de Mayo 757 (open 0900-1700). The set menu with the meal-of-the-day makes an ideal lunch in a renovated old house. Risottos and salads are very good.

Y Gran Victoria, Suipacha 783. Good value *tenedor libre*, including parrilla, in a cheery though not elegant atmosphere, also cheap set price meals.

Y La Casona del Nonno, Lavalle 827. Popular with tourists for its cheap set price menu, Italian-style food, cheap pastas and *parrilla*.

Y Güerrín, Av Corrientes 1368. A Buenos Aires institution, serving incredibly cheap and filling slabs of pizza and *fainá* (chick pea polenta) which you eat standing up at a zinc bar, or at tables, though you miss out on the colourful local life that way. Wonderful.

Tea rooms, café-bars and ice cream parlours

Aroma, Florida y Marcelo T de Alvear. A great place to relax in the centre, with a huge space upstairs, comfortable chairs by big windows onto C Florida, so you can read the papers, and watch the world go by.

Café Tortoni, Av de Mayo 825-9. This most famous Buenos Aires café has been the elegant haunt of artists and writers for over 100 years: Carlos Gardel sang here, and Borges was a regular. It's self conscious of its tourist status these days, but still atmospheric, with marble columns, stained glass ceilings, old leather chairs, and photographs of its famous clientele on the walls. Excellent coffee and cakes, and good tea, all rather pricey, but worth a visit for the interesting *peña* evenings of poetry and music, and jazz and tango.

Clásica y Moderna, Av Callao 892. One of the city's most welcoming cafés, with a bookshop at back, lots of brick and wood, this has a great atmosphere, good for breakfast through to drinks at night, with live music Thu to Sat. Highly recommended.

Confitería Ideal, Suipacha 384. One of the most atmospheric cafés in the city. Wonderfully old-fashioned 1930's interior, almost untouched, serving good coffee and excellent cakes with good service. Upstairs, tango is taught in the afternoons and there's tango dancing at a *milonga* here afterwards, from 2200. Highly recommended.

El Gato Negro, Av Corrientes 1669. A lovely old traditional café serving a wide choice of

coffees and teas, and good cakes. You can also buy a big range of spices here.
Florida Garden, Florida y Paraguay. Another well-known café, popular for lunch, and tea.
Richmond, Florida 468, between Lavalle and Corrientes. Genteel, old-fashioned and charming place for tea with cakes, and a basement where chess is played daily between 1200-2400.

Markets and supermarkets

For quick cheap snacks the markets are recommended. Also huge choice in basement of **Galerías Pacífico**, Florida y Viamonte. Some supermarkets have good, cheap restaurants: **Coto supermarket**, Viamonte y Paraná, upstairs. Many supermarkets have very good deli counters and other shops sell *fiambres* (smoked, cured meats) and cheeses and other prepared foods for quick, cheap eating. Good snacks all day and night at Retiro and Constitución railway termini. The snack bars in underground stations are also cheap. **Güerrin**, Corrientes 1368, is a fabulous atmospheric place for cheap tasty pizzas and *faina*, standing at the zinc bar. A Buenos Aires institution. **Delicity bakeries**, several branches, have very fresh *facturas* (pastries), cakes, breads, and authentic American donuts. Another good bakery for breakfasts and salads is **Bonpler**, Florida 481, 0730-2300, with the daily papers, classical music. Other branches throughout the city.

La Recova

Three blocks west of Plaza San Martín, under the flyover at the northern end of Av 9 de Julio, between C Arroyo and Av del Libertador, are several recommended restaurants.
TTT El Mirasol, Posadas 1032. Serves top quality parrilla in an elegant atmosphere.
TTT La Tasca de Plaza Mayor, Posadas 1052. Good Spanish food.
TTT Piegari, Posadas 1042. Great Italian food.
TT Juana M, Carlos Pellegrini 1535 (downstairs). This is an excellent choice, very popular with locals for a good range of dishes, and salads in a spacious basement.
TT Winery, Paseo La Recova, off Libertador 500. A great place to sample the best of Argentina's fine wines, in a chic wine bar with light dishes such as salads and gourmet sandwiches. Also at Av Alem 880.

Puerto Madero *p77*

The revamped docks area is an attractive place to eat, and to stroll along the waterfront before dinner. It's not the city's cheapest area, since it's long been popular with businessmen and tourists, but the best restaurants here are popular with locals too, and there's lots of choice. Heading along Av Alicia Moreau de Justo (from north to south), the following are recommended. The cheapest places are next to the boat, **Fragata Sarmiento** on Dique 3.
TTT Bice, No 192. Italian-influenced food.
TTT El Mirasol del Puerto, No 202. Well known and loved for a broad menu.
TTT Katrine, No 138. Delicious fish and pasta.
TTT Las Lilas, No 516. Excellent *parrilla*, popular with Porteños, and often recommended.
TT La Parolaccia, 2 sister restaurants: a general bistro at No 1052, and the best seafood restaurant in Puerto Madero, at No 1160, serving fresh and deliciously cooked seafood in a lively brasserie atmosphere. Indeed both places are very stylish, and very popular with Porteños. Bargain lunches during the week, and also superb pastas. Recommended.

Recoleta *p78, map p79*

TTT Lola, Roberto M Ortiz 1805. Well known for superb pasta dishes, lamb and fish. Recommended.
TTT Sirop, Pasaje del Correo, Vte Lopez 1661, T011-4813 5900. Delightful chic design, delicious French-inspired food, superb patisserie too. Highly recommended.
TT El Sanjuanino, Posadas 1515. Atmospheric place offering the best of Argentina's typical dishes from the northwest: *humitas*, *tamale*, and *empanadas*, as well as unusual game dishes.
TT Rodi Bar, Vicente López 1900. Excellent *bife* and other dishes in this typical *bodegón*, a welcoming unpretentious place.
T Güerrin, Corrientes 1368. A fabulous atmospheric place for cheap tasty pizzas and *faina*, standing at the zinc bar. A Buenos Aires institution.
T La Madeleine, Av Santa Fe 1726. Great for cheap pastas in a bright cheerful place, open 24 hrs. Recommended.

Tea rooms and ice cream parlours

Café Victoria, Roberto M Ortiz 1865. A wonderful old-fashioned café, popular with marvellous perfectly-coiffed ladies sipping

tea in a refined atmosphere, great cakes.
Ice Cream Freddo, on Av Quintana on Recoleta parks, Av Callao y Juncal, in Puerto Madero on Dique 4, and at shopping malls. Popular choice, and the city's leading brand. Very good ice cream.
Persicco, Salguero y Cabello, Maure y Migueletes and Av Rivadavia 4933. 'The best ice cream in the world'. You haven't tasted ice cream until you've had Persicco's Mascarpone, or their Flan de Dulce de leche. Exquisite chocolate flavours and fruity ice creams and sorbets too. Also delivery: 0810 333 7377. Branches in upmarket areas, but most convenient is Salguero (near Alto Palermo shopping centre) Salguero 2591 y Cabello, Free wi-fi in their shops which also sell coffee. You could sit and eat ice cream all day.

Palermo *p80, map p81*

There are lots of chic restaurants and bars in Palermo Viejo and the Las Cañitas district, (see below). It's a sprawling district, and lovely to walk around in the evenings. Take a taxi to one of these restaurants, and walk around once you're in the area, before deciding where to eat. Palermo has lots of good cafés opposite the park, including the fabulous ice creams at **Un' Altra Volta**, Av del Libertador 3060, T011-4805 1818.

Palermo Viejo *p82, map p81*

TTT Cabernet, Jorge Luis Borges 1757, T011-4831 3071. The smoked salmon and caviar blinis starter here is unmissable. Dine outside in the elegant terrace, fragrant with jasmine, and heated in winter, or in the more traditional clubby interior in this traditional *chorizo* house, given a cosmopolitan twist with purple walls. Sophisticated traditional cuisine, a great wine list and good service. Worth the price for a special dinner.
TTT Dominga, Honduras 5618, T011-4771 4443, www.domingarestaurant.com. Excellent cuisine with an Asian influence, and sushi too, served in elegant surroundings, muted lighting with bamboo paneling, good professional service and a good wine list. Highly recommended for a romantic evening or a treat. Lunch menu Mon-Fri US$7, closed Sun. Reservations needed for dinner.
TTT Lomo, Costa Rica 4661, T011-4833 3200. The best steak in Palermo in this famous and posh *parrilla*, deservedly popular with stylish Porteños. Highly recommended.
TT Bar 6, Armenia 1676 T011-4833 6807. One of the best chic, modern bars serving food in laid back spacious surroundings in this large airy space, with bare concrete, bold colours and sofas upstairs for relaxing on. Excellent lunches, friendly atmosphere, good for a drink in the evening. Closed Sundays. Recommended.
TT Bio, Humboldt 2199, T011-4774 3880. Delicious gourmet organic food, on a sunny corner where you can sit outside. Fresh lime green decor and a friendly atmosphere. Open daily, but closed Mon for dinner.
TT Cluny, El Salvador 4618, T011-4831 7176. A great place for lunch: the menu is as stylish as the black and cream surroundings, from the excellent home made bread to the exquisite combinations of flavours of sauces for fish and pasta. One of Palermo's classiest restaurants, whether you dine in the bistro at the back, or chic white armchairs in the middle. Friendly staff, mellow music. Recommended.
TT El Diamante, Malabia 1688, 1st floor, T011-4831 5735. Great loud music in this cosy first floor restaurant and bar with a terrace upstairs for a party atmosphere, gay-friendly. Closed Sun.
TT El Manto, Costa Rica 5801, T011-4774 2409. Mon-Sat lunch and dinner. The usual chic concrete look, but the food is exceptional: delicious Armenian dishes cooked by a real Armenian chef, in this spacious relaxed restaurant, where the service is friendly. Good for a quiet evening.
TT Eterna Cadencia, Honduras 5574, T011-4774 4100. A real find: this is a fabulous small bookshop with a wonderful selection of English classics and contemporary literature, which has a great little café in beautifully designed high ceilinged rooms with comfortable sofas at the back, great for a light lunch. Open 0900-2400, closed Mon.
TT Garum, Malabia 1721, T011-4831 6203. Elegant restaurant and wine bar in imaginatively redesigned old house offering wine tastings and good Mediterranean food in its spacious rooms decorated with contemporary art exhibitions.
TT Janio, Malabia 1805, T011-4833 6540. With a great position overlooking Plaza Palermo Viejo and a lovely upstairs terrace,

this was one of the first Palermo restaurants. Open from breakfast until the early hours, this is a lively laid back place for lunch, with good fixed price menu US$5, and more sophisticated Argentine cuisine in the evenings. A great place to meet for a drink.

Miranda, Costa Rica y Fitz Roy, T011-4771 4255. Traditional parrilla in hip surroundings, with simple rustic design and a lively atmosphere in the evenings. Also pasta and a good wine list. Good value for lunch.

Omm, Honduras 5656, T011-4774 4224. Hip, cosy wine and tapas bar with great wines and good food. Open daily from 1800, Happy hour from 1800-2100. Sister restaurant Omm Carnes, Costa Rica 5198, T011-4773 0954, for steak and meat dishes in a similarly trendy environment, Open daily from 1100 but closed for dinner on Sun.

Social Paraiso, Honduras 5182. A real find for a great lunch. Simple delicious dishes served in a relaxed chic atmosphere in this friendly place run by art collectors. Groovy paintings on the walls and a lovely little patio hidden at the back. Good fish and tasty salads. Recommended.

Las Cañitas *p80, map p81*

Northeast of Palermo Hollywood, separated from it by a railway track, this has developed into a popular little area for eating, with a huge number of restaurants packed into a few blocks along C Baez. Most open around at 2000, and also for lunch at weekends:

Baez, next door to Morelia. Very trendy, with lots of orange neon, serving sophisticated Italian-style food, delicious goat's cheese ravioli.

Campo Bravo, Baez y Arevalo. A stylish minimalist place serving superb steaks and vegetables on the *parrilla*, in a friendly atmosphere. Popular and recommended.

De la Ostia, Baez 212. A small and chic bistro for tapas and Spanish-style food, with a good atmosphere.

Eh! Santino, Baez 194. A trendy small restaurant for Italian style food and drinks, dark and cosy with lots of mirrors.

Morelia, Baez 260. Cooks superb pizzas on the *parilla* or in wood ovens, and has a lovely roof terrace for summer.

Novecento. Across the road from **De la Ostia** is a lively French-style bistro, stylish but unpretentious and cosy, serving good fish dishes among a broad menu.

El Primo, on the opposite corner from Campo Bravo. A popular and buzzing *parrilla* for slightly older crowd. Cheap set menus in a relaxed atmosphere with fairy lights.

La Fonda del Polo, on the opposite side of Baez. Serves standard meat dishes in an intimate environment with lots of polo bric-a-brac on the walls, great value set menus, wine included.

San Telmo *p83, map p84*

There are plenty of restaurants along C Defensa, and in the surrounding streets, and new places are opening all the time.

La Brigada, Estados Unidos 465, T011-4361 5557. The best choice in San Telmo, this is a really superb and atmospheric *parrilla*, serving excellent Argentine cuisine and wines in a cosy buzzing atmosphere. Very popular, and not cheap, but highly recommended. Always reserve.

Brasserie Petanque, Defensa y México, T011-4342 7930. Very good french cuisine at affordable prices, and set lunch Mon-Fri. It's an appealing little place, a tasteful combination of Paris and Buenos Aires.

Café San Juan, Av San Juan 450, T011-4300 1112. Not a café but a very small *bodegón* – looking just like a typical *restaurant de barrio* (local dive) but with an excellent cook. A short menu includes delicious *tapas de salmón*. It's very popular, book ahead.

La Casa de Esteban de Luca, Defensa 1000. *Parrilla* and pastas in a lively café atmosphere, though service is slow.

El Desnivel, Defensa 855. Popular for cheap and basic food, jam packed at weekends, good atmosphere.

La Trastienda, Balcarce 460. Theatre café with lots of live events, also serving meals and drinks from breakfast to dinner, great music. A relaxed and cool place to hang out, with an arty crowd. Recommended.

La Vieja Rotiseria, Defensa 963. Cheap café for bargain *parrilla*, packed at weekends, so come early.

Lezama, Brasil 359 (on Parque Lezama). A typical *bodegón*, popular with families, typical Argentine menu, huge portions, though the service is rather slow.

Sumo, Independencia y Piedras. Good ice cream.

Bars and clubs

City centre *p70, map p72*
See also under Live music, below.
The Kilkenny, MT de Alvear 399 esq Reconquista. Open 1730-0600 (Sat opens at 2000), happy hour 1730-2100. Very popular Irish bar. **The Shamrock**, Rodríguez Peña 1220. Irish-run, popular, expensive Guinness, happy hour for ISIC card holders. Also **Druid In**, Reconquista 1040. Live music weekly, English spoken. Next door is **Porto Pirata**. **Celta Bar**, Rodríguez Peña y Sarmiento. **The Temple Bar**, MT de Alvear 945. **La Cigale**, 25 de Mayo 722, T011-4312 8275. A popular place after office hours that's usually crowded by 2400. Very good music, recommended for Tue evenings with guest DJs. **Milion**, Paraná 1048. A French-style residence with lots of space, sitting areas, cushions and tables in the sumptuous halls. It has also a garden and serves very good drinks. A mixed clientele, between 25-40 years old, recommended Fri after midnight.

Recoleta *p78, map p79*
Buller Brewing Company, Roberto M Ortiz 1827. Happy hour till 2100.

Palermo *p80, map p81*
Mundo Bizarro, Guatemala 4802. This hugely popular bar gets its name from bizarre films shown on a big screen. People usually come here for dinner first, and the food is American style, then they stay all night. Electronic music on Fri and Sat; 1960s and 1980s rest of the week. For a 20- to 35-year-old crowd.

Las Cañitas district is especially good on Thu evenings, when it's noisier and there are more people. though it's really not appealing at weekends. Try **Soul Café**, Báez 246, for 1970's style, and a good atmosphere with soul and funk music, a 25- to 40-year-old crowd.

San Telmo *p83, map p84*
There are good bars around Plaza Dorrego. **Boquitas Pintadas**, Estados Unidos 1393 (Constitución), T011-4381 6064. Bar and hotel, German-run.

Clubs

Generally it is not worth going to clubs before 0230 at weekends. Dress is usually smart. **Club 69 (at Niceto Club)**, Niceto Vega 5510, T011-4779 9396, www.nicetoclub.com or www.club69.com.ar. On Thu, for a 20-something crowd, good music with live shows, packed after 0200. Few foreigners. **El Living**, MT de Alvear 1540, T011-4811 4730. As small, cosy and relaxed as a living room gets.
Mint, Av Costanera Norte y Sarmiento (in Punta Carrasco). On Sat, Latin and electronic music. Mostly 20-somethings. Attractive terrace on the river.
Opera Bay, on Dique 4, Puerto Madero, www.operabay.com. A classic in Puerto Madero with huge rooms, several bars, and a variety of music, attracting a 25-to-40-year-old crowd. Popular after office on Wed. Also popular Fri-Sat after 0200.
Pacha, Av Costanera Norte y Pampa, www.pachabuenosaires.com. A big place, upmarket feel, 20- to 30-year-olds, electronic music.

Gay bars and clubs

Most gay clubs charge US$10 entry on door. **Amerika**, Gascón 1040, T011-4865 4416, www.ameri-k.com.ar.
Palacio, Alsina 940, www.palaciobue nosaires.com. Best on Fri.
Sitges, Av Córdoba 4119, T011-4861 2763, www.sitgesonline.com.ar. Gay and lesbian bar, near **Amerika**.

Entertainment

Details of most events are given in the 'Espectáculos' section of newspapers, *La Nación* and *Clarín*, and the Buenos Aires Herald (English) on Fri, and also in www.laguia.clarin.com

Cinemas

The selection of films shown in Buenos Aires is excellent, ranging from new Hollywood releases to Argentine and world cinema;

details are listed daily in all main newspapers. Films are shown uncensored and in the original language, with most foreign films subtitled, rather than dubbed into Spanish: only children's films are dubbed. Tickets are best booked in the early afternoon to ensure good seats (average price US$4, more expensive at weekends; there are discounts on Wed and for first show daily; other discounts depend on cinema). Most shopping malls have cinemas and these tend to show more mainstream Hollywood movies, but you can find recent European or non-Hollywood films elsewhere, mostly in the Atlas chain of cinemas: **Arteplex**, Av Cabildo 2829, T011-4781 6500, Belgrano; **Cineduplex**, Av Rivadavia 5050, T011-4902 5682; and **Lorca**, Av Corrientes 1428. Old movies, classics, curiosities and experimental cinema are shown at **MALBA art gallery**, Av Figueroa Alcorta 3415, T011-4808 6500, and at **Sala Leopoldo Lugones** (Teatro San Martín), Av Corrientes 1530, 10th floor, T011-4371 0111. Most Argentinean movies are shown at **Complejo Tita Merello**, Suipacha 442, T011-4322 1195, and at **Gaumont**, Av Rivadavia 1635, T011- 4371 3050.

For what's on in all cinemas throughout Buenos Aires, see any daily paper or websites such as www.lanacion.com.ar, www.buenos airesherald.com or www.terra.com.ar. Independent foreign and national films are shown during the **Festival de Cine Independiente**, held every Apr.

Cultural events and activities

Centro Cultural Borges, Galerías Pacífico, Viamonte y San Martín, T011-5555 5450. Music and dance concerts, special exhibitions, some shows with students discounts.
Centro Cultural Recoleta, Junín 1930, next to the Recoleta cemetery. Many free activities.
Fundación Proa, Av Pedro de Mendoza 1929, T011-4303 0909. Contemporary art in La Boca.
Luna Park stadium, Bouchard 465, near Correo Central, T011-4312 2135, www.lunapark.com.ar. Pop/jazz concerts, sports events, ballet and musicals.
Palais de Glace, Posadas 1725, T011-4804 1163. Temporary art exhibitions and other cultural events.
Teatro Gen San Martín, Corrientes 1530, T011- 4371 0111, www.teatrosan martin.com.ar. Organizes many cultural activities, many free, including concerts, 50% ISIC discount for Thu, Fri and Sun events (only in advance at 4th floor, Mon-Fri). The theatre's **Sala Leopoldo Lugones** shows international classic films, daily, US$1.

Live music

La Peña del Colorado, Güemes 3657, T011-4822 1038. Argentinean *folclore* music played live in this atmospheric and cheerful place, where regional food is served. Recommended.
La Trastienda, Balcarce 460. This popular venue attracts a mixed crowd for very different types of music.
Maluco Beleza, Sarmiento 1728. Live Brazilian dance music.
ND Ateneo, Paraguay 918. A small theatre for a great variety of Latin American music.
Niceto, Niceto Vega 5510 (Palermo Hollywood district) and La Cigale, 25 de Mayo 722, T011-4312 8275.

Jazz

Café Tortoni, Av de Mayo 825, T011-4342 4328, www.cafetortoni.com.ar. Features the Fénix Jazz Band(dixieland), Sat 2300.
La Revuelta, Alvarez Thomas 1368, T011-4553 5530. Live jazz, bossa nova and tango.
Notorious, Av Callao 966, T011-4813 6888, www.notorious.com.ar. Music shop, live music.
Thelonious, Salguero 1884, T011-4829 1562.

Salsa

La Salsera, Yatay 961. Highly regarded.

Tango

There are basically 2 ways to enjoy Buenos Aires' wonderfully sensuous and passionate dance: watch superb tango at a show, or learn to dance at a class, and then try you're your new steps at a *milonga* (tango club). Tango may seem impossibly complicated, but it's the key to the Argentine psyche, and you haven't experienced the dance unless you've tried it on the dancefloor. There are now so many schools and *milongas* offering classes, where tourists blend in happily with locals, that you won't feel awkward for long. There is a tango information desk at the **Centro Cultural San Martín**, Sarmiento 1551, T011-4373 2829, open 1400-2100. and a useful website: www.tangodata.com.ar. Look out for the latest leaflet listing tango classes and milongas, *Passionate Buenos Aires*, produced by the city tourist board, and available from tourist information kiosks.

Events culminate in **National Tango Day** (11 Dec), and there are free events all over the city, details from tourist offices.

Tango shows

This is the way to see the finest expression of tango dancing at its best. Most shows pride themselves on a very high level of dancing, and although they're not cheap, this could be the unforgettable highlight to your visit.

Bar Sur, Estados Unidos 299, T011-4362 6086. 2000-0300, US$45 including all-you-can-eat pizza, drinks extra. Good fun, and the public sometimes join the professional dancers.

Café Tortoni, see cafés above. Daily tango shows from 2030, US$10.

El Cabaret at Faena Hotel and Universe, Martha Salotti 445, T011-4010 9200. A glamorous show, charting tango's evolution, daily at 2030.

El Querandí, Perú 302, T011-5199 1770. Tango show restaurant, daily, dinner 2030, show at 2215, US$65 for both.

El Viejo Almacén, Independencia y Balcarce, T011-4307 7388. The best place of all. Daily, with dinner from 2030, show at 2200, US$67 with all included. Very impressive dancing from the city's best dancers, excellent live band, and great singing from some of tango's great names. Highly recommended.

La Cumparsita, Chile 302, T011-4302 3387, 2200-0300. Authentic, small venue, just US$17 including drink and some food.

La Esquina de Carlos Gardel, Carlos Gardel 3200, T011-4867 6363, www.esquinacarlos gardel.com.ar. Dinner at 2030, and show at 22.15, US$70 for both. Recommended.

La Ventana, Balcarce 431, T011-4331 0217. Daily dinner from 2000 (dinner and show US$70) or show with 2 drinks, 2200, US$50, touristy but very good, and the only show to include some of Argentina's traditional folklore music.

Piazzolla Tango, Florida 165 (basement), Galería Güemes, T011-4344 8200, www.piazzollatango.com. A beautifully restored belle époque hall hosts a smart tango show; dinner at 2045 (dinner and show US$60), show at 2215 (show only US$40).

Tangol, Florida 971, p 1, T011-4312 7276, www.tangol.com, see also Tour operators, page . Runs trips to tango shows.

Milongas and tango classes

Milongas are extremely popular among younger Porteños, since tango went through a revival a few years ago. You can take a class, and get a good feel for the music, before the dancing starts a couple of hours later. Both traditional tango and milonga (a more cheerful style of music with a faster rhythm) are played, and venues occasionally have live orchestras. Cost is usually around US$3-4, and even complete beginners are welcome. Tango classes are also given all over the city, but you might find milongas more fun, and they're better places to meet people.

Central Cultural Torquato Tasso, Defensa 1575, T011-4307 6506. Daily evening classes, dancing Sun at 2100. English spoken.

Confitería Ideal, Suipacha 384, T011-5265 8069. Dancing Mon, Wed, Sat and Sun. Daily classes from 1500.

Dandi, Piedras 936, T011-4361 3537, www.mansiondandiroyal.com. Excellent teaching with Noelia and Nahuel or Rodolfo and Irma. Mon, Tue, Fri 1900, Wed 1800, Sat 1700, Sun 1930, 2200.

La Viruta, Armenia 1366, Palermo Viejo, T011-4774 6357, www.lavirutatango.com. Most popular among a young trendy crowd. Wed, 2300, Fri and Sat 2400. Classes Wed 2130, Thu 2000 (includes tango and milonga lessons), Fri and Sat 2230, Sun 2000 (includes milonga and tango lessons).

Porteño y Bailarín , Riobamba 345, T011-4932 5452, www.porteybailarin.com.ar. Tue and Sun class 2100, dancing 2300.

Theatre

About 20 commercial theatres play all year, and there are many amateur theatres, with a theatre festival at the end of May. You are advised to book early for a seat at a concert, ballet, or opera. Tickets for most popular shows (including rock and pop concerts) are sold also through **Ticketek**, T011-5237 7200, **Entrada Plus**, T011-4324 1010, or **Ticket master**, T011-4321 9700, www.tm.com.ar. See www.alternativateatral.com or www.mundoteatral.com.ar. For listings, see www.terra.com.ar, www.lanacion.com, www.buenosairesherald.com

The following is a selection that includes the main theatres, almost all of them in the centre. Look for more places in Abasto, Palermo and San Telmo. **Beckett Teatro**, Guardia Vieja 3556, T011-4867 5185. **Broadway**, Av Corrientes 1155, T011-4381 1180. **Centro Cultural Borges**, Viamonte y San Martín, T011-5555 5359. **Centro Cultural de la Cooperación**, Av Corrientes 1543, T011-5077 8077. **Ciudad Cultural Konex**, Sarmiento 3131, T011-5237 7200. **Coliseo**, Marcelo T de Alvear 1125, T011-4816 3789. **El Nacional**, Av Corrientes 960, T011-4326 4218. **General San Martín**, Av Corrientes 1530, T0800-333 5254. **La Plaza**, Av Corrientes 1660, T011-6320 5350. **Liceo**, Rivadavia y Paraná, T011-4381 5745. **Lola Membrives**, Av Corrientes 1280, T011-4381 0076. **Maipo**, Esmeralda 443, T011-4322 4882. **Multiteatro**, Av Corrientes 1283, T011-4382 9140. **Nacional Cervantes**, Libertad 815, T011-4816 4224. **Ópera**, Av Corrientes 860, T011-4326 1335. **Payró**, San Martín 766, T011-4312 5922. **Regina**, Av Santa Fe 1235, T011-4812 5470. **Teatro del Globo**, Marcelo T de Alvear 1155, T011-4816 3307. **Teatro del Pueblo**, Av Roque Sáenz Peña 943, T011- 4326 3606.

Shopping

Buenos Aires is such a great place for shopping that it's getting a reputation for being as good as New York for shopping trips. Contemporary Argentine design is excellent, with fashionable cuts and fabrics which would hold their own in London or Milan but at a third of the price. Argentine designers make the most of the superb quality leather for jackets, shoes and bags, ranging from the funky to the classic and traditional. **Palermo** is the best place for chic little boutiques and some well-known international names, with shops spread out through pleasant leafy streets with lots of cafés – see below for details. For the major names, head straight to **Patio Bullrich** indoor shopping mall. In the centre of town, the main shopping streets are the pedestrianized **C Florida**, stretching south from Plaza San Martín, and the whole of **C Santa Fé**, between Av 9 de Julio to Av Pueyrredon, though some blocks are more upmarket than others, and there are some obviously cheaper zones. But if your time is limited, go straight to one of the indoor shopping malls, known here as '*shoppings*' where you'll find all the major Argentine names. Palermo is so full of boutiques and chic interiors shops, you will be spoilt for choice, and it's hard to know where to start. The 2 main shopping streets to head for, then, are **Honduras** and **El Salvador**, between Malabia and Serrano, with more options further south on Gorriti and along Costa Rica.

To get the tax back on purchases over US$100 (100 pesos), see Essentials, page 54.

Antiques

There are many high quality antiques for sale around Recoleta: a stroll along the streets around Callao and Quintana will yield some great buys. For cheaper antiques, and second-hand bric-a-brac, San Telmo is the place. The market on Sun is a good place to start, but on other days all the shops along Defensa are still open, and it's worth searching around for bargains. China, glass, rugs, old silver *mates*, clothes and jewellery are among the goodies you can pick up. **Pasaje de la Defensa**, Defensa 1179. A beautifully-restored 1880s house containing small shops.

Books

You'll find most bookshops along C Florida, Av Corrientes or Av Santa Fé, and in shopping malls. Secondhand and discount bookshops are mostly along Av Corrientes and Av de Mayo. Rare books are sold in several specialised stores in the Microcentro (the area enclosed by Suipacha, Esmeralda, Tucumán and Paraguay). The main chains of bookshops to look for, usually selling a small selection of foreign books, are: **Cúspide**, with several branches on Florida, Av Corrientes and some malls, and the biggest store at Village Recoleta, Vicente López y Junín; **Distal**, Florida 738 and more branches on Florida and Av Corrientes; **Yenny-El Ateneo**, in all shopping malls, and also sell music too. Biggest stores in Florida 340 and Av Santa Fé 1860.

Every Apr a huge book fair, **Feria del Libro**, is held at the Rural Society grounds, on Plaza Italia; exhibitions, shows and books for sale in all languages. Foreign newspapers are available from news stands on Florida, in Recoleta and the kiosk at Corrientes y Maipú. For a larger selection of books in English, try the following:

ABC, Maipú 866. Also books in German. Acme Agency, Suipacha 245 p 1, Arenales 885. Joyce, Proust & Co, Tucumán 1545 p 1 A. Also books in other European languages. Kel, Marcelo T de Alvear 1369. LOLA, Viamonte 976 p 2, Mon-Fri 1200-1830. Small publishers specialised in Latin America natural history. Also used and rare editions, most in English. Librería Rodríguez, Sarmiento 835. Walrus Books, Estados Unidos 617. Used books in English, including Latin American authors.

Asociación Dante Alighieri, Tucumán 1646. Italian books.

Crack Up , Costa Rica 4767, T011-4831 3502. Funky open plan book shop and café which extends to the street. Open Mon-Wed till 2230, and till the early hours the rest of the week. Good place to meet interesting people.

El Libro Francés, Oficina del Libro Francés, Esmeralda 861. Books in French.

Eterna Cadencia, Honduras 5574, T011-4774 4100 Great bookshop with excellent selection of novels in English: classics, contemporary fiction and translations of Spanish and Argentine authors. Highly recommended for its café too.

Camping equipment

Good equipment available from **Buenos Aires Sports**, Panamericana y Paraná, Martínez (Shopping Unicenter, 2nd level). Good equipment. **Fugate** (no sign), Gascón 238 (off Rivadavia 4000 block), T011-4982 0203. Also repairs equipment. **Outside Mountain Equipment**, Otero 172 (Chacarita), T011-4856 6204, www.outside.com.ar. **Cacique Camping**, Esteban Echeverría 3360, Munro, T011-4762 4475, caciquenet@ciudad.com.ar. Manufactured clothing and equipment. **Ecrin**, Mendoza 1679, T011-4784 4799, www.ecrin.com.ar. Imported climbing equipment. **Angel Baraldo**, Av Belgrano 270, www.baraldo.com.ar. Imported and Argentine stock. **Montagne**, Florida 719, Paraná 834, www.montagenoutdoors.com.ar, and **Camping Center**, Esmeralda 945, www.camping-center.com.ar. Good selection of outdoor sports gear and equipment. **Jorge Gallo**, Liniers 1522, Tigre, T011-4731 0323. For GPS repair service. Camping gas available at **Britam**, B Mitre 1111. **Todo Gas**, Sarmiento 1540, and **El Pescador**, Paraguay y Libertad.

Clothes and accessories

The following can all be found in Palermo.

Men's clothes and accessories

Airborn, Gurruchaga 1770, T011-4831 5465. Informal and more formal clothes.

Balthazar, Gorriti 5131, T011-4834 6235. Smart men's clothes and accessories.

Boating evolution , El Salvador 4603. Updated trainers with a twist.

Il Reve, Gurruchaga 1867, T011-4834 6432. Smart, well-tailored and original menswear.

Postman, Armenia 1555, T011-4833 4818. Great leather postman's bags and wallets.

Sartori, Gurruchaga 1538, T011-4831 2071. Shoes with a baseball/camper feel.

Women's clothes and accessories

Caro Cuore, Armenia 1535. Great underwear, alluring and beautifully designed, and much cheaper than in Europe, in this vast calm shop where the staff are really helpful.

Colombas, Jorge Luis Borges 2029, T011-4833 4664. Fabulous hand made jewellery, eclectic, hippy and very original styles, as well as lovely chic hand knitted jumpers.

Elementos, El Salvador 4817, T011-4832 6971. Soft minimalist suede and leather bags.

Josefina Ferroni , Armenia 1471, T011-4831 4033. Chic shoes.

María Blizniuk, Costa Rica and Borges. Lovely feminine designs, cute shoes too.

Mariana Dappianno , Honduras 4932, T011-4833 4731. Serious interesting and elegant designer, using novel textiles.

Mariano Toledo, Armenia 1564, T011-4831 4861. Very elegant, unusual and feminine modern designs, innovative fabrics and cuts. See www.marianotoledo.com for inspiration.

Nueveveinticinco (925), Honduras 4808, T011-4833 5343, www.nueve veinticinco.com.ar. Fabulous jewellery shop where the owners create wonderful

contemporary designs around stunning rocks of all kinds, and also to your specifications. Incredible value.
Rapsodia , El Salvador 4757, T011-4832 5363. Great range of this best selling eclectic brand of eccentric clothes, wonderful jeans, helpful staff who rush around and get your size.
Renzo Rainero , Gurruchaga y Honduras, T011-4832 5267. High-quality leather and interesting designs.
Uma, Honduras 5225, T011-4832 2122. Stylish contemporary leather.

Handicrafts

Alhué, Juncal 1625. Very good aboriginal-style crafts.
Art Petrus, Florida 969, and **Hotel Panamericano** at Carlos Pellegrini.
Arte y Esperanza, Balcarce 234, and Artesanías Argentinas, Montevideo 1386. Excellent little shop selling an impressive range of very good indigenous crafts from all over Argentina, particularly from the north west. Chaguar bags, masks and weavings. Ethical owners give most of the profits back to the communities who make the goods. The standard is high and prices are reasonable. Highly recommended.
Business Design Centre, Recoleta. High-quality northern Argentine handicrafts.
El Boyero, Galería Larreta, Florida 953, T011-4312 3564. High quality silver, leather, wood work and other typical Argentine handicrafts.
Martín Fierro, Santa Fe 992. Good handicrafts, stonework etc. Recommended.
Plata Nativa, Galería del Sol, Florida 860, local 41, T011-4312 1398, www.platanativa.com. For Latin American folk handicrafts.

Interiors

There are fabulous interior design shops throughout **Palermo**, of which just a couple are mentioned, since it's assumed you won't be able to take much home with you. Look out for the free shopping guides which list the Palermo shops and show them on a map.
Arte Étnico Argentino, El Salvador 4600, T011-4833 6661. Great collection of indigenous art from all over Argentina, high quality and reasonable prices, given that they're a little higher than you'd pay in the place of origin. Weavings, especially, are superb.
Calma Chicha, Honduras 4925, and a smaller branch at Gurruchaga 1580, T011-4831 1818, www.calmachicha.com. The name means calm before the storm, and this is the one place you should browse in for gifts to bring home. Wonderful minimalist cowhide postman's bags and wallets, seats and table mats - or buy an entire cowhide! Also loads of chic kitsch, like the 'Hand of God' flick books which endlessly replay Maradona's immortal moment, plus tin mates and cute toys.

Leather

As you'd expect from all the cattle, Argentina produces, leather is cheap and of very high quality here.
Aida, Galería de la Flor, shop 30, Florida 670. Here you can have a leather jacket made to measure in the same day.
Campanera Dalla Fontana, Reconquista 735, is a leather factory producing fast, efficient and reasonably-priced made-to-measure clothes.

Casa López, MT de Alvear 640/658. The most traditional and finest leather shop, expensive, but worth it.
Galería del Caminante, Florida 844. A variety of good shops with leather goods, arts and crafts, souvenirs, etc.
Prüne, Florida 963, and in many Shoppings. Fashionable designs for bags, boots and shoes. Lots of choice, very reasonably priced.
Uma, in shopping malls and at Honduras 5225 (Palermo Viejo). The trendiest of all.

Quality inexpensive leather goods are available at **All Horses**, Suipacha 1350, and at **La Curtiembre**, Juncal 1173, Paraguay 670.

Markets

Markets can be found all over Buenos Aires, since many plazas and parks have fairs at weekends where you can find almost the same kind of handicrafts everywhere. These are recommended for something different:
Feria de Las Artes, on Defensa, around Alsina. Fri 1200-1700. A few stalls selling crafts.
Feria de Mataderos , Av de los Corrales 6436, T011-4687 1949, Sun 1200-1800. Traditional gaucho crafts and games.
Mercado de las Luces, in the Manzana de las Luces, Perú y Alsina, Mon-Fri 1100-1900, Sun 1400-1900. Handicrafts.
Parque Centenario, Díaz Vélez y L Marechal. Sat market, with local crafts, good, cheap hand-made clothes.
Parque Rivadavia, Rivadavia 4900. Books and magazines (daily), records, toys, stamps and coins, Sun 0900-1300.
Plaza Dorrego, San Telmo. A wonderfully atmospheric market for souvenirs, antiques, some curious bric-a-brac. With free tango performances and live music, Sun 1000-1700.
Plaza Italia, Santa Fe y Uriarte (Palermo). Secondhand textbooks and magazines are sold daily, and handicrafts market on Sat 1200-2000, Sun 1000-2000.
Recoleta, just outside the cemetery. At weekends, this huge crafts Market is held, with lots of street performers, and food on sale too. Recommended.

Shopping malls

Alcorta, Salguero 3172, T011-5777 6500. Massive mall with everything, plus supermarkets, and some cheaper shops. Hard to reach without a car, though.
Alto Palermo, Av Santa Fé and Coronel Díaz, T011-5777 8000, Nearest Subte: opposite Bulnes, Line D. Great for all the main clothes chain stores, and about 10 blocks' walk from Palermo's boutiques.
Galerias Pacificos, Corner of Florida and Cordoba, T011-5555 5110, nearest Subte Plaza San Martín on Line C, Mon-Sat 1000-2100, Sun 2100-2100. Has a good range of everything, and a good food court in the basement.
Patio Bullrich, Posadas 1245, T011-4814 7400, nearest Subte 8 blocks from Plaza San Martín, Line C. The city's most upmarket mall, with all the international designer names and the best Argentine designers too. Also valet parking, taxi service and small food court in very elegant surroundings.
Unicenter, Paraná 3745, Martínez, T011-4733 1166. With everything you could possibly imagine in one overwhelming place. Take a flask of brandy. No Subte anywhere near. Taking a taxi is the only option; ask them to wait for you a few hours later, as taxi queues to leave are endless.

Activities and tours

Cricket

Cricket is played Nov-Mar. More information at **Asociación de Cricket Argentino**, Paraguay 1270, T011-4816 3569.

Football and rugby

Fans of the beautiful game should see Boca Juniors, matches every second Sun 1500-1900 at their stadium, La Bombonera, Brandsen 805, La Boca, www.bocajuniors.com.ar. Cheapest tickets US$5. For details for the museum, see page 85. Try to see the murals; along Av Almirante Brown. Take buses 29, 33, 53, 64, 86, 152, 168; along Av Patricios buses 10, 39, 93. Do not take a bus if traveling alone: call a radio taxi, or their arch-rivals, **River Plate**, www.carp.org.ar (to stadium take bus 29 from centre going north). Soccer season Mar-Jul, Aug-Dec, matches on Sun and sometimes on Wed, Fri or Sat. Rugby season Apr-Oct/ Nov. See also **Tangol** under Tour operators.

Golf

Visitors wishing to play at the private golf clubs should bring handicap certificate and make telephone booking. There are about a dozen clubs. Weekend play possible with a member. Good hotels may be able to make arrangements. **Campo de Golf de la Ciudad** in Palermo, open to anyone, US$7. For information contact, **Asociación Argentina de Golf**, T011-4325 1113.

Horse racing

At **Hipódromo Argentino de Palermo**, a large, modern racecourse, popular throughout the year, and at **San Isidro**. Riding schools at both courses.

Motor racing

There are stock racing and Formula 3 competitions Mar-Dec, and drag racing year round, Fri evenings, from US$1 at the **Oscar Alfredo Gálvez Autodrome**, Av Coronel Roca y Av General Paz, T011-4605 3333.

Polo

Argentina has the top polo players in the world. The high handicap season is Sep-Dec, but it is played all year round (low season: May- Aug). A visit to the national finals at Palermo in Nov and Dec is recommended. For information, **Asociación Argentina de Polo**, T011-4777 6444, www.aapolo.com.

Swimming

Public baths near **Aeroparque**, Punta Carrasco, and Parque Norte, both popular. At **Club de Amigos**, Av Figueroa Alcorta y Av Sarmiento, T011-4801 1213, US$7 (including entrance), open all year round.

Tour operators

An excellent way of seeing Buenos Aires and its surroundings is by a 3-hr tour, especially for those travelling alone, or concerned about security. Longer tours might include dinner and a tango show, or a trip to an estancia (farm or ranch), with excellent food. Bookable through most travel agents.

ATI, Esmeralda 567, T011-4329 9000, www.ativiajes.com. Mainly group travel, very efficient, many branches.

Barbacharters, T011-4824 3366, www.barbacharters.com.ar. Boat trips and fishing in the Delta and Tigre areas.

BAT, Buenos Aires Tur, Lavalle 1444, office 10, T011-4371 2304, www.buenosaires tur.com. City tours (US$6.50) twice daily; Tigre and Delta, daily, 6 hrs (US$15).

Buenos Aires Vision, Esmeralda 356 p 8, T011-4394 4682, www.buenosaires-vision.com.ar. City tours (US$8.50), Tigre and Delta, Tango (US$60-70, cheaper without dinner) and Fiesta Gaucha (US$40).

Cicerones de Buenos Aires, J J Biedma 883, T011-4330 0800, www.cicerones.org.ar. Non-profit organization offering volunteer "greeting"/guiding service for visitors to the city, free, safe and different.

Class Adventure Travel, Av Presidente Roque Saenz Peña 615, office 718, www.cat-travel.com. Dutch-owned and run, with 10 years of experience. Excellent for tailor-made travel solutions throughout the continent.

Eternautas, Av Roque Sáenz Peña 1124, p 4B, T011-4384 7874, www.eternautas.com. Historical, cultural and artistic tours of the city and Pampas guided in English, French or Spanish by historians and other social scientists from the University of Buenos Aires, flexible. Highly recommended.

Exprinter, San Martín 170 p 1 office 101, T011-4341 6600, Galería Güemes, www.exprinter viajes.com. Especially their 5-day, 4-night tour to Iguazú and San Ignacio Miní.

Eves Turismo, Tucumán 702, T011-4393 6151, www.eves.com. Helpful and efficient, recommended for flights.

Flyer, Reconquista 617, p 8, T011-4313 8224, www.flyer.com.ar. English, Dutch, German spoken, repeatedly recommended, especially for estancias, fishing, polo, motorhome rental.

Horseback Riding, T011-4896 2188, www.horsebackridingbsas.com.ar. Specialises in horse rides, polo lessons, golf, fishing and tennis, all in or near Buenos Aires.

Horses and Adventures, T011-155048 2758, www.horsesadventures.com.ar. Horse riding all over Argentina and in the Pampas, arranged by knowledgeable and bilingual José Ramón Jiminez de Toro. Recommended

Lan&Kramer Bike Tours, T011-4311 5199, www.biketours.com.ar. Starts daily at 0930 and 1400 next to the monument of San Martín (Plaza San Martín), 3½-4-hr cycle tours to the south or the north of the city (US$25); also to San Isidro and Tigre, 41/2-5 hrs, US$30, and rent bikes at Florida 868, p 14H.

Patagonia Chopper, www.patagonia chopper.com.ar. Helitours of Buenos Aires and its surroundings US$95-130 pp for 15-45 mins.

Pride Travel, Paraguay 523 p 2, T011-5218 6556, www.pride-travel.com. The best choice for gay and lesbian travellers in Argentina; they also rent apartments.

Say Hueque, Viamonte 749, p 6 of 1, T011-5199 2517/20, www.sayhueque.com. Good value tours for independent travellers in Argentina.

Smile on Sea, T15-5018 8662 (mob), www.smileonsea.com. 2-hr boat trips off Buenos Aires coast in the day and at sunset, leaving from Puerto Madero on 32-ft sailing boats (up to 5 passengers, US$165 for the whole). Also 8-hr trips to San Isidro and Delta (US$320 for 5 people) and longer holidays along the Uruguayan coast.

Tangol, Florida 971, p 1, T011-4312 7276, www.tangol.com. Friendly, independent travel agency, specializing in football and tango. Also offers city tours, various sports, such as polo and paragliding, trips to ranches, plane and bus tickets and accommodation. Overland trips to Patagonia Sep-Apr. English spoken. Special deals for students. A reliable and dynamic company. Recommended.

Turismo Feeling, San Martín 969, p 9, T011-4313 5533, www.feelingturismo.com.ar. Excellent and reliable horseback trips in the Andes and adventure tourism.

Urban biking, Moliere 2801 (Villa Devoto) T011-4568 4321, www.urbanbiking.com. 4-hr cycle tours starting next to the English clock tower in Retiro, US$24, light lunch included, also night city tours, US$18, and day tours to San Isidro and Tigre, US$33. They also rent bikes and organize cycle tours in the pampas.

Transport

Air

Airports

Buenos Aires has 2 airports, Ezeiza for international flights and Aeroparque for domestic flights.

Ezeiza (officially Ministro Pistarini), T011-5480 6111, www.aa2000.com.ar, the international airport, is 35 km southwest of the centre (also handles domestic flights to El Calafate and Ushuaia in high season). The airport has 2 terminals: 'A' for all airlines except **Aerolíneas Argentinas**, which uses 'B'. 'A' has a very modern check-in hall. There are duty free shops (expensive), exchange facilities (**Banco de la Nación**; **Banco Piano**; **Global Exchange**) and ATMs (Visa and MasterCard), post office (open 0800-2000) and a left luggage office (US$2 per piece). No hotels nearby. There is a **Devolución IVA/Tax Free** desk (return of VAT) for purchases over AR$90 (see Shopping, page 99). *Locutorios* with limited internet access. Hotel booking service at Tourist Information desk; helpful, but prices are higher if booked in this way. A display in immigration shows choices and prices of transport into the city.

Aeroparque (Jorge Newbery Airport), 4 km north of the centre, T011-5480 6111, www.aa2000.com.ar, is the smart newish airport which handles all internal flights, and **Aerolineas Argentinas and puna** flights to Montevideo and Punta del Este. The terminal is divided into 2 sections, 'A' for all arrivals and **Aerolineas Argentinas** and LAN check-in desks, 'B' for **puna** and **LADE** check-in desks. On the 1st floor there is a **patio de comidas**, several shops and the airport tax counter. At the airport, you'll find tourist information, car rental, bus companies, bank, ATMs, exchange facilities, post office, public phones, Secure Bag (US$5 per piece) and luggage deposit (between sections A-B at the information point), US$4 per piece a day.

Transport to and from the centre

Airport bus The safest way to get between airports, or to get to town, is by an airport bus service run by **Manuel Tienda León**, whose convenient desk in Ezeiza is in front of you as you exit customs into the Arrivals hall. Buses every 30 mins to their new terminal in town, at Av Madero 1299 y San Martín, behind Sheraton Hotel in Retiro, T011-4315 5115, www.tiendaleon.com. You can pay in pesos, dollars, euros, or with credit or debit cards. Buses run to **Ezeiza**: 0400, 0500, then every 30 mins till 2100 and 2200, 2230 (be 15 mins early); and from Ezeiza: 0600- 2400 regular buses at 0400, 0500, then every 30 mins till 2100 and 2200, 2230 (be 15 mins early) to the centre of town, (US$8.50 (US$15 return), 40-min journey.) and then onto the domestic airport Aeroparque (US$5, another 25 mins); buses leave from outside terminal B. **Manuel Tienda León** will also collect passengers from addresses in centre for US$0.35 extra, book the previous day. **Manuel Tienda León** buses to Aeroparque (see above for address), 0710-0255, every hour ; from Aeroparque (departs from sector B, stops at **Aerolineas Argentinas**), 0900-2000 every hour and 2130, 20-min journey, US$3.

Remise taxis *Remises* are operated by **Transfer Express** and **Manuel Tienda León**, from Aeroparque: US$8 to centre, US$23-24 26 to Ezeiza.

Taxi Taxis from Ezeiza to the centre charge US$20 (plus US$1 toll), but do not have a good reputation for security, and you'll have to bargain. Far better to take a *remise* taxi: these charge a fixed fare and can be booked from the **Manuel Tienda León** counter at Ezeiza, US$23 (plus US$1 toll) payable in advance. *Transfer Express* operates on-request *remise* taxis, vans and minibuses from both airports to any point in town and between them; convenient for large groups.

Airline offices

Aerolíneas Argentinas (AR) and **Austral**, Perú y Rivadavia, Av LN Alem 1134 and Av Cabildo 2900, T0810-2228 6527. Air Canada, Av Córdoba 656, T011-4327 3640. **Air France-KLM**, San Martín 344 p 23, T011-4317 4700. **Alitalia**, Av Santa Fe 887, T011-4787 7848. **American Airlines**, Av Santa Fe 881, T011-4318 1111, Av Pueyrredón 1997 and branches in Belgrano and Acassuso. **Avianca**, Carlos Pellegrini 1163 p 4, T011-4394 5990. **British Airways**, Av del Libertador 498 p 13, T0800-666 1459. **Copa**, Carlos Pellegrini 989 p 2, T0810-222 2672. **Cubana**, Sarmiento 552 p 11, T011-4325 0691. **Delta**, Carlos Pellegrini 1141, T0800-666 0133. **Iberia**, Carlos Pellegrini, 1163 p 1/3, T011-4131 1000. **LAB**, Carlos Pellegrini 141, T011-4323 1900. **Lan**, Cerrito y Paraguay, T0810-999 9526. **Líneas Aéreas del Estado (LADE)**, Perú 710, T5129 9000, Aeroparque T011-4514 1524. **Lufthansa**, M T Alvear 590, p 6, T011-4319 0600. **Malaysia Airlines**, Suipacha 1111 p 14, T011-4312 6971. **Mexicana**, Av Córdoba 1131. **puna**, Florida 1, T011-4342 7000. **TAM**, Cerrito 1030, T011-4819 4800. **United**, Av Madero 900, T0810-777 8648. **Varig**, Av Córdoba 972, p 4, T011-4329 9200.

Road

Bus

Note that buses get heavily booked Dec-Mar, especially at weekends. All long-distance buses arrive at the **Retiro** bus terminal at Ramos Mejía y Antártida Argentina. Retiro terminal enquiries: T011-4310 0700. Long distance bus tickets can now be booked by telephone with a credit card. The biggest bus companies are: **Andesmar**, T011-4313 3717, www.andesmar.com; **Chevallier**, T011-4000 5255, www.nuevachevallier.com.ar; **Flecha Bus** T011-4000 5200, www.flechabus.com.ar; **Vía Bariloche** T011-4315 7700, www.viabariloche.com.ar.

The terminal is on 3 floors. Arrivals and departures are on the middle floor, with toilets, cafés, and cheap gift shops; departures are displayed on screens. Ticket offices are on the upper floor, but there are hundreds of them so you'll need to consult a list of companies and their office numbers at the top of the escalator. They're organized by regions of the country, and each region is colour-coded. There are left-luggage lockers, requiring tokens from kiosks, US$2.50. Large baggage should be left at *guarda equipage* on the lower floor. The service of luggage porters is supposed to be free. Buenos Aires city tourist information is at desk 83 on the upper floor. Bus information at the Ramos Mejía entrance on the middle floor. Taxis leave from the official rank on the lower floor, one level below arrivals, but these are not reliable. For security, phone for a radio taxi, eg **Radio Taxi Sur**, T011-4638 2000, quoting your hotel phone number, and tell the company to pick you up at Puente 3, arriba (bridge 3 upper level) for example (there are 5 such bridges leading from the arrivals level). Otherwise, take a *remise* taxi, **Remis La Terminal**, T011-4312 0711, booked from 1 of 2 booths on the bus platform itself, a little more expensive but very secure. There are no direct bus services to either airport. It's not advisable to walk into town from the bus terminal, since the road still rife with thieves, despite having been cleaned up in recent years.

Car hire

Hiring a car is best done on the spot and less expensive than if done from home. Driving in Buenos Aires is no problem if you have eyes in the back of your head and nerves of steel. **Avis**, Cerrito 1527, T011-4326 5542. **AL International**, San Luis 3138, T011-4312 9475. **Budget**, Santa Fe 869, T011-4311 9870. ISIC and GO 25 discount. **Hertz**, Ricardo Rojas 451, T011-4312 1317. There are several national rental agencies, eg **AVL**, Alvear 1883, T011-4805 4403. **Ricciard Libertador**, Av del Libertador 2337/45, T011-4799 8514. **Localiza**, Paraguay 1122, T011-4314 3999. **Unidas**, Paraguay 864, T011-4315 0777.

Sea

The *Buenos Aires Herald* (English language daily) notes all shipping movements.

Ferry

To **Montevideo** and **Colonia del Sacramento** from Terminal Dársena Norte, Av Antártida Argentina 821 (2 blocks from Av Córdoba y Alem). **Buquebus**, T011-4316 6500, www.buquebus.com (tickets from Terminal or from offices at Av Córdoba 879 and Posadas 1452): 1) Direct to **Montevideo**, 1 to 4 a day, 3 hrs, US$53-57 tourist class, US$63-68 1st class one way, vehicles US$74- 84 US$87-97, motorcycles US$55-68, bus connection to Punta del Este, US$8 extra. 2) To **Colonia**, services by 2 companies: **Buquebus**: 2-3 ferry services a day, 3 hrs, US$18-20 tourist class, US$24-26 1st class one way, with bus connection to Montevideo (US$5-6 extra). Motorcycles US$20 25, cars US$36-41. **Ferrylíneas Sea Cat** operates a fast service to Colonia from same terminal, 1 to 3 daily, 1 hr, US$30-34 tourist class, US$36-40 1st class one way, vehicles US$55-61, motorcycles US$31-36 with bus connection to Punta del Este (US$12).

Note: Argentine port taxes are generally included in the fares for Argentine departures. For return tickets, port tax at Colonia is US$1.70 pp (US$16 per vehicle) and at Montevideo, US$4 pp (US$18 per vehicle).

Train

There are 4 main terminals: **Retiro** (3 lines: Mitre, Belgrano, San Martín in separate buildings), **Constitución**, **Once**, **Federico Lacroze**.

Almost the only passenger trains in Argentina today are Buenos Aires commuter trains, and locals feel they're in pretty bad condition, with the exception of the decent Mitre line to Tigre. There are only a few long distance services, all very shoddy, and not to be considered as a serious alternative to long distance bus or plane. Tickets are checked before boarding and on train, and collected at the end of the journey; urban and suburban fares are charged according different sections of each line. For information contact the companies directly: **Ferrobaires**, T011-4304 0028, www.ferrobaires.gba.gov.ar; **Ferrovías**, T011-4511 8833; **Metrovías**, T011-4555 1616, www.metrovias.com.ar; **Metropolitano**, T0800-122 358736, www.metro politano.com.ar; **TBA**, T011-4317 4407, www.tbanet.com.ar; **Trenes Especiales**, T011-4551 1634.

Retiro

Retiro station runs 3 different lines in separate buildings: train information T011-4311 8704.

Mitre line (run by TBA, services to all the suburbs, though you're most likely to use it to get to Tigre, if you want an alternative to the tourist Tren de la Costa. Urban and suburban services: to **Belgrano**, **Mitre** (connection to Tren de la Costa, see below), **Olivos**, **San Isidro**, **Tigre** (see below), **Capilla del Señor** (connection at Victoria, US$0.90), **Escobar** and **Zárate** (connection at Villa Ballester, US$0.90); long-distance services: to **Rosario Norte**, one weekly on Fri evening, 6 hrs, US$3.50, to **Tucumán** via Rosario, Mon and Fri, 2100, returning Mon and Thu 1000, 26 hrs, US$20 sleeper, US$16 pullman, US$13 1st (service run by **NOA Ferrocarriles**, T011-4893 2244).

Belgrano line For trains to the northwestern suburbs (Villa Rosa), run by Ferrovías, T011-4511 8833.

San Martín line run by Metropolitano. Urban and suburban services: to **Palermo**, **Chacarita**, **Devoto**, **Hurlingham** and **Pilar**. Long distance services: to **Junín**, daily, 5hrs, US$4.

Constitución

Train information T011-4304 0028.

Roca line (run by Metropolitano, see above). Urban and suburban services to **La Plata** (US$0.50), **Ezeiza** (US$0.35), **Ranelagh** (US$0.27) and **Quilmes** (US$0.20). Long-distance services (run by **Ferrobaires**, T011-4304 0028/3165): **Bahía Blanca**, 5 weekly, 121/2 hrs, US$7-13; to **Mar del Plata** daily in summer, US$7-13, 5 hrs; to **Pinamar**, 2 weekly, US$7-13, 6 hrs; to **Miramar**, in summer only, daily, 7 hrs, US$7-13; to

Tandil, US$7-13, weekly, 71/2 hrs; to **Quequén**, 2 weekly, 12 hrs, US$7-13.

Federico Lacroze Urquiza
Train line information, and **Metro headquarters** (run by Metrovías, T0800-555 1616 or T011-4555 1616, www.metrovias.com.ar). Suburban services: to General Lemos, and long distance services to Posadas, run by Trenes Especiales.

Once
Train information T011-4861 0043.
Once Sarmiento line (run by TBA, see above). Urban and suburban services: to **Caballito**, **Flores**, **Merlo**, **Luján** (connection at Moreno, US$0.60), **Mercedes** (US$1) and **Lobos**. Long distance services to **Santa Rosa** and **General Pico** can be seasonally interrupted by floods. A fast service runs daily between **Puerto Madero** (station at Av Alicia Moreau de Justo y Perón) and **Castelar**. Tickets checked before boarding and on train and collected at the end of the journey; urban and suburban fares are charged according to different sections of each line; cheapest fare is around US$0.15 (depending on the company).

Directory

Banks
ATMs are widespread for MasterCard or Visa (look for Link ATMs). The financial district lies within a small area north of Plaza de Mayo, between Rivadavia, 25 de Mayo, Av Corrientes and Florida. In non-central areas find banks/ATMs along the main avenues. Banks open Mon-Fri 1000-1500. Use credit or debit cards for withdrawing cash rather than carrying TCs. Most banks charge commission especially on TCs (as much as US$10). US dollar bills are often scanned electronically for forgeries, while TCs are sometimes very difficult to change and you may be asked for proof of purchase. Major credit cards usually accepted but check for surcharges. General MasterCard office at Perú 151, T011-4348 7000, www.mastercard.com/ar, open 0930-1800. Visa, Corrientes 1437 p 2, T011-4379 3400, www.visa.com.ar. For lost or stolen cards: MasterCard T 0800-555 0507, Visa T011-4379 3333 (T0810-666 3368 from outside BA). **American Express** offices are at Arenales 707 y Maipú, by Plaza San Martín, T011-4310 3000 or T0810-555 2639, www.americanexpress.com.ar, where you can apply for a card, get financial services and change Amex TCs (1000-1500 only, T0810-444 2437, no commission into US$ or pesos); no commission either at **Banco de la Provincia de Buenos Aires**, several branches, or at **Banco Columbia**, Perón 350. **Citibank**, B Mitre 502, T0810-444 2484, changes only Citicorps TCs cheques, no commission; branch at Florida 199. *Casas de cambio* include **Banco Piano**, San Martín 345, T011-4321 9200 (has exchange facility at Ezeiza airport, 0500-2400), www.bancopiano.com.ar, changes all TCs (commission 2%). **Forex**, MT de Alvear 540, T011-4311 5543. **Eves**, Tucumán 702. Other South American currencies can only be exchanged in *casas de cambio*. **Western Union**, branches in Correo Argentino post offices (for transfers within Argentina) and at Av Córdoba 975 (for all transfers), T0800-800 3030. Banco Ciudad at Av Córdoba 675 branch is open to tourists (providing passport) for exchange currency and TCs, Mon 1000-1800, Tue-Fri 1000-1700, Sat-Sun 1100-1800.

Cultural centres
British Council, M T de Alvear 590, p 4, T011-4311 9814, (Mon-Thu 0830-1700, Fri 0830-1330). **British Arts Centre** (BAC), Suipacha 1333, T011-4393 6941, www.britishartscentre.org.ar. English plays and films, music concerts, photography exhibitions (closed Jan). **Goethe Institut**, Corrientes 319/43, T011-4311 8964, German library (Mon,Tue,Thu 1230-1930, Fri 1230-1600, closed Jan) and newspapers, free German films shown, cultural programmes, German language courses. In the same building, upstairs, is the German Club, Corrientes 327. **Alliance Française**, Córdoba 946, T011-4322 0068, www.alianzafrancesa.org.ar. French library, temporary film and art exhibitions. **Instituto Cultural Argentino Norteamericano (ICANA)**, Maipú 672, T011-5382 1500, www.icana.org.ar. **Biblioteca Centro Lincoln**, Maipú 672,

T011-5382 1536, www.bcl.edu.ar, Mon-Wed 1000-2000, Thu and Fri 1000-1800 (Jan and Feb Mon-Fri 1300-1900), library (borrowing for members only), English/US newspapers.

Embassies and consulates

All open Mon-Fri unless stated otherwise. **Australia**, Villanueva y Zabala, T011-4779 3500, www.argentina.embassy.gov.au. 0830-1100, ticket queuing system; take bus 29 along Av Luis María Campos to Zabala. **Belgium**, Defensa 113 p 8, T011-4331 0066, 0800-1300, www.diplobel.org/argentina. **Bolivia**, Consulate, Alsina 1886, T011-4381 4171, www.embajadadebolivia.com.ar, 0830-1530, visa while you wait or a month wait (depending on the country of origin), tourist bureau. **Brazil**, Consulate, C Pellegrini 1363, p 5, T011-4515 6500, www.con brasil.org.ar. 1000- 1300, tourist visa takes at least 48 hrs, US$25-110. **Canada**, Tagle 2828, T011-4808 1000, www.dfait-maeci.gc.ca/ argentina. Mon-Thu 0830-1230, 1330-1730, tourist visa Mon-Thu 0845-1130 **Chile**, Consulate, San Martín 439, p 9, T011-4394 6582, www.embajadadechile.com.ar, 0900-1330. **Denmark**, Consulate, Alem 1074, p 9, T011-4312 6901, www.dina marca.org.ar. Mon-Thu 0930-1200. **France**, Santa Fe 846, p 4, T011-4312 2409, www.consulatfrance.int.ar, 0900-1230, 1400-1600 (by appointment). **Germany**, Villanueva 1055, T011-4778 2500, www.embajada-alemana.org.ar. 0830-1100. **Ireland**, Av Del Libertador 1068 p 6, T011-5787 0801, www.irlanda.org.ar. 0900-1300, 1400-1530. **Italy**, consulate at M T de Alvear 1125/49, T011-4816 6133/36, www.consitalia-bsas.org.ar, Mon, Tue, Thu, Fri 0800-1100. **Netherlands**, Olga Cossentini 831 p 3, Puerto Madero, T011-4338 0050, www.embajadaholanda.int.ar, Mon-Thu 0900-1300, Fri 0900-1230. **New Zealand**, C Pellegrini 1427 p 5, T011-4328 0747, www.nzembassy.com/buenosaires. Mon-Thu 0900-1300, 1400- 1730, Fri 0900-1300. **Norway**, Esmeralda 909, p 3 B, T011-4312 2204, www.noruega.org.ar, 0930-1400. **Spain**, Consulate, Guido 1760, T011 4811 0070, www.mae.es/consulados/ buenosaires. 0815-1430. **Sweden**, Tacuarí 147 p 6, T011-4329 0800, www.swedenabroad.com/ buenosaires, 1000-1200. **Switzerland**, Santa Fe 846, p10, T011-4311 6491, www.eda.admin.ch/ buenosaires_emb, open 0900-1200. **UK**, Luis Agote 2412 (near corner Pueyrredón y Guido), T011-4808 2200 (call T15-5114 1036 for emergencies only out of normal office hours), www.britain.org.ar. 0900-1300 (Jan-Feb 0900-1200). **Uruguay**, Consulate, Av Las Heras 1907, T011-4807 3045, www.embajadadeluruguay.com.ar. 0930-1730, visa takes up to 72 hrs. **US Embassy and Consulate General**, Colombia 4300, T011-5777 4533 (for emergencies involving US citizens, call T5777 4354 or T5777 4873 after office hours), http://buenosaires.usembassy.gov/.

Internet

Prices range from US$0.50-1 per hr, shop around. Most *locutorios* (phone offices) have internet access.

Language schools

International Bureau of Language, Florida 165, 8th floor, T011-4331 4250, www.ibl.com.ar. Group and one-to-one lessons, all levels. **Argentina I.L.E.E**, Av Callao 339, p 3, T011-4782 7173, www.argentina ilee.com. Recommended by individuals and organizations alike. **Programa Tango** adds tango lessons to Spanish. Accommodation arranged. **Cedic**, Reconquista 715, p 11 E, T/F011-4315 1156, www.cedic.com.ar. Recommended. **All-Spanish**, Talcahuano 77 p 1, T011-4381 3914, www.all-spanish.com.ar. One-to-one classes. **PLS**, Carabelas 241 p 1, T011-4394 0543, www.pls.com.ar. Recommended for travellers and executives and their families; also translation and interpreting services. **Universidad de Buenos Aires**, 25 de Mayo 221, T011-4334 7512, www.idiomas. filo.uba.ar. Offers cheap, coherent courses, including summer intensive courses. For other schools teaching Spanish, and for private tutors look in *Buenos Aires Herald* in the classified advertisements. Enquire also at *Asatej* (see Useful addresses, below).

Medical services

Urgent medical service: for free municipal ambulance service to an emergency hospital department (day and night) **Casualty ward, Sala de guardia**, T107 or T011-4923 1051/58 (SAME). Inoculations: **Hospital Rivadavia**, Av Las Heras 2670, T011-4809 2000, Mon-Fri, 0700-1300 (bus 10, 37, 59, 60, 62, 92, 93 or 102 from Plaza Constitución), or **Dirección de Sanidad de Fronteras y Terminales de Transporte**, Ing Huergo 690, T011-4343 1190, Mon 1400-1500, Tue-Wed 1100- 1200, Thu and Fri 1600-1700, bus 20 from Retiro, no appointment required (yellow fever only; take passport). If not provided, buy the vaccines in **Laboratorio Biol**, Uriburu 153, T011-4953 7215, or in larger chemists. Many chemists have signs indicating that they give injections. Any hospital with an infectology department will give hepatitis A. **Travel Medicine Service (Centros Médicos Stamboulian)**, 25 de Mayo 464, T011-4311 3000, French 3085, T011-5236 7772, also in Belgrano y Flores, www.viajeros.cei.com.ar. Private health advice for travellers and inoculations centre. Public Hospitals: **Hospital Argerich**, Almte Brown esq Pi y Margall 750, T011-4121 0700. **Hospital Juan A Fernández**, Cerviño y Bulnes, T011-4808 2600, good medical attention. **British Hospital**, Perdriel 74, T011-4309 6400, www.hospitalbritanico.org.ar. US$24 a visit. **German Hospital**, Av Pueyrredón 1640, between Beruti and Juncal, T011-4827 7000, www.hospitalaleman.com.ar Both maintain first-aid centres (*centros asistenciales*) as do the other main hospitals. Dental treatment at Solís 2180, T011-4305 2530. Excellent dental treatment centre at **Carroll Forest**, Vuelta de Obligado 1551 (Belgrano), T011-4781 9037, info@carroll-forest.com.ar.

Post offices

Correo Central, Correos Argentinos, Sarmiento y Alem, T011-4891 9191, www.correoargentino.com.ar, Mon-Fri, 0800-2000, Sat 1000-1300. *Poste Restante* (only to/from national destinations) on ground floor (US$0.25 per letter). Philatelic section open Mon-Fri 1000- 1700, T011-5550 5176. **Centro Postal Internacional**, for all parcels over 2 kg for mailing abroad, at Av Comodoro Py y Antártida Argentina, near Retiro station, helpful, many languages spoken, packaging materials available, open Mon-Fri 1000 to 1700. Post office at Montevideo 1408 near Plaza V López, friendly staff, Spanish only. Also at Santa Fe 945 and many others. **UPS**, T0800-2222 877, www.ups.com. **DHL**, T0810-2222 345, www.dhl.com.ar. **FedEx**, T0810-3333 339, www.fedex.com.

Telephone

International and local calls, internet and fax from phone offices (*locutorios* or *telecentros*), of which there are many in the city centre.

Useful addresses

Migraciones: (Immigration), Antártida Argentina 1355, edificio 4 (visas extended mornings only), T011-4317 0200, 0730-1330, www.migraciones.gov.ar (see also Documents in Essentials). **Central Police Station**: Moreno 1550, Virrey Cevallos 362, T011-4370 5911/5800 (emergency, T101 from any phone, free). See page 40 for **Comisaría del Turista** (tourist police). **Administración de Parques Nacionales**, Santa Fe 690, opposite Plaza San Martín, T011-4311 0303, Mon-Fri 1000-1700, has leaflets on national parks. Also library (**Biblioteca Perito Moreno**), open to public Tue-Fri 1000-1300, 1400-1700. **Aves Argentinas/AOP** (a BirdLife International partner), 25 de Mayo 749 p 2, T011-4312 8958, for information on birdwatching and specialist tours, good library open Wed and Fri 1500-2000 (closed Jan). Student organizations: **Asatej**: Helpful Argentine Youth and Student Travel Organization, runs a Student Flight Centre, Florida 835, p 3, oficina 320, T011-4114 7600, www.asatej.com, Mon-Fri 0900-1900 (and 5 other branches in BA: Belgrano, Montserrat, Palermo, Recoleta, Caballito), www.asatej.net. Offering booking for flights (student discounts) including cheap one-way flights (long waiting lists), hotels and travel; information for all South America, noticeboard for travellers, ISIC cards sold (giving extensive discounts; Argentine ISIC guide available here), English and French spoken; also runs: **Red Argentino de Alojamiento Para Jovenes** (affiliated to HI); **Asatej Travel Store**, at the same office, selling wide range of travel goods. **Oviajes**, Uruguay 385, p 6, T011-4371 6137, Lavalle 477 p 1, and also at Echeverría 2498 p 1, T011-4785 7840, www.oviajes.com.ar. Offers travel facilities, ticket sales, information, and issues Hostels of Americas, Nomads and Hostels of Europe, ISIC, ITIC and G0 25 cards, aimed at students, teachers and independent travellers. Cheap fares also at **TIJE**, San Martín 640 p 6, T011-4326 2036 or branches at Paraguay 1178, p 7, T011-5218 2800 and Zabala 1736, p 1, T011-4770 9500, www.tije.com, and at **STB** (STA representative), Viamonte 577 p 3, T011-5217 2727, www.stb.com.ar. **YMCA**: (Central), Reconquista 439, T011-4311 4785. **YWCA**: Tucumán 844, T011-4322 1550. The South American Explorers organization has opened a new clubhouse in Buenos Aires, Salguero 553, T011-4861 7571, soon to move to bigger premises, so check the website: www.saexplorers.org. Friendly English speaking staff offer really knowledgeable advice and a comfortable gathering place for travellers. Highly recommended.

Around Buenos Aires

While there's plenty to keep you entertained in Buenos Aires for a week at least, there are great places to escape to for a day or two within easy striking distance. So if you don't relish the frenzy of a big city, especially at the end of a trip exploring some of the widest landscapes on earth, you'll be relieved to know there are calm rural estancias (cattle farms), the fascinating Tigre river delta, and cowboy towns which celebrate an authentic gaucho culture – all within an hour or two of the city.

Mataderos is on the western edge of the city, and worth visiting only on Sundays, when it's the site of a wonderful market, with displays of gaucho horsemanship, the air is filled with the smoky aroma of grilling steak on asados, and there's even tango dancing too. If gaucho culture intrigues you, it's worth setting out for the impeccably preserved 1900s gaucho towns of San Antonio de Areco to the west of the city, or to Chascomus in the south (handy for Ezeiza international airport). There are lots of grand estancias near both towns, where you can try horse riding, or simply lap up the luxury. Details on these places are in the next chapter, Buenos Aires Province.

Closer at hand, there two most popular destinations for day trips are north of the city along the coast of the Río de la Plata, easily reached by the Tren de la Costa. San Isidro has smart shops and a charming old quarter, making it a pleasant place to stroll around, especially at weekends when the craft market is on. Even more appealing, though, Tigre river delta is a maze of overgrown waterways which you can explore by boat, and find a waterfont restaurant, or a romantic boutique hotel on stilts hidden away up a lazy river.

Finally, you could take a boat trip across the Río de la Plata to the quaint Portuguese colonial town of Colonia del Sacramento (which is in Uruguay). Stroll around the quaint buildings on this quiet peninsula, or hire a bike: there's nothing much to do here except eat and gaze at the views, but the architecture is very appealing and there's an amazing sense of calm. *►► For Sleeping, Eating and other listings, see pages 116-118.*

Mataderos

On the western edge of the city in an area where historically cattle were slaughtered, there is now a popular market, the **Feria de Mataderos** ⓘ *Lisandro de la Torre y Av de los Corrales, every Sun and holidays from 1100 (Sat 1800-2400 in summer)*. Take subte E to end of line then taxi (US$2.50), or if there's a group of you, take buses 36, 92, 97, 126, 141. A Radio Taxi all the way will cost US$7. It's a long way out of the centre, (some two hours by bus) but worth it to see this fair of Argentine handicrafts and traditional artwork, with music and dance festivals, demonstrations of gaucho horsemanship skills, typical regional food, and games such as *pato*, a game played on horseback, originally with a duck, and *carrera de sortijas* where players on horseback have to spear a ring on a string with their lance. Nearby is the **Museo de los Corrales** ⓘ *Av de los Corrales 6436, T011-4687 1949, Sun 1200-1800.*

San Isidro » pp116-118.

➔ *Colour map 4, B5*

Just to the north of Buenos Aires city, 22km away, San Isidro is an attractive small town with a lovely setting on the coast, easily reached by the **Tren de La Costa** (see below). It's an appealing place to come for an afternoon, for a stroll along the historical old quarter by the river, or to shop in a centre built in the converted old railway station. This is the most sought after residential area in greater Buenos Aires, and there are lots of bars and places to eat along the coast, with pretty green spaces for walking or relaxing. **Tourist information** ⓘ *just off the central plaza Mitre, at Ituzaingo 608, on the corner with Av del Libertador, T011-4512 3209, www.sanisidro.gov.ar* is staffed by extremely helpful bilingual staff.

Start your tour of San Isidro at the Tren de la Costa train station, nicely renovated, and now housing shops where you can pick up good handicrafts as well as clothes and accessories. Walk up into the pretty main **Plaza Mitre**, filled with shady mature trees and fragrant flowers in summer, and where there is a handicrafts market every weekend. From here, have a look at the old Municipal buildings, before walking along Beccar Varela street to look at the aristocratic houses. This was historically the site of country houses for the aristocracy in the late 19th century, and there are a number of fine colonial buildings including several country houses (*quintas*). **Quinta Pueyrredón** houses the Museo Pueyrredón, containing artefacts from the life of General Juan Martín Pueyrredón. The main shopping street, with lots of *locutorios* and places you can download and print photos, as well as the conventional shops, is **Calle Belgrano**, between Avenida del Libertador and Avenida Centenario, the busy main road into Buenos Aires city.

The *Ribera*, the area by the coast stretching southeast of the centre, is green and peaceful, with plenty of park areas where you can sit gazing out at the great view of the Río de la Plata. There are marinas for yachts and windsurfing, and the **Club Náutico San Isidro**, reached from Calle Mitre. There are also plenty of places to eat along here as this is a popular upmarket nightspot for Porteños, all along the coast road south east of the centre of San Isidro from Primera Junta southeast to Calle Paraná. It's worth strolling onto the viewpoint from the Mirador de Roque Sáenz Peña, for the views over to Buenos Aires. Further southeast, there's a small nature reserve right on the Río de la Plata, the **Reserva Ecológica Municipal** *T011-4747 6179, www.geocities.com/riberan, summer 0900-1900, guided visit at 1700; winter 0900-1800, guided visits Sat and Sun at 1600, free entry*, which hosts an impressive array of bird life, with over 200 species. Access is from the coast road, Camino de la Ribera, via Calle Vicente López.

Another interesting example of the country houses which you can visit is the French-inspired **Villa Ocampo** ⓘ *T011-4807 4428, www.villaocampo.org/visitas,* *weekends 1400-1800, US$3, students US$1.50*. Built in 1891, this beautiful house with galleried verandas and attractive gardens was the home of the famous Argentine writer Victoria Ocampo, where she frequently entertained illustrious visitors from Argentina's literary world. Take a taxi as this is 10 blocks north of the centre. Ask the tourist office for precise directions.

San Isidro is most famous for the **Hipodromo San Isidro**, its magnificent turf racecourse. Built in 1935, this immense race course is one of the best known in South America. Races are run every Wednesday, and some Saturdays or Sundays from 1500-2000. Beyond the compact town centre, the residential area is huge and sprawling, and is *the* place to live if you're a wealthy Porteño. Naturally, this is where you find Argentina's biggest shopping mall, the disarmingly immense **Unicenter Shopping**, at Paraná and the Ruta Panamericana. Don't even attempt to get there by bus: take a taxi, ask the driver to collect you at a pre-determined time and allow at least half a day. All the main brands are here, as well as a good range of restaurants in the Patio de Comidas.

Tren de la Costa

→ *T011-4002 6000, www.trendelacosta.com.ar*

One of Argentina's most comfortable trains is this tourist service which whisks visitors from Maipú station in the Vicente López area of Buenos Aires all the way toTigre, via some of the most picturesque spots on the coast of the Río de la Plata. To get to Maipú, take a normal (TBA) commuter train from Retiro in the centre of Buenos Aires and change at Maipú for the Tren de la Costa. San Isidro is the most appealing place to stop on your way to Tigre, but you could also try Borges station, for the pleasant residential area of Olivos, with its waterfront filled with millionaires' homes, and Barrancas, where you can hire roller blades and bikes and visit the second-hand market. You can get off and on as many times as you like for the fixed single ticket price of US$2. Trains leave every 20 minutes. For those on a tight budget, you can also reach Tigre by taking the TBA train all the way from Retiro for US$0.35 (55 minutes). Trains leave every seven minutes Monday to Friday, or every 15 minutes Saturday and Sunday. It takes 25 minutes to reach San Isidro from Maipú, and 60 minutes to reach Tigre. Delta station, for Tigre Fruit Market, is the end of the line, 90 minutes from Maipú.

Tigre » *pp116-118.*

→ *Colour map 4, B5*

Tigre is deservedly the city's most popular weekend destination: a small town based on the edge of the magnificent river delta of the Río Paraná, some 32 km northwest of the city. The delta is a maze of waterways and hundreds of islands, formed by the accumulation of sediment brought down by the mighty Paraná river which runs from the border with Brazil down to the Río de la Plata, slicing between the First and Second sections of the delta. The delta is a natural paradise, mostly wild and untouched, the lush, jungly banks of the islands making picturesque settings for quaint wooden holiday homes on stilts, the odd boutique hotel, and restaurants hidden miles away from the noise of the city, and reached only by boat. In fact, some 3,000 people live in the delta islands, and since there are no paths or bridges, the only way to get around is by boat; bringing services such as supermarkets, banks and libraries to the islanders. Tigre is the perfect place to cool down on a hot afternoon in summer, and even if you only come for a few hours, you can take one of the regular motor launches for a 60- or 90-minute tour of the nearby rivers in the delta for a pleasurable introduction to this watery world. With more time, hire a kayak to see the wonderfully overgrown expanses at more leisure, or try rowing or canoeing. There are many houses you can rent by the night on the islands (from around US$30, 20% more at weekends), reached by the regular motor launch bus service, and visited by a mobile food shop, so you could hide away here for a night or two on a romantic retreat, a peaceful place to escape to. All have electricity and phone, though you'll need to bring mineral water to drink.

There are lots of restaurants scattered throughout the delta, and also *recreos* – little resorts which have facilities such as swimming pools and tennis as well as waterfront bars and restaurants. One of these is **El Alcazar**, just 10 minutes' boat journey from Tigre, with tennis and volleyball, by a sandy beach, where you can bring your own steaks to barbecue on the *parrilla* grills. Tigre itself has a funfair and an excellent fruit and handicrafts market; a short walk from the centre, along Mitre and turn right at the Delta station. The amusement park, **Parque de Diversiones** (open Friday to Sunday only) is immediately on your left, with the Casino next door in a soulless concrete building, and the fruit market, *Puerto de Frutos* (open daily 1100- 2000) is four blocks further along on the left, on Calle Sarmiento. There's a fairly drab town centre with everything you might need, but the riverside area is the most picturesque, and here you'll find one excellent hotel, **Villa Julia**, which also serves superb food (see Sleeping, page 117). Tigre is a great place to visit any time of the year, with a mild climate even in winter, but note that it's quietest midweek: in summer it gets very busy at weekends, though the festive atmosphere is very appealing in itself. Regattas are held in November and March. Remember to bring a hat and insect repellent in summer.

Tigre is easily reached on the Tren de la Costa (see above) and you should get off at Estación Fluvial, not Delta. There is an excellent **tourist office** ⓘ *next to Estación Fluvial, at Mitre 305, www.tigre.gov.ar, T011-4512 4497, 1000-1800*, with incredibly helpful English speaking staff who can show you the huge folder of houses to rent by the night (complete with photographs) and advise you of boat/bus times to reach them. Note that the ordinary TBA train station is across the roundabout in a more modern building. There's one excellent hotel in Tigre itself, and some average hotels among the delta islands, with a gorgeous boutique hotel, **La Pascuala** (see Sleeping, page 116) in the Second Section, on the other side of the Río Paraná.

Before you take a boat trip, have a stroll along the riverside, the path parallel to Calle Lavalle which leads to Paseo Victorica. You'll pass several rowing clubs, some of them in palatial old buildings, such as the British Rowing Club of 1873, the Buenos Aires Rowing Club, and the Italian Club, as well as the Tudor-style half timbered Club Regata opposite. The main tourist centre is around the old railways station, **Estación Fluvial**, the large old building, now tastefully restored, with souvenir shops and many companies selling boat trips: **Sturla** is one of the most reliable, offering a 90 minute trip for US$4, T011-4731 1300. Boats leave from the quayside just by the Estación Fluvial, and you can take your pick from big catamarans or smaller wooden boats. The tour guides on all boats speak English, and give an informative tour.

There's one museum, the **Museo Naval de la Nación** ⓘ *Paseo Victoria 602, T011-4749 0608, Mon-Thu 0830-1230, Fri 0800-1730, Sat/Sun 1000-1830 US$0.60*, which covers the origins and development of Argentine navy, with lots of model ships. There are also relics of the Falklands/Malvinas War on display outside.

Isla Martín García » pp116-118.

→ *Colour map 4, B5 Population: 200*

Situated in the Río de la Plata just off the Uruguayan town of Carmelo and some 45 km north of Buenos Aires, Martín García is now a provincial nature reserve and one of the best excursions from Buenos Aires, with many trails through the cane brakes, trees and rocky outcrops, and interesting birds and flowers.

This was the site of Juan Díaz de Solís' landfall in 1516, and the island's strategic position has given it a chequered history. It was used for quarantining immigrants from Europe, and then as a prison: four 20th-century Argentine presidents have been detained here, including Juan Perón, and in 1914 British sailors were interned here, as were survivors from the Graf Spee in the Second World War. Evidence ranges from stone-quarries used for building the older churches of Buenos Aires, to four gun batteries, and a *faro* (lighthouse) dating from 1890. The **Museo Histórico** in the former *pulpería*, houses a display of artefacts, documents and photos. **Wildlife** is varied, particularly around the edges of the island and includes laurels, ceibo and several species of orchid. Over 200 species of birds visit the island. Take insect repellent.

There are four weekly boat trips, which run from Tigre at 0900, returning 2030, taking three hours. Prices are around US$16 including a light lunch, *asado* and guide (US$33 pp including weekend overnight at inn, full board). Reservations can be made through *Cacciola* (address, Ferries to Uruguay, page 118), who also handle bookings for the inn and restaurant on the island.

Colonia del Sacramento » *pp116-118.*

→ Phone code: +598-(0)52 Colour map 4 B6

A Portuguese colonial town on the east bank of the Río de la Plata, Colonia del Sacramento is a very popular destination for excursions from Buenos Aires. The modern town with a population of 22,000, which extends along a bay, is charming and lively with neat, leafy streets. The small historic section is particularly interesting because there is so little colonial architecture in this part of South America. There is a pleasant Plaza 25 de Agosto and a grand Intendencia Municipal (Méndez y Avenida General Flores, the main street). The best beach is Playa Ferrando, 2 km to the east (buses from Gen Flores every two hours). There are regular sea and air connections with Buenos Aires and a free port.

Sights

With its narrow streets (wander around Calle de los Suspiros), colonial buildings and reconstructed city walls, the Barrio Histórico has been declared Patrimonio Cultural de la Humanidad by UNESCO. The **Plaza Mayor** (Plaza 25 de Mayo) is especially picturesque. At its eastern end is the **Puerta del Campo**, the restored city gate and drawbridge. On the south side is the **Museo Portugués**; see also the narrow Calle de los Suspiros, nearby. At the western end of the Plaza are the **Museo Municipal** in the former house of Almirante Brown (with indigenous archaeology, historical items, paleontology, natural history), the **Casa Nacarello** next door, the **Casa del Virrey**, and the ruins of the **Convento de San Francisco** (1695), to which is attached the *faro* or lighthouse) built in 1857. Free – tip or donation appreciated. Entry to the museums in this historic quarter is by combined ticket bought from Museo Municipal: US$1, opening hours tend to be 1100-1730 every day.

Colonia del Sacramento is in Uruguay. Remember to take your passport with you. There are no transport taxes although you will be subject to immigration formalities if you travel further into Uruguay.

Just north of the Plaza Mayor a narrow street, the Calle Misiones de los Tapes, leads east to the river. At its further end is the tiny **Museo del Azulejo** housed in the Casa Portuguesa. Two blocks north of here is the Calle Playa which runs east to the Plaza Manuel Lobo/Plaza de Armas, on the northern side of which is the **Iglesia Matriz**, on Vasconcellos, the oldest church in Uruguay. Though destroyed and rebuilt several times the altar dates from the 16th century. Two blocks north of the church on the northern edge of the old city are the fortifications of the **Bastión del Carmen**; just east of it is the **Teatro Bastión del Carmen**. One block south of the Bastión, at San José y España, is the **Museo Español**, formerly the house of General Mitre.

Estancias near Buenos Aires

Many of the province's finest estancias can be visited relatively easily from Buenos Aires, either to spend a day (*dia de campo*) or longer. *Dia de Campo* usually includes horse riding, or riding in a horse-drawn carriage over the estancia's lands, followed by lunch. This is usually a traditional *asado*, often cooked outside with half a cow speared over an open fire: quite a spectacle and absolutely delicious. In the afternoon, you may be treated to demonstrations of farm life, music and dancing from the region, or you might just choose to walk in the beautiful grounds of the estancia, read under a tree, or swim in the pool. To really appreciate the luxury or peace of an estancia, an overnight stay is recommended. Most places are still run as working farms by their owners, who will welcome you personally, and staying with them gives you a unique insight into Argentine rural life and history. Several good websites gives details of estancias: www.turismo.gov.ar, www.caminodelgaucho.com, wwww.raturestancias.com.ar.

There are many estancias grouped around the attractive towns of **San Antonio de Areco** (see page 123), **Chascomús** (see page 127) and **Dolores** (see page 128), all listed under Buenos Aires Province.

Sleeping

San Isidro *p112*

AL Del Casco, Av Libertador 16, 170, T/F011-4732 3993, www.hoteldelcasco.com.ar. Perfectly situated gracious colonial style country house built in 1892, now beautifully converted into a intimate boutique hotel in the excellent New Age Town and Country Hotels chain (www.newage-hotels.com). *Casco* is the word for the main house in a country estancia and this is a grand example, with a grand classical entrance portico and rooms coming off an elegant courtyard with mosaic tiled floor. The bedrooms are huge and tastefully decorated with old furniture and with luxurious bathrooms. The service, from a young bilingual staff, is excellent, and the breakfasts are enormous. All highly recommended. A peaceful alternative for exploring the city than a hotel in the centre.

B Posada de San Isidro Apart Hotel, Maipú 66, T011-4732 1221, www.posadasan isidro.com.ar. Pleasant modern functional rooms in a new building, offering impeccable and good value self catering accommodation. Small pool, breakfast available, handy for the main line train station.

Tigre *p114*

There's just one excellent hotel in Tigre itself, but many more on the islands of the delta, and an exquisite boutique hotel in the Second Section on the other side of the Río Paraná.

LL N/A Town & Country Hotels, Coronel Pizarro 1538, T011-4004 0050, www.newage-hotels.com. 19 upmarket hotels throughout Argentina.

AL La Pascuala, 'la segunda seccion', an hour by motor launch, arrange with reception, T011-4378 0982, www.lapascuala.com. One of Argentina's most delightful places to stay, this is an exclusive and intimate boutique hotel hidden far away from civilization in the wild further reaches of the Second Section of the Tigre delta, but easily reached by motor launch from Tigre in an hour. The hotel consists of 15 individual suite-lodges on stilts in the water, connected by wooden walkways, each one consisting of a huge and luxurious bedroom with its own veranda looking over the river, and an immense bathroom, all beautifully designed for maximum calm and relaxation, equipped with everything you could possibly need. The main public area has an intimate dining room, and lounges, as well as a small pool and Jacuzzi, surrounded by trees. The price is high, but all meals, wine and afternoon tea are included, and the service is top notch. Highly recommended.

AL Rumbo 90 Delta Lodge and Spa, in the eastern area of the delta, 45 minutes by launch from Tigre, T 011-155 8439454. In a glorious natural setting, with 100 acres of rainforest to wander around in, this is a comfortable hotel, bedrooms have smart bathrooms with Jacuzzi, and there is a spa offering facial treatments. Not as luxurious as La Pascuala, but a lovely setting.

AL **Villa Julia**, Paseo Victorica 800, T011-4749 0642, www.villajulia.com.ar. Also part of the New Age Town and Country hotels chain, www.newage-hotels.com, this beautiful villa, built in 1906 on the waterfront, has now been tastefully converted into a chic little boutique hotel with just 9 rooms. There are superb views from the upper rooms, but all are decorated in the original style of the hotel, with incredibly comfortable beds and lots of treats in the bathrooms, many of them having the original bathroom furniture and pretty Art Nouveau tiles. The sitting room downstairs is calm and elegant, and the peaceful dining room is a really special place for dinner with a small but imaginative menu. Open to non-residents too.

C **TAMET Tigre Delta Youth Hostel**, Río Luján y Abra Vieja, T011-4728 0396. Clean, 3-ha park, hot showers, doubles with bath, including breakfast, table tennis, volleyball, canoes, restaurant, basic cooking facilities.

Isla Martín García *p114*

C **Hostería Martín García**, owned by Cacciola. For bungalow rental, T0315-24546. **Camping Martín García**. Also has hostel accommodation.

Colonia del Sacramento *p115*

L-AL **Plaza Mayor**, Del Comercio 111, T/F+598 (0)52-3193. Lovely, English spoken.

AL **Posada del Gobernador**, 18 de Julio 205, T+598 (0)52-3018. Breakfast included, charming. Recommended.

A **Hostal del Sol**, Solís 31, T+598 (0)52-23179, in Buenos Aires T011-154 4152605. A beautiful small hotel, with luxurious rooms in a lovely 300-year-old building, in a quiet position on the coast. Highly recommended.

A **Posada Los Linajes**, Washington Barbot 191, T+598 (0)52-24181. Central, a/c, TV, cafeteria, warmly recommended.

A-B **Italiano**, Lobo 341, T+598 (0)52-22103. With or without bath, good restaurant, hot water but no heating. Recommended.

A-B **Leoncia**, Rivera 214, T+598 (0)52-22369. A/c, modern, good.

B **Hostal de los Poetas**, Mangarelli 675, T/F+598 (0)52-25457. With bath, quiet, pleasant. Recommended.

C-D **Hospedaje Colonial**, Flores 436, T+598 (0)52-22906. Recommended but noisy, restaurant below.

Youth hostel

Hotel del Prado, C Nueva Helvecia, T0554 4169. Open all year, 15 beds, family rooms, no cooking facilities.

Camping

Municipal site, Real de San Carlos, T+598 (0)52-24444. US$3.50 per person, **C** in mini-cabañas, electric hook-ups, 100 m from beach, hot showers, open all year, safe, excellent. Recommended.

Eating

Tigre *p113*

¥¥ **Gato Blanco**, 40 mins drive by regular motor launch bus from Tigre. Good international menu, as well as more traditional Argentine staples such as steak, pasta and pizza, and a bar, and tea room, in elegant surroundings on terraces on the banks of the river.

Colonia del Sacramento *p115*

¥ **El Aljibe**, Flores 248 e Ituzaingó. Good fish dishes.

¥ **El Asador**, Ituzaingó 168. Good *parrilla* and pasta, nice atmosphere, value for money.

¥ **El Frijol Mágico**, Galería Americana at Rivadavia y Méndez. Open 1130-1400. Good vegetarian food.

¥ **La Torre**, Av Gral Flores y Santa Rita. In old town, bar and restaurant, loud disco music, but fine panoramic views especially at sunset.

¥ **Mercado del Túnel**, Flores 227. Good meat dishes, fresh vegetables.

¥ **Pulpería Los Faroles**, just off Plaza Mayor, old town. Recommended, friendly.

Activities and tours

Tigre *p113*

Boat trips

Interisleña, Río Tigre, T011-4731 0261 and **Río Tur**, Puerto de Frutos, T011-4731 0280. Tourist catamarans, 5 services daily, 1 to 2-hr trips, US$2.50-3.50.

Catamarán Libertad, Puerto de Olivos. At the weekends, longer trips (4½ hrs) to the open Río de la Plata estuary.

Transport

San Isidro *p112*

Taxi

Turismo York, T011-4743 0561, turismoyork@aol.com. Friendly and reliable taxi company, cheaper than getting a Buenos Aires company to come out to San Isidro.

Tigre *p113*

Bus

Take No 60 from Constitución: the 60 'bajo' takes a little longer than the 60 'alto' but is more interesting for sightseeing.

Ferry

To **Carmelo**, Uruguay (3 hrs, twice a day, US$25 return plus port tax) leaves from Cacciola dock. Overnight trips to **Carmelo** (from US$50 including accommodation) and bus connections to **Montevideo** (6 hrs from Tigre, US$35 return plus port tax) are also available from Cacciola. **Cacciola** office: Florida 520, p 1 oficina 113, T011-4393 6100 and international terminal, Lavalle 520, Tigre, T011-4749 0329, www.cacciolaviajes.com. Credit cards accepted. It is advisable to book in advance; connecting bus from offices to port and from Carmelo to Montevideo.

Train

Take train from Retiro station, Buenos Aires, (TBA Mitre section) to Tigre or to Bartolomé Mitre and change to the Maipú station (the stations are linked) for the **Tren de la Costa**, T011-4002 6000, www.trendelacosta.com.ar. US$2 fixed price one way from Maipú station to Tigre, get on and off as many times as you like en route, every 20 mins Mon-Thu 0710-2300, Fri 0710-2400, Sat-Sun 0830-0010, 25 mins journey to San Isidro, 60 mins to Tigre. (Buses to Tren de la Costa are 60 from Constitución, 19 or 71 from Once, 152 from centre.)

Colonia del Sacramento *p115*

Book in advance for all sailings and flights in summer, especially at weekends.

Air

Flights to Aeroparque, **Buenos Aires**, most days, generally quicker than hydrofoil. The airport is 17 km out of town along Route 1; for taxi to Colonia, buy ticket in building next to arrivals, US$2.

Bus

Bus company offices: COT, Flores 432, T+598 (0)52-23121; **Tauril**, Flores y Suárez; **Tauriño**, Flores 436. To **Montevideo**, 2½ hrs, COT and Tauril, ½ hrly service, US$7; to **Carmelo**, 1½ hrs, **Tauriño**), 4 per day (not Sun), US$2.50 Chadre/Agencia Central.

Car hire

Budget, *Flores 472*; **Punta**, Paseo de la Estación L, on Méndez near Flores; also car hire at airport.

Ferry

Ferries to **Buenos Aires** are operated by Buquebus (T+598 (0)52-22975) and Ferryturismo (T+598 (0)52-42919). See under Buenos Aires for details.

Motorcycle and bicycle hire

Flores y Rivera, and outside ferry dock, US$5per hr, US$15 per day, recommended as a good way of seeing the town, traffic is slow.

Directory

Colonia del Sacramento *p115*

Banks Open pm only. Banco Comercial, on plaza, gives cash against Visa. **Cambio Viaggio**, Flores 350 y Suárez, T+598(0)-5222070, Mon-Sat 0900-1200, 1300-1800, Sun 1000-1800 (also outside the ferry dock, with car hire). **Cambio Colonia** and **Banco de la República Oriental del Uruguay** at the ferry port (dollars and South American currencies).
Tourist offices Flores y Rivera, T+598 (0)52- 23700, Mon-Fri 0800-1830, Sat and Sun 0900- 2200, good maps of the Barrio Histórico. Also at passenger terminal at the dock, T+598 (0)52-4897.

Buenos Aires province

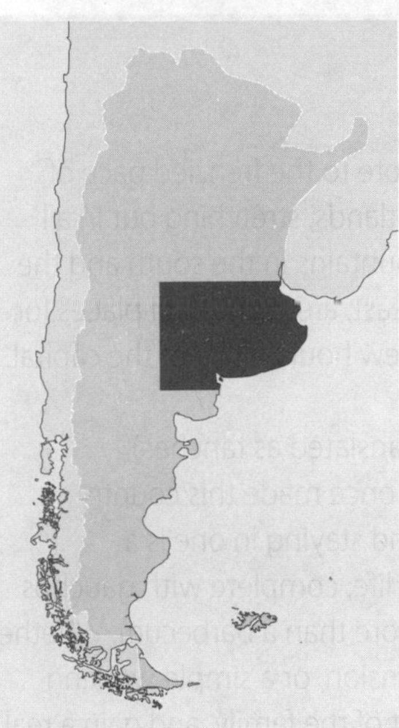

Footprint features

Introduction

The Pampas is the perfect antidote to the frenzied pace of Buenos Aires. These peaceful flatlands, stretching out in all directions towards dramatic mountains in the south and the unspoiled Atlantic coast to the east, are wonderful places for escape and relaxation within a few hours' drive of the capital.

Argentina's estancias (loosely translated as ranches) produce the superb beef which once made this country the breadbasket of the world, and staying in one is a quintessential part of Argentine life, complete with gauchos (cowboys) and *asados* (much more than a barbecue). Whether you choose a grand colonial mansion, or a simple working farm, you'll be welcomed as part of the family, and gain a real insight into Argentine culture, while enjoying the pleasure of life on the land. Ride your horse across the plains, and then tuck into an *asado* of succulent home grown beef cooked on an open fire under the stars: an unforgettable experience. Gauchos are still very much part of Argentine rural life and you can enjoy their music and fine horsemanship in quaint Pampas towns such as San Antonio de Areco and Chascomús, unchanged since the early 1900s.

The Atlantic beaches are a great way to cool down in the summer. Avoid the tawdry casinos of famous Mar del Plata and head instead for the chic resorts of Pinamar and Cariló; chill out in Villa Gesell or escape to Mar de las Pampas where you can walk the shore for miles without seeing a soul. Two of the oldest mountain ranges in the world pop up from the flat pampas at Tandil and Sierra de la Ventana, attracting climbers and hikers, and anyone looking for a relaxing weekend in beautiful countryside.

★ Don't miss...

1 **Gaucho towns: San Antonio de Areco and Chascomús** Watch the original cowboys at traditional rodeo, pages 123 and 127.

2 **Estancias** The most quintessential Argentine experience. Try Dos Talas for its history, Juan Gerónimo for horse riding along the beach, Ave María for luxury – great for your last night before heading home, page 124.

3 **Pinamar** Chic beach resort with live music on summer evenings, page 135.

4 **Sierra de la Ventana** Hike up, or abseil down. The mountain with a hole gives tremendous views for miles, page 155.

The Pampas

The pampas is home to one of the most enduring images of Argentina: the gaucho on horseback, roaming the plains. All over the pampas there are quiet, unspoiled towns where gaucho culture is still very much alive. Two impeccably preserved gaucho towns very much worth visiting are San Antonio de Areco and Chascomús. The former is home to expert craftsmen, working silver and leather in the traditional gaucho way. Near here there are many of the finest and most historical estancias within easy reach: two are recommended, El Ombú and La Bamba. Further southeast, Chascomús is similarly charming, a traditional cowboy town come to life, with pristine examples of 1870's architecture, a good museum of the pampas and gauchos, and a lake for water sports in summer. There are fine estancias here too: friendly, relaxed La Fé, and best of all, Dos Talas, with its extraordinary history and beautiful grounds. Further inland, there are three more fine estancias, La Concepción, Santa Rita, and the Loire chateau-style La Candelaria. Whether you stay the night or just visit for an afternoon to eat lunch and ride, you'll get an unforgettable taste of life on the land. The pampas is also rich in wildlife and on lakes and lagunas you're likely to spot Chilean flamingos and herons, maguari storks, white-faced Ibis and black-necked swans. Ostrich-like greater rheas can also be seen in many parts. ➧ *For Sleeping, Eating and other listings, see pages 129-132.*

Ins and outs

Getting around It's easy to get around the province with a network of **buses** to and from Buenos Aires, and between towns. **Train** lines operate to Mar del Platao, and to Chascomús and Tandil, stopping at many coastal towns on the way. You'll need to hire a car to reach the more remote estancias, and there are good fast toll roads radiating out from the capital to Mar del Plata, via Chascomús, San Antonio de Areco, and Lobos. Check out www.chascomus.com.ar, www.lobos.gov.ar, www.sanantoniodeareco.com/turismo and www.probairesturismo.gba.gov.ar; www.turismo.gov.ar also has links to all these small towns. ➧ *For further details, see Transport, page 132.*

Background

Travelling through these calm lands you wouldn't think they'd had such a violent past; but these are the rich fertile plains that justified conquering the indigenous peoples in the bloody 19th-century Campaign of the Desert. Once the Spanish newcomers had gained control, their produce made Argentina the 'breadbasket of the world', and the sixth richest nation on Earth, exporting beef, lamb, wheat and wool when a growing Europe demanded cheap food and clothing. When you see these vast perfect wheat fields, and superbly healthy Aberdeen Angus cattle roaming vast plains, you might wonder how a country with such riches can possibly have suffered an economic crisis. It's one of the great enigmas of Argentina. To get an idea of Argentina's former wealth, visit an estancia with history, like Dos Talas, and ask their owners what went wrong. Some blame Perón, and now Kirchner, for encouraging passivity in the lazy populace, or Menem for resorting to desperate measures to keep up with the US dollar by selling the nationalized industries. Farmers complain the government imposes impossible taxes for those who produce from the land. The fields of Buenos Aires province provide more than half of Argentina's cereal production, and over a third of her livestock, but many estancias' owners have had to turn to tourism in order to maintain the homes, built by their ancestors in more affluent times. Still, staying in an estancia is a rare privilege, to be wholeheartedly enjoyed.

Gaucho life

The gaucho is the cowboy of Argentina, found all over the country, and one of Argentina's most important cultural icons. Gauchos emerged as a distinct social group in the early 18th century. They were brought over by the Spanish to tend cattle, and combined their Moorish roots with Argentine Criollo stock, adopting aspects of the indigenous peoples' lifestyle, but creating their own particular style and dress. The gaucho lived on horseback, dressing in a poncho, *bombachas* (baggy trousers) held up by a *tirador* (broad leather belt) and homemade boots with leather spurs. He was armed with a *facón* or large knife, and *boleadoras*, a lasso made from three stones tied with leather thongs, which when expertly thrown would wrap around the legs of animals to bring them swiftly to the ground. Gauchos roamed the pampas, hunting the seemingly inexhaustible herds of wild cattle and horses in the long period before fencing protected private property. The gaucho's wild reputation derived from his resistance to government officials who tried to exert their control by the use of anti-vagrancy laws and military conscription. Much of the urban population regarded the gaucho as a savage, on a par with the 'indians'.

The gaucho's lifestyle, was doomed, of course, in the advent of railways, fencing, and the redistribution of land which followed the massacre of indigenous peoples. Increasingly the term gaucho came to mean an estancia (ranch) worker who made a living on horseback tending cattle. As the real gaucho disappeared from the pampas, he became a major subject of Argentine folklore and literature, most famously in José Hernández' epic poem of 1872, *Martín Fierro* and in Güiraldes' later novel *Don Segundo Sombra*. But you can still see gauchos in their traditional dress at work today in any estancia. Visit Mataderos, Chascomús, or San Antonio de Areco, for displays of traditional gaucho horsemanship and music, silversmithing and leatherwork.

San Antonio de Areco » *pp129-132.*

→ *Phone code: 02326. Colour map 4, B5. Population: 15,000*

San Antonio de Areco, 113 km northwest of Buenos Aires, is *the* original gaucho town and makes a perfect escape from the capital. Built in the late 19th-century, much of its charm lies in the authenticity of its crumbling buildings surrounding an atmospheric plaza filled with palms and plane trees, and the streets lined with orange trees. The attractive *costanera* along the river bank is a great place to swim and picnic. There are several estancias nearby, and the town itself has several historical *boliches* (combined bar and provisions stores), where you can lap up the atmosphere, listen to live music and meet locals. Gaucho traditions are on display in the many weekend activities, and the town's craftsmen produce wonderful silver work, textiles and traditional worked leather handicrafts of the highest quality. Annual events include the *pato* games in January, a poncho parade in February and the **Fiesta Criolla** in March. Most important of all, however, is the **Day of Tradition**, in the second week of November (book accommodation ahead), where you will see traditional parades, gaucho games, events on horseback, music and dance. The **tourist information centre** ⓘ *Parque San Martín, Zerboni y Arellano, T02326-453165, www.sanantoniodeareco.com*, has friendly, helpful English-speaking staff who can advise on gaucho activities in the town, accommodation and transport. Other useful websites include www.pagosdeareco.com.ar and www.arecotur.com.ar.

Estancias

Argentina's estancias vary enormously from ostentatious mansions to simple colonial-style ranches that still work as cattle farms. Many now open their doors to tourists as paying guests, enabling you to experience traditional Argentine rural life. There are two main types of estancia: those that function as rural hotels, and those where you're welcomed as a guest of the family. The latter are particularly recommended as a great way to meet Argentine people. You dine with the owners and they'll often tell you about their family's history and talk about life on the farm, turning a tourist experience into a meeting of friends. Some estancias offer splendid rooms filled with family antiques. Others are simple affairs where you'll stay in an old farm house, and the focus is on peace and quiet. They can be the perfect place to retreat and unwind for a few days or to try an activity such as horse riding or birdwatching. Whichever kind you choose, a good estancia will give you an unparalleled taste of traditional Argentine hospitality: welcoming strangers is one of the things Argentines do best.

Activities These depend on the estancia, but almost all provide horse riding, which is highly recommended even if you've no experience. Galloping across the plains on a *criollo* horse has to be one of the biggest thrills of visiting the country. If you're a beginner, just let your hosts know beforehand so that they can arrange for you to ride an especially docile creature. The horse-shy might be offered a ride in a *sulky*, the traditional open horse-drawn carriage, more relaxing but just as much fun. Cattle mustering, meanwhile, may sound daunting but is the best way to get into life on the *campo*. You'll help your hosts move cattle around while sitting astride your trusty steed. Gauchos will be on hand to guide you and by the end of the day you'll be whooping and hollering with the best of them.

Prices Usually around US$150 per person per night for the most luxurious to US$50 for the simpler places, but bear in mind that all meals, and often drinks, as well as fabulous activities such as horse riding are also included. And you can't put a price on the warm hospitality of the owners. If this is outside your budget, consider coming for a day visit (*día de campo*), which usually costs around US$50 per person. Many establishments will pick you up from the nearest town if you don't have a car.

Access As estancias are inevitably located in the country, you'll need to hire a car. If you're visiting for a few days ask your hosts to arrange a remise taxi. Many estancias are within easy access of Ezeiza International Airport in Buenos Aires, so it can be an ideal way to relax after a long flight at the start of your trip, or to spend your last couple of nights, allowing you to return home feeling refreshed and with vivid memories of generous Argentine hospitality.

Recommended estancias include **Dos Talas** (page 128), **Juan Gerónimo** (page 130), **Casa de Campo La China** (page 130), **Santa Rita** (page 130), **Palantelén** (page 144), **Siempre Verde** (page 157) and **Ave María** (page 157).

A few useful websites are: www.probairesturismo.gba.gov.ar, www.guiatierrabuena.com.ar, www.caminodelgaucho.com.ar, www.ripioturismo.com.as, www.raturestancias.com.ar and www.horseadventures.com.ar.

The **Museo Gauchesco Ricardo Güiraldes** ⓘ *Camino Güiraldes, daily except Tue, 1100-1700, US$0.70*, is a replica of a typical estancia of the late 19th century, and houses impressive gaucho artefacts and displays on the life of the celebrated writer who was a sophisticated member of Parisian literary circles, and an Argentine nationalist who romanticized gaucho life. Güiraldes spent much of his early life on **Estancia La Porteña**, 8 km from San Antonio, and settled there to write his best-known book, *Don Segundo Sombra* (1926), which was set in San Antonio. The estancia and sights in the town such as the old bridge and the Pulpería La Blanqueada (at the entrance to the museum), became famous through its pages.

Superb gaucho silverwork is for sale at the workshop and **Museo de Juan José Draghi** ⓘ *Alvear 345, T02326-454219, daily 0900-2000*. Excellent chocolates are made at **La Olla de Cobre** ⓘ *Matheu 433, T02326-453105*, with a charming little café for drinking chocolate and trying the most amazing homemade *alfajores*. There is a large park, **Parque San Martín**, spanning the river to the north of the town near the tourist information centre. While you're here, you should visit one of the old traditional bars, or *pulperías*, many of which have been lovingly restored to recreate the 1900's ambience, and are brought to life by a genuine local clientele every night. Try **La Vieja Sodería**, on Gral Paz and Bolivar, or **El Almacén de Ramos Generales Parrilla**, at Zapiola 143. Two blocks west of here, there's a small zoo **Parque de Flora y Fauna Carlos Merti** ⓘ *opposite the old bridge Puente Viejo, summer 1000-1300, 1700-1900, winter 1000-1700, US$0.70*. Also on Alsina 66 is the city museum, **Centro Cultural y Museo Usina Vieja** ⓘ *Tue-Fri 0800-1400, Sat, Sun, holidays 1100-1700, free*. There are ATMs on the plaza, but nowhere to change travellers cheques. At the country club you can play golf (green fees US$7), or watch a polo match, in restful surroundings, ask at the tourist office for directions.

Some of the province's finest estancias are within easy reach of San Antonio for day visits, offering an *asado* lunch, horse riding and other activities. One such place is La Cinacina (T02326-452045, www.lacinacina.com.ar), which charges US$40pp for a day visit. For a list of those offering accommodation, see page 130.

La Plata » pp129-132.

→ *Phone code: 0221. Colour map 4, B6. Population: 642,000*

The capital of Buenos Aires province is La Plata, a modern university city with a lively student population, and consequently good nightlife, with lots of good restaurants and bars. There's no particular reason to visit as a tourist, but if you're passing through, you'll appreciate the broad avenues, leafy plazas, and elaborate public buildings. It's a young and vibrant place, where football and rugby are major passions. At the east of the city there's a beautiful park, **Paseo del Bosque**, popular at weekends with families for *asados*, with its famous science museum, the magnificent Museo de Ciencias Naturales.

Ins and outs

Getting there La Plata is 56 km southeast of Buenos Aires, 45 minutes by **car**. There are frequent **trains**, taking one hour 10 minutes. **Buses** from Buenos Aires leave every 30 minutes, taking about 1½ hours (from Retiro all day and night and from Plaza Constitución daytime only). Long-distance buses arrive here from all major cities. The terminal is at Calle 4 and Diagonal 74, and a taxi into the central area costs US$3.30.

Getting around The city is easy to get around, but note that the streets have numbers, rather than names, and diagonal streets cross the entire city, which can be very confusing. When you approach one of these crossroads with six choices, make sure you remember the number of the street you're on. There's an efficient network of buses all over the city, and taxis are safe, cheap and plentiful.

High stakes

So how did Argentina come to be synonymous with great beef? Cattle certainly aren't indigenous to the Pampas. But after Juan de Garay's expedition in 1580 brought cattle from Paraguay, the animals roamed wild on the fertile plains, reproducing so quickly that by the time the Spanish returned in 1780, there were 40 million of them. But by then, local indigenous groups were making a roaring trade, driving herds of cattle through the Andean passes to sell in southern Chile. Gauchos, meanwhile, were hunting cattle with the use of *boleadoras* (a lasso with three stone balls), and slaughtering them by the thousand for their hides alone, leaving the meat to rot. When salting plants – *saladeros* – arrived in 1810, the hides were transported to Europe, together with tallow for candles. The meat was turned into *charqui*, cut into strips, dried and salted, sold to feed slaves in Brazil and Cuba. It was only with the invention of refrigerated ships that Argentina's produce was exported to meet the growing demand for beef in an expanding Europe. Cattle-farmers introduced new breeds to replace the scrawny pampas cattle, and sowed alfalfa as richer fodder than pampas grasses. Today Herefords and Aberdeen Angus are still bred for meat.

And why is Argentine beef so succulent? Because these cows are fit! With such vast expanses of land to roam, the cattle burn off any fat, and are well-toned and lean: the meat is even high in Omega 3. So head straight for the best parrilla in town, and, unless you're vegetarian, try a few different cuts. Better still, stay at an estancia to try home reared beef cooked on the *asado* the traditional way over an open wood fire. Delicious.

Tourist information The main tourist office is **Dirección de Turismo** ⓘ *Palacio Campodónico Diag 79 between 5 and 56, Mon-Fri 1000-1800, T0221-4229764, www.cultura.laplata.gov.ar*. There are also **tourist offices** at ⓘ *Pasaje Dardo Rocha, Calle 50 between 6 and 7, T0221-4271535, daily 1000-1700*, and in the bus terminal ⓘ *Calle 42 between 3 and 4, Mon-Fri 0930-1330*. The provincial tourism website is www.probairesturismo.gba.gov.ar (also in English). A helpful office for exploring estancias, stables and for visiting craftsmen in the pampas is **Camino del Gaucho** ⓘ *Calle 57 No 393, T0221-4257482, www.caminodelgaucho.com.ar*. The English-speaking staff are extremely informative and will help you arrange your own itinerary.

Sights

The major public buildings are centred around two parallel north-south streets, Calles 51 and 53, which run north from the Plaza Moreno to the Plaza San Martín, and from there to the Paseo del Bosque at the north of the city centre. On the west side of Plaza Moreno is the enormous brick neo-Gothic **cathedral** ⓘ *daily 0900-1300, 1500-1800*, built between 1885 and 1936, and inspired by Cologne and Amiens, but a little lacking in elegance. Opposite is the large white building of the **Muncipalidad**, in German Renaissance style, with a striking clock tower. Plaza San Martín, six blocks east, is bounded by the **Legislature**, with its huge neoclassical façade and, opposite, the **Casa de Gobierno** is a mixture of French and Flemish Renaissance styles. On the north side of the plaza is the lovely **Pasaje Dardo Rocha**, designed as the main railway station in Italian Renaissance style. It now houses the **Centro Cultural** ⓘ *Calle 50 between 6 and 7, T0221-427 1843, www.cultura.laplata.gov.ar, gallery Mon-Fri 1000-1300, 1500-1800, Sat and Sun 1500-1800, free*, with a gallery of contemporary Latin American art, a café and two theatres. East of the Municipalidad, **Teatro Argentino** has its own orchestra and ballet company. Nearby on Calles 6 and 7 are the imposing **Universidad Nacional** and the **Banco Provincial**. The main shopping streets are on Calles 8 and 12. A good market selling handicrafts and local artesania is in Plaza Italia at weekends.

If you do find yourself in La Plata at the weekend, or on a sunny evening, head straight for **Paseo del Bosque**, a pretty public park of woodlands and an artificial lake, where all the locals head for *asados* and picnics. There's also a **Zoological Gardens**, an astronomical observatory and the Hipodromo, dating from the 1930s and one of the most important racecourses in the country. The **Museo de Ciencias Naturales** ⓘ *T011-425 7744, www.fcnym.unlp.edu.ar, daily 1000-1800, closed 1 Jan, 1 May, 25 Dec, US$1.50, free guided tours, weekdays 1400 and 1600, Sat-Sun hourly, in Spanish and in English (phone first to request)*, is one of the most famous museums in Latin America. It houses an outstanding collection, particularly on anthropology and archaeology, with a huge collection of pre-Columbian artefacts including pre-Incan ceramics from Peru, and beautiful ceramics from the northwest of Argentina. Highly recommended.

Around La Plata

Eight kilometres northwest of the city, the **República de los Niños** ⓘ *Col Gral Belgrano y Calle 501, T011-484 1409, 1000-2200, US$1, children free, parking US$1, train to Gonnet station*, is Eva Peron's legacy, built under the first Perón administration. A delightful children's village, with scaled down castles, oriental palaces, boating lake, cafés and even a little train, it's a fun place for families to picnic.

This area of the country has some lovely rural accommodation. A delightful option close to La Plata is the **Casa de Campo La China** (www.casadecampolachina.com.ar), a charming 1930's adobe house set in eucalyptus woods, with beautifully furnished accommodation and far-reaching views. Stay with the charming English speaking family, or visit for the day, ride horses and enjoy carriage rides. For further information, see Sleeping, page 130.

Parque Costero Sur Reserve and Estancia Juan Gerónimo

Parque Costero Sur is a large nature reserve 110 km south of La Plata, and 160 km south of Buenos Aires – just two hours' drive away. Declared a UNESCO Biosphere Site in 1997, it extends along 70 km of the coastline of Bahía Samborombón, and was created to protect a wide range of birds that come here to breed. There are several estancias inside the reserve including the beautiful 1920's Tudor-style **Estancia Juan Gerónimo** ⓘ *Punta Indio, www.juangeronimo.com.ar*. The 4000-ha estancia is magnificently situated right on the coast, and from here you can enjoy walking or horse riding in total peace and quiet – you can ride for three days here without ever repeating a route. The estancia is more of a village than a house, with a collection of Tudor-style buildings in the lovely grounds, including a tea house, a little cabin, stables and a rural school. The main house has a wonderful old library with an extensive collection of books on pre-Colombian culture, as well as literature in French, English and German. Its 11 guest bedrooms are beautifully decorated but best of all is the warm welcome you'll receive from the relaxed owner, Florencia Molinuevo. As well as horse riding along the coast, dunes and pampas, there's superb birdwatching and opportunities for swimming. For further details, see Sleeping page 130.

Chascomús » *pp129-132.*

→ *Phone code: 02241. Colour map 4, B6 . Population: 40,000*

This quaint historical town, 126 km south of Buenos Aires, is worth visiting to enjoy the vibrant combination of gaucho culture and fine 19th-century architecture, creating an atmosphere of colonial refinement with a Wild West feel. Chascomús was founded in 1779, when a fort was built as protection against the indigenous tribes. In 1839, it was the site of the Battle of the Libres del Sur (the Free of the South), and its streets are full of well-preserved buildings dating from the mid-1800s, and lined with mature trees. Despite the strong historical significance, the town has a lively feel and its position along the eastern edge of the huge Laguna Chascomús gives it an attractive *costanera*, which comes to life in summer. The main **tourist office** ⓘ *Libres del Sur 242, 1st floor, T02241-430405, www.chascomus.com.ar and www.chascomus.net, daily 0900-1900*, is four blocks from the main avenue, Las Astras. There is also an office on the *costanera* and Espana 12. You can take a boat out on the laguna, or head to a couple of fine estancias nearby.

Sights

Around the quiet Plaza Independencia are the fudge-coloured colonial-style **Palacio Municipal** and **Iglesia Catedral**. Southeast of the plaza is the extraordinary **Capilla de los Negros** (1862) ⓘ *daily 1000-1200, 1700-1900*, a small brick chapel with earth floor, built as a place of worship for black slaves who were bought by wealthy families in the early 1800s; it's an atmospheric place that still holds the slaves' offerings. A highly recommended museum for an insight into gaucho culture is the **Museo Pampeano Av Lastra y Munoz** ⓘ *T02241-425110, Tue-Fri 0800-1400, Sat-Sun 0900-1300, 1730-1930, free*, which has lots of information on gaucho traditions, fabulous maps of the Spanish conquest, furniture, and all the evident wealth of the early pioneers.

To the south of the town lies the **Laguna Chascomús**, one of a chain of seven connected lakes; the *costanera* is a pleasant place to stroll, you can sail and windsurf in the summer, and there are frequent regattas. It's also an important breeding site for *pejerrey* fish, with amateur fishing competitions held from November to March. The delightful estancia, **La Fé**, is nearby. See Sleeping, page 131, for further information.

Dolores

» *pp129-132.*

→ *Phone code: 02245. Colour map 4, C6 . Population: 30,000.*

Dolores is a pretty, sleepy little town, 204 km south of Buenos Aires. Founded in 1818, it was the first town in independent Argentina, and its attractive old buildings would be perfect as a film set for a 19th-century drama. There's an interesting little museum, **Museo Libres del Sur** ⓘ *Parque Libres del Sur, daily 1000-1700*, with good displays on local history, in particular about the Campaign of the Desert and the subsequent revolt against Rosas. It also contains lots of gaucho silver, plaited leather *tableros*, branding irons, and a huge cart from 1868. There's a charming plaza at the heart of the town, with a central obelisk and impressive classical-style church, the **Iglesia Nuestra Senora de Dolores**. In mid- to late February, the **Fiesta de la Guitarra** is held, with performances from internationally famous musicians, dancing and processions. This is a good time to visit, but book ahead. For further information, contact the **tourist office** ⓘ *T02245-442432, www.dolores.gov.ar.*

Estancia Dos Talas

The main reason to visit Dolores is its proximity to one of the oldest and most beautiful estancias in the pampas, **Dos Talas** ⓘ *10 km south of Dolores, 2 hrs' drive from Buenos Aires, T02245-443020, T15513282, www.dostalas.com.ar*. The fabulously elegant house is set in grand parkland designed by Charles Thays, with a lovely chapel copied from Notre Dame de Passy and a fascinating history. Come for the day or, even better, stay. You'll be warmly welcomed by the owners, who are descendants of the estancia's original owner, Pedro Luro. This beautifully decorated home is one of Argentina's really special places to stay. See Sleeping page 131.

The Conquest of the Desert

Until the 1870s, the Pampas, and indeed most of Argentina, was in the hands of indigenous tribes. After independence, President Rosas (see Background, page 587) launched the first attempt to claim territory in Buenos Aires province in his 1833 Campaign of the Desert. But in the 1870s, pressure grew for a campaign to defeat the 'indians', since the withdrawal of Argentine troops to fight in the War of Triple Alliance had led to a series of increasingly audacious raids by malones, the indigenous armies. War minister Alsina planned a series of forts and ramparts to contain the indigenous peoples, and defend the territory won from them. But his successor General Julia Roca found these plans too defensive, and called for a war of extermination, aiming to make the whole of Patagonia available for settlement. Roca's Conquest of the Desert was launched in 1879, with 8000 troops in five divisions, one of them led by Roca himself. Five important indigenous chiefs were captured, along with 1300 warriors. A further 2300 were killed or wounded. Roca's view was that 'it is a law of human nature that the Indian succumb to the impact of civilized man'. He destroyed villages and forced the inhabitants to choose between exile in Chile, or life in a reservation. After the campaign, mountain passes to Chile were closed, and any remaining indigenous groups were forced onto reservations.

Although Roca claimed victory in the Conquest of the Desert as a personal triumph, he was helped by technological advances: the telegraph gave commanders intelligence reports to offset the indigenous peoples'knowledge of the terrain and enabled them to co-ordinate their efforts. Railways moved troops around swiftly, and Remington repeating rifles enabled any one soldier to take on five indigenous people and kill them all.

Roca was hailed as a hero, elected president in 1880, and dominated Argentine politics until his death in 1904. The land he conquered was handed out mainly to Roca's friends, since the campaign had been funded by mortgaging plots in advance, with bonds worth 25,000 acres being bought by only 500 people. Argentina has yet to come to terms with this shameful part of its history.

Sleeping

San Antonio de Areco *p123*

C **Paradores Draghi**, Lavalle 385, T02326-454219, paradores@sanantoniodeareco.com. Beautifully renovated old colonial building, with traditional-style rooms, very comfortable, with kitchen and bathroom. Recommended.

C **Posada del Recuerdo**, Vagues, T02326-452715, T02325-15 68 4606, www.posadadelrecuerdo.com.ar. Charming relaxed *casa de campo* (house in the country) where you'll be welcomed by the owners. Nothing flash or fancy, but a relaxing place to stay.

D **Hostal de Areco**, Zapiola 25, T02326-456118, info@hostaldeareco.com.ar. Popular place with a warm welcome, very good value.

D **Los Abuelos**, Zerboni y Zapiola T02326-456390, Modern, neat hotel with well-equipped rooms and a small pool. Simple but comfortable.

D **Posada del Ceibo**, Irigoyen y Smith, T02326-454614, www.laposadadelceibo.com.ar. Old-fashioned family place that looks like a bit like a 1950's motel. Basic rooms, and a pool in the garden.

Camping

Auto-camping La Porteña, 12 km from town on the Güiraldes Estancia, good earth access roads. A beautiful spot with many *parrilladas* at picnic spots along the bank of the Río Areco.

Club River Plate, Av del Valle y Alvear, T02326-452744, is the best of 3 sites in the park by the river. It's an attractive sports club offering shady sites with all facilities, a pool and sports of all kinds, US$3 per tent.

Estancias

Some of the province's finest estancias are within easy reach of San Antonio for day visits but it's best to stay overnight to appreciate the peace and beauty of these historical places. The following are recommended:

LL El Ombú, T02326-492080, office in Buenos Aires, T011-4710 2795 Mon-Fri only, www.estanciaelombu.com. A fine Italian neoclassical house with magnificent terrace, dating from 1890, with comfortable old-fashioned bedrooms, furnished with antiques. Offers horse riding and a warm welcome from English-speaking owners, the Boelcke family. The price includes meals, drinks and activities, but not transfer. *Día de Campo* (day on the ranch) US$50 pp. Taxi from Ezeiza US$60, from Buenos Aires centre or internal airport Aeroparque, US$50.

LL Santa Rita, near Lobos, 120 km west of Buenos Aires, T02227-495026, www.santa-rita.com.ar. Spectacular building in gorgeous lakeside setting where the Nüdemberg family make you extremely welcome in their eccentric late 18th-century home. Great fun and highly recommended. US$47 pp for a day visit.

L El Rosario de Areco, T02326-451000, www.rosariodeareco.com.ar. A 19th-century house in lovely parkland, this is a traditional estancia for breeding polo ponies, and the children of the owners are keen polo players. Not surprisingly, there's excellent horse riding here, as well as a high standard of accommodation in pretty rooms, and superb food. Also 2 swimming pools.

L La Bamba, T02326-456293, office in Buenos Aires: T011-4732 1269, www.la-bamba.com.ar. A plum-coloured colonial-style building dating from 1830 with a fascinating history. The building was originally a posthouse on the Camino Royal (royal road) connecting Buenos Aires with the north of the country. It was the first estancia to open to guests in the 1930's, and has attracted many famous visitors since then. It's set in beautiful parkland, with charming rooms and welcoming English-speaking owners, the Aldao family, who have lived here for generations. It's very relaxing and highly recommended. Serves superb meals.

La Plata *p125*

Most hotels here are business-orientated.

B Hotel Corregidor, Calle 6, No 1026, entre 53 y 54, T0221-425 6800, www.hotelcorregidor.com.ar. An upmarket modern business hotel, with well-furnished rooms with bath, pleasant public rooms. Good value.

C Hotel Argentino, Calle 46 No 536, entre 5 y 6, T0221-423 4111, www.hotelargentino.com. Comfortable and very central, with bright modern rooms, all with bath. Also has apartments to rent.

D Catedral, Calle 49, No 965, entre 14 y 15, T0221-483 0091. Modest but very welcoming. Small modern rooms with fan and bathroom, breakfast included. Good value.

D Del Sol, Calle 54, No 754, y 10, T0221-421 6185, www.hotel-delsol.com.ar. Modest but useful for the centre.

D La Plata Hotel, Av 51 No 783, entre 10 y 11, T/F0221-422 9090. Slightly more comfortable than the **Catedral** with more spacious rooms, and better bathrooms.

Estancias

L Estancia Juan Gerónimo, T(011) 4804 9777, www.juangeronimo.com.ar. 170 km south of Buenos Aires, 2 hrs' drive. The perfect place to relax in really elegant accommodation, this is a beautiful Tudor- style house right on the shore of the Río de la Plata, set in its own nature reserve, with 3238 ha of beach, dunes, forest and pampas to explore. You'll be personally welcomed by the charming owner Florencia and her family, who will take you riding or birdwatching, and share with you the estancia's interesting history. Wonderful riding and food. Full board US$150 pp, all meals and activities included. English and French spoken. Day visit US$50. See also page 127.

A Casa de Campo La China, 60 km from La Plata on Route 11, T0221-421 2931, www.casadecampolachina.com.ar. Beautifully decorated spacious rooms off an open gallery, with great views. Day rates (US$25). Charming hosts speak perfect English. Delicious food. Highly recommended.

Chascomús *p127*

There are a few, very reasonably priced places to stay in town with more upmarket accommodation is to be found in the apart hotels and *cabañas* near the lake shore. There are also several wonderful estancias nearby

A La Posada, on the lake, Costanera Espana, T02241-423503. Delightful, very comfortable.

A Torre Azul, Mercedes y Tandil, T02241-422984, torre_azul@topmail.com.ar. Pool, spa.

C Chascomus, Lastra 367, T02241-4222968, www.chascomus.com.ar/establecimientos. The town's most comfortable hotel, with its stylish turn of the century public rooms, and lovely terrace, this is an atmospheric and welcoming place to stay. Breakfast is included and the staff are friendly.

D El Mirador, Belgrano 485, T02241-422273. An attractively-renovated old building, with simple rooms, but lovely original details in the public rooms. A spotlessly clean and simple place to stay.

E pp **Colón**, Libres del Sur 70 T02241-422977. Decent rooms with TV and bath.

Estancias

LL Estancia La Fé, T02241-1554 2095, www.estancialafe.com. A charming and very typical place to come for a few days to get a feel for life on the land. Friendly hosts María Inés and Carlos Ricci provide a warm welcome. Activities include horse riding, riding in carriages, and walking in the grounds. Simple comfortable rooms, wide open views from the grounds, great *asado*.

LL Haras La Viviana, 45 km from Chascomús, T011-4791 2406, www.laviviana.com. Perfect for horse riding, as fine polo ponies are bred here. Tiny modern cabins in gardens by a huge laguna where you can kayak or fish. Very peaceful, good service, and a welcome from the lady novelist owner, quite a character, who speaks fluent English. Can arrange collection from Chascomús.

AL La Horqueta, 3 km from Chascomús on Route 20, T011-4813 1910, www.lahorqueta.com. An 1898 Tudor-style mansion in lovely grounds with a laguna for fishing, horse riding, bikes to borrow. Sadly, you may not be welcomed by the owners themselves, but it's a good place for children, with safe gardens to explore. Comfortable rooms, though the food is nothing special.

Camping

There are 7 sites all with good facilities. **Monte Corti** is closest, 2.2 km away, T0221-430767, but there are 5 on the far side of the laguna, including **La Alameda**, 12.6 km away, T0221-15684076, and **Mutual 6 de Septiembre**, 8 km away, T011-1551 823836, which has a pool.

Dolores *p128*

L Estancia Dos Talas, 10 km from Dolores, T02245-443020, www.dostalas.com.ar. One of the oldest estancias, you are truly the owners' guests here. The rooms and the service are impeccable, the food exquisite; stay for days, and completely relax. Pool, riding, English spoken. See also page 128.

D Hotel Plaza, Castelli 75, T02245-442362. The only recommendable place to stay in town. Comfortable and welcoming old place on the plaza, all rooms with bath and TV, breakfast extra, good *confitería* downstairs. There's another good café next door.

Cabañas

There are *cabañas* at the aerodrome, **Cabañas Aero Golf Club**, T02245-446681.

Camping

Camping del Náutico, Lago Parque Náutico.

Eating

San Antonio de Areco *p123*

ǂǂ Al Almacén de Ramos Generales, T02326-456376, Zapiola 143, www.ramosgeneralesareco.com.ar. Historical and very atmospheric old bar, or *pulpería*, dating from 1850; the perfect place to have a superb *asado*, or try regional dishes such as *locro*.

ǂǂ El Almacén, Bolivar 66. Popular with locals, serving good food in a characterful original 1900's store.

ǂǂ La Costa Reyes, Zerboni y Belgrano, on the costanera near the park. Delicious *parrilla*.

ǂǂ La Filomena, Vieytes 395. An elegant modern restaurant serving delicious food, with live music at weekends. Recommended.

ǂ La Vuelta de Gato, opposite the park. Good pizzas, local salami and *patero* wine.

La Plata *p125*

ǂǂ El Modelo, Calle 54 y 5. A traditional *cervecería*, with a good range on its menu, and great beer in German-style surroundings.

🍴🍴 **Los Discos**, C 48, No 441, T0221-424 9160. The best *parrilla* in town, superb steaks.

🍴 **Don Quijote**, Plaza Paso. A very good restaurant, delicious food in welcoming surroundings. Well known and loved.

🍴 **El Gran Chaparral**, C 60 y 117 (Paseo del Bosque). Another, more basic *parrillada* situated in the lovely park.

🍴 **La Aguada**, C 50, entre 7 y 8. The oldest restaurant in town is more for *minutas* (light meals) than big dinners, but famous for its *papas fritas* (chips); the chip souffle is amazing.

Two fashionable places include: **La Banda**, Calle 8 and 54, T0221- 4259521, and **El Abaco**, Calle 49 entre 9 y 10. Both serve superb food.

Cafés

Confitería Paris, C 7 y 49. The best croissants, and a great place for coffee.

Chascomús *p127*

🍴🍴 **El Viejo Lobo**, Mitre y Dolores. Good fish.

🍴 **El Colonial**, Lastra y Belgrano. Great food, and very cheap, at the traditional old parilla.

Dolores *p128*

The following selection are all recommended:

🍴🍴 **Restaurant La Farola**, C Buenos Aires 140.

🍴 **Parilla Don Pedro**, Av del Valle y Crámer;

🍴 **Pizzeria Cristal**, C Buenos Aires 226.

Bars and clubs

San Antonio de Areco *p123*

Pulperia La Ganas, Vieytes y Pellegrini. An atmospheric place in an authentic traditional old bar, full of ancient bottles, with live music at weekends, from 2200 onwards.

La Plata *p125*

The following bars are popular and lively.

Block, Calles 122 y 50, and **Rita Bacalao**, in Gonnet, a pleasant residential area to the north of the city.

Wilkenny, Calles 50 y 11. Hugely popular. Irish-style pub.

The Grants, Calles 49 y 9. Lively bar with cheap *tenedor libre* food.

Entertainment

La Plata *p125*

El Viejo Almacén, Diagonal 74, Calle 2. Tango and tropical music.

Teatro Martín Fierro, Paseo del Bosque. Free concerts during the summer.

Activities and tours

San Antonio de Areco *p123*

At the country club (Ruta 8, Km 11, T02326-453073), you can play golf (US$7), or watch a polo match, in restful surroundings. Good food is also served. Ask tourist office for directions.

Transport

San Antonio de Areco *p123*

Bus From **Buenos Aires** (Retiro bus terminal): 2 hrs, US$5 leaving every hour with Chevallier or Pullman General Belgrano.

La Plata *p125*

Bus The terminal is at Calle 4 y Diagonal 74. To **Buenos Aires**, 1½ hrs, US$3.70, about every 30 mins. From **Buenos Aires**, from Retiro day and night, and from Plaza Constitución, daytime only. If you arrive on an overnight bus at 0600, the *confitería* opposite the bus terminal (T0221-427 3186) is safe and will be open.

Train To/from **Buenos Aires** (Constitución) run by TMR, frequent, 1 hr, 10 mins, US$2. The ticket office is at Constitución, hidden behind shops opposite platform 6.

Chascomús *p127*

Bus Terminal, T02241-422595. Frequent services, several per day, to **Buenos Aires**, US$4.50, **La Plata**, **Mar del Plata**, and daily to **Bahía Blanca**, **Tandil** and **Villa Gesell**, with El Cóndor and El Rápido. To **Río de la Plata** with La Estrella.

Train Station, T02241-422220. To **Buenos Aires** (Constitución), 2 daily, US$5, 1st class. Also 1 a week to **Tandil** and daily to **Mar del Plata**.

Dolores *p128*

Bus Terminal, T02245-440351, El Rápido T02245-441109. To **Buenos Aires**, 3 hrs, US$5, and to **La Plata**, US$4.50.

Taxi There is a stand at Belgrano y Rico, 1 block from plaza, T02245-443507.

Train Station 15 mins from centre; daily service to **Buenos Aires**, US$6 .

Atlantic Coast

There are 500 km of beautiful beaches and some splendid resorts spread out along the great sweeping curve of coastline between La Plata and Bahía Blanca. Closest to Buenos Aires, there's a string of sleepy seaside towns known collectively as the Partido de la Costa, popular with older retired Argentines and better for sea-fishing than beachcombing. For more beautiful beaches, head further southwest to upmarket Pinamar, the jewel of the whole coast with its excellent hotels and fine restaurants. Its neighbour, smarter still, is chic Cariló, where the balnearios *are exclusive and the* cabañas *luxurious. Nearby Villa Gesell was created as an ecological resort in the 1930s and despite being over-run with students in January, it retains a relaxed and friendly village feel for the rest of the year. Nearby are two quieter resorts becoming known for their natural beauty and complete peace: in Mar Azul and Mar de las Pampas, you can find* cabañas *set in idyllic woodland right next to the sea.*

Argentina's most famous resort, Mar del Plata was the very height of chic in the 1920s, but it's now a slightly seedy seaside city, with packed beaches and casinos – not the best place to relax. To the west, two old-fashioned resorts are rather more appealing: Miramar is quiet and low-key, good for young families; and larger Necochea has an appealing woodland park along its coastline, with a vast stretch area of unspoilt dunes, perfect for exploring on horseback. The southern stretch of beaches ends in the major port of Bahía Blanca, a useful transport hub if you're heading south, with an attractive town inland from the sea. ▸▸ *For Sleeping, Eating and other listings, see pages 143-153.*

Ins and outs

Getting there and around All resorts on the coast are linked to each other and to Buenos Aires by frequent bus services. Trains also leave to Mar del Plata, stopping at many coastal towns. If you're combining beaches and estancias, it's best to hire a car. The main artery south is the fast privatized toll road Route Provincial 2 (with US$1 tolls every 100 km), from Buenos Aires to Mar del Plata, via Chascomús and Dolores, with another fast road branching off to Pinamar from Dolores: take Routes 63 and then 56. Alternatively, head along the coast from La Plata on Route Provincial 11, also fast and with tolls, to San Clemente del Tuyú and then parallel to the coast to Mar del Plata. Route Provincial 88 links Mar del Plata and Necochea, further southwest. Mar del Plata also has a domestic airport with flights from BA. ▸▸ *For further information see Transport, page 152.*

Best time to visit Avoid January if you can, when the whole coast is packed out. December and late February are ideal for hot weather and fewer crowds. Many resorts are very pleasant in spring and autumn.

Tourist information There are well-organized tourist information offices in all resorts with complete lists of places to stay. There's plenty of accommodation along the coast, so only a small selection is listed. There's a useful provincial website, www.probairesturismo.gba.gov.ar, in Spanish only. Each town has its own website: **Partido de la Costa** www.lacosta.gov.ar and www.lacostaturismo.com.ar; **Pinamar** www.pinamar.gov.ar and www.pinamarturismo.com.ar; **Villa Gesell** www.gesell.gov.ar; **Mar de las Pampas** and **Mar Azul** www.mardelaspampas.com.ar; **Mar del Plata** www.mardelplata.gov.ar; **Miramar** www.miramar-digital.com; **Necochea** www.necochea.gov.ar and www.necocheanet.com.ar; and **Bahía Blanca** www.bahiablanca.gov.ar.

Traveller's cheques cannot easily be changed, but there are plenty of ATMs in each town. Remember to have small change for the tolls as they will not give change for large bills, and do not take plastic.

Partido de la Costa » pp143-153.

Heading south from Buenos Aires, San Clemente del Tuyú is the first of a string of 14 small seaside towns, known as Partido de la Costa, stretching down to Mar de Ajó. First built in the 1930s, they lost popularity when the more glamorous resorts were built further south. It's not the best part of the coast and can't be recommended as most of the resorts are slightly run-down with peeling 1950's seafront hotels and tacky attractions, though they're also rather cheaper than the more upmarket resorts. The beaches are crowded in January but absolutely deserted at other times and particularly forlorn in winter. However, there is an interesting nature reserve and excellent sea fishing. The Río de la Plata has gained international recognition as the widest freshwater river in the world, and here at its mouth, you can fish for shark, pejerrey and brotola from piers or from boats. Fish can often be bought on the beach from local fishermen. See www.lacosta.gov.ar for information on all the towns in this stretch of coastline.

San Clemente del Tuyú → *Phone code: 02252. Colour map 4, C6*

Some 320 km south of Buenos Aires, San Clemente's main attraction is **Mundo Marino** ⓘ *Av Décima No 157, signposted from the main road into town, T02252-430300, www.mundomarino.com.ar, daily Jan-Feb 1000-2000, Mar, Jul, Dec 1000-1800, off season weekends only, US$11, children US$7.* This is the biggest sea life centre in South America, where you can watch performing seals, dolphins, whales and penguins go through their completely unnatural routines; it's fun for children. There's also a smaller, far less spectacular theme park, **Termas Marinas** ⓘ *take the road to Faro San Antonio at the far south of Bahía Samborombón, T02252-423000, www.termasmarinas.com.ar, daily summer 0900-1900, closing earlier off season, US$6.50, children US$5,* where children can swim in thermal pools, identify birds and, for a small extra fee, ascend to the top of a historical lighthouse, which has impressive views.

Even more appealing is the unspoilt wildness of **Reserva Natural Punta Rasa** ⓘ *2 km from San Clemente, take the road to Faro San Antonio and follow signs, free, managed by the Fundación Vida Silvestre, www.vidasilvestre.org.ar/aguadulce, www.rpm-net.com.ar/puntarasa.* This is a private reserve protecting a special area at the southernmost point of the Bahía de Samborombón, where a long tongue of dense sand stretches into the bay where the Río de la Plata meets the sea. Vast numbers of migrating birds and a resident population of crabs and shellfish make this an interesting place to spend an afternoon. It's a great place for a walk, with a short self-guided trail and a lighthouse to visit. It's also a world-famous sea fishing site; the water around the peninsula can be up to 20 m deep, attracting large specimens of corvina negra weighing over 20 kg. Visit www.welcomeargentina/pesca/samborombon for further information. It's possible to drive along the 5-km peninsula but watch out for the tides. Information is available from *guardaparques* at the entrance and at the tip of the peninsula.

San Clemente has a busy fishing port, with yolk-yellow boats characteristic of the area, and the **Club Náutico**, at Tapera de López, offering all kinds of watersports. South of the centre, there's an attractive area of woodland, **Vivero Cosme Argerich** ⓘ *T02252-421103, daily 0800-1900, free, guided visits offered*, a 37-ha park, with woodlands, a plant nursery and sports centre. For further information on activities in the area, visit the **tourist office** ⓘ *Calle 2 Sur y 63 Sur, San Clemente, T02252-430718, also at the bus terminal, T02252-422525, www.lacostaturismo.com.ar.*

Santa Teresita → *Phone code: 02246. Population: 13,000*

From San Clemente, drive through Las Toninas and Costa Chica to reach Santa Teresita, where the biggest attraction is fishing, though there's also a good golf course, tennis and horse riding on offer. The **pier**, entrance US$1.70, is one of the largest on the coast, and is lit for night fishing. There are plenty of boats offering fishing trips off the coast, costing around US$20 per person for three to four hours; book ahead. **Christian Maurs** ⓘ *Calle 8, No 1043, T02246-430461, elcapitanpesca@telpin.com.ar*, and **Choco** ⓘ *Calle 38, No 1642, T02246-421730*, are recommended.

There's a **motor museum** ⓘ *Av 32, No 1550, entre 15 y 16, T02246-525786, summer only 0930-2000, US$2, children US$1*, which has some stylish 1920's models and is fun for enthusiasts. The **tourist office** ⓘ *Calle 3 y 42, T02246-420542, www.santateresita.com.ar*, can advise on accommodation.

Mar del Tuyú → *Phone code: 02246. Population: 6,900.*

Approximately 20 km south of San Clemente del Tuyú, Mar del Tuyú is the administrative centre of Partido de las Costa. It's a tranquil place to visit in February, with a little more life than the other resorts nearby in winter. Boat trips are organized along the coast in summer, all the way to **Faro San Antonio**, where you can see whales basking at close proximity in August and September. Fishing is also a big attraction, see Activities and tours page 151. The **tourist office** ⓘ *town hall, Av 79 y Calle 13*, is helpful.

Mar de Ajó → *Phone code: 02257. Colour map 4, C6. Population: 13,800.*

Another quiet old fashioned resort, 40 km south of San Clemente del Tuyú, Mar de Ajó has a couple of natural attractions as well as motor racing, a shipwreck and casino. The **Autódromo Regional** ⓘ *follow signs from the access roundabout for Mar de Ajó, T02257-423342*, holds important motor racing championships every summer. You can dive or swim at the *Naufragio Margarita*, a large German ship, wrecked off the coast here in 1880, and one of the oldest in the region. Mar de Ajó has one of the largest fleets of small fishing boats in the region, as well as the largest pier. Boat trips to fish for *corvina, pescadilla*, and *cazón* sharks are offered by the best guide in the area, **Lopecito** ⓘ *Av Costanera No 870, T15638093*. A half-day trip including all equipment costs US$20 per person.

The most spectacular part of this area of coastline is **Altos Médanos**, a long stretch of high sand dunes that are, apparently, constantly changing shape. It's one of the wildest and most unspoilt areas of the coast, bordered along the shore by a wide flat beach, perfect for walking, horse riding or 4WD.

The best way to enjoy this area is by visiting one of the few estancias near the coast. **Estancia Palantelén** ⓘ *15 km south of Mar de Ajó, T011-1553424120 or T02257-420983, www.palantelen.com.ar*, is owned by descendants of a pioneering Pampas family, whose atmospheric old house has views of the sea and is beautifully furnished and lined with mahogany panels salvaged from a shipwreck. Walk onto the sands, birdwatch or gallop across the miles of beaches, either on horseback or in a *sulky* (open horse-drawn carriage). Spend a few days here and absorb the complete peace, you could even have private tango lessons on the terrace under the stars. All highly recommended. Owner, María Laura Viñales de Ramos Mejía, speaks perfect English and is utterly charming. See also Sleeping, page 144.

Pinamar → *Phone code: 02254. Colour map 4, C6. Population: 20,600.*

The two most desirable resorts on the coast are right next to each other, with the quieter old-fashioned **Ostende** in between (see below). Both Pinamar and Cariló are upmarket places to stay, attracting wealthy Argentines, and have far smarter hotels here than elsewhere on the coast, not to mention sophisticated bars, fine restaurants and plenty of trendy beach bars and nightclubs. Pinamar is perfect for young people and families, with live bands playing at its chic beach clubs in the evenings in high season (these are also quiet and elegant places to dine with superb seafood). Pinamar is also one of the most attractive resorts on the whole coast with stylish architecture and mature trees lining its avenues.

Access to the beach is mostly by day membership to a *balneario* (beach club). You pay a fee of US$15-20 per family of group or friends per day, and then you can make use of all the *balneario's* facilities. You can rent a *carpa* – little wooden beach huts, built in tightly packed rows perpendicular to the sea, and furnished with tables and chairs to use when you retreat from the hot sun. Alternatively, you can rent a big beach umbrella, and stake a claim on an area closer to the sea. Renting either will allow you to use the *balneario's* showers, toilets, restaurants, and even beach games. Pinamar's *balnearios* range from chic, quiet places with superb restaurants, to very trendy spots with loud music, beach parties and live bands at night. There is free public access to the beach between the *balnearios*, but it's worth visiting one for a day to enjoy beach life. Their restaurants are open to those not renting *carpas* too.

The town also has fine golf courses and tennis courts, and there are fine hotels and smart restaurants along the main street, Avenida Bunge, running perpendicular to the sea. Explore the dunes at **Reserva Dunícola**, 13 km north, by horse or 4WD. The **tourist office** ⓘ *Av Bunge 654, T02254-491680, www.pinamar.gov.ar, www.pinamar turismo.com.ar*, is helpful and can arrange accommodation. English spoken.

Cariló

Cariló is the most exclusive beach resort in Argentina, and you'll soon see why. It's a huge area of mature woodland right on the beach, where luxury apart-hotels and very chic *cabañas* are all tastefully concealed, so that its visitors have complete privacy – something which inevitably appeals to the many celebrities, sports stars and politicians who visit. The *balnearios* are neat and exclusive – **Hemingway** (T02254-470578) is *the* place to be seen for wealthy Porteños. Around the tiny centre, on Cerezo and Carpintero, there are good restaurants and chi-chi arcades with upmarket clothing shops where you can browse for top Argentine fashions among the usual international designers. You might find Cariló less friendly than Pinamar if you're in search of nightlife, since the emphasis is on exclusivity, but it's a good place for couples or for a quiet retreat. The **tourist office** is at ⓘ *Boyero y Castaño, T02254-570773*, www.pinamarturismo.com.ar/carilo.

In between Pinamar and Cariló is **Ostende**, a small town founded by Belgian entrepreneurs in 1908. Little remains of the original resort as it was abandoned when the settlers returned to Belgium on the outbreak of the First World War. The only building surviving from that period is the **Viejo Hotel Ostende**, formerly the **Hotel Termas**, which was a favourite of Antoine de Saint-Exupéry. This is a wilder part of the coast and there are plenty of campsites. Another old hotel, **Atlantic City**, unfinished in 1914, now functions as a youth hostel. On the beach is the much-photographed old stone and wooden walkway, the *rambla*.

Around Pinamar and Cariló

General Madariaga is a quaint 1900's town, 28 km inland, definitely worth visiting for the **Fiesta Nacional del Gaucho**, on the second weekend in December, when there are processions, singing and dancing. From General Madariaga, fishing enthusiasts could visit the **Laguna Salada Grande**, the largest lake in the province with a nature reserve and excellent *pejerrey* fishing. The **tourist office** ⓘ *municipalidad Guerrero 2039, T02267-421058, www.madariaga.gov.ar*, can advise on where to stay.

Villa Gesell → *Phone code: 02255. Colour map 4, C6. Population: 24,000*

In complete contrast to over-developed Mar del Plata, and upmarket Pinamar, Villa Gesell, 22km north, was planned by the brilliant German inventor, Carlos Gesell, as an eco resort. He came to live here in 1931 with the aim of growing trees for wood on the barren sand dunes. His project then evolved into an ecological holiday retreat and the first guests were invited in the 1940s. He planned and built the town along environmentally friendly lines, and in harmony with nature, planting thousands of shady trees that would draw water to the surface, and constructing roads around the sand dunes, rather than imposing on the traditional grid. The result is charming and the town has retained its relaxed, unpretentious atmosphere – although Gesell would probably be aghast at the seaside-town feel of the main street, Avenida 3, filled with arcades, street performers and noisy cafés. The beaches are lovely, with good sand, stretching for miles in both directions with far more space than in Mar del Plata. Look out for the main **tourist office** ⓘ *right-hand side of the road as you enter the town, Av de los Pioneros 1921, T02255-458596, daily summer 0800- 2200, off season 0900-1900*. The English-speaking staff are helpful and can offer advice on accommodation. Other tourist offices can be found on ⓘ *Av 3, entre 108 y 109, T02255 478042*, and ⓘ *Blvd Silvio Gesell y Av Buenos Aires, T02255-456859*. There's a good website with lots of accommodation and other information: www.gesell.gov.ar. Villa Gessell is best avoided in January, when thousands of students descend on the town, and best in December and late February, when it's particularly popular with families. If you visit in March and April and you'll have a very peaceful time.

The **Reserva Forestal y Parque Cultural Pinar del Norte**, at the eastern end of Avenida 3, is where Carlos Gesell built his first house in the woods. It's now a museum, **Museo Casa Histórica** ⓘ *T02255-468624, summer daily 1400-2100, winter Tue-Fri 1000-1600, Sat-Sun 1100-1700*, with inspiring biographical information (in English) and an interesting daily tour. Gesell's second house, **Chalet Don Carlos Gesell**, is now a cultural centre for exhibitions and concerts.

Mar de las Pampas and Mar Azul

Just 5 km south of Villa Gessell, two quieter resorts are developing: **Mar de las Pampas**, and **Mar Azul** are wilder and quieter places than anywhere on the coast, but have some appealing accommodation in more natural surroundings. There are lots of *cabañas* for rent and an increasing number of hotels. The beach here is broad and uncrowded, so although there is less to do than in Pinamar or Mar del Plata and no nightlife to speak of, you can completely relax and enjoy the sea in peace. It's a perfect retreat for writing or reflecting, or a cosy hideaway for couples. Mar de las Pampas has a **tourist office** ⓘ *Av 3 y Paseo 173, T02255-470324*. See also www.mardelaspampas.com.ar.

Mar del Plata and around » *pp143-153.*

→ *Phone code: 0223. Colour map 4, C6. Population: 542,000.*

The oldest and most famous Argentine resort – built in 1874 – has lost much of its charm since its heyday in the 1930s. It's now a big city with plenty of entertainment, but unless you're a lover of crowds or casinos, there are better beaches elsewhere. There are some good new bars and cafés, however, along Calle Güemes, and Alem, near the cemetery, and superb fish restaurants by the port. There are hundreds of hotels, all busy and overpriced even in low season (although prices double in January and February), as this is a popular conference city. Winter is the best time to visit if you want to see the town itself.

Ins and outs

Getting there There are daily flights from Buenos Aires (several in summer) to the airport, 10 km north of town. In summer there are also flights to towns in Patagonia. Regular buses run from the airport into town, or it's US$5 in a taxi. The **bus** terminal is very central but squalid; avoid going there alone at night. **Trains** from Buenos Aires and Miramar and arrive at Estación Norte, on Luro 4599 (T0223-475 3311), about 13 blocks northwest of centre. Buses to/from centre 511, 512, 512B, 541. In general, buses are quicker and more comfortable.

Tourist information The city's **tourist office** ⓘ *San Luis 1949, T0223-494 4140 (ext 130 or 131) or, more conveniently, next to Casino Central, on Blvd Marítimo 2270, T0223-495 1777, daily 0800-2200, off-season Mon-Sat 0800-2000, Sun 1000-1700, www.mardelplata.gov.ar, English spoken*, is very helpful and can provide good leaflets on events, information on bus routes and lists of hotels and apartment/chalet letting agents, including family homes (when everywhere else is full). There's another tourist office at the airport. For what's on see www.todomardelplata.com.

Best time to visit There are several festivals through the summer, with live music shows, parades and the coronation of all kinds of carnival queens. The **Fiesta del Mar**is one of the biggest, in mid-December and the **National Fishing Festival** in mid- to late January. The famous **International Film Festival** is held in the first half of March showing new Argentine films and attracting some good premières from all over the world. But if you're coming for the beaches, January is best avoided, because of overcrowding; December or late February are much more pleasant and it's still warm.

Sights

The city centre is around **Playa Bristol**, where a broad promenade, the Rambla, runs past the fine casino (upper floor open to the public) and the abandoned **Gran Hotel Provincial**, both of which were designed by famous Argentine architect Bustillo, and date from the late 1930s. Six blocks north along San Martín is the Plaza San Martín, a

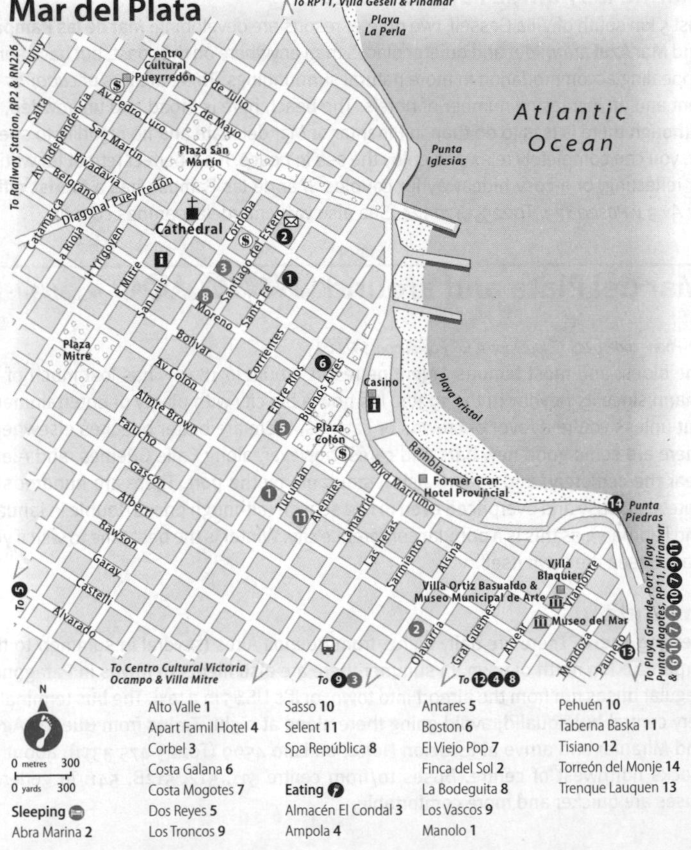

good place for shopping, and flanked by the attractive **cathedral**. Ten blocks southwest, at the end of Avenida Colón there are some impressive and attractive mansions dating from Mar del Plata's heyday, from mock Tudor **Villa Blaquier** to **Villa Ortiz Basualdo** (1909), inspired by a Loire chateaux, now the **Museo Municipal de Arte** ⓘ *Av Colón 1189, summer daily 1700-2200, winter Wed-Mon 1200-1700, US$0.70, including tour*, with rooms furnished in period style. Nearby is the splendid **Museo del Mar** ⓘ *Av Colón 1114, T0223-451 3553, www.museodelmar.org, summer daily 1000- 2300, winter Mon-Thu 1000-1800, Fri-Sun 1000-2000, US$1.70*, an imaginatively designed place on several levels, with a vast collection of 30,000 sea shells, small aquarium, café and roof terrace. The **Centro Cultural Victoria Ocampo** ⓘ *Matheu 1851, T0223-492 2193, daily in summer, Tue and mornings closed off season; ring to check current opening times, US$0.70*, is in a beautiful 1900's wooden house in lovely gardens, where the famous author entertained illustrious literary figures. In summer concerts are held in the grounds. Nearby is the **Villa Mitre** ⓘ *Lamadrid 3870, summer Mon-Fri 0900-2000, Sat and Sun 1600-2000, closes at 1700 in winter, US$0.70*, owned by a son of Bartolomé Mitre; with an eclectic collection of artefacts including old photos of the city. There's no shortage of entertainment in the city, with lots of theatres and cinemas, live music and the casino. See Entertainment, page 151.

Beaches and port area

There are several beaches along this stretch of coast, each with a different feel. Fashionable **Playa Grande** has the best hotels and shops, as well as the famous golf course, with private *balnearios* attracting wealthy Porteños, and a small area open to the public. **Playa La Perla** is packed in summer and far from relaxing, while **Playa Punta Mogotes**, further west, is by far the most appealing beach. The **port area**, south of Playa Grande, is interesting when the old orange fishing boats come in, and this is the place to head to at night, as there are many seafood restaurants gathered in one place; be selective as some are very touristy. A sea lion colony basks on rusting wrecks by the **Escollera Sur**, the southern breakwater which stretches out into the sea. Fishing for *pejerrey*, *corvina* and *pescadilla* is good all along the coast. Beyond the port are the **Punta Mogotes lighthouse**, built in 1891, and the **Bosque Peralta Ramos**, a 400-ha forest of eucalyptus and conifers. If you want sea and sand, rather than bars and entertainment, the best beaches are further southwest of the city, along the road to Miramar. Here you'll find several fine broad beaches interrupted by high cliffs, and all easily reached by regular buses from the terminal.

Around Mar del Plata

Santa Clara del Mar is a low-key family resort 18 km north of Mar del Plata, and has *balnearios* and a relaxed feel. Though it's far from chic, it's a welcoming place. For further information, contact the **tourist office** ⓘ *T0223-460 2433, www.marchiquita digital.com.ar*. Beyond, some 34 km northeast of Mar del Plata, is the **Mar Chiquita**, a lagoon joined to the sea by a narrow channel, with huge dunes in between, offering good beaches, sailing, fishing and boating, and rich bird life. For excursions to the Laguna de los Padres and to Balcarce, see page 151.

Balcarce, 68 km northwest and inland from Mar del Plata, is an attractive small town, with some splendid art-deco buildings, and a leafy central plaza. The main reason for visiting though, is to see the famous **Museo Juan Manuel Fangio** ⓘ *Dardo Rocha 639, T02266-425540, daily summer 0900-1900, winter 1000-1700, US$3.30, children US$1.70*. Argentina's most loved racing driver was born here, and the municipalidad on the plaza has been turned into a great museum, housing all his trophies, and many of the racing cars he drove. Recommended for car enthusiasts. For further information, contact the **tourist office** ⓘ *Calle 17 No 671, T02266-425758, www.balcarce.gov.ar.*

The **Laguna La Brava**, 38 km away, at the foot of the Balcarce hills, offers *pejerrey* fishing, and plentiful birdlife in lovely wooded surroundings. Visit **Estancia Laguna La Brava** ⓘ *RN 226, Km 37.5, T0223-460 8002*, for horse riding, trekking, mountain biking and water sports on the lake with fine views of Sierra Brava. For fishing contact **Club de Pesca Balcarce**, Villa Laguna Brava, T0223-460 8019.

Miramar → *Phone code: 02291. Colour map 4, C6. Population: 24,500.*

A delightful, low-key alternative to Mar del Plata, Miramar, lies 47 km southwest along the coast road, and is a rather charming old-fashioned little resort, known as the 'city of bicycles', and orientated towards families. It has a big leafy plaza at its centre, a good stretch of beach with soft sand, and a very pleasant relaxed atmosphere providing a quieter, low-key alternative to Mar del Plata. The most attractive area of the town is away from the high rise buildings on the sea front, at the **Vivero Dunícola Florentino Ameghino**, a 502-ha forest park on the beach, with lots of walks, restaurants and picnic places for *asado* among the mature trees. There's also a small **Museo Municipal**, with displays of animal fossils and indigenous Querandí artefacts. Further east is the dense wood of the **Bosque Energético** possessed of an allegedly magical magnetic energy, which both attracts large twigs to hang from tree trunks, and groups of meditators to sit in hopeful silence. Golfers will enjoy the fine Scottish links-style course at **Golf Club Miramar** ⓘ *4.5 km away from the centre on RP 11, T02291-420833*, unique in the Americas for its rough terrain, with no notable landmarks. There are plenty of banks with ATMs around the plaza. The **tourist office** ⓘ *northern corner of the plaza, Calle 28 No 1086, T02291-420190, www.miramar-digital.com, Mon-Fri 0700-2100, weekends in summer 0900-2100,* has helpful accommodation lists and maps.

From here, you can easily visit **Mar del Sur**, 14 km south, a peaceful resort with good fishing in a lagoon and bathing on the beach among dunes and black rocks.

Necochea → *Phone code: 02262. Colour map 4, C5. Population: 65,000*

One of the most surprising resorts on the whole Atlantic coast, Necochea, 100 km west of Miramar, is a well-established town, famous for its enormously long (74 km) beach. While the central area is built up and busy in summer months, further west is a spectacular expanse of sand with high dunes, perfect for exploring on foot, horseback or 4WD. There's also a huge forest park, a golf club and rafting on the river Quequén.

Ins and outs There are several buses daily from Mar del Plata, Buenos Aires and Bahía Blanca to Necochea's **bus terminal** ⓘ *Av 47 y Av 58, T02262-422470, take local bus 513 to the beach area,* rather inconveniently northeast of the centre. There's a good bus network all over the city. There is also a train station at Calle 580 y 563 in Quequén, east of Necochea across the bridge. The town lies on the west bank of the Río Quequén, and is in two parts, with its administrative centre 2 km inland from the seafront area. On the opposite bank of the river, Quequén (population 15,000), is mostly a residential area, with one of the most important grain exporting ports in the country. The two towns are linked by three bridges, one of them, Puente Colgante, a 270-m suspension bridge built in Cherbourg and opened here in 1929.

Tourist information There are two helpful centres: on the seafront ⓘ *opposite main Av 79, which runs down to the sea, T02262-438333, T02262-430158, www.necochea.gov.ar, www.necocheanet.com.ar*, useful for accommodation and entertainment; also at the municipalidad ⓘ *Calle 56, No 2945, T02262-431153*. There are plentiful banks with ATMs and *locutorios* along the pedestrianized shopping street, Calle 83.

Sights The **Parque Miguel Lillo** (named after the Argentine botanist) is a wonderful dense forest of over 500 ha with more than a million trees, open to the public for all kinds of activities. It starts three blocks west of Plaza San Martín, and stretches all along the seafront. There are lovely walks, many campsites and picnic spots, a swan lake with paddle boats, an amphitheatre, lots of restaurants, a couple of tiny museums and places to practise various sports.

West of Necochea, there's a natural arch of rock at the **Cueva del Tigre**, and beyond it stretches vast empty beach, separated from the land by sand dunes up to 100 m high, the **Médano Blanco**. This is an exhilarating area for walking or horse riding and the dunes are popular for 4WD, riding and sandboarding. Vehicles and buses stop where the road ends at **Parador Médano Blanco** ⓘ *T15568931*, a good place for lunch where you can rent 4WDs (US$50, jeep for four). If you fancy exploring the distant sand dunes and far flung beaches in 4WDs, head for **Expediciones del Este** ⓘ *central balneario Palmeras del Este on Av 2 y Calle 83, T02262-526900, www.expedicionesdeleste.com.ar.*

East of Quequén harbour there are equally tranquil beaches, particularly **Balneario La Virazón**, and a lighthouse built in 1921, with a good 18-hole golf course.

Around Necochea

You can go rafting on the **Río Quequén**, and visit to the **Cascadas de Quequén**, small waterfalls 13 km north. Nearby is the forested **Parque Cura-Meucó**, 70 km north, on the river, with the splendid **Balneario Puente Blanco**. There's also diving off the coast to a submerged diving park at **Parque Subacuático Kabryl**, www.kabryl.com.ar, just 1500 m from the coast. More information on diving is available at www.buceoprofundo.com.ar.

Bahía Blanca and around

» pp143-153.

➔ Phone code: 0291. Colour map 4, C4. Population: 275,000

The province's most important port and a big naval base, Bahía Blanca is a busy city, and yet it's a relaxed and attractive place with some fine early 20th-century architecture around its large plaza. There's not much to attract tourists, but it's a useful stopping point on the route south, or a base for exploring the beautiful mountains 100 km north at Sierra de la Ventana. It's a city with the feel of a small town, where people are friendly and everyone knows everyone else.

Ins and outs

Getting there There are several flights daily from Buenos Aires to the airport 11 km north of town, and weekly flights with **LADE** to many places in Patagonia. There are **buses** from all over the country to the terminal, 2 km east of the centre, US$2 in a taxi. There are also **trains** to the station, six blocks east of the plaza, from Buenos Aires.

Getting around The city is pleasant to walk around, with a small centre, and most things you'll need on streets Alsina or San Martín north/east of the plaza. There's a good network of local buses, taking *tarjebus* cards rather than cash (available from shops and kiosks), which you'll need to take if you want to get to the shopping mall 20 blocks north. Taxis are cheap, plentiful and safe.

Tourist information The **tourist office** ⓘ *municipalidad, main plaza, Alsina 65, through a small door on the outside of the building to the right, T0291-459 4007, www.bahiablanca.gov.ar, Mon-Fri 0730-1900, Sat 1000-1300*, is very helpful.

Background

Bahía Blanca was founded in 1828 as a fort, the Fortaleza Protectora Argentina, both to control cattle rustling by the indigenous population, and to protect the coast from Brazil whose navy had landed in the area in 1827. Though the indigenous people of the area were defeated in the campaigns of Rosas, the fortress was attacked several times, notably by 3000 Calfucurá warriors in 1859. An important centre of European immigration, it became a major port with the building of railways connecting it with grain-producing areas of the pampas. The biggest industry now is a huge petrochemicals plant 8 km from town at the port.

Sights

Bahía Blanca is a pleasant walk around, with well-preserved architecture from the early 20th century. At the city's heart is the large **Plaza Rivadavia**, a broad, well-kept leafy space, with a striking sculpture. On the west side is the Italianate **Municipalidad** (1904), and to the south the impressive French-style **Banco de la Nación** (1927); it's worth popping in to see its perfectly preserved interior. Three blocks north there's the classical **Teatro Municipalidad** (1922), T0291-456 3973, which hosts regular theatre, live music and dance. At the side of the theatre, at Dorrego 116, the **Museo Histórico** ⓘ *T0291-456 3117, Tue-Sun 1500-2000*, has interesting displays on the city's history.

To the northwest of the centre, along the attractive Avenida Além, the **Parque de Mayo**, is filled with eucalyptus trees, children's play areas, bars. Nearby there's a golf course, sports centre and a long area for walking by the river through a sculpture park.

Not to be missed is the **Museo del Puerto** ⓘ *Torres y Carrega, 7 km away at the port area Ingeniero White, open weekends, summer 1700-2030, winter 1500-2000, and weekdays by arrangement, free, bus 500A or 504 from the plaza, hourly at weekends, or a taxi; US$3*. Set in a former customs building, this has entertaining and imaginative displays on immigrant life in the early 20th century, with witty photographs, evocative music and sound. And there's a great café in one of the exhibition spaces on Sundays. Highly recommended. The port also has a couple of fine fish restaurants in its red light district: take a taxi.

Around Bahía Blanca

Bahía Blanca has both mountains and beach within an hour's drive. At **Pehuén-Có**, 84 km east, there's a long stretch of sandy beaches and dunes, all relatively empty and unspoilt (beware of jellyfish when wind is in the south), signposted from the main road 24 km from Bahía Blanca. It has a wild and un-touristy feel, with a single hotel, several campsites well shaded by pine trees, and a couple of places to eat.

There's a more established resort at **Monte Hermoso**, 106 km east, with good hotels and better organized campsites, but still a quiet, family feel, and wonderful beaches for bathing. It's claim to fame is that it's one of the few places where the sun rises and sets over the sea (here too, don't swim when wind is in the south, because of jellyfish). To get there, **Combis Ariber** ⓘ *T0291-456 5523, US$3.50*, runs a door-to-door minibus service; they will collect you from anywhere in town.

Santa Rosa de la Pampa → *Phone code: 02954. Colour map 4, C2. Population: 102,000.*

Santa Rosa is the capital of La Pampa province, founded in 1892, an important administrative centre 663 km from Buenos Aires. It's not a wildly exciting destination but it's a friendly place. There aren't really any tourist sights, though the **Teatro Español**, Lagos 44, dates from 1908, and ten blocks west of the Plaza San Martín is **Laguna Don Tomás** and a park with sports facilities. There's a **tourist office** ⓘ *San Martín y Luro, www.santarosa.gov.ar*, opposite the bus terminal.

The main reason to stop over here is to visit the **Parque Nacional Lihué Calel**, (see below). But closer still, there's **Parque Luro**, 32 km south of Santa Rosa, which covers over 6500 ha (two buses a day from Santa Rosa). This provincial park occupies the former estate of Pedro Luro124, who created his own hunting grounds for aristocratic friends visiting from Europe, introducing red deer and wild boar, running wild in the park, with many species of birds. Luro's mansion, a French-style chateau, has been turned into a museum, and opposite is a **Centro de Interpretación Ecológico**, with displays on the flora and fauna of the Pampas.

Parque Nacional Lihue Calel → *Information: www.parquesnacionales.gov.ar.*

ⓘ *T02952-436595, T02952-432639, lihuecalel@apn.gov.ar.*

The Lihue Calel National Park is situated 240 km southwest of Santa Rosa and 120 km from General Acha and reached by paved Route 152. The name derives from the Mapuche for 'place of life', and you can understand why when you see its low vegetated hills rising out of rather arid desert. Its microclimate allows it to support a wide variety of plant species, including a number of unique species of cactus in its rocky terrain. Wildlife includes pumas, but you're more likely to spot *maras* (Patagonian hare), vizcachas, guanacos and rheas as well as a wide variety of birds. The area was home to various groups of indigenous peoples 2000 years ago; there are geometric cave paintings in the **Valle de las Pinturas** and the **Valle de Namuncurá**, seen on one of two self-guided trails through the park. The other trail **El Huitru**, climbs the highest hill in the park and introduces some of its flora. The park is best visited in Spring. At the administrative centre for the park, there's a camping area and toilets.

Sleeping

San Clemente del Tuyú *p134*

B **Fontainebleau**, C 3, No 2294 , T02252-421187, www.fontainebleau.com.ar. Comfortable 4-star hotel on the coast, good value, with an elegant entrance and light airy rooms. There is a pool and a restaurant.

C **Morales**, C 1, No 1856, T02252-430357, www.hotelmorales.com.ar. A very welcoming option that has also a large pool and a restaurant. Rooms are plain but comfortable.

C **Solmar**, Av Costanera y 50, T02252-421438, www.hotelguia.com/hoteles/solmar. A 3-star hotel with decent simple rooms, some with balconies with sea views, in a modern block.

D **Sun Shine**, Av Talas del Tuyú No 3025, T02252-430316, www.rpm-net.com.ar/sunshine. The most recommendable of the cheaper places to stay.

E **Sur**, C 3 No 2194, T02252-521137, www.serviciosdelacosta.com.ar/hotelsur. A central location with simple accommodation. A good budget choice.

Campsites

ACA, Av II No 96, T02252-421124, and Cetan, Av IX y Calle 45, T02252-421487.

Santa Teresita *p134*

B **Hostería Santa Teresita**, Av Costanera No 747, T02246-420202, www.go.to/hosteria. A nicely maintained simple family chalet-type hotel by the sea.

B **San Remo Resort**, C 35 No 344, T02246-420215, www.sanremohoteles.com. The best of the 3-stars, this is a huge holiday hotel catering largely for families.

C **Sorrento**, C 37 No 235, entre 2 y 3, T02246-420 0298, www.santateresita2000.com.ar/sorrento. 3-star hotel with a smart entrance and pleasant rooms, though somewhat on the kitsch side.

D **Turista**, Av 32 No 464, T02246-430334, www.santateresita.com.ar/turista. Rather basic, with simple rooms around a central courtyard, but clean and friendly.

Campsites

Estancia El Carmen, C 23 y Playa, T02246-420220, www.estanciaelcarmen.com.ar. A really excellent site on the beach, but with grassy shaded areas, and all facilities, including **D** cabañas for rent. Recommended.

Mar del Tuyú *p135*

There's little on offer in Mar del Tuyú itself, but Costa del Este next door has a couple of places, both comfortable;

B **Seaside Forest Inn**, Av Costanera No 355, T02246-434173.

B **Terrazas al Mar**, Av Costanera entre 1 y 2, T02246-434840, www.club52.com.ar.

Campsites

El Refugio, C 94, entre 2 y 3, T02246-435195, gen@sinectis.com.ar.

Mar de Ajó and San Bernardo *p135*

This town has a couple of recommendable places to stay, but there is better accommodation offered at the next resort along, San Bernardo.

B Bel Sur, Mitre y Esquiú, San Bernardo, T02257-460368, www.hotelbelsur.com.ar. A huge, busy holiday hotel in season, with pool.

B Neptuno Plaza, Hernández 313, San Bernardo, T02257-461789, www.neptunoplaza.com.ar. A well-equipped 4-star place with good service.

C Gran Playa Hotel, Costanera 190, Mar de Ajó, T02257-420001, www.hotelgranplaya.com.ar. The best choice in town and also the oldest, still in the family of the original owners. A comfortable beachfront place, recently modernized it. All rooms have bathrooms and sea views, some have jacuzzis too: good buffet breakfast.

C Hostería Mar de Ajó, Av Costanera Norte 205, Mar de Ajó, T02257-420023, www.hosteriamardeajo.com. The best option after the **Gran Playa**, a modest but comfortable beachfront *hostería*.

Camping

ACA, Javier de Rosas y Melón Gil, T02257-420230.

Estancias

L Estancia Palantelén, 15 km south of Mar de Ajó, T011-1553424120 or T02257-420983, www.palantelen.com.ar. The best place to stay for miles around. A delightful house close to the beach, where you can go horse riding, and even learn tango. Charming owner María Laura makes you extremely welcome and she speaks perfect English. Highly recommended. See also page 135.

Pinamar *p135*

There are over 150 hotels in Pinamar of a high standard, all 4-stars have a pool. Book ahead in Jan and Feb.

AL Del Bosque, Av Bunge 1550 y Júpiter, T02254-482480, www.hotel-delbosque.com. Smart large 4-star hotel in the woods with very attractive, minimalist and comfortable rooms. Although it's quite a way from the beach, it does have a pool, tennis courts, a good restaurant and a casino.

AL Reviens, Burriquetas 79, T02254-497010, www.hotelreviens.com. Right on the beach, this is a modern, international-style hotel with luxurious rooms. Recommended.

AL Terrazas al Mar, Av del Mar y De las Gaviotas, T02254-480900, www.terrazasalmar.com. A large luxurious chain hotel with very comfortable apartments with sea views in a prime position on Pinamar's most central beach. A spa, 2 pools, and a restaurant.

B La Posada, Del Tuyú y Del Odiseo, T02254-482267, www.pinamar.com.ar/laposada. Very comfortable and spacious hotel with renovated rooms on the first floor, and a quiet location next to the sea with a pretty garden for breakfasts by a small pool. Excellent and a very attractive place. Recommended.

B Las Araucarias, Av Bunge 1411, T02254-480812, www.pinamarturismo.com.ar. Attractive rather cottagey rooms in this smaller hotel with pretty gardens.

B Playas, Av Bunge y De la Sirena, T02254-482236, www.playashotel.com.ar. A lovely setting for this old-fashioned large hotel with spacious stylishly-decorated rooms, and comfortable lounge, a small pool, and really good service. Recommended.

B Soleado, Sarmiento y Nuestras Malvinas, T02254-490304, www.pinamarturismo.com.ar. A lovely bright welcoming beachfront hotel with elegant entrance and cosy spacious rooms. Recommended.

B Viejo Hotel Ostende, Biarritz y El Cairo, T02254-486081, www.hotelostende.com.ar. This attractive smallish hotel has been open since 1913, and Antoine de Saint-Exupéry was among its many renowned guests. Although it's now been renovated, the place retains some old-fashioned flavour, and it's comfortable in a simple way. There's a pool, the service is excellent, and the hotel has its own *balneario*. Open summer only.

C Trinidad, Del Cangrejo 1370, T02254-488983, hoteltrinidad@telpin.com.ar. A lively welcoming little hotel with simple rooms, open all year round.

Camping

There are several well-equipped sites (US$11-13 per day for 4-people in 2 tents) near the beach at Ostende.

Estancias

AL Rincón de Cobo, access on RP 11, 30 km north of Pinamar, T02257-15638903, www.rincondecobo.com.ar. Just 3 secluded houses by the sea, separated from each other, and offering rustic comfort, the kind of services you'd expect in a hotel and all the usual calm of the pampas. It has its own airstrip in case you're tempted to fly here yourself.

Cariló *p136*

Most of the accommodation is in apart hotels and timeshares.

LL Marcin, Laurel y el Mar, T02254-570888, www.hotelmarcin.com.ar. Modern and large very swish complex, right on the beach, with a spa and a restaurant.

AL Cariló Village, Carpintero y Divisadero, T02254-470244, www.carilovillage.com.ar. Well- designed, cottagey, attractive, but not luxurious rooms and apartments; there is a very good restaurant and a spa with 2 pools.

Villa Gesell *p136, map p145*

There are many hotels scattered over the town, many between Av 3 and the beach. The tourist office has a complete list and a map showing where they are.

AL Hotel Terrazas Club, Av 2, entre 104 y 105, T02255-462181, www.terrazasclub hotel.com.ar. The most luxurious option in town is a modern tower right by the beach. It's not particularly attractive from the outside, but has very well-equipped apartments, great service, huge breakfasts, a restaurant and a pool, and access to the marvellous **Azulmarina Spa**, T02255-461245, www.spaazulmarina.com.ar. Closed off season.

A Delfín Azul, Paseos 104 No 459, T02255-462521, www.hoteldelfinazul.com.ar. Very cosy with attractive rooms and a pool in a large garden. Closed off season.

B Atlántico, Av Costanera y Paseo 105, T02255-462561, www.atlanticohotel.com.ar. A rather charming and old-fashioned seafront hotel that's been nicely modernized, with comfortable rooms, some with sea views, and all with bathrooms. A relaxing welcoming place, open summer only.

B Playa, Alameda 205 y Calle 303, T02255-458027, www.playahotelgesell.com.ar. Villa Gesell's first ever hotel, situated in the wooded old part of town, now renovated and very comfortable with spacious, attractively decorated simple rustic rooms. Closed off season.

C De la Plaza, Av 2, entre 103 y 104, T02255-468793, www.delaplazahotel.com. A small spotless, very welcoming hotel with excellent service, open all year round. Rooms are plain but very comfortable. Excellent value. Across the garden there are also fully equipped apartments for 2-4, and a small pool.

C Merimar, Costanera y Paseo 107, T02255-462243, hotelmerimar@hotmail.com. This 1970's-style hotel with a seafront location is a very good value choice for its spacious and comfortable rooms, several with balconies with sea views. Its *confitería* on the ground floor is very attractive, with wide windows on the beach. Open all year round.

D Hostería Gran Chalet, Paseo 105, No 447 y Av 4-5, T02255-462913, www.gesell.com.ar/granchalet. You couldn't wish for a warmer welcome here: spacious comfortable rooms, a good breakfast, and the charming owner Mariana knows all

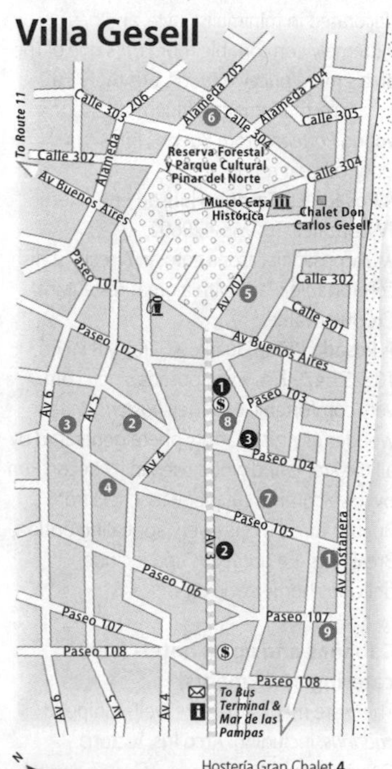

Not to scale

Sleeping
Atlántico **1**
De la Plaza **8**
Delfín Azul **2**
Hospedaje Aguas Verdes **3**
Hostería Gran Chalet **4**
Inti Huasi **5**
Merimar **9**
Playa **6**
Terrazas Club **7**

Eating
Cartagena de Indias **1**
El Ventanal **2**
La Delfina **3**

about the area. Good value. Highly recommended. Closed off season.

E Hospedaje Aguas Verdes, Av 5, entre 104 y 105, T02255-462040, clo@terra.com.ar. A nice airy place with a little garden for drinking beer or barbecuing fish. Rooms for 2-6, very welcoming owners speak some English. Closed off season.

E Inti Huasi, Alameda 202, entre Av Buenos Aires y Calle 301, T02255-468365. A friendly little *hospedaje* in a chalet-style building, in woodlands right on the edge of Parque Pinar del Norte, near the museum. With bath (cheaper without), breakfast included, and a bar for drinks on the terrace.

Mar de las Pampas *p137*

L La Mansión del Bosque, Juez Repetto y R Peñaloza, T02255-479555, www.lamansiondelbosque.com.ar. Just 150 m away from the sea, this attractive large house is beautifully decorated in minimalist style, and has extremely comfortable rooms. It's one of the area's more pricey options, but there's a great spa that attracts affluent stressed young *Porteños* from Buenos Aires. Open all year round.

A Posada La Casona, Hudson entre Roca y JV González, T02255-479693, www.posadalacasona.com.ar. A really stylish, comfortable place with a great restaurant. Excellent value.

A Posada Piñen, Juan de Garay y R Payró, T02255-479974, www.posadapinen.com. A very comfortable cottagey *hostería*, with a wonderfully rustic atmosphere generated by all the stone and wood used in its decor. Run by a welcoming couple of teachers from Buenos Aires, this is a very appealing option. Breakfasts are gorgeous and include delicious homemade pies.

Cabañas and apart hotels (self catering apartments)

There are many attractive well-equipped *cabañas*, including: **Arco Iris**, Victoria Ocampo entre Los Alamos y Ombú, T02255-479535, www.mardelaspampas.com.ar/arcoiris.

There are many apart hotels in the woods, of which **Village de las Pampas**, Corvina y Roca, T02255-454244, www.villagedelaspampas.com.ar, is recommended, with several apartments of different sizes, all very comfortable and attractively designed, and only a few metres from the sea.

Mar del Plata and around *p137, map p138*

Busy traffic makes it impossible to drive along the coast in summer from beach to beach, so choose a hotel near the beach you want. There are over 700 hotels. During the summer months it is essential to book in advance. Many hotels open in season only.

L Costa Galana, Blvd Marítimo 5725, T0223-486 0000, www.hotelcostagalana.com. The best by far, a 5-star tower at Playa Grande with everything you'd expect from a modern luxurious hotel.

AL Dos Reyes, Av Colón 2129, T0223-491 0383, www.dosreyes.com.ar. Long-established but newly modernized town-centre hotel with smart, well-equipped rooms. Guests have automatic access to a *balneario*, and the hotel offers big breakfast, good service, and is very good value off season.

AL Hotel Spa República, Córdoba 1968, T0223-492 1142, www.hotelsparepublica.com.ar. Friendly modern hotel with attentive service and slightly overpriced rooms (all with their own kitchen), a swimming pool and spa, good restaurant.

A Sasso, Av Martínez de Hoz 3545, T0223-484 2500. Welcoming older place, with comfortable rooms and pool, near Playa Punta Mogotes.

B Corbel, Córdoba 1870, T0223-493 4424, www.hotellasrocas.com.ar/hotelcorbel. A modernized 1960s building with very pleasant rooms, good service, and useful central location. Recommended. Closed off season.

C Alto Valle, Buenos Aires 2338, T0223-495 8743, www.altovallegranhotel.com.ar. Beyond the 1980s entrance foyer, with its mirrors and cream vinyl, there are simple but decent rooms in this modest but well-maintained central hotel.

C Apart Hotel Family, Av Martínez de Hoz 1837, T0223-485 0253, www.aparthotelfamily.com.ar. A good place for groups or families in well maintained little apartments facing the sea. Nothing fancy, but good value and comfortable.

C Los Troncos, Rodríguez Peña 1561, T0223-451 8882, www.hotellostroncos.com.ar. A small chalet-style place with a homely

atmosphere and a neat garden, in a nice and quiet residential area, handy for the restaurants and bars along Güemes.
C Selent, Arenales 2347, T0223-494 0878, www.hotelselent.com.ar. This small and central family owned hotel is great value, with warm and welcoming staff and owners on hand, and quiet, very neat rooms, with good bathrooms. Open all year round. Highly recommended.
D Costa Mogotes, Av Martínez de Hoz 2401, T0223-484 3140. A neat and modern hotel, with airy *confitería*, on the main drag, but in the quiet area of Playa Punta Mogotes. Closed off season.
E Abra Marina, Alsina 2444, T0223-486 4646. Basic clean rooms with TV, bath and breakfast lie behind the colourful lobby of this central small place, owned by Italians. A good budget choice open all year round.

Apartment rental

Prices vary a lot, with higher rates in January, slightly lower in Feb and even lower in Dec and Mar. Prices rise again at Easter and in long weekends through the summer months; cheap deals off season. The tourist office has a list of agents, and a helpful section in English on their website, www.mardelplata.gov.ar. Try **Gonnet**, Corrientes 1987 (y Moreno), T0223-495 2171, www.gonnet.com.ar.

Camping

Many on the road south of the city, but far better sites at Villa Gesell.

Around Mar del Plata *p139*

D Balcarce, Calle17 y 16, Balcarce, T0223-422055. Next to the museum, this is the most comfortable option, with friendly service.

Campsites

Campsites are plentiful.
Club de Pesca Balcarce , at Laguna La Brava, RN 226, km 39.4, T0223-460 8019. Well-organized site, with all facilities, and good fishing.
Municipal, R55, Km 63.5, south of centre in Parque Cerro El Triunfo. Pools and good facilities, all kinds of sports too.
Parque Idoyaga Molina, at San Agustín, 25 km south of Balcarce, T0223-491075. A lovely park with mature trees and a pond, with the calm atmosphere of an old village in the hills: the perfect site for camping.

Miramar *p140*

There are dozens of hotels and apartments between Av 26 and the sea.
B América, Diag Rosende Mitre 1114, T02291-420847. One of the most attractive places to stay. Located in a Spanish colonial-style building, surrounded by trees, with lots of games for children, bikes for hire, and lovely gardens. Open all year round. Recommended.
C Gran Rex, Av Mitre (Calle 23) No 805, T02291-420783. A rather austere block, old-fashioned but with comfortable rooms, and good bathrooms. Summer only.
D Brisas del Mar, Calle 29 No 557, T02291-420334. Seafront, family-run hotel with plain, very neat rooms, a cheery restaurant, welcoming attention, good value. Summer only.

Camping

Lots of sites, including:
F pp **El Durazno**, RP 11, T02291-431984, 2 km from town, with good facilities, shops, restaurant and *cabañas*. Take bus 501 marked 'Playas'.

Necochea *p140*

Many hotels close off-season, when it's worth bargaining with those remaining open. Most hotels are in the seafront area just north of Av 2 with at least 100 within 700 m of the beach. There are many apartments for rent; ask the tourist office for a list.
A Ñikén, Calle 87 No 335, T02262-432323, www.hotelniken.com.ar. The best hotel in the seafront area, just 2 blocks from the sea, a very comfortable 4-star with a small pool, good facilities, a good restaurant and excellent service.
B Bahía, Diagonal San Martín No 731, T02262-423353. A really welcoming place with kind service from the friendly owners, comfortable rooms and a pool in neat gardens. Recommended.
B España, Calle 89 No 215, T02262-422896, (ACA affiliated). Less luxurious, but a more modern option open all year round, well suited to families, with warm attentive staff.

B Hostería del Bosque, Calle 89 No 350, T/F02262-420002. 5 blocks from beach, a quiet comfortable place with a lovely atmosphere. The attractive house, now renovated, was formerly the residence of a Russian princess in exile. Now it has rustic rooms, individually designed, and with old furniture, and a great restaurant.

B León, Av 79 No 229, T02262-424800. There are lots of reasonably priced 3-star hotels, but this smart hotel, with business facilities is the best option, next to the beach, with plain spacious rooms and some rather kitsch suites. Open all year round.

B Presidente, Calle 4 No 4040, T02262-423800, www.presinec.com.ar. Another 4-star hotel, recommended for excellent service, comfortable rooms and pool.

B San Miguel, Calle 85 No 301, T/F425155, affiliated to ACA. Just 2 blocks from the sea, this offers good service, and simple comfortable rooms: good value.

C Marino, Av 79 No 253, T02262-524140. Open summer only, this is a historic place, one of the first hotels in town built in the 1920's. It has a wonderful staircase and patios, and although it's faded grandeur and a bit run down, it's full of character.

Camping

The following are recommended:

Camping UATRE, Av 10 y 197, T02262-438278. The best site, a few kilometres west of town towards Médano Blanco, with great facilities, and beautifully situated *cabañas* too; US$1.70 pp per day.

Río Quequén, Calle 22 y Ribera Río Quequén, T02262-428068, www.cabaniasrioquequen.com.ar. Sports facilities, pool, bar, cycle hire, well-maintained in attractive setting on the river. US$5 for 2 people per day.

Bahía Blanca and around *p141*

B Argos, España 149, T0291-455 0404, www.hotelargos.com.ar. 3 blocks from the plaza, the city's finest is a smart 4-star business hotel with comfortable rooms, and good breakfast. Also a restaurant.

B Austral, Colón 159, T0291-456 1700, www.hoteles-austral.com.ar. A friendlier 4-star with plain spacious rooms, good bathrooms, and good views over the city, very attentive service, and very decent restaurant. Good position just a couple of blocks from the plaza.

C Bahía Hotel, Chiclana 251, T0291-455 0601, www.bahia-hotel.com.ar. A new modern business hotel, this is good value for well-equipped rooms, though they're comfortable rather than luxurious, with a bright airy bar and *confitería* on street level. Recommended.

C Italia, Brown 181, T0291-456 2700. Set in a lovely 1920s Italianate building, this is one of the town's oldest, full of character, but the rooms are badly in need of a face lift. There's a good *confitería*, and it's very central.

D Barne, H Yrigoyen 270, T0291-453 0294. A friendly low-key family-run place, good value, and welcoming.

Camping

Best to head for Pehuen Có or Monte Hermoso – both lovely beach places an hour away by bus, with plentiful campsites.

Around Bahía Blanca *p142*

Monte Hermoso

B La Goleta, Av Pte Perón y C 10, T0291-481142. In the town, this is a modern upmarket place. Lovely rooms with sea views and balconies, in a central part of the beach.

D Hotel Cumelcan, Av San Martín y Gonzalez Martines, T0291-497048. A simple 2-star, but in a great position overlooking the beach, with a restaurant providing simple meals, price given is for half board.

D Petit Hotel, Av Argentina 244, T0291-491818. Simple rooms with bath, modernized 1940s style in this friendly family-run place right on the beach, with relaxed atmosphere, and cheap restaurant, El Faro, on the beach (breakfast extra), is recommended.

Camping

There are many sites around Monte Hermoso with good facilities.

Camping Americano, T0291-481149, www.campingamericano.com.ar, signposted from main road 5 km before town (bus or taxi from town). A lovely sprawling shady site by a quiet stretch of beach, with excellent facilities, hot showers, pool, electricity, restaurant, fireplaces, food shop, *locutorio*. Recommended. US$10 for 2 per day.

Santa Rosa de La Pampa *p142*

B Calfucura, San Martín 695, T02954-433303, www.calfucurah.com.ar. A smart modern 4-star, business-oriented place with well-decorated comfortable rooms, pool and restaurants, and a few apartments to rent.
B Club de Campiña, R5, Km 604, T02954-456800, www.lacampina.com. A rather more appealing option if you have transport, attractive gardens, with a pool, gym and spa.
C Lihuel Calel, Av Santiago Marzo 2535, T02954-423001, www.cpenet.como.ar. Back in town, this is a good value option with attractive rooms, and a restaurant.

Camping

There is a municipal site near the Laguna Don Tomás.

Parque Nacional Lihue Calel *p143*

ACA Hostería, RN 152, Km 152, T/F02952-436101. There are 8 decent rooms with TV, and a restaurant, on the road in an attractive setting in open landscape, 2 km south of park entrance. There is a camping site near the park entrance, good facilities.

Eating

Mar de Ajó *p135*

¥ **El Quincho**, Francisco de las Carreras No 800 and ¥ **Parrilla San Rafael**, Av Libertador 817, are both recommended.

If self-catering, buy fresh fish on the beach when the fishermen come back at 1000.

Pinamar *p135*

The restaurants listed here are the best options in town.
¥¥ **Tante**, De las Artes 35, T02254-482735. A small, elegant place – and one of the most expensive – serving a good variety of dishes. Often recommended.
¥ **Tulumei**, Av Bunge 64. A nautical theme in the decor goes with the excellent fish served in this small and popular place.
¥ **Viejo Lobo**, Av del Mar y Av Bunge, T483218. Good seafood and international menu, on the beach.

Villa Gesell *p136, map p145*

¥¥ **Cartagena de Indias**, Av 3 y 102. Good pasta and fish in a quaint place with an eclectic array of objects hung on the walls.
¥ **El Ventanal**, Av 3, 105 y 106. Picturesque café, bookshop, tiny museum and active cultural centre, all in just a few rooms, where you can enjoy deliciously rich cakes and good coffee.
¥ **La Delfina**, Paseo 104 y Av 2. Large, very welcoming place serving simple and very good meals, such as a range of *milanesas*.

Mar de las Pampas *p137*

¥¥ **Marechiare**, Julio Roca y Corvina, T02255-453061. Next to the sea, with an excellent range of fish and seafood dishes.
¥¥ **Viejos Tiempos**, Leoncio Paiva entre Cruz del Sur y Peñaloza, T02255-479524. This is owned by local pioneers, who also serve some Mexican and German specialities together with more refined meals, homely surroundings. This is *the* place to come for tea – worth a detour for the gorgeous cakes.

Mar del Plata and around *p137, map p138*

Besides the city centre, there are lots of seafood restaurants concentrated next to the fishing port, and in the **Centro Comercial del Puerto**. There are cheap pasta and *parrilla* restaurants along **Rivadavia**. But for more modern and chic places to eat and drink, head for 2 more areas which have become popular for attractive smaller shops, trendy bars, pubs and restaurants; Calle Güemes, and the western end of Alem, next to cemetery, which is popular with young crowds late in the evening:
¥¥ **Pehuén**, Bernardo de Irigoyen 3666. Eclectic and attractive decor in this very good and popular parrilla.
¥¥ **Tisiano**, San Lorenzo 1332. Good pasta in this attractive place with a leafy patio.
¥ **Almacén El Condal**, Alsina y Garay. A charming old corner bar, popular with a young crowd for *picadas* and drinks.
¥ **Ámpola**, Güemes 3064. Tiny chocolate shop and slightly larger tea room upstairs serving delicious biscuits, cakes and pastries.
¥ **La Bodeguita**, Castelli 1252. A Cuban bar with food, live music and an excellent place for a drink: great atmosphere.

Centre of town

¥¥ **Trenque Lauquen**, Av Colón y Paunero. A traditional *parrilla*.

Antares, Córdoba 3025. About 15 blocks west of the centre, this very popular brewery and restaurant attracts an eclectic crowd for its excellent beers and imaginative, good value food. Live shows every Mon.

Boston, Buenos Aires 1927 y Blv Marítimo 3887. A slightly old-fashioned *confitería* for very good set menus and a great range of excellent sandwiches and pastries.

Finca del Sol, San Martin 2459. Cheap tenedor libre with vegetarian choices.

Manolo, Rivadavia 2371, and on the coast at Blvd Marítimo 4961. Famous for *churros* (the sausage-shaped doughnuts), with hot chocolate for party-goers in the early hours. Lively atmosphere, packed in high summer, tasty pizzas with a sea view.

Torreón del Monje, Paseo Galíndez. A picturesque stone-building on a rocky point at the southern end of Bristol Beach, this is an unbeatable spot for its attractive terraces on the beach, serving decent food all-day long. Recommended for breakfast.

Port area and Centro Comercial del Puerto

Good for seafood restaurants, although many are brightly lit and not very atmospheric.

El Viejo Pop, Av Martínez de Hoz 599, Candlelit and designed like a ship, this is the best option, and serves superb paella.

Los Vascos, Av Martínez de Hoz 643. A long-established atmospheric place for fish and seafood.

Taberna Baska, 12 de Octubre 3301. Another recommended option for good seafood next to the port.

Miramar *p140*

Lots of restaurants along Calle 21, and at the *balnearios*, on the sea front.

Cantina Italiana, 9 de Julio y Calle 32. As its name suggests, this is a recommended place for good pasta, and seafood too; also delivery.

El Pescador Romano, Calle 22 No 1022. Excellent fish in this popular family restaurant.

Mickey, Calle 21 No 686. A lively long-established *confitería* serving cheap meals.

Necochea *p140*

Cantina Venezia, Av 59 No 259, T02262-424014. This is the most famous of the excellent seafood restaurants near the port, not to be missed.

La Casona de Rocco, Calle 8 y 81. A large house, popular with families, homemade pastas and seafood, both recommended.

Chimichurri, Calle 83, No 345. A popular place, recommended for parrilla.

Parrilla del Loco, Calle 56, No 3202, T02262-437094. Classic *parrilla*, deservedly popular for superb steaks.

Pizzería Tempo, Calle 83 No 310, T02262-425100. A lively traditional place serving good pizzas.

Bahía Blanca and around *p141*

Lola Mora, Av Alem and Sarmiento. The city's most sophisticated restaurant serves delicious Mediterranean-style food, in an elegant colonial-style house. Excellent.

Micho, Guillermo Torres 3875, Ingeniero White, T0291-457 0346. There are several good fish restaurants in the port area, but this elegant restaurant is the best. Take a taxi at night as it's in an insalubrious area.

El Mundo de la Pizza, Dorrego 53. Fabulous pizzas, made with thin bases loaded with toppings, big atmospheric place, the city's favourite. Unbeatable.

Santino, Dorrego 38. Italian-influenced menu, with a relaxed but sophisticated atmosphere, and a welcoming glass of champagne, very good value. Recommended.

Cafés and ice cream parlours

La Piazza, on the corner of the plaza at O'Higgins and Chiclana. Great coffee in a buzzing atmosphere, good salads and cakes.

Lepomm, Alsina 390. The best place for ice cream, especially their chocolate *amargo* and *flan de dulce de leche* – quite delicious.

Muñoz, O'Higgins and Drago. Sophisticated café for reading the papers.

Around Bahía Blanca *p142*

Marfil, Valle Encantado 91, Monte Hermoso. The smartest option in town, serving delicious fish and pastas.

Pizza Jet, Valle Encantado y Int. Majluf, Monte Hermoso. Hugely popular for all kinds of food, arrive before 2130 to get a table.

Bars and clubs

Mar del Plata *p137, map p138*

Many bars and **nightclubs** are on Alem or its surroundings and start at around 0200:

Bikein, Formosa 254 and Mr Jones, Alem 3738, are both for trendy under 25s crowds. La Llorona, on Olavarría, near Blv Marítimo and the Torreón del Monje. This is the place if you're not 25 any more.

Bahía Blanca *p141*
Lots of **discos** on Fuerte Argentino (along the stream leading to the park) mainly catering for under 25s: Chocolate, Bonito and Toovaks. The best place for anyone over 25 is La Barraca.

Entertainment

Mar del Plata *p137, map p138*
On Wed 50% discount at all cinemas. Lots more listed in the free leaflet *Guía de Actividades* from the city tourist office. Reduced price theatre tickets are often available for theatre performances etc from Cartelera Baires, Santa Fe 1844, local 33 or from Galería de los Teatros, Santa Fe 1751, and some others on Santa Fe. Many shows, comedy especially, in summer. See *Guía de Actividades*.
Casino central, Dec-Apr, 1600-0500; May-Nov, Sun-Thu 1500-0230; Fri-Sat 1500-0330, free; minimum bet for roulette, US$0.70. 3 other casinos operate nearby in summer.
Centro Cultural Pueyrredón, 25 de Mayo 3102, T499 7893. Every day screenings, music shows, plays or conferences, mostly free or for a small fee.

Shopping

Bahía Blanca and around *p141*
There's a smart modern shopping mall Bahía Blanca Plaza Shopping, 2 km north of town on Sarmiento. Cheap food hall, cinema (0291-T453 5844) and supermarket. Also supermarket Cooperativa on Donado. Plenty of clothes and shoe shops on Alsina and San Martín within a couple of blocks of the plaza.

Activities and tours

Mar del Tuyú *p135*
Fishing Excellent fishing either from the pier, and or on a boat trip.
El Pescador II, Calle 2, entre 67 y 68, T02246-434728. Organizes day trips to Laguna La Salada, as well as the usual sea excursions.
Tiburon II, Av 1 BIS No 7503 y Calle 75, T02246-434698, eltiburon@infovia.com.ar. 3-hr boat trips, leaving daily at 0700.

Villa Gesell *p136, map p145*
Horse riding **Tante Puppi**, Blvd y Paseo 102, T455533. Every day on summer afternoons, offering horse rides in the dunes and also moonlit rides on the beach.

Mar del Plata *p137, map p138*
Cycling **Bicicletería Madrid**, Hipólito Yrigoyen 2249, on Plaza Mitre, T0223-494 1932, (take buses 573, 551 or 553). US$6 per day, also bikes for 2, US$12 per day.
Fishing There is good fishing all year along the coast from the shore, and off shore in hired boats: *pejerrey*, and *corvina* abound; you can charter a private launch for shark fishing. Offshore fishing is best in Nov and Dec, when *pescadilla* are plentiful: winter is ideal for *pejerrey*. Deep sea fishing yields high salmon and sea bass. Contact tourist office for advice: T0223-495 1777, www.mardelplata.gov.ar. Fishing licences are available from Dirección de Fiscalización Pesquera, Mitre 2853, T0223-493 2528, and fishing gear shops.
Golf **Mar del Plata Golf Club**, is a great course, and deservedly famous, in a wonderful elevated position by the beach. Aristóbulo del Valle 3940 (near Playa Grande), T0223-486 2221.
Horse riding **El Cobijo**, Camino JM Bordeu, Km 2 (Sierra de los Padres), T0223-463 0309. Lovely horse riding in the picturesque hilly setting of Sierra and Laguna de los Padres.

Tour operators
City tours leave from Plaza España and Plaza Colón. Tours also to Miramar and the sierras. 1-hr boat trips along the city coast on the *Anamora*, several times daily in summer, weekends only in winter, from Dársena B, Muelle de Guardacostas in the port, US$7, T0223-489 0310.

Necochea *p140*
Bike hire Several options in the park Av Pinolandia entre 2 y 10.
Fishing For boats contact: Melluso Brothers, Calle 26 No 4044, T02262-426065,

for 1-hr tours or full-day fishing trips. Fishing shops: Gómez Pesca, Av 59 No 1168, T02262-427494. Also splendid *pejerrey* fishing on beautiful lagunas at Estancia La Pandorga, T02262-15504419, near Energía (70 km west of Necochea), and at Laguna Loma Danesa, near La Dulce (60 km northwest of Necochea), T02262-15506504.

Golf **Golf club**, Armada Argentina y 575, Quequén, T02262-450684.

Horse riding **Caballo's**, Villa Marítima Zabala y Av 10, T02262-423138.

Bahía Blanca and around *p141*

Tour operators

ASATEJ, Zelarrayán 267, T0291-456 0666, bblanca@asatej.com.ar.

Transport

San Clemente del Tuyú *p134*

Bus To **Mar del Plata** (and to resorts in between) services are frequent, **El Rápido**, El Rápido Argentino, US$5.50, 5 hrs. To **Buenos Aires**, several companies, US$12-16.

Pinamar *p135*

Bus The terminal is near the access road into town, a 20 min walk to the beach , at Av Bunge y Intermédanos, T02254-403500. To **Buenos Aires**, US$12-15, 4-5 hrs, several companies.

Train The station is a few kilometres away, but there are free bus transfers from town. To **Buenos Aires** (Constitución), US$ 11 Pullman, US$9, the cheapest class.

Villa Gesell *p136, map p145*

Bus Terminal at the southern end of town, Av 3 y Paseo 140, information, T02255-477253. To **Buenos Aires**, with Plusmar, Plaza, El Rápido Argentino 5hrs, US$12-15. To **Mar del Plata**, with El Rápido and El Rápido Argentino, 1½ hrs, US$2.50-2.80.

Mar del Plata *p137, map p138*

Air Camet Airport 10 km north of town. Daily flights to **Buenos Aires**, Aerolíneas Argentinas/Austral (T0223-4960101). LADE flies in summer to towns in **Patagonia** once a week. Remise taxi from airport to town, US$5, also bus 542 (signed Aeropuerto), US$0.40.

Airline offices Aerolíneas Argentinas, Austral, Moreno 2442, T0223-496 0101; LADE, Rambla Casino Loc 5, T0223-493 8211.

Bus The bus terminal, T0223-451 5406, in a former railway station, is central at Alberti y Las Heras, but it's really squalid and short on facilities, though well-connected for bus services. Not a place to hang around at night.

Local El Rápido del Sud line 212 from Terminal goes south along the coast via Miramar up to Mar del Sud; line 221 goes north from the southern beaches and Punta Mogotes up to Mar Chiquita.

Long distance To **Buenos Aires**, 5-6 hrs, US$11-16, many companies. To **San Clemente del Tuyú**, El Rápido, frequent, 5 hrs, US$ 5.50. To **Pinamar**, 2 hrs, US$3 and to **Villa Gesell**, 1½ hrs, US$2.50-2.80 with El Rápido and El Rápido Argentino. The former company also goes southwest to **Miramar**, hourly, 45 mins, US$1.10, to **Necochea**, 2 hrs, US$3.50 and to **Bahía Blanca**, 6 daily, 7 hrs, US$12. To **Bariloche**, Vía Bariloche, 20 hrs, US$48. To all Patagonian towns along RN 3, ending at **Río Gallegos**, 36 hrs, US$80, with Transportadora Patagónica. To **Mendoza**, Andesmar, daily, 19-22 hrs, US$43-57. To Posadas, **Tigre Iguazú**, 20 hrs, US$47.

Car hire Hertz, Córdoba 2149, T0223-496 2772; **Localiza**, Córdoba 2270, T0223-493 3461; **Avis**, at airport, T0223-470 2100.

Train To **Buenos Aires** (Constitución) daily, 5½ hrs, US$10 Pullman, US$ 7 the cheapest class. Also services to **Miramar**.

Around Mar del Plata *p139*

Bus Frequent services to Balcarce from **Mar del Plata**, El Rápido, T0223-451 0600 (in Mar del Plata).

Miramar *p140*

Bus Terminal at Calle 34 y Av 23, T02291-423359. To **Buenos Aires**, several companies , 6 hrs, US$ 12-16. To **Mar del Plata**, 45 min, US$ 1.10. El Rápido del Sud.

Train The station is at Av 40 y Calle 15, T02291-420657. To **Buenos Aires** (Constitución) , via **Mar del Plata**, daily in summer, once a week off season, US$8.

Necochea *p140*

Bus The terminal at Av 47 y Av 58, 3 km from the beach, T02262-422470; take bus 513 from outside the terminal. Taxi to beach area US$ 1.50. To **Buenos Aires**, 8 hrs, US$15-18, La Estrella/El Cóndor, Plus-Mar, Parque; to **Mar del Plata**, El Rápido, US$ 3.50; to **Bahía Blanca**, El Rápido US$ 8.50.

Train Check at www.ferrobaires.gba.gov.ar, to see if there are regular train services from Buenos Aires to Quequén, as they've been stopped for several years.

Bahía Blanca and around *p141*

Air Airport Comandante Espora, lies 11 km northeast of centre, US$5 in a taxi. Airport information T0291-486 1456. Daily flights to **Buenos Aires** with AR/Austral (T0291-456 0561/T0810-2228 6527), LADE (T0291-4521063). LADE has weekly flights to **Bariloche**, **Mar del Plata**, **Neuquén**, **Puerto Madryn**, **San Antonio Oeste**, **San Martín de los Andes** (may involve changes). Book ahead in summer.

Airline offices Aerolineas Argentinas, San Martín 198, T0291-426934. LADE, Darregueira 21, T0291-437697.

Bus

Local US$0.50, not cash, you need to buy *tarjetas* (Tarjebus cards) from kiosks for 1, 2, 4 or 10 journeys.

Long distance Terminal in old railway station 2 km from centre, at Estados Unidos y Brown, T0291-481 9615, connected by buses 512, 514, or taxi US$3, no hotels nearby. To **Buenos Aires** frequent, several companies, 8½ hrs, US$15-18, shop around. Most comfortable by far is Plusmar suite bus, T0291-456 0616, with completely flat beds, US$25. To **Mar del Plata**, El Rápido, US$12, 7 hrs. To **Córdoba**, US$21, 12 hrs. To **Neuquén**, 6 a day, 8 hrs, US$12. To **Necochea**, El Rápido, 5 hrs, US$10. To **Viedma** Ceferino, Plusmar and Río Paraná (to **Carmen de Patagones**), 4 hrs, US$6-8. To **Trelew**, Don Otto and others, US$30, 10½ hrs. To **Río Gallegos**, Don Otto US$36. To **Tornquist**, US$3, Río Paraná and La Estrella/El Cóndor, 1 hr 20 mins; to **Sierra de la Ventana** (town) La Estrella/El Cóndor and Expreso Cabildo, US$4.50. Also *combi* (minibus service like a shared taxi) with Geotur, T0291-450 1190, terminal at San Martín 455. Companies: **Andesmar**, T0291-481 5462, **Ceferino**, T0291-481 9566, **Don Otto**, T0291-481 8585, **Rápido del Sur**, T0291-481 3118.

Taxi

Taxi Universitario, T0291-452 0000/453 0000.

Trains

The station is at Av Gral Cerri 750, T0291-452 9196. To **Buenos Aires** 3 weekly, 12½ hrs, Pullman US$12, own room.

Santa Rosa de la Pampa *p142*

Bus The terminal at San Martín y Luro, 7 blocks east of Plaza San Martín. To **Buenos Aires** US$17, 8 hrs. To **Neuquén**, 8 hrs, US$15. Andesmar, T432841, El Valle (Via **Bariloche**) T02954-423554.

Directory

Mar del Plata *p137, map p138*

Banks Many ATMs all around the central area, along Peatonal San Martín, at Santa Fe y Rivadavia and 2 close together around the casino. Casas de Cambio Jonestur, San Martín 2574, and Av Luro 3181, gives the best rates for TCs and all cash exchange. **Cultural centres** Centro Cultural Pueyrredón, 25 de Mayo y Catamarca, T0223-499 7893. A cinema, theatre and lots of cultural activities. **Internet** Broadband internet is available in most places. **Post office** Av Luro 2460, also international parcels office (open till 1200). **Telephone** There are many *locutorios* around the town.

Bahía Blanca *p141*

Banks Many ATMs on plaza (all major cards). Lloyds TSB Bank, Chiclana 299, T0291-455 3263. Citibank, Chiclana 232. Pullman, San Martín 171, changes TCs. **Consulates** Chile, Güemes 102, T0291-455 0110; Italy, Colón 446, T0291-454 5140; Spain, Drago 70, T0291-422549. Migraciones, Brown 963. **Internet** Try places along Estomba and Zelarrayand near plaza. **Laundry** Laverap, Av Colón 197; Las Heras, Las Heras 86. **Post office** Moreno 34. **Telephone** Big *locutorio* at Alsina 108, also internet.

Southern Sierras

The south of Buenos Aires province has two ranges of ancient mountains rising suddenly from the flat pampas; both are easily accessible and offer great opportunities for a weekend escape. The Sierra de Tandil range, due south from Buenos Aires, is 340 km long and 2000 million years old – among the oldest in the world. The beautiful, curved hills of granite and basalt offer wonderful walking and riding, with the pleasant airy town of Tandil as a base. There are plenty of small hotels, though nearby estancias offer the best way to explore the hills.

Farther west, the magnificent Sierra de la Ventana is the highest range of hills in the pampas, and so called because craggy Cerro de la Ventana has a natural hole near its summit. Next to the Parque Provincial Ernesto Tornquist, it is within easy reach of Bahía Blanca for a day or weekend visit, and the attractive villages of Villa Ventana and Sierra de la Ventana nearby are appealing places to stay, with plenty of accommodation options. These mountains are not quite as old as those in Tandil, but offer more demanding hikes in wilder terrain, with stunning views from their summits. There are daily buses and combis *from Bahía Blanca, but you could break the journey at the quaint sleepy town of Tornquist.* ⏩ *For Sleeping, Eating and other listings, see pages 156-158.*

Tornquist → *Phone code: 0291. Colour map 4, C4. Population: 6066*

Tornquist, 70 km north of Bahía Blanca, is a pretty, sleepy rural town that you will pass through if travelling to Sierra de la Ventana via Route 33. It has an attractive church on the large central plaza (which is more like a tidy park), a strangely green artificial lake, and a big children's play area. It's not a touristy place, but that's precisely its appeal, and it's a good starting point for excursions into the sierra. About 11 km east of town is the Tornquist family mansion (not open to tourism), built in a mixture of French styles. The town is named after Ernesto Tornquist (1842-1908) the son of a Buenos Aires merchant of Swedish origin. Under his leadership the family established an important industrial investment bank and Tornquist helped to establish the country's first sugar refinery, meat-packing plant and several chemical plants. There's a **tourist office** ⓘ *Plaza Ernesto Tornquist, 9 de Julio y Alem, T0291-494 0081*, for information.

Parque Provincial Ernesto Tornquist → *Phone code: 0291*

The sierras are accessed from the Parque Provincial Ernesto Tornquist which is 25 km east of Tornquist on Route 76. There are two main access points, one at the foot of Cerro Ventana and the other one, further east, at the foot of Cerro Bahía Blanca. It's US$1 to enter the park. Other than the Campamento Base (see below), the nearest places for accommodation are the two pretty towns of Sierra de la Ventana and Villa Ventana. ⏩ *For transport to the park see under Activities and tours and Transport, page 158.*

Cerro Ventana section To enter this section of the park, turn left after the massive ornate gates from the Tornquist family home. There is an **information point** ⓘ *Dec-Easter 0800-1700*, and *guardaparques* who you can ask for advice and register for the longer walks. There are also baths and a food kiosk. Nearby is the hospitable **Campamento Base,** T0291-156495304, with hot showers, dormitory accommodation and an attractive campsite. From this entrance, it's a three-hour walk, clearly marked, but with no shade, up **Cerro de la Ventana** (1136m), which has fantastic views from the 'window' in the summit ridge. Register with *guardaparques* and set off no later than midday. Alternative hikes are a gentle stroll to **Garganta Olvidada,** (one hour each way) where you can set off up to 1700, to the **Piletones**, small pools (two hours each way), and **Garganta del Diablo** (six hours return) a wonderful narrow gorge with waterfalls. Guides are available for the walk to Garganta Olvidada, for a minimum of 10 people.

Cerro Bahía Blanca section The entrance to this section is 4 km further east along Route 76. There's a car park and **interpretation centre** ⓘ *T0291-491 0039, Dec-Easter 0800-1800*, with *guardaparques* who can advise on walks. From here you can go on a guided visit to Cueva del Toro (only with own vehicle, four to five hours), natural caves, and the Cueva de las Pinturas Rupestres which contains petroglyphs. There are also good walks, including up Cerro Bahía Blanca (two hours return), a gentle climb, rewarded with panoramic views, highly recommended. There's lots of wildlife to spot, but you're most likely to see grey foxes, guanacos, wild horses and red deer.

Villa Ventana

Some 10 km further from the park's second entrance (Cerro Bahía Blanca section) is an attractive laid-back wooded settlement with weekend homes, *cabañas* for rent, and a municipal campsite by the river with all facilities. There's an excellent teashop, **Casa de Heidi**, and good food served in rustic surroundings at **Las Golondrinas**. The pretty village is the base for climbing Cerro Tres Picos (1239 m), to the south of the park, which is the highest peak the province. The ruins of the **Hotel Club Casino** (1911) can be still seen; once the most luxurious hotel in Argentina, it burned down in 1983. There's a helpful **tourist office** at the entrance to the village, T0291-491 0095.

Sierra de la Ventana → *Phone code 0291. Colour map 4, C4. Population: 1800*

Continuing east, the town of Sierra de la Ventana is a good base for exploring the hills, with a greater choice of hotels than Villa Ventana, and wonderful open landscapes all around. There is a 18-hole golf course, and good trout fishing in the Río Sauce Grande. There's also a wonderful tea shop, **La Angelita**, in the leafy lanes of Villa Arcadia (across the river), and several places on the river to bathe. The helpful **tourist information** ⓘ *Av Roca, just before railway track, T0291-491 5303, www.sierradelaventana.org.ar*, has a complete list of all hotels, *cabañas* and campsites with availability and prices.

Tandil » *pp156-158.*

→ *Phone code: 02293. Colour map 4, C5. Population: 101,000*

Tandil is an attractive town, with a light breezy feel, and a centre for outdoor activities, making it a good base for exploring the nearby sierras. There are a couple of marvellous estancias in the area and a clutch of restaurants, cafés and bars within the town. On the south side of the main Plaza Independencia are the neoclassical **Municipalidad** (1923), the former **Banco Hipotecario Nacional** (1924) and the **Iglesia del Santísimo Sacramento** (1878), inspired (apparently) by the Sacre Coeur in Paris. Six blocks south of the plaza, up on a hill, is the **Parque Independencia**, with a granite entrance in Italianate style, built by the local Italian community to celebrate the town's centenary. Inside the park, the road winds up to a vantage point, where there's a Moorish-style **castle**, built by the Spanish community to mark the same event, with marvellous views over the surrounding sierras. At the base of the hill is an amphitheatre, where a famous community theatre event takes place during Easter week (book accommodation ahead). South of the park is the **Lago del Fuerte**, a popular place for watersports; bathing is possible at the Balneario del Sol in a complex of several swimming pools.

West of the plaza on the outskirts of town is **Cerro Calvario**, an easy walk leading to the **Capilla Santa Gemma** at the top. Further away, 5 km from town, **Cerro El Centinela** has a large attractive family-oriented tourist complex that includes a 1.2-km cable car ride, a good restaurant (book your table in advance) and swimming pools.

It's easy to get out of the city to explore the hilly countryside on foot or by bike. Heading south past the lake, follow Avenida Don Bosco or one of the nearby tree-lined roads, into the beautiful surroundings. Note that you should not enter any private land without permission. Instead, contact local tour operators who have arranged exclusive access with the land owners. The main **tourist information office** ⓘ *at the access to town (next to RN 226), Av Espora 1120, T02293-432073, Mon-Sat 0800- 2000, Sun 0900-1300*, is very well organized and has good brochures and urban maps. There are other offices in the main plaza ⓘ *near the corner of General Rodríguez y Pinto, Mon-Fri 0600-1300, 1800-2000, www.tandil.gov.ar*, and at the bus terminal.

Six kilometres south is the 140-ha **Reserva Natural Sierra del Tigre**, with good views over Tandil from **Cerro Venado**. Foxes and guanacos can be seen occasionally, as well as exotic llamas, and there is a small **zoo** ⓘ *1000-1700, US$1*.

Sleeping

Tornquist *p154*

D San José, Güemes 138, T0291-494 0152. A small central hotel with good, simple rooms.

Villa Ventana *p155*

C El Mirador, RP 76, Km 226, before reaching Villa Ventana, T0291-494 1338, complejoelmirador@infovia.com.ar. Great location at the foot of Cerro Ventana with comfortable rooms and a good restaurant.

C San Hipólito, RP 76, Km 230, T0291-156428281, campoequino@laredsur.com.ar. A few fully-furnished small comfortable houses in a large ranch with welcoming owners, Polito and his wife. Ideal for families with kids. Enjoyable horse rides in the hills.

Sierra de la Ventana *p155*

B Cabañas La Caledonia, Los Robles y Ombúes, on leafy Villa Arcadia, T0291-491 5268. Well-equipped and comfortable *cabañas* in large, pretty gardens.

B Las Vertientes, RP 76, Km 221, T0291-491 0064. A long-established ranch with charming hosts and an attractive main house. A beautiful location for outdoor activities or just for relaxing in peace and lovely surroundings.

C Provincial, Drago 130, T0291-491 5024, hotelprovincial@laredsur.com.ar. An old 1940's state-owned hotel, more quaint than comfy, but with good views, restaurant and a pool. Very good value.

D Alihuen, Calle Frontini, T0291-491 5074. A delightful old place near the river. Recommended.

Tandil *p155, map p157*

A Las Acacias, Av Brasil 642, T02293-423373, www.posadalasacacias.com.ar. Charming *hostería* in a restored 1890's dairy farm in the Golf Club area, with very comfortable rooms on large gardens with a splendid pool. Friendly owners, who speak English and Italian, and excellent staff help to create a welcoming and homely atmosphere for a delightful stay. Recommended.

B Cabañas Brisas Serranas, Scavini y Los Corales, T02293-406110, www.brisasserranas.com.ar. Very comfortable and well-furnished *cabañas*, pool, lovely views and welcoming owners.

B Dior, General Rodríguez 475, T02293-431901, www.hoteldior.com. Modernized 1970s place with a light airy foyer and lounge with views over the pretty plaza, and has the town's most attractive comfortable rooms with modern bathrooms – the ones at the front have splendid views – good breakfast. Friendly staff, and good value.

B Hostal de la Sierra del Tandil, Av Avellaneda 931/41, T02293-422330, www.hostaldeltandil.com.ar. Attractive, modern Spanish-style building, with boldly designed rooms with bath, and appealing areas to sit, a good restaurant for residents only, and a covered pool.

C Bed and Breakfast, Belgrano 39, T02293-426989, www.cybertandil.com.ar/byb. Quite the most welcoming place in town, charming and helpful English owners. This has 2 comfortable secluded rooms for couples or families, one modern double and the large apartment **la Torre** for up to 6, in an idyllic walled garden with small pool. Breakfasts are gorgeous. Warmly recommended.

C Hermitage, Av Avellaneda y Rondeau, T02293-423987, www.hermitagetandil.com.ar. Good value in this quiet old-fashioned hotel in a good position next to the park. There are some smart modernized rooms, though these aren't very different to the standard ones, all very simple, but the service is welcoming.

C Plaza de las Carretas, Av Santamarina 728, T02293-447850, www.plazadelascarretas.com.ar. An early 20th-century family house is now a homely and quiet place to stay, with good rooms with eclectic decor and a nice garden at the back.

Estancias

The real experience of Tandil lies in the beauty of its surroundings, best explored by staying in an estancia. There are 2 quite different places:

L Ave María, 16 km from Tandil, past Cerro El Centinela, T02293-422843, www.avemaria tandil.com.ar. One of the most exquisite small hotels in the whole province, this may call itself a *hostería*, but the splendid Norman-style building set in beautiful gardens overlooking the rocky summits of the sierras is much more like an estancia. Charming owner Asunti encourages you to feel completely at home, and ramble around the place as you please. There are only 8 rooms, all impeccably designed with everything you could possibly need, some having doors opening directly onto the gardens. The discreet staff speak perfect English. A great place to relax and swim in the pool or walk in the grounds, hills and woodland. Prices are half-board and discounts apply Mon-Thu. Highly recommended. Not to be missed.

L Siempre Verde, 45 km southwest of Tandil (next to Barker), T02292-498555, lasiempreverde@dilhard.com.ar. With the most magnificent setting amongst the sierras, this typical 1900's house has a long history. Traditional style rooms with wonderful old fashioned bathrooms and lots of antiques have good views over the grounds, and the owners, descendants of one of Argentina's most important families, are very hospitable and helpful. Staying here provides a real insight into traditional estancia life. Extensive horse riding and walking among the magical sierras in the estate, fishing, *asados* on the hill side. Also camping. Highly recommended.

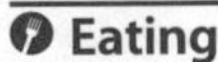

Eating

Tandil *p155, map p157*

Local produce here traditionally includes cheese and sausages, both excellent and

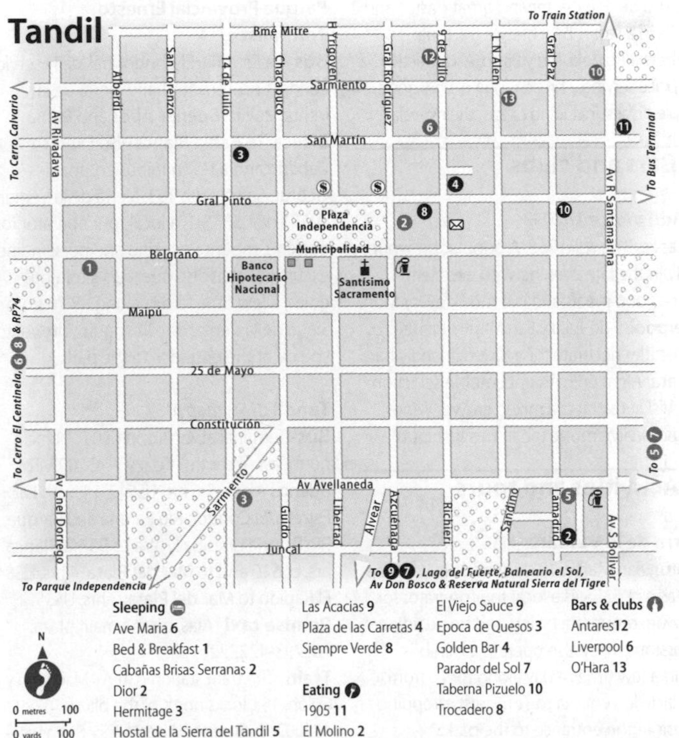

served as part of the *picadas* (nibbles with drinks) served in local bars and restaurants, or available to take away in several good delis in town, such as **Syquet**, General Rodríguez y Mitre or **Epoca de Quesos**.

1905, Av Santamarina y San Martín. A minimalist setting in a charming old house that serves excellent finely elaborate meals.

El Molino, Juncal 936. A small, simple place with a little windmill, which specializes in different cuts of meat cooked traditionally *al disco* – in an open pan on the fire.

El Viejo Sauce, Av Don Bosco y Suiza. Next to the Reserva Sierra del Tigre, in attractive natural surroundings, this is an ideal stopover at tea time for its superb cakes and homemade jams.

Epoca de Quesos, San Martín y 14 de Julio, T02293-448750. An atmospheric 1860's house serving delicious local produce, wines, home-brewed beers and memorable *picadas* to share, which include a great range of cheeses, salami, sausages and traditional pampas bread. Recommended.

Parador del Sol, Zarini s/n, T02293-435697. Located in the attractive *balneario* by Lago del Fuerte, serving great pastas and salads in a smart beach-style trattoria.

Taberna Pizuela, Paz y Pinto. An attractive old place serving a broad range of very good simple dishes, including pizzas, their speciality.

Bars and clubs

Tandil *p155, map p157*

Antares, 9 de Julio 758. A popular brewpub, lively in the late evening with excellent beers, good meals and live music every Mon.

Liverpool, 9 de Julio y San Martín. Pictures of the Beatles decorate this relaxed, friendly bar.

O'Hara, Alem 665. An unbeatable selection of whiskies attracts a mixed crowd. Wines, *tapas* and live music too in this Irish pub.

Activities and tours

Sierra de la Ventana *p155*

Geotur, San Martín 193, Sierra de la Ventana, T0291-491 5355, is a local tour operator for trekking, mountain biking and horse riding excursions. They also operate a minibus going a few times a day along RP 76 from Sierra de la Ventana to Tornquist, dropping you off at the entrance to the park.

Tandil *p155, map p157*

Golf Tandil golf club, Av Fleming s/n, T02293-406976.

Hiking To find an approved guide who will take you to otherwise inaccessible land for trekking, see www.guiasdetandil.com.ar.

Eco de las Sierras, Maipú 714, T02293-442741, T15621083 run by Lucrecia Ballesteros a highly recommended guide, young, friendly and knowledgeable.

Kumbre, Av Alvear 488, T02293-434313, www.kumbre.com. Trekking, mountain biking and some climbing guided by experienced Carlos Centineo.

Valle del Picapedrero, T02293-430463, www.valledelpicapedrero.com.ar. Guided walks along a beautiful nearby valley with Ana Maineri, a geology expert.

Horse riding Gabriel Barletta, Avellaneda 673, T02293-427725 or T15509609. Recommended rides with Gabriel, expert on native flora, who might end your tour with an informal acoustic guitar session.

Transport

Parque Provincial Ernesto Tornquist *p154*

Bus La Estrella/El Cóndor has daily services connecting Tornquist and Sierra de la Ventana with **Buenos Aires** and **Bahía Blanca**. To **Bahía Blanca** also Expreso Cabildo and a few minibus companies. Geotur, San Martín 193, Sierra de la Ventana, T0291-491 5355, is a local tour operator for trekking, mountain biking and horse riding excursions that also operates a minibus going a few times a day along RP 76 from Sierra de la Ventana to Tornquist, dropping you off at the entrance to the park.

Tandil *p155, map p157*

Bus Terminal at Av Buzón 650 (12 blocks northeast of centre), T02293- 432092. To **Buenos Aires**, 5-6 hrs, US$12-14, with La Estrella/El Cóndor, Río Paraná and Parque. Río Paraná goes daily also to **Bahía Blanca**, 6 hrs, US$10 and to **Mar del Plata**, 4 hrs, US$4. El Rápido to **Mar del Plata**, 3 hrs, US$5.

Remise taxi Alas, on the main plaza, T02293-422222.

Train The train station is at Av Machado y Colón, 15 blocks north of the plaza, T02293-423002. To **Buenos Aires**, US$5-8, 1 a week.

Córdoba and the Central Sierras

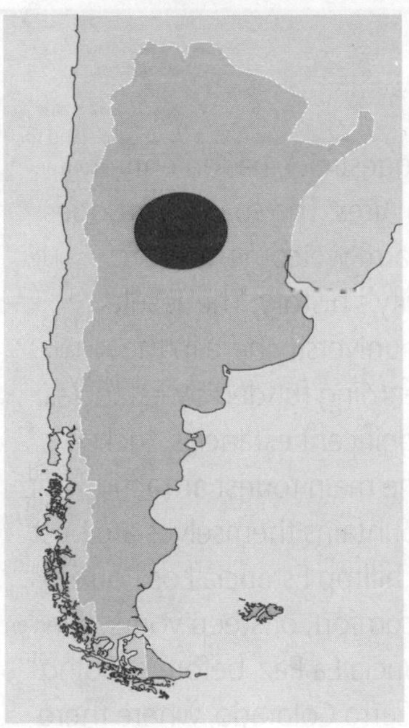

Footprint features

Introduction

Córdoba, Argentina's second biggest city, has an entirely different character from Buenos Aires. The sparky Córdobes are known for their quick wit, warm welcome, and are understandably proud of their city's history. The Jesuits established the country's oldest university here in the 17th-century, with a centre of learning funded by estancias all over the province. These magnificent estancias, tucked away in the Sierras Chicas, are the main tourist attraction and best visited by car, while the mountains themselves are best explored on horseback. Here, at hilltop Estancia Los Potreros, you can live the real gaucho in comfort, or steep yourself in presidential luxury at grand estancia La Paz, before heading north to the remote reaches of Cerro Colorado, where there are amazing displays of rock art in a bizarre rocky landscape.

South of the city in Alta Gracia is Ché Guevara's childhood home, but don't miss the best Jesuit museum inside the spectacular estancia. Nearby Villa General Belgrano remains a German stronghold, with cute chalet-style architecture and endless microbreweries and apfelstrudel. Escape from the crowds to Córdoba's most stunning scenery, high along the Camino de las Altas Cumbres into the Traslasierra valley. Hike into the mountains and gaze at condors in flight at the Parque Nacional Quebrada del Condorito, where majestic birds wheel above the dramatic peaks, and teach their young to fly.

Further west, the sleepy provincial capital of San Luis lies at the foot of its own magnificent sierra which intrepid travellers can explore in Parque Nacional Sierra de las Quijadas, with its dramatic red sandstone canyon. And at sleepy villages El Trapiche and Carolina, you can even mine for gold.

★ Don't miss …

1 **Córdoba city's Jesuit heritage** See the university and the chapels, but don't miss the ancient books in the incredibly extensive library, page 162.

2 **The Jesuit 'estancia' trail** Start at Santa Catalina and end up at Alta Gracia and see the province's fabulous landscapes in between, page 170.

3 **Estancia Los Potreros** Learn to play polo or ride like a gaucho, with native English-Argentines. Heavenly horse riding at the top of the world, page 174.

4 **Paraglide in La Cumbre** Leap off from this charming small town in the mountains, with fabulous big drops for paragliders, page 180.

5 **Villa General Belgrano** Avoid Oktoberfest, but do try the beer in this pretty mountain town inhabited by descendants of *Graf Spee* veterans, page 186.

6 **Cerro Champaquí** Climb up Cerro Champaquí from the tiny village of Villa Alpina, page 187.

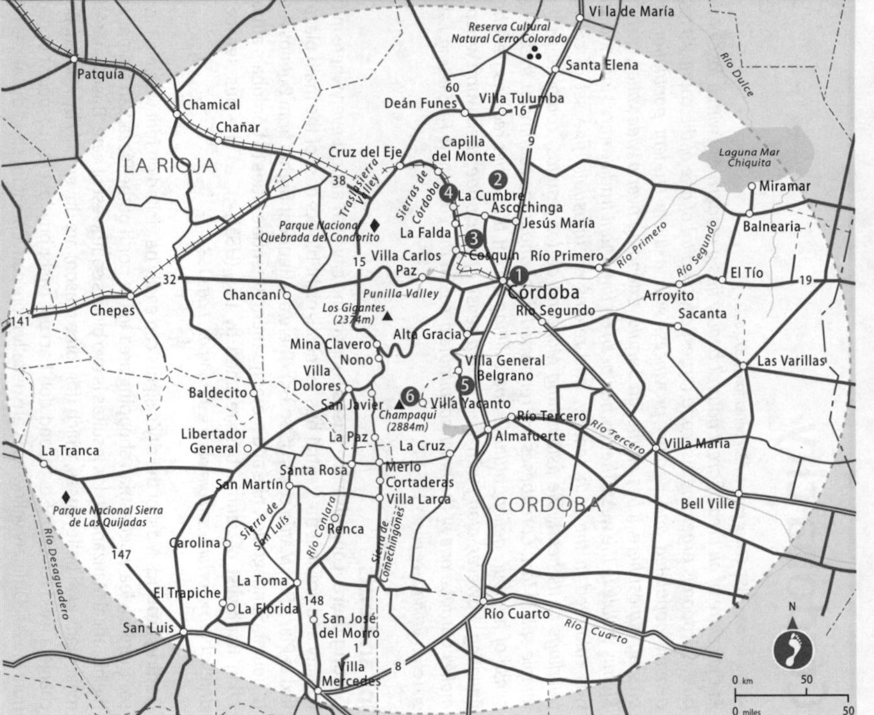

Córdoba city

➔ Phone code: 0351 Colour map 4, A2 Population: 1,370,000.

At the centre of an area of great natural beauty lies a modern city with a fascinating past. Córdoba is Argentina's second largest city, capital of one of the country's most densely populated and wealthy provinces, with a lively student population and buzzing atmosphere. It lies on the Río Suquía, extending over a wide valley, with the Sierras visible in the west. The city has been an important trade centre since the area was colonized in the 16th century, and retains an unusually fine set of colonial buildings at its heart, the astonishing Manzana de los Jesuitas, complete with its temple still in tact. Cordobéses are renowned throughout the country for their sharp sense of humour, defiant attitude and a lilting accent that other regions delight in imitating. However, along with their strong sense of civic pride, their warm welcome makes Córdoba one of the most hospitable areas in the country. *» For Sleeping, Eating and other listings, see pages 165-169.*

Ins and outs

Getting there Long-distance **buses** connect the city with almost everywhere in the country and arrive at the central bus terminal, eight blocks east of the main plaza (a taxi to Plaza San Martín costs US$0.65). There are frequent **flights** from Buenos Aires (2 hours), Santiago de Chile and major northern Argentine cities to Córdoba's airport, 12km northwest of centre, best reached by taxi (US$3-5), as the bus service is unreliable. *» For further information see Transport, page 168.*

Getting around Most of the city's sights can easily be visited on foot within a day or so. There's a leafy pedestrian shopping area to the north of the Plaza San Martín, and the historical Manzana de los Jesuitas is two blocks southwest of here. Buses share the main roads with trolleybuses, which (for some reason) are driven only by women. Both charge a fixed fee of US$0.30, and don't accept cash; buy tokens (*cospeles*) or cards from kiosks. Ordinary yellow taxis are usually more convenient for short distances than green *remise* taxis, which are better value for longer journeys. Tourists are allowed to park free in the centre, but must display a sticker, free from hotels and tourist offices, valid for a week and easily renewable.

Best time to visit Avoid the hot and stormy summer months from December to February, when daytime temperatures are around 30°c. The dry season is April to September, with clear skies, cooler temperatures, but still pleasantly warm.

Tourist information There are tourist offices at several points in the city: ⓘ *Cabildo, Deán Funes 15, T0351-428 5856, Mon 1400-2100, Tue-Sun 0900-2100*, with a small gallery, restaurant and bookshop. Also at ⓘ *Centro Obispo Mercadillo (on Plaza San Martín), Rosario de Santa Fe 39, T0351-428 5600*, or at ⓘ *Patio Olmos Shopping Mall, Av San Juan y Vélez Sarsfield, T0351-420 4100*, as well as at the bus terminal and at the airport. All open early morning to late at night, with useful city maps and information on guided walks and cycle tours. Take the City Tour, leaving daily from the Centro Obispo Mercadillo (Rosario de Santa Fe 39); ask at tourist offices for details. For the best information on the province, head 8 km northwest of centre to **Complejo Ferial** ⓘ *Av Cárcano, Chateau Carreras, T0351-434 8260, dacyt.turismo@cba.gov.ar*. See also websites www.cordobatrip.com and www.cordoba.net in Spanish, for information on the whole province.

Background

Founded in 1573 by an expedition from Santiago del Estero led by Jerónimo Luis de Cabrera, Córdoba was the most important city in the country in colonial times. During the late 16th and 17th centuries, the Jesuit Order made the city their headquarters for the southern part of the continent and founded the first university in the country, giving the city its nickname 'La Docta' (the Learned). In 1810 when Buenos Aires

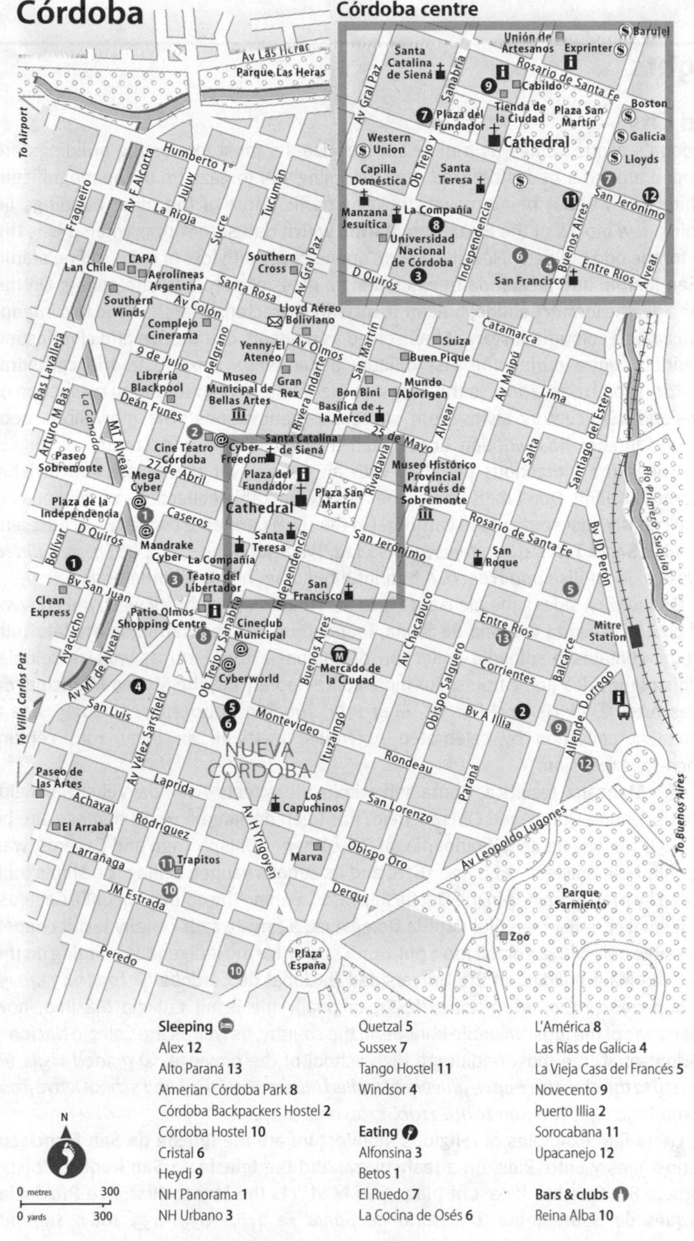

backed independence, the leading figures of Córdoba voted to remain loyal to Spain, and after independence the city was a stronghold of opposition to Buenos Aires. It's remained fiercely independent ever since, supporting many Radical party governments, and in May 1969, disturbances in the city ignited opposition to military rule throughout the country. Since the 1940s Córdoba has grown from a cultural, administrative and communications centre into a large industrial city, though in the last four years, recession has resulted in growing unemployment. However, the city has an upbeat feel and a fabulous nightlife.

Sights

Old City

Córdoba's centre comes as a pleasant surprise. Its most interesting buildings are grouped around a pedestrianized area, enabling you to gaze up at the magnificent architecture without being mown down by traffic. Most of the older buildings lie within a few blocks of the **Plaza San Martín**, which dates from 1577 when it was the site for the odd bullfight. Now it's a wide open space, with lots of cafés, a fine statue of San Martín, and Jacaranda trees creating a mass of purple in late spring. On the west side, the former **Cabildo**, built in 1610, with characteristic arches and two interior patios, has a colourful history. It has served as a prison, courthouse and clandestine detention centre during the last military dictatorship. Next to it, the **cathedral** ⓘ *0800-1200, 1630-2000*, is the oldest in Argentina, an extraordinary confection of 17th- and 18th-century styles from successive renovations. The marvellous neo-baroque interior has wooden doors from a Jesuit temple and statues of angels resembling the indigenous peoples, with an 1800 silver tabernacle and lavishly decorated ceiling. Don't miss one of the most remarkable collections of religious art in the country, just south of the cathedral in the 1628 **Carmelite convent** and adjacent chapel of **Santa Teresa** ⓘ *Independencia 122, Wed-Sat 0930-1230, US$0.35. Guided visits also in English and French*. A beautiful building; highly recommended.

On the west side of the pleasant Plaza del Fundador, one block west, the convent and church of **Santa Catalina de Siena**, founded in 1613, but rebuilt in the late 19th century, contains a splendid collection of paintings from Peru as well as colonial Spanish tapestries and carpets. For more contemporary art, the **Museo Municipal de Bellas Artes** ⓘ *Av General Paz 33, T433 1512, Tue-Sun 0900-2100, US$0.35*, has a permanent collection by celebrated Argentine artists in an early 20th century French-style mansion.

The **Manzana Jesuítica**, contained within the streets Avenida Vélez Sarsfield, Caseros, Duarte Quirós and Obispo Trejo, has been declared a world heritage site by UNESCO. The **Iglesia de la Compañía**, at the corner of Obispo Trejo and Caseros, was originally built between 1640 and 1676, and its curious vaulted ceiling is a ship's hull, created by a Jesuit trained in the Dutch shipyards. Behind the church, on Calle Caseros, is the smaller, most beautiful **Capilla Doméstica**, a private 17th-century Jesuit chapel, accessible only with a guided tour, but worth seeing for the indigenous painting on the altar. The main building of the **Universidad Nacional de Córdoba** ⓘ *T0351-4332075, Tue-Sun 0900-1300, 1600-2000, US$1*, originally the Jesuit Colegio Máximo, now houses one of the most valuable libraries in the country, as well as the Colegio Nacional de Montserrat, the most traditional high school of the province. ⓘ *guided visits (in English) to the church, chapel, university (called Museo Histórico) and school leave from Obispo Trejo 242, Tue-Sun 1000, 1100, 1700 and 1800.*

Other fine examples of religious architecture are the **Iglesia de San Francisco**, Buenos Aires y Entre Ríos, on a leafy plaza, and the **Iglesia de San Roque**, Obispo Salguero 84. One block east of plaza San Martín is the **Museo Histórico Provincial Marqués de Sobremonte** ⓘ *Rosario de Santa Fe 218, T0351-433 1661, summer*

Mon-Fri 0900-1500, Tue-Sat 1000-1600, US$0.35, texts in English and German, the only surviving colonial family residence in the city, dating from 1760, and a labyrinth of patios and simply decorated rooms. The **Basílica de La Merced**, at 25 de Mayo 83, has a fine gilt wooden pulpit dating from the colonial period and beautifully carved wooden doors, with fine ceramic murals revealing Córdoba's history on the outside by the local artist Armando Sica.

Other sights

Attractive areas for a stroll are along **La Cañada**, a stream running a few blocks west of the plaza, and the **Nueva Córdoba** district, south of the plaza San Martín, with cafés and an eclectic mix of building styles along Avenida Hipólito Yrigoyen. The neo-Gothic **Iglesia de los Capuchinos** ⓘ *T0351-433 3412, Tue-Sun 1100-1900*, displays the night skies for every month of the year. **Parque Sarmiento** is the largest green area of the city, laid out by French architect Charles Thays in 1889 with small lakes, a neat rose garden and a **zoo** ⓘ *0900-1800, US$1.20*, set among steep hills. The magnificent **Mitre railway station**, near the bus terminal, has a beautiful tiled *confitería*, still in use for Sunday evening tango shows (see Entertainment page 167). The lively crowded market, **Mercado de la Ciudad**, provides a taste of local urban culture.

Sleeping

Córdoba city *p162, map p163*

Good value accommodation is hard to find. There are several small places next to the bus terminal, but they're unreliable.

A Amerian Córdoba Park, Blv San Juan 165, T0351-420 7000, www.amerian.com. Swish, modern hotel with marbled foyer and professional service. Rooms are hardly inspired in their decor, but they are very comfortable, the breakfasts are superb and this is a convenient and reliable place to stay. Also has a business centre, spa and pool.

A NH Panorama, Marcelo T de Alvear 251, T0351-410 3900, www.nh-hoteles.com Situated on La Cañada stream, this 4-star has comfortable business-style rooms and excellent views of the sierras from its upper floors. Small pool, gym and a restaurant. The NH Urbano, a block further south on Marcelo T de Alvear(La Cañada) 363, T0351-410 3960, nhurbano@nh-hotels.com, is more central, if a little more business-like. Both are recommended.

A Windsor, Buenos Aires 214, T0351-422 4012, www.windsortower.com. A small, smart 4-star, with a warm atmosphere, large breakfast, and use of sauna, gym and pool.

C Cristal, Entre Ríos 58, T0351-535 5000, www.hotelcristal.com.ar. Comfortable rooms with a/c and a large breakfast served in this welcoming and nicely maintained and central hotel.

C Sussex, San Jerónimo 125, T0351-422 9070, www.hotelsussexcba.com.ar. Rooms are basic with flouncy bedspreads, but it's clean, and there's a family welcome, some rooms have lovely views of Plaza San Martín. Pool, breakfast included.

D Alto Paraná, Paraná 230, T0351-428 1625, www.hotelguia.com/altoparana. Very nice 2-star hotel with good rooms and attentive staff.

D Heydi, Blv Illia 615, T0351-423 3544, www.hotelheydi.com.ar. By far the best value accommodation in town, this spotless, quiet 3-star has pleasant rooms with TV and homely decor, breakfast included.

E Alex, Blv Illia 742, T0351 421 4350, www.alexhotel.com.ar. A good value hotel, modern and cosy inside the slightly off-putting exterior. All rooms have bath, and include breakfast and a mate kit, in case you feel the need. Staff are very friendly, and it's very close to the bus station.

E Quetzal, San Jerónimo 579, T/F0351-422 9106. Refurbished with dubious taste, this is good value, spotless rooms with bath; breakfast extra.

E Córdoba Backpackers Hostel, Deán Funes 285, T0351-422 0593, www.cordobabackpackers.com.ar. The best located hostel in town, with friendly staff, family atmosphere, and a nice common room with pool table and bar. Dorms with shared bathrooms, some double rooms. Discount for HI members.

E Tango Hostel, Fructuoso Rivera 70, T0351-425 6023, www.latitudsurtrek.com.ar.

This is the best hostel accommodation in the Nueva Córdoba district, right in the heart of student heaven, with nightclubs and bars all around. Breakfast is included, any time of day, rooms sleep 2-5, kitchen, library, dinner also offered, and lots of trips in and around Córdoba city with the good company **Latitud Sur**. Recommended. Friendly staff.

F pp **Córdoba Hostel**, Ituzaingo 1070, T0351-468 7359, www.cordoba hostel.com.ar. Excellent well-run hostel located in the Nueva Córdoba district. Small with decent facilities and large breakfasts. Small discount for HI members.

Eating

Córdoba city *p162, map p163*

TT L' América, Caseros 67, T0351-427 1734. A small but imaginative menu with modern twists on traditional dishes from sushi to French food, all beautifully cooked in an open kitchen, in a stylishly renovated old house. Large selection of wines, homemade bread and excellent service, in minimalist surroundings, with cheap set menus. Recommended.

TT La Cocina de Osés, Independencia 512, T0351-483 0032. Formal and well decorated, this is a good place for fish, meat dishes and homemade pastas.

TT Betos, Blv San Juan 450, T0351-469 2774. Large, popular *parrilla* serving the best *lomitos* in town.

TT La Vieja Casa del Francés, Independencia 508. Delicious grills in an inviting atmosphere, where you can have a chat with the French expat owners.

TT Las Rías de Galicia, Montevideo 271, T0351-428 1333. Superb seafood.

TT Novecento, at the Cabildo, T0351-423 0660. A smart lively place, with a lovely light patio, and appealing decor with dark wooden tables and immaculate tablecloths. Superb fresh Mediterranean-style cooking, lots of fish and pasta, and excellent service. Lunch only, bar open 0800-2000. Recommended.

TT Upacanejo, San Jerónimo 171. Theme restaurant based on a popular Argentine comic character, with friendly staff dressed accordingly, this is actually an unpretentious parrilla serving excellent beef and chicken.

T Alfonsina, Duarte Quirós 66, T0351-427 2847. Young urban crowds flock to this inviting old house, for food and music, great simple meals, pizza, *empanadas árabes*, *milanesas* or breakfasts with homemade bread. Warm atmosphere.

T La Casa de Salta, Caseros 80, T0351-429 0045 Delicious specialities from North west Argentina, such as locro, empanadas, humitas, in a lively place near the Jesuit block - gets noisy later on, but a good atmosphere.

Cafés

El Anden, Buenos Aires y Entre Ríos. Tasty *facturas* and good music.

El Ruedo, Obispo Trejo y 27 de Abril. Lively confitería, also serving light meals.

Mandarina, Obispo Trejo 171, T0351-426 4909. Central, very welcoming place with lovely leafy decor, lots of great breakfasts, and good for lunch and dinner too. Friendly staff, highly recommended.

Puerto Illia, Blv Illia 555. Next to the bus terminal. Breakfasts and simple meals – great if you arrive at night or have a long wait.

Sorocabana, Buenos Aires y San Jerónimo. Great cheap breakfasts for US$1, in this popular place on plaza San Martín.

Bars and clubs

Córdoba city *p162, map p163*

Córdoba has a rich and varied nightlife, with young crowds gathering in different areas of the city mainly on Fri and Sat, but on weekdays too during holidays. Northwest of town Cerro Las Rosas, locally referred to as Cerro, has a lively area of bars and clubs (US$3.50 pp) along Av Rafael Núñez: **Arcimboldo**, Av Rafael Núñez 4567; **Factory**, Av Rafael Núñez 3964, a club for all ages mixing electronic with Latin dance music; **Villa Agur**, José Roque Funes y Tristán Malbrán. Rock and roll with food and live music. Another popular nightlife area lies further northwest in Chateau Carreras: **Carreras**, Av Ramón J Cárcano, is the most popular club, frequented by trendy crowds in their 20s.

The Nueva Córdoba district is near the city's huge University, 7 blocks from the main plaza towards Parque Sarmiento, with lots of nightclubs and cheap places to eat. Head here if you want to meet young people. A couple of good choices are: **Reina Alba**, Obispo Trejo y Fructuoso Rivera, a re-designed old house, open after sunset, with a happy mix of trendy clothes and books where the chic people drink; and **Rita**, Independencia 1162, another refurbished old house with a trendy clientele.

There are studenty bars along Rondeau between Av Hipólito Yrigoyen and Chacabuco. The less noisy places are: **Alfonsina**, Duarte Quirós 66, if you need to express yourself on a piano or guitar; **Posh**, Av Hipólito Yrigoyen 464, for live jazz, blues and bossa nova after 2400; and **Johnny B Good**, Av Hipólito Yrigoyen 320. El Abasto district, on the river (about 8 blocks north of plaza San Martín) has several good, cheap places: **Casa Babylon**, Bv Las Heras 48, has a disco night on Fri and rock music on Sat; and in **Divino**, Pasaje Agustín Pérez 32 (behind Puente Alvear), .you can enjoy wine tasting before 1900.

Entertainment

Córdoba city *p162, map p163*

See free listings magazines *La Cova* and *Ocio en Córdoba*, local newspaper *La Voz del Interior*, and www.cordoba.net for events.

Cinema

Mainstream films at **Complejo Cinerama**, Av Colón 345 and **Gran Rex**, Av General Paz 174. Independent, old and foreign language films at **Cineclub Municipal**, Bv San Juan 49 and at **Cine Teatro Córdoba**, 27 de Abril 275.

Cuarteto

Very definitively a Cordobés invention, this tropically inspired music has given fame to 'La Mona' Giménez, and many impersonators, whose gigs are attended by hysterical crowds. (Also described as 'worse than cumbia' – the other Colombian-inspired Cordobés musical tradition).

The most popular venues are **Asociación Deportiva Atenas**, Aguado 775, **Estadio del Centro**, Santa Fe 480, and **La Vieja Usina**, Av Costanera y Coronel Olmedo.

Tango

This Buenos Aires tradition also has a home in Córdoba, every Sun from 2000 at **Confitería Mitre**, Blv Perón 101 (in the railway station), tango class before *milonga* (public place to dance) begins, US$1.30. **El Arrabal**, Belgrano y Fructuoso Rivera, is a restaurant with a tango show after 2400, Fri and Sat, US$1.70 extra.

Theatre

The Festival of Latin American Theatre is held every Oct. The **Teatro del Libertador**, Av Vélez Sarsfield 367, T0351-433 2312, is traditional and sumptuous with a rich history. On Plaza San Martín is **Real**, San Jerónimo 66, T0351-433 1669. Smaller places next to Puente Alvear include **Espacio Cirulaxia**, Pasaje Agustín Pérez 12, and **Quinto Deva**, Pasaje Agustín Pérez 10.

Shopping

Córdoba city *p162, map p163*

The main shopping area is along the pedestrian streets north of the plaza. On Belgrano, 700 and 800 blocks, there are several antique shops.

Shopping malls

Córdoba Shopping, José de Goyechea 2851 (at Villa Cabrera), T0351-420 5001.
Dinosaurio Mall, Rodríguez del Busto 4086, T0351-526 1500.
Nuevocentro, Av Duarte Quirós 1400, T0351-482 8193.
Patio Olmos, Av Vélez Sarsfield y Blv San Juan, T0351-420 4100.

Handicrafts

Mundo Aborigen, Rivadavia 155.
Paseo de las Artes, Achával Rodríguez y La Cañada, Sat and Sun 1600-2200 (in summer 1800-2300). Market selling ceramics, leather, woodcrafts and metalware.
Unión de Artesanos, San Martín 42 (Galería San Martín, local 22).

Bookshops

Librería Blackpool, Deán Funes 395. Imported English books.
Tienda de la Ciudad, on a patio at the Cabildo. Specializes in local and regional interest books.
Yenny-El Ateneo, Av General Paz 180. English language titles.

Outdoor equipment

Buen Pique, Rivadavia 255.
Suiza, Rivadavia y Lima.

Activities and tours

Córdoba city *p162, map p163*

Tour operators

On average, operators charge around US$10 pp for half-day excursions and US$17 pp for a full-day trip. Main destinations are in the Punilla, Calamuchita and Traslasierra valleys and all Jesuit-related places. The city tourist office offers city tours on foot or bike, as well as cheap guided visits to the Jesuit estancias in Jesús María and Alta Gracia. Red double-decker buses leave once or twice a day from Plaza San Martín for a 1½-hr city tour with bilingual guides, US$3.

Bon Bini, San Martín 180, p 1, T0351-428 1857.

Itatí, 27 de abril 220, T0351-422 5020. Good company with tours in the province

Nativo, 27 de abril 11, T0351-424 5341 www.cordobanativoviajes.com.ar. Huge range of tours, very professional and reliable.

Southern Cross, Av General Paz 389, p 3, T0351-424 1614, www.terraargentea.com. Off the beaten track.

Transport

Córdoba city *p162, map p163*

Air

Pajas Blancas Airport, T0351-475 0392, 12 km northwest of centre, is reached by taxi (US$5) or (less reliable) bus. There are several daily flights to **Buenos Aires**, about 2 hrs, with Aerolíneas Argentinas. Aerolíneas Argentinas also flies daily to **Mendoza**, **Tucumán** and **Ezeiza airport**, and 3 times weekly to **Jujuy** and **Salta**. Lan Chile has daily flights to **Santiago de Chile**, 1½ hrs. Lloyd Aéreo Boliviano flies weekly to **Santa Cruz de la Sierra**, via Salta. Sol flies daily to Rosario. Gol has weekly flights to Brazil and Uruguay.

Airline offices Aerolíneas Argentinas/ Austral, Av Colón 520, T0351-410 7600. **Lan Chile**, Figueroa Alcorta 206, T0351-475 9555. **Lloyd Aéreo Boliviano**, Av Colón 166, 3rd floor office 1, T0351-421 6458. **Southern Winds**, Figueroa Alcorta 192, T0810-7777979. **Gol**, T0810-266 3232, www.vogol.com. **Sol**, T0810-4444 765 www.sol.com.ar.

Bus

Buses and trolleybuses charge US$0.30, only payable in tokens (*cospeles*) or cards from kiosks. The terminal at Blv Perón 250, T0351-434 1700 or T0351-434 1692, has restaurants, internet facilities, a supermarket, left-luggage lockers, US$0.65 per day (2 coins of 1 peso); *remise* taxi desk, ATM and a tourist office on the lower level, where the ticket offices are. To leave the terminal go upstairs and cross bridges towards city centre. A taxi charges US$0.65 to plaza San Martín. Minibuses, *diferenciales*, have better services to the Sierras and depart from a nearby platform; tickets can be bought on the bus or from offices at Terminal, 1st floor.

Provincial services To **Alta Gracia**, SATAG and Sarmiento, Sierras de Calamuchita (stops at El Crucero on route, 30-min walk from centre), 1 hr, US$0.70. To **Cerro Colorado**, Ciudad de Córdoba, 3 weekly, 4½ hrs, US$5. To **Jesús María**, Ciudad de Córdoba, Colonia Tirolesa, 1 hr, US$1. To **Laguna Mar Chiquita**, Expreso Ciudad de San Francisco goes to Miramar, 3½ hrs, US$3.50. Transportes Morteros goes to **Balnearia**, 3 hrs, US$3.80. To **Punilla valley**, Ciudad de Córdoba, TAC, (La Falda, US$1.70; La Cumbre, US$2) and La Calera, El Serra, Transierras, Lumasa. To **Río Ceballos**, La Quebrada, 1 hr, US$0.70; Ciudad de Córdoba goes also to **Río Ceballos** and continues north to **Ascochinga** and then, **Jesús María**. To **Río Cuarto**, TUS, 3-3½ hrs, US$5. To **Traslasierra valley**, Ciudad de Córdoba, TAC, (**Mina Clavero**, 3 hrs, US$4) and Sierra Bus and Panaholma minibus services. To **Villa Carlos Paz**, Ciudad de Córdoba, also Car-Cor and El Serra minibus services, 45 mins, US$0.80. To **Villa General Belgrano**, TUS, Sierras de Calamuchita (runs also minibus services, like Lep, La Villa and Pájaro Blanco), 1½-2 hrs, US$3.

Long-distance services To **Buenos Aires**, Chevallier, General Urquiza, TAC, 9-11 hrs, US$12-17 (coche cama). To **Catamarca**, General Urquiza, TAC, 5-7 hrs, US$7. **Jujuy**, Balut, TAC, 12 hrs, US$15. To **La Rioja**, Chevallier, General Urquiza, Socasa, 6-7 hrs, US$7. To **Mendoza**, Andesmar, Autotransportes San Juan-Mar del Plata, CATA, Expreso Uspallata, TAC, 10-12 hrs, US$10-12. To **Puerto Iguazú**, Expreso Singer, 20 hrs, US$27-30, and Crucero del Norte. To **Rosario**, General Urquiza, TAC, 5-6 hrs, US$7-8. To **Salta**, Chevallier, La Veloz del Norte, 12 hrs, US$18. To **San Luis**, Andesmar, Autotransportes San Juan-Mar del Plata, TAC, 7 hrs, US$6-8. TAC and Andesmar have connecting services to several destinations in Patagonia.

International services To **Santiago** (Chile), US$20, 17-19 hrs, CATA, TAC. To **Tacna** (Peru), US$75, with change at Mendoza and Santiago de Chile. For **Bolivia** take Balut or Andesmar services to the border at **La Quiaca** (19 hrs, US$20) or **Pocitos** (17 hrs, US$20-23).

Car hire

Avis Bv San Juan 137, T0351-424 3565. Europcar, Entre Ríos 70, T0351-422 4867, www.europcar.com.ar. Four Way, T0351-499 8436, fourway@arnet.com.ar.

Remise taxis

Alta Córdoba Remis, T0351-471 0441. Auto Remis, T0351-472 7777.

Train

There are weekly trains from the Mitre station, Bv Perón 371 (next to bus terminal) to **Villa María** and Buenos Aires, T0351-426 3565.

Directory

Córdoba city *p162, map p163*

Banks Open in the morning. Lloyds Bank, Banco de Galicia, Boston Bank and Banco de la Nacion, all on Plaza San Martín, all have ATMs. Exchange and TCs at Exprinter, Rivadavia 47, only Amex TCs (low commission) or at Barujel, Rivadavia y 25 de Mayo, Amex TCs (15% commission), VISA TCs; also Western Union branch. **Consulates** Dirección Nacional de Migraciones, Caseros 676, T0351-422 2740. Bolivia, San Jerónimo 167, 6th floor, T0351-424 5650. Chile, Crisol 280, T0351-469 0432. **Internet** Many places charging US$0.35/hr including: Cyber Freedom, 27 de Abril 261, Cyber world. Obispo Trejo 443. Mandrake Cyber, Marcelo T de Alvear 255. Mega Cyber, Marcelo T de Alvear 229. Open until 0500. **Post office** Av Colón 210, parcel service on the ground floor beside the customs office. **Useful addresses** Hospital Córdoba, Av Patria 656, T0351-434 9000. Hospital de Clínicas, Santa Rosa 1564, T0351-4337010. Nuevo Hospital de Niños Santísima Trinidad, Bajada Pucará 1900, T0351-434 8800, children's hospital.

Northern Córdoba province

Stretching north from Córdoba city are two parallel chains of mountains known as the Sierras Chicas, with wonderfully wild landscapes to explore. There are two main routes north offering quite different pleasures. Head up Route 9, named by the tourist board as the Camino de la Historia, to visit Jesús María and the Jesuit estancias, the cultural highlights of Córdoba province. Hiring a car is the best way to really enjoy them, as you can stop off at the more attractive villages in the hills and stay at rural estancias too, such as luxurious La Paz in Ascochinga. North of here, Route 9 leads to the Reserva Natural Cerro Colorado, where there are extraordinary pre-historic paintings in red rocky landscapes, or further northwest, the old Camino Real, now Route 60, leads you to quaint unspoiled villages where you can hide away in remote estancia San Pedro Viejo. The alternative route north along the Punilla Valley (Route 38) takes you through depressing built-up tourist towns, so keep going until you reach the pretty little mountain town of La Cumbre, which offers spectacular paragliding, golf and the laid-back, friendly villages of Capilla del Monte and San Marcos Sierras nearby are great bases to explore the mountains.

The region's most interesting rural landscapes lie between these two valleys, where there's a beautiful and surprisingly unspoiled land of rolling mountains, best explored on horseback from the traditional rural estancia, Los Potreros; just an hour from Río Ceballos in the valley. You could easily spend a week here and not exhaust the places to explore. Birdwatchers would be entertained here too, though keen twitchers should head east to Laguna Mar Chiquita, a lake the size of a small sea, which is a paradise for migratory birds. ▸▸ *For Sleeping, Eating and other listings, see pages 176-181.*

Jesuit estancias: Camino de la Historia

» pp176-181.

→ *Visit www.sierraschicas.net and www.delnortecordobes.com.ar*

The real jewel in the crown of Córdoba province is the collection of fine 17th-century Jesuit estancias in the hilly, rural areas to the north of the provincial capital. Three of the oldest estancias lie close to what used to be the **Camino Real** (the 'royal road'), used by the Spanish to link the Córdoba with Lima and the Alto Perú mines. The Jesuit missionaries established huge, enterprising estancias in the country that were used to finance their educational and artistic work in the city. The elegant residences and beautiful chapels built for the priests (see box page) still remain, complete with some wonderful art and walled gardens. These can be explored at **Jesús María**, 40 km north of Córdoba, **Estancia Caroya** nearby, and **Santa Catalina** 20 km further northwest. You could visit all three Jesuit estancias in a long day's drive from Córdoba, but part of the charm of exploring the sierras is to enjoy a night or two in the area's marvellous estancias – the kind where you're offered fine wine with dinner and horse riding, rather than religious instruction!

Jesús María

→ *Phone code: 03525 Population 27,000 Colour map 4, A3*

The sleepy town of Jesús María, with its avenues lined with plane trees, is a good base for exploring two of Córdoba's oldest Jesuit estancias. It's typical of towns that grew through a wave of immigration from Friuli in the north of Italy, starting with 60 families in 1878. There's a distinctly Italian influence to the food, with some superb salamis to be found in the cafés and shops. Jesús María itself has little to offer tourists, but during the first half of January it hosts the **Festival de Doma y Folclore**, a popular *folclore* music and gaucho event whose profits benefit local schools (entry US$2-2.50).

There are two **tourist offices** ⓘ *at the bus station, Belgrano 580, T03525-426113; and on the way into town on R9, T03525-426773, www.cerrocolorado.infoturis.com.ar*, which provide useful information. Ask for the leaflet *Caminos de las Estancias Jesuíticas*, which includes a handy map of the estancias in relation to Córdoba, a plan and some information on each estancia (in Spanish). From the main road into town, Estancia de Jesús María and Estancia Caroya are clearly signposted.

Estancia Jesús María

ⓘ *1 km northeast of Jesús María, T03525-420126. Mon-Fri 0800-1900, Sat and Sun 1000-1200, 1400-1800 (1500-1900 in spring and summer). US$0.65, Mon free.*

This is a well-conserved example of a Jesuit-built estancia, whose production supported the schools in Córdoba. Argentina's first vineyards were created here, and wine from Jesús María was reputed to have been the first American wine served to the Spanish royal family. The residence and church, built mainly in 1618, form three sides of a square enclosing a neat garden with pleasing cloisters on two sides. The imposing façade of the church is in good condition, with tall, plaster-covered pillars contrasting with the stone work of the main building, but it's a sober affair compared with the opulent interior of the church, with its finely decorated cupola. In the adjoining **Museo Jesuítico**, beautiful Cuzco-style paintings, religious objects and a curious collection of plates are on display, together with artefacts from early wine-making. There are no longer remains of the housing for slaves and indigenous workers, or the cultivation areas but, with its lovely pond underneath mature trees and a small graveyard to the left of the church, the whole place is very attractive and peaceful. Highly recommended for a few hours' visit.

To get there take a taxi ($1), or it's an easy 15-minute walk from the Jesús María bus station: take Avenida Juan B Justo, north, turn left at Avenida Cleto Peña, cross bridge on river and follow a dirt road right about 300 m.

Estancia de Caroya

ⓘ *In the southern suburbs of Jesús María, T03525-426701. Daily 0900-1300, 1400-1800 (1500-1900 in spring and summer). US$1.*

Estancia de Caroya, dating from 1616, was the first of the Jesuit establishments to be built in the area and has an interesting history. It was acquired in 1661 by the Jesuit founder of the Colegio Convictorio de Montserrat (in Córdoba city) and while its agricultural activities funded the college, it was also used as a holiday home for the students. Between 1814 and 1816, it was used as a weapons factory for the Army of the North fighting in the Wars of Independence, and then in 1878 the first Italian immigrants stayed here. A simpler construction than Jesús María, Santa Catalina consists of single-storey cloisters around a central patio, with access to kitchens, dining rooms, and a simple stone chapel. The fascinating history is well presented in the displays here, including a room with artefacts from the Italian immigration, and though the tour is informative your guide may not speak English. Ruins of a dam and a mill can be seen in the surrounding gardens.

Take a taxi ($1.30) or it's a 20-minute walk from the bus station: take Avenida Juan B Justo, south, and turn right at Avenida 28 de Julio. After 500 m, gates of the estancia are on the left side of the road. Tourist information T03525-466305.

Around Jesús Maria

Next to Jesús María, **Colonia Caroya** was the heart of the Italian immigration, and you can taste delicious salami at any of the local restaurants. The long access road is beautifully lined by an uninterrupted avenue of mature sycamore trees, where you'll find **Bodegas La Caroyense** ⓘ *Av San Martín 2281, T03525-466270, Mon-Fri 0800-1200, 1500-1900, Sat and Sun 1000-1800, free*, a winery offering guided visits.

Set picturesquely among hills, 22 km west of Route 9, the attractive village of **Villa Tulumba** has hardly changed since colonial times. It's worth visiting for the beautiful 17th-century baroque tabernacle in its church, crafted in the Jesuit missions.

Estancia Santa Catalina

ⓘ *T03525-424467. Winter Tue-Fri 1000-1300, 1400-1800; summer Tue-Fri 1000-1300, 1500-1930, Sun 1000-1800, Only open at weekends during Jan, Feb, July, Easter and bank holidays. US$2.*

This is the largest of the estancias, beautifully located in rolling fertile countryside northwest of Jesús María, and not to be missed. It is the best preserved of all the estancias, and the only one that remains in private hands. It also has the added advantage of being close to Ascochinga (see below), which has some good accommodation.

The house is still in use by the extended Diaz family as their weekend and summer home, but the church and all the outbuildings are open to the public. The guided tour (Spanish only) is included in the entrance price and provides lots of information on the way of life here, as well as allowing you to visit the seminary buildings and the second and third patios, which are rich in architectural detail. Access is by a 14-km dirt road branching off route E66 to Ascochinga, 6 km west of Jesús María (signposted, 20 km in total). From Jesús María bus station, remise taxis charge US$10 return including 2 hours waiting time at the estancia. Good lunches are available at La Ranchería de Santa Catalina, a simple rustic restaurant on the right as you approach the estancia. It also has two small guests rooms with shared bathroom.

Built in 1622, the church has the most wonderful baroque façade, with swooping curves and scrolls in white plaster, and twin bell towers. The beautifully maintained interior has a fabulous gold pulpit and retable, brought from Alto Perú, with religious figures made by indigenous craftsmen betraying certain anatomical details of their makers, such as their big knees and robust workmen's thighs. There are superb Cuzco-school paintings representing the Passion and, opposite the retable, an intriguing articulated sculpture of Jesus on the cross. This was used by the Jesuit priests as a teaching device to evangelize the indigenous peoples, and unlike most such figures, this Jesus has his eyes open: his arms could be lowered to enact scenes from his life, pre-crucifixion, and then raised as he was mounted on the cross. A moving and fascinating figure.

The house has a beautiful central patio, where just three priests lived in spacious splendour, organizing a staff of 600, and a workforce of thousands of African slaves and local indigenous peoples. Santa Catalina was the most important of the estancias economically, with its 25,000 head of cattle and extensive agriculture. To the right of the church is a huge vegetable garden and, further out, a little brick building with six tiny rooms where novice priests were trained. The slaves' quarters were even more miserable and can be found on the road leading to the estancia, now converted into a restaurant (see Eating page 179). The servants for the main house were housed in the second patio, and in the third patio were wood and metal workshops. In the lovely surrounding parkland, you can see the *tajamar* – a reservoir used for the sophisticated watering system for crops.

Ascochinga and Estancia La Paz

The upmarket little village of **Ascochinga**, 13 km west of Santa Catalina, is full of second homes for rich Córdobes, a couple of shops, a part-time locutorio, an ACA petrol station and there are plenty of accommodation options. A fabulously opulent place to stay is the historical **Estancia La Paz** ⓘ *Ashcochinga, www.estancialapaz.com*, which was owned by President Roca from 1872 until his death in 1914, and remains almost untouched. Just try not to think about him planning the massacre of the indigenous peoples in the Conquest of the Desert when he stayed here. Roca added the neoclassical Italianate touches to the building, and commissioned a splendid 100-ha park from Argentina's most famous landscape architect Charles Thays, whose work includes the parks at Palermo, Tucumán and Mendoza. There are grand bedrooms, with enormously high ceilings, coming directly off a long terrace with wonderful views across the huge ornamental lake where you can go rowing if the mood takes you. There are immense groves of exotic trees and blissful, private places to sit in the 1930's garden furniture and order tea from the impeccable staff. Old-fashioned opulence is combined with more modern luxuries such as an Olympic-sized pool, tennis courts, a spa with expert masseuse and a superb restaurant, making this a real treat.

Asochinga to La Cumbre

From Asochinga a spectacular route heads over the mountains to La Cumbre (see page 175). The road courses through wonderful landscapes of rounded mountain ridges and deep valleys and is much loved by rally drivers and cyclists in training. This winding dirt road, full of hair-pin bends, is probably best not attempted in the dark or bad weather. Keep your speed below 40 kph, watch out for hares and perdis crossing the road, and allow at least two hours for the journey. The vegetation varies from lush subtropical woodlands, to lush scrub on the summits, and there are consistently great views on a fine day.

Northeast of Córdoba → *Phone code: 03563 Colour map 4, A3*

From Route 9 north of Ascochinga you can head east to Argentina's largest inland sea, the **Laguna Mar Chiquita** ('Lagoon of the Small Sea'), set on the borders of the pampas and the chaco, 192 km northeast of Córdoba. The lake is very shallow (maximum depth 12 m) and has no outlet into any rivers, so its size varies (from 65 km by 80 km, to 30 km by 40 km) according to rainfall patterns. At times, the water is apparently so salty, you can float in it.

A reserve, called the Reserva Natural Bañados del Río Dulce y Laguna Mar Chiquita, has been created to protect the huge numbers of migratory birds which flock here in summer from the northern hemisphere, So far, over 300 species of bird have been spotted here, returning to different parts of the lagoon each year. There are also large resident populations of flamingos representing all three species extant in South America. It's the site of greatest biodiversity in the province, and is also popular for fishing *pejerrey* all year round. During the summer, human visitors flock here too, since the salty waters are used in the treatment of rheumatic ailments and skin diseases. It's a singular and spectacular landscape and, although you may not feel it's not worth a big detour, if you're spending some time in the area, it would make a good relaxing day out. Park administration is in Miramar on the southern shore, the only settlement nearby, where there are a few hotels and campsites. There's a tourist office at Libertad 351, T03563-493003.

Córdoba Norteña » *pp176-181.*

If you're enjoying getting off the beaten track and want to see where the Camino Real leads, keep going northwest from Jesús María along Route 60 into the northernmost extreme of the province. In **Deán Funes** (118 km from Córdoba), you'll find a couple of decent hotels, plenty of places to eat and a **tourist information office** ⓘ *municipalidad, Sáenz Peña 466, T03521-420020, www.deanfunes.gov.ar.*

From Deán Funes head east on Provincial Road 16 to find **San Piedro Viejo**. This tiny hamlet has a beautiful little church, built in adobe with a squat square bell tower, and an *estancia* where you can stay for a few nights to completely unwind and explore the rolling land on foot or horseback. This place has a history: it was an important staging post on the royal road between the Río de la Plata and Perú, and such illustrious figures as General San Martín and President Belgrano stayed in the building which is now a chic and rustic boutique hotel (see Sleeping page 177).

Reserva Cultural y Natural Cerro Colorado

ⓘ *Summer daily 0700-1300, 1400-2000, winter daily 0800-1900. US$1.*

Some 104 km north of Jesús María, reached by an unpaved road (12 km) which branches off R9 at Santa Elena (see Transport, page 181) is this provincial park covering 3000 ha of rocky hills and woodlands protecting some 35,000 rock paintings in around 200 sites, some of them underground. It's thought that they were painted by the indigenous Comechingones peoples sometime between the 10th century and the arrival of the Spanish. The strikingly bold paintings, in red, black and white, portray animals and plants, hunting scenes, magic rituals and dancing; even battles against the Spanish, mounted on horse-back. There are lots of more enigmatic paintings with geometric patterns, open to wildly imaginative interpretations. There are two small museums: **Museo Arqueológico** ⓘ *daily 0700-1300, 1400-2000, guided visits leave at 0830, 1030, 1600 and 1800*, at the foot of Cerro Intihuasi, has information on the site itself; **Museo Atahualpa and Yupanqui** ⓘ *T0351-155198715, daily 0900-1300, 1600-2000*, at the end of the winding road to Agua Escondida, also offers guided tours. The vegetation is interesting with lots of ancient algarrobo trees, molles and a rare *mato* forest in the park, where you can also spot small armadillos.

The park can only be visited as part of a guided tour which lasts 1-1½ hours and is included in the entry fee. For tours, ask in the administration building, or for private guides contact **Ramón Bustos**, T03522-15515069, **Justo Bustamante**, T0351-156820866 or **Luis Martínez**, T0351-156522480. There's a hotel and a few cabaña complexes nearby in the sprawling villages at the foot of the Cerro, and plenty of handicrafts for sale. Useful websites include www.infoturis.com.ar and www.cerrolcolorado.infoturis.com.ar. A helpful leaflet, *El Chasqui de Cerro Colorado*, is available from tourist offices in Córdoba city.

Sierras Chicas and Estancia Los Potreros

To really get into the wild, remote country which is the Sierras Chicas, you need to spend a few nights away from civilization, and the best way to do this is to stay at an estancia such as **Estancia Los Potreros** ⓘ *T03548-452121, T15566628, www.ride-americas.com, see Sleeping page 177, for further details*. One of Argentina's finest riding estancias, this is situated in the middle of its own range of peaks, yet it's easily accessible: just an hour from the airport. It's run by a British family, Robin and Kevin Begg, who were brought up on this land and who breed fine horses and offer a wonderful mixture of real gaucho Argentine ranch culture and British hospitality. If you're not a rider, you can walk, birdwatch, swim or simply relax and enjoy the peace and immense vistas. If you'd like to learn to ride, the Beggs are the most patient teachers, and the horses very tame and sure-footed. It's best to stay for at least three nights to get the feel of the place but for those with more time, a riding tour of the sierras taking several days can be arranged. As well as enjoying spectacular scenery, a longer tour allows you to explore remote mountain villages with their tiny churches and schools and stay at other mountain estancias in the region, gaining invaluable insights into the local culture and communities that you could never otherwise access. You can also learn how to play polo here, and learn all about the processes of breeding horses and cattle, joining in the cattle-mustering and branding activities if you hit the right time of year. The Beggs are great hosts, charming, very relaxed and down to earth and the riding here is incomparable. This is an unmissable experience of the Córdoba sierras.

Punilla Valley to La Cumbre » pp176-181.

→ *www.sierrascordobesas.com.ar, www.lacumbre.gov.ar, www.alacumbre.com – all in Spanish.*

The Punilla Valley, situated between the Sierra Chica to the east and the Sierra Grande to the west, was the first area of the Sierras to become populated by weekend and summer visitors from the cities of Córdoba and Buenos Aires back in the 1920s. Sadly, these once-idyllic weekend retreats have now developed into one long string of built up urban areas alongside Route 38: **Villa Carlos Paz**, **Cosquín**, **Valle Hermoso** and **La Falda**. There's no real reason to stop, unless you're keen to visit Cosquín's famous *folclore* music festival, which is held every year in January and attracts the country's best musicians and budding talent. The whole valley is unbearably busy during the Argentine holiday periods of January, February and Easter, when it is best avoided. Any time of the year, it is preferable to head straight for **La Cumbre** further north (see page 175), where there's a more civilized pace of life and plenty of appealing places to stay in this pretty hillside town. A brief description of the main Punilla Valley towns is followed by a more complete description of La Cumbre.

Villa Carlos Paz and around

→ *Phone code: 03541 Colour map 4, A2 Population: 56,000*

Ghastly Villa Carlos Paz, 35 km west of Córdoba, is a large and over-populated resort, crammed with hotels and brimming with Argentine tourists in summer. There are lots of activities on offer and a chair-lift runs from the Complejo Aerosilla to the summit of the Cerro de la Cruz, but your only reason to come here would be if everywhere else is full, or to use as a base for the area's superb trekking. There are plenty of hotels, and some quieter places to bathe and hang out, such as the *balnearios* along Río San Antonio, such as **Villa Las Jarillas**, 15 km south of town.

Villa Carlos Paz is on the road to Traslasierra further west (see page 190). If you're not going that far, and are into hiking or climbing, it's certainly worth heading for **Cerro Los Gigantes** (2374 m), 39 km west of Villa Carlos Paz, with spectacular views and challenging walks. To get there, take the unpaved Route 28 via **Tanti** over the

Pampa de San Luis towards **Salsacate**. Los Gigantes is signposted at Km 30, where you turn off left; here you'll find the nearest base for climbing the granite massif. By public transport, you'll need to get a local bus from Villa Carlos Paz to Tanti, and from there to Los Gigantes. Daily buses with TAC to Salsacate stop at Los Gigantes. Remise taxi charges about US$11. There is **tourist information** at Tanti, T03541-498250.

Cosquín and around → *Phone code: 03541 Colour map 4, A2 Population: 18,800*

Cosquín, 20 km north of Carlos Paz, is not an attractive town, but its setting on the banks of the wide Río Cosquín, gives it several *balnearios*, of which **Pan de Azúcar** is the quietest option. Cosquín is also known as the national *folclore* capital, and Argentina's most important folklore festival is held here in the last two weeks of January. The country's most famous bands and singers play every night on **Plaza Próspero Molina**, and there are plentiful food and handicrafts stalls. An increasingly popular rock festival is held here in early February so that accommodation is almost impossible to find between 10 January and 10 February. There is also a **tourist office** ⓘ *Av San Martín 560, Plaza Próspero Molina, T03541-453701.*

La Falda and around → *Phone code: 03548 Colour map 4, A2 Population: 16,000*

La Falda, 20 km north of Cosquín, is another seething and tawdry tourist town, once the destination of Argentina's wealthy and influential who all stayed at the magnificent Hotel Edén. The hotel is now sadly in ruins but the bar gives you a flavour of its former grandeur, with an exhibition of old photographs. The town is known for its nightlife, and bars and casinos abound, but it's really a place to avoid unless you want to use it as a base for hiking in the surrounding hills and pampas. The **tourist office** ⓘ *Av España 50, T03548- 423007*, is at the former railway station.

The sierras to the east of La Falda are a good place for hiking. **Cerro La Banderita** (1350 m), also popular with paragliders, is a 1½-hour walk from the town centre: leave the left side of Hotel Edén, taking Calle Austria, for panoramic views of the valley. Ask at tourist office for map and directions. From La Falda you could also head out west to the pampas: an 80-km rough, winding road goes to La Higuera, on the west side of the Cumbres de Gaspar. It crosses the vast **Pampa de Olaén**, a grass-covered plateau at 1100 m, where you'll find the tiny Capilla de Santa Bárbara (1750), 20 km from La Falda, and waterfalls Cascadas de Olaén, 2 km south of the chapel. There are more beautiful rivers and waterfalls at **Río Pintos** (26 km from La Falda) and **Characato** (36 km from La Falda). Jesuit **Estancia La Candelaria** lies further along this road, 53 km west of La Falda. This is a great area for cycling, although there are no facilities, so take water.

La Cumbre and around → *Phone code: 03548 Colour map 4, A2 Population: 7200*

By far the most attractive town in this whole area, La Cumbre sits at the highest point of the Punilla Valley at 1141 m. It's only 1½ hours' drive from Córdoba, if you head straight here without stopping on the way. It was founded by the British engineers and workers who built the railway here in 1900 and who have given the place its distinctive flavour, with trees lining the avenues in the attractive residential area to the east of town, where you'll find the best hotels. **Golf Club La Cumbre** ⓘ *T03548 -451170, US$12 for a round,* to the southeast of town was built 90 years ago and is beautifully landscaped, with mature trees and a quaint Tudor-style clubhouse. Further east you'll find lots of craftsmen selling their wares, particularly in the summer months. Unlike the rest of the valley, this friendly little town still feels authentic and the town centre bustles busily just before midday. There are some classy shops, as well as lots of places to eat and a couple of tea rooms selling superb cakes. For the more adventurous, there's excellent paragliding nearby in **Cuchi Corral** southwest of the town (see Activities and tours, page 180). There are also plenty of places to walk in the mountains, with access from residential areas **Cruz Chica** and **Cruz Grande**, on the road to **Los Cocos**.

The **tourist office** ⓘ *Av Caraffa 300, T03548-452966, daily from early morning until late in the evening*, is in the old train station, and many of the friendly staff speak English. They'll give you a very helpful map listing all the hotels and restaurants.

As a visitor to Argentina, you might not have noticed the national obsession with *alfajores*, the soft cakey biscuits made of a double layer of corn flour sponge, and sandwiched with *dulce de leche*. The chocolate-covered ones from **Havanna** *alfajores* shops in any town centre are particularly recommended. While you're in La Cumbre, you could visit the famous *alfajores* factory **Estancia El Rosario** ⓘ *R66, 5 km east of town, daily 0800-1900*, to see them being made and try a fine specimen or three. The factory has been operating since 1924 and was, for many years, a major tourist attraction (which says something for the Argentine lack of appetite for hill walking, given the splendour of the surroundings). These days there are still free guided visits to the small factory where fruit preserves and other sweet delicacies are also made.

Head east from the golf course along Route 66 for the spectacular mountain crossing which leads to Ascochinga (for a route description, see page 172). North of La Cumbre, there are more hotels in the lovely leafy residential areas of Cruz Chica, Cruz Grande and Los Cocos. Further along this picturesque road are two popular places for families: **El Descanso,** with its well-designed garden and maze, and **Complejo Aerosilla**, with a chairlift to the nearby hills (US$2).

Capilla del Monte and around

→ *Phone code: 03548 Colour map 4, A2 Population: 8940*

Capilla del Monte is a quiet town and not wildly appealing, but it does offer a base for good trekking and paragliding and for exploring nearby rock formations, see www.cordobaserrana.com.ar/capilla/aguadelospalos.htm for details. The landscapes are hilly and scrubby, with places rather reminiscent of the lunar landscapes in Ischigualasto – Valle de la Luna in San Juan (see page 230). The **tourist office** ⓘ *T03548-481903, www.capilladelmonte.com.ar*, is at the end of the diagonal Calle Buenos Aires. The town is overlooked by dramatic **Cerro Uritorco,** 1979 m, which you can climb: head 3 km east of town and it's another 5 km to the summit, though be warned that this is a four-hour climb with no shade (US$2 entry).

UFO-spotters flock to the amazing landscape of **Quebrada de la Luna, Los Terrones** and **Parque Natural Ongamira,** where there are curious rock formations. Ask in the tourist office for more information and for a *remise* to take you there.

Sleeping

Jesús María *p170*

D La Gringa, Tucumán 658, T03525-425249, one block across the railway lines from the bus station. A/c, breakfast included.

D Napoleón, España 675, T03525-421273, hotelnapoleon@coop5.com.bar . The best option, only 2 blocks from bus station, with a/c and a pool.

Estancia Santa Catalina *p171*

A Posada Camino Real, 10 km from Santa Catalina, T0351-156134287, T155525215 www.posadacaminoreal.com.ar. Descendants of the original owners of this estancia, the Díaz family, have made this a welcoming and comfortable place to stay with 8 elegant stylish rooms and a pool complex, offering all the usual estancia pursuits: walking, riding, picnics, plus the less common *asado* of local kid and llama. Massages also on offer.

C La Ranchería de Santa Catalina, 10 m before the entrance to Estancia Santa Catalina, on the right-hand side, T03525-424467, T15538957. Basic, but convenient for visiting the Jesuit estancia. 2 small rooms in the former slaves' quarters, next to the restaurant. Separate bathroom.

Ascochinga *p172*

LL Estancia La Paz, Ruta E66, Km 14, a few kilometres from Ascochinga, signposted, but ring for directions, T03525-492073, 424468, www.estancialapaz.com. Opulence and splendour, presidential style, but this is a warmly welcoming luxury estancia with impeccable service, beautiful parkland, and offering golf, horse riding and a spa. Bilingual reception staff. Recommended.

B Golf, right in the middle of Ascochinga village. One of the many hotels built by Perón in the 1940s to allow workers' unions to go on holiday economically, this has been converted into a comfortable place to stay, but remains slightly institutional in its neatness.

Córdoba Norteño *p173*

AL Estancia San Pedro Viejo, RP16, San Pedro Norte, San Pedro Viejo, T0351-155293682, www.sanpedroviejo.com.ar. A quaint historical post house converted into a chic boutique hotel, with 1-m-thick walls, old fireplaces, and ancient trees near a charming lake. 6 bedrooms decorated with antiques and rustic furniture, some with jacuzzi, great food and wines, relaxing walks and horse riding in the nearby hills. A lovely retreat.

C San Jorge, España y Buenos Aires, Deán Funes, T03521-421873, hotelsanjorge@intinet.com.ar. Drab modern exterior, but reasonably comfortable rooms with a/c, TV, and a snack bar in the ground floor.

Cerro Colorado *p173*

There are several places to stay in the hamlets around the foot of the *cerro*, and you can also stay with local families if the hotel is full. The tourist office produces a helpful free leaflet, *El Chasqui de Cerro Colorado*, available in Córdoba city before you set off. A few to try (all **D**) are **Cerro Colorado** (T03522-15648990), **Complejo Argañarez** (T0351-156466778) and **La Italiana** (T0351-4246598).

Sierras Chicas *p174*

L Estancia Los Potreros, Sierras Chicas, either take a bus to the nearest town, Río Ceballos, or the owners will arrange a taxi from Córdoba city or the airport, 1 hr , T03548-452121, www.ride-americas.com. Warm hospitality from this exceptional English Argentine family who grew up on these lands, and now offer extremely comfortable rooms in their beautifully restored 1900s house, in a remote hilltop location in the middle of the sierras, for superb horse riding on their impeccably trained and calm polo horses. Learn to play polo, relax by the pool, go birdwatching, enjoy delicious food and wines – all included in the price. 3 nights minimum stay. Highly recommended. See also page 174.

Cosquín and around *p175*

C La Puerta del Sol, Perón 820, T03541-452045, lapuertadelsol@hotmail.com. This hotel quite undeservedly has the best reputation in town. Still, it's a decent choice if you want to use the pool or take advantage of the half board deals or car hire.

E Siempreverde, Santa Fe 525 (behind Plaza Molina), T03541-450093, siempreverde hosteria@hotmail.com. Spotless place run by welcoming and informative owner María Cristina. Some rooms are small, but still comfortable and there's a gorgeous garden with a huge tree. Breakfast included.

Camping

There are several campsites but San Buenaventura, 8 km west on Río Yuspe, is in the nicest location with shady trees, beaches and places for a good swim, US$2.30 per group (*remise* taxis charge US$7 for an open return trip from Cosquín).

La Falda and around *p175*

About 80 hotels in all categories, all full in holiday season.

D La Asturiana, Av Edén 835, T03548-422923, hotellaasturiana@yahoo.com.ar. Simple and comfortable rooms, a pool and a superb breakfast including rice pudding. Welcoming owners.

D L'Hirondelle, Av Edén 861, in the same block as La Asuriana, T03548-422825. Some rooms retaining their original parquet floor, a large garden with a pool, and a restaurant. Welcoming owners.

E El Colonial, 9 de Julio 491, T03548-421831. Though lacking comfort, there's well-preserved early 1950s decor in the reception and dining room with magnificent wooden-framed windows. Includes the use of a large pool at the back.

Camping

Balneario 7 Cascadas, next to the dam and the seven falls (west of town), T03548-425808. Nicely located site with hot showers, electricity and a food shop, US$1.30 a day pp. *Remise* taxi charges US$1.70.

La Cumbre and around *p175*

There are plenty of hotels but you're likely to want to stay in *cabañas* here, as these are particularly high quality and in attractive settings, ideal for larger groups who want the flexibility of self-catering. Cruz Chica is a lovely place to stay, but you'll need a car or taxi to get there.

A Cabañas Villa Benitz, Av Benitz 102, T03548-451597, www.villabenitz.com.ar. Very stylish high quality houses, all individually designed, make a very upmarket place to stay and very good value for 4 or more. All houses have everything you need: TV, grills for barbecues, and breakfast is delivered to your door in the mornings. Also a pool and restaurant for guests. Recommended.

B Gran Hotel La Cumbre, Posadas 680, T03548-451550, www.granhotella cumbre.com.ar. Alpine style on top of a hill, and rather impressive, this hotel has wonderful views from its comfortable rooms. Larger rooms with balcony are 20% extra and a good breakfast is included here. Pool and restaurant.

B Los Mimbres, Runciman s/n, T03548-451039, www.losmimbres.com.ar. Pretty location in a large garden, this attracts an older crowd - popular with retired folks, and owned by Brits. Very sedate place to stay, but comfortable enough.

C Cabañas Del Golf, JL Cabrera, T03548-452008, www.cabanasdelgolf.com . Attractive well-equipped *cabañas* arranged in nice parkland with lush vegetation and lovely views.

C Cruz Chica, Cruz Chica, 3 km north of town, T03548-452780, hotelcruzchica@ digitalcoop.com.ar, mediterraneaturismolyf@ digitalcoop.com.ar. A charming old stone building dating from 1886, in pleasant gardens, this has a spa (extra cost) and attractive rooms.

C Hostal Toledo, Bartolome Jaime 1150, T03548-452898, www.hostaltoledo.com.ar. One of a pair of hotels owned by the same people on opposite sides of the road leading to Cruz Chica in an attractive area, this is an attractive Spanish-style stone building, with traditionally decorated interiors, but very comfortable and rooms are of a high standard.

C Posada Lambare, Bartolome Jaime 880, on the right-hand side, high up on the road to Cruz Chica, T03548-451054, www.lambare.com.ar. In gorgeous gardens with huge cedars and pines, a grand staircase leads up to the elegant main house

For an explanation of the Sleeping and Eating price codes used in this guide, and other relevant information, see Essentials, pages 48 and 51.

with rustic rooms, and pretty views. Pool, no restaurant, very relaxing.

C **Posada los Cedros**, Av Argentina 837, T03548451028, posadaloscedros@arnet.com.ar. A lovely old house set in the leafy residential area, close to the golf club, this is set in attractive gardens and good service. An appealing option.

C **Posada San Andres**, Av Benitz and Montcagudo, T03548 451165, www.posadasanandres.com. Popular with couples and families, this is a lovely old stone house, set back from the road in lovely gardens with a pool, and mountains behind, great for walks. The owners are on hand to welcome guests, and good dinners are served in the restaurant.

D **Cabañas Villa Bosque**, Benitz s/n, T03548-452295, villabosquelacumbre@yahoo.com.ar. These yellow houses are closer together than some, but still offer very comfortable accommodation. Reasonably well equipped, and good value for larger groups.

E **Residencial El Condor**, Bartolome Jaime and Irigoyen, well signposted from the road, T03548-452870, el_condor_2001@yahoo.com.ar. Very popular with Europeans and backpackers who use this as a base before going hiking and climbing, this is a basic but welcoming place with European owners who give advice on hikes and tours too. Beds in rooms for 4-7, very good value. English spoken, nice laid-back atmosphere.

Camping

Carpa Verde, Paraje Balata, 4 km from the centre of La Cumbre, T03548-15633395, www.geocities.com/carpaverde. US$2 pp per day, or US$3 in the *refugio*. You can also rent tents here, and there are excursions offered directly from the campsite. Hot water but no electricity.

Capilla del Monte and around *p176*

D **La Casona**, Pueyrredón 774, T03548-482679, silviadon48@hotmail.com. This 19th-century villa has a distinctly haunted house look. At the top of a hill, surrounded by palm trees, there is a pool and the best views of the sierras. The interior retains some magnificent examples of former opulence and the welcoming owners also offer homemade meals, including smoked hams and cheeses; English spoken. Recommended.

D **Petit Sierras**, Pueyrredón y Salta, T03548-481667, petitsierras@capilladelmonte.com.ar. A renovated hotel with clean and comfortable rooms. The owners run the restaurant **A Fuego Lento**, on the edge of town, with good local trout. Discounts and free transport for guests.

Camping

G pp **Calabalumba**, 600 m north of the centre, T03548-481903. Municipal shady site with pool, hot water, *cabañas* for 4-6.

Eating

Jesús María *p170*

Fertilia, signposted from Av San Martín 5200, Colonia Caroya, T03525- 467031, buses stop on the main road, from here it's a 15 min-walk along a dirt road to the farm. An unmissable treat. Welcoming farmers serve excellent quality salamis and ham accompanied by delicious local red wine.

Viejo Comedor, Tucumán 312. Popular for cheap meals, including local specialities.

Estancia Santa Catalina *p171*

See **La Ranchería de Santa Catalina** in Sleeping above.

Cerro Colorado *p173*

El Arco de Noe, in Las Galerias, T03522-15456517. Bar and restaurant.

Inti Huasi, in the visitor centre for Córdoba Ambiente agency. More of a café with food.

Purinqui Huasi, opposite the archaeological museum, T03522-15648705. A *parrilla* with barbecued kid as the house speciality, also serves good pastas and salads.

Cosquín and around *p175*

La Encrucijada del Supaj-Ñuñú, on the way to the Cerro Pan de Azúcar, T3541-15532267. Pleasant restaurant, tea house and brewery, serving a variety of meals as well as fondue, cakes or sandwiches at moderate prices.

Wissen, Av Juan B Justo y Ruta 38 (100 m north of bridge), T03541-454097. Open for lunch and dinner, this former German family residence with sumptuous decor and a pleasant terrace offers an unpretentious menu, with excellent homemade pastas, and several meat-based dishes at moderate prices with a wide selection of wines.

La Falda and around *p175*

¶¶ **Hotel L'Hirondelle**. This hotel, see Sleeping, above, has a moderately priced restaurant open to non-residents, offering good set menus.

¶ **El Cristal**, San Lorenzo 39. Very good cooking, where the locals eat.

¶ **Pachamama**, Av Edén 127. If you're tired of eating beef, there is a health food shop with a few neat tables at the back, where you can have cheap organic vegetable pies, or wholemeal pizzas and *empanadas*.

La Cumbre and around *p175*

¶ **Dany Cheff**, opposite the tourist office, Av Caraffa y Belgrano, T03548-451379. The best place for afternoon tea, this serves delicious pastries and cakes, and there's a lively buzz mid-morning when locals flock there.

¶ **El Enkuentro**, 25 de Mayo 283, T03548-452053. Fabulous family restaurant and useful meeting place, this is central and well run. The homemade pastas are superb, and there are lots of excellent meat dishes on the menu too, including game. Highly recommended.

¶ **La Casona del Toboso**, Belgrano 349, T03548-451439. Also highly recommended for excellent food across a wide menu, including *parrilla*.

Activities and tours

La Falda and around *p175*

Tour operators

Turismo Talampaya, T03548-470412, turismotalampaya@yahoo.com.ar. Run by Teresa Pagni who guides 4WD full-day trips to the Pampa de Olaen and Jesuit Estancia La Candelaria for US$15 pp.

VH, T03548-424831/T15562740, vhcabalgatas@hotmail.com. 1-hr horse rides to nearby hills from US$5 pp.

La Cumbre and around *p175*

Golf

Golf Club La Cumbre, Posadas, T03548-451170/ 452283/452284, www.lacumbregolfclub.com.ar. Follow Belgrano from the town centre, opposite the tourist office, to reach the corner of the golf course, then turn left onto Posadas. Very attractive 18-hole golf course, with caddies and coaching. Also putting green and Olympic-sized pool.

Horse riding

Chachito Silva, T03548-451703/T15635673. Hires horses and offers half-day, 1- and 2-day guided horse-riding trips to the sierras and Candonga.

La Chacra, Pasaje Beíro s/n, T03548-451703/15570847. US$2.50 per hr, also half-day rides or rides for several days with guides.

La Granja de los Gringos, Route 38, T03548-15574317, cabalgatascumbre@yahoo.com. US$2.50 per hr, guides accompany your rides, longer rides also offered.

Paragliding

See www.sierrascordobesas.com.ar. The world-renowned paragliding site of **Cuchi Corral** is just 9 km west of La Cumbre on an unpaved road. From a natural balcony overlooking the Río Pintos, a few hundred metres below, northwest winds generate thermal currents, which collide with the mountains and make a superb place to practise paragliding if you're already expert, or to try for the first time if you're a novice. Several local companies offer flights, which start at US$50 for your first flight, the *Vuelo Bauptismo*, 20 mins, accompanied by a trained paragliding instructor in tandem. A 1-hr flight with instructor is US$85.

Operators include **Fechu**, T03548-15570951, parapentefechu@yahoo.co.ar; **Toti López**, T03548-494017, T15636592, toti_lopez@hotmail.com; **Mariano Baccola**, T0351-156548009; or Andy Hediger at **Aero Club La Cumbre**, T03548-452544, aerotelier@agora.com.ar.

Trekking

Escuela de Montaña y Escalada, T03548-492271, georgmallo@yahoo.com. Run by Jorge González, for parapenting, but also climbing and mountain trekking courses and excursions, eg to the Cascada de los 70 pies in Cruz Grande. Equipment hire.

Tour operators

These operators all go to Cuchi Corral and Río Pintos: **4x4 Turismo Aventura**, T15566664; **Cerro Uritorco**, Corrientes 96, T03548-451470; **Gonzalo Gili**, T03548-492201.

Aventura Family Club, T03548-423809, www.estanciapuestoviejo.com. Covers the area, as part of a day trip to a remote estancia, northwest of La Cumbre.

Transport

Jesús María *p170*
Bus Direct to **Córdoba**, Ciudad de Córdoba, Colonia Tirolesa, 1 hr, US$1, or minibus Fono Bus, US$1.10. To **Córdoba** via Ascochinga, Ciudad de Córdoba, 2½ hrs, US$1.90. To **Colonia Caroya**, Ciudad de Córdoba, Colonia Tirolesa, US$0.30.

Cerro Colorado *p173*
Bus Buses Ciudad de Córdoba, T0351-424 0048 go to/from Córdoba 3 times weekly, but check for current days 4½ hrs, US$5. There are also combis to **Santa Elena** with El Tatú, T0351-423 6335, and Río Seco, T0351-424 5610.

Laguna Mar Chiquita *p172*
Bus To/from **Córdoba**, Expreso Ciudad de San Francisco (from **Miramar**), 3½ hrs, US$3.50 and Transportes Morteros (from **Balnearia**), 3 hrs, US$3.80.

Cosquín and around *p175*
Bus Terminal at Perón y Salta. La Calera, TAC and Ciudad de Córdoba run frequent buses along the **Punilla Valley** and to **Córdoba**: to **La Falda**, US$0.70, to **La Cumbre** US$1, to **Capilla del Monte** US$1.40. Several minibuses do same route. To **Córdoba**, 1-1½ hrs, US$1.50.

Mountain bike hire
Centro, Perón 937, T03541-15622983.

Remise taxis
El Cerro, Av San Martín 1036, T03541-450444.

La Falda and around *p175*
Bus
Terminal at Av Buenos Aires (R38), 5-min walk north of Av Edén. Chevallier, General Urquiza and Sierras de Córdoba go daily to **Buenos Aires** and to several other national destinations. La Calera and Ciudad de Córdoba run frequent buses along the **Punilla Valley** and to **Córdoba**: to **Cosquín**, US$0.70, to **La Cumbre** US$0.60, to **Capilla del Monte** US$1. Several minibuses also do the same route. To **Córdoba**, US$1.70-2.

Mountain bike hire
Club Edén 201, Av Edén 201, US$3.50 per day.

Remise taxis
Casa Blanca, 9 de Julio 541, T03548-426323.

La Cumbre and around *p175*
Bus
Bus terminal just round the corner from the tourist office at Juan José Valle and Ruznak, T03548-452442. Daily buses to **Buenos Aires** with El Práctico, T03548-452442, General Urquiza / Sierras de Córdoba, T03548-452400, 11 hrs, US$30 . To **Córdoba** Ciudad de Córdoba, T452442, La Calera, T03548-452300.

Car hire
Reynas, 25 de Mayo 448, T03548-452107, gustavobecker2003@hotmail.com. US$30 per day. Ask for a discount if you hire for several days. Bring your credit card.

Taxis
Taxi Victoria 25 de Mayo 260, T03548-452150. Auto Remis, López and Planes 321, T03548-451800/ T0800-4447040.

Capilla del Monte and around *p176*
Bus Daily buses to **Buenos Aires** and to **Córdoba** (US$3). Ciudad de Córdoba and La Calera and minibuses El Serra run services along the **Punilla valley**. Twice a day, Ciudad de Córdoba goes to **Traslasierra valley** via Cruz del Eje.

Mountain bike hire
Claudio, Deán Funes 567.

Remise taxis
El Cerro, Pueyrredón 426, T03548-482300.

Southern Córdoba province: Calamuchita Valley

South of Córdoba, there's another fascinating and well-preserved Jesuit estancia in the unprepossessing town of Alta Gracia, which is the gateway to a picturesque hilly area between the high peaks of the Sierra Grande and Sierra de Comechingones. Fans of that great 20th century icon Che Guevara will also want to visit his childhood home. Further south still, there's superb walking in the wooded countryside, near the quaint Germanic town of Villa General Belgrano and prettier still, the mountain town, La Cumbrecita. It's well worth spending two or three days combining the Jesuit heritage with some walking or relaxing in the hills, to gain the essence of Córdoba's history and landscapes. ⏩ *For Sleeping, Eating and other listings, see pages 187-190.*

Alta Gracia ⏩ *pp187-190.*

→ *Phone code: 03547 Colour map 4, A2 Population: 42,600, 36 km from Córdoba, www.calamuchita.com.*

Alta Gracia's great attraction is the wonderful 17th-century **Estancia Jesuítica Alta Gracia** (see below), whose church, residential buildings, and a small lake make a splendid hill-top centre to the town, around the scrappy Plaza Solares. The rather tawdry main commercial area spills down Calle Belgrano, with everything you need, but no charm whatsoever. Head instead to the pretty residential area west of centre **El Alto**, where the most appealing restaurants are to be found. El Alto was built when the British came here to build the housing which the locals describe as typically 'British': two stories with corrugated tin roofs. The rather grand **Hotel Sierras**, stylishly built in 1907 as Argentina's first casino, was made popular by the rich upper classes who flocked to the area for the summer in the 1920s when Alta Gracia was in its heyday. It's currently being restored and should soon be a desirable place to stay. There's also an attractive golf course in this area, whose club has one of the town's most recommendable restaurants, open to non-members (see Eating, page 189). All this aristocratic pleasure might sound an unlikely environment for the early years of Che Guevara, but his family house can now be visited, see the **Museo Casa de Ernesto Che Guevara**, page 184.

Ins and outs

Tourist information ⓘ *corner of Molino and Padre Viera, at the top of Av Belgrano, T03547-428128, www.altagracia.gov.ar*, is at the base of the clock tower on the corner of the Jesuit reservoir, the Tajamar. Staff don't speak much English, but are helpful and will give you a map and a useful *Guia Turistica*.

Estancia Jesuítica Alta Gracia and Museo Casa de Virrey Liniers

ⓘ *Plaza Solares, Av Padre Viera 41, T03547-421303, www.museoliniers.org.ar, summer Tue-Fri 0900-2000, Sat-Sun 0930-2000; winter Tue-Fri 0900-1300, 1500-1700, Sat- Sun 0930-1230, 1530-1830. Closed 1 Jan, Good Friday, 1 May, 25 Dec. US$1, free on Wed.*

Part of the same development of Jesuit establishments at Jesús María and Santa Catalina, which were declared a World Heritage Site by UNESCO in 2000, Alta Gracia is a fascinating testimony to the Jesuits' culture, and the entire estancia is now an excellent museum. If you visit only one Jesuit estancia in Córdoba, make it this one. There's added interest in the life of Viceroy Liniers, who owned the house form 1810. An excellent guided tour is included in the entry ticket, but ask in advance for an English/French/German speaking guide. There are also informative laminated cards in several languages in each room.

Alta Gracia dates from 1643, when Córdoba was the capital of the Jesuit province of Paraguay, and this estancia – one of their most prosperous rural establishments – was built to fund the religious education of their young men in the Colegio Maximo in Córdoba city. The centre comprised a Residence (now a museum), the Obraje (industrial workshops), the Rancheria (where the black slaves lived), the Tajamar (built by the Jesuits as a water reservoir), the water mill and the church. This latter was started in 1659, and completed only in 1723, has a splendid baroque façade and a grand cupola, which is the only part which has been renovated. The rest is all now sadly a little dilapidated, but it's the only Jesuit church which still functions today as the parish church. It is open daily 0900-2000, but closed 1200 1300, and you can attend Mass.

Córdoban Sierras

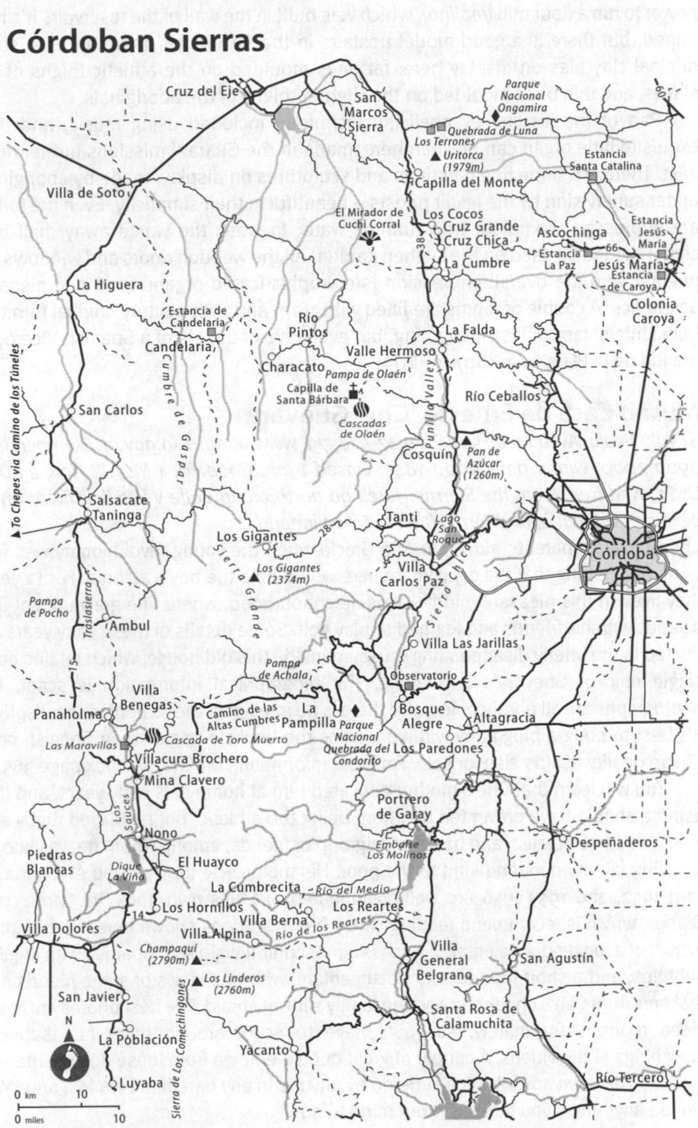

The Jesuits built their ambitious project in two stages: first they lived in an adobe building while the main house was constructed of brick. This first building then became the *herrería* (smithy), where iron was smelted with the aid of bellows, and workers made all the tools they needed for construction. There are impressive locks, keys and nails on display, testimony to their fine metal working skills. Just three Jesuit priests lived in the Residence, which was built on two floors around an enclosed patio; the lower floor was used only for storage. All the aboriginal workers lived outside the estancia, but 310 African slaves lived on the premises in the Ranchería. They were of great importance to the Jesuits, as they were used as overseers in the ranches, and did carpentry, brickwork, and blacksmithing. In the Obraje, African women and girls learned to spin and knit. The Jesuits built canals to bring water here to the Tajamar, a large reservoir outside the estancia, which supplied them with the power to run a flour mill (*molino*), which was built in the wall of the reservoir; it's now ruined, but there is a good model upstairs in the Residence. There are also some original clay tiles on display here: fat ones moulded on the athletic thighs of the slaves, and thin ones moulded on the slighter thighs of the aboriginals.

Part of the Jesuits' evangelizing technique included using music, and their exquisite little organ can be seen here, made in the Guaraní missions further north east. There are some fine paintings and sculptures on display, made by aboriginals under supervision by the Jesuit priests – beautiful in their simplicity. Even the toilets are impressive, complete with running water to wash the waste away, half of it channelled to be used on the kitchen garden. All the wooden doors and windows are original, and the overall impression is of sophisticated organization and pleasing aesthetics. A couple of rooms are filled with 18th- and 19th-century original furniture from Liniers' family, less interesting, but evocative of the life of a Spanish Viceroy of the Río de la Plata from 1807 to 1809.

Museo Casa de Ernesto 'Che' Guevara

ⓘ *Villa Nydia, Avellaneda 501, T03547-428579, www.altagracia.gov.ar. Summer daily 0900-2000; winter daily 0900-1845; closed 1 Jan, Good Fri, 1 May, 8 Nov, 25 Dec. US$1, Wed free. From the Sierras Hotel, go north along Calle Vélez Sarsfield, which becomes Quintana, and turn left on to C Avellaneda.*

Che Guevara's parents moved to Alta Gracia when the young revolutionary was four years old, hoping that the dry climate here would help the boy's asthma. For 12 years they lived in this pleasant middle-class neighbourhood, where Che grew up, got into scrapes with his friends and learned to play golf. Some details of these early years are related in the utterly disappointing museum inside this old house, which retains not a single relic of Guevara's upbringing. The biographical information is scant, the photographs are all photocopies, and there is no intelligent thesis behind the displays. It's best to bring a biography with you, since the books on sale are in Spanish only. Cheap quality t-shirts also for sale. For more information on Che, see box page 365.

You will learn that Che's mother educated him at home in is early years, and that asthma should have prevented him from being too athletic, but he played rugby and golf, was a keen cyclist, and had a wide group of friends, among whom he was known as being fair-minded, and kind to the poor. His motorcycle trips around Argentina, in 1951-1952, and 1953-1956 are well-documented in Che's own book *The Motorcycle Diaries*, which is recommend reading. There are two videos shown here, a ten minute extract of a longer documentary, which is almost unintelligible, in Spanish with English subtitles, and a short introductory documentary, with interviews of some friends and teachers from Che's childhood and the family's former maid. The best photos are in the video room, unfortunately, so you'll have to scoot around them fast between screenings of the videos. A couple of great quotes emerge from these documentaries: "Feel as your own any injustice suffered by anyone in any part of the world", and "You can do anything if you make up your mind to do it".

Graf Spee

The famous *Graf Spee* was a German 'pocket' battleship, successful because she was of cruiser size and speed, but with the fire power of a battleship. Early in World War II, in 1939, the *Graf Spee* sank nine merchant ships in the Atlantic before being cornered outside Uruguay on 13 December by three British cruisers. After the 14-hour Battle of the River Plate, in which one British ship was badly damaged, the *Graf Spee's* commander Captain Hans Langsdorff retreated into the neutral port of Montevideo, where he landed most of his crew, and the 36 dead German crewmen were buried. Langsdorff was granted just two days to repair his ship, by the Uruguayan government, under British pressure, and on 17 December, the *Graf Spee* sailed out to sea. Crowds lined the shore expecting to see another battle, but watched the vessel sink within minutes. All the remaining crew and 50 captured British seamen on board were rescued. Langsdorff has been trapped into believing that a superior British force was waiting for him over the horizon and Hitler had given him the order to scuttle the vessel rather than allow it to be captured. Two days later in Buenos Aires, Langsdorff wrapped himself in the flag of the Imperial German Navy and committed suicide.

Most of the crew were interned in Argentina and warmly welcomed by the German community of Buenos Aires, but British pressure forced the Argentine government to disperse them. In Mendoza, they were stoned by the locals and beaten up by the police. In Córdoba they were welcomed by the governor, while the German embassy tried to enforce military discipline and prevent the men from getting too friendly with local women.

In 1944, the US and British governments demanded the repatriation of all the men to Germany. Nearly 200 managed to avoid this by marrying Argentine women, and another 75 escaped: after six years in Argentina, many had no wish to return to a country shattered by defeat. German communities created a distinctive culture in many areas, no more so than Villa General Belgrano in Córdoba, with its German architecture, beer festival and superb chocolate and pasties, where many members of the *Graf Spee* crew made their homes.

Other sights

If you've time and energy for more museums, you might be interested in **Museo Manuel de Falla** ⓘ *Carlos Pellegrini 1100, T03547-429292, museofalla altagracia@yahoo.com, daily 0900-1900, free*, the charming home of the famous Spanish composer in the last four years of his life from 1942 to 1946. It's an attractive Spanish-style house with great views from its beautiful garden. There are concerts from April to November, and the **Festival de Falla** in November attracts some fine musicians.

There's an easy 5-km walk to **Los Paredones**, with the remains of a Jesuit mill in a rocky section of the river. To get there, follow Avenida Sarmiento to the west and cross the river, passing the bus station on your left. On the way is the **Gruta de Lourdes**, where, every 11 February, hundreds of pilgrims arrive on foot from Córdoba city. Nearby lies the **Laguna Azul**, a small lake surrounded by impressive cliffs. From Alta Gracia take Avenida Sarmiento, turn right at Vélez Sarsfield and left at Carlos Pellegrini until the end of the road, where you turn right and follow the road, passing Parque García Lorca on your left.

Some 21 km northwest of Alta Gracia is the **Observatorio Bosque Alegre** ⓘ *summer Tue-Sun 1000-1300, winter Fri-Sun 1000-1300, 1500-1800; remise US$5 plus waiting time*, built in 1942 for astrophysics research. At 1250 m, it offers good views over Alta Gracia, Córdoba and the Sierra Grande. Visits are guided by astronomers.

Villa General Belgrano

» pp187-190.

→ *Phone code: 03546 Colour map 4, A2 Population: 6500*

Imagine a German theme park, Disneyland-style, with bierkellers and chocolate shops, carved wooden signposts everywhere and cute Alpine architecture, and you get an idea of what the centre of Villa General Belgrano is like. It's a pretty mountain town, with leafy avenues and wonderful views of the sierras beyond, and although it's extremely touristy, it's a lovely place to spend a few days.

The town was founded in 1932 when two German immigrants bought land and sold it off through advertisements in the German newspapers, with the intention of starting a German colony. Its German character was boosted by the arrival of 155 sailors from the *Graf Spee* in 1939 (see box, page 185), many of whom later settled here. Plagues of locusts and heavy rainfall meant that the colony grew slowly at first, and so children from German schools in Buenos Aires were encouraged to come here for holidays, bringing the very first influx of tourists to the town. German is still spoken by older inhabitants, and the architecture along the main street, Avenida Julio Roca, is dominated by Swiss chalet-style buildings and German beer-houses. You can find genuine German smoked sausages and a wide variety of German breads, delicious Viennese cakes and locally brewed beer. You can even celebrate **Oktoberfest** from 12 October, when the town is packed with 12,000 tourists. This is not the best time of year to appreciate the town, but the **Viennese Pastry Festival** in Easter week and the **Alpine Chocolate Festival** during the July holidays, are certainly worth a visit. Book accommodation in advance at these times.

The town makes a great centre for hikes in the nearby hills, with plenty of places to stay and good restaurants. The souvenir shops along the main street are crammed with Tirolean hats, beer mugs and *Graf Spee* memorabilia, however there are also fine chocolates for sale and a handicrafts market near the small oval plaza on Sundays and in the holidays. Note that Calle Julio Roca changes its name to Calle San Martín at the oval plaza, half way along.

Ins and outs

To reach Villa General Belgrano from Alta Gracia, take the new faster route via Portrero de Garay. The **tourist office** ⓘ *Av Roca 168, T03546-461215, or free T125 from inside the town, www.vgb.org.ar, www.vgb.gov.ar, www.elsitiodelavilla.com, daily 0830-2030*, has friendly English- and German-speaking staff, who'll give you a great map, accommodation list and a free booklet with loads of tourist information.

Walks around Villa General Belgrano

There are plenty of walks in and around the town itself; a map is available from the tourist office, ask for directions before setting off. Two rivers run through the town, **La Toma** and **El Sauce,** and a lovely shaded area for walking has been created along their banks. You could also hike up the **Cerro de la Virgen** (one hour), the hill to the east of town. Start at Calle Ojo de Agua, 200 m east of Avenida Julio Roca. Walk along Calle Ojo del Agua, and turn right on the main road, Route 5, then left where signposted. It's a steep walk, but there are rewarding views. Alternatively, a lower and easier hike is up to **Cerro Mirador**, northeast of town. To get here, walk along Avenida las Magnolias, turn left on the main road and then right along Pozo Verde (one hour). From the top there are great views of the valley and the town. A recommended guide is Diego Chaliari, see Activities and tours for Villa General Belgrano, page 189.

La Cumbrecita and Sierra villages » p187-190.

→ *Phone code: 03546*

To get right into the mountain scenery, head west from Villa General Belgrano via the tiny hamlet of **Los Reartes** with its old chapel, to **La Cumbrecita**, a charming, Alpine-style village hidden away in the forested hills, where there are no cars (see Transport page 190). Although crowded in summer, life here is very tranquil indeed and if you visit during spring or autumn to walk in the surrounding mountains, you'll probably have them all to yourself. It's an excellent centre for trekking or horse riding, with walks from half a day to three days, including to **Cerro Champaquí**, though this peak is better accessed from Villa Alpina (see below). There are short walks to a 14-m high waterfall **La Cascada**, and to a small lake of cystralline water, **La Olla**, a natural pool with sandy beaches which is good for swimming. Longer walks or horse rides follow footpaths or 4WD vehicle tracks to the **Cerro Cristal**, the pools along **Río del Medio**, or for spectacular panoramic views, hike up **Cerro Wank** (1715 m), two hours' return. A footpath leads south to another quaint village, Villa Alpina, but it's a six-hour walk (return) and you should take a guide. You can also go horse riding, try rappelling, or explore the area with 4WDs. Many visitors in summer just come for the day, but there are plenty of places to stay and eat including *cabañas* for hire, and tasty food in chalet-style restaurants with lovely settings and great views.

There's a **tourist office** ⓘ *T03546-481088*, where staff can advise on walking guides and where to get information on riding and other activities. A useful website with information in English and German is www.lacumbrecita.info.

Villa Alpina and Cerro Champaquí

South of La Cumbrecita is another quaint mountain village, **Villa Alpina**, a small remote resort set in the forested upper valley of **Río de los Reartes**. On the map it looks close to La Cumbrecita, but there's no road connecting the two so the only direct way to get there is to walk, which takes three hours. By vehicle, you'll need to head back to pretty wooded Villa Berna, and from there it's 38 km west, along a poor gravel road.

Villa Alpina is the best base for the three-day trek to **Cerro Champaquí** (2790 m), 19 km from the village. It's possible to take a 4WD almost to the summit, but the longer walk is much more rewarding for the superb mountainous scenery and the chance to meet local inhabitants as you stop at the *puestos* on the way. You'll need an all-season sleeping bag to stay in the *puestos*, and be aware that it can snow even in summer. Take a local guide to avoid getting lost. Information is available from Villa General Belgrano tourist office (see page 186), or in La Cumbrecita (see above). A recommended guide is Diego Chaliari, see Activities and tours for Villa General Belgrano, page 189

There are more picturesque hilly landscapes with streams and falls close to **Yacanto de Calamuchita**, a village in the mountains, reached via Santa Rosa de Calamuchita, the largest town in this part of the valley, and a very popular, but drab resort. From Yacanto de Calamuchita you can drive almost to the summit of Cerro Champaquí, thanks to a dirt road climbing up to Cerro de los Linderos, leaving you with only a 40-minute walk. Regular minibuses go to Los Reartes, Villa Berna, La Cumbrecita, Villa Alpina, Santa Rosa and Yacanto de Calamuchita.

Sleeping

Alta Gracia *p182*

A El Potrerillo de Larreta, on the road to Los Paredones, 3 km from Alta Gracia, T03547-423804, www.potrerillodelarreta.com. Old-fashioned, fabulous 1918 resort and country club in gorgeous gardens with wonderful views. Tennis courts, 18-hole golf course, swimming pool, grand grounds. Great service.

A-B **Fincas del Virrey**, Las Rosas 970, near the golf course, T03547-423913, www.fincasdelvirrey.com.ar. Extremely smart self-catering houses, a bit sparse, but well-equipped, with lovely pool and TV, games for kids, and private gardens.
C **Solares del Alto**, Bv Pellegrini 797, T03547-429042, www.solaresdelalto.com. Modern and comfortable, this smart little hotel on the edge of the lovely residential district is recommended for its friendly bilingual staff, pool and spa (extra cost) and neat rooms with good bathrooms. **Leyendas** sports bar and café is part of the hotel, and serves good lunches and snacks.
D **Asturias**, Vélez Sarsfield 127, T03547-423668. Welcoming owners have clean but cramped rooms on a small building at the back of the old house; breakfast extra.
D **Hispania**, Vélez Sarsfield 57, T03547-426555. Run by a Spanish family, this old residence with neat garden offers very comfortable and spotless rooms with breakfast. Indulge yourself by sitting at the veranda enjoying a fine panoramic view of the sierras while trying some excellent tapas.
D **Savoy**, Av Sarmiento 418, T03547-15578263. This 1970s hotel has seen better days, but still has decent rooms, though rather noisy if on the street; breakfast extra.

Camping

Los Sauces, Parque Federico Garcia Lorca, northwest corner of town, T03547-420349/T15577786. The site goes down to a river. Lots of facilities including hot showers, food shop, restaurant, volleyball and pool, bike park.

La Cumbrecita *p187*

Lots of *cabañas*, ask in the tourist office.
B **Cumbrecita**, T03546-481026/T481052, hotelcumbrecita@cumbrecita.info. Charming chalet-style building with plain rooms, but lovely setting. Horse riding and fishing.
C **Cabañas Amancay**, by the car park at the town entrance, T03547-15482234, amancay@lacumbrecita.info. A cute chalet-style building where *alfajores* are made, also *cabañas*.
C **Cabañas de la Compañía**, call Débora or Marcelo Lancellotta T03564-481102, www.delacompania.com.ar. By far the nicest *cabañas* in town with great views of the river. These are beautifully designed, chic and spacious, with wood stoves and TVs.
C **Las Verbenas**, T03546-481008, lasverbenas@lacumbrecita.info. A traditional chalet hotel with a pretty pool, and welcoming service from its owners.
C **Solares Cumbrecita**, 2 blocks from the main street, contact the **Solares de Alto** in Alta Gracia (see page 188), T03547-429042, www.solaresdelalto.com. A lovely old Sierras hotel with pool and great views, modernized, also 4 apartments. Restaurant, spa, massage centre. Horse riding and hiking arranged.
D **El Ceibo**, T03546-481060, elceibo@lacumbrecita.info. Neat clean rooms for 2-4, near the entrance to the town, bathrooms, TV, great views, access to the river.

Villa General Belgrano *p186*

Endless *cabaña* complexes here, but book ahead in Jan, Feb, July and Easter.
A **Posada Chamonix**, 2 km out of town on the quiet road to Los Reartes, T03546-464230/T464231, www.chamonixposada.com.ar. This is a beautiful, chic chalet-style building with splendid views across the valley, attractive rooms, and luxurious accommodation, indoor and outdoor pools, tennis, spa,
B **Berna**, Vélez Sarsfield 86, T03546-461097, bernahotel@vgb.org.ar. Next to the bus station, this vast agency hotel is Swiss-owned, with good service, tidy rooms, ample breakfast and a large garden with a pool.
B **Bremen**, Cero Negro 173, T03546-461133, www.hotelbremen.com. Huge, chalet-style hotel with lots of amenities and attractive gardens with pool, tennis, and pretty rooms.
B **Edelweiss**, Ojo de Agua 295, T03546-461317, www.edelweissresort.com. Huge chalet-style place with pool, volley ball and tennis, dated decor, but everything you need.
C **Baviera**, El Quebracho 21, T03546-461476, www.bavierahotel.com. Just off Av San Martín, with a leafy garden and a large pool, this modern, family-orientated, motel-like place has an unbelievably kitsch Bavarian interior, but rooms are spotless and the hosts are very charming. The splendid breakfast includes homemade cakes and jams. Fabulous.
C **La Posada de Akasha**, Los Manantiales 60, T03546-462440, www.elsitiodelavilla.com/akasha. Extremely comfortable, spotless chalet-style house with small pool and welcoming owners.
G pp **El Rincón**, Fleming 347, T03546-461323, www.calamuchitanet.com.ar/

elrincon. The only hostel in town is beautifully set in hills with dense forests and green spaces. Welcoming owners offer dormitories, very good double or single rooms with bath for US$50 and camping (US$3 pp). US$1 extra either for bed linen or superb breakfasts. Meals for US$4 on request. 20% ISIC and HI discounts available, half price for children under 16. 10 min-walk from bus terminal. Recommended.

Eating

Alta Gracia *p182*

Morena, Av Sarmiento 413, T03547-426365. Excellent menu of imaginative contemporary Argentine cuisine in the welcoming atmosphere of an old house. Recommended. Also delivers.

Alta Gracia Golf Club, Av Carlos Pellegrini 1000, T03547-422922. Superb food in elegant surroundings in this charming neighbourhood golf club, with the added advantage that you can watch the machinations of small town upper echelons social life unfold around you. Recommended.

Betos, Av del Libertador 917, T03547-430996. Great value *parrilla*, plus pizzas, *empanadas* and snacks, as-much-as-you-can-eat deals including drinks and dessert.

Hispania, Urquiza 90. Excellent restaurant serving fish and seafood, including paella and *fidebua*, with sangría and occasionally gazpacho. Desserts, such as *crema catalana* are fabulous.

Leyendas, Bv Pellegrini 797, T03547-429042. This American-style sport-inspired bar has cosy nooks to sit in, and really good hamburgers and snacks. A buzzing atmosphere, with friendly welcoming staff. Recommended.

Villa General Belgrano *p186*

Bierkeller, Av Las Magnolias and RN 5, T03546-461425. Look for the giant beer bottle outside. A chalet- style building with a welcoming family feel. Goulash and spatzle recommended, trout too. Slow service but the staff wear jolly Tirolean outfits. Recommended.

Blumenhaus, Roca and Bolivia, where Roca divides, T03546-462568. Touristy but with nice gardens. Pretty place to sit outside.

El Clervo Rojo, Av Julio Roca 210, T03546-461345. This unmissable Alpine-style building on the main street is the most typical German beer house in town, with a Tirolean band playing on Sat and dancing. Lots of typical German food.

El Viejo Munich, Av San Martín 362, T03546-463122, www.cervezaartesanal.com. The first brewery in the town, serving superb beer. There are 9 different kinds of the stuff on draft (ask for 'Chopp') and legendary cold cuts of meat (*fiambres*), superb smoked meats, hams and trouts, in charming rustic Bavarian-style interiors. Recommended.

La Casa de Dina, Los Incas 463, T03546-461104. Superb cakes and fondues in this cheery and welcoming place.

La Posta del Arroyo, Ojo de Agua 174, T03546-461767. Smart *parrilla* that also serves such delicacies as kid and frogs. Good pastas, welcoming atmosphere.

Ottilia, Av San Martín y Strauss. A traditional cosy Austrian tea room. Delicious apfelstrudel and kirschtorte.

Activities and tours

Alta Gracia *p182*

Golf Alta Gracia Golf Club, T03547-422922, www.aggc.com.ar. Beautifully landscaped 9-hole golf course, with a fine restaurant (see under Eating).

Paragliding Fly Experience, T0351-156315016, flyexperience@argentina.com. Daily flights in tandem over the valley, US$20 for 2 people.

Villa General Belgrano *p186*

Aero Club, Av Jorge Newbery, T03546-462502. Short flights over the valley, US$20 for 2 people.

DAPA, Av Roca 76, T03546-463417, dapaturismo@calamuchitanet.com.ar. Day trips to La Cumbrecita and guided walks in the surroundings for US$7 pp; Cerro Champaquí in 4WD and a 40-min walk to the summit for US$13 pp; to El Durazno or San Miguel de los Ríos for US$7 pp.

Diego Caliari, T03546-461510/ T15475576, mlturismo@yahoo.com.ar. An excellent, trained, friendly young guide who has worked extensively in Traslasierra, and who can take you hiking up Champaquí or on other walks, or arrange horse riding trips in the area.

Friedrich, Av Roca 224, T03546-461372, www.elsitiodelavilla.com/excursiones.

Reliable company offering adventure tourism, 4WD hire and day trips to La Cumbrecita or Yacanto de Calamuchita. Also a 10-hr walk across Sierras Chicas along Camino de los Chilenos.

Peperinatur, Julio Roca 235, T03546-461800, peperinatur@vgb.org.ar. Great company organizing trekking to Champaquí, Traslasierra and trips in 4WD.

Transport

Alta Gracia *p182*

Bus Terminal some 10 blocks from the centre on the river at Butori and Perón 1977, T03547- 427000. For **Villa General Belgrano** and other towns in Calamuchita valley, buses also stop at El Crucero roundabout, a 30-min walk from centre. To **Córdoba**, buses leave every 15 mins with one of the following: Empresa La Serranita T03547- 420369, Sarmiento T03547-426001, Sierras de Calamuchita T0351-4226080 (from El Crucero), 1 hr, US$1.20. To **Villa Carlos Paz**, Sarmiento, 1 hr, US$1.50. To **Villa General Belgrano**, Sierras de Calamuchita 1 hr, US$2.50. To **Buenos Aires**, Chevallier, T03547-425585), Valle de Calamuchita, Sierras Cordobesas, TUS, T03547-429370, 10-11 hrs, US$20.

Car hire Rodar Rent a car, T03547-15579927, www.autosrodar.com.ar.

Villa General Belgrano *p186*

Bus To/from **Córdoba**, Pájaro Blanco, La Villa, Lep, Sierras de Calamuchita, 1½-2hrs, US$5. To **Buenos Aires**, Chevallier, Valle de Calamuchita, Sierras Cordobesas, TUS, 10-11 hrs, US$20. To **La Cumbrecita**, Pájaro Blanco, every 2-4 hrs, 1½ hrs, US$5.50 return. Pájaro Blanco, (office at Av San Martín 105, T03546-461709) also goes to the nearby villages of **Los Reartes**, **Villa Berna**, **Villa Alpina** and **Yacanto de Calamuchita**.

Car and mountain bike hire

Friedrich, see under Tour operators. Fly Machine, Av Roca 50, T03546-462425.

Remise taxi

Central de Remises, Av Roca 95, T03546-462000.

La Cumbrecita *p187*

Bus There's a reliable daily bus service to **Córdoba city** (2½ hrs) or from **Villa General Belgano** (1½ hrs).

Traslasierra Valley

→ *For further information, try www.traslasierramix.com.ar*

Situated west of the Sierra Grande, Traslasierra (literally, 'across the mountains') is far less developed for tourism than neighbouring valleys, but ideal for those looking for an adventure. With its drier climate and generally slower pace of life, it's also a perfect place to relax for a few days. It can either be accessed from Córdoba city by the camino de las Altas Cumbres from the north, via the long but not uninteresting Route 15 across the pampa de Pocho, or from the south, via Villa Dolores into San Luis province. ▸▸ *For Sleeping, Eating and other listings, see pages 193-194.*

Camino de las Altas Cumbres ▸▸ *pp193-194.*

→ *Phone code: 03544*

The first town you reach, Mina Clavero, is probably too busy if you've come to escape the crowds, but further south, Nono and Los Hornillos are far more appealing. They and San Javier, even further south, both make a great base for hiking. The main road to the Traslasierra valley from Córdoba is the most spectacular route in the Sierras. Running southwest from Villa Carlos Paz, the road passes Villa Icho Cruz before climbing into the Sierra Grande and crossing the Pampa de Achala, a huge granite plateau at 2000 m, and descending into the Traslasierra valley near Mina Clavero.

Mina Clavero → *Phone code: 03544 Colour map 4, A2 Population: 6,800*

Mina Clavero (915 m) has the best nightlife and most raucous atmosphere in the entire valley, with nightclubs, theatres, a casino and dozens of hotels, restaurants and small shops. Though not the most appealing place in high season, it's a good base for trips into the surrounding natural beauty. It lies at the foot of the **Camino de las Altas Cumbres** and at the confluence of the Río Panaholma and Río Mina Clavero, which form many small falls among impressive rocks right in the town centre, and there are attractive views along the riverside. The large **tourist office** ⓘ *next to the intersection of Av San Martín and Av Mitre, T03544-470171, mclavero.turismo@traslasierra.com, daily 0900 until very late,* has an ATM.

On the other side of the rivers is the quieter **Villa Cura Brochero**, named after Father Brochero who built schools, roads and aqueducts here at the end of the 19th century. Every March, around the 20th, he is remembered with the *Cabalgatas brocherianas*, a gaucho procession on horses and mules that follows a section of the former road he helped to build across the mountains.

Around Mina Clavero

Nearby rivers offer several attractive places for swimming among huge rocks and waterfalls, all busy in high season. About 5 km north of Villa Cura Brochero, a dirt road passing San Lorenzo branches east to the **Cascada de Toro Muerto**, where icy water falls into a 7-m-deep pool. The *balneario* (bathing area) serves very good meals.

Las Maravillas, a *balneario* set in a deep ravine, is 4 km north of San Lorenzo, and it's another 7 km to the hamlet of Panaholma with its old chapel. The **Camino de los Artesanos** is an 18-km stretch of road from Mina Clavero to Villa Benegas along which a dozen families offer hand-woven handicrafts and distinctive black ceramics.

North of Villa Cura Brochero, Route 15 crosses the vast **Pampa de Pocho**, a strange landscape covered by palm trees, with small inactive volcanoes in the background. At Taninga, Route 28 branches off east across the Sierra Grande and the northern edge of Reserva Hídrica Pampa de Achala to Villa Carlos Paz.

Nono and around → *Phone code: 03544 Colour map 4, A2 Altitude 900 m*

Nono, 8 km south of Mina Clavero, is an attractive little town, so far unspoilt by increasing tourism. On the plaza there is a handicraft market in summer and a lovely little church. Among other well-conserved houses is the historic **Casa Uez**, which serves as a shop, café and basic hotel and has been the lively meeting point for locals since 1931. **Traslasierra Tur** runs an excellent **tourist office** ⓘ *T03544-498310, www.traslasierra-info.com.ar, daily 0900-1500, 1600-2200*, at a wood cabin next to the petrol station, with internet facilities. The most visited sight is the extraordinary **Museo Rocsen** ⓘ *5 km east, following Av Los Porteños, T03544- 498218, www.museorocsen.org, daily 0900 till sunset, US$1, US$1.30 by taxi*. This eclectic selection of fabulously bizarre objects spanning archaeology, anthropology and human history is the personal vision of Frenchman Juan Santiago Bouchon. Not to be missed.

A network of minor roads east and southeast link the town with the foot of the mountains across a pretty landscape of rivers and hamlets, such as **Paso de las Tropas** and **El Huayco**. To the west, a dusty road leads from the church to the sandy beaches of **Río Los Sauces** and 11 km beyond to the village of **Piedras Blancas**. Cerro Champaquí is accessible from Nono (via San Javier) but you need to take a guide.

Los Hornillos and around → *Phone code: 03544*

South of Nono, Route 14 skirts the base of some imposing mountains amid lush vegetation and there are scattered villages offering some accommodation. At Los Hornillos (15 km from Nono) there are good walks 500m east of the road (left of camp site), along Río Los Hornillos. From there, footpaths lead to the nearby summits, such as the five-hour trek to **La Ventana** (2300 m) passing a 50m fall halfway. A 1½-hour

Parque Nacional Quebrada del Condorito

Covering 37,000 ha of the Pampa de Achala and the surrounding slopes at altitudes of between 1900 and 2300 m, the park was created in 1996 to protect the central section of Córdoba's sierras, including the spectacular Quebrada del Condorito. This 800-m deep gorge is the easternmost habitat of the condor. Since you're at the same level as the top of the gorge, it's possible to see fledgling birds taking their first flying lessons. Though condors are elusive and sightings are not guaranteed, you may be lucky enough to see them take a bath under the waterfalls. It takes about three hours to get to the first vantage point – Balcón Norte – and two more hours to the Balcón Sur, by crossing the Río de los Condoritos. Tours are available from Villa Carlos Paz. There's great trekking on the pastizal de altura (high altitude grassland) which is the furthest south that rare tabaquillo trees can be found. The only accessible section of the park is its northeast corner, reached by a short walk from La Pampilla (well signposted), on Route 34, 55 km southwest of Villa Carlos Paz. The landscapes are superb. The climate is warm sub-tropical but take a warm jacket.

Park information Ciudad de Córdoba and TAC buses will both stop at La Pampilla on their way from Villa Carlos Paz to Mina Clavero, 1 hr, US$1.90. If you go with your own vehicle, park it at the NGO Fundación Cóndor (9 km before La Pampilla), beside the handicraft shop (1 km before La Pampilla) or at El Cóndor (7 km after La Pampilla). There are three camping areas with no facilities, along the path to Balcón Norte and Balcón Sur. There's a national park administration office in Villa Carlos Paz at Sabattini 33, office 2, T03541-433371. For an excellent guide for trekking and horse riding, contact Diego Caliari T03546- 461510, mlturismo@yahoo.com.ar.

walk upstream along the riverbed takes you to **Piedra Encajada**, a huge rock supported by two other blocks with waterfalls. At **Los Hornillos**, the Von Ledebur family has run the lovely hotel **Alta Montaña**, since 1947, see Sleeping page 193. Ten kilometres northwest is **Dique La Viña** with a large reservoir and an impressive 106-m-high dam, not recommended for vertigo sufferers.

West of the sierras the main town is **Villa Dolores**, a useful transport hub, with a couple of banks and a few hotels, though there's no reason to stop here, unless you're keen to see the potato festival in January. There's an informative **tourist office** ⓘ *T03544-423023*, at the bus station.

San Javier and Yacanto → *Phone code: 03544*

These two neighbouring villages lie at the foot of the **Cerro Champaquí** (2790 m) the highest peak in the sierras. They are both very pleasant, peaceful places to stay, with old houses under mature trees, and even if not keen to climb the peak itself, you could relax by the streams or stroll around the picturesque area. The ascent up the Champaquí takes about seven hours from San Javier along the Quebrada del Tigre, but take a guide, as many people get lost. For more information, contact the Municipalidad, T03544-482041.

Further south there are more small resort towns where tourism is developing, such as **La Población, Luyaba, La Paz** and nearby **Loma Bola**, which lie along the road to Merlo, 42 km of San Javier. All these towns are linked by regular TAC buses services, which run between Villa Dolores and Merlo (via San Javier).

Sleeping

Mina Clavero *p191*

There are over 70 hotels in Mina Clavero and Villa Cura Brochero, though many are closed in the off season.

D Abuelo Juan, Los Pinos 1919 (take Calle Bolívar to the west from Av Mitre), T03544-470562. In a leafy residential area south of town, next to the amphitheatre. Run by artists, there is a large garden with a pool and 8 spotless, cosy rooms with a large breakfast. It is oriented to guests with no kids. Recommended.

Remnants from better days, 2 central hotels have retained their distinctive character and decent rooms with bath and breakfast: **D Porteño**, Av San Martín 1441, T03544-470235, and **E Oviedo**, Av San Martín 1500, T03544-15571719.

Camping

Several sites in Mina Clavero, but better to go to the less crowded Villa Cura Brochero.

Nono and around *p191*

Several family houses next to the plaza have signs offering rooms for rent by the day.

A Gran Hotel Nono, Vicente Castro 289, T03544-498022, www.granhotelnono.com.ar. On the riverside with views of the sierras and surrounded by a large and leafy park with a pool and tennis courts, this is a very comfortable and welcoming place, with attractive rustic decor. It has a restaurant and breakfast is included with lots of fruit. Rates are for half-board accommodation.

B La Gloria, on the way to Museo Rocsen, 800 m from Calle Sarmiento, T03544-498231, www.hostal-lagloria.com.ar. On the rural outskirts set in 5 ha of park, this old house has comfortable though not luxurious rooms in a relaxed atmosphere. It has a pool and access to the river. Delicious breakfast included.

E Lo de Teresita López, Sarmiento 216 (no sign, just knock), T03544-498030. A welcoming former head teacher offers several comfortable rooms and kitchen in her home, whose garden has a beautiful view of the sierras. Recommended.

Camping

A road to the left of the church goes west to the river where are 3 sites, of which **Los Canadienses**, T03544-498259, is the best choice. A well-kept shady place with clean bathrooms and electricity supply; no pets or large groups allowed. Open high season only. From US$5 a day per tent.

Los Hornillos *p191*

D pp **Alta Montaña**, 300 m east of route (signposted), T03544-499009 (in Buenos Aires, T011-4768 5075), www.hosteria altamontania.com. Neat, comfortable rooms and splendid views from the grounds to the sierras. It also has a pool, a restaurant and 8 ha of virgin land by the river. Rates are for half board accommodation; 50% discount for children under 7. Recommended.

Parque Nacional Quebrada del Condorito *p192*

A La Posta del Qenti, 19 km west of La Pampilla, T03544-426450, www.lapostadel qenti.com.ar. A pricey but comfortable resort at 2300 m offering rooms and dormitory accommodation together with outdoor activities. Book in advance, and ask about full-board promotional offers.

San Javier and Yacanto *p192*

B San Javier, T03544-482006, www.hosteria sanjavier.com.ar. Lovely gardens, a pool and good rooms with a large breakfast. Several excursions can be arranged.

B Yacanto, T03544-482002, www.hotelya canto.com.ar. A traditional 1920s hotel with comfortable rooms and a beautifully situated 9-hole golf course. In low season there is only half board accommodation.

Eating

Mina Clavero *p191*

Rincón Suizo, down by the river, on Calle Recalde, 1 block off Av San Martín. This is an unmissable treat. While it's basically a cosy tea room serving rich strudel or chocolate cakes, if you book in advance, you can be served delicious French meals such as coq au vin.

Nono and around *p191*

La Casona de Nono, Sarmiento 302. Less attractive, but offers *pollo al disco* (grilled chicken) and *humita* as its specialities.

🍴 **La Pulpería de Gonzalo**, on the plaza, opposite the church. Alfresco dining in the wonderful, romantically lit patio. *Parrilla* dishes are the speciality, but fish is also recommended.

Activities and tours

Mina Clavero *p191*
Short half-day trips to the surrounding area cost about US$4-5 pp and the longer Camino de los Túneles costs US$7 pp.
Andar, T03544-471426, andar@arnet.com.ar.
Conocer, behind bus station, T03544-472539.

Nono and around *p191*
Camp Aventura, T0351-156535014. An old lorry is used for weekend short trips to the surroundings of Dique La Viña, leaving from 1 block east of plaza.
Traslahuella, Vicente Castro 210, T03544-498084/T15610621, traslahuella@yahoo.com.ar. Local guide Martín Zalazar runs half-day guided treks and mountain bike tours along the river and to the nearby mountains for US$5-8 pp. Also available is a day walk to the summit of Cerro Champaquí for US$20 pp with a meal included.

Transport

Mina Clavero *p191*
Bus Terminal in centre at Av Mitre 1191. To **Córdoba**, Ciudad de Córdoba (via Altas Cumbres), 3 hrs, US$4, (via Cruz del Eje), 6 hrs, US$6 and TAC (stopping at villages in **Pampa de Pocho**), 6 hrs, US$5; to **Buenos Aires**, Chevallier, Expreso del Oeste, TAC, 12 hrs, US$17; to **Mendoza**, Andesmar, 9 hrs, US$11; to **Merlo**, Expreso del Oeste, Monticas, 2 hrs, US$3. Minibuses Expreso Mina Clavero goes to **Villa Cura Brochero** and south to **Nono** and **Villa Dolores**, calling at villages in between. Panaholma and Sierra Bus go direct to **Villa Dolores** (45 mins, US$1) and **Córdoba** (3 hrs, US$4).

Mountain bike hire Available at Urquiza 1318, US$4 per day.

Remise taxis Servicar, T03544-471738. Valle, T03544-472145.

Around Mina Clavero *p191*
Bus TAC buses go to **Panaholma** and some villages in the **Pampa de Pocho**. Other nearby places are only accessible with own vehicle or with a *remise* taxi (eg to **Toro Muerto** US$10; to **Villa Benegas** US$9). No buses go along the Camino de los Túneles, only tour operators.

Nono and around *p191*
Bus Expreso Mina Clavero going to **Villa Dolores** (50 mins, US$0.90) or up to **Villa Cura Brochero** (15 mins, US$0.45) runs the only bus and minibus services that stops hourly at Nono centre (stop on Calle Sarmiento next to tcol for both directions). Other companies stop on route.

Mountain bike hire From Traslahuella (see Activities and tours), US$4.50 per day.

Remise taxis Tele Taxi, Sarmiento 94, T03544-498115.

Los Hornillos *p191*
Bus Expreso Mina Clavero stops at Los Hornillos on its way between **Villa Dolores** and **Villa Cura Brochero**.

San Luis province

The province of San Luis has always been considered Córdoba's poorer sister: it's further from Buenos Aires, lacking a grand city centre and is not popular with tourists, apart from the over-visited resort town of Merlo on the border. However, there's a spectacular national park, Sierra de las Quijadas, with a great red sandstone canyon and fossil-strewn lunar landscape and you can still find remote places where rural life is sleepy and traditional. ▸▸ *For Sleeping, Eating and other listings, see pages 197-200.*

San Luis city » pp197-200.

→ *Phone code: 02652 Colour map 4, B2 Population: 162,000*

The city of San Luis was founded in 1594, but it wasn't until the late 19th century that it really started to grow, with a flood of European immigration. There was further development in the 1980s when tax incentives encouraged industry to the area. The result is a modern city with a few colonial buildings, but little to attract visitors. However, it is a friendly place with decent accommodation and food, and is a good starting point for exploring the Sierras de San Luis and the Parque Nacional Sierra de las Quijadas.

Sights

The centre of the city is the attractive, leafy **Plaza Pringles**, filled with beautiful jacarandas and palm trees and thronging with young crowds after sunset. It's worth popping into the **cathedral** ⓘ *daily 1000-1300, 1830-2000, US$1*, with its slender towers and sumptuous interior, to see replicas of famous Murillo paintings and an extraordinary *pesebre electrónico* – a personal vision of the birth of Christ, with moving figures to the accompaniment of Beethoven's *Ninth Symphony* and Scottish pipes; kitsch and marvellous. Northwest of the plaza, there's a magnificent, decaying former railway station. At the corner of Avenida Illía and Junín the large **tourist office** ⓘ *T02652-423479, www.turismoensanluis.gov.ar*, has little information.

For hotels and bars, stroll along Avenida Illia, which becomes very lively at night. There's a tiny **Museo de Historia Natural** ⓘ *university campus, Italia y Ejército de los Andes, T02652-423917 (ext 43); Tue, Wed, Sat, Sun and bank holidays 0900-1300, Thu-Fri 1330-1730; US$0.35*, which traces the evolution of San Luis, including the fossil of an alarming giant spider and a dinosaur footprint. The main commercial heart of the city is on Rivadavia, and three blocks away there's the quieter Plaza Independencia, with its extraordinary Moorish Dominican temple, with a Moorish façade. You can see rugs being woven at the **Centro Artesanal San Martín de Porres** ⓘ *25 de Mayo 955, T02652-424222, Mon-Fri 0800-1300.*

Sierras de San Luis » pp197-200.

Northeast of the city of San Luis, there's a beautiful range of hills which remains little known to travellers, and where there are just two frequently visited resorts, the small town of El Trapiche and the reservoir in La Florida. The rest of this vast hilly region is sparsely inhabited, with quiet villages which maintain old rural traditions and a simple way of life. The eastern edge of the sierras and the upper valleys and high pampas around Carolina, can be visited by taking Route 9 north from San Luis. Regular buses go up to Carolina and Intihuasi.

El Trapiche → *Phone code: 02651. Altitude 1050 m*

At Km 40, El Trapiche is an attractive village set on the Río Trapiche in wooded hills. There are summer homes, hotels and picnic sites and some good easy walks to **Los Siete Cajones** on the sparkling waters of Río Grande and 6 km west, to pleasant surroundings of rivers **Virorco** and **De las Aguilas**.

Carolina → *Phone code: 02651 Population: 200 Colour map 4, A2*

Carolina is a former gold-mining town founded in 1792 at the foot of Cerro Tomolasta (2018 m) which offers great views from its summit. It's a picturesque village with stone houses and a goldmine, which can be visited through San Luis tour operators (see page 199). The local **Huellas** agency, T02651-490224, huellashuellas@hotmail.com, dresses you up as a miner and guides you along 300 m tunnel for about 1½ hours

Parque Nacional Sierra de Las Quijadas → *Phone code: 02652*

Situated 125 km northwest of San Luis in the northwestern corner of the province, the park covers 150,000 ha of wonderful scenery, in one of the hottest and most arid areas of Argentina. Its only accessible area, **Potrero de la Aguada**, is an immense natural amphitheatre of nearly 4000 ha surrounded by steep red sandstone walls, eroded into strange shapes. There's a small archaeological site next to the access road, and the fossil-rich field of Loma del Pterodaustro shows intriguing evidence of dinosaurs and pterosaurs (winged reptiles). The vegetation is largely scrub, and *jarillas* are very common though there are trees such as the *quebracho blanco*. Wildlife includes guanaco, collared peccaries, pumas, tortoises, crowned eagles, peregrine falcons and condors.

Near the park warden's office is **Mirador de Elda**, the first of the two vantage points on the Potrero. From here two optional footpaths go to **Mirador Superior** (an easy 45-minute return) or down to the *huella* (a more demanding two-hour return walk to a dinosaur footprint). This path also leads to the impressive cliffs of **Farallones**, reached by a five-hour return walk and only advisable well after midday.

Ins and outs

Open from dawn till dusk. Visit early in the morning or late afternoon for the best views and to avoid the heat. T02652-490182, www.parquesnacionales.gov.ar. To get there, take the 6-km unpaved road that turns off from Route 147 (San Luis to San Juan) at Hualtarán. Only two bus companies with very few daily services link San Luis and San Juan (Autotransportes San Juan and Del Sur y Media Agua) and stop at Hualtarán, US$3 and US$2, respectively. Tour operators in San Luis and Merlo run half or full day tours to the park. Entry costs US$4. Accommodation is available at **Complejo La Aguada**, T02652-15650245, www.laaguada.com. The only site for camping (free) is 100 m from the park warden's office next to a basic canteen. Visit early in the morning or late in the afternoon for better views and to avoid the heat.

(English spoken), and provides tools in case you suddenly feel the desire to dig. From Carolina a rough track leads north over the Cuesta Larga to San Francisco del Monte de Oro, on Route 146. Two other roads in better condition cross attractive scenery of undulating pampas and volcanic peaks to Libertador General San Martín or to La Toma. **Tourist information** is available in the Municipalidad ⓘ *16 de Julio s/n, T02651-490214, www.slcarolina.com.ar.*

Eastern San Luis » *pp197-200.*

Villa Mercedes → *Phone code: 02657 Colour map 4, B2 Population: 90,000*

Founded in 1856 as a fortress, Villa Mercedes is an important route centre and an alternative transport hub, though of little of interest to the tourist. It lies on Route 7, 100 km southeast of San Luis. Accommodation is mainly found along Avenida Mitre (six blocks east of the bus terminal). The bus terminal, T02657 -428035 and **tourist office** are both at Avenida 25 de Mayo 1500. Villa Mercedes is also the gateway to the southern plains with dozens of small lakes, attractive for anglers. *Pejerrey* is the main catch and the fishing season runs from November to August. Accommodation is available offered at local estancias (ask at tourist office).

Conlara Valley → *Phone code: 02656 Population: 90,000*

Lying east of the Sierra de San Luis and west of the Sierra de Comechingones, this broad valley runs into the Traslasierra Valley to the north, with a number of attractive places to visit and stay. **San José del Morro**, has an 18th-century chapel in its blissful traditional village. Nearby, the **Sierra del Morro** (1639 m), is the remains of a collapsed volcano; inside its crater are small volcanic cones, and lots of rose-quartz can be found here (access through Estancia La Morena). On 3 May, at tiny **Renca**, one of the most popular religious festivities in the region, **El Señor de Renca**, is celebrated. **Santa Rosa del Conlara** is a pleasant small town by a river, a good alternative for accommodation when Merlo is packed (reached by bus or *combi* from San Luis). A more scenic journey is via Provincial Route 1, which runs parallel to the east of Route 148 along the base of the Sierra de Comechingones through a string of pretty villages: **Papagayos**, surrounded by natural palm tree groves of '*Trithrinax campestris*'; **Villa Larca**, where the waterfall **Chorro de San Ignacio** and upper natural pools offer lovely walks; **Cortaderas**; **Carpintería** and up to the well-promoted Merlo.

Merlo → *Phone code: 02656 Colour map 4, A2 Population: 11,000 Altitude 895 m*

Situated almost at the San Luis-Córdoba border, Merlo is a popular holiday centre on the steep western slopes of the Sierra de Comechingones. It has lost much of its charm in recent years, due to mass tourism which has made it busy and overpriced. It claims to have a special microclimate, and sunny days can certainly be enjoyed throughout the year. The town was founded in 1797, but the **church** on the plaza, said to be of Jesuit origin, dates from the early 18th-century, and is soon to be replaced by the huge new redbrick church behind. There's a brand new airport and bus terminal and two **tourist offices**: ⓘ *at the busy roundabout on R5 and R1; and next to the plaza at Coronel Mercau 605, 0800-2000 (closing at 2200 in summer), T02656-476079, www.lavillademerlo.com.ar, www.merlo-online.com.ar.*

Merlo's surroundings are still pleasant for walking at the foot of the mountains or to their summits (the **Circuito de Damiana Vega** takes three to four hours). The slopes are covered with woods and scrub and there are numerous refreshing streams with falls. Higher up there are some are excellent sites for paragliding; an experienced pilot recently reached heights of 5000 m. A paved road (15 km long) leads to the top of the sierras at **Mirador del Sol**, where there are wonderful panoramic views, best at sunrise or sunset. The mirador is accessible by bus and is the starting point for a rough track leading across 82 km of pampas and sierras de Córdoba to Embalse del Río Tercero.

Quieter places to stay are spread in the neighbouring small settlements of **Piedra Blanca** (4 km north) or **Rincón del Este** (4 km east), but book ahead in high season.

Sleeping

San Luis city *p195*

C Gran Hotel San Luis, Av Illia 470, T02652-425049, hotelsanluis@hotmail.com. 3-star hotel with traditional decor. Good pool, breakfast.

D Aiello, Av Illia 431, T02652-425609, www.hotelaiello.com. Best value in town: good rooms with a/c, welcoming staff, breakfast included, good pool; internet access.

D Grand Palace, Rivadavia 657, T02652-422059. Lively atmosphere and friendly staff. Rooms are not spectacular but have attractive parquet floors and some have a/c. Breakfast included, and there is a good restaurant at the back.

E Belgrano, Belgrano 1440, T02652-435923. This is probably the best budget option with welcoming staff, renovated rooms with fan and bath and breakfast included.

Around San Luis

There are a few camp sites in El Volcán on the river bank (20 km from San Luis).

C Campo La Sierra, 19 km east of San Luis (access via R20), T02652-494171, www.campolasierra.com.ar. A warm welcome at this Swiss-owned 70-ha farm with native flora (cacti experts visit annually). German-style cooking, breakfast, pool and archery.

C Hotel Potrero de los Funes, R18, Km 16, T02652-440038/T02652-423898, hpfreser@sanluis.gov.ar. Set in a mountainous area, this lakeside resort offers affordable rooms, some with splendid views (slightly pricier). A pool and sport facilities are included (also ATM), as well as a large breakfast.
C Los Tamarindos, Balde, T02652-442220. Rates at this attractive spa resort include breakfast and rooms with a/c in small flats for up to 6; there are both indoor and outdoor pools accessible to non-guests for US$3 pp. Also cabins with a/c where you can rest after the baths for US$4/hr.

El Trapiche *p195*
D Villa Alinor, T02652-493038. Price is per house. A group of small houses at the most attractive location on a natural rocky balcony next to the river. Each house sleeps 4-6 with kitchen, fridge and phone; bed linen and towels extra. Delightful. Recommended.
F pp **El Parqu**, T02651-493176. A family-orientated hotel with full or half board accommodation; children under 5 free.
F pp **La Adolfina**, next to the school, T02651-493009. A decent place to stay with leafy gardens, a pool and clean rooms, breakfast included. Open only in summer.

Camping
At the north end of town, to the right side of the bridge. Nearby is the La Florida reservoir which offers good fishing, accessible via a paved road encircling the lake. On its northern shore there is a small natural reserve, intended to preserve the original flora and wildlife.

Carolina *p195*
D pp **Hostería Las Verbenas**, 10 km south of Carolina, T02652-15669797, www.lasverbenas.com.ar. Situated in the beautiful Pancanta Valley, this is an ideal base for walking and horse riding or for enjoying a relaxing stay. Price is for full board.
D La Posta del Caminante, RP 9, Km.83, T02651-490223, www.lapostadelcaminante.com.ar. Housed in a former residence for mining engineers. Offers comfortable rooms with bath and breakfast (cheaper with shared bath), pool in natural setting, and has a small restaurant next door; walks to the mines and horse-riding excursions are also arranged.

Conlara Valley *p197*
E Cerro Blanco, T02656-492012. Next to a nicely-maintained *balneario*, where the river was dammed, this place has clean and comfortable rooms; with breakfast.

Merlo *p197*
Book in advance for high season: Jan and Feb, Easter, Jul and Aug. Dozens of recently opened places all with garden and pool, varying only in size and quality of service. Prices rise 10-20% in high season.
B Villa de Merlo, Pedernera y Av del Sol, T02656-475335. Comfortable rooms with splendid views of the sierras, and a large garden with pool. There are sport facilities, though the quiet atmosphere of this rather exclusive 3-star hotel is more appealing for a relaxing holiday. Moderately priced restaurant.
D Colonial, Av Dos Venados y P Tisera, T02656-475388, hotelcolonial@hotmail.com. Probably the best value, in a quiet residential area not far from the centre. An attractive neo-colonial building has simple rooms on a patio with an incredibly small pool. Breakfast is included, internet access (not free).

Camping
Las Violetas, Chumamaya y Av Dos Venados, T02656-475730, lasvioletas@merlo-sl.com.ar. The closest site to centre has a small shady area for tents, pool, canteen, grocery and clean but not spotless bathrooms. US$4 per campsite plus US$0.35 per day.

Eating

San Luis city *p195*
Chivito (kid) is the main local dish. Its usual accompaniment is *chanfaina* (a stew whose main ingredients are the goat's entrails).
La Porteña, Junín y General Paz, T02652-431722. Simple meals such as the *plato del día* and prepare for enormous portions in the enjoyable atmosphere of this popular place.
Crocantes, San Martín 630. A bakery where cheap and superb sandwiches are prepared at your request and with your chosen bread.
Grand Palace, Rivadavia 657. At the hotel of the same name (see Sleeping), the experienced chef Pedro Pardo offers a selection of very good dishes based on grilled meats, fish or pork with scrumptious homemade desserts.

¥ **La Pulpería del Arriero**, 9 de Julio 753, T02652-432446. With tasty regional specialities and live folk music in the evenings, this is the place for trying *empanadas* or *asado* during a lively night out. The set menus are good value.
¥ **Los Robles**, Colón 684, T02652-436767. Formal atmosphere and very good food, you can eat very well at moderate prices at this smart *parrilla*. There is a wide choice of meat dishes (*bife de chorizo* is great), including *chivito* and trout. Recommended.

Cafés and bars

There's a cluster spread along Av Illia and Calle Rivadavia entre 800 y 1000. During the daytime 2 enjoyable cafés on the plaza are **Aranjuez** and **Ocean**. Try also **Liberato**, Av Illia 378, popular with young crowds by night; and **Macedonio**, San Martín 848, a laid-back café-bookshop.

Conlara Valley *p197*

¥ **Manía**, San Martín 199. Very good pizza and simple and cheap meals.

Merlo *p197*

¥¥ **El Ciprés**, Av del Ciprés 114. Popular with locals, so good filling meals are guaranteed though the menu is pretty standard.
¥¥ **El Establo**, Av del Sol 450. Handsome *parrilla*, where the grill or *asador* is strangely trapped in a glass enclosure. Try *chivito* here.
¥¥ **La Vieja Posada**, Av del Sol 2. A simple place with more than 30 different pizzas with a folk music show on Saturday evenings.
¥ **La Estrella de Merlo**, Becerra y Av del Sol. Locals come here for tasty homemade pastas.

Festivals

San Luis province *p195*

3 May The popular religious festival of **Cristo de la Quebrada** takes place at nearby Villa de la Quebrada.
25 Aug A religious procession commemorates the day of **King Saint Louis** and it is a national holiday across the province.

Activities and tours

San Luis city *p195*

All agencies offer similar tours at standard rates (rates in leaflets usually do not include fees to national parks). A half-day tour to Sierra de las Quijadas is the most popular (US$12 pp plus entry) and includes a walk to Los Miradores (1-1 ½ hrs) and to La Huella (2-2½ hrs). Weather permitting (usually not in summer), a more demanding walk to Los Farallones (4-5 hrs) is organized (US$13 pp plus entry). The Circuito Serrano Chico (US$7 pp) is a short walk around El Volcán, Potrero de los Funes and the town itself, while the Circuito Serrano Grande (US$10 pp) adds El Trapiche and La Florida. Circuito de Oro (US$12 pp) goes up to Carolina and Intihuasi and may include the Circuitos Serranos. There are also tours are to religious sites in Suyuque and Villa de la Quebrada and to the hot springs of Balde and the salt flats in Salinas del Bebedero. A day trip to Merlo via La Toma is also available (US$17 pp).
Bruno Aliberti, T02652-426021/ T15502971. Guide only, for those with their own vehicle.
Dasso, Rivadavia 540, T02652-421017, T15645410.
Gimatur, Av Illia y Caseros, T02652-435751, gimatursl@hotmail.com. English spoken.
Luciano Franchi, Chile 1430, T02652-420345/T15657441.
Remises Sur, T02652-455000. Good-value trips if there are 3 or 4 of you.

Merlo *p197*

Paragliding

El Nido, San Martín 370, T02656-475994, elnidoparapente@yahoo.com.ar. This paragliding school offers courses all year round (accommodation provided) and jumps for beginners (with instructor) from a platform at 2020 m (1100 m above Merlo). Usually lasting 15-20 mins, each flight costs US$23.

Tour operators

Excursions to local sights and provincial attractions, including full-day tours to Sierra de las Quijadas (US$13 pp plus entry fee). Closer destinations include half-day trips to Mina Los Cóndores (US$8 pp plus entry fee) and to Bajo de Véliz, an over promoted palaeontological site, where giant spiders used to live million of years ago (US$6.50 pp). Surrounding villages may also be explored for a few hours (US$5-7 pp). These more conventional tours are organized by **La Plaza**, Becerra y Av del Ciprés, T02656- 476853, and **Sol** Av del Sol 171, T02656-475346.

More demanding activities like climbing hills, visiting a remote ghost mining town, sleeping in caves or crossing rivers are also on offer. These activities are run by **Cimarrón incursiones**, Av del Sol 300, T02656- 478934, T02652-15664251; **Juan Carlos Sciamarella**, T02652-15548536; or **Los Tabaquillos**, Av de los Césares 2100, T02656-474010.

Transport

San Luis city *p195*

Air Airport, T02652-422427, 3 km northwest (access via Colón, Av Justo Daract and Sargento Baigorria); ordinary and *remise* taxis charge about US$1-1.20 from centre. To **Buenos Aires**, 1¼ hrs, CATA (from Merlo).

Airline offices CATA, Av España 950, T02652-439156.

Bus Terminal at Av España 990, T02652-424021. Triangular shaped building with offices and bus stops on all sides (check at office where your bus leaves). To reach the centre (10- min walk from plaza), take Calle Rivadavia. Left luggage at Kiosko Portos (facing University), open 24 hrs, US$0.65 per item half day. To **Buenos Aires**, several companies, 10-11 hrs, US$13-18. To **Lima** (Perú), **El Rápido Internacional** (direct), 2½ days, US$100. To **Santiago** (Chile), **Tur Bus, Tas Choapa, Cata**, 9-10 hrs, US$12-15. To **La Rioja**, **Socasa**, 7½, US$9. To **Mendoza**, several companies, 3-4 hrs, US$6. To **Córdoba**, several companies, 6-7 hrs, US$6-8. To **San Juan**, **Andesmar, Autotransportes San Juan, Autotransportes San Juan-Mar del Plata, TAC, Del Sur y Media Agua**, 4 hrs, US$7. To **Santa Rosa** (La Pampa), **Dumas**, 10 hrs, US$8.50; also to destinations in southern San Luis. To **Merlo**, **Expreso Uspallata, TAC, SENA, Automotores Merlo** (usually packed minibuses), 3 hrs, US$3. To **Balde** and **Salinas del Bebedero**, **Dasso**, 2 daily Mon-Fri, 45 mins (US$0.45) and 1 hr (US$0.75), respectively. To **El Trapiche**, **María del Rosario, San José**, US$0.65; same services go to La Florida and Río Grande. To **Carolina** and **Intihuasi**, **Polos**, 3 daily (unreliable timetable), US$1.70 and US$2.10, respectively.

Car hire Avis, Belgrano 1440, T02652-440288. **Localiza**, Chacabuco 649, T02652-438500, localizasanluis@ciudad.com.ar.

Remise taxis Cosmos, Chacabuco 1151, T02652-440000. **Zoo**, Bolívar y Falucho, T02652-421000.

Merlo *p197*

For frequent services to destinations in Córdoba province, go to Villa Dolores.

Air Airport, on R148, T02656-492840, 23 km west of Merlo T02656-422427. To/from **Buenos Aires**, 1 hr 50 mins, **CATA** (stops at San Luis), desk at tourist office (at Merlo roundabout), T02656-478460. *Remise* taxis charge US$5. Bus Terminal on R1, next to roundabout, 10-min walk from plaza. Frequent services to **San Luis**, **Expreso Uspallata, TAC, SENA, Automotores Merlo**, 3 hrs, US$3. To **Buenos Aires**, **TAC, Expreso del Oeste, Autotransportes San Juan-Mar del Plata, Sierras Cordobesas and Chevallier**, US$15-18, 10-12 hrs. To **Córdoba**, **TAC, Expreso Uspallata, Andesmar, Monticas**, 5 hrs, US$6. To **Mina Clavero**, **Monticas, Expreso del Oeste**, 2 hrs, US$3. To **Villa Dolores**, **TAC**, 2 hrs, US$1.70 (via San Javier) or **Sierras Cordobesas and TAC**, 1 hr, US$1.30-2 (via R148). Urban bus station, on C Pringles y Av Los Almendros (2 blocks south of plaza). **La Costa** goes daily along R1 to Cortaderas, Villa Larca and Papagayos. **STU** runs frequent services to **Mirador del Sol**, stopping there for 10 mins, US$1.20 return.

Bicycle hire Sis, Coronel Mercau y Los Huarpes (2 blocks north of plaza).

Remise taxis Avenida, Becerra 575, T02656-476031. **Unión**, Videla 114, T02656-478444.

Directory

San Luis city *p195*

Banks Banex, Rivadavia y Pringles, T02652-440004. Changes US$ and TCs, but these take 3 days, with a 1.5% commission for Amex TCs. Exchange available at **Banco de Galicia**, Colón y Pringles, and at **Montemar**, Belgrano 980. **Internet** Cyberclub Buskar, Pedernera 1305, US$0.35/hr (US$0.25/hr after 2400). **Ego!**, Av Illia 320. US$0.65/hr (US$0.35/hr after 2200). **Telecentro**, Av Illia 127, US$0.65/hr. **Post office** San Martín y Av Illia; Western Union branch. **Telecommunications** Telecentros on C San Martín and on Av Illia.

Mendoza and the west

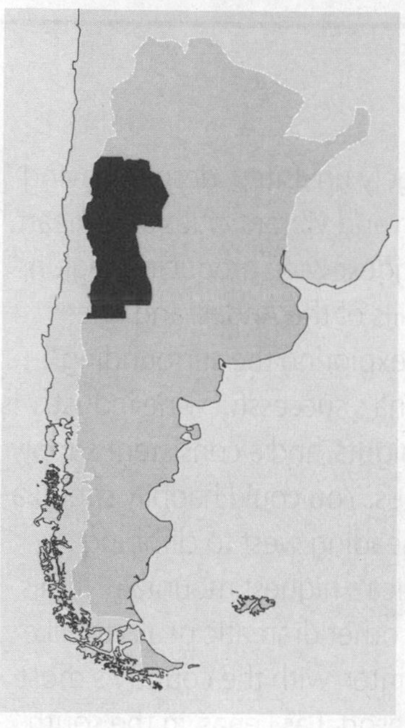

Footprint features

Introduction

Argentina's west is wild and largely unvisited, despite having one of the country's most stylish and vibrant cities at its heart. Mendoza is the centre of the biggest wine producing region, and with its setting at the foothills of the Andes, and fine restaurants, it's a great base for exploring the surrounding vineyards. The secret to Argentina's successful wine industry is the climate: hot days and cool nights, and a consistent supply of pure snowmelt from the Andes. You could happily spend a week visiting bodegas, before heading west to climbing Mount Aconcagua, South America's highest mountain. If this is too daunting, there are many other dramatic peaks to hike up in summer, or ski down in winter, with the country's most famous ski and snowboarding resort, Las Leñas, in the south of the province.

South of Mendoza, find Champagne producers in San Rafael, or set off for adventures in the wild landscapes beyond. Go rafting in the eerie ravine of Cañón del Atuel or find yourself seduced by the quieter charms of Llancanelo where thousands of flamingos rise from the Prussian blue waters. Ride a horse through the starkly beautiful volcanic landscape of La Payunia, where guanacos roam unhindered. A spirit of adventure is definitely needed to explore the quieter provinces of San Juan and La Rioja, but the intrepid will be rewarded with forgotten valleys offering perfect peace and natural beauty. But the undoubted stars of the region are two national parks; likely to make you feel dwarfed by both time and space. The 'Valley of the Moon' at Ischigualasto is indeed an other-worldly landscape: a 200-million-year-old lake-bed, strewn with fossils from first life forms to dinosaurs. And Talampaya's vast canyons of terracotta rock, eroded by wind into gigantic sculptures, are magnificent at sunset when they turn a vivid red.

★ Don't miss...

1 **Mendoza's fine wineries** Enjoy some free tastings then dine at 1884, or stay in luxury at Tapiz, page 209.

2 **Aconcagua Provincial Park** Visit the highest peak in the world outside the Himalayas, page 224.

3 **Las Leñas** One of the southern hemisphere's best winter sports resorts, page 232.

4 **La Payunia** Ride horses across the volcanic plains beside herds of wild guanacos, page 233.

5 **Ischigualasto Provincial Park** Walking on the moon in the ancient Ischigualasto park, page 240.

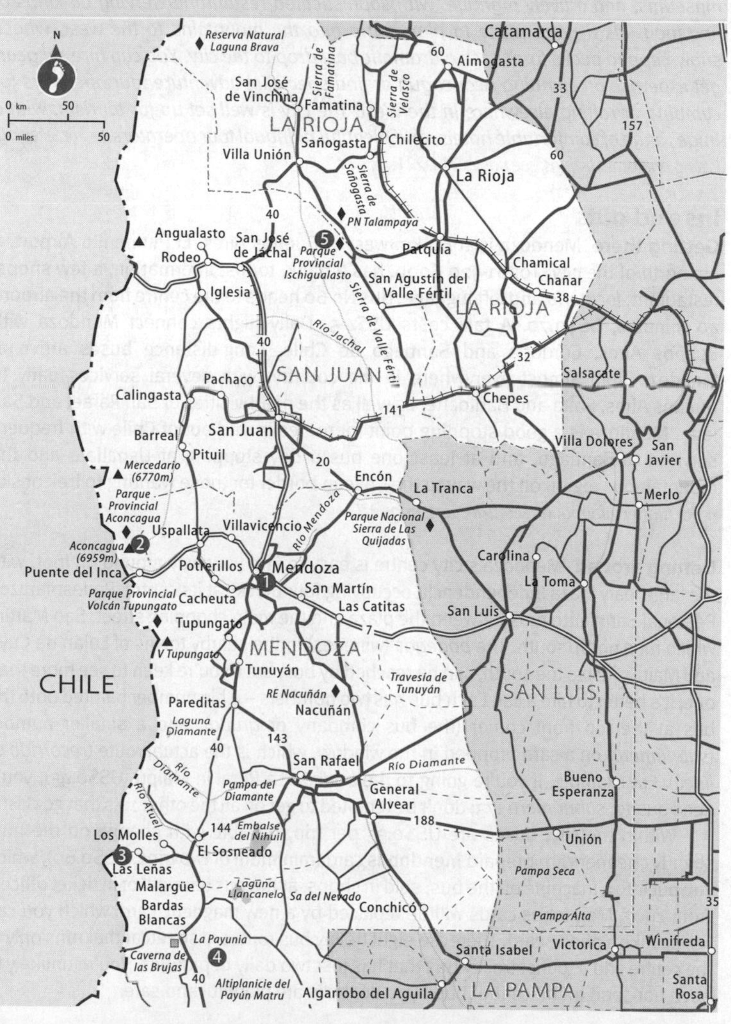

Mendoza city

→ *Phone code: 0261 Colour map 3, A2 Population Greater Mendoza: 849,000.*

Mendoza is undoubtedly the tourism centre of the west of Argentina, and a good place to spend a few days, with its pretty plazas, wide boulevards and sophisticated nightlife. Its flourishing economy is entirely based around wine, as it's the centre of Argentina's rapidly growing wine industry. Any trip to the city should include a tour of some of the vineyards at Maipú and Luján de Cuyo, to the south of the city. There are large flashy commercial bodegas and smaller family wineries, and after seeing the process of wine making, you'll be treated to a generous tasting to appreciate why Argentina's wine is receiving such worldwide acclaim. Wine is a part of the city's culture too, in the profusion of wonderful vinoteques where you can taste fine wines, and in the spectacular festival held to celebrate the wine harvest every March in Mendoza's splendid park Parque San Martín. The city has some small interesting museums, and a lively nightlife, with sophisticated restaurants serving all kinds of fine food. It's a good place to plan a trip into the mountains to the west, whose snow-capped peaks form such a dramatic backdrop to the city. You can hire ski gear, get expertise on climbing Aconcagua or find specialist adventure tour operators for climbing or rafting elsewhere in the West. The city is well set up for tourism, with a huge range of comfortable hotels, and plentiful bilingual tour operators. ▸▸ *For Sleeping, Eating and other listings, see pages 214-221.*

Ins and outs

Getting there Mendoza is 1060 km west of Buenos Aires. **El Plumerillo Airport**, 8 km north of the city, T0261-520 6000, has a bank, tourist information, a few shops, restaurant, *locutorio* and left luggage. Bus No 60 heads to the centre from the airport; 40 minutes, US$0.70. A taxi costs US$4-5. Daily flights connect Mendoza with Buenos Aires, Córdoba and Santiago de Chile. Long-distance **buses** arrive at Mendoza from almost everywhere in the country, with several services daily to Buenos Aires, Salta and Bariloche, as well as the nearby cities of San Rafael and San Juan. Mendoza is a good stopping point for routes in and out of Chile with frequent services to Santiago, and at least one bus a day stopping at Uspallata and the mountainous region on the way to the Chilean border for those wanting to trek or ski. ▸▸ *For further information see Transport, page 220.*

Getting around Mendoza's city centre is easy to find your way around on foot, with the large leafy Plaza Independencia occupying four blocks at its centre. Pedestrianized Peatonal Sarmiento runs between the plaza and the main shopping street, San Martín, which runs north/south. The *bodegas* (wineries) in the nearby towns of Luján de Cuyo and Maipú, just to the south, can be reached by bus, but if you're keen to see more than one, it's better to hire a car. Each bus has two numbers – a big number painted onto the bus at the top front corner (the bus company or *grupo*), and a smaller number (*subnúmero*) on a card propped in the window, which is the actual route (*recorrido* or *línea*). For example, if you're going to the *bodega* La Rural in Maipú (US$0.45), you'll need bus 10, *subnúmero* 173; don't be tempted to get on all the other 10's that go past.

Within the city, buses are US$0.35 per trip, payable with change on the bus, slightly cheaper with prepaid **Mendobus** card (minimum of two trips, US$0.60), which you put into a machine on the bus; sold in shops, at the bus terminal or in ticket offices. From 2007, Mendobus cards will be replaced by a new magnetic card, which you can top up, like a phone card. There are eight trolley bus routes, a streetcar that runs only in the centre and a tourist trolley bus that has just two daily departures. You're unlikely to need transport in the centre, but if you do, taxis are plentiful and safe.

San Martín El Libertador

If you only learn about one Argentine hero on your trip, make it San Martín, one of the greatest independence heroes of South America. Celebrated in statues in every town in the country, José Francisco de San Martín hoped to unite Spanish America after independence, and though he failed to achieve this aim, his military genius played a major role in securing independence. He possessed a tremendous organizational ability, even when leading troops scattered over large distances and mountainous terrain, and his epic crossing of the Andes in 1817 was a turning point in the Wars of Independence, and the campaigns that followed in Chile and Peru ended Spanish rule in South America.

Born in Yapeyú, Corrientes, in 1778 and educated in Spain, San Martín served in the Spanish army in North Africa, Spain and France from the age of 15. In 1811 he resigned from the army and made contact with Francisco de Miranda and other supporters of South American independence, returning to Buenos Aires in 1812 to train the new cavalry regiment. The following year, he replaced Belgrano as commander of the northern armies and once appointed governor of Cuyo province, spent the next two years preparing to capture Peru from his base in Mendoza, means of a giant flanking movement through Chile and up through the coast to Lima. His 'Army of the Andes' was drawn from regular troops sent by Buenos Aires, but San Martín personally reconnoitred the mountain passes to plan the crossing to Chile himself. He also planned a brilliant deception, calling a meeting of Pehuenche chiefs to ask their permission to cross their territory to invade Chile via mountain passes south of Mendoza. As he'd expected, spies carried this news across the Andes, leaving San Martín free to use a more northerly route, with the main force crossing by Los Patos and Uspallata passes. Some 3778 men set out on 18-19 January 1817, with equipment and 10,791 horses and mules, and crossed the Andes in 21 days, arriving on time at their intended destinations. Within days, the army defeated the Spanish at Chacabuco and entered Santiago, Chile, in triumph, though the conclusive victory was at the Battle of Maipú in April 1818.

With Chilean independence secure, San Martín led his forces by sea to Peru in 1820. Avoiding battle against the larger Spanish forces, he negotiated a truce, and encouraged army desertions. Finally entering Lima in triumph in July 1821, he assumed political and military command of the new republic of Peru. Afterwards, San Martín resigned his post and returned to his small farm in Mendoza, before travelling to Europe in 1824 to settle in Brussels and then Grand Bourg, France. He died in Boulogne-sur-Mer in 1850, and his remains lie now in Buenos Aires cathedral. Symbolizing to many Argentines the virtues of sacrifice, bravery and the lack of personal gain, he's remembered by street names in even the smallest towns.

Best time to visit The biggest festival of the year **Fiesta de la Vendimia** is held from mid-February to mid-March to celebrate the start of the wine harvest. The festival includes a carnival queen, a procession of floats and outdoor extravaganzas in the park – but little wine-tasting. A parallel event is the less-promoted but equally entertaining **Gay Vendimia Festival** with parties, shows and the crowning of the Festival Queen. *Bodegas* can be visited all year round and at harvest time (March and April) you'll see the machinery in action. If you're heading beyond Mendoza to explore the landscape, trekking in the mountains is only possible from November to April, when the snow has melted. The most pleasant time for trekking is December to February, which is the only feasible season for trekking at higher altitudes. Skiing at Los Penitentes (on the road to Chile) is from July to October, though Las Leñas further south is open from mid-June.

Tourist information Mendoza has a well developed tourism infrastructure, with tourist offices all over the city. The city's **main office** ⓘ *San Martín 1143, opposite Peatonal Sarmiento, T0810-666 6363, or T0261-420 2800, daily 0900-2200*, provides information on the whole province. There's also a useful booth on the street outside, for city information only. Both offices have English-speaking staff who can provide city maps, information on *bodegas* and explain the buses. Smaller offices open Monday to Friday 0800-1300 and can be found in the civic centre ⓘ *9 de Julio 500, T0261-449 5185*, and at Las Heras and Mitre ⓘ *T0261-429 6298*. There are two small but very helpful kiosks at the airport and at the bus terminal, and another extremely helpful office at the entrance to Parque San Martín ⓘ *daily 0800-1800*. For online information visit www.turismo.mendoza.gov.ar, www.mendoza.com.ar and www.vendimia.mendoza.gov.ar. For city information, try www.ciudaddemendoza.gov.ar. Another very useful site, designed by English expats, is www.welcometomendoza.com.ar.

Background

Mendoza was founded by Pedro del Castillo in 1561, when he was sent from the Spanish colony in Chile by Captain General García Hurtado de Mendoza to cross the 4000-m pass over the Andes, and found a new city. Mediterranean fruits were introduced to the region soon afterwards, and thrived in its sunny climate, aided by pre-Hispanic irrigation channels that are still used today to water the dry lands with abundant snow-melt from the Andes. The city's wealth grew, although it remained

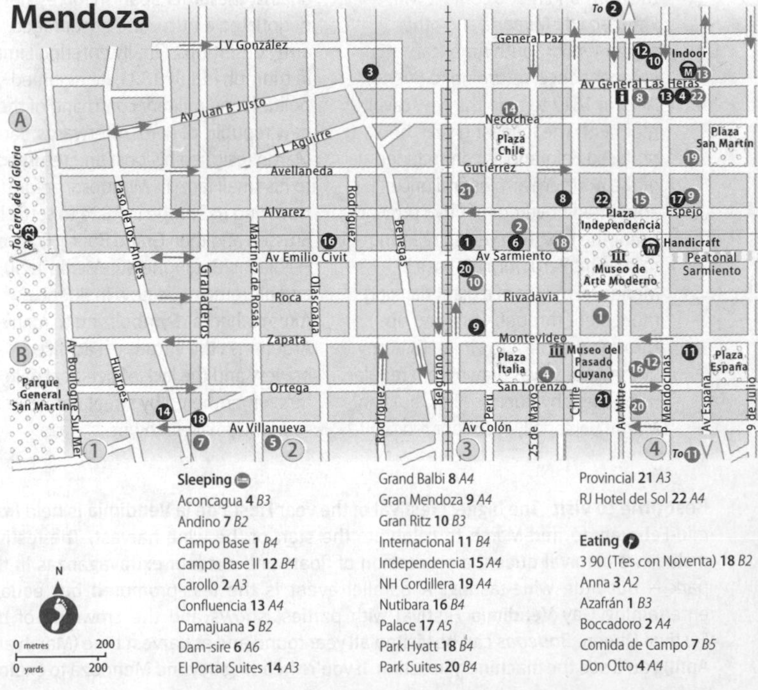

largely isolated throughout the colonial period, being governed from Chile and having little contact with modern-day Argentina. The city's greatest blow came on Easter Saturday in 1861 when it was completely destroyed in a devastating earthquake which killed some 4000 of its 12,000 inhabitants. Very quickly, a new centre was built by the French architect Ballofet, several blocks to the southwest of the original. This modern city was designed with low, quake-proof buildings and broad avenues with many plazas to aid evacuation in case of further tremors. Plane trees were planted on all the streets, watered by a network of irrigation channels which still gush with water every spring. Nowadays, Mendoza's main industry is wine, though a busy university and, increasingly, tourism help to sustain its wealth and lively character.

Sights

The large **Plaza Independencia** is a popular meeting place for *mendocinos* with its shady acacia and plane trees and pretty fountains. In the middle is the small **Museo de Arte Moderno** ⓘ *Mon-Sat 0900-2100, Sun 1600-2100, US$0.70*, originally designed to be an emergency bunker for victims of future earthquakes, now housing temporary exhibitions. On the western side is the new and luxurious **Park Hyatt Hotel**, once a splendid 1920's palace where Juan Perón and Evita stayed. The eastern side of the park is filled with a handicrafts market at weekends, where Peatonal Sarmiento runs to Calle San Martín. Around the four corners of this central plaza, just a block further out are four smaller plazas. The most attractive is the **Plaza España**, to the southeast. Its floor and benches are beautifully tiled and it's a lovely place to sit under the trees and gaze at the rather sentimental mural displaying historical episodes as well as scenes from *Don Quijote* and the famous gaucho poem, *Martín Fierro*. Four blocks west along Montevideo, with its pretty Italianate and colonial-style buildings, is **Plaza Italia**, with wonderful mature tipa trees. Nearby it's worth visiting the small **Museo del Pasado Cuyano** ⓘ *Montevideo 544, T0261-423 6031, Mon-Fri 0900-1230, US$0.35*, housed in a beautiful 1873 mansion owned by the Civit family. There's lots of San Martín memorabilia, and an exquisite Spanish 15th-century carved altarpiece. The director will give you an excellent tour and insights into the city's history.

The original city centre, destroyed by the earthquake in 1861, was located 12 blocks to the northeast of today's Plaza Independencia, and is now known as the **Area Fundacional**. Here there is a broad tranquil plaza and a beautifully designed **museum** ⓘ *Beltrán and Videla Castillo, T0261-425 6927, Tue-Sat 0800-2000, Sun 1500-2000, US$0.70 (underground chamber, extra US$0.20), kids under 6 free, buses 1 (line 13) and 3 (line 112)*, whose glass floor reveals continuing excavations of foundations from the old Cabildo and the buildings that followed, with an array of objects salvaged from the rubble. The informative free tour is highly recommended to give you a picture of Mendoza's history. Under the plaza you can see the first fountain to bring running water to the city, and nearby, at the corner

El Mesón Español 11 *B4*
Facundo 6 *B3*
Ferruccio Soppelsa 17 *A4*
Francesco 8 *A4*
Il Dolce 19 *B5*
La Marchigiani 10 *A4*
La Mora 9 *B3*
La Sal 20 *B3*
Mi Tierra 21 *B4*
Montecatini 12 *A4*
Mr Dog 13 *A4*
Por Acá 14 *B1*
Quinta Norte 22 *A4*
Sr Cheff 15 *B5*
Terrazas del Lago 23 *A1*
Vía Civit 16 *B2*

of Ituzaingó and Beltrán are the ruins of the Jesuit **Iglesia de San Francisco**. **Plaza Pellegrini** is another attractive little plaza, at Avenida Alem y Avenida San Juan, where wedding photos are taken on Friday and Saturday nights, and there's a small antiques market on Friday lunchtimes.

Ten blocks west of Plaza Independencia, wrought iron gates mark the entrance to the great **Parque General San Martín**, 350 ha of lavishly planted parkland designed by famous Argentine landscape architect Charles Thays, with sports facilities, a big lake where regattas are held, a sports stadium, and an amphitheatre. On a hill in the park is the **Cerro de la Gloria**, popular with paragliders, giving splendid views of the Andes to the west. There's also a monument to San Martín, showing various episodes of his leading his army across the Andes to liberate Argentina and Chile from the Spanish. From the east end of the park, on Avenida Libertador, an hourly bus ('Oro Negro') runs to the top of the Cerro de la Gloria – otherwise it's a long walk (45 minutes). On the side of the Cerro is the **Jardín Zoológico** ⓘ *T0261-427 1559, Tue-Sun 0900-1800, US$1.35*, one of the country's best zoos. There's a helpful **tourist information office** next to the main gates. The lakeside restaurant **Terrazas del Lago** is open from breakfast to the early hours of the morning. At the south end of the lake is the **Museo de Ciencias Naturales y Antropológicas** ⓘ*T0261-428 7666, Mon-Fri 0800-1300, 1400-1900, Sat-Sun 1500-1900, US$0.70*, with an ancient female mummy amongst its fossils and stuffed animals. Not far from the Area Fundacional, at the southern end of Parque O'Higgins, kids might enjoy the small aquarium **Acuario Municipal** ⓘ *Ituzaingó y Buenos Aires, daily 0900-1900, US$0.70*. Across the street is a small **Serpentario** ⓘ *daily 0930-1300, 1500-1930, US$1*, with plenty of snakes and lizards.

The city's best art gallery is in the nearby suburb of **Luján de Cuyo**, where there's a small, charming collection of Argentine paintings in the house where Fernando Fader painted his beautiful murals, at the **Museo Provincial de Bellas Artes** ⓘ *Casa de Fader, Carril San Martín 3651, Mayor Drummond, T0261-496 0224, Tue-Fri 0800-1800, Sat-Sun 1400-1900, free. Reached by bus 1 (line 19) Empresa Trapiche, 40 mins*. There are also sculptures in the lovely gardens. For the **Museo Nacional del Vino**, see Maipú page 213.

Around Mendoza

The sight of distant purple mountains is bound to draw you from the city sooner or later up into the dramatic Andes to the west, on the road to Chile. This area, known as Alta Montaña, is the undoubted highlight of the region, with Mount Aconcagua at its heart, and plenty of other places for walking in Parque Provincial Aconcagua. These are described in the next section, but if you're thinking of taking a day trip from Mendoza city, bear in mind that you'll get very little chance to walk around, and that you'd be better off hiring a car and spending a few days exploring. You'll pass through the pretty town of Uspallata reached by two possible routes west: either Portrerillos or Vallecitos. These routes and town are described in more detail in the next section, but just to whet your appetite: there are thermal springs and a good place for lunch at the pretty village of Cacheuta, 40 km west of Mendoza city, which also has a good hotel. At **Potrerillos**, 68 km west of Mendoza on route 7, you could do a day's rafting, walking or horse riding, but if you're driving, note there's no road between the two since the river was dammed, even though they're only 10 km away from each other.

The alternative route to Uspallata takes you up to **Villavicencio**, 47 km north, where there are gentle walks and a charming rustic restaurant in spectacular mountain scenery, though the famous hotel you see on all the bottles of Villavicencio water is still awaiting renovation. Further west, the road climbs up to Paramillos at 3,200 m, a spectacular and much more adventurous route to reach Uspallata valley and the Alta Montaña circuit. This is offered in some tours, but more fun in your own transport, (See page 218 for more details). For watersports, **Embalse El Carrizal**, an artificial lake 60 km south of Mendoza, has yachting and fishing, campsites and picnic areas. For skiing in the winter, you can do two resorts in day trips. **Los Penitentes**, 183 km away, is by far the better of the two, but since there's plenty of accommodation there, it's better to go for a couple of days. Vallecitos is closer, at 95 km, but it's a very basic little ski resort and the *ripio* roads can be tricky.

Wine region » pp214-221.

No trip to Mendoza is complete without a tour of the local wineries. Wine is at the heart of Mendoza's landscape and industry, and the bodegas are beautiful places to visit. Surrounded by semi-arid lands with little vegetation, the rich green vineyards

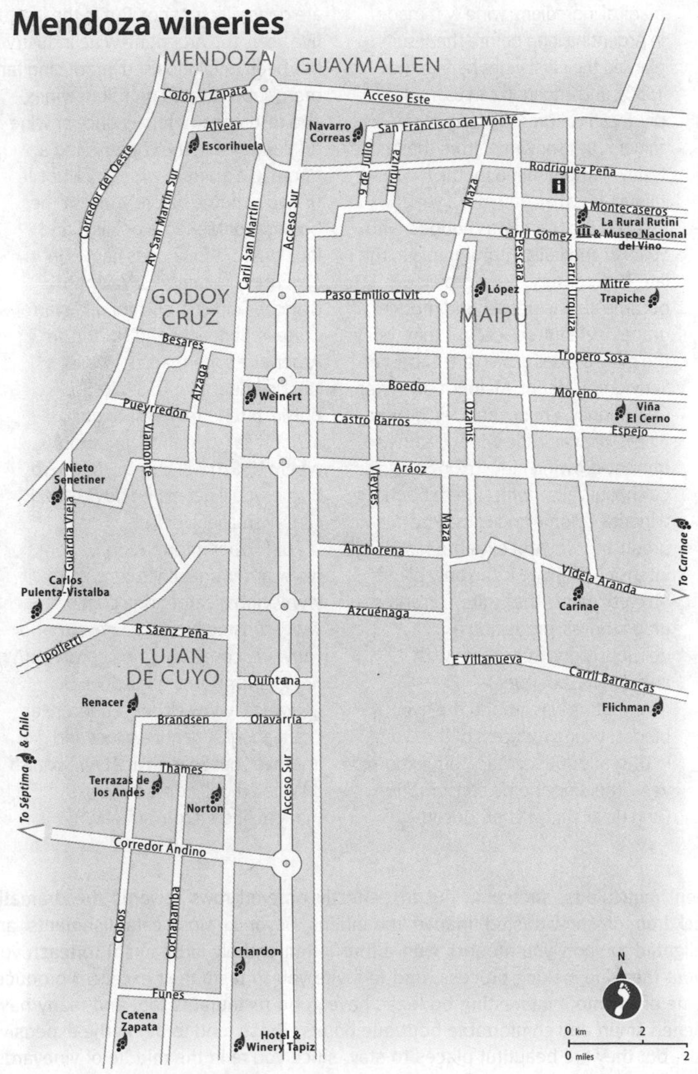

Argentine wine

Wine is grown in Argentina along the length of the Andean foothills, from Cafayate in Salta to the Río Negro valley in Neuquén, with the oldest and most famous wine- producing areas in Mendoza and San Juan provinces, where the climate is ideal: warm, almost consistently sunny days, and cold nights, with a 'thermal amplitude' of 15 degrees which gives grapes such a rich flavour. Water is the other magical ingredient: wine was made in Argentina long before the Jesuits planted their first vines here in the 1550s, and irrigation canals made by pre-Incan cultures still carry pure, mineral-rich snowmelt from the Andes today, compensating for the low rainfall, less than 200 mm a year.

When Argentina was flooded with Spanish and Italian immigrants in the late 19th century, wine-growing became an imperative, and modern grapes were introduced, so that today the main grapes grown are Cabernet Sauvignon, Merlot, Malbec and Syrrah; Chardonnay, Chenin and Sauvignon Blanc. 'High altitude wine' is a tiny, but fast-growing industry in Salta's Calchaquí Valley, with superb boutique wineries Colomé and El Estecco producing wines of extraordinary intensity. Cafayate is the only place on earth where the white Torrontés grape thrives, producing a deliciously dry, fruity wine with an aromatic bouquet.

Argentina was among the five biggest wine producers of the world in the early 20th century, but exported very little, since home consumption used up all that was produced. However, in the 1970s, after market became glutted with cheap wine – much of it inferior quality – wine-drinking slumped, Argentines preferring beer and soft drinks with their steaks. In the 1990s, Chile's vigorous marketing campaign secured their wines a place on every European supermarket shelf, but Argentina failed to compete, despite the fact that their wines, particularly their reds, are generally superior. But in the last five years the Argentine wine industry has been revolutionised, producing far more sophisticated premium wines, and resulting in a renaissance of wine drinking within the country, and a boom in exporting wine. Try a bottle or two at home before you visit the bodegas of Mendoza or Salta, and look out for the famous names in Argentine restaurants: Valentín Bianchi, Trapiche, Flichman, Navarro Correas, Senetiner and Norton. In Argentine supermarkets, wines can be bought for US$1.50-5 a bottle, but better by far to go to a Vinoteca (specialist wine shop) where US$10 will buy you a superb bottle, you'll get expert advice, and can try smaller labels.

Fur further information: www.argentinewines.com/ing/, www.vinosdeargentina.com, www.turismo.mendoza.gov.ar/vino, www.welcomeargentina.com/vino/index_i.html, and magazines *El Conocedor* www.elconocedor.com.ar. Learn about Argentine wines and improve your Spanish at AEAV Spanish & Wine School, http://cablemodem.fibertel.com.ar/aeav.

seem miraculous, stretching out in perfectly ordered rows towards the dramatic backdrop of snow-dusted mauve mountains beyond. Most establishments are delighted to show you around, with a tour (often entirely in Spanish) to teach you about the wine making process, and to invite you to taste their excellent produce. Some of the more interesting bodegas have good restaurants too, and many have opened smart and comfortable boutique hotels. These tend to be on the expensive side, but they are beautiful places to stay, since you're in the middle of vineyards, with the added advantage that you can enjoy superb wine with your meal and not have to worry about driving. **Tapiz**, www.tapiz.com, is one of the best and gaining a reputation for excellence. **Cavas Wine Lodge**, www.cavaswinelodge.com, is also frequently recommended.

There are three main wine-producing areas in Mendoza province. The **High zone of Río Mendoza**, the oldest wine producing area, is immediately to the south of Mendoza city with bodegas sprinkled among two towns, Maipú and Luján de Cuyo. Wineries in this region are described in more detail below. The second region is the **Uco Valley**, to the south of the small town of Tupungato which lies southwest of Mendoza in the foothills of the Andes. And the third region is around **San Rafael** (286 km south of Mendoza city). Only the first region is described here, since both Tupungato and San Rafael are described in Southern Mendoza (see page 229).

Argentina's wine industry has grown considerably in recent years (see box on facing page). Now it's being shaken up by the arrival of foreign investors who have bought extensive vineyards in the region: and as well as British, French, Dutch, Spanish, American and Australian wine growers, there are other enthusiasts who have settled down here and started up more related businesses, running bodega tours, wine clubs, wine magazines and opening restaurants. This area of tourism is bound to change dramatically in the next few years, so check for new information if you're serious about your wine. For more information on the wine-growing region in general, see the following websites: www.bestofmendoza.com; www.turismo.mendoza.gov.ar/vino (has maps and information on the Camino del Vino); www.mendoza.com.ar (in Spanish and English with lots of information); www.vendimia.mendoza.gov.ar (covers the annual wine harvest festival in Mendoza); www.welcometomendoza.com.ar (another very useful site, designed in English by expats with a good general overview); and www.welcomeargentina.com/vino/mendoza_i.html.

While you're on your way around Argentina, perhaps anticipating a trip to Mendoza, it's a good idea to try some of the famous brands in restaurants so that you know what you like when you're choosing vineyards to visit. This is a list of the best known and longest established names whose wineries you can visit in Mendoza province: López, Valentín Bianchi, Escorihuela, J&F Lurton, Trapiche, Flichman, La Rural, Norton, Félix Lavaque, Navarro Correas, Nieto Senetiner, Chandon, Weinert. See the Map of Mendoza wineries to find these bodegas in Maipú and Luján de Cuyo

Visiting bodegas

Transport There are plenty of tours on offer from agencies in Mendoza city, allowing you to visit a couple of bodegas in an afternoon. These are fine if you haven't got a car, but it's much more interesting to go independently, so that you can choose the bodegas you'd like to visit, and take your time over the visits. Touring wineries by bus really isn't an option, since almost all the bodegas are some way out of any town, it's easy to get lost in labyrinthine rural roads with little signposting, and you might waste a lot of time waiting for buses. Cycle tours are an appealing alternative to exploring one limited area, such as Mapiú, with a couple of specialized agencies based in the wine regions, and reasonable distances to cover: you could put together a tour of bodegas that are a five to 20-minute ride from each other.

Reserve ahead However you choose to visit the bodegas, remember always to ring and book your tour first, and if you don't speak Spanish, ask if they have an English-speaking guide. You'll be able to get a vague idea of the process but it will be far more interesting if you understand the detail. Many wineries are closed on Sundays.

Map Get hold of a map of the wine region: there are lots of maps available in free tourist brochures, but the best is the *Winemap Turístico* sold in some restaurants and wine stores: very good and informative.

Variety Limit yourself to four or five bodegas in a day, especially if you're driving. (Drink-driving laws are only rarely enforced in Argentina, but for your own safety – so you can find your way around the badly-signposted streets – it's best to limit your intake if you're driving). It's worth trying to see both a big modern winery and smaller and more intimate places, since their processes are quite different, and often a smaller winery will take even more time and trouble to share their produce with you.

Try it at home One of the great things about visiting these bodegas is that often you'll be trying wines that are available in your own country, so that even if you can't carry a crate home with you, you can buy the same wine from your home wine supplier, and share it with friends as you show them the photos of where the wine was grown.

Zona Alta del Río Mendoza

The area immediately to the south of Mendoza city, around the sprawling centres of Maipú and Luján de Cuyo, contains the oldest and some of the most famous vineyards in the province, producing wines with a high concentration of fruit. Malbec, particularly, thrives here, in altitudes between 650 and 1050 m, and it's said that although the grape was brought from France, it is in Argentina that it's found its real home, and in Zona Alta del Río Mendoza that it's at its best. Wine growing styles are eclectic in the various vineyards here, but this area produces premium wines, thanks to the unique combination of soil and climate. Other grape varieties grown here are Cabernet Sauvignon, Merlot, Chardonnay, Syrah and Tempranillo, among others. This is the closest region to the city of Mendoza, and easily visited in a few hours. But since the wineries are spread out along pretty country roads, with few signs to guide you, it's worth taking a map, and contacting the bodegas ahead of your visit.

Escorihuela

ⓘ *Belgrano 1188, Godoy Cruz, T0261-424 2282, www.escorihuela.com.ar.*
Before you reach Maipú or Luján de Cuyo, it's worth stopping to visit one of the most famous bodegas in the country, in the suburb of Godoy Cruz. The closest winery to the city is the historical Escorihuela. Founded in 1884 by Spanish immigrants, it retains its traditional atmosphere in the original buildings. They export wine to the UK under the Gascón label and still produce Pont L'Eveque, which was Perón's favourite brand. The winery is only about 20 blocks south of the centre, five minutes away by taxi, or easily reached by all buses going south along Avenida San Martín. Belgrano runs parallel to Avenida San Martín, one block east. Escorihuela also has an excellent and expensive restaurant, **1884 Francis Mallman** (see Eating, page 217) with a superb menu – the perfect complement to the bodegas fine wines, and run by the famous chef Francis Mallman. The stunning centrepiece of your tour is in the cellars, where there's an ornately carved barrel from Nancy. If your Spanish isn't strong, you might like to visit this bodega before the others for its helpful brochure explaining the whole process in pictures!

Maipú

The satellite town of Maipú sprawls immediately southeast of Mendoza (take bus No 10, subnumero 173, at Rioja y Garibaldi). You may find it useful to collect information from the local **tourist office** ⓘ *Urquiza y Montecaseros, Plazoleta Rutini, T0261-497 7437, where bus No 10 (173) stops*. There are many famous brands in this area, and some more intimate bodegas described here.

If you've only time for one bodega, make it **La Rural** ⓘ *Montecaseros 2625, Coquimbito, T0261-497 2013, www.bodegalarural.com.ar. Bus No 10 (subnúmero*

173) stops by the tourist information centre in Maipú, not far from the bodega. This is a large traditional bodega founded in 1885 by Felipe Rutini, that has been modernized recently with the latest technology allowing it to bottle 6000 units per hour. This bodega is renowned not only for its excellent wines but also for the marvellous **Museo Nacional del Vino** ① *Mon-Sat 0900-1700, Sun 1000-1400*, where you can see the history of winemaking through an amazing display of implements dating back to the pre-Colombian skin of an entire cow where grapes were trodden in the belly so that juice flowed out of its neck. Wonderful. Felipe Rutini and Trumpeter labels are exported worldwide: look out for the San Felipe bottles in the UK.

Quite a long way east of Maipú town centre, and 35 km east of Mendoza, is the large and highly developed **Familia Zuccardi** winery ① *RP 33, Calle Las Margaritas, Km 7.5, San Roque, T0261-441 0000, www.familiazuccardi.com, Mon-Sat 0900-1730, Sun 1000-1630*. This is an exceptionally welcoming winery with a good restaurant, extensive wine tasting, a tea room, and occasional music concerts on offer. Anyone wanting to pick grapes during the harvest is always welcome, and cookery lessons are available with the restaurant's chef. Their wines are easily found abroad, where they're known as Q and Santa Julia.

There are also several wineries in Coquimbito district, immediately east of Maipú. Two smaller family-owned wineries, both delightful for a visit, lie very close to each other. **Tempus Alba** ① *Perito Moreno 572, Coquimbito, T0261-481 3501, www.tempusalba.com*, is a modern bodega where the Biondolillo family takes great pride in their attention to detail and happy to share it with you. **Viña El Cerno** ① *Perito Moreno 631, Coquimbito, T0261-481 1567, www.elcerno.com.ar*, has a lovely country house, a restaurant and olive groves. Founded in 1887, the historic bodega of **Inti Huaco** ① *Carril Gómez 3602, Coquimbito, T0261-155652630, www.bodegaintihuaco.com*, has elegant mid-range rooms coming off a central courtyard in beautiful surroundings. Contact Juan Morales.

Another charming, small and welcoming winery is the French-owned **Carinae** ① *Videla Aranda 2899, Cruz de Piedra, south of Maipú town centre, T0261-499 0470, www.carinaevinos.com, daily 1000-1800*. As the name might suggest, wines aren't the only passion of Philippe and Brigitte, but astronomy too. They have an interesting collection of telescopes, which you can use. They produce Malbec, Syrah and Cabernet Sauvignon under the Carinae name (for export), and Octans and El Galgo labels (within Argentina).

Luján de Cuyo

Southwest of Maipú, **Luján de Cuyo** is another wine producing area in whose leafy suburb, Chacras de Coria, you'll also find restaurants and small hotels. For information, contact the local **tourist office** ① *Roque Sáenz Peña 1000, T0261-498 1912, www.lujandecuyo.gov.ar*.

The large and impressively modern Mayan-pyramid like bodega, **Catena Zapata** ① *C Cobos, Agrelo (see map), T0261-490 0214, www.catenawines.com*, lies in one of the most beautiful settings in the region. It's owned by a traditional family who produce outstanding wines that are exported under the names Catena Alta, Álamos, Nicolás Catena Zapata and Catena. There is a restaurant too. Another large, modern bodega with fantastic mountain views is **Séptima** ① *RN 7, Km 6.5, Agrelo (see map), T0261-498 5164, www.bodegaseptima.com.ar, Mon-Fri 1000-1700 (Tue and Thu also open for amazing sunset tasting sessions)*. Ask about the unique architectural design which is based on ancient stone building techniques developed by the indigenous Huarpe people.

There are now several wineries which offer accommodation, but the most famous and deservedly popular is the exquisite **Tapiz** ① *C Pedro Molina, Russell, T0261-496 3433, www.tapiz.com*, a small winery that owns a *finca* in Luján de Cuyo. There's a restored 1890's main house, beautifully decorated with impeccable taste, which is on the region's an most exclusive hotel and has one of the finest restaurants in Mendoza. See also Sleeping page 216.

A smaller winery, but also highly developed, **Carlos Pulenta-Vistalba** ⓘ *Roque Sáenz Peña 3135, Vistalba (west of Luján de Cuyo town centre), T0261-498 9400, www.carlospulentawines.com*, is renowned for its marvellous Vistalba wines and for having on its ultra-modern premises, *La Bourgogne*, one of the best restaurants east of the Andes.

The Malbec grape flourishes wonderfully at **Renacer** ⓘ *Brandsen 1863, Perdriel (south of Luján de Cuyo town centre), T0261-488 1247, www.bodegarenacer.com.ar*, which produces Punto Final Reserva, one of the top Argentine Malbec wines. Quite close to here, you'll find **Achával Ferrer** ⓘ *C Cobos by the Mendoza river, Perdriel (southwest of Luján de Cuyo town centre), T0261-498 4874, www.achaval-ferrer.com.* A young, modern and repeatedly prize-winning boutique bodega which produces the finest quality red wines, including the great Finca Altamira. **El Lagar de Carmelo Patti** ⓘ *Av San Martín 2614, Mayor Drummond (north of Luján de Cuyo town centre), T0261-498 1379*, is highly recommended for its welcoming owner, who personally leads the tours, and takes pride in serving his excellent Cabernet Sauvignon or his Gran Assemblage for tasting, even straight from the barrel. Spanish only.

Sleeping

Mendoza city *p204, map p206*

Like all tourist areas in Argentina, hotels fill up quickly in the holiday periods of Jan, Jul and Easter, and during the Vendimia festival from mid-Feb to mid-Mar.

LL Park Hyatt, Chile 1124, on main plaza, T0261-441 1234, www.mendoza.park.hyatt.com. Extremely swish and very comfortable with an excellent and affordable restaurant, pool, spa and casino.

AL NH Cordillera, España 1324, on plaza San Martín, T0261-441 6464, www.nh-hotels.com. A modern business hotel with smart, comfortable, well-equipped minimalist rooms, a small heated pool and a restaurant. Superior rooms have their own stylish terraces (some looking onto the plaza).

A Aconcagua, San Lorenzo 545, T0261-520 0500, www.hotelaconcagua.com. A large business hotel offering comfort and good service in functional rooms, next to the quiet Plaza Italia.

A El Portal Suites, Necochea 661, T0261-438 2038, www.elportalsuites.com.ar. Stylish, spacious and very comfortable rooms in this small apart hotel on Plaza Chile. Excellent value.

A Park Suites, Av Mitre 753, T0261-413 1000, www.parksuites.com.ar. Very comfortable apartments in this excellent modern 15-storey tower block business hotel, with a restaurant, pool, conference rooms, gym and sauna. All rooms are warmly decorated and have a small kitchen, and great views from the top floors. Larger apartments with 2-3 bedrooms are fully equipped and incredibly comfortable.

B Carollo, 25 de Mayo 1184, T0261-423 5666, www.hotelcarollo.com.ar. Comfortable place, though slightly old fashioned, and very welcoming, this hotel shares its pool and facilities with the newer Gran Hotel Princess next door.

B Grand Hotel Balbi, Av Las Heras 340, T0261-423 3500, www.hotelbalbi.com.ar. Old-fashioned splendour, now rather fading, in what was once one of Mendoza's finest hotels. You can still find elegance in some fine details; the rooms are spacious and simply decorated, but the rates are too high.

B Gran Hotel Mendoza, España 1210 y Espejo, T0261-425 2000, www.hotelmendoza.com. Spacious rooms and stylish decor make this an appealing though slightly pricey option. However, it's very central and there are larger rooms for families. Splendid views from its small restaurant El Mirador on the 10th floor.

B Gran Hotel Ritz, Peru 1008, T0261-423 5115, www.ritzhotelmendoza.com.ar. Highly

For an explanation of the Sleeping and Eating price codes used in this guide, and other relevant information, see Essentials, pages 48 and 51.

recommended for its excellent service, and good value in comfortable rooms. Great location, within quick reach of the centre.

B Nutibara, Av Mitre 867, T/F0261-429 5428, www.nutibara.com.ar. Welcoming, slightly old fashioned place, with eclectic decor but a lovely pool, a leafy patio, comfortable rooms, and a quiet but central location.

B Provincial, Belgrano 1259, T0261-425 8284, www.hotelprovincialmza.com. Welcoming spotless small hotel, though a bit pricey. The best feature is the great view of the Andes Cordillera at breakfast.

C Palace Hotel, Av Las Heras 70, T0261-423 4200, www.hotelpalace.com.ar. An Italian-owned small hotel, with 1960's Italian decor in its comfortable rooms. A central good value place with a popular restaurant.

C RJ Hotel del Sol, Av Las Heras 212, T0261-438 0218, hoteles@ciudad.com.ar. Most of this old house has been renovated, adding some comfort to the basic but decent rooms. A smart entrance, and lovely balconies (looking out onto noisy streets) remain from the original building. In summer, breakfast is served on the terrace.

F pp **Dam-sire**, Viamonte 410, San José, Guaymallén, T0261-431 5142, 5 mins from bus terminal. A family-run place with spotless rooms, breakfast included.

Youth hostels

F/E pp **Confluencia**, España 1512, T0261-429 0430, www.hostal confluencia.com.ar. This central hostel has a quiet small hotel atmosphere with immaculate simple rooms for 2-4 with own bath, and breakfast included, free internet access and cooking facilities. An excellent budget choice, recommended for its quietness, tidiness and friendly staff.

F/E pp **Damajuana**, Arístides Villanueva 282, T0261-425 5858, www.damajuana hostel.com.ar. Recommended for its stylish comfortable rooms and shared dorms , with pool in a lovely garden, and a small restaurant.

F pp **Andino (or Arístides)**, Arístides Villanueva 470, T0261-420 2486, www.mendozahostel.com. The quietest of the 3 hostels run by **Campo Base** (see below) lies in the lively bar area of Mendoza. The staff are friendly, though accommodation is basic, but there is a large nice garden which unfortunately separates some rooms at the back from their bathrooms.

F pp **Campo Base**, Mitre 946, T0261-429 0707, www.hostelcampobase.com.ar. A livelier and sometimes rowdier option than **Andino** above, with cramped rustic-style rooms for 2-9 people with shared bath, offering guests lots of parties and barbecues. Particularly ideal if you're planning to climb Aconcagua, as it's owned by friendly and expert mountain guide Roger Cangiani who also runs a travel agency in town. Discounts to HI members. Very similar in style and also central, is **Campo Base II**, Patricias Mendocinas 876, T0261-429 0775, www.hihostels.com.ar. It's larger and rooms have their own bath. There's also a small pool.

F pp **Independencia**, Mitre 1237, T0261-423 1806, www.hostelindependencia.com.ar. A lovely Tudor-style house in an attractive central location. Wooden floors add warmth to the spartan dorms and double rooms, all with own bath, and breakfast included. There is a huge kitchen and organic wines for sale. A travel agency organizes excursions to Aconcagua: see www.aconcagua-xperience.com.ar.

F pp **Internacional**, España 343, T0261-424 0018, www.hostelmendoza.net. In a quiet residential area, next to the civic centre (15 mins' walk from plaza Independencia), this is a very good and comfortable hostel with friendly staff, dorms for 4-6 and 1 double room, all with their own bathroom, and breakfast included. There is a bar and barbecues are held on Fris. The same owners run **Cuyo Aventuras** travel agency (see Activities and tours).

Camping

Camping Suizo, Av Champagnat, El Challao, 6 km from city, T0261-444 1991, www.alojar.com.ar/campingsuizo. Modern with pool, barbecues, hot showers, nice leafy surroundings, friendly, recommended.

Churrasqueras del Parque, T0261-452 6016, T0261-155123124. Right in the centre of the beautiful Parque General San Martín (next to the football stadium), at Bajada del Cerro de la Gloria.

Saucelandia, Tirasso 5165, 9 km east at El Sauce, Guaymallén, T0261-451 1409. Large pool and a restaurant. Take insect repellent.

Zona Alta del Río Mendoza *p212*

LL Cavas Wine Lodge, Costaflores, Alto Agrelo, Luján de Cuyo, T0261-410 6927, www.cavaswinelodge.com. A pricey but heavenly experience, ideal for a romantic and wonderfully relaxing stay. Just 14 incredibly spacious rooms in a rural mansion now beautifully restored to a very high standard with creativity and impeccable taste. Each room has a fireplace and its own little terrace, with a pool for a cool dip, in addition to the main swimming pool, with the most wonderful views of the Andes. Everywhere here you'll find that styles have been cleverly combined, so that Moorish patios sit beside little Mediterranean areas in a residence that feels like an Italian villa. A restaurant and a spa complete this unique place. Highly recommended.

AL Club Tapiz, C Pedro Molina, Russell, Maipú, T0261-496 3433, www.tapiz.com. Surrounded by vineyards, Tapiz is a small, beautifully restored neo-Renaissance Italian-style villa, where the minimalist style helps you unwind in the delightful comfort of the 7 guest rooms. A spa and superb cuisine in the **Terruño** restaurant make this unquestionably one of the top hotels in Mendoza. A member of the impressive chain of quality **NA Town and Country Hotels** www.newage-hotels.com. See also page 213.

A Casa Glebinias, Medrano 2272, Chacras de Coria, Luján de Cuyo, T0261-496 2116, www.casaglebinias.com. 2 detached houses set in large landscaped gardens are delightful places to stay. Decoration is simple, but there's a homely feel, a tempting swimming pool and beautiful trees and flowers in the grounds, looked after by an art historian and a scientist, the very welcoming owners of this charming rural hotel.

A Parador del Ángel, 100 m from main plaza, Chacras de Coria, Luján de Cuyo, T0261-496 2201, www.paradordel angel.com.ar. This 100-year-old adobe house has been restored with traditional materials and decorated in tasteful rustic style, making this a thoroughly relaxing place to stay surrounded by gardens, with a pool. Daniel, the owner, is an experienced mountain climber.

Eating

Mendoza city *p204, map p206*

There are 2 main areas to eat in the centre of the city: around the main Plaza Independencia with restaurants along Sarmiento and around Las Heras; or along C Arístides Villanueva, just a 10-min walk southwest of the main plaza where Mendoza's hipper crowd hang out in lively bars and chic restaurants. If you have your own transport, there are also excellent restaurants throughout the wine region. It's essential to book a table for the top restaurants.

City centre

TTT Bistro M, Park Hyatt Hotel, Chile 1124, T0261-441 1200. Recommended for its impeccably stylish setting, imaginative menu, and offering cheaper choices too.

TT Azafrán, Sarmiento 765. A fine-wine lover's heaven, with an extensive range from all the best bodegas, expert advice on wines and a fabulous delicatessen where you can enjoy superb *picadas*. Its menu changes with the season: basically Argentine style with some international touches. Recommended.

TT Boccadoro, Av Mitre 1976. Renowned locally for its *parrilla*.

TT El Mesón Español, Montevideo 244. Authentic Spanish food, great paella and live music at weekends. Cheap lunch menus.

TT Facundo, Sarmiento 641. A welcoming and friendly *parrilla* with lots of other choices and a good salad bar.

TT Francesco, Chile 1268, T0261-425 3912. A smart old town house with a wonderful garden at the back where you can try excellent Italian food, prepared by the Barbera family, and to accompany your meal, choose from over 350 different wines.

TT La Marchigiana, Patricias Mendocinas 1550. One of Mendoza's best restaurants and great value. Wonderful Italian food served in spacious surroundings with charming old-fashioned service. Popular with everyone from families to glamorous couples. Fantastic *parrilla*, home made *pastas caseras* and delicious puddings. Recommended.

TT La Mora, Perú 928, T0261-438 1044. A small quiet dining room with an intimate atmosphere, a limited but imaginative menu and a good wine list. Delicious dishes, such as the *ravioles negros* filled with salmon. Booking recommended.

La Sal, Belgrano 1069. Stylish and lively atmosphere for a creative menu which changes with the seasons. The wine list is extensive and there's good live music here too.

Mi Tierra, Mitre y San Lorenzo. Recommended for wine tasting with expert advice, this is an elegantly restored 1890's house with four rooms, each devoted to a different *bodega*: Norton, Catena Zapata, Chandon and Terrazas de los Andes. A limited menu with traditionally cooked meat-based dishes.

Montecatini, General Paz 370. Good Italian food is the speciality here, and also *parrilla* and seafood. The decor has been smartened, but this is slightly lacking in atmosphere. Popular with families.

Por Acá, Arístides Villanueva 557. The most original place in the area, a cosy and stylish place serving pizzas and drinks til late, and often noisier with crowds of people partying.

Sr Cheff, Primitivo de la Reta 1071. One of the city's longest established restaurants with a good reputation for *parrilla* and fish.

Terrazas del Lago, Av Las Palmeras s/n, T0261-428 3438. The main reason to come here is for the really splendid setting by the lake in Parque San Martín. The food is fine, too.

Anna, Av Juan B Justo 161, T0261-425 1818. One of the most attractive restaurants in town, this is an informal French-owned place, cleverly designed and very welcoming, with good food and drink at all times. The short menu combines French and Italian flavours, open for lunch and dinner. Excellent value, and open till late for laid-back drinking. Recommended.

Comida de Campo, Sarmiento 55. Resist the first café along Peatonal Sarmiento and head here instead for good set menu lunches and a vast range from pastas caseras to great traditional *Mendocino* steaks. Recommended. Groups are welcome.

Don Otto, Av Las Heras 242. Cheap, small and unsophisticated, but central.

Ferruccio Soppelsa, Espejo y Patricias Mendocinas, Plaza Independencia, and other branches. For the best ice cream with a great range, including wine flavours!

Il Dolce, Sarmiento 81. A friendly place for inexpensive set lunches and dinners, and good vegetarian options.

Mr Dog, Av Las Heras y Patricias Mendocinas. This local chain is better than average for fast food.

Quinta Norte, Mitre y Espejo. Attractively set in an old family mansion, this is a great informal place for good cheap meals that come in generous portions. Very good service.

Via Civit, Emilio Civit 277. Wandering back to town from the park, try the wonderful sandwiches, tasty tarts and exquisite pastries in the relaxed but refined atmosphere of an elegant traditional bakery. Open from breakfast time onwards.

Also try the atmospheric indoor market on Las Heras at nights for cheap and delicious pizza, *parrilla* and pasta. Also heaps of cured meats, dried fruits, pastries, wines and herbs and a cheap snack bar.

Arístides Villanueva is the area for an evening stroll and to find Mendoza's more exciting bars and restaurants, popular with a younger crowd, and just 10 mins' walk southwest of the main plaza. (Note that this street changes its name to Colón at Belgrano). You'll find it pretty quiet if you're heading out for an early dinner, but it really livens up after 2400.

3 90 (Tres con Noventa), Arístides Villanueva 451. Unbeatable for all the pasta possibilities imaginable, with any combination of sauce, all tasty. The atmosphere is friendly and studenty.

Zona Alta del Río Mendoza *p212*

1884 Francis Mallman, Bodega Escorihuela, Belgrano 1188, Godoy Cruz, T0261-424 2698. This is the place to go for a really special dinner. Mallman is one of the country's great chefs and here he's created an exotic and imaginative menu. Open for lunch and dinner, but reservation is advisable. Highly recommended.

See also page 210.

ΨΨΨ **La Bourgogne**, Bodega Carlos Pulenta, Roque Sáenz Peña 3531, Vistalba, Luján de Cuyo, T0261-498 9421. Top French cuisine using the best local ingredients, served in the stylish new ultra-modern premises of the Pulenta winery. See also page 214.

ΨΨΨ **Terruño**, Bodega Tapiz, Calle Pedro Molina, Russell, Maipú, T0261-496 3433. Refined minimalist decor in beautifully restored rooms of an Italian-style residence. Exquisite dishes such as Mediterranean flavours with a dash of Asian style, and high-quality local produce. Recommended. See also page 213.

ΨΨ **Almacén del Sur**, Zanichelli 709, Maipú, T0261-410 6597. A restored farmhouse surrounded by delightful gardens, with leafy patios makes an attractive setting for this delightful restaurant, where your vegetables are grown close to where you eat them. A good range of delicious and imaginative dishes beautifully served. Lunches are particularly recommended: 4-courses. Unforgettable.

ΨΨ **Karma**, Italia 6076, Chacras de Coria, Luján de Cuyo, T0261-496 1731. A truly exotic little gem. Owned by one of the Tibetan actors who filmed *Seven Years in Tibet*, which was filmed in Uspallata, there's an Asian atmosphere here both in the ambiance and the tasty food.

O Shopping

Mendoza city *p204, map p206*

Shops usually close for siesta 1300-1600, when the city centre is completely dead. The best area for clothes shopping is Av San Martín and Av Las Heras, where there are good souvenir, leather and handicraft shops, and vast sports emporia. Further north on San Martín are cheap fabric shops and old department stores, such as **C&A**. Las Heras has an attractive indoor market for good food, next to the corner of Patricias Mendocinas.

Books

Centro Internacional del Libro, Lavalle 14. Small selection of classics and paperbacks in English and *Buenos Aires Herald* usually available from kiosks on San Martín.

SBS, Gutiérrez 54. For more books in English.

Camping equipment

Casa Orviz, Juan B Justo 536, T/F0261-425 1281, www.orviz.com. Sales and rental of camping and climbing equipment; also provides climbing information.

Handicrafts

There are handicrafts markets on the eastern side of Plaza Independencia at weekends, and on Plaza España, Thu-Sun.

El Turista, Av Las Heras 351. Sells most of the traditional local souvenirs, piled high and pretty cheap.

Las Viñas, Av Las Heras 399. Good range of t-shirts, *ponchos* and ornate *mates*.

Mercado Artesanal, Av San Martín 1133. Traditional leather, baskets, and weaving.

Raíces, España 1092, just off Peatonal Sarmiento. High quality goods.

Shopping centres

Centro Comercial Mendoza Plaza, about 5 km east in Guaymallén, T0261-449 0100, 1000-1200. Known as **Mendoza Plaza Shopping**, this is the best indoor shopping mall with supermarkets, shops, fast food and cinemas, and a play area for kids. Free transfers from town; call to arrange.

Palmares, 7 km south in Godoy Cruz, is much smaller than the **Mendoza Plaza**, but includes a supermarket, shops, cinema and restaurants. Arrange a free transfer from the centre or your hotel by calling Palmares shopping centre office, T0261-43199052.

Wine stores/vinotecas

All the *bodegas* sell their produce 10% cheaper than in shops, and stock many wines you can't find elsewhere. But there are an increasing number of *vinotecas* in town: specialist wine stores that stock bottles from many bodegas together, and offer expert advice on what to buy. The following are recommended:

Central, Mitre y Espejo, T0261-459 0658, www.centralvinoteca.com. English spoken, tastings are arranged in advance.

Marcelino, Tiburcio Benegas y Martín Zapata, T0261-429 3648, Mon-Fri only. Also offers courses on wine tasting.

Puracepa, Av Sarmiento 644, T0261-423 8282. English spoken; offers delivery service worldwide. Stocks an incredible range of wine from US$3-230.

The Vines, Espejo 567, T0261-438 1031, www.vinesofmendoza.com, daily 1100-2200, booking advisable. Unique in its type and highly recommended. A lovely restored house with a peaceful atmosphere with a leafy patio create the perfect atmosphere where you can try a selection of premium wines, and wines from the top boutique bodegas in chic minimalist wine tasting rooms. Bottles are not sold on the premises, but they can be shipped to North America and Europe. An office next door takes reservations for visiting bodegas. Not to be missed.

▲ Activities and tours

Mendoza city *p204, map p206*

Mountain climbing

Club Andinista, F L Beltrán 357, Guaymallén, T0261-431 9870, www.clubandinista.com.ar. See also page 222 for more information on climbing Aconcagua.

Skiing

There are 3 resorts within reach of Mendoza. Equipment can be hired from **Piré**, Av Las Heras 615, T0261-425 7699, and other agencies. For useful information, see www.mendozaski.com.

Las Leñas, T02627-471 100, www.laslenas.com, 440 km from Mendoza, southwest of San Rafael. A world-class resort with by far the best skiing in the region. See page 227 for further details.

Los Penitentes, T02624-420110 (or Mendoza T0261-424 5648), www.penitentes.com, 183 km west on the road to Chile. A quiet family resort with a satisfying range of pistes, plus hotels and restaurants and affordable equipment hire. It's too far for a day trip from Mendoza but there is good accommodation.

Vallecitos, 95 km from Mendoza, on the winding road from Potrerillos, T02622-4236569, www.skivallecitos.com. A tiny ski centre and very basic place with simple accommodation but it can be reached on a long day trip from Mendoza.

Swimming pools

Gimnasia y Esgrima, Gutiérrez 261, T0261-425 0315. Indoor swimming pool, Turkish baths and sauna.

Marina Natación, San Lorenzo 765, T0261-423 6065. Indoor swimming pool.

Tour operators

There are lots of operators, especially on Peatonal Sarmiento. Most go to the same places but shop around for the best deals. As a rough guide: Mendoza city tour US$8, wine tour US$10, Alta Montaña US$25. There are also longer excursions including a long trip to the Valle de la Luna, US$50 (more comfortable from San Juan) and to Cañón del Atuel, US$30 (easier from San Rafael). The following companies are recommended.

A, Espejo 228, T/F0261-4291911. A good range of tours and some cheap deals.

Asatej, Peatonal Sarmiento 223, T/F0261-429 0029, www.asatej.com. Enormously helpful offering lots of trips and cheap travel deals.

Aymara Turismo, 9 de Julio 1023, T0261-420 5304, www.aymara.com.ar. Excellent, professional company offering a huge range of activities such as adventure tourism, rafting, climbing Aconcagua and the spectacular 10-day Andes horseback crossing to Chile every summer, as well as more conventional excursions to *bodegas* and Alta Montaña.

Bikes and Wines, Plazoleta Rutini, Maipú, T0261-410 6686, www.bikesandwines.com. Cycle tours to Maipú wineries including lunch; also bike rental, 1000-1800.

Campo Base, Peatonal Sarmiento 229, T0261-425 5511, www.youthtravelargentina.com. The same company that owns a chain of youth hostels offers wine tours oriented to younger travellers as well as much more demanding 3 and 6 day-long summer treks to Aconcagua base camps.

Cuyo Aventuras, in **Internacional** youth hostel (see Sleeping above), España 343, T0261-424 0018, www.cuyoaventuras.net.. Discounts to HI members.

El Cristo, Espejo 228, T/F0261-429 1911, www.turismo-elcristo.com.ar. A good range, including Valle de la Luna and some cheap deals for the usual tours.

The Grapevine, Peatonal Sarmiento 133, Galería San Marcos local 12, T0261-429 7522, www.thegrapevine-winetours.com.ar. British and Irish owned, the company organizes personalized tours in the wine region, including flights, combined with bodega visits and lunch. They also organize their own wine club meetings and publish a very informative free magazine, which is available everywhere.

Huentata, Las Heras 699, T0261-425 3108, www.huentata.com.ar. The usual short tours plus full-day excursions to Villavicencio and all the way up to Cruz de Paramillo, and then down to Uspallata, and another tour to Cañón del Atuel.
Inka Expediciones, Juan B Justo 345, T0261-425 0871, www.inka.com.ar. Bespoke climbing expeditions, including treks to Aconcagua base camps and alternative routes to the summit. Highly professional. Fixed departure dates. Mules for hire.
Mancagua, España 967, T0261-429 7398, www.mancaguaviajes.com.ar. Recommended for its friendly staff and many wine tour options, combining different *bodegas* with lunches, wine included.
Mendoza Viajes, Peatonal Sarmiento 129, T0261-461 0210, www.mdzviajes.com.ar. Imaginative tours in comfortable coaches, including to the valleys of Uspallata and Calingasta. Professional service cheap deals.

Whitewater rafting

The most popular place for rafting is on the challenging Río Mendoza at Potrerillos (see page 208, but there's also quieter rafting for beginners among the colourful green rocks of Río Atuel, to the south near San Rafael (see page 227). Further south still, there are more remote sites for rafting along the upper Ríos Atuel, Diamante, Grande and Andinos in southern Mendoza. Ask at one of the tour operators, such as **Ríos Andinos**, Sarmiento 717, T0261-429 5030, www.riosandinos.com. They are the most experienced operator for rafting on Mendoza river. They also run horse back rides and do some rock climbing.

Transport

Mendoza city *p204, map p206*

Air

To **El Plumerillo Airport**, 8 km north of centre, take bus No 60 from Alem y Salta, every hour at 35 mins past the hour, 40 mins journey, US$0.70; make sure there is an 'Independencia- Aeropuerto' sign on the driver's window. Taxi to/from centre US$4-5. Daily flights to **Buenos Aires**: 1 hr 50 mins, **Córdoba**, Aerolíneas Argentinas/Austral, **Santiago** (Chile) and **Buenos Aires**, Lan.

Airline offices Aerolíneas Argentinas/ Austral, Sarmiento 82, T0261-420 4100. **Lan** , España and Rivadavia, T0261-425 7900.

Bicycle hire

Hire companies include: **Cycles El Túnel**, at the exit of the subway passage coming from bus terminal, buys and sells cycles, also repairs, friendly. **Indiana Aventuras**, Espejo 65, T0261-429 0002, info@indianaventuras.com.ar. Also at **Adventure World**, Sarmiento 231, T0261-429 0206.

Bus

Long distance Beware of thieves at all times in the bus station. The big terminal is on the east side of the major road Av Videla or Costanera, 15 mins' walk from centre, via an underpass which leads from the corner between platforms 38 and 39 to Calle Alem. A taxi to the centre costs US$2-2.50. Call the helpful information centre for all companies and times, T0261-431 5000. There is an ATM, a locutorio, confiterías, lockers (AR$2 in 2 AR$1 coins), left luggage, US$1 (next to platform 52) and a travel agency opposite the information desk. Ticket offices for national and some provincial services are along a corridor behind the information desk; for the closer provincial destinations, including **Expreso Uspallata** services for Alta Montaña, go to the left (facing the information desk) and for Chile, Perú and Uruguay, go to the right.
Andesmar, España y Espejo, T0261-429 3894, and at the bus terminal, T0261-432 4800.
Provincial services To **San Rafael**, many daily, **Expreso Uspallata, TAC**, 3½ hrs, US$5-6. To **Malargüe**, **Expreso Uspallata**, 6 hrs, US$10, also **combi** service, **Transporte Viento Sur**, 3 a day (Mon-Fri), 2 on Sat, 1 on Sun, 4½ hrs, US$10. To **Cacheuta**, Expreso Uspallata, 5-7 daily, 1 hr, US$1.20. To **Alta Montaña** destinations, only with Expreso Uspallata, T432 5055: to **Potrerillos**, 6 daily, 1½ hrs, US$1.50; to **Uspallata**, 6 a day, 2-2½ hrs, US$4. To Los Penitentes or Puente del Inca, 3 a day, 3 hrs, US$4.50. To Las Cuevas, 2 a day, 4 hrs, US$4.60. Fewer services in winter. To Tunuyán, ECLA, several a day, 1-1½ hrs, US$2.50. To Tupungato, Empresa Mitre 380, several a day, 1½-2 hrs, US$3.

National services To **Buenos Aires**, 13-17 hrs, US$24-45, companies include **Chevallier, TAC, El Rápido, Tramat, Sendas, Andesmar, Central Argentino**. To **Bariloche**, Andesmar, one daily, US$38, 19 hrs, book ahead (or an alternative is TAC to Neuquén, and change).

To **Córdoba**, TAC, Chevallier, San Juan Mar del Plata, Tramat, Mercobus Plus Ultra, 9-12 hrs, US$12-18. To **San Luis**, TAC frequent, other companies including **San Juan Mar del Plata**, US$7-8, 3-3½ hrs. To **San Juan**, TAC, frequent, San Juan Mar del Plata, Andesmar, US$3.50-4.50, 2-2½ hrs, and others.

To **Tucumán**, 12-15 hrs, US$24-42, **Andesmar, Flecha Bus, TAC, Tramatall** via **San Juan, La Rioja** (US$17, 6-7 hrs) and **Catamarca** (8-9 hrs, US$19-20). To **Salta**, **Andesmar, Flecha Bus, Tramat** (via San Juan, La Rioja and Catamarca), 17-19 hrs, US$28-45.

To **Mar del Plata**, TAC, San Juan Mar del Plata daily, 17-19 hrs, US$38-45. To **Neuquén**, Andesmar, TAC, Del Sur y Media Agua 5 daily, 11-12 hrs, US$21-28. To **Comodoro Rivadavia**, Andesmar, 3 a day, 30-31 hrs, US$61. To **Río Gallegos**, Andesmar one daily, 40 hrs, US$86-112. To **Santa Fe**, TAC, 13 hrs, US$22-24. To **Rosario**, TAC US$18-22, 12 hrs.

International services To **Santiago**, Chile: several daily, US$15-20, 6-7 hrs depending on border crossing, **CATA, El Rápido, Tur Bus, Chile Bus, Tas Choapa, Ahumada**. There are also minibus services at similar rates, run by **Chiar, Nevada** and **Radio Móvil**. Passport required when booking, tourist cards given on bus. Children under 8 pay 60% of adult fare, but no seat. Book at least 1 day ahead, shop around.

The journey over the Andes is spectacular (see page 227 for a description). If you want to return, buy an undated return ticket Santiago-Mendoza; it is cheaper. Almost all the same companies also go to **Viña del Mar**. **Tas Choapa** goes to Valparaíso, 1 daily. **CATA** and **Chile Bus** go to La Serena, 3 a week, 12-16 hrs, US$27-30. **CATA** goes weekly to Arica, 1½ days, US$50.

To **Lima**, 2½ days, US$125-150, one service almost daily, with **El Rápido** and **Ormeño**. To **Montevideo**, 20-21 hrs, **El Rápido**, US$40, on Tue, also **EGA**, US$60, on Sun.

Car

Shop around and barter for cheap car hire since international tourists are charged double the Argentines' rate. Sometimes you'll find several companies at Calle Primitivo de la Reta, next to Plaza Pellegrini. **Avis**, Primitivo de la Reta 914, T0261-429 6403, www.avis.com.ar, or at airport, T0261-447 0150. Reliable and efficient. **Dollar**, Gutiérrez 567, T0261-425 0430, www.dollar.com.ar. **Hertz**, Espejo 415 and at the airport, T0261-423 0225, www.hertzargentina.com.ar. **Localiza**, Primitivo de la Reta 936, T0261-429 6800, www.localiza.com.ar.

Motorcycle

Motos Parra, Av Zapata 344, T0261-429 0340, motosparra@yahoo.com.ar, for repairs.

Directory

Mendoza city *p204, map p206*

Banks Most have branches with ATMs on plaza San Martín, or on nearby streets. Many *casas de cambio* on San Martín, corner with Espejo/Catamarca. **Consulates** Spain, Agustín Alvarez 445, T0261-425 3947; **Italy**, Necochea 712, T0261-423 1640; **France**, Av Houssay 790, T0261-423 1542; **Germany**, Montevideo 127, 2nd floor, D1, T0261-429 6539; **UK**, Bodega Domaine Vistalba, T0261-498 3504; **Israel**, Lamadrid 738, T0261-428 2140. **Chile**, Belgrano 1080, T0261-425 4844. **Internet** Find the largest places along Av Las Heras or Av San Martín. **Medical services 24-hr pharmacies** Del **Aguila**, Av San Martín y Buenos Aires. **Del Puente**, Av Las Heras 201, T0261-423 8800. **Mitre 2**, San Martin 701. **Emergencies** T428 0000. **Central hospital** near bus terminal, Alem y Salta, T0261-420 0600, T0261-449 0500. **Lagomaggiore**, public general hospital at Timoteo Gordillo s/n, T0261-425 9700. **Hospital Pediátrico Humberto Notti**, Bandera de los Andes 2603, Guaymallén, T0261-445 0045. **Post office** San Martín y Colón, T0261-429 0848. Mon-Fri 0800-2000, Sat 1000-1300. **United Parcel Service**, 9 de Julio 803, T0261-423 7861. **Telephone** There are many *locutorios* around the centre: a huge one on Av San Martín y Garibaldi, also at Av San Martín y Lavalle.

Alta Montaña

The high Andes to the west of Mendoza City are the world's highest mountains outside the Himalayas, and offer some of the country's most amazing scenery. The spectacular setting offers hiking, mountain climbing and adventures of all kinds, and is easily accessible from Route Nacional 7 to Chile, and simply driving west along Route 7 is an unforgettable experience. Alta Montaña is an essential part of any trip to the province, even if you're not crossing the border, or planning to climb Aconcagua. From the pretty oasis town of Uspallata, the road to Chile climbs up between the jagged snow-capped mountains, with staggering views of Volcán Tupungato in the distance to the south and Aconcagua closer at hand to the north. In winter, you'll quickly reach the snowline, the charming small ski resort of Los Penitentes and, beyond it, the natural wonder of the bridge at Puente del Inca, near the base for climbing Aconcagua. The road climbs finally to the border crossing at Túnel Cristo Redentor, and if you continue to Chile, the steep descent on the other side offers yet more superb views. In winter, this road is sometimes blocked by snow, so check conditions from Mendoza or Uspallata before setting off. Snow can lie as late as September and October, so bring appropriate clothing, even if you're just going for a day trip. » *For Sleeping, Eating and other listings, see pages 227-228.*

Mendoza to Upsallata » *pp227-228.*

There are two ways to reach Uspallata from Mendoza, both offering great views. Most dramatic is the climb north via many hairpin bends past the (abandoned) spa resort of Villavicencio (104 km, of which 52 km is on unpaved roads), or alternatively, you can head south from Mendoza to pleasant Potrerillos (102 km, all paved roads) and take a short detour to the thermal springs at Cacheuta.

Villavicencio → *Phone code: 0261 Colour map 3, A2*

Famous to all Argentines from the image of its Alpine-style 1940's hotel seen on bottles of the ubiquitous mineral water, Villavicencio (1800 m, Km 47) is reached by a wonderful drive. From Mendoza, head north along Route 52, across flat plains growing nothing but scrubby *jarilla* bushes, and following the *pre-cordillera* mountains on your left. The road rises steeply to climb through thickly forested mountains to the beautiful old spa resort, closed for many years, and now the centre of its own little nature reserve – a good place for a picnic and a stroll. The reserve protects the sources of mineral water and the whole area is owned by the French company Danone, who run a smart information centre on the local wildlife and employ *guardaparques* who can direct you to nearby walks. You can also stroll around the splendid grounds of the hotel, visit its chapel and eat at the **Hostería Villavicencio**, T0261-424 6482, run by a friendly local family who offer good value lunches and teas with fine local produce such as *jamon crudo* (prosciutto) and *chivo* (goat), which you can enjoy at tables outside.

Beyond Villavicencio the *ripio* road climbs up over the spectacular **Cruz de Paramillo**, via Caracoles de Villavicencio, the many (allegedly 365) hairpin bends which give the road its name *La Ruta del Año* (Route of the Year). At an altitude of 3050 m there are breathtaking views all around, and this is a marvellous introduction to the vast peaks of Aconcagua, Tupungato and Mercedario. Descending to the fertile valley of Uspallata, there are rocks popping up like jagged teeth through the earth, in extraordinary colours from aubergine through to oxidized copper green, orange and creamy white. There are no bus services, but many tour operators include this trip. With your own transport, this makes for a great route to Uspallata. Cyclists should carry plenty of water and be warned of the dangers of altitude and lack of shade. Take your time.

Cacheuta

An alternative route to Uspallata and into the Andes is via the pretty villages of Cacheuta and Portrerillos, offering thermal spa and watersports respectively. If you're driving, note that since the river has been dammed there is no direct road between Cacheuta (1245 m) and Potrerillos, so you need to take a detour to get to Cacheuta. From Mendoza, head south out of the city by Avenida J Vicente Zapata, Access Route 7, leading to Route 40. Follow signs to Cacheuta, passing the area's biggest petrochemical plant, before you climb up into the hills. Cacheuta's pretty setting in a narrow valley merits the extra journey to reach it. There's a huge complex of several thermal pools where you can spend a day, and next to this, a fine hotel in attractive gardens with a good restaurant. It's better to stay at least a night to really enjoy the mountain scenery. See Sleeping, page 227, for details.

Potrerillos → *Phone code: 02624 Colour map 3, B1*

Potrerillos (1354 m, Km 68), just 10 km further on from Cacheuta, is a charming laid-back village sprawling among the foothills of the Cordón del Plata mountains. In the summer it's a popular retreat among *Mendocinos*, but it's excellent for a weekend's walking or horse riding at any time of year, though particularly lovely in spring, or in autumn, when the avenues of alamo trees are a rich yellow against the mauve haze of mountains beyond. From December to February, you can go rafting and kayaking on Río Mendoza, which runs through the valley below the village. The water level depends on the time of year and the amount of snowmelt swelling the river, so that the high season varies from year to year. In summer you can hike from Potrerillos to Vallecitos over two days. There's also a lovely walk to Cascada del Salto, but the path isn't marked, so take a guide (see Activities and tours, page 228).

From Potrerillos' centre – where there's little more than a hotel, campsite and YPF station on a crossroads – you could take the road south up to Vallecitos via the little hamlets of El Salto, Las Vegas and San Jorge, where there's a small *cervecería* (microbrewery). There are *parrilla* restaurants, tea rooms and lots of *cabañas* for hire around these areas, and the views are wonderful.

Vallecitos → *Phone code 02622*

This tiny hamlet (2900 m) is 27 km west of Potrerillos along a madly winding *ripio* road, certainly not to be attempted in poor weather conditions. There's little here apart from a couple of *refugios* with hostel accommodation and a rather basic family ski resort, but it's popular as a day trip from Mendoza. The **ski centre** ⓘ *Valles del Plata Centro de Esqui, T02622-488810, www.skivallecitos.com, lift pass US$17 pp per day, equipment hire US$12*, has 4.7 km of pistes, mostly intermediate standard, seven ski lifts and a ski school. Vallecitos is used as a base camp by climbers for training in the nearby peaks, before attempting Aconcagua. Contact **Expediciones El Plata**, T02622-488810, www.expedicioneselplata.com.ar to take part in a climbing expedition to the beautiful summits of the Cordón del Plata range. They're less well known than Aconcagua, but also spectacular.

Uspallata → *Phone code: 02624 Colour map 3, A2 Population: 3,400*

The picturesque village of Uspallata (1751 m, 120 km from Mendoza and 52 km from Potrerillos) lies in its own wide valley, very close to the high Andes and so it's become a popular stopping point on the road to Chile. All routes pass through it, and yet it has retained a rather charming unspoilt atmosphere – out of peak season at least. With distant mountains glimpsed through a frame of *álamo* (poplar) trees, it is reminiscent of the Himalayas and was the setting for *Seven Years in Tibet*. Stay for a day at least to explore the mysterious white egg-shaped domes of **Las Bóvedas** ⓘ *2 km on R39 north, US$0.30*, built by the indigenous Huarpes people, under instruction by the Jesuits, to melt silver. There is a small, interesting museum.

Aconcagua Provincial Park

The Aconcagua Provincial Park is 190 km west of Mendoza city, and apart from Aconcagua itself – the highest peak in the world outside Asia, at 6959 m – it includes 30 other peaks over 4000 m, nine of them over 5000 m, making it a great centre for hiking and climbing. Mount Aconcagua gets its name from the Quechua for 'stone sentry', and it is indeed a majestic peak with five great glaciers hanging from its slopes. It's a demanding climb even for the experienced, and it's absolutely essential to take at least eight to 10 days just to adapt to the altitude before you ascend. Pulmonary and cerebral oedema are serious risks and the dangers should not be under-estimated: climbers die on the mountain every year. The north face was first climbed by Zurbriggen of the Fitzgerald Expedition in 1897, and in 1985, a complete Inca mummy was discovered at 5300 m: a sacred offering to the mountain. If you're planning to climb Aconcagua, it's essential to seek expert advice and plan your trip carefully. Below is a brief resume. See the official website, www.aconcagua.mendoza.gov.ar, for more details.

Access Valle de los Horcones (2950 m), 2 km west of Puente del Inca and another 2 km off RN 7: *guardaparque* (ranger station) and free camping, open in the climbing season. This is the last accessible point for vehicles. No permits are required for the short walk to the mirador on Laguna Horcones, where you have excellent views of Aconcagua's southern face, especially in the morning.

Advice Climbers are advised to make use of medical services where available in some base camps to check for early symptoms of altitude sickness and oedema. For more advice, and online discussion, see www.aconcagua.org.ar and www.aconcagua.com.ar. Tents must be able to withstand 160-kph winds. Clothing and sleeping gear for temperatures below -40°C. Always carry plenty of water, as there are very few sources. Take all your rubbish out with you: no litter is to be thrown away in the park, and bags are handed out at the park entrance to be collected when you leave. Bring stove and sufficient fuel: No wood is to be used for lighting fires. For emergencies only, use the guardaparques radio frequency 142.8 Mhz.

Permits It's essential to obtain a permit for trekking or climbing at any time of year: pay a fee (much cheaper for Argentine nationals) and fill in a form. You'll need to submit certain other documents for some specific activities. The rules vary according to time of year and activity. For climbing in the high season (15 December-31 January) you must obtain a permit in person in Mendoza, at the Subsecretaría de Turismo, Avenida San Martín 1143. In the winter season (1 April-14 November) permits to climb Aconcagua are sold at Dirección de Recursos Naturales Renovables, next to the gates of Parque General San Martín in Mendoza. Permits vary in price, depending on the season and the activity. An ascent permit lasts for 20 consecutive days from the moment it is stamped at the park entrance, and prices vary from US$330 (US$500 via Plaza Guanacos) in high season, to US$400 (for any route), in winter. Fees are much lower in mid season (1-14 December and 1-20 February), low season (15-30 November and 21 February-31 March), and in the special winter season (April). Be warned that places selling the permits, and fees, may change, so it's vital to check the official website. Trekking permits are needed for all walks up to any of the base camps (excepting Plaza Guanacos camp, at the end of the only ascent trek) and are sold near the park itself at Horcones ranger station. These cost: US$70 for seven consecutive days; US$50 for three consecutive days in high season, US$30 the rest of the year. Day permits are also available for US$10.

Trekking and climbing routes

There are two access routes to Aconcagua's summit: Río Horcones and Río de las Vacas, which lead to the two main base camps, Plaza de Mulas and Plaza Argentina respectively. For climbing Aconcagua, allow two weeks for the complete trip. Getting to the summit is not technically difficult: the problem is in taking sufficient time for your body to adjust to the high altitude. Most people fail simply because they take it too fast. All climbers should allow at least one week for acclimatization at lower altitudes before attempting the summit. Allow another few days for the weather. The best time is from the end of December to end of February.

Day permits allow you to walk from Horcones 4 hours up to Confluencia Base Camp (3390 m), where the upper Horcones meets the lower Horcones river, and then two hours back, all along the Quebrada del río Horcones. The walk presents no difficulties, except for the high altitude – so be prepared to take your time, and don't be surprised that some people in your group will be affected more than others.

Confluencia Base Camp can get horribly crowded in summer, but has an interesting international atmosphere: dozens of climbers and many more mules. Ranger station, public showers and medical services (in high season). From here you can either take the North Face route, used by 80% of climbers to Plaza de Mulas (4365 m), in eight hours, or the South Face Route to Plaza Francia (4250 m), in five hours. It's a tiring, rather monotonous walk or up to Plaza de Mulas, another busy camp, full of climbers and mules, with ranger station, medical services and the highest hotel in the world another 20-minute walk away.

South Face route leads from Confluencia to Plaza Francia base camp (five hours), with a mirador after about four hours looking over the lower Horcones glacier, with an outstanding view of the 3000-m high rock and ice walls of Aconcagua's south face. Plaza Francia Camp is less crowded, but has no services at all.

Route via the Polish Glacier: This little-used route starts at Punta de Vacas (2400 m), 16 km east of Puente del Inca, (also used to reach the Falso de los Polacos route that connects with the normal route). Plaza Argentina (4200 m) is the base camp with intermediate camps at Pampa de Leñas (2900 m), with ranger station, reached after four hours of easy walking from Punta de Vacas, and Casa de Piedra (3240 m), reached after a further moderate 6-hour walk along the same Quebrada del río de las Vacas, also with ranger station. From here, it's a steep seven-hour walk to Plaza Argentina, where there is a ranger station and medical services.

Facilities and services

Mules are available from Puente del Inca: about US$120 for 60 kg of gear one way to Plaza de Mulas or US$240 for 60 kg one way to Plaza Argentina; arrange return before setting out for a reduced two-way price. Organized trekking expeditions and tours can be booked in Mendoza, whether several days' trekking or climbing to the summit, with all equipment and accommodation / camping included (see Tour operators, Mendoza, and the official website).

From Uspallata, the Route Provincial 39 leads north to **Barreal** and **Calingasta** (see pages 230 and 239), unpaved for its first part and tricky when the snowmelt floods it in summer. Here you'll find the remains of the Inca road, one of the most important archaeological sites in the region, with foundations of an Inca Tambo (post house) too; look for signs on the left-hand side of the road. Uspallata has a few hotels, a hostel, food shops, bakeries, a post office and a YPF station with restaurant, shop and *locutorio*, open 0900-2200.

Route to Chile via Parque Provincial Aconcagua » *pp227-228.*

→ *Phone code: 02624*

This dramatic road, which runs past the foothills of Aconcagua, is one of Mendoza's most memorable sights and not to be missed. From Uspallata, a good paved road to Chile crosses a broad plain, with maroon and chalk-white rocks stick up from the rolling land. The road winds alongside a ravine with a thread of turquoise water below, before climbing up into a mountain pass with amazing terracotta rock formations and a heart-stopping glimpse of Volcán Tupungato – one of the giants of the Andes, rising to 6600 m. The first tiny village you come to, **Punta de Vacas**, has a large *gendarmería* (police station) but no accommodation. The road continues, climbing quickly beyond the snowline in winter, to the charming small ski resort of **Los Penitentes** (2580 m) ⓘ *Km 183, May-Sep, daily ski hire US$15, lift pass US$33.* Named after the majestic mass of pinnacled rocks on its mountainside, which you might think looks vaguely like a group of cowled monks climbing upwards, this is a low-key family ski resort right by the road, though it's surprisingly quiet. There is good skiing on the 28 pistes (total length of 25 km, with 10 lifts); most of them are graded difficult but there are a couple of long descents of medium difficulty and three beginners' slopes. It's good value and uncrowded.

Another low-key ski resort in the area is **Los Puquios**, 5 km west, www.lospuquios.com.ar. It's small, ideal for beginners and cheap. It's also used as a base camp for climbers for acclimatization to the high altitudes, and as a departure point for mule caravans to higher base camps closer to Aconcagua. On the southern side of Route Nacional 7, opposite, you'll find a cemetery for climbers who have died on Aconcagua's slopes; a reminder that this summit is not to be undertaken lightly.

Puente del Inca → *Phone code: 02624 Colour map 3, B1 Population: 132*

Puente del Inca (2718 m, Km 190), 7 km further on, is set among breathtaking mountains and is a great base for exploring the peaks on foot or on horseback, with access to the Parque Provincial Aconcagua. The naturally formed bridge, after which the village is named, is said to be one of the wonders of South America. Crossing Río Mendoza at a height of 19 m, it is 21-m long and 27-m wide and seems to have been formed by sulphur-bearing hot springs below which have stained the whole ravine an incredible ochre yellow, and left the bridge an eerie orange colour. Underneath the bridge are the ruins of a 1940's spa hotel, destroyed by a snow avalanche and now mostly washed away by the river, but a torrent of hot sulphurous water still gushing from its walls. (Watch your footing on the steps as they are extremely slippery.) The old baths, to the side of the river, between the bridge and the small church, have basic facilities, but are still good for a soak amidst magnificent scenery.

West of the village there is a fine view of Aconcagua, sharply silhouetted against the sky. **Los Horcones**, the Argentine customs post, is 1 km west. To visit the Laguna Horcones in the Parque Provincial Aconcagua, see page 224.

Chilean border

The paved road to the border goes through the 3.2-km **Cristo Redentor tunnel** ⓘ *0900-2100, US$3 for cars, no cyclists*, into Chile. The last settlement before the tunnel is tiny forlorn **Las Cuevas,** 16 km from Puente del Inca, offering only a kiosko, café and hostel accommodation. In summer you can take the old road over La Cumbre pass, to **El Cristo Redentor** (Christ the Redeemer), an 8-m-high statue erected jointly by Chile and Argentina in 1904 to celebrate the settlement of their boundary dispute. If you want to see this, take an all-day excursion from Mendoza, or drive up in a 4WD, after the snow has melted, or walk from Las Cuevas, (4½ hours up, two hours down – only to be attempted by the fit, in good weather). Expreso Uspallata runs buses to here from Mendoza.

The Chilean border is beyond Las Cuevas, but customs is back near **Los Horcones,** 2 km west of Puente del Inca. No fresh food is to be brought into Chile. Hire cars need special papers, and the number plate engraved in the window: tell your hire company if you plan to take the car into Chile.

Sleeping

Cacheuta *p223*

AL Hotel & Spa Termas Cacheuta, R82, Km 38, T02624-490152, www.termascacheuta.com. A warm and inviting place with comfortable rustic style rooms and thermal water piped into the private bathrooms. There's a large swimming pool, a good restaurant and access to the lovely spa included. Prices are full board. Recommended.

Potrerillos *p223*

C Cabañas Andinas, Av Los Cóndores y El Plata, El Salto, T0261-438 0505 www.cabanasandinas.com. Very comfortable with fabulous views, and beautiful gardens. Recommended.

C Gran Hotel Potrerillos, RN 7, Km 50, T02624-482130. A large faded 1940's resort hotel in a lovely hilltop location with simple rooms and a pool. Rates are for half-board.

Camping

ACA campsite, RN 7, Km 53, T02624-482013. Excellent, nicely maintained well-shaded site, with a pool, and hot water after 1800. US$ 5 per tent and car. Public phone on the road outside.

Vallecitos *p223*

C Refugio San Antonio, T0261-423 7423, www.sanantoniomendoza.com.ar. Down the hill from the ski centre this cosy *refugio* has been converted into an attractive hostel with a few warm simple rooms with their own baths. Full board optional. They also run excursions through their own travel agency **Cordón del Plata**, www.cordondelplata.com. There's no public transport to the resort.

Uspallata *p223*

A Valle Andino, RN7, T02624-420095, www.hotelvalleandino.com. The town's best. A modern airy place with good functional rooms, a heated pool and a restaurant.

B Hotel Uspallata, RN 7, Km 1149, towards Chile, T02624-420066, www.atahoteleria.com.ar/uspallata. One of several hotels built in Perón's post-war era, now modernized and spacious, in a lovely location with big gardens and a pool, all a couple of kilometres from the centre. Cheap restaurant.

D Los Cóndores, T02624-420002, www.hostalloscondores.com.ar. Great value, bright neat rooms, good restaurant with tasty pasta and cheap set menu. Highly recommended.

E pp **Viena**, Las Heras 240, T02624-420046. Small, family-run place with good little rooms, breakfast included.

F pp **Hostel Uspallata**, RN 7, Km 1141.5 (south of centre), T0261-154667240, www.hosteluspallata.com.ar. A large house with mature trees in quiet, attractive surroundings. Rooms are basic and clean, sleeping 4-8, some with bathroom. Lively bar and restaurant. Tours arranged. Discounts to HI members.

Aconcagua Provincial Park *p224*

AL Hotel Plaza de Mulas. Full-board or **B** without meals, good food, information, medical treatment, recommended, also camping area, open high season only.

Route to Chile via Parque Provincial Aconcagua: Los Penitentes *p226*

Hotels on the same side of the road as the ski resort offer a 20% reduction in ski passes.

AL Hostería Penitentes, T02624-420110. A cheery place near the slopes offering cheap deals for several nights. Good café, the friendly owner speaks perfect English. Recommended.
A Apart Hotel Las Lomas Blancas. Modern, functional units, clearly visible from the road, handy for the ski lifts, and there's lively laid-on nightlife. Prices are for an apartment for 4.
A Ayelén, opposite side of the road to the ski resort, T02624-420229. A huge, old fashioned, and shabby place, usually filled with groups of students. Convenient but overpriced, poor restaurant, terrible service. Last resort.
E pp **Campo Base Penitentes**, T0261-425 5511, www.penitentes.com.ar. One of the cheapest options in the Andes for staying at a ski resort. Lively atmosphere. Slightly cramped dorms with shared bath, bar and restaurant and all the usual hostel facilities. Minibus transfers to Mendoza. Ski programmes in season, though the hostel is open all year.

Puente del Inca *p226*
C Hostería Puente del Inca, RN 7, Km 175, T02624-420 5304. Next to the small ski centre at Los Puquios, has doubles and rooms for 4-8, huge cosy dining room, helpful advice on Aconcagua, good atmosphere. Warmly recommended. Full board optional.
F pp **Hostel La Vieja Estación**, 100 m off the road next to the bridge, T0261-4521103, www.viejaestacion.com. Basic but cheery hostel, cheap meals, use of kitchen.
Camping At Los Puquios and at Laguna Horcones inside the park.

Chilean border: Las Cuevas *p227*
F pp **Arco de las Cuevas**, T0261-426 5273, www.arcodelascuevas.com.ar. Set right above the old road to Cristo Redentor on a picturesque old Alpine-like stone and wooden-arch, this has spartan though comfortable dorms, a restaurant, and a bar that mostly attracts climbers, some skiers and mountain guides. Transfer to access to Aconcagua Provincial Park.

Eating

Potrerillos *p223*
El Futre, opposite the ACA campsite. Typical Cuyo food, vegetarian dishes and homemade pizzas. Open all day, summer only.
Los Pinos, Av Los Cóndores, on the left hand side as you go up the hill. Recommended for trout.
Tomillo, Av Los Cóndores, El Salto. Open all day for excellent homemade cooking in a welcoming simple place.

Uspallata *p223*
There are several reliable *parrillas* in town; the cheapest is **La Estancia de Elías**, opposite the YPF station. Right on the crossroads, **Pub Tibet** is a welcoming bar with photos from the filming here of *Seven years in Tibet*, and a warm atmosphere.

Activities and tours

Potrerillos *p223*
Argentina Rafting, Ruta Perilago, T02624-482037, www.argentinarafting.com. Reliable company. Guide Rodolfo Navio can organize all kinds of activities including mountain biking, climbing and a 2-day hike from Potrerillos to Vallecitos in summer. Rafting costs around US$30 for 2 hrs rafting, with all equipment and transport included.

Uspallata *p223*
Desnivel Turismo Aventura, C Ejército de los Andes, T02624-420275, desniveltursimo aventura@yahoo.com.ar. Rafting, mountain biking, trekking, riding, climbing and skiing.

Transport

Alta Montaña *p222*
Expreso Uspallata, T0261-432 5055, has daily services to and from **Mendoza** with stops at all towns along RN 7. Fewer services in winter, when roads can be blocked by snow, west of **Uspallata**. Between Uspallata and **Mendoza**, there are 6 services a day; between **Puente del Inca** and **Mendoza**, 3 a day, and between **Las Cuevas** and **Mendoza**, 2 a day. From **Potrerillos** to **Mendoza**, 1½ hr, US$1.50; from **Uspallata**, 2-2½ hrs, US$4; from **Puente del Inca**, 3 hrs, US$4.50; from **Las Cuevas**, 4 hrs, US$4.60. Buses going to Chile do not pick up passengers on their way.

Cacheuta *p223*
Daily **Expreso Uspallata** service to/from **Mendoza**'s terminal.

Southern Mendoza province

The southern half of the province is wilder and less visited by tourists than the area around Mendoza city, and it's well worth taking a few days to explore. There are two main centres, the closest of which and most appealing, is the charming town of San Rafael, the centre of its own wine-growing region, with tree-lined streets and excellent bodegas. Near here, there's rafting heaven in the extraordinary Cañón del Atuel, a canyon of weird rock formations with a wonderful fast flowing river running through it. The other centre, much further south, is the fledgling tourist town of Malargüe, which you could use as a base for skiing at Las Leñas, or for visiting remote areas of natural beauty at La Payunia and Llancanelo. There are two possible routes to the south of the province: you can take the fast Route 40 directly to San Rafael, or the picturesque route from Potrerillos along the Cordon del Plata to Tupungato, a sleepy place with superb wineries and the starting point for long excursions into Tupungato Provincial Park. An appealing detour here is to scenic Manzano Histórico, right in the foothills of the Andes. ▸▸ *For Sleeping, Eating and other listings, see pages 234-237.*

Tupungato ▸▸ *pp234-237.*

→ *Phone code: 02622 Colour map 3, B2 Population: 11,700*

To reach the quiet little town of Tupungato (1050 m), take the picturesque road from Potrerillos (Route 89), descending along the Córdon del Plata mountain range, with splendid views of the mountains, and through the fertile fruit- and vine-growing Uco Valley. Otherwise, take Route 86 from Route Nacional 40, south of Mendoza. Nearby are the stunningly wild mountain landscapes of Tupungato Provincial Park, named after the imposing peak of its volcano, 6600 m, and inaccessible to the public unless you go with an approved guide, see page 227. There are also superb wild landscapes on the upper Río de Las Tunas, to the west of town; contact the tourist office at Tupungato to stay overnight at the nearby Refugio Santa Clara (they'll direct you to the army for the key). The best way to get to the park is to go on a trip with Rómulo Nieto's company (see Tour operators, page 236). **Tourist information** on Tupungato and the surrounding area is available from the foyer of **Hotel Turismo**, Belgrano 348, T02622-488007. Ask them about nearby bodegas and estancia visits for horse riding.

There are many vineyards around Tupungato; one of the most famous is **Bodega Salentein** ⓘ *Los Árboles, 15 km south, T02622-429000, www.bodegasalentein.com, tours of the bodega daily 1000-1600*, whose fine wines you may have noticed in many restaurants. With a beautiful setting against the foothills of the Andes, the bodega produces some of the country's finest wine (the Malbec is exquisite) and you can stay in **Posada Salentein** (L) which has comfortable rooms, extremely welcoming hosts, and there's perfect peace in which to walk, ride, and relax. Recommended.

A much newer winery also worth visiting is the Spanish-owned **O Fournier** ⓘ *Calle Los Indios, La Consulta, west of San Carlos, T02622-451088, www.ofournier.com*. Its output is dedicated mainly to Tempranillo grapes, and here you can admire both the vines and the avant-garde architecture of the winery building, which is strictly functional and state of the art.

Continue south from Salentein to **Manzano Histórico**, a tiny hamlet in fabulous scenery, where a statue of San Martín marks his victorious return via this route from Chile. A *hostería* and campsite make this a good base for trekking, and there's a little shop and bar for provisions.

San Rafael » pp234-237.

→ Phone code: 02627 Colour map 3, B2 Population: 107,000

San Rafael (688 m, 236 km south of Mendoza) is a charming, quiet, airy town in the heart of fertile land which produces wine, fruit and olives in abundance. It's a relaxed place, smaller and less sophisticated than Mendoza but with a good range of accommodation. It makes an ideal base for exploring the vineyards and for trying adventure sports at nearby Cañón del Atuel or more challenging activities further west. There are lovely, leafy boulevards of French-influenced buildings, thanks to the arrival of a significant French community here in the early 1900s, and it's a trim and well-maintained place, where everyone cycles around – there are more bicycles than cars on the streets. The main street is Avenida Hipólito Yrigoyen, changing names at the central north/south street Avenida San Martín (called Avenida El Libertador south of Avenida H Yrigoyen).

There are ATMs and *locutorios* all along Yrigoyen, and a friendly and helpful **tourist office** ⓘ *7 blocks west of San Martín at Av H Yrigoyen y Balloffet, T02627-437860, www.sanrafael.gov.ar and www.sanrafael-tour.com.*

Sights

Río Diamante runs just south of the town, with a lovely park, **Parque Mariano Moreno**, 2 km from the centre, on an island, the Isla del Río Diamante. Among its attractions are a zoo and a small museum, the **Museo Municipal de Historia Natural** ⓘ *Tue-Sun 0800-2000, free, take Iselin bus along Av JA Balloffet.* San Rafael is at the heart of an important wine-producing region, whose wines are at least as excellent as those around Mendoza. One of the country's most important bodegas is **Bianchi** ⓘ *T02627-422046, www.vbianchi.com*, which can be visited on a commercialized tour.

The **Bianchi** champagne house ⓘ *RN 143, 5 km west of town*, is also worth seeing for the fascinating process and rather over-the-top pseudo-classical building (take a taxi as buses are infrequent). Their more traditional bodega is in town, at Comandante Torres y Ortiz de Rosas, and also gives an excellent and detailed tour, and sells the top wines at reduced prices after a generous tasting. Look for their exported wines abroad under the names Elsa, Elsa's vineyard or Valentín Bianchi Premium. There's a smaller, more intimate bodega **Jean Rivier** ⓘ *H Yrigoyen 2385, T02627-432675*, which also produces excellent wine, and can be visited Monday to Saturday.

Around San Rafael

San Rafael is a great centre for all kinds of activities including rafting, horse riding, trekking, climbing and fishing. The most spectacular place for adventure is the nearby **Cañón del Atuel**, 35 km southwest. It's an atmospheric drive along the *ripio* road through this 20 km long ravine of extraordinary rock formations, of cream and pink, and metallic sulphurous greens next to vivid terracotta. There are constantly changing views and an eerie feel in places, in the darker recesses of the canyon, where birds of prey wheel overhead. The gorge lies between two lakes, 46 km apart, **El Nihuil** (9600 ha), and **Valle Grande** (508 ha) ⓘ *from San Rafael 3 buses (Iselin, T02627-435998) a day go to the Valle Grande at the near end of the gorge, 35 km, US$1.40. There is no public transport through the gorge to the El Nihuil dam*. The best place for rafting is near Valle Grande, 2 km down the river from the Valle Grande dam (about 40 km from San Rafael). On the south side of the river, near the bridge, you'll see plenty of adventure tour operators (see page 236 for the most reliable ones). Many offer river rafting (grade 2 for beginners) and horse riding, and several offer excursions to places further afield for more challenging rafting, such as the upper Atuel or Diamante river (up to grade 5, experience required). There are plenty of hotels

Alive

Some 8 km from Hotel Termas El Sosneado, a plaque marks the site of a crash of an Uruguayan airforce plane in October 1972. The plane, a Fairchild F-27 en route from Montevideo to Santiago, was carrying 45 passengers and crew, including the members of the Uruguayan rugby team. The pilot, co-pilot and several passengers died on impact and despite the efforts of the Chilean and Argentine airforces, the wreckage was not found. Two of the survivors, Nando Parrado and Roberto Canessa, crossed the mountains to Chile, by an incredibly arduous journey, and finally found a local man who told them that they'd been within 17 km of a settlement to the east in Argentina. They brought help to the remaining passengers and crew who had spent 70 days on the Las Lágrimas glacier, substantially extending all known capacity for the human body to survive, by eating the flesh of their dead companions. The incident inspired the best selling book *Alive!* by Piers Paul Read, and the films *Survive* (1976) and *Alive!* (1992). Better still, read Nando Parrado's own account, *Miracle in the Andes: 72 Days on the Mountain and My Long Trek Home*.

Today, you can go on a spectacular three-day horseriding expedition from Malargüe to visit the crash site, which will give you an appreciation of a struggle for survival at high altitudes in austere, outstandingly beautiful landscape.

and campsites lining the pretty river banks on the north side of the river, in a 13-km stretch from this bridge back in the direction of San Rafael.

Lago Los Reyunos is another popular excursion, 35 km west of San Rafael, a lake in barren rocky landscape, which can only be reached on a tour, as there are no buses. But far more spectacular is the **Laguna Diamante**, 200 km northwest of San Rafael, an ultramarine blue expanse of water, whipped by perpetual winds, set against the craggy backdrop of the Andes and the perfectly conical Volcán Maipo. Only 4WD vehicles will make it over the last 60 km or so of track, and it's best to go on an excursion from San Rafael with **Taiel Viajes** (see page 237). There is some superb horse riding in the region into the Andes. You could take an excursion from El Sosneado (see below) or Tupungato to the place where the Uruguayan plane crashed into the mountains, subject of the book and film *Alive!* (see box above). This is less gruesome than you might think, since the landscapes are amazing: stark and very beautiful. **Laguna del Atuel**, 200 km west of San Rafael, has incredible turquoise water lapping against ochre mountains, and makes for another fabulous five-day horse riding trip.

El Sosneado and around » pp234-237.

If you're heading south to ski or hike in Las Leñas, or explore the area around Malargüe, you might like to stop off at El Sosneado. A good paved road (the 144 and then the 40) leads west from San Rafael across the vast plain of the Río Atuel, passing saltflats and marshland as you head towards stark snow dusted mountains rising steeply out of the ochre coloured land. **El Sosneado**, at Km 138, is the only settlement, with a service station, *hostería* and a small shop for fine home cured hams and olives, where you can also take away delicious sandwiches. The **YPF** station sells snacks and hot drinks. El Sosneado is also the starting point for good rafting and treks into the mountains, but there is little infrastructure in the village itself, and most visitors prefer to arrange their trips before coming here, in San Rafael or Malargüe. However, if you're feeling spontaneous, tours can be arranged at **Hostería El Sosneado** (see Sleeping, page 235).

Nearby there's a good lake for trout fishing, **Laguna El Sosneado**, 42 km away, reached by a *ripio* side road following the valley of the Río Atuel northwest. Some 13 km or so further on from the lake, there are natural thermal pools, the **Termas el Sosneado**, where you can bathe in the sulphurous waters for free, since there's no organization here, and the **Hotel Termas El Sosneado** is in ruins. Ahead, you'll see the Overo volcano (4619 m).

Los Molles → *Phone code: 02627 Colour map 3, B1*

The greatest attraction in the area is the superb ski resort of Las Leñas, reached by a road 21 km southwest of El Sosneado and 156 km southwest of San Rafael following the Río Salado west into the Andes. After 30 km, the road passes through the tiny hamlet of Los Molles, a small, faded old thermal resort, now little more than a cluster of hotels, the oldest of which has access to thermal springs. None of these establishments is luxurious but they offer an alternative to expensive Las Leñas hotels, plus some adventure tourism trips in the summer that mainly include horse riding to nearby sites. Opposite Los Molles a *ripio* road leads to the *refugio* of the **Club Andino Pehuenche** and 8 km further on, to the **Laguna de la Niña Encantada**, a beautiful little lake and shrine to the Virgin. Continuing towards Las Leñas, there are the strange **Pozo de las Animas** (Well of the Spirits), two natural circular pits, filled with water (the larger is 80 m deep); where wind blowing across the holes makes a ghostly wail, hence the name. They're a curious sight if you happen to be passing, but don't quite merit a special excursion.

Las Leñas → *Phone code: 02627 Colour map 3, B1*

ⓘ *T02627-471100, www.laslenas.com, lift pass in high season US$46 per day, equipment hire US$23 daily, 13 ski-lifts.*

Las Leñas (2250 m), 49 km off the San Rafael-Malargüe road, is internationally renowned for its excellent skiing and snowboarding. As a result, it's one of the most expensive resorts in the country, full of beautiful people in trendy bars and wealthy Argentine families. Set at the end of a spectacular valley, in the middle of five snow-capped peaks, it has powder snow throughout the season on 27 pistes with a total length of 64 km and despite the frequent bad weather and lack of tree cover, its steep slopes, with a vertical drop of some 1230 m, and the fact that you can walk straight out of your hotel and onto the pistes, make it the best resort in South America. A constantly circulating free bus service picks up guests from further flung hotels in the resort. The season runs mid June to early October but the busiest and most expensive time is throughout July and August, when prices are at least 50% higher. The resort also has a ski school, a special snowboard park, many cafés, bars and restaurants (several right on the pistes), a useful information point where there are lockers, banks, doctors, and tourist information. There are also many ski patrol units all over the pistes, so you are in very safe hands here. In summer, Las Leñas also operates as a resort for adventure sports, such as trekking and climbing. Beyond Las Leñas the road continues into **Valle Hermoso**, a beautiful valley accessible from December to March only.

Malargüe

» pp234-237.

→ *Phone code: 02627 Colour map 3, B2 Population: 18,100*

Situated 186 km southwest of San Rafael in reach of really spectacular unspoilt landscapes, Malargüe (1426 m) is slowly developing as a centre for hiking and horse

riding. It promotes itself rather grandly as the national centre for adventure tourism
but the standard of accommodation and service is still very disappointing here. However, it's certainly a cheap alternative to Las Leñas in the ski season when there are frequent minibus services between the two and there is a 50% reduction on your ski pass if you stay in a Malargüe hotel. However the best time to come is from spring to autumn, when you can make the most of the landscape for walking and riding. The **Fiesta Nacional del Chivo** (locally produced kid, a local delicacy) is held in the first fortnight of January, with live music and partying, attracting national *folclore* stars, as well as Chilean performers and public from across the Andes.

Malargüe has a broad main street, San Martín, with an assortment of small shops, *locutorios*, cafés and the odd run-down hotel, but the best accommodation is in the outskirts, north of the centre. On the way into town from the north, there's an impressive modern conference centre on the right, built for conventions of the nearby Philip Auger Observatory of Cosmic Rays, but mostly used for showing films. It has a smart bar. Next to it is the helpful **tourist office** ⓘ *T02627-471659, 0800-2300, www.malargue.gov.ar*, which can arrange for you to visit the nearby provincial parks.

Around Malargüe

The wild untouched landscape around Malargüe is surprising and extraordinarily beautiful. There are three main places to visit, all pretty remote and with no public transport, so unless you have your own vehicle, they can only be visited on a tour. Even if you do have your own transport, you must be accompanied by an authorized guide, which must be arranged in advance, and which requires a certain amount of planning.

La Payunia Reserve, 208 km south, is the most remarkable of the three, and dominated by the majestic peaks of several snow-capped volcanoes. The vast expanse of seductive altiplanic grasslands, is riven with volcanic peaks, and deep red and black crags of extraordinary sculpted lava. The appearance of hundreds of guanaco running wild across your path adds to the magic. The entrance is 100 km south of Malargüe on sandy *ripio* roads. You can bring your own vehicle here and the *guardaparques* will show you around in their 4WD. Ask at the tourist office in Malargüe for directions; they will also radio the *guardaparques* to expect you. The best way to enjoy the reserve is on horseback, on a three-day expedition or you can take a tour from Malargüe with **Karen Travel**, see Activities and tours, page 237.

The **Laguna Llancanelo** (pronounced *shancannELLO*), 65 km southeast, is filled with hugely varied birdlife in spring, when 150 species come to nest on its lakes. At any time of year you'll see Chilean flamingoes, rising in a pink cloud from pale turquoise waters where volcanic peaks are perfectly reflected. You may also see tern, curlews, grebes, teal and black-necked swans, among others. To get there, contact the Llancanelo *guardaparques* via the tourist office, or go on a trip from Malargüe with **Karen Travel.**

At **Caverna de las Brujas** ⓘ *2- to 3-hr guided tours, lights and helmets provided, children over 7 welcome*, there are 5 km of underground caves to explore, taking you through different eras of the earth's development from the Jurassic period onwards, and a fantastic variety of elaborate stalactites and stalagmites. There is no independent access to the caves, and all visits must be arranged with one of the authorized tour operators in Malargüe. The tourist office in Malargüe will show you pictures of the caves, and recommend a tour operator. See also Activities and tours, page 237.

Border with Chile

Paso Pehuenche (2553 m) is reached by a *ripio* road which branches off Route 40, 66 km south of Malargüe. On the Chilean side the road continues down the valley of the Río Maule to Talca. The border is open from December to March 0800-2100 and April to November 0800-1900.

Sleeping

Tupungato and around *p229*

AL Chateau D'Ancon, RP 89, San José, Tupungato, T02622-488245, www.estanciancon.com. At the foot of the mighty Tupungato volcano, a 1933 French-style rural mansion is at the heart of a traditional estancia owned by the Bombal family, who were originally French, but have been living in Mendoza since 1760. The magnificent park was designed by famous Argentine landscape architect Charles Thays and all the fruit and vegetables used for meals here are grown in nearby orchards and kitchen gardens. A wonderfully comfortable place to stay, with elegant decor inside the house, and excellent service. Open mid Oct-Apr.

D Hostería Don Romulo, Almirante Brown 1200, T02622-489020, www.donromulo.com.ar. This *hostería* is owned by Rómulo Nieto, who runs his own tour company (see Tour operators, page 236). There are simple rooms with TV and bath for 2-4 with a cosy lounge to relax in and decent, very inexpensive, food from pasta to *parrilla* in the restaurant. Recommended. .

D Hotel Turismo, Belgrano 1060, T02622-488007. A slightly modernized 1940's place, basic but comfortable rooms with wonderful kingfisher blue tiles in the bathrooms, some family rooms, a pool and a good restaurant.

Camping

Patios de Correa, T02622-15673299, Calle La Costa, El Peral, 4.3 km northwest of Tupungato. A good site in woods of willow and walnut trees, on the river bank, also a good picnic spot.

Camping San Antonio, RP 94, Km 27.5, T0261-4294099, www.campingsanantonio.com.ar. There are various attractive spots in the Manzano Histórico, but this one is particularly recommended for its good, well-kept facilities, including a large pool.

San Rafael *p230*

There are lots of appealing small hotels here.

A Tower, Av Yrigoyen 774, T02627-427190, www.towersanrafael.com. The smartest option is this international-style hotel easily spotted in the main street, an 8-storey peachy yellow building. It's slightly soulless, but has luxurious rooms, great bathrooms, very professional service, a small pool and spa.

B Family Inn, Av Yrigoyen 5501, T02627-431451, www.familyinnsanrafael.com.ar. This modern roadside hotel is conveniently located next to the airport, in the western outskirts of town. Rooms are spacious, functional and open directly onto neat gardens, with a pool. There's also a restaurant and a gym.

B Kalton, Av Yrigoyen 120, T02627-430047, www.kaltonhotel.com.ar. The oldest, and still the most welcoming hotel in town, with comfortable rooms, a small cheery bar and excellent service. Highly recommended.

B Nuevo Mundo, Av Balloffet 725, T02627-445666, www.hnmsanrafael.com.ar. This small, modern business-hotel has minimalist decor in its rooms, good service, and is great value. There is a restaurant and a spa, and it's close to the town centre.

B San Rafael, C Day 30, T/F02627-428251, www.hotelsanrafael.com.ar. A decent option with plain comfortable rooms and welcoming bar area, and very reasonable prices.

C Regine, Independencia 623, T02627-430274, www.reginehotel.com.ar. A delightful rustic place, with its pool in the garden. It's slightly eccentric, and popular with older guests, but there's a relaxing atmosphere. Rooms with pastel decor have TV and bath and there's a *quincho* for *parrillas*. Good value.

D Jardín, Av Yrigoyen 283, T02627-434621. Welcoming modern place with stylish rooms off a lovely patio. A bargain, with breakfast, included.

D Tonin, Pellegrini 330, T02627-422499, www.sanrafael-tour.com/tonin. A lovely quiet family-run place, with modern spacious rooms, TV and bath. Good location next to the plaza.

Youth hostels

F pp **Tierrasoles**, Alsina 245, T02627-433449, www.tierrasoles.com.ar. Convenient for its proximity to the bus station, this is a lively, welcoming well-kept house with all the usual hostel facilities, basic dorms, also doubles, all with shared bath, and lots of excursions and activities on offer, including bikes for hire.

Camping

El Parador, at the park on Isla Río Diamante, 5 km southeast, T02627-420492, www.complejoelparador.com.ar. There are also many sites at Valle Grande in the Cañón del Atuel.

Around San Rafael *p230*

B **Valle Grande Hotel & Resort**, T02627-15580660, www.hotelvallegrande.com. Well situated on the banks of the river in the Cañón del Atuel with a big terrace and good views from its restaurant, this has smart rooms, a pool, and friendly service, and there are lots of activities laid on for guests. Also *cabañas* for hire, popular with families and very lively in summer.

El Sosneado and around *p231*

D pp **Hostería El Sosneado**, T02627-421551, www.sanrafael-tour.com/elsosneado. Half board, simple clean rooms with rustic furniture, and 5 cabañas, sleeping 4-6, with breakfast included, and welcoming owners, who also organize summer horse-riding excursions to the 'Avión de los Uruguayos', where the Uruguayan plane crashed (see *Alive!* box, page 231) or to Laguna del Atuel, rafting and 4WD trips.

Los Molles *p232*

Accommodation here is much cheaper than at Las Leñas, but it's all very basic.

B-C **Lahuen-Co**, on left-hand side of road, T02627-499700. The most welcoming hotel here, built in 1938, is still pretty kitsch. Its special feature is the sulphurous thermal baths, in private cabins in a decaying extension at the back.

Las Leñas *p232*

Budget travellers should consider staying in Malargüe or Molles. Most of the accommodation is expensive, although some cheaper apart-hotels and dorm houses are available. For further information, T02627-471100, www.laslenas.com. The following options are all **L-A** and have restaurants: **Piscis**, 5-star with exceptional facilities and pools, including an outdoor heated pool, fine restaurants, casino and shows; **Aries**, 4-star, with a sauna, gym and pool; **Escorpio**, great views; **Acuario** right in the thick of the action; **Geminis**, an apart-hotel, also with pool and sauna.

Malargüe *p232*

Guests staying for more than 2 nights are issued with a voucher for 50% discount on a Las Leñas ski pass.

B **Microtel Inn & Suites**, R40 Norte (north of centre), T02627-472300, www.microtelinn.com.ar. By far, the best option in town with very comfortable rooms and also well-equipped *cabañas*, all very functional and simply decorated. It has a heated pool, sauna and a large restaurant.

B **Rincón Sur**, R40 Norte (north of centre), T02627-15514816, www.posadarinconsur.com. In attractive setting near the river, this is a small complex of simple though reasonably comfortable cabañas, brightly painted inside.

B **Río Grande**, R40 Norte (north of centre), T02627-471589, hotelriogrande@infovia.com.ar. A good value place with renovated rooms.

E **La Posta**, Av San Martín 646, T02627-472079, laposta_malargue@yahoo.com.ar. A welcoming cheap place with wood-panelled entrance hall and rooms. Also has a *parrilla*, a few blocks away, serving good kid and trout.

Youth hostels

F pp **Campo Base**, Telles Meneses 897, T02627-471534, www.backpackersmalargue.com.ar. A lively hostel with basic comfort in its dorms and doubles, all with shared bath. Excursions arranged.

F pp **Internacional**, Prolongación Constitución Nacional (Finca No 65), 2 blocks from R40 Norte, south of town, T02627-470391 or T15402439, www.hostelmalargue.net. An appealing eco-hostel in rural surroundings. It has its own farm with dairy production and where organic fruit and vegetables are grown for delicious meals and breakfasts. Basic, comfortable accommodation in dorms and doubles. They run their own travel agency.

Camping

Castillos de Pincheiras, 27 km west of town, office in town at Rufino Ortega 423 , T02627-471283, www.pincheira.com.ar. In wonderful wild surroundings by the river and at the foot of strange rock formations, this is a complex with campsite, a restaurant serving regional specialities and a tea room, and a base for lots of excursions, including a fabulous horse riding trip to a remote mountain hut.

Around Malargüe *p233*

D pp **Puesto La Agüita**, RP 186, 140 km southeast of Malargüe, T02627-15588635, or T011-4299 2577 (in Buenos Aires), www.kinie.com.ar. At the edge of La Payunia reserve, this lovely country house is set in a remote and unbeatably beautiful location, where the welcoming Sagal family offer all kinds of excursions into Payunia's volcanic world. The house is decorated in rustic style offering comfortable accommodation, and guide **Ariel Sagal** organizes guided walks, 4WD excursions or horse riding into the park. Call in advance. Price is for full board.

Eating

Tupungato *p229*

Apart from the hotels' restaurants, there are just a few pizzerias to choose from on the main street, Belgrano.

ΨΨ **La Posada del Jamón**, RP 92 Km 14, Vista Flores, Tunuyán, T02622-492053. Pork rules on the menu here, in this charmingly rustic and very popular roadside restaurant. There are other tasty dishes on offer, though, and the wine list is for sampling the excellent local wines.

San Rafael *p230*

San Rafael is rather lacking in exciting places to eat but most are clustered along the western end of Av H Yrigoyen, and you won't have to walk far for a steak. All are mid-range to cheap.

ΨΨ **El Restauro**, Comandante Salas y Day, T02627-445482. A really outstanding restaurant, and an exception in this town, this is the one elegant place to eat, where chef Ana Paula makes the most of regional ingredients, served in the minimalist rooms of a lovely restored house.

ΨΨ **La Fusta**, Av H Yrigoyen 538. A smart traditional restaurant with really delicious Italian style food, superb *parrilla* and good home-made pastas. Warmly recommended.

ΨΨ **Tienda del Sol**, Av H Yrigoyen 1669. The town's busiest place serves everything in a cheery family atmosphere, recommended for pizzas and pastas.

Ψ **Pagoda**, Av Mitre 216. This Chinese *tenedor libre* is a bright place with a huge variety, and very cheap.

Cafés

There are lots of cafés but most appealing for a drink or coffee is **Nina**, Chile y San Martín, with tables outside and a cosy woody interior. Fantastic *lomitos*, too.

Malargüe *p232*

Ψ **El Bodegón de María**, Rufino Ortega y Villegas. A cosy, simple place for home-cooked food, pizzas and pastas, lunch and dinner. Very welcoming. Recommended.

Ψ **Puli Huen**, Av San Martín 224, at the otherwise not recommendable **Hotel de Turismo**. Unpretentious traditional place for good food.

Bars and clubs

Malargüe *p232*

The impressive conference centre, next to the tourist information office, has an attractive bar for an evening drink.

Activities and tours

Tupungato *p229*

Tour operators

A highly recommended guide is **Rómulo Nieto**, www.donromulo.com.ar. He organizes trekking and horse riding excursions into the provincial park, where he also runs the base camp Refugio El Cóndor in a magnificent mountain setting. There are day trips from town to this refugio and excursions to nearby sites; and also 6-day trips for a fabulous approach to Volcán Tupungato. In summer, Rómulo also offers trekking to the summit and horse riding along the old path to Chile from Manzano Histórico to Portezuelo de los Piuquenes, in incredibly stirring landscapes. Also contactable through his *hostería* in Tupungato, see Sleeping page 234.

San Rafael *p230*

Travel agencies run all-day excursions to Cañón del Atuel and there are several rafting companies at Valle Grande, all of whom charge around US$9 for 20 mins rafting.

Cañón del Atuel, C Day 45, T02627-424871.

Conventional tours to local *bodegas*, to Los Reyunos lake, and through the cañon itself.
Raffeish, Valle Grande, T02627-436996, www.raffeish.com.ar. Recommended for being very professional, offering a range of rafting from very secure family trips to more adventurous expeditions for the experienced. Their greatest attraction is the bizarre variety of different floating craft you can try – great fun. Also rock climbing and rappel, and a great trekking excursion too, returning by boat.
Portal de Atuel, Valle Grande, T02627-15586662, www.portaldelatuel.com. Rafting and catamaran trips across Lago Grande and 4WD excursions to nearby sand dunes.
Sport Star, Valle Grande, T02627-15581068, www.sportstar.com.ar. Another good company, which also offers whitewater rafting excursions on the upper Atuel and Diamante rivers, among other adventures.
Taiel Viajes, Av H Yrigoyen 707, T02627-427840, www.taiel.com.ar. Runs both conventional and adventure tours of all kinds. Wonderful 7-day horse-riding trip to Laguna del Atuel, 4WD trips to sand dunes and to Laguna el Diamante and Volcan Maipo, and rafting of all grades. Very helpful and professional.

Malargüe *p232*
Choique, Av San Martín y Rodríguez, T02627-470391, www.choique.net. A great range of excursions to all nearby sites and provincial parks. Also daily transfers to Las Leñas ski resort.
Karen Travel, San Martín 54, T02627-470342, www.karentravelcom.ar. Highly recommended for excursions to all the nature reserves above and also horse riding trips, such as the 4-day excursion to the crashed Uruguyan plane site known as *Viven* (*Alive!*). Their amazing photos of the spectacular landscapes will convince you it has to be done.

Around Malargüe *p233*
Horse riding
Kiñe tourism, www.kinie.com.ar. Unique horse riding in La Payunia reserve, and accommodation at the delightful *hostería*, Puesto La Agüita, see Sleeping above for details.

Transport

Tupungato and around *p229*
Bus Daily buses to/from **Mendoza** and the bus terminal at Las Heras and D Chaca, with Empresa Mitre 380, 1½-2 hrs, US$3.

San Rafael *p230*
Air Airport at Las Paredes, a few kilometres west of town, access from RN 143, 6 flights a week to/from **Buenos Aires**, one stop at San Luis, 2½ hrs, with **Aerolíneas Argentinas**, T02627-435156; office in town: Av H Yrigoyen 395, T02627-438808.
Bus Central terminal at Coronel Suárez y Avellaneda. To **Mendoza**, **Expreso Uspallata** and **TAC**, frequent, 3-3½ hrs, US$ 5-6; to **Neuquén**, Andesmar, 8-9 hrs, US$ 18-23. To **Buenos Aires**, TAC, Andesmar, **La Unión** and **Chevallier**, US$ 24-45, 12-13 hrs. To **Malargüe**, Expreso Uspallata , daily, 2½ hrs, US$4.50.

El Sosneado and around *p231*
Bus Buses that pass daily to **Malargüe** from **San Rafael** stop at El Sosneado, and you can pick up buses from either places passing through to **Los Molles** and **Las Leñas**.

Las Leñas *p232*
Bus Bus to/from **San Rafael**, 2 companies **Isolin** and **Butini** go daily in winter only (no buses the rest of the year): both US$15. This service varies from year to year, so check first. Bus to/from **Malargüe**, **Autotransportes Malargüe**, runs a daily service, winter only: US$5 return. There's no regular bus service to Las Leñas off season, other than minibuses run by tour operators. To/from **Buenos Aires**, 15 hrs, in skiing season only.

Malargüe *p232*
Air The airport is on southern edge of town, T02627-471600. There are only charter flights to/from **Buenos Aires** in the skiing season.
Bus The terminal is at Aldao y Beltrán. Daily buses to/from **Mendoza** with **Expreso Uspallata**, 6 hrs, minibuses with **Transporte Viento Sur**, 4½ hrs, both US$10.

San Juan province

The province of San Juan extends north and west from the capital, San Juan city, which lies in the broad valley of the Río San Juan, and is the centre of a wine-producing area as big as Mendoza's but not of the same quality. The city itself is sleepy and not wildly interesting for visitors, but there are two areas in the province which might lure you here. San Juan's jewel is the little-visited west of the province, where the foothills of the Andes rise in ranges separated by beautiful, lush valleys such as the lovely Calingasta. There is great climbing and trekking here, with several Andean peaks to explore, including the mighty Mercedario (6770 m) and incredibly peaceful ancient hamlets provide charming places to completely unwind. The northeast of the province near the border Rioja offers two more famous attractions: Ischigualasto Provincial Park, often known as the Valle de la Luna (valley of the moon), where millions of years of the planet's history, and dinosaur fossils are on display in dried out lagoons; and Talampaya National Park, just over the border in La Rioja, with fabulous dramatic canyons and eroded rocks. This northern region is almost inhospitably hot and dry almost all year round, but the landscapes are impressive: empty and starkly beautiful.

▸▸ *For Sleeping, Eating and other listings, see pages 242-244.*

San Juan city ▸▸ *pp242-244.*

→ *Phone code: 0264 Colour map 3, A2 Population of Greater San Juan: 422,000*

The provincial city, 177 km north of Mendoza, is much less inviting than the marvellous landscapes all around and you're most likely to arrive here on the way to the Calingasta Valley or the parks further north. However, it's a good base for organizing those trips as there are several good places to stay and eat, and some good *bodegas* for wine tasting. There's also one sight of fascinating cultural interest in the shrine to pagan saint La Difunta Correa. Although the city was founded on its present site in 1593, little of the original settlement remains since the most powerful earthquake in Argentine history struck in 1944, killing over 10,000 inhabitants. Though it's been rebuilt in modern style, San Juan has not yet recovered, unlike Mendoza. It was at a fundraising event at Luna Park in Buenos Aires for the victims of the tragedy that Juan Perón met Eva Duarte, the radio actress who became his second wife.

Sights

This is an important wine-producing area and there are lots of *bodegas* to visit, if you haven't seen those in Mendoza. Those offering tours include: **Santiago Graffigna** ⓘ *Colón 1342 N, Desamparados, northwest of centre, T0264-421 4227, Tue-Fri, Sun, mornings only, Sat all day, Mon closed*, the oldest in San Juan, with an interesting museum displaying wine making machinery and old photos, and a wine bar. **Fabril Alto Verde** ⓘ *RN 40, entre Calle 13 y 14, Pocito, south of centre, T0264-492 1905, closed on Sun*, is an organic winery with a smart showroom and small bar. **Antigua Bodega** ⓘ *Salta 782 (N), near the ring road, northwest of centre, T0264-421 4327, closed on Mon*, has a museum, underneath where the champagne is made. **Viñas de Segisa** ⓘ *Aberastain y Calle 15, La Rinconada, Pocito, south of centre, T0264-492 2000, www.saxsegisa.com.ar*, is a small boutique bodega with attractively renovated buildings. Not far from here is the charming small family-run bodega **Las Marianas** ⓘ *C Nueva, La Rinconada, Pocito, south of centre, T423 1191*. **Cavas de Zonda** ⓘ *RP 12 Km 15, Rivadavia, west of centre, T0264-494 5144*, has an interesting setting right inside a mountain and a champagne house at the end of a tunnel carved into the rocky hills, where wines are made following traditional Spanish and French methods. The **Mercado**

Artesanal Tradicional ⓘ *España y San Luis, T0264-421 8530*, sells the woven handicrafts, such as blankets and saddlebags, for which the province is famous. If you haven't time for a bodega tour, there are a few wine stores where you can buy the local produce, such as **La Bodega** ⓘ *25 de Mayo 957 Este*, or **La Reja** ⓘ *Jujuy 424 Sur*.

San Juan's museums are mostly rather dry, but if you're interested in Argentine history, pop into **Museo Casa Natal de Sarmiento** ⓘ *Sarmiento 21 Sur, summer daily 0900-1300, also Tue-Fri and Sun 1700-2000; winter Tue-Fri and Sun 0900-1900, Mon, Sat 0900-1400, US$0.70, free on Sun*, dedicated to the important Argentine President and educator, Domingo Sarmiento. The **Museo de Ciencias Naturales** ⓘ *Predio Ferial, España y Maipú, T0264 421 6774, daily 0930 1330, US$1.70*, has some of the fossils from Ischigualasto Provincial Park, which you won't see at the site itself. There is a basic **tourist office** ⓘ *Sarmiento Sur 24 y San Martín, T0264-421 0004, www.turismo.sanjuan.gov.ar or www.ischigualasto.com, daily 0800-2000, also at the bus terminal.* Note that the main street, Avenida San Martín, is often called Libertador.

Around San Juan → *See page 238 for Parque Provincial Ischigualasto.*

There's a wonderful collection of pre-Hispanic indigenous artefacts including several well-preserved mummies at the **Museo Arqueológico** ⓘ *University of San Juan, Acceso Sur entre Calle 5 y Progreso, Rawson, a few kilometres south of centre, T424 1424, Mon-Fri 0800-2000, Sat-Sun 1000-1800, US$0.70, buses 15, 49, 50 from centre*. The museum offers fascinating insights into the culture of the indigenous Huarpe peoples and into the Incan mountain top sacrifice practices.

About 26 km north of centre, there are inexpensive open-air thermal baths at **Baños Termales La Laja** ⓘ *daily 0800-1700, from US$1.70, bus No 20 from San Juan*, where you can stop for a quick dip, or spend a day in the spa, enjoying the very smelly but apparently healing sulphurous water.

At **Vallecito**, 64 km east of San Juan city, the famous shrine to Argentina's most beloved pagan saint, **La Difunta Correa** ⓘ *buses from San Juan to la Rioja stop here for 5 mins, or Vallecitos runs a couple of services a day*, has to be seen to be believed, and will give you far more insight into the Argentine character than any cathedral. By now, you'll have noticed piles of bottles at roadside shrines all over Argentina. The legend goes that the beautiful young Correa was making the long walk to reclaim the body of her young husband, killed in the wars of independence, when she fell by the roadside and died of thirst. No one would help her. But by some miracle, the baby she was carrying suckled at her breast and survived, and thus La Difunta Correa became the pagan patron saint of all travellers. People leave bottles of water by her shrine to quench her thirst, and to thank her for her protection on their journey. During Holy Week, 100,000 pilgrims visit this extraordinary series of shrines at Vallecito, to make offerings to splendidly florid effigies of Difunta and her child. Testimony to their faith is a remarkable collection of personal items left in tribute, filling several buildings, including cars, number plates from all over the world, photographs, stuffed animals, tea sets, hair (in plaits), plastic flowers, trophies, tennis rackets and guitars – and vast numbers of bottles of water (which are used for the plants, and the plastic recycled). There are cafés, toilets, a hotel and souvenir stalls. Bizarre and fascinating.

Calingasta Valley » *pp242-244.*

The most beautiful part of the province, this long fertile valley lies 100 km west of San Juan between the jagged peaks of the snow-capped Andes *cordillera* and the stark crinkled range of the Sierra del Tontal, west of San Juan city. Inhabited since at least 10,000 BC, the Calingasta Valley was once the route of the Camino del Inca and though little of this history remains today, it still carries a compelling attraction. Its few oasis villages are charming places to stay to explore the hills, utterly tranquil and unspoilt.

Parque Provincial Ischigualasto → *Colour map 3, A2*

Popularly known as the Valle de la Luna (Valley of the Moon), this protected area covers 62,000 ha of spectacular desert landforms, and is the site of important palaeontological discoveries. Named after a Huarpe Indian chief, the site occupies an immense basin, which was once filled by a lake, lying, at an average altitude of 1200 m, between the scarlet red Barrancas Coloradas to the east and the green, black and grey rocks of Los Rastros to the west. The vegetation is arid scrub and bushes; you may be lucky enough to see guanacos, vizcachas, Patagonian hares or red foxes and rheas. For many visitors, the attraction lies in the bizarre shapes of massive hunks of rock eroded into fantastical shapes, dotted throughout the park's other worldly terrain. With the Argentines' charming penchant for naming all natural structures after things that they resemble, these are signposted accordingly: 'The Submarine', 'The Kiosk', 'Gusanos' (Worms), and 'La Cancha de Bochas' (the Bowling Green) – extraordinary spheres of fine compacted sand. Sadly, 'El Hongo' (the Mushroom) has fallen over. However, the park's real fascination lies in the 250 million years of strata that you can see in the eroded cliffs of the rocks where fossils from all the geological periods have been found, among them fossils of the oldest dinosaurs known, including *Eoraptor*, 225 million years old and discovered in 1993. Your tour guide will show you the extraordinary strata, but you'll be disappointed to discover that there's no evidence of the dinosaur fossils here: you'll have to go to the Museo de Ciencias Naturales in San Juan (see page 239). The views throughout the park are impressive though, and the span of time you can witness here is mind-blowing. Highly recommended.

Tours and access Entrance costs US$8, including a tour. There is only one tour route about 40 km long, lasting three hours, visiting only a part of the park but encompassing the most interesting sites. If you're in your own vehicle, you'll be accompanied by one of the rangers, whose knowledge and

The valley is reached from San Juan by the scenic paved Route Provincial 12. About halfway between Calingasta and Barreal, this passes, to the east, the Cerros Pintados, a range of red, white and grey stratified hills, striped like toothpaste. There are beautiful views of the whole valley here with its meandering river, a ribbon of green running through the dusty plain between cordillera and Sierra del Tigre.

Calingasta → *Phone code: 02648 Population: 2100*

The road from Pachaco to Calingasta follows the winding course of the Río San Juan, through a steep sided gorge of astonishingly coloured and stratified rock. After Pachaco, the landscape opens out, and Calingasta village lies at the confluence of the Ríos de los Patos and Calingasta, a vivid green splash on the otherwise arid landscape. This idyllic, secluded little village (1430 m, 135 km west of San Juan) is a delightful place to rest for a few days or plan a trek into the mountains. The Jesuit chapel, **Capilla de Nuestra Señora del Carmen**, is worth seeing, a simple adobe building dating from the 1600s, with the ancient original bells. There is a **tourist information office** ⓘ *Av Argentina s/n, T02648-421066, or at the Municipalidad in Tamberías, Lavalle y Sarmiento, T02648-492005.*

interest vary greatly: with luck you'll get a knowledgeable one (though none speak English). There's no fee but a tip is appreciated. It can be crowded at holiday times, January, Easter and July. There are no regular buses that reach the park, so your only alternative is to take an excursion, either from San Juan or San Agustín. From San Juan, tours cost around US$50 (including breakfast and lunch) and take 14 hours. In San Agustín, there are a couple of small agencies (Paula Tour, T420096; you'll see them at bus terminal) charging US$15-20, and giving you less time in the bus (ask at tourist office); they also offer a useful day trip combining Ischigualasto with Talampaya Park. Talampaya Park (in La Rioja province) lies only 94 km away from Ischigualasto, and some agencies organize a combined visit to both parks in one intense day: explore this option before you set off, and plan accordingly).

A taxi to the park costs US$30 from San Agustín (recommended if there are four to five people), more expensive out of season. If you are travelling in your own transport, plan to overnight at San Agustín or the less lovely Villa Unión, as the drive is long, hot and tiring. From San Juan, both Ischigualasto and Talampaya can be reached by taking Route 20 east through Caucete and joining Route 141, via Difunta Correa to Marayes, then turning north onto Route 510 (paved but poor in parts) for 174 km northwest up to Los Baldecitos, and from here it's 17 km to the entrance to Ischigualasto. If you're driving, beware of the donkeys and goats wandering across the roads.

Accommodation You can camp opposite the ranger station in the park, which has a small museum, but bring all food and water as there's only an expensive *confitería* here, and nothing else for miles.

Further information Visit www.ischigualasto.org , a really excellent website full of interesting research and articles about the park, well worth a look before you come.

Barreal → *Phone code: 02648 Colour map 3, A2 Population: 2400*

Another peaceful oasiincluding s, Barreal (1650 m) offers more accommodation and services than Calingasta, and is the best base if you plan to trek into the Andes. However, it's still small and quiet enough to feel like a village, and offers spectacular views of the peaks all around. From here you can explore the mountains of **Sierra del Tontal**, which rise to 4000 m and give superb views over San Juan, Mercedario and Aconcagua, or climb the mighty **Cerro Mercedario** (6770 m) itself, one of the Andes' greatest peaks. For all mountain expeditions, contact Ramón Luis Ossa at **Fortuna** tour agency (see Activities and tours, page 244). For information, contact the **tourist office** ⓘ *Calle Las Heras s/n, T02648-441066*, in Barreal.

Barreal is famous for *carrovelismo* (wind-car racing), thanks to its vast expanse of flat land known as Barreal del Leoncito, parallel to the main road, south of town. Another, more tranquil attraction, are the two space observatories at nearby **El Leoncito** (2348 m) ⓘ *T02648-441088, www.casleo.gov.ar, daily 1000-1200, 1400-1800*. The observatories were built here because the climate is so sunny, with 320 clear nights a year, making it a perfect place for observing the stars and planets. The observatories are set within an immense nature reserve, covering 76,000 ha of the western slopes of the Sierra del Tontal and rising to over 4000 m. To the west there are fine views of Mercedario and other peaks in the *cordillera* with the flat plain and lush valley between. But hiking in the reserve is limited to one short walk to a small waterfall, near the entrance. Fauna includes suris (rheas), guanacos, red and grey foxes and peregrine falcons. There's no public transport except remise taxis from Barreal; take the partly paved road (17 km) that turns off the R412, 22 km south of Barreal. The administrative office is in Barreal, Calle Belgrano, T02648-441240, elleoncito@apn.gov.ar. There's also a ranger post at the observatory entrance; but no facilities, so if you if you want to camp, take all supplies.

Cerro Mercedario

Known in Chile as El Ligua and rising to 6770 m, the mighty peak of Mercedario, southwest of Calingasta, is considered by many mountaineers to be a more interesting climb than Aconcagua. It was first climbed in 1934 by a Polish expedition which went on to climb the nearby peaks of Pico Polaco (6050 m), La Mesa (6200 m), Alma Negra (6120 m) and Ramada (6410 m). This is a serious climb, and requires the same time to adjust to the altitude and the careful preparation as Aconcagua. You must not consider this expedition without hiring an experienced mountain guide (*baqueano*), who can provide mules if necessary, as there are no facilities and no rescue service. The best time to climb is from mid-December to the end of February. To join an organized expedition, contact Ramón Ossa at **Fortuna** tour agency (see Barreal Tour operators, page 244). No authorization is required to climb but it is advisable to inform the *Gendarmería Nacional* at Barreal. Note that the mountain passes to Chile here are not officially open, making the crossing illegal.

San Agustín del Valle Fértil → *Phone code: 02646 Population: 3900*

San Agustín is a rather charming little town, 250 km northeast of San Juan, and is definitely the best base for exploring the Ischigualasto park, with several good places to stay and eat. You could also fish in the Dique San Agustín, and buy ponchos and blankets from the local weavers here. There's a very helpful **tourist information office** ⓘ *municipalidad, on the plaza, Gral Acha 64, T02646-420104 , 0700-2200*, who can give you a map and advise on accommodation.

Sleeping

San Juan *p238*

Hotels in the **A** to **C** range all include breakfast and parking.

A Alkázar, Laprida 82 Este, T0264-421 4965, www.alkazarhotel.com.ar. A well-run central 4-star hotel with very comfortable rooms, pool and gym. Also an excellent restaurant, where you can eat well for US$11 including wine.

C Alkristal, Av de Circunvalación 1055 Sur , T0264-425 4145, www.alkazarhotel.com.ar. One of the city's best bargains can only really be enjoyed if you have your own transport. Very comfortable well-equipped rooms in a new high-rise international-style hotel with a pool. Poor breakfast but otherwise recommended, good value. Also smart apartments, very cheap for groups.

C Capayán, Mitre 31 Este, T0264-421 4222, hcapayan@infovia.com.ar. Next to cinema on the plaza with a rather sombre foyer downstairs, but this is a welcoming place with comfy rooms and good service and a restaurant too.

D América, 9 de Julio 1052 Este, T0264-427 2701, www.hotel-america.com.ar. A smart, modern hotel, nicely designed and very comfortable with good service, tours arranged. Recommended.

Youth hostels

F pp **Triásico**, Pedro Echagüe 538 Este, T0264-421 9528, www.triasicohostel.com.ar. There's a homely feel in this house with simple dorms and doubles, some with own bath, and a large patio with a pool in summer. Free transfer from bus station. They run their own travel agency (see Activities and tours, below).

F pp **Zonda**, Laprida 572 Oeste, T0264-420 1009, www.zondahostel.com.ar. This is a central spotless hostel with a neat backyard. Rooms are simple, light, for 2-6, all with shared bath, and breakfast at any time is included. There is a comfortable kitchen for communal use, though dinners are served on request. Excursions arranged.

Calingasta *p239*

E Hotel de Campo Calingasta, take the left fork from the *gendarmería*, cross the river and continue 2 km, hotel is up a hill on your right, T0264-421220. A restored colonial- style building with airy rooms coming off a colonnaded patio, with open views to the mountains, and a pool in the garden. Very tranquil. Meals also available. Recommended.

Barreal *p241*

B La Querencia, C Florida, T154364699, www.laquerenciaposada.com.ar. The upmarket choice is a small, homely place in rural surroundings with 6 comfortable rooms decorated in rustic style, all with a fireplace and beautiful views.

C Posada San Eduardo, Av San Martín s/n, T0264-441046. Charming colonial-style house, whose rooms open onto a courtyard. Very pleasant and relaxing. Also has a good restaurant. Recommended.

E Cabañas Doña Pipa, Mariano Moreno s/n, T0264-441004, www.fortunaviajes.com.ar. Attractive cabañas sleeping 6-8, well-equipped, breakfast included, with a swimming pool, and great views to the mountains, open all year. Owned by the charming mountain guide Ramón Luis Ossa. Highly recommended.

E Hotel de Turismo Barreal, San Martín s/n, T0264-441090, hotelbarreal@yahoo.com.ar. Nicely refurbished 1940's place with slightly plain rooms and some hostel space but a good restaurant and friendly service. Also has a pool, and can organize riding.

Camping

There is a municipal site in El Barreal, Calle Belgrano, T0264-441241, which is well maintained with shady sites, *cabañas* and a pool, open all year.

San Agustín del Valle Fértil *p242*

During Easter all accommodation is fully booked. There are a couple of good hotels, and lots of cabañas, but these are recommended:

C Hostería Valle Fértil, Rivadavia s/n, T02646-420015, www.alkazarhotel.com.ar. Smart, very comfortable hotel with fine views from its elevated position above the town, also has *cabañas* and a good restaurant open to non residents.

F pp **Campo Base**, Tucumán between San Luis and Libertador, T02646-420063, www.hostelvalledelaluna.com.ar. Lively, cheerful hostel with basic dorms with shared bath. Discounts to HI members. Tours arranged to Ischigualasto, see page 238.

F pp **Los Olivos**, Santa Fe y Tucumán, T02646-420115, posada_losolivos@hotmail.com. Welcoming and simple with hostel accommodation and a good restaurant.

Camping

There are several campsites, of which the most highly recommended is **La Majadita** in a lovely spot on the river 8 km to the west of town with hot showers and great views. There's a municipal campsite in the town, on Calle Rivadavia, 5 blocks from the plaza, T02646-420104 (municipal office for information on both sites).

Eating

San Juan *p238*

Club Sirio Libanés, Entre Ríos 33 Sur. A large, long-established place with pleasant decor, and good tasty food that includes some Middle Eastern dishes.

Las Leñas, San Martín 1670 Oeste. For superb steak, head straight to this popular and atmospheric *parrilla* in *quincho* (ranch) style with rustic wooden interior. Arrive at 2100 to avoid queues later in the evening. Next door Las Leñas has another vegetarian restaurant at Rincón Verde.

Remolacha, Santa Fé 1232 (oeste). Stylish, warm and welcoming place with superb

For an explanation of the Sleeping and Eating price codes used in this guide, and other relevant information, see Essentials, pages 48 and 51.

Italian inspired menu, delicious steaks and pastas. Recommended.

Soychú, Av de la Roza 223 Oeste, T422 1939. Excellent vegetarian food. Highly recommended, very good value.

San Agustín del Valle Fértil *p242*

El Astiqueño, Tucumán next to the Dique. Good regional specialities.

Noche Azul, Gral Acha s/n. *Parrilla*, just off the plaza, offering local *chivito* (kid).

Activities and tours

San Juan *p238*

Tour operators

Nerja Tours, Entre Rios 178 Sur, T0264-421 5214, www.nerja-tours.com.ar. Conventional tours, local trips and combined visits to Valle de la Luna (Ischigualasto) and Talampaya.

Triásico, Pedro Echagüe 520 Este, T0264-421 9528, www.triasico.com.ar. Day tours to Valle de la Luna (Ischigualasto), Calingasta and Las Quijadas Park in San Luis.

Valley Moon, Rivadavia 414 Oeste, www.valleymoon.com. Excellent alternatives to conventional tours, and offering activities such as rafting and windsurfing at Rodeo, horseback rides in remote valleys, climbing expeditions into the Andes peaks, including a 14-day ascent to Mercedario and also tours to Calingasta and Valle de la Luna (Ischigualasto), all with highly experienced guides. Recommended.

Barreal *p241*

Tour operators

Fortuna, C Mariano Moreno, T0264-4040913, www.fortunaviajes.com.ar. Ramón Ossa is an expert guide for 1- to 15-day treks, horse-riding expeditions, and 4WD excursions into the Andes including up Mercedario and into the Cordón del Plata. Highly recommended.

Transport

San Juan *p238*

Air

Chacritas Airport, on RN 20, 11 km southeast. No regular buses go to the airport, but a remise to/from city costs US$2-3. To **Buenos Aires** Aerolíneas Argentinas/Austral, T0264-425 0487, daily, 1½ hrs.

Bus

Terminal information, T0264-422 1604, Estados Unidos y Santa Fe, 9 blocks east of centre. Bus 33 and 35 for city centre, US$0.40. Hourly departures to/from **Mendoza** with TAC and Media Agua and others, 2-2½ hrs, US$3.50-4.50.To **La Rioja**, 5-6 hrs, US$10-15, 6 companies including Andesmar and Flechabus. **Catamarca**, 6 companies, 7-8 hrs, US$14-20. **Tucumán**, 6 companies, 10-12 hrs, US$20-30. **Córdoba**, (Socasa, 20 de Junio, San Juan-Mar del Plata, Cata, Chevallier), 8-9 hrs, US$13-18. **Buenos Aires** (Autotransporte San Juan, TAC, San Juan-Mar del Plata, 20 de Junio), 14-16 hrs, US$25-40.

Local To **San Agustín** with Vallecito, 3 a day, 4 hrs, US$6. Also daily services in the afternoon (plus a morning bus on Mon, Fri, Sat) to **Barreal**, 5 hrs, US$8, and **Calingasta**, 4 hrs with El Triunfo, T0264-421 4532.

Car hire

Parque Automotor, Av San Martín 685 Oeste, T0264-422 6018. **Avis**, Av Lib San Martín 163, T0264-422 4622.

Barreal *p241*

Bus There is at least 1 bus daily to **San Juan** , El Triunfo, 5 hrs, US$8. Also minibus run by José Luis Sosa, T02648-441095.

San Agustín del Valle Fértil *p242*

Bus Empresa Vallecito runs few services a day to **San Juan**, 4 hrs, US$6, and also 3 buses a week to **La Rioja**, 3 hrs, US$5.

Directory

San Juan *p238*

Banks Open 0800-1300. Many, Banelco and Link, ATMs accept international credit cards in the centre. **Cambio Santiago**, General Acha 52 Sur, T0264-421 2232, weekdays until 2100, Sat until 1300.

Internet Several *locutorios* have internet, those at Rivadavia y Acha, on the plaza, and Mendoza 139 Sur are open on Sun.

La Rioja province

La Rioja is usually visited for the wonderful Parque Nacional Talampaya, a vast canyon of rock sculpted by wind and water into fantastic shapes, declared a world heritage site by UNESCO. However, there's also stunning scenery beyond the national park and places where you can find perfect tranquility, since the area is sparsely populated and little-visited. Between the mountain ranges of the west are the extended Famatina and Vinchina valleys with verdant oasis villages at the foot of colourful eroded hills. In the arid southeast are the plains known as Llanos de los Caudillos, with the beautiful Sierra de los Llanos and extraordinary saltflats nearby. The city of La Rioja itself has two fine museums of indigenous art. ▸▸ *For Sleeping, Eating and other listings, see pages 250-252.*

La Rioja city ▸▸ *pp250-252.*

→ *Phone code: 03822 Colour map 1, C2 Altitude 498 m Population: 147,000*

Though not obviously touristy, the capital of the province does offer decent accommodation and is a good starting point for a trip to more remote parts of the province. Founded in 1591 at the edge of the plains, with views of Sierra de Velasco, La Rioja has a few interesting museums, some neo-colonial houses and the oldest building in the country. Sleepy, and oppressively hot from November to March, the town becomes very lively every day after siesta time and during the celebrations of the local carnivals such as 'chaya' and the 'Tinkunaco'.

Sights

The centre of the city is **Plaza 25 de Mayo** with its shady tipas, sycamores, araucarias and pine trees. Here, in 1637, the head of the native leader of an insurrection was exhibited as a trophy by the Spaniards. On the plaza is the early 20th-century **cathedral** with the image of San Nicolás de Bari and a room full of silver offerings.

Other interesting sights on the plaza are the neo-colonial government buildings, **Casa de Gobierno** and **Poder Judicial**, together with the pink building of the **Club Social**. The oldest surviving church in Argentina is one block northeast, the **Church of Santo Domingo** ⓘ *Pelagio B Luna y Lamadrid*. It's a quaint stone temple, sparsely decorated inside but with magnificent carved wooden doors, dating from 1623, and renovated in later centuries. There is a lovely patio in the adjacent convent.

By far the most interesting sight in the town is the the **Museo Arqueológico Inca Huasi** ⓘ *Alberdi 650, Tue-Sat 0900- 1300, US$0.50*, which houses one of the most important collections in the country of pre-Hispanic ceramics in Argentina. These beautiful pieces were made by the ancient cultures who originally inhabited the region, and include a remarkable funerary urn from the Aguada culture 1500 years ago.

The **tourist office** ⓘ *Pelagio B Luna 345, Mon-Sat 0800-1300, 1600-2100, Sun 0800-1200, T03822-426384, www.larioja.gov.ar*, is friendly, helpful and hands out a map of the city. Ask here about accommodation, including rooms with families (*casas de familia*).

Around La Rioja city

The **Quebrada del Río Los Sauces** is the fastest escape from the heat of the city, 10 km west via Route 75. There's a shaded river with campsites and a reservoir amidst lovely mountain scenery. From there, a 13-km dirt track (no shade) leads to the summit of the **Cerro de la Cruz** (1648 m) with great panoramic views, popular with hang gliders. Seven kilometres west of La Rioja is **Las Padercitas**, where there is a large, stone temple protecting the adobe remains of what is supposed to have been a Spanish fortress in the 16th century. Route 75 continues north and passes Las Padercitas, before following the Quebrada for 4 km to the reservoir of Dique Los Sauces. Regular minibuses or *diferenciales*, as they're called here, with **Transal**, T03822-421577, to Villa Sanagasta from Rivadavia 519, take you to Quebrada and **Dique Los Sauces**, US$1. *Remise* taxis charge US$5-7. Some tour operators also run excursions.

Northeastern La Rioja (La Costta) » *pp250-252.*

If you have time and want a tranquil place to hang out or retreat to for a few days, with no distractions, head for the long narrow strip of land known as La Costa, lying at the edge of the plains at the foot of the Sierra de Velasco mountains. There are delightful small villages dotted about, green oases with old chapels, surrounded by vineyards, orchards and olive groves. Two roads head north from La Rioja. Route 75 to Aimogasta, is the more interesting of the two, passing through Villa Sanagasta, Aminga and Anillaco and all the small towns of La Costa. Alternatively, Route 38 runs northeast to Catamarca and you could take a detour to visit thermal baths at **Termas Santa Teresita** ⓘ *at Km 33 take RP 9 (later 10) to Villa Mazán, Km 99*. The termas are some 7 km north and there's a budget **Hostería Termas Santa Teresita**, T03827-420445, which has open-air thermal pool, thermal baths in all rooms, and breakfast included.

The first town you'll come across on the way to La Costa, is **Villa Sanagasta**, nicely set among orchards and where, on the last Friday in September, there is a big religious procession to La Rioja. A few kilometres further, at **Agua Blanca**, there is a lovely Alpine-style cabin, **El Alpino** where good meals are served.

There are a few curious sights near Anillaco: a house which looks like a fairy tale or horror story (depending on your mood), called **Castillo de Dionisio** at Santa Vera Cruz, built on a rock and surrounded by cacti; the massive **Señor de la Peña**, a naturally shaped rock and very popular religious sanctuary during Holy Week, lying in a desert plain 30 km east of Anillaco; and the 18th-century **chapel of Udpinango**. The largest town in the area, at the heart of the olive production, is **Aimogasta**, which serves as a good transport with links to several towns in the province of Catamarca.

Famatina Valley » *pp250-252.*

One of the richest areas of the province and only a few hours west of the capital, this immense valley is attractively flanked to the west by the magnificent Famatina Mountains, 6000 m high, and to the east by the Sierra de Velasco, rising to 4000 m. Once an important mining area, it's now famous for its tasty wines, olives and walnuts. You can combine the most challenging treks in the region with a relaxing stay in a calm, rural *finca*.

Chilecito → *Phone code: 03825 Colour map 1, C2 Altitude 1074 m Population: 30,000*

The second biggest town in the province and certainly the most attractive, Chilecito lies at the foot of the snow-capped Famatina Mountains in an area of vineyards and olive groves, and is the best base for exploring the hills and nearby villages. Founded in 1715, its name derives from the influx of Chilean miners in the 19th century. The town centre, with lots of cafés and a modern church, is centred around Plaza de los Caudillos, beautifully shaded with mature pine and red gum trees, and two pergolas covered with grapevines. Each February the plaza is the focus of the *chaya* celebrations (see La Rioja's festivals, page 244) and the anniversary of the town's foundation.

There is good local wine to sample at the **Cooperativa La Riojana** ⓘ *La Plata 646, T03825-423150, www.lariojana.com.ar, free 45-min guided visits and a smart wine shop open in the morning*, you can watch local grapes being processed to make a wide variety of red and white wines, including organic products, many of which are exported to Europe under the labels Inti, 7 Days, Pircas Negras or Santa Florentina. For an easy five-minute walk from plaza, head along Calle El Maestro, past the pleasant Parque Municipal and up to the **Mirador El Portezuelo** where there are splendid panoramic views of the town and the Velasco and Famatina mountains. Another delightful nearby attraction is the botanical garden at **Chirau Mita** ⓘ *Av Primera Junta Km 0.25, take Calle Arturo Marasso northwards, turning right at Primera Junta, and it's on the way to La Puntilla, T03825-424531, www.chiraumita.com.ar*. The beautiful private garden has an incredibly rich collection of over 1500 cacti and succulent plants (native and non native species) growing on terraces on the rocky slopes, and using the same techniques ancient Andes people used for cultivation. Not to be missed. For further information contact the **tourist office** ⓘ *Castro y Bazán 52, T03825-422688*. A useful website is www.chilecitotour.com.

One of the pleasures of Northwestern Argentina is a visit to a *finca*, or farm. **Finca Samay Huasi** ⓘ *San Miguel, 3 km southeast of town, T03825-422629, Mon-Fri 0800-1300, 1330-1930, Sat-Sun 0800-1200, 1500-1900 (till 1800 in winter), closed 22 Dec-6 Jan, US$0.35*, is an attractive place to come and relax for a day, or stay overnight. The estate was once the summer residence of Joaquín V González, founder of La Plata University, who designed the gardens using native trees, and strange stone monoliths expressing his love of ancient cultures. There's also a small natural history museum.

Around Chilecito

While the Famatina Mountains are best explored on a guided tour, you can amble to the villages around Chilecito quite easily, with their old adobe houses and historical chapels. In **Famatina**, Good Friday and Christmas Day are celebrated with fabulous processions, and there's also a good site for paragliding. At **Santa Florentina** (8 km northwest of Chilecito), the impressive remains of a huge early 20th-century foundry can be reached from Chilecito and La Mejicana mine by cable car. A few kilometres west of Sañogasta, Route 40 leads to the eroded red sandstone rocks of **Cuesta de Miranda**, one of the most spectacular routes in the province. Winding its way between Sierra de Famatina and Sierra de Sañogasta, it rises to 2020 m and drops again, passing through 320 bends in 11,500 m.

Western La Rioja » pp250-252.

Western La Rioja is remote and undiscovered, but you might want to visit to base yourself in the town of La Unión for Talampaya park, or to visit the strange otherworldly landscapes of the Reserva Natural Laguna Brava. The westernmost inhabited valley in La Rioja (also known as Valle del Bermejo) follows the **Río Vinchina** which flows along the western side of the Sierra de Famatina. The valley can be reached from La Rioja city along Route 26 via the Parque Nacional Talampaya, or from Chilecito by Route 40, via the spectacular **Cuesta de Miranda**.

Villa Unión and around

→ *Phone code: 03825 Colour map 1, C1 Population: 4700*

Some 92 km west of Nonogasta, Villa Unión (1240 m) is the largest settlement in the valley and is another base for visits to the Parque Nacional Talampaya, 67 km south. North of Villa Unión, paved Route 76 heads along the arid valley to **Villa Castelli** and **Vinchina** (70 km north of Villa Unión) offering the last comfortable accommodation option before the high mountains, (E) **Corona del Inca**, T03825-15675945.

An extraordinary testament to ancient cultures, on the west side of Route 76, on the northern outskirts of town, there is the **Estrella de Vinchina**, the only surviving star-shaped stone mosaic made by ancient settlers centuries ago. Immediately north of Vinchina, Route 76 enters the spectacular **Quebrada de la Troya** and 36 km

Parque Nacional Talampaya → *Phone code: 03825*

Extending over 215,000 ha at an altitude of 1200 m, Talampaya is a remarkable natural phenomenon for its impressive rock formations, of which the main feature is the 4-km canyon of the River Talampaya. A stroll through this vast chasm gives you the unforgettable experience of being entirely dwarfed by the landscape. Though some sections of the park are only accessible by vehicle, guided walks and cycle rides are possible.

The park and circuits

The park itself occupies a basin between the Sierra Morada to the west and the Sierras de Sañogasta to the east. This is the site of an ancient lake, where piled up sediments have since been eroded by water and wind for the last 200 million years, forming a dramatic landscape of pale red hills named **Sierra de los Tarjados.** Numerous fossils have been found, and some 600 year-old petroglyphs can be seen not far from the access to the gorge. As in Ischigualasto, along the canyon there are extraordinarily shaped structures which have been given names such as 'the balconies', 'the lift', 'the crib' or 'the owl'. At one point, the gorge narrows to 80 m wide and rises to 143 m deep. A refreshing leafy spot in the centre of the gorge has been named 'the botanical garden' due to the amazing diversity of plants and tree specimens living here. The end of the *canyon* is marked by the imposing cliffs of 'the Cathedral' and the curious 'King on a camel'. 'The chessboard' and 'the monk', 53 m high, lie not far beyond the gorge, marking the end of the so-called **El Monje circuit**. Only accessible with 4WD vehicles, another circuit, **Circuito Los Cajones** continues in the same direction up to 'los pizarrones', an enormous wall of rock covered with petroglyphs, and then to '*los cajones*', a narrow pass between rock walls. Two other circuits in other areas within the Park are organised from another entrance on RN 76 Km 133.5: **Ciudad Perdida**, southeast of the gorge, accessible only with 4WD vehicles, leads to an area of high cliffs and a large number of breathtaking rock formations, and the **Arco Iris circuit** leads to a multi-coloured canyon.

Access and information

The park is reached by Route 76: turn off at Km 144 (217 km from La Rioja), 61 km north of the police checkpoint at Los Baldecitos and 55 km south of Villa Unión, onto a paved road, 14 km long.

Accommodation

The only option inside the park is a basic campsite, next to the

northwest of Vinchina, it reaches **Jagüe** (1900 m), with food and basic facilities, and where you will be approached by park wardens of the nearby Reserva Natural Laguna Brava (see below). This is the starting point for a 154 km long road to Chile through the Andean mountain pass of **Pircas Negras** (4165 m). About every 20 to 30 km you'll see stone huts, built in the 19th century to shelter cattle wranglers on their way across the Andes. The road gives also access to a vast, empty territory of the **Reserva Natural Laguna Brava.**

Reserva Natural Laguna Brava → *Colour map 1, C1*

ⓘ *Entry US$1.70 per person.*

This reserve protects Laguna Brava, a salt lake, 4271 m, 16 km long, 3 km wide, and some 405,000 ha of mountains and a high plateau, rising from 3800m to 4360m. The lake lies further northwest beyond the Portezuelo del Peñón, with superb views administration office (US$1 pp). The closest base for visiting the park is the small town of La Unión, 67 km north, see under Western Rioja, page 247.

Tour operators
Tour operators in La Rioja and Chilecito organise tours into the park, sometimes combining a visit with nearby Ischigualasto (Valle de la Luna), which is otherwise difficult to access. Check when you book that both the entrance fee and guides' fees are included in the cost of your tour). Independent access is possible, since buses or combis (minibuses) linking La Rioja and Villa Unión stop at the park entrance, but note that it's a long (14 km), lonely and unshaded walk to the administration building. No private vehicles are allowed beyond the administration building, where you have to park, and arrange alternative transport around the park: either a park vehicle, walking, or bicycle.

Tours of the park along the **El Monje**, and the **Circuito Los Cajones** circuits can be arranged at the administration office, but not for the **Ciudad Perdida** and **Arco Iris** circuits. These both take 4½ hours and cost US$8 pp each; tours start from RN76, Km 133.5. For more information, call T03822-15681114.

Guided walks, cycle rides and tours
Guides for both walks and rides speak English.
Guided walks to Quebrada Don Eduardo, a secondary gorge, next to the canyon, (about three hours, US$10 pp).
Guided bike rides (three hours, US$10 pp, cycle and helmet provided) follow the whole length of the cañón up to 'la catedral'. A shorter journey is also on offer up to 'the botanical garden'.
Guided visits in a park vehicle for **El Monje** circuit (two hours, US$12 pp), **Circuito Los Cajones** circuit (four hours, US$15 pp).

Best time to visit
The best time to visit is in the morning, when the natural light is at its best, and avoiding the strong winds in the afternoon.

Entry cost
US$4, September to April 0800-1800, May to August 0830-1730.

Further information
Call the park administration T0351-5709909 for more information on these excursions and for advance bookings. A small restaurant, toilets, public telephones are in the same park administration office.

over the lake, and some of the mightiest volcanoes on earth in the background. From the left, these are: the perfect cone **Veladero** (6436 m), **Reclus** (6335 m), **Los Gemelos** (6130 m), **Pissis** (6882 m) the highest volcano in the world, though inactive, and **Bonete** (6759 m) which is also visible from Villa Unión and Talampaya. The park is home to thousands of flamingoes and vicuñas, the more elegant cousins of the llama. There are many organized 4WD tours on offer here, which take you to the high plateau, the Laguna Brava itself and occasionally, the small lagoon Corona del Inca lying at the crater of a volcano at 5300 m. See tour operators in La Rioja and Chilecito below. The nearest settlement is Jagüe, at the western end of Route 76, and from here, 4WD or mountain bike are essential to enter the park. The nearest accommodation is at Villa Unión. Access is limited by summer rainfall and winter snow, so the best times for a visit are April and early May.

Sleeping

La Rioja city *p245*
A fan or a/c are essential for hot summer nights. High season is during Jul and the winter holidays.
B King's, Av Quiroga 1070, T03822-422122. A pricey 4-star hotel with buffet breakfast included, a/c gym, pool and fine rooms, car rental.
B Plaza, San Nicolás de Bari y 9 de Julio (on Plaza 25 de Mayo), T03822-425215, www.plazahotel-larioja.com. Functional 4-star place with a pool on the top floor and breakfast included; all rooms with a/c. Some have good plaza views but can be noisy.
C Vincent Apart Hotel, Santiago del Estero y San Nicolás de Bari, T03822-432326. Spotless new flats for up to 4 people with a/c, including a dining room, a small kitchen and fridge; breakfast is also included. Excellent value for a group of 3-4. Recommended.
D Savoy, San Nicolás de Bari y Roque A Luna, T03822-426894, hotelsavoy@infovia.com.ar. Located in a quiet residential area, this is a neat, comfortable hotel with breakfast and a/c included, though it has some strangely shaped rooms, and it's worth paying the extra 30% for more spacious rooms with renovated bathrooms on the 2nd floor.

Camping
There are several sites along Av Ramírez de Velasco, in the northwest suburbs on the way to Las Padercitas and Dique Los Sauces, but the most appealing with pool, hot water and electricity is the one belonging to Sociedad Sirio-Libanesa at Quebrada de los Sauces, 13 km west of town.

La Costa *p246*
E Hostería Anillaco (ACA), T03827-494064. The best place to stay in the area. Breakfast included, a pool and also a decent restaurant.

Chilecito *p246*
D Finca del Paimán, Mariano Moreno y Santa Rosa (at San Miguel, 3 km southeast of town), T/F03825-425102, www.fincadel paiman.com.ar. The friendly owners, Alejo Piehl and Marisa, have opened their own renovated adobe house, where they welcome guests to share their spacious rooms and kitchen, and perhaps even the fruit harvest or making jam. Accommodation rates include breakfast and transport to/from Chilecito. The *finca* is a delightful 4½-ha farm where you can just chill out or plan an excursion to the mountains, led by Alejo. Warmly recommended, book in advance.
D Mary Pérez, Florencio Dávila 280, T03825-423156, hostal_mp@hotmail.com. Best value in town for its comfortable rooms. Good breakfast. Recommended (though check if the nearby sports club is holding a party).
F pp **Hostel del Paimán**, El Maestro 188, T03825-425102, www.fincadelpaiman.com.ar. This is the best budget choice, with the same owners as **Finca del Paimén**, above. An old house in the town centre, friendly and welcoming, with dorms, singles, doubles and rooms for 3-4, with or without own bath, all basic and open onto a lovely and peaceful garden. Discounts to HI members.

Camping
There are 3 sites at Santa Florentina and Las Talas, 8 km northwest of Chilecito (*remise* taxis charge US$ 3.50).

Villa Unión and around *p247*
B Pircas Negras, R76, T03825-470611, www.hotelpircasnegras.com. Easy to spot as it stands out a mile: the only large building at the side of the road amongst the other more humble dwellings, this modern place is the most comfortable in town, with good rooms, a restaurant, a pool and lots of excursions on offer.
D Noryanepat, Joaquín V González 150, T03825-470133. A small, modern family-run hotel; good value, although rooms are a bit cramped, but they do have a/c and breakfastis included.
E Dayton, Nicolás Dávila 115, T03825-470640. Basic but decent, with breakfast.

For an explanation of the Sleeping and Eating price codes used in this guide, and other relevant information, see Essentials, pages 48 and 51.

Eating

La Rioja city *p245*

El Corral, Av Quiroga y Rivadavia. Try the traditional rustic *comidas de campo*, a rich *locro* (traditional stew) or a *puchero, asado* (barbecued meat) or *pollo al disco* (chicken cooked in an open pan on the fire); there are good local wines too.

La Vieja Casona, Rivadavia 427, T03825 425996. A popular smart *parrilla*. The *lechón a la parrilla* (pork) with apple sauce is superb.

La Aldea de la Virgen de Luján, Rivadavia 756, T03825-460305. Fill up cheaply in a small and popular place and try also the Middle Eastern dishes.

Chilecito *p246*

Capri, 25 de Mayo y Joaquín V González. Traditional *confitería* on the plaza serving snacks and some basic meals.

Club Arabe, 25 de Mayo, entre Zelada y Dávila and Famatina. Despite its name, Middle Eastern food only available on request, but you can eat the usual dishes on tables outside under thick grapevines.

El Rancho de Ferrito, Pelagio B Luna 647, T03825-422481. A very popular *parrilla*, where grilled meats and regional dishes such as *locro* can be enjoyed with local wines.

Festivals and events

La Rioja city *p245*

It's worth planning your visit to coincide with one of La Rioja's 2 lively festivals. At the very popular **chaya** in early Feb, flour and basil are thrown around, while percussion music is played for 4 nights at the Estadio del Centro. Beginning on New Year's Eve and lasting 4 days, **Tinkunaco** is a vestige of the peacemaking efforts of San Francisco Solano; a colourful procession accompanies the meeting of the images of San Nicolas de Bari and the Niño Alcalde in front of the cathedral.

Activities and tours

La Rioja city *p245*

The most common destination, Talampaya, is usually offered together with Valle de la Luna (Ischigualasto Provincial Park) in one long day-tour, plus occasionally Cuesta de Miranda in 1 or 2 days. Check if park entry, IVA (VAT) and meals are included in the price. Trips to the high mountains and plateaux in the west are restricted to good weather conditions, Sep-Apr.

Aguada, D Vélez Sarsfield 742, T03822-433695, www.aguadatransporte.com.ar. Highly professional services for full-day excursions to Talampaya, combined either with Valle de la Luna or Chilecito, or consider an amazing 4-day trip, including Talampaya, Valle de la Luna, Laguna Brava and Chilecito. Some English and French spoken.

Corona del Inca, Pelagio B Luna 914, T03822-450054, www.coronadelinca.com.ar. A wide range of excursions including Talampaya and Valle de la Luna, and also including outstanding 4WD expeditions to the Corona del Inca lake at 5300 m. English spoken.

Extreme, T03822-437690 or T15661189 www.expedition-extreme.com.ar. Several excursions to the Parks and the provincial valleys, and climbing expeditions in the Andes plus a trip to the Sierra de los Llanos to spot condors in a deep ravine.

Néstor Pantaleo, Ecuador 813, T03822-422103. Pantaleo is an experienced photographer and runs 4WD trips to La Costa, Talampaya, Valle de la Luna and the mountainous west.Several languages spoken.

Chilecito *p246*

Chilecito is an excellent base not only for amazing treks in the Famatina mountains, but also for day trips to Talampaya and Valle de la Luna.

Alejo Piehl, T/F03825-425102, www.fincadel paiman.com.ar. Experienced guide Alejo offers all-inclusive 1-day tours to Talampaya and Valle de la Luna for US$60 pp and a variety of unforgettable 2- to 3-day treks (US$35-130 pp) to the colourful slopes of nearby Famatina, visiting abandoned cable car stations on the way to the summit. Also 1-day 4WD trips to El Oro or La Mejicana (at 4400 m). Recommended.

Inka Ñan, T03825-423641. Organizes excursions to the main attractions in the province.

Transport

La Rioja city *p245*

Air

Airport VA Almonacid, T03822-427239, 5 km northeast (access via San Nicolás de Bari and Route 5); taxi charges US$ 3-50 from centre. To/from **Buenos Aires**, Aerolíneas Argentinas, flights usually stop at **Catamarca**.

Airline offices Aerolíneas Argentinas, Belgrano 63, T03822-426307, F03822-426385.

Bus

Terminal 7 blocks south of the cathedral at Artigas y España, information T425453. Left luggage, 0600-2100, US$0.70 a day. To **Buenos Aires**, General Urquiza and Chevallier, 15-17 hrs, US$40-45. To **Catamarca**, many companies, 2 hrs, US$4-8. To **Córdoba**, General Urquiza, Socasa, Chevallier, 6½ hrs, US$10-12. To **Mendoza**, many companies, 6-7 hrs, US$17 and **San Juan**, same companies, 5-6 hrs, US$10-15. To **Tinogasta**, and **Fiambalá**, Robledo, 3 weekly, 5-6 hrs, US$8-10. To **Tucumán**, several companies, 5-6 hrs, US$10-14. To **San Agustín del Valle Fértil**, Vallecito, 3 hrs, US$5. Facundo and Nuevo Cuyo go daily to several provincial destinations, mainly **Chilecito** (3 hrs, US$4), **Villa Unión** (4 hrs, US$4.50), **Vinchina** (5 hrs, US$6), and **San Blas de los Sauces** (referred to as Los Sauces).

Minibus (diferenciales or combis)

Popular alternative to buses, booked in advance, and costing a few extra pesos, but usually faster and more frequent (though fewer on Sun) than ordinary buses. All arrivals and departures are from their offices: El Zonda, Dorrego 79, T03822-421930; to Pagancillo, Villa Unión and Vinchina. Transal, Rivadavia 519, T03822-421577; to **Villa Sanagasta** (via **Dique Los Sauces**). La Riojana and Family Bus, El Maestro 61, T03822-435279 or T03822-420222; to **Chilecito** and **Aimogasta** (via **La Costa**) Maxi Bus, Rivadavia y Dávila (Esso petrol station), T03822-435979; to **San Blas de los Sauces**.

Car hire

King's, at the King's Hotel (see Sleeping page 250), T03822-422122.

Taxi

Remise taxis Libertad, T03822-432000..

Around La Rioja *p245*

Regular minibuses, or *diferenciales*, run to Las **Padercitas** with **Transal**, T03822-421577. Buses to **Villa Sanagasta** leave from Rivadavia 519, and take you to **Quebrada** and **Dique Los Sauces**, US$1. *Remise* taxis charge US$5-7. Some tour operators also run excursions.

Chilecito *p246*

Bus

Station on Av Perón (on the south access to town) . To **Buenos Aires**, General Urquiza, T03822-423279, 17 hrs, US$35, via **Córdoba**, 7 hrs, US$12. To **La Rioja**, Facundo and Nuevo Cuyo, 3 hrs, US$4.

Remise taxis

San Cayetano, T03822-424848. San Roque, T03822-425002.

Around Chilecito *p247*

Minibus

Daily service with several minibuses (*combis*) from **Chilecito** to many of the villages in the valley.

Directory

La Rioja city *p245*

Banks US$ cash changed at Banco de Galicia, Buenos Aires y San Nicolás de Bari. More ATMs along San Nicolás de Bari. **Internet** A handful of good broadband centres in the plaza 25 de Mayo surroundings. **Post office** Av Perón 258; Western Union branch.

Chilecito *p246*

Banks US$ cash only changed at Banco Macro, Castro Barros 50 (on plaza). **Internet** Telecentro with internet on the plaza. **Post office** Joaquín V. González y Pelagio B Luna; Western Union branch.

The Northwest

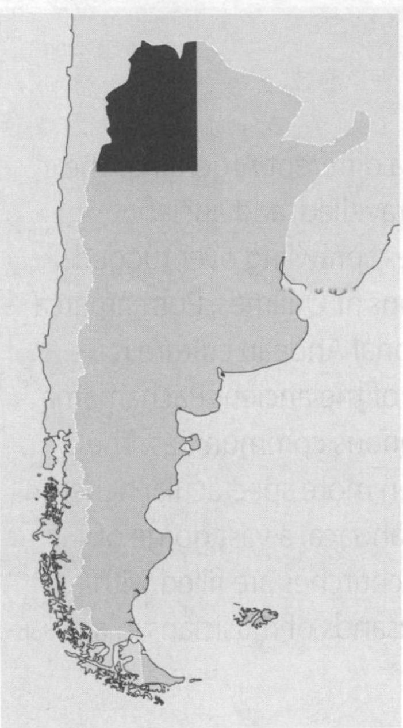

Footprint features

Introduction

The northwest of the country is a different Argentina. The Andes here are wilder and less travelled, and ancient civilizations have left ruined cities sprawling over rugged mountainsides in the vast canyons at Quilmes, Purmamarca and Santa Rosa de Tastil. Traditional Andean culture is thriving, with lively celebrations of the ancient Pachamama festivities throughout the indigenous communities. The poorer province of Jujuy has even more spectacular riches in the stunning Quebrada de Humahuaca, a vast gorge of stratified rock, where tiny white churches are filled with treasures, and Easter draws thousands of musicians in a moving procession.

Landscapes of the northwest are among Argentina's most breathtaking: winding roads snake up the Quebrada del Toro, steep gorges clad with cloudforest, though terracotta canyons dotted with giant cactus and then streak across the endless expanse of the high-altitude puna, with its shimmering salt flats and vast skies. Set off up the dramatic Cuesta del Obispo to the magical Valles Calchaquíes, to find giant cactus against snow capped mountains, and tranquil villages at Cachi and Molinos, or sophisticated wineries at Colomé and Cafayate – a wine-growing region to rival Mendoza.

Salta is the splendid colonial city at the heart of the region, with fine hotels in its plazas of crumbling buildings and waving palm trees, vibrant *peñas* where passionate folklore music is sung live, and luxurious *fincas* all around for great hospitality and unforgettable horse riding up into the cloudforest.

★ Don't miss …

1 **Salta's fincas** Explore the estancias and *bodegas* of the northwest including Los Los, El Molino de Cachi, Colomé and Santa Anita, page 260.

2 **Peñas on Calle Balcarce, Salta** Listen to stirring *folclore* music, played live by local bands, page 264.

3 **Santa Rosa de Tastil, Quebrada del Toro** Visit the ancient ruined city left by great civilizations, pre dating the Incas, page 268.

4 **Los Valles Calchaquíes** Visit the oasis villages Cachi and Molinos with expert local guides, descendants of the ancient inhabitants, page 271.

5 **Quebrada de Humahuaca** Head for Purmamarca to explore the salt flats, go wild at the Pachamama fiesta, page 293, or seek perfect peace at the rock of seven colours, page 291.

6 **Horse riding in cloudforest** The jungle landscape of Calilegua National Park is made accessible on horseback from Portal del Piedra, page 305.

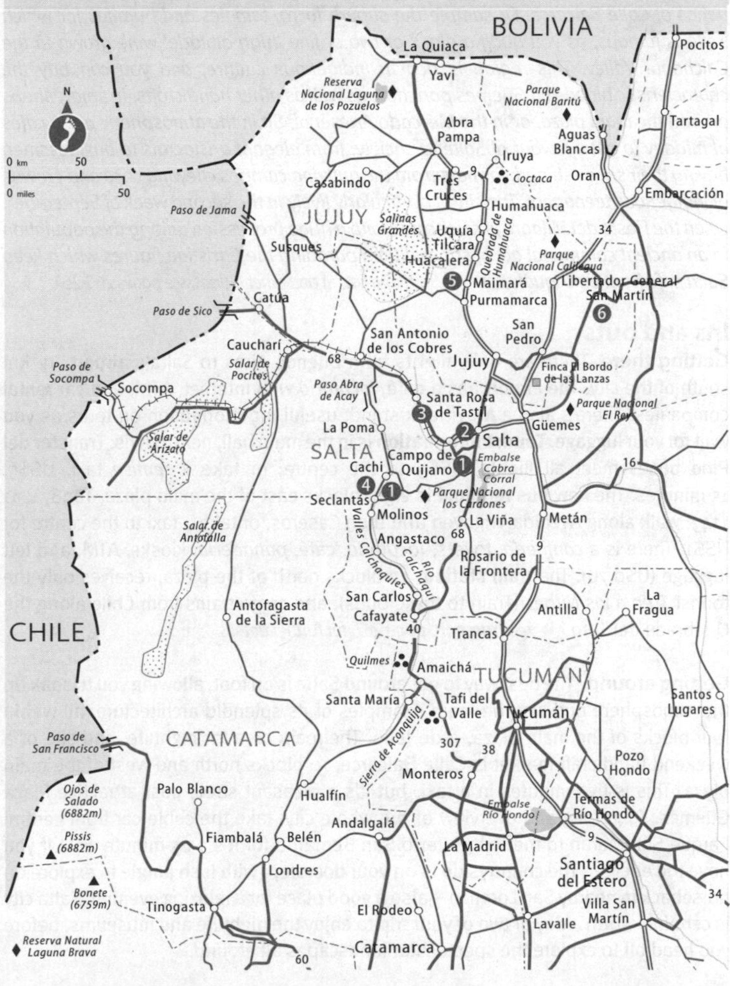

Salta

→ *Phone code: 0387 Colour map 1, B3 Population: 470,000. Altitude: 1190 m*

Salta is one of Argentina's most charismatic and historical cities; its colourful past is tangible in palm-filled plazas lined with crumbling 17th-century buildings, such as the plum-coloured Iglesia San Francisco and the handsome colonial Cabildo. Its fine museums chart the city's fascinating past, and the amazing finds from an Inca burial on remote Mount Llullaillaco. Salta's tourist infrastructure is well established, and agencies offer trips south to the beautiful Calchaquí Valley, where oasis villages are timeless retreats, and there are splendid wineries around Cafayate. You could take the train to the clouds into the dramatic Quebrada del Toro, or take your time to explore the ancient archaeological site of Santa Rosa de Tastil. Head further west into the shimmering salt flats, and discover the ancient way of life of the puna (high-altitude desert).

Salta city is worth at least a day of your trip. It buzzes with life in the mornings, comes to a complete halt at lunchtime and comes alive again at night. Balmy evenings are perfect for wandering the streets to find live music played with passion in the local peñas of Calle Balcarce. Or sample the superb locro, tamales and humitas for which Salta is famous, as you quaff a glass or two of fine 'high altitude' wine grown in the Calchaquí Valley. This region is rich in indigenous culture, and you can buy the characteristic blood-red Güemes ponchos, as well as other handicrafts, in smart shops around the main plaza, or in the Mercado Artesenal. Sit in the atmospheric plaza cafés at midday to get a flavour of Salteño society: from elegant aristocrats to businessmen having their shoes shined, farmers from the outlying campos chewing coca and crowds of indigenous teenagers. The city is particularly lively in the second week of September, when the Fiesta del Milagro is celebrated with a huge procession uniting the population in an ancient communal act of superstition: parading the Christian figures which keep Salta safe from earthquakes. ▸▸ *For Sleeping, Eating and other listings, see pages 260-267.*

Ins and outs

Getting there There are daily flights from Buenos Aires to Salta's **airport**, 12 km south of the city. The airport has a café, *locutorio* with internet, ATM, and car rental companies. There's also a **Movitrack** stand, useful for information on tours as you wait for your luggage. **Tourist information** is in the main hall, next to **Avis**. **Transfer del Pino** buses meet all flights, US$3 to the centre; or take a *remise* taxi, US$5, 15 minutes. The new **bus terminal** is eight blocks east of the main plaza, T0387-401 1143; walk along Avenida Yrigoyen and then Caseros, or take a taxi to the centre for US$1. There is a *confitería*, toilets, *locutorio*, café, *panadería*, kiosks, ATM, and left luggage (U$0.70). The **train station**, 10 blocks north of the plaza, receives only the tourist *Tren a las Nubes* (Train to the Clouds), and cargo trains from Chile along the Quebrada del Toro. ▸▸ *See Transport, page 267, for further details.*

Getting around The best way to get around Salta is on foot, allowing you to soak up the atmosphere and see the main examples of its splendid architecture, all within four blocks of the main plaza, 9 de Julio. The main area for nightlife, and site of a weekend handicraft market is Calle Balcarce, 10 blocks north and west of the main plaza. This is five minutes in a taxi, but it's a pleasant stroll, past attractive Plaza Güemes. To get a grand overview of the whole city, take the cable car from central Parque San Martín to the top of Cerro San Bernardo (or it's a 25-minute walk if you have the energy). The countryside is on your doorstep, with lush jungle to explore on horseback in nearby San Lorenzo – also a good place for a relaxing evening. Salta city is certainly worth a day or two of your trip to enjoy the nightlife and museums, before you head off to explore the spectacular landscapes all around.

Tourist information The **provincial tourist office** ⓘ *Buenos Aires 93 (1 block from main plaza), T0387-431 0950, www.turismosalta.gov.ar, Mon-Fri 0800-2100, Sat and Sun 0900-2000*, is helpful and provides free maps both of the city and the province, as well as offering advice on accommodation and tours. Staff speak English. The **municipal tourist office** ⓘ *San Martín y Buenos Aires, T0387-437 3340, Mon-Fri 0800-2100, Sat and Sun 0900-2100*, is for Salta city only. There is also a **national parks office** ⓘ *España 366, 3rd floor, T0387-431 2683, Mon-Fri 0800-1500*. Useful websites include www.iruya.com and www.redsalta.com.

Background → *See also History, page 582.*

The first Spanish expedition, led by Diego de Almagro from Cuzco (Peru), entered Argentina in 1536 and soon a busy trade route was established through the Quebrada de Humahuaca (now Jujuy). Along this route the Spanish founded a group of towns: Santiago del Estero, Tucumán, Salta and Jujuy. Throughout the colonial period these were the centres of white settlement and *encomiendas* were established to subdue the indigenous population. Jesuit and Franciscan missions were also attempted, but resistance was fierce, especially in the Calchaquí and Humahuaca valleys and, as a result, this is one of the few areas in Argentina which retains a rich indigenous culture.

The city of Salta was founded in 1582 and became one of the viceroyalty's most important administrative centres, governing a wide area, and gaining considerable wealth from the fertile outlying areas. The city also had an important role in the Wars of Independence between 1810 and 1821, when General Güemes led gaucho anti-Royalist forces to victory, utilising their detailed knowledge of the terrain and inventing the now famous red poncho which his men wore. Through the 19th century, Salta suffered a decline, since trade went directly to the country's new capital, Buenos Aires. Relatively little immigration and expansion allowed the city's colonial buildings to survive, boosted by neo-colonial architecture in the 1930s when there was a large influx of newcomers. Today, Salta retains its old aristocratic upper class population, but has a more affluent middle class than its neighbour, Jujuy. Tourism has taken off since devaluation in 2002, and is now the province's main source of income.

Sights

Plaza 9 de Julio and around

In just a few hours you can get a feel for the city. The heart is the **Plaza 9 de Julio**, richly planted with wonderful tall palm trees, orange trees and surrounded by colonial-style buildings. The whole area has been spruced up and three sides of it are now pedestrianized, with cafés where you can sit and watch teenagers hanging out in the plaza and smart business men having their shoes shined. There's an impressive **Cabildo** built in 1783, one of the few to be found intact in the whole country, and behind its pleasingly uneven arches is an impressive museum, the **Museo Histórico del Norte** ⓘ *Tue-Sat 0930-1330, Tue-Fri 1530-2030, Sat 1630-2000, Sun 0930-1330, US$0.70*. In a series of rooms around two open courtyards, the collection charts the region's history from pre-Hispanic times, with particularly good displays on the Wars of Independence and on Güemes leading the gauchos to victory. Upstairs, among some lovely religious art, is a fine golden 18th-century pulpit and some Cuzco school paintings, while outside are carriages and an ancient wine press. Fascinating and informative.

Opposite the museum, on the north side of the plaza, is the **cathedral**, built 1858-1878, now painted pastel pink, and open mornings and evenings so that you can admire a huge baroque altar (1807) and the images of the Cristo del Milagro and of the Virgin Mary. These are central to Salta's beliefs and psyche, and the focus of Salta's biggest mass ritual. In 1692 Jesuit priests were amazed to discover that two statues, of

 Christ and the Virgin of Rosario, had survived a severe earthquake intact. During a series of tremors they paraded them through the streets in procession, and the following day, the 14 September, the tremors stopped. The **Milagro** (miracle) is now the biggest event of Salta's year, when thousands of pilgrims walk to the city from hundreds of kilometres away.

Ironically, these images are now just a stone's throw from the precious beings involved in the Incas' attempts to avert earthquakes and volcanic eruptions. The *Niños de Llullaillaco*, a sacred burial unearthed by a National Geographic expedition in 1999, are now housed in the **Museo de Arqueología de Alta Montaña** (MAAM) ⓘ *Plaza 9 de Julio at Mitre 77, next to the cathedral, T0387-437 0499, www.maam.org.ar, Tue-Sun 0900-1300, 1600-2100, shop and café*. At the time of writing, the children's bodies are not yet on display, but it's expected that one of them at least will be visible in 2007, though this is the subject of considerable controversy. Meanwhile, you can see many of the other fabulous objects found in the burial, well displayed in this museum, with texts in English and a guided tour included in the entry price. Take time to watch the short videos on the ground floor and the longer film on the mezzanine floor, with fascinating insights from several scientists involved in examining the children and their funerary bundle. The guides are trained by resident archaeologist Christian Vitry, and if you speak any Spanish, you can also talk to two experts in Andean culture: Katia Gibaja and her husband (T0387-437 0499, katiagibaja@hotmail.com). There's a fine library, too.

Near the plaza, there are also a couple of historical houses worth visiting for a glimpse of wealthy domestic life, of which the best is **Museo Histórico Uriburu** ⓘ *Caseros 421, Tue-Fri 0930-1330, 1530-2030, Sat 0930-1330, 1630-2000, Sun 0930-1300, US$0.35*, situated in the former mansion of the Uriburu family, the most distinguished of *Salteño* families, containing furniture, clothes and paintings.

A block west of the Cabildo, on one of the main pedestrian streets, are a couple of interesting museums housed in colonial mansions. The **Casa Leguizamón**, Caseros y Florida, has interesting architecture and the **Casa Arias Rengel**, next door, now houses the **Museo de Bellas Artes** ⓘ *Florida 20, T0387-421 4714, Mon-Sat 0900-1300, 1600-2030, US$0.70*, which has the city's finest collection of paintings, including superb Cuzqueño school works and small exhibitions of Salteño painters and sculptors.

Across the street is the **Museo de la Ciudad 'Casa de Hernández'** ⓘ *Florida 97 y Alvarado, T0387-437 3352, Mon-Fri 0900-1300, 1530-2030, US$0.35*, in a fine 18th-century mansion with a collection of old furniture, musical instruments and dull portraits, but a marvellous painting of Güemes.

East of Plaza 9 de Julio

Walk east from the plaza, along Caseros, an appealing street full of slightly crumbling buildings. After a block, you'll come to the **Iglesia San Francisco** (1796) ⓘ *Caseros y Córdoba, 0730-1200, 1700-2100*, one of the city's landmarks, with its magnificent plum coloured façade ornately decorated with white and golden stucco scrolls, and its elegant tower (1882) rising above the low city skyline. The interior is relatively plain, but there are some remarkable statues to admire, such as the rather too realistic San Sebastián. Two blocks further east is the **Convento de San Bernardo** ⓘ *Caseros y Santa Fe*, built in colonial style in 1846, with an exquisitely carved wooden door dating from 1762. Sadly, you can't enter the convent as it's still the home to nuns, but they'll open up the little shop for you, with a little collection of quaint handicrafts.

Continuing along Caseros for two blocks and turning right at Avenida Yrigoyen, you come to the wide open green space of **Parque San Martín**, where you'll find the **Museo de Ciencias Naturales** ⓘ *Tue-Sun 1530-1930, US$0.20*, with various stuffed animals. It's not a particularly elaborate park, but there's a boating lake, and from here you can take the teleférico (cable car) up to **Cerro San Bernardo** (1458 m) ⓘ *daily 1000-1930, US$ 2.70 return, children US$ 1.35*, whose forested ridge looms over the east of the city centre. The top of the hill can be climbed by a steep path (which starts beside the

Museo Antropológico, see below). At the top there is a great café with deck chairs and fabulous views.

At the base of the hill, is an impressive **statue** of General Güemes by Victor Gariño. His gaucho troops repelled seven powerful Spanish invasions from Bolivia between 1814 and 1821. The nearby **Museo Antropológico** ⓘ *follow Paseo Güemes behind the statue, and up Av Ejército del Norte, Mon-Fri 0830-1830, Sat 0900-1300, 1500-1900, closed Sun, US$0.35, www.antropologico.gov.ar*, makes a good introduction to the pre-Hispanic cultures of the region. It has a superb collection of anthropomorphic ceramics and beautifully painted funerary urns. There's also an exhibition on high-altitude burial grounds, complete with mummies, objects found at the ancient ruins of Tastil (see page 268) and, most mysteriously, skulls flattened during the owner's life by wearing boards to squash the head (thought to confer higher intelligence). It's all very accessible and well laid out.

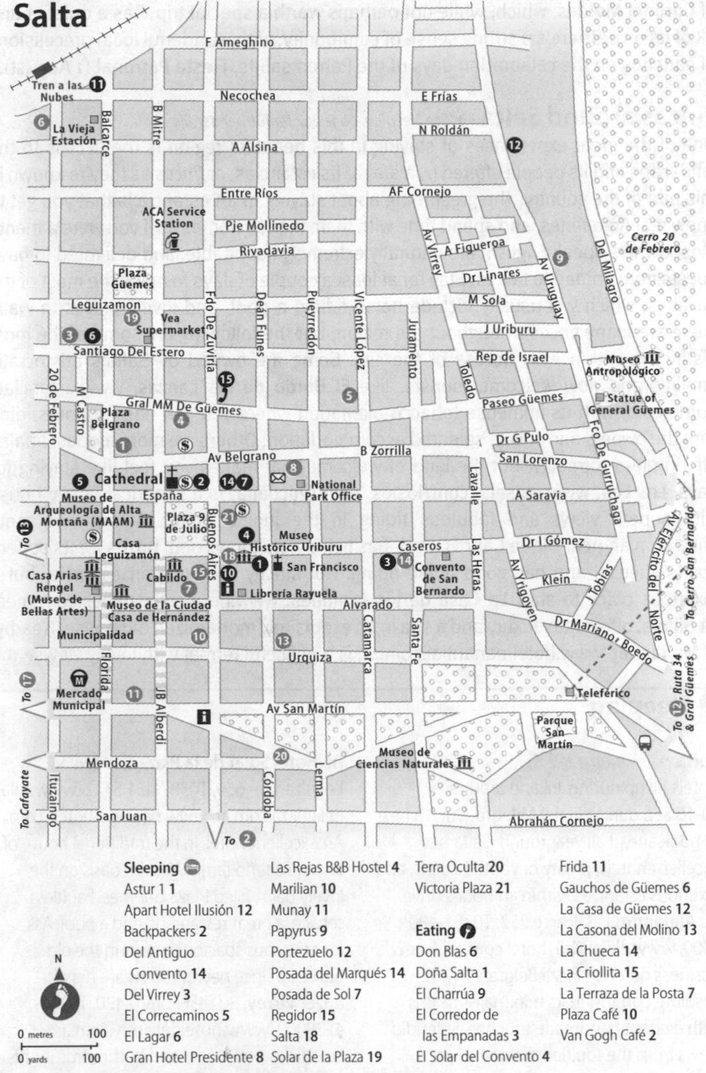

Around Salta city ➡ pp260-267

There are many lovely places close to Salta where Salteños go to relax: the smart leafy suburbs of **San Lorenzo,** 11 km to the west, or the **Dique Cabra Corral** for fishing and watersports, or jungly **Campo Quijano** on the way to Quebrado del Toro (see page 268).

Dique Cabra Corral

Salta makes a big deal of its only big lagoon – one of the largest artificial lakes in Argentina, the Dique Cabra Corral. It's a popular place for fishing pejerrey, the tasty local delicacy, and for enjoying a bit of beach life, with water-skiing, fishing, camping and restaurants also on offer. There's one really comfortable place to stay, the **Hostería Cabra Corral,** 4 km from the lake, and the **Finca Santa Anita** is nearby and also gives you ready access to the water. The nearest town is the quaint gaucho town of **Coronel Moldes,** which, while not perhaps worth a special trip, has a quiet charm all of its own. There's a strong sense of community, with wonderful local precessions of gauchos on the celebration days of the Patron saints, **Fiesta Patronal** (1 August).

Fincas around Salta → *See Sleeping, page 262 for further details.*

One of the great experiences of staying in this beautiful region is the access to the landscape and its people offered by a stay at its estancias, or *fincas* as they're known in this part of the country. The great thing about staying in an estancia is that you get to know real Argentines, and spend time with them in their homes as if you were a friend. Most owners speak English, are naturally extremely hospitable, and delighted to have guests from abroad to talk to. Stay for at least a couple of days to make the most of the facilities, which will usually include horse riding, a pool, and lovely places to walk. There are many *fincas* throughout the region, but the following are some of the most distinctive within easy access of the city. Some are owned by Salta's aristocratic families and now welcome tourists, like **El Bordo de las Lanzas,** www.estanciaelbordo.com, with its immense tobacco plantation where you can ride for hours, dine with the owners and stay in splendid accommodation. Others are more modest affairs, offering less formality, but the kind of welcome that makes you feel like staying for days. **Los Los,** www.redsalta.com/loslos, near Chicoana, is a historical family house with superb views and fabulous riding in the jungle. **Santa Anita,** www.santaanita.com.ar, near Dique Cabra Corral, has twice won 'Slow Food' prizes for its superb goat's cheese, and has good horse riding. Not strictly speaking an estancia, but a luxurious place to stay, **La Casa de los Jazmines,** www.houseofjasmines.com, near La Silleta, offers utter luxury and a spa in an exquisitely modernized old house. Nearby, **El Manantial,** www.hotelmanantial.com.ar, is a peaceful retreat with lovely views.

Sleeping

Salta *p256, map p259*

Hotels fill up during Jul and around 10-16 Sep during **El del Milagro**. But it's best to book ahead all year round. Salta has excellent hotels, plenty of youth hostels, and luxurious estancias within an hour's drive.

AL Alejandro I, Balcarce 252, T0387-400 0000, www.alejandro1hotel.com.ar. A new business hotel on Plaza Belgrano, with absolute comfort in its minimalist rooms with elegant handmade touches. Splendid views from the top floors of the tower.

AL Hotel Solar de la Plaza, Juan M Leguizamon 669, T0387-431 5111, www.solardelaplaza.com.ar, www.newage-hotels.com. An excellent hotel, in the traditional house of an old Salteño family. A calm oasis on the lovely palm-filled Plaza Güemes. Faultless service, a great restaurant, and a pool. Ask for gorgeous spacious rooms in the old building, since newer rooms are noisy.

A Del Virrey, 20 de Febrero 420, T0387-4228000, www.hoteldelvirrey.com.ar. Luxurious bedrooms and bathrooms in this classy colonial-style hotel, well situated for the nightlife of Balcarce.

A **El Lagar**, 20 de Febrero 877, T0387-431 9439, ellagar@arnet.com.ar. A wonderful boutique hotel, beautifully decorated rooms filled with fine paintings, an excellent restaurant (guests only), wine tasting cellar, library and gardens with pool. Impeccable service. Complete peace, comfort and privacy, though noisier at weekends with Balcarce's nightclubs. Email or phone to reserve in advance. Closed 20 Dec-20 Jan. Highly recommended.

A **Gran Hotel Presidente**, Av Belgrano 353, T/F0387-431 2022, reservas@grhotel presidente.com.ar. Central and very comfortable, with stylish entrance and very plush rooms. Bar, excellent restaurant with great value fixed-price menu for US$8, pool and gym. Open all year round.

A **Papyrus**, Pasaje Luis Linares 237 (no sign on this street, turn right at Repsol, top of hill), T0387-422 7067, www.hotelpapyrus.com.ar. A luxury boutique hotel offering peace and great comfort in stylish chic bedrooms (ask for the modern ones), and gracious lounge with antique furniture. Central but away from the bustle, this has a small pool and excellent restaurant (by arrangement). Recommended.

A **Portezuelo**, Av Turística 1, T0387-431 0104, www.portezuelohotel.com. Great views over Salta from its hill top position, but tatty 1960s rooms. Come here for the setting, the pool and a good restaurant. Also offers cheap deals (check website) excellent excursions.

A **Salta**, Buenos Aires 1, T/F4310740, www.hotelsalta.com. This famous plaza-side Salta institution, with its neo-colonial public rooms and splendid mosaics, has dull but comfortable bedrooms, some with charming views of the mountains. The suites overlooking the plaza are marvellous.

C **Apart Hotel Ilusión**, next to Hotel Portezuelo, José Luis Fuentes 743, T154-060379, T0387-4321081, www.aparthotel ilusion.com.ar. As the name suggests (*ilusión* means dream), these stylish modern apartments for 2-4 really are something special. Beautifully decorated with Latin American art, and well equipped with everything you need for total independence, they're just a few blocks from the centre, but elevated in the peaceful leafy residential area of Portezuelo Norte, with great views over the valley. Charming owner Sonia Alvarez makes you feel completely at home. Excellent value, and reductions for longer stays. The most appealing self-catering option in town. Highly recommended.

C **Hotel del Antiguo Convento**, Caseros 113, T0387-422 7267, www.hoteldel convento.com.ar. A new, small and very welcoming hotel. Lovely old-fashioned rooms around a neat patio at the front side of this 100-year-old house large rooms on the modern side are merely functional. An unbeatable central location between San Francisco and San Bernardo churches make this one of the best choices in town.

C **Marilian**, Buenos Aires 176, T/F0387-421 6700 www.hotelmarilian.com.ar. Of the many **C** price range options, this is recommended for its excellent service. Modern and central, and though the rooms are simple, the bathrooms are smart and breakfasts are great.

C **Posada del Marqués**, Córdoba 195, T0387-431 7741, www.posadadel marques.com.ar. Peaceful and quiet, this small colonial-style house is charming for its simplicity and comfort. With lovely patios where you can unwind in central Salta. An excellent choice.

C **Posada del Sol**, Alvarado 646, T0387-431 7300, www.hotelposadadelsol.com. This is a good choice in this category, with good service although the rooms are dated.

C **Regidor**, Buenos Aires 8, T0387-431 1305, www.hotelregidorsalta.com.ar. Smart wood panelling everywhere, and though the rooms are small, this is a welcoming place and has a very decent restaurant.

C **Victoria Plaza**, Zuviría 16, T0387-431 8500, www.hotelvictoriaplaza.com.ar. The plaza side location is the best thing about this hotel. Rooms are tolerable, well equipped but unmodernized, and not all have plaza views.

D **Las Rejas B&B**, Gral Güemes 569, T0387-421 5971, www.lasrejashostel.com.ar. A lovely family house with just a few comfortable rooms, and warm attentive service from the friendly English speaking owners, who'll go out of their way to make you feel at home. Central, peaceful, and highly recommended.

D **Munay**, San Martin 656, T0387-422 4936, www.munayhotel.jujuy.com. This hotel is by far the best of the budget hotels. Nicely decorated with small but smart bathrooms, warmly welcoming staff, and breakfast included. Highly recommended.

Youth hostels

F Backpackers, Buenos Aires 930, T/F0387-423 5910, www.backpackerssalta.com. The official HI youth hostel is 9 blocks or 30 mins walk from the plaza – or take bus No 12 from the terminal. It's well run, has small dorms, a laundry and kitchen and budget travel information. Noisy, crowded and popular.

F pp **El Correcaminos**, Vicente López 353, T0387-422 0731, www.correcaminos.com.ar. A well-kept and lively hostel, 4 blocks from plaza. Basic 8 and 4 bed dorms, and 2 small double rooms, all with shared bathrooms, laundry, modern kitchen, free internet and a pleasant garden. Safe place to arrive at night.

F pp **Las Rejas Hostel**, Gral Güemes 569, T0387-421 5971, www.lasrejashostel.com.ar. This quiet family house offers the best hostel accommodation in central Salta with friendly English-speaking owners. All rooms (for 2-6) have their own bath, free internet and there are cooking facilities. Breakfasts for US$1. Recommended.

F pp **Terra Oculta**, Córdoba 361, T0387-421 8769, www.terraoculta.com. More of a party atmosphere with friendly small dorms of 8 and 4, and doubles, a homely kitchen, laundry, free internet and a lively rooftop bar.

Around Salta *p260*

It's worth considering staying outside Salta if you're in search of more tranquillity, at San Lorenzo (11 km), at the Dique Cabra Corral or at Campo Quijano, or one of the many fincas within an hour of the city.

A-B Hostería Punta Callejas, in Campo Quijano, Route 51, 30 km west at the entrance to the Quebrada del Toro, T0387-490 4086. With breakfast, very clean and comfortable, a/c, pool, tennis, horse riding, excursions, meals. There are also several campsites including a municipal site at the entrance to Quebrada del Toro gorge, with hot showers, bungalows, with plenty of room for pitching tents.

B Hotel del Dique, Dique Cabra Corral, Route 47, T0387-490 5112, www.hotel deldique.com. Extremely comfortable, great lakeside position, with a pool and good food.

C Hostería de Chicoana, on the way to Cachi, on the plaza in Chicoana at Espana 45, 47 km south, T0387-4907009, T154081493, www.newsendas.com. A pretty colonial building, though now slightly faded, but with the added advantage of expert guide Martin Pekarek who runs wonderful adventure trips.

C Selva Montana, Alfonsina Storni 2315, T0387-492 1433, www.iruya.com/ent/ selvamontana. Most highly recommended. Nestling high up in the lush leafy hills of San Lorenzo, just 15 mins by car from Salta. Complete comfort and peace in stylish rooms, with a pool, horses and walking on offer. Attentive service, helpful staff, wonderful. Take a taxi or bus **El Indio interurbano** from terminal.

Estancias/fincas

See also page 260.

L pp **Finca El Bordo de las Lanzas**, 45 km east of Salta, T0387-490 3070, www.estanciaelbordo.com. Formal and luxurious, a taste of aristocratic life, with splendid horse riding and charming hosts. Highly recommended.

L La Casa de los Jazmines, Route 51, 11 km south towards La Sileta, T0387-4972005, www.houseofjasmines.com. Not exactly an estancia, but a beautiful place to unwind: old finca building exquisitely redesigned to the height of luxury and good taste, perfumed with roses and jasmines, with a pool and superb spa offering great range of treatments. Excellent food and service. Recommended.

A Los Los, Chicoana, just 40 km from Salta at the entrance to the Valles Calchaquies, T0387-431 7258, www.redsalta.com/loslos. Open Mar-Dec. Most welcoming and highly recommended, beautifully situated on a hilltop with fabulous views from the colonial style galleried veranda, a charming place, where you can completely relax. Spacious rooms, prettily decorated with old furniture, beautiful gardens with a pool. Includes unforgettable horseriding into the forested mountains of the huge *finca*, where you will be cooked lunch in a remote rustic lodge. Handy for the airport and Cachi. Warm welcome from friendly hosts Sara and Guillermo. Reserve in advance.

A-B pp **Finca El Manantial**, La Silleta, 25 km from Salta, T/F0387-439 5506, www.hotel

manantial.com.ar. Beautiful views from the superbly decorated rooms in this historical estancia, offering swimming walking and riding on the estate. Gorgeous.

A-B Finca Santa Anita, Coronel Moldes, 60 km from Salta, on the way to Cafayate T/F0387-490 5050, www.santaanita.com.ar. The whole family makes you welcome on this prize-winning organic farm with superb goat's cheese. great organic food and all activities included in the price. A real traditional colonial-style finca, Beautiful views, swimming, guided walks to prehistoric rock paintings, and horse riding in wonderful landscapes. A complete delight. Highly recommended.

B Finca Quisto, T0387-424 3607, www.fincaquisto.com.ar, close to Parque Nacional El Rey. Offers horse riding amidst sub-tropical vegetation, with English speaking owners.

Eating

Salta *p256, map p259*

There are lots of great *peñas* for live music, and serving good regional food at night along the north end of C Balcarce. The cheapest *empanadas* and *humitas* are available from stalls in the lively municipal market, at San Martín y Florida, but there are also lots of good places around the Plaza 9 de Julio.

TT El Solar del Convento, Caseros 444, T0387-421 5124. One of Salta's finest restaurants and yet reasonably priced. You're greeted with a glass of champagne, the surroundings are elegant, and there's delicious *parrilla* and a fine wine list. Service is excellent. Recommended.

TT Gauchos de Güemes, Uruguay 750. Excellent regional specialities at this *peña*

TT Hotel Portezuelo, Av Turística 1, T0387-431 0104. Eat delicious food in this hotel restaurant with great views over the city.

T Doña Salta, Córdoba 46 (opposite Iglesia San Francisco, with gaudy sign). In a 1820s house, serving delicious *carbonada, locro* and other regional delicacies in attractive rustic surroundings, recommended and cheap.

T El Charrúa, Caseros 221. A good, brightly lit family place with a reasonably priced and simple menu where *parrilla* is particularly recommended.

T El Corredor de las Empanadas, Caseros 117, T0387-422 0345. Justifiably renowned, serves fabulous *empanadas* and delicious local dishes.

T Frida, Balcarce 935, T0387-432 0771. Great place for a drink or dinner, with vaguely Mexican-inspired food and all the local delicacies, superb wine list, friendly staff and cosy interior, with sofas and booths, and chic eclectic decor. Recommended.

T La Casa de Güemes, España 730. Atmospheric house where Güemes lived, serving *empanadas, tamales, humitas*, and *asado*, cooked in the traditional way.

T La Casona del Molino, Caseros 2500. Another *peña* in a crumbling old colonial house with good food and drink. Popular with *folclore* stars who often burst into song.

T La Chueca, España 476, T0387-422 0653. Appealing place selling regional food and excellent *empanadas*, despite the bright lighting the staff are friendly, and the food is good and reasonably priced.

T La Criollita, Zuviría 306. Small and unpretentious, this is a traditional place for juicy and tasty *empanadas*

T La Terraza de la Posta, España 456. A large touristy place with a patio, but it's reliable, great for *parrilla* and pastas, good atmosphere and friendly service, with an excellent value fixed price menu.

Cafés

There are lots of cafés on Plaza 9 de Julio, a great place to sit now that it's largely pedestrianized. Note the 2 cafés outside MAAM, Havana and El Palacio, are very touristy.

Don Blas, Balcarce 401. A lovely old corner of Balcarce serving good coffee.

MAAM, inside the museum MAAM, Plaza 9 de Julio. Lovely airy café for meals and drinks.

Plaza Café, next to **Hotel Salta**. This elegant café is popular with *Salteños* late morning, when the centre is buzzing, a nice spot for breakfast.

Time, Plaza 9 de Julio, corner with Alberdi. Avoid the tourist cafés outside MAAM, and go where the *Salteños* go. Great juice, salads, and light meals.

Van Gogh Café, north side of plaza, España y Zuviría. Bright and popular with tourists. Good for coffee and breakfast.

Around Salta *p260*

Lo de Andrés, Juan Carlos Dávalos y Gorritti (at San Lorenzo), T0387-492 1600. Fabulous restaurant. Great steaks and pasta.

Castillo de San Lorenzo, on the road up to the Quebrada, just before the car park at the top, T0387-492 1052. Fabulous interior in this castellated building, delicious meals, stylish setting. Recommended.

Entertainment

Salta *p256, map p259*

No trip to the northwest is complete without sampling its stirring *folclore* music. You can eat *empanadas* while watching great musicians playing live in Salta's *peñas* or listening to spontaneous performers in the crowd. Most are concentrated in the north end of C Balcarce, where you will find many peñas within 3 blocks. This area also has a number of popular rock and jazz bars, such as **Macondo** or **Café del Tiempo**, as well as intimate restaurants and nightclubs. The result is an entertaining and noisy mix, though there are quieter bars here too.

Balderrama, San Martín 1126, T0387-421 1542, 2200-0200. Famous from the popular *folclore* song Unless you're in a huge coach party and fond of audience participation, avoid this place. The entrance is expensive the food is poor, and the music is inauthentic.

La Casa de Güemes, España 730. Close to Plaza 9 de Julio, recommended for shows, and frequented by *Salteños*.

La Casona del Molino, Caseros 2500, T0387-434 2835, daily, and at lunchtime. West of the centre (reached by taxi), this is the most authentic place for spontaneous *peña*, where guests help themselves to guitars on the walls and play.

La Vieja Estación, Balcarce 885, T0387-421 7727. Particularly recommended *peña* for a great atmosphere; shows and sometimes spontaneous performances from the crowds.

Festivals and events

Salta *p256, map p259*

Feb/Mar Salta celebrates **Carnival** with processions on the 4 weekends before Ash Wed at 2200 along C Ibazeta; also on **Mardi Gras** (Shrove Tue) there is a procession of decorated floats and dancers with intricate masks of feathers and mirrors. It is the custom to squirt water at passers-by and *bombas de agua* (small balloons to be filled with water) are on sale for dropping from balconies.

16-17 Jun **Commemoration of the death of Martín Güemes**. Folk music in afternoon and gaucho parade in mornings around his statue.

1 Aug, and throughout the month, **Fiesta de la Pachamama**. A wonderful tradition of the indigenous peoples of the north and entire Andean region, giving thanks to the mother earth, La Pachamama, with offerings of drinks and food, in fascinating ceremony which binds the whole community. Go to San Antonio de los Cobres, Tolar Grande, and other villages in the puna.

6-15 Sep **Cristo del Milagro**, Salta's biggest event, where thousands of pilgrims add to the city's population in a grand procession around the town, with the Virgen and Señor del Milagro, an amazing act performed since the 17th century to prevent earthquakes. All accommodation is heavily booked ahead of time, so reserve at least a month in advance.

Shopping

Salta *p256, map p259*

The best place for shopping are the parallel pedestrianized streets of Alberdi off Plaza 9 de Julio, and Florida, a block to the west. There are pricey but high-quality local goods on C Buenos Aires near the plaza, and in the shopping centre next to MAAM on the plaza.

Librería Rayuela, Alvarado 570. Excellent bookshop, with foreign-language media.

Mercado Artesanal, Calle Balcarce. Weekends and Fri evenings, an informal market of local handicraft makers, some interesting jewellery, wood and mates.

Mercado Municipal, San Martín y Florida. Wonderful place for cheap food; great fruit and veg and some handicrafts, is wonderful. Closed 1400-1700, and after 2100.

Samponia, Caseros 468, Mitre 994, T0387-422 8333. High quality crafts and locally made things for the home.

Vea, Florida, entre Caseros y Alvarado, and Mitre corner with Santiago del Estero. Big supermarket.

Around Salta *p260*

Mercado Artesanal, San Martín 2550, on the western outskirts of the city in the Casa El Alto

Molino, T0387-434 2808, 0900-2100. Take bus No 5a from Av San Martín in centre and get off as bus crosses the railway line. If you're short of time, head straight for this lovely 18th-century mansion, selling beautiful handicrafts made by craftsmen in the surrounding areas. Perhaps a little more expensive than if you buy them from a tiny village, but superb quality, and all under one roof. Look out for soft and warm llama wool socks, wonderful handwoven ponchos, delicate carved wood and weavings. Highly recommended.

▲ Activities and tours

Salta *p256, map p259*

Unless you hire a car, you'll probably need to take a tour of some kind to visit the Valles Calchaquíes and the puna. But bear in mind that distances are huge here, you're going to end up spending many hours in a minibus, and it's much better to take 3 days, go by bus and spend proper time in a place than just visit for an hour or 2. There is lots of adventure tourism on offer including horse riding, rafting and trekking. All agencies charge similar prices for tours: Salta City US$13, Quebrada del Toro and San Antonio de los Cobres US$42, Cachi US$35, Quebrada de Humahuaca US$40, 2-day tour to Cafayate, Angastaco, Molinos, Cachi, US$70.

Adventure tourism

Check out the association of approved adventure tour operators: www.adopata.org.ar

Bici Tours, T0387-439 4887, www.bicinorte.com.ar. Bike trips around the city, and to the Valles Calchaquíes and the puna.

Hernán Uriburu (HRU), Leguizamón 446, T0387-431 0605, www.hru.todowebsalta.com.ar, The original tour guide to the area, Hernán organizes trekking and horse-riding expeditions, and is highly professional and charming. His son, Marcos, is also a mountain guide, and speaks English: hru@arnet.com.ar

Norte Rafting, T0387-424 8474, www.noreterafting.com. Fun and professional rafting trips along the Río Juramento to see dinosaur footprints.

Norte Trekking, T0387-436 1844, www.nortetrekking.com. Enormously experienced Federico Norte offers great trips to experience the Valles Calchaquíes, puna into Chile or Bolivia, mountains and *selva* in depth. He's one of the few authorized guides into El Rey cloudforest park, and his trips can combine trekking with 4WD, horse riding and rafting, personally tailored to the group's needs, and not expensive. Highly recommended.

Puna Expediciones, Agustín Usandivaras 230, T0387-434 1875, www.punaexpeditions.com.ar. Well qualified and experienced guide Luis H Aguilar organizes treks in remote areas, US$25 a day including transport to trekking region, food, porters. Recommended.

Clark Expediciones , Caseros 121, T0387-421 5390, www.clarkexpediciones.com. Specialist tours for birdwatchers, natural history and cultural tailored tours; they also offer a half day-tour to Reserva El Huaico (in San Lorenzo), the closest cloudforest reserve to Salta, English spoken.

Salta Rafting, T0387-401 0301, www.saltarafting.com. A wide range of rafting and kayaking excursions in the Río Juramento, canopying and rappel, professionally run. Also arranges accommodation.

Socompa, Caseros 266, T0387-422 8471, www.socompa.com. Excellent company specializing in trips to the *puna*, 1-3-day trips to giant salt flats and mighty volcanoes based at the beautiful and remote hamlet of Tolar Grande. English and Italian spoken by the knowledgeable guides, who will inform you all about the culture and history of the places you'll visit. Unmissable. Highly recommended.

Turismo San Lorenzo, Dávalos 960 (San Lorenzo), T0387-492 1757, www.turismosanlorenzo.com. Excellent horse riding in nearby San Lorenzo, but also mountain bike excursions, trekking, 4WD and paragliding.

Tour operators

There are plenty of conventional agencies on C Buenos Aires, first couple of blocks from the main plaza, get a list in the tourist office.

MoviTrack, Buenos Aires 28 (and desk at airport), T0387-431 6749, www.movitrack.com.ar. A dynamic and well-organized company offering imaginative trips in special 4WD vehicles. Highly recommended is their alternative to the *Safari a las Nubes* , US$100, which follows the same route as the train, either in an open bus or with the ultra-

modern Oxy Bus (altitude-sickness-proof with pressurized and dust-free cabin) for a fantastic range of landscapes from *selva* to puna all in one day. Friendly informative bilingual guides. Great 1- to 4-day trips, some getting off the beaten track.
Saltur, Caseros 485, T0387-421 2012, saltursalta@arnet.com.ar. Efficient and recommended for local tours.
TEA, Buenos Aires 82, T0387-421 3333, www.teaturismo.com. Offers well-organized tours to the usual places. Recommended.
Yaco, Buenos Aires 39, T0387-401 0970, yacotour@hotmail.com. Offers a wide range of trips including a 2-day trip to Salinas Grandes, Humahuaca and Iruya; always small groups, English spoken.

Transport

Salta *p256, map p259*

Air

The airport is 12 km south of the city, T0387-424 3115, reached by vans run by **Transfer del Pino**, US$3. A taxi from the bus station to the airport is US$5. **LAB** to **Santa Cruz** (Bolivia) twice a week, once via Tarija. **Aerolíneas Argentinas** flies to **Buenos Aires**, 2 hrs. Note that **Aerolíneas Argentinas** is currently the only Argentine airline, also working under the name **Austral**, Caseros 475, T0387-431 0862. **Lloyd Aéreo Boliviano**, Caseros 529, T0387-431 1389.

Bus

Local The main bus terminal is 8 blocks east of the main plaza, information T0387- 401 1143. Buses to local destinations, such as **Coronel Moldes** can be caught next to the cable car office, the *teleférico* on the corner of San Martín y Yrigoyen. To **Campo Quijano** via **Silleta**, hourly. El Indio, T0387- 431 9389 goes to **Cafayate**, US$7, 3½-4 hrs, 3-4 daily, to **Santa María**, US$10, 5½ hrs, daily, to **Angastaco**, US$9.50, 5½ hrs, Mon-Fri, to **Belén**, US$18, 13 hrs, Wed. To **Cachi**, US$7, 4-4½ hrs, 1-2 daily, with **Marcus Rueda**, leaves 0700. Spectacular journey. Usually continues to **Molinos**, US$10, 6½ hrs, every 2 days and to **La Poma**, US$9, 6½ hrs, 4 weekly (Marcos Rueda, T0387-421 4447). To **Rosario de la Frontera**, US$6, 2½-3 hrs. To **San Antonio de Los Cobres**, 5 hrs, El Quebradeño, Mon-Sat 1500, Sun 1910, US$6.

Long distance To **Buenos Aires**, several daily, US$ 35-63, 17-20 hrs, **Flecha Bus**, **La Veloz del Norte**, **Brown**, **Chevallier** and other companies. Choose *coche cama* for maximum comfort and reclining seats. To **Córdoba**, several daily, 12-13 hrs, US$25-28, **Flecha Bus**, **Tramat**, **La Veloz del Norte**. To **Santiago del Estero**, 6-7 hrs, US$16. To **Tucumán**, 4-4½ hrs, several companies, including **Flecha Bus, Andesmar** or **La Veloz del Norte** recommended, US$ 10-14. To **Mendoza** via Tucumán, several companies, daily, 16-18 hrs, US$ 35-60. To **Jujuy**, **Balut Hnos**, **La Veloz del Norte**, **Andesmar**, **Flecha Bus** and others, hourly between 0600 and 2200, 'directo', US$ 3.50, 2 hrs. To **La Rioja**, US$ 18-26, 10-11 hrs. To **Resistencia**, US$25-37, 13-16 hrs. To **Puerto Iguazú**, US$ 48-60, 24-25 hrs, daily.

International To **Chile** Géminis and Pullman Bus go on Tue, Thu and Sun to **San Pedro de Atacama**, US$40, 10-11 hrs and to **Arica**, US$54-60, 24 hrs. To **Bolivia** La Veloz del Norte goes to **Santa Cruz de la Sierra** (connection at General Güemes), or go to **La Quiaca**, on Bolivian border, several daily, **Andesmar**, **Flecha Bus**, **Balut**, US$8.50, 7 hrs or to **Pocitos** or **Aguas Blancas**, both on Bolivian border, several companies daily.

Car hire

Avis, at the airport, Route 51, T0387-424 2289, salta@avis.com.ar. Efficient and very helpful, recommended; **Hertz**, Caseros 374, T0387-421 6785, foarentacar@arnet.com.ar. **NOA**, Buenos Aires 1, T0387-431 7080, www.noarentacar.com, in **Hotel Salta**, helpful.

Train

The station is at 20 de Febrero y Ameghino, 9 blocks north of Plaza 9 de Julio, taxi US$1. The only train running is the **Tren a las Nubes** ('Train to the Clouds'), which usually runs between Salta and La Polvorilla viaduct once a week from Apr to Nov, weather permitting, and on additional days in the high season (Jan/Feb and Jul/Aug). It departs promptly at 0705, returning to Salta 2200. At the time of writing, services have been suspended, but it's due to reopen in 2007. The price may come down from the previous US$120 for foreigners. Be warned: it's a very touristy experience (see box, page 269) Consider the alternatives.

Directory

Salta *p256, map p259*
Banks Banks are open 0900-1400, all have ATMs (many on España). Banco de la Nación, Mitre y Belgrano, Banco de Salta, España 550 on main plaza, cashes TCs. **Consulates** Bolivia, Mariano Boedo 34, T0387-421 1040. Mon-Fri, 0900-1400 (unhelpful, better to go to Jujuy). Chile, Santiago del Estero 965, T0387-431 1857. **Cultural centres** Alliance Française, Santa Fe 20, T0387-431 2403. **Internet** There are many fast and cheap internet places and *locutorios* in the centre: Cibercom, next to the tourist office on Buenos Aires, is one of the best and sells drinks. **Immigration office** Maipú 35, T0387-422 0438, 0730-1230. **Medical services** Hospital San Bernardo, Tobías 69. Emergencies T911.

Northwest Salta and the Quebrada del Toro

The landscapes of northwestern Salta province are utterly spectacular. In one simple, unforgettable journey up the Quebrada del Toro from Salta city to the town of San Antonio de los Cobres, you'll travel through an extraordinary spectrum from dense forest, gorges of brightly coloured rock strewn with cactus, to the silent expanses of high altitude desert in the puna. This is the route of Argentina's famous narrow gauge railway, Tren a las Nubes (train to the clouds), but it's a long, frustrating and very touristy experience. Far better to take a minibus tour or hire a car, and take time to pause and explore on the way. You might stay a night in the forested weekend resort of Campo Quijano, and don't miss the superb ruined city of Santa Rosa de Tastil, one of Argentina's archaeological gems. Set in stunning rocky landscapes, there's fascinating evidence of ancient pre-Inca and Inca civilizations here, and a local guide will bring it all alive. At the top of the gorge, the quiet mining town San Antonio de los Cobres is at its best for the Fiesta de la Pachamama in August, and a good stopping point before setting off into the puna. To offset altitude sickness, stop off for coca tea with typical puna family Sandro Yampa at el Mojón, and then be dazzled by the shimmering white expanse of the Salinas Grandes salt flats. From here you could drop to Purmamarca in the Quebrada de Humahuaca down the thrilling Cuesta de Lipán road. Or head west, further into the puna to discover tranquil isolation at Tolar Grande. ▸▸ *For Sleeping, Eating and other listings, see page 270.*

Ins and outs

This part of Salta has traditionally been the sole preserve of the Tren a las Nubes, but in the last few years, another tour operator **Movitrack** has run very successful tours along the same route which actually allow you to see far more of the impressive engineering of the train track, and certainly absorb more of the landscape. Inevitably, other tour operators followed, and along Salta's Calle Buenos Aires, you'll find plenty of tours on offer, though Movitrack is the only company to have pressurized oxygen pumped vehicles to counter the inevitable effects of altitude. It's well worth hiring a car to explore the Quebrada del Toro, and to make time to see Santa Rosa de Tastil, which few agencies include in any detail. Ask the tourist office for latest information on local guides at the site, since there is a new project to put trained locals in place. There is comfortable accommodation at **San Antonio de los Cobres**, but very little on the way. If cycling, note that much of the road is *ripio* (gravel), that there is no shade, and it's extremely cold at nights. However you travel, the effects of altitude are not to be underestimated, since you'll be climbing to nearly 4000 m. You must take time for your body to adjust if you're going to exert yourself beyond a gentle stroll. Drink plenty of water, avoid alcohol, and don't over-eat. Take it easy and you should feel fine.

Quebrada del Toro and Tren a las Nubes » p270.

The route for the Train to the Clouds is the same as the road through the Quebrada del Toro. The only difference is that travelling by road gives you the chance to get out and walk around – and to examine the spectacular feat of engineering of the train track – which of course you can't see from the train itself. You'll leave Salta's subtropical valleys via the jungly weekend retreat of **Campo Quijano**, at Km 30, which lies in a beautiful, thickly vegetated valley at the entrance to the gorge and is an attractive place for a stop. The road and track then climb along the floor of the Quebrada del Toro, fording the river repeatedly amidst densely growing pampas grass and *ceibo*, Argentina's national flower, with its striking fringed red blossoms. At **Chorrillos**, you'll see one of several identical wooden 1920's train stations along the route, with outside ovens built to heat steel fixings during the building of the track. From here the train track zig-zags as it climbs past tiny farmsteads lined with alamo trees, and up into the dramatic **Quebrada Colorada** – so called because of its bright red, pink and green stratified rock – to Ingeniero Maury at an altitude of 2350 m, Km 65, where there is a police control point. From Km 96, now paved, the road climbs the **Quebrada de Tastil**, parting company from the railway which continues through the **Quebrada del Toro**. The road passes through the tiny hamlet of Santa Rosa de Tastil, where there are marvellous pre-Inca ruins, and the only accommodation before San Antonio de los Cobres.

Santa Rosa de Tastil

→ Phone code: 0387 Colour map 1, A2

This picturesque little hamlet (3200 m, Km 103) lies near the site of one of Argentina's most important pre-Hispanic settlements which once contained well over 400 houses and over 2000 people, believed to have been inhabited from AD 1336 to 1439. There is a small **museum** ⓘ *at the side of the road, daily 1000-1800, US$1*, which is recommended. It has some of the finds from this intriguing culture, among them a well preserved mummy, delicate jewellery and a xylophone of sonorous rocks. The museum's guide may treat you to a rendition of *Für Elise*, a wonderful anachronism. The remains of this ancient city are extraordinarily beautiful; a vast expanse of regular walls and roads, stretching out on an exposed hillside with views along the entire gorge. The ruins themselves are well worth visiting, but be sure to ask for a local guide, since there the site is extensive, and you'll get more out of it with a little interpretation. Guides will show you around, but are unpaid so appreciate a tip.

San Antonio de los Cobres *→ Phone code: 0387 Colour map 1, B2*

Beyond Tastil the road climbs through green hanging valleys where cattle roam, and then up over the **Abra Blanca Pass** (4050 m) where the landscape changes dramatically, suddenly becoming vast, open and eerily empty. At the top of the pass, the road drops and runs across the *puna*, offering views of Mount Chañi (5896 m) to the right, Acay (5716 m) to the left, and Quewar (6102 m) in the far distance.

San Antonio de los Cobres (3774 m, 168 km northwest of Salta) is a simple remote mining town of low adobe houses situated in a shallow hollow. There's nothing much to do here but it's a good introduction to the reclusive life of the puna, and it does have its subtle charms. It's also one of the few places here which retains authentic indigenous culture, and where the **Pachamama festival** is celebrated in style every August. Tourists are welcome at this great event which is not to be missed. People are friendly and the handicrafts on offer are of high quality, and incredibly cheap. You may want to experience real puna life, and 35 km beyond the town, on the way to Salinas Grandes, you can visit Sandro Llampa and his family at **El Mojón**. Look out for signs on the main road, or take a tour with Socompa (see Salta tour operators,

Train to the clouds

The famous narrow gauge *Tren a las Nubes* is extraordinary feat of engineering, and a good way to experience the dramatic landscape up to the puna.

Built to enable commerce over the Andes to Chile, the track, which runs 570 km from Salta to Socompa on the Chilean border, was the outstanding achievement of Richard Maury, an engineer from Pennsylvania. Work started in 1921, and took 20 years. The track starts in Salta at 1200m above sea level, rising to 4200m, up through the impossibly rocky terrain of the steep gorge Quebrada del Toro, with several switchbacks ('zig-zags') and 360 degree loops to allow diesel engines to gain height over a short distance with a gentler gradient. One thousand men worked with only the most basic tools through inhospitable conditions, detonating rock, and carving away at steep mountainsides through howling winds and snow. Many died in the attempt. The destination of the tourist Tren (passengers no longer being allowed on the weekly cargo trains) is La Polvorilla viaduct, near San Antonio de los Cobres, a delicate bridge across a mighty gorge, spanning 224m long and 63 m high; it feels like you're travelling on air, both scary and exhilarating.

The tourist train is a comfortable ride, though a long day out. Leaving Salta at 0700, (cold and dark in winter) to the cheerful accompaniment of *folclore* singers on the platform, the train edges to the entrance of Quebrada de Toro, steep forested mountains tinged with pink on top as the sun rises, and a light breakfast is served. The landscape changes as you climb through the gorge, dotted with farms and adobe houses, to arid red rock where giant cacti perch, past sculptural mountains, coloured terracotta to chocolate, ochre and pink, to the staggeringly beautiful puna. The seven hours of the ascent are kept lively by chats from bilingual guides (English spoken, but French, Portuguese too, on request), and the serving of lunch. The puna (altitude sickness) hits many people, and oxygen is on hand. At La Polvorilla viaduct, you can get out briefly to admire the construction, and buy locally made llama wool goods from the people of San Antonio. Don't bother haggling: these shawls and hats are beautifully made, and these people's only source of income. At San Antonio, the Argentine flag is raised to commemorate those who worked on the railway, and the national anthem is sung, in a rather surreal ceremony. The descent, however, is tedious beyond belief, despite the constant stream of entertainment from folclore singers and Andean bands. Consider returning by road instead, to see the ruins at Santa Rosa de Tastil.

page 265). However, altitude sickness can strike heavily here, so avoid eating too much or drinking alcohol until acclimatized.

From here you could head back south along Ruta 40 to La Poma and Cachi over the mighty Paso Abra del Acay (4900 m), see page 272. This road should only be attempted in a 4WD as it is very rough in places. Or you could head north to the fabulous salt flats at Salinas Grandes, and on to Purmamarca in the Quebrada de Humahuaca – a spectacular journey, see below. About 14 km west of San Antonio de los Cobres, there is a road which runs below the famous **La Polvorilla** railway viaduct, giving you the chance to photograph it.

San Antonio to Chile

From San Antonio there are two possible crossings to Chile. The best, closest, and most used, is the **Paso de Sico**, due west on Route Nacional 51. Alternatively, at Cauchari, take Route Provincial 27 southwest across the giant Salar de Arizaro to the Chilean border at the **Paso de Socompa** (not recommended). The road runs through very beautiful scenery including salt flats and desert, but be warned that is extremely isolated, and there are no services whatsoever. Make sure you stock up on drinking water and fuel before setting out from San Antonio. Only for the very intrepid.

Border crossing Paso de Sico ⓘ *T0387-498 2001, daily 0800-2000*. The Argentine immigration offices are at the pass itself and in San Antonio de los Cobres at the other end of town from *aduana* (customs house). There is a police checkpoint at Catúa, 26 km east of Paso de Sico. There is a police checkpoint in Toconao but customs and immigration for Chile is in San Pedro de Atacama. No fresh food may be taken into Chile (there is a search 20 km west of Paso de Sico). From **Paso de Socompa** a poor road runs to Pan de Azúcar, with roads west to the Pan-American Highway, or north via the Salar de Atacama to San Pedro de Atacama. No fuel is available until San Pedro or Calama.

San Antonio to Purmamarca

Another road, the Ruta 40, leads north from San Antonio to Abra Pampa, or curves around to join a good route to Purmamarca in the Quebrada de Humahuaca (see page 292) which is recommended for a taste of the extraordinary landscapes. The road continues dead flat across the scrubby yellow puna – its horizons edged with pinkish mauve or bronze mountains, with the occasional flock of llamas or cows grazing. It's either wonderfully meditative or unbearably monotonous, depending on your point of view, but the salt flats, **Salinas Grandes**, which you'll reach in two hours from San Antonio, are certainly worth seeing. The huge expanses of dazzling white salt, crazy paved with crusted lines, are silent and other worldly. There are crossroads some 20 north of the salt flats, where you could head west to Susques (in Jujuy, see page 278), up to Abra Pampa or follow the spectacular road to Purmamarca down the broad slalom bends of **Cuesta de Lipán** with breathtaking views of the valley below.

Sleeping

Santa Rosa de Tastil *p268*
Basic accommodation in shared dorms is available in the village for US$2 pp – ask at the museum.

San Antonio de los Cobres *p268*
C Hostería de las Nubes, on the eastern outskirts, T0387-490 9059. A smart, well-maintained place with lovely comfortable rooms, including breakfast, and a good restaurant. Staff are friendly and can advise on routes nearby. Recommended.
F Belgrano, T0387-490 9025. Very friendly, basic rooms, evening meals also offered.
F El Palenque, Belgrano s/n, T0387-490 9019. Also a café, family run.

Eating

Santa Rosa de Tastil *p268*
Posta de los Cardones, RN 51, T0387-499 1093. Tasty food by chefs Erick and Paula.

San Antonio de los Cobres *p268*
El Mojón, 35 km from San Antonio on RN40 to Salinas Grandes. Sandro Llampa and his family serve coca tea or lunch and will show you around their farm.

Transport

Santa Rosa de Tastil *p268*
Bus El Quebradeño bus for **San Antonio de los Cobres** leaves Salta at 1500, but arrives too late to see the ruins. Best to take a tour.

Los Valles Calchaquíes

Dramatic, constantly changing and stunningly beautiful, the Valles Calchaquíes are perhaps the most captivating part of Salta province. The river Calchaquí springs 5000 m up on the slopes of the Nevado de Acay, just south of San Antonio de los Cobres, and flows, via a series of timeless oasis villages through a spectacularly long and broad valley, to Cafayate and beyond. The first village is La Poma, set in wide open red rocky land, but you're more likely to start exploring at the pretty town of Cachi, reached from Salta by a breathtaking drive up the Cuesta del Obispo and through the giant cactus park, Parque Nacional los Cardones. Cachi is set against the massive range of the Nevado de Cachi mountains, with a hidden valley, Cachi Adentro, irrigated since pre-Inca times to produce the bright red peppers which you'll see drying in the sun in April. Head south from Cachi, and there are unspoilt villages dotted along the valley: Seclantás, with its poncho weavers, Molinos, with its lovely church and Bodega Colomé to the west, Angastaco and San Carlos, all reached by the rough ripio Ruta 40. There are extraordinary rock formations at Quebrada de las Flechas, just north of the more established wine-growing centre of Cafayate. South of here, the valley and Ruta 40 continues to heavenly Santa María (Catamarca) and Amaichá del Valle (see page 315). The sun shines here all year, and there is minimal rainfall, making it perfect to visit in the winter. » *For Sleeping, Eating and other listings, see pages 278-283.*

Ins and outs

It's possible to travel in the valleys using public transport, with buses from Salta to both Cachi and Cafayate. There are two different routes. To reach Cafayate quickly, there are several buses daily along the fast, paved Route Nacional 68. South of Cafayate, there are buses to Santa María (Catamarca) and Amaichá del Valle. If you're short of time, there are one or two day tours from Salta to the Cafayate and Calchaquíes valleys, but they are frustratingly brief, with many hours spent cooped up in a mini bus.

Alternatively, the more scenic route through the valley is the iconic Ruta 40. One bus a day goes from Salta to Cachi and Molinos along the nail-biting Cuesta del Obispo, Route Nacional 33, and the beautiful Ruta 40, quite an experience in itself. It's worth taking the extra time to explore the villages and stay the night in Cachi or Molinos. However, from Molinos there's only one bus a week along the Calchaquí Valley to Angastaco, leaving you stranded for days. The best way to see this region is to hire a car in Salta, preferably a 4WD for the rough stretch between Cachi and Cafayate and essential in summer, when rains swell the rivers. The road is rough along this stretch, just about passable in an ordinary vehicle but easier in a 4WD, especially during the rainy season in January and February, when the road is often flooded.

Background

The whole vast Calchaquí Valley was densely populated in pre-Hispanic times, by sophisticated peoples who built stone dwellings in large organized 'cities', the impressive remains of which you can see still at Las Pailas near Cachi, and at Quilmes further south. Much archaeological work has yet to be done to establish more detail about their daily lives, and there are currently digs at Las Pailas and La Borgata, near Cachi Adentro. Often referred to as 'Diaguitan', the Diaguita were just one of several tribes in the valley. They left a rich legacy of ceramics which you can see today in all the small museums throughout the region. From beautifully painted urns made to contain the bodies of their dead children, to simple cooking pots, and glazed black polished vessels, these artefacts speak of sophisticated peoples with a high degree of social organization.

After the defeat of the indigenous population in the Calchaquí Wars, the Spanish established missions and *haciendas* in the valley, which were run along feudal principles – some until as recently as the 1980s. During the colonial period the valley prospered, providing pasturage for mules and herds of cattle en route to the mountain passes into Chile and Alto Perú (Bolivia). After independence, lower parts of the valley became the primary wheat-growing and wine-producing area for Salta city, but the local economy declined in the late 19th century when the railway brought cheap wheat from the pampas and wine from Mendoza. Salta's endemic racism, and the feudal legacy has meant that the indigenous peoples in the valley are only recently coming to value their own cultural inheritance. Rather than taking a commercial group tour from Salta, seek out local guides who will tell you about their fascinating history.

La Poma to San Antonio de los Cobres

La Poma (3015 m), with its modern adobe houses and a population of 600, lies beneath the massive Cumbre del Libertador General San Martín (6380 m). It's the first village in the valley but not the original one. The old village was destroyed by an earthquake in 1930; its ruins lie 2 km north at La Poma Vieja. North of La Poma, Route 40 continues over the **Paso Abra del Acay** (4900 m), Km 282, the highest pass in South America negotiable by car. Road conditions vary depending on the weather and whether the roads have been recently cleared; a high clearance 4WD vehicle is advised. The critical part of the route is south of the pass at **Mal Paso**, Km 257, where summer rains can wash the road away. Buses do not travel on this road and anyone tempted to try it on a bicycle should think twice. There is no shade, night temperatures are several degrees below freezing, and you need to be well adapted to the altitude. Take plenty of water and an arctic sleeping bag. North of the pass, the road runs across the puna to San Antonio de los Cobres.

To explore La Poma in a day trip from Cachi, contact local guide, **Santiago Casimiro**, T03868-15638545, who can bring you here in your car or taxi, via the fascinating Inca grain storage caves at **Los Graneros**, and visiting the ex-feudal village of Palermo, with lots of interesting history and culture thrown in.

Chicoana and the journey from Salta to Cachi

Cachi is 170 km west of Salta, along one of the most unforgettable routes in Argentina. Head south from Salta on Route Nacional 68, and turn right at El Carril, to the quaint little colonial town of **Chicoana**, where you could stay the night in the splendid **Finca Los Los** (see page 278). There's not much to do in Chicoana, but it's an interesting example of a colonial-style town, sitting amidst some of the finest tobacco-producing land in the world, and with lots of buildings dating from the 1900s and a peaceful way of life. Religious festivals are celebrated with much enthusiasm, and the **Carnaval** (February) and the **Fiesta Patronal** (16 July) are particularly recommended for a fun day out. Easter celebrations are impressive too, with the Passion re-enacted throughout the town. The weekend afterwards (around 23 July) is the town's famous **Fiesta de Tamales** when regional delicacies such as meat and corn tied up in corn-husk bundles, are traditionally made on a massive scale, famous *folclore* musicians come to sing, and gauchos compete in Doma contests – roughly equivalent to rodeo and very impressive.

From Chicoana, the road enters the fertile **Quebrada de Escoipe**, and a good wide road hugs the mountains as it snakes up the breathtaking **Cuesta del Obispo**. The road here is mostly still *ripio*; paving is in progress but taking many years. There are two places to stop for tea roughly half way to Cachi. At **El Maray** (70 km from Salta), there's a nice *confitería* in a yellow building on the right and, opposite, delicious jams and walnuts are sold; ask for hot corn on the cob. Further on, **Café Margarita** serves coffee and layered *tortillas* for bus passengers. Throughout the journey, you'll pass tiny hamlets of adobe houses shrouded in low cloud. As the cloud clears, you'll glimpse dramatic views of the vast bronze green velvety mountains, and there's a fantastic panorama as you round the head of the valley. From here you might like to take the turning off down to the **Valle Encantado**, an eerie fascinating place for a picnic amongst bizarre wind-sculpted terracotta rocks. Take great care if you drive the Cuesta del Obispo in fog, which often hangs in the valley in the early mornings, or in rain. It is not advisable at night.

Beyond the arid **Piedra del Molino Pass** (3347 m), where you'll want to stop for photos, the road runs west along a dead-straight stretch known as **La Recta del Tin-Tin**, passing through the **Parque Nacional Los Cardones**, at altitudes between 2700 and 5000 m, an astonishing landscape of huge candelabra cacti. Walking amongst these giant sentinels, their arms thrust up to the cloudless sky, and a backdrop of stratified bright pink rock, is extraordinary experience. There are occasionally *guardaparques* at Recta del Tin-Tin, but no services. Camping is officially not allowed. About 11 km before reaching Cachi is the small village of **Payogasta**, with the national park **administrative office** ⓘ *T03868-496005, loscardones@apn.gov.ar*, and the **Hostería de Payogasta**, T03868-496034.

Cachi → *Phone code: 03868 Colour map 1, B2 Population: 7200, altitude 2280 m, 180 km from Salta*

Cachi is a beautiful, tranquil town in a wide green valley at the foot of the majestic Nevado del Cachi, whose nine peaks are snow-covered for much of the year, and whose highest summit is **San Martín** (6380 m). Founded in 1694, it had been a Diaguita settlement long before the Incas arrived in 1450, and the extensive irrigation channels they built to channel the Nevado's snowmelt are still used today to make the valley so green and to grow huge fields of peppers. These are an amazing sight when harvested in April and laid out to dry in huge scarlet squares which stand out against the arid mountains beyond. The **tourist office** ⓘ *on the plaza, opposite side to the church, T03868-491053, www.salnet.com.ar/cachi, daily 0900-1200, 1500-2000*, can provide a basic leaflet and map. No one speaks English, but they are well-meaning and will give advice if you're patient. A private tourist office has opened, **Casa de Turismo de Cachi** ⓘ *by the entrance to the town on the left*. Local guide Susana can be found here, and they sell crafts.

Cachi has a pleasingly simple church, the **Iglesia de San José**, whose roof and lecterns are made of cactus wood. Next door, there's a fascinating survey of pre-colonial Calchaquí culture in the **Museo Arqueológico** ⓘ *Mon-Fri 0830-1930, Sat and Sun 1000-1300, US$0.30, T03868-491080*, with impressive painted funerary urns and an intriguing cat/man petroglyph. With its sunny climate, Cachi is the perfect place for a few days' rest, but there are satisfying walks into the mountains, to see extraordinary pre-Inca ruins, and there are panoramic views from its spectacularly sited hill-top cemetery, just 20 minutes' walk from the plaza.

The town feels more like a small village and has a lively community life, with fiestas throughout the year, where you can hear traditional folclore music as well as the *bagualas*, and *coplas* coming from the indigenous traditions. The **Fiesta de la Tradición Calchaquí**, held in the third week in January, and the **Carnaval** in February, are particularly worth experiencing. **Pachamama** is celebrated in August. Cachi has a special advantage in being one of the few original towns in the region with trained local guides: Susana, Santiago and Hilda lead fascinating tours around Cachi and the surrounding areas. See Tour operators, page 282. Don't miss **Las Pailas** archaeological site. **Cerro de la Virgen** makes a satisfying day's hike. Serious climbers should plan to spend a week or so to climb the spectacular Nevado de Cachi.

Cachi has a great tradition in weaving, and you can buy beautiful handmade ponchos, shawls, rugs and wall hangings at the government run **handicrafts shop** in the same room as the tourist office on the plaza. But these are more expensive than if bought directly from weavers, and they receive hardly any of the profit. Instead, go up the street, and find the workshop of **Oscar Cardozo** ⓘ *Juan Calchaquí, opposite the monument, T03868-491037*. Oscar teaches weaving and can direct you to other weavers in his association. There's an ATM on the plaza at Güemes and Ruiz de los Lanos, and several restaurants and cafés on the plaza too.

Around Cachi

There are walks to **La Aguada**, 6 km southwest along the lush valley fringed with Alamo trees, and dotted with lovely adobe farm houses. Leave town by Calle Benjamín Zorrilla at the southwest of the plaza, and walk along the *ripio* track. There's wonderful accommodation here at the *finca* **El Molino** (see Sleeping page 279), with its superb tiny *bodega*, and charming hospitality.

But you shouldn't miss the ancient ruins at **Las Pailas**, 16 km northwest of Cachi (via Cachi Adentro), with intriguingly complex circular dwellings, long irrigation channels and worked stone cultivation terraces. The views are breathtaking, with huge cacti set against the snow-topped Nevado de Cachi behind. To get there, take a bus to Las Arcas, from where it's a two-hour walk. The bus leaves Cachi early in the morning (check the current timetable with the tourist office) and returns in the afternoon. However, it's better to go with one of the local guides such as Santiago Casimiro, see Activities and tours, page 282.

Cerro de la Virgen is another rewarding day hike near Cachi, up through a pretty hanging valley and slopes strewn with giant boulders to a peak which gives wonderful views over the Calchaquí valley beyond. The hamlet **Cachi Adentro**, on the opposite side of the valley from La Aguada, has more fine views, a school, church and dairy farm, **El Tambo**. To climb any of the peaks in the **Nevado de Cachi**, you must take a mountain guide who is trained and familiar with the route. Do not attempt these peaks alone: a tourist lost his life here recently, and the danger is not to be under-estimated. See Activities and tours, page 282, for recommended guides, or ask in the tourist office.

Seclantás and Molinos → *Phone code: 03868 Colour map 1, B2 Population: 900*

The road continues from Cachi on the west side of the river, via the hostería **Casa de Campo La Paya** (see Sleeping, page 279), 9 km from Cachi, where there are interesting archaeological ruins of an important pre-Inca town and administrative centre. For a pretty detour via the hamlet of **Seclantás**, cross the river and follow signs. This is a quaint tranquil village with simple colonial-style houses, and an interesting church dating from 1835. Seclantás' weavers are among the finest in the land, and sell ponchos directly from their workshops on the side of the road; look for the looms strung up between the pillars on a porch. The quality is higher and prices are much lower than in the Cachi tourist office shop, and you have the satisfaction of knowing that the profits go directly to the weavers. Wander down the main street, and ask around for *telares* (weavers), as there are few signs. There's currently nowhere to stay in Seclantás, but a couple of places sell food and snacks.

Some 52 km from Cachi, you come to the village of **Molinos** (2000 m), hidden away 1 km off Route 40 at Km 118. Set in a bowl of craggy mountains, with a wide plaza and neat adobe houses, it's a peaceful place and an idyllic retreat for relaxing and doing very little. Founded in 1659, it has a fine church dating from 1692, with a simple gold *retablo*, containing the mummified body of the last Royalist governor of Salta, Don Nicolás Severo Isasmendi. The house he built, opposite the church, is now the **Hostal Provincial de Molinos**. There are a couple of satisfying two-hour walks: either across the river bed (usually dry) and then up the hill opposite; or up to the Cross above the town. Both offer fine views of Molinos and the surrounding country. Visit the *vicuña* farm, **Asociación de Artesanos y Productores San Pedro Nolasco** ⓘ *T0387-154 071259, daily 0800-1300, 1630-2100*, for fine weavings, some made of the light and unbelievably soft *vicuña* wool.

Accommodation is limited in Molinos, but the nuns opposite the church have pristine little rooms to rent, and there are several families who rent rooms in the village. There are a few very simple places to eat, near where the bus to Cachi stops – ask around, or at the basic **tourist office** ⓘ *municipalidad, on the plaza at 9 de Julio s/n, 0800-2200, low season 0900-1300 and 1600-2100*. No one speaks English here but they are kind and want to help. Molinos celebrates **La Virgen de la Candelaria** in February, with processions, music and handicrafts.

Just 20 km from Molinos along a road running west into the mountains, is the extraordinary and fabulous winery, **Colomé** ⓘ *4 hrs from Salta, 2½ hrs from Cafayate via a short cut, T03868-494044, www.bodegacolome.com*. Owned by charming art collector Donald Hess and his wife Ursula, this remote retreat is more than just a swish place to stay. As well as having a stunningly lovely setting, the *bodega* produces the highest altitude wines in the world, at 2300m. In an arid valley of red and grey rock, surrounded by mountains, there are hundreds of hectares of rare pre-Phylloxera vines, producing Malbec-heavy wines of exquisite intensity – and all grown on organic and biodynamic principles. A Spanish-style house with nine rooms provides ultra luxurious accommodation, delicious meals, and there is great walking and riding in the extensive *finca*. It's impressive in terms of social responsibility too, since the Hesses have built a church, clinic and community centre for the 400 families living on their land, and take great care of their well-being.

Angastaco → *Colour map 1, B2 Population: 900*

From Molinos, Ruta 40 weaves its way through some of the most exquisite scenery in the region. But the road is rough *ripio*, and only manageable in an ordinary hired car as long as it hasn't rained. Consider hiring a 4WD for safety. The landscape is beautiful: tiny settlements with green fields and orchards, against the constant backdrop of the rugged Andes. Angastaco (1900 m) is a modern village, 2 km off Route 40, at Km 77, less picturesque than Cachi, but it does have an **archaeological museum** in the Centro Cívico. The church is modern, so it's worth the trek to the much older one, the **Iglesia del Carmen de Angastaco** (1800) about 8 km further north on the **Finca El Carmen**. Stop in Angastaco to try the *vino patero*, for which the town is famous. This sweet red or white wine is traditionally made by treading the grapes in the traditional manner – hence the name (*pata* is the informal word for leg). Sample it at Señor Flores' house close to the bridge in Angastaco. The **Fiesta Patronal Virgen del Valle** is held on the second weekend of December, with processions, music, dancing, gauchos and rodeos. Information is available from the **tourist office** ⓘ *in the municipalidad on the plaza, Mon-Fri 0900-1300*.

San Carlos and the Quebrada de las Flechas → *Colour map 1, B2*

The highlight of your trip on this fabulous route will probably be the next stretch of road through the **Quebrada de las Flechas** (the gorge of arrows) to San Carlos. You'll find yourself surrounded by massive rocks, eroded into complex forms and massive sharp peaks towering above you, and jutting like giant vertical valleys into the blue sky. All very photogenic. **San Carlos** (1710 m, Km 24) is a pleasant place and was the most important village in the valley until the growth of Cafayate. The main buildings are on the pretty plaza, including the church, the largest in the valley, which was built between 1801 and 1860. Nearby, there's a small **archaeological museum** ⓘ *daily 1000-1400*, which contains some superb archaeological finds from the region, including some fine funerary urns. Also on the plaza are artisans' shops and workshops and a craft market.

Cafayate and around » pp278-283.

→ *Phone code: 03868 Colour map 1, B2 Population: 10,700*

Cafayate (1660 m) is beautifully situated in a broad stretch of the valley at the confluence of the Santa María and Calchaquí rivers. There are mountains on all sides, and the valley is filled with vineyards, which have long produced wine to rival Mendoza in quality, if not in quantity. There's lots of accommodation, with one exquisite place to stay – **Patios de Cafayate** (see Sleeping, page 280) – making this a good base for exploring the dramatic scenery all around, or just relaxing for a couple of days, though the centre might be a little too touristy for those who like to get off the beaten track. Cafayate has long been a popular excursion destination for visits to the handful of *bodegas* which open their doors to tourists, with free tours and tastings for you to try their produce. There are superb red grapes grown at high altitude here, and it's worth asking specifically to try the white *torrontes* grape, which is grown in few places other than Argentina, and flourishes in the annual 350 days of sunshine, and the cool nights.

Ins and outs

Getting there and around There are several buses daily from Salta along the fast Route Nacional 68, and it's an easy drive in a hire car, though the road is winding for the last 30 km as you enter the amazing rock formations of the Quebrada de las Conchas. Alternatively, and even more scenic, is the Ruta 40 via Cachi and the Valles Calchaquíes (see above) but the road is rough *ripio* and there's only one bus a week between Molinos and Angastaco. There are many excursions on offer from Salta to Cafayate US$30, including lunch and visit to a *bodega*, with brief stops to see the strange rock formations in the Quebrada de las Conchas. But these make for a long day, and you'll miss the chance to walk around the region. Cafayate is easy to get around on foot, with restaurants and shops located around the main plaza, but you'll need transport to reach many of the *bodegas* further out. Find a taxi in the plaza.

Tourist information There's a tiny but informative centre in a hut on the northeast corner of the plaza, T03868-422223 (daily 0800-2200). They have a basic sketch map with the *bodegas* marked, and an accommodation list. Tour operators can be found along Calle Gral Güemes – note that this street changes names from Norte to Sur across the plaza, and, confusingly, identical numbers can be found on both sides.

Sights

Conventional sights aren't Cafayate's strong point; it's much more interesting to explore the landscape and the *bodegas*. The **Museo de la Vid y El Vino** ⓘ *Güemes Sur, 2 blocks south of the plaza, Mon-Fri 0800-2000, Sat-Sun 0800-1300, 1400-2000, US$0.35*, contains old wine-making equipment and a display on the history of wine. The **Museo Arqueológico Rodolfo I Bravo** ⓘ *Colón 191, T03868-421054, Mon-Fri 1100-2100, open on request at weekends, US$1*, is tiny but has some beautiful funerary urns, black ceramics from the fifth century, and Inca pieces too – well worth seeing if you haven't come across them elsewhere.

Bodegas

Cafayate's wines are sophisticated and generally of very high quality, with intense high-altitude reds (Malbec and Cabernet sauvignon predominate), and the famous white Torrontes. This superbly fruity dry wine with delicious floral aromas, is grown only in the Valles Calchaquíes, and makes an excellent aperitif (it also goes particularly well with carrot and coriander soup). There are several *bodegas* that can be visited and all are shown on the tourist office's map; the best are described below.

Tours usually take around 45 minutes, are free, and are followed by a free tasting. Ask if the guides speak English.

The most highly recommended *bodega*, with an informative tour, is **El Esteco** ⓘ *junction of R68 and R40, T03868-421283, www.elesteco.com.ar, Mon-Fri 0900-1200, 1400-1600, Sat-Sun 0900-1300*. There are hourly tours (request Carolina Martín, the excellent English-speaking oenologist), and visitors can learn more about the process of wine making and tasting in one of the courses on offer. Next door is Cafayate's best accommodation: the sumptuous **Patios de Cafayate** (see Sleeping, page 280), formerly a part of the *bodega* and now with luxury spa. It's also a great place for lunch.

Another excellent *bodega* is **Etchart** ⓘ *2 km south on R40, Km 1047, T03868-421310, www.prargentina.com.ar, tours daily on demand, open Jan, Feb, July Mon-Sat 0900-1700, Sun 0900-1300, otherwise Mon-Fri 0900-1700, but closed for lunch; book in advance*, which produces high-quality wines, some of which are exported to Britain and can be sampled here.

The diminutive **San Pedro de Yacochuya** ⓘ *8 km behind Cafayate, take R40 in the direction of Cachi, after 2 km turn left on R2, follow this for 6 km until you reach the bodega, T03868-421233, www.yacochuya.com, phone to arrange a tour*, is a boutique *bodega*, beautifully situated high up into the hills, making exquisite wines.

Once you've visited the best three, you could go to **Finca de las Nubes** ⓘ *3 km above Cafayate, on the Camino al Divisadero, beyond Hotel Viñas de Cafayate, T03868-422129, japmounier@yahoo.com.ar, guided visits are available Mon-Sat 0930-1700 and Sun 1000-1500*, dramatically set against the mountains. This is a small family *bodega*, which produces fine wines, and offers simple meals so you can sit and enjoy a bottle of wine on the terrace.

Then there are two mass-production bodegas that can also be visited: **Domingo Hermanos** ⓘ *3 blocks south of the plaza on 25 de Mayo, T03868-*

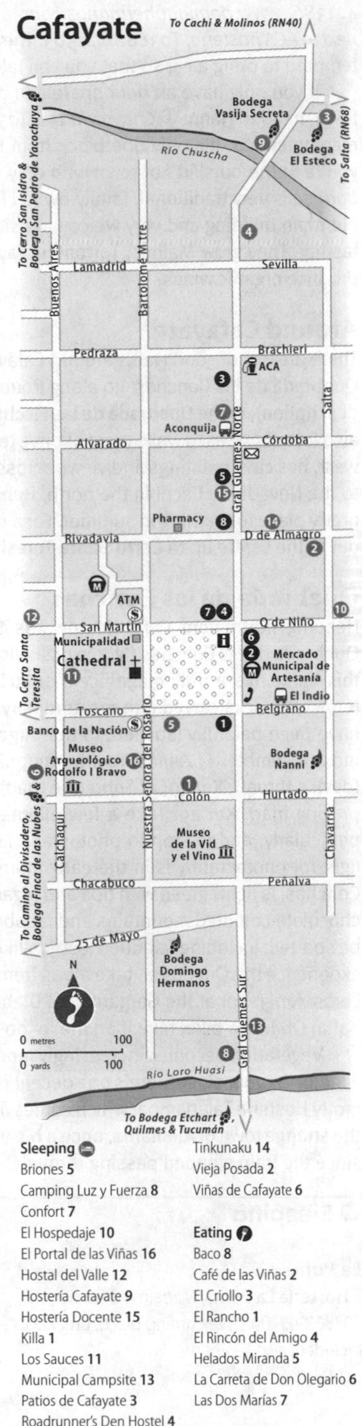

 421386, www.domingohermanos.com, and **Vasija Secreta** ⓘ *outskirts of Cafayete, next to ACA hostería, T03868-421503*. They're still interesting to visit and you might be tempted to bring a car so that you can take plenty of bottles away with you.

If you only have an hour spare and don't want to wander far from the centre of town, head to **Nanni** ⓘ *Chavarría 151, T03868-421527, www.bodegananni.com*, also recommended. It's only one block from the plaza, but once you're inside, you feel you're in the outskirts of town with only vineyards and the mountains in sight. The *bodega* is very traditional, family-owned for over 100 years. It's a small place with an old main building and very welcoming staff who guide you around and offer a good tasting. They grow Malbec, Torrontés, Tannat, Cabernet and Sauvignon grapes, and produce organic wines.

Around Cafayate

There are lots of good walks around Cafayate. To see the amazing rock formations of Quebrada de las Conchas, go along Route Nacional 68 towards Salta (see above for description), or the **Quebrada de las Flechas** on Ruta 40 towards San Carlos. There are also lots of places to walk, cycle or drive to from the town itself. **Cerro San Isidro,** 5 km west, has cave paintings and views across the Aconquija mountains in the south and to the Nevado de Cachi in the north. Behind it, the waterfalls of **Río Colorado** are a pretty place for bathing in summer. For a stroll and a good view, take V Toscano west out of the centre up to **Cerro Santa Teresita**, 2 km each way.

Quebrada de las Conchas

Heading north from Cafayate towards Salta, the Route Nacional 68 enters the Quebrada de las Conchas ('gorge of shells'), though no one seems to know why it has this name. It's a truly magnificent stretch of road, with huge ochre, burgundy and terracotta rocks carved into extraordinary forms by wind and rain. These formations have been helpfully labelled, in true Argentine style, with the names of things they most resemble: *El Anfiteatro* (the amphitheatre) Km 48; the *Garganta del Diablo* (devil's throat), Km 49; *El Sapo* (the toad), Km 35; and *El Fraile* (looks vaguely like a praying friar), Km 29. Take a few minutes to walk inside the Garganta del Diablo, particularly, and to stop to photograph *Los Castillos* (the castles), Km 20. The best light for photography is in the early morning. The valley floor beside the Río de las Conchas, is richly green with tipa and algarrobo trees, contrasting beautifully with the chocolate-coloured mountains and raspberry ripple strata. There's lots of bird life to be spotted, including ñandúes (ostrich-like rheas). If you haven't got a car but want to experience the Quebrada, take a bus from Cafayate towards Salta, and get off at Los Loros, Km 32, or at the Garganta del Diablo, walk back, and catch a return bus from Salta. Or, hire a bike, take it on the 0500 El Indio bus and cycle back.

Vegetation becomes increasingly more dense as you approach Salta, with a river winding by your side. There's one decent place to stop: the **Posada de las Cabras** (not grotty Hostería Talapampa, which comes first if you're heading south) and look out for the strange town of **Alemania**, once a busy trading place on the train line but deserted since the train stopped passing through.

Sleeping

La Poma *p272*

F Hostería La Poma, Madelmo Díaz s/n, T03868-491003. Welcoming place, breakfast included, also serves meals.

Chicoana *p272*

A Los Los, Chicoana, just 40 km from Salta at the entrance to the Valles Calchaquíes, T03868-431 7258, www.redsalta.com/loslos, open Mar-Dec. Most welcoming and highly recommended, beautifully situated on a hilltop with fabulous views from the colonial-style galleried veranda, a charming place, where you can completely relax. Spacious rooms are prettily decorated with old furniture, beautiful gardens with a pool. Includes unforgettable horse riding into the forested mountains of the huge *finca*, where you will be cooked lunch in a remote rustic lodge. Handy for the airport and Cachi. Friendly hosts, Sara and Guillermo. Book in advance.

C Hostería de Chicoana, on the right-hand side of the plaza in Chicoana, at Espana 45, T03868- 4907009, www.newsendas.com. A pretty colonial building, though now slightly faded, but with the added advantage of expert guide Martin Pekarek on hand, and horses for hire.

Cachi *p273*

A El Molinode Cachi Adentro, 4 km out of Cachi on the road to La Aguada, T/F03868-491094, www.elmolinodecachi.com.ar. The most luxurious choice in the area, this is a beautiful place to stay, with 6 exquisitely tasteful rooms around a restored 300-year-old mill. Lovely views down the valley from the garden and pool, and superb food. Nuny and Alberto Durand are charming (and bilingual) hosts, and make sure every detail is perfect. They'll happily collect you from Salta airport, arrange personally designed tours on horseback or 4WD. Their miniature *bodega* produces wonderful wines, and there are lovely places to walk and sit all around. Heaven. Highly recommended.

A Finca Santana, take the road to Cachi Adentro, and ask for Camino to Finca San Miguel, on right at top, T03868-1563 8762, www.fincasantana.net. Just 2 lovely rooms in this beautifully situated boutique B&B right in the heart of the valley, with spectacular views, and complete sense of privacy and silence. Friendly young owner Adriana makes you feel at home in this stylish house, with spacious living room, terrace and garden. Twin or double both with private bath, gourmet breakfast, trekking can be arranged. Wonderful.

B Casa de Campo La Paya, 12 km south of Cachi at La Paya, clearly signposted from the road, T03868-491139, www.casadecampo lapaya.com.ar. A restored 18th-century house with a pool, all the elegant rooms with bathroom, also serves excellent dinners, with friendly welcome from the owners. Recommended.

B El Cortijo, just opposite the ACA, on Av Automóvil Club s/n, T03868 491034, www.hostalelcortijo.com.ar. Small, family-owned boutique hotel, with delightful rooms decorated simply in great style, with lovely paintings and religious icons from Peru and local areas. There's a lovely sitting area downstairs, and charming courtyard with lovely water sculpture. A special place to stay. Recommended.

C ACA Hostería Cachi, at the top of Juan Manuel Castilla, up a steep slope behind the monument from Av Automóvil Club Argentina, T03868-491904, www.soldel valle.com.ar. Very comfortable, modern rooms with wheelchair access, great views from its hilltop position, and a pool. The restaurant serves excellent food – the best in Cachi by far – with friendly staff, and a warm welcome from the delightful English-speaking manager Veronica. Recommended.

C Hostería Llaq'ta Mawka, Colonel Ruiz de los Llanos s/n (20 m from the plaza), T03868-491016, hostal_llaqta_mawka@ hotmail.com. An old building, nicely renovated, with comfortable rooms, pool, good breakfasts, and helpful local owners who can give tourist information and arrange collection from Salta, trekking and horse riding.

D Cabañas Inti Killa, opposite the municipal campsite, T0387-4340476, T1568533377, intikillacachi@yahoo.com.ar. *Cabañas* for 4-6, with heating and TV, and views of the Nevado de Cachi.

D Samay Huasi, on the road to La Aguada, just 1 km further on from El Molino, T15639729, reservas@samayhuasi.com. Great views but the rooms are run down, and very basic. A laid-back place.

E Hospedaje Don Arturo, C Bustamente s/n, T03868-491087. Homely, and welcoming,

For an explanation of the Sleeping and Eating price codes used in this guide, and other relevant information, see Essentials, pages 48 and 51.

with small but very clean rooms on a quiet old street, signposted from the plaza, and very sweet owners who don't speak English but make you feel at home.

G Hospedaje El Nevado de Cachi, Ruiz de los Llanos y Federico Saurez, T03868-491912. The cheapest option, right next to the bus stop. Characterful with impeccable small rooms, all with bathrooms, arranged around a central courtyard.

Camping

Municipal campsite, at the end of the Av Automóvil Club Argentina s/n, T03868-491902. With pool and sports complex, also has basic *cabañas* and hostal.

Molinos *p274*

L Colomé, 20 km west of Molinos, T03868-494044, www.bodegacolome.com. Leave town via the vicuña farm and follow signs, or phone for directions from Cafayate. The most luxurious place to stay in the Valles Calchaquíes, this winery is beautifully set in the mountains, and has wonderful accommodation in 9 gorgeous rooms with spectacular views, great horse riding and walks, *bodega* tours and wine tastings that attract world-class connoisseurs for the excellent Estate wines. The entire *finca* is biodynamic, all the food is organic, the power is hydroelectric. Owners Donald and Ursula Hess are charming, warm and welcoming. One of Argentina's best places to stay. Highly recommended.

B Hostal Provincial de Molinos, T03868-494002, hostaldemolinos@arnet.com.ar. Huge simple rooms arranged around big courtyards in this historic house, recently under new management. Not luxurious, but elegant, and the public rooms are welcoming. The restaurant serves the only decent food in Molinos, but don't expect anything fancy. A quiet charming place to stay.

E Cardones de Molinos, Sarmiento y San Martín, T03868-494061, cardonesmolinos@salnet.com.ar. Real family experience in this haphazard but welcoming home run by the charming young owner, Miriam. Don't expect luxury, but this is the real thing.

F pp **Hospedaje San Agustín**, Sarmiento y Abraham Cornejo, T03868-494015. The nuns here have small but impeccably clean neat rooms for rent, some with private bathroom. They don't like them to be advertised, though, so just ask around in a gentle way for 'las monjas' in the street behind the church, and someone will come and give you a key.

Camping

Municipal campsite, in the sports complex, Alvarado y Mitre, T03868-494037. Hot showers, electricity, US$1 per tent, There are various simple restaurants around the plaza.

Angastaco *p275*

E Hostería de Angastaco, T15639016. Breakfast included, and prices are negotiable in low season. Rooms are basic but comfortable and this is especially recommended for its warm welcome from reception staff, very helpful with information on the region. Pool, and meals on request.

E pp **Los Cardones**, towards the bridge off the plaza, T03868-491123. Breakfast extra, good, clean rooms and hospitable owners.

San Carlos *p275*

D La Casa de Los Vientos, Las Alfareras s/n, T03868-495075, casadelosvientos@yahoo.com.ar. Comfortable accommodation in a colonial-style house built almost entirely of adobe, recreating a traditional Calchaquí residence. Just 8 rooms, and it's rustic but very welcoming with the friendly Swiss owner on hand to make your stay enjoyable. Excellent value, with breakfast included.

Camping

Municipal campsite, Rivadavia and San Martín, T03868-495110. Well tended with plenty of shade.

Cafayate *p276, map p277*

There's lots of accommodation here but Cafayate is popular, so book ahead in holiday periods (Jan, Easter and late-Jul), and it's all much cheaper off season .

L Patios de Cafayate, Rutas 68 and 40, T03868-421747, www.luxury collection.com/cafayate or www.elesteco.com.ar. A stunningly lovely hotel, in the converted building of the old winery (now El Estecco, see page 277 for visits to the *bodega*), with beautifully designed rooms, sumptuous lounges, and set in gorgeous gardens, with lovely pool. There are interesting wine-oriented treatments in their spa (T03868-421753) and the restaurant serves really fine food, with a lovely terrace for lunches, and excellent wines. Highly recommended.

A Viñas de Cafayate, R21, Camino al Divisadero, T03868-422272, www.cafayate wineresort.com. High up on a hillside above Cafayate, this new hotel is built in colonial style, with large airy public rooms, and pretty, spacious bedrooms, some with stunning views. The restaurant looks simple, but the chef (ex-Marriott) is excellent, and there are superb local delicacies on the menu, open to non-residents too, with reservation. Full buffet breakfast. A calm, welcoming place. Recommended.

B Killa, Colón 47, T03868-422254, www.killacafayate.com.ar. A delightfully restored colonial house with an imaginatively rustic decor in all the well- equipped rooms. Pleasing views, tranquility, comfort and Martha, the lovely owner makes you feel absolutely at ease and keeps a fascinating collection of plants growing in the marvellous garden. Breakfasts are just great.

C Hostería Cafayate, T03868-421296, www.soldelvalle.com.ar. There's still a slightly institutional feeling to this large ACA hostería (it used to be a school) at the northern access to town, but it's still a pleasant place to stay. Rooms are comfortable, although waiting for renovation and all open onto a tree-filled patio. Reasonably priced restaurant and pool (summer only). Discounts to other international automobile clubs members.

C Los Sauces, Calchaqui 62, T03868-421158, lossauces@arnet.com.ar. Modern and very functional, this hotel lies behind the cathedral. The neat garden, accessible directly from some of the rooms, is very attractive, and there are lovely views from the upper rooms.

C Vieja Posada, Salta 70, T03868-422251, www.viejaposada.com.ar. A lovely 1900's house with a quiet courtyard and simple attractive rooms all around. An ideal place to unwind.

D Briones, Toscano 80, on the main plaza, T03868-421270. A colonial-style place with simple rooms, open in high season only. Welcoming.

D Tinkunaku, Diego de Almagro 12, 1 block from plaza, T03868-421148. Simple, rather pleasant rooms in this small central hotel.

E Confort, Güemes Norte 232, T03868-421091. Friendly people in this slightly kitsch place with simple rooms, also has well-equipped cabañas Chalets Seis (**A-B**), sleep 6, with kitchen, pool, heating.

E El Portal de las Viñas, Nuestra Señora del Rosario 165, T03868-421098, www.portal vinias.com.ar. This is the loveliest budget place to stay, thanks to its owner, charming schoolteacher Mirta. The spotless rooms, all have bath, and there are generous breakfasts served under the grapevines.

E Hostal del Valle, San Martín 243, T03868-421039, www.nortevirtual.com. Highly recommended for comfort and great value, this homely place has beautifully maintained spacious rooms, all with bath, around lovely plant-filled patio. A new living room at the top offers splendid views of the valley. And for extra few pesos, the upper rooms have really nice views.

F pp **Roadrunner's Den Hostel**, Güemes Norte 441, on the left as you enter the town, T03868-421440. Small, but welcoming, with a nice patio with grapevines. Simple dorms and a few doubles with shared bath with hot water, English and Italian spoken. Organizes excursions.

F pp **El Hospedaje**, Quintana de Niño y Salta, T03868-421680, elhospedaje@ nortevirtual.com. A large colonial-style house with simple but very pleasant dorms and double rooms around patios in one of which there is a wonderful pool, good value. Discounts to HI members.

F Hostería Docente, Güemes Norte 160, T03868-421810. A great cheap place to stay with kitchen facilities. Clean rooms, some with bath, but not breakfast. Central.

Camping

Camping Luz y Fuerza, T03868-421568, also on RN 40, south of the town. More appealing than the municipal site and quieter .

Municipal site, on the southern outskirts of RN 40, T03868-421051, well maintained with hot water, a pool, and bungalows for rent, **E** for 4 people.

Eating

Cachi *p273*

ACA Hostería Cachi, at the top of town, T03868-491904. By far the best choice.

Confitería El Sol, on the plaza, next to Olivier. Good cheap regional food, big groups at lunchtimes in high season.

El Aujero, on the corner by the bus station. Interestingly decorated with old farm tools, the food is average but it's a good place to hang out and meet people, and you can try regional specialities or European classics.

Oliver Café, on the plaza. Sandwiches, juices and ice creams in a friendly tiny café. Good for breakfast or tea and pizzas.

Cafayate *p276, map p277*

Cafayate has lots of choices around the plaza, most of them huge and prepared for coach parties. In summer, many provide live music. The following are recommended.

El Rancho, Toscano 4. The best mid-range option. A traditional restaurant serving *parrilla* and good regional dishes.

La Carreta de Don Olegario, Güemes Sur y Quintana de Niño. Huge, but does good set menus for the usual meat dishes and pastas.

Viñas de Cafayate, R21, Camino al Divisadero, T03868-422272. Elegant food, simple surroundings, but lovely views from this hotel. Book ahead.

Baco, Güemes Norte y Rivadavia. An attractive corner and a lively place serving basic sandwiches and pizzas and also trout-based dishes with a great range of local wines.

Café de las Viñas, Güemes Sur 58. Open all day, serving everything from breakfast to cheap *lomitos*.

El Criollo, Güemes Norte 254. A small *parrilla*, recommended.

El Rincón del Amigo, on the plaza at San Martín 25. A small cheap place with great set menus and *empanadas*.

Las Dos Marías, next door to El Rincón del Amigo. Cheap, small and unimposing, but serves good food, and loved by locals.

Ice cream parlours

Helados Miranda, Güemes Norte 170. Cafayate's unmissable treat is this fabulous homemade ice cream. The creative owner makes wine-flavoured ice cream among many delicious flavours.

Shopping

Cachi *p273*

Artesanía Juan Calchaquí, near the monument at the bottom of the hill from the service station, T03868-491037. Oscar Alfredo Cardozo is the leading weaver and teacher in Cachi, and promotes local weavers through this shop which sells their work at far lower prices than the government shop in the tourist office. He'll also tell you where all Cachi's weavers are, so that you can go off and find them at work for yourself.

Artesanía Kuyaymasi, opposite the ACA hostería, T03868-15639615, oscartesano@yahoo.com. Oscar Valenzuela works with Alpaca and also makes fine jewellery but also sells a good selection of local weavings, leather and wood work. He's also a good tourist guide and leads conventional trips to Las Pailas, La Paya and La Poma.

Cafayate *p276, map p277*

Lots of fairly trashy souvenir shops have opened recently on the plaza, but there are some fine handicrafts shops to be found if you dig around. There's the **Calchaquí tapestry exhibition** of Miguel Nanni on the main plaza, silver work at **Jorge Barraco**, Colón 157, T03868-421244. Oil paintings, woodcarving, metalwork and ceramics by **Calixto Mamani** can be seen in his gallery, Rivadavia 452, or contact him at home (Rivadavia 254). Ceramics are also made by **Manuel Cruz**, Güemes Sur 288 (the building itself is worth seeing). Local pottery is sold in the **Mercado Municipal de Artesanía** on the plaza.

Activities and tours

Cachi *p273*

Horse riding

Ask Ariel Villar at **Hostería Llaq'ta Mawka**, T03868-491016, arielvillar@hotmail.com, see Sleeping, above.

Tour operators

Cachi has 3 excellent local guides, Susana, Santiago and Hilda, who can give you the best insight into the culture and history and take you around the town on foot, and further afield either in your hire car, or in a taxi. Rates are very reasonable, though you have to be able to speak some Spanish, and it's infinitely better than a commercial tour from Salta.

Fernando Gamarra, corner of Benjamín Zorrilla y Guemes, T0387-4317305, laspulgas@copaipa.org.ar. More conventional trips around Cachi with genial Fernando, who is good company, to Las Pailas, La Poma and Seclantás, including the beautiful Laguna de Brealito. Knowledgeable, reasonably priced, especially if divided amongst a group.

Hilda, ask at main tourist office, T03868-491053, cachi@salnet.com.ar. Hilda leads walking tours around Cachi, leaving from the main tourist office every afternoon at 1630. Just wait for her by the information desk, or call the tourist office for information.

Martín Oliver, T03868-491052, cafedecachi@yahoo.com.ar. Martín organizes a week-long horse ride to the Nevado de Cachi at the end of the year.

Santiago Casimiro, T03868-15638545. Particularly recommended for all mountain hikes; he's a nurse trained in mountain rescue, and has lived in the valley all his life. He'll take you to La Poma, Cerro de la Virgen, and up the Nevado peaks, all very reasonable. He even shows you what all the medicinal plants are for, and will sing haunting bagualas in the mountains, if asked. Highly recommended.

Susana Guantay, T0387-154134135. Charming local Susana will take you on informed walks around the town, to La Poma and Las Pailas. Also informed guide on the archaeological museum.

Cafayate *p276, map p277*

Cycling

There are many places to hire a bike; ask the tourist office for a list.

Tour operators

Turismo Cordillerano, C Quintana de Niño 59, T03868-422137, www.turismo cordillerano.com.ar.

Transport

Cachi *p273*

Bus To **Salta**, Marcos Rueda, T03868-491063, leaves daily (not on Sun) at 0900 and Mon, Thu, Fri, Sun 1500, 4½ hrs, US$7. To **Molinos** daily at 1200.

Remise taxis San José, T03868-491907, Los Calchaquies, T03868-491071.

Molinos *p274*

Bus To **Salta** via Cachi, Mon, Tue, Thu, Sat, at 0645, also Sun 1245. Marcos Rueda; 2 hrs to **Cachi**, US$3, 7 hrs to **Salta**. In Salta T0387-421 4447. From Salta to **Molinos**, Sun, Mon, Wed, Fri, 0700, arriving Molinos 1330. US$10.

Angastago *p275*

Bus To **Salta** (US$9.50), Mon-Fri. To **Cafayate** via San Carlos, El Indio, Mon-Fri Taxi to **Molinos** US$20.

San Carlos *p275*

Bus 5 services a day to **Cafayate**, El Indio, 30 mins, US$1.50.

Cafayate *p276, map p277*

Bus There are 2 bus terminals: for **Salta**, go to **El Indio** bus terminal on Belgrano, half a block from the plaza, T03868-421002, and for **Tucumán**, to the **Aconquija** terminal at Güemes Norte y Alvarado, T03868-422175. To **Salta**, via the Quebrada de Las Conchas, **El Indio**, 3-4 a day, US$7 (worth travelling in daylight to see the rock formations), 3½- 4 hrs. To **Angastaco**, El Indio, one daily Mon-Fri, US$3, 1½-2 hrs, but note this bus does not go further north along the RN 40 to Molinos and Cachi. To **Santa María**, (for **Quilmes**) El Indio, Aconquija, 4 daily. To **Tucumán**, 3 daily (more services added from Santa María), 5½ hrs (6½-8½ hrs via Santa María), US$9 and **Tafí del Valle**, 3 daily (more connecting at Santa María), 3 hrs (5½ hrs via Santa María), US$5.50, with **Aconquija**,

Directory

Cafayate and around *p276, map p277*

Banks Banco de la Nación, Toscano y NS del Rosario. ATM, but no TCs. There is another ATM at **Banco Salta**, Mitre y San Martín. Open all year, good service.

Pharmacy F Pastor, Rivadavia 35.

Jujuy province

→ *Phone code: 0388 Colour map 1, A3 Population: 278,000*

The beautiful province of Jujuy lives slightly under wealthier Salta's shadow, but it has some of the richest culture of the whole country, thanks to its large population of indigenous peoples, or what most Argentines refer to as 'los indios'. Absorb the lively street life in Jujuy City, take part in a Pachamama ceremony, or witness the vibrant festival remotest Casabindo, and you'll feel the palpable energy of the authentic Andean culture which has survived over 300 years of colonial rule. So while Jujuy is less developed in tourist infrastructure, it's definitely worth making the effort to explore, and as tourism brings more income to the region, bus services and hotels are opening up fast in response.

Jujuy's great attraction is the Quebrada de Humahuaca, recently made a World Heritage Site by UNESCO for its spectacular beauty. A broad gorge of stratified vividly coloured rock, its pretty towns and oasis villages contain wonderful colonial churches, and there's a marvellous hilltop fort built in pre-Hispanic times at Tilcara. Easter and Carnival are celebrated here in exuberant style which combines Christian traditions with the pre-existing Andean religious beliefs. Dotted along the Quebrada there are pleasant towns to hang out for a few days for walking and exploring. Purmamarca is most appealing: famous for its Cerro de Siete Colores, there are now some fine hotels here, walks to the stratified rocks of seven colours behind the town, and a dramatic drive up to the salt flats. Tilcara is probably the best base for exploring the area, with lots of good accommodation, a lively market, a museum and the Pucará, the ruined hill-top town. From here the adventurous could trek west into the subtropical cloudforest park of Calilegua, or into the stunning Garganta del Diablo.

The Quebrada villages all have characteristic squat white adobe churches, but Uquía's is the most impressive, with an extraordinary collection of Cuzqueño school paintings. Further north, Humahuaca is less welcoming, but take the bus from here to the exquisite remote hamlet of Iruya, just over the border into Salta. At the northernmost end of the Quebrada, off the road to Bolivia, the church in the village of Yavi is the country's most exquisite colonial treasure, its gold decoration seen in the lemony light from onyx windows. And east from here, there's the stunningly located village of Nazareno (Salta).

East and west of the province are two contrasting landscapes: In Jujuy's expanse of puna in the west, you'll find fascinating small villages of Susques and Casabindo, famous for its bullfight in August. There are old Jesuit gold mines and Laguna de los Pozuelos with its wealth of birdlife. To the east, find cloudforest in Calilegua National Park, accessible from Libertador General San Martín. Or stay at eco-finca Portal del Piedra for incredible horse riding into the same landscapes with greater comfort.

▸▸ *For Sleeping, Eating and other listings, see pages 288-290.*

Jujuy city ▸▸ *pp288-290.*

→ *Phone code: 0388 Colour map 1, A3 Population: 278,000*

Often overlooked by tourists, the city of Jujuy (pronounced Choo-Chooey, with ch as in Scottish loch), may be Salta's poorer sister, but it has plenty of life and culture to make it a good starting point for the Quebrada de Humahuaca which stretches northwest from here. Properly referred to by locals by its full name, San Salvador, it's the capital of Jujuy province, and sits at 1,260 m in a bowl of lushly wooded mountains, 100 km north of Salta. Jujuy was founded in 1593, between two rivers, the Río Grande and Chico, or Xibi Xibi, but it's sprawled south, supporting a growing population on dwindling industry. Wars and earthquakes have left the city with few colonial buildings, but there's some fine architecture around its plaza, and from the bridge over the Río Xibi Xibi, with its brightly coloured market stalls, you have wonderful views of the dramatic purple mountains, contrasting with the thick green vegetation that fills the river bed. Although more chaotic than Salta, Jujuy has some lively bars where you can hear the region's wonderful folklore music, and its history is worth exploring, with two fine churches, a packed archaeological museum, and a fabulous market. All this makes a good introduction to the province's rich indigenous culture and a handy base for exploring a variety of landscapes within easy reach. The region's most accessible cloudforest park, Calilegua, is just 125km east from here.

Ins and outs

Getting there Jujuy's airport, **El Cadillal** is 32 km southeast of the capital. Minibuses (US$2.50) run between the airport and the **Aerolíneas Argentinas** office in town; a taxi costs US$10. The bus terminal is six blocks south of the main street, Belgrano, over the river on Dorrego and Iguazú. The terminal serves the whole province including all destinations north of the city and border towns with Bolivia, as well as south to Salta and from there to most major destinations. There are direct buses to Buenos Aires taking at least 19 hours. ▸▸ *For further details, see Transport, page 290.*

Getting around The city is pleasant to walk around, and is particularly interesting around the plaza, the market opposite the bus terminal, and on the bridges. The most interesting sites are within six blocks and could comfortably be visited in a day.

Tourist information The **city tourist office** ⓘ *on the plaza at Gorriti y Belgrano, Mon-Fri 0700-2200, Sat-Sun 0900-2100*, has a helpful accommodation leaflet and a map, but little information about the rest of the province or transport. There is another office ⓘ *at the bus terminal, T0388-422 1343, www.turismo.jujuy.gov.ar (also in English), daily 0700-2100*, offering helpful advice on accommodation, though few staff speak English

Background

Jujuy has an extraordinary history. The Spanish wanted to found a city to link the chain of settlements connecting Alto Perú with Córdoba, but met extreme resistance from the indigenous peoples, who destroyed their first two attempts, in 1561 and 1575. The city was finally established in 1593, and prospered until the 18th century, but the province of Jujuy bore the brunt of fighting during the Wars of Independence: between 1810 and 1822 the Spanish launched 11 invasions down the Quebrada de Humahuaca from Bolivia. Then, in August 1812, General Belgrano, who was commander of the Republican troops, demanded an incredible sacrifice of Jujuy's people when he ordered the city to be evacuated and destroyed before the advancing Royalist army. They left, the city was razed to the ground, but the people of Jujuy survived, and remain proud of their sacrifice. This event is marked on 22-23 August by festivities known as **El Exodo Jujeño** with gaucho processions and military parades. As a tribute to the city for obeying his orders, Belgrano donated a flag which is displayed in the lavish Casa de Gobierno in Plaza Belgrano.

Jujuy has experienced growing poverty in recent years, since its industries – traditionally sugar and tobacco – suffered in the economic crisis, with resulting widespread unemployment. It's one of the few Argentine cities where the population is largely indigenous, boosted in the last 20 years by considerable immigration from Bolivia. You may well find bus journeys in the region delayed en route by peaceful demonstrations of *piqueteros* blocking the road, protesting about job and benefit cuts. Tourism is the main growing industry in the area, as the city is slowly waking up to its huge natural asset, the extraordinary beauty on its doorstep.

Sights

If you arrive in the city by bus, you will be greeted by a perfectly typical example of the usual mayhem of *boleterías* (ticket offices) for 20 different bus companies, crowds waiting with huge packages to be carried to remote parts of the puna, and people selling balloon-like plastic bags of pink popped corn. To get into town from the bus station, walk along Dorrego/Lavalle, crossing the bridge across the thickly vegetated river bed, where the city teems cheerfully with life, and you'll pass the fabulous fruit and vegetable market, with delicious *empanadas* and stalls selling razors and peaches, tights and herbal cures, pan pipes and plimsols.

In the eastern part of the city is the tranquil **Plaza Belgrano**, a wide square planted with tall palms and lined with orange trees, with a striking equestrian statue of Belgrano at its centre. On the south side stands the **Casa de Gobierno**, a cream French-style neoclassical building built in 1927. Inside, you can see the very flag that Belgrano gave the city in recognition of their great sacrifice, in a sumptuously decorated long hall with pleasing art nouveau statues representing Justice, Liberty, Peace and Progress, by the Argentine sculptor, Lola Mora.

On the west side of the plaza is the **cathedral**, whose neo-classical façade – built in the late 19th century to replace the original, which was built in the early

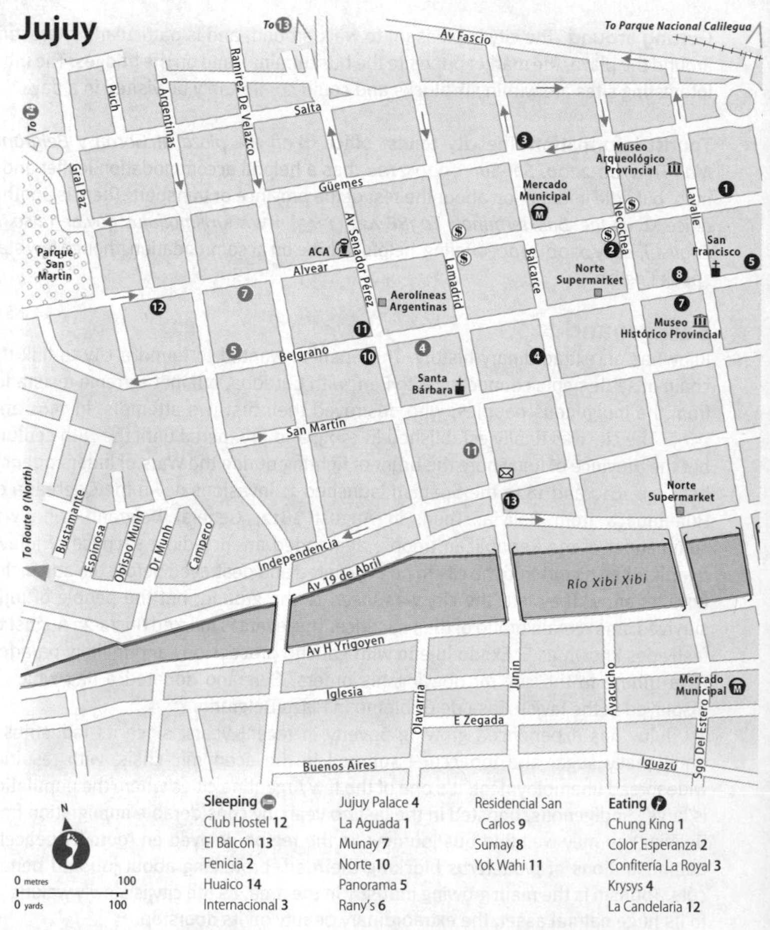

1600s and destroyed by an earthquake – contains an exquisite jewel: a gold plated wooden pulpit, carved by indigenous tribes in the Jesuit missions. Its elegant and naïve biblical illustrations are very moving, and the delicate modelling of the dove overhead and on the angels' faces, is stunning. It's one of Argentina's finest colonial treasures. There are also several fine 18th-century paintings. On the north side of the plaza is the **Cabildo**, built in 1867 and now occupied by the police, with a rather dull police museum inside.

The **Iglesia de San Francisco** ⓘ *Belgrano y Lavalle, 2 blocks west of the plaza, daily 0730-1200, 1730-2100 (Thu till 2200), well informed guides*, is modern but has a graceful, calm interior, and contains another fine gilded colonial pulpit, with ceramic angels around it, like that at Yavi (see page 295). The **Iglesia de San Bárbara** (1777), San Martín y Lamadrid, is similar in style to the colonial churches in the Quebrada de Humahuaca,

The **Museo Arqueológico Provincial** ⓘ *Lavalle 434, Mon-Fri 0800-2100, Sat-Sun 0900-1300, 1500-1900, US$0.35*, has some superb ceramics from the pre-Inca Yavi and Humahuaca cultures, and beautifully painted funerary urns made, sadly, some containing the tiny bones of children. The museum may be under-funded, and poorly displayed, but it's definitely worth visiting – particularly for a fabulous 2500-year-old sculpture of a goddess giving birth, and the rather gruesomely displayed mummified infant.

If you like military portraits, you could visit the **Museo Histórico Provincial** ⓘ *Lavalle 252, Mon-Fri 0800-1330, 1500-2000, Sat-Sun 0900-1300, 1400-2000, US$0.35*, though it's pretty dry, and a whole room is dedicated to the death of Gral Lavalle which occurred in this house, a turning point in the civil war between Federalists and Unitarists. There are also a couple of fine Cuzco-school paintings dating from 1650.

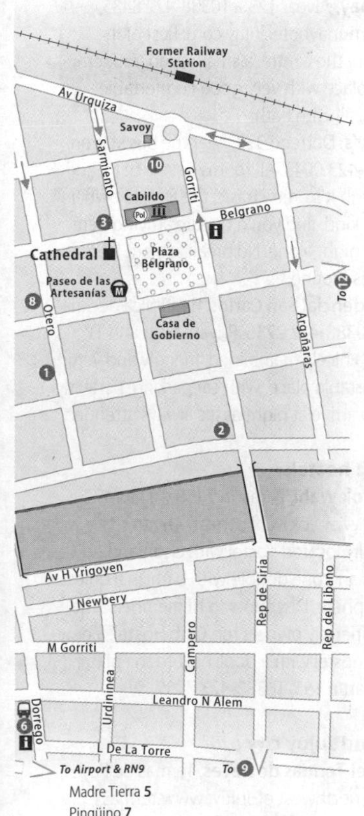

Madre Tierra **5**
Pingüino **7**
Ruta 9 **8**
Sociedad Española **10**
Tío Bigote **11**
Viracocha **13**

Around Jujuy city

There's plenty of accommodation in Jujuy itself or you could head out to the **Termas de Reyes**, for the thermal baths. Tour operators offer full-day excursions from Jujuy into the puna and the Quebrada de Humahuaca, but it's far better to take at least a couple of days to explore both areas properly. Jujuy is also the starting point for the cloudforest park of **Calilegua**, by bus via Libertador General San Martín. To explore similar landscapes, head to **Finca Portal del Piedra**, in the middle of a reserve between Parque Nacional Calilegua and Parque Nacional El Rey, with fabulous horse riding and an eco-cabin, see Sleeping, below.

Sleeping

Jujuy city *p284, map p286*
All hotels will be fully booked for the festival of El Exodo Jujeño, 22-23 Aug: book ahead. Near the bus terminal there are a number of cheap places, those listed here are the best, though the area is not safe at night.

B Fenicia, Av 19 de Abril 427, T/F0388-423 1800, www.quintar.com.ar. A welcoming place, despite the 1980's decor in the foyer. Lots of marble, swirly chairs and swagged curtains, but the rooms are spacious and very nicely decorated (ask for the ones with swish bathrooms), some with great views over the city. Recommended for its friendly welcome.

B Internacional, Belgrano 501 (on Plaza Belgrano), T0388-423 1599, www.hinternacionaljujuy.com.ar. On the northwest corner of the plaza, this quiet hotel has comfortably decorated rooms all with bath and TV, and though they're smallish, many have great views over the city, with modern bathrooms. Elegant public rooms, a *confitería*, and very friendly service, recommended.

B Jujuy Palace, Belgrano 1060, T/F0388-423 0433, jpalace@imagine.com.ar. Top of Jujuy's range is this popular conference hotel, with cool, plain decor in the well-equipped bedrooms, and spacious bathrooms. The restaurant has a good reputation, though it's rather squashed.

B La Aguada, Otero 170, T0388-423 2034, www.laaguadahosteria.com.ar. A charming family owned small house with only 3 minimalist rooms, decorated with paintings by the owner's father. A stylish living room and a beautifully kept patio make this an excellent choice in central Jujuy.

B Norte, Alvear 444, T0388-424 0903, www.hotelnorte.com. A tastefully restored colonial house made of adobe, this boutique hotel has a wonderful old palm-tree in its graceful patio. Extremely comfortable, with wonderful attention to detail.

C Panorama, Belgrano 1295, T0388-423 2533, hotelpanorama@imagine.com.ar. Another business hotel, but much more appealing than most, just, and a couple of blocks further away from the hubbub. Better value, with rather more stylish rooms and a restaurant.

D Sumay, Otero 232, T0388-423 5065, www.sumayhotel.com.ar. Rather dark and pokey, the rooms are nevertheless clean, with bathrooms, and this place is very central, with friendly staff.

E El Balcón, El Fortín 12, Los Perales district, T0388-426 0520, hotelelbalcon@noroestevirtual.com.ar. This quiet place has simple and comfortable rooms, some for 4, in a quiet district, 15 mins from the centre, with attractive views over the valley.

E Huaico, Av Bolivia 3901, T0388-423 5186, hotelhuaicojujuy@arnet.com.ar. 1.5 km from the centre, near the park, this is a great place to sleep surrounded by tropical gardens, and it's convenient if you're heading north. A very pleasant place with a pool, breakfast included, and special rates for students.

E Munay, Alvear 1230, T0388-422 8435, www.munayhotel.jujuy.com. Best of its range in the centre, a small, clean, modern, quiet place with very good comfortable rooms, all with bath.

F Rany's, Dorrego 327, near the bus station, T0388-423 0042. All rooms have a bath, and although it's pretty basic, the female owner is very kind, and you'd be safe arriving here late at night alone. No breakfast, but loads of cafés around.

F Residencial San Carlos, República de Siria 459, T0388-422 2286. Private bath and TV, this is a nicely maintained, friendly and very comfortable place, with car parking, perfectly safe to arrive at night as it's always attended.

Youth hostels

F pp **Yok Wahi**, Lamadrid 168, T0388-422 9608, www.yokwahi.com.ar. An attractive, centrally located hostel with clean and tidy dorms and one double with bath, in a quiet atmosphere. Discounts to HI members. The same friendly owners run **Club Hostel**, a new larger hostel with a pool, next to the plaza, San Martín 155, T0388-423 7565.

Around Jujuy city *p287*

A Hotel Termas de Reyes, Termas de Reyes, 19 km northwest of Jujuy, www.termasdereyes.com, 6 buses a day from Jujuy bus terminal 0630-1945, returning 0700-2040, US$1, 1 hr. This sumptuous thermal spa resort with a grand neo-classical hotel is set among magnificent mountains at an altitude of 1800 m. A first-class hotel offering comfort, relaxation and great views. in this. Rates include the use of the thermal pools. No children allowed. Recommended for a relaxing couple of days' rest.

Cabañas

El Caserío, Finca Cerro Chico, Bárcena, 32 km north of Jujuy on RN9, T0388-156825257. www.caseriojujuy.com. Beautiful *cabañas* and a house available for rent in lovely wild parkland, with wide open views.

Camping

If you keep going north from Jujuy, up in the Quebrada de Humahuaca, there's a campsite in every town.

E pp **El Refugio**, T/F0388-4909344, elrefugio@ arnet.com.ar. This is the nearest campsite to the city is actually at Yala, over the bridge in a pretty spot on the banks of the river, 14 km north of Jujuy city on RN9. There's also a youth hostel, pool, restaurant and trekking and horse riding excursions are on offer. Highly recommended, a great place to relax.

Serranías de Zapla, T0388-427 7881, www.turismopalpala.com.ar. An attractive campsite also with cheap dorms, slightly further afield at 24 km in the dull town of Palpalá.

Eating

Jujuy city *p284, map p286*

Following Lavalle across the bridge to the bus terminal (where it changes names to Dorrego) there are lots of cheap places selling *empanada*.

TT Chung King, Alvear 627. A *Jujeño* institution (although the accommodation upstairs can't be recommended), this is an atmospheric and good-value place for regional food, and its sister restaurant next door serves '50 kinds of pizza'.

TT Krysys, Balcarce 272. A popular bistro-style *parrilla* restaurant with excellent steaks.

T La Candelaria, Alvear 1346. A welcoming choice for *parrilla*, with good service.

T Madre Tierra, Belgrano 619. A great place for vegetarians (or if you want a break from all the meat). Behind the wonderful wholemeal bakery of same name, a cool oasis serves delicious food (closed dinner).

T Ruta 9, Belgrano 743. Another great place, lively and popular with a wide range of regional meals including a few good Bolivian dishes.

T Viracocha, Independencia y Lamadrid. Recommended for regional and spicy delicacies.

Cafés

There are several good cafés on the same busy block of Belgrano between Lavalle and Necochea, including **Pingüino**, the best *heladería* in the town.

Confitería La Royal, Balcarce y Güemes. A classic café serving good coffee and pastries, slightly pricey lunches, and a great place to watch Jujuy bustle past.

Color Esperanza, Necochea 376. A small café also serving cheap *lomitos* and hamburgers.

Sociedad Española, opposite Tío Bigote, on the same corner. Serves good, cheap set menus with a Spanish flavour; *mariscos con arroz* and paella.

Tío Bigote, Av Senador Pérez y Belgrano. A hugely popular café and pizzeria.

Entertainment

Jujuy city *p284, map p286*

Head for a *peña* to hear the region's passionate folklore music played live here. **La Casa de Jeremías**, Horacio Guzmán 306; **La Juntada**, Brown 1769; and **Savoy**, Alvear y Urquiza, all have live music and dancing at weekends, and during the week in busy holiday periods.

Shopping

Jujuy city *p284, map p286*

Camping and fishing equipment

This can be hired at **Tierrita**, Necochea 508.

Food

You can't beat the colourful **Municipal market**, Dorrego y Alem, near the bus terminal. Outside it, women sell home baked *empanadas* and *tamales*, and delicious goat's cheese, as well as all kinds of herbal cures. There is a **Norte** supermarket, Belgrano 825, and a bigger branch at 19 de Abril y Necochea.

Handicrafts

Handicrafts are sold from stalls on Plaza Belgrano near the cathedral. There's a better range in the old train station north of the plaza on Urquiza, and from the rather limited **Paseo de las Artesanías** on the west side of the plaza. Try also **Regionales Lavalle**, Lavalle 268, and **Mercado Municipal**, Balcarce 427.

Activities and tours

Jujuy city *p284, map p286*

Tour operators

For visiting Calilegua under your own steam, see Transport, below.

Be Dor Turismo, Lavalle 295, T0388-402 0242, be-dor@imagine.com.ar. Conventional tours, student reductions.

Horus Turismo, Belgrano 722, T0388-422 7247, horus@imagine.com.ar. Good for the more predictable trips.

NASA, Av Senador Pérez 154, T0388-422 3938. Guided tours to Quebrada de Humahuaca (US$30 pp, minimum 2 people), Iruya (US$83 pp), Calilegua NP (US$47 pp); 4WD, and attractive and well-equipped cabañas near Yala for rent.

TEA Turismo, Belgrano 775, p1, T0388-423 6270, teajujuy@imagine.com.ar. Recommended for professional trips to the Quebrada over 2 days, with guides and accommodation included.

Transport

Jujuy city *p284, map p286*

Air

Aeropuerto El Cadillal, 32 km southeast, T0388-491 1505. Minibuses (US$2.50) to/from **Aerolíneas Argentinas** office in town; taxi, US$10. Flights to **Buenos Aires** and **Córdoba** with **Aerolíneas Argentinas** .

Airline offices Aerolíneas Argentinas, Av Senador Pérez 355, T0388-422 7198.

Bus

Long distance The bus terminal is at Iguazú y Dorrego, 6 blocks south of the centre, information T0388-422 1373. Buses go almost hourly up the Quebrada de Humahuaca – several companies. Via Tucumán to **Córdoba**, Panamericano and La Veloz del Norte, daily; to **Tucumán**, 5 hrs, US$10, and **Córdoba**, 13-14 hrs, US$24.

To **Salta** hourly, 2 hrs, US$ 3.50. To the Bolivian border **La Quiaca**, 4-6 hrs, US$5-7, Panamericano, Balut, El Quiaqueño. Several rigorous luggage checks en route for drugs, including coca leaves. To **Humahuaca**, Evelia and others, US$3.50, 2½-3 hrs, several daily, via **Tilcara**, 1½-2 hrs, US$2.50.

To **Buenos Aires**, 19-23 hrs, US$45-63 , several daily with Flecha Bus, La Veloz del Norte, Panamericano. To **Orán** and **Aguas Blancas** (border with Bolivia), daily with Balut, Flecha Bus and Brown, via San Pedro and Ledesma. To **Purmamarca**, Cotta Norte, El Vallisto, Panamericano, Evelia (check they call at Purmamarca village, off the main road). To **Susques**, **Purmamarca**, and Andes Bus, T0388-425 7845, US$6, 4-6½ hrs, daily (except Mon). To **Calilegua**, various companies to Libertador Gral San Martín (also called Ledesma) almost every hour, eg Balut, from there take Empresa 23 de Agosto or Empresa 24 de Septiembre buses, leaving 0830 to Valle Grande, across Parque Nacional Calilegua. All **Pocitos** or **Orán** buses pass through **Libertador San Martín**.

Car hire

At the airport: Hertz, T0388-155801383, foarentacar@arnet.com.ar. Also in town Noroeste, T0388-423 3205 and Localiza, T0388-491 2734, www.localiza.com.ar.

Directory

Jujuy city *p284, map p286*

Banks There are ATMs at: Banco Macro, Alvear y Lamadrid, changes dollars. Banco Río, Alvear y Necochea; Banco Galicia , Alvear y Necochea, Banco Francés, Alvear y Lamadrid. TCs can be changed at travel agencies, **Horus**, Belgrano 722, **Be Dor**, Lavalle 295. **Consulates** Bolivia, Av Senador Pérez and Independencia, open 0900-1300. **Pharmacy** Del Pueblo, Alvear 927, T0388-422 2339. **Post office** Independencia y Lamadrid. Many *locutorios* with internet in the centre.

Quebrada de Humahuaca

Since it was declared a world heritage site by UNESCO, the Quebrada de Humahuaca has attracted a deluge of visitors, and while a couple of its main towns are becoming transformed by tourism beyond recognition, much of the area retains its ancient authentic life. Starting at the city of Jujuy, the main route heading north to the Bolivian border is quite one of the most dramatic areas of natural beauty in the country, passing through a long gorge of intensely coloured rock, arid mountains of terracotta, yellow, orange, pink, cream and malachite green strata, speckled with giant cacti. In the fertile valley floor of the Quebrada are several small historic towns, some with their neat adobe houses now mingled with modern new developments, but all centred around the characteristic simple squat white 18th-century churches of the region. The pretty village of Purmamarca, with its backdrop of the Cerro de Siete Colores, Tilcara with its handicraft market and restored hill fort town, Maimará with its hillside cemetery and La Paleta del Pintor, and the more introverted Humahuaca, all make good places to stay, to walk and to absorb the ancient history of the area. The indigenous culture is particularly rich here: there area pre-Incan ruins at Tilcara, and throughout the Quebrada there are weeks of riotous pre-Lent carnivals. Tilcara's Easter celebrations are justifiably famous: a traditional procession on Holy Thursday night is joined by thousands of pan pipe musicians making a huge procession down from the mountain into the town: an overwhelming experience. ▸▸ *For Sleeping, Eating and other listings, see pages 297-301.*

Ins and outs

Getting around Public transport is easy to use and a number of bus companies go up and down the Quebrada from Jujuy to Humahuaca, stopping at Purmamarca, Tilcara, Maimará and Uquía. **El Quiaqueño, Panamericano** and **Balut** go all the way to La Quiaca on the Bolivian border. If driving, fuel is available at Volcán, Tilcara, Humahuaca and Abra Pampa, so you might need to take a spare can if you're heading far into rural areas. It's a good area for cycling, preferably away from the Route Nacional 9, where there can be a lot of traffic through the valley and there's not much shade.

Purmamarca → *Phone code: 0388 Colour map 1, A3 Population: 500, Altitude 2200 m*

The first village you come to in the Quebrada, just off Route Nacional 9 at Km 61, Purmamarca is a perfect place to rest and acclimatize to the altitude. It's a tiny, peaceful village with a choice of comfortable places to stay and a stunning setting at the foot of the Cerro de los Siete Colores – a mountain striped with at least seven colours, from creamy pink to burgundy, and copper to green, best seen in the morning light. Once the steady trickle of tour buses has left, Purmamarca retains its own quiet rhythm of life. There's a good market in the plaza, selling a mixture of locally made llama wool good, but lots of alpaca spoons and weavings are imported from Bolivia. At the top of the plaza, there's a beautiful church, **Iglesia de Santa Rosa** (1648, rebuilt in 1778) typical of those you'll see elsewhere in the Quebrada, with its squat tower, white-washed adobe walls and simple, well-balanced construction. Inside there's a splendid time-darkened cactus roof and pulpit, and a series of exquisite paintings depicting the life of Santa Rosa. Next to the church is an algarrobo tree thought to be 500 years old. There's a tiny, helpful **tourist office** on the plaza, which can provide maps, information on accommodation and bus tickets.

Maimará → *Population: 2200, Altitude 2383 m*

About 12 km from Purmamarca at Km 75, Maimará is a lovely, tranquil oasis village. Its green fields of onion and garlic are set in contrast with the backdrop of richly coloured marbled rock, known as La Paleta Del Pintor, to the east of the village. For an enjoyable walk in the low evening light, when the colours of the rock are at their warmest, walk along the old road to the east of Maimará, and take your camera: it's a beautiful sight. Just off the road, 3 km south, is **La Posta de Hornillos**, one of the chain of colonial posting houses which used to extend from Buenos Aires to Lima, also the scene of several battles, and where Belgrano stayed. Now restored, the building houses a historical **museum** with a collection of 18th- and 19th-century furniture as well as weapons and historical documents. North of Maimará, there's a huge cemetery on the hillside, brightly decorated with paper flowers at Easter.

Tilcara → *Phone code: 0388 Colour map 1, A3 Population: 4400, Altitude 2461 m*

Tilcara lies 22 km north of Purmamarca at Km 84. It's the liveliest Quebrada village, and the best base for exploring the area, with plenty of places to stay and to eat. There's an excellent handicrafts market around its pleasant plaza, though be discerning as lots of the goods are mass produced in Bolivia. For fine local weavings, visit the women's weaving co-operative, **La Flor del Cardón** next to the **tourist office** ⓘ *Belgrano, next to Hotel de Turismo, T0388-495 5720, daily 0800-2130*, which has very helpful staff. Useful websites include www.quebradaypuna.org.ar and www.turismo.jujuy.gov.ar.

Tilcara is the site of an important pre-Hispanic settlement, and you can visit the **Pucará** ⓘ *daily 1000-1800 but varies with time of year (summer closed for lunch)*, a restored hilltop fortress above the town, with panoramic views of the gorge from its complex web of low walled dwellings, made more splendid by mighty cacti. To get there, turn right off Belgrano where signposted, head up the hill, and across the metal bridge over the Río Huasamayo. At the entrance to the Pucará, there's also a small handicrafts shop, where you can get helpful information, and a small botanical garden, with many species of cactus. On the plaza is a superb **Museo Arqueológico** ⓘ *daily 0900-1230, 1400-1800, US$1.70 including entry to Pucará, and vice versa*, with a fine collection of pre-Columbian ceramics, masks and mummies. There are four art museums in town, of which **Museo Regional de Pintura**, Rivadavia 459, is worth a look, with paintings on the customs and traditions of Tilcara. There are some good walks in all directions from the village, but those to **La Garganta del Diablo** (see page 329) and **Cerro de la Virgen** are particularly recommended. There are fiestas throughout an extended **Carnival** period. At Easter, there's a famous gathering of thousands of pan-pipe musicians, who play as they follow the procession of the Virgen de Copacabana down the mountain. It's an extraordinary, noisy and moving sight. Book accommodation well in advance.

Huacalera and Uquía

Huacalera lies 2 km north of the Tropic of Capricorn; a sundial 20 m west of the road marks the exact location. The church, several times restored, has a roof made of cactus wood and a small museum. **Uquía** is one of the smaller villages along the Quebrada, and totally untouristy with a tranquil atmosphere and a narrow street of adobe houses. Close to the road, there's one of the valley's finest churches, its beautifully proportioned white tower very striking against the deep red rock of the mountain behind. Built in 1691, **Iglesia San Francisco de Paula** contains an extraordinary collection of Cuzqueño paintings of angels in 17th-century battle dress, the *ángeles arcabuceros*. Painted by local indigenous artists under the tuition of Jesuits, the combination of tenderness and swagger in these winged figures, brandishing their weapons, is astonishing.

Humahuaca and around → *Phone code: 03887 Colour map 1, A3 Population 8000*

Although Humahuaca (2940 m) was founded in 1591 on the site of a pre-Hispanic settlement, it was almost entirely rebuilt in the mid-19th century. There's something strangely insular about the atmosphere here, with its labyrinth of narrow streets of low adobe houses around a small central plaza. Despite having been the most popular tourist destination for Argentines along the Quebrada, it retains its own

Pachamama and festivals of the northwest

Throughout the Andean region, indigenous people worship La Pachamama. Loosely translated as 'Goddess of the earth', Pachamama also refers to time and place in the cosmos, the sky and the sea too. Fundamental to our very survival, Pachamama inspires a series of festivals throughout August when offerings are made to 'feed the earth', as seeds are planted, and to thank Pachamama in advance for a good yield. Fires are burned all over the countryside, and even in Salta city, as the earth is burned or purified in preparation, and you'll smell *saumerio* resin or fragrant herbs being added to create smoke, which carries prayers to the gods in the sky realm.

Andean people believe that there are gods in all three realms: in the sky, on the earth's surface and under the earth. The serpent is the symbol of Pachamama because it can exist in all three levels, and you'll find serpent imagery on ceramics all over the northwest region. You'll see piles of rocks too: *apachetas*, which are also believed to be sacred, since they reach into the sky from beneath the earth, and this is where offerings are made. On 1 August, the traditional offerings are coca leaves, cigarettes, all kinds of liquids including wine and all manner of foods, to encourage Pachamama to yield such riches again. Often a young llama is slaughtered and laid in the earth as a sacrifice. Even the Spanish conquistadores realised that these piles of stones were significant, and built their churches on top of them.

Traditionally, the August Pachamama celebrations are quiet family affairs, but in recent years, communities are welcoming tourists to join in their fiestas. You'll be welcomed in San Antonio de los Cobres, Cachi, Tolar Grande and in the Quebrada de Humahuaca: ask tourist offices for details, and remember that these rituals hold great significance for their participants: don't take photos without asking first. The Christian calendar is maintained here too, with big celebrations for Carnival for two weeks in February, and for Easter, when Tilcara has a famous procession of thousands of pan pipe musicians down the mountain. This is not to be missed, but book accommodation ahead.

culture. Accommodation here is more limited than at Tilcara, but once the coach trips have left, it's quiet, and is a useful stopping point for travelling north up to the *puna*, or to Iruya. **La Candelaria** festival is celebrated on February 2, and the beginning of carnival here is famously lively with **Jueves de Comadres,** and **Festival de las Coplas y de la Chicha,** when everyone throws flour and water at each other and gets very drunk. Book accommodation ahead.

On the tiny plaza is the church, **La Candelaria**, originally constructed in 1631, rebuilt 1873-1880, containing wonderfully gaudy gold *retablos* and 12 fine Cuzqueño-school paintings. Every day at 1200, tourists gather outside **El Cabildo**, the neo-colonial town hall on the plaza, to watch a large mechanical figure of San Francisco Solano emerge to bless the town from his alcove high in the wall. You may find this kitsch rather than spiritually uplifting, but it's quite a sight. Overlooking the town is the massive and uninspiring, **Monumento a la Independencia Argentina**, commemorating the scene of the heaviest fighting in the country during the Wars of Independence. There is a good **Feria Artesanal** on Avenida San Martín (on the far side of the railway line) and a fruit market at Tucumán y Belgrano. Several new restaurants have opened recently, with decent choices to eat.

About 10 km northeast of Humahuaca, near **Coctaca**, there's an impressive and extensive (40 ha) series of pre-colonial agricultural terraces, the largest archaeological site in Jujuy, though you'll have to go with a guide to find them. Ask in the tourist office and give local guides a bit of business. Or contact **Ser Andino** ⓘ *Jujuy 393, Humahuaca, T03887-421659, www.serandino.com.ar*, who offers two- to three-hour tours to Coctaca from Humahuaca, US$7 per person. Highly recommended is a night or two at least in the peaceful hamlet of **Iruya** (see below), reached by a breathtaking (or hair-raising) three-hour bus ride. Ask the tourist office about trips over the mountains to enter **Parque Nacional Calilegua**, via the beautifully situated little hamlet of Abra Zenta

Iruya → *Colour map 1, A3*

To reach Iruya, a rough *ripio* road 25 km north of Humahuaca runs northeast from the Route Nacional 9, 8 km to Iturbe (also called Hipólito Irigoyen). The bus stops here for five minutes, giving you a chance to glimpse captivating rural life and perhaps buy a woven hat from women waiting by the bus stop. There are no facilities here. The road then crosses the broad river (manageable in an ordinary car only if it hasn't rained heavily) and climbs up over the 4000 m pass, Abra del Cóndor, where you have panoramic views, before dropping steeply, around an amazing slalom of many hairpin bends, into the Quebrada de Iruya.

Iruya is an idyllic small hamlet tucked into a steep hillside, remote and hidden away, but full of warm and friendly inhabitants. In recent years, its character has started to change due to the influx of wealthier tourists staying at the *hostería* at the top of the town and, more damagingly, the huge invasion of backpacking Argentines, *'los hippies'*, each January, whose loud music and sunbathing offends local inhabitants. This is one of many examples in the northwest of tourism not bringing benefits to local people.

The village still retains its festivals, with a colourful **Rosario** festival on the first Sunday in October, and lively Easter festivities, when accommodation is booked up in advance. It's worth spending a few days here to lap up the tranquil atmosphere, and to go horse riding or walking in the beautiful valleys nearby. The hike to the even more remote hamlet of **San Isidro** (seven hours return) is unforgettable. At **Titiconte**, 4 km away, there are some unrestored pre-Inca ruins, though you'll need to take a guide to find them. Iruya has no ATM or tourist information, but has a *locutorio* and food shops. Wander up the tiny narrow main street to find a post office, a shop selling wonderful herbal teas of all kinds and dried peaches from a local co-operative, and another selling superb woven and knitted goods. Not to be missed.

La Quiaca and into Bolivia → *Phone code: 03885 Colour map 1, A2 Population: 3800*

La Quiaca (3442 m) lies on the border with Bolivia, linked by a concrete bridge to **Villazón** on the Bolivian side. Neither town is appealing, but if you have to stay the night, La Quiaca is definitely preferable: there are a few decent places to stay, and if you're around here on the third weekend in October, you can see the three-day **Fiesta de la Olla** when villagers from the far reaches of the remote *puna* arrive on donkeys and in pickups to sell their ceramic pots, sheepskins and vegetables during a colourful festival that involves a lot of dancing and drinking *chicha*. Argentine time is 1 hr later than Bolivia. Do not photograph the border area.

Border with Bolivia The border bridge is 10 blocks from La Quiaca bus terminal, 15 minutes walk (taxi US$1). Argentine office open 0700-2400; on Saturday, Sunday, and holidays there is a special fee of US$1.50 which may or may not be charged. If leaving Argentina for a short stroll into Villazón, show your passport, but do not let it be stamped by Migración, otherwise you will have to wait 24 hours before being allowed back into Argentina. Formalities on entering Argentina are usually very brief at the border but thorough customs searches are made 100 km south at Tres Cruces. Leaving Argentina is very straightforward, but travellers who need a visa to enter Bolivia are advised to get it before arriving in La Quiaca. **Villazón** (Phone code: +591-(0)2) is a grim place, little more than the centre of commercial activity in an otherwise remote and uninhabited area. The road from the border bridge, Avenida República de Argentina, is lined with shops and stalls selling sandals, kids' toys, underpants and calculators, sunglasses and paper flowers, sacks of pink puffed corn, and armfuls of coca leaves. Women in traditional Bolivian dress, with their enormous skirts, spin wool and weave vividly coloured textiles on the pavement, and there's plenty of fresh orange juice and cheap ice cream for sale. However, there's nowhere decent to stay and no tourist information.

Note that Argentine time is one hour behind Bolivian time.

Yavi and around

By far the best place to stay around here is Yavi, 16 km east, which has a couple of good *hosterías*. Yavi is an intriguing *puna* village with a beguiling, hidden quality. Consisting of little more than a few streets of uniformly brown adobe dwellings, most often deserted, it was founded in 1667 and was the crossing point to Bolivia until rail and road connections were built through La Quiaca. The surrounding landscape is wide open with the distinctive swooping stratified hills of the Siete Hermanos to the east. These have long been an important landmark and their stark beauty immediately calls your attention, even before you stumble across the pre-historic petroglyphs on the rocks at the foot of the hills. Ask at **Hostal de Yavi** for a tour, see page 299.

Yavi also has perhaps the finest church in the northwest, well worth the detour from La Quiaca. The **Iglesia de Nuestra Señora del Rosario y San Francisco** ⓘ *Mon 1500-1800, Tue-Fri 0900-1200, 1500-1800, Sat-Sun 0900-1200*, was built 1676-1690, a sturdy, white construction with buttresses and a single tower. Inside is the most magnificent gold retablo and pulpit, made by artisans who were brought, like the gold, from Peru. The retablo is adorned with a gold sculpture of an angel in 18th-century battle dress (like a three dimensional version of the paintings of Uquía) and the tabernacle is lined with mirrors to make candlelight within glow like the sun. Above the exquisite pulpit, decorated with ceramic cherubs, flies a golden dove. All this splendour is seen in the yellowy light from windows made of transparent onyx, giving the beautiful Cuzqueño paintings even more power. It's an impressive and moving sight. The caretaker, Lydia, lives opposite the police station and will show you round the church.

Opposite the church is the 18th-century **Casa del Marqués Campero y Tojo** ⓘ *Mon-Fri 0900-1300, 1400-1800, Sat-Sun 0900-1800*, the austere former mansion of the family who were granted large parts of the *puna* by Philip V of Spain. It's an imposing building with empty courtyards, whose one-room museum houses a strange and eclectic collection of 18th-century bedsprings, arrowheads and candelabras. There's a small but excellent selection of handicrafts for sale inside, and some nicely carved local slate with petroglyphs on a stall outside. There is a colourful evening procession during Easter week.

For a really marvellous experience of the wild beauty and isolation of this region, make time to visit the remote town of **Nazareno**, a four-hour drive east of La Quiaca. The road crosses astonishingly bold rolling hills, before climbing up to the dramatic Abra del Cóndor, and then dropping thousands of metres to find Nazareno nestled in a crown of vermillion mountains. There are some wonderful walks along old Inca roads to Cuesta Azul and to Milagro. Accommodation is with local families; the hospitality is warm and the landscapes are unforgettable. If you speak Spanish, and can chat to the people living here, you'll be able to get a real taste of fascinating Andean culture.

Puna Jujeña » pp297-301.

The Puna Jujeña (3700 m, Km 213) covers all the area to the west of the Quebrada de Humahuaca. It's a spectacularly remote and bleak place with few settlements, but extraordinary salt flats, lakes full of bird life, and plenty of history to be explored. If you have time it's definitely worth spending a few days in the area, The *puna* is high altitude (between 3000 and 4000 m) and it's an inhospitable area to travel alone, so although you could hire a 4WD vehicle and be independent, consider trips with adventure travel company **Socompa** (see Salta tour operators, page 265), which enable you to explore the *puna* in the company of expert guides without having to worry about practicalities.

There are two main areas to explore. **Salinas Grandes** and **Susques** can be reached either from San Antonio de los Cobres in Salta, or from Purmamarca in the Quebrada de Humahuaca. The second area, in the far north, is the **Monumento Natural Laguna de los Pozuelos**, reached by turning west from Abra Pampa. You could do one round trip (now offered by **Movitrack** and other tour companies), setting off from Salta, climbing the Quebrada del Toro to San Antonio de los Cobres, and reaching the Salinas Grandes (Route 40), before descending via the spectacular **Cuesta de Lipán** (Route 52) to Purmamarca in the Quebrada de Humahuaca. Diego Bach runs trips from La Quiaca, see Activities and tours below.

Susques and Salinas Grandes → *Phone code: 03887 Colour map 1, A2*.

The main crossing to Chile is via Route 52 which links Purmamarca and the Salinas with the little village of **Susques**, and on to the **Paso de Jama** (see below) over the awesome Abra Potrerillos pass (4170 m). Susques is the only settlement between Purmamarca and the border, lying in a hollow at the meeting of the Río Susques and Río Pastos Chicos. It has a stunning little church, dating from 1598 – one of the outstanding examples of colonial architecture in the region, with a roof of cactus-wood and thatch. Inside is an old bellow-organ. There are regular buses from Jujuy, with Andes Bus and Purmamarca, (four hours), but it's best to hire a car or join a tour for safety. There are a few basic places to stay and eat in Susques, see listings below.

The salt flats of Salinas Grandes are astonishing – a seemingly endless perfectly flat expanse of white, patterned with ruckled eruptions of salt around regular shapes, like some kind of crazy paving. Against the perfectly blue sky, the light is dazzling. It's safe to walk or drive onto the surface, and you'll find men mining salt, creating neat oblong pools of turquoise water where salt has been cut away, and stacking up piles of white and brown salt blocks, ready for refining. There are plans to create a museum and restaurant on the side of the road: look out for signs.

Casabindo → *Colour map 1, A3*

Heading north from Susques on Route 11, you'll reach the tiny hamlet of **Casabindo** (3500 m), founded in 1602. It can also be approached by travelling 63 km southwest from Abra Pampa – quite a trip over the *puna*. There's a magnificent church, one of the finest in the whole region, with twin towers dating from 1772. It's beautifully proportioned and contains a superb series of 16th-century paintings of *angeles arcabuceros* (archangels in military uniforms) like those at Uquía. It's worth trying to visit on 15 August, when there's a lively celebration of the **La Ascensión de la Virgen**, accompanied by the last remaining *corrida de toros* (running with bulls) in Argentina. **El Toreo de la Vincha** takes place in front of the church, where a bull defies onlookers to take the ribbon and medal it carries: a symbolic offering to the virgin rather than a gory spectacle. The only place to stay is at the village school, which offers basic dorm accommodation, T03887-491129. However, most visitors come in a day trip from Tilcara and return there to sleep at night.

Paso de Jama Border with Chile

Paso de Jama, (4750 m) 360 km west of Jujuy, is reached by a 60 km road which branches off Route 70. Argentine customs and immigration are at Susques. On the Chilean side the road continues (unpaved) to San Pedro de Atacama (Km 514), where fuel and accommodation are available, and Calama. Chilean customs and immigration are at San Pedro de Atacama.

Monumento Natural Laguna de los Pozuelos → *Phone: 03887 Map 1, A3*

ⓘ *Park office in Abra Pampa, T03887-491048, www.parquesnacionales.gov.ar.*

Monumento Natural Laguna de los Pozuelos (3650 m) is a nature reserve 50 km northwest of Abra Pampa and centred around the lake. Laguna de los Pozuelos hosts 44 species of birds, and is visited by huge colonies of up to 25,000 flamingos. It's a stunning landscape, well worth exploring if you have a few days. Be warned though that this is high-altitude *puna*, and temperatures can drop to -25°C at nights in winter; don't attempt camping, unless you have high mountain gear and all the food, warm clothing and drinking water you're likely to need, plus spare supplies. There is a ranger station at the southern end of the Laguna with a campsite nearby. At **Lagunillas**, further west, there is smaller lagoon, which also has flamingos. There are no visitor services and no public transport. Unless you have your own car, the only real option is to go with a guide. Try **Socompa** or Diego Bach (see above)..

If you're keen to explore the wild *puna* further, you could head for the tiny village of **Santa Catalina**, 67 km west of La Quiaca, along *ripio* Route 5. There's a *centro artesanal*, La Negra, and a 19th-century church with a dazzling gold and red interior (ask Doña Pascuala to let you in) and a small museum of artefacts from local history housed in the oldest building in the village.

Sleeping

Purmamarca *p291*

A El Manantial del Silencio, RN52, Km 3.5, T0388-490 8081, www.hotelmanantial.com.ar. Signposted from the road into Purmamarca. The most luxurious option in the Quebrada, this is an elegant traditional *estancia* building, with beautifully designed comfortable minimalist rooms, grand spacious sitting areas, a huge fire, pool, and wonderful views all around. Good service from the professional staff. The restaurant (residents-only) serves superb food and wine, and the breakfasts are sumptuous. Recommended.

A Hostería del Amauta, C Salta, T0388- 490 8043, www.hosteriadelamauta.com.ar. Not quite as sophisticated as **La Comarca** or **El Manantial**, but this central option offers spacious and functional rooms with attractive rustic decor, and also has a restaurant. Perfectly comfortable.

A La Comarca, RN52 Km 3.8, T0388-490 8001, www.lacomarcahotel.com.ar. A small complex of very comfortable rooms plus a few *cabañas*, all built with local materials in rustic style in this bright pink building. The location is unbeatable, amidst colourful mountains on the outskirts of Purmamarca. Rooms are comfortable, service is excellent, there's a heated pool, a mini spa, and a restaurant serving regional cuisine.

C La Posta de Purmamarca, C Santa Rosa de Lima, T0388-490 8029, www.postade purmamarca.com.ar. Highly recommended, with a beautiful elevated setting against the mountain, just 4 blocks up from the plaza. All of its standard rooms are spacious and comfortable, with modern bathrooms. Beautiful cacti plants for sale.

C Terrazas de la Posta, beside La Posta, above, T0388-490 8053, terrazasdelaposta@ yahoo.com.ar. Very good rooms that open onto a veranda with wonderful views over the little town.

D El Viejo Algarrobo, just behind the church, T0388-490 8286, elviejoalgarrobo@ hotmail.com. Modest, but recommended, with small but pleasant rooms, cheaper with shared bath.

Maimará *p291*

C Posta del Sol, Martín Rodríguez y San Martín, T0388-499 7156, www.posta

delsol.com. Lovely comfortable *hostería*, with a good restaurant. The owner is a tourist guide, can take you on a tour of the area, and has helpful information.

Tilcara *p292*

B-C Posada de Luz, Ambrosetti y Alverro, T0388-495 5017, www.posadadeluz.com.ar. The gorgeous views of the Quebrada from the private terraces behind each room are really striking in this small, comfortable and rustic hotel surrounded by large gardens. There's a relaxed atmosphere, with comfortable leather sofas for hanging out on, and occasional live music in the bar. Book ahead for the llama caravan excursions to the *puna*. Recommended.

B-C Quinta La Paceña, Padilla y Ambrosetti, T0388-495 5098, www.quintalapacena.com.ar. This architect-designed traditional adobe house is a peaceful haven and the nicest place to stay in Tilcara. Restored rooms of the old farm are smaller and cheaper than the stylish and very comfortable newer ones. The garden is gorgeous and wonderfully kept, and Lili, the owner, gives wonderful attention to detail. Recommended.

C Los Establos, Gorriti s/n (next to **Con los Angeles**, below), T0388-495 5379. Pretty, rustic rooms, decorated in local style, and well-equipped *cabañas* for 2-6.

C Posada con los Angeles, Gorriti 153 (signposted from access to town), T0388-495 5153, www.posadaconlosangeles.com.ar. A much-recommended favourite with charming rooms, each in a different colour, all with fireplace and door to the garden with beautiful mountain views. A calm atmosphere throughout, and kind attentive service. Warmly recommended.

E pp **Malka**, San Martín s/n, 5 blocks from plaza up steep hill, T0388-495 5197, www.malkahostel.com.ar. Quite the most welcoming place to stay in Tilcara is its superb youth hostel, one of the country's best. It has beautifully situated rustic *cabañas*, dorms for 4 people and doubles with bath. Kitchen and laundry facilities, HI-affiliated. Owner and guide, Juan, is wonderfully helpful and informative, and he and his wife Tere are great company. Highly recommended.

E La Morada, Debenedetti s/n, T/F0388-495 5118, lamorada@imagine.com.ar. An attractive budget option with quite good rooms for 2-5, with own bath and cooking facilities.

Camping

Camping El Jardín, access on Belgrano, T0388-495 5128. Camping US$2 pp, with hot showers (only in the afternoon). Also **E** pp basic but clean rooms available, with bath.

Huacalera and the Uquía *p292*

C Hostal de Uquía, next door to the Iglesia San Francisco de Paula, T0388-490523, hostaluquia@yahoo.com.ar. Simple rooms around a courtyard, and very good food.

D Hostal La Granja, Huacalera, T0388-426 1766. A welcoming rustic place with pool, outstanding food and service, a good base for exploring the region.

Humahuaca *p292*

B Camino del Inca, Calle Ejército del Norte s/n, signposted on the other side of the river, T0388-421136, hosteriainca@imagine.com.ar. A smart well-built modern hotel in traditional style with large rooms coming off colonnaded galleries, all rather over-priced. Good restaurant.

D Hostal Azul, over the bridge and 500 m further, Barrio Medalla Milagrosa, T0388-421596, www.hostalazulhumahuaca.com.ar. This new house is a good choice with simple rooms with bath, around a central patio and an agreeable dining room. It lies in a quiet semi-rural area on the outskirts of the town, and the owners are young and friendly.

E Residencial Humahuaca, Córdoba 461, 1 block from bus terminal, T0388-421141. Good clean *residencial* with rooms with bath. Breakfast extra.

F pp **El Cardón**, next to the river, across the bridge, T0388-421625, www.elcardon.8K.com. Rural *cabañas* with rooms for up to 4 people, all facilities, regional meals and horse-riding excursions offered by the charming family owners.

F pp **Posada el Sol**, over the bridge and 500 m further, signposted, Barrio Medalla Milagrosa, T0388-421466, www.posada

For an explanation of the Sleeping and Eating price codes used in this guide, and other relevant information, see Essentials, pages 48 and 51.

elsol.com.ar. Friendly, comfortable hostel in a small rustic house, by far the best budget accommodation near Humahuaca. The surroundings are lovely and peaceful, on the semi-rural outskirts of town, and there are some doubles as well as small dorms with shared bath, plus a well-equipped apartment for 6 with bath and breakfast. Discounts to HI members.

Iruya *p294*

A Hostería de Iruya, T03887-482002, www.hosteriadeiruya.com.ar. Extremely comfortable hotel with beautifully simple rooms, smart bathrooms, and excellent food, this has great views from the top of the village. Highly recommended.

F pp **Hostal Federico Tercero**, at Café del Hostal, at the bottom of the steep main street, T03887-15629152. Owned by delightful singer Jesús, simple rooms (some with bath), good food from breakfast to dinner, and frequent live music.

F pp **Hospedaje Tacacho**, T03887-15629350. A welcoming family owned house, with simple rooms, tremendous views over the valley, and a *comedor* on the plaza.

La Quiaca and into Bolivia *p294*

D Turismo, Siria y San Martín, T03885-422243, intenmun@laquiaca.com.ar. The smartest place to stay, this has comfortable rooms with TV, a heated pool, and a good restaurant.

E Cristal, Sarmiento 539, T03885-422255. Basic functional rooms with bath, in this old fashioned place, not far from the bridge.

E Hostería Munay, Belgrano 51, T03885-423924, www.munayhotel.jujuy.com. A very pleasant place to stay with comfortable and spotless rooms. Very good value. Recommended

F La Frontera, Belgrano y Siria, T03885-422269. This hotel and restaurant has good cheap food, basic but decent rooms with shared bath. The owner is very hospitable.

Camping

Camping Municipal, on the route to Yavi, T03885-422645.

Yavi and around *p295*

D Hostal de Yavi, Güemes 222, T03887-490523, hostaldeyavi@hotmail.com. Simple bedrooms with bath, and some hostel space, with a cosy sitting room, good food cooked by the hospitable Javier and Gino, and a welcoming relaxed atmosphere. Tours also arranged to see cave paintings, moonlight walks, trekking and trips to the Laguna de los Pozuelos. Recommended.

E La Casona 'Jatum Huasi', Senador Pérez y San Martín, T03887-422316, mccailsaya@laquiaca.com.ar. Homely and welcoming.

Susques and Salinas Grandes *p296*

D Pastos Chicos, R52, Km 220 (at Casas Quemadas, 3 km west of Susques), T03887-423 5387, www.pastoschicos.com.ar. A rustic building providing comfortable accommodation. Good value. Its restaurant serves delicious regional specialities, open to non-residents. Phone for pick-up.

D El Unquillar, R52, Km 219 (2 km west of Susques), T03887-490201, www.elunquillar.com.ar. An attractive *hostería* decorated with local weavings, with very good rooms. Also has restaurant, open to non-residents. Phone for pick-up.

F Residencial Las Vicuñitas, San Martín 121, T03887-490207, opposite church. This very basic budget accommodation is the only place to stay in Susques itself.

Casabindo *p296*

The only accommodation here is in the local school, T03887-491129. Basic hostel-type beds, with shared bath and breakfast for US$7 pp.

Eating

Purmamarca *p291*

ΨΨ Los Morteros, C Salta (behind the church). A smart restaurant, combining chic and traditional style with a high standard of regional cuisine. Open lunch and dinner. Often recommended.

Ψ Arte y Té, C Sarmiento. Ideal for tea, or for regional *picadas* with a drink, in the informal atmosphere of an artist's home.

Ψ La Posta, on the plaza. Excellent local dishes – *humitas* and *tamales* especially recommended. Touristy, but the service and the food are good. A small handicrafts shop next door sells high quality goods.

Ruta 52, opposite where the bus stops. Very cheap and delicious food.

Tilcara *p292*

Posada con los Angeles, Gorriti 153, T0388-495 5153, resto@posadaconlos angeles.com.ar. A few blocks from the plaza, this charming bed and breakfast also serves dinner. Few choices but superb food with well-balanced flavours, based on the best local ingredients (quínoa, llama meat, Andean potatoes, lamb, goat cheese and herbs), excellently prepared and served by chef José María. For desserts, the *budín del cielo* is gorgeous. Often mellow live music. Book ahead. Recommended.

Pucará, C Padilla, at the top of the hill on the right on the road to the pucará. The best restaurant in town, with really imaginative twists on traditional dishes, such as llama quinoa and risotto, all served in a rustic intimate atmosphere and really delicious. Excellent desserts; try the exquisite chocolate pudding. Dinner, also open lunchtime in high season. Highly recommended.

El Patio Comidas, Lavalle 352. The best option in the town itself, this is a popular place, with rustic tables and chairs in a few small rooms, where simple tasty Andean meals are served. Great atmosphere, and charming owner, María Mercedes, an anthropologist. Recommended.

Música Esperanza (Bar del Centro), Belgrano 547, T0388-495 5462. A small restaurant and café serving delicious local dishes in a small elegant patio. It's a lovely place to eat, but not always open, and the service varies so you may be lucky or might have to wait for ages. Both the restaurant and crafts shop next door sustain an NGO that organizes free art and music workshops for local children.

Humahuaca *p292*

El Portillo, Tucumán 69. A simply decorated room, but serves slightly more elaborate regional meals than the usual, such as llama with a fine plum sauce.

La Cacharpaya , Jujuy y Santiago del Estero. This brightly lit large place lacks sophistication, but it's central and the food is good. Attracts an interesting mix of clientele.

Iruya *p294*

All hotels have their own restaurant with prices reflecting the room rates, see Sleeping, above. They all serve regional meals (*locro, empanadas, humita, tamales*). **Hostal Federico Tercero** (on the plaza at the bottom of the hill) is the most welcoming place to hang out, but the most sophisticated and elegant place to eat is the pricey **Hostería de Iruya** (at the top of the town).

La Quiaca and into Bolivia *p294*

La Frontera, Belgrano y Siria. An atmospheric place, where the generous set menu will cost you around US$2.

Ruta 9, R9, on the way out of town to the south. The best place to eat in town.

Bars and clubs

Tilcara *p292*

For a taste of Tilcara's culture, there are a couple of places not to be missed:

El Cafecito, on the plaza. Serves good coffee and wonderful locally grown herbal teas during the day, and has superb live folklore and jazz music at weekends from celebrated local musicians.

Lapeña de Carlitos, on the plaza. Regional music from the charismatic and delightful Carlitos, also cheap meal-of-the-day, *empanadas*, and drinks. A selection of all the typical music of the area, with bits of history and culture thrown in, in a great show by the inimitable Carlitos.

Activities and tours

Tilcara *p292*

Cycling

Malka youth hostel, T0388-495 5197, rents bikes to guests and friends.

Tour operators

Ariel Mosca, T0388-495 5119, arielpuna@ hotmail.com. A recommended historian and guide for informative trips to the *puna*, Iruya, Salinas Grandes, and archaeological sites. He will take you out I your own vehicle, is very well informed, and speaks English.

Caravana de Llamas, T0388-495 5017, www.caravanadellamas.com.ar. Hiking into the mountains while llamas carry your belongings, reviving the ancient tradition.

Magnificent mountainous landscapes you can explore, from half- to 3-day excursions. A great way to see the landscape. He can also be contacted at Posada de Luz.

Máximo Ezcurra, T0388-495 5053, maxezcurra@imagine.com.ar. Máximo arranges amazing horse-riding trips from easy half-day tours to the nearby mountains to unforgettable 4-day rides from the Quebrada to Calilegua.

Oscar Branchesi, T0388-495 5117, branchesi_guia@arnet.com.ar. Oscar will take you to meet locals and gives you great insight into indigenous culture. Recommended. He also rents *cabañas* for rent up to 6 people.

Humahuaca *p292*

Tour operators

Ser Andino, Jujuy 393, T03887-421659, www.serandino.com.ar. Really nice people offering an attractive range of trips along the Quebrada plus Iruya, and to the *puna* including to Laguna de los Pozuelos. And they also go to Coctaca in 2- to 3-hr tours from Humahuaca, US$7 pp.

Iruya *p294*

Tour operators

For local guides for walking and mules in the surrounding area, ask at the tourist office in Iruya, T03887-482001. If you're short of time, it's probably a good idea to contract a guide in Humahuaca or Salta.

Norte Trekking, T0387-436 1844, www.nortetrekking.com. The region's most experienced guide, Federico Norte, runs small tours to Iruya, including other adventurous options, according to the groups needs. Highly recommended.

Puna Jujeña *p296*

Diego Bach, T03885-422797, T156860691, punatours@hotmail.com. Diego leads excellent and highly informed excursions, from day trips to several days, and may include panning for gold, as the Jesuits did. Recommended is a 5-day trek on horseback to the cloudforest Parque Nacional Baritú.

Transport

Purmamarca *p291*

Bus Cotta Norte, El Vallisto, Panamericano and Evelia all run several buses a day to **Jujuy** US$2, 1 hr, and up to **Humahuaca**, buses to **Susques**, daily (not on Mon), US$4.

Tilcara *p292*

Bus There are frequent services to all towns on the **Quebrada** and to **Jujuy**, and at least 3 buses a day to and from **La Quiaca** on the Bolivian border.

Iruya *p294*

Bus There are 2 or 3 daily buses from **Humahuaca**, with Empresa Mendoza (T03887-421442), 0830, 1030, 2100 (not on Sat), takes 3 hrs, US$5.50 return, returning to Humahuaca 0600 (not on Sun) and 1515. Also excursions of several days organized by tour companies. Tickets from the bus station, and from the food shop round the corner from the church.

La Quiaca and around *p294*

Bus Terminal at España y Belgrano, luggage storage. Taxi to border US$0.70. There are several buses a day to **Salta** (US$8-10) with Balut (7-7½ hrs), **La Veloz del Norte** and **Andesmar**. Several daily to **Humahuaca**, US$3-4, 3-3½ hrs, and to **Jujuy**, US$5-7, 5-6½ hrs. Take your own food, as there are sometimes long delays. Buses may be stopped for routine border police controls and searched for coca leaves; don't carry any drugs. Note that overnight buses from Jujuy may arrive in the early morning when no restaurants are open and it's extremely cold outside. To **Buenos Aires**, via Jujuy, US$40-50 including meals, 26-28 hrs. **Andes Norte** links several villages west of R9, including **Santa Catalina**, Mon-Fri, US$2.

Yavi *p295*

No buses go to Yavi. You can hitchhike from the exit to R5 (US$1 pp is expected) or take a *remise* taxi for US$9 return, including ½ hr stay. **Remises La Quiaca**, Belgrano 169 (round the corner from terminal), T03887-423344.

Las Yungas

In complete contrast to the puna and the Quebradas, the Yungas (pronounced shungas, with sh as in measure) are areas of cloudforest jungle lying along the eastern edges of the Salta and Jujuy provinces. Receiving heavy rainfall, these forests support an incredible wealth of wildlife and vegetation, together with fragile indigenous communities. Hence three national parks were created to protect them: Baritú and El Rey in Salta, and Calilegua in Jujuy. All three are very much worth visiting, but you'll need to be determined. Access is limited, and planning is required as infrastructure is still limited. If you don't have a 4WD vehicle, contact one of the few adventure tourism agencies who are allowed to operate in the parks. *» For Sleeping, Eating and other listings, see page 305.*

Best time to visit

All three parks are difficult to access during the rainy season, January to March, when the roads are mostly impassable. There are lots of mosquitoes all year round so take plenty of repellent. The prevalence of malaria varies from year to year so check with your doctor about medication, especially in mid-summer.

Accommodation

There is no accommodation inside the parks themselves, except for very basic campsites with few facilities. However, there are some highly recommended places to stay nearby that can also arrange trips into the parks. See Sleeping, page 305.

Parque Nacional Calilegua » p305.

The park protects an area of peaks, sub-tropical valleys and cloudforest on the eastern slopes of the Serranía de Calilegua. There are some surprisingly high peaks including **Cerro Amarillo** (3720 m), which you can climb in a three-day trek round trip, starting from the entrance, and **Cerro Hermoso** (3200 m), which lies closer to the road, but is attempted by few visitors as you must go with a guide. Several rivers flow southeast across the park into the Río Ledesma. The wildlife is wonderful with at least 300 species of bird including the red-faced guan and the condor, and over 60 species of mammal. You're likely to see tapirs, otters, taruca (Andean deer) and perhaps even pumas. The unpaved Route 83 runs through the park climbing from southeast to northwest and affording splendid views, before reaching Valle Grande beyond the park's borders. From Valle Grande there is a basic road leading via Aparzo to the Quebrada de Humahuaca. Or you could hike west from the park to Humahuaca and Tilcara (allow at least four days); you'll need to take a guide.

Ins and outs

Parque Nacional Calilegua is 125 km northeast of Jujuy and the most accessible of the three cloudforest parks in the region. The park entrance is at Aguas Negras, 12 km northwest of Libertador General San Martín, reached by Route 83, which runs off Route 34 just north of town. There are frequent buses, including **Balut**, T03886-422 2134, from Jujuy's terminal to Libertador General San Martín (also called Ledesma). From there, buses run to the park, where you'll be met by the *guardaparque* guides. Hitching is also possible. **Park headquarters** ⓘ *San Lorenzo s/n, Calilegua, 4 km northeast of Libertador, T03886-422046, calilegua@apn.gov.ar*. There is another *guardaparque* at Mesada de las Colmenas, 13 km further northwest along Route 83. The climate is subtropical with average temperatures ranging from 17°C in winter to

28°C in summer. Mean annual rainfall is 2000 mm, falling mainly in summer (November to March).

Walks

Within the park, there are 22 km of trails for trekking, most of which are close to the Aguas Negras ranger station. There are also some roads crossing the park for cars and bikes, but note that horse riding is not allowed.

A good tourist circuit is to **Calilegua** and then on to **Aguas Calientes**, a very rural place, where there are *hosterías* and a covered pool. You can do this in a day, if it hasn't rained, and it is accessible in an ordinary vehicle.

Cerro Amarillo (3720 m) is a three-day trek starting from the entrance. Ask the *guardaparques* for advice on directions.

At **Alto Calilegua** near the base of Cerro Amarillo, you could walk to an interesting shepherds' hamlet, at 2700 m. It's actually outside Calilegua park, but close to its northern border and only accessible on foot (eight to 10 hours, one way) or on horse back horses (six hours, one way). Mules can be hired from San Francisco (contact Luis Cruz). There are some small pre-Hispanic ruins near the hamlet, but the main point of visiting is to witness a culture which has remained isolated for centuries, in a picturesque mountainous setting. Locals will tell you they're tired of transporting everything by mules, and long for a road to be built. Visit now, before the road comes.

Parque Nacional Baritú » p305.

Baritú is Argentina's only tropical park, lying north of the Tropic of Capricorn. It protects several species close to extinction, such as the yaguarete which lives only in a few eco-regions of this kind, and whose only rival carnivore is the puma. There is rich bird life, and there are also rare plant and tree species here, making the park a great destination for serious nature lovers. Although the park lies entirely within Salta province, to reach it you'll have to go into Bolivia first, on Route 50 via Aguas Blancas (see below). The climate here is wet and hot, with summer rains bringing between 900 and 1300 mm, making roads completely impassible in January and February. This makes Baritú one of the most inaccessible parks in the country, and you'll have to be determined to make a visit. But it's spectacularly beautiful, covering 72,439 ha of the eastern slopes of the Andean foothills and with peaks rising to around 2000 m, mostly covered by cloudforest. You'll see many of the same birds and animals as in Calilegua. Fauna is also abundant and varied. There are no facilities apart from ranger posts, campsites at the entrances and rustic *cabañas* It's the hottest of the three parks, with average temperatures in summer of 21°C in winter and 30°C in summer.

Ins and outs

Access is only now possible through Bolivia. Start in Orán (full name San Ramón de la Nueva Orán) and travel up Route 50 to Aguas Blancas region. Then drive 110 km through Bolivian territory – a beautiful winding road through hills – to reach the international bridge El Condado-La Mamora. Take Route 19 south (now back in Argentina), and after 14 km, you'll reach the region known as Los Toldos, and keep heading south for a further 26 km until you reach the northern boundary of the park. Remember to bring your passport and, if hiring a car in Argentina, warn the hire company that you plan to take it into Bolivia. Fill up with fuel in Orán or Aguas Blancas. Check the state of the roads before setting off at Salta's tourist office, T0387-4310950, or call the park directly T03878-1540 1537. Information in English is also available on the website www.parquesnacionales.gov.ar; follow links to the 'Protected areas' to find.

Walks

▲ There are many walks in the northeast area of the park, allowing you could close contact with the many species of birds in the park. A recommended walk is to **Termas de Cayotal**, two hours' walk from the *guardaparque's* office in El Lipeo. Another is to the settlement of **Campo Grande**, where you can meet local indigenous peoples living in the park, and get a glimpse of their rich culture. From here, you could also walk the seven hours to **Angosto del Río Lipeo**.

Parque Nacional El Rey

Parque Nacional El Rey is the closest of the three cloudforest parks to Salta city (196km), though still not easily accessible unless you go with a specially arranged expedition. Covering 44,000 ha, it was once a privately owned estate, 'El Rey' (the king), on the eastern border of the Spanish territory. It belonged at one time to Coronel Fernández Cornejo, who had carried out the expulsion of the Jesuits, and the remains of his 18th-century house can still be found in the park. With a warm climate, and relatively high average rainfall, the park's vegetation is extremely varied, since the landscape stretches from arid steppe in the east at 750 m above sea level, to mountainous regions at over 2000 m. So in the east, you can find Chaqueño-serrano forest, then transition jungle in the middle, and high mountain forest at the most western extreme. The natural amphitheatre formation of the park's landscape is created by the horseshoe-shaped ridge of the Sierra de la Cresta del Gallo, northwest of the park, reaching heights of around 1700 m, and from it there are rivers descending through lush jungle to the Río Popayán flowing below. There's abundant wildlife, much of it easily spotted, since visitors to the park are few and far between, and there's little vehicular access. Toucans abound, and other birdlife too, though these are rather more shy, but you might be lucky enough to spot wild cats and tapirs.

Ins and outs

Getting there The park entrance is 46 km off RP 5, but no public transport reaches the park so it's best to take a tour from Salta city with one of the three operators licensed to take groups into the park: **Federico Norte, Movitrack** and **Clark Expediciones** (see Salta tour operators, page 265). These are highly recommended, with expert guides to the interesting flora and fauna in the park, offering one and two-day trips in 4WD vehicles with walks in the Park, and camping. No other accommodation possible in the park.

Park information The best time to visit is May to November, avoiding the very rainy season of January-March. There is a rangers office near the entrance with a clearing where you can camp. This is a simple campsite, but has drinking water and bathrooms. Park office in Salta: España 366, 3rd floor (4400) Salta T03487 4312683. More information at Parques Nacionales website: www.parquesnacionales.gov.ar

Walks

▲ There are several good paths you can take to explore the park's varied landscapes, and accompanying wildlife. **Los Patitos** is a small lake, 1½ km from the *guardaparques* centre, and a great one-hour walk for spotting aquatic birds and mammals. **Popayán River** is 10 km (two hours) from the *guardaparques* centre. **Pozo Verde** path is 12 km from the *guardaparques* centre and challenging for the first 3 km. Part of the way there's a footpath with interpretation information, called 'Los ocultos'. **Santa Elena Field and Los Lobitos waterfall** is a challenging hike but good for seeing transition jungle; 4km from the *guardaparques*, two hours each way; you'll need a guide. **Chorro de los loros** is a pedestrian path of medium-high difficulty. It is 10 km long and crosses the transition jungle. It starts in the *guardaparques* centre.

Sleeping

Parque Nacional Calilegua *p302*

A-B Finca Portal de Piedra, Villa Monte, Santa Bárbara, 12 km south of Palma Sola, via paved roads either by leaving RN 34, 10 km south of San Pedro, or 17 km north of Libertador General San Martín, T03886-156820564, www.portaldepiedra.netfirms.com. Convenient for Parque Nacional El Rey and Parque Nacional Calilegua. This fabulous eco-run finca is located inside its own nature reserve, Reserva Provincial Las Lancitas, which has been reclaimed from cattle-grazing and hunting ground which was being devastated by deforestation by the owners. Bilingual guides Carlos and Silvia run a guesthouse, and also a self-contained eco-cabin in the hills, and offer really superb horse riding and excursions into the cloud forest, trekking in Calilegua, birdwatching, and archaeology. The food is simple, the welcome warm. It's worth staying for 3 days to learn all about the wildlife and medicinal plants, and about the culture of the indigenous people who live here, and to go on longer rides into the parks. It's a great adventure for children too. Highly recommended. Portal de Piedra can be reached by bus from Jujuy via San Pedro and Palma Sola.

C Posada del Sol, Los Ceibos y Pucará, Barrio La Loma, Libertador General San Martín, T03886-424900, www.posadadelsoljujuy.com.ar. Comfortable and functional hotel with good rooms in exuberant gardens with a pool. The best place to stay close to Calilegua National Park. Trip advice and, excursions to the Yungas.

D Termas de Caimancito, Aguas Calientes, on RP 1, T03886-15650699, www.termasdecaimancito.com.ar. A beautiful and tranquil place in tropical surroundings, owned by a welcoming English speaking family. Simple rooms with bath, a campsite, thermal pools and a small restaurant. The Familia Strelkov are excellent guides to Calilegua. Ask about excursions and trekking into the park, just a 30 min drive from here.

Camping

There is a campsite at Aguas Negras, near the first rangers station and you'll find when entering Calilegua from RN 34. There is drinking water from the river nearby, and some cooking facilities and tables. To camp at Mesada de las Colmenas ask permission at Aguas Negras

Activities and tours

Parque Nacional Calilegua *p302*

Clark Expediciones, in Salta (see page 265), T0387-421 5390, www.clarkexpediciones.com. Specialist tours for birdwatchers, natural history and cultural tailored tours.

Posada del Sol, Libertador General San Martín, T03886-424900, www.posadadelsoljujuy.com.ar. Tours offered if you stay in the hostería, see Sleeping.

Tony Strelkov, T03886-15650699, www.termasdecaimancito.com.ar. Runs bilingual excursions, and runs the Termas de Caimancito in Aguas Calientes (see Sleeping).

Parque Nacional Baritú *p303*

Only **Movitrack** and **Clark Expediciones**, both in Salta (see page 265)) are authorized to take visitors into the park. Both are recommended for specializing in natural history, with 1- to 2-day trips in 4WD vehicles, camping and walking inside the park

Transport

Parque Nacional Calilegua *p302*

Various companies go from San Salvador de Jujuy to Libertador General San Martín (also called Ledesma) almost every hour, eg **Balut**. From there, take **Empresa 23 de Agosto** or **Empresa 24 de Septiembre** buses, leaving 0830 to **Valle Grande**, across Calilegua national park. All Pocitos or Orán buses pass through **Libertador General San Martín**.

Catamarca province

Most of the population of this large province lives in the capital, leaving the stunning countryside to the north and west virtually empty of people. Catamarca city is hot and dull, livening up each July for the hugely popular poncho festival, an excuse for a big forlclore music festival, food and dancing. There is a great tradition of weaving – wool, alpaca and llama – throughout the province of Catamarca, and while you can find them in the handicrafts centre in the city, you might want to explore the wild remote villages to the west, where you'll many local weavers.

The small towns of Belén and Andagalá are animated oases on the way to the puna, where the tiny hamlets of Fiambalá and Tinogasta are fascinatingly remote last outposts, and possible bases for climbing Mount Pissis in the highlands to the far west. The province has one really impressive archaeological find: the ruined Inca town of El Shincal, close to Londres, but accessible on a tour from Belén. With evidence of extensive Inca conquest and a sophisticated infrastructure, this is well worth visiting. From Belén, a lonely road leads north across the puna to remotest Antofagasta de la Sierra, surrounded by a vast expanse of salt flats. Catamarca's most appealing place to stay is the charming hilltop town of El Rodeo; a popular weekend retreat for Catamarqueños, with its refreshing microclimate and good walks. Further north, on the border with Tucumán, is the delightful village of Santa María, a lovely place to rest on the way to Salta, near the spectacular ruins at Quilmes.

The province is not the northwest's most accessible and the infrastructure can be frustratingly basic, but you'll be warmly welcomed in the remotest reaches; and you'll want to stuff olives, walnuts and superb woven textiles in your bag to bring home.

▸▸ *For Sleeping, Eating and other listings, see page 309-311.*

Catamarca city ▸▸ *pp309-311.*

➔ *Phone code: 03833 Colour map1, C3 Population: 172,000*

The provincial capital is a sleepy, traditional, and rather run down place. Unless you're here for the poncho festival in mid-July, there's little to draw you to the city, or keep you here. There are some attractive 19th-century buildings grouped around a large central plaza, and a wonderful museum, but the accommodation is poor, and the summers are unbearably hot with temperatures up to 45°C. El Rodeo, an hour away by regular minibus, makes a far more appealing alternative if you're on the way to the *puna* or Chile.

Ins and outs

Getting there Catamarca's airport, 20 km south, has a daily flight to and from Buenos Aires. Alternatively, there are several daily buses from Buenos Aires, taking at least 14 hours. Buses also go regularly to Salta, Tucumán, Mendoza and La Rioja. The route to Santiago del Estero is longer, to avoid high mountains, and only one bus a day operates. The bus terminal is seven blocks southeast of the main plaza.

Getting around The city is small enough to walk around, with most hotels situated on Sarmiento, northwest of the plaza. Shops and banks are mostly on the pedestrianized street Rivadavia, which runs down the eastern side of the plaza and continues to the south. Buses link the city to outlying areas of the province, and there are many minibuses a day to Villa El Rodeo.

Tourist information The **tourist office** ⓘ *by the plaza, República 446, T03833-437791, www.turismocatamarca.gov.ar, daily 0800-2100*, is helpful but no one speaks

English. There's also a **provincial tourist office** ⓘ *Roca y Virgen del Valle, T03833-437594, Mon-Fri 0800-1300, 1500-2000*, and information point at the airport.

Best time to visit The best time to visit is during the *Poncho* festival in mid July, though do book accommodation ahead, and it's best to avoid the summer, when temperatures exceed 40°. Very sensibly, the siesta is strictly observed here, and everything closes down from 1230 to 1700.

Sights

The central, leafy **Plaza 25 de Mayo** was designed by the illustrious Charles Thays and contains tall trees of unusual species, providing much needed shade from the scorching summer heat, and a rather striking equestrian sculpture of San Martín. There's the white stuccoed **Casa de Gobierno** (1891), designed by Caravati and, to the west, the faded red bulk of his neo-classical **cathedral** (1878), looking rather forlorn but sporting a pair of fine mosaic tiled cupolas on its towers. The interior is a rather uncelestial, peeling *eau de nil*, but the scenes from the life of Christ painted on the ceiling are lovely. In a chapel high above and behind the altar, you can visit the much worshipped Virgen del Valle all dressed up, on a mighty gilded pedestal. Access is up a double staircase system to the *Camarín*, where the walls of the chapel are lined with plaques of offerings and cases crammed with thousands of silver arms, legs hands and eyes offered by her followers over the years. One block north of the plaza, the **Iglesia de San Francisco** (1882), has an impressive colonial-style façade. Five blocks west of the plaza, the **Paseo General Navarro**, is a rather scrappy park surrounded by huge trees, with good views over the town, but not recommended for a quiet picnic.

For weavings and other handicrafts, try the **Mercado Artesanal** ⓘ *Av Virgen del Valle 945, Mon-Fri, 0800-1200, 1500-2030*, in the 'Manzana de Turismo' (a 'block' for tourists, with no other obvious attractions), which is also a carpet factory.

The must-see of the city is the incredible **Museo Arqueológico** ⓘ *Sarmiento 446, T03833-437413, Mon-Fri 0700-1300, 1430-2030, Sat-Sun 0830-1230, 1530-1830, US$0.30*, containing an enormous collection of artefacts from the sophisticated pre-Hispanic cultures who inhabited the area from around 1000 BC. There are carved stone vessels with animal figures leaping off their sides, beautifully painted funerary urns, deliberately flattened skulls (compressed by the owners by wearing wooden boards), a comical two headed pot with a smiling llama at one end and an anxious looking man the other, and quite a shocking mummified baby, naturally conserved above 5000 m. Allow at least an hour to discover the many fascinating finds. Highly recommended.

Around Catamarca city

» *pp309-311.*

Heading north, towards El Rodeo, you'll pass through the **Valle de Catamarca**, with a series of attractive churches, built mostly in the 19th century. Look out for the ones at **San Isidro**, 5 km east, **Villa Dolores**, 1 km further north, and at **San José**, a further 4 km north, whose colonial church dates from 1780. Oldest of all is **La Señora del Rosario**, 2 km east of the city, a simple white building dating from 1715.

Some 25 km north of Catamarca, the **Dique Las Pirquitas** lake has good fishing and watersports, as well as trekking and mountain-biking. To get to the lake, take bus No 1A from the bus terminal (every 30 minutes) to the **Hostería de Turismo** at Villa Pirquitas, from where it is about 45-minute walk.

However, the best place to head to escape from the city is the pretty weekend retreat of **El Rodeo**, some 37 km north of Catamarca in lovely mountain setting with a cool microclimate and lots of good walks and horse riding. There's a great two-day hike to Cerro el Manchao, 4550 m above sea level, and trout fishing in the Río Ambato. Ask for advice at the friendly **tourist information** ⓘ *T03833-490043*. It's easy to get here by bus or hire car, and there are plenty of delightful *hosterías*, which make this a pleasant alternative to staying in the city. **El Rodeo Bus** runs several combis a day (minibuses) from the car park Estacionamiento San Martín, half a block east of the plaza on San Martín. US$5 each way, return buses the same day.

Las Juntas, a further 20 km away on the same road, is another rural retreat from the city, also in attractive mountainous countryside. **Los Hermanos Vergara** run buses from Catamarca terminal Monday to Saturday at 0800 and 2000.

Northeast of Catamarca, there are fine panoramic views over the Valle de Catamarca at the **Cuesta del Portezuelo**, along the road snaking up the Sierra de Ancasti, 20 km northeast of the town. The Cuesta rises through 13 hairpin bends to 1680 m and, from the summit, with a vista over the city and valley below, the road continues via El Alto (950 m). There's a reservoir nearby, **Dique Ipizca**, good for *pejerrey* fishing.

Belén and around → *Phone code: 03835 Colour map 1, B2 Population: 11,000*

From whichever direction you approach Belén (1240 m) – whether from Andagalá on Route 46, or along the equally poor Route 40 – you'll be very relieved to arrive. Route 40 takes you across vast open plains fringed with chocolate-coloured flaking mountains, and through the desolate little village of **Hualfin**, with thermal baths in summer at **Pozo Verde**, to the north. This is a better road than the Route 46, but still should not be attempted in the rainy season (February to March) when the rivers crossing the roads are high. Both roads are easier and safer in a 4WD.

There are good views from the **Cerro de Nuestra Señora de Belén**, a hill above the town, where a newly constructed Virgen (the last one was struck by lightning) watches over the place. Information is available from the small **Dirección de Turismo** ⓘ *at the bus terminal a block from the plaza on Rivadavia y Lavalle, T03835-461539, daily 0900-1300, 1600-2000, turismobelencat@hotmail.com*. For excursions in 4WD, go to the friendly and extremely helpful **Ampujaco** Gral Roca 190, T3835-461189, or ask at **Hotel Belén**, Belgrano y Cubas, T03835-461501, www.belencat.com.ar This young agency organizes interesting tours to El Shinkal with tour guides and possibly an archaeologist, though you should ask specifically for this, and request in advance.

Londres → *Population: 2100*

South of Belén, Route 40 is paved to Chilecito via **Londres** (1300 m), a pretty and quiet village, with a remote feel. Founded in 1558, it is the second oldest town in Argentina, though its site was moved several times. It was named in honour of the marriage of Mary Tudor and Philip II. The municipalidad displays a glass coat-of-arms of the city of London and a copy of the marriage proposal. There are important Inca ruins at **El Shincal**, see below; they are signposted from the second plaza you come to after entering the village from Belén. Londres celebrates its walnut festival in January. There are no hotels here, but several *hospedajes* and a campsite T03835-491019) on the route to Shincal. Food can be bought from the few shops around the plaza.

El Shincal

ⓘ *7 km from Londres, Mon-Fri 0730-1330, 1700-1900. Cóndor buses linking Belén and Londres stop 100 m from the ruins, US$0.50. Tours are run by the helpful Ampujaco Tur in Belén, T03835-461189, Gral Roca 190, or at Hotel Belén, Belgrano y Cubas, T003835-461501. A tour for 4 with guide costs US$7 pp. In Spanish only.*

This ruined town is one of the most astonishing remains of the Inca occupation of Argentina, from the 1470s to their demise in 1532. The setting is superb, in a flat area between a crown of mountains and the river – a place the Incas clearly recognised as having sacred significance. Their religious beliefs were deeply entwined with their worship of mountains and their modification of natural forms – the most extreme example of which is Machu Picchu in Peru. Cuzco, too, follows strict conventions, siting the town to line up auspiciously with sacred hills, water sources and the home of the ancestors. According to expert Ian Farrington, El Shincal is a 'little Cuzco', following precisely the same rules of orientation to mountains and water sources. There are large kallankas (thought to be either grain stores or military barracks), sleeping areas and a central plaza, lined up between two artificially shaped hills and perfectly aligned with the rising and setting sun at the solstice. In the middle of the plaza is a sacred platform with a specially designed trough for sacrifices, where Professor Raffino and the La Plata University have been excavating for many years. Raffino's book on the site is available in bookshops in Catamarca and has fascinating information on their finds and on Inca culture (in Spanish). It's best to visit El Shincal with a guide, but you'll be lucky to find one in Londres so take a tour from Belén. It's a remarkable site, well worth visiting.

North of Belén

There are two routes north to Salta. The most direct is via Route 40 which runs northeast via Santa María (176 km, see page 315) and Cafayate (page 278). The alternative is via Route 43, which branches west off Route 40 at a point 52 km north of Belén and runs across the high *puna* to Antofagasta de la Sierra and San Antonio de los Cobres (see page 268). This route is challenging at the best of times, and impassable for ordinary cars after heavy rains. The stretch just after the junction with Route 40 is very difficult, with 37 km of fords. At Km 87 is Cerro Compo (3125 m), from which the descent is magnificent. At Km 99 the road turns right to Laguna Blanca, where there is a museum and a small *vicuña* farm (don't go straight ahead at the junction). There are thermal springs along this road at **Villavil**, 13 km further north, open from January to April, and a *hostería* (D). Drivers should note that you'll need enough fuel for 600 km on unmaintained roads, with fuel consumption being double at high altitudes. Fill up at Hualfín and San Antonio de los Cobres.

Antofagasta de la Sierra → *Colour map 1, B2 Population 900 Altitude 3365 m*

Antofagasta de la Sierra is the main settlement in the sparsely populated northwest corner of Catamarca province, situated on the Río Punilla, 260 km north of Belén and 557 km northwest of the provincial capital. With its low pinkish adobe buildings, surrounded by vast empty lunar landscapes and massive volcanoes, it's a wonderfully remote place. To the west are the salt flats of the **Salar de Antofalla**, though these are inaccessible. The **Salar del Hombre Muerto** on Route 43 can be visited, but it's best to hire a guide. It's a wonderful journey. There's nothing at all to do here, and that's just the point. There are few places on earth that remain so wild and untouched, and the other-worldly landscapes are a paradise for photographers. If you're attracted to wild immense open spaces and long roads leading apparently to nowhere, you'll love it. A decent *hostería* makes it feasible to stay here.

Within reach are of Antofagasta de la Sierra are several interesting archaeological sites including the ruins at **Campo Alumbreras**, in the shadow of the volcano of the same name. There's a pre-Columbian *pucará* (fort) and some nearby petroglyphs. Guides can be found at the small but wonderful museum **Museo del Hombre**, which contains incredibly well preserved pre-Hispanic textiles, and a mummified baby, 2000 years old. There's no petrol station, but fuel can be bought from the *intendencia*.

Sleeping

Catamarca city *p306*

Hotels are pricey and overcharge for singles.

A Amerian Park, República 347, T03833-425444, www.amerian.com. The best option in town is this modern but expensive business hotel, with spacious, attractively decorated and very comfortable rooms, a large restaurant and a pool at the top.

C Ancasti, Sarmiento 520, T03833-435952, www.hotelancasti.com.ar. Next best option in Catamarca, aspiring to be a business hotel. The modernized rooms are comfortable but drab and the bathrooms are tiny. There are sometimes cheaper deals to include dinner in the pleasant airy restaurant.

C Arenales, Sarmiento 542, T03833-431329/330, www.hotel-arenales.com.ar. Welcoming, but slightly institutional in feel. Pleasant plain rooms with well-equipped bathrooms, minimalist though not stylish exactly, but the most comfy in the range.

D Grand Hotel, Camilo Melet 41, T03833-426715, www.grandhotelcatamarca.com.ar. You'll get the friendliest welcome here and it's a real pleasure to walk into such a nicely maintained place, with spacious and comfortable rooms, all with bath TV and a/c, reductions for cash. Recommended.

D Hotel Casino Catamarca, Pasaje Cesar Carman s/n, T03833-432928. A smart place to stay with its discrete casino, large pool (summer only), cheerful bright restaurant, and well-decorated rooms, all with minibar, TV cable, hidden away behind the ACA service station, 4 blocks from the centre. It's peaceful and very welcoming, but beware that in peak summer months of Jan and Feb partying goes on till the early hours and the hotel is very popular. The best in its range by far.

D Pucara, Caseros 501, T03833-431569, T03833-430688. If you've a taste for kitsch you'll love the hideously bold decor in the entrance lounge. The bedrooms are comfortable, if you can cope with pink satin bedspreads and flamenco prints.

E Residencial Shinkal, Vicario Segura 1120, T03833-421083. There are no youth hostels in the city, so your cheapest option is this *residencial*, not recommended for single women. It's the best and newest of the lot, but doesn't include breakfast.

Around Catamarca *p307*

C Hostería El Rodeo, T03833-490296, RP 4, www.hotelguia.com/elrodeo. Lovely spacious rooms, pool, good restaurant, and great views. Climbing, 4WD trips and excursions for children. Highly recommended.

D La Casa de Chicha, Los Gladiolos s/n, T03833-490082, la_casa_de_chicha@yahoo.com.ar. With fewer facilities than El Rodeo, but with a more idyllic setting right in the mountains, and rooms with antique furniture. Try the excellent restaurant for lunch and dinner, or have tea in the beautiful garden, filled with pear trees.

Belén *p308*

D Belén, Belgrano y Cubas, T03835-461501, www.belencat.com.ar. The most comfortable place to stay. Recently refurbished with stylish plain rooms in a modern block in a little leafy garden, and also a tour operator.

E Samay, Urquiza 349, T03835-461320. Old fashioned but very welcoming, and its homely little rooms have bathrooms and fans.

Antofagasta de la Sierra *p309*

Several family houses have cheap, basic but very welcoming accommodation, some rooms including private bath and breakfast.

D Hostería Municipal de Antofagasta, T03835-471001, hosteriaantofagasta@yahoo.com.ar. This is the only really comfortable accommodation, and though it's rooms are simple, they're perfectly decent, and the owners also have a restaurant and offer travel advice.

Eating

Catamarca city *p306*

There are few good restaurants in Catamarca, many cheap ones around the Plaza 25 de Agosto and the bus terminal but this area is not safe at night.

La Tinaja, Sarmiento 533. T03833-435853. The best eating choice by far, this delicious *parrilla* does really excellent pastas. Slightly pricey, but worth it. Deservedly popular.

Salsa Criolla, República 546, on the plaza. Traditional and popular *parrilla*. Sloppy service, but the beef is recommended. The same owner runs Italian-style **Trattoria Montecarlo** next door, whose speciality is pasta, but also has a *parrilla*.

Sociedad Española, Av Virgen del Valle 725, near the Paseo, T03833-431897. Recommended for its quality and variety, serving paella, seafood and other Spanish specialities, with friendly service, and worth the 5-block walk from the main plaza.

Belén *p308*

The best *parrilla* is **El Unico**, and for a drink or *lomitos*, **Bar El Seminario** is a great meeting point for the whole town, especially at weekends, when its customers spill out onto tables in the plaza.

Festivals and events

Catamarca city *p306*

Mar-Apr In the week following Easter, there are pilgrimages to the **Virgen del Valle.** Hotel rooms are hard to find.

Jul Festival Nacional del Poncho, the city's major festival, is the held in the 3rd week in Jul, it includes a huge *feria artesanal* with the best of the province's handicrafts, as well as those from other parts of the country, and 10 nights of excellent *folclore* music.

Nov29-Dec 8 There are pilgrimages to the Virgen del Valle. Hotel rooms are hard to find.

Belén *p308*

20 Dec-6 Jan Fiesta de Nuestra Señora de Belén, the town's most important fiesta.

Feb Carnival is celebrated in style.

Mar/Apr At Easter there are processions for the Virgin.

Shopping

Catamarca city *p306*

Catamarca specialities are available from Cuesta del Portezuelo, Sarmiento 571, T03833-452675, and **Fábrica Valdez**, Sarmiento 578, T03833-425175. There's a range of handicrafts and you can see carpets being woven at the **Mercado Artesanal**, Av Virgen del Valle 945. The carpet factory is open Mon-Fri 0800-1200, 1500-2030.

Activities and tours

Catamarca city *p306*

Tour operators/guides

Tours are offered to El Rodeo and there are various opportunities for adventure sports.

Aníbal Vázquez, T03835-471001. Walking expeditions in Antofagasta de la Sierra.

Inca Viajes, T03833-422064. Conventional tours to main sights in the eastern valleys of Catamarca.

Transport

Catamarca city *p306*

Air

Aeropuerto Felipe Varela, 20 km south, T03833-430080. Aerolíneas Argentinas, to **Buenos Aires** and **La Rioja**.

Airline offices Aerolíneas Argentinas, Sarmiento 589, T03833-424460.

Bus

Modern terminal is 7 blocks southeast of plaza at Av Güemes y Tucumán T03833-437578, with shops, café, ATM and *locutorio*. The entrance is mysteriously through a car park. Taxi to/from Plaza 25 de Mayo US$0.50. To **Tucumán**, several companies, 3½-4hrs, US$6. To **Buenos Aires**, 4 companies daily, 14-18 hrs, US$22-53. To **Córdoba**, 6 companies daily, 6 hrs, US$10-12. To **Santiago del Estero**, just one daily service, 3½ hrs, US$5. To **Mendoza**, several companies, daily, 10 hrs, US$18-35. To **La Rioja**, several companies, daily, 2 hrs, US$4-7. To **Tinogasta**, Robledo, Gutiérrez, 5 hrs, US$6. To **Belén** via Aimogasta and Londres, 3 companies, 4-6 hrs, US$5-6; To **Andagalá**, 4 companies including Marín (via Aconquija), 4½-6 hrs, US$6.50.

Belén *p308*

Bus

To **Santa María**, **San Cayetano** and **Parra** (connection there with other companies to Cafayate and Salta), daily, 5 hrs, US$7. To **Tinogasta**, **Robledo**, 4 weekly, 2-3hrs, US$4. To **Antofagasta de la Sierra,** El Antofagasteño, 2 weekly, 11 hrs, US$15. For more frequent services to **Catamarca** or **La Rioja**, take bus to **Aimogasta**, 1 hr, US$2.

Antofagasta de la Sierra *p309*

Bus

Buses from **Belén** and **Catamarca** with El Antofagasteño arrive in Antofagasta Wed, Fri evening, and return on Mon and Fri 0800. Or hire a pickup or hitch.

Directory

Catamarca city *p306*

Banks Many ATMs for all major cards, along Rivadavia and at bus terminal, and Banco de la Nación, San Martín 632. TCs can only be cashed at BBVA Banco Francés, Rivadavia 520. **Internet** and **telephone** Several *locutorios* with broadband access in the centre. **Post office** San Martín 753, slow, open 0800-1300, 1600-2000.

Tucumán province

One of the country's largest cities lies in one of its smallest provinces. Its subtropical climate is ideal for growing sugar, tobacco and lemons. Outside the modern provincial capital, in the surrounding mountains to the north and west, is the popular weekend retreat of Tafí del Valle, with its cool microclimate. Further northwest, on the route to Cafayate in Salta, are the delightful small towns of Amaichá del Valle and Santa María, over the border in Catamarca, both good bases for exploring Quilmes – one of Argentina's most important archaeological sites. Here you can wander around the extensive remains of a city of 5000 Calchaquíes, built into the side of a mountain amidst breathtaking scenery. Combine Tucumán with Salta via the spectacular drive from Tafí del Valle and Amaichá, stopping at Quilmes, and then up the Valle Calchaquí along Route 40. It's an unforgettably beautiful experience. ➡ *For Sleeping, Eating and other listings, see pages 316-322.*

Tucumán city ➡ *pp316-322.*

➔ *Phone code: 0381 Colour map 1, B3 Population: 740,000*

The city of San Miguel de Tucumán, known simply as Tucumán, lies almost equidistant between Catamarca and Salta on a broad plain just east of the massive Sierra de Aconquija. It's the largest and most important city in the north of the province, though it has suffered economically in the recent recession. Visually, the city lacks Salta's style or architectural splendour, despite being one of the first cities to be founded by the Spanish, and few of its colonial buildings remain. However, it's a busy centre with plentiful restaurants and a huge park designed by Charles Thays. There are few attractions for visitors, and it's overwhelmingly hot in summer – the siesta is strictly observed from 1230 to 1630 – but it does have a couple of good museums and lively nightlife.

Ins and outs

Getting there The airport, 10 km east of town, is linked to the city by **Transfer Express** buses or taxis. There are daily flights from Buenos Aires (via Córdoba). This is one of the few places reached by long-distance train from Buenos Aires. There's a huge bus terminal, seven blocks east of the plaza, where long-distance buses arrive from all parts of the country, as well as Chile and Peru.

Getting around The plaza is the city's heart along with the busy pedestrianized shopping streets to the north and west It's an easy place to get around on foot, but taxis are cheap and reliable. There are several good accommodation options, but if this is a strategic stopover for you, it be better to retreat to the cooler mountains of Tafí del Valle, as the *Tucumanos* do at weekends.

Best time to visit The city's big festivals are the **Day of Independence,** 9 July, when Tucumán is capital of the country for the day. On September 24, the city celebrates the day Belgrano won the Battle of Tucumán, with a huge procession. Summer is best avoided because of the heat, especially January and February.

Tourist information There's a very helpful **tourist office** ⓘ *on the plaza, 24 de Septiembre 484, T0381-430 3644, www.tucuman turismo.gov.ar, Mon-Fri 0800-2200, Sat-Sun 0900-2100*. Also in the bus terminal and airport.

Background

Tucumán was an important city in Spanish colonial times. Founded in 1565 and transferred to its present site in 1685, it was a strategic stop for mule trains on the routes from Bolivia to Buenos Aires and Mendoza. With a colonial economy based on sugar, citrus fruit and tobacco, it developed an aristocracy distinct from those of Buenos Aires and Córdoba. The city was the site of an important battle during the Wars of Independence. Belgrano's victory here in 1812 over a royalist army ended the Spanish threat to restore colonial rule over the River Plate area. Tucumán's wealth was derived from sugar, and it remains the biggest industry, though lemons have also become vital exports in recent decades. The province has suffered badly in the recent recession, with rising unemployment and child poverty. The town has consequently a rather neglected air.

Sights

Plaza Independencia in the city's commercial centre, with many tall palms and mature trees giving welcome shade in the sweltering heat. At night it's full of *Tucumanos* eating ice cream from one of the many *heladerías*. Among its attractive buildings are the ornate **Casa de Gobierno** (1910), with tall palms outside and art-nouveau balconies. Next door is a typical *casa chorizo* (sausage house), **Casa Padilla** ⓘ *25 de Mayo 36, Mon-Sat 0900-1230, 1600-1900, closed Sun*, a series of skinny rooms off open patios, whose collection of china and paintings belonging to a wealthy Tucumán family gives you a flavour of 19th-century life. Across the road, the **Iglesia San Francisco** (1891) has a rather gloomy interior, but a picturesque façade and tiled cupola. On the south side of the plaza, the neoclassical **cathedral** (1852) has a distinctive cupola, but disappointingly bland modern interior, the ceiling painted, uninspiringly, with rainbows and whales.

South of the plaza, on Calle Congreso, is the **Casa Histórica** ⓘ *Mon-Fri 1000-1800, Sat-Sun 1300-1900; July daily 0900-1900, US$1; Fri-Tue son et lumière show (except in Jul) at 2030, US$1.35, children US$0.70*. Rooms are set around two attractive patios, filled with old furniture, historical documents and some fine Cuzqueño school paintings. The highlight is the actual room where the Declaration of Independence was drafted, with portraits of the Congressmen lining the walls. Next to it is a room full of interesting religious artefacts.

It's also worth visiting the small **Museo Arqueológico** ⓘ *25 de Mayo 265, in university building, T0381-4221692 (ext 211), Mon-Fri 0800-1200, 1700-2100, US$0.35*, with it's fine collection of artefacts from the pre-Hispanic cultures of the Calchaquí valleys. The **Museo Folklórico Provincial** ⓘ *24 de Septiembre 565, Mon-Fri 0900- 1300, Sat 0930-1230*, has an impressive collection of silverwork from Peru and musical instruments in an old colonial house.

Tucumán's enormous park, **Parque Nueve de Julio**, east of the centre, is a much-used green space, designed by French landscape architect Charles Thays who also designed the Parque Tres de Febrero in Buenos Aires. With many subtropical trees, it was once the property of Bishop Colombres who played an important role in the development of the local sugar industry, and whose handsome house is now the **Museo de la Industria Azucarera** ⓘ *0820-1830, free*, with a display on sugar-making. The park also has a lake and lots of sports facilities.

Northwest Tucumán province

» *pp316-322.*

Tucumán has stunning mountain scenery to the west and north of the province, along the Nevados de Aconquija, where there are several attractive small towns to visit on the way to Salta. Of the two possible routes, Route 9, via Rosario de la Frontera and Güemes is far quicker, but by far one of the most spectacular routes in the whole area is the Route 40 to Cafayate and up into the Valles Calchaquíes. The road rises up though verdant Tafí del Valle, over the massive Infiermillo pass and then there are spectacular landscapes all the way to the archaeological site of Quilmes, with the added charms of small towns of Santa María and Amaichá del Valle on the way.

Tafí del Valle → *Phone code: 03867 Colour map 1, B3 Population: 3300*

The journey from Tucumán to Tafí is very satisfying. Route 307 leads northwest towards Cafayate, climbing through sugar and citrus fruit plantations, and then jungly subtropical forest, before entering the wide Valle de Tafí, surrounded by mountains densely covered in velvety vegetation. At Km 69 there is a statue to 'El Indio', with good views from the picnic area.

Tafí (2000 m) is a popular weekend retreat from the heat of the city for *Tucumanos*, since it has a cool microclimate, and makes a good base for walking, with several peaks of the Sierra de Aconquija providing challenging day-hikes. Within the sprawling town itself, you can walk by the Ríos El Churqui and Blanquito and to the Parque de los Menhires, where a collection of 129 engraved granite monoliths stand to the south of an attractive reservoir, the **Embalse Angostura**, in the valley below. For hikes into the mountains, it's best to go with a guide, available from **La Cumbre**, see Activities and tours, page 321. There's some excellent accommodation, especially at the upper end of the market, making this an appealing alternative to staying in Tucumán. There are also a couple of very fine estancias, such as **Las Carreras**, www.estancialascarreras.com. Most shops are on the main streets, Avenida Gobernador Critto (becoming Los Faroles to the west near the plaza) and Avenida Perón. At the junction you can buy good locally made cheese and delicious bread, while there's a basic **tourist office** ⓘ *daily 0800-2200*, to the south of the semi circular plaza. You'll have to pay for a map, US$ 1.40, but they do have lists of accommodation, if you're persistent.

Sights

Tafí's most historic building is the attractive **Capilla Jesuítica y Museo de La Banda** ⓘ *Mon-Sat 0900-1900, Sun 0900-1600 (closing early off season), US$0.70 including a guided tour*. This 18th-century chapel and 19th-century estancia has a small museum with interesting finds from the valley and 18th-century religious art. Cross the bridge over Río Tafí southwest of town, and the museum is on your left after 500 m. **Parque de los Menhires** lies in an attractive spot at the south of the Dique la Angostura, 10 km south of the centre of Tafí del Valle. The *menhires* are 129 granite stones, engraved with designs of unknown significance, said by some to symbolize fertility. They are undeniably intriguing, however, it's not quite the mystical sight the tourist brochures claim it is, since the stones were unearthed in various places in the valley and put here in 1977. There's a decent campsite nearby and windsurfing and sailing are available on the reservoir in summer.

Five kilometres further west, **El Mollar** is another weekend village with campsites and *cabañas*, and popular with teenage and student crowds.

Northwest of Tafí del Valle

One of Argentina's most memorable journeys is along Route 307 northwest from Tafí, climbing out of the valley up to the mountain pass **Abra del Infiernillo** (3042 m) at Km 130. There are panoramic views south over the **Cumbres de Mala Mala**, the steeply sided deep green valley below, then breathtaking vistas as you emerge over the pass, looking north over the **Cumbres Calchaquíes**, purple veiled in the distance, and finally over the dramatic Valles Calchaquíes. The road descends along hairy zigzags to the beautiful rocky landscape of the valley of the **Río de Amaichá**.

Amaichá del Valle → *Phone code: 03892 Colour map 1, B2 Population: 1100*

Claiming rather grandly to have the best climate in the world, Amaichá (1997 m) is a lovely tranquil little place that does indeed always seem to be sunny. There's a splendid museum, the **Complejo Pachamama** ⓘ *T03892- 421004, daily 0830-1200, 1400- 1830 (Sun closed in low season), US$2, explanations in English, guided tour in Spanish*, also known also as Casa de Piedra. The museum was designed by the well- known Argentine sculptor Héctor Cruz, who uses the iconography of the region's pre- Colombian art with bold flair in his own ceramics and weavings. It's part gallery, part archaeological museum, and a great place to relax for a couple of hours, with wonderful views from the mosaic cactus gardens. Outside, Cruz's dramatic Pachamama figures frame the surrounding mountains beautifully. The shop sells an extensive range of handicrafts and wonderfully bold rugs and hangings, designed by Cruz and made by local weavers. There's an important Pachamama festival at end of Carnival.

The road forks at Amaichá for Quilmes and Cafayate. Take Route 357 north for 14 km to the junction with Route 40 then follow it north. For Santa María and western Catamarca, take Route 307 south to join Route 40 heading south.

Santa María → *Phone code 03838 Colour map 1, B2 Population: 10,800*

With its lively village feel, still untainted by tourism, Santa María (1880 m) makes a very attractive place for a stopover on the road to either Tucumán or western Catamarca. There's a lovely plaza full of mature trees, several friendly places to stay and to eat, and a wonderful small museum. The **Museo Arqueológico Eric Boman** ⓘ *Centro Cultural Yokavil, on the plaza, Mon-Fri 0900-2000, Sat 1000-2000*, houses a fine collection of sophisticated ceramics tracing the development of the various indigenous cultures who lived in the Calchaquí valleys. Ask the well-informed staff to show you around. In the same building is a handicrafts gallery selling weavings, wooden objects, and the delicious local *patero* wine. There is a helpful **tourist kiosk** ⓘ *on the plaza, T03838-421083*, which can provide a map and a full list of places to stay.

In January the town has handicrafts fairs and a live music festival, with the crowning of *la reina de Yokavil* (the old indigenous name for Santa María). For the **Fiesta de San Roque** on August 16, thousands of pilgrims descend on the town, and accommodation fills up fast. There's a *locutorio* on the plaza, the only ATM for miles around on Mitre and Sarmiento, taking Visa and MasterCard, a post office and several service stations. Buses arrive at Avenida 9 de Julio and Maestro Argentino, eight blocks south of the plaza.

Quilmes → *Colour map 1, B2*

ⓘ *32 km north of Santa María, 5 km along a dirt road off R40 (no shade, tiring walk up hill), 0800-1830, US$1 including guided tour and museum. There is a hotel with restaurant, see Sleeping, page 319, and a good café, open until 1830.*

Quilmes is one of the most important archaeological sites in Argentina, sadly little known by most Argentines, who are more likely to associate the name with the country's most popular lager, see box page . Located on the slopes of the Sierra de Quilmes, at an altitude of 1850 m, it has commanding views over the entire valley. The city was home to 5000 Diaguitan people, who lived here peacefully for hundreds of years until the Incas and then the Spanish arrived. What remains today is an extensive network of thousands of roofless rooms bordered with low walls, mostly heavily reconstructed, but walk up to the top of the mountain, and you'll see a beautiful and elaborate lacework which continues right up from the valley to the higher slopes. It's a spectacular site, especially early or late in the day, when the silvery walls are picked out against the pale green of the enormous cacti growing throughout the valley.

South of San Miguel de Tucumán » pp316-322.

Santiago del Estero

→ *Phone code: 0385 Colour map 1, B3 Population: 328,000*

This quiet, provincial town makes a handy stopping point if you're heading from the flat landscape of the Chaco to explore the northwest corner of Argentina but little of the architectural heritage of Argentina's oldest city remains. There are, however, some comfortable places to stay and a couple of museums worth seeing, and the people are among Argentina's most friendly and welcoming.

Santiago was founded in 1553 and was an important base for establishing other major cities in the northwest. As the other cities grew, Santiago was left behind and the town is now a rather impoverished older neighbour. It's a bit run-down, with its plaza and bus station in a shambolic state of affairs, but it has a warm, laid-back atmosphere and the siesta here is legendary.

On the Plaza Libertad stand the **Municipalidad** and **Jefatura de Policia**, built in 1868 in the style of a colonial *cabildo*. On the west side is the **cathedral**, the fifth on the site, dating from 1877. Two blocks southeast of the plaza is the **Convento de Santo Domingo** ⓘ *Urquiza y 25 de Mayo*, containing one of two copies of the 'Turin Shroud', but otherwise unremarkable. Six blocks east of the plaza is the welcome greenery of the **Parque Francisco de Aguirre** which stretches to the river, and includes the town's campsite. There's also a **tourist office** ⓘ *Plaza Libertad, T0385-421 4243*.

The best museum is the **Museo de Ciencias Antropológicas y Naturales** ⓘ *Avellaneda 353, T0385-421 1380, Tue-Sun 0800-2000, free,* with the wonderfully eclectic collection of pre-Hispanic artefacts by brothers Emilio and Duncan Wagner, now sadly haphazardly presented and badly conserved. Amongst the stuffed armadillos, bone flutes, delicate spindles and board-flattened skulls, is a quite breathtaking quantity of beautifully decorated funerary urns, some rare bronze ceremonial *hachas*, and anthropomorphic pieces. Mysterious and amazing.

Termas de Río Hondo

→ *Phone code: 03858 Colour map 1, B3 Population: 28,000 Altitude 265 m*

Argentina's most popular spa town, 65 km northwest of Santiago del Estero, is also its most dreary. It was very popular in the 1950s but much of it remains unmodernized from that era, and the only real reason to visit is if you want to take advantage of the warm mineral-laden waters, which are piped into every hotel in the city. Older Argentines hold it in fond regard and it's a Mecca for visitors with arthritic or skin conditions in July and August, when you'll need to book in advance. Out of season, it's a desperately depressing place. With the cream bulk of the casino dominating the scruffy triangular plaza, the resort consists of 160 hotels interspersed with *alfajores* shops (the much-loved Argentine chocolate maize flour biscuit), mostly in run-down and flaking buildings. Even in high season, there's little to make you feel better here, and nibbling another biscuit is hardly likely to help.

Sleeping

Tucumán city *p312, map p318*

A Catalinas Park, Av Soldati 380, T0381-450 2250, www.catalinaspark.com. The most comfortable place to stay is this luxurious hotel, overlooking Parque 9 de Julio, with comfortable minimalist decor in the bedrooms, outstanding food and service, and pool (open to non-residents), sauna and gym. Good value and highly recommended.

A Suites Garden Park, Av Soldati 330, T0381-431 0700, www.gardenparkhotel.com.ar. The competition next door is this smart and welcoming 4-star, with views over Parque 9 de Julio, pool, gym, sauna, restaurant. Also apartments.

B Swiss Hotel Metropol, 24 de Septiembre 524, T0381-431 1180, www.swisshotelmetropol.com.ar. Central, chic and modern,

Quilmes: not just a lager

Of all the indigenous peoples of Argentina, perhaps the most tragic was the fate that awaited the inhabitants of Quilmes. This ancient city, now an intricate lacework of terraces climbing high up the mountainside, housed around 5000 people from 5000 years ago until AD 117, with a well developed social structure, and its own language, kakán, now extinct. The Quilmes people lived in the plains, but built the site as a defensive stronghold to retreat to in times of attack, since the whole Calchaquí valley was the site of frequent warfare between rival clans. Added to this excellent strategic position, the Quilmes were hard to dominate thanks to their sophisticated weaponry: with *boleadoras* made from stones tied with llama hide thongs, and slings of plaited lambswool, they hurled egg-shaped stones with great accuracy over long distances. Their houses consisted of adjacent dwellings buried some way into the earth, and lined with stone walls, which also served as walkways between houses. Posts of sturdy algarrobo wood were used to support pitched roofs (now vanished), and they lived in clans or family groups. The higher social orders and those who held shamanic or religious positions in the community occupied dwellings highest up the mountainside – closest to the gods.

They cultivated fruit in the valley, beans, potato, pumpkins and maize, using irrigation canals to redirect snowmelt from the mountain tops. Chicha was the popular mildly alcoholic drink made from ground and fermented algarrobo seeds, and their Shamen cured people using local herbs and plants, as they do today.

The Incas were the first to dominate the Quilmes clan, in the late 15th century, but the Quilmes adapted and survived. It was the arrival of the Spanish in the 17th century which proved fatal. After resisting Spanish attacks for many years, the Spanish finally besieged them and cut off all their supplies. Their hillside position proved to be their downfall. In 1668, the Quilmes surrendered, the community was broken up, and the largest group was made to walk to a suburb of Buenos Aires, named Quilmes, after their home. In1812, the last descendent died, and Argentina's most popular lager brewery was later built in the town. Few Argentines are aware that its namesake was this sophisticated civilization.

this is primarily a business hotel, but with its comfortable well-designed rooms, a pool and an excellent restaurant. Good service, highly recommended.

C Carlos V, 25 de Mayo 330, T0381-431 1666, www.redcarlosv.com.ar. Central traditional hotel, in need of renovation but with good service and a civilized restaurant.

C Dallas Hotel, Corrientes 985, T0381-421 8500, www.dallashotel.com.ar. Quite a way from the centre, this is a very welcoming place with large rooms and good bathrooms.

C Premier, Crisóstomo Alvarez 510, T/F0381-431 0381, www.redcarlosv.com.ar. The rooms are spacious and comfortable, and those next to the street are noisy, but the bathrooms are modern, and the staff helpful.

C Francia, Crisóstomo Alvarez 467, T/F0381-431 0781, www.franciahotel.com. A centrally located hotel with plain but comfortable high-ceilinged rooms and renovated bathrooms; cheap apartments for 5 too. A good budget option.

C Versailles, Crisóstomo Alvarez 481, T0381-422 9760, www.hotelversaillestuc.com.ar. A touch of class in this rather charming older place, a lovely open entrance with reproduction furniture, good service and comfortable beds in rather small rooms. Ask for the renovated ones Recommended.

C Miami, Junín 580, T0381-431 0265, hotelmiami@hotmail.com. This is a good small place, 8 blocks away from the plaza. Rooms are plain with a/c and TV, a little overpriced. There is a pool and they offer small discounts for HI members.

E Petit, Crisóstomo Alvarez 765, T0381-421 3902, www.redcarlosv.com.ar.
A rather eccentric hotel, this is a spacious old house with small rooms at the back coming off a modern patio. Pretty basic, but quiet, and cheaper rooms without bath, or fan.

Youth hostels

G pp **Argentina Norte**, Laprida 456, T0381-430 2716, www.hostel.argentinanorte.com. Basic dorms in this central 1920's restored house, with a quiet atmosphere and lovely patios. Free internet, a small travel agency and a double room **E** with its own bath add to the usual hostel services.

G pp **Tucumán Hostel**, Buenos Aires 669, T0381-420 1584, www.tucumanhostel.com. The striking point of this old and quiet house is its beautiful **Parador Tafinisto**, at the bottom of Av Perón. Recommended for *parrilla* with plenty of regional dishes, and live folklore music at the weekends.

Tafí del Valle *p314*

There's lots of comfortable accommodation in Tafí, tending towards the more expensive, with a good range of mid-price hotels, most of them with great views. There's a good value estancia, though, right in the centre of town, and a welcoming small hostel.

B Hostería Tafí del Valle, Av San Martín y Gobernador Campero, T03867-421027, www.soldelvalle.com.ar. Right at the top of the town, on the apex of the semicircular plaza, with splendid views, a pool and an airy restaurant. Its standard rooms are comfortable though rather small, worth paying extra for the larger special ones. As an ACA hotel, there are discounts to members of international automobile clubs, like the AA.

B La Rosada, Belgrano 322, T03867-421323, miguel_torres@sinectis.com.ar. Huge, functional and overpriced rooms, and just off to the west of the plaza with lots of excursions on offer and bikes to borrow.

B Lunahuana, Av Gobernador Critto 540, T03867-421330, www.lunahuana.com.ar. This is the most comfortable and best value hotel in Tafí centre with splendid views from its stylish rooms. There are spacious 2-floor 'duplex' rooms for 4, and a restaurant.

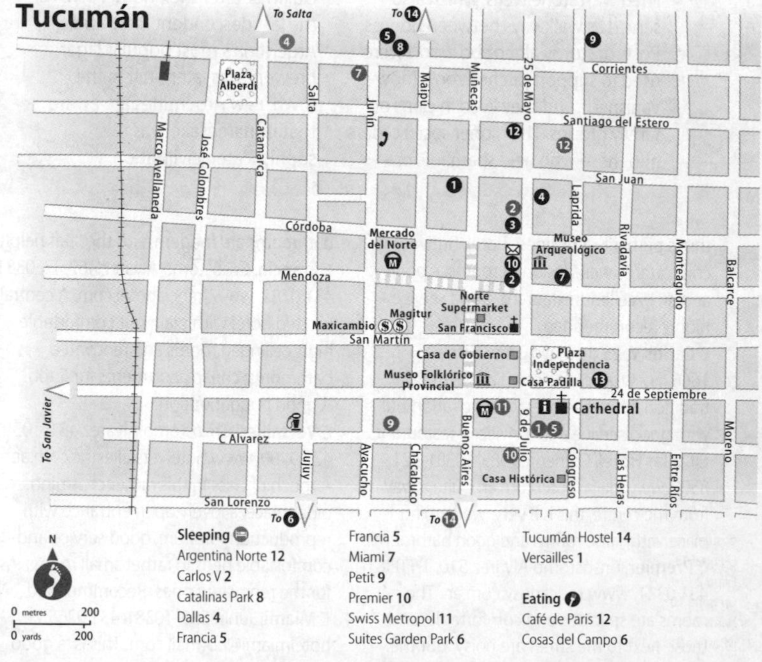

B Mirador del Tafí, on the RP307 just east of the town, T03867-421219, www.miradordeltafi.com.ar. This is the best option in the valley, comfortable and spacious with spectacular views, a fine restaurant, and wonderful service. Recommended.
C Tafí, Av Belgrano 177, T03867-421007, www.hoteltafiweb.com.ar. Simple, welcoming and comfortable rooms in a central location make this a very good choice among mid-range hotels.
D Estancia Los Cuartos, on Av Gobernador Critto y Av Juan Calchaquí, T0381-155874230, www.estancialoscuartos.com. Very good value, and full of character, this 200 year old estancia is right in the middle of town. There are three original rooms, hardly restored, and which retain an eclectic collection of antiques. New rooms fit in well with the old style, but benefit from touches of modern comfort. Recommended. They also offer a day at the estancia, with lunch, excursion and horse riding and a great *té criollo*, US$ 4, with farm cheese that can also be bought at the cheese shop on Av Gobernador Critto. Very welcoming.
F La Cumbre, Av Perón 120, T03867-421768, www.lacumbretafidelvalle.com. Basic and cramped rooms with views to a grey patio make this a most uninspiring place to stay. However, this hostel is centrally located and the helpful owner runs a very active tour agency (see Activities and tours below).

Amaichá del Valle *p315*
F El Portal de Amaichá, on the main road, next to the petrol station, T03892-421140, www.elportaldeamaicha.0m.com. Quiet and comfortable accommodation with great views either in simple rooms or in cabañas.

Santa María *p315*
D Hotel de Turismo, San Martín 450, T03892-420240, cielosdeloeste@yahoo.com.ar. Occupying a block of its own 2 blocks east of the plaza, this large institutional place is the best option, with several newer and very comfortable rooms. Free internet, a restaurant and a pool surrounded by a large garden.
D Plaza, San Martín 258, on the plaza, T03892-420309. Small, simple and rather dark but comfy rooms all with bath and TV, breakfast included.
E Inti-Huaico, Belgrano 146, T03892-420476, pirka@cosama.com.ar. A bargain with nice clean rooms with bath, friendly owners, and lovely gardens.

Camping
Municipal campsite at end of Sarmiento, about 6 blocks east of the plaza, T03892-421083, with **F** albergue and restaurant too.

Quilmes *p315*
B Parador Ruinas de Quilmes, T03892-421075. Make the most of the site by staying in this peaceful, very comfortable hotel. Its spacious, stylish interior was boldly designed by Héctor Cruz (see Amaichá above), and filled with his weavings and ceramics, and there's a good restaurant, and free camping. Best of all, there are great views of Quilmes: get up early and have them to yourself. Recommended. Restaurant open to residents only.

Santiago del Estero *p316*
B Carlos V, Independencia 110, T0385-424 0303, www.carlosvhotel.com. On the corner of the plaza. The most expensive and luxurious hotel is still good value for a really

Costumbres Argentinas **1**
El Portal **13**
Filipo **2**
Gregorio **10**
Harris **7**
Il Postino **3**
Klo y Klo **5**
La Leñita **4**
Los Negros **9**
Panadería Villecco **8**
Sir Harris **7**

comfortable international-style hotel with an all year round pool, a good restaurant, and elegant rooms ; go for the spacious superior rooms if you can afford it.

C **Hotel Libertador**, Catamarca 47, T0385-421 9252, www.hotellibertadorsrl.com.ar. This smart place has a spacious light lounge and plain well equipped rooms. There's an attractive leafy patio with pool (summer only) and a very elegant restaurant, also open to non residents. A peaceful place to stay 5 blocks south of the plaza in the better-off part of town.

C **Hotel Centro**, 9 de Julio 131, T0385-422 4350, www.hotelcentro.com.ar. Light, prettily decorated rooms, all with good bathrooms and minibar and an airy first floor restaurant. Recommended.

D **Nuevo Hotel Santiago**, Buenos Aires 60, T0385-421 4949, nuevohotelsantiago@arnet.com.ar. Modernized and comfortable, this is the better of the remaining decent budget choices. The rooms are small but well equipped and it's quiet for such a central location, a block from the plaza.

D **Savoy**, Tucumán 39, T0385-421 1234. Cheapest and with most character is the faded grandeur of this central wonderful art nouveau building with swirling stairwell. Rooms are large, simple, and airy, an excellent budget option.

Camping

Las Casuarinas, Parque Aguirre, T0385-421 1390. Insect repellent essential.

Termas de Río Hondo *p316*

Ask the helpful tourist office for accommodation advice, at Caseros 268, T03858-421969 or at Av Alberdi 245, T03858-421571, or www.lastermasderiohondo.com

L **Hotel de los Pinos**, Maipú 201, T03858-421043, www.lospinoshotel.com.ar. The best option, in an attractive Spanish-style building a little removed from the centre in a huge park, with pools, and great comfort, including rooms with private thermal baths. Rates are for all-inclusive stays.

B **Hotel Termal Rio Hondo**, Sarmiento 119, T03858-421455, www.hoteltermalriohondo.com.ar. Most comfortable in centre with modern rooms, medical services, pool for thermal baths and a good restaurant too.

Eating

Tucumán city *p312, map p318*

There are plenty of places to eat along 25 de Mayo, which stretches north from the west side of the plaza.

TT **La Leñita**, 25 de Mayo 377. Highly recommended for excellent *parrilla*, and superb salads, one of the best on the street, also offering live folklore music at weekends.

TT **Il Postino**, 25 de Mayo y Córdoba. A hugely popular pizza place and café, stylishly designed, with lots of brick and wood, and a buzzing atmosphere. Generous pizzas, plus tapas and tortillas too. Recommended.

TT **Harris**, Mendoza y Laprida. A Tucumán institution, serving really good imaginative dishes, some vegetarian choices, pizzas and sandwiches.

TT **Los Negros**, Laprida 623. Good for *parrilla* and *tenedor libre* for US$9.

T **Cosas del Campo**, Lavalle 857. South of centre, next to Plaza San Martín, this small place is becoming an unmissable point in town for its delicious *empanadas*. Also for take-away at T0381-420 1758.

T **El Portal**, 24 de Septiembre 351 (at the back of a crafts market). Unpretentious and popular, this large place and its attractive patio makes an ideal start for gorgeous *empanadas*, *locros*, *humitas* and *tamales*.

T **Klo y Klo**, Junin 657. A wide variety of excellent dishes, in a welcoming rather charming environment. Closed on Sun evenings and Mon.

Cafés

Café de Paris, Santiago del Estero 502, (25 de Mayo corner). A tapas bar and stylish little restaurant.

Costumbres Argentinas, San Juan 666. Good atmosphere in this intimate bar for late drinks.

Filipo, Mendoza y 25 de Mayo. A very popular smart café, with a nice atmosphere. Good place for a coffee or a drink.

Gregorio, on 25 de Mayo, 2 blocks north of Plaza Independencia. Another pleasant place for a coffee, good salads and pasta.

Panadería Villecco, Corrientes 751. Superb bread, pastries, and *pan integral* (wholemeal).

Plaza de Almas, Santa Fe y Maipú. North of centre, this bar attracts young crowds in the late evenings.

Tafí del Valle *p314*

El Mangrullo, opposite Hotel Mirador del Tafí. A good mid-range family *parrilla* with pastas too, and a play area for kids.

Hotel Mirador del Tafí, see above. Good value, and excellent food at this hotel.

El Pabellón, corner of Critto. Cheapest of all, recommended for pasta.

El Portal de la Villa, Av Perón. Very good food, excellent empanadas.

Parador Tafinisto, at the bottom of Av Perón. Frequently recommended for *parrilla* with plenty of regional dishes, and live folklore music at the weekends.

Santa María *p315*

There are some good and lively places on the plaza, including:

El Colonial del Valle. Serves *empanadas* and other meals, and it is also a nice *confitería*.

Jandar. Serves excellent and cheap *empanadas* pizzas and salads.

Santiago del Estero *p316*

The better restaurants at **Libertador** and **Carlos V** hotels.

Mia Mamma, on the plaza, 24 de Septiembre 15. Often recommended this is a cheery place for *parrilla* and tasty pastas, with good salad *libre* starters, and friendly service.

Periko's, on the plaza. Lively and popular, for *lomitos* and pizzas, popular with a younger crowd.

Cafés, bakeries and heladerías

Cerecetto, a couple of blocks from the plaza, Córdoba y Libertad. Best ice cream in town.

Termas de Río Hondo *p316*

San Cayetano or homely Renacimiento, both on the main drag Sarmiento, and reasonably priced for *parrilla*.

El Chorizo Loco, Alberdi and Sarmiento. A very cheap lively pizzeria.

Activities and tours

Tucumán city *p312, map p318*

Duport Turismo, Congreso 160, T0381-422 0000, duporttur@tucbbs.com.ar. Same tours as Turismo del Tucumán plus a circuit of the local valleys, 6 hrs, US$17, Parque Alpa Puyo, half-day US$12, El Cadillal, half-day US$15.

Turismo del Tucumán, Crisóstomo Alvarez 435, local 2, T0381-422 7636, www.turismodeltucuman.com. Informative tours to local places, Quilmes, full day, US$35, and Tafí del Valle, full day US$22.

Tafí del Valle *p314*

Tour operators

El Puesto, Av Lola Mora (at La Costa district), T03867-421241, jjcritto@hotmail.com. Jerónimo Critto organizes horseback excursions to the nearby mountains from a few hours long to several-day journeys.

La Cumbre, Av Perón 120, T03867-421768, www.lacumbretafidelvalle.com. An energetic and friendly company who offer 4WD excursions, and full-day walks to all the nearby peaks, to waterfalls Cascada lo Alisos and ruins at Valle de la Ciénaga. Also a recommended trek to Cerro Muñoz, (4437 m), with an *asado* at the summit.

Transport

Tucumán city *p312, map p318*

Air Aeropuerto Benjamín Matienzo is 10 km east of town. **Transfer Express** buses meet all flights, charging US$1.70 from airport to Plaza Independencia or US$3.35 to/from hotels in town, office at the airport, T0381-426 7945. Taxi US$4. To **Buenos Aires** via **Córdoba**, AR/Austral, T0831-431 1098.

Bus Local bus services operate on *cospeles*, US$0.35, which you buy in advance in kiosks. For long-distance services, the modern terminal has 70 ticket offices. There is a helpful information kiosk opposite **Disco** T0381-422 2221. The terminal is 6 blocks east of Plaza Independencia on Av Brígido Terán, with huge shopping complex, left luggage lockers (US$1), tourist information office (by *boletería* 1), *locutorios*, toilets and an ATM. Bus No 4 goes to the centre from outside terminal (on Av Benjamín Aráoz), to Córdoba y 25 de Mayo. Taxi to centre US$0.50-1.

To **Buenos Aires**, many companies, 14-16 hrs US$28-50. To **Tafí del Valle**, Aconquija 2½ hrs, US$4. To **Salta** direct (not via Cafayate), 4-4½ hrs, several companies US$10-14. To **Cafayate**, Aconquija, 5½ hrs (6½ hrs if via Santa María), US$9. To **Posadas**, Vosa, 16 hrs, US$27. To **Mendoza**, 14 hrs, US$26-34, via **Catamarca**, **La Rioja**, and **San**

Juan. To **Catamarca**, Aconquija and other companies, 4 hrs, US$6. To **Andalgalá**, Gutiérrez, 1 daily, US$7. To **Córdoba**, 8 hrs, US$13-17. To **Santiago del Estero**, 2 hrs, US$4-5. To **La Quiaca** (border with Bolivia), Balut and Andesmar, 10-11 hrs, US$16. To **Santiago** (Chile) via **Mendoza**, Andesmar and El Rápido Internacional, daily, 22-24 hrs, US$35-50. To **Lima** (Perú), **El Rápido Internacional**, 3 a week, 3½ days via **Mendoza**, US$145.

Car hire Movil Renta, San Lorenzo 370, T0381-431 0550, www.movilrenta.com.ar, and at airport. Donde Rent a Car, Gob Gutiérrez 1383, T0381-428 3626.

Train To **Buenos Aires** via **Rosario** with Ferrocentral, T0381-430 9220, for more information see Buenos Aires Mitre line, page 107.

Tafí del Valle *p314*
Bus There's a smart Aconquija terminal on Av Critto, which you might mistake for another hotel, with café, toilets, luggage lockers and helpful information, T0381-421025. To/from **Tucumán**, Aconquija, 8 daily, 2½ hrs, US$4. To **Cafayate**, 3 a day, 2½ hrs, US$5.50 (4 hrs via **Santa María**). To **El Mollar** several daily, US$0.70. Buses to **Tucumán** stop at El Mollar on request.

Amaichá del Valle *p315*
Bus to **Tucumán**, 5 hrs, 6 daily , US$4.50, sit on the right for best views. To **Santa María**, Gutiérrez, 15 mins, US$0.70.

Santa María *p315*
Bus To **Tucumán**, Aconquija, 4½-5 hrs, US$5, 5 daily. To **Cafayate**, 2 hrs, Aconquija and El Indio, daily, US$3. To **Salta**, El Indio, 5-6 hrs, daily, US$10. Parra and Cayetano to **Belén**, 4 hrs, US$7, check with tourist office for current times. To **Amaichá del Valle**, Gutiérrez, 15 mins, US$0.70. To **Catamarca**, Gutiérrez, daily (except Sat), US$10.

Quilmes *p315*
Bus For a day trip take 0600 Aconquija bus from **Cafayate** to **Santa María**, after an hour get off at stop, 5 km from site, or take 0700 (not on Thu) El Indio bus from Santa María. Either way you'll have to walk the 5 km up the hill. Take 1130 bus back to Cafayate, US$1.60. Or take a tour from Cafayate (see page 283).

Santiago del Estero *p316*
Air Mal Paso airport is on the northwestern outskirts. Aerolíneas Argentinas/Austral to **Buenos Aires** and **Tucumán**. Aerolíneas Argentinas, 24 de Septiembre 547, T0385-422 4335 .

Bus The renovated terminal at Gallo 480 has toilets, a *locutorio*, basic café and *kioskos*, as well as stalls selling food. **Córdoba** 6 hrs US$8-10; **Jujuy**, 8 hrs US$13; **Salta** 6-6½ hrs US$ 11; **Tucumán** 2 hrs, US$4-5; to **Catamarca** go via Tucuman.

Taxi Very cheap, US$0.80 into town, to save you the 8 block walk, though if you find a taxi little further from the terminal, you'll avoid being surcharged by some taxi drivers.

Termas de Río Hondó *p316*
Bus The terminal is at Las Heras y España, 8 blocks north of centre near R9, but buses will drop you at the plaza, on Alberdi, opposite the casino. To **Santiago del Estero**, 1 hr, US$1.70 and to **Tucumán**, 2 hrs, US$3; several to **Buenos Aires**, 13-14 hrs, US$25-40.

Directory

Tucumán city *p312, map p318*
Banks Most banks are along San Martín especially the 700 block between Junín and Maipú. **Maguitur**, San Martín 765, T0381-431 0127, accepts TCs. **Maxicambio**, San Martín 779, T0381-431 0020, for currency exchange. **Post office** Córdoba y 25 de Mayo, Mon-Fri 0800-1400, 1700-2000, Sat 0900-1300. **Telephone** Lots of *locutorios* all over the centre, many with broadband internet access.

Tafí del Valle *p314*
Banks ATM at Banco de Tucumán, Miguel Critto 311, T03867-421033. All the major international cards accepted.

Santiago del Estero *p316*
Banks Banco Francés, 9 de Julio y 24 de Septiembre.

The Northeast

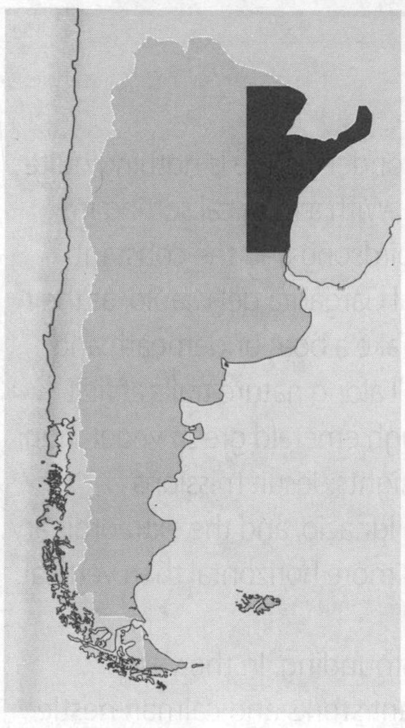

Footprint features

Introduction

Of all Argentina's many natural wonders, there is nothing quite as spectacular as the Iguazú Falls . With a magical setting in subtropical rainforest, alive with birdsong and the constant dancing of butterflies, the colossal Garganta del Diablo at their centre is an unforgettable sight. Take a boat underneath and get drenched in the spray, or stroll along nature trails at first light. Along red earth roads through emerald green vegetation, Minions province holds other delights: Jesuit missions unearthed from the jungle at San Ignacio, and the extraordinary Saltos de Moconá, 3000 m of falls more horizontal than vertical.

El Litoral's wealth of wildlife is astounding. In the vast wetlands of Esteros del Iberá, giant storks and caiman nestle between floating islands and water lilies. In Mburucuyá tall palms wave in grasslands and passion flowers thrive in abundance. In the Chaco, watch out for pumas and monkeys, while the palm forests of Entre Rios are centuries old. Stop on the lazy Paraná river for relaxed, pretty Colón with its port and sandy beaches and the faded splendour of Paraná . For more stimulation, historical Corrientes is a riot at Carnival time, and lively Rosario's hotbed of culture produces the country's finest musicians.

The northeast's rich culture stems from its indigenous peoples, the Guaraní and Wichí, who produce beautiful art. The gently meandering rivers set the pace, giving the land its lush vegetation and generating in its people a charming laid-back warmth. *Yerba mate* is grown for the nation's favourite drink, and everywhere you'll encounter friends gathered on riverbanks on balmy afternoons sipping from their *mate* gourd.

★ Don't miss ...

1 **Yacutinga Lodge** A real taste of life in the subtropical jungle, an eco-lodge with excellent guides for walks and boat trips, page 334.

2 **Surubí** The delicious river fish, cooked to perfection at La Rueda restaurant in Puerto Iguazú, page 335.

3 **Jungle Explorer** Take the fast boat rushing underneath the Iguazú Falls for a real sense of the mighty power of the water, page 335.

4 **Jesuit missions** See the ruins at San Ignacio Mini, where thousands of Guaraní worked in relative harmony with their Jesuit masters, page 344.

5 **Esteros del Iberá** Estancias Posada de la Laguna and Rincón del Socorro take you to see the fabulous birdlife, butterflies and basking caiman on these vast wetlands, page 351.

The Northeast

Iguazú Falls

Any trip to Argentina should include the Iguazú Falls. They're the biggest falls in South America – half as high again as Niagara – and a spectacular experience. You can get right up close to the water as it gushes down, along paths which enable you to enjoy the natural splendour of their subtropical setting, filled with birdsong and vividly coloured butterflies. In all, there are 275 falls stretching over 2.7 km but the main attraction is the Garganta del Diablo, where walkways take you right above the falls to see the smooth river transformed in an instant into a seething torrent as the water crashes 74 m over a horseshoe-shaped precipice onto basalt rocks below, filling the air with bright spray and a deafening roar. The whole chasm is filled constantly with billowing clouds of mist in which great dusky swifts miraculously wheel and dart, and an occasional rainbow hovers. Then you can walk close to the bottom of the immensely wide Saltos Bossetti and Dos Hermanos, or take a boat trip which speeds you beneath the falling water to get a total drenching. Viewed from below, the rush of water is unforgettably beautiful, falling through jungle filled with begonias, orchids, ferns, palms and toucans, flocks of parrots, cacique birds and myriad butterflies. There are some longer trails enabling you to enjoy the diverse flora and fauna in this national park, and several excellent guides on hand whose expertise will considerably add to your pleasure. The whole experience is uplifting and easily worth at least a couple of days of your itinerary.

Argentina shares the falls with Brazil and you can visit them from either side for two quite different experiences. The Brazilian side has a smaller, more restricted park, and offers a panoramic view from its limited trails but you're kept at a distance from the falls themselves. If you have to choose just one, go for the Argentine one side, where you can get closer to the falls, walk in the jungle and explore the rainforest. Allow at least two days to see both sides, or to return to the park a second time in Argentina (half price). The most pleasant place to stay is undoubtedly the laid-back Argentine town of Puerto Iguazú, where hotels are cheaper and the streets are far safer than in the Brazilian city of Foz do Iguaçu, where accommodation is plentiful but there is a serious crime problem. On either side, most establishments will accept Brazilian reais, Argentine pesos or dollars. In this chapter the Argentine side of the falls is described first, with the national park, then Puerto Iguazú, and all the listings information. Then the Brazilian side follows, with Foz do Iguaçu and its listings. » *For Sleeping, Eating and other listings, see pages 332-337.*

Ins and outs

Getting there and around The falls on both sides are contained within national parks, both of which charge entry fees and have well organized free transport to take you to the waterfalls. **In Argentina**, park entry costs US$10 (Argentines pay US$4), and you should allow at least a day (it takes six hours to see the main attractions if you go fast), starting early (park opens at 0800). If you find a brisk pace exhausting in the heat of summer, you can revisit the park the next day at half the price. Just opposite a free entrance, a free train takes you from the visitor centre to Estación Garganta, where a 1-km long walkway leads to the Garganta del Diablo falls and then to Estación Cataratas, where two trails, taking at least an hour each, offer great views of the falls and a free boat crossing to Isla San Martín for even closer views. **On the Brazilian side**, park entry costs US$6.50 and a visit takes around two hours, with free buses taking you to the start of a walkway with steps down to the falls.

On both sides there are optional extra boat trips right up to the falls themselves: **Jungle Explorer** (see page 335) on the Argentine side is best, with a great trip that takes you rushing right underneath the falls. Both parks have visitor centres, though the Argentine centre is far superior. There are also cafés and restaurants.

Dos and don'ts

- Get to the park as early as you can in the morning to spot wildlife.
- Wear a hat, good sunscreen and sunglasses: the sun is fierce here.
- In the rainy season, when water levels are high, wear waterproof coats or swimming costumes for some of the lower catwalks and for boat trips.
- Bring insect repellent.
- Wear shoes with good soles, as the walkways can be very slippery.
- Protect cameras and binoculars from the spray with a plastic bag.
- Take all rubbish out of the park with you, or use the bins.
- Don't feed animals or birds, don't damage the flora, and walk quietly so as not to disturb wildlife.

When to visit The falls can be visited all year round. There's officially no rainy season, though it tends to rain more in March and June and there can be heavy downfalls in summer. The average temperatures are 25°C in summer and 15°C in winter. The busiest times are the Argentine holiday periods – January, Easter week and July – when you must book accommodation in advance, and on Sundays when helicopter tours over the falls from the Brazilian side are particularly popular (and noisy). Remember that between October and March Argentina is one hour behind Brazil (daylight saving dates change each year) and, from December to March, one hour behind Paraguay.

Background

The first European visitor to the falls was the Spaniard Alvar Núñez Cabeza de Vaca in 1542, on his search for a connection between the Brazilian coast and the Río de la Plata: he named them the *Saltos de Santa María*. Though the falls were well known to the Jesuit missionaries, they were forgotten until the area was explored by a Brazilian expedition sent out by the Paraguayan president, Solano López in 1863.

Parque Nacional Iguazú (Argentina) ▲ ▸▸ *pp332-337.*

➔ *www.parquesnacionales.gov.ar, www.iguazuargetina.com*

Created in 1934, the park extends over an area of 67,000 ha of dense subtropical rainforest. There is excellent access to the falls themselves from various angles and along two further trails that wind through the forest to give you an experience of the wildlife. Visits begin at the visitor centre, with free transport by mini train to the start of the walkways and trails.

Ins and outs

Getting there The park lies 20 km east of the town of Puerto Iguazú along Route 12. **El Práctico** buses, T03757-420377, run from the Hito Tres Fronteras junction in Puerto Iguazú, 0700-1930 on the hour and 30 minutes past, stopping at the main bus terminal 10 minutes later, and arriving at the visitor centre after 45 minutes, US$1.50. Buses return from the park 0750-2020. You can get on or off the bus at any point in the journey. For transport between the Argentine and Brazilian sides see Foz do Iguaçu, page 338, and Border with Brazil, page 331. In case of emergency, call T03757-420180, or go to the emergency centre near the Old Hotel; turn left at the tower heading from Circuito Superior to Inferior. ▸▸ *For further information, see Transport, page 336.*

Park information The park is open every day of the year: 1 April to 31 August 0800-1800, and 1 September to 31 March 0800-1900. Entry US$10 for all foreign visitors. Get your ticket stamped as you leave for half-price entry next day.

There's an excellent **visitor centre (Centro de Interpretación)** on the right after you enter, with information and photographs of the flora and fauna, and the history of the area from the earliest settlers. Opposite, you'll find plenty of places to eat in the **Patio de Comidas**, including a pizzeria, parrilla (steak) and snack bar. As you walk towards the barriers where you pay the entry fee, there are excellent souvenir shops selling both commercial souvenirs and local Guaraní handicrafts (though these are cheaper when bought from the Guaraní people themselves, just inside the entrance). These shops will also download digital photos to CD. Opposite are clean toilets, *locutorio* (public phone centre) and ATMs. Further along the 'Sendero Verde' towards the start of the 'Circuitos Inferior' and 'Superior' there's a great open-air café (fresh orange juice and fruit salad recommended), *locutorio* and *parrilla* (US$6 for *parrilla tenedor libre*). At the **Estación Garganta** there's another little café and shop selling postcards, water and film.

The **guardería** (ranger station) is next to the Estación Cataratas, on the way to the Circuitos Inferior and Superior. The *guardaparques* are hugely knowledgeable about the park and will give you detailed information on wildlife and where to spot it, and will even accompany you if they're not too busy. They also hand out a helpful leaflet with a clear map of the park, and another in English, *Birds of Iguazú*.

Recommended books *The Laws of the Jungle* by Santiago G de la Vega, and *Iguazu Life and Colour*, both around US$6, available in English from visitor centres throughout Puerto Iguazú. Also, *Birds of Southern South America and Antarctica*, by De la Peña and Rumboll, published by Harper Collins, 1998.

Around the Iguazú Falls

Wildlife

You'll see amazingly rich wildlife whatever time you visit the park: there are more than 430 species of birds, 70 species of mammals and over a hundred species of butterflies. But you'll need to come in the early morning or late afternoon to stand a good chance of seeing the more elusive species: pumas and tapirs. Look out for restless and curious brown capuchin monkeys, seen in groups of around 20, howler monkeys and friendly coati with their striped tails. Toucans are ubiquitous, with their huge orange cartoon beaks, and also the curious plush crested jays, black with pale yellow breasts, who perch inquisitively around the park's restaurants. You'll also see two kinds of vultures wheeling above the falls themselves, both with fringed wing tips: the red-headed turkey vulture, and the black vulture whose wing tips are white. You should spot blue-winged parakeets, the red-rumped cacique which builds hanging nests on *pindo* palms, and fruit-eaters like the magpie tanager and the colourful purple-throated euphonia. The butterflies are stunning: look out for electric blue *morpho* butterflies, as big as your hand, the poisonous red and black *heliconius* and species of *Papilionidae* and *Pieridae*, with striking black and white designs.

Trails

Garganta del Diablo From the visitor centre a small gas-run train (free), the *Tren de la Selva*, whisks visitors on a 25-minute (2.3 km) trip through the jungle to the Estacíon Garganta, from where it's a 1-km walk along walkways (fine for wheelchairs) across the wide Río Iguazú to the park's centrepiece, the Garganta del Diablo falls. Trains leave Estación Central, just beyond the Visitor Centre, on the hour and 30 minutes past the hour, and leave Estación Cataratas (see map) at 15 and 45 minutes past the hour (either direction). Allow two hours for the whole trip: train, walking, watching the falls and photos.

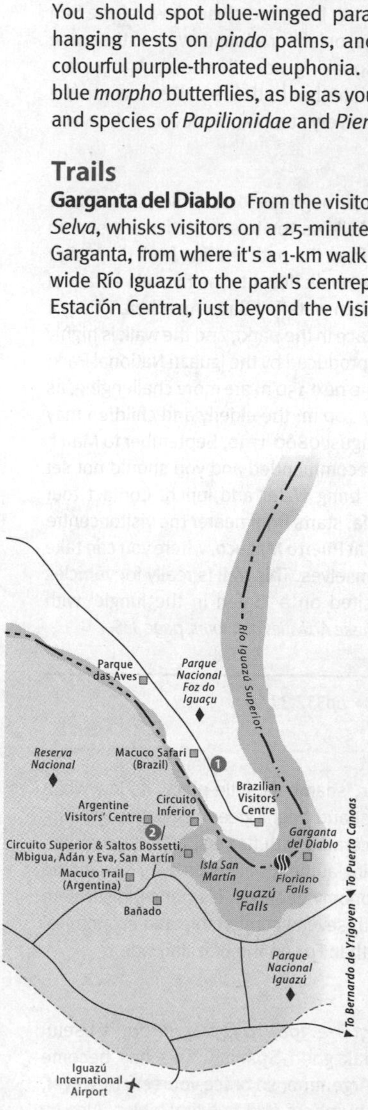

Circuito Inferior and Circuito Superior There are excellent views of the wider range of falls, from Salto San Martín to Salto Dos Hermanos, from the two well-organized trails along sturdy catwalks: the **Circuito Superior** (650 m) and **Circuito Inferior** (1400 m), both taking around 1½ to two hours to complete. To reach these, get off the train at the Estación Cataratas (after a 10-minute journey) and follow signs a short distance to where the trails begin. Alternatively, you can walk from the visitor centre along the Sendero Verde to the Estación Cataratas, which takes 10-15 minutes and avoids waiting for the next train.

Start with the **Circuito Superior**, a level path which takes you along the westernmost line of falls – Saltos Dos Hermanos, Bossetti, Bernabé Mendez, Mbigua (Guarani for cormorant) and San Martín – allowing you to see these falls from above. This path is safe for those with walking difficulties, wheelchairs and pushchairs, but you should wear supportive non-slippery shoes.

The **Circuito Inferior** takes you down to the water's edge via a series of steep stairs and walkways with superb views of both San Martín falls and the Garganta del Diablo from a distance, and then up close to Salto Bossetti. Wheelchair users, pram pushers, and those who aren't good with steps should go down by the exit route for a smooth and easy descent. There's a café on the way down and plenty of shade. You could then return to the **Estación Cataratas** to take the train to Estación Garganta, at 10 minutes and 40 minutes past the hour, and see the falls close up from above.

Isla San Martín An optional extra hour-long circuit is to take the free two-minute ferry ride (leaves every 10 minutes, or on demand) at the very bottom of the Circuito Inferior, which crosses to the small hilly island of Isla San Martín where two trails lead to *miradores* (viewpoints): take the right-hand path for good close views of the San Martín Falls and straight ahead to Salto Rivadavia, or left for a longer walk to the same place. Bathing on the beach here is strictly speaking not allowed, but there are usually a few Argentines sunning themselves. Note that both the paths down to the ferry and up on to the *miradores* on the island are very steep and uneven. Take water to drink, as there are no services.

Alternative trails The park offers two more trails through the forest which allow you to get closer to the wildlife: the **Macuco Nature Trail** allows you to see particularly superb bird life, 7 km return, (allow seven hours) starts from the path leading from the Visitor Centre to the Sheraton Hotel, and is a magnificent walk down to the river via a natural pool (El Pozón) fed by a slender, ice-cold, 20-m-high waterfall **Salto Arrechea**. This is a good place for bathing (and the only permitted place in the park), and the walk is highly recommended. See the helpful leaflet in English produced by the Iguazú National Park: *Macuco Nature Trail*. The first 3 km are easy but the next 150 m are more challenging, as the path descends steeply, before the final easy 200 m; the elderly and children may find this route tough. The path is open April to August 0800-1730, September to March 0800-1830, but leaving in the early morning is recommended and you should not set out later than 1500. There are no services, so bring water and lunch. Contact tour agencies for guided walks. The **Sendero Yacaratía**, starts from nearer the visitor centre and reaches the river by a different route, ending at **Puerto Macuco**, where you can take the *Jungle Explorer* boat to the see the falls themselves. This trail is really for vehicles and less pleasant for walkers, so it's best visited on a 'Safari in the Jungle' with **Explorador Expediciones.** » *For further information see Activities and tours, page 335.*

Puerto Iguazú » *pp332-337.*

→ *Phone code: 03757 Colour map 2, A3 Population: 19,000*

Puerto Iguazú (210 m) is a friendly, atmospheric, shambolic little place, its low white buildings splashed with the red dust from roads, and bright green vegetation growing abundantly everywhere. Its houses are neat, decorated with flowers, and although the centre is slightly chaotic, the town has an appealing authentic life of its own, despite the massive daily influx of tourists on whom the economy depends. It's not sophisticated, but it's a pleasant place to walk around, and with several comfortable and economical places to stay, it's a much more appealing base than Foz on the Brazilian side.

Ins and outs

The **tourist information office** ⓘ *Av Victoria Aguirre 396, T03757-420800*, is useful only for the very patient and those who speak good Spanish. This has become notorious as the rudest and most unhelpful in Argentina, so brace yourself. However, they do have a basic map with useful phone numbers and bus timetables. Also try www.misiones.gov.ar and www.iguazuturismo.gov.ar.

Sights

The town's main street is Avenida Victoria Aguirre where, at No 66, you will find the Iguazú National park information office, **Parque Nacional Iguazú** ⓘ *T03757-491444, T03757-420382, 0900-2200, www.iguazuargentina.com, in park T03757-420180*. This avenue runs northwest from the entrance to the town to the little plaza at its hub, and changes names to Avenida Tres Fronteras as it turns east and heads to the spectacular viewpoint *mirador* high above the meeting of rivers Paraná and Iguazú, known as the **Hito Tres Fronteras** (three borders landmark). You can also reach this point via an attractive *costanera*, running above the Río Iguazú, past the small port where boats leave for cruises along the Paraná and to Paraguay. At the Hito, there's a string of touristy souvenir stands, where children will press you to buy orchid plants, and little rolls of the local *chipita* bread, made from mandioc root, and very tasty. The views over the rivers and neighbouring Paraguay and Brazil are impressive, and you can enjoy them at leisure over a beer at the atmospheric **La Reserva** pub opposite, (see Bars and clubs, page 335).

There a couple of interesting projects worth visiting for a greater appreciation of the area. **La Aripuca** ⓘ *T03757-423488, www.aripuca.com.ar, US$1.30, turn of Ruta 12 at km 4.5 just after Hotel Cataratas; or get off the bus here and walk 250 m*, is a charming centre for appreciation of the native trees of the forest – a good option for families if it's raining. Aripuca is a traditional Guaraní trap for birds, and a giant version of the pyramidic structure has been made from the fallen logs of 30 ancient trees of different species. A 30-minute guided tour (English, Spanish or German) explains all about the tree life, and then you can clamber up their trunks, or enjoy the sculpture from enormous chairs made from tree roots. In a traditional *choza* (hut) there's excellent produce and high quality handicrafts for sale, made by the nearby Andresito community. Sponsor a living tree in the forest to protect it! Recommended. Nearby, **Güira Oga** (Casa de los Pájaros) ⓘ *daily 0830-1800, US$1, turn off Ruta 12 at Hotel Orquídeas Palace; T03757-423980, mobile T15670684, and the entrance is 800 m further along the road from Aripuca*, is a sanctuary for birds that have been injured, or rescued from traffickers. Here, they are cured and reintroduced to the wild; exquisite parrots, magnificent birds of prey. A 1 km-long trail from the road winds through forest, and through the large aviaries, with families of monkeys in trees overhead. Endangered species are bred here, and eagles and hawks are taught to hunt, in an entirely self-funded family enterprise. Inspiring and informative. A guided visit in English or Spanish takes 40 minutes, after which you can wander around at your leisure, and enjoy the peace of the place.

Border with Brazil

This crossing via the Puente Tancredo Neves is straightforward, and if crossing on a day visit no immigration formalities are required, so you should state clearly if you need your passport stamped on re-entry for another three months in the country. Argentine immigration is at the Brazilian end of the bridge, and if entering Argentina buses stop at immigration. The Brazilian consulate is in Puerto Iguazú, Córdoba 264, T03757-421348.

Border with Paraguay

The ferry service from the port in Puerto Iguazú to Tres Fronteras is for locals only (no immigration facilities). Crossing to Paraguay is via Puente Tancredo Neves to Brazil and then via the Puente de la Amistad to Ciudad del Este. Brazilian entry and exit stamps are not required unless you are stopping in Brazil. There is a US$3 tax to enter Paraguay. The Paraguayan consulate is at Bompland 355.

Iguazú means 'big water' in the local Guaraní language (i = water, guazú = big)

Sleeping

Puerto Iguazú *p330, map p332*
The Brazilian side is favoured by tour operators because of the profusion of large hotels, but the city is dangerous at night, so it's much better to stay on the Argentine side. Puerto Iguazú is cheaper, the town is definitely safer and access to the more interesting Argentine side of the falls is naturally much easier. Hilton and Hyatt hotels are under construction at the time of going to press. Also consider staying at the **Yacutinga Jungle Lodge** nearby.

LL Iguazú Grand Hotel Resort and Casino, RN12, Km 1640, on the road to the border, T03757-498050, www.iguazugrand hotel.com. 5-star luxury and elegant style in this opulent modern palace, with delightful gardens, pool, and casino. Sumptuous rooms, superb restaurant (US$22 for buffet dinner). Also a fitness centre and beauty salon. The most luxurious hotel on the Argentine side.

LL-L Sheraton Internacional Iguazú Resort, T03757-491800, www.sheraton. com/iguazu. The only hotel within the park itself, with unsurpassable wonderful views of the falls from half of the stylish rooms (the others have attractive forest views) and open access to all the trails directly from the gardens, so that you can even visit the park and its wildlife before breakfast. It's the standard international style, but access to nature makes it the best place to stay in the area. The service is excellent, there's a good restaurant (dinner buffet US$12) and breakfasts. There's a pool, tennis courts, putting green, sauna, bikes for hire (US$2.50, half a day). Transfer to airport, taxi US$12.

L Esturión, Av Tres Fronteras 650, T03757-420100, www.hotelesturion.com. On the road to Hito Tres Fronteras, above the river, with panoramic views from its pool, a 1970's hotel smartly renovated to a luxurious standard. Comfortable modern rooms, and great for families, with nightly entertainment, pool, tennis courts, volley ball and football.

AL Cataratas, RN 12, Km 4, T03757-421100, www.hotelcataratas.com. Not the 5-star it claims to be, but a standard modern hotel popular with agencies, who offer more economical packages with flight included (see *Clarin* newspaper on Sun). There's a pool, gym and tennis courts, nightly

Puerto Iguazú

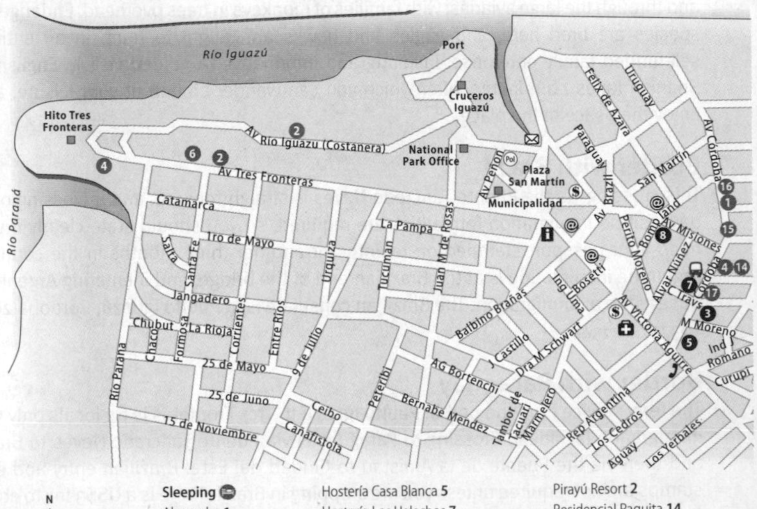

Sleeping
Alexander **1**
Correcaminos **4**
El Güembe **18**
Esturión **6**
Hostel Park Iguazú **3**
Hostería Casa Blanca **5**
Hostería Los Helechos **7**
Iguazú Grand Hotel Resort & Casino **8**
Iguazú Jungle Lodge **9**
Lilian **12**
Noelia **10**
Pirayú Resort **2**
Residencial Paquita **14**
Residencial San Fernando **15**
Saint George **17**
Tierra Colorada **16**

entertainment on offer, and trips arranged to the falls.

A Saint George, Córdoba 148, T/F03757-420633, www.hotelsaintgeorge.com. The most presentable hotel in the centre of town, this has comfortable modern-ish rooms (ask for the most luxurious ones) around a leafy pool area, attentive service and a friendly atmosphere. Good breakfast included. Good restaurant La Esquina (see below) too. Tours arranged. Recommended.

C Alexander Hotel, Av Córdoba 222, T03757-420249, www.hotelguia.com/hoteles/alexander. Inauspicious from the outside, but this is a smart modern place with simple clean rooms, really welcoming staff and excellent value. TV, A/C, pool, good breakfast included. Handy for the bus terminal.

C Hostería Los Helechos, Amarante 76, T03757-420338, www.hosterialoshelechos.com.ar. Another warmly welcoming place, this popular hostería has a relaxed easy-going atmosphere and friendly owners, nicely maintained rooms with TV and A/C, restaurant and a pool. Good value.

C-D Hostería Casa Blanca, Guaraní 121, 2 blocks from bus station, T03757-421320, www.casablancaiguazu.com.ar. Good value with breakfast included in this conveniently central, family-run place with impeccably clean pleasant spacious rooms, simple but beautifully maintained. Breakfast included.

C-D Tierra Colorada, Córdoba y El Urú 28, T03757-420649. Located in a quiet area, with basic, slightly gloomy rooms, TV and a/c in some rooms only, though this is welcoming, and breakfast included.

D Hotel Lilian, Beltrán 183, T03757-420968, hotellilian@yahoo.com.ar. One of the most charming cheaper options, this is impeccably maintained with bright modern rooms, in a quiet location, just 2 blocks from bus terminal, with breakfast included, and helpful owners.

D Noelia, Fray Luis Beltrán 119, T03757-420729. Also very welcoming, this is a beautifully neat house with pleasant rooms, a lovely garden, and friendly family service, very good value rooms with bathrooms, and breakfast included. Recommended.

D Residencial Paquita, Córdoba 158, , opposite the bus terminal, T03757-420434. A simple but rather appealing place, some rooms modernised, and with balcony, all with new bathrooms and air conditioning. No breakfast but there's a bakery next door.

D Residencial San Fernando, Córdoba y Guaraní, near terminal, T03757-421429. A popular place, and good value, with bathrooms, and breakfast included.

Eating
La Esquina **3**
La Rueda **5**
Parilla El Quincho de Tío Querido **8**
Pizza Color **7**

Bars & clubs
La Barranca **2**
La Reserva **4**

Cabañas

A Iguazú Jungle Lodge, Hipolito Iyrigoyen and San Lorenzo, T03757-420600, www.iguazujunglelodge.com. Quite the most luxurious place in the town itself is this beautifully designed complex of cabañas and loft apartments, just 7 blocks from the centre, by a river, with lovely pool. Each self-contained apartment is incredibly comfortable and stylish, equipped with everything you need, a/c, wi-fi, DVDs to borrow, and very good value. Great service, warmly recommended. Lofts are US$80 for 2, breakfast included. Houses sleep 7, good value if you fill them up.

C Pirayú Resort, Av Tres Fronteras 550, on the way to the Hito, T03757-420393, www.pirayu.com.ar. A beautifully built complex of comfortable and well-equipped cabañas, with lovely river views, and sports of all kinds, lots of games for children, attractive pool, and entertainment. Recommended.

Estancias

LL Yacutinga Lodge, 30 km from town, Mickie and Charlie will collect visitors in their jeep, www.yacutinga.com. A really wonderful experience of the jungle, staying in this beautifully designed lodge in the middle of the rainforest, with activities filling your 2-day stay so that you get the most out of the incredible location and learn about the bird and plant life as well the culture of the Guaraní people living in harmony with the reserve. Accommodation is in rustic adobe houses in lovely tropical gardens, superb food and drinks included, as well as boat trips and walks to spot wildlife and plant trees. Highly recommended as the perfect complement to seeing the Iguazú falls.

Youth hostels

Most charge US$7 pp per night in shared dorms, some offer double rooms for couples, though these cost more. You might find a residencial quieter and more comfortable, and only slightly more expensive.

Correcaminos, Amarante 45, T03757-420967, and another hostel at El Mensú 38, T03757-424336, www.correcaminos.com.ar. A noisy friendly place with open sitting area which incorporates kitchen, bar and games room, this also has a pool and double rooms with TV and bathroom for US$20 each. No breakfast, but tours organized to the park. Friendly atmosphere.

El Güembe, El Urú 120, T03757-421035, www.elguembe.com.ar. 3 blocks from the bus station this is the nicest and quieter of 2 hostels owned by the same people, very welcoming and appealing. The other, El Güembe House, www.elguembehouse.com.ar, is much noisier, but still recommended for its friendly atmosphere, parties and music. Sheets and breakfast included in both places. Double rooms US$20.

Hostel Inn Iguazú, Ruta 12, Km 5 (3370), T03757-421823/420156, www.hostel-inn.com. 20% discount to HI members and 10% on long-distance buses.

Hostel Park Iguazú, Amarante 111, T03757-424342, www.hostelparkiguazu.com.ar. Two blocks from the bus station, and newly built, small neat rooms for 2-4 with own bathroom, breakfast, small pool, helpful staff.

Camping

Viejo Americano, RN12, Km 5, T03757-420190, www.viejoamericano.com.ar. The town's best site with 3 pools in pleasant, nicely tended wooded gardens, 5 km from town, and also cabañas and a hostel too, camping US$3 per person, food shop, electricity, games area, pool, barbecue places. Recommended.

Eating

Puerto Iguazú *p330, map p332*

Take a break from steak and try the delicious local fish which is the speciality here: surubí, pacú and dorado.

TTT Iguazú Grand Hotel Resort and Casino, RN12, Km 1640, T03757-498000. The swanky hotel's swish restaurant is open to non-residents if you book in advance. Posh food and international cuisine for an elegant night out.

TT El Encuentro, Av Eva Perón and RN12, T03757-424235, Go by car or taxi, it's worth the effort to get to this place for above average food and service. Steaks are recommended.

TT La Esquina, corner of Av Córdoba 148. Very good restaurant next to Hotel Saint George. Good beef, salads and local fish. Warm friendly service.

TT La Rueda, Córdoba 28, T03757-422531. By far the best restaurant in town, this family run restaurant has a warm and lively atmosphere inside a cosily decorated rustic cabin, often with mellow live music. There's delicious food throughout the superb menu, including well-prepared locally caught surubí and pacú fish, steaks and pastas. Great, professional service, charming welcoming owners. Good wine list. Highly recommended.

T Parrilla El Quincho de Tío Querido, Bompland 110, T03757-420151. The best parrilla in town, and much loved by locals. Great value. Live music in high season.

T Pizza Color, Córdoba 135, T03757-420206. Nothing special, but great for pizzas, and also *parrilla*. Reasonably priced and very central.

T Pizzería La Costa, Av Río Iguazú on the Costanera. Popular with locals, this is an informal pizzeria high above the river on the coast road. Looks basic, but the pizzas are really superb.

Bars and clubs

Puerto Iguazú *p330, map p332*

La Reserva, around Hito Tres Fronteras, the landmark above the meeting of the rivers. Great place for an evening drink or dinner, in a big wooden building, with a warm atmosphere, good live music.

Cuba Libre, Av Brasil y Paraguay, T03757-422531. Just a block from the newly popular area of town for eating out, this is a fun place for a drink, or if you fancy dancing salsa. Owned by a Cuban, the music is great and the atmosphere lively at weekends.

Activities and tours

Parque Nacional Iguazú *p327, map p328*

A day trip from Puerto Iguazú to the Argentine side of the falls, including transfer from your hotel and guide (request English speakers) costs US$15, and to the Brazilian side is US$15, but neither includes park entrance fee. The tour to the Brazilian side of the falls will inevitably stop at the Duty-Free Shop, a large flash indoor mall between the two customs points. Perfumes and cosmetics, electrical goods, spirits and cigarettes at reduced prices. Open 1000-2100. If you want to visit the Jesuit ruins at San Ignacio Mini, 250 km away, a trip to an open mine for semi-precious stones at Wanda, 60 km away, is likely to be included. Full day US$30, plus park entrance to the Jesuit ruins US$5. For Tour operators in Puerto Iguazú, see page 336.

Boat trips

Jungle Explorer , T03757-421696, www.iguazujunglexplorer.com, run a series of fabulous boat trips, all highly recommended. Paseo Ecológico takes you floating silently 3 km down the river from Estación Garganta to appreciate the wildlife on its banks: basking tortoises, caiman, monkeys and birdlife. A wonderful and gentle introduction to the river; 30 mins, US$8. Aventura Náutica, is a fast and exhilarating journey by launch along the lower Río Iguazú, from opposite Isla San Martín right up to the San Martín falls and then into the Garganta del Diablo, completely drenching passengers in the mighty spray. Great fun; not for the faint-hearted. 12 mins, US$15. Gran Aventura combines the Aventura Nautica with a longer boat trip along rapids in the lower Río Iguazú to Puerto Macuco, followed by a jeep trip along the Yacaratiá trail, 1 hr, US$30. Also recommended. Other combinations at reduced prices, and tailor- made tours. An excellent company. Tickets available at all embarkation points or at the Sheraton Hotel.

Other tours

Cruceros Iguazú T03757-421111, www.crucerosiguazu.com, or visit the office in the park area of Puerto Iguazú. Run short cruises along the Río Paraná, US$22, including lunch/dinner, visiting an indigenous Guaraní group at night, very touristy, and during the day to visit the mines at Wanda. Lunch or dinner and live musical show included.
Iguazú Forest, www.iguazuforest.com, offers a half- or full-day's adventure in the jungle offering the chance to try canopying, climbing waterfalls, rapelling and mountain biking. Great for kids and teenagers. US$30 for half a day.

There are also **Full Moon Walks:** night-time walking tours to the falls when the moon is full. See the *guardaparques*, or www.iguazuargentina.com. The **Sheraton** also hires mountain bikes, for US$2.50 for a couple of hours. T03757-491800.

Wildlife safaris

Explorador Expediciones, T/F03757-424055, www.rainforestevt.com.ar. Offers two good tours in small groups: *Safari a la Cascada* which takes you by jeep to the waterfall Arrechea, stopping along the way to look at plants, bird and animal life, identifying tracks, and involving a short walk to the falls, 2 hrs US$15. And *Safari in the Jungle* with more in-depth interpretation of the natural life all around, in open jeeps along the longer version of the Yacatariá trail, 2 hrs, US$25. Daily at 1030 and 1600, though you can request special departures. Both trips will give you fantastic insights into the jungle from expert guides who really bring the natural world alive. The company is run by expert guide Daniel Somay who also leads excellent **Birdwatching trips**, completely accessible for those who have never done it before, and for expert twitchers too. Daniel recognizes the bird call, and plays it back from a concealed CD and speaker to bring an amazing variety of birds flocking to the nearby trees. Astonishing and highly recommended. T/F03757- 424055/ 421632, www.rainforestevt.com.ar.

Puerto Iguazú *p330, map p332*

Tour operators

Turismo Cuenca del Plata, Amarante 76, T03757-421062, cuencadelplata@ cuencadelplata.com
Turismo Dick, Av Victoria Aguirre 226, T03757-420778, turismodick@zipfoz.com.
Four Tourist Travel, Av Misiones 177, T03757-422962, fourtourist@arnet.com.ar.
Aguas Grandes, Mariano Moreno 58, T03757-421140, www.aguasgrandes.com.ar, runs conventional tours to both sides of the falls and Iguazú Forest (as above), adventure activities in the forest, including US$20 half day, good fun.
Cabalgatas por la Selva, Ruta 12, just after the Rotonda for the road to the international bridge, mobile T15 542180. Highly recommended for 3-hr horse riding trips in the forest, US$12.

Transport

Puerto Iguazú *p330, map p332*

Air

The airport is some 20 km southeast of Puerto Iguazú near the falls, T03757-420595. A bus service runs between airport and bus terminal to connect with plane arrivals and departures, US$3, and will drop you at / collect you from your hotel. Check times at Aerolíneas Argentinas office. Taxis charge US$10 to Hotel Sheraton, and around US$15 to **Puerto Iguazú**, US$16 to **Foz do Iguaçu** and US$25 to the **Brazilian airport**. Aerolíneas Argentinas flies direct to **Buenos Aires**, 1hr 40mins, flights fill up fast in Jan, Feb, Easter and Jul.

Airline offices Aerolíneas Argentinas, Brasil y Aguirre, T03757-420168.

Bus

Terminal Av Córdoba y Av Misiones, has a locutorio, restaurant, various tour company desks (see below) and bus company offices, who might look after your luggage if you ask nicely. Bus terminal information T03757-423006 (Crucero del Norte). To **Buenos Aires**, 18 hrs, US$45 for the nearly horizontal comfortable seats in Suite Bus, with Crucero del Norte Tigre Iguazú, Via Bariloche, daily, US$30 semi cama. To **Posadas**, stopping at San Ignacio Miní, hourly, 5 hrs, US$10, **Corrientes**, 10hrs, US$16 servicio común, and **Santa Fé**, 14 hours, US$30 servicio común; all with Empresa Horianski T03757-454559. To **San Ignacio Miní**, US$9 servicio común. Agencia de Pasajes Noelia, local 3, T03757-422722, can book tickets beyond Posadas for other destinations in Argentina, very helpful, ISIC discounts available.

Car hire

Avis at airport, T03757-422397. Localiza, at airport and Aguirre 279, T0800-9992999. Cars may be taken to the Brazilian side for an extra US$5.

Taxi

Fares: to **airport** US$15, to **Argentine falls** US$16, to **Brazilian falls** US$20, to **centre of Foz** US$20, to **Ciudad del Este** US$25, to **Itaipu** US$45 return, to **Wanda gem mines** with wait. El Sol is a very reliable company, T03757-421532; call Ruben on 15415560.

Border with Paraguay *p331*
Direct buses (non-stop in Brazil), leave Puerto Iguazú terminal every 30 mins, US$2, 45 mins, liable to delays especially in crossing the bridge to **Ciudad del Este**. **Taxi** from Puerto Iguazú to **Ciudad del Este**, US$70 one way.

Directory

Puerto Iguazú *p330, map p332*
Banks Many ATMs in town, including at Macro Misiones and Banco Nación, T03757-420150, banks are generally open 0800-1300. TCs can be changed at Libres Cambios in the Hito Tres Fronteras, T03757-421566, open 0800-2200, or Cambios Links, Av Victoria Aguirre 226, T03757-423332. **Communications** Plenty of *locutorios*, but Telecom, Victoria Aguirre y Los Cedros is central, open all afternoon, and has Internet too. **Embassies and consulates** Brazilian, Av Córdoba 264, T03757-421348. **Internet** Several places at the town's hub, Aguirre and Brasil, opposite tourist office. **Medical services** T03757-420288.

Parque Nacional Foz do Iguaçu (Brazil)

The Brazilian National Park was founded in 1939 and declared a World Heritage Site in 1986. The park covers 170,086 ha, extending along the north bank of the Rio Iguaçu, then sweeping northwards to Santa Tereza do Oeste on the BR-277. The experience is less impressive than on the Argentine side since you are not immersed in the jungle, and can't get close to the falls but it's interesting to see the whole panorama from a distance. ▸▸ *For Sleeping, Eating and other listings, see pages 339-341.*

Ins and outs

Getting there It is 17 km from the city of Foz do Iguaçu to the park entrance. Buses leave Foz do Iguaçu, from the Terminal Urbana on Avenida Juscelino Kubitschek and República Argentina every 40 minutes 0730-1800, and are clearly marked number 400, *Parque Nacional*. You can get on or off at any point on the route past the airport and **Hotel das Cataratas,** 40 minutes US$0.80 one way, payable in *reais* only. The driver waits at the park entrance while passengers purchase entry tickets, which are checked by a park guard on the bus. Taxi US$4, plus US$5.50 per hour for waiting. ▸▸ *For further information, see Transport, page 340.*

Getting around From the entrance, shuttle **buses** leave every 10-15 minutes for the 8 km journey to the falls, stopping first at the start of the Macuco Safari. From there it's another 10-minute drive to the **Hotel Tropical das Cataratas,** and a short walk to the falls.

 Park information Entry is US$6.30, payable in pesos, reais, dollars or euros, and the park is open daily, apart from Monday mornings 0800-1700 in winter, and to 1800 in summer. At the entrance to the park there's a smart modern visitors centre here, with toilets, ATM, a small café and a large souvenir shop, but little information on the park or wildlife. Also a **Banco do Brasil** *câmbio* (0800-1900). If possible, visit on a weekday when the walks are less crowded.

Wildlife

Most frequently encountered are the little and red brocket deer, South American coati, white-eared opossum, and a brown capuchin monkey. Much harder to see are the jaguar, ocelot, puma, white-lipped peccary, bush dog and southern river otter. The endangered tegu lizard is common. Over 100 species of butterflies have been identified, among them the electric blue *Morpho* and the poisonous red and black *heliconius*, and the bird life is especially rewarding for the birdwatcher. Five members of the toucan family can be seen including toco and red-breasted toucans.

Trails

The 1.2 km paved walk from **Hotel Tropical das Cataratas** to the falls is an easy walk, taking you high above the Río Iguazú, giving splendid views of all the falls on the Argentine side from a series of galleries. At the end of the path, you can walk down to a viewing point almost right under the powerful **Floriano Falls**, a dramatic view, since you're in the middle of the river. A catwalk at the foot of the Floriano Falls goes almost to the middle of the river to give a good view of the **Garganta del Diablo**. From here, there are 150 steps up to the **Porto Canoas complex**, a quick and easy walk, but for those who find stairs difficult, you can return the way you came, and walk a little further along the road. The Porto Canoas complex consists of a big souvenir shop, toilets, a café, a fast food place (cheeseburger US$1.50) and smart restaurant (full three-course lunch US$7.30, Tue-Sun 1130-1600), all recommended, good value, and all with a good view of the river above the falls. Return to the visitor centre and entrance either by the free shuttle bus, or walk back along the forest path as far as **Hotel Tropical das Cataratas**, (where you can also eat a good lunch with a view of the falls for US$13) and take the bus from there. The visit will take you around two hours, plus time for lunch.

Foz do Iguaçu (Brazil) » *pp339-341.*

→ *Phone code: +55-(0)45 Colour map 2, A3 Population: 232,000*

A small modern city, Foz lies 28 km from the falls, with a wide range of accommodation and good communications by air and road with the main cities of southern Brazil and Asunción in Paraguay. It's not a particularly attractive town, and Argentina's Puerto Iguazú makes a better base, with cheaper hotels and better access to the falls. Street crime has increased in Foz in recent years, but the inhabitants are friendly and welcoming, and there are some good places to eat.

Ins and outs

Getting there Buses leave Puerto Iguazú terminal for Foz do Iguaçu every 20 minutes, US$2, but do not wait at the border so if you need exit and entry stamps, keep your ticket and catch the next bus (bus companies do not recognize each other's tickets). Taxis between the border and Puerto Iguazú, US$15.

Tourist information The main tourist office is at Praça Getúlio Vargas 69, a small plaza at the corner of Avenida JK and Schimmelpfeng, T0800 451516 (freephone 0700-2300). The staff are extremely helpful and well organized, and speak English. There's also a tourist office at the bus terminal at the end of Avenida José María de

Brito, and at the airport open for all arriving flights, with map and bus information. A newspaper, *Triplice Fronteira*, carries street plans and other tourist information. Tourists are warned not to stray from the main roads in the town, not to wear jewellery, to leave a copy of your passport in your hotel, and to avoid the river area south of Avenida JK. Take taxis or tours wherever possible. Avenida Kubitschek and the streets south of it, towards the river, have a reputation as being unsafe at night as there is a favela nearby. Take care if walking after dark.

Sights

Apart from the Parque Nacional do Iguaçu there are a couple of other attractions. The world's largest hydroelectric dam at **Lago Itaipu** ⓘ *15 km away, T+55-(0)45 520 6999, www.itaipu.gov.br, buses run from Terminal Urbano, Av JK and República Argentina to a village 200 m away from the visitor centre, US$0.50*, is quite a feat of human achievement, an interesting contrast to the natural wonder of the falls. Check times with tourist office, and take passport. There are also attractive artificial **beaches** on Lake Itaipu, good places for relaxing in the summer. **Bairro de Três Lagoas**, at Km 723 on BR-277, and in the municipality of **Santa Terezinha do Itaipu**, 34 km from Foz. The **Parque das Aves** ⓘ *US$8, next to the visitor centre at Rodovia das Cataratas Km 18, just before the falls*, contains some local and Brazilian species, but most of its beautiful caged birds are from Africa and Asia. It's a picturesque setting, particularly the butterfly house, with hummingbirds whirring about, but it's far more satisfying to spot birds in the wild, or at Güira Oga on the Argentine side of the falls. There's a café and shop.

Border with Paraguay

The Ponte de Amizade/Puente de Amistad (Friendship Bridge) over the Río Paraná, 12 km north of Foz, leads straight into the heart of Ciudad del Este. Crossing is very informal but keep an eye on your luggage and make sure that you get necessary stamps – so great is the volume of traffic that it can be difficult to stop, especially with the traffic police moving you on. It is particularly busy on Wednesday and Saturday, with long queues of vehicles. Pedestrians from Brazil cross on the north side of the bridge allowing easier passage on the other side for those returning with bulky packages.

Immigration Paraguayan and Brazilian immigration formalities are dealt with at opposite ends of the bridge. There is a US$3 charge to enter Paraguay. Remember to adjust your watch to local time.

Transport Buses (marked Cidade-Ponte) leave from the Terminal Urbana, Avenida Juscelino Kubitschek, for the Ponte de Amizade (Friendship Bridge), US$0.60. Crossing by private vehicle: if only visiting the national parks, this presents no problems.

Sleeping

Parque Nacional Foz do Iguaçu *p337*

There is a good selection of hotels and many also offer excursions to the falls. The excellent tourist office has a full list.

L-AL Tropical das Cataratas, directly overlooking the falls, 28 km from Foz, T+55-(0)45 521-7000, www.tropicalhotel.com.br. Elegant pale pink colonial-style building with a pool in luxuriant gardens, where you might spot wildlife at night and early morning. The rooms are disappointingly plain and sombre, but there's a small terrace with views of the falls to the front of the hotel, and a restaurant, also open to non-residents; lunch and dinner buffet, US$14 also à la carte dishes and dinner with show.

Foz do Iguaçu *p338*

D Pousada Evelina Navarrete, Rua Irlan Kalichewski 171, Vila Yolanda, T+55-(0)45574 3817. Lots of tourist information, English, French, Italian, Polish and Spanish spoken, helpful, good breakfast and location, near Chemin Supermarket, near Av Cataratas on the way to the falls. Recommended.

D Tarobá, Rua Tarobá, 1048 T+55-(0)45 523 9722, www.hoteltaroba.com.br. Highly recommended, as a good value central place, with a/c, a small indoor pool, good breakfast. Recommended.

Eating

Foz do Iguaçu *p338*

Many restaurants stay open till midnight and accept a variety of currencies. There are lots of restaurants along Av JK.

Bufalo Branco, Rebouças 530. Sophisticated surroundings and attentive service, and a superb all-you-can-eat *churrasco* for US$15, including filet mignon, bull's testicles, and a good salad bar.

Rafain, Av das Cataratas, Km 6.5, T523 1177. A touristy but entertaining affair, extravaganza with live folklore music from all over South America, dancing, and buffet, US$12.

Galletos, Av JK and Jorge Sanwais. Good food, on a weigh-and-pay basis, tasty and good value. Recommended.

Bars and clubs

Foz do Iguaçu *p338*

There are lots of bars concentrated along the 2 blocks of Av Jorge Schimmelpfeng from Av Brasil to R Mal Floriano Peixoto. Wed and Sun are the best nights.

Amazém, R Edmundo de Barros 446. Intimate and sophisticated, attracts discerning locals, good atmosphere, mellow live music, US$1 cover, recommended.

Bier Garten, No 550. Pizzeria and *choparía*, beer garden in name only, but there are some trees, and a lively rowdy atmosphere in peak season, as this is hugely popular.

Capitão Bar, Schimmelpfeng 288 y Almte Barroso. Large, loud and popular nightspot for drinks, nightclub attached.

Oba! Oba!, Av das Cataratas 370, T+55-(0)45 529 6596, (Antigo Castelinho). Live samba Mon-Sat 2315-0015, very popular, US$11 for show and a drink. Also known as Coopershow.

Pizza Park, opposite Bier Garten on Av Jorge Schimmelpfeng, open from 2000. Good pizzas in a lively atmosphere, popular with tourists and residents.

Rafain Cataratas, Av das Cataratas, Km 6.5. With floor show and *churrascaria* dinner.

Activities and tours

Parque Nacional Foz do Iguaçu *p337*

Macuco Safari Tour (1 hr 40 mins, US$33) leaves from the first stop on the free shuttle bus service. Ride down a 3-km-long path through the forest in open electric jeeps, and then a motor boat takes you close to the falls themselves, similar to **Jungle Explorer** on the Argentine side, but it's more expensive, and the guides aren't as good. Portuguese, English and Spanish spoken, take insect repellent.

Helicopter tours over the falls leave from near the entrance and Parque das Aves, US$20 pp, 8 mins. The altitude has had to be increased to avoid disturbing bird life and visitors, making the flight less attractive. Lots of companies organize conventional tours to the falls – convenient as they collect you from your hotel. Half day, US$10, plus park entrance.

Foz do Iguaçu *p338*

Tour operators

Caribe Tur, at the international airport, and **Hotel Tropical das Cataratas**, and **Hotel Bourbon**, T523 1612, run tours from the airport to the Argentine side, and **Hotel das Cataratas**, **STTC Turismo**, **Hotel Bourbon**, Rodovia das Cataratas, T529 8580. Cruises on the Río Paraná, with dinner and show, T03757 421111, ventas@crucerosiguazu.com.

Transport

Foz do Iguaçu *p338*

Air Iguaçu international **Airport** is 18 km south of town near the falls, T+55-(0)45 521 4200. In Arrivals is **Banco do Brasil** and **Caribe Tours e Câmbio**, car rental offices, tourist office and an official taxi stand, US$12 to town. All buses marked Parque Nacional, No 400, pass the airport in each direction, US$0.50 to anywhere around town, allows backpacks but not lots of luggage. Many hotels run minibus services for a small charge. Daily flights to **Rio de Janeiro**, **São Paulo**, **Curitiba** and other Brazilian cities.

Airline offices Rio Sul, and Varig, J Sanways 779; **TAM**, T+55-(0)45 574 6080, (free transport to Ciudad del Este for its flights, all border documentation dealt with); **Varig**, Kubitschek 463, T+55-(0)45 523 2111; **Vasp**, Brasil 845, T+55-(0)45 523 2212 (airport T529 7161).

Bus
For transport to the falls see above under Parque Nacional Foz do Iguaçu, page 337.
Long distance Terminal (*Rodoviária*) at Av Costa e Silva, 4 km from centre on road to Curitiba, T+55-(0)45 522 2590; bus to centre, any bus that says 'Rodoviária', US$0.65. Book as far ahead as possible. There's a tourist office 0630-1800, **Cetreme** desk for tourists who have lost their documents, *guarda municipal* (police) and luggage store. To **Curitiba**, Pluma, Sulamericana, 9-11 hrs, paved road, US$15. To **Guaíra** via Cascavel only, 5 hrs, US$10. To **Florianópolis**, Catarinense and Reunidas, US$22, 16 hrs; Reunidas to **Porto Alegre**, US$28. To **São Paulo**, 16 hrs, new buses Kaiowa, and Pluma US$28, *executivo* 6 a day, plus one *leito*. To **Rio de Janeiro**, 22 hrs, several daily, US$38. To **Asunción**, Pluma, RYSA (direct at 1430), US$11.

Car hire
Localiza at the airport, T+55-(0)45 523 4800, Av Juscelino Kubitschek 2878, T+55-(0)45 522 1608, and Rodovia das Cataratas Km 2.5, in Hotel Bourbon, (see Sleeping, above).

Directory

Foz do Iguaçu *p338*
Banks There are plenty of banks and travel agents on Av Brasil. **Banco do Brasil**, Brasil 1377. Has ATM, high commission for TCs. **HSBC**, Av Brasil 1151, MasterCard ATM **Bradesco**, Brasil 1202. Banco 24 Horas at Oklahoma petrol station. **Itaú** ATM at Kubitschek e Bocaiúva and airport. Exchange at **Vento Sul**, Av Brasil 1162, no TCs. Also Corimeira, Av Brasil 248. **Embassies and consulates** Argentine, Travessa Eduardo Bianchi 26, T+55-(0)45 574 2969, open Mon-Fri 1000-1430. **Internet** Net pub @, Av JK and Rua Rui Barbosa 549, **Zipfoz.com**, R Barão do Rio Branco 412 and Av JK, Smart, a/c, US$2.50 per hour. Fast but noisy at **L@n Zone**. **Post office** Praça Getúlio Vargas 72. **Telephone** Posto 1, Edmundo de Barros 281, Calçadão y Brasil.

Misiones province and the Jesuit missions

There are wonderfully evocative remains of several Jesuit missions in the south of picturesque Misiones province. Testimony to their great organization and extensive expansion in the early 17th century, they make a worthwhile stop on your way south from the Iguazú Falls. And if you're interested in seeing more, there are the ruins of San Ignacio Mini, Santa Ana, and Loreto, all are within reach of the provincial capital Posadas, or in a long day trip from Iguazú. Misiones' lush landscapes of red earth roads cutting through fecund green jungle, and forest plantations are matched by a rich culture, generated by the mix of indigenous Guaraní and European immigrants, particularly from Eastern Europe, together with a constant flow of Paraguayans and Brazilians from over the borders. The fertile land produces pine forests for wood, huge plantations of tea, and most important of all, the yerba for mate, the Argentine drink without which the country would grind to a halt. It's a fairly wet region: the annual rainfall exceeds 2000 mm, generating hundreds of rivers and waterfalls, the most magnificent of which are the overwhelming Iguazú Falls, at the province's northernmost tip. But there are more falls, the Saltos de Moconá, almost as spectacular and staggeringly wide, on the southeastern-most edge of the province and accessible for those adventurous enough to make the trip. With time to spare, you could head inland to Oberá, whose 35 churches represent immigrants from an amazing 15 countries, but beyond the laid-back way of life, there's little to hold you in the province for long. The climate might be uncomfortably hot for much walking in summer, but it's pleasantly warm in winter, while flowers and bird life are most abundant in spring. ▸▸ *For Sleeping, Eating and other listings, see pages 348-351.*

Ins and outs

Getting there and around The Jesuit missions at San Ignacio are near the southwestern-most end of the province, and while you could visit these on a long day trip from Puerto Iguazú, you'll see more of the region's lush landscapes if you stop off at the city of Posadas – also a stop if you're combining a trip to Iguazú with the Esteros del Iberá further south. From Posadas, two parallel roads run northeast to the Iguazú Falls, but only Route 12, the northernmost one is tarmacked and negotiable in an ordinary vehicle. The Jesuit ruins at San Ignacio are 60 km north of Posadas and the road continues, via a series of small towns such as Eldorado, to Wanda, famous for its open mines of semi-precious stones, to Puerto Iguazú, the best base for visiting the falls. The other road, Route 14, runs parallel and south along the interior of the province, via Oberá to Bernardo de Irigoyen. It's paved but there are no buses. To visit the Saltos de Moconá, you'll need to take a rough road further south, Route 2, which is unpaved from Alba Posse onwards (about halfway), so you'll need a 4WD vehicle. » *For further information, see Transport, page 350.*

Best time to visit Summers are incredibly hot here, with temperatures reaching 40°C from November to March, but winters are warm and sunny.

Posadas and around » *pp348-351.*

→ *Phone code: 03752 Colour map 2, B2 Population: 280,500*

Posadas is the lively capital of Misiones, set on a bend on the southern bank of the Río Paraná, with excellent views over the river from its attractive *costanera* (river banks). It was founded in 1814, and developed after the War of Triple Alliance as a useful strategic post. It's a modern city, and though there aren't any particularly remarkable sights, Posadas is a pleasant place for a stop if you're on your way from the Esteros del Iberá to the missions or Iguazú. The bus terminal is 3 km south of the centre – take a taxi. The **tourist office** ⓘ *2 blocks south of the Plaza 9 de Julio at Colón 1987, T03752-447540, www.posadas.gov.ar, daily 0800-2000*, can provide a basic map. For information on the whole province visit www.misiones.gov.ar .

Sights

The centre of the city is the Plaza 9 de Julio, with its French-style cathedral and government building, and several hotels. Banks and ATMs can be found one block west on San Martín, or one block south on Félix de Azara. Two blocks southeast, there's a peaceful spot at Paseo Bosetti, a quiet plaza with mural paintings. There are a couple of rather old-fashioned museums near the Plaza, the **Museo de Ciencias Naturales e Historia** and the **Museo Regional de Posadas** with the obligatory collection of stuffed animals. There's also a cultural centre and arts exhibition hall at **Museo de Arte Juan Yaparí** ⓘ *Sarmiento 317*, a block north of the plaza, and next door, a **Mercado de Artesanías**, where Guaraní handicrafts are for sale, and the **Museo Arqueológico** ⓘ *General Paz 1865, T03752-435845*.

Posadas' main feature is the long and attractive Costanera, extending northeast of the centre alongside the board river Paraná and a good place for a stroll. Avenida **Andrés Guaçurarí** (referred to also as Avenida Roque Pérez) is a pretty boulevard which becomes livelier by night with several popular bars. A few blocks northwest is the small **Parque Paraguayo** and the **Museo Regional Aníbal Cambas** ⓘ *Alberdi 600, T03752-447539, Mon-Fri 0700-1900*. This is Posadas' most interesting museum with a permanent exhibition of Guaraní artefacts and pieces collected from the nearby Jesuit missions, including the façade of the temple at San Ignacio Mini.

The **port** lies at the eastern end of the Avenida Costanera and you can still see the two ferries, built in Glasgow in 1911, that operated the river crossing for train coaches until 1990. Nearby, the **Mercado La Placita**, daily 0630-2030, is a colourful market, its inner corridors buzzing with life, offering a great selection of intriguing goods for sale.

The Jesuit mission

Jesuits were the religious force which accompanied the Spanish conquest of much of northern Argentina, and though their impact on indigenous culture was far more positive, their rule remains controversial. Were they pioneers of a primitive socialism or merely exploiting the local Guaraní in the name of religious enlightenment?

Between 1609, when they built their first *redacción* or mission, in present day Brazil, and 1767 when they were expelled, the Jesuits founded about 50 missions around the upper reaches of the Ríos Paraná, Paraguay and Uruguay. In 1627, they were forced to flee southwards, when their northern missions were attacked by slave-hunting Bandeirantes. The priests led some 1000 converts down the Río Parapanema into the Paraná on 700 rafts, only to find their route blocked by the Guaíra Falls. They pushed on for eight days through dense virgin forest, built new boats below the falls and continued their journey. Some 725 km from their old homes, they re-established their missions, and trained militias to protect them from further attacks.

The missions prospered on agricultural produce, which raised profits to fund religious teaching. The Guaraní grew traditional crops such as manioc (the local root vegetable), sweet potatoes and maize, plants imported from Europe, such as wheat and oranges, and they also kept horses and herds of cattle and sheep. The missions became major producers of *yerba mate* (see page 53) favoured by the Jesuits as an alternative to alcohol. Apart from common lands the Guaraní also farmed their own individual plots.

The decision by Carlos III to expel the Jesuits from South America in 1767 was made under the conditions of highest secrecy: sealed orders were sent out to the colonies with strict instructions that they should not be opened in advance. On the appointed date, over 2000 members of the order were removed by force and put on ships for Italy. Jesuit property was auctioned, schools and colleges were taken over by the Franciscans and Dominicans, and many missions fell into disuse, or were destroyed.

The Jesuits had attracted many enemies since their wealth and economic power angered landowners and traders, and their control over the Guaraní irritated farmers short of labour. Rumours circulated that the missions contained mines and hoards of precious metals. But however the Jesuits may have exploited their Guaraní manpower, they certainly defended the Guaraní from enslavement by the Spanish and Portuguese, and many feel their societies were a vanished arcadia.

Only four of the missions retain their former splendour: San Ignacio Mini in Argentina, Jesús and Trinidad in Paraguay, and São Miguel in Brazil. The first three can be visited with ease from Posadas, along with several others, including Santa Ana and Loreto.

Around Posadas

The only real reason to stop in Posadas is to visit the Jesuit missions of San Ignacio Mini (60 km) and two others. There is a marvellous traditional estancia nearby, **Estancia Santa Inés** ⓘ *RN105, Km 8.5, 20 km south of Posadas, T03752-436194, estanciasantaines"arnet.com.ar*, a traditional estancia of 2000 ha, growing *yerba mate*. Activities include walking, horse riding and, between February and October, helping with mate cultivation. Half-day activities US$20, taxi from Posadas, US$15. However, if you're here in July, you might like to visit the **Fiesta Nacional de la Yerba**

 Mate (mate festival) in **Apóstoles** a prosperous town 65 km south of Posadas, founded in 1897 by Ukrainian and Polish immigrants on the site of a Jesuit mission dating from 1633. The festival attracts folclore singers, to this town set in the heart of *yerba mate* plantations in a picturesque hilly region – reached by regular buses.

The **Museo Histórico Juan Szychowski** ⓘ *13 km further at La Cachuera, follow the 6 km dirt road, branching off Route 1.7 km south of Apóstoles*, is worth a trip if you have a car. It displays tools and machinery invented by a young Polish immigrant, including a cute pram used by all his children, mills for processing rice, corn and *yerba mate*, and his hydraulic works, which can be seen in the grounds still amaze engineers. He was the founder of a *yerba mate* processing plant, **La Cachuera** ⓘ *T03758-422443, www.yerbamanda.com.ar, Mar 21-Sep 20 Wed-Fri 0800-1130, 1430-1730, Sat-Sun 1000-1730; Sep 21-Mar 20 Wed-Fri 0700-1130, 1500-1730, Sat-Sun 0800-1200, 1530-1900*, still operating, now under the brand name of *Amanda*.

For Esteros del Iberá, see page 351, and see Posadas tour operators, page 350, to arrange transfer to *estancias* or to Colonia Carlos Pellegrini. You could also cross the border to Encarnación in Paraguay to visit more Jesuit missions at Trinidad and Jesús.

Border with Paraguay

A bridge, the Puente San Roque, links Posadas with Encarnación. Pedestrians and cyclists are not allowed to cross the bridge; cyclists must ask officials for assistance. Pesos are accepted in Encarnación, so there is no need to change them. Paraguay is one hour behind Argentina, except during Paraguayan summer time.

Immigration and customs Formalities are conducted at respective ends of the bridge. The Argentine side has different offices for locals and foreigners, T03758-435329; Paraguay has one for both. Formalities for boat crossing are carried out at both ports. The Argentine consulate is at Mallorquín 788, T03758-3446.

San Ignacio and the Mini Jesuit Mission

» pp348-351.

➔ Phone code: 03752 Colour map 2, B2 Population: 6,300

The tiny town of San Ignacio is the site of the most impressive Jesuit mission in Misiones province, 63 km northeast of Posadas. The site, together with the nearby Jesuit missions of Loreto and Santa Ana, has been declared a World Heritage site by UNESCO. It's a very sleepy place, but useful for lunch or a night's stay if you're seeing the missions.

Ins and outs

Getting there San Ignacio Mini Jesuit Mission is located six blocks from Avenida Sarmiento on the northwest side of town, entrance at Calle Alberdi, exit to Calle Rivadavia. A bus from Posadas or Puerto Iguazú will drop you off at the entrance to the town. Walk straight ahead of you down Sarmiento, and you'll see sign posts 'To the Ruins'. Keep walking and you'll find the ruins on your right. Note that the entrance is 200 m further on than the exit, round the corner of the block to your right. There are plenty of restaurants and cafes along this road near the ruins.

Tourist information Open daily except Christmas Day 0700-1900, T03752-470186, US$4 with a 30-minute guided tour included (ask for English), which leaves the entrance every 20 minutes. Tip appreciated. A free leaflet gives basic information in English and Spanish. You can reliably leave your luggage in a room behind the ticket office – give a tip for this too. Basic toilet facilities, though there are plenty of cafés across the road. Keep hold of your ticket, as it gives you entrance to the other Jesuit ruins at Santa Ana, Santa María La Mayor, and Loreto, within a 15-day period.

Background

San Ignacio Mini ('small' in comparison with San Ignacio Guazu – 'large' – on the Paraguayan side of the Río Paraná) was originally founded in 1610 near the river Paranapanema in the present Brazilian state of Paraná, but frequent attacks from the *bandeirantes* (hunting for slaves as workers) forced the Jesuits to lead a massive exodus south together with the neighbouring Loreto mission. Taking their massive Guaraní population down the river by a series of rafts, they established San Ignacio on the river Yabebiry, not far from its present site, which was definitively settled in 1696.

At the height of its prosperity in 1731, the mission housed 4356 people. Only two priests ran the mission: a feat of astounding organization. Latin, Spanish and Guaraní were taught in the school, and nearly 40,000 head of cattle grazed in the surrounding land, where *yerba mate* and cotton, maize and tobacco were also cultivated. The mission itself once covered around 35 acres: today you can see remains on only 16 – still an impressive sight with the immense central plaza lined with buildings in dramatic red sandstone. For almost a hundred years, the Jesuit 'reducciones' operated successfully, growing in size from a population of 28,000 in 1647 to 141,00 in 1732. But after the expulsion of the Jesuits in 1767, the mission rapidly declined. By 1784 there were only 176 Guaraní, and by 1810 none remained. In 1817, by order of the Paraguayan dictator, Rodriguez de Francia, San Ignacio was set on fire. The ruins, like those of nearby Santa Ana and Loreto, were lost in the jungle until the late 19th century when attempts at colonization forced the founding of new towns, and San Ignacio was founded near the site of the former mission. It wasn't until the 1980s that there was some attempt to give official protection to the ruins, which were declared a national monument at last in 1943.

The mission

Like other Jesuit missions, San Ignacio Mini was constructed around a central plaza: to the north, east and west were about 30 parallel one-storey buildings, each with a wide veranda in front and each divided into four to 10 small, one-room dwellings for slaves. Guaraní communities lived in the surrounding areas. The roofs of these buildings have gone, but the massive 1-m-thick walls are still standing except where they have been destroyed by the *ibapoi* trees. The public buildings, some still 10 m high, are on the south side of the plaza: in the centre are the ruins of the church, 74 m by 24 m, finished about 1724. To the right is the cemetery, which was divided for men and women, priests and children, to the left are the cloisters, the priests' quarters, guest rooms and the workshops for wood and metal work, gold and silver. Sculpture was of particular significance in San Ignacio, and some of the most pleasing details are to be found in the red sandstone masonry. While the architecture is the traditional colonial baroque style found in all Jesuit public buildings, the influence of the Guaraní culture can be seen in the many natural details in bas-relief on walls and lintels: elegantly entwined grapes, fruit and flowers, together with naïve human forms and angels, so that even the buildings reveal a harmony between the Jesuit priests and their Guaraní workers. The chapel was designed by two Italian sacerdotes, and it took 36 years to build. Along the same stretch of terrace, you will see the remains of the music conservatory, library, kitchen. Many of the porticos and windows are elaborately carved, testimony to the highly trained work force, and high standards of aesthetics. The whole area is excellently maintained and is a most impressive sight.

Just 200 m inside the entrance to the ruins is the **Centro de Interpretación Jesuítico-Guaraní**, with a fine model of the mission in its heyday, and an exhibition which includes representations of the lives of the Guaraní before the arrival of the Spanish, displays on the work of the Jesuits and the consequences of their expulsion. Next to the exit, to the left, there is also a small **Museo Provincial**, which contains a collection of artefacts from the Jesuit missions, some beautiful examples of stone carving, and a bas-relief of San Ignacio de Loyola, founder of the Jesuit order.

Other sights

Follow Avenida Sarmiento to its very end and turn right for a picturesque view of a row of wooden houses on a reddish road amidst lush vegetation. Next to the Jesuit missions site entrance is **Galería Bellas Artes**, at La Casa de Inés y Juan, San Martín 1291, where painter Juan Catalano exhibits and sells his works which feature geometrical motifs, or typical local scenes, mounted on wooden boards.

On the opposite side of the town, there's a really delightful stroll to the house of celebrated Uruguayan writer Quiroga's, a 20-minute walk (with little shade) along San Martín, in the opposite direction to the ruins. Walk to the end of the street, past the *Gendarmería*, and two attractive wooden and stone houses. After 200 m the road turns left and 300 m later, a signposted narrow road branches off leading to the **Casa de Horacio Quiroga** ⓘ *T03752-470124, 0800-1900, US$2 including a 40-min guided tour; ask for an English guide*, the home of the Uruguayan writer (1878-1937) who lived there part of his tragic life as a farmer and carpenter between 1910-1916 and again in the 1930s. Many of his fantastical short stories were inspired by this subtropical region and its inhabitants. The scenery is beautiful, with river views, a garden with palms and an amazing bamboo forest planted by Quiroga. There's a replica of his first house, made for a movie set in the 1990s, while his second house is still standing, and contains an exhibition of a few of his belongings. Return to the main road, follow it down the slope amongst thick vegetation for a gorgeous riverside (25-minute) walk.

Other missions: Loreto and Santa Ana

If you have transport, and plenty of time, it's interesting to complement your visit to San Ignacio with a trip to see the ruins of two other Jesuit missions nearby. The mission of **Loreto** ⓘ *0700-1830, US$1, or free with your ticket from San Ignacio, within 15 days*, has far fewer visitors than San Ignacio, and under thick shady trees, the silence of the still air and the refreshing darkness add an attractive touch of mystery. The mission was moved to its present site in 1631, after the exodus from the former Jesuit province of Guayrá, and more than 6000 people were living here by 1733. It's thought that this was the site of the first printing press in the Americas, and of an extensive library, as well as being impressively productive: cattle and *yerba mate* were grown here, and ceramics were made. Little remains of this once large establishment other than a few walls, though excavations are in progress. Note the number of old trees growing entwined with stone buttresses. Access is via a 3-km dirt road (signposted) off Route 12, 10 km south of San Ignacio; no public transport enters Loreto, but buses will drop you off on Route 12, otherwise take a tour from Posadas or a remise taxi.

Some 16 km south of San Ignacio at **Santa Ana** ⓘ *0700-1900, US$1, or free with your ticket to San Ignacio, within 15 days, regular buses stop on RN12*, are the ruins of another Jesuit mission, not as extensive as San Ignacio, but revealing interesting architectural adaptation to the terrain, and founded much earlier, in 1633. Moved to its present site in 1663, Santa Ana housed the Jesuit iron foundry. In 1744 the mission was inhabited by 4331 people. The impressively high walls are still standing and there are beautiful steps leading from the church to the wide open plaza. The ruins are 700 m along a path from Route 12 (signposted).

You could also explore the ruins of **Santa María la Mayor**, 76 km southwest, on paved Route 2 linking San Javier and Concepción de la Sierra, 9 km west of Itacaruare. It dates from 1637 and never restored. Remains of the church and a jail are still standing, and a printing press operated there in the early 18th century.

Oberá → *Phone code: 03755 Colour map 2, B3 Population: 51,400*

Oberá is the second largest town in Misiones, located amongst tea and *yerba mate* plantations, with factories open for visits. It's one of the province's biggest centres of 20th-century European immigration, and there are around 15 different nationalities here, including Japanese, Brazilian, Paraguayan and Middle Eastern communities, represented every September in the annual *Fiesta Nacional del Inmigrante*, held at the Parque de las Naciones. The town has over 35 churches and temples, but there's little reason to make a special trip. Oberá's **tourist office** ⓘ *Plazoleta Güemes, Av Libertad 90, T03755-421808, Mon-Fri 0700-1900, Sat-Sun 0800-1200, 1500-1900*, has information on local estancias open to visitors. There is a **zoo** ⓘ *Italia y Alberdi, Tue-Sun 0900-1200*, with the **Jardín de los Pájaros** ⓘ *1500-1900 (in winter until 1800), US$0.35, T03755-427023*, which houses native birds.

Monte Aventura ⓘ *Tue-Sun 1000-1800, US$0.35, T03755-422430, access from Av José Ingenieros*, is a park with forest trails and entertainment for kids. If you're more interested in tea, you could head for **Campo Viera**, 21 km north of Oberá on Route 14. The 'national capital of tea', it has about 8,000 ha of tea fields and 25 processing plants. The **Fiesta Nacional del Té** is held here every September with the Queen of Tea coronation (for more information, go to the **Casita del Té**.

There's a dazzling array of **orchids** some 28 km southwest of Oberá on Route 14 at Leandro N Alem (regular public transport from Oberá), where **Blumen Haus** (T03755-497090), is a nursery and an arboretum of 36 ha with native trees.

The route from San Ignacio to Puerto Iguazú

From San Ignacio Route 12 continues northeast, running parallel to Río Alto Paraná, towards Puerto Iguazú, through appealing landscapes of bright red soil and green vegetation: plantations of *yerba mate*, manioc and citrus fruits can be seen as well as timber yards, and *yerba mate* factories. The road passes through several small modern towns including Jardín America, Puerto Rico, Montecarlo and Eldorado, but the only place worth stopping at is the wonderful traditional cattle ranch **Estancia Las Mercedes**, see Sleeping page 349. If you're driving and feel like an extra stop you could consider the **Salto Capioví**. Just 100 m from Route 12 in Capioví, 60 km from San Ignacio, this 7 m-waterfall is immersed in a patch of jungle, with a campsite. Nearby, there's the **Parque Natural Las Camelias**.

At 100 km south of Puerto Iguazú is **Eldorado**, a quaint, friendly and typical little Misiones town with an interesting archaeological collection at the **Museo Municipal** ⓘ *T03751-430788, Thu-Sun 1500-1800*. The bus stops here between Puerto Iguazú and San Ignacio, and it's the closest to town for **Estancia Las Mercedes**. This marvellous cattle farming ranch remains almost unchanged since it was built in the 1900s. The lovely traditional main house is set amidst beautiful parkland and offers fascinating insights into life on the land. Charming owner, Edie Lowe who speaks excellent English. The best way to explore this lovely landscape is on horseback from Las Mercedes. For information visit the **tourist office** ⓘ *Av San Martín 2060, 2nd floor, T03751-421152*.

If you're interested in seeing how amethyst and quartz are mined, you might like to stop off at **Wanda**, 50 km north, a famous open-cast mine, which also sells precious gems. There are guided tours to two mines, Tierra Colorada and Compañía Minera Wanda, daily 0700-1900. Consult tour operators in Eldorado or Puerto Iguazú.

Saltos del Moconá » *pp348-351.*

While the main tourist route through Misiones runs along Route 12, if you have time, a 4WD and a spirit of adventure, you might well want to get off the beaten track and explore Misiones' hilly interior. Beautiful waterfalls are hidden away in the dense subtropical forests, and, at the furthest end of the track, you'll find the remote Saltos de Moconá. Tourist services are less well developed here, but you can stay next to the falls or in San Pedro or El Soberbio.

For a staggering 3 km, on the Argentine side of the Río Uruguay, water falls over a vast shelf of rock from 18 m up to 120 m, creating one of the most magnificent sights in the region. The rocky edge is quite easily reached on foot from the bank of the river, in an area surrounded by dense woodland, and protected by the Parque Estadual do Turvo (Brazil) and the Parque Provincial Moconá, the Reserva Provincial Esmeralda and the Reserva de la Biósfera Yabotí (Argentina). The **Parque Provincial Moconá** covers 1,000 ha with vehicle roads and footpaths, and accommodation nearby, where all activities are arranged, including excursions to the falls. In all three natural reserves the hilly forested landscape offers tremendous trekking, kayaking, birdwatching and exploring in 4WD vehicles. Alternative bases for exploring the remains are the small towns of **El Soberbio** (70 km southwest) or **San Pedro** (92 km northwest). Roads from both towns to Moconá are impassable for ordinary vehicles after heavy rains. There are regular bus services from Posadas to El Soberbio and San Pedro and from Puerto Iguazú to San Pedro, but no public transport reaches the falls.

Sleeping

Posadas *p342*

If you just need somewhere to stay near the missions, try the hotels in San Ignacio.

B Julio César, Entre Ríos 1951, T03752-427930, www.juliocesarhotel.com.ar. Large 4-star with pool and gym and spacious rooms. Breakfast included.

C Continental, Bolívar 1879 (on plaza 9 de Julio), T03752-440990, www.hoteleramisiones.com.ar. Comfortable standard rooms, plainly decorated, but more spacious **B** VIP rooms, some with river views. Restaurant on first floor.

C Posadas, Bolívar 1949, T03752-440888, www.hotelposadas.com.ar. Business-oriented hotel with good standard rooms and bigger especial rooms. Restaurant, gym, free internet access.

D City, Colón 1754, T03752-433901, citysa@arnet.com.ar. Gloomy reception area, but good a/c rooms, some overlooking the plaza. Breakfast included, restaurant on 1st floor.

D Le Petit, Santiago del Estero 1630, T03752-436031. Very good value small hotel a short walk from the centre on a quiet and shady street. Spotless rooms have a/c and breakfast is included. Recommended.

E Residencial Misiones, Félix de Azara 1960, T03752-430133. Very welcoming owners offer pleasant rooms with fan and bath in a centrally located old house with a patio. No breakfast is served, but cooking and laundry facilities are available. Popular with Europeans.

San Ignacio *p344*

Easier and cheaper than staying in Posadas.

D pp **Club de Río**, 3km from San Ignacio (ring for directions), T03755-404828, www.clubderio.com.ar. Cabañas in rural setting.

D El Descanso, Pellegrini 270, T03755-470207. Appealing and comfortable with small detached houses, 5 blocks southwest of main Av Sarmiento, and campsite.

D San Ignacio, San Martín 823, T03755-470047, hotelsanignacio@arnet.com.ar. Most recommendable place in town, this is very welcoming. The informative owner Beatriz offers very good rooms with a/c and nice self catering apartments for 4-5. Breakfast US$2. Phone booths and an interesting aerial view of town from the reception. Recommended.

E pp **Residencial Doka**, Alberdi 518, T03755-470131, recidoka@yahoo.com.ar. Simple but comfortable rooms, handy for the ruins.

G pp **La Casa de Inés y Juan**, San Martín 1291 (no sign and no phone). A warm and laid-back artist's house, very quaint, with 2 rooms, a small library and a backyard for pitching tents (US$1.30 pp per day), where there's also a small but delightful pool and a curious bathroom. Meals on request. Recommended.

Camping

Two sites on the river are splendidly situated and very well-kept on a small sandy bay among rocky promontories. They are reached by 45-min walk from town at the end of the road leading to Quiroga's house: **Club de Pesca y Deportes Náuticos**, on hilly ground with lush vegetation at Puerto Nuevo, 3km from San Ignacio, www.pescasanignacio.netfirms.com. US$1.50 pp per day plus US$1 per tent.

Playa del Sol, T03752-470207. On the beach side. US$1.50 pp per day plus US$1 per tent.

Oberá *p346*

Ask the tourist office for details of farms run by host families of different nationalities.

C Cabañas del Parque, Ucrania y Tronador, T03755-426000, cabanas@arnet.com.ar. Situated next to the Parque de las Naciones, is this tourist complex of several houses or rooms for 2 to 8 people with kitchen and a/c, breakfast included. Large swimming pool and a restaurant. Also more luxurious accommodation, **B** rooms.
C Premier, 9 de Julio 1114, T03755-406171, hpremier@hotmail.com. A good central option, with a/c, but no breakfast.
D Cuatro Pinos, Sarmiento 453, T03755-425102. A well-located hotel.

The route from San Ignacio to Puerto Iguazú: Eldorado *p347*
A Estancia Las Mercedes, just south of Eldorado, 120 km from Iguazú, T03751-431511, is a great place for a couple of nights. A traditional Argentine estancia founded by British pioneers, it has a quaint historical old house, gorgeous grounds with pool, horse riding through virgin rainforest, and rafting on the river. Owner Edie Lowe makes you extremely welcome. Recommended. Price is for full board, all activities included. **Delmonte** travel agency in Eldorado (see page 350) can arrange transfer from the falls.

Saltos del Moconá *p347*
D pp **El Refugio Moconá**, 3 km from access to the reserve, 8 km from the falls (or contact at Pasaje Dornelles 450, in San Pedro), T03751-470022, www.mocona.com. Rustic rooms for 4-5 with shared bath, campsite for US$4.30 a day per tent, tents for rent (US$8.50 a day), meals for US$4.30-6 and many activities, such as 30-min boat trips to the falls (US$63 per group of up to 5), 1-hr walk to the falls (US$21 per group), and several other excursions on foot and by 4WD vehicles. There is also a kayak journey down the river Yabotí (US$29 pp). Transfer with sightseeing to/from San Pedro, 2 hrs, US$85 for up to 8.
D Hostería Puesta del Sol, C Suipacha s/n, El Soberbio, T03755-495161 (T011-43001377 in Buenos Aires). A splendid vantage point on the town, with swimming pool and a restaurant. The rooms are comfortable with breakfast and a/c. For full board add US$6.50 pp. Boat excursions arranged to the falls, 7-8 hrs, landing and meal included, US$20 pp (minimum 4 people). The journey to the falls is by a boat crossing to Brazil, then by vehicle to Parque do Turvo, 7 hrs, meal included, US$20 pp. Otherwise, a 4WD journey on the Argentine side with more chances for trekking takes 7 hrs, with a meal included, US$20 pp.

Eating

Posadas *p342*
Most places offer the *espeto corrido* system, as much *parrilla* as you can eat for a fixed price: pork, beef, sausages, entrails or chicken, grilled and brought to the table speared on a long brochette or *al galeto*. Instead of the usual potato or bread with meat, in Misiones it's common to eat *mandioca*, a potato-like root. The typical dessert is *mamón en almíbar* (papaya in syrup). If you haven't already tried chipá, small bread rolls made with manioc flour, there are lots to try in Posadas. Delicious.
De La Costa, Av Costanera. Hugely popular with locals, this place on the river banks has 2 floors, with great views from the upper floor, and a cheerful buzz on Sat.
Diletto, Bolívar 1729. A rather formal atmosphere, good for fish such as surubí and, curiously, rabbit as the house speciality.
El Mensú, Fleming y Coronel Reguera (in the Bajada Vieja district). A very attractive house in the picturesque old port area with a varied menu with fish, pastas and a large selection of wines included. Closed Mon.
Espeto del Rey, Ayacucho y Tucumán. A *parrilla* with *espeto corrido*, which serves good food at moderate prices. Try *mandioca frita* (fried manioc).
La Querencia, Bolívar 1849 (on plaza 9 de Julio). A large traditional restaurant offering *parrilla* served *al galeto*, surubí and pastas.
La Rueda, Av Costanera. A quiet smart place on the banks of the river.

San Ignacio *p344*
There are also several restaurants catering for tourists (eg La Carpa Azul) at Rivadavia 1295, on the streets by the Jesuit ruins.
Pizzería La Aldea, Rivadavia y Lanusse, right opposite the entrance to the ruins. A friendly place serving good cheap pizzas, empanadas and other simple meals, also will make sandwiches to take away. Recommended.
Hotel San Ignacio, San Martín 823, see above. Restaurant at the hotel offers simple meals are also offered 1700. Closed Mon

Oberá *p346*

🍴 **Engüete**, Cabeza de Vaca 340. Good food and a varied menu is available.

🍴 **El Lapacho**, Sarmiento 1230 and Juan Alfredo, Av Libertad y Ralf Singer.

Festivals

Oberá *p346*

Sep The vibrant **Fiesta Nacional del Inmigrante** lasts a week around Sep 4 (Immigrant's Day). In the Parque de las Naciones houses built in various national styles are the attractive setting for folk dances, parades, tasting national dishes and the election of a Queen. Very popular..

Activities and tours

Posadas *p342*

Abra, Colón 1975, T03752-422221, abramisiones@arnet.com.ar. Runs tours to San Ignacio, including Santa Ana Jesuit ruins (US$20 pp), to Jesuit ruins in Paraguay (US$23 pp) and in Brazil (US$48 pp), to Jesuit ruins in Misiones and waterfalls (US$47 pp), to Saltos del Moconá (a 2-day trip, US$136 pp).

Guayrá, San Lorenzo 2208, T03752-433415, www.guayra.com.ar. Tours to Iberá (US$50-65 pp if 4 people), to Saltos del Moconá (US$80 pp if 4 people), both sites in a 5-day excursion for US$240 pp (if 4 people). Also car rental and transfer to Colonia Carlos Pellegrini (for Esteros del Iberá).

Oberá *p346*

Transit 21, Ucrania y Tronador, 1st floor, T03755-402121, www.transit21.com.ar Ask here for a transfer to the Saltos de Moconá.

The route from San Ignacio to Puerto Iguazú: Eldorado *p347*

Delmonte, Av San Martín 1734, Km9, T03751-422113, cebrera@ceel.com.ar. Transfers from Iguazú to San Ignacio, and to estancias like Las Mercedes. Incredibly friendly and helpful. Recommended.

Transport

Posadas *p342*

Air General San Martín Airport is on RN12, 12 km west, T03752-457413, reached by Bus No 8 or 28 with stops along C Junín in centre, 40 mins, US$0.23, remise taxi (takes 25 mins)US8$. To **Buenos Aires**, twice daily with **Aerolíneas Argentinas**, 1 hr 25 mins (if direct), some flights call at **Corrientes** or **Formosa**, 1 hr 50 mins.

Airline offices Aerolíneas Argentinas, Ayacucho 1728, T03752-432889

Boat At Río Paraná, port access from Av Costanera y Av Andrés Guaçurarí, T03752-425044 (**Prefectura**). Boat crossing to Encarnación (Paraguay), 6-8 mins, almost every hour Mon-Fri 0800-1800, US$1. Ticket office at main building.

Bus The terminal is 5 km out of the city on the road to Corrientes at Av Santa Catalina y Av Luis Quaranta, T03752-456106. Reached by Bus No 4, 8, 15, 21, with stops along C Junín in centre, 20 mins, US$0.23, remise taxis charge US$2. Platforms at both levels, so check. Left luggage, Mon-Fri 0730-2100, Sat 0730-2000, US$0.35. To **Buenos Aires**, with **Crucero del Norte** T03752-455533, **Expreso Tigre Iguazú** T03752-455200, **Vía Bariloche** T03572- 45300, **Expreso Singer** T03572-455800, **Río Uruguay**, T03572-455833, 12-13 hrs, US$17- 25. Choose *coche cama* for real comfort.

To **Mendoza**, **Autotransportes Mendoza**, (T03752-454833), 30 hrs, US$36 . To **Tucumán**, **La Nueva Estrella** (**T03752-455455**), **Autotransportes Mendoza**, 16-18 hrs, US$18-21. To **Salta**, **La Nueva Estrella** (change at Resistencia), 18 hrs, US$30 (coche cama). To **Puerto Iguazú**, **Horiansky, Kruse, Expreso Singer, Aguila Dorada Bis**, hourly, 5-6 hrs, US$8. Several companies run frequent services to almost all main provincial destinations, including San Ignacio (1 hr, US$1.30), Oberá (1½ hrs, US$2), El Soberbio (3½-4½ hrs, US$5).

To **Encarnación** (Paraguay), **Servicio Internacional**, 50 mins, US$0.65, leaving at least every half an hour from platforms 11 and 12 (lower level), tickets on bus.

If going to **Esteros del Iberá**, there are more frequent services via Corrientes to **Mercedes**, which is the nearest town. You may have to take a transfer from Posadas – your estancia in Iberá can arrange this.

Car rental Hertz, San Lorenzo 2208 (at Guayrá travel agency), T03752-433415. **Avis**, at airport T03752-596660, or San Martín, T03752-15561430.

Remise taxi JC, Entre Ríos 1945, T03752-431185. Nivel, Córdoba 194, T03752-428500.

San Ignacio *p344*
Bus Buses stop in front of church, leaving every hour to **Posadas** (US$2.50) or to **Puerto Iguazú** (US$5-6) and all towns along Route 12. Don't rely on the terminal at end of Av Sarmiento, as only a few buses actually stop here. More buses stop on Route 12 at the access road (Av Sarmiento). **Remise taxis** stop at Av Sarmiento and San Martín.

Oberá *p346*
Bus To **Posadas**, Horiansky, Expreso Singer, Capital del Monte, Don Tito, 1½ hrs, US$2. Capital del Monte goes also to **Campo Viera**, **Aristóbulo del Valle, Leandro N Alem**. Don Tito goes to **El Soberbio**.

Directory

Posadas *p342*
Banks Banco de La Nación, Bolívar 1799. Round the corner on Félix de Azara are Banco Río and HSBC. Citibank, San Martín y Colón. Mazza, Bolívar 1932. For money exchange, all TCs accepted. **Consulates** Paraguay, San Lorenzo 179, T03752-423858. Mon-Fri 0730-1400. All visas in general on the same day. **Immigration** Dirección Nacional de Migraciones, Buenos Aires 1633, T03752-427414. **Internet** Anyway, Féliz de Azara 2067. Cheaper evenings and weekends. Cyber Nick, San Luis 1847. Mateando, on Félix de Azara, next to San Martín. US$0.35/hr. Misiol@n, San Lorenzo 1681. Open 24 hrs, US$0.35/hr. **Medical emergencies** Hospital Dr Ramón Madariaga, Av L Torres 1177, T03752-447000. **Post office** Bolívar y Ayacucho. Also Western Union branch.

Esteros del Iberá

Still one of Argentina's secret natural wonders, the Esteros del Iberá is a vast nature reserve of lagoons and marshes, home to an astonishing array of bird and animal life. The area has been loved by ornithologists for some time, and they still come here in great groups to tick off rare species which can't be seen elsewhere, and certainly not at such close quarters. But you don't have to be an expert to appreciate this natural paradise. Among the 370 species of birds, herons and egrets soar elegantly from bush to bush, swifts and kingfishers swoop low on the water, giant storks nest on the many floating islands, rich with plant life, and there are tiny bright red headed federal birds, long tailed flycatchers, families of southern screamers – chajá –with their fluffy heads and rasping cry, amongst many species.

These immense and beautiful wetlands are among the largest expanse of virgin lagoons in South America, bettered only by the far more famous Pantanal in Brazil. Fed by an expanse of freshwater the size of Belgium, the Esteros (marshes) del Iberá host an incredible diversity of bird and animal life in one of Argentina's most exquisite landscapes. Great stretches of water are interrupted by embalsados, huge floating islands where marsh deer can be glimpsed among lush foliage, and on whose banks alligators wait, half submerged, for something to eat. The great appeal of a stay here is that you don't have to be an expert bird-watcher to find the varied bird life fascinating. Stay in one of the estancias at Colonia Carlos Pellegrini, or further south at Rincón del Socorro, and your accommodation includes at least one boat trip on the lagoons, with a guide who can tell you all about the flora and fauna. In this country of so many natural wonders, it's one of the most unforgettable experiences. Come here soon before everyone else does.

On the western side of the region, in an area of lowlands and higher woodlands, is the Parque Nacional Mburucuyá, where natural conditions are ideal for a close view of the local wildlife. ▸▸ *For Sleeping, Eating and other listings, see pages 354-356.*

Ins and outs

Getting there and around Part of the magic of the Esteros del Iberá is that they are isolated, and though it takes a while to get here, transport can be organized by the estancias. The quickest way is to fly from Buenos Aires to Posadas (twice daily, 1½ hours) but the flight leaves Buenos Aires at 0600. A better option may be to take the overnight bus (*coche cama*, 10 hours) from Buenos Aires to **Mercedes**, and ask your estancia or hotel to arrange a 4WD remise transfer from there. There's a bus from Merdedes to Colonia Carlos Pelegrini but it takes forever and leaves at inconvenient times. From **Posadas**, the 200-km journey takes four to five hours as the roads are earth and gravel after the first 60 km, and negotiable only in a 4WD vehicle, impassible after heavy rain. It's best not to hire a car. The hotels are all near the Iberá Lagoon, the easiest lagoon to access in the Esteros, reached by boat from one of several small hotels and estancias with their own stretch of waterfront in the sleepy little village of **Colonia Carlos Pellegrini. Estancia Rincón del Socorro**, 30 km south of Pellegrini, is the most beautiful of all the estancias, and slightly closer to Mercedes. They will arrange transfers. ▸▸ *For further information, see Transport, page 356.*

Best time to visit Autumn, winter or spring, avoiding the intense heat of mid-summer, with more chance of rain and thunderstorms.

Background

This beautiful area at the heart of Corrientes province has only just opened to tourism, since it was until recently a rich territory for hunters and grazing land for cattle ranchers. Since the creation of a nature reserve here in 1983, several local estancias have opened to guests, keen to enjoy the perfect tranquillity here as much as the bird life. The Esteros have yet to gain national park status, however, which would ensure their greater protection. North American conservationist Douglas Tompkins is campaigning for this, and has been buying up huge sections of the land from private owners, in order to rescue it from cattle farming and rice growing which pollute the pristine waters. Though he's a controversial figure, his aims are sincere: he plans to give all the land to Argentina if it can be guaranteed national park status. You can visit his own estancia Rincón del Socorro, 30km south of Colonia Carlos Pellegrini.

Mercedes → *Phone code: 03773 Colour map 2, B1 Population: 30,900*

Mercedes is the most convenient access point for Colonia Carlos Pellegrini and the Esteros del Iberá, with regular overnight buses from Buenos Aires. It is 120 km from Pellegrini (but note that this takes two hours on the gravel roads) and 250 km southeast of Corrientes. A chirpy little town, with some quaint 1900's buildings, there are a couple of decent places to stay overnight, and a few restaurants, internet facilities and ATMs around the plaza, where there is also a small **tourist office**. Both Calle Pujol and Calle San Martín lead from the bus station to the plaza, and you're likely to see gauchos hanging around here in the distinctive outfits of Corrientes province, with their red berets. A few kilometres west of the town, on the road to Corrientes, is a shrine to **pagan saint Gauchito Gil** at the place where it's said he was killed. Shrines to Gil can be seen all over the country, with their distinctive red flags.

Colonia Carlos Pellegrini → *Phone code: 03773 Colour map 2, B2 Population: 600*

With a remote setting on the beautiful Laguna Iberá 120 km northeast of Mercedes, the sprawling village of Pellegini is the only base for visiting Los Esteros del Iberá. A quiet, very laid-back place of 600 inhabitants, there are just a few blocks of earth roads, and all the hotels are just a few hundred metres away from each other. There is no bank, no ATM, no restaurants, and no shops to speak of so make sure you bring everything you need. There are, however, eleven hotels and estancias, most very comfortable, and these all offer full board, or a picnic if you're out during the day. They also offer boat trips on the lake as part of your accommodation, and some estancias offer walking and horse riding too. A two-night stay allows you to do at least one two-hour boat trip, and you might be offered a walk to see the howler monkeys in a patch of lovely jungle near the visitors' centre, but you may want to plan to stay for three or four nights to really unwind and lap up the tranquil atmosphere. There are few streetlights in the village so carry a torch at night, and ask anyone for directions to get back to your hotel. Bring a hat, mosquito repellent, plenty of sun block, and binoculars too if you're keen to spot the more distant birds as well as those right by your boat.

Reserva Natural del Iberá

This reserve protects nearly 13,000 km sq of wetlands known as the Esteros del Iberá, a vast flat flooded plain which is one of the most important natural areas in all Argentina for its superb wildlife. The area is really only accessible to visitors from the little village of Colonia Carlos Pellegrini, from where excursions depart. There's a **Park Rangers office and visitors centre** ⓘ *by the bridge at the access to Colonia Carlos Pellegrini, 0730-1200, 1400-1800*, where you can chat to the *guardaparques*, see a map of the natural reserve, and get more information on the flora and fauna. They also sell an excellent guide to all the plants, birds and animals you'll find here – *Iberá, Vida y Colour*, in Spanish and English with the Latin names noted as well – which is indispensable if your guide on the boat trip doesn't speak English. Opposite the visitor centre is a stretch of jungle where howler monkeys hang out – a *guardaparque* may accompany you if your trip doesn't include this.

The Esteros del Iberá – 'shining water' in the Guaraní language – are fed exclusively by fresh water from rain: no rivers flow into it. The marshes extend 250 km northeast to Ituzaingó on the Alto Paraná, and are some 70 km wide at their broadest. Clear waters cover between 20 to 30% of the protected area, and there are over 60 *lagunas*, or small lakes, astonishingly no more than a few metres deep, the largest being the **Laguna Iberá** and **Laguna de la Luna**. The area is rich in aquatic plants, including the beautiful purple *camelote*, tiny cream coloured star-shaped flowers, *irupé* (*Victoriana cruziana*) which forms a kind of floating plate supporting animal and birdlife, and when it stretches along the shoreline, it's hard to differentiate the land from the lake. The area owes its rich animal life to the profusion of *embalsados*, which sit like islands in the *lagunas*, but are just floating vegetation, dense enough to support large animals, such as the marsh deer, and sizeable trees and bushes. *Carpinchos* (capybaras) make their homes along the edges, and alligators can be seen basking on any protruding clump of mud. Watch out for the ghastly but ingenious colonial spiders, working together to weave enormous horizontal nets for unsuspecting insects in the later afternoon. Prolific bird life is all around. The boat trip is at its most exciting when you travel down narrow creeks between these *embalsados*, and when you're invited to walk on them – they are amazingly stable, but yield subtly to your feet with a pleasing springiness. In case you don't understand your guide's instructions in Spanish – if you suddenly start sinking, you're advised to spread out your arms before the *embalsado* closes in over you. But don't worry – this is very unlikely to happen.

Boat trips Your hotel or estancia will offer at least one boat trip included in your accommodation into Laguna Iberá to visit areas where there are lots of birds, alligators and capybaras. Depending on the time of day, these usually take two to three hours, and in summer it's best to go out in the early morning or later evening, to avoid the intense heat and to stand more chance of seeing more birds. Do ask your hotel or estancia at the time of booking if there are guides who speak your language: many of the local guides are excellent and know the lagunas like the back of their hands, complete with all the resident wildlife, but speak little English. You can be guaranteed English speaking guides at **Posada de la Laguna** and **Rincón del Socorro**. If you're lucky, your trip will be timed to return as the sun sinks on the water – sun sets here are really spectacular, when the whole world of water and sky is tinted vivid vermillion, an unforgettably moving sight. Some estancias also offer walks to the jungle to see – and hear howler monkeys, swinging off the trees, and roaring, especially when rain is approaching. Night safaris are fun too: see cute mammals, vizcachas, owls and lots of capybaras running around by the light of your guide's lamp.

Parque Nacional Mburucuyá

If you can't make it over to the Esteros del Iberá and are in Corrientes city, you might like to visit this park, which stretches north from the marshlands of the Río Santa Lucía. It's 180 km southeast of Corrientes, 12 km east of the small town of Mburucuyá (where there are two places to stay overnight), accessible by a 47 km-long road branching off at Saladas. Unpaved Route 86 (later Route 13) links Mburucuyá with the park and this sandy road leads northeast to Itá Ibaté, on Route 12, 160 km east of the provincial capital.

The land was donated by Danish botanist Troels Pedersen, whose long research had identified 1300 different plants, including some newly discovered species. There's a variety of natural environments, ranging from savanna with *yatay* palms and 'islands' of wet Chaco forest, with *lapacho* trees (with purple blossom in late winter) and *timbó* trees to the aquatic vegetation of the *esteros*. You'll also see *mburucuyá* or passionflower that gives its name to the park. Lots of interesting wildlife too: capybaras, the rare *aguará guazu* (maned wolf) and the *aguará pope*, similar to the North American raccoon – though these are both nocturnal animals – deer such as *corzuela parda* (*Mazama gouazoubira)* and *ciervo de los pantanos*, foxes *aguará-í*, monkeys and many bird species, such as the lovely *yetapá de collar* (*Alectrurus risora*) or strange-tailed tyrant, with its beautiful double tail.

Provincial Route 86 (unpaved) crosses the park for 18 km, to the **information centre** and free **campsite** (hot water and electricity) at the centre of the park. From there, two footpaths branch off the access road. The **Sendero Yatay** goes south to a vantage point on Estero Santa Lucía, winding 2.5 km through gallery forests and grassland with mature palms. The Sendero Aguará Popé goes north 1.2 km, through thick vegetation and wet Chaco forests and near the western access to the park, the road crosses the *arroyo Portillo*, where 2-m-long *yacarés negros* alligators are often spotted.

Sleeping

Mercedes *p352*

D La Casa de China, call for directions, T03773-15627269. A delightful historical old house with clean rooms and a lovely patio, breakfast included. Recommended.

Colonia Carlos Pellegrini *p352*

AL pp **Rincón del Socorro**, T03782-497073, T011-48112005 (in Buenos Aires), www.rincondelsocorro.com. Incredibly luxurious, this estancia is part of an impressive conservation project by North American millionaire Douglas Tompkins, who is buying up large tracts of cattle farming land to protect it and donate it to the Argentine government. Beautifully set in its own 12,000 hectares 35km south of Carlos Pellegrini, there is impeccable taste throughout: 6 spacious bedrooms, each with bathroom and little sitting room, 3 cabañas, and elegant sitting rooms and dining rooms. Delicious organic food is grown in the kitchen garden, and a charming welcome from Leslie and Valeria, who speak perfect English, and organise excellent trips on the lagunas with expert, bilingual guides, asados at lunchtime, night safaris and wonderful horse riding. Gorgeous gardens, pool with superb views all around. Highly recommended.

A pp **Hostería Ñandé Retá**, T/F03782-499411, T011-48112005 (in Buenos Aires), www.nandereta.com. The first house to receive guests at the Esteros, this big old wooden house is set under shady trees and offers friendly and relaxed accommodation in 9 rooms, full board with excursions included, as well as a playroom on the upper floor: ideal for long rainy afternoons. Good family cooking from owner Estrella Losada.

App **Posada Aguapé**, T03782-499412, T/F011-47423015 (in Buenos Aires), www.iberaesteros.com.ar. Named after the pale yellow water lilies which abound nearby, this estancia combines relaxed living with extremely good food and a very high standard of activities. Run by a welcoming couple, Rafael and Elena, accommodation is in high ceilinged traditional galleried rooms, with big windows directly onto the simple gardens going down to the lagoon. Rafael speaks good English and is an excellent guide to the local wildlife, but note that other guides speak little English. Canoeing and horse riding are also on offer. Recommended.

App **Posada de la Laguna**, T/F03782-499413, T011-4807 3740 (in Buenos Aires), www.posadadelalaguna.com Quite the loveliest place to stay in Pellegrini, this charming little estancia was built by the current owner, Elsa Güiraldes, granddaughter of one of Argentina's great writers. She's created a stylish and welcoming home here, where guests share the spacious sitting and dining rooms, but have their guest house with elegant bedrooms coming off a terrace with open views onto the laguna. Here there is direct access to the water from the lovely gardens, and a pool. Price includes all boat trips and use of the canoes, and all the delicious meals. Elsa speaks fluent English and some French, and makes you feel entirely at home. She also guides the boat trips, and will arrange transfers. A beautiful place. Highly recommended.

Bpp **Irupé Lodge**, T15402193, www.irupe lodge.com.ar. Newly built right on the laguna, with great views from the first floor dining room, this is a rustic place with simple rooms, offering the usual trips, as well as some less conventional ones: camping on remote islands, asado with local musicians playing chamamé, and diving and fishing piranha! Several languages spoken, including English.

Dpp **Posada Ypa Sapukai**, T03782-420155, www.ypasapukai.com.ar.This cosy house is the best value place to stay, run by friendly Pedro Noailles, who has lived here for 10 years and is an expert guide to the lagoon's wildlife. His wife, Claudia, speaks English, and they offer excellent excursions to the laguna. Rates are for full board and include two 3-hr boat trips, or a walk/ horse riding. Recommended.

Fpp **San Cayetano**, T03773-15628763. A very basic place run by local guide Roque Pera, also with campsite.

Estancias

Bpp **San Juan Poriahú**, at Loreto, T03781-15608674, T011-47919511 (in Buenos Aires). An old estancia with an attractive house run by Marcos García Rams, situated at the northwestern edge of the Esteros del Iberá, next to the village of Loreto, and accessible by a paved road from nearby Route 12. Rates include full board accommodation (half rate for under 12s) and activities such as horse riding and boat trips to appreciate the rich wildlife in an area where there has been no hunting at all. Closed in Jan, Feb and Jul holidays. Recommended.

Bpp **San Lorenzo**, at Galarza, T03756-481292, www.iberaargentina.com.ar. Set next to 2 of the biggest lakes of the Iberá (at the northeast edge of the region), this estancia is in a splendid place for wildlife watching, especially rare deer venado de las pampas. Welcoming, full board, activities (riding, walking, boat trips to Lagunas de Luna and Galarza) are all included in the rates. Boat excursions by night are charged separately. Access from Gobernador Virasoro (90 km away), via Routes 37 and 41. Transfers can be arranged to/from Gobernador Virasoro or Posadas for an extra charge. Closed in Jan-Feb.

Eating

There aren't any good restaurants in Coloni Carlos Pellegrini, since all hotels and estancias offer full board. There are a couple of kioskos selling cold drinks and snacks on the road leading to the bridge, unreliable opening times.

Mercedes *p352*

There are several places around the cheery plaza, including:

Café de la Plaza, next to the casino. Very popular, 'where the well-off people go'.

El Quincho. Upmarket, but still very inexpensive and serves delicious food.

Pizza Libre, opposite the main church, serves great pizzas as well as parrilla and lomitos. A simple place but excellent value for a filling meal.

Transport

Mercedes p352

Bus

To **Colonia Carlos Pellegrini**; Itatí II combi provides the only service but check as times change. Used to leave daily at 1130 (or 1200) from Pujol 1166, T03773-420184, T15629598, 3-5 hrs, US$3.30. Note that it spends an hour picking up passengers from the whole of Mercedes after leaving the office. Returns from Pellegrini the next day at 0400. A new trial service leaves Mercedes at 0700, returning from Pellegrini at 1700. Ask in bus terminal. Your best bet is organizing a transfer with local taxi company who have 4WD vehicles. See below. To **Buenos Aires**, Flecha Bus, Itatí, Nuevo Rápido Tata, Aguila Dorada Bis, San Cristóbal, 9-10 hrs, US$12-14. To **Corrientes**, several companies, 3 hrs, US$3.30-4. To **Puerto Iguazú**, there are two options: via Corrientes; or via any major town along Route 14, where you can take a bus going north. The first takes longer, but there's more chance of a bus.

Colonia Carlos Pellegrini p352

Bus

To **Mercedes** Itatí II combi, 3-5 hrs, US$3.30, departs daily at 0400. Booking is required before 2200 on the night before at the office in a local grocery (ask for directions). Their bus departs Mon-Sat at 0430. To **Posadas**, the only way is to organize a transfer through your hotel or estancia (4-5 hrs) impassable after heavy rain). Your hosts will be happy to sort this out by email before you arrive. Or try **Fermin Cruz**, T15403967, ferbenitezcruz@hotmail.com. Transfer prices are per vehicle, so much cheaper if there are a few of you. **Mercedes to Colonia Carlos Pellegrini** US$60; **Pellegrini to Corrientes** US$220. From Posadas see under Posadas tour operators.

Parque Nacional Mburucuyá p354

Buses

San Antonio from Corrientes goes daily to **Mburucuyá**, 2½ hrs, US$2.30. **Remise taxis** from there to the park, US$5. Free entry, T03782-498022.

Along the Río Uruguay

The mighty Río Uruguay is over 1600 km long, and a staggering 10 km wide in places. It forms Argentina's eastern boundary with Uruguay and Brazil, and along the Argentine side are dotted a few interesting towns and cities. With time to spare you could return from the northeast to Buenos Aires via the river. Gualeguaychú is so keen to party, it celebrates its carnival every weekend for two months, but you can calm down in Concepción del Uruguay, with attractive old buildings, or Colón, with its historic port area and sandy beaches. There's a national park protecting splendid palm forests, though the reserve La Aurora del Palmar is more accessible. You can stay on colonial estancias, jungle islands, and with small communities at Irazusta and Arroyo Barú. The section that follows takes you from south to north along the Río Uruguay. *» For Sleeping, Eating and other listings, see pages 360-363.*

Gualeguaychú → *Phone code: 03446 Colour map 4, A5 Population: 74,700*

The first town of any size on the route north, Gualeguaychú is famous for its extended carnival. It's lively throughout the summer, with an attractive *costanera* on the Río Gualeguaychú, where there are several *balnearios* and restaurants, a pleasant place for a stroll with views of the picturesque port. Carnival is celebrated at the local *corsódromo* (arena), a hugely popular event, lasting well beyond the usual fortnight to fill every weekend for a couple of months. The port and *balneario municipal* (town bathing spot) are the departure points for short boat excursions and city tours, T03446-423248 (only in high season). About 200 m south of the port in Plazoleta de los Artesanos, local handicrafts are sold at weekends in summer, and a vast green area, a thatched hut houses the local **tourist office** ⓘ *T03446-423668, www.gualeguaychuturismo.com 0800-2000 (closing later in summer).*

On the *costanera* at Gervasio Méndez is **El Patio del Mate** ⓘ *T03446-424371, www.elpatiodelmate.com.ar, daily 0800-2100*, a workshop where dedicated craftsmen make the cups from which *mate* is drunk, varying widely from simple dyed gourds to ornate silver goblets.

Around Gualeguaychú

Villa Paranacito, is a village set in the delta islands, 100 km south of Gualeguaychú, where houses are built on tall stilts and boats are the essential means of transport. It's popular with anglers in the waters of the nearby Río Uruguay (half an hour farther by boat), and anyone looking for a quiet place to stay, immersed in the islander culture. There are campsites, a youth hostel and *cabañas* offering boat excursions. There's delicious local fish at **Villa Paranacito Annemarie**.

Estancia La Azotea ⓘ *10 km north of Villarancito, on Route 12 in Ceibas, T03446-492007 (or in Buenos Aires, T011-4393 8057)*, is a 19th-century house popular for day visits, with cattle ranching, horseriding, an *asado* lunch, and the use of a pool in summer. At US$10pp it's very good value.

West and northwest of Gualeguaychú, there are a string of small **eco communities** near Larroque and Urdinarrain, newly opened to tourism both to share the tranquillity of these peaceful rural places and to meet their inhabitants. At **Aldea San Antonio**, 41 km northwest, you can visit a German settlement and tour in a horse drawn carriage. Contact Señora Susana Schaaf, T03446-497045 and Señora Mercedes, T03446-497055 at **Casa Alamana**. At the tiny community of **Irazusta**, 63 km west, there's a community of just 350 inhabitants, where Señora Eufemia, T03446-491530 and Señor Abel, T03446-491524 (ask also at local railway station) provide accommodation and meals at family houses, an enriching experience for both guests and hosts. This is a pilot project, intended to stop the depopulation process of small communities: for more information visit www.responde.org.ar. So far it's been very successful.

Border with Uruguay

Situated 33 km southeast of Gualeguaychú, the Libertador General San Martin Bridge (5.4 km long) provides the most southerly route across the Río Uruguay, to Fray Bentos. Customs and immigration are at opposite ends of the bridge and it's an uncomplicated crossing; formalities take about 10 minutes. Passport details are noted when booking bus tickets and passed to officials at the border, and passports are inspected on the bus. Note that pedestrians and cyclists can only cross on motor vehicles, though officials may arrange lifts. Vehicle toll is US$4. Don't carry any dairy products, meat, fruit and vegetables, flowers, plants and seeds, or animals (as if you would!). The Argentine consulate is at 18 de Julio 1225, T+598-(0)562 3225, Fray Bentos.

Into Uruguay: Fray Bentos

➔ *Phone code: +598-(0)562 Colour map 4, A6 Population: 22,000*

Fray Bentos is the main port on the east bank of Río Uruguay, a friendly little town with an attractive *costanera*. The main reason to visit is to see the meat-packing factory. The name Fray Bentos was synonymous with corned beef in Britain throughout the 20th century, and the factory (*frigorífico*) known as El Anglo, which produced *Oxo* for many years has been beautifully restored as the **Museo de La Revolución Industrial** ⓘ *daily except Mon, entry by guided tour only, US$1, 1000, 1430 (1000, 1130 and 1700 in summer), tour 1½ hrs in Spanish, may provide leaflet in English, T+598 (0)562- 3607*, and business park, with a restaurant, *Wolves*, and a disco. The office block in the factory has been preserved with some of the old machinery. See also the *Bovril* estancia, *Vizcacheras*, below. The **tourist office** is at Puente General San Martín, T+598 (0)562-2369.

Concepción del Uruguay

» pp360-363.

→ *Phone code: 03442 Colour map 2, C1 Population: 64,500*

Concepción del Uruguay lies on the western shore of the Río Uruguay 74 km north of Gualeguaychú, with views of islands in the river opposite. Founded in 1783, it was capital of Entre Ríos province between 1813-21 and 1860-1883, and retains some fine architecture in its public buildings, and has a distinctively lively character, thanks to a young student population. The **tourist office** ⓘ *9 de Julio 844, T03442-425820, Mon-Fri 0700-1300, 1400-2000, and weekends from 0700-2200 in high season*, is two blocks from the plaza. There is another information point on the access road at Galarza y Elías ⓘ *T03442-440812, daily 0800-2000.*

The old town is centred on beautiful **Plaza Ramírez**, with the Italian neoclassical-style **Basílica de la Inmaculada Concepción**, containing the remains of General Urquiza on its western side. Next to it is the **Colegio Superior Justo José de Urquiza**, the first secular school in the country, although its 19th-century buildings were largely replaced in 1935. One block northeast of the plaza is **Museo Casa de Delio Panizza** ⓘ *Galarza y Supremo Entrerriano, daily 0900-1200, 1400-1800 (1800-2100 in summer)*, in a mansion dating from 1793 and containing 19th-century furnishings and artefacts.

Around Concepción del Uruguay

Palacio San José ⓘ *32 km west of the town, www.palaciosanjose.com, Mon-Fri 0830-1230, 1400-1830, Sat-Sun 0900-1745, US$1, information in Spanish, French and English, free guided visits at 1000, 1100, 1500, 1600,* is the former mansion of General Urquiza, which dates from 1848, built in Italian style with 38 rooms and a chapel. It was once the country's most luxurious residence. Now a museum with artefacts from Urquiza's life, the palace stands in a beautiful park with an artificial lake.

Basavilbaso, 68 km west, is a historical small town which in the early 20th century was an urban centre for Lucienville, inhabited by Jewish immigrants from Russia. There's a **tourist office** at Lagocen e Hipólito Yrigoyen, T03445-481015; information also at *Asociación Israelita*, T03445-481908. There are three well-preserved synagogues, of which the **Tefila L Moises** has a beautifully painted wooden ceiling. It's also worth visiting the **Navibuco synagogue**, 2.5 km of town, dating from 1895, and two Jewish cemeteries nearby. Basavilbaso was a busy transport hub. Though the last passenger train left in 1992, the station houses a museum where the rich history of the local railway history can be explored.

Colón

» pp360-363.

→ *Phone code: 03447 Colour map 2, C1 Population: 19,200*

One of the prettiest towns on the river, Colón was founded in 1863 as a port for the Swiss colony of San José, 9 km west, and it's an excellent base for several very interesting places nearby, including the Parque Nacional El Palmar. It is also linked by a bridge to the Uruguayan city of Paysandú, with its interesting old buildings (see below). Colón itself has many well preserved early 19th-century houses, and a beautiful riverbank with long sandy beaches and shady streets.

Sights

The most attractive part of town is the port district, next to the Plaza San Martín, with fine old houses on the plaza and nearby streets leading down to the riverside. The former passenger boat terminal, now houses the **tourist office** ⓘ *Av Costanera Quirós y Gouchón, T03447-421233, www.colonentrerios.com.ar, Mon-Fri 0630-2100, Sat 0700-2100, Sun 0800-2100.*

At the corner of Avenida 12 de Abril and Paso is **La Casona**, (1868), where there's a handicrafts exhibition and shop. North of the port, Calle Alejo Peyret gives access to the *balnearios* and their sandy beaches on the river and Calle Belgrano leads to the **Complejo Termal** ⓘ *daily 0900-2100, US$1.30, T03447-424717*, where there are 10 thermal pools (ranging from 34-40°C), in an attractive setting, very popular for treating a variety of ailments. Most shops and banks can be found on Avenida 12 de Abril, with the old **Teatro Centenario**, opened in 1925.

Excursions

Some 40 km north of Villa Elisa is **Arroyo Barú**, a rural village whose inhabitants have opened their houses to visitors who want to enjoy the tranquility of its small community. This place, together with Irazusta (west of Gualeguaychú), are both study cases for an NGO research. Contact Señora Marta, T03447-496048, turismoenbaru@hotmail.com. It is reached via a 35 km long dirt road, branching off Route 130, 5 km west of Villa Elisa, where remise taxis (T03447-496010) and combis (T03447-496013), will take passengers in good weather.

Border with Uruguay

Seven kilometres southeast of Colón, the General José Artigas Bridge gives access to the Uruguayan city of Paysandú. Toll US$4. Argentine and Uruguayan formalities are both dealt with at Uruguayan end of the bridge. *Migraciones* officials board the bus, but non-Argentine/Uruguayans should get off bus to have their passports stamped. The Argentine consulate is at Gómez 1034, T03447-22253 (Monday-Friday 0800-1300).

Parque Nacional El Palmar → *Colour map 2, C1*

ⓘ *T03447-493049. Entry: Argentines: US$2; foreigners; US$4.*

On west bank of the Río Uruguay 51 km north of Colón and 53 km south of Concordia, this park covers 8,500 ha of gently undulating grassland and mature palm forest, including *Yatay* palms hundreds of years old. These graceful trees were once found all over the pampas, until the introduction of cattle, who found the young seedlings irresistible. Growing in *palmares*, or groves, mature trees may reach 12 m in height, with fronds some 2 m in length. Along the Río Uruguay, and the *arroyos* streams which flow into it, there are gallery forests of subtropical trees and shrubs. You'll find indigenous tombs hidden away on the edge of the Río Uruguay there are **beaches** and the remains of an 18th-century quarry and port. Look out for capybaras, foxes, lizards and vizcachas as well as rheas, monk parakeets and several species of woodpecker.

The entrance gates to the park are on Route 14, where you are given a map and information on walks, and a *ripio* road leads to the administration centre, in the east of the park, near the Río Uruguay, with access to several viewpoints: **Mirador de La Glorieta, Mirador del Arroyo El Palmar, Mirador del Arroyo Los Loros** and to the coast of the Río Uruguay. There are walks between 300 m and 1000 m and you are free to walk around the main roads, though there's little shade. The administration centre is the departure point for guided walks and cycle tours run by *Capybara Aventura* (English spoken). Nearby there's camping (US$2 pp plus US$1.70 per tent in high season, electricity, hot water) with restaurant opposite, and a small shop. Visit at any time of year, but note that the park is very popular at weekends in summer and Easter week, and in summer there are more chances of thunderstorms and very hot weather.

Refugio de Vida Silvestre La Aurora del Palmar

More accessible than the National Park, the wildlife reserve of La Aurora del Palmar was created to protect a similar environment. Situated 3 km south of Ubajay, on Route 14, Km 202, it covers 1,150 ha, of which 200 are covered with a mature palm forest. There are also gallery forests along the streams and patches of *espinal*, or scrub. There's lots of birdlife, but capybaras also can be spotted along the streams. The administration centre is only 500 m from Route 14, and it offers far more organized services for visitors. Since entry is free, you could reach the vantage point of the *quincho panorámico* for a drink (try the *yatay* spirit), while enjoying the view of the palm forest. Guided excursions include horse riding into the palm forest and the *arroyo de los Pájaros* (two hours, US$5 pp, minimum two people), canoe journeys along *arroyo El Palmar* (US$5 pp, minimum two people) and walks to the Mirador del Cerro de Piedra (US$3.35 pp, minimum three people, only at weekends). All recommended.

Sleeping

Gualeguaychú *p356*

C Puerto Sol, San Lorenzo 477, T/F03446-434017, www.puerto-sol.com.ar. Appealing place to stay with good rooms with a/c, next to the port. The hotel runs a small resort in a nearby island (transfer and access included in room rates) where you can spend the day relaxing.

C Tykuá, Luis N Palma 150, T03446-422625, hoteltykua@arnet.com.ar. Brand-new place with breakfast included, lying 3 blocks from the bridge. Rooms are rather small for 3 people (**D** in low season).

D Bonanza, T03446-495199. These houses by the river are for 6, with cooking facilities and rates are negotiable if there are fewer people. There is also a campsite with hot showers and electricity for US$5 a day per tent up to 4 people.

E pp **Rose Marie**, T03446-495204. A beautiful house set in a remote position at the mouth of arroyo (stream) Martínez (1 km from Río Uruguay and at a 25-min boat journey from the village). Transfer from the village can be arranged in advance or through the local Guardería Náutica Los Pinos for an extra US$27. **D** for full board accommodation, and boat or fishing excursions are on offer.

F pp **Top Maló**, T03446-495255, topmalo@infovia.com.ar. Affiliated to Hostelling International (discounts for members), this place has **E** houses, built on stilts 3 m above ground, for 2 and 4 people with cooking facilities, shared rooms for up to 5 people, kitchen and bed linen included, and a campsite with hot showers and electricity for US$3.50 a day plus US$0.35 pp payable only for the first day. An attractive rustic style and a warm atmosphere. Short boat excursions from US$2 pp are on offer together with half-day fishing trips. The welcoming owners speak some English, but fluent German and Danish.

Camping

There are several sites along Río Gualeguaychú's banks, next to the bridge and north of it.

Costa Azul, 200 m northeast of bridge, T03446-423984. A shady willow grove, and a good location on the riverside. Camping (US$4 a day for a 2 man-tent) and also new wooden cabins (US$13 for 4 people) and small flats with cooking facilities (US$20 for 4 people).

El Ñandubaysal, T03446-423298, www.nandubaysal.com.ar. The smartest campsite and the only one on the beautiful Río Uruguay, 15 km southeast, with very good facilities (US$5.50 per tent plus access fee) and a 'VIP' sector (US$7.50 per tent plus access fee).

Concepción del Uruguay *p358*

D Grand Hotel, Eva Perón 114, T03442-422851, www.palaciotexier.com.ar. Originally a French-style mansion with an adjacent theatre built in 1931 for the Texier family, it retains some of its former splendour, especially in the hall and casino. Superior rooms (25% more expensive) have a/c and TV but are otherwise similar. Both include a large breakfast.

Estancias

Founded by Urquiza, these offer excellent accommodation and all meals included:

AL pp **Estancia San Pedro**, Near Villa Mantero, 39.5 km west of Concepción del Uruguay. T03442-428374, esanpedro@ciudad.com.ar. Owned by descendants of Urquiza, this has old rooms full of antiques, very good accommodation.

AL pp **Estancia Santa Cándida**, T03442-422188. Offers half-board accommodation at US$90 pp.

Colón *p358*
A Quirinale, Av Costanera Quirós y Noailles, T03447-421133, www.hquirinale.com.ar. A large, rather overpriced, 5-star overlooking the river. Panoramic views from some of the rooms, spa treatments charged separately. Restaurant, a casino, open-air and indoor pools, the latter with thermal waters.
D Hostería Restaurant del Puerto, Alejo Peyret 158, T03447-422698, hosteriadel puerto@ciudad.com.ar. By far the nicest and best value place to stay. This old building has been redecorated offering comfort, and retaining the period-style atmosphere. Rooms for 4 at the front on first floor have balconies overlooking the river, but off-season are also offered as doubles. Breakfast is included.
D La Chozna, Colonia Hocker, T03447-421912. This posada is in one of the colony's oldest houses, retaining its old style with very comfortable rooms. Breakfast included.
D La Posada de David, Alejo Peyret 97, T03447-423930. A pleasant family house with a garden. Welcoming owners offer very good double rooms with breakfast and one with cooking facilities.
E Hostería Liebig, Eric Evans 223, Pueblo Liebig, T03447-492049. Very kind hosts at this very pleasant family house with a splendid garden and spacious rooms. Breakfast is included and excellent meals are available. Single occupants pay double at weekends. Recommended.
F pp **Casamate**, Laprida 128, T03447-422385, www.casamate.com.ar. Affiliated to Hostelling International (discounts for members), this is a renovated old house with a nice backyard and a pleasant sitting room with a fireplace. The very welcoming young owners provide excellent information on local sights and on bus connections. Good rooms with shared baths (bed linen provided), as well as **D** doubles with own bath. Breakfasts are superb (US$1.50 if you add scrambled eggs); other meals on request. Cooking and laundry facilities and free use of cycles are also available. German and English spoken. Recommended.
F pp **Sophie Hostel**, Laprida 128, T03447-424136, www.hostels.org.ar. Affiliated to Hostelling International (discounts for members), this is an attractively renovated old house with a nice backyard for relaxing siestas and a pleasant sitting room with a fireplace. The very welcoming young owner Marcela provides excellent information on local sights and on bus connections. Good rooms with shared baths (bed linen provided), as well as **D** doubles with own bath. Breakfasts are superb; other meals on request. Cooking and laundry facilities. German and English spoken. Recommended.

Camping
Consult the tourist office for their extensive list, as there are many campsites along the riverside, getting quieter the further you go from the centre, as well as some on nearby rivers. They all charge about US$3 a day per tent for up to 2 people.
Camping Municipal Playa Norte, T03447-422074. A few blocks north of the port.
Piedras Coloradas, T03447-421451. Lies on the river a few hundred metres south of Av 12 de Abril.

Refugio de Vida Silvestre La Aurora del Palmar *p359*
Camping
There is a campsite (US$1.70-2 pp a day plus US$1.30 per tent) and one of the most extraordinary places to stay; converted train carriages: T03447-421549, www.aurora delpalmar.com.ar. (**G** pp, shared room and bath, bed linen extra; **D** doubles with bath and breakfast provided, also for 3 to 6 people). Book in advance or check availability for the excursions. Surplus charged for tours for 1 person.

Eating

Gualeguaychú *p356*
ΨΨ Campo Alto, San Lorenzo y Concordia. A large *quincho* (rustic place to eat) at the end of the *costanera*, lots of local fish *suchas surubí*, *boga*, *dorado* and *patí* on the menu.
Ψ Dacal, Av Costanera y Andrade. A traditional restaurant, serving good food; the surubí is recommended.
Ψ La Solapa, 3 de Febrero 126. Serves good homemade pastas in warm family atmosphere, where decoration includes some carnival costumes.

Concepción del Uruguay *p358*
Ψ El Remanso, Rocamora y Eva Perón. Good food, popular and moderately priced parrilla.

La Cosquilla de Angel, Alejo Peyret 180. The smartest place in town with attractive decor, live piano music in the evenings and tables outside at lunchtime. Varied and moderately priced meals, including fish of the day and also a reasonable set menu.

Viejo Almacén, Urquiza y Paso. A cosy place offering very good cooking and excellent service. The *surubí* is tasty *al limón* or with a delicate sauce. In the basement, there's a great place for trying wines and *picadas* (nibbles of cheese and ham).

Festivals

Gualeguaychú *p356*

Jan/Feb Local teams or *comparsas* compete in colourful parades, to the powerful drumbeats of the *batucada*, with the spectacularly decorated *carrozas* and dancers dressed in brightly coloured costumes and feathers. Carnival is celebrated every weekend throughout Jan and Feb at the corsódromo, a purpose-built carnival parade ground with grandstand, at the back of the former railway station, Piccini y Maipú. It's US$7 for a seat, and while the spectacle is quite amazing, it lacks the spontaneity of a street festival.

Colón *p358*

Feb The Fiesta Nacional de la Artesanía is held over 9 evenings in Feb in Parque Quirós, where craftspeople from Argentina display a wide variety of handicrafts. There are also folklore and pop music concerts.

Activities and tours

Gualeguaychú *p356*

Landaburo, Eva Perón 444 (next to Av Aristóbulo del Valle), T03446-428668. Hires mountain bikes.

Concepción del Uruguay *p358*

Mirst Travel, Colón 301, Villaguay, T03455-423790, www.mirsttravel.com.ar. Operates tours to the Jewish colonies.

Colón *p358*

Cycling

Bici Fabián, on C Sourigues, between Av 12 de Abril and San Martín. Mountain bike hire.

Tour operators

Cambá, Martín Reibel 79, T03442-422114. Offers 3-hr guided birdwatching walks in small groups of people to nearby sites in the riverside (US$6.50 pp).

Ita i Cora, San Martín 97, T03442-423360, www.itaicora.com. Very welcoming and informative people run boat trips on the Río Uruguay, where you can lie on the huge beaches or take long walks in shallow waters, stopping off at islands to give you a taste of trekking through jungle. Recommended (45 mins-2½ hrs, US$5-17 pp). Also short 4WD trips, including a visit to Pueblo Liebig (1½-2½ hrs, US$6.50-10). Boat departures from Av Costanera Quirós y Noailles; children under 10 half price.

Parque Nacional El Palmar *p359*

Capybara Aventura T03442-15580220, pnpalmar@ciudad.com.ar (at park administration), T03447-493053, capybara aventura@ciudad.com.ar. Guided walks (1-3 hrs, US$1-1.70 pp), cycle tours with mountain bikes and helmets (1½-3 hrs, US$1.70-3.35). Call first in low season.

Transport

Gualeguaychú *p356*

Bus

Terminal at Blv Artigas y Blv Jurado, T03446-440688 (30-min-walk to centre along Av Artigas and Av Aristóbulo del Valle to the east; remise taxi charges US$1.20 to centre). The terminal has tourist information and a post office, phones, a small restaurant and 24-hr left luggage (US$0.35 per day).

To **Buenos Aires**, Flecha Bus, Nuevo Expreso, Nuevo Rápido Tata, 3-3½ hrs, US$7-8. To **Paraná**, Nuevo Expreso, Ciudad de Gualeguay, Jovi Bus, 4½-5 hrs, US$6.

To **Concepción del Uruguay**, Flecha Bus, Nuevo Expreso, Jovi Bus, 1 hr, US$1.50.

To **Colón**, Flecha Bus, Nuevo Expreso, Jovi Bus, 1½-2 hrs, US$2-2.50. To **Fray Bentos**, Ciudad de Gualeguay, 2 daily (1 on Sun), 1 hr 15 mins, US$2.30 (arrive half an hour before departure to do the border paperwork proceedings). To **Villa Paranacito**, Nuevo Expreso, daily, 2 hrs, US$3.50. To **El Ñandubaysal**, Expreso Ñandubaysal, several daily in high season, US$1.70 open return includes entry fee.

Remise taxi
San José, San José y Rivadavia (on plaza), T03446-431333.

Around Gualeguaychú *p357*
Villa Paranacito is accessible only via a 22 km dirt road, branching off Route 12, 10 km south of **Ceibas**. Daily buses Nuevo Expreso to/from **Gualeguaychú**, **Zárate** and **Buenos Aires**. Buses to **Zárate** or **Buenos Aires** stop at **Ceibas**, not far from Estancia La Azotea, and there are regular buses from **Gualeguaychú** to **Larroque** and **Urdinarrain**, where remise taxis will take you to **Irazusta** and **Aldea San Antonio**.

Concepción del Uruguay *p358*
The bus terminal is at Rocamora y Los Constituyentes, T03442-422352, 11 blocks west of Plaza Ramírez (remise taxi to centre, US$0.40). Left luggage, free at information desk. To **Buenos Aires**, Flecha Bus, Nuevo Rápido Tata, 4 hrs, US$8-9.

To **Paraná**, Flecha Bus, Nuevo Rápido Tata, Itapé, 5 hrs, US$7. To **Colón**, several companies, 45 mins, US$1. To **Palacio San José**, Itapé, Paccot, San José (stopping at El Cruce or at Caseros), 30 mins, US$0.80. To **Gualeguaychú**, several companies, 1 hr, US$1.50.

Around Concepción del Uruguay *p358*
Palacio San José can be reached by taking Route 39 west and turning right after Caseros train station. Buses going to **Paraná** or **Rosario del Tala** will stop at **El Cruce** or **Caseros**, and from here, the palacios are 4 and 8 km away, respectively (take *remise* taxi from Caseros). *Remise* taxis charge about US$8 with 1½ hrs wait. Tour operators run combis (minibuses) only in high season for about US$5 including entrance (check companies at tourist office, since they change every year). A train service arrives on Sat from **Villa Elisa** (see under Colón). **Basavilbaso** has regular buses which link **Concepción del Uruguay** and **Paraná** or **Rosario del Tala**.

Colón *p358*
Bus
Not all long-distance buses enter Colón. Buses going north from Colón will stop at **Ubajay**. Terminal at Paysandú y Sourigues (10 blocks north of main plaza), T03447- 421716. There is a 24-hr bar where luggage is kept for US$0.35 a day; and the owner provides information on bus timetables. At Ubajay, Parador Gastiazoro, T0345-4905026 {CHECK CODE}, is a busy bus stop where you can take daily **Expreso Singer** to **Puerto Iguazú** (US$27).

To **Buenos Aires**, Flecha Bus, Nuevo Expreso, Nuevo Rápido Tata, 5-6 hrs, US$8-10. To **Mercedes** (for getting to Iberá), Nuevo Rápido Tata, Flecha Bus, 6-7 hrs, US$6-8. To **Paraná**, Flecha Bus, Paccot, 4-5 hrs, US$7. To **Concepción del Uruguay**, several companies, 45 mins, US$1. To **Gualeguaychú**, several companies, 1½-2 hrs, US$2-2.50. To **San José**, Paccot, 20 mins, US$0.50. To **Pueblo Liebig**, Paccot, 45 mins, US$0.50.

Access to **Parque Nacional El Palmar**, Flecha Bus, Itapé, Jovi Bus, 1 hr, US$1.50.

To **Villa Elisa**, Itapé, Mitre Bus, Transporte Ogara, 1 hr, US$1-1.20. To **Paysandú** (Uruguay), Copay, 45 mins, US$2-2.30.

Remise taxi
Palmar, Laprida 37, T03447-421278.

Parque Nacional El Palmar *p359*
Buses from **Colón**, 1 hr, US$1.50, or coming from the north will drop you at the entrance, from where you can walk or hitch the last 12 km to the park administration.

Remise taxis from **Colón** or from **Ubajay** also offer tours (eg from Colón, US$15 for a 4-hr round trip, including a tour or waiting time in the park. Enquire in Ubajay at bus stop Parador Gastiazoro or at petrol station for park wardens who might be going to the park.

Refugio de Vida Silvestre La Aurora del Palmar *p359*
Buses from **Colón** or from the north will drop you at the entrance. Remember to tell the driver you're going to La Aurora del Palmar, to avoid confusion with the national park.
Remise taxis from **Ubajay** charge US$1.70.

Directory

Gualeguaychú *p356*
Banks Banco de la Nación, 25 de Mayo y Alberdi. Credicoop, Rivadavia y Perón.
Uruguayan consulate, Rivadavia 810, T03446-426168, Mon-Fri 0800-1400.

Río Paraná

Running parallel to the Río Uruguay, the Río Paraná weaves its lazy course right across the northeast of Argentina, from Misiones to Buenos Aires where it forms a vast delta. If you have time for a road trip from Buenos Aires to Corrientes, you will pass through the major cities of Rosario and Santa Fé. There are two main routes north: an interesting journey is along the eastern banks of the river, through Paraná via small towns with wildlife spotting and fishing and onwards to Goya and Corrientes; or the more major route north along the western banks, through the cities of Rosario and Santa Fe to Reconquista and Resistencia. This chapter explores the western route first, as far as Santa Fe, and then crosses to the eastern bank to the city of Paraná, and areas north and south. ▸▸ *For Sleeping, Eating and other listings, see pages 370-377.*

Rosario ▸▸ *pp370-377.*

→ *Phone code 0341 Colour map 4, A5 Population: 1,159,000*

Rosario is Argentina's third largest city, renowned for its rich cultural life, since it's home to many famous artists and pop musicians. Although little visited by travellers, it has some fine buildings in its attractive centre, and a well-kept costanera alongside the Paraná river. The nightlife is lively, with plenty of cafés, restaurants and nightclubs, and there are daily theatre and live music shows at venues all around the city. To recover from all that entertainment, the nearby islands in the river, just minutes away from the centre, you can relax on sandy beaches.

Background

Unlike most Spanish American cities, Rosario was never officially founded. Though a fort was established in 1689 by Luis Romero de Pineda, it was just a place to export mules and tobacco throughout the 18th century. However, it grew rapidly in the late 19th century, with the opening of a railway line to Córdoba in 1870 and the increase of shipping along the Paraná: its port became a major exporter of grain and beef, while new industries were established, including breweries, grain mills, and leather industries. In the late 20th century, Rosario attracted thousands of immigrants from northern provinces of Argentina who settled on the outskirts, later forming one of the largest deprived communities in the country. The main **tourist office** ⓘ *Av Belgrano y Buenos Aires, on the riverside park next to the Monumento a la Bandera, T0341-4802230, www.rosarioturismo.com,* has very efficient staff and a free tourist card is given for discounts at several hotels, restaurants and other services.

Sights

The old city centre is on the Plaza 25 de Mayo, just a block south of the Parque a la Bandera which lies along the riverside. Around it are the cathedral, in somewhat eclectic style and containing the *Virgen del Rosario*, and the Palacio Municipal. On the north side is the **Museo de Arte Decorativo** ⓘ *Santa Fe 748, T0341-4802547, Thu-Sun 1600-2000, free,* a sumptuous former family residence housing a valuable private collection of paintings, furniture, tapestries, sculptures, and silver, brought mainly from Europe. To the left of the cathedral, the **Pasaje Juramento** is the pedestrian access to the imposing **Monumento a la Bandera** ⓘ *T/F0341-4802238, Mon 1400-1800, Tue-Sun 0900-1800 (in summer till 1900), US$0.35 (tower), free (Salón de las Banderas).* An austere monument built on the site where General Belgrano raised the Argentine flag for the first time in 1812. The tower has a vantage point 70 m high with excellent panoramic views over the city.

Che!

If you haven't seen the film, Che Guevara's *Motorcycle Diaries* makes an entertaining read to accompany your travels to Argentina. The enduring image of youthful revolutionary zeal, Che stands proud, implacable and defiant beneath his black beret on many a student wall. The future revolutionary was born into a middle class family in Rosario in 1928, but his parents soon moved with their asthmatic son to the healthier climate of the Sierras of Córdoba. You can visit the house where they lived in Alta Gracia (see page 182).

Che's eyes were soon opened to the plight of South America's poor during his journey around the continent on a beaten-up old motorcycle. Rather than pursue a career in medicine, which he'd started studying, he decided to dedicate the rest of his life to the flight for the 'liberation of the American continent'.

In 1956 he met Fidel Castro in Mexico, and together they planned to create the ideal Socialist model in Cuba, as well as establish links with other sympathetic nations. Che's overriding ambition had always been to spread the revolutionary word, and take the armed struggle to other parts – particularly in his own country. But conditions in Argentina were not right, and so Fidel and Che began their mission to liberate America in Bolivia. Che spent a little time in La Paz, and then travelled to a guerrilla base at Nanchuazú. However the constant movements of the group aroused the suspicion of neighbours and the army were alerted. Fidel and Che fled and spent several months wandering the steep valleys of eastern Bolivia. In August 1967, when Che was just 39, they were ambushed by Bolivian troops. Che was executed and buried in an unmarked grave. In 1997 his body was exhumed and taken to Cuba.

From Plaza 25 de Mayo, Calle Córdoba leads west towards Plaza San Martín with the **Paseo del Siglo**, the largest concentration of late 19th- and early 20th-centuries buildings in the city. The palm-lined **Boulevard Oroño** leads north to the riverside parks, the Rosario Norte railway station and south to the **Pichincha district**, popular for nightlife, and to **Parque Independencia** at the south end. This beautiful 126-ha park was designed by the famous landscape architect Charles Thays. It has a large lake and a **tourist information** ⓘ *Mon-Fri 1500-2100, Sat-Sun 1300-1930*. There are gardens with fountains and fine statues, shady avenues, the Newell's Old Boys football club stadium and three museums in the area.

Just outside the park, the **Museo de Bellas Artes** ⓘ *J B Castagnino, Av Pellegrini 2202, T0341-4802542, Wed-Mon 1400-2000, US$0.35*, is considered one of the best fine arts museums in the country, with a large collection of European paintings, particularly French Impressionist, Italian Baroque and Flemish works, and one of the best collections of paintings and sculpture works by renowned Argentine artists.

Next to the stadium is the **Museo Histórico Provincial** ⓘ *T034-4721457, Tue-Fri 0900-1700, Sat 1500-1800, Sun 1000-1300 (in summer Thu-Sun 1000-1300), free*, which has a very well displayed collection of Latin American aboriginal artefacts and valuable pieces of religious art including Cuzco school paintings and a magnificent altar covered with silver plaques, which was used by Pope John Paul II in 1987.

The riverside is lined with several parks, making it a very attractive place to walk. Eight blocks south of the Monumento a la Bandera is the **Parque Urquiza** ⓘ *T0341-4802533, shows on Sun 2000, US$0.65; museum open Sat-Sun 1830-2100,*

 US$0.65, with sports facilities, an open-air theatre and the **Complejo Astronómico Municipal** with an observatory, a planetarium and a small science museum.

Further north is the **Estación Fluvial** where boats leave for excursions around the islands, containing the **Museo del Paraná y las Islas** ⓘ *T0341-4400751, Wed-Sun 1600-1930, US$0.35*, which gives an insight into islander culture through local art and artefacts. At the foot of the monument, is the **Parque a la Bandera**, one of the most appealing parks, and the tourist office beyond which is the **Parque de España**, a modern red-brick development which incorporates the old railway arches as an exhibition centre and offers fine views over the Río Paraná.

The most popular destination for locals as well as visitors are the dozens of riverside resorts on the islands and sandy banks opposite Rosario. These have restaurants and bars, and most have comfortable facilities for an enjoyable day's stay, with woods, beaches and lagoons. There are campsites and *cabañas* for rent in some of them. Boats depart daily in summer from *La Fluvial* or from *Costa Alta* to the island resorts, each with its own transfer service. Weekend services run throughout the rest of the year.

Santa Fé » *pp370-377.*

→ *Phone code: 0342 Colour map 4, A5 Population: 451,600*

Santa Fé is capital of its province, one of the oldest cities of the country, though there's little architectural evidence and this is not really a tourist destination. It lies near the confluence of the Ríos Santa Fé and Salado in a low-lying area with lagoons and islands just west of the Río Paraná and was severely flooded in May 2003, one of Argentina's most shocking disasters. It is connected to the smaller city of Paraná, on the east bank of the river, by road bridges and a tunnel.

Sights

The city's **commercial centre** lies a few blocks southwest of the bus terminal, along the partially pedestrianized San Martín. This street leads southwards to the historic centre, with the oldest buildings and a few museums. On the plaza itself is the cathedral, dating from 1751 but remodelled in 1834, its twin towers capped by blue tiled cupolas.

Southeast of the plaza is the **Museo Histórico Provincial** ⓘ *3 de Febrero 2553, T0342-457 3529, all year round Tue-Fri 0830-1200; Jan-Feb Tue-Fri 1600-2030, Sat-Sun 1730-2030; Mar-Apr Tue-Fri 1500-1900, Sat-Sun 1600-1900; May-Sep Tue-Fri 1400-1830, Sat-Sun 1500-1800; Oct-Dec Tue-Fri 1430-1930, Sat-Sun 1630-1930, free*, in a former family house dating from 1690 (one of the oldest surviving civil buildings in the country), worth visiting for the house itself rather than the exhibition of two 17th-century Cuzco school paintings. About 100 m south is the **Iglesia y Convento de San Francisco** built between 1673 and 1695. The church has walls nearly 2m thick and fine wooden ceilings, built from timber floated down the river from Paraguay, carved by indigenous craftsmen and fitted without the use of nails. The pulpit and altar are 17th-century baroque.

On the opposite side of the park is the superb **Museo Etnográfico y Colonial** ⓘ *all year round Tue-Fri 0830-1200; Jan-Feb Tue-Sun 1700-2000; Mar-Apr Tue-Fri 1530-1900, Sat-Sun 1600-1900; May-Sep Tue-Fri 1530-1900, Sat-Sun 1530-1830; Oct-Dec 1530-1900, Sat-Sun 1600-1900, US$0.20*, with a chronologically ordered exhibition of artefacts from aboriginal inhabitants from 2000 BC to the first Spanish settlers who lived in Santa Fe la Vieja, the town's original site. The most remarkable objects are delicate zoomorphic ceramic pots, Spanish amulets and board games, and a model of both Santa Fé towns, showing that the distribution of the main buildings remained unchanged after the moving.

The city has three very good **tourist information** points: at the bus terminal (T0342-4574123, 0700-1300, 1500-2100); at Paseo del Restaurador, Bulevar Pellegrini y Rivadavia (T0342-4571881, 0700-1900); and at Boca del Tigre, Avenida Paso y Zavalía (0700-1900, www.santafeciudad.gov.ar).

Paraná

» pp370-377.

➔ Phone code: 0343 Colour map 4, A5 Population: 247,600

Capital of Entre Ríos province, Paraná stands on the eastern bank of a bend in the Río Paraná, opposite Santa Fé. Its centre lies on a hill offering fine views over the river, and if you're travelling up the Paraná river, it is a good place to stop on a journey north. It was founded in 1649, when Santa Fe was moved from its original spot and settlers crossed the river in search of higher ground for cultivation, and a suitable port. In the mid-19th century it gained importance as capital of the Argentine Confederation and a subsequent period of growth left some sumptuous public buildings. The city's faded splendour creates a quiet, rather melancholic atmosphere but there is an appealing calm pace of life here.

Ins and outs

Getting there and around The city can easily be visited on foot, since the most interesting sights lie around the two main plazas, Plaza 1 de Mayo and three blocks north, Plaza Alvear.

Tourist information Paraná has four city tourist offices (all open daily 0800-2000): in the centre at ⓘ *Buenos Aires 132, T0343-4230183*; at the bus terminal ⓘ *T0343-4201862*; at Parque Urquiza ⓘ *Av Laurencena y Juan de San Martín, on the east side, T0343-4201837*; and at the Hernandarias tunnel, www.turismoenparana.com.

Sights

From Plaza Alvear, Avenida Rivadavia leads to the beautiful **Parque Urquiza** and the riverside. Though nothing remains from the colonial period, the city retains many fine 19th- and 20th-century public buildings, centred around the Plaza Primero de Mayo. On the east side is the impressive **Cathedral**, built in 1883 in Italianate neoclassical style, with a fine dome and colonnaded portico, though the interior is plain. Also on the plaza are the **Municipalidad** (1890) with its distinctive tower, and the **Club Social** (1906), for years the elite social centre of the city. Take pedestrianized San Martín half a block west of the corner with 25 de Junio, to see the fine **Teatro 3 de Febrero** (1908). Two blocks north is the **Plaza Alvear**, and opposite one of its corners, the provincial **tourist office** ⓘ *Laprida 5, T0343-4222100, www.vivientrerios.com, Mon-Fri 0800-2000, Sat 0800-1400*. On the same block is the mildly engaging **Museo Histórico Martiniano Leguizamón** ⓘ *Laprida y Buenos Aires, T0343-4312735, museo leguizamon@ciudad.com.ar, Tue-Fri 0800-1200, 1530-1930, Sat 0900-1200, 1600-1900, Sun 0900-1200 (Jan-Feb, Mon-Fri 0800-1200), US$0.35*.

On the west side of the plaza is the **Museo de Bellas Artes** ⓘ *Buenos Aires 355, T0343-4207868, Tue-Fri 0700-1300, 1500-1900, Sat 1000-1400, 1700-2000, Sun 1000-1300, US$0.35*, housing a vast collection of Argentine artists, with many works by painter Cesáreo Bernaldo de Quirós. On the north side of the plaza is the **Museo de Ciencias Naturales y Antropológicas** ⓘ *Carlos Gardel 62, T0343-4208894, Tue-Sat 0800-1230, 1400-1800, Sun 0900-1200, US$0.35*, particularly appealing for kids, with an insect collection (see the 25-cm-wide moth), and lots of stuffed animals. Among fascinating artefacts by Guaraní people are a rare urn, with red geometrical paintings and small utensils made by groups of indigenous peoples to the north, and a rather alarming display of jars containing human foetuses, from five weeks to six months old.

From the northwestern corner of the plaza, it's a pleasant stroll along tree-lined Avenida Rivadavia, with the monumental **Escuela del Centenario** (1910), Avenida Rivadavia 168, to reach the city's pride and joy, the **Parque Urquiza**. Extended along the low cliffs of the Paraná river, with wonderful views and many fine statues, the park is well planted with *lapachos*, *palos borrachos* and pines. There's an open-air theatre, and steps to the Avenida Costanera. The cobbled street **Bajada de los Vascos**, which in the 19th century gave access to the port area, is now known as Puerto Viejo and retains some original buildings. The Avenida Costanera is lively, with restaurants, sports clubs and sandy beaches on the river. The **Paraná Rowing Club**, T0343-4312048, charges US$3.50 per day for beach access, including the use of its pool.

North of Paraná

» pp370-377.

Heading north from Paraná along the Río Paraná, you can take monotonous Route 11 to Resistencia on the western bank, or Route 12 north to Corrientes which closely follows the eastern banks of the river through varied landscapes, giving access to two small attractive towns on the coast with good fishing: Santa Elena and La Paz, and a marvellous traditional estancia, Vizcacheras.

Santa Elena

→ *Phone code: 03437*

Santa Elena lies on the Río Paraná about 150 km north of the capital. It is a small port whose fishing attracts many anglers and its history has been associated with that of its meat-packing factory run by British firms from the late 19th century, before it closed down in 1993. The red brick buildings of the *frigorífico* can still be seen in town, and the superb estancia built by the *Bovril* company can be visited nearby. At the end of the *costanera* is the Paseo La Olla, with beautiful views over the river. The **tourist office** is at Eva Perón y 9 de Julio, T03437-481223.

La Paz

→ *Phone code: 03437 Colour map 4, A5 Population: 22,700*

La Paz, 68 km north of Paraná, is a small port in an area popular for fishing, where the fishing festivals *Fiesta Provincial del Surubí* and the *Fiesta Provincial del Dorado* are held respectively every April and September. The undulating terrain and the cliffs above the river make a picturesque setting for the old houses still standing in the town. The **tourist office** is at Vieytes y España, T03437-422389 (ask for information on accommodation at few nearby estancias).

There is a **Museo Regional**, a small history museum at the Parque Berón de Astrada, from where there are fine views, while another park, the **Parque de la Aventura**, has trails along the riverside for walking or cycling. Access is on the way to La Armonía, reached by Bulevar 25 de Mayo and then Yrigoyen.

Corrientes

» pp370-377.

→ *Phone code: 03783 Colour map 1, B6 Population: 316,500*

Capital of Corrientes province, some 30 km southwest of the meeting of the rivers Paraná and Paraguay, the city is mainly a service centre for its agricultural hinterland which produces beef, cotton, tobacco, rice and *yerba mate*. Although Corrientes is less important transport hub than Resistencia, it is a pleasant place for a stopover. The city centre, with its peaceful traditional streets and squares, is well preserved and its *costanera* is one of the most attractive in the country. The national capital of Carnival, the city is also famous as the location of Graham Greene's novel *The Honorary Consul*. In summer the air can oppressively hot and humid, but in winter the climate is pleasant.

Wife savers

Ask your guide about the identity of people from Corrientes, and he's likely to tell you with great pride that Corrientes is a separate republic from Argentina. It has its own culture and laws, and its men – the Correntinos – are kind and noble but known for their strong personalities. And polygamy is still a way of life here. You heard right. Many men have several wives and lovers, and lots of women have children by several men. And they all live happily together. Rural myth? There's certainly a distinctive flavour to life here. Ask one of the locals.

Ins and outs

The **city tourist office** is on the central Plaza Cabral, T03783-428845, with two more information points at Parque Camba Cuá, T03783-423779, and at punta Tacuara, on Avenida Costanera, T03783-464504, where you can ask for a good map; open daily 0700- 2100. The **provincial tourist office** ⓘ *25 de Mayo 1330, T03783-427200, www.corrientes.com.ar, Mon-Fri 0700-1300, 1500-2100*, also provides information on the city, as well as other destinations in Corrientes province.

Background

Founded in 1588 on the Paraná river, next to seven relatively high *puntas*, or promontories, by an expedition from Asunción, led by Juan Torres de Vera y Aragón, Corrientes became important as a port on the Route between Buenos Aires and Asunción. Numerous shipyards led to the development of a naval industry that endured for centuries. The Guaraní population that inhabited the region were mainly absorbed into the Jesuit missions or became workers for the estancias. They progressively mixed with the Spanish newcomers giving the local society a distinctive character, still evident today in the faces of the inhabitants, and also in the daily use of Guaraní words and a particular accent in the spoken Spanish.

Sights

The main Plaza 25 de Mayo, one block inland from the *costanera*, is a beautiful shady space. You could take a pleasant stroll from here around the surrounding blocks, with their fine old houses and river views, and to the Avenida Costanera. On the north side of the plaza is the **Jefatura de Policía**, built in 19th-century French style. The **Museo de Artesanías** ⓘ *Quintana 905, Mon-Fri 0800-1200, 1600-2000, free*, is a large old house with an exhibition of handicrafts made from the most diverse materials imaginable, by indigenous groups, as well as by contemporary urban and rural artisans. Tiny skeleton-shaped images represent San La Muerte, a popular devotion that ensures the bearer a painless death. A large room at the front is a workshop where you can watch the patient work of the local craftspeople. On the east side of the plaza are the Italianate **Casa de Gobierno** (1881-1886) and the **Ministerio de Gobierno**. On the south side is the church **La Merced**, where there are confessionals carved by the indigenous inhabitants of Misiones in the mid-18th century, and a colonial-style altar. The **Casa Lagraña**, a huge building with three interior patios, built in 1860 for the governor, lies one block south. At 9 de Julio 1044 is the **Museo Histórico** ⓘ *Tue-Fri 0800-1200, 1600-2000, free*, displaying among other pieces a collection of religious objects dating from the 18th and 19th centuries. Only two blocks north is the **Teatro Juan de Vera**, San Juan 637, T427743, a lively cultural centre and a beautiful building itself (1913). Across the road is the **Museo de Bellas Artes** ⓘ *San Juan 634, Tue-Fri 0800-1200, 1630-2030, free*, a small arts museum with temporary exhibitions and a permanent collection including valuable works by the painters Petorutti, Fader and Quinquela Martín. The quite impressive **Iglesia y Convento de San Francisco**, Mendoza 450, was rebuilt in 1861 on the site of the original which dated from 1608. Six blocks south of the Plaza 25 de Mayo is the leafy Plaza de la Cruz and opposite, the church of **La Cruz de los Milagros** that houses the Santo Madero, a miraculous cross placed by the founder of the city, the miracle occurring, allegedly, when the indigenous residents who tried to burn it were killed by lightning from a cloudless sky. Near the plaza, the **Museo de Ciencias Naturales 'Amadeo Bonpland'** ⓘ *San Martín 850, Mon-Sat 0900-1200, 1600-2000*, has a large collection of archaeology and plants with a remarkable display of 5,800 insects including a huge wasp nest.

The attractive Avenida Costanera, lined with *lapachos* and *palos borrachos*, leads along the Río Paraná from its southwestern end, next to the bridge, to **Parque Mitre**, from where there are good views of sunsets over the river. On the intersection with Junín, there is a small **zoo** ⓘ *Tue-Sun 0900-1830*, set by the river, with animals of the region.

Sleeping

Rosario *p364*

A-B Riviera, San Lorenzo 1460, T/F0341-4242058, www.solans.com. A 4-star hotel, whose **A** superior rooms are very good, and more business style, while the cheaper standard rooms are smaller but still comfortable, with warmer decor. Both include a large breakfast, and there are sauna, gym and restaurant. The same chain as the Riviera owns 3 more similar upmarket hotels all offering very good accommodation often promotional prices: **Libertador**, Av Corrientes 752, T/F0341-4241005; **Presidente**, Av Corrientes 919, T/F0341-4242789; **República**, San Lorenzo 955, T/F0341-4248580.

C Garden, Callao 39, T0341-4370025, www.hotelgardensa.com. This is a good though pricey option a little way from the centre, in the Pichincha district (next to Blv Oroño) with very good **B** superior rooms and smaller, but comfortable standard rooms. Also restaurant and children's play area.

C Plaza del Sol, San Juan 1055, T/F0341-4219899, plaza@satlink.com.ar. Very comfortable, spacious rooms and a pool on the 11th fl with splendid views. A large breakfast is included.

D Rosario, Cortada Ricardone 1365 (access from Entre Ríos 900 block), T/F0341-4242170, hrosario@infovia.com.ar. A central place with good rooms with a/c and breakfast. Larger **C** rooms in the annexe.

E Savoy, San Lorenzo 1022, T0341-4480071. This early 20th-century mansion is the most appealing place to stay and the best value by far. Once Rosario's best hotel, it now has a charming faded grandeur and welcoming service. Don't miss the sumptuous fumoir on the first floor. Breakfast included.

Sante Fé *p366*

All listed hotels lie within 10 blocks of the bus terminal.

C Conquistador, 25 de Mayo 2676, T/F0342-4001195, linverde@gigared.com. Worth the price only if you use the pool, the sauna and the gym, all included in the rate.

C Riogrande, San Gerónimo 2580, T0342-4500700, riogrande@santafe.com.ar. Santa Fe's best hotel has very good rooms, with slightly smaller standard ones. A large breakfast is included.

D Castelar, 25 de Mayo y Peatonal Falucho, T/F0342-4560999. On a small plaza, this old-style hotel built in the 30s with quality materials is a good value option, offering comfortable accommodation in a formal atmosphere. Breakfast is included. It has a smart but welcoming restaurant on the ground floor.

D Hostal Santa Fe de la Veracruz, San Martín 2954, T/F0342-4551740, hostal_santafe@ciudad.com.ar. Traditionally one of the top hotels in town, with 2 types of room categories **C** superior rooms), both good value, including a large breakfast and checkout at 1800. It has a restaurant and the sauna is for an extra fee.

Paraná *p367*

A Marán Suites & Towers, Av Rivadavia y Mitre, T0343-4235444, www.maran.com.ar. An impressive modern tower on Parque Urquiza with very comfortable, light, functional and simply decorated rooms, whose splendid views over the park and the river are the main reasons for choosing this pricey hotel. There is a restaurant and a fitness room.

B Mayorazgo, Av Etchevehere y Miranda, T0343-4230333, www.mayorazgohotel.com. A large upmarket hotel on Parque Urquiza with casino, pool, gym, restaurant and four types of room (the standard ones are fine) with good views over the river.

C Gran Hotel Paraná, Urquiza 976, T0343-4223900, www.hotelesparana.com.ar. Overlooking Plaza Primero de Mayo, this large hotel offers 3 types of room, (all with breakfast included), pricey standard rooms, but very comfortable and spacious **B** superior ones. It has a gym and the smart restaurant La Fourchette. Guests get discounts for using the facilities of Club Atlético Estudiantes.

C Marán Apart-Hotel, Buenos Aires y Malvinas, T/F0343-4235444, www.maran.com.ar. Comfortable small apartments for 1 to 6 people located in a nice residential area next to the park.

D San Jorge, Belgrano 368, T/F0343-4221685, www.sanjorgehotel.com.ar. With palm trees growing on the street outside, this is an attractive renovated house, made welcoming by friendly staff and owners. There are cheaper old-style rooms (avoid noisy rooms closer to reception) or modern ones at the back with renovated bathrooms and TV. A light breakfast is included, and there are cooking facilities.

Santa Elena *p368*

L Estancia Vizcacheras, Route 12, km 554,5, T011-4719 5613 (in Buenos Aires), www.vizcacheras.com.ar. South of Santa Elena, the Bovril estancia was built in the early 1900's in British colonial-style with Argentine touches. The owners are extremely hospitable, making guests feel at home in luxuriously furnished bedrooms, all with their own bathroom (some with old fashioned bathtubs) and private verandas. Drinks on the terrace with splendid views of the gardens and grasslands beyond, and delicious dinner served under the stars. You'll be invited to see the daily routines of the working cattle ranch, with walking and horse riding, fishing and birdwatching also arranged. Highly recommended.

La Paz *p368*

D Milton, Italia 1029, T03437-422232, www.miltonhotel.com.ar. A central place with comfortable enough rooms; a/c and breakfast extra.

D Posta Surubí, España 224, T03437-421128. Nicely located by the river with good rooms with breakfast and fine views; it has a restaurant.

Corrientes *p368*

Good value accommodation is non-existent in Corrientes. It is worth while paying extra pesos to avoid a slew of rather scrappy and overpriced places. All hotels below have a/c in their rooms.

B Corrientes Plaza, Junín 1549, T/F03783-466500, www.hotelplazactes.com.ar. A business oriented large hotel with plain comfortable rooms, gym and a small pool; larger rooms with bigger beds available for an extra 15%.

C Gran Hotel Guaraní, Mendoza 970, T03783-433800, www.hguarani.com.ar. A 4-star business-oriented hotel with restaurant, pool and gym. 4 types of room, slightly differing in comfort, all functional, well-equipped but with plain decor. Large breakfast included.

D Hostal del Río, Plácido Martínez 1098, T/F03783-436100, www.hotelguia.com/hostaldelrio. Standard rooms are pleasant enough, but the superior ones for an extra 30% are certainly more comfortable. There's a small pool on the roof and a restaurant, and breakfast is included.

D Turismo, Entre Ríos 650, T/F03783-433174. By far the most appealing hotel in town, for its riverside location and its homely style though the rooms have seen better days, they're comfortable enough, with ancient a/c. There is a smart restaurant, a large swimming pool and an adjacent casino. Breakfast included.

Eating

Rosario *p364*

ΨΨ **Amarra**, Av Belgrano y Buenos Aires. Good food, including fish and seafood, served in a formal atmosphere. Cheap set menus Mon-Fri lunchtimes.

ΨΨ **Alvear y Nueve**, Alvear y Nueve de Julio. Good for grilled meat.

Ψ **Bruno**, Montevideo y Av Ovidio Lagos. For homemade pastas.

Ψ **Club Español**, Rioja 1052. Doesn't exactly serve up Spanish specialities, but the usual menu is given a vague Spanish flavour, and it's a nice place to eat.

Ψ **Escauriza**, Bajada Escauriza y Av Colombres, north of centre at La Florida. The most traditional fish restaurant in Rosario serving tasty dorado, surubí, pacú or boga.

Ψ **La Estancia**, Av Pellegrini y Paraguay. Another typical parrilla a few blocks east of Parque Independencia.

Ψ **Pampa**, Moreno y Mendoza. A good *parrilla* with attractive Argentine-style 1940's decor.

Ψ **Rich**, San Juan 1031, www.richrestaurante.com.ar. This is a classic in Rosario, and indeed, one of the finest restaurants in the whole country. The food is superb. There's a widely-varied menu and good set meals including delicious pastas, excellent meats and many different salads. Rarities such as *milanesa de yacaré* (alligator milanesas) are occasionally served. Recommended.

Ψ **Gigante**, San Martín 946. This large and popular restaurant offers generous helpings of good food at incredibly low prices.

Cafés

Aux Deux Magots, Av Belgrano y Entre Ríos, at the northern end of Parque de España. Emulates a Parisian café, overlooking the river, and popular at weekends till the small hours, with cheap set menus.

Café de la Opera, Mendoza y Laprida (next to the access to the Teatro El Círculo). Regular performances of jazz, tango, Russian folk music, poetry and storytelling in this pretty café, open afternoons and evenings.

Kaffa, Córdoba 1473. For good coffee served inside the large bookshop El Ateneo.

La Favrika, Tucumán 1816. A fashionable café and restaurant with evening shows, also popular at lunchtimes.

La Sede, San Lorenzo y Entre Ríos. An extremely popular café, crowded at lunchtimes with office workers having lunch.

Victoria, Jujuy y Bv Oroño. One of the oldest cafés in town and most traditional.

Sante Fé *p366*

Ψ **Baviera San Martín**, San Martín 2941. A traditional place in the centre with a varied menu and good food.

Ψ **Club Sirio Libanés**, 25 de Mayo 2740. Very good Middle Eastern dishes, reasonably priced; popular with families on Sun lunchtime.

Ψ **El Brigadier**, San Martín 1670. This colonial-style place next to the Plaza 25 de Mayo serves superb *surubí al paquete* (stuffed fish) and many parrilla dishes.

Ψ **El Quincho de Chiquito**, Av Almirante Brown y Obispo Príncipe, next to boxer Carlos Monzón's statue (on Costanera Oeste). A classic fish restaurant, excellent food and good value, with huge helpings.

Ψ **España**, San Martín 2644. An elegant place in town, serving good food.

Ψ **Rivadavia**, Rivadavia 3299. A traditional parrilla for excellent grills.

Ψ **Tasca Real**, 25 de Mayo 3228. A Spanish bar de tapas with a good selection of its specialities at a low price.

Paraná *p367*

ΨΨ **Giovani**, Urquiza 1047. A popular place in centre, good for pasta.

ΨΨ **La Fourchette**, Urquiza 976 (at Gran Hotel Paraná). The finest restaurant in town is a small, stylish place: choose from a small menu of really fine dishes. Perfect for a sophisticated intimate dinner.

Ψ **Club de Pescadores**, access from Av Estrada at Puerto Viejo. Another good traditional fish restaurant in the old and picturesque section of the port.

Ψ **Coscoino**, Corrientes 373. A relaxed family place serving good and very filling homemade pastas, tenedor libre, except Sat evenings and Sun lunches.

Ψ **El Viejo Marino**, Av Laurencena 341, on the opposite extreme of the Av Costanera. Well prepared fish dishes.

Ψ **Nos sobran los motivos**, Colón y San Juan, for very good tapas in a cheerful atmosphere that includes live shows on Thu and Sun.

🍴 **Playa**, Av Costanera (at Club Atlético Estudiantes). Nicely situated on a sandy beach with fine views of the river, a good place for fish such as surubí, boga or pejerrey (caught upstream in Corrientes or Misiones).

Cafés

There's an appealing café **Viejo Paraná**, Buenos Aires y Av Rivadavia (on Plaza Alvear).

Corrientes *p368*

Most options are in the centre and on the *costanera*.

🍴🍴 **El Mirador**, Av Costanera y Edison. A large place, good for parrilla, and local fish.

🍴 **El Solar**, San Lorenzo 830. With an informal atmosphere, and busy at lunchtime, this self-service restaurant serves decent and cheap salads, pastas and milanesas.

🍴 **Club Regatas de Corrientes**, at north end of Av Costanera, on Parque Mitre. Attractively set by the river, this is an excellent and deservedly popular place for fish, ask for the superb milanesa de surubí.

🍴 **Las Brasas**, Av Costanera y San Martín (near beach). Another large place good for *parrilla*, and local fish.

Cafés

Martha de Bianchetti, 9 de Julio y Mendoza. A smart café and bakery.

Panambí, on pedestrianized Junín, near Córdoba. A traditional central confitería, ideal for delicious pastries and the regional bread-like speciality, *chipá*.

Bars and clubs

Rosario *p364*

Bars

Albaca, Italia y Mendoza. This attractive bar is open during the day, and has live music in the evenings.

La Traición de Rita Hayworth, Dorrego 1170. A café/concert venue named after a novel by the Argentine writer Manuel Puig offering live comedy and music shows (usually Wed-Sun evenings, US$1-2) with good food.

Piluso, Catamarca y Alvear. A lively meeting point at night, also open during daytime.

Rock & Feller's, Córdoba 2019. Expensive theme bar, with a mix of pop icons and the sumptuous art deco design of an old house.

Victoria, Jujuy y Bv Oroño. One of the oldest cafés in town and most traditional.

Sante Fé *p366*

Santa Fé has a long tradition of brewing, and is one of the few places where local lagers can compete with the big national monopoly, Quilmes. Beer is usually sold in a liso (not a very large glass). There are lively areas of bars and nightclubs, popular with young crowds, all along the Costanera Este, beyond the bridge on Laguna Setúbal, in the Recoleta district, north of centre, around plaza Los Constituyentes, and next to Blv Pellegrini and to Bv Gálvez.

Don Ernesto, San Martín y General López. A traditional café in the civic centre.

Las Delicias, Hipólito Yrigoyen y San Martín. A well-preserved early 20th-century café and bakery, with beautiful decor, serving a wide variety of coffees and sweet pastries. Try their speciality, the alfajorsantafesino.

Tokio, Rivadavia y Crespo (on Plaza España). Another café with a rich history in Santa Fé.

Entertainment

Rosario *p364*

A good listings guide can be found in a section of daily paper Pagina 12: Rosario 12, as well as www.viarosario.com

Cinema

In centre are **El Cairo**, Santa Fe 1120, El Patio, Sarmiento 778, and **Del Siglo**, Córdoba y Presidente Roca (at the Shopping Mall Del Siglo).

Cultural centres

Centro Cultural Bernardino Rivadavia, San Martín 1080, T0341-4802401. A large centre holding all year round art exhibitions, video screenings, plays, music shows, seminars and a puppet theatre.

Centro Cultural Parque de España, on Parque de España, T0341-4260941. Shows temporary art exhibitions, photography, and plays at the Teatro Príncipe de Asturias.

Centro de Expresiones Contemporáneas, Sargento Cabral y el río (on the riverside, opposite Ex Aduana building), T0341-4802245. A large warehouse with almost daily music, theatre and cinema events.

Theatre

El Círculo, Laprida 1235, T0341-4245349.
Lavarden, Mendoza y Sarmiento, T0341-4721462.
De la Comedia, Cortada Ricardone y Mitre, T0341-4802597.

Festivals and events

Rosario *p364*

Jun 20 Flag Day, it is worth going to the Monumento a la Bandera at the swearing-in ceremony made by hundreds of school pupils to the country's flag.
Nov **Fiesta de las Colectividades**, every year during the first half of Nov at the Parque a la Bandera (opposite the monument) the town celebrates the diverse origins of the inhabitants, offering food, folk music and dancing from 1800 onwards. The main show is on Nov 11, the **Day of Tradition**.

Corrientes *p368*

Feb **Carnival** has been one of the most popular celebrations for decades in Argentina and is celebrated on Fri and Sat evenings throughout Feb at the **Corsódromo**. This stadium lies a little distance from the centre reached by bus No 105 along 9 de Julio. The colourful parade opens the competition among the different comparsas, passionately supported by the audience as football teams. Tickets are not sold in the stadium, but in many shops in the centre. For more information on Carnival see www.faeventos.com.
Dec/Jan The regional music chamamé has its own festival in Corrientes at Anfiteatro Tránsito Cocomarola, Barrio 1000 Viviendas, 10 blocks south of Av 3 de Abril. This cheerful music is danced in couples with the upper body close, legs far apart. Join in!

Shopping

Rosario *p364*

The main shopping street is the pedestrianized Córdoba.

Books

Balcarce, San Lorenzo 1576. A massive place for second-hand books and vinyl records.
El Ateneo, Córdoba 1473.
Stratford, Santa Fe 1340. English books.

Markets

Feria del Boulevard, Blv Oroño y Rivadavia, a weekend handicraft market.
Mercado Retro La Huella, Av del Valle y Callao (next to Rosario Norte railway station at Pichincha district). Every Sun and bank holidays, this is a large flea market where you can find some valuable antiques.
Mercado de Pulgas. Flea market at weekends, next to the tourist office on the riverside.

Outdoor gear

Central de Pesca, San Juan 1089.
El Combatiente, San Martín 816.

Shopping malls

Del Siglo, Córdoba y Presidente Roca.
Palace Garden, Córdoba 1358.

Activities and tours

Rosario *p364*

Swimming On Laguna Setúbal, from **El Espigón**, the **Club de Regatas**, next to the bridge or from **Piedras Blancas** on Costanera Este.

Tour operators

For city tours check agencies at Asociación Rosarina de Agencias de Viaje, T0341-4213554.
Barco Ciudad de Rosario, T0341-4498688. A large passenger boat leaves from the pier next to Estación Fluvial for 2-hr excursions on the river on weekend afternoons.
Catamarán Victoria Austral, leaving on weekend afternoons from Estación Fluvial.
Transporte Fluvial del Litoral, T0341-4544684. This operator used to run the regular boat service to Victoria (check if it's still running; recommended) from Estación Fluvial; also has boats for rent at US$17/hr for up to 10 people.

Paraná *p367*

Costanera 241, Buenos Aires 212, T/F0343-4234385, www.costanera241.com. City tours and boat excursions on the Paraná river.
Equilibrio, General López 3697, T0343-4599663.

Transport

Rosario *p364*

Air

Fisherton airport is located 15 km west of centre, T0341-4511226. Daily flights to/from **Buenos Aires** with Aerolíneas Argentinas and Aerovip, 45 mins. Remise taxis to town charge US$4-5. Transfers also arranged with the airline companies.

Airline offices Aerolíneas Argentinas, Santa Fe 1410, T0341-4249517. **Aerovip**, Mitre 830 local 32, T0341-4496800.

Boat

Modern terminal called **Estación Fluvial**, (known as La Fluvial), Av de los Inmigrantes 410, opposite Monumento a la Bandera, T447 3838. The main departure point for boat transfer to the island resorts. Cafés and restaurants on an attractive terrace overlooking the river, as well as a museum.

At **Costa Alta**, situated between La Florida and the suspension bridge, is a pier also used for passenger boats going to the island resorts. Tickets US$1-3 return, boat services every 30 min in the summer to some resorts, with a few weekend services during the rest of the year.

Bus

The terminal is at Santa Fe y Cafferata, about 30 blocks west of the Monumento de la Bandera, T437 2384. For local buses a magnetic card must be bought at kiosks in the centre or near bus stops (US$0.25 per trip).

Several bus lines to centre with stops on Córdoba (eg 101, 103, 115), US$0.25; from centre, take buses on Plaza 25 de Mayo, via C Santa Fe, remise taxi US$1.50. The terminal has an information point, post office, shops and restaurants; also sells cards for buses, and left luggage, open 24 hrs, (US$0.70 a day per piece). Several companies going to main destinations. To **Buenos Aires**, 4 hrs, US$7. To **Córdoba**, 6 hrs, US$8.50. To **Santa Fe**, 2 hrs 20 mins, US$4-5.

Car rental

Localiza, T0342-4351234, Olé, T438 6593, Avis, T0342-4352299.

Taxi

Radio taxis (painted in black and yellow), T0342-482 2222. **Remise taxis** Primera Clase, T0342-4545454. Nuevo Estilo, T0342-4543000.

Train

Rosario Norte station, Av del Valle y Av Ovidio Lagos. The **Buenos Aires-Tucumán** service operated by TBA, T0800-3333822, stops weekly in Rosario, though at inconvenient times in the day and tickets are only sold just before departures, at the station. To **Tucumán**, US$12; to **Buenos Aires**, US$3.50. Taxis charge US$0.80.

Sante Fé *p366*

Air

The airport, Sauce Viejo, is located 17 km southwest, T0342-4995064. Daily flights to and from **Buenos Aires** with Aerolíneas Argentinas and Aerovip. Taxis charge US$4 from bus terminal. A bus with a yellow 'L', signed Aeropuerto, stops on C San Luis (one block from bus terminal), 20 mins journey, US$0.40.

Airline offices Aerolíneas Argentinas, Lisandro de la Torre 2635, T0342-4599461. **Aerovip**, Lisandro de la Torre 2570, T0342-4522491.

Bus

The terminal is located near to the centre at Belgrano 2910, T457 4124. City tourist information desk with bus information. Taxis charge US$0.65 to centre. Luggage lockers for US$0.65 (insert two $(peso)1 coins).

To **Buenos Aires**, several companies, 6 hrs, US$11-13. To **Córdoba**, several companies, 5 hrs, US$8.50. To **Paraná**, ETACER, Fluviales, 50 mins, US$1. To **Rosario**, several companies, 2 hrs 20 mins, US$4-5. To **Cayastá** (marked Helvecia), Paraná Medio, 1 hr 40 mins, US$1.70.

Car hire

Localiza, Av Alem 19098, T0342-4534300.

Taxis (Radio and remise)

Cooperativa Radio Taxi Santa Fe, T0800-5555444. Santa Fe, Moreno 2512, T0342-4595906.

Bus

The bus terminal is at Av Ramírez 2598, T0343-4221282, 10 blocks southeast of Plaza Primero de Mayo; leave the small plaza on your right and take Av Echagüe right to centre, or buses No 1, 6 to/from centre, US$0.40, remise taxis, US$2-2.50. Left luggage, Mon-Sat 0700-2300, Sun 0800-1200, 1730-2300, US$ 0.70 a day per piece. To **Buenos Aires**, Flecha Bus, San José, Basa, 6-7 hrs, US$ 15-22. To **Santa Fe**, ETACER, Fluviales, every 20 mins, 50 mins journey, US$1. To **Corrientes**, Flecha Bus, 8-9 hrs, US$ 20. To **Puerto Iguazú**, Expreso Singer, 15 hrs, US$ 30. To **Colón**, Flecha Bus, Paccot, 4-5 hrs, US$ 8. To **Diamante**, several companies, 1 hr, US$ 1.50. To **La Paz**, ETA, 3 hrs, US$4.50. To **Victoria**, several companies, 2-3 hrs, US$2.50-3.50.

Car hire

Localiza, 25 de Mayo y Arturo Illia, T0343-423 1707.

Remise taxis

Ciudad Paisaje, T0343-423 2100. Tele-Radio, T0343-424 6565.

Corrientes *p368*

Air

Camba Punta airport is 10 km east of city reached by RN 12, T0343-458684. Minibus pick ups from hotels, T0343-450072, US$1.30 (US$2.70 to Resistencia airport). Remise taxis charge US$4. Flights to/from **Buenos Aires** with Aerolíneas Argentinas, 1 hr 20 mins.

Airline offices Aerolíneas Argentinas, Junín 1301, T0343-428678.

Bus

From the town centre, several buses or *combis* go to nearby towns from the centre, with stops around Plaza Cabral or along central streets. To **Santa Ana**, Bus No 11 (Santa Ana), from *9 de Julio y Catamarca*, 30 mins, US$ 1. To **Paso de la Patria**, Mir, office in Paso de la Patria at La Rioja y 12 de Octubre, T0343-494654, or Silvitur, 8 de Diciembre 234 (in Paso de la Patria), T0343-494260; both charge US$1.70. To **Empedrado**, Empedrado minibus, Mendoza 837, T15687431, US$2. All these destinations also have regular buses from terminal. The port area around Av Costanera y La Rioja is another transport hub with buses Chaco-Corrientes leaving regularly to **Resistencia**, 40 mins, US$ 0.70 return.

The bus terminal is at *Av Maipú, 5 km southeast of centre*; take bus No 103 (check with the driver, as same line has many different routes) from Carlos Pellegini y Córdoba (or any stop along Carlos Pellegrini and Salta), 20 mins, US$0.35. From terminal to centre, take bus No 103 stopping outside, next to the parking area, on Av Maipú. **Left luggage** at Crucero del Norte office, US$0.65 a day, open 0530-0100. Tickets can be bought at same prices at many offices other than the company's own.

To **Empedrado**, López, San Justo, Nuevo Expreso, US$ 2. To **Mburucuyá**, San Antonio, 2½ hrs, US$4. To **Mercedes**, many companies, 3 hrs, US$8-11. To **Paso de la Patria**, Paso de la Patria, US$2 (tickets on bus), 5 daily.

To **Santa Ana**, Bus No 11 (Santa Ana), US$1 (tickets on bus), every 2 to 3 hrs. To **Posadas**, several companies, 3½-4 hrs, US$ 8-13. To **Puerto Iguazú**, Aguila Dorada Bis (change at Posadas), Expreso Singer, Crucero del Norte, Autotransportes Mendoza, 8-9½ hrs, US$ 16-25. To **Resistencia** bus terminal, Puerto Tirol, 30 mins, US$1 (for going to city centre, get off at traffic lights immediately after supermarket Libertad and take bus No 9, US$0.23, stopping there; not recommended at night).

To **Buenos Aires**, several companies, 11-12 hrs, US$20-30. To **Salta**, Norte Bis or La Nueva Estrella (change at Resistencia), 13-14 hrs, US$25. To **Tucumán**, La Nueva Estrella, Nuevo Rápido Tata, Vosa, 12-15 hrs, US$21-24. To **Asunción** (Paraguay), Crucero del Norte, El Pulqui, 5-7 hrs, US$7-8.

Taxi

Remise taxi Interprovincial, Av Costanera y La Rioja.

Directory

Rosario *p364*

Banks Many banks along C Córdoba, east of plaza San Martín. Money exchange at **Transatlántica**, Mitre y Rioja. TCs cashed at Banex, Mitre y Santa Fe; 2% or US$10 min commission. **Western Union** at Laprida y San Juan. **Internet** Several places in centre charging US$0.35/hr. **Medical services**

T107, T0341-4351111. Hospital de Emergencias Clemente Alvarez, T0341-4808111. Hospital de Niños Víctor Vilela (Children's Hospital), T0341-4808133. **Police** T101, T0341-448 6666. **Post office** Córdoba y Buenos Aires.

Sante Fé *p366*
Banks Banking district around San Martín y Tucumán. Exchange money and TCs at Tourfe, San Martín 2500, or at Columbia, San Martín 2275. **Internet** El Shuk, San Martín y Corrientes, US$0.50/hr. Xiver, 9 de Julio 2344, US$0.40/hr. **Laundry** Lavarfe, 25 de Mayo 2879. San Martín, San Martín 1786. Lavamax, 9 de Julio 2138. **Post office** C San Martín between Tucumán and La Rioja; Western Union branch.

Paraná *p367*
Banks Banco de la Nación, San Martín 1000. Banco Francés, San Martín 763. Banco Río, Pellegrini 29. **Internet** Several broadband places in the centre and along Av Rivadavia. **Medical services**, Hospital San Martín, Perón 450, T0343-4312222. **Police** T0343-420 9038. **Post office** 25 de Mayo y Monte Caseros; Western Union branch.

Corrientes *p368*
Banks Banco de la Nación, 9 de Julio y Córdoba. Bank Boston, San Juan y Carlos Pellegrini. El Dorado, 9 de Julio 1343, exchanges money and accepts all TCs; Western Union branch. **Internet** Brujas, Mendoza 787, US$0.35/hr. **Post office** San Juan y San Martín. **Medical servcies** T107. Hospital Escuela General San Martín, Rivadavia 1250, T03783-420695. Sanatorio del Norte, Carlos Pellegrini 1358, T03783- 421600. **Police** T101. **Telecommunications** Several *locutorios* in centre.

The Argentine Chaco

Little visited by travellers, the Argentine Chaco is just part of an immense sprawling lowland some 900 km wide, covering half of Paraguay and huge areas of Bolivia and Brazil. Rising gently from east to west, it's crossed by meandering rivers, and filled in central parts with cattle and cotton fields, soya and sunflowers. Though much of the Chaco is inaccessible, with little public transport, and rough roads which become almost impassable after heavy rains, two national parks can easily be reached all year round, both hosting a rich diversity of wildlife largely uninterrupted by human activity: Parque Nacional Chaco reached from Resistencia, and Parque Nacional Río Pilcomayo reached from Formosa. These are the region's two main cities, both close to Río Paraguay, and the only other settlement is uninspiring Presidencia Roque Sáenz Peña 170 km northwest of Resistencia, though its thermal waters are among the country's finest.

The most fascinating aspect of the Chaco is its pure and extensive indigenous population. Two of the largest groups are the Toba, mainly settled in towns next to the Paraná river, and the semi-nomadic Wichí in the west, who maintain their traditions of fine weaving, woodwork and ancient fishing techniques. ▸▸ *For Sleeping, Eating and other listings, see pages 380-382.*

Ins and outs

Getting there From Resistencia and Formosa, parallel Routes 16 and 81 head dead straight northwest across the plains, until they encounter the first hills of eastern Salta, which mark the border of this vast territory. Buses to Salta take Route 16, while Route 81 has long unpaved sections west of the small town of Las Lomitas, making the journey tough going after heavy rains.

Background

The Chaco falls into two distinct zones along a line south of the boundary between Chaco and Formosa provinces: the Wet Chaco and the Dry Chaco. The **Wet Chaco** spreads south from the Río Pilcomayo (the border with Paraguay) and west of the Río Paraguay, fertile wetlands supporting rich farming and abundant vegetation, marshlands with savanna and groves of *Caranday* palms, hosting many species of birds. Further west, as rainfall diminishes, the **Dry Chaco** is arid and wild, with little plant life, or indeed human life. Scrub vegetation, dotted with the algarrobo trees, white quebracho, the spiny bloated trunks of palo borracho and various types of cacti. This is one of the hottest places in South America, the western part of the Chaco has been known as 'El Impenetrable'.

Resistencia » *pp380-382.*

→ *Phone code: 03722 Colour map 1, B6 Population: 359,100*

The hot and energetic capital of the Province of Chaco, Resistencia is the commercial centre for the Chaco region together with the port of Barranqueras, just to the south on the Río Paraná. It's a modern city, not architecturally rich, but boasting an impressive number of sculptures by renowned artists, earning it the title of 'city of statues'. There's also a splendid central plaza, a nature reserve and the lovely **Isla del Cerrito** within easy reach, making it an appealing alternative stopover to neighbouring Corrientes on the journey between Iguazú and Salta.

Sights

The large Plaza 25 de Mayo occupies four blocks in the centre of the city, with a variety of indigenous plants and palms turning it into a mini botanical garden. Here, you'll find the city **tourist office** ⓘ *Mon-Fri 0800-2000, T03722-458289*. If they can't give you a map try the **provincial tourist office** ⓘ *Santa Fe 178, T03722-423547, www.chaco.gov.ar/turismo, Mon-Fri 0630-2000, Sat 0800-1200*, where you can get information on other destinations.

Five blocks from here, there's an informal cultural centre, **Fogón de los Arrieros**, (literally, 'the hearth of the muleteers') ⓘ *Brown 350, (between López y Planes and French), T03722-426418, open to non-members Mon-Sat 0900-1200, Mon-Fri 2100-2300, US$1.70*. This rather wonderful institution was formed by artists in the late 1960's, who decided to make the city an open air gallery, with public spaces filled with sculpture and murals. The centre itself still operates as a meeting place and exhibition space. Inspiring, and highly recommended. In the surrounding streets, you'll find more than 175 pieces of art by the country's finest artists.

Take López y Planes (later Sáenz Peña) and turn right at Juan B Justo to reach the **Museo Del Hombre Chaqueño** ⓘ *Juan B Justo 280, Mon-Fri 0800-1200, 1600-2000, free*. This small anthropological museum covers the story of colonization in the region, with a fine exhibition of handicrafts by native Wichi, Toba and Mocoví peoples, together with a fascinating mythology section in which small statues represent the Guaraní peoples' beliefs. Many of the rituals detailed are still practised in rural areas today, and are characterized by creatures of the marsh and woodland.

The **Isla del Cerrito**, a beautiful island northeast of Resistencia at the confluence of the Ríos Paraná and Paraguay, has a provincial nature reserve of 12,000 ha, covered mainly with grassland and palm trees. At the eastern end of the island (51 km from Resistencia), on the Río Paraná, in Cerrito, there's an attractive tourist complex with white sand beaches, a history museum, accommodation and restaurants, all very busy during the *Fiesta Nacional del Dorado* on the opposite shores in Paso de la Patria. Follow Route 16 east and turn north 3 km before the bridge to Corrientes: from here a road, the last 20 km of which are dirt (difficult after heavy rain), leads to a bridge, from where it is 17 km unpaved further to Cerrito. **Combi Arco Iris** has three daily services (0600, 1100, 1900) to Cerrito, an hour's journey and stopping half an hour there, US$1.20, leaving from bus stop at Juan B Justo y Avenida Alberdi (off Banco Hipotecario).

Parque Nacional Chaco → *Colour map 1, B6*

The Chaco National Park, 115 km northwest of Resistencia, extends over 15,000 ha and protects one of the last remaining untouched areas of the Wet Chaco with its exceptional *quebracho colorado* trees, *Caranday* palms and dense riverine forests, with orchids growing along the banks of the Río Negro. It is a very good place for birdwatching, with 340 species having been sighted in the park, including the parrot *loro hablador*. You're certain to be woken in the morning by the loud screams of *Carayá* monkeys, though other mammals living in the park may be less obtrusive, like the collared *peccary*, the *corzuela parda, the puma and the yaguarundí cat (Felis jaguamindi).*

At 300 m from the park's entrance there's a visitor centre and a free campsite with hot showers and electricity. There you can hire bicycles or horses for US$1.30/hr and move freely along the park's inner roads. Two short footpaths, *sendero del puente colgante* and *sendero del abuelo*, respectively lead to the banks of the Río Negro, and to an 800-year-old specimen of the *quebracho* tree. A vehicle road goes north 6 km up to two high *mangrullos* or view points, overlooking the two lakes, Laguna Carpincho and Laguna Yacaré, where, with a bit of patience, you'll see *yacarés* (alligators). Another track, suitable only for 4WD vehicles, goes south, through a forest of *quebracho* trees and after 9 km reaches the peaceful Laguna Panza de Cabra. There is a campsite by the lake, without facilities, and where you'll often hear the rare Maned wolf *(aguará guazú)* at night. Tour operators run day-long excursions to the park from Resistencia. Access to the park is free, open 24 hrs, T03725-496166.

Paved Route 16 goes northwest from Resistencia and after about 60 km Route 9 branches off it, leading north to Colonia Elisa and beyond to Capitán Solari, which lies 5 km east of the park entrance via a dirt road. If there's a group of you, call the park in advance to be picked up at Capitán Solari. Regular buses La Estrella daily link Resistencia and Capitán Solari, where *remise* taxis should not charge more than US$1 for the short journey to the park, which can also be made on foot.

North of Resistencia » *pp380-382.*

Route 11 runs north to Formosa and then onwards to the Paraguayan border near **Clorinda**, with the city of Asunción just over the border. Crossing low lying pastures with streams and *Caranday* palms, this route offers views of the diverse birdlife of the Wet Chaco, and is beautiful in the evening.

Formosa → *Phone code: 03717 Colour map 2, A1 Population: 198,100*

Formosa is the capital of its province and the only Argentine port of any note on the Río Paraguay. Oppressively hot from November to March, the city is the base for boat trips along the rivers in the eastern part of the province during the winter, when the weather is mild. It's also a possible stopover on the way to the **Parque Nacional Río Pilcomayo** or the **Bañado La Estrella**, and it's close to the Paraguayan capital, Asunción. From the town's small port, boats cross the river to Alberdi, a Paraguayan duty-free spot (only if you have a multiple entry visa).

Tourism is not well developed here yet, but increasingly activities are offered: guided excursions and accommodation at estancias; ask at the **tourist office** ⓘ *José M Uriburu 820 (on Plaza San Martín), T03717-420442, Mon-Fri 0700-1300, 1600-2000.*

Parque Nacional Río Pilcomayo → *Best visited in winter*

This park, 162 km north of Formosa, covers 48,000 ha of Wet Chaco environment bordering Paraguay on the southern bank of the Río Pilcomayo. The lower parts may be flooded during the rainy season and the resulting lakes and *esteros*, or marshlands, create the park's most beguiling landscapes. The rest is grassland with *Caranday* palm forests, where rheas can be seen, with some Chaco forest in the upper lands, habitat of three monkey species and several types of woodpecker. Due to its significance as a natural wetland, the park is a Ramsar site with diverse birdlife, including herons and three different species of stork. Anteaters, capybaras, coatis, two species of yacarés and aguará guazu are on the list of animals protected within the park.

Ins and outs From Formosa, take Route 11 to Clorinda, and from there take Route 86 going west. After 47 km, a 5 km dirt road leads north to the entrance to the Laguna Blanca area. Follow Route 86 for a few kilometres further for the 5 km access dirt road to the entrance to the Estero Poí section. Buses Godoy run from Formosa or Resistencia to the small towns of Laguna Naick-Neck, 5 km from the park (for going to Laguna Blanca) and from Laguna Blanca, 8 km from the park (for going to Estero Poí). Remise taxis from both towns should charge no more than US$3 for these short journeys. Access to the park is free and open 24 hours, administration centre at town of Laguna Blanca, Avenida Pueyrredón y Ruta 86, T03718-470045, Monday-Friday 0700-1430.

The park has two entrances leading to different areas. The most visited and easier to reach if you are on foot is Laguna Blanca, where there's an **information point** and a free campsite with electricity and cold water. From there, a footpath leads to the **Laguna Blanca**, the biggest lake in the park where you'll spot alligators among the rich aquatic plant life. The lake is not recommended for swimming, since the resident piranhas have a penchant for human toes. The second of the entrances, leads to **Estero Poí**, another information point and a campsite without facilities. Here take the 1,200-m footpath, with informative signs on the botany of the upper areas of the park. A vehicle road goes into the park up the Río Pilcomayo and the international border, but can only be used with special permission.

Border with Paraguay

There are two routes into Paraguay. The easiest crossing is by road via the Puente Loyola, 4 km north of Clorinda. From Puerto Falcón, at the Paraguayan end of the bridge, the road runs 40 km northeast, crossing the Río Paraguay to reach Asunción, (*Empresa Falcón* US$0.50, every hour, last bus to the centre of Asunción 1830).

Immigration Formalities for entering Argentina are dealt with at the Argentine end, at Puerto Pilcomayo, closed at weekends for tourists, and for those for leaving Argentina at the Paraguayan end at Itá Enramada, easy crossing, open 24 hrs. The other route is by ferry from Puerto Pilcomayo, close to Clorinda, to Itá Enramada (Paraguay), US$0.50, five minutes, every 30 minutes. Then take bus 9 to Asunción.

Sleeping

Resistencia *p378*

C Covadonga, Güemes 200, T03722-444444, hotelcovadonga@infovia.com.ar. The city's top hotel offers comfortable rooms with a/c. Pool, sauna and gym, breakfast included.

D Gran Hotel Royal, Obligado 211, T03722-443666, www.granhotelroyal.com. Reasonably good value, with comfortable rooms with a/c and breakfast included.

E Bariloche, Obligado 239, T03722-421412, jag@cpsarg.com Definitely the best value place in town, with a welcoming owner and decent rooms with bath and a/c. Unfortunately no breakfast here, but there's a nearby café at Gran Hotel Royal.

Formosa *p379*

B Turismo, San Martín 759, T03717-431122, hoteldeturismoformosa@arnet.com.ar. A large, strangely-shaped building by the river offering good views, though the rooms are pricey, all have a/c and breakfast is included.

C Casa Grande Apart-Hotel, Av González Lelong 185, T03717-431573, www.casagrandeapart.com.ar. Situated 8 blocks north of Av 25 de Mayo and next to the river, these are good 1 and 2-room apartments, with kitchen, a/c and breakfast, a gym and pool.

D Colón, Belgrano 1068, T03717-426547. Comfortable rooms, a/c, breakfast included.

D Plaza, José M Uriburu 920, T03717- 426767. On Plaza San Martín, this is a good choice for a swim in the pool. Breakfast included.

Eating

Resistencia *p378*
There is a lack of choice when it comes to restaurants but these can be recommended:
Kebon, Don Bosco y Güemes.
San José, Roca y Av Alberdi, Plaza 25 de Mayo. A popular café and *confitería* with excellent pastries (try the *medialunas*) and ice creams.

Formosa *p379*
Asador Criollo, Av Gutnisky. A popular parrilla where chivito (kid) is on the menu.
El Fortín, Mitre 602. A traditional place, good varied local fish dishes.
El Tano Marino, Av 25 de Mayo 55. An Italian restaurant, fine homemade pastas.
Yayita, Belgrano 926. Regional dishes such as *soyo*, or *sopa paraguaya* are offered in this central restaurant.

Festivals and events

Resistencia *p378*
Oct Fiesta Nacional de Pescado de los Grandes is celebrated every 10-12 Oct in the Río Antequeros, 14 km away from Resistencia.

Formosa *p379*
Easter The world's longest **Via Crucis** pilgrimage with 14 stops all the way along Route 81 (already registered in the Guinness Book of Records) takes place every Easter week, starting in Formosa and ending at the border with the province of Salta, 501 km northwest.
Jul On the night of the last day of Jul, the **Festival de la Caña Con Ruda** is held, when a drink of the Paraguayan *caña* flavoured by the ruda plant is taken as a protection for the mid-winter blues. The celebration is very popular and organized annually by the local authorities (ask at tourist office about the venue). It's also a good chance to try regional dishes.
Nov The **Festival Provincial de Folklore** held at Pirané (115 km northwest) is the major music festival in the northeast, attracting national stars of stirring folklore music.

Shopping

Resistencia *p378*
Fundación Chaco Artesanal, Carlos Pellegrini 272. A charity selling fine handicrafts made by Toba, Wichi and Mocoví native groups in varied materials, whose profits return to those communities.

Activities and tours

Resistencia *p378*
Sudamericana, San Buenaventura del Monte Alto 866, T/F03722-435954, sudevt@ciudad.com.ar. One-day tours to nearby sights all for a minimum of 5 people (Isla del Cerrito, US$9 pp, lunch included; Parque Nacional Chaco, US$8 pp).

Formosa *p379*
Domínguez Excursiones, San Martín 1577, T03717-421264, dominguez_excursiones@yahoo.com.ar. Excursions to all sights in the province, including the National Parks and Bañado La Estrella.
La Corvina, Mitre 164, T03717-423702, corvinaderio@hotmail.com. Reinaldo Saporiti is a fishing guide running excursions to Herradura on Paraguay river.
Pedro Iznardo, Paraguay 520, T03717-420780, iznardo@uol.com.ar. Freddy is a knowledgeable guide specializing in canoeing, who runs very interesting excursions down the nearby rivers lasting several days, such as the Riacho Monte Lindo Grande, north of Formosa. Good for birdwatching. He also runs excursions to Bañado La Estrella.

Transport

Resistencia *p378*
Air
Airport 8 km west of town (no bus), T03722-446009. Flights to/from **Buenos Aires** only with **Aerolíneas Argentinas**, 1 hr 15 mins. Taxis charge US$2.50-3.
Airline offices Aerolíneas Argentinas, Juan B Justo 184, T03722-445550.

Bus
The terminal is on Av Malvinas Argentinas y Av MacLean, on the western outskirts, far

from centre, T03722-461098. Buses No 3 and 10 from Oro y Perón, 1 block west of plaza, 20 mins, US$0.23. Taxis charge US$1.70 from centre. Left luggage: on platform, open 24 hrs US$0.35 a day. Tickets can be bought at same prices at several offices.

To **Corrientes**, Chaco-Corrientes buses stop opposite Norte supermarket on Av Alberdi e Illia, 40 mins, US$0.40 return. To **Capitán Solari** (for going to Parque Nacional Chaco), **La Estrella**, 3¼ hrs, US$2. To **Corrientes** bus terminal, **Puerto Tirol**, 30 mins, US$0.65 (drops you off at a small plaza at Av 3 de Abril y Av España; Corrientes centre lies six blocks north on Av España).

To **Buenos Aires**, several companies, 12-13 hrs, US$13-26. To **Puerto Iguazú**, **Aguila Dorada Bis** (change at Posadas), **Expreso Singer, Río Uruguay, Autotransportes Mendoza**, 8-10½ hrs, US$11-12.

To **Salta**, **Flecha Bus, La Nueva Estrella**, 12½ hrs, US$17-19. To **Tucumán**, **Almirante Brown, Vosa**, 12 hrs, US$16. To **Formosa**, several companies, 2-2½ hrs, US$2.70-3.50. To **Laguna Blanca** or **Laguna Naick-Neck** (for Parque Nacional Río Pilcomayo), **Godoy**, 8 hrs, US$5.70.

To **Asunción** (Paraguay), **El Pulqui, Brújula, Godoy, Crucero del Norte**, 5-5½ hrs, US$5.50-6.

Taxi
Radio taxi, T03722-438535.

Formosa *p379*
Air
El Pucu Airport is 5 km southwest, T03717-452490; **Aerolíneas Argentinas** to **Buenos Aires**, direct 1 hr 30 mins (2 hrs 20 mins when calling at Corrientes or Resistencia). Remise taxi, US$1.70.

Airline offices Aerolíneas Argentinas, Av 25 de Mayo 601, T03717-429314.

Bus
The terminal is at Av Gutnisky y Av Antártida Argentina (15 blocks west of plaza San Martín), T03717-430817. Remise taxis to centre, US$0.65. To **Asunción**, **Godoy, El Pulqui, Brújula**, 3 hrs, US$5. To **Resistencia**, several companies, 2½ hrs, US$2.70-3.50. To **Buenos Aires**, **El Pulqui, Flecha Bus, Puerto Tirol, Godoy**, 15-17 hrs, US$16-28. To **Laguna Blanca** or **Laguna Naick-Neck** (for **Parque Nacional Río Pilcomayo**), **Godoy**, 3 hrs, US$3. To **Las Lomitas** (for Bañado La Estrella), **Giroldi Travel**, 4 hrs, US$7.

Taxi
Remise taxi **Libertad**, José M Uriburu 750, T03717-420700.

Directory

Resistencia *p378*
Banks Banco de la Nación, Güemes y Av 9 de Julio. **Banco de Galicia**, Mitre 153. **El Dorado**, J M Paz 50. For money exchange: **Western Union** branch and TCs (bring high denomination US$ cheques, as commission is charged per cheque). **Internet** Klap, Illia 12. US$0.40/hr, open 24 hrs. **Medical services** Hospital Perrando, Av 9 de Julio 1101, T03722- 425050. **Hospital Pediátrico** (Children's Hospital), Juan B Justo 1136, T03722-441477. **Police** T101, T03722-432002. **Post office** Av Sarmiento e Hipólito Yrigoyen on Plaza 25 de Mayo.

Formosa *p379*
Banks Banco de la Nación, Av 25 de Mayo 602. **Banco de Galicia**, Av 25 de Mayo 160. **Medical services** T110. **Hospital Central**, Fotheringham 550, T03717- 426194. **Hospital de la Madre y el Niño** (for children), Ayacucho 1150, T03717-426097. **Police** T101, T03717- 429000.

Lake District

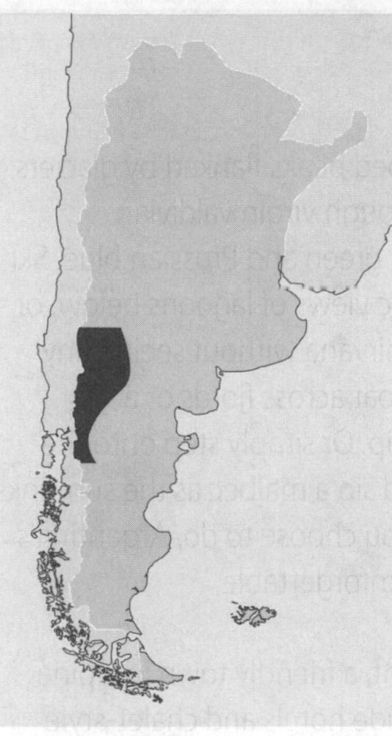

Footprint features

Introduction

Trek amongst craggy snow-capped peaks flanked by glaciers, and crystalline rivers running through virgin valdivian rainforest to lakes of peppermint green and Prussian blue. Ski down long pistes with panoramic views of lagoons below, or hike for days in a mountain top nirvana without seeing any sign of civilization. Take a slow boat across fjords or a hair-raising whitewater rafting trip. Or simply step onto the terrace of your lakeside hotel and sip a malbec as the sun sinks over the mountains. Whatever you choose to do, Argentina's Lake District is spectacular, and unforgettable.

Bariloche is the best starting point, a friendly town in alpine style with chocolate shops, lakeside hotels and chalet-style restaurants selling wild boar and smoked trout. Towering above is a range of peaks where you can hike, ski, or cycle. Or just take a cable car and admire the incredible views. Bariloche could easily entertain you for a week. A magical road winds through seven lakes and three national parks to the pretty tourist town of San Martín de los Andes. Retreat to Lago Huechulafquen, where perfectly conical volcano Lanín is reflected in cobalt blue waters. North of here, it's wilder and less visited. Pehuenia is a quiet haven with its forests of pre-historic monkey puzzle trees, broad lagoons, and the rich culture of the native Mapuche people. At the southern end of the lakes, El Bolsón is a wonderfully relaxed place for a few days' hiking, where the mountains are magnificent, and the local *cerveza* is excellent. Take the *Old Patagonian Express*, try a Welsh tea in quaint Trevelin, and then explore the region's most unspoilt national park, Los Alerces. A jade green river flows between the cinnamon trunks of Arrayanes trees and 1000-year-old alerces trees tower above you. And if you come in March, you'll have all this to yourself.

★ Don't miss...

1 **Bariloche** Sample wild boar or stuff yourself with chocolate, page 392.
2 **Estancia Huechahue** Ride into Lanín National Park on a trusty steed, page 430.
3 **Villa Pehuenia** Wander through mystical silent Araucaria forests, page 434.
4 **Mount Tronador** Borrow crampons and climb the glacier, page 448.
5 **Jauja ice cream in El Bolsón** Sample the best ice cream in Argentina, page 449.
6 **Estancia Peuma Hue** A lakeside paradise for hiking, peace and luxury, page 455.
7 **Los Alerces National Park** Hike up Cerro Dedal or take a boat trip to see 2600-year-old alerce trees, page 463.

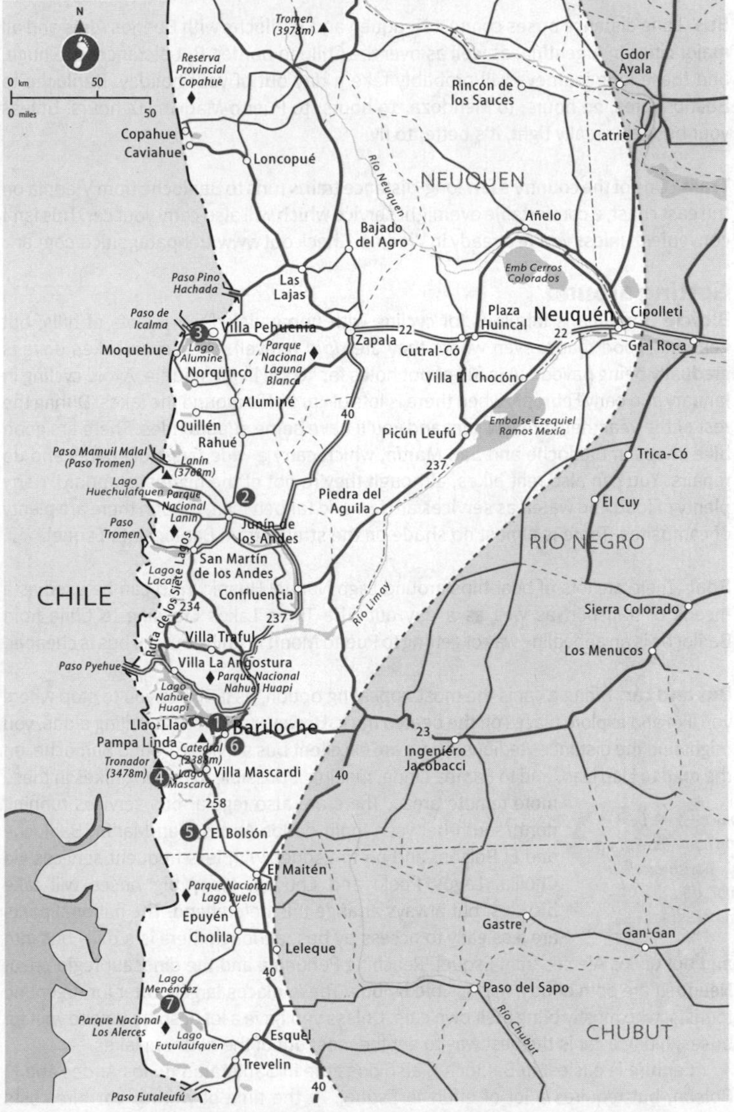

Ins and outs

Getting there

Air There are several flights daily from Buenos Aires to Bariloche, or Esquel (for the southern lakes) and San Martín de los Andes (for the northern lakes), as well as flights from Santiago in Chile to Bariloche. In addition, the army airline **LADE** runs weekly flights connecting Bariloche with other Patagonian towns. If you're short on time, flying is preferable to long bus journeys, and it's relatively inexpensive. Consider buying two singles (same price as a return), flying to San Martín de los Andes in the north and leaving from Esquel in the south, allowing you to see the whole area by hired car or bus. Book well in advance December-March.

Bus Long distance buses connect Neuquén and Bariloche with Buenos Aires and all major cities in Argentina, as well as over the Chilean border. But distances are huge, and these long journeys will probably take a day out of your holiday. Bariloche to Buenos Aires, 22 hours; to Mendoza, 19 hours; to Puerto Madryn, 14 hours. Unless your budget is really tight, it's better to fly.

Train One of the country's few long-distance trains runs to Bariloche from Viedma on the east coast, a comfortable overnight service which will also carry your car. This isn't convenient unless you're already in Viedma. Check out www.trenpatagonico.com.ar.

Getting around

Bicycle The area is fabulous for cycling with unparalleled views, lots of hills, but generally good roads, even where they are *ripio* (gravel). The Seven Lakes drive is gradually being paved but is full of pot holes for 50 km in the middle. Avoid cycling in January and early February when there is lots of car traffic around the lakes. During the rest of the year there are few cars and you'll have some superb rides. There are good bike shops in Bariloche and San Martín, which carry a wide range of spares and do repairs. You can also rent bikes, although they're not of the highest standard. Carry plenty of food and water, as services are few and far between, though there are plenty of campsites. There is almost no shade on the stretch from Bariloche to Esquel.

Boat There are lots of boat trips around Lago Nahuel Huapi which can be used as a means of transport as well as a day out. The Three Lakes Crossing to Chile from Bariloche is an appealing way of getting to Puerto Montt in Chile, but the bus is cheaper.

Bus and car Hiring a car is the most appealing option, as it allows you to stop where you like and explore places off the beaten track. However, if you're travelling alone, you might find the distances tedious. There are excellent bus services around Bariloche, on the road to Llao Llao, and to Pampa Linda, making it possible to do long hikes in these more remote areas. There are also regular bus services running north/south between Junín de los Andes, San Martín, Bariloche and El Bolsón, and on to Esquel, with less frequent services via Cholila, Lagos Puelo and Epuyen. Many big buses will take bicycles, but always arrange this beforehand. The national parks are less easy to access by bus, although there is a daily bus into and out of Los Alerces from Esquel. Reaching Pehuenia and the dinosaur region near Neuquén are both almost impossible by bus. These places largely cater for Argentine tourists, who mostly bring their own cars. Unless you have a lot of spare time to wait for buses, hiring a car is the best way to get the most out of the northern lakes.

> *Bariloche is the best starting point for visiting the lakes, with excellent transport and accommodation.*

Car hire is easiest in Bariloche, also possible in San Martín de los Andes and El Bolsón, but requires a lot of effort in Esquel. At the time of writing, car hire costs around US$40 a day; for an extra charge of around US$35, the better companies will allow you to drop the car off at a different town from where you hired it. If you plan to take a hire car over the border into Chile, let the car hire company know ahead of time, as by law the vehicle must have its registration number etched on the windows.

Walking There are plenty of *refugios* in the mountains behind Bariloche, making it possible to plan four- or five-day hikes. They vary in quality but most will provide hot meals and advice on routes. There are more *refugios* near Pampa Linda, in the hills around El Bolsón, and a couple in both Los Alerces and Lanín national parks. Get advice from park offices or **Club Andino Bariloche** (see page 393). Bus services around Bariloche are well set up to help hikers get about; again, ask in Club Andino.

Best time to visit

Summer (December to February) is the obvious time to come, but beware that January is impossibly busy throughout the region, as this is when Argentines take their holidays *en masse*, and accommodation is hard to find. Come in March and early April instead, when days are still likely to be clear and there are far fewer visitors, making it much easier to get flights and be spontaneous with accommodation. Late spring and early summer (October/November) can be lovely, though cool. Autumn is the most beautiful time of year to visit, with brilliant displays of autumn leaves in late April to early May. The skiing season runs from late June to September and is busiest in July, when prices rise, and Bariloche is inundated by Brazilians. Outside the peak season, transport services are fewer, requiring more flexible schedules, but well worth it to enjoy greater tranquility. Hotels are all more expensive in peak periods, with the highest in January and July.

Tourist information

The best centre is in Bariloche. It is well set up for tourism with good tour operators and well-organized boat and cable car services to make the most of the stunning mountain landscape nearby. Tourist offices are given for each town, but to plan your trip and for more information before you come, check out these sites: www.neuquentur.gov.ar; www.barilochepatagonia.info (a great site in English, French, Portuguese and German); www.elbolson.gov.ar; www.naheulhuapi.gov.ar; www.junindelosandes.gov.ar; www.visitchile.org; www.parquesnacionales.gov.ar; www.parquenacionallanin.gov.ar; www.interpatagonia.com (excellent site for general information on the area); www.clubandino.org (for walks and mountain climbing); www.activepatagonia.com.ar (hiking and trekking expeditions); www.huala.com.ar and www.alsurnh.com (adventure tourism) and www.revistapatagonia.com.ar (a useful magazine).

National parks

There are no less than four national parks covering enormous swathes of the Lake District, and these areas are generally where you'll find the best hiking, rafting and horse riding, in the most unspoiled forests and mountain landscapes you can imagine. The area's main centre, **Bariloche**, is inside **Parque Nacional Nahuel Huapi**, and has well developed infrastructure for activities in the park, see page 392. Inside this park is another, tiny park, **Parque Nacional Los Arrayanes**, accessed from **Villa La Angostura**. Immediately to the north of Nahuel Huapi is **Parque Nacional Lanín**, which contains the town of **San Martín de los Andes**, and has also superb hiking, especially around **Volcán Lanín** (see page 422). South of Bariloche, there is the tiny but beautiful **Parque Nacional Lago Puelo**, just south of **El Bolsón**. Finally, **Los Alerces** is the most pristine of all the parks, with just one road running through it, and most areas accessible only on foot. The nearest towns are **Esquel** and **Trevelin**, see page 460. Each park has a rangers station, where *guardaparques* will give you a map and advise on walks in the park, as well as on accommodation and state of the paths.

Parque Nacional Nahuel Huapi

Nahuel Huapi is the national park you're most likely to visit since Bariloche is right at its heart. It stretches along the Andes for over 130 km, from south of Lago Mascardi to north of Villa Traful, and so there are no official entry points, like most of the other national parks. It was Argentina's first ever national park, created in 1934, from a donation made to the country by naturalist Francisco Perito Moreno of 7500 ha of land around Puerto Blest. Extending across some of Argentina's most dramatic mountains, the park contains lakes, rivers, glaciers, waterfalls, torrents, rapids, valleys, forest, bare mountains and snow-clad peaks. Among those you can climb are Tronador (3478m), Catedral Sur (2388m), Falkner (2350m), Cuyín Manzano (2220m), López (2076m), Otto (1405m) and Campanario (1052m). The outstanding feature is the splendour of the lakes, and the pristine nature of the virgin forests. ▸▸ *For Sleeping, Eating and other listings, see pages 400-409.*

Ins and outs

Tourist information

There are many centres within the park, at Villa la Angostura, and at Villa Traful, for example. But Bariloche is the usual first port of call for activities within the park, and here you can equip yourself with information on transport, walks and maps. The **Nahuel Huapi National Park intendencia** ⓘ *San Martín 24, T02944-423111, www.parquesnacionales.com.ar, daily 0900-1400*, is pretty unhelpful, with no real precise information. Much better information on walks, *refugios* and buses, with great maps is available from the trained guides and mountaineers at **Club Andino Bariloche (CAB)** ⓘ *20 de Febrero 30, T02944-422266, www.clubandino.org, Mon-Fri 0900-1300, plus 1600-2100 high season only*.

You can also contact the **Association of Guides** (aguiasdeturismoula@yahoo.com.ar), all of whom are trained, and know the geography, flora and fauna. Ask for English speakers. They sell excellent maps showing walks, with average walking times, and refugios, and can advise on which have room. Ask for the *Sendas y Bosques* (walks and forests) series, which are 1:200,000, laminated and easy to read, with good books containing English summaries of the walks, www.guiasendasybosques.com.ar, the *Active Patagonia* map, with fabulous detail, and the *Carta de Refugios, Senderos y Picadas* for Bariloche. They can also tell you about transport: services vary from year to year and high/low season, so it's best to check.

Around the park

Lago Nahuel Huapi

The centrepiece of the park is its largest lake, Lago Nahuel Huapi, a huge 531 sq km and 460 m deep in places, particularly magnificent to explore by boat since the lake is very irregular in shape and long fjord-like arms of water, or *brazos*, stretch far into the west towards Chile, where there is superb virgin Valdivian rainforest, and north towards the Parque Nacional Los Arrayanes, (a park inside a park) which contains a rare woodland of exquisite arrayán trees with their cinnamon-coloured flaky bark. There are many islands: the largest is Isla Victoria, with a luxurious hotel. The tourist town of Bariloche is the best base for exploring this area, with plentiful accommodation all along the southern shore of Lago Nahuel Huapi, and hiking, rafting, tours and boat trips on offer.

North of Bariloche

North of the upmarket tourist village of Villa La Angostura (see page 411), a winding road takes you through spectacular and largely unspoiled landscapes on the famous Seven Lakes Drive (see page 410) to San Martín de los Andes (see page 423). The northernmost stretch of this drive, and three of its lakes, are in Parque Nacional Lanín (see page 418), which borders Nahuel Huapi National Park. Lagos Correntoso and Espejo both offer stunning scenery, and tranquil places to stay and walk. Another tiny

Parque Nacional Nahuel Huapi

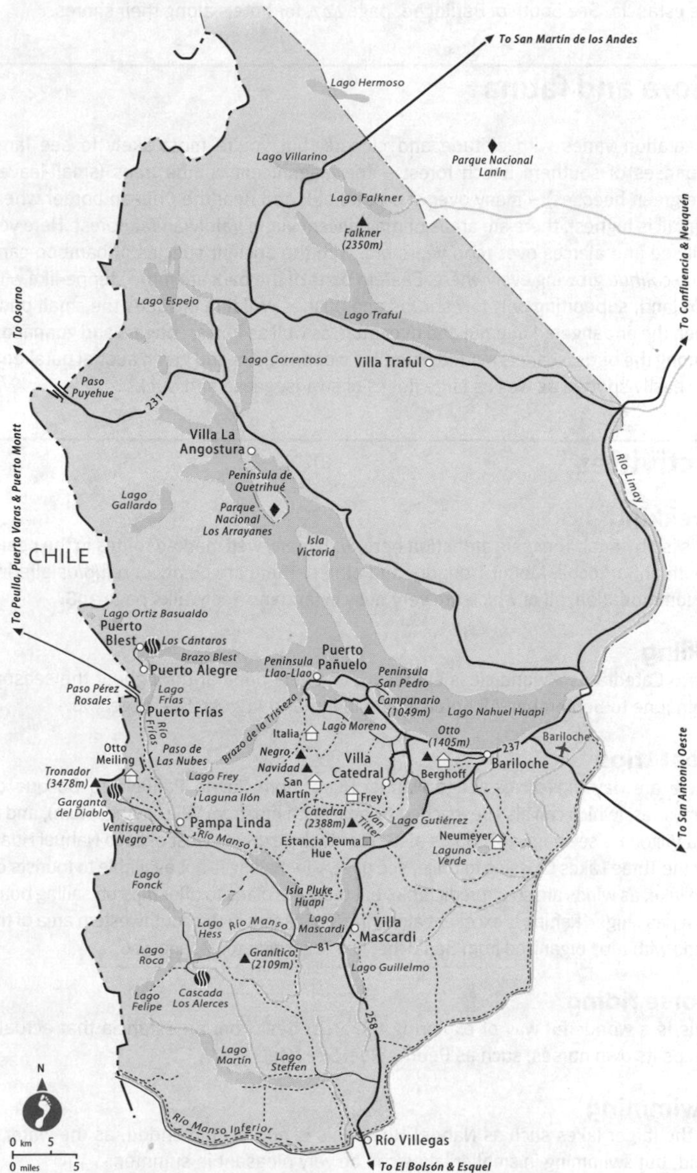

 centre, Villa Traful (see page 412), lies on the shore of navy blue Lago Traful, the perfect place to escape to, with fishing, camping and walking.

South and west of Bariloche

West of Bariloche, there are glaciers and waterfalls near Pampa Linda, the base for climbing Mount Tronador, and starting point for the trek through Paso de las Nubes to Lago Frias. South of Lago Nahuel Huapi, Lagos Mascardi, Guillelmo, and Gutiérrez have even grander scenery, offering horse riding, trekking, and rafting along the Río Manso. An excellent base for exploring this area is **Estancia Peuma Hue** on the southern shore of Lago Gutiérrez, with great walking, riding and rafting arranged by the estancia. See South of Bariloche, page 447, for hotels along their shores.

Flora and fauna

Vegetation varies with altitude and climate, but you're most likely to see large expanses of southern beech forest – the magnificent coihue trees (small-leaved evergreen beeches) – many over 450 years old, and near the Chilean border where rainfall is highest, there are areas of magnificent virgin Valdivian rainforest. Here you will see and alerces over 1500 years old, with the ancient species of bamboo cane *caña colihue* growing everywhere. Eastern parts of the park are more steppe-like with arid land, supporting only low shrubs and bushes. Wildlife includes the small pudú deer, the endangered huemul and river otter, as well as foxes, cougars and guanacos. Among the birds, scarlet-headed Magellan woodpeckers and green austral parakeets are easily spotted as well as large flocks of swans, geese and ducks.

Activities

Trekking

This is obviously the main attraction here, with many well marked routes in the peaks south of Bariloche, Mount Tronador and others. There are plenty of *refugios* offering accommodation, all of which are very busy in January. See Walks page 398.

Skiing

Cerro Catedral is a world-class ski resort, and very popular throughout the season, from June to September. All hotels fill up in July and August. See page 396.

Boat trips

There are day trips across Lago Nahuel Huapi from Puerto Pañuelo to Bosque de Arrayanes, (which can also be reached by boat or on foot from Villa La Angostura), and to Isla Victoria – see page 397. Boats also cross to the extreme west of Lago Nahuel Huapi for the Three Lakes Crossing to Chile, see page 399. Sailing is not available to tourists on the lake, as winds are so unpredictable, but there are plans to offer trips on sailing boats as a passenger. Rafting is excellent along the Río Manso, in the southwestern area of the park, with trips organized from Bariloche; see Tour operators, page 406.

Horse riding

This is a wonderful way of exploring the area: best from an estancia that actually keeps its own horses, such as Peuma Hue. See page 455.

Swimming

In the larger lakes such as Nahuel Huapi this is not recommended, as the water is cold, but swimming in smaller lakes can be very pleasant in summer.

Parque Nacional Los Arrayanes

This park covers the Quetrihué Peninsula, which dips south from Villa La Angostura into the Lago Nahuel Huapi, and lies within the Parque Nacional Nahuel Huapi. It was created to protect a rare forest of arrayán trees, since it's one of the few places where the arrayán grows to full size, and some of the specimens are 300 years old. This myrtle-like tree, grows near water in groves, and likes to have its roots wet, since it really has no bark. The trunks are extraordinary: a smooth powdery or peeling surface, cinnamon in colour and cold to the touch. They have no outer bark to protect them, but the surface layer is rich in tannins which keep the tree free from disease. They have creamy white flowers in January and February, and produce blue-black fruit in March. The sight of so many of these trees together, with their twisting cinnamon-coloured trunks creates a magical light, and is really fairy tale wonderful. The most rewarding way to see the wood is to take the boat trip across the sparkling deep blue lake, fringed with spectacular peaks, to the tip of the peninsula, and then take a leisurely walk along the wooden walkways through the trees, waiting until the guided tour has left. Then stroll back to the port through the mixed forest, passing two pretty and secluded lakes, Laguna Patagua, and Laguna Hua Huan.

Ins and outs

The entrance to the park lies 2 km south of the port area of Villa la Angostura, known as La Villa, Bus company **15 de Mayo** runs buses from El Cruce to la Villa every two hours and takes 15 minutes. There's a *confitería* in the park, selling drinks and confectionery. Entrance costs US$4, and a taxi to the Villa costs US$3. The **park office** is at Calle Inacayal 13, 2nd floor, T02944-494004, www.bosquelosarrayanes.com.ar.

Walking/cycling

There's a clear path all the way from the tip of the Quetrihué Peninsula where the boat arrives, through the prettiest part of the arrayán forest, and then running the length of the peninsula back to La Villa. You can walk or cycle the whole length: three hours one-way walking; two hours cycling.

Boat trips

There are two companies running catamarans that run from the pier in La Villa to the end of the peninsula, and take passengers on a short guided tour through the forest before allowing time for a drink at the small *confitería* and then taking the boat back to La Villa. **Greenleaf Turismo** runs *Catamarán Futuleufu*, T02944-494004, angosturaturismo@netpatagon.com. Also **Catamarán Patagonia Argentina**, T02944-494463. Tickets from **Hotel Angostura**, US$12 return with the catamaran. Boats also run from Bariloche, via Isla Victoria, with **Turisur**, T02944-426109, www.barilche.com/turisur.

Bariloche and around

➔ *Phone code: 02944 Colour map 5, B2 Population: 100,000*

Beautifully situated on the steep and wooded southern shore of Lago Nahuel Huapi, surrounded by high peaks, San Carlos de Bariloche (it's official name) is an ideal base for exploring the Lake District. It's right in the middle of Nahuel Huapi National Park, and there's so much on offer from the town itself that you'd be quite content to spend a week or so around here. There's hiking and adventure sports of all kinds in the mountains behind the town, a fabulous estancia and some wonderful boutique hotels on the lakeshore heading west.

The town was founded in 1902 but really took off in the 1930s when the national park was created. The chalet-style architecture was established at this time by early German and Swiss settlers. Hotel Llao Llao and the Civic Centre were designed by major Argentine architect Bustillo, who set the trend for 'Bariloche Alpine Style', with local stone, brightly varnished wood and cute carved gable ends, now ubiquitous throughout the region.

Bariloche is well set up for tourism, with the main street, Mitre, bustling with tour operators, outdoor clothing shops and chocolate makers. There are also many restaurants serving fondue as well as delicious local trout and wild boar, some of them bordering on kitsch, but appealing nevertheless. There are plenty of hotels and restaurants in the town centre, but the best places are sprinkled along the shore of lake Nahuel Huapi, towards Llao Llao, where Argentina's most famous hotel enjoys a spectacularly beautiful setting. To the immediate south of Bariloche there are fabulous walks in the mountains, and up giant Mount Tronador, reached from Pampa Linda further south. On the way are two gorgeous lakes: Gutiérrez, with Estancia Peuma Hue on its shores for excellent horse riding and relaxing; and Mascardi, with access to rafting on the Río Manso. In summer there are good bus and boat services to reach these mountains and lakes as well as cable cars up two of the peaks behind Bariloche. Ski resort Cerro Catedral is arguably the best in South America, and makes a great base for trekking in summer. ►► *For Sleeping, Eating and other listings, see pages 400-409.*

Ins and outs

Getting there The airport is 15 km east of town, taxis charge US$5. A bus service meets each arriving flight. US$2.30. Bus and train stations are both 3 km east of town; taxi US$1.50, frequent buses 10, 20, 21. If you are staying in one of the many hotels on the road to Llao-Llao, west of town, expect to pay a little more for transport to your hotel.

Getting around Bariloche is an easy city to walk around and to orient yourself in, since the lake lies to the north, and the mountains to the south. The main street is Calle Mitre running east-west, and unmistakable with its souvenir and chocolate shops. Here you'll find all the tour operators, *locutorios* and internet cafés, as well as banks and some food shops. The tourist information office (see below) is in the distinctive chalet-style Centro Cívico, with an open space giving good views onto the lake, and most hotels and restaurants are gathered in three or four blocks around here, with cheaper accommodation and youth hostels tending to be a few blocks further south on the upper slopes of town. More upmarket hotels and many restaurants are spread out on along Avenida Bustillo, the road running the southern shore of Lago Nahuel Huapi for some 25 km, as far as the famous **Hotel Llao-Llao**, and in an area known as Colonial Suiza. This is a viable place to stay even if you haven't got a car, since frequent local buses, run by **3 de Mayo**, run along its length. Take number 20 to Llao Llao, for lakeside hotels and restaurants and Puerto Pañuelo, 10 to

Colonia Suiza and Bahia Lopez for trekking, 50 to Lago Gutiérrez, via the base for cable car to Cerro Otto, and the bus labelled 'Catedral' for Cerro Catedral.

Tourist information The **tourist office** ⓘ *Centro Cívico, T02944-429850, www.barilochepatagonia.info, daily 0900-2100*, has helpful staff who speak English, French and German, and have maps showing the town and whole area to Llao Llao, with bus routes marked. They can also help with accommodation and campsites in the area. **Nahuel Huapi National Park intendencia** ⓘ *San Martín 24, T02944-423111, www.nahuelhuapi.gov.ar, daily 0900-1400*, is pretty unhelpful; far better to go straight to **Club Andino Bariloche** (CAB) ⓘ *Just above the Centro Cívico, T02944-422266, www.clubandino.org, 0900-1300, 1600-2100, high season only*, for information on walks, hikes, mountain climbs refugios, and buses to reach all the local areas for walking. Excellent maps, advice and current information given. All staff know the mountains well and some of them speak English, French or German.

Best time to visit Argentina's favourite holiday destination is busiest in the school holidays of January and July, but it's also the destination for all graduating secondary school students in August, September and January, though these groups are now confined to special hotels (not listed here!), and rarely stray beyond the city's bars and nightclubs for their inevitable rites of passage. Trekking is possible between mid-December and the end of April , but some longer treks are impassable until late January and February when the paths have been cleared of winter snow and fallen trees. Email ahead to get weather and path conditions. Accommodation is cheaper outside of the peak periods, and paths are less busy. But beware that bus services are less frequent once the schools restart in early March, and that the weather becomes unpredictable at the end of April. For skiing, July and August are best, though hotels are packed with mass tourism from Chile and Brazil. Try June or September instead, and always book well ahead.

Sights

At the heart of the city is the **Centro Cívico**, designed by Bustillo in 'Bariloche Alpine style' on an attractive plaza above the lake, where there's also a small museum, **Museo de La Patagonia** ⓘ *Tue-Fri 1000-1230, 1400-1900, Mon-Sat 1000-1300, US$1*, with some indigenous artefacts and material from the lives of the first white settlers. Mitre is the main commercial area, and here all the chocolate shops are clustered – a sight in themselves, and not to be missed. **Abuela Goye** and **Mamushka** are most highly recommended. The **cathedral**, built in 1946, lies south of Mitre and opposite is a huge rock left in this spot by a glacier during the last glacial period. On the lakeshore is the **Museo Paleontológico** ⓘ *12 de Octubre y Sarmiento*, which has displays of fossils mainly from Patagonia including an ichthyosaur and replicas of a giant spider and shark's jaws. Bariloche's real sights are the mountains themselves, and don't miss a trip up to one of their peaks in cable cars to either **Cerro Otto** or **Cerro Campanario** to see lakes and mountains stretching out in front of you as far as the eye can see.

The road to Llao Llao

» pp400-409.

To really appreciate the splendid setting of Bariloche, you need to get out of town, and head west along **Avenida Bustillo** running parallel to the lakeshore to the area known as **Llao Llao**, where the hotel is, and where boats leave from Puerto Pañuelo. Frequent buses run along this road, so it's easy to explore even without your own transport. Parallel to Avenida Bustillo, **Avenida de los Pioneros** runs above, with more hotels, but mostly residential areas. There's easy access to the mountains above these roads, by driving to, or getting off the bus at, the kilometre stop you want. The free tourist office map, *Circuito Chico* shows the stops clearly. For a

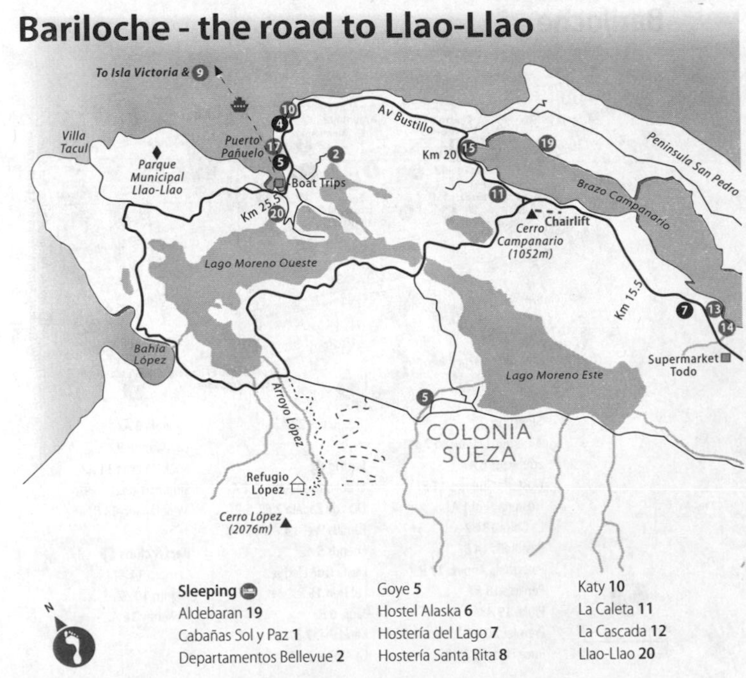

summary of some of the many excellent hikes in the area, see Trekking and climbing, page 407. Cyclists beware that this is a busy road, and drivers will show you no mercy, expecting you to pull over onto the gravel verges as they pass.

Llao Llao

Llao Llao, named after the exquisitely pretty hotel, is a charming area 25 km west of Bariloche, and a lovely place for walking with gorgeous views. It's at the end of Avenida Bustillo, which runs along Lago Nahuel Huapi to the port (Puerto Pañuelo), where boat trips leave. **Hotel Llao-Llao** itself is one of Argentina's finest, and worth the extortionate rates for the view, spa and restaurant. The hotel was designed by Bustillo, and opened in 1937, originally almost entirely a wooden construction. It burned down within a few months of opening and was rebuilt using local stone. Superbly situated on a hill with incredible views over the lake, it's a good place for tea on the terrace. Even if luxury hotels aren't your thing, it's still worth coming to the area, as there are superb walks in beautiful virgin forest, rich in wildlife, at **Parque Municipal Llao Llao**, just off the road west of the hotel. This small peninsula juts into the lake, with a small hill, and a little beach, **Villa Tacul**, both offering good views. Take bus No 20, a lovely 45-minute ride, US$0.70. Buses leave from the big bus stop on Moreno y Rolando. For information, T02944-425648. Alternatively, take a half-day tour to 'Circuito Chico', but beware that you won't get much time for walking, see below, or take a full day to cycle.

Cerro Campanario

At Km 17.5, a **chairlift** ⓘ *T02944-427274, daily 0900-1800, 7 mins, US$5, extended opening in summer*, goes up to Cerro Campanario (1049 m) with superb views of the lake, edged with mountains, as well as San Pedro Peninsula below and Lago Moreno. Take bus 20, 10 or 22 to Km 17.5. Restaurant and bar at the top with fabulous views.

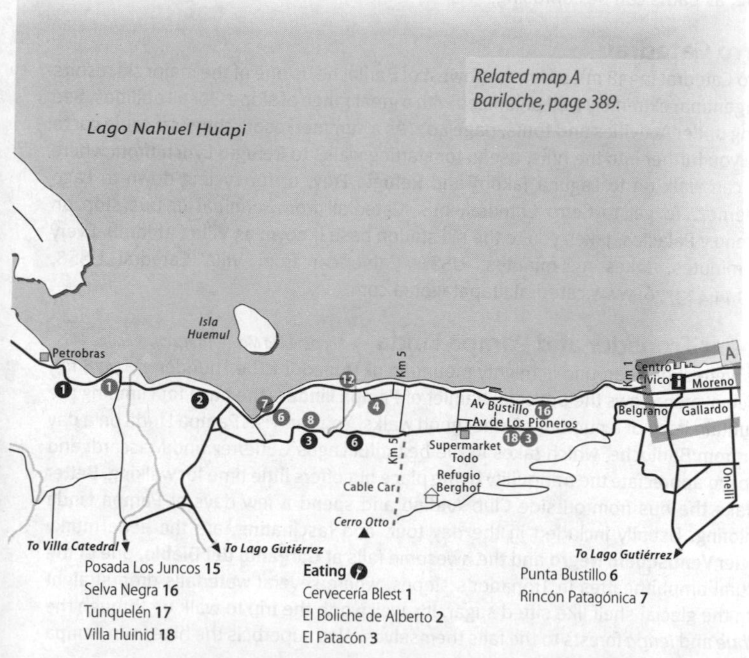

Posada Los Juncos 15
Selva Negra 16
Tunquelén 17
Villa Huinid 18

Eating
Cervecería Blest 1
El Boliche de Alberto 2
El Patacón 3
Punta Bustillo 6
Rincón Patagónica 7

Circuito Chico

Circuito Chico is the classic old Argentine tour: you sit in the car and gaze at the view. These days, you're more likely to want to stop, hike, take photos and find somewhere to eat, so the tour as offered by tour operators is a frustrating experience. Drive or cycle instead. The circuit itself is a great introduction to the area. Start by travelling along Avenida Bustillo, and turn off at Km 18.3 to go around Lago Moreno Oeste, past Punto Panorámico (with really great panoramic views) and continue around **Bahía Lopez**, through the Parque Municipal Llao Llao with lovely walks, and on to Hotel Llao Llao and Puerto Pañuelo. You could extend the circuit by returning via **Colonia Suiza** and ski resort **Cerro Catedral** (2388 m), both of which are possible starting points for longer treks. This is a satisfying all-day cycle ride, see page 447, but beware impatient drivers who will expect you to get off the road onto the gravel verge. Take bus 10 to Colonia Suiza, Bus 'Catedral' to Catedral. All buses from the big bus stop on Moreno y Rolando, information T02944-425648.

Southwest of Bariloche

» *pp400-409.*

Cerro Otto

→ *For skiing on Cerros Catedral and Otto, see Activities and tours, page 407*

At Km 5 on Avenida de los Pioneros, a cable car (known here as *teleferico*) goes up to Cerro Otto, (1405 m) with its revolving restaurant and really wonderful views over the lakes and mountains all around. Alternatively, 20 minutes walk away on the summit at **Refugio Berghof** is a *confitería* belonging to Club Andino Bariloche. Highly recommended. Take the free hourly bus service from Mitre y Villegas, running from 1030 to 1730, returning hourly 1115 to 1915. Cable cars run from 1000-1800. A combined ticket for both bus and cable car is US$10 return, T02944-441035. By car, take Avenida de los Pioneros, then the signposted dirt track 1 km out of town. To climb Cerro Otto on foot (two to three hours): turn off Avenida de los Pioneros at Km 4.6, then follow the trail past Refugio Berghof, with splendid views. Not recommended alone, as paths can be confusing.

Cerro Catedral

Cerro Catedral (2338 m), 21 km southwest of Bariloche, is one of the major ski resorts in Argentina; extremely well organized with a great range of slopes for all abilities. See skiing under Activities and tours, page 407. As a summer resort, there's a cable car to take you further into the hills, useful for starting walks to **Refugio Lynch** (from where you can walk on to Laguna Jakob) and **Refugio Frey**, or for cycling down to Lago Gutierriez. To get to Cerro Catedral, bus 'Catedral' from terminal or bus stop on Moreno y Palacios, takes you to the ski station base (known as Villa Catedral). Every 90 minutes, takes 35 minutes, US$1. Cable car from Villa Catedral US$8, T02944-423776, www.catedralaltapatagonia.com.

Mount Tronador and Pampa Linda

→ *For climbing Mount Tronador, see page 448.*

The highest peak around is mighty mountain of Tronador ('The Thunderer', 3478 m), which overshadows the peaceful hamlet of **Pampa Linda** – the base for climbing the mountain itself or a number of other good walks. You can visit Pampa Linda on a day tour from Bariloche, which takes in the beautiful Lagos Gutiérrez and Mascardi and stops to appreciate the tranquility of the place but offers little time for walking. Better to take the bus from outside Club Andino and spend a few days at Pampa Linda exploring. Usually included in the day tour, and fascinating, are the eerie murky glacier **Ventisquero Negro** and the awesome falls at **Garganta del Diablo**, one of the natural amphitheatres in Tronador's slopes, where several waterfalls drop straight from the glacial shelf like sifted sugar. It's well worth the trip to walk up through the *coihue* and *lenga* forests to the falls themselves. Also superb, is the hike from Pampa

Linda to **Refugio Otto Meiling,** where you can hire crampons and walk on the glacier. The lower sections of these paths are great for mountain biking in the forest. More spectacular walks to Lago Blest along the **Paso de los Nubes**, and **Laguna Ilon.** A good way to make the most of the area is to take a tour with an agency, and then stay on at Pampa Linda to start trekking, returning with the minibus service run by **Transitando lo Natural**, 20 de Febrero 25, T02944-527926, transitando1@hotmail.com. Buses to Pampa Linda run daily at 0900 in season, US$7.50. Alternatively, **Expreso Meiling** also run buses in season, leaving Club Andino Bariloche at 0830, and returning from Pampa Linda at 1700 (T02944-529875). There's a great simple *hostería* at Pampa Linda, offering lunches. » *For Pampa Linda listings, see page 455.*

Boat trips on Lago Nahuel Huapi

Bosque de Arrayanes

A popular boat trip is across to Lago Nahuel Huapi to **Isla Victoria** and Bosque de Arrayanes, where these rare myrtle trees with their twisting cinnamon-coloured trunks create a magical fairy tale atmosphere. The *bosque* can also be visited by boat or on foot from **Villa La Angostura** which allows you more time in the forest, and a good 13-km hike back. There are half-day excursions (1300-1830) from Puerto Pañuelo (bus 10, 20 or 21 to get there) and on to Parque Nacional Los Arrayanes, on the Quetrihué peninsula further north in a full-day excursion (either 0900-1830, or 1300 till 2000 in season) costing US$18; take a picnic lunch.

Puerto Blest

The other great boat trip in the area is the all-day excursion to Puerto Blest, and **Cascada los Cantaros,** at the western end of Lago Nahuel Huapi, and **Lago Frías,** visiting native forest and Valdivian rainforest. Highly recommended. This is usually done as a nine-hour trip from Bariloche, leaving at 0900 from Puerto Pañuelo (Km 25.5), and sailing down to fjord-like Puerto Blest, where there's a good *hostería*, and restaurant at the end of the lake. *Coihue*-clad mountains drop steeply into prussian blue water, and it's usually raining, but very atmospheric. The tour then continues by short bus ride to **Puerto Alegre** on Lago Frías, and you cross the still, peppermint green lake by launch. From Puerto Blest, the walk through beautiful forest to the **Cascada de los Cántaros** (one hour) is absolutely superb. Set off while the rest of the party stops for lunch, and you'll have time for your picnic by the splendid falls before the crowd arrives by boat. Or walk beyond them up to quiet **Lago de los Cantaros,** enclosed by vertical granite cliffs. This is one of only four places in Argentina where you can see Valdivian rainforest in unspoilt state, as it only grows in areas of heavy rainfall, here around 4000 mm a year.

Boats fill up entirely in high season, and are much more pleasant in December and March. Boat trips cost US$18 plus extra US$4 for a bus transfer from Bariloche, or slightly cheaper if you take the 0730 bus (US$0.70) from the centre of town to Puerto Pañuelo where boat excursion leaves for Puerto Blest at 0900. Tours are run by **Catedral** and **Turisur**. Boats are comfortable with a good (but expensive) *cafetería* on board. Stock up on picnic provisions from the shop next to the Shell garage just before you reach Puerto Pañuelo at Km 24.6. Set lunch at **Hostería Blest** is US$8; cheaper sandwiches from the snack bar next door. The **Hotel y Restaurant Puerto Blest** (C) is a small cosy hotel built in 1904, with homely rather than luxurious rooms. It's worth staying a night if you want to try any of the treks from here, or fish trout, and the only other option is camping *libre* with no facilities. The *guardaparques* at Puerto Blest can advise on the many walks from here (and their state), but the seven-hour, 15-km trek to **Lago Ortiz Basualdo** is recommended (mid-December to March only).

Walks around Bariloche

There are many superb walks in this area, and there's not space here to do justice either to their descriptions or to detailed instructions. For all walks, contact **Club Andino Bariloche** (see page 393) who sell the excellent *Carta de Refugios, Senderos y Picadas* maps for Bariloche and the book *Infotrekking de la Patagonia*, which gives great detail on all the possible walks, times, distances and *refugios* where you can stay, with satellite-based maps to guide you. Ask at **CAB** to check paths are open before you set off: crucial in spring when snow may not have cleared the upper slopes. You could also consider also contacting a trekking company such as **Active Patagonia** (www.activepatagonia.com.ar) to take you on guided hikes rather than setting off alone. In summer *tábanos* (horseflies) are common on the lake shores and at lower altitudes; their bites are very annoying but not harmful, and the only solution is to climb higher.

Below is just a small selection of walks of various grades of difficulty, recommended for the surrounding natural beauty:

▲ **Around Llao Llao** There are several easy and very satisfying walks from LLao Llao: a delightful easy circuit in virgin Valdivian rainforest in the Parque Municipal Llao Llao (turn left off the road, just past the golf course, two hours), or the small hill Cerrito Llao Llao (900 m), for wonderful views (turn right off the road and follow signs – one to two hours), or a 3-km trail through to Brazo de la Tristeza (turn right off the road opposite the *guardebosque*), via tiny Lago Escondido, with magical views. Bus 20 to Llao Llao, every 20 minutes.

▲ **Refugio López** (2076 m, five to seven hours return) This is a great hike with some of the most wonderful views of the whole area. Starting from the southeastern tip of Lago Moreno, go up alongside Arroyo López, and then along a ridge to the distinctive rose-coloured **Refugio López,** with its fabulous views. From Refugio López, you could do some climbing, or continue to make this a three- to four-day trek: head south to **Refugio Italia,** which is on the shores of the incredibly calm Laguna Negra at the foot of Cerro Negro. Then from here, you could hike on via Cerro Navidad to Laguna Jakob and **Refugio San Martín**. But note that this section is poorly signposted, and advisable only for very experienced walkers, who are well-equipped, and can use a compass. Take a trekking guide if in any doubt, and always ask at CAB for the conditions of the paths. Bus 10 to Colonia Suiza and Arroyo López (check return times), bus 11 in summer only. Refugio López is the only refugio which is privately owned, and not part of CAB's chain. The owners may charge you to use the paths.

▲ **Refugio Frey** (1700 m) From the ski station at **Villa Catedral**, there are two ways up: 1) Walk up to Refugio Frey, or take the cable car to **Refugio Lynch** (check before you set off, as precise cable car routes change each year) and from here walk along the ridge of Cerro Catedral to Refugio Frey with a beautiful setting on a small lake (two to four hours one-way); or 2) from Villa Catedral, walk south and up alongside the Arroyo Van Titter to **Refugio Piedritas,** a very basic emergency shelter with no services, to reach Refugio Frey (three to six hours to climb one-way). The area around **Refugio Frey** is the best area for practising climbing in the whole region, with innumerable options in the granite walls around. From Refugio Frey there are several possibilities: walk on to Refugio Piedritas (four hours each way), and then down the Arroyo Van Titter to reach Lago Gutiérrez. Once you reach the lake, you could either walk around the southern head of the lake to join the Route 258 which runs from Bariloche to El Bolsón, or ask **Estancia Peuma Hue** (see page 455) to collect you at the start of a few night's stay there. (The same is also possible in reverse). To reach the ski station at Villa Catedral, take bus 'Catedral' from terminal or bus stop on Moreno 480, takes you to the ski station base. Every 90 minutes, takes 35 minutes, US$1.

▲ **Lago Gutiérrez** You can reach this grand lake southwest of Bariloche, by walking 2 km downhill from the ski base at Cerro Catedral, and along the northern lake shore, reaching the El Bolsón road (Route 258) where you can take a bus back to Bariloche (six hours). Or arrange with **Estancia Peuma Hue** (see Sleeping, page 455) to collect you by boat from the shore of Lake Gutiérrez, and stay a couple of nights at the estancia for more great walks.

▲ **Refugio Neumayer** Some 12 km south of Bariloche, this offers a really charming centre for exploring the area, with eight paths to walk, information and guides on offer. Two are particularly recommended, to **Laguna Verde**, and to a mirador through Magellanic forest at **Valle de los Perdidos**. This is a cosy friendly *refugio*, very well set up for walkers and families and offering a wonderful range of activities. Office in town ⓘ *Diversidad, 20 de Junio 728, T02944 420995, www.eco-family.com.*

▲ **Around Pampa Linda** This blissful setting for a *hostería* and campsite is also the starting point for a number of truly spectacular walks. Firstly for climbing mighty Mount Tronador, or up to **Refugio Otto Meiling** (five hours each way), or to tranquil **Laguna Ilon** (5½ hours each way), or across Paso de las Nubes to **Puerto Frias**, where you can get the boat back to Bariloche (two days). For all of these, you must check with the excellent *guardaparques* in Pampa Linda on the state of paths – the Paso de las Nubes is often closed when boggy).

Into Chile » *pp400-409.*

The three lakes crossing to Chile → *No cars carried on the ferries on this route*

This popular route to Puerto Montt, with ferries across Lago Nahuel Huapi, Lago Frías and Lago Todos Los Santos, is outstandingly beautiful whatever the season, though the mountains are often obscured by rain and heavy cloud. It's a long and tiring journey, however, and is not recommended in really heavy rain. Book well ahead in high season (you can reserve online), and take your passport when booking from a tour operator. The journey can be done in one or two days: the one-day crossing (1 September-30 April) arrives Puerto Varas at around 2000 and does not allow a return to Bariloche next day, and you miss the walk to see Cascada de los Cantaros. For the two-day crossing (operates all year round), there is an overnight stop in Peulla.

Tickets are sold by various operators, but all trips are run by **Turismo Catedral** ⓘ *Palacios 263, T02944-425444, www.crucedelagos.com/tickets/publico/ index.shtml.* See also www.goargentina.net/cruce/indexENG.shtml for detailed description of the journey, prices and photos. Cost is US$165, plus cost of lunch at Peulla (US$20), credit cards accepted. No student reductions. Book before 1900 the day before, and further in advance during the high season; and beware the hard sell. Take your own lunch, but eat it before you reach Chile, as no fresh food can be taken over the border.

Border with Chile

The three lakes crossing enters Chile via the Paso Perez Rosales. **Argentine immigration and customs**, at Puerto Frías (open all year). **Chilean immigration and customs** at Peulla, open daily 0800-2100 summer, 0800-2000 winter. The launches (and hence the connecting buses) on the lakes serving the direct route via Puerto Blest to Puerto Montt generally do not operate at weekends, but check (T02944-425216). There is a ban in Chile on importing any fresh food – meat, cheese, fruit – from Argentina. Chilean currency can be bought at Peulla customs at a reasonable rate.

Puerto Montt → *Phone code: +56-(0)65 Population: 110,000.*

Puerto Montt is a popular centre for excursions to the Chilean Lake District, and departure point for boats to Puerto Chacabuco and Puerto Natales. A paved road runs 55 km southwest to Pargua, where there is a ferry service to the island of Chiloé. The little fishing port of **Angelmó**, 2 km west, has become a tourist centre with many seafood restaurants and handicraft shops (reached by Costanera bus along Portales and by *colectivo* Nos 2, 3 or 20 from the centre, US$0.30 per person). See *Footprint South American Handbook* and *Footprint Chile* for further details. Accommodation is expensive in season, much cheaper off season. Details are available from **Sernatur** (Chilean tourist authority) in the Intendencia Regional ⓘ *Av Décima Región 480, 3rd floor, Casilla 297, T065-254580, Mon-Fri 0830-1300, 1330-1730*. There is also a kiosk on Plaza de Armas run by the municipality, open till 1800 on Saturday.

Sleeping

Bariloche *p392, map p393*

Prices rise in 2 peak seasons: Jul and Aug for skiing, and mid-Dec to February for summer holidays. It's essential to book accommodation ahead in summer, but if you do arrive in the high season without a reservation, the tourist office can help.

L Edelweiss, San Martín 202, T02944-445500, www.edelweiss.com.ar. More than just a smart international 5-star, there's real attention to detail here, and excellent service from bilingual staff, well furnished, spacious and comfortable rooms. Restaurant La Tavola indoor pool and beauty salon, wi-fi, good suites for families. Reliable and good value in low season when prices are halved.

A- C Hostería Tirol, Libertad 175, T02944-426152, www.hosteriatirol.com.ar. Very neat and friendly family-run hotel just a block from the Civic Centre, with nice Tirolean touches in the clean welcoming rooms, and warm attention from the owners. Wi-fi. Excellent value in low season.

B La Pastorella, Belgrano 127, T02944-424656, www.lapastorella.com.ar. A cosy, quaint little hostería, whose welcoming owners speak English.

B Tres Reyes, 12 de Octubre 135, T02944-426121, www.hoteltresreyes.com. Traditional lakeside hotel with spacious rooms (allegedly modernised) and lounge with splendid views, but it's all a bit dated. Still the friendly professional staff speak English, and . It's cheaper on the spot than if you reserve by email.

C Premier, Rolando 263, T02944-426168. www.hotelpremier.com. Good economical choice in centre of town, with a light spacious entrance and gallery, and neat modern rooms with bath and TV, friendly young owners are very welcoming, wi-fi, English spoken. Recommended.

D Hostería Güemes, Güemes 715, T02944-424785. The charming Berlusconis welcome you here in this lovely quiet bed and breakfast in a residential area, with lots of space in the living area with views of the lake and TV, all the simple rooms have bath, breakfast is included, and Mr Berlusconi is a fishing expert, and gives lots of advice on the local area. Warmly recommended.

D Piuké, Beschtedt 136, T02944-423044. A delightful little bed and breakfast centrally located in town, with simple, nicely decorated rooms with an Alpine flavour, all with bath, breakfast included. Excellent value. German, Italian spoken.

D Refugio Neumeyer, 20 de Junio 728, T02944-428995, www.eco-family.com. run by **Diversidad**. Not quite as luxurious as an estancia, but with many of the benefits, this is a mountain lodge with comfortable shared accommodation and rooms for families, just 12 km south of Bariloche, where you can do all kinds of activities, with expert bilingual guides and with Patagonian regional cooking in their restaurant. Recommended.

E Res No Me Olvides, Av Los Pioneros Km 1, T02944-429140, 30 mins' walk or Bus 50/51 to corner of C Videla then follow signs. Beautiful house in quiet surroundings, use of kitchen, camping.

Youth hostels

Bariloche has many good quality hostels, all charging around US$8 for a bed in a shared dorm. These are the best:

E pp **La Bolsa**, Palacios 405 (y Elflein), T02944-423529, www.labolsadeldeporte.com. Recommended for its friendly relaxed atmosphere, homely rustic rooms (some with lake views), and a great deck to sit out on.

E pp **Patagonia Andina**, Morales 564, T02944-421861, www.elpatagonia andina.com.ar. A quiet place with comfortable dorms, and **E** double/twin rooms with shared bath. Well equipped small kitchen, TV area, sheets included, breakfast extra, internet, advice on trekking, good atmosphere.

E pp **Periko's**, Morales 555, T02944-522326, www.perikos.com. A warm and friendly atmosphere, with an *asado* every Friday, but it's otherwise a quiet calm place, since groups tend to go to the sister hostel, Alaska on Av Bustillo (see below). Towels and sheets included, but breakfast extra. Use of kitchen, and washing machine, nice airy rustic rooms, either all girls or boys, all shared rooms are for 4, and have their own bathroom. Also **E** double with own bath, garden, free internet access, can also organize horse riding, rent mountain bikes. Excellent service. Highly recommended.

E pp **Ruca Hueney**, Elflein 396, T02944-433986, www.rucahueney.com. A lovely calm place, with very comfortable beds and duvets. Spotless kitchen, quiet dining area, and very welcoming bilingual owners. Good double bedroom **E** with extra bunk beds, bathroom and great view. Also Spanish school. Highly recommended.

F pp **Albergue El Gaucho**, Belgrano 209, T02944-522464, www.hostelgaucho.com.ar. Welcoming modern place in quiet part of town, run by great German couple, very friendly, offering some doubles with own bath, **E** pp. English, German and Italian spoken.

Estancias near Bariloche

A Estancias Patagónicas, 20 km east of Bariloche in the steppe, www.estancias patagonicas.com. Offering riding, hunting and other estancia activities, this is more of a traditional estancia based in the historical Fort Chacabuco. The landscape is less dramatic, but it's interesting to see a working ranch.

The road to Llao Llao *p394, map p394*

There are lots of great places to stay all along the shore of Lago Nahuel Huapi, on the way to Llao Llao, many of them very close to centre, and all reachable with buses, which run every 20-30 mins.

LL Llao Llao, Bustillo, Km 25, T02944-448530, www.llaollao.com. Deservedly famous, one of the world's most wonderful hotels in a superb location, with panoramic views from its perfect gardens, golf course, gorgeous spa suite, pool[s] sports, superb restaurants. Excellent but some complaints about tiny ro[...] the extra for more space and a view.

L Aldebaran, on Península San Pedro, reached from Av Bustillo km 20,4, T02944-465132, www.aldebaranpatagonia.com. At last a hotel that's not chalet style. Exquisite taste in warm stylish minimalist rooms in this modern boutique hotel right on the rocky lake shore, where your every need is catered for, and there are superb views across the lake. Chic food in the rustic style restaurant, wonderful sauna and spa with outdoor pool, so you can bask under the stars. Great service from young helpful bilingual staff. Highly recommended.

L Design Suites, just 2.5 km from Bariloche centre, Av Bustillo, T02944-457000, www.designsuites.com. Refreshingly modern, with wonderful bold design in glass and wood in the stylish bar and restaurant area, this is a great place to stay. Huge spacious rooms with modern bathrooms, some with windowside jacuzzis, and all very comfortable, this has a great spa and gym, kids' room, friendly bilingual staff, and excellent food in the bar and restaurant. Warmly recommended. Book ahead.

L Isla Victoria Resort, T011-439499605 (Buenos Aires), www.islavictoria.com. On Isla Victoria just off the coast, this is really something special, and recommended for an escape from it all, amidst its own spectacular island scenery, a resort with pool, sauna, spacious and cosy places to sit and relax, riding and trekking organised all over the beautiful island, good food. A fabulous and romantic treat.

L La Cascada, Bustillo Km 6, T02944-441088, lacascada@infovia.com.ar. A traditional hotel with a really stunning lakeside position, and terrace going down to water, and a good, reasonably priced restaurant (3 courses US$7). Not quite luxurious but comfortable.

L Posada Los Juncos, Av Bustillo Km 20, T02944-448107, www.bariloche.org/losjuncos. A member of the exclusive Rusticae chain, this is a charming luxurious place on the lake shore, with just a few beautifully designed rooms.

For an explanation of the Sleeping and Eating price codes used in this guide, and other relevant information, see Essentials, pages 48 and 51.

L Tunquelén, Bustillo Km 24.5, T02944-448400, www.tunquelen.com. A real alternative to its close neighbour, Llao Llao, this is a comfortable 4-star hotel, on the lakeside with really splendid views and a secluded feel, wilder and closer to nature than its more famous cousin. Nicely decorated cottage-style rooms, attentive service, superb food, warmly recommended. Much cheaper if you stay 4 days.
L Villa Huinid, Km 2.5, T02944-523523, www.villahuninid.com.ar. Luxurious *cabañas* for 2-8, and well furnished rooms, though the service is variable.
AL Peñon del Lago, Av Bustillo, Km 14, T02944-463000, or in Buenos Aires T011-4790 7979, www.penondellago.com.ar. Hidden away in a forested park on the lake shore, this is stylish and bold design in chalet style comfort, with a relaxed atmosphere, and a hip international feel. Rates include breakfast, transfers from the airport, and to the ski centre in season.
A Hostería del Lago, Av Bustillo, Km 7.8, T02944-525044, www.hosteriadel lago.com.ar. Lovely traditional and welcoming chalet style hostería, on the beach, with great views of Isla Huemul, and Península San Pedro, this is particularly good value in low season, and a charming place to stay.
A-B Departamentos Bellevue, Av Bustillo, Km 24.6, T02944-448389, www.belle vue.com.ar. A dream come true: the famous tea room with the most beautiful view in Bariloche has become three cabañas where you can stay, with access to beaches on the lake, incredible views, and gorgeous gardens and native forest. High quality furnishings, extremely comfortable and well equipped self catering cabañas, with lovely views, and a delicious breakfast included. Highly recommended.
B Cabañas Sol y Paz, Av Bustillo, Km 10.63, T02944-462784, www.solypaz bariloche.com.ar. Pretty cabañas in chalet style with lovely views of mountains around. Welcoming owner.
B La Caleta, Av Bustillo, Km 1.9, T02944-443444, bungalows@bariloche.com.ar. English-owned and very well-run, these cabañas sleep 4, with open fire, and are excellent value.
C Hosteria Santa Rita, Av Bustillo, Km 7.2, T/F02944-461028, www.santarita.com.ar. Close to the centre, but with peaceful lakeside views, comfortable rooms, lovely terrace, and great service from the friendly family owners. Warmly recommended. Bus 10, 20, 21 to Km 7.5.
C Katy, Av Bustillo, Km 24.3, T02944-448023 www.gringospatagonia.com. Delightful peaceful place in a garden full of flowers, charming family welcome, breakfast included. Also offers adventure tourism. Recommended.
E pp **Hostel Alaska**, (Hostelling International), Av Bustillo, Km 7.5, T02944-461564, www.alaska-hostel.com. To get there, take bus 10, 20, 21, to Km 7.5). Well run, cosy chalet-style hostel open all year, doubles and dorms. Kitchen facilities, internet access, rafting and riding.

Camping

Complete list of camp sites is available from the tourist office, with prices and directions, www.bariloche.org. These are recommended for attractive sites and good facilities: For Av Bustillo, towards Llao Llao take buses 10, 11, 20, 21.
El Yeti, Km 5.8, T02944-442073, gerezjc@bariloche.com.ar. Pretty place, which also has *cabañas*.
Goye, Colonia Suiza, T02944-448627, camping_goye@hotmail.com, and **Hueney Ruca**, T02944-436190, omar@bariloche.com.ar, Colonia Suiza, buses 10 and 11 in season. These 2 sites both have *cabañas* and lots of facilities.
Petunia, Km 13.5, T02944-461969, www.campingpetunia.com. Well protected from winds by trees, a lovely shady lakeside site with beach, all facilities and restaurant, and shop, recommended, also *cabañas*.
Selva Negra, Km 2.95, T02944-441013, campingselvanegra@infovia.com.ar. Very attractive well-equipped site, highly recommended.

Southwest of Bariloche *p396*

For details of accommodation on Lago Gutiérrez, see page 455.
LL Catedral Ski, Villa Catedral, T02944-460006, hcatedral@bariloche.com.ar. Large, very touristy place, pretty luxurious, with pool, restaurant, sauna, gym, also apartments, discount for one week stay.

LL Pire-Hue, Villa Catedral, T011-4807 8200 (Buenos Aires), www.pire-hue.com.ar. Exclusive 5-star hotel with beautifully decorated rooms and all the facilities.

Into Chile *p399*

LL Hotel Peulla, PO Box 487, Puerto Montt, T+56 (0)65-258041. Includes dinner and breakfast, cheaper out of season, beautiful setting by the lake, restaurant and bar, good but expensive meals, cold in winter, often full of tour groups (tiny shop at back of hotel).

D pp **Res Palomita**, 50 m west of Hotel Puella. Half board, family-run, simple, comfortable but not spacious, separate shower, book ahead in season, lunches.

Camping

There is a site opposite the Conaf office, US$1.50, and a good campsite 1¾ hrs' walk east of Peulla, take food.

Eating

Bariloche *p392, map p393*

Bariloche is blessed with superb food: famous for locally smoked trout and salmon, and for wild boar, there are other delicacies to be sampled too, like the berries in season, and the fine chocolate.

YYY **Cassis**, opposite Arelauquen golf club, just off Route 82, call first for directions, T02944-431382, www.cassis-patagonia.com.ar. This is without doubt Bariloche's finest restaurant, with a stunning setting right on the waterfront of Lake Gutiérrez, in secluded gardens, and amazing food. Local delicacies, exquisite dishes. Highly recommended. Open evenings only except in high season, it's always worth reserving ahead.

YYY **Chez Philippe**, Primera Junta 1080, T02944-427291. Delicious local delicacies, really fine French influenced cuisine, and delicious fondue, in this cosy place with a living room feel. Book ahead.

YY **Dias de Zapata**, Morales 362, T02944-423128. Great on atmosphere, don't expect anything too authentic in the Mexican food, which isn't remotely spicy, or the Margaritas, which look like Slush Puppies. But the staff are welcoming, there's lots of choice, and the meals are tasty. Fun, friendly. Recommended.

YY **Familia Weiss**, also Palacios y VA O'Connor. Don't let the Heidi exterior put you off: entire trees, highly varnished, in chalet-style splendour. But there's excellent local cuisine, and live music in high season. So although this feels touristy, the food is great. The wild boar and salmon-filled pasta are particularly recommended.

YY **Hasta Que Llegue el Tren**, next to the train station 3km from centre, 12 de Octubre 2,400, T02944-457200. Really sophisticated food, including Patagonian ostrich, lamb and quail, with great wine list. Very tasty, frequently recommended.

YY **Jauja**, Quaglia 366, T02944-422952. Specializing in local delicacies, this is a consistently pleasing place with a quiet welcoming atmosphere, and great local trout and wild boar. Friendly and good value. Recommended.

YY **Kandahar**, 20 de Febrero 698, T02944-424702. Best in town, and most highly recommended for its excellent food and intimate warm atmosphere. A romantic and charming place to eat. Tasty Argentine dishes, and other imaginative cuisine served in style, in a cosy place, run by ski champion Marta Peirono de Barber, superb wines and the pisco sour are recommended. US$9 for 2 courses. Wonderful. Dinner only. Reserve ahead in high season.

YY **La Marmite**, Mitre 329, T02944-423685. Going to seed a little, this is a central place good for a huge range of fondues, wild boar and delicious cakes for tea too.

YY **Vegetariano**, 20 de Febrero 730, T02944-421820, www.vegetarianpatagonia.com.ar. There are fish options too in the excellent set menu here, beautifully served in a warm friendly atmosphere. Highly recommended.. Dinner only except in high season.

Y **Dazzler**, San Martín 441, T02944-456900. Dreadful name, but funky place, with cool modern design, and happy hour 1800-2000.

Y **Friends**, Mitre 302, T02944-423700. Seething with gringos in summer, this is a good lively café on the main street, convenient for lunch or a beer, open 24 hrs.

Y **La Jirafa**, Palacios 288. A cheery family run place for good food, good value.

Y **Rock Chicken**, Rolando. Small, busy, good value fast food (also take away).

Y **Simoca**, Palacios 264. Recommended for delicious and cheap Tucumán specialities, such as *humitas* and *locro*, and huge *empanadas*

Cafés

La Alpina, Moreno 98. Charming old fashioned Alpine style place, as you'd expect, with delicious cakes, great for tea.

The road to Llao Llao *p394, map p394*

Il Gabbiano, Av Bustillo, Km 24.3, T02944-448346. Really excellent Italian food here in this intimate restaurant on the lakeside. Delicious trout and sea food, and wild boar, and extensive wine list. Booking essential. Closed Tue. No credit cards. Highly recommended.

Punta Bustillo, Av Bustillo, Km 5.8, T02944-442782, www.puntabustillo.com.ar. Very cutesy chalet style exterior, but don't be put off: the food is great. Lots of steak, Patagonian lamb, wild boar, smoked delicacies, and the locally brewed beer, as well as pastas for vegetarians. Cosy, welcoming and a great wine list.

Rincón Patagónico, Av Bustillo, Km 14, T02944-463063. Traditional *parrilla*, with tasty Patagonian lamb cooked *al palo* speared over an open fire. Come out of season when there aren't huge coach loads.

Tarquino, 24 de Septiembre y Saavedra, T02944-434774. Warm welcoming design with trees growing through the boldly coloured room, and friendly service, this is great for steak, and tasty pasta, with a good wine list.

Cerveceria Blest, Km 11.6, T02944-461026, open 1200-2400. The only pub in Bariloche to brew its own beers, this is a great place to come at lunch time or for dinner in the evening, with delicious beers – try their *La Trochita* stout, and imaginative local and German dishes and, incredibly, steak and kidney pie! in a warm rustic atmosphere. Come with friends and order their superb *picadas* with a selection of beers. Recommended.

El Boliche de Alberto, Villegas 347, T02944-431433. Very good steak and live folklore music. So popular that you'll have to queue in summer.

El Patacón, Km 7, T02944-442898. This was a chic place until it became popular with agencies who bring huge groups here. The food is good, but it's pricey and not particularly welcoming.

Meli Hue, Km 24.7, T02944-448029. Another tearoom, and B&B, in a lavender garden and selling fragrant produce, also has lovely views.

Bars and clubs

Bariloche *p392, map p393*

Only 2 recommendable places in Bariloche for clubbing, and don't expect too much.

Cerebro, JM de Rosas 406, T02944-424948, www.cerebro.com.ar. Same hours as Roxy below. This is where everybody who doesn't go to Roxy goes.

La Esquina, Moreno 10. Another traditional pub with good food and a relaxed atmosphere.

Pilgrim, Palacios 167, between O Connor and Mitre. One of 2 Irish theme pubs in town, this serves a good range of beers in a lively pub atmosphere, also regional dishes, reasonably priced too.

Roxy, San Martín 490, T02944-400451. Food, and then dancing from 0130. It's where everybody goes.

Wilkenny, San Martín 435, T02944-424444. The other Irish pub, also lively.

Shopping

Bariloche *p392, map p393*

The main commercial centre is on Mitre between the Centro Civíco and Beschtedt.

Bookshops

Cultura, Elflein 78, T02944-420193. A good range, some in English and German.

La Barca Libros, Quaglia 247, and another branch on Mitre 534, T02944-423170, www.patagonialibros.com. Mon-Fri 0930-2100, closed for lunch on Sat. For a wonderful range of books on Patagonia, and an excellent bookshop: the Mitre branch has a good selection of books in English.

Clothing and outdoor equipment

Arbol, Mitre in the 400 block. Sells good quality outdoor gear, lovely clothes and interesting gifts.

Cardon, San Martín 324, T02944-439997, www.cardon.com.ar. Reliable chain of shops all over Argentina selling quality leather and clothing.

Huala, San Martín 86. Excellent range of walking and climbing equipment from the adventure travel company Huala.

Martin Pescador, Rolando 257, T02944-422 2275, also at Cerro Catedral in winter. Fly shop with fishing, camping and skiing equipment.
Patagonia Outdoors, Elflein 27, T02944-426768, www.patagonia-outdoors.com.ar. Maps and equipment, everything you might need, plus adventure tourism organized, trekking and rafting especially.
Scandinavian, Mitre 219, T02944-433170.Skiing and outdoors clothes, plus climbing gear – very reasonable prices.

Food and drink

The local chocolate is excellent, and there are many shops along Mitre.
Abuela Goye, Mitre 258, Quaglia 221, www.abuelagoye.com. Open 0800-2330. Delicious chocs. A personal favourite. Also a cosy café in the Quaglia branch, where you can sit and plan which chocolates to eat next.
Ahumadero Weiss, Mitre 131, T02944-435874 www.ahumaderoweiss.com. Just pop in to look around and you won't be able to resist buying some smoked trout, or local wild boar, jam, beer, or fine wine. A great little shop selling the home-smoked goods for which the Familia Weiss restaurant is famed.
Fenoglio, Mitre 301 y Rolando. A bigger place, handy if you want to buy pre-packaged chocolates rather than choose your own. Superb chocolate ice cream.
Jauja, Moreno y Quaglia, above. A smaller selection of the famous and most excellent ice creams in Patagonia (or indeed the world), made in El Bolsón, from organic milk and using local berries and handmade chocolate. Open till late.
Mamushka, corner of Mitre y Rolando. 0830-2230. 'The best'. No mistaking the quality here in the handmade chocolate bars. Try a piece for free as you're waiting to be served: the filled chocolates are delicious, US$16 a kilo. Nice little café here too.
Uno, Moreno 350 and **Todo**, Moreno 319. Supermarkets which both have a good selection, and are reasonably cheap.

Handicrafts

Burton Cerámica, Av Bustillo 4100. Makes and sells the renowned handmade Patagonian pottery.
Feria Artesanal Municipal, Moreno y Rolando, daily 0900-2100.

▲ Activities and tours

Bariloche *p392, map p393*

Rafting, horse riding, birdwatching, hiking, climbing and skiing can all be arranged through tour operators. There are many along Mitre, but best to use one that's recommended to you, or those below. Excellent trout fishing Nov-Apr; arrange boat hire with tackle shops. There are lots of conventional tours, and prices are regulated by the tourist office, so tour operators charge the same price. It is best to buy tickets the night before, rather than far in advance, although they get very booked up in season, and many trips only run in Jan and Feb or when there is enough demand. Many Argentines enjoy seeing their scenery from a bus with commentary and you may find that too much time is spent sitting: check the itinerary before you book.

Tours include: San Martín de los Andes, (360 km) US$25, via the Seven Lakes Drive and returning via Paso de Córdoba and the Valle Encantado, twelve-hour minibus excursions. There are also tours around the Circuito Chico (60 km), US$8, half-day. 'Cerro Tronador' (they mean a view of Tronador, not climbing it) and Cascada los Alerces full day (255 km) U$20, El Bolsón full day (300 km, including Lago Puelo) US$22. Whole-day excursions to Lagos Gutiérrez, Mascardi, Hess, the Cascada Los Alerces and Cerro Tronador and the Ventisquero Negro, leaving at 0800, US$32, lots of time spent on the bus. Useful as a way to get to walks at Pampa Linda if the bus from CAB isn't running.

Boat trips

Isla Victoria and Bosque de Arrayanes full day US$20, Puerto Blest, Cascada de los Cantaros and Lago Frias full day, including buses US$22.
Cau Cau, Mitre139, T02944-431372, www.islavictoriayarrayanes.com. Specializing in the trip to Isla Victoria and the Bosque de Arrayanes, these are fast modern boats with good catering facilities, and professional guides.
Catedral Turismo, Palacios 263, T02944-425444, www.lakecrossing.cl. This company has the monopoly on the famous Three Lakes Crossing to Puerto Montt in Chile (see below), but you can buy it at any agency. US$140.

Del Lago Turismo, Vilegas 222, T02944-430056, www.dellagoturismo.com.ar. Helpful and friendly, and speaks fluent English. Offers all the conventional tours, and lots of more adventurous options, horse riding and kayaking. Also a fabulous boat trip up Lago Mascardi (summer only) to Cascada de los Césares and Hotel Tronador.
Tronador Turismo, Quaglia 283, T02944-425644, www.tronadorturismo.com.ar. Tours, trekking and rafting to Refugio Neumeyer. Expeditions to the Chilean border, and more adventurous great winter sports options.
Turisur, Mitre 219, T02944-426109, www.bariloche.com/turisur. Boat trips to Bosque de Arrayanes, Isla Victoria and Puerto Blest, and conventional tours.

Cycling

This is a great area for mountain biking, with some fabulously challenging descents from the peaks around Bariloche, also easily reached by bus. Even the basic tourist information map shows the main routes, but **Club Andino** (see Trekking and climbing below) has more detailed maps and advice.
Bariloche Bikes, Moreno 520, T02944-424657.
Dirty Bikes, V O'Connor 681, T02944-425616, www.dirtybikes.com.ar. Very helpful for repairs– if pricey, and also offer guided excursions on bikes, with bikes for hire. Recommended.
Diversidad, 20 de Junio 728, T02944-428995, www.eco-family.com. Excellent mountain biking around the beautiful Refugio Neumeyer.
Huala, San Martín 66, T02944-522438, www.huala.com.ar. All the usual circuits, with the back-up of guides, and also more unusual rides onto the steppe with trips to see Patagonian inhabitants and their chacras (farms) – very interesting. Plus amazing 12 day bike expedition to Traful via Villa la Angostura. Book well ahead as this is very popular. Also crossing by bike to Chile.

Fishing

Excellent trout fishing Nov-Mar (permits required). For Information, see www.interpatagonia.com/pesca/index_i.html.
Baruzzi Deportes, Urquiza 250, T02944-424922, www.baruzzi.com. Fly shop and offers guided fishing excursions in the whole area (flycast, trolling, spinning) for experts and newcomers; US$150-300 (Trout Unlimited membership discounts).
Fishing and Company, T02944-1558 4296, www.fishingandcompany.com. Bilingual guides can take you to all the good rivers nearby for fly fishing.
Martin Pescador, Rolando 257, T02944-422275, martinpescador@bariloche.com.ar. A great shop for fishing supplies (as well as camping and skiing) and experts there can organize all kinds of fishing expeditions.

Horse riding

Diversidad, 20 de Junio 728, T02944-428995, www.eco-family.com. Great 2-day ride to Pampa Linda, US$200 per person, everything included, or longer rides into the Steppe. Great all-round company.
Estancia Peuma Hue, T02944-501030, www.peuma-hue.com. The best riding in the region, starting at the beautiful estancia on the head of Lago Gutiérrez, with luxurious accommodation, and fine horses, with your own guide and horse whisperer. Day-long rides into the mountains all around, or longer rides to Pampa Linda and across the border into Chile. Highly recommended. See below under Lago Gutiérrez.
Estancia Fortín Chacabuco, T02944-441766, www.estanciaspatagonicas.com. Superb riding for all levels, with bilingual guides, in the rugged steppe, filled with wildlife, east of Bariloche.
Los Baqueanos, T02944-1555 4362. Based on the shore of Lago Gutiérrez, offering trips up to Refugio Frey.
Tom Wesley, country ranch by the lake at Km 15.5, T02944-448193, www.tomwesley.com. A relaxed place with tuition and full day's riding offered.

Paragliding

Parapente Bariloche, T02944-462234, parapente@bariloche.com.ar. Gliding at Cerro Otto.

Rafting

Río Manso, south of Bariloche, from the road which skirts Lago Mascardi, offers some of the best rafting in Argentina, with sections of river suitable for all levels. There are 2 main trips offered by the best companies, and

they vary very little in what's on offer:
Aguas Blancas, Morales 564, T02944-432799, www.aguasblancas.com.ar. Also offer full day excursions, 'Duckies (inflatable kayaks) for beginners, and the trip to Chile.
Extremo Sur, Morales 765, T02944-427301, www.extremosur.com. Offering both trips for beginners and the more experienced, this is a very professional company with an excellent reputation. They also offer the longer trips to Chile.
Huala, San Martín 66, T02944-522438, www.huala.com.ar. Superb company offering all kinds of rafting, both Río Manso and also up to the Chilean border, with the added pleasure of a traditional *asado* on the beach. Great care taken of children, and also more challenging rafting offered for the more experienced. Bilingual guides, great value. Warmly recommended.

Skiing

One of South America's most important ski resorts centres is just above Bariloche, at **Cerro Catedral**, with 70 km of slopes of all grades, allowing a total drop of 1010 m, starting at 2000 m, and 52 km of cross-country skiing routes, all with utterly spectacular views. There are also snowboarding areas and a well equipped base with hotels, restaurants and equipment hire, ski schools and nursery care for children. Open mid-Jun to end Sep, busiest from 15 Jun to 15 Aug for school holidays. Ski lifts open 0900 to 1700. Price of ski lift pass adults US$20 per day, ski school, US$30 per hour individuals. Bus run by 3 de Mayo 'Catedral', leaves Moreno 480 every 90 mins approximately, T02944-425648, US$1. Taxi costs US$5. Cable car for Catedral, T02944-460090, www.catedralpatagonia.com. There is also superb cross country skiing (called Nordic skiing here) around the wonderful **Refugio Neumeyer**, where you can also try out snowshoe walking, and stay the night or for dinner. Bilingual guides and equipment for hire. Great fun. Contact **Diversidad** (see Trekking, below).
Cerro Otto also has skiing. Cable car passengers can take a free bus leaving from hut at Civic centre, hourly 1030 to 1730, returning hourly 1115 to 1915. Ticket for both costs US$8 pp, T02944-441031 there's a revolving *confitería*, craft shop, great views. Also **Club Andino confitería**, 20 mins' walk from main confitería on summit. Ski equipment can also be rented by the day from **Martín Pescador** (see Fishing above), **Cebron** Mitre 171, or **Milenium**, Mitre 125.

Trekking and climbing

There are fabulous peaks around Bariloche, allowing you to walk for an afternoon, or several days, staying at mountain *refugios* which provide beds and food, but cannot be booked. These are run by **Club Andino Bariloche**, and 1 is privately owned. The season runs from Dec to Apr, and note that winter storms can begin as early as Apr at higher levels, making climbing dangerous. The best information is available from **Club Andino Bariloche**, 20 de Febrero 30, T02944-422266, www.clubandino.org. (the website lists areas to walk, in Spanish), Mon-Fri 0900-1300, and also 1600-2100 in high season only. CAB sell excellent maps and books for walks, *Infotrekking* produced by trekking company Active Patagonia is detailed, has great maps and is highly recommended. It's advisable to go with a guide. You should always check with *guardaparques* that paths are open where you're intending to walk. For climbing, get hold of the booklet *Guia de Escalada (climbing) en Roca*, by Eduardo (Tato) López, with translations in English and explanations of all the areas to climb. Horseflies (*tábanos*) frequent the lake shores and lower areas in summer: bring insect repellent. For trekking guides, see below.
Al Límite, Salta 215, T02944-435362, www.allimitepatagonia.com.ar. Climbing company selling clothing and camping gear.

Tour operators and trekking guides

Active Patagonia, Ask in Club Andino Bariloche, T02944-527966, www.active patagonia.com.ar. Excellent company with very knowledgeable and well-trained guides. Ask for English speakers. Also produce good maps and walking books. Recommended.
Diversidad, 20 de Junio 728, T02944-428995, www.eco-family.com. Riding, walking, skiing, all kinds of great adventures offered by this friendly company with a great base in Refugio Neumeyer, 12 km south of Bariloche. Tremendous long treks can be tailor made for you with bilingual guides

adapted to your level. Highly recommended.
Extremo Sur, Morales 765, T02944-427301, www.extremosur.com. Professional company offering rafting and kayaking, all levels, full day all-inclusive packages offered, and longer trips including accommodation, check web for more details.
Huala, San Martín 66, T02944-522438, www.huala.com.ar. Excellent company with all kinds of adventure tourism on offer: rafting, riding, climbing, biking, and more. English speaking guides. Highly recommended.
Sebastian de la Cruz, Pampa Linda Hostería (see page 455), in Bariloche T02944-442038, pampalindaa@bariloche.com.ar. Renowned mountaineer, who lives at the base of Tronador and owns the Pampa Linda Hostería. Enormously knowledgeable.
Transitando lo Natural 20 de Febrero 25, T02944-527926, transitando1@hotmail.com. Buses to Pampa Linda daily at 0900 in season, US$7.50, plus rafting, Ruta 40, paragliding, horse riding and more.

Transport

Bariloche *p392, map p393*

Air

Airport, 15 km east of town, T02944-426162. Bus service into town meets all flights. US$2.60 **Aerolíneas Argentinas** runs several flights a day to **Buenos Aires**, and to **El Calafate** too in summer. Chilean airline **LAN** also run flights to **Buenos Aires** and Chilean cities, excellent service. LADE flies weekly to many destinations in Patagonia, including **Bahía Blanca, Comodoro Rivadavia, Mar del Plata, Puerto Madryn**; book well in advance in peak seasons.

Airline offices Aerolíneas Argentinas, in airport T02944- 422144, in town at office on corner of Mitre and Villegas, T02944-423682, free phone from anywhere in Argentina: T0810-222 86527, www.aerolineas.com, ask for English speaking assistants. LADE, Mitre 531, 1st floor, T02944-423562, or in airport T02944-423161. LAN, Moreno 234, 2nd floor, T02944-431043, www.lan.com.

Bus

The bus terminal, T02944-432860, has toilets, small *confiteria*, *kiosko*, no *locutorio* but public phones. Left luggage US$1 per day. To get there: Buses 10, 20, 21 frequent service from bus / train station to centre of town, US$1. Taxi US$3. Bus company offices in town: **Vía Bariloche/El Valle**, Mitre 321, T02944-429012, bus station T02944-432444, free phone T0800-333 7575, www.viabariloche.com; **Andesmar/Albus**, Mitre 385, T02944-430211, bus station T02944-430211; **Chevallier/La Estrella/Ko Ko**, Moreno 105, T02944-425914; **TAC**, Moreno 138, T02944-434727; **Cruz del Sur**, T02944-437699; **Don Otto/Río de La Plata**, 12 de Octubre T02944-437699; **Flechabus**, Moreno 107, T02944-423090, www.flechabus.com; **3 de Mayo**, for local services, Moreno 480, T02944-425648.

Local Frequent buses run by **3 de Mayo**, Moreno 480, T02944-425648, from terminal into town and along Av Bustillo: Bus 20 to **Llao Llao**, for lakeside hotels and restaurants, Bus 10 to **Colonia Suiza** and **Bahia Lopez** for trekking, Bus 50 to **Lago Gutiérrez**, and the bus labelled 'Catedral' for Cerro Catedral.

Long distance To **Buenos Aires**, 6 companies daily, 22½ hrs, US$60 *coche cama*, **Andesmar**. To **Bahía Blanca**, 3 companies, US$38. To **Mendoza**, US$38, TAC and **Andesmar**, 19 hrs, via Piedra de Aguila, Neuquén, Cipolleti and San Rafael. To **Esquel**, via El Bolsón, **Don Otto, Mar y Valle, Vía Bariloche, Andesmar**, 4 hrs, US$8. To **Puerto Madryn**, 14 hrs, US$35 with **Mar y Vale** and **Don Otto**. To **San Martín de los Andes**, Ko Ko, 4 hrs, US$10. No direct bus to **Río Gallegos**; you have to spend a night in **Comodoro Rivadavia** en route: **Don Otto** daily, US$5514½ hrs. To **Calafate**, ask at youth hostel **Alaska**, or **Periko's** about Safari Route 40, a 4-day trip down Ruta 40 to **Calafate** via the Perito Moreno National Park, Cueva de Las Manos and Fitz Roy, staying at Estancia Melike and Río Mayo en route, US$128 plus accommodation at US$10 per day, www.visitbariloche.com/alaska.

To Chile To **Osorno** (4-6 hrs) and **Puerto Montt**, 7-8 hrs US$30, daily, **Bus Norte, Río de la Plata, TAS Choapa, Cruz del Sur, Andesmar** (sit on left side for best views). For **Santiago** or **Valdivia** change at Osorno.

Car hire

Let your hire company know if you're planning to drive over the border into Chile, as they'll need to rent you a vehicle which has its registration number engraved on the windows, by law. Give 24 hrs. Rates are around US$40 a day. You can arrange to drop the car at San Martín de los Andes, or Esquel for an extra charge, from US$35. **Budget** , Mitre 106, 1st floor, T02944-426700, www.budget bariloche.com.ar. **Localiza**, O' Connor 602, T02944-435374, localiza@autosur patagonia.com.ar. Reliable, English spoken. **Rent a Car Bariloche**, Rolando 258, T02944-426420, www.rentacar bariloche.com. Reliable and good value.

Taxi
Melipal Remises, T02944-442300, Puerto Remises, T08009-990885 (freephone), T02944-435222, Radio Taxi Bariloche, T02944-422103; Remises Bariloche, T02944-430222. Remises del Bosque, T02944-429109.

Train
Station 3 km east of centre, near bus terminal. Booking office T02944-423172. Closed 1200-1500 weekdays, Sat afternoon and all Sun. Information from the tourist office. Tourist service to **Viedma** (16 hrs, US$35 *turista*), also with sleeper section, and carries cars, T02944-423172, www.trenpatagonico.com.ar. See bus section above for transport to the centre.

Southwest of Bariloche *p394*
To **Pampa Linda** and **Tronador**: minibuses run by **Transitando lo Natural**, 20 de Febrero 25, T02944-527926, transitando1@ hotmail.com. Buses to Pampa Linda daily at 0900 in season, US$7.50. Alternatively, **Expreso Meiling** also run buses in season, leaving Club Andino at 0830, and returning from Pampa Linda at 1700, T02944-529875. Alternatively, **Expreso Meiling** also run buses in season, leaving Club Andino at 0830, and returning from Pampa Linda at 1700, T02944-529875.

Puerto Montt *p399*
Air
El Tepual Airport, 13 km northwest of town. ETM bus from terminal 1½ hrs before departure, US$2. To **Santiago** and **Punta Arenas** several daily flights by LanChile, Lan Express and **Aero Continente**. To **Temuco**, **Lan Chile** daily. Flights fully booked in advance in summer: worth asking at the airport for cancellations.

Bus
The terminal is on the sea front at Portales y Lota. Facilities include, telephones, restaurants, *casa de cambio*, left luggage (US$1.50 per item for 24 hrs). There are services to all parts of the country.

Sea
Shipping offices Cruce de Lagos, www.lakecrossing.cl, includes departures to **Puerto Vargas** and **Bariloche**.

Directory

Bariloche *p392, map p393*
Banks ATMs at many banks along Mitre: Bansud at Mitre 27, **Banco Nación Argentina** at Mitre 180. **Banco Galicia**, Moreno y Quaglia, **Banco Patagonia**, Moreno 127, **Banco Frances**, San Martín 332. Exchange and TCs, best rates and service at Casas de Cambio: **Sudamérica**, Mitre 63, T02944- 434555. **Consulates** Austria, 24 de Septiembre 230, T424873. **Chile**, Rosas 180, T02944-422842. **France**, T02944-441960. **Germany**, Ruiz Moreno 65, T02944-425695. **Italy**, Beschtedt 141, T02944-422247. **Switzerland**, Quaglia 342, T02944-426111. **Customs** Bariloche centre T02944-425216, Rincon (Argentina) T02944-425734, Pajarito (Chile) T002944-236284. **Internet** Many places along Mitre, and in the first block of Quaglia. **Immigration office** Libertad 191, T02944-423043, Mon-Fri 0900-1300. **Language schools** La Montana, Elflein 251, 1st floor, T02944-156 11872, www.lamontana.com. Spanish language school. **Medical services** Dial 107 for emergencies, or San Carlos Emergencias, T02944-430000, Clinic: **Hospital Zonal**, Moreno 601, T02944-426100. **Post office** Moreno 175, Mon-Fri 0800-2000, Sat 0830- 1300. **Telephone** Many *locutorios* along Mitre, Telecom at Mitre y Rolando is helpful.

North of Bariloche and the Seven Lakes Drive

The journey north from Bariloche along the celebrated Seven Lakes Drive is a magical experience: a winding road through a wonderland of lakes embedded in forest-covered mountains. On the way to picturesque San Martín de los Andes, there are two good bases for further adventures. First, on the northern side of Lake Nahuel Huapi, is the pretty, upmarket town of Villa la Angostura. Much loved by wealthier Argentines, you might find it's rather too developed for tourism, but there's no shortage of smart places to stay and eat, such as famous and blissful boutique hotel, Las Balsas. From Villa la Angostura you can visit the tiny national park, Los Arrayanes, created to protect a rare forest of Arrayanes trees with their cinnamon-coloured bark, and twisting trunks: a fairy tale woodland where you can walk or take a boat. Further along the Seven Lakes Drive, is another more remote village, Villa Traful. Tucked into a deep fold between dramatic, spired mountains, on the side of a navy blue sliver of lake, this is a peaceful place for a few days rest, with a couple of good walks, and some appealing places to stay.

Drive up through ever-changing combinations of lakes and mountains to find San Martín de los Andes sitting proudly at the head of Lake Lacar. No shortage of chalet style cabañas here, this is a very comfortable base for exploring another fine national park, Lanín, whose conical volcano is visible for miles around, and which you can climb, if you have a few days free. It's well worth hiring a car here to explore the park in detail, especially Lagos Huachulafquen and Paimun. Junín de los Andes makes an alternative base, much more down to earth than San Martín but with some good hotels. Estancia Huechahue is nearby, with superb horse riding into the park and across the Andes to Chile. Heading further north still, you'll come eventually to Villa Pehuenia, a fledgling village in a spectacular setting on Lake Aluminé, with some superb accommodation and its own resident Mapuche community who will take you riding and skiing in season. Sleepier Lake Moquehue is a great place to hang out and do nothing. » *For Sleeping, Eating and other listings, see pages 413-418.*

La Ruta de los Siete Lagos » *pp413-418.*

The Seven Lakes Drive is the most famous tourist route in the Argentine Lake District. It follows Route 234 through the Lanín and Nahuel Huapi national parks, and passes seven magnificent lakes, all flanked by mixed natural forest and is particularly attractive in autumn (April/May) when the forested slopes turn red and yellow. The road is only partially paved, and mostly decent, apart from a very pot holed stretch in the middle, not recommended after heavy rain or snowfall.

The seven lakes are (from south to north): Nahuel Huapi, Correntoso, Espejo, Villarino, Falkner, Machónico and Lácar. Leaving Villa la Angostura, you'll be treated to a superb view of Lago Correntoso, then turn off to reach gorgeous secluded Lago Espejo ('mirror'), or stop for a picnic at least, off the road a few kilometres, with lovely beaches on the lakeshore, before passing the northwestern corner of Lago Traful at Km 58. At Km, 77 Route 65 branches off to the east, running along the south shore of Lago Traful through Villa Traful to meet the main Neuquén-Bariloche highway (Route 237) at Confluencia. If you have a couple of days to spare, this is a lovely place to stop. At Pichi Traful, a beautiful spot by the wide green banks of the aquamarine blue river, there's a campsite and picnic ground amidst little beech trees by turquoise water with steeply rising mountains on all sides. Carry on though for the pretty, if exposed, free campsite (with no facilities) by the deep green Río Villarino, and as the road emerges to climb up overlooking the shores of Lago Villarino, you're suddenly shown a welcome open vista of the lake and from here the road is paved. Popular with fishermen, Lago Falkner opposite is wide and open with thickly forested fiord-like mountains descending steeply into it. There's a long narrow sandy beach on the roadside, a good place for a picnic stop, and wild camping, with no facilities, though **Camping Lago Falkner** nearby does have facilities.

You can see the route from the windows of a bus on a round trip excursion from either Bariloche or Villa la Angostura, but they take five hours, and it's far better in your own transport, as you'll want to stop and explore. Buses will stop at campsites on the route, see under San Martín, page 432, for companies. It's a good route for cycling, when you can really appreciate the beauty of the ever-changing landscape, though note that there's more traffic in January and February.

The direct route to San Martín de los Andes

There's a quicker route to San Martín and Neuquén if you're in a rush, or for the way back, when you've already seen the view. Further west, via **Confluencia**, it's also attractive. Take Route 237 from Bariloche to Confluencia running through the astounding **Valle Encantado**, where there are weird rock formations including El Dedo de Dios (The Finger of God) and El Centinela del Valle (The Sentinel of the Valley), and then north on Route 63, over the **Paso de Córdoba**, Km 77, (1300 m), and along the tranquil shore of Lago Meliquina. You could turn off to isolated Lago Filo-Hua-Hum at Km 54 (unpaved track).

Villa La Angostura and around

» pp413-418.

→ Phone code: 02944 Colour map 5, B2 Population: 8000

This is a hugely popular holiday resort for wealthier Argentines, who pack it out in January, when it's pretty unbearable. Any other time of year, it's an appealing place to stay, especially for those who like their nature seen from the comfort of a luxurious hotel. There are some really superb restaurants here and some seriously chic hotels, like the exquisite **Las Balsas**, with the best cuisine in Patagonia, and a superb spa. *Cabaña* complexes have mushroomed up everywhere, so there's no shortage of places to stay. And there are some good walks nearby, excellent fly fishing, and a golf course, as well as skiing in winter. The area is divided into several different *barrios*: around the sprawling town centre, **El Cruce**, around the lakeside area of **Puerto Manzano**, and around the picturesque port, known as **La Villa,** which is 3 km away at the neck of the Quetrihué Peninsula.

Ins and outs

Tourist information The **tourist office** ⓘ *on the left-hand side of the road heading north, just opposite the bus terminal, at Av Siete Lagos 93, T02944-494124, www.villalaangostura.gov.ar, high season 0800-2100, low season 0800-2000*, is busy and helpful office, with lots of information, and accommodation prices marked on a board inside. English spoken.

Sights

Villa La Angostura's great attraction is the **Parque Nacional Los Arrayanes**, at the end of the Quetrihué Peninsula, which dips into the northern end of Lago Nahuel Huapi, and can be reached on foot or by boat from the port area of La Villa. Also from La Villa, a short walk leads to lovely **Laguna Verde**, an intense emerald green lagoon surrounded by mixed *coihue* cypress and arrayán forests, where there's a 1-km self-guided trail, taking about an hour. A bus runs from El Cruce to La Villa every couple of hours, taking 15 minutes, but it's a pleasant walk.

There are no services in La Villa apart from a *kiosko* and tea room in high season, and the restaurant at **Hotel Angostura**. About halfway between the two centres there is a chapel (1936), designed by Bustillo, the famous architect who gave this region's buildings their distinctive style and nearby is **El Messidor** (1942), the summer resort of Argentine presidents, where you can visit the beautiful gardens with lake views.

In winter, there's good skiing at Villa La Angostura's popular ski resort **Cerro Bayo** ⓘ *9 km north of town, T02944-494189, www.cerrobayoweb.com*, with 24 pistes, many of them fabulously long, and all with excellent views over the lakes below, 20 km in total, and a great area for snowboarding. This is one of Argentina's pricier resorts; a ski pass costs US$15 for adults for the day in high season. There's also a tiny museum, **Museo Regional** ⓘ *on the road to La Villa, Mon 0800-1400, Tue-Fri 0800- 1630, Sat 1430-1700*, with interesting photos of the original indigenous inhabitants.

Walks around Villa La Angostura

▲ **Parque Nacional Los Arrayanes** For an easy flat walk, take the boat to the head of the Quitrihue Peninsula and walk the 13 km back. See box page 391.

▲ **Mirador Belvedere** Offers fine views of Lagos Correntoso and Nahuel Huapi. It's a 3-km drive or walk up the old road, northwest of El Cruce; and from the *mirador* a path to your right goes to **Cascada Inacayal**, a waterfall 50 m high, situated in an area rich in native flora and forest.

▲ **Cascada Río Bonito** A delightful walk leading to a beautiful waterfall, lying 8 km east of El Cruce off Route 66. The steep path gives tremendous views, and the falls themselves are impressive, falling 35 m from a chasm in basalt cliffs to an emerald green pool. Further along the same path, you can reach the summit of Cerro Bayo 1782 m. Alternatively, 1 km further along the road, a ski lift takes you to the platform at 1500 m, where there's a restaurant with great views, and from here, it's a short trek to the summit. The ski lift runs all year; cyclists can take bikes up in the lift and cycle down.

Border with Chile → *This route is liable to closure after snow*

Officially known as Paso Samore, **Paso Puyehue** (1280 m) lies 125 km northwest of Bariloche by Route 231, which is unpaved from Villa La Angostura, a spectacular six-hour journey, with plenty of buses from Bariloche, making it a cheaper alternative to the expensive Three Lakes Crossing from Bariloche.

The road is rough *ripio* here, with the occasional paved stretch. **Argentine customs and immigration** ⓘ *winter 0900-2000, summer 0800-2100*. It's another 50 km to Chilean customs over a wonderful mountain pass. On the Chilean side the road is paved via Entre Lagos and Lago Puyehue to Osorno. **Chilean immigration** ⓘ *mid-Oct to 1 May 0800-2100, winter 0900-2000, but liable to be closed after snowfalls*, is in the middle of a forest at Anticura, Km 146, 22 km west of the border. For vehicles entering Chile, formalities take about 30 minutes, and include the spraying of tyres and wiping of shoes on a mat (US$2 fee) and should have Chilean pesos ready. No fresh food is to be taken over the border to Chile, and Argentine hire cars must have necessary documentation, and the car's number plate etched on the windows. Tell your car hire company you plan to cross to Chile 24 hours in advance.

Villa Traful → *Phone code 02944*

If you want to get off the beaten track, Villa Traful is ideal. It was created after the Nahuel Huapi National Park was set up, with the aim of giving visitors the greatest possible contact with nature. Approaching from the west, the winding road passes through forests of lenga and tall coihue trees, their elegant trunks creating a woody cathedral, with idyllic spots to camp all along the shore. The quiet pretty village sprawls alongside the narrow deep-blue sliver of Lago Traful, enclosed on both sides by stunning sharp peaked mountains. There's not much to do here, but it's popular with fishermen, and there are a couple of wonderful walks and waterfalls to see, and it's a pleasant place to unwind. Best in December or late February/March when the only two restaurants aren't full of tourists, Traful is prone to mercurial winds, so check the forecast if you're coming for a few days. It's miserable being stuck here in bad weather, and the buses are infrequent. At the heart of the village opposite the main pier is a payphone, a kiosk selling basic supplies and bus tickets, and the best restaurant. There's a small but very helpful **tourist office** ⓘ *on the lakeshore, just past Aiken cabañas, T02944-479099, www.neuquen.gov.ar/muni/villa_traful, www.interpatagonia.com/traful*, which has information on walks, riding and fishing. The national park *guardería* is opposite the pier, open only in high season, with advice on walks.

Walks around Villa Traful

A 1½-hour walk from the village centre there are lovely **Cascadas dal Arroyo Coa Có y Blanco**, waterfalls thundering down through beech forest and *cañas colihues* bamboo. Walk up the hill from the **Ñancu Lahuen** restaurant and take the left-hand path to the mirador over Cascada Coa Có, and from here take the right-hand path through coihue forest to **Cascada Blanco**. A lovely ride by horse or mountain bike. Bikes can be hired at **Del Montanes** T02944-479035, along the road running up the slope behind the centre of the village. Better still, there's a satisfying hike up to **Cerro Negro** (2000 m) five hours up, following uncertain yellow markers. Ask at the national park office to get the best advice on the route. It's a stiff climb to start with, through gorgeous coihue and lenga forest, and the views as you clear the tree line are unbelievable, with the dramatic spired peaks visible on the northern side of Lago Traful. There's a lot of scree near the summit, but the views of Lanín, Tronador and the others make it all worthwhile. Alternatively, cross the lake (15 minutes) by boat leaving from the main pier, to reach a sand beach from where you can walk up a steep path to twin lagoons, and some superbly well conserved pre-historic cave paintings nearby. Ask in the tourist office to see which companies are currently running trips.

Sleeping

La Ruta de los Siete Lagos *p410*

B pp **Hostería Los Siete Lagos**, in a secluded spot on the shore of Lake Correntoso, T02944-15497152. A lovely *hostería* with just 5 small, very simple rooms, but some with great views of the lake. You'll be welcomed by Mariana Quintupuray and her family, who have lived here for generations. There is only electricity in the evenings, but there's excellent food served in the restaurant with homemade bread for sale. Also a campsite, summer only, no facilities, free. The bus from San Martín to Villa La Angostura stops here for a coffee break, so you can easily get off and take another bus the next day.

C Hostería Lago Villarino, Lago Villarino. A lovely setting, good food, also camping.

C Lago Espejo Resort, at tranquil Lago Espejo, set a little way off the road. A beautifully situated hotel, though not quite a resort as the name suggests, with simple camping area on the tranquil and secluded shore of the lake, surrounded by *coihue* trees. Lovely in good weather, and out of season.

D Hostería Lago Espejo. Old fashioned and comfortable, with good food in the restaurant, open Jan-Mar only.

Camping

The campsite Lago Espejo Resort is open all year. Facilities include toilets, drinking water, fireplaces, no showers, US$1pp. Further along an earth track is the lovely **Lago Espejo Camping**, a magical spot on quiet shores of the lake and its incredibly blue-grey river. Open all year, mostly visited by fishermen in the season (from Nov to end Apr), US$1pp, no showers, but toilets, drinking water and fireplaces. Also picnic spots, busy Jan, less so in Feb. Recommended.

The direct route to San Martín *p411*

C Hostería La Gruta de las Virgenes, Confluencia, T02944-426138. On a hill with views over the 2 rivers, very hospitable.

D Hostería ACA Confluencia, T02944-490800, at the ACA service station, with a *confitería*.

Villa La Angostura *p411*

Accommodation is good here, but pricey. It's much more pleasant, and cheaper, outside of Jan and Jul peak seasons

L Cabañas La Ruma Andina, Blv Queitrhué 1692, La Villa, T02944-495188, www.ruma adina.com.ar. Top-quality rustic *cabañas* with lots of stone and wood, and cosily furnished, in a lovely setting with pool. Recommended.

L Correntoso, discreetly hidden off the road, Route 231, and Río Correntoso, T02944-15619728, www.correntoso.com. Really fabulous setting for this intimate and stylish hotel with a really superb restaurant. Very special. Often recommended.

L El Faro, Av 7 Lagos 2345, T02944-495485, www.hosteriaelfaro.com.ar. Swish and stylish. Recommended.

L Las Balsas, on Bahía Las Balsas (signposted from Av Arrayanes), T02944-494308 (Buenos Aires T011-4700 1417), www.lasbalsas.com. One of the best hotels in Argentina, with fabulous cosy rooms, warm relaxed public areas, impeccable service, and a wonderfully intimate atmosphere in a great lakeside location with its own secluded beach. The chef, Pablo Campoy, creates really fine cuisine from top local produce. There's a beautiful lakeside pool (indoor and outdoor, both heated), and quite the best spa in the Lake District. Trips and excursions arranged, or transfers to the ski centre in season. This cannot be recommended highly enough.

A Cabañas Aries, Los Coihues 141, on the road towards Algo Correntoso, T02944-494648, www.cabaries.com.ar. Attractive rustic *cabañas*, well equipped, with lake views.

A Casa del Bosque, Los Pinos 160, Puerto Manzana, T02944-475229, www.casadelbosque.com. Luxury and style in these wonderfully designed *cabanas*, lots of glass, with jacuzzis and all possible comforts, in secluded woodland.

A Hostal Las Nieves, Av 7 Lagos 980, T02944-494573, www.lasnieves.com. Chalet-style splendour, high standard of service and cuisine.

A Hostería Pichi Rincón, RN 231, Km 64, 2 km northwest of the Cruce, T02944-494186, www.pichirincon.com.ar. Attractive wood and stone chalet in woodland elevated above the lake, with cottagey wood-lined rooms, and comfortable lounge with wood fire. Attentive service, and good restaurant.

A Hotel Angostura, T02944-494224, www.hotelangostura.com. Open all year, and beautifully situated on the lakeside at the port, La Villa, this handsome stone and wood chalet was designed by Bustillo in 1938, and retains a rather charming old- fashioned feel, with lovely gardens, and an excellent restaurant, open to residents in high seasons.

A La Posada, RN 231 km 65, a few kilometres west of town on RN 231 towards Chile, T02944-494450, www.hosterialaposada.com. In a splendid elevated position off the road and with clear views over the lake, this is a welcoming, beautifully maintained hotel in lovely gardens, with pool and fine restaurant; a perfectly peaceful place to relax.

A Portal de Piedra, RN 231, Km 56.7 y Río Bonito, T02944-494278, www.portal depiedra.com. A welcoming *hostería* and tea room in the woods, with tastefully decorated wood-panelled rooms, pool, and attractive gardens. Guests-only restaurant, excursions and activities.

C Verena's Haus, Los Taiques 268, T02944-494467, www.verenashaus.com.ar. A quaint and welcoming wooden house, with accommodation for adults and non-smokers only, cosy rooms with a pretty garden, delicious breakfasts. German and English spoken. Recommended.

D Hostería Del Francés, Lolog 3057, located in a great position on shore of Lago Correntoso, T02944-488055, lodelfrances@ hotmail.com. Excellent value in a lovely house, chalet-style with great views from all the rooms, with facilities. Recommended.

F pp **Bajo Cero Hostel**, Av 7 Lagos, T02944-495454, www.bajocerohostel.com. Well situated in town, neat rooms for 2-4 with private bath, linen and breakfast included.

F pp **Hostel la Angostura**, Barbagelata 157, T02944-494834, www.hostel laangostura.com.ar. 300 m up the road behind the tourist office is this warm, luxurious and great value hostel, beautifully run and impeccably clean. All the small dorms have bathrooms, and the friendly young owners organize trips too. Pool, internet, bar, TV, bikes for hire. Highly recommended.

Camping

There are many sites, with good facilities along RN 231.

Osa Mayor, signposted off main road, close to town, T02944-494304, www.campingosa mayor.com.ar. Highly recommended is this delightful leafy site on a hillside with good, shaded levelled camping spots, and all facilities and clean bathrooms, run by a friendly family. US$4 pp. Also rustic *cabañas* with heating and good views. Lovely apart from in Jan, when the place is packed.

Border with Chile *p412*

AL Termas Puyehue, RN 215, Km 76, T(56-2) 293 6000, www.puyehue.cl. Luxurious accommodation and excellent thermal baths at a huge complex set in beautiful open parkland, framed by mountains, with an impressive spa. Recommended.

Villa Traful and around *p412*

There are just a few places to stay clustered around the lake shore; most of them basic.

B-D Ruca Lico, T02944-479004, www.inter patagonia.com/rucalico. Luxurious *cabañas*, in woodland above the lake shore, lavishly furnished in rustic chic style, with jacuzzi and balcony with splendid views. Good value for 6, a fabulous treat for 2. Highly recommended. Horse riding is also organized.

C Marinas Puerto Traful, T02944-475284, www.marinastraful.com.ar. Gorgeous uninterrupted views of the lake from this recently modernized place, now bizarrely painted bright blue. Comfortable.

D Aiken, T02944-479048, or in Buenos Aires, T011-4568 2107, www.aiken.com.ar. Rustic and compact, but well-decorated *cabañas* in spacious gardens with old trees, with lovely open views of the lake below. All have *parrilladas* outside, so you can grill your own steaks, and a feeling of privacy. Cheap for 4 or 5. Also a restaurant. Recommended.

D Cabañas del Montañes, up behind the village, T02944-479035. Accommodation in *cabañas,* offered by the company that makes *alfajores*. Lovely setting.

D Hostería Villa Traful, T02944-479005. A delightful place to stay, this simple *hostería* is elevated above the lakeside, in pretty gardens. Separate cabins, with comfortable furnishings, and ample bathrooms. There are also pretty *cabañas* for up to 6, US$50. Charming hospitality from the owner, whose son Andres Quelin, T02944-479005, also organizes fishing and boat trips.

F Vulcanche, T02944-494015, www.vulcanche.com. An attractive chalet-style hostel and 2 *cabañas* (**D**), very comfortable and set in lovely open gardens with good views. Also simple camping in a pleasant open site, US$4 pp with hot showers, phone, *parrilladas*.

Camping

There are many sites along the lakeshore.

Camping Traful Lauquen, on the shore, T02944-479030, www.interpatagonia.com/ trafullauquen. With 600 m of beach on the lake, this is among the loveliest of the many sites all along the lake. Facilities include hot showers, light, fireplaces, restaurant, US$2.30 pp, open Nov-Mar. A really calm and beautiful site, much favoured by families wanting a quiet time.

Costa Traful, T02944-479049. If you're under 30 and you've got a guitar, or would like to meet somebody who has, camp at this lively place with 24-hr hot showers, restaurant, fireplaces, *proveduria*, popular with backpackers, US$4 pp, open Dec-Apr. Also restaurant, and shared bunk rooms. Basic but rustic *cabañas* for hire (**B**). Also fishing and horse-riding trips as well as trips to see cave paintings on the other side of the lake (3-hr trek each way), US$12, full day, also boat trip to see a submerged cypress forest, diving for those with experience.

Eating

Villa La Angostura *p411*

Plenty of places are to be found on the main Av Arrayanes, lots of them chalet-style, and open all day from breakfast onwards. Prices reflect the fact that this is a popular tourist town. Don't miss out on some really excellent places for fine cuisine here.

TTT Cocina Waldhaus, Route 231, Puerto Manzano, T02944-475323, www.sabores deneuquen.com.ar. Much recommended, this is 'auteur cuisine' with gorgeous local delicacies created by Chef Leo Morsella, served in a charming chalet-style building.

TTT Las Balsas, T02944-494308, www.lasbalsas.com. The chef Pablo Campoy creates really special food here: possibly the best in all Argentina. The wines are superb too, and the whole atmosphere is a real treat. Non-residents are only admitted if the hotel is quiet, and you should book well in advance, and dress up a bit. It's going to be an amazing night. Highly recommended.

TTT Tinto Bistró, Blv Nahuel Huapi 34, T02944-494924. An interesting, eclectic menu, but it's really the royal connections here which make is so trendy among Argentines: the owner is the brother of the famous Maxima, married into Dutch royalty. Very chic, great wine list. Good fun people-watching in season.

TT Correntoso, Hotel Corentoso, Av 7 Lagos, T02944-1561 9727. Another gourmet restaurant, this one specializing in Mediterranean cuisine, with Patagonian touches, like lamb and trout. Great wine list, gorgeous setting on the lakeside.

TT Los Pioneros de la Patagonia, Av Arrayanes 263, T02944-495525. Famous for fine local dishes in a chalet style building and great Argentine steaks, this is widely recommended.

TT Los Troncos, Av Arrayanes 67, T02944-495035. More chalet style, and more of the same but this is good for high-quality smoked fish and meats, and the trout and apple strudel are really tasty. Warm and cosy setting. With a warm atmosphere and live music at weekends.

TT Nativa Café, Av Arrayanes 198. This is the most relaxed and welcoming of those on the main drag with a high-ceilinged chalet feel, good music playing, and a menu which manages to be international and individual. Excellent pizzas – try the smoked goat topping – and a good place to hang out. Friendly efficient staff and a mixed clientele: couples and families of all ages. Pizza for 2 US$3-8, huge salads. Recommended.

TT Rincon Suizo, Av Arrayanes 44. Open only in high season for delicious regional specialities with a Swiss twist, in a rather more authentic chalet-style building.

T El Esquiador, Las Retames 146 (behind the bus terminal). Your best bet on a budget is this *parrilla*. Cheap fixed price 3-course menu.

T Gran Nevada, opposite **Nativa Café**. Good for cheap *parrilla* US$4, and *noquis* US$2.20 in a cheery friendly atmosphere.

T Hora Cero, Av Arrayanes 45. Hugely popular, heaving in summer, this serves a big range of excellent pizzas, and *pizza libre* (as much as you can eat for US$2) on Wed and Sat, a great deal.

T TemaTyCo , Route 231 and Mirlo, T02944-475211. Chic tea room serving amazing range of teas, *mate*, and delicious cakes. Charming, welcoming, recommended.

Villa Traful and around *p412*

T Ñancu Lahuen, T02944-479179. Quite the best restaurant for miles around, this is a delightful tea room and restaurant serving excellent trout and homemade pastas, all reasonably priced, and in a cosy setting. Great cakes and delicious home made chocolates, a homely place to hang out if it's raining, with a big open fire.

T Parrilla La Terraza, T02944-479073. Recommended for delicious locally produced lamb and kid on the *asado*, with panoramic lake views.

Activities and tours

Villa La Angostura *p411*

Bike hire

Expect to pay around US$7 per day.

Free Bike's, Las Fucsias y Los Notros, T02944-495047, info@freebikes.com.ar. Also arranges spares and repairs.

Boat trips

There are 2 companies running catamarans: **Greenleaf Turismo**, runs *Catamarán Futuleufu*, T02944-494004, tickets from Hotel Angostura, US$12 return. **Turisur**, T02944-426109, www.barilche.com/turisur, runs boats from Bariloche, via Isla Victoria

Barco Anna, T02944-155 53363, veleroanna@gmail.com, and **Velero Luz de Luna**, T02944-1551 3716, both offer trips on sailing boats with a special meal on board, or have a drink with picadas of smoked meat and fish.

Catamarán Patagonia Argentina , T02944-494463, also runs trips.

Canopying

The new craze in the lakes is this terrifying (or exciting) business of hanging from a harness rolling along wires strung up high in the forest to get an adrenalin-filled ariel view.

Canopy Villa la Angostura, Curruhué and Melinquina, T02944-1541 7817, www.canopyargentina.com.ar, runs a great trail in the forest nearby, with over 1400 m of cable to zoom along.

Climbing

Club Andino Villa La Angostura, Cerro Bayo 295, T02944-494954. Excursions, maps and information.

Fishing

The season runs from mid-Nov to May. For permits and a list of fishing guides, ask at the tourist office.

Angler's Home Fly Shop, Belvedere 22, T02944-495222. Arranges fishing trips.

Banana Fly Shop, Av Arrayanes 282, T02944-494634. Fly shop.

PatagonFly, www.patagonfly.com. A fly shop and association of local fishing guides, also runs trips.

Horse riding

Rates are usually about US$10 per hr.

Los Saucos, Av Arrayanes 1810, T02944-494853.

Cabalgatas Correntoso, Cacique Antrao 1850, T02944-1551 0559, info@cabalgatacorrentoso.com.ar. Offers horseback excursions in the surrounding area and to Villa Traful.

Cabalgatas Millaqueo, Av 7 Lagos 655, T02944-1556 6054.

Mountain biking

Free Bike's, Las Fucsias y Los Notros, T02944-495047, info@freebikes.com.ar.

Pegaso, Inacayal 44, T02944-495562, pegasovla@speedy.com.ar.

Skiing

Cerro Bayo, T02944-494189, although smaller and more popular with families than the famous Cerro Catedral in Bariloche, is also very well worth visiting, with a 700-m drop, and more than 20 pistes of 4 levels of difficulty, there are spectacular views of the mountains and lakes all around.

Tour operators

Bayo Turismo, Av Arrayanes 282, T02944-494920.

Correntoso Travels, Av Arrayanes 21, 1st floor, T02944-494803, www.correntosotravels.com.ar.

Rucan Turismo, Av 7 Lagos 239, T02944-495075, www.rucanturismo.com. Skiing, riding, mountain biking and conventional tours.

Terpin Turismo, Los Notros 41, T02944-494551, www.terpinturismo.com. Trips to Chile and surrounding areas, car hire.

Trekking

Alma Sur, T02944-1556 4724, www.almasur.com. Great trips in the local area and further afield, with bilingual, knowledgeable (and handsome) Anthony Hawes. A trained guide of Nahuel Huapi National Park, he creates really imaginative walks, which can include boats, climbing and hiking way off the beaten track. Recommended.

Villa Traful and around *p412*

Fishing

Andres Quelin, T02944-479005. A fishing guide who organizes boat trips to see a submerged cypress wood. Find him at Hostería Villa Traful.

Osvaldo A Brandeman, Bahía Mansa, T02944-479048, pescaosvaldo@mail.com. Fishing expert and excellent guide. Find him on the lakeshore 200m from Arroyo Cataratas. Horse riding and boat trips are organized by Camping Costa de Traful.

Transport

La Ruta de los Siete Lagos *p410*

Round-trip excursions along the Seven Lakes route, 5 hrs, are operated by several companies, but it's better in your own transport, as you'll want to stop and explore. **Buses** will stop at campsites on the route – see under San Martín, page 431, for companies. It's a good area for **cycling**, though there is more traffic in Jan/Feb.

Villa La Angostura *p411*

Bus The terminal is at the junction of Av 7 Lagos and Av Arrayanes, opposite the ACA service station. For bus network information, Albus, T02944-1561 7578, 15 de Mayo T02944- 495104, Andesmar, T02944-495247, Via Bariloche/El Valle, T02944-495415. To/from **Bariloche**, 1¼ hrs, US$4, several companies, several daily. If going on to **Osorno** (Chile), you can arrange for the bus company to pick you up at **La Angostura**, US$8 to **Osorno**. Daily buses to **San Martín de los Andes** with Ko Ko and Albus. For other destinations, change at San Martín de los Andes and Bariloche.

Car hire Angostura Rent a Car, T02944-424621, info@angosturarentacar.com.ar. Reliable company, offering accessories such as baby seats and ski racks at no extra charge. Good value. **Giminez Vidal**, Las Muticias 146, T02944-494336. **Terpin Turismo**, Los Notros 41, T02944-494551, www.terpinturismo.com.
Taxi Juan Carlos Pinuen, T02944-494221.

Border with Chile *p412*
Bus For bus services from Bariloche to **Osorno**, **Puerto Montt** and **Valdivia**, see page 399.

Villa Traful and around *p413*
Bus In high summer, a daily bus between **Villa la Angostura** and **San Martín** stops here, but in low season, buses run only 3 times a week. **Kiosko El Ciervo**, by the YPF service station, sells tickets and has the timetable.

Directory

Villa La Angostura *p411*
Banks Andina, Arrayanes 256, T02944-495197. For cash and TC's. **Banco de Patagonia**, Av Arrayanes 275, and **Banco Prov de Neuquén**, Av Arrayanes 172. Both with ATMs. **Internet** Punta Arrayanes, Av Arrayanes 90, T02944-495288. **Medical services** Hospital Rural Arraiz, Copello 311 (at *barrio* Pinar), T02944-494170. **Post office** Siete Lagos 26. **Telephone** Several *locutorios* along Av Arrayanes.

Parque Nacional Lanín

Some of the most beautiful sights in the Lake District are to be found in one of the country's largest national parks, Lanín, which stretches north from Nahuel Huapi National Park all the way to Lago Norquinco, to the west of Aluminé, and along the border with Chile for some 200 km. The park's centrepiece, and its most climbed peak, is the magnificent extinct snow-capped volcano Lanín. The ascent takes two days, and starts from close to the border at Paso Tromen (also known as Paso Mamuil Malal). Lanín forms a dramatic backdrop to the beautiful landscapes all around the park, and is especially superb seen from two connected lakes, which make the most beautiful places in the park to visit: Lagos Huechulafquen and Paimún stretch west from Junín de los Andes, with great hiking, fishing and camping. Both lakes have shores of volcanic black sand, and there are comfortable hosterías, and basic campsites, as well as marked paths for several rewarding hikes. A new boat trip allows you to see the spectacular heart of the park from the water, and access to Lago Epulafquen. These are the easiest parts of the park to visit, with a good road leading from Junín de los Andes. Southernmost parts of the park can be visited easily from San Martín de los Andes, which sits at the head of picturesque Lago Lacar (well set up for tourism), with boat trips and several beaches where you can bathe and rent canoes. Quiet Lago Lolog further north also offers good fishing, and it's worth the drive to find two more tranquil and very pretty lakes hidden away in mountains: Lagos Curruhué Grande and Chico. Further along the same road, there are thermal waters at Lahuen-Co, at the western end of Lago Epulafquen, which you could also reach in a spectacular two-day hike from Lago Paimún. Northernmost areas of the park are harder to access, and infrastructure here is building only slowly. But there are several Mapuche communities living in the park who organize campsites and horse riding, and sell homemade bread and other provisions, making this area interesting to visit. The whole park is definitely more rewarding if you visit in your own transport, as bus services are sporadic at best, and there is a great deal of unspoilt landscape to explore, varying from lowland hills in the east to steep craggy mountains in the west, all heavily clad in native beech trees coihue, lenga and ñire. ▸▸ *For Sleeping, Eating and other listings, see pages 426-433.*

Ins and outs

Getting there

Bus transport into the park is tricky, with services usually running to Lago Huechulafquen from San Martín de los Andes with **Ko Ko Bus**, but the timetable varies from year to year. There are boat trips along Lago Lacar from San Martín de los Andes, and rafting at its western end on the River Hua Hum: contact tour operators in San Martín for information (see page 432). There are *guardaparques* (rangers) offices at Huechulafquen, and Tromen who can advise on hikes. There park can be entered at two points: **San Martín de los Andes** is the main tourist centre and within the park itself. It gives easy access to Lago Lacar the River Hua Hum on its western end, with plenty of tourist services, and further north, to remoter Lago Lolog. There are more good walks at the natural thermal pools at **Termas de Lahuen-Co** further west, accessed from Route 62, starting either south of Junín, or from Lago Lolog.

Lago Huechulafquen, further north, provides the easiest access to beautifully situated lakes, with some accommodation. Go to Junín de los Andes, and take the good dirt road Route 61 west, past the fishing spot at the mouth of the Chimehuín river, 22 km further on. Stop off here for a moment, to appreciate one of Argentina's most celebrated fly-fishing spots, and the heavenly turquoise water, with black sandy shore. As soon as you cross the river, you'll be asked to stop at the *guardaparque's* office, where you can get free maps and information on hikes. From Lago Huechulafquen there are fabulous walks up into the hills and along the shore, and along beautiful Lago Paimún further west. Three *hosterías* and great campsites offer accommodation, and there are simple food shops and places to eat. The very north of the park is hard to access, since the roads are poor, but it's possible to reach Quillén from Rahue by heading west along Route 46, where signposted on Route 23. Roads are poor, and there's little infrastructure when you reach Quillén, but there are Mapuche communities to visit and some rural campsites.

Park information

Park entry is US$4 (paid at entry point). The park administration is at San Martín de los Andes, Emilio Frey 749. You're supposed to register here before setting out on any major treks at Huechulafquen, although this is obviously impractical. There is now a *guardaparques* office at the entrance to the park at the eastern end of Lago Huechulafquen, and they can advise on walks and should always be notified before you set off for a hike. Ask them about your route, and if paths are open. They have two really good free leaflets: one on the park itself, and another on climbing Lanín, both with sections in English. Check out www.parquenacionallanin.gov.ar. Having a good map is essential: look out for the *Sendas y Bosques* (walks and forests) map for Parque Nacional Lanín, 1:200,000, laminated and easy to read (US$3), with a book containing English summaries of the walks, 'Lanín/Villarica', (US$5.50) www.guiasendasybosques.com.ar.

Around the park

There are some delightful walks here, with guides only needed for the longer treks where paths are not marked. (For these, ask in the Junín park office or at San Martín de los Andes, address above.) Yellow arrows indicate the paths; allow plenty of time to return before dark. Ask *guardaparques* for advice on routes before setting off. To cross to other side of Lago Paimún at La Unión, there's a boat operated by **Mapuches**; just ring the bell. Wherever you are in the park, fires are a serious hazard here: always put out with lots of water, not just earth. Take all rubbish away with you.

Trekking routes

▲ **El Saltillo Falls** Two hours return, fabulous views. Start from campsite **Piedra Mala** (where you can stock up on provisions) at Lago Paimún, and head west towards the Paimún *guardaparque's* office. From here you can also walk on to Río Paimún, three to four hours one way, from Piedra Mala campsite.

▲ **Termas at Lahuen-Co** It's well worth getting to beautiful Lago Curruhué and the rustic Termas. You could walk it from Lago Paimún: it's eight hours to reach the end of Lago Paimún, walking along the northern side, then four more to reach the Termas, best done over two days. You must consult the book of walks *Sendas y Bosques* for Parque Nacional Lanín, and notify *guardaparques*. It's a beautiful walk, and you'll be rewarded by a soak in these simple rustic pools. Start from beautiful **La Unión**, where Lago Huechulafquen meets Lago Paimún. If you can't face the two-day hike, go west along Route 62 south of Junín de los Andes on a good dirt road, passing the turning to Lago Lolog, Lagos Curruhué Chico and Grande, through ancient pehuén forests along the southern shores, and then past the impressive lava field at Laguna Escorial. It's worth checking in San Martín's tourist office before you set off. **Camping Agreste Lanín** is a lovely shaded spots with hot showers, toilets, *parrilladas* and places to wash, well run by friendly people; open December to April, US$2 pp.

▲ **Base of Volcán Lanín** Eight hours return, a satisfying walk. Start from Puerto Canoa.

▲ **Cerro El Chivo** (2064 m) eight to nine hours return. A more challenging walk through forest. Note that heavy snow can lie till January. Set off early, and register in campsite at Bahía Cañicul. Potentially dangerous without a guide. Consult *Sendas y Bosques* book for Parque Nacional Lanín, and notify *guardaparques*.

Horse riding

You can explore much of the area on horseback, including the trek to the base of Volcán Lanín. Five places along the lake hire horses: ask *guardaparques* for advice, or ask at Mapuche communities where you see the signs, *cabalgatas* (horse rides). Also recommended for longer rides, and really fine horses, is **Estancia Huechahue** ⓘ *reached from north of Junín de los Andes, T02944-491303, www.ridingtours.com,* *see also page 430*. Unbeatable riding and hospitality, and excellent rides into the park, enabling you to reach areas completely inaccessible otherwise.

Boat trips

A new boat trip offers the chance to see Lanín and the beautiful surrounding mountains from the water, and to reach the relatively inaccessible Lago Epulafquen with its impressive 6-km lava deposit. Trips on the comfortable catamaran *José Julián*, T02972-421038, www.catamaranjosejulian.com.ar, start at Puerto Canoa, on the northern shore of Lago Huechulafquen, and there are some refreshments available on board.

Paso Tromen/Mamuil Malal border with Chile

Paso Tromen – known in Chile as Paso Mamuil Malal – is 64 km northwest of Junín de los Andes and reached by *ripio* Route 60 which runs from Tropezón on Route 23, through Parque Nacional Lanín. Some 3 km east of the pass a turning leads north to Lago Tromen, and south of the pass is the graceful cone of the Lanín volcano. This is the normal departure point for climbing to the summit (see page 422). This crossing is less developed than the Hua Hum and Puyehue (now known as Paso Cerro Samore) routes further south; it is unsuitable for bicycles and definitely not usable during heavy rain or snow (June to mid-November), as parts are narrow and steep. Ring to check: *gendarmería*, T02972-491270, or customs, T02972-492163. This is a beautiful spot, with a good campsite, and some lovely walks: From the *guardaparque* centre, footpaths lead to a *mirador* (1½ hours round trip), or across a grassy prairie with magnificent clear views of Lanín and other jagged peaks, through ñirre woodland and some great araucaria trees to the point where Lago Tromen drains into Río Malleo (4 km).

Parque Nacional Lanín

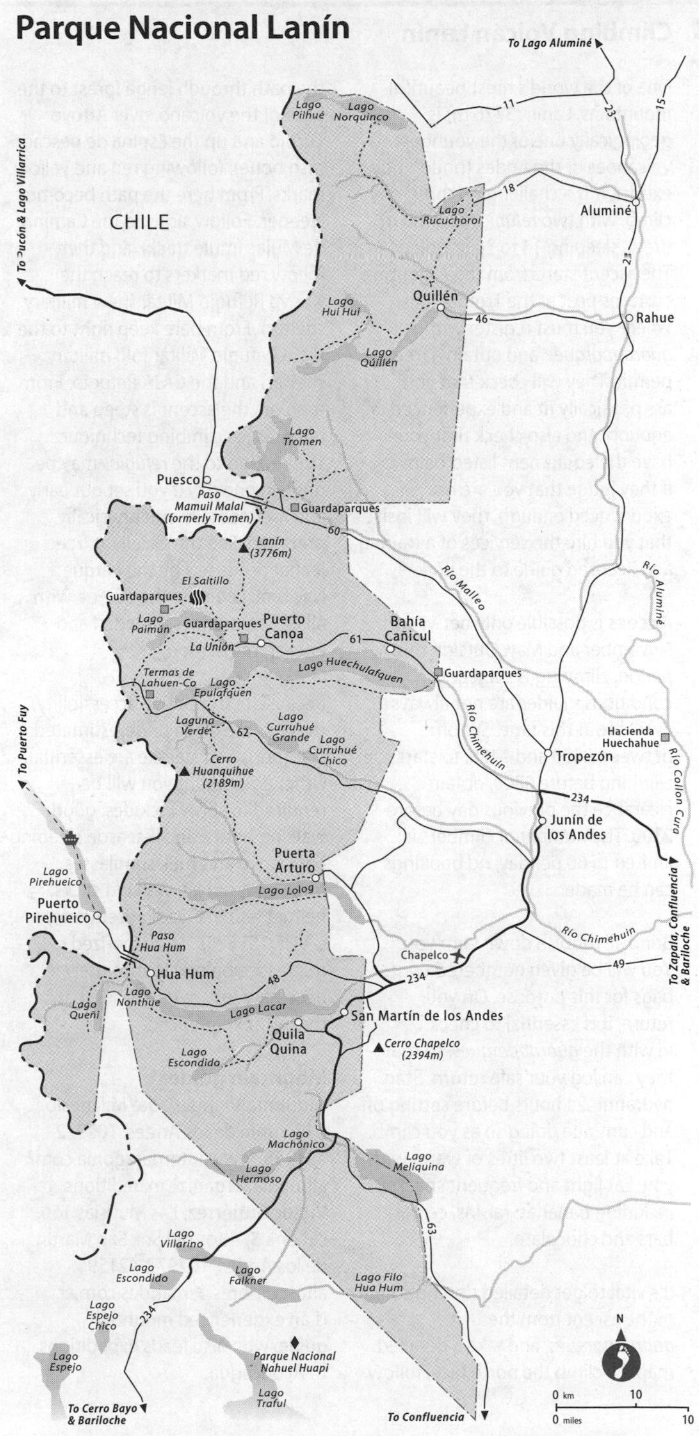

Climbing Volcán Lanín

One of the world's most beautiful mountains, Lanín (3776 m) is geologically one of the youngest volcanoes of the Andes though now extinct. It is a challenging three-day climb, with two *refugios* at 2400 m (free), sleeping 14 to 20 people. The ascent starts from the Argentine customs post at the Tromen pass, where you must register with *guardaparques*, and obtain a free permit. They will check that you are physically fit and experienced enough, and also check that you have the equipment listed below. If they judge that you are not experienced enough, they will insist that you hire the services of a trained and licensed guide to the park.

Access is possible only between November and May. Outside this period, climbing is subject to conditions; guides are not always available at this time. Set off between 0800 and 1400; to start climbing before 0800, obtain clearance the previous day before 2100. The number of climbers is limited to 60 per day; no bookings can be made.

Bring all rubbish down with you. You will be given numbered waste bags for this purpose. On your return, it is essential to check in with the *guardaparques*, so that they can log your safe return. Start hydrating 24 hours before setting off and continue doing so as you climb. Take at least two litres of water with you. Eat light and frequent snacks, including bananas, raisins, cereal bars and chocolate.

It's vital to get detailed descriptions of the ascent from the *guardaparques*, and take a detailed map. To climb the north face, follow the path through lenga forest to the base of the volcano, over Arroyo Turbio and up the Espina de pescado (fish bone), following red and yellow marks. From here the path becomes steeper. Follow signs to the Camino de Mulas (mule track), and then follow red markers to reach the Nuevo Refugio Militar (new military shelter). From here keep right to the Viejo Refugio Militar (old military shelter) and the CAJA Refugio. From then on, the ascent is steep and requires ice climbing technique. The section to the *refugios* may be done in one day if you set out early and are mentally and physically prepared. See the excellent free leaflet produced by the Parque Nacional Lanín on the ascent, with all GPS references provided and English translation.

Because of its relative accessibility, the risks are often underestimated: crampons and ice-axe are essential. Other equipment you will be required to show includes: good walking boots, an all-season sleeping bag, stove and fuel, sunglasses, torch, first-aid kit, walking sticks, helmet and VHF radio (frequency is VHF 155675). An authorized guide (see below) is absolutely necessary for anyone other than the very experienced.

Mountain guides

Alquimia Viajes, Padre Milanesio 840, Junín de los Andes, T02972-491355, www.interpatagonia.com/alquimia, organize expeditions.
Víctor Gutiérrez, Las Mutisias 150, cabaña 5, Altos del Sol, San Martín de los Andes, T02972-421595, altascumbres@smandes.com.ar, is an experienced mountain guide, who also leads expeditions to Aconcagua.

Argentine immigration and customs ⓘ *Puesto Tromen, 3 km east of the pass, open 0800-2000 all year.* **Chilean immigration and customs** ⓘ *Puesco, 8 km west of the pass, Dec-Mar 0800-2100, Apr-Nov 0800-1900.* On the Chilean side the road continues through glorious scenery, with views of the volcanoes of Villarrica and Quetrupillán to the south, to Pucón, 40 km west of the pass, on Lago Villarrica. Hire cars will need special documents (ask when you rent), no fruit or vegetables are to be taken into Chile, and the car's number plate must be etched into all windows.

San Martín de los Andes ›› *pp426-433.*

➔ *Phone code: 02972 Colour map 5, A2 Population: 20,000*

San Martín de los Andes is a charming upmarket tourist town in a beautiful setting on the edge of Lago Lacar, with attractive chalet-style architecture and lots of good accommodation. It's an excellent centre for exploring southern parts of the Parque Nacional Lanín and nearby lakes Lolog and Lacar, where there are beaches for relaxing and good opportunities for rafting, canoeing, mountain biking and trekking. There is also excellent skiing at Chapelco resort 10 km south, and Chapelco Airport, 12 km north, receives daily flights from Buenos Aires. ›› *For further information, see Activities and tours page 431.*

Ins and outs

Getting around It's easy to orientate yourself here, as the town nestles in a valley surrounded by steep mountains at the eastern end of Lago Lacar. The bus terminal is

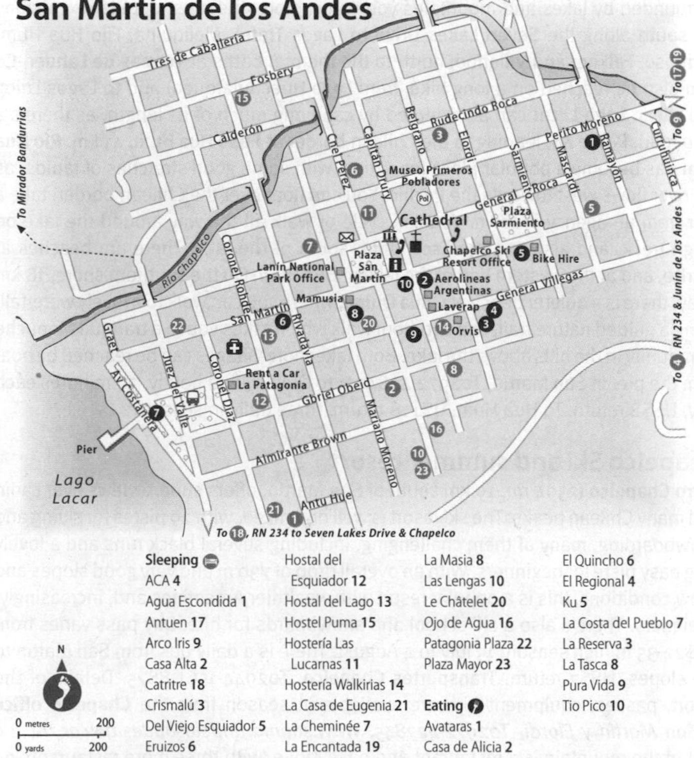

 just off the *costanera* (shore road) at Juez del Valle and Villegas. Beware of confusing street names: Perito Moreno runs east-west, crossing Mariano Moreno which runs north-south, and Rudecindo Roca which is two blocks north of General Roca.

Tourist information The **tourist office** ⓘ *San Martín y Rosas 790, on the main plaza, T02972-427347, open all year 0800-2100*, hands out maps and has lists of accommodation, with prices up on a big board. Helpful staff speak English and French, but are very busy in summer, when it's advisable to go early in the day, before they get stressed. The **Parque Nacional Lanín office** is at ⓘ *E Frey 749, T02972-427233, www.parquenacionallanin.gov.ar*. Also, check out www.chapelco.com.ar, www.sanmartindelosandes.gov.ar.

Sights

The main street, San Martín, runs perpendicular to the *costanera*, and here you'll find most shops and plenty of places to eat. Of the two plazas, the more interesting is Plaza San Martín, which has a sporadic crafts market. It's a pleasant 1½-hour walk north and west up the hill to **Mirador Bandurrias** with great views, and a great *quincho*-like restaurant, **Lola Mora** run by a Mapuche community. Start at the far northernmost end of the *costanera*, passing the fish trap (open winter 1100-1630, summer 1000-1300, 1600-1900) and walk along the shore before ascending the path, 40 minutes up. Even lovelier, set off from the costanera up to **Mirador Arrayán,** where there's a gorgeous tea room **La Casa de Té Arrayán,** and restaurant with spectacular views over the lake.

Around San Martín de los Andes

Surrounded by lakes and mountains you can explore, the most popular excursions are south along the **Seven Lakes Drive** to Lagos Traful, Meliquina, Filo Hua Hum, Hermoso, Falkner and Villarino, north to the thermal baths at **Termas de Lahuen-Co** (can also be reached on a long hike from Lago Huechulafquen) and to Lagos Lolog and Lacar. **Lago Lacar** can be explored by car along much of its length, as there's a *ripio* road, Route 48, leading to the Chilean border at **Paso Hua Hum**, 41 km. **Río Hua Hum** has become a popular place for rafting, with some good stretches of rapids, as the river flows west towards the Pacific. You can float over the Chilean border: take a tour from an agency in town. You can cycle or walk all the way around the lake on rough track, and also to **Lago Escondido**, south of the lake. There are beaches at **Catrite**, and at the western end of the lake at **Hua Hum**. On the southern shore, 18 km away, there is a quieter beach at **Quila Quina**, where you can walk to a lovely waterfall, along a guided nature trail, or a two-hour walk which takes you to a tranquil Mapuche community in the hills above the lake. Both lakeshore villages can be reached by boat from the pier in San Martín, T02972-428427; to Quila Quina hourly, 30 minutes each way, US$8 return. To Hua Hum, US$18 return, three daily in season.

Chapelco Ski and summer resort

Cerro Chapelco (2394 m), 19 km south of San Martín, offers superb views over Lanín and many Chilean peaks. The ski resort is well organized, with 29 pistes for skiing and snowboarding, many of them challenging, including several black runs and a lovely long easy piste for beginners. With an overall drop of 730 m and very good slopes and snow conditions, this is a popular resort with wealthier Argentines and, increasingly, foreigners. There's also a ski school and snowboards for hire. Day pass varies from US$22-35 in high season, 15 July to 4 August. There is a daily bus from San Martín to the slopes, US$3 return. **Transportes Chapelco**, T02944-1561 8875. Details of the resort, passes, equipment hire are available in season from the **Chapelco office** ⓘ *San Martín y Elordi, T02972-427845, www.sanmartindelosandes.gov.ar*. At the foot of the mountain is a restaurant and base lodge, with three more restaurants on the mountain and a small café at the top. In summer this is a good place for cycling (take your bike up on the cable car, and cycle down), trekking, archery or horse riding.

There are also trips to **Lago Curruhué** and **Termas de Epulafquen** or **Lahuen-Co**, are offered by tour operators, but could also cycle or drive along *ripio* roads from Lago Lolog. See Parque Nacional Lanín, page 418. There's no public transport to these places at present.

Border with Chile

Paso Hua Hum is usually open all year round and is an alternative to the route via the Paso Tromen/Mamuil Malal (see page 420). Paso Hua Hum (659 m) lies 47 km west of San Martín de los Andes along Route 48 (*ripio*) which runs along the north shore of Lago Lacar and crosses the border to Puerto Pirehueico. Buses leave early morning daily, two hours, US$4, check terminal for schedule (T02972-427044); they connect with boat across Lago Pirehueico. Bikes can be taken. The Argentine and Chilean immigration is open summer 0800-2100, winter 0900-2000.

Into Chile The road (*ripio*, tough going for cyclists) continues on the Chilean side to Puerto Pirehueico at the southern end of Lago Pirehueico, a long, narrow and deep lake, totally unspoilt except for some logging activity. At its northern end lies Puerto Fuy. Accommodation is available in private houses in both Puerto Pirehueico and Puerto Fuy. Ferries cross the lake between the two ports (from January to February, three daily, and from November to December and March to April, two daily, and from May to October they are daily except Sunday). Buses connect Puerto Pirehueico with Panguipulli, from where transport is available to other destinations in the Chilean Lake District.

Junín de los Andes » pp426-433.

→ *Phone code: 02972 Colour map 5, A2 Population: 9000*

Situated on the beautiful Río Chimehuín, the quiet town of Junín de los Andes (773 m) is justifiably known as the trout fishing capital of Argentina. It offers some of the best fly fishing in the country, and the fishing season now runs from mid November to May. Junín is also an excellent base for exploring the wonderful Parque Nacional Lanín and for climbing the extinct volcano itself, while there is excellent riding at **Estancia Huechahue** just to the north, and rafting on Río Aluminé further north still.

Founded in 1883, Junín is a real town; not as picturesque or tourist-orientated as its neighbour, San Martín – there are far fewer chalet-style buildings, and few chocolate shops here – but it's a quiet neat place with genuinely friendly people. The hotels are not as upmarket as San Martín, but **Estancia Huechahue** nearby (see Sleeping, page 430) is superb, and there are some decent family-run hotels here, plus one excellent restaurant make it worth stopping over night to get a feeling of real life trundling by in a Patagonian town, where you can try the celebrated local trout.

Sights

Most of what you need can be found within a couple of blocks of the central Plaza San Martín with its fine araucaria trees among mature *alerces* and cedars. The small **Museo Salesiano** ⓘ *Ginés Ponte y Nogueira, Mon-Fri 0900-1230, 1430-1930, Sat 0900-1230*, has a fine collection of Mapuche weavings, instruments and arrowheads, and you can buy a whole range of excellent Mapuche handicrafts in the **Feria Artesanal** behind the tourist office. There's an impressive sculpture park **El Via Christi** ⓘ *just west of the town, T02972-491684*, from the plaza walk up Avenida Ant Argentina across the main road, Route 234, to the end. Situated among pine forest on a hillside, the stations of the cross are illustrated with touching and beautifully executed sculptures of Mapuche figures, ingeniously depicting scenes from Jesus's life together with a history of the town and the Mapuche community. The sculptures are to be found along trails through the pine woods. A lovely place to walk, and highly recommended. The church, **Santuario Nuestra Senora de las Nieves y Beata Laura Vicuña,** also has fine Mapuche weavings, and is a pleasing calm space.

Some 7 km away, clearly signposted, on Route 61 towards Lago Huechuflafquen, is the **Centro Ecologico Aplicado de Neuquén** (CEAN) ⓘ *Mon-Fri 0900-1300, US$0.30*, where trout are farmed, and ñandus and llamas can be seen; a good place for kids.

Fishing is undoubtedly one of the great attractions of Junín, and the best fishing is at the mouth of the river Chimehuin on the road to Lago Huechulafquen, although there are many excellent spots around; see guides below. In the town itself, there are pleasant places to fish and picnic along the river, while there are several fishing lodges in the area which cater for the expert, with guides whose services you can hire.

The **tourist office** ⓘ *T02972-491160, www.junindelosandes.gov.ar, summer 0800-2200, rest of year 0800-2100*, on the plaza has friendly staff who can advise on accommodation, and hand out maps.

Sleeping

Parque Nacional Lanín: Lago Huechulafquen *p418*

LL Hostería San Huberto, Route 60, Km 33, T02972-491238, rolsen@smandes.com.ar. Fishing lodge, also offers meals.

L Hostería Paimún, Route 61, Km 58, T02972-491201. Best location, nicely decorated, but the staff aren't friendly. Meals offered.

L Refugio del Pescador, Route 61, Km 57, leave messages at T02972-490210. The most basic, and popular with fishermen. Full board offered, small golf course.

A Huechulafquen, Route 61, Km 55, T002972-427598, (price for half-board). The most recommendable, and welcoming of the three options, with comfortable small rooms lined with wood and well heated, with gardens going down to the lakeside, very peaceful. The owner is a fanatical fisherman, and there's an expert native fishing guide on hand too (extra charge for this). In high season, lunches are served to non-residents here. Other choices for eating are limited, best to take a picnic.

Camping

There are lots of sites, all along the lake sides, run by local Mapuche communities, and often selling delicious *pan casero* (homemade bread), or offering horse riding. Easiest if you have your own transport, and can keep going till you find one you like. They're all beautifully situated.

Bahía Cañicul, 48 km from Junín. All the facilities you'll need, including places to bring your boat on shore.

Camping Lafquen-co, 53 km from Junín, just after the sign to Bahía Coihues. This campsite is highly recommended for its friendly welcome and facilities: hot showers, fireplaces, toilets. Wild camping is also possible in a beautiful spot nearby, but there are no facilities. Lafquenco is run by friendly and helpful Juan Andres, with a good open spot on the lakeside and lots of room, $2.30 pp.

Piedra Mala, 65 km from Junín, on the shores of Lago Paimún. Hot showers, toilets, fireplaces, picnic tables, restaurant offering local dishes, good facilities and beautiful setting. Sites are spread under araucaria and beech trees by 2 beaches, with lovely walks along the water's edge to the end of the lake. $2.30pp. This is where the bus stops (when it's running).

There are 3 more campsites beyond Hostería Paimún, including **Mawizache**, just beyond the picturesque little chapel. This has a great little restaurant serving fabulous local dishes very inexpensively, hot chocolate and cakes, offers fishing trips with expert Raúl Hernández (US$13 per hr), and also picnic places in an amazing spot. Raúl and his wife Carmen have lived on the land all their lives, and know it well. Open all year.

For an explanation of the Sleeping and Eating price codes used in this guide, and other relevant information, see Essentials, pages 48 and 51.

San Martín de los Andes *p423, map p423*
Single room rates are expensive. There are 2 high seasons, when rates are much higher, and you must book ahead: Jan/Feb and Jul/Aug.

L La Casa de Eugenia, Coronel Díaz 1186, T02972-427206, www.lacasadeeugenia.com.ar. Quite the most charming B&B in San Martín, this beautifully renovated 1900's house is more like an exclusive boutique hotel, but completely relaxing and unsnobby. Rooms are beautifully designed, incredibly cosy, and very welcoming. Breakfasts are luxurious, including home made cakes, and the Rocas, friendly family owners, go out of their way to make you feel at home. Highly recommended.

L Las Lengas, Col. Pérez 1175, T02972-427659, www.hosterialaslengas.com.ar. You'll get a friendlier reception here than at La Cheminée. A large airy spacious hotel, with plain attractive rooms, all individually designed, and a warm relaxing atmosphere, in a peaceful part of town. Recommended.

AL La Cheminée, Gral Roca y Mariano Moreno, T02972-427617, www.hosterialacheminee.com.ar. One of the most luxurious options, with pretty and cosy cottage-style rooms, spacious bathrooms, and a small pool. Breakfast is included, but no restaurant. Overpriced in high season, but reasonable otherwise. English spoken.

AL Le Châtelet, Villegas 650, T02972-428294, www.hotellechatelet.com.ar. Really chic and luxurious, everything in this beautiful chalet-style hotel has been thought of to make you feel utterly pampered. Cosy wood lined living room, and gorgeous bedrooms, video library, excellent service, spa and pool with massage and facial treatments. Also some suites.

AL Patagonia Plaza, San Martín and Rivadavia, T02972-422280, www.hotelpatagoniaplaza.com.ar. Centrally situated, and very comfortable but slightly s oulless, this is a standard modern international hotel, with good rooms, a café and restaurant and spa which is free for guests (apart from massages). All rooms have jacuzzi.

A Hostería Walkirias, Villegas 815, T02972-428307, www.laswalkirias.com. A lovely place, homely but smart, with very spacious and well furnished, tasteful rooms with big bathrooms, breakfast and free transfer from the airport included, sauna and pool room, charming owners. Great value off season.

A Hostal del Esquiador, Col Rhode 975, T02972-427674. Well decorated rooms, and a sitting room, good service. Great value low season.

A Hotel Del Viejo Esquiador, San Martin 1242, T02972-427690, www.delviejoesquiador.com. Very comfortable rooms with good beds, in traditional hunting lodge-style, excellent service. English spoken. Recommended.

A Plaza Mayor, Coronel Pérez 1199, T02972-421929, www.hosteriaplazamayor.com.ar. A chic and homely *hostería* in a quiet residential area, with traditional touches in the simple elegant rooms, all decorated to a high standard. Pool, quincho, parking. Great homemade breakfast is included. English, French and Italian are spoken by the helpful staff. Very welcoming, and recommended.

B La Masia, Obeid 811, T02972-427879. Spacious high-ceilinged rooms, in this simple chalet-style place with lots of dark wood, and nice little bathrooms, lots of cosy places to sit in the evenings in bar and lounge.

C Casa Alta, Obeid 659, T02972-427456. Deservedly popular, this is a welcoming B&B with charming multilingual owners, who will make you feel at home. Comfortable rooms, most with bathrooms, lovely gardens, and delicious breakfast. Closed in low season, book in advance.

C Crismalú, Rudecindo Roca 975, T02972-427283, crismalu@smandes.com.ar. Simple rooms in attractive chalet-style place, good value with breakfast included.

C Hostería Las Lucarnas, Pérez 632, T02972-427085. Really good value, this central and pretty place with simple comfortable rooms, and friendly owner, who speaks English.

D-E pp **Hostería Bärenhaus**, Los Alamos 156, Barrio Chapelco (8370), T/F02972-422775, www.baerenhaus.com. Welcoming English- and German-speaking young owners have thought of everything to make you feel at home here: excellent breakfast, very comfortable cosy rooms with bath and heating, or great value shared dorms. Highly recommended. 5km outside town, free pick-up from bus terminal and airport.

D Hostal del Lago, Col Rhode 854, T02972-427598, hostalago@hotmail.com. A relaxed

homely place, the rooms have basic bathrooms, but a good breakfast is included.
E pp **Hostel Puma**, Fosbery 535 (take Rivadavia to the north, 2 blocks after crossing the bridge), T02972-422443, www.pumahostel.com.ar. HI discounts. The cheapest in town is this excellent, really lovely hostel, warm, friendly, and clean, run by an enthusiastic mountain guide who organizes treks to Lanín, rooms for 4 with private bathroom, also twin and double rooms with bath **D**, kitchen facilities, laundry, information on local trails, internet, cycle hire. Taxi US$1.30 from terminal. Highly recommended.

Cabañas

Plentiful *cabañas* are available in 2 main areas: up Perito Moreno on the hill to the north of town, and down by the lakeside. Prices increase in high season, but are good value for families or big groups.
Agua Escondida, Rhode 1162, T02972-422113, www.aguaescondida.com.ar. Very luxurious aparthotel, very comfortable, nicely designed, spacious apartments, great breakfasts, cosy, wood fires, internet access.
Antuen, Perito Moreno 1850, T/F02972-428340, www.interpatagonia.com/antuen.j Modern well equipped luxurious *cabañas* for 2-7, with jacuzzi, pool, games room for kids, with views from elevated position above the valley.
Arco Iris, Los Cipreses 1850, T02972-429450,www.arcoirisar.com. You couldn't wish for a warmer welcome in these comfortable and perfectly equipped, spotless *cabañas* in a quiet area of town. Beautifully situated, with their own access to the river, so you can fish before breakfast, or enjoy a drink on the water side in the evening. Each has 2 bathrooms, cosy living rooms with TV, and spacious kitchen. Friendly owners Ida and Hector Scagnetti are very knowledgeable about the area and incredibly helpful. Very good value at US$35 for 4 in high season. Highly recommended.
Eruizos, Perez 428, T02972-425856, www.eruizos.com.ar. Plainer *cabañas* in rustic but comfortable style.
La Encantada, Peritor Moreno y Los Enebrs, T/F02972-428364, www.laencantada.com. In a spectacular position above town in wooded surroundings, large, beautifully furnished cosy *cabañas* for 2 or more families, with all possible comforts, and pool, games room, fishing guides offered too.
Ojo de Agua, Perez 1198, T/F02972-427921, www.interpatagonia.com/ojodeagua. Well-equipped *cabañas* for 2-7, more like little urban chalet-style houses, crammed next to each other in quiet part of town near the lake.

Camping

ACA, Koessler 2176 (on the access road), T02972-429430. Hot water, laundry facilities.
Catritre, Route 234, Km 4. On the southern shore of the lake, T02972-428820. Good facilities in a gorgeous position on the shore.
Quila Quina, T02972-426919. A pretty spot and a peaceful place (out of peak season) with beaches and lovely walks, 18 km from San Martín. Recommended.

Estancias

A Estancia Lemu Cuyén, 60 km south via Lago Melinquina, T02972-428360, www.lemucuyen.comar. Chalet-style *cabañas* for rent and restaurant serving great food made by the owner-chef, great fishing, riding, and lovely forests for walks. *Cabaña* for 5, US$60.

Junín de los Andes *p425, map p429*

If there are several of you and you have your own transport, there are several new *cabaña* complexes; ask at the tourist office.
L Rio Dorado Lodge and Fly Shop, Pedro Illera 448, T/F02972-491548, www.riodorado.com.ar. Expensive fishing lodge, with comfortable, spacious rooms in log-cabin style, with huge beds and private bathrooms, lovely gardens and attentive service. Big 'American' breakfast included. Good fly shop.
B San Jorge, at the very end of Antártida Argentina, Chacra 54, T/F02972-491147, www.7lagos.com/ hotelsanjorge. Open Nov-Apr. A big, recently modernized 1960's hotel, beautifully located with lovely views and large gardens, homely well furnished rooms, all with bath and TV. Very good value, with good restaurant and internet access. English spoken. Recommended.
C Hostería Chimehuín, tucked away at the end of the road by the river on Suárez y 25 de Mayo, T02972-491132, www.hosteriachimehuin.com.ar. The best value choice in town, a long-established classic fishing

hostería with beautiful gardens, and friendly owners, quaint cosy decor, and comfortable rooms all with bath and TV. Ask for the spacious newer rooms with balconies in the block next to the river. Good breakfasts, open all year. Recommended.

C Milla Piuke, set back from the road RN 234, at Gral Roca y Av los Pehuenes, T/F02972-492378, millapiuke@ fronteradigital.net.ar. Absolutely delightful and welcoming *hostería*, with tastefully decorated and stylish rooms all with bath and TV, and apartments for families, very warm hospitality from the radiant owner Vilma. Breakfast included. Highly recommended.

D Posada Pehuén, Col Suárez 560, T02972- 491569, posadapehuen@ fronteradigital.net.ar. A lovely quiet bed and breakfast with pretty, rather old-fashioned rooms, all rooms with TV and bathroom, charming owners, good value.

E Res Marisa, Juan Manual de Rosas 360, T02972-491175, residencialmarisa@ deandes.com.ar. A simple place, and the best value in town, with plain clean rooms with TV and bathroom, and cheery family owners. *Confitería* downstairs, but breakfast is US$1 extra. It's on the main road, so a little noisy during the day, but handy for the bus terminal and cheap eating places.

Camping

There are many sites in the area with 2 good ones in town:

La Isla, T02972-492029. Also on the river. US$2.30 pp.

Mallin Laura Vicuña, Ginés Ponte 861, T02972-491149, campinglv@ jandes.com.ar, on the river, with hot showers, electricity, small shop, discounts for stays over 2 days, also very good value *cabañas* for 4-7.

Junín de los Andes

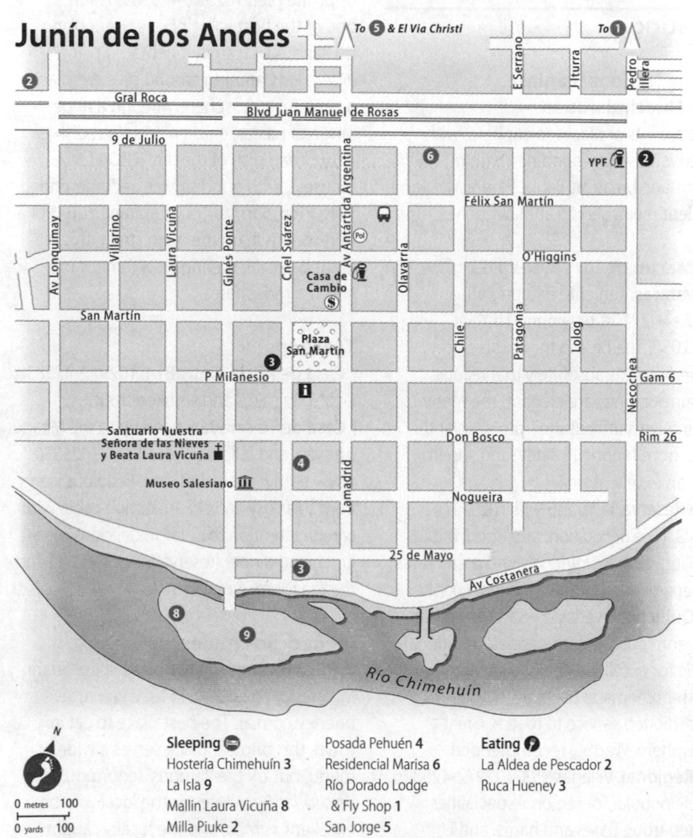

Sleeping
Hostería Chimehuín 3
La Isla 9
Mallin Laura Vicuña 8
Milla Piuke 2
Posada Pehuén 4
Residencial Marisa 6
Río Dorado Lodge & Fly Shop 1
San Jorge 5

Eating
La Aldea de Pescador 2
Ruca Hueney 3

Estancias

L **Estancia Huechahue**, north of town, off RN 234 (reached from the Junín-Bariloche bus), T02972-491303, www.huechahue.com. The best riding in the lake district can be experienced at this marvellous self-sufficient, traditional Patagonian *estancia*, where Jane Williams breeds horses, and cattle, and welcomes guests to stay in very comfortable wooden cabins. Evenings are spent dining together with delicious food and plentiful wine. There's unbeatable horse riding into Parque Nacional Lanín, as well as watching condors and exploring the beautiful wilderness nearby, cattle mustering for the adventurous, or longer pack trips over the mountains to Chile. Superb horses, great *asados* in the open air, even a jacuzzi under the stars to rest tired muscles. The atmosphere is lively and welcoming, the riding exhilarating. Highly recommended.

Eating

Parque Nacional Lanín: Lago Huechulafquen *p418*

There are lots of places to eat here, with *provedurías*, selling good *pan casero*, homemade bread, at Bahía, Piedra Mala and excellent meals served at Mawizache.

San Martín de los Andes *p423, map p423*

TTT **Avataras**, Teniente Ramon 765, T02972- 427104, only open Thu-Sat from 2030. The best in town, this pricey, inspired place is absolutely marvellous. The surroundings are elegant, the menu imaginative, with cuisine from all over the world, from fondue to satay, and superb wine, an excellent treat.

TTT **La Reserva**, Belgrano 940, T02972-428743. Nice decoration, tasty food, but appalling service. Unfriendly and pretentious. Be prepared for a long wait: bring a book.

TT **El Quincho**, Rivadavia y San Martín. An excellent, much-recommended traditional *parrilla* for excellent steaks, also offering superb homemade pasta, with good old-fashioned service to match. Great atmosphere. Warmly recommended.

TT **El Regional**, Villegas 953, T02972-425326. Hugely popular for regional specialities – smoked trout, pâtés and hams, and El Bolsón's homemade beer, all in cheerful German-style decor.

TT **La Tasca**, M Moreno 866, T02972-428663. A great atmospheric family restaurant with superb food, and a wonderful wine list of good Argentine wines, perfect with their tasty picadas. Fascinating paintings and bottles line the wood panelled walls. The food is traditional but with something extra, and the smoked boar and trout-filled pasta are both excellent. Friendly service. Recommended.

TT **Pura Vida**, Villegas 745. The only vegetarian restaurant in town, small and welcoming, also serves fish and chicken dishes.

T **Ku**, San Martín 1053, T02972-427039. An intimate *parrilla*, also serving delicious homemade pastas and superb mountain specialities. Excellent service and wine list.

T **La Costa del Pueblo**, on the *costanera* opposite pier, T02972-429289. This is one of the best value places overlooking the lake. A big family-orientated place, where kids running around give the place a cheerful atmosphere, offering a huge range of pastas, chicken and trout dishes. Very cheap dish of the day (US$4 for 2 courses), with good service, recommended.

T **Tio Pico**, San Martin y Capitan Drury. For a drink or lunch on the main street, this is a great bar-café, serving tasty *lomitos* in a warm atmosphere.

Teashops

T **Casa de Alicia**, Drury 814, T02972-425830. Delicious cakes and smoked trout.

T **Casa de Té Arrayán**, head up to the Mirador Arrayán, and follow signs, T02972- 425570, www.tenriverstenlakes.com. Fabulous views from this cosy and chic-rustic log cabin with careful attention to detail in delicious meals, lunch and dinner (reservations essential) and the tea room. A real treat.

Junín de los Andes *p425, map p429*

TT **Ruca Hueney**, on the plaza at Col Suárez y Milanesio, T02972-491113, www.ruca-hueney.com.ar. The best place to eat in town, this popular place serves a wide menu, but try the 'famous' (enormous) *bife de chorizo Ruca Hueney*, the local wild boar, excellent *parrilla*, and the locally caught trout: all are delicious. Also Middle eastern dishes US$10 for 2 courses. Great atmosphere, and wonderful old-fashioned service. Highly recommended.

La Aldea de Pescador, RN 234 y Necochea, on the main road by the YPF station. This is great place for *parrilla* and trout, very cheap.

La Posta de Junín, Rosas 160 (RN 234), T02972-492303. Good steaks, local trout, tasty home made pastas and good wine list. Also take away.

Festivals and events

Junín de los Andes *p425, map p429*

Jan At the end of the month is the Agricultural show and exhibition of flowers and local crafts.

Feb The Fiesta Provincial de Puestero in mid-Feb sees the election of the queen, handicrafts, *asados* with local foods and fabulous gaucho riding, the most important country fiesta in the south of Argentina.

Mar Carnival.

Jul Festival of aboriginal arts, mid-month.

Nov Opening of the fishing season, 2nd Sat.

Dec Inauguration of the church of Laura Vicuña, with a special mass on the 8th and singing to celebrate the life of Laura Vicuña.

Shopping

San Martín de los Andes *p423, map p423*

A great place for shopping, with chic little shops selling clothes and handmade jumpers, and a handicraft market in summer in Plaza San Martín. Lots of outdoor shops on San Martín sell clothes for walking and skiing.

Aquaterra, Villegas 795, T02972-429797. Outdoor equipment and clothing.

La Oveja Negra, San Martín 1025, T02972-428039. Wonderful handmade scarves and jumpers, esoteric crafts to a high standard, interesting souvenirs.

Mountain Ski Shop, San Martín 861.

Nomade, San Martín 881. Outdoor gear and camping equipment.

There are 2 recommended places for chocolates, among the many on San Martín: **Mamusia**, No 601, T02972-427560, which also sells homemade jams, and **Abuela Goye**, No 807, T02972- 429409, which also serves excellent ice creams.

Junín de los Andes *p425, map p429*

Crafts stalls behind the tourist office sell good-quality local weavings and wood work.

Patagonia Rodeo, Padre Milanesio 562, 1st floor, T01972-492839. A traditional shop selling what real gauchos wear in the field, plus quality leather work: belts, wallets, saddlery. Look like the real thing before you turn up at the *estancias*.

Activities and tours

San Martín de los Andes *p423, map p423*

Cycling

Many places rent mountain and normal bikes along San Martín, all charging more or less the same.

Enduro Bikes, Elordi and Pto Moreno, T02972-427093.

HG Rodados, San Martin 1061, T02972-427345, hgrodados@smandes.com.ar, rents mountain bikes at US$8 per day, also sells spare parts and offers expertise.

Fishing

The season runs from mid-Nov to May. For guides contact the tourist office or the park office. See www.turismo.gov.ar/pesca, www.neuquentur.gov.ar/guias2.htm or send an email to camguiasneuquen@ smandes.com.ar for more information in English. The following outlets sell equipment and offer fishing excursions: **Fly Shop**, Pedro Illera 378, T02972-491548; **Jorge Cardillo Pesca Fly shop**, Villegas 1061, T02972-428372; **Los Notros**, P Milanesio y Lamadrid, T02972-492157; **Orvis Fly shop**, Gral Villegas 835, T02972-425892; **Patagonian Anglers**, M Moreno 1193, T02972-427376, patagoniananglers@ smandes.com.ar. **Rosario Aventura**, Av Koessler 1827, T02972-429233.

Flying

Aeroclub de los Andes, T02972-426254, aeroclubandes@smandes.com.ar. For flights in light aircraft.

Skiing

Chapelco has 29 km of pistes, many of them challenging, with an overall drop of 730 m. Very good slopes and snow conditions make this a popular resort with foreigners and wealthy Argentines. At the foot of the mountain are a restaurant and base lodge, with 3 more restaurants on the mountain and a small café at the top. To get to the slopes, take the bus from San Martín, US$2 return, **Transportes Chapelco**, T02944-1561 8875. Details, passes, equipment hire from office at San Martín y Elordi, T02972-427845, www.sanmartindelosandes.gov.ar.

Tour operators

Many are advertised on a helpful board in tourist information. These are the most professional (prices quoted are standard):
El Claro, Coronel Díaz 751, T02972-429363, www.interpatagonia.com/elclaro. Trips to the lakes, and also paragliding, horse riding, and other adventure trips.
El Refugio, Access from upstairs on C Pérez 830, just off San Martín, T02972-425140, www.elrefugioturismo.com.ar. Excellent company with friendly bilingual guides, offering conventional tours and boat trips: visiting Lagos Huechulafquen and Paimún, US$18, Villa la Angustura via Seven Lakes US$18, Boat trip to Quila Quina US$12, mountain bike hire US$23 for the day, rafting at Hua Hum US$33 for the day, horse riding US$20, and trekking US$20. Lots more on offer. Recommended.
Lucero Viajes, San Martín 826, 2nd floor, office B, T02972-428453, www.lucero viajes.com.ar. Rafting at Hua Hum, horse riding, 4WD trips, and conventional tours to Hua Hum, Quila Quina, as well as selling ski passes in winter.

Junín de los Andes *p425, map p429*

Fishing

The season runs from 2nd Sat in Nov to May. For fly casting and trolling the best place are Lagos Huechulafquen, Paimún, Epulaufken, Tromen, Currehue, Rivers Chuimehuin, Malleo, Alumine, Quilquihue. See www.turismo.gov.ar/pesca for more information in English.
Alquimia Viajes and Turismo, Padre Milanesio 840, T02972-491355, www.alquimia turismo.com.ar. Offers fishing excursions, with expert local guides, among a range of adventure tourism expeditions, including climbing Lanín, climbing in rock and ice, rafting, and transfers.
Estancia Quillén, further north, at Aluminé, T02942-496196, www.interpatagonia.com/quillen/index.html. Offers fishing on the *estancia* as well as trips to rivers and lakes in the surrounding area.
Jorge Trucco, based in fly shop **Patagonia Outfitters** in San Martín de los Andes, Perez 662, T02972-427561, www.jorgetrucco.com. Expert and professional trips, good advice, and many years of experience on the lakes and rivers around.
Pesca Patagonia with Alejandro Olmedo, JM Rosas 60, T02972-491632, www.pesca patagonia.com.ar. Guides, tuition and equipment.
Río Dorado Lodge, Pedro Illera 448, T02972-491548, www.riodorado.com.ar. The luxury fishing lodge at the end of town has a good fly shop, and organizes trips, run by experts and passionate fishermen.

Tour operators

Alquimia Viajes and Turismo, Padre Milanesio 840, T02972-491355, www.alquimia turismo.com.ar. Offers fishing excursions, with expert local guides, among a range of adventure tourism expeditions, including climbing Lanín, climbing in rock and ice, rafting, and transfers.

Transport

San Martín de los Andes *p423, map p423*

Air

The nearest airport is Chapelco, 20 km away on RN 234, see Junín de los Andes, below.

Bus

Information, T02972-427044. The bus terminal is reasonably central, at Villegas and Juez del Valle, with all the usual services, luggage store, toilet facilities, kiosk, *locutorio*. Bikes can be carried on most routes, wheels removed, but consult first to be sure. To **Buenos Aires**, 20 hrs, US$55 *coche cama*, daily, 6 companies. To **Bariloche**, 3½ hrs (not via 7 Lakes Drive), US$8.30, many daily, via Bariloche, T02972-425325, **Albus**, T02972-428100, minibus along the 7 Lakes Drive via Traful and La Angostura, 4 hrs, US$7. **Ko Ko**, T02972-427422, daily, fast route via Confluencia. Over the border, **Koko** goes to Chile, via boat crossings to **Lago Pirehueico**, leaving Puerto Fuy at 1230 and boat leaving Pirehueico at 1600 daily (boat takes bikes US$1, cars US$5). **Puerto Madryn** (changing Neuquén) US$32. To **Neuquén** with Albus 2 daily, takes 6½ hrs, US$14.

To Chile **Temuco** with Empresa San Martín, T02972-427294, Mon, Wed, Fri, Igi-Llaima, T02972-427750, Tue, Thu, Sat, US$11, 6-8 hrs (heavily booked in summer), via Paso Hua Hum.

Boat

The boat which crosses the pass to Chile at Hua Hum also takes cars daily in summer from Puerto Fuy to Puerto Pirehueico tourist office in Panguipuli, T(63)311311, www.panguipuli.com.

Car hire

Hansen Rent a Car, San Martín 532, T02972-427997, www.hansenrentacar.com.ar. Reliable, friendly, and very professional company with excellent rates. Mario Hansen is very helpful. Recommended.
Hertz, San Martín 831, 1st floor, T02972-420820.
Nieves Rent a Car, Villegas 668, office 2, T02972-428684, nievesrentacar@smandes.com.ar.
Rent a Car La Patagonia, Villegas 305, T02972-421807.

Taxi

Eco Taxi, also known as Lacar, T02972-428817. Very helpful and efficient. If in town, find them on main street San Martín, or give Abuela Goye as useful meeting point.

Junín de los Andes *p425, map p429*

Air

Chapelco Airport, 19 km southwest on the road to San Martín de los Andes (can be reached by taking any bus to San Martín). Taxi US$10. Flights to **Buenos Aires**, Austral, LADE weekly from **Bahía Blanca**, **Esquel**, and **Bariloche**.

Bus

The terminal is at Olavarría y Félix San Martín (do not confuse with Gral San Martín), with public phone, and other basic facilities. Information T02972-492038. To **San Martín de los Andes**, 45 mins, US$4.50, several a day, Centenario, Ko Ko, Airén. To **Neuquén**, 7 hrs, US$23, several companies. Ask about buses to **Huechulafquen**; every year a different company. To **Tromen**, Mon-Sat 1½ hrs, US$5.50. To **Caviahue** and **Copahue**, change at Zapala. 3½ hrs, US$12. To **Bariloche**, 3 hrs US$9, Via Bariloche, Ko Ko. To **Buenos Aires**, 21 hrs, US$35, several companies. To **Chile**: Service Temuco (5 hrs) US$11 via Paso Tromen/Mamuil Malal , daily service with either Empresa San Martín 3 a week, Igi Llaima, 4 a week.

Directory

San Martín de los Andes *p423, map p423*

Banks Many ATMs along San Martín: Banelco, at the tourist office, San Martín 1093 y Rosas. **Banco Nación**, San Martín 687. Casas de cambio at **Banco de la Nación**, San Martín 687, **Andina Internacional Cambio y Turismo**, Cap. Drury 876. **Banco de la Provincia de Neuquén**, Obeid y Belgrano, also has ATM, T02972-427243. **Internet** Lots of broadband services, **Punto.Com**, inside *galería* at San Martín 866, **Punto.Net**, Galería Azul, **Terminal**, Vilegas 150. **Laundry** Laverap, Drury 880, daily 0800-2200. Marva, Drury y Villegas, and Perito Moreno 980. Fast, efficient and cheap. **Medical services** Hospital Ramón Carrillo, San Martín y Coronel Rodhe, T02972-427211. **Post office** General Roca y Pérez, Mon-Fri 0800-1300, 1700-2000, Sat 0900-1300. **Telephones** Cooperativa Telefónica, Drury 761, **Terminal**, Villegas 150.

Junín de los Andes *p425, map p429*

Banks TCs can be cashed at Western Union, Milanesio 570, 1000-1400, 1600-1930; and money changed at Banco Provincial Neuquén, San Martín y Lamadrid, also has ATM. **Internet** in the *galería* behind tourist office. The Parque Nacional Lanín office is in same building as tourist office, T02972- 491160, and is very helpful. **Post office** Suárez y Don Bosco. **Telephone** *Locutorío* near tourist office on plaza at Milanesio 540.

Pehuenia and northern Neuquén

At the northern end of the Lake District, Pehuenia is a wonderful expanse of unspoilt wilderness, which is only now opening up to visitors, around the picturesque villages of Villa Pehuenia and Moquehue. The area due west of Zapala, running along the border with Chile, is quite different from the southern lakes, thanks to its large forests of ancient pehuén, or araucaria – monkey puzzle trees. These magnificent silent forests exert a mysterious force, and give a prehistoric feel to the landscapes, while the sleepy backwaters feel of the villages makes them appealing for a few days' rest or gentle walking. Further north there are two little-visited tourist centres, useful stopping points if you're heading north to Mendoza. Caviahue is good for walking in rugged and unspoilt landscape or skiing in winter, while bleaker Copahue is known for its high-quality thermal waters. » *For Sleeping, Eating and other listings, see pages 438-440.*

Pehuenia » *pp438-440.*

→ *Phone code 02942*

The magical and unspoilt area of Pehuenia is named after the country's unique forests of *pehuén* trees, which grow here in vast numbers. Covering a marvellous open mountainous landscape, these ancient, silent trees create a mystical atmosphere, especially around the lakes of Aluminé and Moquehue, where a pair of small villages provide good accommodation. Villa Pehuenia is the best set up for tourism, with its picturesque setting on the lakeside, and a whole cluster of upmarket cabañas have opened here in recent years, with one exceptionally lovely boutique hotel, **La Escondida**. Moquehue is quite different in style: more sprawling and relaxed. There are more *cabañas*, excellent hiking up La Bella Durmiente, and good fly fishing. You'll need to hire a car to get the best out of the area. You can approach from Neuquén city, or, even closer, from Temuco over the border in Chile.

Villa Pehuenia

Getting there To reach Villa Pehuenia, it's best to hire a car. There are daily buses from Neuquén city via Zapala, but these take a long time, and once you're here you'll want to explore the area in your own transport. Consider approaching from Temuco in Chile, which is just 1½ hours across the border, or hire a car in Neuquén (3½ hours' drive) and drop it off in San Martín or Bariloche afterwards. Route 13 continues to the Paso de Icalma crossing to Chile, just a few kilometres from Villa Pehuenia, with easy access to Temuco, 130 km further, on the other side.

Getting around The centre of the village is just off the main road, Route 13, where you'll find a service station, *locutorios*, food and handicrafts shops and a pharmacy. There are two tour operators who can arrange trekking, boat trips on the lake and bike hire, and there is another area of restaurants and tea rooms by the lake side.

Tourist information There is a **tourist kiosk**ⓘ *off the main road, by the turning for Villa Pehuenia, T02942-498044, www.villapehuenia.gov.ar*, which, along with most hotels, has the excellent free leaflet showing a detailed map of Villa Pehuenia with all the hotels and restaurants marked. In March, the harvest of the *piñones* is celebrated in the **Fiesta del Pehuén** with horse-riding displays and live music.

Sights This pretty village on sprawling Lago Aluminé's northern shore, is picturesquely set amongst steep wooded hills, and makes a lovely base for a few days' relaxation or gentle walks in the hills and forests around. This is Mapuche land and was chosen for a settlement when the Mapuche were flushed out of Buenos Aires province in the late 19th century. It has special significance because eight volcanoes in a chain are visible from here, and because the area abounds with *pehuén* (monkey puzzle) trees, which are sacred to the Mapuche (see box on page 436). With the rapid building of *cabaña* complexes in recent years, tourism is slowly taking off here, and at the moment you have the best of both worlds: an unspoilt feel but enough tourist infrastructure to stay in comfort, with good restaurants the excellent hotel, **La Escondida**. Walk onto the peninsula stretching out into the lake from the village for wonderful walks along the araucaria-fringed shore, and up to the **Mirador del Cipres** with fabulous views.

There is skiing and winter sports at the **Parque de Nieve Batea Mahuida** winter sports area (turn right just a few kilometres further along the main road, signposted). This reserve was created to protect an area of *pehuén* trees and the majestic volcano Mahuida (1900 m) which is regarded by the Mapuche peoples as sacred. This sports area is one of the few businesses in the area run by Mapuche people, and is a lovely place for walking in summer, with tremendous views of all seven volcanoes around, and good for limited skiing in winter, with snowmobile and snowshoe walking. Delicious homecooked food is served. Contact the Mapuche Puel community at the entrance. It's a lovely walk up here (three hours), or one hour by bike.

Walks

For lovely walks through the araucaria forests, drive west from Villa Pehuenia towards Chile and continue 4 km further along the road until you reach the end of the lake, where you turn left at the *gendarmería*, following a dirt road across the bridge over a narrow strip of water, La Angostura. Follow the arrow to a campsite 50 m further on, **El Puente** (delightful: recommended). Continue past it and, when you come to a little hut and a sign to Lago Redonda, take the right fork and follow the track. Park or leave your bike at the the largest of the three small lagunas, and take the path due south when the track comes to an end at a farmstead by a large lagoon. Climb from here to a ridge with great views, and then take the path which drops and skirts around **Lago Moquehue**. Awe-inspiring. You could walk to Moquehue from here, but you need a map. Ask for the *Sendas y Bosques* map of Norte Neuqino, which shows the Pehuenia-Moquehue area, and some paths. This whole area is the heart of the Mapuche community: many houses offer *pan casero* (homemade bread), horse riding, or walking guides. Alternatively, head further north to the weird other worldly landscapes of **Paso de Arco**.

Lago Moquehue → *Phone code 0299*

Another 10 km on Route 13 brings you to the sprawling village of Moquehue. It's a wilder, more remote place than Villa Pehuenia, spreading out on the shores of its lake, with a lovely wide river. Famous for fishing, this is a beautiful and utterly peaceful place to relax and walk, and it has a less cultivated feel, inspiring adventurous treks. A short stroll through araucaria forests brings you to a lovely waterfall; a longer hike to the top of **Cerro Bandera** (four hours return) gives wonderful views over the area, and to Volcán Llaima. There are fine camping spots and a couple of comfortable places to stay.

Aluminé → *Population 5000 Colour map 5, A2 Phone code 02942*

In the splendid Aluminé Valley, on Route 23 between Pehuenia and Junín, lies the area's self-proclaimed rafting capital, the tiny town of Aluminé (see Activities and tours, page 440). There is indeed superb rafting (grades II or IV to VI, depending on rainfall) nearby on Río Aluminé. There are places to stay, but despite the lovely setting, it's a drab place with earth roads: far better to keep going to Villa Pehuenia unless you are here to go rafting. There's a very friendly **tourist office** ⓘ *C Christian Joubert 321, T02942-496001, www.alumine.net, daily 0800-2100 all year*. There's a service station too, the last before Villa Pehuenia.

Monkey puzzle trees

The stunningly beautiful area of Pehuenia is remarkable for its forests of araucaria, or monkey puzzle trees (Araucaria araucana). Growing slowly to a mighty 40 m high, the trees exert a powerful presence when seen en masse, perhaps because their forests are silent, moving little in the breeze. A true conifer, the araucaria is a descendent of the petrified pines found in Argentina's Bosques Petrificados. For centuries the pehuén or araucaria have been revered by indigenous peoples, and the local Mapuche still eat its pine nuts, rich in vitamins and fats. The custom of collecting their nuts, around which a whole array of foods, and a celebratory harvest festival are based, has been the source of a bitter territory dispute in parts of the northern Lake District. The Mapuche feel that they have a natural right to harvest the fruits of their trees, and local landowners, backed by local government, clearly don't agree.

In recent years though, there's a growing respect for the Mapuche in the area, and they are beginning to get involved in the provision of basic tourist services with great success. You'll see *pan casero* (homemade bread), *tortas fritas* (fried pastries) and handicrafts for sale on roadsides, as well as the fledgling winter sports centre near Villa Pehuenia, all run by Mapuche. These small enterprises enable them to survive financially, while retaining their traditions and customs, and with luck, access to the magnificent araucarias which they hold so sacred.

Rucachoroi

From Aluminé there is access to Lago Rucachoroi, 23 km west, the biggest Aigo Mapuche community inside the national park Lanín, in gentle farmland surrounded by ancient *pehuen* forests. Access is by a rough *ripio* road, best in a 4WD in winter, and spectacular in autumn when the deciduous trees are a splash of orange against the bottle green araucarias. The only accommodation is in two campsites, both offering Mapuche food, and horse riding. Here too, there's a *guardería* where you can ask about a possible trek to Lago Quillén. The landscape is very beautiful and you will want to linger, but bring provisions and camping gear. Private transport is essential.

Lago Quillén

At the junction by the small town of Rahue, 16 km south of Aluminé, a road leads west to the valley of the Río Quillén and the exquisite Lago Quillén, from where there are fine views of Volcán Lanín peeping above the mountains. The lake itself is one of the region's most lovely, jade green in colour, with beaches along its low-lying northern coast. Further west, where annual rainfall is among the heaviest in the country, the slopes are thickly covered with superb Andean Patagonian forest. There's no transport, and the only accommodation is at **Camping Pudu Pudu** (with food shop and hot showers) on the lake's northern shore, just west of the *guardería*. Here you can get advice about walks, and register with *guardaparques* if you plan to hike to Rucachoroi. There's another walk to the remote **Lago Hui Hui** 6 km north from the second campsite, (3½ hours return). For fishing, contact **Estancia Quillén** (see Sleeping, page 439).

Border crossings with Chile

Paso Pino Hachado (1864 m) lies 115 km west of Zapala via Route 22, which is almost completely paved. On the Chilean side a *ripio* road run northwest to Lonquimáy, 65 km west of the border. Temuco lies 145 km southwest of Lonquimáy. **Argentine immigration and customs** ⓘ *9 km east of the border, open 0700-1300, 1400-1900.*

Chilean immigration and customs ⓘ *Liucura, 22 km west of the border, Dec-Mar 0800-2100, Apr-Nov 0800-1900.* Very thorough searches and two- to three-hour delays reported. Buses from Zapala and Neuquén to Temuco use this crossing.

Paso de Icalma (1303 m) lies 132 km west of Zapala and is reached by Route 13 (*ripio*). On the Chilean side this road continues to Melipeuco, 30 km west of the border, and thence to Temuco. **Argentine immigration and customs** ⓘ *9 km east of the border, 0800-2100 in summer, 0900-1900 approximately in winter.* All paperwork to be carried out at the customs office, clearly signposted. **Chilean immigration and customs** ⓘ *Dec-Mar 0800-2100, Apr-Nov 0800-1900.*

Copahue and Caviahue » pp438-440.

→ *Phone code 02948 Colour map 3, C1*

The extraordinary landscape of **Reserva Provincial Copahue** at the heart of this region is formed by a giant volcanic crater, whose walls are the surrounding mountains. An arid, dramatic and other-worldly landscape, the park was created to protect the araucaria trees which grow on its slopes, and there are some wonderful walks that take you to unexpectedly stunning landscapes. About 150 km from Zapala, **Caviahue** is by far the most attractive of the two, with an appealing lakeside setting, and the best base for walking and horse riding; it converts into a skiing and winter sports centre from July to September. It has three ski lifts, excellent areas for cross-country skiing, snow-shoeing and snowmobiling, all with tremendous views, and it's one of cheaper resorts in the Lake District. **Copahue** (altitude 1980 m) is a thermal spa resort enclosed in a gigantic amphitheatre formed by mountain walls and boasting the best thermal waters in South America, though it's decidedly the bleaker of the two towns.

Ins and outs

Getting there Both towns are easily reached by public transport from Zapala, 150 km southeast, or by flying to Neuquén, 300 km southeast.

Tourist information In Caviahue, the **tourist office** is at ⓘ *8 de Abril, bungalows 5 and 6, T02948-495036, www.caviahue-copahue.com.ar.* For information on the thermal waters check out www.caviahuetours.com/esqui.htm. To find out about the ski centre, contact **Caviahue Base**, T02948-495079. There's an ATM at the *municipalidad*, several restaurants and a tea room, as well as some decent accommodation. In Copahue, the **tourist office** is on the approach road into town, Route 26.

Around Caviahue

The Volcán Copahue last erupted, smokily, in 2000, destroying the bright blue lake in its crater, but it's still a popular destination for horse riding, and the views of the prehistoric landscape are astounding. Most highly recommended, though, is **El Salto del Agrio**, 15 km northeast along Route 27. This is the climax in a series of delightful falls, approached by a road passing between tall, ancient araucaria trees poised on basalt cliffs; a wonderful excursion by horse to see all seven falls. Other fantastic walks in the area are to the extraordinary **Las Máquinas**, 4 km south of Copahue, where sulphurous steam puffs through air holes and against a panoramic backdrop, making the weirdest noises. And at **El Anfiteatro**, there are thermal waters reaching 150°, in a semicircle of rock edged with araucaria trees. Just above Copahue, there is a steep climb up to **Cascada Escondida**, a torrent of water falling 15 m over a shelf of basalt into a pool surrounded by a forest of araucaria trees; above it Lago Escondida is a magical spot.

Villa Pehuenia *p434*

There's one superb boutique hotel, and plenty of *cabañas*, many with good views over the lake and set in idyllic woodland. Email or ring first for directions, since there are no road names or numbers here.

AL La Escondida, western shore of the Península, T02942-1569 1166, www.posadalaescondida.com.ar. By far the best place to stay in the whole area, this is a really special boutique hotel, run with style by the welcoming and friendly Marcelo and Cristina, with just 9 rooms in an imaginatively designed building right on the rocky lakeside. Each room is spacious and beautifully considered, with smart bathrooms (all with jacuzzi), and private decks, all with gorgeous views over the lake. There are lovely places to sit all over the hotel, and the restaurant is superb. Really imaginative cuisine turns fine local produce into sensational delights with eclectic touches. Non-residents can dine here with a reservation. The whole place is relaxing and welcoming. Highly recommended.

A Altos de Pehuén, T02942-1566 6849, www.altosdepehuen.com.ar. Very comfortable *cabañas* with lovely views, and a *hostería* too.

A Complejo Patagonia, T02942-1557 9434, or in Buenos Aires T011-4637 9100, www.complejopatagonia.com.ar. Very comfortable indeed, these lovely *cabañas* are traditionally designed and the service is excellent. Recommended.

C Cabañas Bahía Radal, T02942-498057, bahiaradal@hotmail.com, on the peninsula (ask the tourist office for directions). Luxurious *cabañas*, with clear lake views from its elevated position.

C Cabañas Caren, T02942-1557 4133, www.cabanias.com/caren. Simple A-frame *cabañas*, but with open views and balconies, and made especially welcoming by the warm friendly owner Walter.

A-C Puerto Malén Club de Montaña, T02942-498007, T011-4226 8190 (Buenos Aires), www.puertomalen.com. Well built wooden *cabañas* with lake views from their balconies, and the highest quality interiors. Also a luxurious *hostería*. Recommended.

C Las Terrazas, T02942-498036, www.lasterrazaspehuenia.com.ar. Warmly recommended: the owner is an architect of Mapuche origin, who has retained Mapuche style in his beautiful design of these comfortable *cabañas*, tasteful, warm and with perfect views over the lake, with also **D** bed and breakfast. He can direct you to magical places for walking, and to Mapuche communities to visit.

D La Serena, T011-1547 940319, www.complejolaserena.com.ar. Beautifully equipped and designed *cabañas* with lovely uninterrupted view, gardens going down to beach, sheltered from wind, furnished with rustic-style handmade cypress furniture, and wood stoves, all very attractive.

Camping

Camping Agreste Quechulafquen, at the end of the steep road across La Angostura. Situated among lovely steep hills and dense vegetation, run by Mapuche Puels.

Camping El Puente, at La Angostura. US$2 pp, with hot showers, is a simpler site, in beautiful surroundings.

Las Lagrimitas, just west of the village, T02942-498003. A lovely secluded lakeside site on the beach, with food shop, US$2 pp, hot showers and fireplaces.

Lago Moquehue *p435*

C Hostería Restaurante Moquehue, set high above the lake with panoramic views, T02946-1566 0301, www.hosteriamoquehue.netfirms.com. Cosy, stylish, rustic rooms, nicely furnished with good views, and excellent food. Try the superb Moquehue trout and local *chivito*. Charming family hosts. Recommended.

D La Bella Durmiente, T0299-496172. In a rustic building with no heating, summer only, the welcoming owner offers good food and also offers trekking, horse riding, diving in lake, mountain bikes. Call for directions.

Cabañas

Along RN 13, 11 km to Lago Ñorquinco, past mighty basalt cliffs with *pehuéns* all around, there's idyllic camping. Also idyllic, reached by RN 11 are the smaller campsites of **Lagos Pilhué** and **Ñorquinco Camping**.

A Cabañas Los Maitenes, T0299-421681, T1566 5621, losmaitenes@infovia.com.ar.

Right on the lake, well-equipped *cabañas*, with breakfast included, and friendly owners. Recommended.

A La Busqueda, T0299-4481552, www.labusquedamoquehue.com.ar. Just north of the lake, before you reach the head of Lago Moquehue. Interesting design in these well-equipped *cabañas* with TV, including breakfast. Recommended

C-D Cabañas Melipal, T0299-432115. Very attractive, rustic stone-built *cabañas* in secluded sites right on lake side. Lovely old-fashioned style, well-equipped and warm, fabulous views from balcony, use of boats. Highly recommended.

D Cabañas Huerquen, T0299-1564700, huerquen_patagoni@hotmail.com. Beyond Moquehue on the road to Norquinco, these lovely secluded stone *cabañas* are in beautifully tranquil surroundings.

D Ecocamping Ñorquinco, T0299-496155, ecocamping@hotmail.com. There is one amazing rustic *cabaña* right on the lakeside, with a café by the roadside, $6.50 pp per night $3 for under 12, Dec or Mar, Apr to Easter. Great fishing, hot showers and a *proveduría*. This is a lovely place to eat and drink if it rains.

Camping

Good camping on the lake shores.

Camping Trenel, in a fabulous site elevated on the southern shore of Lago Moquehue, just beyond the Hostería Moquehue. Beautiful, well-kept shady sites in the thick of little *nirre* trees, with seats and *parrillas* overlooking lake, Recommended, smart, hot showers, good restaurant, food shop, information and excursions run by mountain trekking guide Fernando López.

Los Caprichosos, on Lago Ñorquinco. Open Nov-April only, with water and food shop.

Aluminé *p435*

A Estancia Quillén, RN 46 near Rahue, near the bridge crossing Río Aluminé, T02942-496196, www.interpatagonia.com/quillen/index.html. A comfortable, traditionally furnished house, with spacious rooms, and a restaurant, where you'll be welcomed by the estancia owners. Open Dec-Apr. Great for fishing and hunting.

C Pehuenía, just off RN 23 at Crouzeilles 100, T02942-496340, www.hotelpehuenia.com.ar. A huge tin chalet-style building, not attractive, but with great views over the hills opposite. The rooms are comfortable and simple, the staff are friendly, and it's good value; by far the town's best choice. Horse riding, bike hire and canoeing at the owner's campsite, **Bahía de los Sueños**, 6 km from the red bridge north of Aluminé.

D Aluminé, Joubert 336, T02942-496174, hosteriaalumine@hotmail.com. In the middle of town, opposite tourist information, this is a drab 1960's place, with clean, functional rooms. There's an excellent little restaurant next door, however, **La Posta del Rey**.

Camping

There are campsites all over the area.

La Vieja Balsa, T02942-496001, just outside of Aluminé on RN 23 on the Río Aluminé. A well-equipped site offering rafting and fishing, US$1 pp per day to camp, hot showers, shop, fireplaces, open Dec to Easter.

Rucachoroi *p436*

Camping

There are 2 sites: **Rucachoroi 1** or **Rucachoroi 1** (as they're called) are respectively before and after the lake; open all year, but really ideal only Dec-Feb. The first has more facilities, with toilets, but no hot water, some food supplies, including Mapuche homemade bread and sausages, and offers horse riding.

Copahue *p437*

A Aldea Termal, T0299-442 5605, www.aldeatermal.com. Very attractively decorated chalet-style wood and stone apartments. Recommended.

C Hotel Copahue, Olascoaga y Bercovich, T0299-495117. This lovely old place where you'll be warmly welcomed by Pocho and Moriconi is the most recommended place in Copahue. There are well built wood and stone *cabañas*, at **A-C** (depending on season).

Caviahue *p437*

B Lago Caviahue, Costanera Quimey-Co, T02948-495110, www.hotellago caviahue.com. Better value than the Nevado above; comfortable lakeside apartments with kitchen, also a good restaurant, great views, 2 km from the ski centre.

B Nevado Caviahue, 8 de Abril s/n, T02948-495042, www.caviahue.com. Plain rooms, but modern, and there's a restaurant, and

cosy lounge with wood fire. Also **A-B** for 6 *cabañas*, well-equipped but not luxurious.
C La Cabaña de Tito, Puesta del Sol s/n, T02948-495093. *Cabañas* near lake, excellent meals.
C Farallon, Caviahue Base, T02948-495085. Neat apartments, some with kitchens.

Camping
Copahue, T02948-495111, Hueney Municipal.

Eating

Villa Pehuenia *p434*
TTT La Escondida, on the western shore of the Península, T02942-1557 0420, www.posadalaescondida.com.ar. By far the best in town. Only open to non-residents with a reservation, this is really special cuisine, all local ingredients, imaginatively prepared and served. Highly recommended.
TT Anhedonia, on the lakeside, T02942-1566 9866. Fondue, beef and pasta.
TT Gnaien Chocolateria and tea room, on the lakeside, T02942-498082. Good for tea, with lovely views of the lake, chocolate delicacies, picadas and range of wines.
TT La Cantina del Pescador, on the lakeside, T02942-498086. Fresh trout.
T Costa Azul, on the lakeside, T02942-498035. Tasty local dishes and pasta; *chivito* (kid) *al asado* is the speciality of the house.

Aluminé *p435*
T La Posta del Rey, next to the service station, opposite the plaza, Cristian Joubert, T02942-496248. The best place by far, with friendly service, great trout and local kid, delicious pastas, sandwiches. Recommended.

Caviahue *p437*
T Copahue Club Hotel, Valle del Volcán. Serves good *chivito al asado* and local trout.
T Hotel Lago Caviahue. The most stylish place to eat with an inspired *chivo a la cerveza* (kid cooked in beer) on the menu, along with more traditional favourites and local specialities.

Activities and tours

Villa Pehuenia *p434*
Los Pehuenes, T02942-498029, www.lospehuenesturismo.com. Excellent company offering wide range of excursions and adventures, from trekking in the mountains, to rafting (US$30, for full day, grade 4), horse riding (US$30 for full day with lunch), visits to the local Mapuche communities, with kid *asado*, and fascinating local history and culture, fishing and boat trips. Professional, helpful and friendly. Ask for Fernando. Can also arrange transfers to Pehuenia from San Martín and Neuquén.

Aluminé *p435*
Aluminé Rafting, Ricardo Solano, T02942-496322. US$9-15, depending on grade of difficulty, for 3 hrs rafting, grades 2-6. All equipment included. **Circuito Abra Ancha** 2½ hrs, grade 2, 6 km, very entertaining, suitable for everyone. **Circuito Aluminé Superior**, 12 or 15 km run, 5-6 hrs, grade 3/4, very technical river leaving Lago Alumine, for those who like a thrill, passing little woods of araucarias and nirres, family trips grades 1 and 2, costs US$20 pp for Abra Ancha, US$60 pp for higher level. Trekking US$80 per day, trekking in Cordon de Chachil, US$120 per day, 2 days minimum, but can be up to a week, also kayaking, and biking.

Caviahue *p437*
Caviahue Tours, San Martín 623, Buenos Aires, T02948-4314 1556. Good information on the region.

Transport

Villa Pehuenia *p434*
There are 3 buses weekly to Villa Pehuenia and **Moquehue** from **Neuquén** (less predictable in winter, when the roads are covered in snow) and **Aluminé**, 5½ hrs.

Aluminé *p435*
There are buses daily to and from Zapala, with either **Aluminé Viajes** (T02942-496231), or **Albus** (T02942-496368), 3 hrs, US$4.50. Twice a week to **Villa Pehuenia**, 1 hr, US$2.50. Twice a week to **San Martín de los Andes**, 4 hrs, US$7, with **Tilleria**, T02942-496048.

Caviahue *p437*
Bus
To/from **Neuquén**, El Petroleo and **Centenario**. Daily, 6 hrs, US$13, via Zapala (US$7). **El Centenario**, T02948-495024.

Western Neuquén

The northern half of the Lake District falls into the province of Neuquén, encompassing an enormous region from just north of Bariloche to beyond Copahue and Caviahue, and ending at the border with Mendoza. The provincial capital is the pleasant modern city of Neuquén, centre of an important fruit-growing area, providing most of Argentina's apples, pears and grapes. You're likely to stop off only briefly here on the way to greater adventures in the mountains further west, but it's worth making time for a brief encounter with dinosaurs at several sites easily reached from Neuquén city. There are incredibly huge dinosaur footprints at Villa El Chocón, and you'll want to see the skeleton in the museum there as proof that the hugest carnivores ever known actually stomped around these lands 100 million years ago. You could also try a spot of excavation yourself at Valle Cretacico, and not only dinosaur fans will be impressed by the skeleton of the largest herbivorous dinosaur on earth in Plaza Huincul. *» For Sleeping, Eating and other listings, see pages 445-446.*

Neuquén city and around » *pp445-446.*

→ *Phone code: 0299 Colour map 5, A3 Population: 260,000*

The provincial capital is at the eastern tip of the province of Neuqúen, an attractive industrial town, founded in 1904, just after the arrival of the railway. It's on the opposite side of the Río Neuquén from Cipolletti, a prosperous centre of the Río Negro fruit-growing region and while it has no major tourist attractions, it's a useful stopping point for the lakes, but it's also a good base for exploring the dinosaur finds in the area to the immediate southwest. There's even a *bodega* you can visit: **Bodega del Fin del Mundo** ⓘ *RN 8, Km 9, near San Patricio de Chañar, T0299-485 5004, turismo@bdfm.com.ar, Mon-Fri 1000-1600, weekends and bank holidays 1000-1700*. Free tours take an hour and include a tasting.

Ins and outs

Getting there There are daily flights from Buenos Aires to the airport 7 km west of town, T0299-444 0245. Take a local bus into town for US$0.40 (*tarjeta* bus card needed), or taxi US$6. There are frequent long-distance buses to the central terminal at Mitre 147 from Buenos Aires and towns throughout the Lake District as well as north to Mendoza and west to Chile. No terminal number, but useful companies are: **Andesmar,** T0299-442 2216, and **Via Bariloche** T0299-442 7054.

Getting around The town can easily be explored on foot in a few hours, with most hotels and restaurants around the main street Avenida Argentina, which runs north from the disused railway track running east-west across the town, just south of Gral San Martín. Don't get confused with the street Félix San Martín, three blocks further south.

Tourist information The **tourist office** ⓘ *Félix San Martín 182, T0299-442 4089, www.neuquentur.gov.ar, turismo@neuquen.gov.ar, Mon-Fri 0700-2200, Sat-Sun 0800-2000*, provides helpful lists of accommodation and a map.

Sights

At the northern end of Avenida Argentina at the Parque Centenario there is the **Mirador Balcon del Valle** with panoramic views over the city and the confluence of the rivers (be sure not to take the bus to Centenario industrial suburb). In the university buildings at the entrance of the park is the **Museo Paleontológico de Ciencias**

Naturales ⓘ *Argentina 1400*, which includes exhibitions of dinosaur fossils found in the region. The **former railway station**, at Olascaoga y Pasaje Obligado, has been converted into a cultural centre and exhibition centre. South of the centre there is also a pleasant walk along the Río Limay. Facing Neuquén and connected by bridge is **Cipolletti**. All the towns in the valley celebrate the **Fiesta Nacional de la Manzana** (apples are the main local crop) in the second half of March.

Routes to the lakes

From Neuquén, there are various ways to approach the lakes. An attractive route involves continuing due west to Zapala on the Route 22, and then south to Junín de los Andes on Route 40. Or from Zapala, you could continue west to Villa Pehuenia, or north to Caviahue and Copahue. For the direct route to Bariloche, Route 237, via **Piedra del Aguila** and the astounding scenery of the **Valle Encantado**, with mountains whipped into jaggy peaks rising surprisingly from rolling scrubby land, and Río Limay appears, a mysterious milky turquoise as it flows into Embalse Alicura (dammed lake), and rocks are stacked up high, eroded into fantastical shapes. The road continues to Lago Nahuel Huapi where there are fine views over Cerros Catedral and Tronador.

West of Neuquén » *pp445-446.*

To the southwest of Neuquén lies the huge lake **Embalse Ezequiel Ramos Mexía** in an area which has become famous in recent years for the wealth of dinosaur fossils found here from the Cretacic period (100 million years ago). There are a number of places where you can see the finds, and even walk close to the footsteps of dinosaurs, and although the towns themselves are not appealing, they could make convenient stopping points along the road from Neuquén to the lakes, with a good museum at Villa El Chocón. You can even take part in dinosaur excavation at the Centro Paleontológico at Lago Barreales.

Villa El Chocón and around → *Phone code 0299 Colour map 5, A3*

Your only reason to visit Villa El Chocón at the northern end of Lago Ezequiel Ramos Mexía, 72 km from Neuquén, is to see the remains of dinosaurs. It's a neat, rather uninspiring town, a strictly functional place built for workers on the hydroelectric dam, but worth a stop for the amazing evidence of **dinosaurs**: take Route 237 towards Piedra del Aguila, and turn left at Barrio Llanquén, where indicated, to the lake shore. Red sedimentary rocks have preserved, in relatively good condition, bones and even footprints of the creatures which lived in this region during the Cretaceous period about 100 million years ago. For information on how to reach the footprints, and how they were formed, see www.interpatagonia.com/paseos/huellas/index_i.html. Some of the fossils can be seen in the **Museo Paleontológico Ernesto Bachmann** ⓘ *civic centre, El Chocón, T0299-490 1223, daily 0900-1900 winter 0800-2100 summer*. Guides in museum give very good tours. See also www.interpatagonia.com/paseos/ernestobachmann/index_i.html, for more information in English. Exhibits include fossils of the mighty 10-ton, 15-m long *Gigantosaurus carolinii*, a carnivorous dinosaur larger than the more famous *Tyrannosaurus rex*. There's a well laid-out and informative display with information on these quite mind-boggling finds. Alejandro París of **Aventura Jurásica** ⓘ *El Chocón, T299-490 1243*, offers guided two- to three-hour visits to the museum and surroundings from US$3 pp not including transfers.

Excavation at Valle Cretacico

The lunar landscape around Villa El Chocón is rather amazing and contains surprising amounts of dinosaur remains. So much so that an area has been named 'Cretacious Valley'. The website www.interpatagonia.com/paseos/valle_cretacico1/index_i.html,

Walking with dinosaurs

Few countries are as important as Argentina for palaeontologists. The relative abundance of fossils near the surface has made the country one of the most important for the study of dinosaur evolution. The Ischiqualasto and Talampaya parks (San Juan and La Rioja respectively) have yielded rich evidence of dinosaurs from the Triassic period (225-180 million years ago), among them, the small *Eoraptor lunensis*, 220 million years old. Ask your Ischigualasto tour guide to find some fossilized dinosaur bones for you to hold: quite a sensation.

Patagonia was home to Jurassic dinosaurs (180-135 million years old), with some outstanding examples found here: Cerro Cóndor in Chubut is the only site of Middle Jurassic dinosaurs found in the Americas, and has given palaeontologists an important breakthrough in understanding the evolutionary stages of the period. Finding five examples of *patagosaurus* indicated that these dinosaurs were social creatures, perhaps uniting for mutual defence. In Santa Cruz, traces of dinosaurs from the Upper Jurassic period have been found in rocks which indicate that the climate was arid and desert-like at the time, surprising palaeontologists with the news that dinosaurs could live and breed in such adverse conditions.

Head for Neuquén and Chubut, where the most important discoveries of dinosaurs from the Cretacic period (135-70 million years ago) have been made. Dating from the period of separation of the continents of South America and Africa, these provide evidence of the way in which dinosaurs began to evolve differently due to geographic isolation. The *Carnotaurus sastrie* has horns and small hands, for example, whereas the Patagonian dinosaurs are huge. The carnivorous *Gigantosaurus carolinii*, found near Neuquén city, was larger even than the better known *Tyranosaurus Rex*, discovered in North America. You'll find huge dinosaur footprints, eerily well-preserved, near Villa Chocón, southwest of Neuquén city, and more finds in the local museum. You can even take part in excavation at a site in 'Cretacious Valley', and there are remains of the largest herbivorous dinosaur on earth at Plaza Huincul's famous museum. Trelew on the Atlantic coast, has the country's finest dinosaur museum, and there's an excellent site with 40 million years of history near the Welsh village of Gaiman: www.interpatagonia.com has great information in English.

has information in English. The valley lies 18 km south of Villa El Chocón, near the Dique and has improbably shaped pedestals of eroded pink rock coming out of the blue water. There are two walks beside the lake to see the dinosaur footprints, which are amazingly well preserved.

If you're really into dinosaurs, you should consider visiting the **Centro Paleontológico at Lago Barreales**, T15-4048614, where you can even take part in dinosaur excavation. A team of paleontologists is currently working on a large site, where some 30 fossils of dinosaur vertebrates have already been found, some of them belonging to a small dinosaur so far unnamed. Leave Neuquén on Route 7 and then take Route 51 towards Añelo. Before reaching this district, and after having passed Lake Mari Menuco, you'll find Lake Barreales. The entrance to the paleontological centre is located in the detour towards the lake. For more information and pictures visit www.interpatagonia.com/paseos/megaexcavacion_dinosaurios/index_i.html.

Plaza Huincul → *Colour map 5, A2 Population: 11,000*

There are more dinosaur remains at a quite impressive little museum in the otherwise rather dull town of **Plaza Huincul**. The road to Zapala, Route 22, leaves Neuquén and passes through the fruit-growing region of the Río Limay and the much duller oil-producing zone. Situated 107 km west of Neuquén, Plaza Huincul was the site of the country's first oil find in 1918. The **Museo Municipal Carmen Funes** ⓘ *on the way into Plaza Huicul, at the crossing of RN22 y RP17, T0299-496 5486 for opening times*, includes the vertebrae of *Argentinossaurus huinclulensis*, believed to have weighed over 100 tons and to have been one of the largest herbivorous dinosaurs ever to have lived on earth, as well as a nest of fossilized dinosaur eggs. It's mainly a centre for research, and you can see the results of the fieldwork in fossils, photographs and videos, as well as the skeletons themselves. For information in English, see: www.interpatagonia.com/paseos/carmen_funes/index_i.html.

Zapala → *Phone code: 02942 Colour map 5, A2 Population: 35,000*

Zapala (1012 m) lies in a vast dry plain with views of snow-capped mountains to the west. It's a modern and rather unappealing place, but you'll need to stop here if you want to take buses to Pehuenia, Copahue and Caviahue, or to cross the border into Chile at the Icalma Pass. There is a **tourist information** ⓘ *San Martín y Mayor Torres, T02942-421132, (summer) Mon-Fri 0700-1930, Sat-Sun 0800-1300, 1600-1900, closes earlier off-season.*

The **Museo Mineralógico Dr Juan Olsacher** ⓘ *Etcheluz 52 (next to the bus terminal), neumin@zapala.com.ar, Mon 0900-1500, Sat, Sun 1600-2000, free,* is one of the best fossil museums in South America; it contains over 2000 types of mineral and has the finest collection of fossils of marine reptiles and marine fauna in the country. On display is the largest turtle shell from the Jurassic period ever found and an ophthalmosaur, as well as photos of an extensive cave system being excavated nearby.

Parque Nacional Laguna Blanca → *Colour map 5, A2*

Covering 11,250 ha at altitudes of between 1200 m and 1800 m, this park is one of only two reserves in the Americas created to protect swans and is 35 km southwest of Zapala. This is a rare example of high arid steppe, and its 1700-ha lagoon is one of the most important nesting areas of the black-necked swan in Argentina. Other bird life includes several duck species, plovers, sandpipers, grebes and Chilean flamingos, with birds of prey such as the red-backed hawk and the peregrine falcon nesting on the steep slopes of the laguna. It's best visited in spring, when young can be watched at many sites around the laguna. The landscape is indeed very dry, and rather bleak, with fierce winds, encouraging only the lowest and most tenacious plant life. A rough track runs round the lake, suitable for 4WD vehicles only. Nearby the **Arroyo Ñireco** has eroded the volcanic rock to form a deep gorge, and it's worth seeking out a small cave, inhabited in pre-historic times, with cave paintings. Southwest of the park Route 46 continues through the spectacular Bajada de Rahue, dropping 800 m in under 20 km before reaching the town of Rahue, 120 km southwest of Zapala.

Park information The park entrance is 10 km from the junction of Route 46, (which runs across the park) with Route 40. The laguna itself lies 5 km beyond this. There's no public transport, so without your own vehicle the only option is a tour from Zapala. There's a *guardería* post near the southeast corner of the laguna, with a visitors' centre and picnic area. Take drinking water and a hat for the heat. There's a hiking trail which takes in 10 lagoons in all Entry US$2. Free camping by the *guardaparque*, otherwise Zapala has the nearest accommodation, see www.parquesnacionales.gov.ar.

Sleeping

Neuquén *p441*
AL Hotel del Comahue, Av Argentina 377, T0299-443 2040, www.hoteldelcomahue.com.ar. The most comfortable by a long way is this international-style, elegant modern 4-star, with spa and pool, an excellent restaurant, very good service and facilities.
B Amucan, Tucumán 115, corner with Rivadavia, T0299-442 5209, www.amucanhotel.com.ar. Smart modern place with nice rooms and good breakfast.
C Alcorta, Alcorta 84, T0299-442 2652. Also flats for 4, breakfast, TV in rooms, good value.
C Royal, Av Argentina 143, T0299-448 8902, www.royalhotel.com.ar. A smart modern hotel, not grand or luxurious, but with welcoming rooms, car parking and breakfast included, good value.

Camping
There's no site in the town.
Las Araucarios, 16 km away, before Plottier on RN22. Enjoythe activities of the *chacra* (farm) and pool, a great place for kids.

Villa El Chocón and around *p442*
B La Posada del Dinosaurio, on the lakeshore in Villa El Chocón, Costa del Lago, Barrio 1, T0299-490 1200, www.posadadinosaurio.com.ar. Convenient for dinosaur hunting, a modern place with plain but comfortable modern rooms, all with views over the lake, and a restaurant.
D La Villa, Club Municipal El Chocón, T0299-490 1252. The only decent budget choice.

Camping
Club Chocón Lauquen, T156-318719.
Las Flores, T0299-490 1155.

Plaza Huincul *p444*
C Hotel Tortorici, Cutral-Co, 3 km west, Av Olascoaga y Di Paolo, T0299-496 3730, www.hoteltortorici.com. The most comfortable option is this newly built hotel with neat rooms, a restaurant, which can arrange golf on a nearby course.

Zapala *p444*
A Hostal del Caminante, 13 km south of Neuquén towards Zapala,T02942-444 0118. Popular in summer, with pool and garden.
C Hue Melén, Brown 929, T02942-422414. Good value 3-star hotel, with decent rooms, and a good restaurant serving the town's best food, including local specialities.
C Huincul, Av Roca 311, T02942-431422. A spacious place with a cheap restaurant, serving good homemade regional food.
D Coliqueo, Etcheluz 159, T02942-421308. Conveniently opposite the bus terminal, if the 2 options above are full (unlikely).
D Pehuén, Elena de Vega y Etcheluz, T02942-423135. Comfortable, 1 block from bus terminal. Interesting display of local maps.

Camping
Hostería Primeros Pinos, RP13, T02942-422637 primerospinos@yahoo.com.ar. Municipal site.

Eating

Neuquén *p441*
TT 1900 Cuatro, at the Comahue Hotel, Av Argentina 377. Posh and a little pricey, but serves superb food.
T Anonima, corner of Av Olascoaga y Félix San Martín. This supermarket has a good *patio de comidas* (food hall), and games to amuse the kids.
T El Reencuentro, Alaska 6451. A popular *parrilla* recommended for delicious steaks in a warm atmosphere.
T Fatto Dalla Mama, 9 de Julio 56. Fabulous filled pasta.
T La Birra, Santa Fe 23. Lots of choice and very welcoming, with chic modern surroundings.
T Rincón de Montaña, 9 de Julio 435. Recommended for delicious local specialities and cakes.
T Tutto al Dente, Alberdi 49. Recommended for tasty homemade pasta.

Cafés
There are lots of cheap cafés opposite the bus terminal on Mitre. The following are recommended.
Café El Buen Pan, Mitre y Corrientes, open 0600-2300. A bright modern place for snacks and good bakery too.
El Patagonia, Bartolomé Mitre between Corrientes y Río Negro. *Lomitos* and sandwiches, with cheap(ish) deals.

Living Room, Pte Rivadaria. A lovely comfortable bar-café, with armchairs and table outside, a great place to relax.

Zapala *p444*
See Sleeping, above, for hotel restaurants.
El Chancho Rengo, Av San Martín y Etcheluz, T02942-422795. This is where all the locals hang out.

Activities and tours

Neuquén *p441*
Gondwana Tour, Córdoba 599 T0299-496 3355, geoda@copelnet.com.ar. Excursions to dinosaur sites nearby, and accommodation.

Zapala *p444*
Mali Viajes, Alte Brown 760, T02942-432251.
Monserrat Viajes y Turismo, Etcheluz 101, T02942-422497.

Transport

Neuquén *p441*
Air
The airport is located 7 km west of centre, T0299-444 0245. Regular local buses 10 and 11 go to the airport, but you must buy a *tarjeta* (bus card); US$0.40 for this journey. Taxi US$4. To **Buenos Aires**, daily with AR, Austral, and Aerolíneas Argentinas.

Airline offices Aerolíneas Argentinas/ Austral, Santa Fe 52, T02942-442 2409, Lapa, Argentina 30, T02942-448 8335. **Southern Winds**, Argentina 237, T02942-442 0124.

Bus
The terminal is at Mitre 147. Left luggage: US$0.70 a day per item. **Andesmar**, T0299-442 2216, **Via Bariloche**, T0299-442 7054, **El Valle**, T0299-443 3293.

About a dozen companies to **Buenos Aires**, daily, 12-16 hrs, US$25-35. To **Zapala** daily, 3 hrs, US$5. To **San Martín de los Andes**, 6 hrs, US$11 To **Bariloche**, many companies, 5-6 hrs, US$13,. To **Mendoza**, Andesmar, and 3 others, daily, 12 hrs, US$22. To **Junín de los Andes**, 5 hrs, US$9, many companies.

To **Aluminé**, 6 hrs, US$10, many companies. To **Zapala**, 3 hrs, US$5, **Albus**, Centenario. To **Plaza Huincul**, 1½ hrs, US$3, same companies. To **Caviahue** (6 hrs, US$11) and **Copahue**, 6½ hrs, US$12, Centenario.

To Chile Services to **Temuco** stop for a couple of hours at the border, 12-14 hrs, US$22. Some companies offer discount for return, departures Mon-Thu and Sat; 7 companies, some continuing to destinations en route to **Puerto Montt**.

Taxi
Confluencia, T0299-443 8880. Radio Taxi, T0299-442 2502.

Zapala *p444*
Bus
The terminal is at Etcheluz y Uriburu, T02942-423191. To **Neuquén**, 3 hrs, US$5, Albus, Centenario, several daily. To **San Martín de los Andes**, 3-4 hrs, US$10. To **Junín de los Andes**, 3 hrs, US$9 with Albus, Centenario, several daily. To **Aluminé**, 2½ hrs, US$5, several companies, daily. To **Villa Pehuenia**, 2½ hrs, US$7, daily in summer, 4 a week winter, most go on to **Moquehue**, but check first, 5-6 hrs, US$8. To **Caviahue**, (3 hrs, US$8) and **Copahue** (3½-4 hrs, US$8) daily with **Centenario**. To **Bariloche**, **Albus**, **TAC**, **Vía Bariloche** change at San Martín. To **Buenos Aires**, 18 hrs, US$25-35, many companies. To **Temuco** (Chile), US$16, Mon/Wed/Fri, **Centenario** (buy Chilean currency before leaving).

Directory

Neuquén *p441*
Banks Lots of ATMs along Av Argentina. Casas de cambio at: **Pullman**, Alcorta 144, Exterior, San Martin 23. **Consulates** Chile, La Rioja 241, T02942-442 2727. **Internet** Near the bus terminal at Mitre 43, T02942-443 6585, a block from bus station. **Post office** Rivadavia y Santa Fe. **Telephone** Many *locutorios* in the centre, often with internet access. **Telecom**, 25 de Mayo 20, daily till 0030, and Olascoaga 222, open till 2345. Cheap.

Zapala *p444*
Banks Three banks including **Banco de la Nación Argentina**, Etcheluz 465, but difficult to change TC's, **Bansud**, Etcheluz 108.
Internet Instituto Moreno, Moreno y López y Planes. **CPI**, Chaneton y Garayta.

Bariloche to El Bolsón

Some of Argentina's most spectacular and unspoilt scenery lies south of Bariloche, where tourism has developed more recently and there is a wilder, more relaxed feel to the landscape. Route 258 , the road south from Bariloche to El Bolsón, is breathtaking, passing the picturesque lakes of Gutiérrez and Mascardi, lying below a massive jagged range of mountains. There are some fabulous, peaceful places to stay here and wonderful hikes and horse riding. From Villa Mascardi, a road leads west along the Lago Mascardi's southern shore to glorious Pampa Linda, where there is enough excellent trekking to entertain you for several days, including access to climb Mount Tronador. Further south, Río Manso Medio has become famous for whitewater rafting, and at Lago Hess there is a hostería and the lovely Cascadas Los Alerces. El Bolsón is a pretty and relaxed town, sprawled out between two mountain ranges, with superb hikes nearby and beautiful rivers, waterfalls and mountains to explore. The town itself is a laid-back place which started as a hippy community in the 1970s. Now there are several micro-breweries converting local hops into fine handmade beers, and craftsmen supplying the local market with wood and leather work, as well as delicious jams from the abundant soft fruits in summer. Further south, Lago Puelo is a tiny national park, offering great fishing some good walks, and a boat trip to the Chilean border. As you head south, Cholila might attract Butch Cassidy fans, but the cabin where he and the Sundance kid hid out has been brutally reconstructed. And though Cholila feels authentically like the wild west, there's little appeal here now. ▸▸ *For Sleeping, Eating and other listings, see pages 455-460.*

Lago Gutiérrez → *Phone code: 02944*

Easily accessible by bus from Bariloche, Lago Gutiérrez feels like a fjord, with mountains dropping steeply into its western side, and spectacular views all around. There are many ways to access the lake, and it can be explored on foot or bike almost all the way round. There are many campsites, a youth hostel and fine hotels at its northern end, or a fabulous comfortable estancia, **Peuma Hue** (see Sleeping, page 455) on the southern lakeshore and the base of the mountain, with great trekking and horse riding.

For an adventurous approach, you could hike down from **Refugio Frey** or walk or cycle down the stony track from Cerro Catedral (which can be reached by bus). Or just get off any bus headed from Bariloche to El Bolsón to explore either end. Water sports can be practised on the lake in summer, and there's a golf course at Arelauken on th northern shore.

Lago Mascardi → *Phone code: 02944 Colour map 5, B2, Km 35*

At the southern end of Lago Mascardi, **Villa Mascardi** is a small village from where the *ripio* Route 81 runs towards Lago Hess and Cascada Los Alerces. This road operates a one-way system: going west 1000-1400, east 1600-1800, two-way 1900-0900; times may vary, check with Bariloche tourist office, T2944-423022. From this road, another *ripio* road runs along the lake side to reach Pampa Linda, with access to climb Mount Tronador. Bariloche to El Bolsón buses can be taken to and from here, enabling you to visit the lake itself. Park entry costs US$4.

Along Lago Mascardi, there are several beautifully situated places to stay, all easily reached by car, or bus when the service is running in summer, including the luxurious **Hotel Mascardi**, with biking, rafting and horse riding. Opposite the lovely straight beach of Playa Negro, handy for launching boats and fishing, is the peaceful **Camping La Querencia**, at Km 10 on Route 258 to Tronador. Shortly afterwards, the road forks, with the left-hand branch following the crystalline Río Manso Medio to Lago Hess. This is a beautiful spot for a picnic, and there is also good camping at **Camping Los Rapidos**. For further details on accommodation at the lake, see page 455. The **Río Manso** is popular for rafting (arranged through tour operators in Bariloche, see page 406). At **Lago Hess** is **Hostería Lago Hess,** T02944-462249, piccino@bariloche.com.ar. The right fork follows a narrow arm of Lago Mascardi, with a viewpoint in lovely woodland to see Isla Piuke Huapi in the centre of the lake. A few kilometres further on is the lakeside paradise of Hotel Tronador before reaching Pampa Linda at the end of the road.

Pampa Linda and Mount Tronador → *Phone code: 02944*

Pampa Linda lies 40 km west of Villa Mascardi in the most blissfully isolated location, with spectacular views of Cerro Tronador towering above. There's a *guadería* (ranger station) with very helpful *guardaparques* who can advise on walks, and whom you must consult about the state of the paths before setting out, and register your name. From Pampa Linda, a lovely track (*ripio*) continues to **Ventisquero Negro** (black glacier), which hangs over a fantastically murky pool in which grey icebergs float. The colour is due to sediment, and while not exactly attractive, the whole scene is very atmospheric. The road ends at the awesome **Garganta del Diablo,** one of the natural amphitheatres formed by the lower slopes of Mount Tronador. A beautiful walk (90 minutes' walk there and back) from the car park through beach forest takes you to a more pristine glacier, and up to the head of the gorge, where thin torrents of ice melt from the hanging glacier above fall in columns like sifted sugar.

From Pampa Linda two other paths lead up **Cerro Tronador** (3478 m): the first is 15 km long and leads to **Refugio Otto Meiling** (2000 m), in itself a wonderful walk (five hours each way), situated on the edge of the eastern glacier. Another hour from the *refugio*, a path takes you to a view over Tronador and the lakes and mountains of **Parque Nacional Nahuel Huapi**. The other path leads to a *refugio* on the south side of the mountain. Otto Meiling is a good base camp for the ascent, with lots of facilities and activities, including trekking and ice climbing; always ask the *guardaparques* in Pampa Linda if there's space (capacity 60) US$7 per person per night, dinner US$5 (let them know in advance if you're vegetarian).

Paso de los Nubes

Pampa Linda is the starting point for a 22-km walk over Paso de los Nubes (1335 m) to **Laguna Frías** and **Puerto Frías** on the Chilean border. Allow at least two days; start the walk at Pampa Linda, rather than the other way around, as there's a gentler rise to the pass this way. There is camping at **Campamento Alerce** (after four hours) or **Campamento Glacier Frías** (after seven hours); from here it's another five hours to Puerto Frías. You'll see a spectacular glacial landscape, formed relatively recently (11,000 years ago), and the pass lies on the continental divide, with water flowing north to the Atlantic, and south to the Pacific. Views from the Río Frías Valley are tremendous, and from Glacier Frías you enter Valdivian rainforest. Boats cross Lago Frías three times a day in summer at roughly 1115, 1315 and 1630, but check this before leaving Bariloche. You must register with *guardaparques* at Pampa Linda before setting out, and check with them about conditions. The route is not always well marked and should only be attempted if there is no snow on the pass (it's normally passable only between December and February) or if the path is not excessively boggy. Do not cross rivers on fallen bridges or trees. Get advice from the very helpful *guardaparques* here, and buy the map produced by Infotrekking for Mount Tronador/ Paso de las Nubes before you leave Bariloche (available from **Club Andino Bariloche,** see page 393). See the excellent leaflet for *Paso de las Nubes* produced by Parque Nacional Nahuel Huapi. From Puerto Frías a 30-km road leads to Peulla on the shore of Chilean Lago Todos Los Santos. Or you can take a boat back to Bariloche; highly recommended. Another pleasant walk is to tranquil **Laguna Ilon** (5½ hours each way), with bathing on the shore in summer. Also to **Refugio Otto Meiling.** Check with *guardaparques* before setting out.

Río Manso Medio and Lago Hess

Some 9 km west of Villa Mascardi, a road runs 18 km through the beautiful valley of the Río Manso Medio to Lago Hess and on to the nearby **Cascada Los Alerces**. This is the starting point for trekking excursions in a more remote area of small lakes and forested mountains, including Lagos Fonck, Roca, Felipe and Cerros Granito and Fortaleza. Check with *guardaparques* at Lago Hess about the conditions of the paths. There is also wonderful rafting here, but you have to take a trip starting in Bariloche. Contact a reputable company such as **Extremo Sur**, or **Huala** (see page 406). Note that there is also rafting on the **Río Manso Inferior**, further south, heading west from **Villegas**, on Route 258. This is the place for wilder rafting, and the trip to the Chilean border, run by the same rafting companies.

Lago Steffen and Lago Martín → *Phone code: 02944*

About 20 km south of Villa Mascardi, another one-way dirt road leads to Lago Steffen, where a footpath runs along both northern and southern shores (of Lago Steffen) to Lago Martín. Both lakes are quite outstandingly lovely, fringed with beech and *alamo* trees, with far-off mountains in the distance, and pretty beaches where you can sit at the water's edge. There's also great fishing here. Paradise. The *guardería* is at Lago Steffen, and further north, wild camping is possible on the lake shore. Further south, a road leads west along the Río Manso Inferior towards Chile. There is excellent rafting on the river, and several places where you can buy homemade produce.

El Bolsón » *pp455-460.*

→ *Phone code: 02944 Colour map 5, B2 Population: 18,000*

El Bolsón is a very seductive little place. With its laid-back atmosphere, sprawled out in a broad fertile valley 130 km south of Bariloche, it is contained within huge mountain ranges on either side (hence it's name 'the big bag'),and it makes a great base for relaxing for a few days, and for hiking in the tempting peaks around. The great serrated ridge of Cerro Piltriquitrón (2284 m) dominates the town, apparently emitting healthy positive ions, which might be why you feel so relaxed while you're here. Certainly it's a magical setting, and it's not surprising that it inspired thousands of hippies to create an ideological community here in the 1970s. What remains is a young, friendly place where the young population make lots of handicrafts, and with the sparkling Río Azul running close by, and a warm sunny microclimate, you're likely to want to stay for a few days, to try the homebrewed beers and fruit for which the town is famous. A craft market is held in the semicircular plaza on Tuesday, Thursday and Saturday 1000-1600 in season. Argentina's finest ice cream is made at **Jauja**, also the town's best restaurant, with organic milk and local berries: there are 11 flavours of chocolate alone.

Nearby, there are many beautiful mountain walks, a couple of waterfalls and rafting on the Río Azul. The small national park of Lago Puelo is within easy reach 18 km south, for fishing, swimming and walking. And there's a small family orientated ski centre in the winter, at Centro de Ski Perito Moreno.

Ins and outs

Getting there There are hourly buses from Bariloche (two hours) and buses every two hours from Esquel (2½ hours) to El Bolsón, arriving off the main street at **Via Bariloche**'s offices at Sarmiento and Gral Roca. Also buses to and from Parque Nacional Los Alerces, and from destinations in Chile. There are equidistant airports at Bariloche and Esquel.

Getting around El Bolsón sprawls out from the spine of Avenida San Martín which runs through the town, where you'll find places to eat, and there are lots of places to stay dotted around the town, though the prettiest cabañas are in Villa Turismo up the hill. There are buses to Lago Puelo, but buses to other sights are infrequent, and geared to locals rather than tourists. However, El Bolsón is a lovely place to walk around, you can hire bikes, and there are plenty of cheap *remises*.

Tourist information The **tourist office** ⓘ *San Martín y Roca opposite the big post office (Correo), T02944-492604, www.elbolson.gov.ar, daily 0900-2100, all year, till 2400 in summer*, is on the side of the semicircular plaza. Staff are helpful and friendly (with plenty of English speakers). They'll give you an excellent map of the town and the area and suggest places to stay. If you want to walk in the mountains, you must go to **Club Andino Piltriquitrón** ⓘ *Sarmiento y Roca, T02944-492600, daily 0800-2200 in summer till 31 Mar, otherwise closed*, who will advise on hikes, and registers all walkers before setting off. The tourist office can also give limited advice on hikes and sells two quite useful maps, but you will need more detailed advice.

Best time to visit Summer is obviously the best time to visit, when you can take full advantage of the blissful rivers and mountains, and there's a lively atmosphere in the plaza with live music at nights. But it´s very busy here in January, so try to come in February or March, or even in April, when autumn turns the trees brilliant yellow and orange, and there are sunny days but cold nights. Winter is very rainy, and best avoided, though there is a basic ski resort at Cerro Perito Moreno.

Around El Bolsón

El Bolsón's great attraction – apart from the pleasure of being in the town itself – are the superb hikes up to the mountains west of the town which start from the other side of turquoise Río Azul, where there are lovely places to sunbathe, camp and picnic. For a pleasant hour-long walk, with views over the town, climb **Cerro Amigo**. Follow Calle Gral Roca east until it becomes Islas Malvinas and continue up the hill. Better still are the panoramic views from **Cerro Piltriquitrón**, the jagged peak looming over the town, from where you can paraglide in summer. Drive, take a tour, or take a taxi 10 km east of the town up winding earth roads. Then it's an hour's walk to the sculpture park of the **Bosque Tallado**, sculptures carved from fallen trees by local craftspeople, to the *mirador* with fabulous views over the valley to the Andes beyond. A six- to seven-hour round trip walking all the way. Food and shelter are available at the *refugio* (1400 m), and from there it's three hours' walk to the summit. A useful map, *Sendas y Bosques El Bolsón and Los Alerces*, is available from the tourist office. You can also do paragliding from here. Contact tour operator **Grado 42**, see Activities and tours, page 459.

There are also good views from **Cabeza del Indio**, so called because the rock's profile resembles a face, a good 6-km drive or bike ride from the centre. Take Calle Azcuénaga west to cross the bridge over Río Quemquemtreu, follow signs to Cabeza del Indio. From here, there's a new walk marked leading to **Cascada Escondida**.

To the north of the town, in woods reached from winding gravel roads, there's an impressive sweep of waterfalls at **Cascada Escondida**, 10 km northwest, a good place for a picnic, with a botanical garden. This area is also worth visiting for a good rustic *parrilla* **El Quincho**, for local lamb and great meat (vegetarians: don't even think about it) signposted from the road. There are rather less exciting falls at **Cataratas Mallín Ahogado**, a little further north, but it's still a pleasant spot for a stop. **La Golondrina** runs three buses daily Monday to Friday from the plaza to the loop around Mallin Ahogado, but extra walking is required to reach both falls. See the tourist office map for details. There are many micro-breweries dotted around town – **Cerveceria El Bolsón** ⓘ *RN 258, Km 123.9, just north of town, www.cervezaelbolson.com*, is particularly worth a visit, with brief guided tour, restaurant and no fewer than 18 different beers on offer, including three for celiacs. You could also try **Otto Tipp**.

Butch Cassidy and the Sundance Kid

Near Cholila, south of El Bolsón, is a wooden cabin which was home to Butch Cassidy (Robert LeRoy Parker) and the Sundance Kid (Harry Longabaugh). In the late 1890s, the two were part of a loosely-organized gang, known variously as the Train Robbers' Syndicate, the Hole in the Wall Gang and the Wild Bunch, which carried out hold-ups on railway payrolls and banks in the borders of Utah, Colorado and Wyoming. In 1900, the gang celebrated the wedding of one of their colleagues by having their photo taken: a big mistake. The photo was recognized by a Wells Fargo detective, and with their faces decorating Wanted posters across the land, Cassidy, Sundance and his girlfriend Etta Place escaped to Argentina in February 1901.

Using the names Santiago Ryan and Harry Place, the outlaws settled on government land near Cholila and applied to buy it, but Pinkerton detectives hot on their trail soon tracked them down and informed the Argentine authorities. The three lay low in their idyllic rural retreat until 1905, when, needing money to start up elsewhere, the gang raided banks in Villa Mercedes and a particularly audacious job in Río Gallegos. Posing as ranching company agents, they opened a bank account with US$7000, spent two weeks at the best hotels and socialized with the city's high society, and then entered the bank to close their accounts and empty the safe before escaping to Chile. Then Etta returned to the United States, and disappeared from the history books.

Butch and Sundance moved to Bolivia, and worked at the Concordia tin mine, disappearing occasionally to carry out the occasional hold-up. Lack of capital to settle as respectable ranchers was, however, their undoing. In 1908, near Tupiza in southern Bolivia, they seized an Aramayo mining company payroll, but gained only a fraction of the loot they expected. With military patrols in pursuit and the Argentine and Chilean forces alerted, they rode into the village of San Vicente and were recognized. Besieged, they did not, as in the film, run into the awaiting gunfire. Their deaths were not widely reported in the United States until the 1930s, and rumours abounded: Butch was said to have become a businessman, a rancher, a trapper and a Hollywood movie extra, while Sundance had run guns in the Mexican Revolution, migrated to Europe, fought for the Arabs against the Turks in the First World War, sold mineral water, founded a religious cult, and still found time to marry Etta.

Their ramshackle wooden cabin was, until June 2006, an evocative place to visit. Now the owner has restored it with brand new bright orange wood, ruining the outlaw hide-out feel. The location is still spectacular, however, and worth the trip for fans.

The famous narrow gauge railway **La Trochita** (also known as the *Old Patagonian Express*) is definitely worth it, as a novel way of seeing the landscape and a glimpse into Patagonia's past. As well as the better known route from Esquel, there's another journey from at El Maitén, near El Bolsón, where you can see the fascinating steam railway workshops too. Contact **Grado 42**, see page 459.

El Bolsón benefits from a gentle microclimate which means it's warmer than most of the lakes region, even in winter. However, there is a ski centre, **Centro de Ski Perito Moreno**, on the upper slopes of Cerro Perito Moreno (2216 m). With good snow and no wind, its 720 skiable metres are good for families. It's a newish centre and the only place to stay at the moment is the **Refugio Perito Moreno**, with 120 beds, but there are three ski lifts and ski instructors too. Ask the tourist office for more information. Leave town by Route 258, and take the left hand turn to Rio Azul. Follow signs to Refugio Perito Moreno.

Walks → *For Parque Nacional Lago Puelo, see below.*

There are wonderful treks to the mountains west of the town. For all walks, get the *Sendas y Bosques* (walks and forests) map and book for El Bolsón, Lago Puelo and Los Alerces. Maps are 1:200,000, laminated and easy to read, and the book is full of great walks, with English summaries. Register for all walks before setting off at the **Club Andino Piltriquitrón** (see Ins and outs, above).

Cerro Lindo Due west of town, there's a great hike up Arroyo Lali to Cerro Lindo (2105 m), in one of the most beautiful mountain landscapes of the whole area, with **Refugio Cerro Lindo** halfway up, after a five-hour walk. From here, you can reach an ancient glacier and climb onwards to several or view points. You'll need a map, and check the rout before setting off. The altitude difference is pretty extreme here, so you're advised to go slowly and steadily.

Cerro Hielo Azul This is a more serious and demanding hike up to Cerro Hielo Azul (2255 m), where you can stay at **Refugio Cerro Azul**, at 1300 m. It's steep and takes six hours one-way, From the comfortable *refugio*, you can also walk to the glacier on the slopes of Cerro Hielo Azul (three hours return), or on to Cerro Barda Negra. It's often suggested that you could walk from here via **Refugio Natación** to **Refugio Cajon de Azul**, but this is really not to be recommended without a local guide. The path can be confusing in places, the area remains marshy well into the summer months, and people have got lost, with dangerous consequences. Ask in the **Club Andino Piltriquitrón** (see page 450).

Cajón de Azul One of the loveliest and most accessible walks can be done in a day, although once you reach the delightful *refugio* (600 m) at Cajón de Azul, you're going to wish you could stay at least a night. It's a fabulous four-hour walk up the Río Azul which flows from a deep canyon. Set off early to allow for a leisurely lunch at the top, or spend the night in the *refugio*, with its lovely gardens, in the company of Atilio and friends, who make a fine dinner with produce from the garden. Take a *traffic* (minibus) to Wharton, leaving El Bolsón at 0900. There's a well-marked path. It's a bit hairy crossing the two wood-and-wire bridges (and only one at a time, so queues actually build up here in January), but worth it for a dip in the sparkling turquoise water on the way down. You'll be collected by the *traffic* at 2000. Buses and information from **Nehuén**, at Belgrano y Perito Moreno, in same office as Andesmar.

Refugio Los Laguitos A wonderful four-day walk that takes you right into the deepest part of the Andes Cordillera, almost to the border with Chile, and through outstanding alerce forests. Allow four hours to **Refujio Cajón de Azul**, another three hours to the Mallín de los Chanchos, and another four hours on from there to reach the basic **Refugio Los Laguitos**, in a beautiful spot on the shore of Lago Lahuán. A map and guidebook are absolutely essential; seek advice before setting out.

Parque Nacional Lago Puelo » pp455-460.

This lovely green and wooded national park is centred around the deep turquoise-coloured Lago Puelo, 15 km south of El Bolsón on the Chilean border, surrounded by southern beech forest and framed with the spikey peaks of snow-dusted far off mountains. It's a blissful spot, out of the busy holiday season. With relatively low altitude (200 m) and high rainfall, the forest is rich in tree species, particularly the cinnamon-bark *arrayán* and the *pitra*, *coihues* (evergreen beech) and cypresses. There's lots of wildlife, including the *huemul*, *pudu* and foxes, and the lake is known for its good fishing for trout and salmon. There are gentle walks on marked paths around the northern shore area, boat trips across the lake, and canoes for rent. *Guardaparques* at the park entrance can advise on these, and hand out a basic map.

Ins and outs

Getting there Entry fee US$4. The main entrance is along a pretty road south from El Bolsón, through *chacras* (small farms) growing walnuts, hops and fruit, to Villa Lago Puelo, 3 km north of the park, where there are shops, plenty of accommodation and fuel. From here the road is unpaved. Entry is also possible at **El Desemboque**, on the eastern side of the park: take the bus from El Bolsón to Esquel, alight at El Hoyo, then walk 14 km to El Desemboque. It's best to come between November and April, though the northern shore of the lake can get crowded in January and February. The lake is glorious in April, when the trees turn a vivid yellow.

Park information The **Intendencía** ⓘ *500 m north of the lake, T02944-499232, lagopuelo@apn.gov.ar, year-round Mon-Fri 0800-1500, with a booth at the pier in summer*, can provide a helpful leaflet and advice on walks. You must register here before embarking on long hikes, and register your return. In the town of Lago Peulo there's a **tourist office** ⓘ *Av 2 de Abril y Los Notros, T02944-499591, www.turismo lagopuelo.com, summer 0900-2100, winter 0900-1900*, on the roundabout as you enter town. Staff are helpful, English-speaking and can advise on accommodation.

Walks

For all walks, get the *Sendas y Bosques* (walks and forests) map and book for El Bolsón, Lago Puelo and Los Alerces. Maps are 1:200,000, laminated and easy to read. The book is full of great walks, with English summaries, www.guiasendasybosques.com.ar.

▲ **Bosque de las Sombras** or Forest of the Shadows, is a delightful overgrown forest which you wander through on wooden walkways, on the way to the shingle beach at 'La Playita', with guided trails and signs telling you what trees you're passing. It's an easy 400-m walk.

▲ **Senda los Hitos,** is a 10-km (four hours each way) walk through marvellous woods, to the rapids at Río Puelo, on the Chilean border, (passport required), and there is some wild camping on the way at **Camping de Gendarmería,** after two hours.

▲ **Cerro Motoco** There's a tremendous two-day hike up Cerro Motoco, with **Refugio Motoco** at the top of the path. Leave Lago Puelo heading north, and cross the hanging bridge to access Río Motoco. It's 25 km altogether, and could be done in seven hours, one way, but you'll want to stay at the top. Take the walks book with you.

▲ **Cerro Plataforma** From the east of the lake, you can hike to **El Turbio** and Cerro Plataforma, crossing the lake first by boat to El Desemboque (or taking the bus and walking 14 km). At Cerro Plataforma, there's a tremendous amount of marine life in evidence, as this was a beach in the ice age. It's about seven hours to Río Turbio, where there's a *guardaparque* and then 12 hours to Cerro Plataforma; allow three days for the whole trip. There's also a three-day trek through magnificent scenery to **Glaciar y Cerro Aguaja Sur**: get advice and directions from the *guardaparques*.

Other activities

There is wonderful **fly fishing** in the park, thanks to the fact that this is the lowest crossing in the whole of the Andes region (at only 190 m) so there is no snow, and with mild warm summers in the microclimate here, Pacific salmon come here in large numbers. Contact fishing guides through the park *guardería*. Also check out **Puelo Trout** for fishing trips. There are boat trips across Lago Puelo with **Juana de Arco,** as well as kayaking with **Kayak Lago Puelo**. For details, see Activities and tours, page 459.

South of El Bolsón » pp455-460.

Epuyén → Phone code: 02944 Colour map 5, B2

Forty kilometres southeast of El Bolsón on Route 258, the little settlement of Epuyén (pronounced epooSHEN) is, so far, undeveloped for tourists, and there's nothing much to do here except stroll around Lago Epuyén. There's a simple *hostería*, which also has rustic *cabañas*, owned by friendly laid-back Sophie, who provides meals on request. A fire destroyed trees all over one hillside a few years ago, making the area less attractive for walks, but there's a good trek around the lakeside, and good fishing in the lake.

Cholila → Phone code 02945 Colour map 5, B2

Cholila is a real Patagonian settlement, which one day will make a great place to stay, with its lovely setting in broad open landscape with superb views of Lago Cholila, crowned by ranges of mountains all around. Cholila lies 76 km south of El Bolsón on Route 71, which branches off Route 258 at Km 179. There's excellent fishing, canoeing and kayaking on rivers nearby, but very little tourist infrastructure. The accommodation is extremely limited, and there's little information.

You might have heard that the reason to visit Cholila is to see the wooden cabins where **Butch Cassidy**, the **Sundance Kid** and Etta Place lived between 1901 and 1905 (see box above). You can understand why they hid out here for so long: Cholila still feels remote and untouched, and the views from their land are breathtaking. The cabins themselves were rather evocative, falling to pieces, patched up with bits of wood and with a lichen-stained slatted roof, but in 2006, the owner of the land started to 'renovate' the cabins, by replacing the tattered timbers with brand new bright orange beams, doors and window frames. As a result, it is unlikely to please visitors keen to see what remained of the authentic cabins where Butch and Sundance lived. It's now not worth the considerable effort required to visit them. To get there make a detour from Route 258 heading south from El Bolsón, towards Los Alerces National Park's northern entrance; 13 km north of Cholila along Ruta 71, look out for a sign on the right, park by the little kiosk and walk 400 m to the cabins. Entry US$1, if anyone's around to charge you.

There is a good walk around **Lago Mosquito**: continue down the road from El Trébol past the lake then take a path to the left, following the river. Cross the river on the farm bridge and continue to the base of the hills to a second bridge. Follow the path to the lake and walk between the lake and the hills, crossing the river via a suspension bridge just past El Trébol – six hours.

Leleque → Colour map 5, B2

Route 40 (paved) is a faster way to get from El Bolsón to Esquel than Route 71 via Cholila, and this is the route the bus takes. You could stop off at Leleque to see the **Museum of Patagonia** ⓘ *off the RN 40, Km 1440, 90 km from Esquel and 80 km from El Bolsón, US$1, Mar-Dec 1100-1700, Jan-Feb 1100-1900, closed Wed and May, Jun and Sep*, in the vast estate owned by **Benetton**, the Italian knitwear company. To their credit, they have created a remarkable museum here. There's a beautifully designed exhibition on the lives of indigenous peoples, with dwellings reconstructed of animal skins, using the original construction techniques, a huge collection of delicate arrowheads and the original *boleadoras* for catching cattle. Other moving exhibits include one on the first pioneers in Patagonia, especially the Welsh. And there's an attractive café in a reconstructed *boliche* (provisions shop and bar).

Sleeping

Lago Gutiérrez *p447*

L Arelauquen Golf and Country Club, on the eastern shore of Lago Gutiérrez, T02944-467626, Buenos Aires T011-4311 1919, www.arelauquen.com. Upmarket golf and country club, with tennis, squash and horse riding too, and luxurious accommodation in a beautiful chalet-style building. Smallish but luxurious rooms, excellent restaurant and golf bar, exclusive atmosphere.

AL El Retorno, Villa Los Coihues, on the northern shore, T02944-467333, www.hosteriaelretorno.com. With a stunning lakeside position, this is a traditional family-run hotel in tasteful hunting lodge style, with lovely gardens running down to the beach, tennis courts, and comfortable rooms, as well as 5 self-catering apartments. Also a restaurant. Very relaxing.

AL Estancia Peuma Hue, on the southern shore of Lago Gutiérrez, 3 km off the road, T02944-501030, www.peuma-hue.com. One of the finest places to stay in the whole area, this estancia combines a gorgeous rural setting on 2 km of private shoreline on Lago Gutiérrez, right up against the foot of Cerro Catedral Sur, with luxurious accommodation in 2 beautifully designed country houses and a mountain cabin. Prices include meals and superb activities such as trekking into virgin forest on the mountain to find waterfalls, and amazing wildlife, great horse riding with the resident horse whisperer, exploring the lake in kayaks, and rafting in Ríos Mansos, massage, yoga. The food is delicious and rooms are individually decorated with great panache, and wonderful views from huge windows. Jacuzzi under the stars in the huge suite is particularly recommended. The charming owner, Evelyn Hoter, makes sure all her guests have a really special experience here. Highly recommended.

Camping

Villa los Coihues, Lago Gutiérrez, T02944-467479. Well equipped and beautifully situated. Take bus 50/51, or take the track down to Gutiérrez from Cerro Catedral (4WD advisable) or the road to El Bolson (RN 258), and follow signs.

Lago Mascardi *p447*

A pp **Hotel Tronador**, T02944-441062, www.hoteltronador.com. A lakeside paradise, mid-Nov to Easter, the lovely rooms have terrific lake views from their balconies, there are beautiful gardens, and the charming owner is truly welcoming. It's a really peaceful place, (especially out of peak season). Can also organize riding, fishing and excursions on the lake. Highly recommended.

B Mascardi, RN 258, Km 36.8, on the road to Pampa Linda and Tronador on Lago Mascardi, T2944-490518, www.mascardi.com. The first you come to, just a few kilometres from the turning off RN 258. is this luxurious place with a delightful setting in lovely gardens on its own beach by lake Mascardi, restaurant and tea room, horse riding, mountains bikes, rafting and fly fishing in the Río Guillelmo can also be arranged.

Camping

Camping La Querencia, T02944-426225, further on towards Pampa Linda, at Km 10. A pretty and peaceful spot on the side of river and on banks of lake, opposite the lovely straight beach of Playa Negro.

Camping Las Carpitas, also on Lago Mascardi, at Km 33, T02944-490527. Set in a great lakeside position, summer only, with *cabañas* and restaurant.

Camping Los Rapidos, T/F02944-461861. Attractive shaded site going down to the lake, with *confitería*, food store and all facilities, US$2.50 pp. Also bunk beds in a basic *albergue* US$3pp (sleeping bag needed). Friendly owners organize trekking, kayaking, fishing and mountain bikes.

Pampa Linda and Mount Tronador *p448*

D Hostería Pampa Linda, T02944-442038, www.tronador.com. This *hostería* is a luxurious base for climbing Tronador, or a comfortable retreat from which to start other treks. Simple comfortable rooms, all with bath, and all with stunning views. The owners are charming; Sebastian de la Cruz is one of the area's most experienced mountaineers. Horse riding can be organized, as well as trekking and climbing courses. Full board, and packed lunches for hiking available.

Camping

Pampa Linda, T02944-424531. Idyllic spacious lakeside site, *confitería* serving good meals and food shop. Excellent service, run by the Club Andino Bariloche.

Río Manso Medio and Lago Hess *p449*

LL Río Manso Lodge, www.riomansolodge.com. Spectacularly set on the bank of the Río Manso in beautiful mountainous scenery, this is a top-class fishing lodge, run by bilingual hosts Sebastian and Eugenia Graziosi, with lovely rooms with great views from their large windows, fine food and great fishing. Loved by experts.

El Bolsón *p449*

There are lots of *cabañas* and *hosterías* up on a hill in the Villa Turismo, 3 km southeast of the centre, a good hour's walk, or a cheap taxi ride. It's difficult to find accommodation in the high season: book ahead.

C Hostería Casa Blanca, José Hernández y Onelli, T02944-493784. Losalerces@elbolson.com. Charming chalet style *hostería* with comfortable rooms with bath, and TV, and good service.

C La Casona de Odile, Barrio Lujan, T02944-492753, odile@elbolson.com. A really special place to stay, in rustic wooden cabins in this idyllic lavender farm by a stream, with delicious French cooking by the wonderful charismatic owner Odile. Ask the tourist office for directions. Recommended.

C Sukal, high on a hill in Villa Turismo, T02944-492438, www.sukalarteyflores.com. Gorgeous bed and breakfast, a haven of peace in a flower-filled garden, with glorious views. Welcoming owners. Delightful.

D Amancay, San Martin y Hernandez, T02944-492222. Central, old-fashioned but comfortable, if a little institutional, all rooms with small bathrooms, breakfast included.

D Hostería Steiner, San Martín 670, T02944-492224. Worth going a little way out of the centre to stay in this peaceful place with huge lovely gardens. Simple plain rooms, wood fires, German spoken. Recommended.

D La Posada de Hamelin, Int Granollers 2179, T02944-492030, www.posadadehamelin.com.ar. One of the most welcoming places in the whole region, run by the charming Gustavo and Silvia, who make a really outstanding breakfast with different treats every day, including homemade jams and cakes. Lovely chalet-style house with quaint and comfortable rooms all with bathroom, very central. Highly recommended.

D Valle Nuevo, 25 de Mayo y Belgrano, T02944-1560 2325. Small and basic rooms in this quiet place, breakfast not included, but good value.

Cabañas

There are many *cabañas* in picturesque settings with lovely views, in the Villa Turistica, costing around US$40 for up to 5 people per night, though prices vary widely between high and low seasons. Call each cabaña complex for directions. Buses to Villa Turismo run by **Comarca Andina**, opposite Via Bariloche, T02944-455400, or take a remis, US$2. The following are recommended:

Cabañas Paraíso, T02944-492766, www.cabaniasparaiso.com.ar. Lovely wooden cabins in a gorgeous setting amongst old trees. Pool, good service.

La Montaña, T02944-492776, www.montana.com.ar. Very well-equipped smart *cabañas* spaced out in a big complex with pool, children's play area, and lovely views of Piltriquitrón. These are the most appealing option.

Lincoln Ranch, T02944-492073, www.lincolnranch.com.ar. Big, modern, well maintained *cabaña* complex with open views, and pool.

Los Teros, ask for the road leading up via Los Tres Cipreses, T02944-455 5569, www.cabañaslosteros.com.ar. Lovely cabins, well spaced in park land with good views of the mountains, these have good service, and complete peace. Recommended,

Youth hostels

E pp **Refugio Patagónico**, Islas Malvinas y Pastorino, T02944-1563 5463, diegogfe@hotmail.com. High quality youth hostel, with small dorms all with bathrooms, in a spacious house set in open fields, where you can also camp, with great views of Piltriquitrón, and just 5 blocks from the plaza. Recommended.

E pp **Sol del Valle**, 25 de Mayo 2329, T02944-492087, T1560 2325. A bright hostel with basic rooms, shared bathrooms, big kitchen and eating space for big groups, sheets/towels extra. Garden with view of Piltriquitrón.

F Altos del Sur, Villa Turismo, T02944-498730, www.altosdelsur.bolsonweb.com.

In a lovely setting in Villa Turismo, with beautiful views from the terrace, and nice welcoming sitting areas, this is a peaceful hostel with shared rooms, and 1 double, **D** with private bath. Dinner available, and breakfast included, lovely welcoming owner Mariela will collect from bus station if you book in advance. Highly recommended.

Camping

There are many good sites, fully equipped and lively particularly in Jan.
Arco Iris, T02944-1555 8330. Blissful wooded setting near Rio Azul, helpful owners.
La Chacra, Belgrano 1128, T02944-492111. 15 mins' walk from town, well shaded, good facilities, lively atmosphere in season.
Quem Quem, on the banks of Rio Quemquemtreu, T02944-493550, quemquem@elbolson.com. Well kept lovely site with hot showers, good walks, free pick-up from town.
Refugio Patagónico, see hostels above. A great open site with hot showers and fireplaces, lovely views.

Parque Nacional Lago Puelo *p452*

There are lots of *cabañas*, shops and fuel. Apart from wild camping, there's no accommodation in the park itself, but plenty in Villa Lago Puelo, just outside, with *cabañas*, restaurants and campsites spread out along RN 16 through the little village.

Cabañas

A Lodge Casa Puelo, RN 16, T02944-499539, www.casapuelo.com.ar. *Cabañas* for up to 6. Beautifully designed rooms and self catering cabins right against forested mountains where you can walk, with good service from friendly English-speaking owner Miguel, who knows the local area intimately. Very comfortable, dinner offered too. Free internet access. Recommended.
B Río Azul, RN 16, T02944-499345, www.complejoazul.com. Beautifully designed rooms in pretty area next to Río Azul, with gardens, Swimming pools, volley ball,
B-C Frontera, isolated in woodland, off the main road heading for Esquel, T02944-473092, www.frontera-patagonia.com.ar. *Cabañas* for 4 and *hostería*, furnished to a very high standard, in a lovely building set in native forest, and offering delicious breakfasts and dinner if required.
C La Granja, 20 m from Río Azul, T02944-499265, www.interpatagonia.com/lagranja. Traditional chalet-style *cabañas* with simple furnishings, nothing out of this world, but there's a pool, and these are good value.
C La Yoica, just off RN 16, Km 5, T02944-499200, www.layoica.com.ar. Charming Scottish owners make you feel at home in these lovely traditional cabañas set in lovely countryside with great views.
C San Jorge, a block from the main street, on Plaza Ilia, T02944-491313, www.elbolson.com/sanjorge. Excellent value, these neat little self-catering apartments in a pretty garden, with friendly helpful owners.

Camping

There are many good sites with all facilities: **La Pasarela**, Km10, T02944-499061; **Los Quinchos**, Km 13; and **Ailin Co**, Km15, T02944-499078. All recommended. There are 2 free sites in the park itself, on Lago Puelo, of which **Camping del Lago** is most highly recommended. All facilities, and also offers rafting, fishing and trekking.

Epuyén *p454*

D Refugio del Lago, T02945-499025, a.sophie@epuyen.net.ar. A relaxed place with rustic comfortable rooms in a lovely wooden house, a short walk from the shore, with breakfast included, also good meals. Owners Sophie and Jacques are mountain guides, and can organize trekking and riding. Also camping and *cabañas*. Recommended. Buses between El Bolsón and Esquel stop (briefly) at Epuyén, though some don't enter the village itself. Sophie will come and meet the bus if you ask in advance.

Eating

El Bolsón *p449*

¶ Cerro Lindo, on the main street, Av San Martín 2524, T02944-492899. A cosy wood-lined place with local paintings on the walls, quiet and welcoming place for dinner, serving Patagonian specialities and delicious pastas.
¶ Jauja, San Martín 2867, T02944-492448. The best place in town by a long way, Jauja is a great meeting place, with a friendly, welcoming atmosphere, good mellow music playing, and really tasty food. Some of the

lovely staff speak English. There's a broad menu, lots of local specialities, but the trout-filled pasta, and apple strudel are particularly fabulous, and whatever you do, don't miss the country's best handmade ice creams, including Patagonian *calafate* berry flavour. All made from organic milk, and locally grown fruit, so that they're entirely natural, with exquisite flavours. There are 11 kinds of chocolate alone. Divine. Also high quality handmade chocolates. Highly recommended.

‡‡ **Martin Sheffield**, Av San Martín 2760, T02944-491920. Conveniently central and serving good food, Patagonian specialities, menu of the day.

‡‡ **Parrilla El Quincho**, 10 mins north of town, signposted from Route 258, near Cataratas del Mallín, T02944-492870. Excellent asado, and delicious lamb are the specialities here at this charming rustic parrilla with garden going down to the river, and tables in the open air. Recommended.

‡‡ **Parrilla Patagonia**, RN 258, 2 km out of town, T02944-492056. Superb *parrilla*, recommended for steak, and excellent Patagonian lamb and kid on the *asado* at weekends. Also a cheap set menu and *parrilla libre*.

‡ **Arcimboldo**, San Martin 2790, T02944-492137. Good value *tenedor libre*, smoked fish and draught beer.

‡ **El Rey de Sandwich**, Roca 345, T02944-491076. The cheapest sandwiches in town at this *rotisería*, next to **Via Bariloche** bus terminal.

‡ **La Tosca**, San Martín y Roca. Café, restaurant in summer, warm atmosphere.

Breweries and tea rooms (Casas de té)

Cerveza El Bolsón, RN 258, Km 123.9, T02944-492595, www.cervezaselbolson.com. The best microbrewery in El Bolsón, and a great place to visit, to see how the beer is made – and sample the 18 varieties. Try the delicious *picadas* served with your beer, sitting outside in the gardens, and take a few bottles away with you. Highly recommended.

Dulcinea, on the main road, RN 258, to El Hoyo at Km 137.5, Debbie_dulcinea@yahoo.com.ar. This delightful tea room is not to be missed. The owner, Debbie (who speaks English) is famous for her cakes and rose hip tea, and there's fondu and *asado* in the evenings in season.

El Mirador, RN 258, Km 137, Las Golondrinas, T02944-473024. Open for breakfast and afternoon tea, with delicious homemade cakes, in pretty gardens.

Parque Nacional Lago Puelo *p454*

‡‡ **Familia von Fürstenberg**, RN 16 on the way to the national park, T02944-499392, www.vonfuerstenberg.com.ar. In a delightful perfectly decorated Swiss-style chalet, try the beautifully presented traditional waffles and homemade cakes. Sumptuous. Also *cabañas* to rent.

‡‡ **Sabores de Patagonia**, RN 16 on the way to National Park, T02944-499532. Good for lunch or tea, locally caught trout, and smoked s. Service is slow, but the food is worth waiting for.

Cholila *p454*

La Casa de Piedra, RN 71 outside village, T02945-498056. Welsh tea room, chocolate cake recommended.

Bars and clubs

El Bolsón *p449*

La Bandurria. Live music at weekends, and dancing. **Bar 442**, Dorrego 442, T02944-492313, for rock. **Life**, M Moreno 3450, T02944-493294, for techno,

Festivals

El Bolsón *p449*

Jan Fiesta de la Fruta Fina (Berry Festival) at the nearby El Hoyo.

Feb At the end of the month is the **Fiesta del Lúpulo** (Hop Festival).

Oct The homebrewed beer festival, **Fiesta de la Cerveza Artesanal**, much more civilised than an Oktoberfest!

Dec The **jazz festival** attracts many famous musicians, for 10 days.

Shopping

El Bolsón *p449*

The handicraft and food market is on Tue, Thu, and Sat in season 1000-1600 around the main plaza. Some fine leather and jewellery, carved wood and delicious organic produce. **Centro Artesanal**, Av San Martín 1866, daily 1000-2000, T02944-491150. If the market's not open, a selection of the best crafts can be bought here: wood, leather, precious stones, ceramics and candles.

Granja Larix, RN 258, Km 118.5, T02944-498018, alejandra@bariloche.com.ar. For fabulous smoked trout and homemade jams.

La Huella, Sarmiento y Dorrego, T02944-491210. For tent hire and outdoor equipment.

Laten K'Aike, T02944-491969. Also known as Piedras Patagonicas, for exquisite semi precious stones.

Mercado Artesanal, Av San Martín 1920, Mon-Fri 0800-1300, 1400-2000, Sat 0900-1300. Wonderful Mapuche weavings can be bought here in this co-operative of local weavers, and you can watch women spin and weave beautiful rugs, scarves and bags, in the traditional way. Also knitted goods, all incredibly high quality and beautifully made. Recommended.

Talabarteria Poyetun, Dorrego 443, T02944-498606. Excellent leather goods: belts, hats, boots and bags, locally made to traditional designs.

Activities and tours

Lago Gutiérrez and Mascardi *p447*

Boat trips

Victoria II Lago Mascardi Paseos Lacustres, T02944-441062, lmascardi@bariloche.com.ar. Trips on Lago Mascardi are a wonderful way to see the mountains in summer.

Horse riding

Los Baqueanos, signposted from RN 258, on the eastern shore of Lago Gutiérrez, T02944-1555 4362, baqueanos@bariloche.com.ar.

Estancia Peuma Hue, see Sleeping above. From the *estancia* on the southern shore of Lago Gutiérrez, you can ride into the mountains, and over to Pampa Linda.

Rafting

Rafting on the Río Manso is arranged through operators in Bariloche; see page 406.

El Bolsón *p449*

Ask at the tourist office for their *Agroturismo* leaflet, with information on the *chacras* (fruit farms) you can visit in summer, for delicious freshly picked soft fruits and berries, jams and other delights. Throughout El Bolsón and El Hoyo further south.

Cycle hire

La Rueda, Sarmiento 2972, T/F02944-492465. US$10 per day, open 0830-1330, 1530-2130.

Tour operators

Grado 42, Av Belgrano 406, on the corner with Av San Martín, T02944-493124, www.grado42.com. Excellent company offering wide range of tours, including La Trochita's lesser-known trip from El Maitén, where there is a superb steam railway workshop and you can learn all about how the trains work. Rafting on the Río Manso, horse riding in glorious countryside at Cajón de Azul, wonderful fishing in Lago Puelo, paragliding from Plitriquitron, helpful information on buses too. Recommended. Ask for Jorge Szwarcnabel.

Juana de Arco, T02944-493415, juanadearco@elbolson.com. Boat trips across Lago Pielo, US$15 for a 3-hr trip to the Chilean border, including walk through Valdivian rainforest. Recommended. Also run fishing trips, email for details.

Kayak Lago Puelo, T02944-499197, www.kayaklagopuelo.com.ar. Kayaking on the lake with guide and instructor Alberto Boyer.

Patagonia Adventures, Pablo Hube 418, T02944-492513, patagoniaadventures@elbolson.com. Horse riding, fly fishing, rafting and boat trips, crossing to Chile.

Puelo Extremo, T02944-499588, www.pueloextremo.com.ar. Trekking and canoeing in the park.

Puelo Trout, T02944-499430. Run boat trips, and all-inclusive fishing trips with equipment included.

Transport

Lago Mascardi *p447*

Bus Bus services from Bariloche to **El Bolsón** pass through **Villa Mascardi**. And buses to **Los Rapidos** run from the terminal in Bariloche at 0900, 1300, 1800 daily in summer. Check with **Vía Bariloche/El Valle**, or Bariloche Bus station for timings (see below).

Pampa Linda *p448*

Bus **Transitando lo Natural**, 20 de Febrero 25, T02944-527926, transitando1@hotmail.com. Buses to Pampa Linda daily at

0900 in season, US$7.50. Alternatively, **Expreso Meiling** also run buses in season, leaving Club Andino at 0830, and returning from Pampa Linda at 1700, T02944-529875. From Pampa Linda you can often get a lift with an excursion trip returning to **Bariloche**, if there's room, US$7.

El Bolsón *p449*

Air The nearest airports are Esquel and Bariloche; see respective sections for flights.

Bus Several daily from **Bariloche** and **Esquel**, with Don Otto, Via Bariloche. Check with **Vía Bariloche/El Valle**, Mitre 321, T02944-429012, or Bariloche Bus station T02944-432444, www.viabariloche.com, for timings. Heavily booked in high season. US$7.50, 2 hrs. Other destinations from these 2 towns. Buses to **Lago Puelo** with Via Bariloche every 2 hrs, 4 on Sun, 45mins, US$1.30. To **Parque Nacional Los Alerces** (highly recommended route), with **Transportes Esquel** (from ACA service station), once a day, US$5, 4-5 hrs, via Cholila and Epuyen.

Taxi

Piltri, T02944-492272.

Parque Nacional Lago Puelo *p452*

There are regular buses, US$2, from Av San Martín y Dorrego in El Bolsón to the lake via Villa Lago Puelo. **Transportes Esquel** run daily buses connecting Lago Puelo with **Cholila**, **PN Los Alerces**, and **Esquel**.

Directory

El Bolsón *p449*

Banks Exchange cash and TCs at **Banco Patagonia**, San Martín y Roca, with ATM outside. **Internet** Various places open and close. Currently functioning: **Ciber Café La Nuez**, Av San Martín 2175, T02944-455182. **Post office** San Martín 1940.

Esquel, Trevelin and Los Alerces National Park

This southernmost area of the lakes is the most Patagonian in feel, with pioneer towns Esquel and Trevelin caught between the wild open steppe to the east and the dramatic mountains of the Andes to the west. Esquel retains the quiet charm of an ordinary country town – with one very famous attraction. It's the starting point for the narrow gauge railway known as La Trochita, an atmospheric way to see the surrounding landscape, but the town also boasts a family ski resort and a few places to trek and mountain bike. Far more tranquil is the village of Trevelin, which still bears signs of its origins as a Welsh colony: Welsh is still spoken in the streets, you can try an enormous 'traditional' Welsh tea, and there's a fascinating old flour mill to visit in the pretty landscape towards the Chilean border. Both towns make good bases for exploring the most unspoilt national park in the Lake District: Los Alerces. With just one road running through it, the park has pristine forested mountains and several stunning lakes, and is best enjoyed on foot. There are wonderful hikes, boat trips to see ancient alerce trees, and some unforgettable views, like Río Arrayanes and Lago Verde. Since this area is less developed for tourism than the rest of the lakes, it's best to hire a car to see it independently. » *For Sleeping, Eating and other listings, see pages 466-470.*

Esquel » *pp466-470.*

→ *Phone code: 02945 Colour map 5, B2 Population: 30,000*

One of the most authentic towns in the Lake District, Esquel is a pleasant, breezy place that still feels like a pioneer outpost, set where the steppe meets the mountains. It's a typical Patagonian country town, with many buildings dating from the early 1900s, and battered pick-ups filling the streets in the late morning bustle when local farmers come into town. There are few tourist sights, but it's all the more appealing for that. But it is the starting point for the narrow gauge railway, 'La Trochita', made famous by Paul Theroux as the *Old Patagonian Express*, which chugs off into the steppe from a charming old-fashioned station just north of town. It's the best base for visiting the Parque Nacional Los Alerces, and for skiing at La Hoya in winter. The tranquil village of Trevelin, where the Welsh heritage is more in evidence, is just 25 km away.

Ins and outs

Getting there and around Esquel has its own airport, 20 km east of town, reached by bus or taxi, and a smart modern bus terminal on Avenida Alvear, six blocks from the main commercial centre around Avenida Fontana. Buses arrive here from Comodoro Rivadavia on the Atlantic coast and Bariloche, with connections from those places to all other destinations in Patagonia and to the north. Buses also run daily into Los Alerces National Park.

Tourist information The **tourist office** ⓘ *in a little hut on the corner of Alvear y Sarmiento, T02945-451927, www.esquel.gov.ar, daily 0800-2000, summer 0730-2200, closed weekends off-season*, is friendly enough, but doesn't seem to have much information. They do hand out a useful town map, however, and another leaflet it's worth asking for, with a yellow map of Los Alerces National Park showing all access and accommodation in the park, as well as crossing to Chile via Paso Futulaeufú. You might have to press them patiently for bus timetables. For further information on Los Alerces see www.comarcadelosalerces.com.ar/lacomarca.htm.

Sights

There aren't any sights, as such, and the whole point of visiting Esquel is to get to Los Alerces, or Trevelin, but it's a pleasant place to walk around. All the food shops and services you need are contained within a few blocks east of Avenida Alvear, between Mitre and the wide Avenida Fontana. The famous narrow gauge railway, **La Trochita** ⓘ *station office Estación Viejo Expreso Patagonico, T02945-451403, www.latrochita.com.ar, US$8.50, children under 6 free, Jan-Feb 5 departures a week, other times Sat only at 1000, tour operators in town sell tickets*, also known in Spanish as *El Viejo Expreso Patagónico*. The train leaves from a pretty little old station six blocks north of the town centre at the corner of Brown and Roggero. While it's obviously a tourist

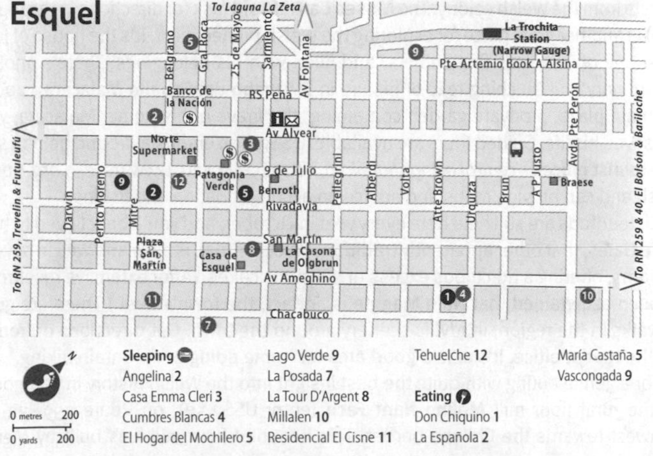

experience, this is a thoroughly enjoyable trip, and as the steam train rumbles across the lovely valleys and mountains of the *precordillera* on tracks just 75 cm wide, you'll find yourself wanting to know how it works. There's Spanish and English commentary along the way, the quaint carriages each have little wood stoves, and there's a small tea room on board. But it's worth waiting for the homemade cakes (and handicrafts) for sale at the Mapuche hamlet of **Nahuel Pan**, where the train stops, and where you'll hear an interesting explanation of how the engine works. Recommended.

There's good skiing on high quality powder snow over a long season at the low-key family resort of **La Hoya**, 15 km north (see Skiing, page 469). There are also some challenging walks and mountain bike trails in the surrounding mountains. See the map *Sendas y Bosques* (walks and forests) for El Bolsón, Lago Puelo and Los Alerces, which has the trails clearly marked. It's an easy climb along a clear path to **Laguna La Zeta**, 5 km from the centre of town, with good views and a lake with bird life. From there, head further north up the Río Percey or towards Cañadón Huemul. The path is signposted from the end of Avenida La Fontana. Another good hike, **Cerro La Cruz**, for spectacular views, five hours return; walk from the centre of town signposted from the end of the street 25 de Mayo. There are longer hikes to **Cerro Veinte Uno**, (five to eight hours return) and the pointy cone of Cerro Nahual Pan (eight hours return).

Trevelin

» pp466-470.

→ *Phone code: 02945 Colour map 5, B2 Population: 5,000*

The pretty village of Trevelin, 25 km southwest of Esquel, was once an offshoot of the Welsh colony Gaiman on the Atlantic coast (see box page), when the Welsh travelled west to find further lands for growing corn. The name means Town (*tre*) of the Mill (*velin*) in Welsh, you can still hear Welsh spoken here, and there is plenty of evidence of Welsh heritage in several good little museums around the town. With a backdrop of snowcapped mountains, the village is an appealing place to rest for a few days, to go fishing and rafting on nearby Río Futuleufu, or see the beautiful waterfalls at the reserve of Nant-y-fall.

Sights

Trevelin remains a quiet village with a strong sense of community, and its history is manifest in several sights. The Welsh chapel of 1910, **La Capilla Bethel**, can be visited, with a guided tour to fill you in on a bit of history. The fine old flour mill of 1918 houses the **Museo Histórico Regional** ⓘ *daily 0900-2100, US$1.30*, which has fascinating artefacts from the Welsh colony. The **Museo Cartref Taid** (ask for directions in the tourist office) is another great place for exploring the Welsh pioneer past. It's the house of John Evans, one of Trevelin's first settlers, and filled with his belongings. There's another extraordinary and touching relic of his life in **El Tumbo del Caballo Malacara** , 200 m from main plaza, a private garden containing the grave of his horse, Malacara, who once saved his life. Guided tours are available, US$2. The enthusiastic and helpful staff at the **tourist office** ⓘ *central octagonal plaza, T02945-480120, www.trevelin.org*, speak English and can provide maps and advice on accommodation and fishing.

Eisteddfods are still held here every year in October, and you'll be relieved to hear that **Té Galés**, that other apparently traditional Welsh ritual, is alive and well in several tea rooms, offering a ridiculous excess of delicious cakes. (After extensive research it has been ascertained that **Nain Maggie** is, in fact, the town's best.) There are good day walks in the region, in idyllic scenery around the town. Get directions on routes from the tourist office. It's also a good area for horse riding or mountain biking.

For a gentle outing with quite the best insight into the Welsh history in Patagonia, visit the rural flour mill **Molino Nant Fach** (entry US$2.50), on Route 259, 22 km southwest towards the Chilean border. This beautiful flour mill was built by Merfyn

Evans, descendant of the town's founder Thomas Dalar Evans, as an exact replica of the first mill built the town in 1899. Merfyn's fascinating tour (in Spanish, but English booklet available to read) recounts a now familiar tale of the Argentine government's persistent mismanagement of natural resources and industry, through the suppression of the Welsh prize-winning wheat industry. It's a beautiful spot, and Merfyn tells the rather tragic story in a wonderfully entertaining way. Highly recommended. On the same road, but 5 km earlier the **Nant-y-fall Falls**, 17 km southwest of Trevelin, on Route 259 heading to the Chilean border, before you reach Molino Nant Fach, are a series of spectacular waterfalls reached by an easy 1½-hour walk along a trail through lovely forest. There's a charge of US$4 pp which includes a guide to take you to all seven falls.

Fishing is popular in many local rivers and lakes, most commonly in Río Futuleufú, and Corintos, and Lagos Rosario and Corcovado. The season runs from the end of November to mid-April, and the tourist office can advise on guides and where to go.

Parque Nacional Los Alerces

» pp466-470.

One of the most magnificent and untouched expanses of the whole Andes region, this national park was established to protect the enormously tall and stately alerce trees (*Fitzroya cupressoides*). The alerce is among the longest living tree species in the world, and there are some specimens in the park over 2000 years old. They grow deep in the Valdivian rainforest which carpets these mountains a rich velvety green, beside vivid navy blue Lago Futalaufquen and emerald Lago Verde. There are several good hikes, rafting and fishing in the park, and idyllic lakeside campsites and *hosterías*, making this a great place to spend a few days.

The park, 60 km west of Esquel, is enormous, over 500,000 acres, and it remains the most virgin park in the whole lake district, since much of it is only accessible on foot. There are four large lakes: navy blue **Lago Futalaufquen**, with fine fishing; **Lago Menéndez**, which can be crossed by boat to visit the ancient alerce trees; the exquisite green **Lago Verde**; and the almost inaccessible **Lago Amutui Quimei**. In order to protect this fragile environment, access by car is possible only to the eastern side of the park, via *ripio* Route 71 which runs between Cholila and Trevelin alongside the eastern side of Lagos Futalaufquen, Verde and Rivadavia, with many good camping spots and small *hosterías* on their shores. The western side of the park, where rainfall is highest, has areas of Valdivian forest, and can only be accessed by boat or by hiking to Lago Krügger. Lago Futalaufquen has some of the best fishing in this part of Argentina (the season runs from end November to mid-April), and local guides offer fishing trips, and boat transport. Ask in the *Intendencia* (see Ins and outs, below), or **Hostería Cume Hue** (see Sleeping, page 467).

Ins and outs

There are two main entrances to the park: Route 71, at the northern end of Lago Rivadavia, and Route 7112 km south of Lago Futulaufquen. At the southern tip of this lake is the park's administration centre, the *Intendencia* (park office) with a visitor centre offering useful information on the park. Helpful *guardaparques* give out maps and advise on walks. Right by the *Intendencia*, and less than 2 km from Route 71, **Villa Futulaufquen** is a little hamlet which is very useful for services. There's a petrol station, *locutorio*, two food shops, and a restaurant, **El Abuelo Monje**. Fishing licences can be obtained either from the food shops, the kiosko or **Hosteria Cume Hue**. Park entrance costs US$4. A daily bus runs along Route 71 in each direction, picking up and dropping off passengers at campsites and *hosterías*, and also at the petrol station, opposite the Intendencia. Ask at the petrol station for bus times, see also Transport page 469. For further information contact T02945-471020, www.parquesnacionales.gov.ar.

Walks

For all walks, get the *Sendas y Bosques* (walks and forests) map and book for El Bolsón, Lago Puelo and Los Alerces. Maps are 1:200,000, laminated and easy to read, and the book is full of great walks, with English summaries, and detailed directions in Spanish. www.guiasendasybosques.com.ar. The park office *Intendencia* also as leaflets listing the walks, but there is insufficient detail.

▲ **Cave paintings** There are *pinturas rupestres* to be found just 40 minutes stroll from the park *Intendencia* (Km 1). Also a waterfall, and a *mirador* (viewpoint) with panoramic views over Lago Futulaufquen.

▲ **Lago Verde** The most beautiful walk in the whole park, and unmissable, no matter how little time you have, is across the suspension bridge over Río Arrayanes (Km 34.3) to heavenly Lago Verde. A self-guided trail leads around a peninsula and to Lago Menéndez, to the pier where boat trips begin, Puerto Chucao. Go in the early evening, to see all kinds of bird life from the beach by Lago Verde, swifts and swallows darting all around you. Signposted off Route 71, Pasarella (walkway) Lago Verde. While you're in the area, take a quick 20-minute stroll up to **Mirador Lago Verde** where you'll be rewarded with gorgeous views up and down the whole valley

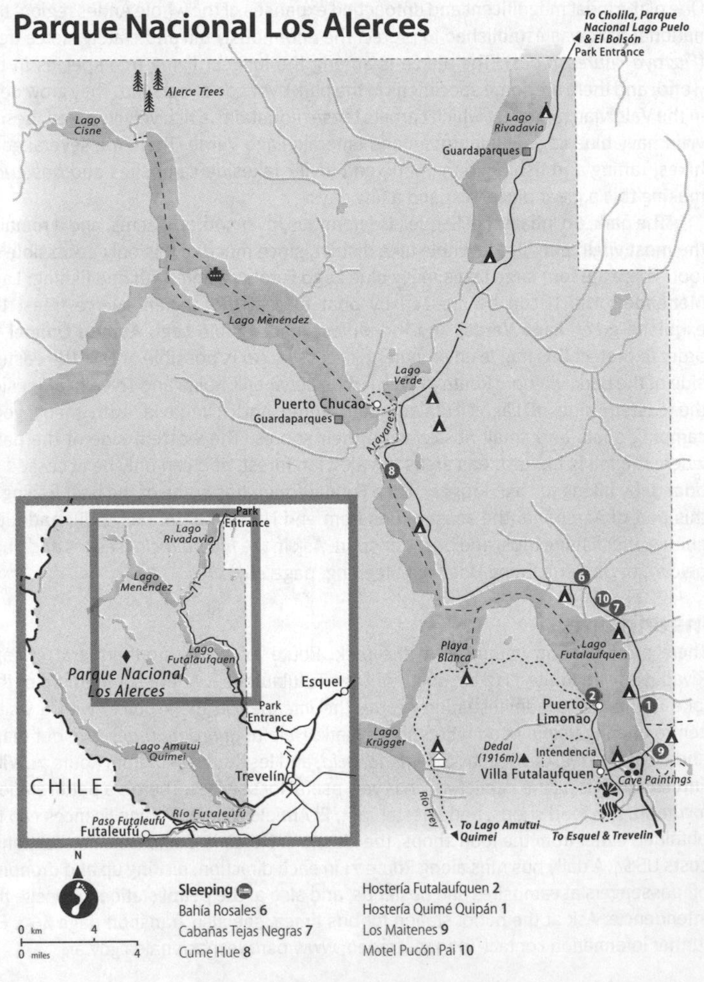

and can appreciate the string of lakes, running from Lago Futulaufquen in the south, Lago Verde, and Lago Rivadavia in the north.

Cerro Dedal For a great day hike, there is a longer trek up Cerro Dedal (1916 m), a circular walk, at least eight hours return, with a steep climb from the *Intendencia*, and wonderful views over the lake and mountains further west. Register with *guardaparques* and get detailed instructions. You're required to start before 1000. Carry plenty of water.

Lago Krügger There is also a but rewarding two- to three-day (12- to 14-hour) hike though *coihue* forest to the southernmost tip of **Lago Krügger**, where there is a *refugio* (open only Jan and Feb), and campsite, as well as a *guardaparque's* office. Here you can take a boat back to Puerto Limonao, but check when the boat is running before you set off, and always register with the park's *Intendencia*. From Lago Krügger, you could walk south along the course of Río Frey, though there is no *refugio* here. For information on the boat service, and the *refugio* contact **Hostería Lago Krügger**, www.lagokruger.com, a little rustic fishing lodge. US$60 for two, full board.

Cascada Arroyo A satisfying and easy four-hour walk to see waterfalls, and passing various miradores.

Boat trips

All boat trips run frequently in high season (1 December to 31 March), and all can be booked through **Safari Lacustre** ⓘ *T02945-471008, www.brazosur.com*, **Patagonia Verde** ⓘ *Esquel, T02945-454396*, or when you get to the piers, though tickets sell out in high season. Boat trips leave from Puerto Limonao at the southern end of Lago Futulaufquen: follow signs up the western side of the lake, just for a few kilometres; or from Puerto Chucao, which is reached from the suspension bridge crossing Lago Verde, half way along Route 71. Trips start at Puerto Limonao, and then call in at Puerto Chucao, before setting off across Lago Futulaufquen and along the pea-green Río Arrayanes, lined with the extraordinary cinnamon-barked *arrayán* trees. Even more spectacular, from Puerto Chucao, across Lago Menéndez (one and a half hours) where you land, and walk a short distance to see a majestic 2,600 year old *alerce* tree, known as 'el abuelo'. From here you walk to the hidden and silent jade-green Lago Cisne, and then back past the rushing white waters of Río Cisne. An unforgettable experience. From Puerto Limonao, cost US$35, set off 1000, return 1900. From Puerto Chucao, cost US$25, set off 1200, return 1700. Boats also go from Puerto Limonao to Lago Krügger or you can trek there, and take the boat back, but check boat times before you set off. Boats sail in summer only.

Border with Chile

There are two border crossings just south of Esquel, the spectacularly beautiful Paso Futaleufú and Paso Palena. On the Chilean side roads from these crossings both link up to the route to Chaitén.

Paso Futaleufú lies 70 km southwest of Esquel via Trevelin and is reached by Route 259 (*ripio* from Trevelin). The border is crossed by a bridge over the Río Futaleufú, and formalities should take no longer than an hour. **Argentine immigration and customs** is on the Argentine side of the bridge. Eat all your fresh food, as no fruit or vegetables may be take into Chile. Cars must have special papers and the numberplate etched into all windows: advise your hire company when booking. **Chilean immigration and customs** is in Futaleufú, 9 km west of the border.

Paso Palena lies 120 km southeast of Esquel and is reached by Route 17 from Trevelin which runs to Corcovado, 75 km east of Tecka (reached by ripio road). From Corcovado it is 26 km west to the border. **Argentine immigration and customs**, is at the border, daily 0900-1800. **Chilean immigration**, is at Palena, 11 km west of border. There are *cabañas* in Corcovado and several *pensiones* in Palena

South of Esquel » pp466-470.

The iconic Route 40 continues (paved) south from Esquel across very deserted landscapes that give you a taste for the full experience of Patagonia. It's a tricky section for travel by public transport, since there are few settlements or services along this section of road until you reach Perito Moreno. At **Tecka**, Km 101, Route 62 (paved) branches off east and follows the valley of the Río Chubut to Trelew: another lonely road. Route 40 continues south to **Gobernador Costa**, a small service centre for the estancias in this area on the Río Genoa at Km 183. Buses go up and down to the town of Perito Moreno, and from here you can take a daily service on to El Chaltén or El Calafate: ask in Esquel's bus terminal.

Río Pico → *Phone code: 02945 Colour map 5, C2 Population: 1,000*

Río Pico lies in a wide green valley close to the Andes and has become quietly known among trout-fishing circles as a very desirable place to fish. It is the site of an early 20th-century German settlement and some old houses remain from that period. Nearby are several lakes, good for fishing and free camping, ask locals for hitching; the northern shore of Lago Tres, 23 km west of town, is a peaceful and remote place, with a rich birdlife and wild strawberries at the end of January. Some 30 km north of Río Pico lies the huge Lago Vintter, reached by Route 44. There are also smaller lakes good for trout fishing. Permits are available from the municipalidad in Gobernador Costa.

South of Gobernador Costa

At Km 221, Route 40 (poor *ripio*) forks southwest through the town of **Alto Río Senguer** from which visits can be made to the relatively unexplored Lago Fontana and Lago La Plata. Provincial Route 20 (paved) heads almost directly south for 81, before turning east towards Sarmiento and Comodoro Rivadavia. At La Puerta del Diablo, in the valley of the lower Río Senguer, Route 20 intersects provincial Route 22, which joins with Route 40 at the town of Río Mayo in Patagonia (see page 508). This latter route is completely paved and preferable to Route 40 for long-distance motorists.

Sleeping

Esquel *p460, map p461*
There are also now many cabañas for rent in Esquel: ask at tourist office for the full list.
A-B Cumbres Blancas, Ameghino 1683, T/F02945-455100, www.cpatagonia.com/esq/cblancas. A little out of the town centre, this lovely *hostería* has great views, comfortable traditional rooms and an airy restaurant serving good food. Recommended.
B Angelina, Alvear 758, T02945-452763. A warm welcoming place, open high season only, serving good food, Italian spoken.
B Canela, C Los Notros, Villa Ayelén, on the road to Trevelin, T/F02945-453890, www.canela-patagonia.com. Comfortable B&B and tea room. English-speaking owners are knowledgeable about Patagonia.
B Tehuelche, 9 de Julio 825, T02945-452420, tehuelche@ar.inter.net. A comfortable redesigned 1970's-style place with modern rooms, breakfast included, and a good restaurant with cheap set menu.
D La Chacra, Km 5 on RN 259 towards Trevelin, T02945-452802. Tranquil place with spacious modern rooms and huge breakfast, Welsh/English spoken.
D La Posada, Chacabuco 905, T02945-454095, laposada@ar.inter.net. A real find, this welcoming, tasteful *hostería* is in a quiet part of town, with a lovely lounge to relax in, and good spacious rooms, breakfast included. Excellent value. Friendly owner Luis Gomez is very welcoming. Recommended.
C La Tour D'Argent, San Martín 1063, T02945-454612, www.cpatagonia.com/esq/latour. With breakfast, the bright plain modern rooms are very good value in this friendly family-run hotel. Recommended.
E Res El Cisne, Chacabuco 778, T02945-452256. With cooking facilities, this quiet and

well-kept family guest house is good value.

F Casa Emma Cleri, Alvear 1021, T02945-452083. Helpful and hospitable.

G pp **Mrs Elvey Rowlands' guesthouse**, behind Rivadavia 330, T02945-452578. With a warm welcome, this is a recommended place, though the rooms are simple with shared bath. Breakfast included, Welsh spoken.

Camping

El Hogar del Mochilero, Roca 1028, T02945-452166. Camping summer only (Jan-Mar), also has laundry facilities, 24-hr hot water, friendly owner, internet, free firewood.

La Rural, 1 km on road to Trevelin, T02945-1568 1429. Well organized and shady site with facilities.

Millalen, Ameghino 2063, T02945-456164. Good services.

Youth hostels

E pp **Casa de Pueblo**, San Martin 661, T02945-450581, www.epaadventure.com.ar. A friendly welcoming hostel with smallish rooms, kitchen, laundry. Also run-rafting, trekking, climbing and mountain biking.

E Lago Verde, Volta 1081, T02945-452251, patagverde@teletel.com.ar. A modern comfortable place, with rooms for 2, breakfast extra, kitchen, laundry. Handy for the bus terminal, and 2 blocks from La Trochita. The owners run a travel company and can organize excursions. Recommended.

F El Hogar del Mochilero, Roca 1028, T02945-452166. Jan-Mar only. Hostel and campsite with laundry, 24-hr hot water, friendly owner, internet, free firewood.

Trevelin *p462*

A Challhuaquen, Los Cipreses, T02945-1550 4072, www.challhuaquen.com. Charming place set high up with beautiful views over the river, and high quality accommodation and food, aimed at the fly fishing market with expert resident fishing guide.

B Patagonia Lodge, RN 71, Km 1, T02945-480752, tom@lapatagnialodge.com. Has been recommended.

D Pezzi, Sarmiento 353, T02945-480146, hpezzi@intramed.com.ar. Open Jan-Mar only, an attractive small hotel, English spoken, and a garden.

D-E Casa Verde Hostal, Los Alerces s/n, T/F02945-480091, www.casaverde hostel.com.ar. 'The best hostel in Argentina' is run by the lovely Bibiana and Charley, who'll make you welcome in their cosy log cabin, with gardens, and views over Trevelin. Comfortable dorms for 4-6 people all have bathrooms. Kitchen facilities, laundry, lounge, HI member, meals available. They also run trekking and rafting excursions into Los Alerces national park. There's also a *cabaña* for hire: very comfortable. All highly recommended.

Cabañas

Ask for a full list at the tourist office. The following are recommended:

A-B Casa de Piedra, Brown 244, T02945-480357, casadepiedratrevelin@yahoo.com.ar.

A-B El Tropezón, San Martín y Saavedra, T02945-480016, eltropezon@ciudad.com.ar.

Camping

There are many sites, especially on the road to Futuleufú and Chile.

Aikén Leufú, on the road to Futaleufú dam, T02945-1568 1398, with full facilities and *cabañas* for 2.

Puerto Ciprés, on the banks of Río Futuleufú, T02945-450913. Peaceful place, right on river bank, simple facilities.

Parque Nacional Los Alerces *p463*

East side of Lago Futalaufquen

L El Aura: Lago Verde Wilderness Resort, T011-4522 7754 (Buenos Aires), www.tenriverstenlakes.com/elaura-i.htm. Exquisite taste in these 3 stone cabins and a guest house on the shore of Lago Verde. Luxury in every respect, attention to detail, ecologically friendly. Impressive place.

AL Cume Hue, T02945-453639. A rather overpriced fishing lodge with spartan rooms and basic bathrooms, and enclosed in woodland, so that only some rooms have views, but great for anglers. You can fish directly from the shore here, or in boat trips organized by the owners. Prices are full board.

A Hostería Quimé Quipán, T02945-454134. Delightful, comfortable rooms, impeccably clean and attractively decorated, with uninterrupted lake views, and dinner included. Wonderfully peaceful. Paths lead down to a small rocky beach, and there are gardens to sit in. Recommended.

C Bahía Rosales, T02945-471044. A welcoming family-run place with spacious *cabañas* to rent, in an elevated position above the lake, also *refugio*-style little *cabañas* to share **F** pp, and camping in open ground with great views, fireplaces and tables and hot showers; restaurant and *quincho*, all recommended.
D Cabañas Tejas Negras, T02945-471046. Next door to **Pucón Pai**, these are really comfortable *cabañas* and good facilities for camping. Also recommended tea room.
D Motel Pucón Pai, T02945-451425, puconpai@ciudad.com.ar. Slightly spartan rooms, but a good restaurant with lovely views, recommended for fishing (holds a fishing festival to open the season); also campsite with hot showers, US$2 pp. Gardens go down to the lake.

West side of Lago Futalaufquen

L Hostería Futalaufquen, just north of Puerto Limonao, T02945-471008, www.brazosur.com. This hotel has an idyllic lakeside setting and architecture, but is woefully maintained, and the service is dreadful: *Fawlty Towers*, but not funny. Rooms are shabby, with ancient bathrooms, and all are overpriced, you'll pay US$250 for those with a lake view, and the food is mediocre. It's even extortionate for tea. Much better on the other side of the lake.

Camping

There are several campsites on the eastern side of the lake, at Lagos Rivadavia, Verde and Río Arrayanes, ranging from free to US$3 depending on facilities. All have marvellous views, lake access and fireplaces, and can be busy in high season. If walking, register with *guardaparques* before you set off, bear in mind that it takes at least 10 hours to reach the *refugio* at Lago Krügger, and camping is possible (one night only) at Playa Blanca, where fires are not permitted.
Krügger Lodge, Lago Krügger has a *refugio* and campsite, with hot showers, food shop, meals provided, fishing guides, and boat trips.
Lago Rivadavia, T02945-454381.
Los Maitenes, Villa Futalaufquen, T02945-451003. Excellent, US$1.50 pp, US$2 per tent.
Pucón Pai, T02945-451425.

Eating

Esquel *p460, map p461*

Don Chiquito, Av Ameghino 1641, T02945-450035. There's a fun atmosphere here, the walls lined with numberplates, and the owner will entertain you with magic and mind-teasing games while you wait for your pasta and pizzas.
Vascongada, 9 de Julio y Mitre, T02945-452229. Fabulous *parrilla*. Good trout and local specialities.
La Española, Rivadavia 740, T02945-451509. Serves excellent beef, with salad bar, and tasty pastas. Recommended.
La Tour D'Argent, San Martin 1063, T02945-454612. Delicious local specialities, good value set meals, and a warm ambience in this popular, traditional restaurant.

Cafés and tea rooms

Maria Castaña, Rivadavia y 25 de Mayo. A popular place for excellent coffee, reading the papers and watching street life.
Melys, Miguens 346 (off Ameghino 2000). Welsh teas and also a good breakfast.

Trevelin *p462*

Patagonia Celta, 25 de Mayo y Molino Viejo, T02945-480722. This is the best place to eat by a long way. Really delicious local specialities, superbly cooked fresh trout, steaks and vegetarian dishes too in elegant stylish surroundings. Very welcoming, and reasonably priced.
Parrilla Mirador del Valle, RN 259, Km 46, T02945-1568 8951. Recommended for excellent *parrilla* and other delicious dishes.
Parrilla Oregon, Av San Martín y Murray Thomas, T02945-480408. Large meals (particularly breakfast).

Cafés and tea rooms

Nain Maggie, P Moreno 179, T02945-480232, www.patagoniaexpress.com/nainmaggie.htm. The best tea room, offering a huge *té galés* and excellent *torta negra*. Recommended.

Shopping

Esquel *p460, map p461*

Benroth, 9 de Julio 1027. Chocolates.
Braese, 9 de Julio 1959. Homemade

chocolates with other regional specialities. **Casa de Esquel**, 25 de Mayo 415. A range of rare books on Patagonia, also souvenirs. **Librería Patagonica**, 25 de Mayo 415, T02945-452544. Rare books on Patagonia and recent editions, with friendly service. **La Casona de Olgbrun**, San Martín 1137. A variety of handicrafts and souvenirs. **Norte**, 9 de Julio y Roca. Huge supermarket.

Activities and tours

Esquel *p460, map p461*

Fishing

Lots of guides and equipment for hire. See Frontera Sur, under Tour operators, below. **Jorge Trucco and Patagonia Outfitters**, Tte Cnel Pérez 662 (San Martín de los Andes) T/F2972-427561, www.jorgetrucco.com.

Skiing

Esquel is a popular resort with Argentines, since it's one of the cheapest and friendliest, **La Hoya**, 15 km north, has 22 km of pistes, many of them suitable for kids or beginners, with good challenging pistes too, and 7 ski lifts. For information, try asking the tourist office, and see www.interpatagonia.com/lahoya/index_i.html There are 3 daily buses to La Hoya from Esquel, US$5 return. A ski pass costs US$12 per day in high season, with reductions for a week or longer, equipment hire from US$6 a day. Contact for equipment: **Sol del Sur**, 9 de Julio y Sarmiento, T02945-452189.

Tour operators

Frontera Sur, Av Alvear y Sarmiento, T02945-450505, www.fronterasur.net. Good company offering adventure tourism of all sorts, as well as more traditional excursions, ski equipment and trekking. **Patagonia Verde**, 9 de Julio 926, T/F02945-454396, patagoniaverde@ciudad.com.ar. Excellent local tours, to Los Alerces, including the wonderful boat trip across Lagos Menéndez and Cisnes, and La Trochita. Also adventure excursions, horse riding (US$12 half day), rafting (US$25 per day, grades 2-4), fishing (US$100 per day, all inclusive), and fabulous 4WD trips to trek in tunnels of ice (US$18 full day). Helpful, professional, English spoken.

Trevelin *p462*

Gales al Sur, Patagonia s/n, in the same building as the locutorio T/F02945-480427, trevelin@galesalsur.com.ar. Tours to Chilean border, Los Alerces National Park and Futaleufú dam; also La Trochita. Recommended for their rafting, trekking, bike, 4WD and horse riding excursions. Friendly, English spoken. Also have internet.

Parque Nacional Los Alerces *p463*

Agencies in Esquel or Trevelin run tours including the boat trip across Lago Menéndez to the alerce trees. For short guided excursions, ask at the *intendencia* in Villa Futalaufquen.

Transport

Esquel *p460, map p461*

Air

Airport, 20 km east, US$9 by taxi, US$3 by bus. For airport enquiries, T02945-451676. To **Buenos Aires** with Aerolíneas Argentinas (agent), Av Fontana408, T453614. LADE, Alvear 1085, T02945-452124, to **Bahía Blanca, Bariloche, Comodoro Rivadavia, El Bolsón, Mar del Plata, Neuquén, Puerto Madryn** weekly.

Airline offices LADE, Alvear 1085, T02945-452124.

Bus

The modern terminal at Alvear 1871, T02945-451584, has toilets, kiosko, *locutorio*, left luggage (US$2 per item per day), and taxis. From **Buenos Aires** travel via Bariloche: Andesmar, T02945-450143, can be booked **Esquel-Buenos Aires**, including change in Bariloche, 24 hrs, *semi cama* US$50. To **Comodoro Rivadavia** 9 hrs US$13, Don Otto, T02945-453012, 4 times a week (but usually arrives from Bariloche full in season).

To **Bariloche**, 4-5 hrs, US$6, **Don Otto**, Andesmar, **Mar y Valle**, T02945-453712, **Vía** Bariloche, T02945-453528. To **El Bolsón**, 2 hrs, US$4, on bus to **Bariloche**, or via **Los Alerces national park**, see below. To **Trelew**, 9 hrs, US$16. Mar y Valle, Emp Chubut, Don Otto, daily. To **Trevelin**, Jacobsen , T02945-453528, Mon-Fri, hourly 0700-2100, every 2 hrs at weekends, US$2. To **Los Alerces National Park**, Jacobsen , T02945-453528, runs a daily bus through the park from Esquel bus terminal at 0930, arriving at **Futulaufquen** (the entrance and *guardería*) 1100, and on to **Lago Verde** 1215You can get on or off at any of the campsites or *hosterías* in park. US$4 each way. Returns to Esquel from **Futulaufquen** at 2000, arriving **Esquel** 2115. Ring to check times as they vary from season to season.

To Chile From Esquel to **Paso Futaleufú**, a bus runs at 0800 daily in Jan/Feb, otherwise Mon, Fri, sometimes Wed, with **Jacobsen**, T02945-453528, US$3.50. At the border a bus will be waiting to go to Futuleufu and onto **Chaitén**, with **Transportes Cordillera** T02945-258633, and **Ebenezer**, between them 4 times a week, and daily Jan/Feb. From Chaitén there are services to **Coyhaique**.

Car hire
Localiza, Rivadavia 1168, T02945-453276. The only agents who have cars for hire, and even then, you can't rely on them. Book way in advance.

Taxi
Unión, Roca 477, T0800-333 2806. **Gerardo Parsons**, T02945-156 87702, gerardoturismo@yahoo.com.ar.

Train
La Trochita – the *Old Patagonian Express* generally runs from Esquel to **Nahuel Pan** (19 km) 5 times a week, and up to twice a day in high season (much less frequent in winter), taking 2½ hrs, US$5, children under 6 free. At wild and remote Nahuel Pan, there's just a small terrace of houses, home to a Mapuche community, who sell delicious home baked cakes, and display their knitwear for you to buy, some of it very fine quality. Sometimes there's an extra service from **El Maitén** at the northernmost end of the line on Sat, taking 6 hrs, US$10, with a dining car. Information, in English including schedules in El Maitén, T02945-495190, and in Esquel T02945-451403. Www.latrochita.com.ar.

Trevelin *p462*
Bus
To **Esquel**, with **Via Trevelin**, T02945-455222, Mon-Fri, hourly 0700-2100, every 2 hrs weekends, US$2. To the **Chilean border**, **Jacobsen** bus from Esquel runs through Trevelin, 0830 daily in Jan/Feb, otherwise Mon, Fri, sometimes Wed, US$3, connecting bus at border to **Futuleufu** and on to **Chaitén**. Ring to check times as they vary from season to season, T02945-453528.

Parque Nacional Los Alerces *p463*
From Esquel there are 2 services running at the time of writing: **Jacobsen**, as described above, and **Transportes Esquel**, T02945-453529, runs daily buses at 0800 from Esquel (returning at 2115) along the east side of **Lago Futalaufquen**, passing **Villa Futalaufquen** 0915 (return 2000), **Lago Verde** 1030 (return 1845), **Lago Rivadavia** 1120 (return 1830), and continuing on to **Cholila**, **El Bolsón** and **Lago Puelo** (return 1500). The driver will drop you at your accommodation, and you can stop the bus at any point on the road. US$4 each way.

South of Esquel *p466*
Bus From Esquel to **Río Pico**, 4½ hrs, Mon/Wed/Sat, **Jacobsen**, T02945-453528.

South of Gobernador Costa *p466*
Bus From Esquel to **Alto Río Senguer**, **ETAP**, Mon, Thu.

Directory

Esquel *p460, map p461*
Banks **Banco de la Nación**, Alvear y Roca, open 0730-1300, ATM accepts all cards. ATMs also at **Banco Patagonia** , 25 de Mayo 739, **Bansud**, 25 de Mayo 752. **Internet** **Best & Best**, Av Fontana y Ameghino, T02945-450632. **Cyberplanet**, San Martin 996, T02945-452228 , lots more in the centre. **Post office** Alvear 1192 y Fontana, Mon-Fri 0830-1300 and 1600-1930, Sat 0900-1300. **Telephone** Many *locutorios* in centre including **Unitel**, 25 de Mayo 528, Central Sur Rivadavia 949, and at bus terminal.

Patagonia

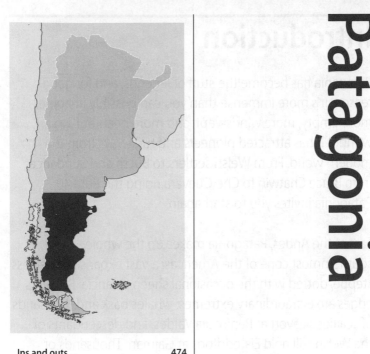

Footprint features

Introduction

Patagonia has become the stuff of legends, and for good reason. It's more immense than you can possibly imagine, more empty, more windswept, and more beautiful. No wonder it has attracted pioneers and runaways from the modern world. From Welsh settlers to Butch and Sundance; from Bruce Chatwin to Che Guevara riding the Ruta 40, Patagonia invites you to start again.

East of the Andes, Patagonia makes up the whole southernmost cone of the Americas: a vast expanse of treeless steppe, dotted with the occasional sheep estancia. But at its edges are extraordinary extremes: whales bask and thousands of sea lions cavort at Península Valdés, and descendants of the Welsh still hold Eisteddfods at Gaiman. Thousands of handprints are testimony to stone age life at Cueva de las Manos, and there are two petrified forests of mighty fallen monkey puzzle trees.

Take the Ruta 40 south, and you'll travel hundreds of kilometres without seeing a soul, until the magnificent granite towers of Mount Fitz Roy rise up from the flat plains: this trekking heaven is far less crowded than Torres del Paine, and on the southern ice field there are no beaten tracks whatsoever. El Calafate is the base for boat trips to the Perito Moreno glacier: put on your crampons and walk their sculpted turquoise curves, or escape to splendidly isolated Estancia Cristina. Once you've seen Upsala Glacier stretching out as far as the eye can see, silent and pristine, calving below you into a milky Prussian blue lake, you'll have forgotten about everything. Allow plenty of time, bring walking boots, and prepare to lose yourself.

★ Don't miss...

1 **Península Valdés** Thousands of sea lions, orcas and southern right whales, page 480.
2 **Real Patagonian estancias** Monte León and Alta Vista, pages 499 and 525.
3 **Ruta 40** Follow in Che's tyre tracks and experience real wilderness, page 506.
4 **Upsala Glacier** Breathtaking views of the immense ice field from Estancia Cristina, page 518.
5 **Trekking at Mount Fitz Roy** Explore the southern ice cap, page 519.

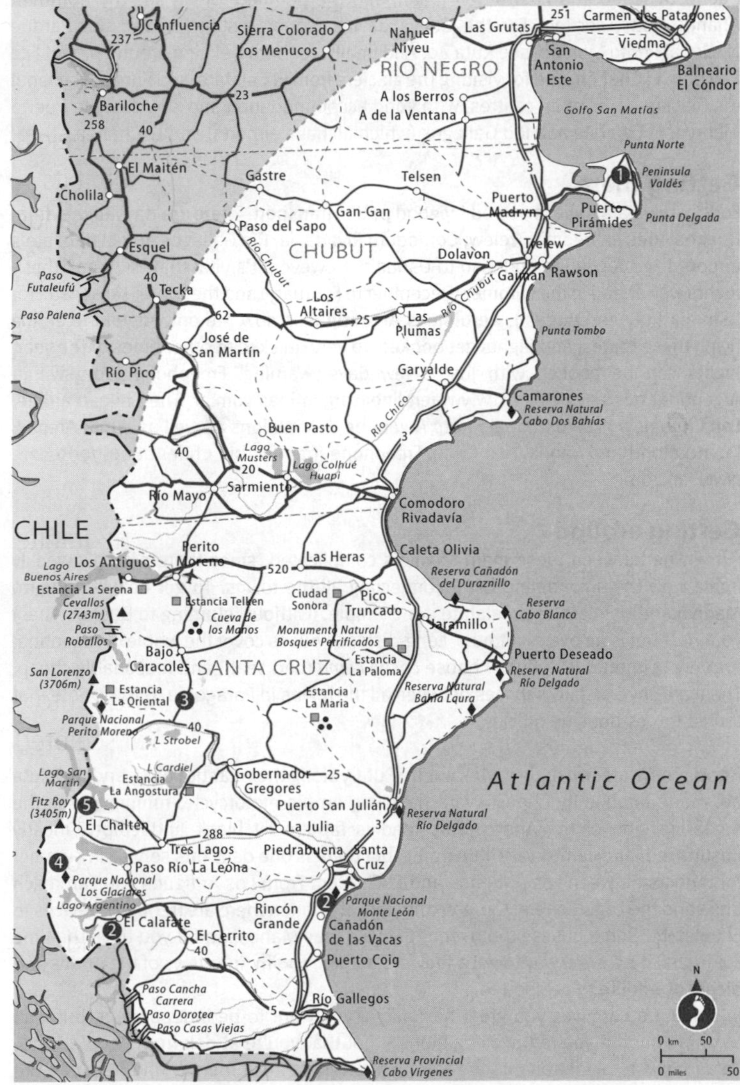

Ins and outs

Patagonia is vast, and it's no surprise that getting around takes some organization. Strictly speaking, Patagonia is the whole southern cone of South America, combining all parts of Argentina and Chile, south of the Río Colorado, which runs from west to east, just north of Viedma. It includes the Andes, running north-south along the extreme west (marking the Chilean border) and therefore the Lake District, which has been given its own chapter in this book, see page 383. The Patagonia chapter, then, includes all of Argentine Patagonia apart from the lakes and Tierra del Fuego, the island at the very bottom, which has its own chapter, see page 557.

For Puerto Madryn, whale watching at Península Valdés, and the Welsh village of Gaiman, see the Northern Atlantic Coast section. For marine wildlife reserves at Puerto Deseado and Puerto San Julián, and the petrified forest, see the Southern Atlantic Coast section. For the Cueva de las Manos, estancias and the Parque Nacional Perito Moreno, see Ruta 40. And finally, for both trekking around Mount Fitz Roy from El Chaltén, and for visiting the glaciers from El Calafate, see Parque Nacional los Glaciares. The main centres, with good accommodation and services, are Puerto Madryn, El Calafate and Río Gallegos (which all have airports) and El Chaltén.

Getting there

Fortunately Patagonia is served by good public transport. There are daily flights from Buenos Aires to Viedma, Trelew, Comodoro Rivadavia, Río Gallegos and El Calafate's airport, Lago Argentino and also to Ushuaia. However, it's vital that you book these flights well ahead in the summer (December to February) and the winter ski season for Ushuaia (July and August). **Aerolineas Argentinas** is now the only Argentine airline flying these routes, and flights get booked up very quickly. At other times of the year, flights can be booked with just a few days' warning. Freephone (from within Argentina) 0810-222 86527, www.aerolineasargentinas.com.ar. The Chilean airline, **Lan Chile** now flies to Ushuaia from Argentine destinations as well as Punta Arenas, Puerto Montt and Santiago in Chile. Freephone (from within Chile) 0800 9999 526, www.lan.com.

Getting around

Air Flying between these main towns is complicated, since there are only weekly fights with the army airline **LADE** connecting all the towns. To get between Puerto Madryn and Ushuaia or El Calafate, for example, (without returning to Buenos Aires) your best bet is an overnight bus. Long-distance buses cover the whole of Argentina, are very comfortable – if you choose *coche cama* (bed seat), and reasonably cheap. There are several daily services between all the towns in Patagonia, though note that tourist routes book up quickly.

Road There are two main routes south: Ruta 3 along the Atlantic coast, and the Ruta 40, made famous by Che Guevara travelling on his motorcycle, running along the Argentine side of the Andes. This road is fabulously bleak and empty, mostly unsurfaced, and carries very little traffic, but there is one daily bus service in summer for tourists between Los Antiguos and El Chaltén. From Los Antiguos you can reach Chile and the Lago General Carrera, and from El Chaltén there are frequent services to El Calafate. Some buses stop over at Cueva de las Manos, and if you have the time (14 hours) it's a great way to get a feel for Patagonia, with fine views of the Andes and plenty of wildlife to be spotted.

Hiring a car gives you great flexibility if you want to be independent, but isn't recommended if you're travelling alone – not that you're at risk from people, since Patagonia's rural inhabitants are among the world's most friendly and helpful – but the elements are harsh, distances are enormous and, if you run out of petrol or get a stone through your windscreen, it's not a place to be stranded alone. However, hire companies will now let you rent a car in one place and drop it off in another, so you could combine flying with driving.

Driving and cycling in Patagonia require care and patience. Most of the roads are *ripio* – gravel – limiting driving speeds to 60 kph, or slower where surfaces are poor, and it's worth driving your hire car very carefully, as there are huge fines for turning them over. Carry spare fuel, as service stations may be as much as 300 km apart, carry warm clothing in case of breakdown at night, and make sure your car has anti-freeze. There are lots of cattle grids (watch out for signs saying *guardaganados*) to be crossed with care. Hitchhiking is difficult, even on Ruta 3 in the tourist season, and hitching along the Ruta 40 is only possible with a lot of luck and a little help from locals; it helps to speak good Spanish. The Ruta 40 has become a favourite long-distance favourite among hardy cyclists, and it is an amazing experience. But do your research first: winds are fierce, there are few places to get food and water, and a complete absence of shade. A tent is essential, with camping allowed pretty much everywhere, but very few *hosterías* or places to stay.

Train There's just one long-distance train across this expanse: a comfortable overnight service between Viedma and Bariloche in the lakes, also taking cars. Check out www.trenpatagonico.com.ar for further information. It's cheap, but takes as long as the bus, and only useful if you happen to be in Viedma in the first place.

National parks

There are many national parks in the region, of which **Parque Nacional Los Glaciares** is the most famous. At the northern end the main centre is El Chaltén for trekking around **Mount Fitz Roy**, and at the southern end are the glaciers at the southern end, reached from El Calafate. Both have good tourist infrastructure, with *guardaparques* offices, where staff speak English and other languages, hand out maps, and can advise on where to walk and camp.

Parque Nacional Perito Moreno is also spectacular, and well worth the considerable effort involved in reaching its remote lakes and mountains. Access is from the Ruta 40, but there is almost no infrastructure whatsoever, little information for visitors, and no services. The best way to see the park is to stay at an estancia, such as **La Maipú** and ride horses into the park: an unforgettable experience of true wilderness.

Marine life abounds on the Atlantic Coast in Península Valdés, reached from an organized tour, or hire car from Puerto Madryn. This is a well organized area for visits and there are also several estancias on the peninsula where you can stay in great comfort. Further south, **Parque Nacional Monte León** is reached from the Ruta 3, where you'll need your own transport: there is a comfortable *hostería* here. There are many other colonies of penguins, and other sea life reserves along the Atlantic Coast. There are two other tourist sights, at **Cueva de las Manos**, and a petrified forest. Unless you have your own transport, it's best to take an organized tour to reach these, as services are few at the sites themselves.

Best time to visit

The summer months from December to April are best for trekking: though avoid January everywhere but the most remote places, if you can, since this is when most Argentines go on holiday, and transport and accommodation are both heavily booked. December and March/April can be lovely, and much emptier. Most hotels are closed between early April and mid-November and many bus services don't operate in this period, since temperatures in the south plummet to minus 20, making it very inhospitable. For Península Valdés, the season for spotting whales is between September to November, when all services are open.

Tourist information

There are tourist offices in even the smallest towns that have any tourist potential, although the best ones are inevitably in El Calafate and El Chaltén, with excellent information centres in Puerto Madryn, Trelew and Río Gallegos. Many have good websites, worth a look before you set off, some with links to hotels for booking accommodation: **Puerto Madryn** and **Península Valdés**, www.madryn.gov.ar; **Chubut province** (northern half of Patagonia), www.chubutur.gov.ar; **Santa Cruz province** (southern half of Patagonia), www.santacruz.org.ar; **El Chaltén**, www.elchalten.com; **El Calafate**, www.turismo.elcalafate.gov.ar. Also worth visiting is the national parks site www.parquesnacionales.gov.ar. For information on all towns and tourist services try www.interpatagonia.com. For articles on specific places www.revistapatagonia.com.ar, and for information on estancias www.lastfrontiers.com and www.estanciasdesantacruz.com. Fly fishing www.interpatagonia.com/pesca/index_i.

Background

Patagonia was inhabited by various groups of indigenous peoples from thousands of years ago until colonization by the Europeans, and the region gets its name from early Spanish settlers' first impressions of these native people: Big Feet (*pata* being the informal word for leg). The first European visitor to the coast of Patagonia was the Portuguese explorer Fernão Magalhães, in 1519, who gave his name to the Magellan straits, by which he discovered a safer route through the southern extreme of the continent, going north of the island of Tierra del Fuego, rather than the perilous route south around Cape Horn. The first to traverse Patagonia from south to north was the English sailor, Carder, who survived a shipwreck in 1578 in the Strait of Magellan, walked to the Río de la Plata and arrived in London nine years later.

For several centuries European attempts to settle along the coast were deterred by isolation, lack of food and water and the harsh climate, as well as understandable resistance from the indigenous peoples. However, they were almost wiped out in the bloody war known as the Conquest of the Desert in 1879-1883 (see box, page 129). Before this there had been a European colony at Carmen de Patagones, which shipped salt to Buenos Aires, and the Welsh settlement in the Chubut valley from 1865. After the Conquest of the Desert, colonization was rapid. Welsh, Scots and English farmers were among the biggest groups of immigrants including sheep farmers from Las Malvinas/Falkland Islands, as well as Chilean sheep farmers from Punta Arenas moving eastwards into Santa Cruz. The discovery of large oil reserves in many areas of southern Patagonia brought wealth to Chubut and Santa Cruz provinces in the 1900s. However, when President Menem privatized the national oil company YPF in the 1990s, much of that wealth immediately diminished. One of the few people to gain from it all was Argentina's current president, Kirchner, who had been governor of Santa Cruz province while it was rich and influential within the country.

Northern Atlantic Coast and Puerto Madryn

The sight of a mother and baby whale basking in quiet waters, just a few metres from your boat is an unforgettably moving sight. Not, perhaps, what you expected to see after travelling for days in the wild unpopulated open desert of Patagonia. But the whole Atlantic coast hosts huge colonies of marine life, and there is no region quite as spectacular as Península Valdés. This wide splay of land stretching into the Atlantic from a narrow isthmus enclosing a gulf of protected water attracts an astonishing array of wildlife who come to breed here each spring, most famously the southern right whales, who can be seen from September to November. The pleasant breezy town of Puerto Madryn is the best base for exploring the peninsula, though there are estancias on Valdés itself. Just to the south, Trelew is worth a visit for its superb palaeontological museum, and to reach the old Welsh pioneer villages of Gaiman and Dolavon further west. If you're heading south by road, consider stopping off at historic Carmen de Patagones, a quaint Patagonian town. Patagonia's fine estancias start here, with riding and sheep mustering at La Luisa. *⏩ For Sleeping, Eating and other listings, see pages 486-494.*

Viedma and Carmen de Patagones

⏩ pp486-494.

➔ Phone code 02920 Colour map 5, A5

These two towns straddle the broad sweep of the Río Negro, about 250 km south of Bahía Blanca, and while neither has any real tourist attractions, you could stop off here on the way south and find warm hospitality, and a couple of decent places to stay. The two towns face each other, and share a river, but little else. Capital of Río Negro province, Viedma, on the south bank, was founded as Mercedes de Patagonia in 1779, but was destroyed almost immediately by floods, after which Carmen de Patagones was founded on higher ground on the north bank later that same year. The towers of a handsome church thrust above the town's roofs, and the little town prospered, since for many years, it was a European colony which shipped salt to Buenos Aires, and in 1827, it was the site of an extraordinary battle. Poor old Viedma was rebuilt, but destroyed again by floods in 1899. Now, it's a rather dull modern place, employing most of its residents in the administrative centre for the province of Río Negro, and rather less attractive than Patagones. However, Viedma does have the perfect bathing place along the shaded south bank of the river, a delightful spot in summer. Patagones (as it's called by the inhabitants) has more tangible history, with charming streets of nineteenth century adobe houses near the river, where the tiny ferry takes you across to Viedma, and there's a fabulous little museum.

Viedma *➔ Population 40,000.*

Viedma is quite different in character from Carmen de Patagones, since it's the provincial administrative centre, rather than the home of farmers and landowners. An attractive *costanera* runs by the river, with large grassy banks shaded by willow trees, and the river water is pleasantly warm in summer and completely uncontaminated. On a calm summer's evening, when groups gather to sip *mate*, the scene resembles Seurat's painting of bathers. There are two plazas, with the cathedral, built by the Salesians in 1912, on the west of Plaza Alsina. The former convent, next door, was the first chapel built by the Salesians in the area, in 1887, is now a cultural centre housing the **Museo del Agua y del Suelo** and the **Museo Cardenal Cagliero**, which has ecclesiastical artefacts. Two blocks east, on the Plaza San Martín, are the French-style **Casa de Gobierno** (1926) and, opposite, the **Museo Gobernador Tello** ⓘ *0900-1230, 1700-1930 in summer*, with fossils, rocks and indigenous *boleadoras*. Most diverting, though, is the **Museo Gardeliano** ⓘ *Rivadavi 34, Mon Wed Fri 0930-1130*, a fabulous collection of biographical artefacts of tango singer Carlos Gardel. Along the attractive *costanera*, the **Centro Cultural**, opposite Calle 7 de Marzo, houses a small **Mercado Artesenal** selling beautifully made Mapuche weavings and wood work. The rather impoverished **tourist office** ⓘ *3 blocks east of Plaza Alsina, T02920-427171, www.rionegrotur.com.ar, 0900-2100*, is also on the *costanera*.

Carmen de Patagones *➔ Population 16,000.*

This is by far the more dynamic of the two places (which isn't saying much) and although you'll still find this is a very sleepy town, there's a feeling of positive bustle on the main street on weekday mornings. The town centre, just east of the river, lies around the Plaza 7 de Mayo, and just west is the **Iglesia del Carmen**, built by the Salesians in 1880. Take a stroll down the pretty streets winding down to the river to find many early pioneer buildings along the riverside. The **Torre del Fuerte**, tower of the stone fortress built in 1780 against indigenous attacks, the **Casa de la Tahona**, a disused 18th-century flour mill, now housing the **Casa de la Cultura**, with another late colonial building, **La Carlota**, one block east. And nearby there's the fascinating **Museo Histórico** ⓘ *Viedma 4, T02920-462729, daily 0930-1230, 1900-2100, Sun afternoon only*, giving a great insight into early pioneer life. There are Tehuelche arrowheads, stone *boleadoras*, silver gaucho stirrups, and great early photos – one of a baptism by Salesians of a 100-year-old Tehuelche man in a field, next to delicate tea cups. Great guided tours too. The **Museo de la Prefectura Naval** ⓘ *Mitre 350, T02920-461742, www.prefecturanaval.edu.ar/museo*, is also worth a look if you're into ships, housed in a building dating from 1886 with a marine history of the area.

Patagones is linked to Viedma by two bridges and a very small ferry which takes four minutes and leaves every 15 minutes, US$0.20. There's a helpful and dynamic **tourist office** ⓘ *Bynon 186, T02920-462054, www.vivalaspampas.com*. The town is packed out for the **Fiesta de 7 de Marzo**, which celebrates the victory at the Battle of Patagones with a week of music and handicrafts, fine food, a huge procession, gaucho horse riding displays, and lots of meat on the asados. Great fun. Book accommodation ahead. For more information, T02920-464360, subcom@patagones.mun.gba.gov.ar.

Around Viedma and Carmen de Patagones

At **El Cóndor**, 30 km south (also known as La Boca) there is a beautiful beach, with the oldest lighthouse in the country, dating from 1887. Facilities include a hotel, restaurants and shops, open January and February only. There's free camping on beach 2 km south. There are three buses a day in summer.

This whole stretch of coast is great for shore fishing, with pejerrey, variada and even shark among many other species. **Playa Bonita**, 12 km further south is known as a good fishing spot, with more good beaches. Equipment is available in Viedma (see Shopping page 491). Ask the tourist office for their leaflet *Lobería Punta Bermeja*; 60 km south is a sealion colony visited by some 2500 sea lions in summer, which you can see at close range (daily bus in summer; but hitching is easy). There's also an impressive visitor centre (with toilets). There's more lovely coastline, and a well- established little fishing resort at **Bahia San Blas**, 100 km from Patagones, renowned for shark fishing area. There's lots of accommodation here, including the plush **Resort Tiburon**, www.tiburonresort.freeservers.com. More information at www.bahiasanblas.com.

Estancia La Luisa ⓘ *T02920-463702 or T15624640, eleri@monline.com.ar*, offers an experience on an old Patagonian estancia, with cattle mustering and riding on polo ponies across farmland, immense dunes and limitless expanses of unspoilt beach. The hosts have another, more remote, estancia offering riding holidays, and a genuine gaucho experience camping out in the bush on the shores of a vast salt lake. The place teems with Patagonian wildlife. Overnight guests are welcome at both. Full board is available with home reared lamb roasting on the *asado*.

Puerto Madryn » *pp486-494.*

→ Phone code: 02965 Colour map 5, B5 Population: 60,000

The undoubted highlight of the whole Atlantic Coast in Patagonia is the splendid array of marine wildlife on Península Valdés, best visited from Puerto Madryn. This pleasant breezy seaside town has a grand setting on the wide bay of Golfo Nuevo, and is the perfect base for setting off to Valdés, just 70 km east, as there are plenty of hotels and reliable tour operators running excursions to the peninsula, including boat trips to see the whales. During the breeding seasons (broadly speaking, September to December) you can see whales, penguins and seals at close range, or go diving to explore life underwater. It's possible to stay on the peninsula if you hire a car, with several estancias right in the middle of the wild nature, and conventional hotels at the small popular resort of **Puerto Pirámides**. Puerto Madryn makes a good place to enjoy the sea for a couple of days, with lots of beachfront restaurants selling superb locally caught seafood.

Ins and outs

Getting there There are weekly flights with **LADE** from Buenos Aires to Puerto Madryn's airport, 10 km west. However, there are more frequent flights with **Aerolíneas Argentinas** from Buenos Aires, El Calafate and Ushuaia to Trelew's airport, some 60 km south, with buses to Puerto Madryn that meet all flights. **Mar y Valle** also runs a bus every hour from Trelew's bus terminal to Puerto Madryn's bus terminal.

Getting around The city centre is easy to get around on foot, with many restaurants and hotels lined up along the seafront at Avenida Roca, and most shops and excursion companies on the streets around 28 de Julio, which runs perpendicular to the sea and past the town's neat little plaza, all contained within four or five blocks.

Best time to visit Much of Península Valdés' wildlife can be enjoyed throughout the year, with sealions, elephant seals, dolphins and many species of bird permanently resident. The bull elephant seals can be seen fighting for females from September to early November, and at this time, too, killer whales can sometimes be sighted off the coast, staying until April. Penguins can be seen from September to March, and the stars of the show, the southern right whales, come to these waters to breed in spring - September to November.

Tourist information One of the country's best **tourist information centres** ⓘ *Av Roca 223, just off 28 de Julio, T02965-453504, www.madryn.gov.ar, Mon-Fri 0700-2300, Sat and Sun 0800-2300*, is found here on the seafront, next to the shopping complex. Its staff are friendly, extremely well organized, and speak English and French. They have leaflets on Península Valdés and accommodation, and can advise on tours.

Background

Puerto Madryn was the site of the first Welsh landing in 1865 and the town is named after the Welsh home of the colonist, Jones Parry. However, it wasn't officially founded until 1889, when the railway was built connecting the town with Trelew, to enable the Welsh living in the Chubut Valley to export their produce. The town is a modern, relaxed and friendly place, and hasn't been ruined by its popularity as a tourist resort, with a large workforce occupied by its other main industry: a huge aluminium plant (which you can visit by arrangement through the tourist office). Accommodation is generally of a high standard, but can be pricey. This is one of several tourist centres in Argentina where higher rates apply for foreigners than Argentines for hotel rooms and some entrance fees. It's hopeless to argue.

Sights

You're most likely to be visiting the town to take an excursion to Península Valdés (see page 480), and it's certainly worth spending at least a day enjoying the wildlife there. You can also spot whales directly from the coast at the long beach of **Playa El Doradillo**, 16 km northeast, along the *ripio* road closest to the coast.

In the town itself, the real pleasure is the sea, and it's a pleasant first day's stroll along the long stretch of beach to **El Indio**, a statue on the road at the eastern end of the bay, marking the gratitude of the Welsh to the native Tehuelche people whose shared expertise ensured their survival. As the road curves up the cliff here, there's the splendid **EcoCentro** ⓘ *Julio Verne 784, T02965-457470, www.ecocentro.org.ar, daily 1000-1800 (Tue usually closed in winter, but check with tourist office as times change), US$6*, an inspired interactive sea-life information centre that combines an art gallery, café, and fabulous reading room with comfy sofas at the top of a turret. The whole place has fantastic views of the bay; great for an afternoon's relaxation reading books on wildlife in English or other European languages. Take bus linea 2 from 25 de Mayo y Belgrano, and walk five minutes from the university.

Just a little closer to town, perched on the cliff, is the tiny **Centro de Exposición de Punta Cuevas** ⓘ*1500-1900 daily, US$1*, of interest if you're tracing the history of the Welsh in Patagonia. It's little more than a couple of rooms of relics, near the caves and basic huts on the cliffs where the settlers first lived, but enthusiastic guides make the visit worthwhile. A more conventional museum, with displays on local flora and fauna, the **Museo de Ciencias Naturales y Oceanográfico** ⓘ *Domecq García y J Menéndez, T02965-451139, Mon-Fri 0900-1200, 1430-1900, Sat 1430-1900, US$1*, is informative and worth a visit.

Excursions

Península Valdés is the main attraction, with whale spotting boat trips leaving from Puerto Pirámides, on the southern end of the peninsula. There's more marine life on the coastline – and both are included in one organized tour from Puerto Madryn. There are also sea lions at the **Punta Loma reserve** ⓘ *US$3.50, child US$1.70*, 15 km southeast of Puerto Madryn, open during daylight hours and best visited at low tide in December and January. Access is via the coastal road from town and, like the road to the north, makes a great bike ride; allow 1½ hours to get there. Puerto Madryn is also Patagonia's **diving** capital, with dives to see wildlife and many off-shore wrecked ships, together with all kinds of courses from beginners' dives to the week-long PADI course on offer from tour operators, such as **Madryn Buceo**, See Activities and tours, page 492. You can also hire mountain bikes and windsurfs here, from many places along the beachfront.

There are several estancias on the peninsula which allow you to really appreciate the space and natural beauty of the land and give you much more access to some of the most beautiful places, with great wildlife to observe. Ask the tourist office for their leaflet and advice. Day trips can also be arranged, which might include wildlife trips with an *asado*, and perhaps horse riding. **Estancia Rincón Chico**, T02965-471733, www.rinconchico.com.ar, is particularly recommended. Also **Estancia La Elvira**, T02965-15669153, www.laelvira.com.ar.

Península Valdés

» pp486-494.

Whatever time of year you visit Península Valdés you'll find a wonderful array of marine life, birds and a profusion of Patagonian wildlife such as guanacos, rheas, Patagonian hares and armadillos. But in spring, this treeless splay of land is host to a quite spectacular numbers of whales, penguins and seals, who come to breed in the sheltered waters of the gulf south of the narrow isthmus Ameghino, and on beaches at the foot of the peninsula's chalky cliffs. The land is almost flat, though greener than much of Patagonia, and at the heart of the peninsula are large saltflats, one of which, **Salina Grande**, is 42 m below sea level. The peninsula is privately owned – many of its estancias offering comfortable and wonderfully remote places to stay in the middle of the wild beauty – but it is also a nature reserve and was declared a World Heritage Site by UNESCO in 1999. The beach along the entire coast is out of bounds and this is strictly enforced. The main tourist centre for accommodation, and whale trips is **Puerto Pirámides**, on the southern side of the isthmus.

Ins and outs

Getting there and around Tour operators in Puerto Madryn offer full-day trips that usually include a whale-watching boat trip, which departs from Puerto Pirámides (see below), together with a stop or two on the eastern coastline, to see sealions, penguins, and other wildlife at close hand. Minibus travel, boat trip, and transfers to your hotel are included, but not lunch or entrance to the peninsula. Alternatively, you could hire a car in Puerto Madryn, and drive yourself. This would allow you more time to gaze at the wildlife, but take care driving on the *ripio* (gravel) roads, as they can be treacherous, and hire companies charge a huge excess for turning cars over. A daily bus service goes from Puerto Madryn to Puerto Pirámides, but this would only allow you to see the whales, since there is no public transport to other areas of the peninsula. The island is almost entirely undeveloped, and the only tourist centre is at Puerto Pirámides, where there's one good hotel, places to camp and many restaurants. Otherwise, the most comfortable accommodation is in one of several estancias on the island, recommended for a longer stay with closer contact with nature and the incredible wildlife.

Tourist information At about 45 km northeast of Puerto Madryn is the entrance to the reserve, where you get the ticket for visiting all the sites within the peninsula. Entry costs (foreigners) US$12 (US$6 for children). Twenty kilometres beyond, on the isthmus, there's an interesting **interpretation centre** with stuffed examples of the local fauna, many fossils and a wonderful whale skeleton, which makes a great complement to seeing the real thing gracefully soaring through the water. Ask for the informative bilingual leaflet on southern right whales.

Wildlife → *These are the main marine wildlife colonies.*

Isla de los Pájaros, is in the Golfo San José, 5 km from the interpretation centre. Its seabirds can only be viewed through fixed telescopes (at 400 m distance). Only recognized ornithologists can get permission to visit. Between September and April you can spot wading birds, herons, cormorants and terns. **Caleta Valdés**, 45 km south of Punta Norte in the middle of the eastern shore, has huge colonies of elephant seals which can be seen at close quarters. In the breeding season, from September to October, you'll see the rather unappealing blubbery masses of bull seals hauling themselves up the beach to make advances to one of the many females in their harem. During the first half of August the bull-seals arrive to claim their territory, and can be seen at low tide engaging in bloody battles over the females. At **Punta Cantor**, just south of here, you'll find a good café and clean toilets. Also three marked walks, from 45 minutes to two hours. **Estancia La Elvira** is a short distance inland from here, clearly signposted.

Punta Delgada, at the southeastern end of the peninsula, 110 km from the entrance, is where elephant seals and sea lions can be seen from the high cliffs in such large numbers that they seem to stretch out like a velvety bronze tide line on the beautiful beach below. It's mesmerising to watch as the young frolic in the shallow water, and the bulls lever themselves around the females. There's a hotel nearby, **Faro Punta Delgada** (see Sleeping page 488), a good base for exploring this beautiful area further.

Punta Norte, at the northern end of the peninsula, 97 km from the entrance, is not often visited by the excursion companies, but it has colonies of elephant seals and sea lions. Killer whales (orca) have also been seen here, feeding on sea lion pups at low tide in March and April. **Estancia San Lorenzo** is nearby (see Sleeping page 488).

Puerto Pirámides → *Colour map 5, B5.*

Puerto Pirámides, 107 km east of Puerto Madryn, is the centre for visits to the peninsula, and whale-watching boat trips leave from its broad sandy beach. Every year, between June and December, 400 to 500 southern right whales migrate to the Golfo Nuevo to mate and give birth. It is without doubt one of the best places in the world to watch these beautiful animals, and in many places these whales come within just a few metres of the coast. From Puerto Pirámides, boat trips take you gently close to basking whales, and if you're lucky, you may find yourself incredibly close to a mother and baby. The sight of them frolicking in the water, nuzzling each other gently, is quite unforgettable. Sailings are controlled by the Prefectura, according to weather and sea conditions (if you're very prone to sea sickness, think twice before setting off on a windy day). There's one decent hotel, right by the beach where boat trips begin, and plenty of places to stay strung out along the road from the beach in this touristy little place, plus a campsite, and a good range of places to eat. All are packed out in January and February. There is a small **tourist office** ⓘ *T02965-495084, www.puertopiramides.gov.ar*, on the edge of Puerto Pirámides, offering useful information for hikes and driving tours.

Welsh colonies in the Chubut Valley

» *pp486-494.*

The Río Chubut is one of the most important rivers in Patagonia, flowing a massive 820 km from the eastern foothills of the Andes into the Atlantic at Bahía Engaño. It's thanks to the Río Chubut that the Welsh pioneers came to this part of the world in 1865, and their irrigation of the arid land around it enabled them to survive and prosper. You can trace their history west along the valley from the pleasant airy town of Trelew to the quiet little village of Gaiman, with a wonderful museum, and *casas de té*. Further west, past little brick chapels sitting amidst lush green fields is the quieter settlement of Dolavon, with an old brick chapel. And if you're keen to investigate further into the past, there's a marvellous museum full of dinosaurs in Trelew, and some ancient fossils in the Parque Palaeontológico Bryn-Gwyn near Gaiman. And from Trelew you could visit South America's largest single colony of Magellanic penguins on the coast at Punta Tombo.

Trelew → *Phone code: 02965 Colour map 5, B5 Population: 90,000*

Some 70 km south of Puerto Madryn, Trelew is the largest town in the Chubut Valley. Founded in 1884, it was named in honour of Lewis Jones, an early settler, and the Welsh colonization is still evident in a few remaining chapels in the town's modern centre. It's a cheerful place with a quietly busy street life, certainly more appealing than the industrial town of Rawson, 20 km east on the coast. Trelew boasts a splendid palaeontological museum, a good tourist office and a couple of fabulous cafés.

Ins and outs There are flights from Buenos Aires, El Calafate and Ushuaia to Trelew's airport, 5 km north of centre. A taxi costs US$3-3.50, and local buses to Puerto Madryn will stop at the airport entrance if asked, and from here it's a 10-minute walk. The bus terminal is northeast of the centre, 10-minute walk from the main plaza, where you'll find the very helpful **tourist office** ⓘ *Mitre 387, T02965-420139, www.trelew.gov.ar, Mon-Fri 0800-1400, 1500-2100, Sat and Sun 0900-1300, 1500-2000*. They'll give you an excellent map, directing you to the town's older buildings. Visit mid-October to see the Eisteddfod.

Sights There's the lovely shady **Plaza Independencia** in the town centre, packed with mature trees, and hosting a small handicraft market at weekends. Nearby is the **Capilla Tabernacle**, on Belgrano between San Martín and 25 de Mayo, a red-brick Welsh chapel dating from 1889. Heading east, rather more impressive is the **Salon San David**, a Welsh meeting hall first used for the Eisteddfod of 1913, and now sadly, used for bingo. On the road to Rawson, 3 km south, you'll find one of the oldest standing Welsh chapels, **Capilla Moriah**. Built in 1880, it has a simple interior and a cemetery with the graves of many original settlers, including the first white woman born in the Welsh colony.

Back in Trelew itself, not the oldest but quite the most wonderful building is the 1920's **Hotel Touring Club**, Fontana 240. This was the town's grandest hotel in its heyday, and politicians and travellers met in its glorious high-ceilinged mirrored bar, now full of old photographs and relics. You can eat lunch and there's simple accommodation here; you should also ask the friendly owner to see the elegant 1920's meeting room at the back: almost perfectly preserved.

The town's best museum – and indeed one of the finest in Argentina – is the **Museo Paleontológico Egidio Feruglio** ⓘ *Fontana 140, T02965-432100, www.mef.org.ar, spring and summer daily 0900-2000, otherwise Mon-Fri 1000-1800, Sat and Sun 1000-2000, US$5, full disabled access and guides for the blind.* Imaginatively designed and beautifully presented, the museum traces the origins of life through the geological ages, displaying dynamically poised dinosaur skeletons, with plentiful information in Spanish. Tours are free, available in English, German and Italian. There's also a reasonably cheap café and shop. Highly recommended, and great for kids. Also ask about the **Parque Paleontológico Bryn-Gwyn**, 8 km from Gaiman, with fossil remains from over the last 40 million years.

The **Museo Regional Pueblo de Luis** ⓘ *Fontana y 9 de Julio, T02965-424062, Sat/Sun 1700-2000, US$ 0.70*, is appropriately housed in the old railway station, built in 1889, since Lewis Jones founded the town and started the railways that exported Welsh produce so successfully. It has interesting displays on indigenous societies, on failed Spanish attempts at settlement and on Welsh colonization.

Around Trelew

The two most popular excursions are to see the penguin colony at **Punta Tombo**, 107 km south, and the Welsh valley towns of **Gaiman** and (less so) **Dolavon**. The **Embalse Florentino Ameghino**, 120 km west, is less interesting. There is a lovely rock

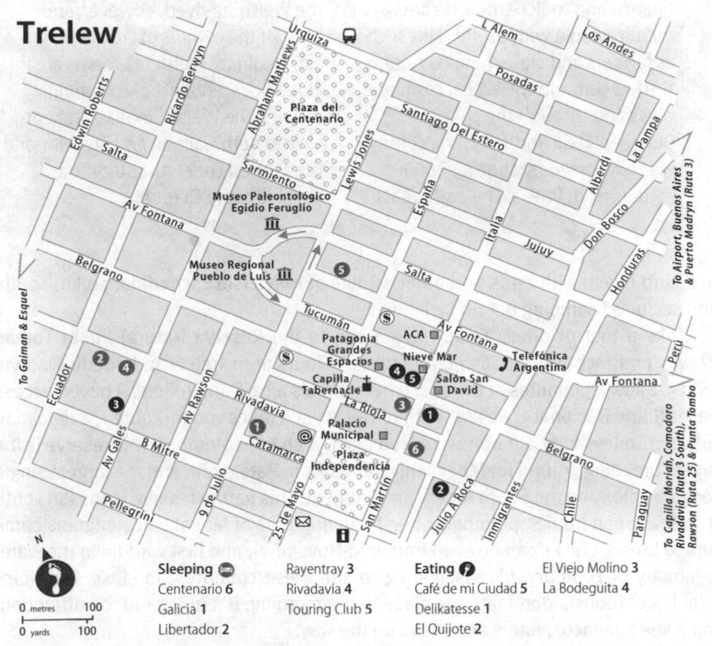

Welsh Patagonia

Among the stories of early pioneers to Argentina, the story of the Welsh emigration, in search of religious freedom, is one of the most impressive. The first 165 settlers arrived in Patagonia in July 1865. Landing on the bay where Puerto Madryn now stands, they went south in search of drinking water to the valley of the Chubut river, where they found cultivatable land and settled. The first ten years were harsh indeed, and they were saved by trade from local Tehuelche indigenous peoples, who taught them essential survival skills, such as irrigation. The British navy also delivered supplies, and there was also support from the Argentine government, eager to populate its territory.

The settlement was partly inspired by Michael D Jones, a non-conformist minister whose aim was to create a 'little Wales beyond Wales', far from the intruding influence of the English restrictions on Welsh religious beliefs. He provided much of the early finance and took particular care to recruit people with useful skills such as farmers and craftsmen, recruiting settlers through the Welsh language press and through the chapels. Between 1865 and 1915, the colony was reinforced by another 3000 settlers from Wales. The early years brought persistent drought, and the Welsh only survived through creating a network of irrigation channels. Early settlers were allocated 100 ha of land, and when, by 1885, all irrigable land had been allocated, the settlement expanded westwards along the valley to the town of Trevelin in the foothills of the Andes.

The Welsh colony was tremendously successful, partly due to the creation of their own Cooperative Society, which sold their excellent produce and bought necessities in Buenos Aires. Early settlers were organized into chapel-based communities of 200 to 300 people, which were largely self-governing, and organized social and cultural activities. The colony thrived after 1880, producing wheat from the arid Chubut Valley which won prizes all over the world. However, the depression of the 1930s drove wheat prices down, and the poor management by the Argentine government resulted in the downfall of the Welsh wheat business. Many of the Welsh survived, however, and most of the owners of Gaiman's extraordinary Welsh tea rooms are indeed descendants of the original settlers. The Welsh language is kept alive in both Gaiman and Trevelin, and the musical concerts Eisteddfods are held every October.

and sand beach with birds and other wildlife at **Playa Isla Escondida**, 70 km south, with secluded camping but no facilities.

Take a tour or drive, if you have a car, to the **Reserva Natural Punta Tombo** ⓘ *park entrance US$7, US$3.50 for children*. Tours from Trelew and Puerto Madryn, US$25, allow 45 minutes at the site, where there's a café and toilets. A paved access leaves Route Nacional 3, 60 km south of Trelew, and takes you to Route 1, a *ripio* road between Trelew and Camarones. Closed late March to September. This reserve is the largest breeding ground for Magallenic penguins in Patagonia, and the largest single penguin colony on the South American continent. This nature reserve is 107 km south of Trelew, open from September, when huge numbers of Magallenic penguins come here to breed. Chicks can be seen from mid-November, and first waddle to the water in January or February. It's fascinating to see these creatures up close, but noisy colonies of tourists dominate the place in the morning; it's quieter in the afternoon. You'll see guanacos, hares and rheas on the way.

Gaiman → *Phone code: 02965 Colour map 5, B4 Population: 4,303,205*

The quaint Welsh village of Gaiman is west of Trelew, in the floodplain of the Río Chubut, is made beautifully green and fertile, thanks to careful irrigation of these lands by the Welsh. After travelling for a few days (or even hours) on the arid Patagonian steppe, it will strike you as a lush green oasis, testimony to the tireless hard work of those hardy Welsh emigrants. Gaiman is the first village you come to on Route 25 which heads past Dolavon before continuing through attractive scenery to Esquel in the Andes, and the other Welsh colony of Trevelin. On the way, you'll find old Welsh chapels tucked away amongst the poplars in this green valley. Gaiman is a pretty little place with old brick houses, which retains the Welsh pioneer feel, despite the constant influx of tourists, and Gaiman hosts the annual **Eisteddfod** (Welsh festival of arts) in October. Around its pretty plaza are several tearooms, many of them run by descendants of the original pioneers, serving delicious and 'traditional' Welsh teas. Before you fill up on all that cake, though, spare a thought for the spartan lives of those idealistic pioneers. There's the wonderful tiny **Museo Histórico Regional Galés** ⓘ *Sarmiento y 28 de Julio, T02965-491007, Tue-Sun 1500-1900, and during school holidays (Dec-Mar, Jul and Easter) 1000-1130, 1600-2000, US$0.70*, with an impressive collection of Welsh artefacts, objects and photographs, all evocative and moving testimony to extraordinary lives in harsh conditions. Curator Mrs Roberts is helpful and hugely knowledgeable, and this is a great resource if you're looking for books on the subject or trying to trace your emigrant relatives.

Many older buildings remain, among them the low stone first house, **Primera Casa** (1874) ⓘ *corner of main street, Av Tello y Evans, daily 1400-1900*; the **old railway station** (1909), which now houses the regional museum (see above) the old hotel (1899), at Tello y 9 de Julio, and the **Ty Nain tea room** (1890), on the Plaza at Yrigoyen 283 (see below). On the south side of the river there are two old chapels: cross the bridge, and then take the first right to find the pretty **Capilla Bethel** (1913) and the **Capilla Vieja**.

A far more recent monument to human energy and inspiration is the extraordinary creation **El Desafío** ⓘ *2 blocks west of plaza, daily until 1800, US$1.70*, an imaginative sculptural world, made entirely from rubbish by the eccentric Joaquín Alonso. Painted plastic bottles, cans and wire form pergolas and dinosaurs are sprinkled liberally with plaques bearing words of wisdom and witty comments. Beginning to fade now, but still good fun. The **tourist office** ⓘ *Av Eugenio Tello, T02965-491571, www.gaiman.gov.ar, Mon-Sat 0900-2000*, is on the plaza.

Some 8 km south of town, there are fossil beds dating back 40 million years at the **Parque Paleontológico Bryn Gwyn** ⓘ *T02965-432100, www.mef.org.ar, Oct-Feb daily 1000-1800; Mar-Sep 1100-1700, US$2.70, taxi from Gaiman US$2*. This is a mind-boggling expanse of time brought to life by a good guided tour. It takes 1½ hours to do the circuit, with fossils to see, as well as a visitor centre where you can experience try some fieldwork in palaeontology. The park is associated with the Museo Paleontológico Egidio Feruglio in Trelew, www.mef.org.ar.

Dolavon → *Phone code: 02965 Colour map 5, B4 Population: 2700*

Founded in 1919, Dolavon is the most westerly Welsh settlement in the valley, and not quite as inviting as Gaiman, though its quiet streets are quite atmospheric, and on a short stroll you can find a few buildings reminiscent of the Welsh past. The main street, Avenida Roca, runs parallel to the irrigation canal built by the settlers, where willow trees now trail into the swiftly flowing water, and there's a Welsh chapel, **Capilla Carmel** at its quieter end. The old **flour mill** at Maipú y Roca dates from 1927 and can be visited (ask for the key at the Municipalidad, Roca 188, in office hours). There's **Autoservicio Belgrano** at the far end of San Martín for food supplies, but there are no tea rooms, and nowhere to stay, though there's a municipal campsite two blocks north of the river, free, with good facilities.

Welsh chapels

If you're in your own transport, it's worth driving on from Dolavon back towards Gaiman via the neat squared fields in this beautiful irrigated valley, where you'll see more Welsh chapels tucked away among poplar trees and silver birches. Follow the main road that leads south through Dolavon, and then turn left and then the next right, signposted to Iglesia Anglicana. The **San David Chapel** (1917) is a beautifully preserved brick construction, with an elegant bell tower, and sturdy oak-studded door, in a quiet spot surrounded by birches. Further on you'll cross the raised irrigation canals the Welsh built, next to them small orchards of apple trees, with tidy fields bordered by alamo trees.

Sleeping

See www.argentinahostels.com for youth hostels, and www.estanciasdesantacruz.com for estancias.

Viedma and Carmen de Patagones *p477*

The best places to stay are all in Viedma.

C Austral, 25 de Mayo y Villarino, T02920-422615, paradoresviedma@infovia.com.ar. Along the *costanera*, this modern hotel has well equipped, if slightly old-fashioned, rooms.

C Nijar, Mitre 490, T02920-422833. Very comfortable, smart modern rooms, a quiet relaxed atmosphere, and good attentive service. Recommended. The best of the 2 decent, modern mid-range hotels.

D Peumayén, Buenos Aires 334, T02920-425222. An old-fashioned friendly place on the plaza.

E Hotel Spa, 25 de Mayo 174, T02920-430459. A real find, this lovely great value hotel in a quiet complex with steam baths has a very relaxing atmosphere and warm staff.

Camping

There's a good **municipal campsite** near the river, T02920-421341, US$2 pp, all facilities including hot showers. Also at the sea lion colony, **La Lobería**, T02920-428883, US$1 pp. **Trenitos**, T02920-497098. US$1 pp, good facilities.

Estancias

AL La Luisa, 40 km away, T02920-463725, eleri@rnonline.com.ar. Highly recommended for its beautiful location, this historic 1900's house, in lovely open land, with excellent horse riding on well trained polo ponies through bush and beaches. Also at the host's even more remote, **San Juan** where you eat *asado*, deep in the bush under the stars. Both are traditional Patagonian estancias with young and friendly English-speaking owners. Great hospitality. Highly recommended. All meals, activities and transfers included. Open Dec-Mar.

Puerto Madryn *p478, map p487*

There is a huge range of hotels, but all are heavily booked ahead in summer.

A Marina, Av Roca 7, T/F02965-454915, www.marinamadryn.com.ar. Great little seafront place with well-equipped apartments for up to 5 people. Welcoming owners will also arrange excursions. Price quoted for 5. Worth booking ahead.

A Península Valdés, Av Roca 155, T02965-471292, www.hotelpeninsula.com.ar. A luxurious place on the seafront, great views from many of its spacious rooms and from the calm minimalist lounge. Spa, sauna and gym. International prices here, plus 30% extra for bookings made from outside Argentina.

A Playa, Av Roca 187, T02965-451446, www.playahotel.com.ar. Good central sea front location with spacious entrance and airy *confitería*. All comfortable, there is a range of rooms and it's worth paying extra for the larger, more modern rooms with sea view. Parking costs US$2 per night.

A Tolosa, Roque Sáenz Peña 253, T02965-471850, www.hoteltolosa.com.ar. An extremely comfortable modern place with faultless personal service and great breakfasts. Note that the superior rooms are much more spacious and have full wheelchair access. Bookings made from outside Argentina will be international tourist prices. Free use of bicycles and internet. Highly recommended.

B Bahía Nueva, Av Roca 67, T/F02965-451677, www.bahianueva.com.ar. One of the best seafront hotels, with a welcoming reception area, and high standards in all details. Rooms are on the small side, but comfortable, breakfasts are generous, and staff are helpful and professional. Cheaper in low season, but be aware that this hotel has higher prices for non-Argentines. Recommended.

Sleeping
ACA Camping 2
Bahía Nueva 1
Casa de Pueblo 15
El Gualicho 3
Gran Palace 14
Hostería Torremolinos 4
Marina 5
Muelle Viejo 6
Patagonia 12
Península Valdés 7
Playa 8
Residencial J'Os 13
Santa Rita 9
Tolosa 10
Villa Pirén 11

Eating
Caccaros 3
Cantina El Náutico 6
Centro de Difusión de la Pesca Artesanal 2
Havanna 4
La Casona del Golfo 5
La Vaca y el Pollito 7
Lizard Café 8
Mitos 10
Nativo Sur 1
Plácido 11
Taska Beltza 12
Yoaquina 13

Bars & clubs
Margarita 9

B-C Villa Pirén, Av Roca 439, T/F02965-456272, www.piren.com.ar. Excellent modern rooms and apartments in smart seafront building with great facilities. Ask for the junior suite, or rooms with a view.

C Casa de Pueblo, Av Roca 475, T02965-472500, www.madryncasadepueblo.com.ar. Once apparently the first brothel in town, now a charmingly renovated seafront chalet with functional rooms and a homely atmosphere. Good value.

C Hostería Torremolinos, Marcos A Zar 64, T02965-453215. Nice modern place with simple, well decorated rooms.

C Muelle Viejo, H Yrigoyen 38, T02965-471284, www.muelleviejo.com. Ask for the stylish, comfortable modernized rooms in this funny old place. Excellent value, large rooms sleep 4 and there are *parrilla* and kitchen facilities if you want to cook.

C Patagonia Hotel and Apart Hotel, Albarracin 45, T/F02965-452103, www.patagoniaaparthotel.com. Modern and spacious rooms and apartments are of a high standard but pricey, since you'll be charged international tourist prices.

D Gran Palace Hotel, 28 de Julio 390, T02965-471009. Attractive entrance to this central and economical place, but rooms are a bit squashed and rather dark, thanks to the mahogany effect wallpaper. But they're clean and have bathroom and TV, making this good value.

D Residencial J'Os, Bolivar 75, T02965-471433. A friendly small *hostería*, all the rooms have private bathrooms, and breakfast is included.

D Santa Rita, Gob Maiz 370, T02965-471050, www.hostelsantarita.com.ar. Welcoming place and comfy rooms with wash basin – this is good value with dinner included, though you can also use the kitchen facilities. Helpful hosts. Often recommended.

E-F pp **El Gualicho**, Marcos A Zar 480, T02965- 454163, www.elgualicho hostel.com.ar. By far the best budget place in Puerto Madryn, this hostel is beautifully designed and run by a friendly and enthusiastic owner. Free pick up from bus terminal, parrilla, breakfast included, garden, some attractive double rooms, and bikes for hire – book ahead. Discounts to HI members. Highly recommended.

Camping

ACA, Blv Brown, 3.5 km south of town centre (at Punta Cuevas), T02965-452952. Sep-Apr, hot showers, café, shop, no kitchen facilities, shady trees, close to the sea.

Península Valdés/Puerto Pirámides *p480*

L Las Restingas, primera bajada al mar, T02965-495101, www.lasrestingas.com. The top hotel in town has an exclusive location on the beach, and 8 of its 12 suites have their own balcony for splendid sea views. All very comfortable, with minimalist decoration and there's a small restaurant serving a sophisticated selection of regional food. The hotel is a member of the excellent NA Town & Country Hotels group, www.newage-hotels.com.

A Cabañas en el Mar, Av de las Ballenas s/n, T02965-495049, www.piramides.net. 5 comfortable 2-6-bed cabañas, well equipped.

A The Paradise, at the far end of the main street, T02965-495030, www.hosteria paradise.com.ar. Huge very comfortable light rooms, smart bathrooms, and splendid suites with jacuzzis. Also a fine restaurant, serving delicious squid, among other seafood.

C Motel ACA, Av de las Ballenas 25, T02965-495004, www.piramides.net. Slightly old fashioned, but still modern in feel, this has welcoming rooms, handy for the beach. Also a good seafood restaurant, from whose terrace you might even spot whales!

Camping

Municipal site, T02965-495084. Near the beach, shop, hot showers in evening only, a bit scruffy and very busy, so get there early to secure a place; do not camp on the beach: people have been swept away by the incoming tide.

Estancias

LL Estancia La Ernestina, T156-61079, www.laernestina.com.ar. Near Punta Norte, very welcoming Familia Copello offers comfortable accommodation in simple rooms, all meals and excursions included. Open from mid-Sep to mid-Apr No credit cards.

L Faro Punta Delgada, T154-06303, www.puntadelgada.com. Comfortable accommodation next to the Punta Delgada's lighthouse, offering also half and full board, excellent food, and horse riding, guided walks. Some activities are included in the basic rate. Recommended

L Rincón Chico, T156-88303 (office in Puerto Madryn: Brown 1783, T02965-471733), www.rinconchico.com.ar. A working sheep farm close to Punta Delgada, still owned by the original pioneer family who built it. Luxurious accommodation in lovely rooms opening onto an attractive veranda. Beautifully situated, and with well-organised circuits for walking and bike riding. Half and full board also available. Recommended.

AL Estancia La Elvira, T156-69153 (office in Puerto Madryn: Av Yrigoyen 257, T02965-474248), www.laelvira.com.ar. Traditional Patagonian dishes, and comfortable accommodation in an outstanding location on Caleta Valdés, near Punta Cantor.

AL San Lorenzo, on RP3, 20 km southwest of Punta Norte (contact through Argentina Visión in Puerto Madryn, see below tour operators). For day excursions to a beautiful stretch of coast to see penguins close up in one of the peninsula colonies.

Trelew *p482, map p483*

Trelew is not a touristy town, and so there's limited choice of accommodation, particularly for low budgets, though there is a good campsite.

B Rayentray, San Martín y Belgrano, T02965-434702, www.cadenarayentray.com.ar. Huge modernized 1960s place with comfortable rooms and professional staff – the spacious 'superior' rooms are worth the extra, with sitting area and good bathrooms, and splendid 70s leather panelling. Swimming pool on top floor is free for guests, but gym, sunbed and sauna are extra.

C Centenario, San Martín 150, T02965-420542, hotelcentenario@yahoo.com.ar. This vast 1970's relic is worth seeing for the untouched decor, though it's more amusing than comfortable, and service is poor. Popular with Argentines, but you can always get a room here; not great value.

For an explanation of the Sleeping and Eating price codes used in this guide, and other relevant information, see Essentials, pages 48 and 51.

C Libertador, Rivadavia 31, T/F02965-420220, www.hotellibertadortw.com. Breakfast is included in this large modern place, highly recommended for its friendly service and comfortable rooms – the newer more spacious rooms are slightly pricier but worth it. Reserve ahead.

D Galicia, 9 de Julio 214, T02965-433802, www.hotelgalicia.com.ar. Breakfast included in this recently refurbished and central hotel, whose smallish rooms don't quite live up to the grand entrance, but are extremely comfortable and well decorated, and the staff are friendly. Excellent value and recommended.

D Rivadavia, Rivadavia 55, T02965-434472, hotelriv@infovia.com.ar. Simple, comfortable rooms with TV and bath, and some even cheaper rather spartan rooms without, in this well-located place. Good value if you can ignore the grumpy owner. Breakfast extra.

D Touring Club, Fontana 240, T02965-433997, htouring@internet.siscotel.com. After the gorgeous faded style of the bar, the vast staircase and light corridors, the rooms here are on the plain side, but they're quiet and spacious with big bathrooms, and well kept. Breakfast is extra, but this is good value, and the bar is marvellous.

Camping

Camping Patagonia, Ruta 7 y Rawson, 11 km from town, T154-06907. US$ 2.50 pp. Pretty site with *parrilla*, hot showers, football pitch and *proveduría* (food shop). Leave Trelew on RN 7 in the direction of Rawson, pass a roundabout, the road bends sharply to the right, take right fork, a *ripio* road, and the campsite is after 3 blocks on the right.

Gaiman *p485*

C Posada Los Mimbres, Chacra 211, 6 km west of Gaiman, T02965-491299, www.posadalosmimbres.com.ar. A farmstead in idyllic surroundings with just a few rooms in the charming old house or in a modern one. Gorgeous meals. A wonderful place to unwind.

C Unelem, Av Tello y 9 de Julio, T02965-491663, www.unelem.com. Priciest, but very comfortable, this is a restored hotel from 1867, whose restaurant serves Welsh cuisine.

D Casa de Té Ty Gwyn, 9 de Julio 147, T02965-491009, tygwyn@cpsarg.com. The next best option in town are the smart new rooms above the tea house.

D Plas Y Coed, Yrigoyen 320, T02965-15585219. A good place run by the charming Marta Rees, descended from a welsh tea pioneer family, with double and twin rooms with bath and TV including breakfast.

E Gwesty Tywi, Jones 342, T02965-491292, gwestywi@infovia.com.ar. A pretty and very well kept bed and breakfast.

Camping

Los Doce Nogales is an attractive site south of the river at Chacra 202, close to **Ty Te Caerdydd** tea room, T155-18030, with showers.

Eating

Viedma and Carmen de Patagones *p477*

Ÿ **Camilla's Café**, Saavedra and Buenos Aires. A smart and relaxing place for coffee, to watch Viedma trundle by on its errands.

Ÿ **La Balsa**, on the river at Colon y Villarino. By far the best restaurant, inexpensive with a pleasant atmosphere. Delicious seafood, and a bottle of superb Río Negro wine, Humberto Canale Merlot, are highly recommended.

Ÿ **Parrilla Libre**, Buenos Aires and Colón. Cheap *tenedor libre* steaks in a cheerful atmosphere, US$2.50 for dinner.

Puerto Madryn *p478, map p487*

One of the unmissable pleasures of Puerto Madryn is its great seafood. While you're here, try at least one plate of *arroz con mariscos* (rice with a whole selection of squid, prawns, mussels and clams). Most restaurants are mid-range and charge around the same price, but differ widely in quality. Without doubt, the best place to eat in town is the wonderful Taska Beltza, though there's plenty of choice along the coast road.

ŸŸŸ **Plácido**, Av Roca 508, T02965-455991. For a special dinner or a romantic place to eat. Overlooking the sea, and beautifully designed, with stylish tables and intimate lighting, this has excellent service and a good range of seafood, with cheaper pasta dishes too, lots of options for vegetarians.

ŸŸ **Caccaros**, Av Roca 385, T02965-453767. Stylish simple place on sea front with relaxing atmosphere, good value seafood menu, and cheap lunch menu.

Cantina El Náutico, Av Roca 790, T02965-471404. Long-established and now resting on its laurels, this is still popular for its seafood, and family atmosphere. The set menu isn't great value, and you're better off choosing individual dishes.

Centro de Difusión de la Pesca Artesanal, Brown, 7th roundabout, T155-38085. Grandly named, but with no sign outside, this is a basic *cantina* on the coast road east, opposite the municipal campsite, where the fishermen's families cook delicious meals with their catch. Hugely popular with locals, so come early. Far more authentic than **El Náutico**.

La Vaca y el Pollito, Av Roca y A Storni, T02965-458486. You can't miss this place as it's partly built into the wooden hull of a boat. A big place but with a cosy atmosphere, the speciality is *parrilla*, very reasonably priced, but there's seafood and pastas too. Great for families, with a big soft play area for kids.

Nativo Sur, Blv Brown 2000, T02965-457403. Smarter than its more popular sister restaurant **Yoaquina**, Nativo Sur is a good place for a quiet dinner on the beach front, with an imaginative menu of local Patagonian produce and seafood.

Taska Beltza, 9 de Julio 345, T02965-474003, closed Mon. Chef and owner 'El Negro' cooks superb seafood with great passion and a Basque influence. Even if you're on a budget, his *arroz con mariscos* is cheap and superb. Highly recommended. Book ahead.

Yoaquina, Blv Brown between 1st and 2nd roundabouts, T02965-456058. Great in the summer when you can eat outside, this is a relaxed spacious beachfront place, serving good seafood, if slightly pricey, and open from breakfast to after dinner. Cheap lunch menu, play area for kids, attentive service. Recommended.

La Casona del Golfo, Av Roca 349. Good value *tenedor libre* with lots of choices including good *parrilla* and seafood, and *helados libre* – as much ice cream as you can eat. Great for families – kids pay half price.

Cafés

Havanna, Av Roca y 28 de Julio. Smart, buzzing café selling the famous *alfajores* you see all over Argentina, coffees and sandwiches *de miga*. Very central, and open from breakfast to the early hours.

Kebom, Av Roca 540. Popular ice cream place with big soft play area for kids.

Lizard Café, Av Roca y Av Gales. Lively funky place with friendly people. Good for cheap and plentiful pizzas or for late night drinks on the seafront.

Mitos, 28 de Julio 80. Friendly and welcoming stylish café with good atmosphere, and pictures of tango stars and jazz musicians on the walls. Great for breakfast, or lunch and open until the early hours. Recommended.

Península Valdés/Puerto Pirámides *p480*

There are many restaurants in the main street. There are reasonably priced restaurants at Punta Norte, at Punta Cantor and at the Faro in Punta Delgada. These are recommendations at the beach itself:

Las Restingas. Perfect for a romantic dinner for the sea views and tranquility. An imaginative menu combines quality local produce with a touch of sophistication.

The Paradise. Just off the beach, good atmosphere and great seafood. Also lamb and a few vegetarian choices too.

Patagonia Franca, T02965-495006. A good seafood restaurant in the new hotel on the beach front, with perfect sea views.

Quimey Quipan, T1569 3100. By the beach, and next to *Tito Bottazzi*, this family-run place specializes in delicious seafood with rice and has a cheap set menu. Recommended. Always open for lunch, ring to reserve for dinner.

Mi Sueño. Close to the beach, good cheap pizzas to share.

Trelew *p482, map p483*

El Quijote, Rivadavia 463, T154-02937. Traditional *parrilla*, popular with locals.

El Viejo Molino, Gales 250, T02965-428019, open 1130-0030, closed Mon. The best restaurant in town, and well worth a visit to see the first flour mill that was built here in 1886, is now beautifully restored with a fine restaurant and café in relaxed and stylish surroundings. There's an imaginative menu with Patagonian lamb and homemade pastas, good value set menu with wine included, and Welsh teas. Recommended.

La Bodeguita, Belgrano 374, opposite the cinema. Serves superb home-made pastas, in a warm and lively atmosphere, with interesting local art on the walls. Recommended.

Norte, Soberanía y Belgrano. Cheap takeaway food is available at this supermarket.

Café de mi Ciudad, Belgrano y San Martín. A smart café serving great coffee; read the papers watching street life.

Delikatesse, Belgrano y San Martín. Serves pizzas in a cheery place, good for families.

Hotel Touring Club, Fontana 240. Open from breakfast to the small hours for sandwiches and drinks, worth a visit to see the splendid 1920's bar.

Gaiman *p485*

There's a stylish small restaurant **El Angel**, Rivadavia 241, serving delicious food in an old-fashioned intimate atmosphere. Also a high quality *panadería* **La Colonia** on the main street, and **Siop Bara**, Tello and 9 de Julio,sells cakes and ice creams.

Welsh teas

You're unlikely to be able to resist the scrumptious Welsh teas for which Gaiman has become famous, though quite how the tradition has sprung up remains a mystery. It's hard to imagine their abstemious ancestors tucking into vast plates filled with seven kinds of cake and scones at one sitting, and inevitably, they're not cheap. Tea is served from 1500, all the tea rooms charge about the same – US$7 – and include the most well known of the Welsh cakes *torta negra* – a delicious dense fruit cake. The first 3 are all near the Plaza:

Plas Y Coed, Yrigoyen 320. The first house to start serving tea, now in renovated premises, its owner Marta Rees is a wonderful raconteur and fabulous cook who can tell you all about her Welsh forebears, married in this very house in 1886. Highly recommended.

Ty Cymraeg, down by the river. Set in a lovely spot is with room for big groups, and selling good cakes.

Ty Gwyn, 9 de Julio 147. This large tea house serves a very generous tea in a more modern place with traditional features; the owners are welcoming. Recommended.

Ty Nain, Yrigoyen 283. Quite the prettiest house and full of history. Owner Mirna Jones is charming; her grandmother was the first woman to be born in Gaiman.

Ty Te Caerdydd, Finca 202, 2 km from the centre, but well sign posted. A quite staggering theme park of its own, with manicured lawns and dressed-up waitresses; its main claim to fame is that Princess Di took her tea here. The atmosphere is entirely manufactured.

Bars and clubs

Puerto Madryn *p478, map p487*

Margarita, RS Peña 15, next to Ambigu on RS Peña and Av Roca. Late night bar for drinks and live music.

Shopping

Viedma *p477*

Patagonia Out Doors Life, 25 de Mayo 340, and **Tiburón**, Zatti 250, both stock fishing equipment.

Puerto Madryn *p478, map p487*

Cardon, is recommended for regional goods and leather bags. You'll find lots more posh clothes, T shirts with whales and penguins on, high quality Patagonian handicrafts and leather goods, and artesanal *alfajores* and cakes in streets 28 de Julio and Av Roca.

Portal de Madryn, 28 de Julio y Av Roca. The sleek new indoor shopping centre has all the smart clothes shops, Café Havanna on the ground floor, and a kids games area with a fast, but not cheap, food place Mostaza on the top floor.

For fishing tackle, guns and camping gear, try **Nayfer**, 25 de Mayo 366. For diving gear, there's **Acquablu**, Av Roca 329, www.acquablu.com.ar, and also at **Pino Sub**, Yrigoyen 200 , www.pinosub.com.

Trelew *p482, map p483*

The main shopping area is around San Martín, and from the plaza to Belgrano, though Trelew can't compare with Puerto Madryn for souvenirs, it has a good little handicrafts market on the plaza.

Norte, Rivadavia y 9 de Julio. Opposite Banco Río. Supermarket.

Activities and tours

Puerto Madryn *p478, map p487*

Diving

Madryn Buceo, Blvd Brown, 3rd roundabout in Balneario Nativo Sur, T(02965) 155 13997, www.madrynbuceo.com. Offer courses of all kinds from beginners' dives to the week-long PADI course, around US$160, or US$30 for a day excursion.
Ocean Divers, Blv Brown (between 1st and 2nd roundabout), T02965-472569. Advanced courses (PADI) and courses on video, photography and underwater communication.
Scuba Duba, Blvd Brown 893, T02965-452699. Courses, excursions, night dives.

Fishing

Raul Diaz, T02965-450812; and **Juan Dominguez**, T156 64772

Horse riding

Huellas y Costas, Blvd Brown 860, T156-80515. Also kayaks and windsurf boards for hire.

Mountain bike hire

El Gualicho, Marcos A Zar 480, T02965-454163. **Vernardino Club Mar**, on beach at Blvd Brown 860, T02965-455633. XT Mountain Bike, Av Roca 742, T02965-472232.

Tour operators

Lots of agencies in Puerto Madryn do tours to Península Valdés, usually taking in the same places: the interpretation centre and viewing point for the Isla de los Pájaros, (both on the narrow isthmus at the entrance to the peninsula), and then Puerto Pirámides, where the boat trip to see the whales costs US$25 extra. They go on to Punta Delgada and Caleta Valdés, with time to look at wildlife. Trips take 12 hrs, so you should bring water and lunch, though there are places to eat in Puerto Pirámides. All charge US$40, plus US$12 entrance to the Peninsula – but shop around to find out how long you'll spend at each place, how big the group is, and if your guide speaks English.

On all excursions take drink, food if you don't want to eat in the expensive restaurants, and binoculars. Most tour companies (addresses above) stay 50-60 mins on location. Usually half price for children under 10, free for under 6s. Tours are also offered to see the penguins at Punta Tombo, or the Welsh village of Gaiman with Ameghino Dam thrown in, but these are both 400 km round trips and better from Trelew.

Alora Viaggio, Av Roca 27, T/F02965-455106. A helpful company which also has an office at the bus terminal.
Argentina Visión, Av Roca 536, T02965-451427, www.argentinavision.com. Offers 4WD adventure trips and can arrange estancia accommodation at Punta Delgada. English and French spoken.
Cuyun Co, Av Roca 165, T02965-451845, www.cuyunco.com.ar. Offers a friendly personal service and a huge range of conventional and more imaginative tours: guided walks with biologists, 4WD expeditions, and also arrange estancia accommodation. Bilingual guides. Recommended.
Flamenco Tour, Av Roca 331, T02965-455505, www.flamencotour.com.ar. For slightly more sedate trips and charming staff.
Golfo Azul, Mitre y H Yrigoyen, T02965-451181. For windsurf boards, kayaks, jet ski, sailing boats for hire.
Hydrosport, near the ACA, T02965-495065, hysport@infovia.com.ar. Rents scuba equipment and boats, and organizes land and sea wildlife tours to see whales and dolphins.
Jorge Schmidt, Puerto Pirámides, T02965-495012. Recommended for whale watching.
Juan Benegas, Puerto Pirámides, T02965-495100. Offers diving expeditions and provides equipment. Tours do not run after heavy rain in the low season.
Tito Botazzi, Blvd Brown y Martín Fierro , T/F02965-474110, and at Puerto Pirámides. Particularly recommended for small groups and well informed bilingual guides; very popular for whale watching.

Trelew *p482, map p483*

Tour operators

Agencies run tours to Punta Tombo, US$22, Chubut Valley (half-day), US$30, both together as a full day US$40. Tours to Península Valdés are best done from Puerto Madryn.

Nieve Mar, Italia 98, T02965-434114, www.nievemartours.com.ar. Punta Tombo and Península Valdés , bilingual guides (reserve ahead). Organized and efficient.
Patagonia Grandes Espacios, Belgrano 338, T02965-435161, infopge@speedy.com.ar. Good excursions to Punta Tombo and Gaiman, but also palaeontological trips, staying in *chacras*; also whale watching. Recommended

Transport

Viedma and Carmen de Patagones *p477*

Air

Aeropuerto Gobernador Castelo, 5 km south. LADE fly to **Buenos Aires**, **Mar del Plata**, **Bahía Blanca**, **Neuquén**, **San Martín de Los Andes**, **Trelew** and **Comodoro Rivadavia**.

Airline offices LADE, Saavedra 403, T/F02920-424420.

Bus

The terminal in Viedma is at Av Pte Peron y Guido, 15 blocks from plaza; take a taxi (US$1). To/from **Buenos Aires** 3 daily, 14 hrs, US$20, Don Otto/La Estrella/Cóndor. To **San Antonio Oeste**, several daily, 2½ hrs, US$4, Don Otto. To **Bahia Blanca**, 4 daily, 4 hrs, US$5, Rio Parana.

Train

A comfortable sleeper train, which also carries cars, goes from Viedma to **Bariloche** overnight once a week, Fri 1800, and arrives in the morning. On board there's a restaurant and a cinema car showing videos. All reasonably comfortable. US$30 for a bed, US$18 for a *semi-cama* seat. T02944-431777, www.trenpatagonico.com.ar. Book ahead.

Puerto Madryn *p478, map p487*

Air

Puerto Madryn Airport is 10 km west of centre, T02965-451909, reached by taxi, US$7. Only LADE operate from here. Flights, once a week to and from **Buenos Aires** . More flights to and from **Buenos Aires** , and from **El Calafate**, and **Ushuaia** from Trelew airport, 5 km north of Trelew, T02965-433443. Buses to Trelew stop at entrance to airport if asked. Taxi US$30. Transportes Eben Ezerrun a bus service to Puerto Madryn's bus terminal.

Airline offices LADE, Roca 119, T02965-451256. **Aerolíneas Argentinas**, Roca 427, T02965-451998.

Bus

The terminal is at Yrigoyen y San Martín (behind the old railway station), with a café, clean toilets, *locutorio*, and a kiosko selling drinks and sweets. Walk 3 blocks down R S Peña to get into town. Terminal information T02965-451789. To **Buenos Aires**, 18-19 hrs US$35-65, several companies, Andesmar recommended. To **Río Gallegos**, 18 hrs; US$38, El Pingüino (connecting to El Calafate, Punta Arenas, Puerto Natales), Andesmar, Transportadora Patagónica/Don Otto. To **Trelew**, 1 hr, every hr, US$2.50 with 28 de Julio, Mar y Valle. To **Puerto Pirámide**, 1½ hrs, US$ 3.50, daily, 28 de Julio. To **Esquel**, 11-12 hrs, US$25-35, daily, Mar y Valle. Companies: **Andesmar**, T02965-473764. **Transportadora Patagónica/Don Otto**, T02965-451675. **El Pingüino**, T456256. **TUS**, T02965-451962. **28 de Julio/Mar y Valle**, T02965-472056.

Car hire

More expensive than other parts of Argentina, and note the large insurance excess for turning the car over. Drive slowly on unpaved *ripio* roads. **Localiza**, Roca 15 , T02965-458000. Recommended for efficient and helpful service. **Madryn Rent a Car**, Roca 624, T02965-452355.

Taxi

Outside the bus terminal, T02965-452966.

Península Valdés/Puerto Pirámides *p480*

Península Valdés can most easily be visited by taking one of the many well-organized full day excursions (see Tour operators above for further details) but if you'd rather see the peninsula independently, you can hire a car relatively inexpensively for a group of 4, and then take just the boat trip to see the whales (Sep-Nov) from Puerto Pirámides with **Jorge Schmidt**, T02965-495012. Note that distances are long on the peninsula, and roads beyond Puerto Pirámides are *ripio*, so take your time – car hire companies charge a heavy excess if you turn the car over. A cheaper option is the daily bus to **Puerto Pirámides** with 28 de Julio, leaving the terminal daily at 0930, returns 1900, 1½ hrs, US$ 3.50 each way.

Trelew *p482, map p483*

Air

Airport 5 km north of centre; taxis about US$3-3.50. Local buses to/from **Puerto Madryn** stop at the airport entrance, turning is 10 mins walk. Aerolíneas Argentinas have flights to/from **Buenos Aires**, and from **El Calafate** and **Ushuaia**.

Airline offices Aerolineas Argentinas, 25 de Mayo 33, T02965-420222.

Bus

The terminal is on the east side of Plaza Centenario, T02965-420121.

Long distance To **Buenos Aires**, 19-20 hrs; US$ 36-67, several companies go daily, inc El Pingüino, Que Bus, Transportadora Patagónica/Don Otto, Andesmar, El Cóndor; to **Comodoro Rivadavia**, 5 hrs, US$ 12, many companies, to **Río Gallegos**, 17 hrs; US$ 40, (from here to **El Calafate, Puerto Natales, Punta Arenas**), many companies. To **Esquel**, 9-10 hrs; US$ 23-30, Mar y Valle, Empresa Chubut, Transportadora Patagónica/Don Otto.

Local Mar y Valle and 28 de Julio both go frequently to **Rawson**, 30 mins; US$ 0.70, to **Gaiman**, 30 mins; US$1, and **Dolavon** 1 hr, US$1.50, to **Puerto Madryn**, 1hr, US$ 2.50, to **Puerto Pirámides**, 2½ hrs, US$5, daily, Mar y Valle.

Bus companies Andesmar, T02965-433535; TUS, T02965-421343; El Pingüino, T02965-427400; Transportadora Patagónica/Don Otto, T02965-429496; El Cóndor, T02965-431675; 28 de Julio/Mar y Valle, T02965-432429; Que Bus, T02965-422760; El Ñandú, T02965-427499.

Car hire

Car hire companies at the airport desks are staffed only at flight arrival times and cars are taken quickly. All have offices in town. AVIS, Italia 98, T02965-436060; Localiza, H Yrigoyen 1416, T02965-430070; Hertz, at the airport, T154-05495.

Gaiman *p485*

Bus Buses to/from **Trelew**, 30 mins, US$1, with company **28 de Julio**, several a day.

Dolavon *p485*

Bus Buses to/from **Trelew**, 1 hr, US$1.50, 28 de Julio, several a day.

Directory

TCs are hard to change throughout Patagonia, and it's easier, and safer, to use credit/debit cards to withdraw cash. There are ATMs in all the main towns, except El Chaltén.

Viedma and Carmen de Patagones *p477*

Banks ATMs at Colon and San Martín in Viedma, and Carmen de Patagones at Bynon and Alsina or Bynon and Paraguay. **Travel agencies** Mona Tour, San Martín 225, Viedma. Sells flights and tickets for the train to Bariloche, www.trenpatagonico.com

Puerto Madryn *p478, map p487*

Banks Lots of ATMs at the following: Banco Nación, 9 de Julio 117. Banco del Chubut, 25 de Mayo 154 and **Río**, 28 de Julio 56. **Internet** Internet Centro Madryn, 25 de Mayo y Belgrano. US$0.60 per hr. Re Creo, Roque Sáenz Peña 101. **Medical services** There are chemists all along 28 de Julio, and a late night pharmacy on Belgrano y 25 de Mayo. **Post office** Belgrano y Maiz, 0900-1200, 1500-1900. **Telephone** Many *locutorios* in the centre.

Trelew *p482, map p483*

Banks Open Mon-Fri 0800-1300. Banco de la Nación, 25 de Mayo y Fontana. Banco del Sud, 9 de Julio 320, cash advance on Visa. Currency changed at Patagonia Grandes Espacios, Belgrano 338. **Internet** 25 de Mayo 219. **Post office** 25 de Mayo and Mitre. **Telephone** Telefónica, Roca y Pje Tucumán, and several *locutorios* in the centre.

Southern Atlantic Coast

Quieter, and much less visited by tourists than Puerto Madryn and Península Valdés, the southern stretch of the Atlantic coastline from Camarones to Río Gallegos is extremely rich in marine life of all kinds. There are several wonderful reserves protecting a wide variety of species of birds and mammals, and a few good bases for exploring them at the coastal towns of Camarones, Puerto Deseado, and Puerto San Julián, with good services and accommodation. If you have your own transport, you could head out to the only national park on the coast, Monte León, where you can walk the shore for miles and stay in a remote but comfortable hostería. And on the last spit of land before Tierra del Fuego, there's ancient history to explore near the coast at Cabo Vírgines.

There are two cities in this huge region, of which by far the most appealing is the southernmost town on the Argentine mainland, Río Gallegos. It's a pleasant place, with good accommodation, and tours offered to penguin colonies, though there's little to draw you here unless you're changing buses. The other city, Comodoro Rivadavia, is probably best avoided, unless you're keen to see the petroleum museum. Aside from coastal attractions, this region also boasts the country's finest petrified forest, the Monumento Natural Bosques Petrificados, difficult to reach on public transport, 250 km west of Puerto Deseado. ▸▸ *For Sleeping, Eating and other listings, see pages 500-505.*

Comodoro Rivadavia and around ▸▸ *pp500-505.*

➔ *Phone code: 02967 Colour map 5, C4 Population: 145,000*

The largest city in the province of Chubut was established primarily as a sheep-exporting port, and early settlers included Boer immigrants fleeing British rule in southern Africa. Its compact centre is at the foot of Cerro Chenque, 212 m high, a dusty bluff overlooking the town unattractively adorned with radar masts, with its own shanty town. The city began to flourish suddenly when oil was discovered here in 1907, bringing in many international companies. However, since the petrol industry was privatized by President Menem in the 1990s, there's been consequent unemployment and now the town has a slightly sad, rather unkempt feel. You're most likely to end up here if you need to change buses, and there's little to make you want to stay. Comodoro Rivadavia has a **tourist office** ⓘ *Rivadavia 430, T02967-4462376, www.comodoro.gov.ar, Mon-Fri 0900-1400, and another in the bus terminal, daily 0800-2100*, which is very helpful, English spoken.

Situated at the end of the Bioceanic Corridor, a fast road to Chile, Comodoro is the hub for terrestrial transport, and a bus nexus from all areas of Patagonia, though there are some smart hotels and a popular beach nearby. If you're really stuck for something to do, you could visit the **Museo del Petroleo** ⓘ *T02967-4559558, Tue-Fri 0900-1800, Sat and Sun 1500-1800, taxi US$43 km north of the centre at San Lorenzo 250*, for a good history of local oil exploitation. Some 20 km north is **Museo Paleontológico** ⓘ *weekends 1400-1800*, has fossils and reconstructions of dinosaurs. There's a good view of the city from **Cerro Chenque**, a dun-coloured hill whose cliffs give the town its drab backdrop. It's interesting to take a taxi up there if you don't feel like the walk, and see the first pioneers' homes, now dilapidated, but with panoramic views of the bay.

There's a good beach at the resort of **Rada Tilly** 12 km south, where you can walk along the beach at low tide to see sea lions (**Expreso Rada Tilly** buses every 30 minutes, packed in summer). You could use Comodoro Ravadavia as a base for exploring a second petrified forest, the Bosque Petrificado Héctor Szlápelis (see page 508), but the little town of **Sarmiento**, some 150 km west, is far more pleasant. There are three buses daily to Sarmiento with Etap, at 0800, 1300, 1900, T02967-447 4841.

Camarones → *Phone code: 0297 Colour map 5, B5 Population: 800*

Camarones is a quiet fishing port on Bahía Camarones, between Comodoro and Trelew, whose main industry is harvesting seaweed. This is prime sheep-rearing land, and Camarones wool is world-renowned for its quality. Aside from the salmon festival in early February, the only real attraction is a penguin colony, which you can walk to from the town. There's another well-known penguin colony with lots more species of marine life, 35km southeast at Reserva Natural Cabo Dos Bahías.

Reserva Natural Cabo Dos Bahías is a small reserve, 35 km southeast of Camerones at the southern end of the bay and reached by a dirt road. It protects a large penguin colony of some 12,000 couples, which you can see close up, but also lots of other marine life; there are sea lions and whales, too, if you're lucky. The reserve is open all year, and you can see seals and sea lions any time, but there are whales from March to November, and killer whales might be spotted from October to April, US$5.

South to Río Gallegos » *pp500-505.*

Caleta Olivia → *Phone code: 0297 Colour map 5, C4 Population: 40,000*

Caleta Olivia lies on the Bahía San Jorge 74 km south of Comodoro Rivadavia. Founded in 1901, it became the centre for exporting wool from the estancias of Santa Cruz. It boomed with the discovery of oil in 1944, but has suffered since the petroleum industry was privatized in the 1990s, and is now a rather sad place with heavy unemployment. However, there's a lovely 70-km stretch of pebbly beach, popular with locals for bathing, and lots of fishing nearby. There's an ATM at **Banco del Chubut**, on San Martín, and **tourist information** ⓘ *Güemes y San Martín, T0297-485 0988, extension 476.*

At **Pico Truncado**, some 50 km southwest, there's the gas field which feeds the pipeline to Buenos Aires, and an enterprising art project, **Ciudad Sonora**, www.ciudadsonora.com.ar, in a spectacular open setting; the wind sings through structures made of metal and marble, producing strange and eerie sounds. There's a daily bus service from Caleta Oliva, and nearby Pico Troncado has a few simple hotels, a campsite, and **tourist information** (T0297-4992202).

Monumento Natural Bosques Petrificados

ⓘ*256 km west of Puerto Deseado, 1000-1800, entry by donation.*

Extending over 10,000 ha in a bizarre, wind-wracked lunar landscape surrounding the **Laguna Grande** this park contains much older petrified trees than the forests further north around Sarmiento. The trunks, mainly of giant araucaria trees, are up to 35 m long and 150 cm in diameter. They were petrified in the Jurassic period 140 million years ago by intense volcanic activity in the Andes cordillera which blew ash over the entire area. It was the silicates in this volcanic ash which petrified the trunks of fallen trees, and creating these strange jasper-like hulks, which were only revealed when other organic matter around them was eroded. The place is more eerie than beautiful, but it does exert a strange fascination, especially when you consider that the fossils of marine animals that you see on the site are a mere 40 million years old, belonging to a sea which covered the land long after the trees had turned to stone. There is a small visitor centre and museum, and a well documented 1-km trail that takes you past the most impressive specimens. You may be very tempted to take away your own personal souvenir: don't.

The only way to visit the park, unless you have your own transport is with a tour from either Comodoro Rivadavia, or the more appealing Puerto Deseado. Recommended companies in Puerto Deseado include **Darwin Expediciones**, www.darwin-expeditions.com, and **Los Vikingos**, www.losvikingos.com.ar. Access is via a small road 49 shooting west from the main route south, the Ruta 3, at Km post 2063, 86 km south of the small town of Fitz Roy. There is no public transport, and no accommodation in the park. Camping is not allowed, and you're advised to bring your own food and drink.

Puerto Deseado » pp500-505.

→ Phone code: 0297 Colour map 6, A4 Population: 7,100

Puerto Deseado is a pleasant fishing port on the estuary of the Río Deseado, which drains, curiously, into Lago Buenos Aires in the west. It's a stunning stretch of coastline, and the estuary has a wonderful nature reserve, Ría Deseado, with Magellanic penguins and several species of cormorants among its inhabitants; as well as being the breeding grounds of Commerson's dolphin. Within reach are more reserves, protecting sea lions and penguins. The **Museo Regional Mario Brozoski** ⓘ *Belgrano y Colón, 1000-1700*, has remains of an 18th-century ship that sank off the coast here in 1770, as well as some evocative photos. Outside the former railway station, a rather fine old building, in vaguely English medieval style, is the **Vagón Histórico** ⓘ *San Martín 1525, T0297-4870220, www.santacruz.gov.ar*, an 1898 carriage now used as the tourist office.

The **Reserva Natural Ría Deseado**, the submerged estuary (*ría*) of the Río Deseado, 42 km long, is an important nature reserve, and a stunning area to visit. Among many varieties of seabird, there's a colony of Magellanic penguins, and the crumbling chalky cliffs, mauve and ochre, splattered with guano (droppings), are home to four species of cormorants including the unique red-legged cormorant, most appealing with their smart dinner-jacketed appearance. These birds nest from October to April in four islands off the shores. The reserve is also the breeding grounds of Commerson's dolphins, beautiful creatures, who frolic playfully around your boat. Excellent boat tours with **Darwin Expediciones**, and **Los Vikingos** (see Tour operators, page 503), run straight from the town's pier, lasting about two hours, and are best in early morning or late evening. There are several other nature reserves within easy reach, all offering good places to walk, if you have transport to take you closer:

North of Puerto Deseado, some 90 km on the northern shore of the peninsula, is **Cabo Blanco**, the site of the largest fur seal colony in Patagonia. It's another magnificent area, a rocky peninsula bursting out from flat lands, with one of the oldest lighthouses on the coast perched on top, and thousands of seals perched on the rocks below. The breeding season is December to January. A little further west, you should also visit **Reserva Cañadón de Duraznillo** in the estancia of **La Madrugada**. Here you'll see lots of guanacos, ñandues, foxes and birds, as well as the largest seal colony in the province on spectacular unspoilt beaches. The estancia is a great place to visit or stay (see Sleeping, page 502).

South of Puerto Deseado are two more reserves, at **Isla Pingüino**, an offshore island with a colony of Magellanic penguins, as well as cormorants and steamer ducks, and the **Reserva Natural Bahía Laura**, an uninhabited bay where black-necked cormorants, ducks and other seabirds can be found in abundance. Isla Pingüino is an offshore island, reached by boat, and Bahía Laura, nearby is 155 km south along *ripio* and dirt roads. **Darwin Expediciones** and **Los Vikingos** both run tours. See Tour operators, page 503.

The **Gruta de Lourdes**, 24 km west, is a cave which attracts pilgrims to see the Virgen de Lourdes. Further south along the same road is the **Cañadon del Puerto**, a mirador offering fine views over the estuary.

Puerto San Julián » pp500-505.

→ Phone code: 02962 Colour map 6, A4 Population: 5,300

The quiet port town of Puerto San Julián, lying on the Bahía San Julián 268 km south of Fitz Roy, is the best place for breaking the 834 km run from Comodoro Rivadavia to Río Gallegos. It has a fascinating history, although little of it is in evidence today. The first

Mass in Argentina was held here in 1520 after the Portuguese explorer Magellan had executed a member of his mutinous crew. Then in 1578, Francis Drake also put in here to behead Thomas Doughty, after amiably dining with him. There's plenty of wildlife to be seen in the area, and a paradise of marine life in the coastal Reserva Natural San Julián, all very accessible from the town.

After the 16th-century visitors, there was an attempt to found a colony here in 1780 which failed due to scurvy. The current town was founded in 1901 on a peninsula overlooking a fine natural harbour, as a port to serve the sheep estancias of this part of Santa Cruz. There's a little regional museum, **Museo Regional at Rivadavia and Vieytes**, which houses the amazingly well preserved dinosaur footprint found in the town. There are superb tours offered to see the wildlife in the reserve, which you can ask about at the **tourist office** ⓘ *Av Costanera y 9 de Julio, or San Martín 1126, T02962-454396, centur@uvc.com.ar, www.santacruz.gov.ar.*

The **Reserva Natural San Julian**, on the shores of Bahía San Julian, includes the islands **Banco Cormorán** and **Banco Justicia**, thought to be the site of the 16th-century executions, where there is a colony of Magellanic penguins and nesting areas for several species of cormorants and other birds. You're also very likely to spot Commerson's dolphins. It's a lovely location and the concentration of marine life is stunning. Highly recommended. There are excellent zodiac boat trips, lasting 90 minutes, run by **Excursiones Pinocho** ⓘ *Av Costanera between San Martín and Mitre, T02962-452856, nonois@sanjulian.com.ar.* The best to visit in December to see dolphins and cormorants, though there's plenty to see from December to April. **Cabo Curiosa**, 15 km north, has fine beaches: there are 30 km of spectacular coastline, and it's a popular bathing place for the whole of the region. You can also visit the ruins of **Florida Blanca**, 10 km west, the site of the failed colony founded in 1870 by Antonio Viedma. It's certainly worth visiting **Estancia La María**, 150 km west, with one of the main archaeological sites in Patagonia. A huge canyon with 87 caves of paintings including human hands and guanacos, 4000-12,000 years old. The estancia offers transport and accommodation. Highly recommended. Contact Fernando Behm, Saavedra 1168, T02962-452328.

Piedrabuena → *Phone code: 02962 Colour map 6, B3 Population: 3300*

Known officially as Comandante Luís Piedrabuena, this quiet town is named after the the famous Argentine explorer and sailor, Piedra Buena, who built his home on Isla Pavón, an island in the river Santa Cruz, in 1859. On this small mound in the deep emerald green fast-flowing river you can visit the **Casa Histórica Luis Piedra Buena**, a reconstruction of the original building where he carried on a peaceful trade with local indigenous groups. However, the island has become most popular as a weekend resort for those fishing steelhead trout. It's a world-renowned fishing spot, and there's a smart four-star *hostería* as well as an attractive campsite to cater for anglers and their families, on weekend breaks (see Sleeping, page 498). In March there's a national trout festival. Piedrabuena is a good base for exploring the **Parque Nacional Monte León**, which protects 40 km of coastline and steppe, 30 km south (see below).

Parque Nacional Monte León

→ *www.parquesnacionales.gov.ar www.vidasilvestre.org.ar*

The only national park on Argentina's long Atlantic coastline, Monte León is a beautiful stretch of steppe and shore, south of Piedrabuena. It includes 40 km of coastline, where there are many species of seabirds, the world's fourth largest colony of penguins and colonies of sea lions in its many caves and little bays, as well as the tiny island Monte León, an important breeding area for cormorants and terns. It was acquired for the Argentine nation by North American millionaire Douglas Tompkins (who also owns Parque Pumalín in Chile, and **El Rincón del Socorro** in Los Esteros del Iberá, see page 354), and looked after by the organization **Vida Silvestre**, before being made a national park in 2004. It's not easy to access the park, but your efforts to get here will be rewarded by wonderful walks along wide isolated beaches with their extraordinary rock formations, and cliffs riven with vast caverns, fabulous at low tide. The park also protects an important habitat of sea-shore steppe, which is home to pumas and wolves as well as guanacos and choiques. Improved access is one part of the plan for the national park, which will also include turning the old shearing shed into a visitor centre.

It's difficult to reach the park unless you have a 4WD vehicle; access is along 23 km of poor *ripio* road which branches off Route 3, 36 km south of Piedrabuena. Fly from Buenos Aires to Río Gallegos, and from there take a taxi (two hours, US$100). The old house at the heart of the estancia has been converted to a *hostería*, and by far the best way to enjoy the park in comfort, is to stay at the traditional but beautifully modernized **Estancia Monte León** ⓘ *RN3, www.monteleon-patagonia.com/hosteria_ml.html, open Nov-Apr*, with four impeccably tasteful rooms, all decorated with Tompkins' considerable style, this is a fantastic place to stay. There's a good library, living room and even a small museum. Fishing is good here, too.

Río Gallegos » pp500-505.

→ *Phone code: 02966 Colour map 6, B3 Population: 75,000*

The capital of Santa Cruz province lies on the estuary of the Río Gallegos, the river famous for its excellent brown trout fishing. It's a pleasant, airy town, founded in 1885 as a centre for the trade in wool and sheepskins, and is by far the most appealing of the main centres on Patagonia's southern Atlantic Coast. It has always been a major transport hub, but receives fewer visitors since the airport opened at El Calafate. However, if you come here to change buses, you could visit the penguin reserve at **Cabo Vírgenes** some 130 km south, or Monte León National Park 210 km north. The town itself has a couple of museums, and boasts a few smart shops and restaurants.

Ins and outs → *Río Gallegos is pronounced rio ga-SHAY-gos*

Getting there Flights arrive at the airport from Buenos Aires, 10 km from centre, Ushuaia and Río Grande, as well as the **LADE** flights connecting all major Patagonian towns. Take a taxi for US$4. The bus terminal is inconveniently 3 km from the centre, at the corner of Route 3 and Avenida Eva Perón. Bus Nos 1 and 12 will take you into town, or take a taxi for US$1.30.

Tourist information ⓘ *Av Roca 863, T02966-438725, www.epatagonia.gov.ar, Mon- Fri 0900-2100, Sat 1000-2000, Sun 1000-1500, 1600-2000*. An excellent and well-organized office with information for the whole province. The staff are extremely helpful, speak English and have a list of estancias in Santa Cruz. They'll also phone round hotels for you. Also at the airport and a small desk at bus terminal, T02966-442159.

Sights

The tidy, leafy Plaza San Martín, two blocks south of the main street, Avenida Roca, has an interesting collection of trees, many planted by the early pioneers, and a diminutive corrugated iron **cathedral**, with a wood-panelled ceiling in the chancel and stained glass windows. The best of the town's museums is the small **Museo de los Pioneros** ⓘ *El Cano y Alberdi, T02966-437763, daily 1000-2000, free*. Set in a house built in England and shipped here in 1890, there are interesting photographs and artefacts telling the story of the first Scottish settlers, who came here in 1884 from the Falklands/Malvinas Islands, by government grants of land. There's an interesting tour given by the English-speaking owner, a descendent of the Scottish pioneers, and great photos of those first sheep-farming settlers. There's work by local artists at **Museo de Arte Eduardo Minichelli** ⓘ *Maipú 13, Mon-Fri 0800-1900, Sat-Sun and holidays 1400-1800. (closed Jan/Feb)*. There's **Museo Regional Provincial Manuel José Molina** ⓘ *Av San Martín y Ramón y Cajal 51, Mon-Fri 0900-2000, Sat 1500-2000,* in the Complejo Cultural Santa Cruz, with some dull rocks and fossils and a couple of dusty dinosaur skeletons. More stimulating is the **Museo Malvinas Argentinas** ⓘ *Pasteur 48, T02966-420128, Mon and Thu 0800-1200, Tue and Fri 1300-1730, 3rd Sun in every month 1530-1800, Wed closed,* which aims to inform visitors, with the historical and geographical reasons, why the Malvinas are Argentine. There's also a library and video archive.

Around Río Gallegos

Laguna Azul, 62 km south near the Monte Aymond border crossing, is nothing more than a perfect royal blue lagoon in the crater of an extinct volcano. But it does have a certain atmosphere, set in arid lunar landscape, and is a good place for a walk. Take a tour, or get off the bus along Route 3, which stops on the main road.

Reserva Provincial Cabo Vírgenes, 134 km south, is a nature reserve protecting the second largest colony of Magellanic penguins in Patagonia. There's an informative self-guided walk to see their nests amongst the *calafate* and fragrant *mata verde* bushes. It's good to visit from November, when chicks are born, with nests under every bush, to January. Fascinating for anyone; wonderful for children. US$3 . You can climb the **Cabo Vírgenes lighthouse** (owned by the Argentine Navy) for wonderful views. Both these are usually included in a tour organized form Río Gallegos. There's a *confitería* close by for snacks and souvenirs. Branch off Route 3 onto Route 1 (unpaved), 15 km south of Río Gallegos, and from here it's 119 km, 3½ hours. South of Cabo Vírgenes are the ruins of **Nombre de Jesús,** one of the two settlements founded by Pedro Sarmiento de Gamboa in 1584 and where, tragically, all its settlers died.

Estancia Monte Dinero, 13 km north of Cabo Vírgenes, is a wonderful base for visiting the reserve, a working sheep farm, where the English-speaking Fenton family offers accommodation, food and excursions; all excellent.

Sleeping

Comodoro Rivadavia *p495*
Hotels are either luxurious or basic, with little in between.

B Lucania Palazzo Hotel, Moreno 676, T02967-4499338, www.lucania-palazzo.com. A stylish and luxurious business hotel, with a lovely airy spacious reception, and superb rooms, many with sea views, good value. A huge American breakfast, and use of the sauna and gym are included. Recommended.

C Comodoro, 9 de Julio 770, T02967-4472300, info@comodorohotel.com.ar. Buffet breakfast included. Larger rooms are worth paying extra for in this slightly unwelcoming place.

D Hotel Azul, Sarmiento 724, T02967-4474628. This is a nice quiet old place, with lovely bright rooms, friendly owners, and great panoramic views from the *confitería*, though breakfast is extra.

D Hotel Victoria, Belgrano 585, T02967-4460725. An old fashioned city *hostería*, mostly used by workers in the oil industry, but it's friendly, and clean and comfortable enough. Breakfast US$1.20 extra.

D Rua Marina, Belgrano 738, T02967-446 8777. All rooms have TV and bath and breakfast is included; the newer rooms are particularly comfortable. Recommended for the friendly welcome. The best budget choice.

E Hospedaje Cari Hue, Belgrano 563, T02967-4472946. Sweet rooms, with separate bathrooms, coming off a central hallway, very nice owners who like backpackers. Breakfast is extra. The best budget choice.

Camping
Municipal site, Rada Tilly, reached by Expreso Rada Tilly bus from town. Hot showers.
San Carlos, 37 km north on RN3, T02967-4560425.

Camarones *p496*
B Kau I Keu Kenk, Sarmiento y Roca. Good food, recommended, owner runs trips to penguin colony. There are 2 others, **C**, the one by the power station is not recommended.

Caleta Olivia *p496*
C pp **Robert**, San Martín 2152, T0297-4851452, hrobert@mcolivia.com.ar. The most comfortable option in town by far. All rooms have bathroom, and breakfast is included.
D Grand, Mosconi y Chubut, T0297-4851393 The other recommendable place: reasonably comfortable rooms.

Camping
Municipal campsite, T0297-4850999, ext 476. Hot showers near beach, US$3 pp.

Monumento Natural Bosques Petrificados *p496*
There are no services, no water source anywhere close by, and no accommodation in the area, apart from camping at **Estancia la Paloma**, 25 km away, T02967-443503. No camping is allowed near the park.

Puerto Deseado *p497*
C Isla Chaffers, San Martín y Mariano Moreno, T0297-4872246, www.islachaffers.wm.com.ar. The town's best, modern and central.
C Los Acantilados, Pueyrredón y España, T0297-4872167, www.pdeseado.com.ar/acantour. Beautifully-located hotel, popular with anglers, comfortable rooms with bathrooms, good breakfast.

Camping
Camping Municipal, on the seafront, T156-252890.
Camping Cañadon Jiminez, 4 km away on RN 281, T0297-4872135.

Estancias

A La Madrugada, situated on the Atlantic coast, 120 km from Puerto Deseado, reached from the RN281 to Km 79, then RN68, T155-94123, walker@caminosturismo.com.ar. Splendid views, and plenty of places to spot wildlife from the estancia itself, good Patagonian home cooking, and comfortable accommodation. The owners also arrange excursions to sea lion colony and cormorant nesting area, English spoken, recommended.

Puerto San Julián *p497*

B Bahía, San Martín 1075, T02962-453144, nico@sanjulian.com.ar. Modern and comfortable rooms, good value.
B Res Sada, San Martín 1112, T02962-452013. Simple rooms, on a busy road.
C Municipal, 25 de Mayo 917, T02962-452300. Attractive rooms, well-run, good value, no restaurant.

Camping

Municipal campsite, Magellanes 650 y M Moreno, T02962-452806. US$2 per site plus US$1 pp, recommended, all facilities.

Estancias

B Estancia La María, 150 km west, contact Fernando Behm, Saavedra 1163, T02962-452328. Simple accommodation in a modern house, with amazing cave paintings. The owners also organize trips to see marine and birdlife.

Piedrabuena *p498*

A-B ACA Motel, T02962-47145. Simple, functional but good, warm and nice food.
A-B Hostería El Alamo, Lavalle 08, T02962-47249. Quiet, breakfast extra. Recommended.
A-B Hostería Municipal Isla Pavon, Isla Pavón,T156-38380. Luxurious 4-star catering to fishermen of steelhead trout.
C Res Internacional, Ibáñez 99, T02962-47197. Recommended.

Camping

Sites south of town on Route 3; also on Isla Pavón.

Río Gallegos *p499, map p501*

Most hotels are situated within a few blocks of the main street, Av Roca, running north west to south east. Do not confuse the street Comodoro Rivadavia with (nearby) Bernardino Rivadavia.
C Apart Hotel Austral, Roca 1505, T/F02966-434314, www.apartaustral.com.ar. A smart newly built apart hotel, with bright rooms, with attractive sunny decor, and very good value, particularly the superior duplexes. The kitchen facilities are a bit basic, but certainly adequate for a couple of nights. Breakfast US$1.50 extra.
C Comercio, Roca 1302, T02966-422458, hotelcomercio@informacionrgl.com.ar. Good value, nicely designed comfortable rooms with bathrooms, and breakfast included. There is an attractive cheap *confitería* on the street.
C Croacia, Urquiza 431, T02966-421218. Cheaper, and one of the best reasonably priced places, with comfortable beds, bright spotless rooms with bath, huge breakfasts, and helpful owners. Recommended.
C Santa Cruz, Roca 701, T02966-420601, www.advance.com.ar/usuarios/htlscruz. This modern city-style hotel is excellent value. Go for the slightly pricier, spacious new rooms with excellent bathrooms and full buffet breakfast included. Highly recommended.
D Covadonga, Roca 1244, T02966-420190. Attractive old 1930s building, the basic rooms have bath and TV, and come off a long corridor to a courtyard. Breakfast is included, and though rooms are small, it's all clean and well maintained.
D Nevada, Zapiola 480, T02966-435790. A good budget option, with clean, simple spacious rooms, nice beds and good bathrooms, and welcoming owners.
D París, Roca 1040, T02966-420111. Fairly simple rooms with bath, set back from the street, a good value choice, though breakfast is extra.

Estancias

A Hill Station, 63 km north of Río Gallegos on RN58. An estancia with 120 years of history, run by descendants of the founder, William Halliday. A sheep farm, also breeding criollo horses, this offers wonderful horse riding to see flora and fauna of the coast, and simple accommodation.
A Monte Dinero, near Cabo Vírgines, T02966-428922, www.montedinero.com.ar. On this working sheep farm accommodation

is comfortable. The house is lined with wood rescued from ships wrecked off the coast, and the food is delicious and home grown. They'll take you on a tour of the reserve, and give you an impressive demonstration of the incredible prowess of their sheep dogs. Highly recommended.

Camping

Camping ATSA, Route 3, en route to bus terminal, T02966-420301. US$2.50 pp plus US$0.50 for tent.

Chacra Daniel, Paraje Río Chico, 3.5 km from town, T02966-423970. US$4 pp per day, is also recommended, with parrilla and full facilities.

Club Pescazaike, Paraje Güer Aike, T02966-421803, some 30 km west of town on Route 3. Well equipped, and an attractive place US$2 pp per day, also *quincho* and restaurant.

Eating

Comodoro Rivadavia *p495*

TT Cayo Coco, Rivadavia 102. A welcoming little bistro, with very cheery staff, and excellent pizzas. Recommended. Good value.

TT Dionisius, 9 de Julio y Rivadavia. A smart and elegant parrilla, popular with a more sedate clientele, serving excellent set menus for US$5.

TT La Barca, Belgrano 935. Welcoming and cheap: *tenedor libre.*

TT La Barra, San Martín 686. A pleasant bright café for breakfast, very good coffee or a light lunch.

TT La Tradición, Mitre 675. Another popular and recommended *parrilla*, for good *asado*.

TT Peperoni, Rivadavia 348. A cheerful modern place with good range of home made pastas, filled with exciting things like king crab, as well as serving seafood and *parrilla*. US$4-7, for main dish.

TT Superquick, La Anónima supermarket, San Martín y Güemes. Quick, cheap food.

Puerto Deseado *p497*

TT El Pingüino, Piedrabuena 958. Established *parrilla* which serves fabulous rice pudding.

TT Puerto Cristal, Espana 1698. Panoramic views of the port, a great place for Patagonian lamb and *parrilla*.

Puerto San Julián *p497*

TT El Muelle Viejo, Mitre 1. Good seafood on this seafront restaurant. The *pejerrey* is recommended. Also bars and tearooms.

TT Rural, Ameghino y Vieytes. Good, but not before 2100.

TT Sportsman, Mitre y 25 de Mayo. Excellent value.

Río Gallegos *p499, map p501*

There are lots of good places to eat here, many serving excellent seafood, and some smart new inexpensive restaurants.

T Buena Vista, Sarmiento y Gob Lista, T02966-444114. Most chic, and not expensive. Near the river, with open views across the Plaza de la República, this has an imaginative menu, and is reasonably priced.

T El Club Britanico, Roca 935. Doing its best to look like a London gentleman's club, though lacking in atmosphere, serves cheap set lunches.

T El Dragon, 9 de Julio 29. Cheap and varied *tenedor libre*.

T El Horreo, Roca 863. Next door to *Puesto Molino*. A more sophisticated option, rather like a bistro in feel, serving delicious lamb dishes and good salads. Recommended.

T La Vieja Esquina, Sarfield 90. For pizzas and pastas.

T Puesto Molino, Roca 862, opposite the tourist office. A relaxed airy place, its design inspired by life on estancias, with bold paintings, wooden tables and excellent pizzas (US$5 for 2) and *parrilla* (US$10 for 2). Recommended.

Activities and tours

Monumento Natural Bosques Petrificados *p496*

The site can be visited in a day trip with a tour from San Julián, or from Puerto Deseado with **Los Vikingos**, Estrada 1275, T0297-4870020, www.losvikingos.com.ar

Puerto Deseado *p497*

Darwin Expediciones, España 2601, T156-247554, www.darwin-expeditions.com and **Los Vikingos**, Estrada 1275, T0297-4870020, both offer excursions by boat to Rio Deseado reserve, and Reserva Provincial Isla Pinguino, as well as trips to see the Monumento Natural Bosques Petrificados .

Puerto San Julián *p497*

Tur Aike Turismo, Av San Martín 446, T02962-452086.

Río Gallegos *p499, map p501*

Fishing

The southern fishing zone includes the Ríos Gallegos, Grande, Fuego, Ewan, San Pablo and Lago Fagnano, near Ushuaia. It is famous for runs of sea trout. Ask the tourist office for fishing guides, and information on permits, or visit www.santacruz.gov.ar /pesca.

Tour operators

Macatobiano Turismo, Roca 908, T/F02966-434201, macatobiano@macatobiano.com. Air tickets and tours to Pingüinero Cabo Vírgenes (see above), all day trip US$20 also to the mystical Laguna Azul, a half-day trip to this beautiful lake in a volcanic crater, and to Estancia Monte León, as well as tickets to El Calafate and Ushuaia. Recommended.

Transport

Comodoro Rivadavia *p495*

Air

Airport, 9 km north. Bus No 6 to airport from bus terminal, hourly (45 mins), US$0.40. Taxi to airport, US$3. To **Buenos Aires**, Aerolíneas Argentinas/Austral. LADE flies once a week to **Puerto Madryn, Esquel, Bariloche**, and **El Calafate**, among other towns in **Patagonia**.

Airline offices Aerolineas Argentinas, 9 de Julio 870, T02967-4440050. LADE, Rivadavia 360, T02967-4476565.

Bus

Terminal, T02967-3367305, is conveniently located in the centre at Pellegrini 730; has luggage store, good *confitería* upstairs, toilets, excellent tourist information office 0800-2100, and a few kiosks. Services to **Buenos Aires**, 2 daily, 28 hrs, US$45. **Chile**: To **Coyhaique**, **Santiago**, 35 hrs $155. Etap Angel Giobbi, US$15, 12 hrs, twice a week. To **Mendoza** 28 hrs, US$42. Andesmar T420139. To **Bariloche**, 14 hrs, US$19 (Don Otto). To **Esquel** (paved road) 8 hrs direct with ETAP and Don Otto, US$18. In summer buses usually arrive full; book ahead. To **Río Gallegos**, Don Otto, Pingüino and TAC daily, 11 hrs, US$9. To **Puerto Madryn**, US$8. To **Trelew**, Don Otto 3 daily 4 hrs US$6, several companies. To **Caleta Olivia**, La Unión hourly, US$1.50. To **Sarmiento**, US$4, 2½ hrs at 3 daily. TAC T02967-4443376, Don Otto, T02967-4470450.

Car rental

Patagonia Sur Car, Rawson 1190, T02967-4466768. Avis, 9 de Julio 687, T/F02967-496382.

Camarones *p496*

Bus Don Otto buses from **Trelew**, Mon and Fri, 2½ hrs, returns to **Trelew** same day 1600. There are buses to **Reserva Natural Cabo Dos Bahías** Mon, Wed, Fri 0800 from **Trelew**, El Nañdu, US$4.20, 2½ hrs, returns same day 1600.

Caleta Olivia *p496*

Bus

To **Río Gallegos**, Pingüino, US$8, overnight. Many buses to **Comodoro Rivadavia**, 1 hr, US$1.70 and 3 daily to **Pto Deseado**, US$5. To **El Calafate**, 5 hrs; to **Perito Moreno** and **Los Antiguos**, 5 hrs, US$7, daily. Bus company La Union, terminal: T0297-4851134. El Pingüino, T0297-4852929, TAC T0297-4853481.

Puerto Deseado *p497*

Sportman, La Unión bus companies, at terminal T155-928598, daily to **Caleta Olivia**, US$5.

Puerto San Julián *p497*

Air

Weekly services (Mon) with LADE to **Santa Cruz**, **Río Gallegos**, **El Calafate**, **Puerto Deseado**, **Gob Gregores**, **Comodoro Rivadavia**, and **Río Turbio**. LADE, San Martín 1552, T02962-452137.

Bus

To **Buenos Aires**, Transportadora Patagónica, T452072, Pingüino, T02962-452425. To **Río Gallegos**, Pingüino, 6 hrs, US$7. To **Mendoza**, US$50, Andesmar, T02962-454403.

Río Gallegos *p499, map p501*

Air

Airport 10 km from centre. Taxi (*remise*) to/from town US$4; Río Gallegos used to be the nearest airport to El Calafate, but there are less flights now that Lago Viedma airport has opened near El Calafate . However, there are still regular flights to/from **Buenos Aires**, **Ushuaia** and **Río Grande** direct with Aerolíneas Argentinas. LADE to **Río Turbio** and **El Calafate**, twice a week, to **Ushuaia** and **Comodoro Rivadavia** once a week. LADE flights should be booked as far in advance as possible. The Ladeco service from **Punta Arenas** to **Port Stanley** on the **Falkland Islands/Islas Malvinas** stops once a month in either direction. Both Pingüino and Interlagos can arrange packages to **Calafate** including accommodation and trip to Moreno glacier from their offices at the airport.

Airline offices Aerolíneas Argentinas, San Martín 545, T02966-422020. LADE, Fagnano 53, T02966-422326.

Bus

Terminal at corner of RN3 and Av Eva Perón, 3 km from centre (crowded, no left luggage, but a *confitería*, toilets, kiosks); taxi to centre US$1.00 also bus Nos 1 and 12 from posted stops around town to/from terminal.

To **El Calafate** 4-5 hrs, US$9, Taqsa and Interlagos, To **Los Antiguos**, Sportman daily at 2100, US$20. To **Comodoro Rivadavia**, Pingüino, Don Otto and TAC, 10 hrs, US$10. For **Bariloche**, Transportadora Patagonica, daily at 2130. To **Buenos Aires**, 33 hrs, several daily, Pingüino, Don Otto, TAC, US$35.00 . To **Río Grande** and **Ushuaia**, Tecni Austral, Tue, Thu Sat, at 1000, US$18-23, 8-10 hrs. To **Chile**: to **Puerto Natales**, Pingüino, Sat, 7 hrs, US$7. Bus-Sur Tue and Thu 1700. To **Punta Arenas**, Pingüino and others, US$11 daily.

Car

Taking a car to Chile Make sure your car papers are in order (go first to tourist office for necessary documents, then to the customs office at the port, at the end of San Martín, very uncomplicated). Let the hire company know, and allow 24 hrs to get the appropriate papers. The car's windows should be etched with the licence plate number. It is essential to book car rental in advance in high season. Localiza, Sarmiento 245, T02966-436717; **Cristina Vehiculos**, Libertad 123, T02966-42570.

Taxis

Hiring a taxi for group excursions may the same price as a tour bus. Taxi ranks plentiful, rates controlled, *remise* slightly cheaper. Also consider hiring a car with driver from Todo Transfer Patagonia www.interpatagonia.com/todotransfer.

Directory

Comodoro Rivadavia *p495*
Banks Many ATMs along San Martín: Banco de la Nación, San Martín 102, Banco del Chubut, San Martín 833. Change money at Thaler, San Martín 270, Mon-Sat 1000-1300, or at weekends ETAP in bus terminal. **Consulates** Chile, Sarmiento 936. **Internet** Rivadavia 201, and along San Martín at Nos 131, 394, 808, 263 and 699. **Post office** San Martín y Moreno.

Puerto San Julián *p497*
Banks Banco de la Nación, Mitre y Belgrano, and Banco de la Provincia de Santa Cruz, San Martín y Moreno. **Post office** Belgrano y San Martín.

Río Gallegos *p499, map p501*
Banks Change TCs here if going to El Calafate, where it is even more difficult. 24-hr ATMs for all major international credit and debit cards all over the centre. Banco Tierra del Fuego, Roca 831, changes TCs. Cambio El Pingüino, Zapiola 469. Thaler, San Martín 484. Both will change Chilean pesos as well as US$. **Consulates** Chile, Mariano Moreno 136, Mon-Fri, 0900-1300; tourist cards issued at border. **Internet** J@va cybercafe (next to British Club on Roca); also various *locutorios* offer internet services US$0.60 per hr. **Post office** Roca 893 y San Martín. **Telephone** *Locutorios* all over town.

Ruta 40

The Ruta 40 – known in Argentina, with affection and awe, simply as 'la cuarenta' – is one of the wildest and least travelled roads on the planet. It runs the whole length of Argentina, from La Quiaca on the border with Bolivia in the north, all the way down to El Chaltén and Río Gallegos in the south. And almost the entire length of the Ruta 40 crosses extraordinarily beautiful countryside: at times dramatic, at times eerily remote. Che Guevara travelled along much of it in his famous motorcycle jaunts, and his experience of the poverty and adversity he encountered helped form his revolutionary spirit. You can get a flavour of the toughest parts by travelling this southernmost stretch through Patagonia on bicycle, motorbike, or by bus, which might be quite enough adversity for some travellers. In the 14 hours it takes to go from Los Antiguos to El Chaltén, you're likely to see no more than a dozen cars, and this experience alone convinces you of the sheer emptiness of Patagonia. You'll also spot condors wheeling high above the Andes, the occasional Patagonian fox, and not much else apart from the clouds, whipped into amazing shapes by the ubiquitous winds.

Along the way you could veer off the battered track to hide out at a number of isolated estancias, visible from miles away where you see a fringe of tall poplars protecting a cluster of buildings from the relentless wind. Many estancias in this area welcome guests, and you can enjoy horse riding, walking and the warm hospitality of their owners, who will share their experience of a hardy life. There's a wonderful national park to explore, Perito Moreno (not to be confused with Glaciar Perito Moreno, which is in Parque Nacional Los Glaciares further south). Estancia La Oriental is the best way to see the park's stark and beautiful landscapes, much of which are inaccessible by car. To the north of this stretch, the Ruta 40 has a couple of strange attractions. One which belies the incredible emptiness of Patagonia is the Cueva de las Manos. Near the small town of Perito Moreno, in the beautiful canyon of the Río Pininturas, are caves containing thousands of human hand prints, made more than eight thousand years ago. Mind blowing, especially after travelling for 12 hours without seeing a soul. Just to the north, near Sarmiento, there's a petrified forest, with huge trunks of monkey puzzle trees turned to stone 140 million years ago.

And when at last you arrive at Mount Fitz Roy, whose great turrets of granite can be seen rising up from the flat steppe from 100 km away, you may well think you've imagined it. It's one of the most magnificent sights in the whole country, made all the more spectacular by hours or days of relentless flat lands, with only condors and the clouds for company. ▸▸ *For Sleeping, Eating and other listings, see pages 511-513.*

Ins and outs

Getting around

Travelling along the Ruta 40 is quite an experience, and unless you're taking the bus, it's one that requires careful planning. Travelling south, the road is paved as far as Perito Moreno, and then good *ripio*, improving greatly after Las Horquetas. From Río Mayo to El Calafate, the wide stony *ripio* track of the Ruta 40 zigzags its way across windswept desolate land. Every few hundred kilometres or so, there will be a small, improbable signpost to an estancia, somewhere off the road unseen, but be warned that not all accept paying guests, and many are just ordinary sheep farms. There are only a few service stations for fuel along the whole stretch, and few places offering accommodation.

Bus The most efficient way to travel this stretch is making use of the bus services offered by two companies, **Chalten Travel** and **Itinerarios y Travesías** who between them run one service daily in each direction between Los Antiguos and El Chaltén. Departure times and the itinerary can change throughout the year, but if you're keen to stop off at Cueva de las Manos, both companies run a service which visits the caves at dawn, at least a couple of times each week. Cueva de las Manos can also be reached with a tour organized from Perito Moreno.

Car/motorbike/bike Hiring a car in one town, and dropping it off in another is possible, and allows great flexibility. But it's only fun if you're not travelling alone. Make sure you know exactly where the next petrol station is, as they can easily be 300 km apart: carry spare fuel, and allow more time than you think before nightfall. It's not advisable to travel faster than 60 kph on *ripio* roads. Take warm clothes, hot drinks and a blanket, in case you become stranded at night. If cycling, note that food and water stops are scarce, the wind is fierce, and there is no shade whatsoever. Hitching along this road is virtually impossible, and can't be recommended, as you could be stranded for days.

Crossing the border from Chile You might be wondering how to start your journey along the Ruta 40. There are several options. Travelling from north to south, you could reach Río Mayo from Comodoro Rivadavia, with regular buses along the Ruta 26. There are also daily buses from Esquel, at the southernmost end of the Lake District. But you may well have crossed from Argentina into Chile at Futuleufú (near Trevelin) and come south along the Carretera Austral in Chile. In this case, take the ferry across Lago General Carrera/Lago Buenos Aires, from south of Coyhaique to Chile Chico, and cross the border back into Argentina at Los Antiguos. This is the starting point of the bus journey south along the Ruta 40.

Accommodation Be warned that there are few decent places to stay along this entire route. The best bases for accommodation are the pretty little town of Los Antiguos, near the border with Chile, and Perito Moreno – both in the north. After that, there are only remote rural estancias, and some very bleak one-horse towns until you reach the tourist haven of El Chaltén. Take a tent if you're on a bike. To get to the estancias, you'll need to have booked in advance, and you'll need your own transport to get to them. Various companies organize tours along the route, with estancia stays and travel included, see www.tierrabuena.com.ar, www.lastfrontiers.com. There's a useful site for information on the estancias in the area, although this organization offers no real logistical help www.estanciasdesantacruz.com.

Colonia Sarmiento and the petrified forests

» pp511-513.

→ *Phone code: 0297 Colour map 5, C3 Population: 7,000*

The vital east–west road link between Chile and the Atlantic is Route 26, also known as the Bioceanic Corridor, which runs east from the Andes across the steppe amid oil wells, from the Chilean border and the Chilean towns of Coyhaique and Puerto Aisén to Comodoro Rivadavia. Mainly used by lorries, it gives access to two unusual sights – the petrified araucaria forests of José Ormachea and Héctor Szlapelis, both within easy reach of the small town Colonia Sarmiento.

Sarmiento lies on the Río Senguer just south of two great lakes and 156 km west of Comodoro Rivadavia, **Lago Musters** and **Lago Colhué Huapi**, both of which offer good fishing in summer. Founded in 1897 and formally known as Colonia Sarmiento, its early settlers were Welsh, Lithuanians and Boers. It's a quiet and relaxed place, sitting in fertile, well irrigated land, and little visited by tourists, though it's the best base for visiting two areas of petrified forest nearby. Most accessible is the **Bosque Petrificado José Ormachea** ⓘ *US$2.50*, 32 km south along a *ripio* road. Less easy to reach is the rather bleaker **Bosque Petrificado Héctor Szlápelis**, some 40 km further southwest along the same road (follow signposts, the road from Sarmiento is in good condition). These forests, 60 million years old, of fallen araucaria trees nearly 3 m in circumference and 15- to 20-m-long, are a remarkable sight, best visited in summer as the winters are very cold. There are *guardaparques* (rangers) at both sites, who can give tours and information. The **tourist office** ⓘ *Av San Martín, almost at Alberdi, T0297-4898220*, is helpful and has a map of the town. A *combi* (minibus) service runs to Bosque Petrificado Héctor Szlápelis twice daily from December to March; contact the tourist office. A taxi from Sarmiento to the forests costs around US$16 (three passengers), including a one-hour wait. Contact Señor Juan José Valero, the *guardaparque*, Uruguay 43, T097-4898407, for guided tours. Ask him about camping.

Río Mayo and routes to Chile » pp511-513.

→ *Phone code: 02903. Colour map 5, C2 Population: 2,600*

Set in beautifully bleak landscape, by the meandering Río Mayo, there's little of tourist interest in this very rural little town, and you're most likely to find yourself here to change for buses or pick up fuel. But every November, it is the site for an extraordinary display of dexterity at the **Fiesta Nacional de la Esquila** (national sheep-shearing competition). Teams of five or six *esquiladores*, who travel around Patagonia from farm to farm in shearing season, compete to shear as many sheep as possible. A good shearer might get through 20 in an hour.

Border with Chile

There are two roads crossing the border into Chile to take you to Coyhaique from here. The southernmost of the two, via Paso Huemules has better roads. Coyhaique Alto is reached by a 133 km road (87 km *ripio*, then dirt) which branches off Route 40 about 7 km north of Río Mayo. On the Chilean side this road continues to Coyhaique, 50 km west of the border. See Transport, page 513, for bus services.

Chilean immigration ⓘ *Coyhaique Alto, 6 km west of the border, May-Jul 0800-2100, Sep-Apr 0700-2100*. Paso Huemules is reached by a road which branches off Route 40, some 31 km south of Río Mayo and runs west 105 km via Lago Blanco (fuel), where there is an estancia community, 30 km from the border. There's no hotel but the police are friendly and may permit camping at the police post. This road continues from Balmaceda on the Chilean side of the border to Coyhaique.

Perito Moreno and routes to Chile » pp511-513.

→ *Phone code: 02963 Colour map 5, C2 Population: 3000*

Not to be confused with the famous glacier of the same name near El Calafate, nor with Parque Nacional Perito Moreno, this Perito Moreno is a spruce little town, 25 km west of Lago Buenos Aires, and the nearest base for exploring the mysterious cave paintings at the **Cueva de las Manos**, to the south. The town has no sights as such, apart from the pleasure of watching a rural community go about its business. But southwest of the town is **Parque Laguna**, where you can see varied bird life including flamingos and black-necked swans, and go fishing. You could also walk to the crater of **Cerro Volcan**, from a path 12 km outside Perito Moreno: ask at the tourist office for directions. The friendly **tourist office** ⓘ *San Martín 1222, T02963-432222, www.epatagonia.gov.ar, 0700-2300,* can advise on tours to the cave and estancias. You could also visit Santa Cruz's tourist office in Buenos Aires (T011-4325 3102, www.estanciasde

santacruz.com). There are two ATMs in the main street, at **Banco de la Provincia de Santa Cruz** and **Banco de la Nación**, but nowhere to change traveller's cheques.

Cueva de las Manos → *Phone code: 02962 Colour map 6, A2*

ⓘ *US$1.50, under 12 free.*

Situated 47 km northeast of Bajo Caracoles, the canyon of the **Río Pinturas** contains outstanding examples of handprints and cave paintings, estimated to be around 8000 years old. In the cave's four galleries, shelves in the rock in a stunning canyon, are over 800 paintings of human hands, all but 31 of which are of left hands, as well as images of guanacos and rheas, and various geometrical designs. Painted by the Toldense peoples in red, orange, black, white and green, the pigments were derived from earth and calafate berries, and fixed with a varnish of guanaco fat and urine. They are mysterious, and rather beautiful, albeit indecipherable. However, the canyon alone is worth seeing, 270 m deep and 480 m wide, with strata of vivid red and green rock, especially beautiful in the early morning or evening light. Access is via an unpaved road which branches east off Route 40, 3 km north of Bajo Caracoles. A *guardaparque* living at the site gives helpful information. The minibus **Itinerarios y Travesias** from El Chaltén to Los Antiguos stops here in the early morning for a couple of hours. See El Chaltén Transport, page 521, for details.

Los Antiguos and border with Chile → *Phone code 02963 Colour map 6, A2*

Though there are two crossings to Chile west of Perito Moreno, the easiest and most commonly used is via the pretty little village of Los Antiguos, which lies just 2 km east of the border. The town lies on the southern shore of Lago Buenos Aires the second largest lake in South America, extending into Chile as Lago General Carrera, where the landscape is very beautiful and unspoilt, and the Río Baker, which flows from the lake is world-renowned for excellent trout fishing.

Los Antiguos is a sleepy little place, but has a pleasant atmosphere, thanks largely to its warm microclimate, and it's certainly a nicer place to stay than Chile Chico. It's a rich fruit-growing area with a popular **cherry festival** in early January, which attracts national *folclore* stars. While you're here, there are two local *chacras* (small farms) worth visiting. You can walk from the main street to **Chacra Don Neno**, where there are strawberries growing and jam for sale. You'd have to drive, or take a taxi, though, to the idyllic **Chacra el Paraiso**, where the charming owners make really exquisite jams and chutney. Recommended. The **parque municipal** at the east end of the town is a pleasant place to walk, along the bank of the river, with bird life to look at, and two blocks down, there's an superb campsite. The small but willing **tourist office** ⓘ *Av 11 de Julio 446, www.losantiguos-sc.com.ar, 0800-2200 in summer, am only at other times.*

Into Chile **Transportes VH** buses cross the border by the new bridge to the drab village of **Chile Chico**, 8 km west, US$2, 45 minutes. The main reason to enter Chile here is either to explore the largely unvisited and lovely southern shore of **Lago Gral Carrera**, or to take the ferry over the lake north to Puerto Ibáñez with bus connections on to **Coyhaique**, the main town for visiting the Carretera Austral. You can also drive to Puerto Ibáñez, via the paved road which goes around the north side of Lago Buenos Aires.

Bajo Caracoles and south to Tres Lagos

→ *Phone code: 0297 Colour map 6, A2 Population: 100*

After hours of spectacular emptiness, even tiny Bajo Caracoles is a relief. It's nothing more than a few houses with an expensive grocery store and very expensive fuel. West of Bajo Caracoles, 72 km along Route 39 are **Lago Posadas** and **Lago Pueyrredón**, two beautiful lakes with contrasting blue and turquoise waters and separated by a narrow isthmus. Guanacos and rheas can be seen and there are sites of archaeological interest.

Border with Chile From here Route 41 goes 99 km northwest to the **Paso Roballos** border with Chile, and from there 201 km onwards to Cochrane. Some 92 km south of Bajo Caracoles is the turning off west to Lago Belgrano and Parque Nacional Perito Moreno (see below). About 7 km east, along Route 521 is **Hotel Las Horquetas** (see Sleeping, page 512) with a café/bar, and 15 km beyond this is the **Tamel Aike** village (police station, water). 'Super' grade fuel is available in most places, but carry extra, since the nearest fuel before Tres Lagos involves a 72-km detour to Gobernador Gregores. From the Parque Moreno junction to **Tres Lagos**, Route 40 improves considerably. Paso Roballos is 99 km northwest of **Bajo Caracoles** via (unpaved) Route 41, which runs past Lago Ghio and Lago Columna. On the Chilean side this road continues to Cochrane, Km 177. Though passable in summer, it is often flooded in spring. No public transport. From Tres Lagos, Route 40 deteriorates rapidly and remains very rugged until after the turnoff to the Fitz Roy sector of Parque Nacional Los Glaciares. 21 km beyond is the bridge over Río La Leona, with delightful **Hotel La Leona** whose café serves good cakes. **Tres Lagos**, at Km 645, is a solitary village with a supermarket and fuel at the junction with Route 288. A road also turns off northwest to Lago San Martín, which straddles the border (the Chilean part is Lago O'Higgins).

South of Bajo Caracoles Route 40 crosses the Pampa del Asador and then, near Las Horquetas, Km 371, swings southeast to follow the Río Chico. At **Tamel Aike**, Km 393, there is a police station and water but little else. At Km 464, Route 25 branches off to **San Julian** via **Gobernador Gregores**, 72 km southeast, where there is fuel and a good mechanic, while Route 40 continues southwest towards Tres Lagos. At Km 531, a road heads west to Lago Cardiel, a very saline lake with no outlet and good salmon fishing.

Parque Nacional Perito Moreno

» pp511-513.

Situated southwest of Bajo Caracoles on the Chilean border, this is one of the wildest and most remote parks in Argentina. There is good trekking and abundant wildlife among this large, interconnected system of lakes, lying between glaciated peaks of astonishing beauty. However, since much of the park is dedicated to scientific study, it's largely inaccessible. **Lago Belgrano**, in the park's centre, is the biggest in the chain of lakes, a vivid turquoise, contrasting with surrounding mountains streaked with a mass of differing colours; on its shores, you might find ammonite fossils.

Ins and outs

The **park office** is 220 km away in the nearest town, Gobernador Gregores, Avenida San Martín 409, T02962-491477, and you can get information here before reaching the park itself. Also check www.parquesnacionales.gov.ar. Entrance to the park from Gobernador Gregores is via the paved Ruta 40, before you turn off west, 100 km south of Bajo Caracoles, onto 90 km of unpaved road. The *guardaparques* office is 10 km beyond the park entrance, and has maps, leaflets on walks and wildlife. It's essential to get detailed maps here and to ask advice about hikes and paths. You should always inform *guardaparques* before setting out on a hike. The park is open all year round, but is most pleasant in the summer. However, the access road may be blocked by snow from November to March. Bring an all-season sleeping bag and plenty of warm clothing: the climate here is mercurial. There is nowhere to buy fuel inside the park, unless you're staying at one of the estancias, and cyclists should bring water: there is no source along the 90 km branch road.

There are two estancias inside the park boundaries (see Sleeping, below): **Estancia La Oriental**, and **Estancia Menelik**, www.cielospatagonicos.com, which is homely and comfortable accommodation in three double rooms with one quadruple, plus a *refugio* where you can sleep with your sleeping bag. If you're coming to stay in **Estancia La Oriental** a taxi costs US$90 from Gobernador Gregores. There are several good sites for camping – all free, although much of the park is closed to visitors. The most accessible part is around Lago Belgrano, 12 km from the entrance.

Around the park

Just outside the park, but towering over it to the north is **Cerro San Lorenzo** (3706 m), the highest peak in southern Patagonia. Between the lakes are other peaks, permanently snow-covered, the highest of which is Cerro Herros (2770 m). The vivid hues of Sierra Colorada runs across the northeast of the park: it's erosion of these coloured rocks that has given the lakes their differing colours. At the foot of Cerro Casa de Piedra is a network of caves containing cave paintings, accessible only with a guide. Wildlife in the park includes guanacos, foxes and one of the most important surviving populations of the rare huemul deer. Birds include flamingos, ñandus, steamer ducks, grebes, black-necked swans, Patagonian woodpeckers, eagles and condors. The lakes and rivers are unusual for Argentina in that only native species of fish are found here, whereas in the rest of the country, trout and salmon have been introduced for fishing.

Hiking

Several good hikes are possible from here. There are also longer walks of up to five days. Ask the *guardaparques* for details, and see the website.

▲ **Lago Belgrano** Follow the Senda Natural Península Belgrano to the peninsula of the lake, 8 km, where there are fine views of Cerro Herros, and an experience of transition landscape from steppe to forest (one to two hours).

▲ **Lago Burmeister** via Cerro Casa de Piedra, 16 km.

▲ **Cerro León** Start at **Estancia La Oriental**, this walk has fabulous panoramic views over the park, and offers the chance to see condors in flight (four hours).

Sleeping

Colonia Sarmiento and the petrified forests *p507*

C Chacra Labrador, 10 km from Sarmiento, T0297-489 3329, agna@coopsar.com.ar. This is an excellent place to stay on a small estancia, breakfast included, other meals extra and available for non-residents. English and Dutch spoken, runs tours to petrified forests at good prices, will collect guests from Sarmiento (same price as taxi).

Camping

Municipal site near Río Senguer, 2 km north of centre on Route 243, basic, no shower, US$3 for tent, US$1 pp.

Río Mayo and routes to Chile *p508*

D Covadonga, San Martín 575, T02903-420014. The oldest hotel in town, established for travelling salesmen in the 1940s, and now restored with comfortable rooms, and a decent restaurant. There is a free camp site on northern outskirts near river.

Perito Moreno and routes to Chile *p508*

B Hostería Cueva de Las Manos, 20 km from the cave, also known as Los Toldos, see below.

D Austral, San Martín 1327, T02963-42042. Bath and breakfast, and a decent restaurant. The slightly better of the two hotels in town.

D Belgrano, San Martín 1001, T02963-42019. Also pleasant, with simple rooms.

Estancias

L Las Toldos, 60 km south on RN40, 7 km off the road to Bajo Caracoles, T02963-432856 (Buenos Aires T011- 4901 0436), www.estanciasdesantacruz.com/lostoldos/lostoldos.htm. The closest estancia for visiting the Cueva de las Manos, a modest building, but set in wonderful landscape, the owners, Alicia and Martín Molina organize trips by horse and 4WD to see the cave paintings, as well as to the lakes and the Perito Moreno park. They also have an albergue. Open Nov-Easter.

L pp **Telken**, 28 km south on RN40, T02963-432079, Buenos Aires T011-4797 7216, jarinauta@santacruz.com.ar. Formerly a sheep station, now aimed at tourism, and providing comfortable accommodation in the farmhouse, wood-lined rooms, and charming simple bedrooms. All meals shared with the warmly welcoming owners, Joan and Reynaldo Nauta, who also offer horse riding. Highly recommended.

Camping

Municipal site 2 km at Laguna de los Cisnes, T02963-432072.

Los Antiguos *p509*

A Hostería La Serena, outside Los Antiguos at Km 29, T02963-432340. Very comfortable accommodation, excellent home-grown food, organizes fishing and trips in Chilean and Argentine Lake District, open Oct-Jun; further details from Geraldine des Cressonières.

B Antigua Patagonia, on the lakeside, signposted from Ruta 43, T491038/491055, www.antiguapatagonia.net. Los Antiguos has one really great hotel, and it's really worth a detour. Luxurious rooms with beautiful views from this modern building on the shore of the lake, with wide open vistas and big skies reflected in its waters. There's also an excellent restaurant. The charming owner Alejandro also arranges small tours to the Cueva de los Manos and nearby Monte Cevallos. Highly recommended.

D Argentino, 11 de Julio 850, T02963-491132. Comfortable rooms, and a decent restaurant.

F pp **Albergue Padilla**, San Martín 44 (just off main street) T02963-491140. The town's cheapest place to stay. Big shared rooms for 4-8 with bathrooms, cosy quincho and garden to sit in, where you can also camp. Very friendly. Recommended. They sell the El Chaltén travel tickets and receive passengers off the bus from El Chaltén.

Camping

Camping Municipal, T02963-491308. An outstanding campsite with hot showers, and every other facility, in lovely grounds 2 km from centre, US$1.25 pp.

Bajo Caracoles and south to Tres Lagos *p509*

L Hostería Lagos del Furioso, Lago Posadas, on the peninsula between the lakes, reached along Route 39, T02963-490253, www.lagosdelfurioso.com. Open Mid Oct-Easter. Extremely comfortable accommodation in cabins in a really incredible setting by the lake shore, offering superb Patagonian cooking with home produced food, and good wines. Also offers horse riding, trekking and excursions in 4WD vehicles. Two nights minimum – you'll want to stay longer.

D Hotel Bajo Caracoles, T02963-434963. Very old fashioned, 1920s building, with plain spacious rooms, but a rather institutional feel, and not quite welcoming. There are meals, and given the wilderness all around you'll probably be glad of a bed.

Camping

G At this campsite, rooms **E** pp, are also available. A simple and welcoming place, also running excursions to Cueva de las Manos, 10 km by vehicle then 1½-to 2-hrs' walk, and to nearby volcanoes by car or horse. Ask for **Señor Sabella**, Av Perón 941, Perito Moreno, T02963-432199.

Estancias

There are some superb estancias in this region: tricky to get to without your own transport, but offering an unforgettable experience of Patagonian life; 55 km from Gobernador Gregores is **A** pp **La Angostura**, T02962-452010. Horse riding, trekking, fishing, recommended.

Parque Nacional Perito Moreno *p510*

B Estancia La Oriental, T02962-452196, elada@uvc.com.ar. Open Nov-Mar, full board. In a really splendid setting, rooms are comfortable, and there's superb horse riding.

Camping

Camping is possible and there are 4 free sites inside the park: **Lago Burmeister, Mirador Lago Belgrano, Cerro de Vasco** and **Alberto de Agostini**. No facilities, no fires.

Eating

Perito Moreno *p508*

There's good food at **Pipach**, next to Hotel Austral, **Parador Bajo Caracoles**, or pizzas at **Nono's**, on 9 de Julio y Saavedra. **Rotiseria Chee's I**, is a cheap and cheery place to eat and does takeaways.

Los Antiguos *p509*

La Perla del Lago, Fitzroy y Perito Moreno. The best *parrilla*.

Activities and tours

Colonia Sarmiento and the petrified forests *p507*

Aonikenk Viajes, Rawson 1190, T0297-4466768, aonikenk@satlink.com. Tours to the petrified forests, with 2 hrs at the site.
Atlas, Rivadavia 439, T0297-4475204.
Monitur, Brown 521, T0297-4471062, monitur@amadeusmail.com.ar.

Perito Moreno and routes to Chile *p508*

Senor Sabella, Av Perón 941, T02963-432199. Trips organized from Perito Moreno. He'll take you to the edge of the canyon, and it's a spectacular 2-hr walk from here to the caves, alongside the river winding through the green base of the valley.
Transporte Terrestre Guanacondór, Juan José Nauto, T02963-432079, and **Transporte Lago Posados**, T02963-432431. All day tour with option of collecting from Bajo Caracoles or **Ea Los Toldos**, US$30-40. Both operators do the Circuito Grande Comarca Noroeste, one of the highlights of Santa Cruz, taking in some of the province's scenery. From Perito Moreno to Bajo Caracoles, Cueva de los Manos, Lago Posada, Paso Roballos, Monte Cevallos, Los Antiguos.

Transport

Colonia Sarmiento *p507*

Bus Overnight services to **Esquel** with Etap (T0297-454756) daily except Sat; take food for journey as cafés are expensive. Frequent buses to **Comodoro Rivadavia**. To **Chile** via Río Mayo, **Giobbi**, 0200, 3 weekly; seats are scarce in Río Mayo.

Río Mayo and routes to Chile *p508*

Bus Giobbi buses from **Comodoro Rivadavia** to **Coyhaique (Chile)**, pass through Río Mayo 3 times a week.

Perito Moreno and routes to Chile *p508*

Air Airport 7 km east out of town, and the only way to get there is by taxi. LADE flies to **Perito Moreno** from **Río Gallegos**, **Río Grande**, **Ushuaia**, **El Calafate** and **Gob Gregores**.

Airline offices LADE, Av San Martín 1207, T02963-432055.

Bus The terminal is on the edge of town next to the EG3 service station, T02963-432072. To **Comodoro Rivadavia**, with **La Union** 6 hrs US$12. If crossing from Chile at **Los Antiguos**, there are 2 buses daily in summer, 1 hr, US$2, **La Union**, T02963-432133. Two companies run to **El Chaltén**, with **Chalten Travel** even days 1000, and **Itinerarios y Travesias** other days at 1800, US$30. It's a 14-hr, 582-km journey over bleak emptiness. Northbound buses with **Itinerarios y Travesias** stop at the Cueva de los Manos for a couple of hours at dawn, and while it's a shame to miss the ride in daylight, it's a great way to see the caves.

Los Antiguos *p509*

Bus To **Comodoro Rivadavia**, US$9, **Co-op Sportman**, from near **Hotel Argentino**, daily, 7½ hrs, via Perito Moreno and Caleta Olivia. To **El Chaltén** and **El Calafate** via Perito Moreno, **Chaltén Travel** every even day, US$40, booked through **Albergue Padilla**, San Martín 44 Sur, T02962-491140. **Itinerarios y Travesias**, run buses along the route every odd day, tickets in **El Chalten**, Perito Moreno 152, T02962-493088, **Albergue Patagonia**, Av San Martín 495 T02962-493088, alpatagonia@infovia.com.ar. To **Chile**, **La Union** buses to **Chile Chico**, 8 km west, US$1, 45 mins.

Parque Nacional Perito Moreno *p510*

There is no transport into the park but it may be possible to get a lift with estancia workers from **Hotel Las Horquetas**, www.parquesnacionales.com also has information.

Parque Nacional Los Glaciares

Of all Argentina's impressive landscapes, [illegible] of these immense glaciers stretching out infinitely and silently before you, may stay with you longest. This is the second largest national park in Argentina, extending along the Chilean border for over 170 km. Almost half of it is covered by the Southern Ice Cap – at 370 km long, it's the third largest in the world. From it, 13 major glaciers descend into two great lakes: Lago Argentino in the southeast, and Lago Viedma to the northeast. Two quite different areas of the park are centres for tourism. At the southern end, the spectacular glaciers themselves can be visited from El Calafate, with bus and boat trips to Glaciares Moreno, Upsala and Spegazzini. At the northern end, there is superb trekking around the dramatic Fitz Roy massif, and ice climbing on glaciers near its summit, reached from El Chaltén, 217 km northwest of El Calafate. The central section, between Lago Argentino and Lago Viedma, is composed of the ice cap on the western side, with a couple of estancias open to tourists. East of the ice fields, there's plentiful southern beech forest, but further east still, the land flattens to the typical wind-blasted Patagonian steppe, with sparse vegetation. Bird life is surprisingly prolific, and you'll spot the scarlet headed magallenic woodpecker, black-necked swans, and perhaps even the torrent duck, diving for food in the streams and rivers. Guanacos, grey foxes, skunks and rheas can be seen on the steppe while the rare huemul inhabits the forest.

▸▸ *For Sleeping, Eating and other listings see pages 523-532.*

Ins and outs

Getting there Access to the park is very straightforward at both El Calafate and El Chaltén. There are regular bus services from El Calafate, as well as many tourist excursions, combining bus access with boat trips, walking and even ice trekking on Glaciar Perito Moreno. There are flights to El Calafate from Buenos Aires, Ushuaia, Río Gallegos, Esquel, Comodoro Rivadavia, Bariloche and Puerto Natales in Chile. All transport gets heavily booked in the summer months of January and February. From El Chaltén you can hike directly into the park, with a well established network of trails leading to summits, lakes and glaciers around Mount Fitz Roy, with many campsites. There are several buses daily to El Chaltén from El Calafate.

Best time to visit Although this part of Patagonia is generally cold, there is a milder microclimate around Lago Viedma and Lago Argentino, which means that summers can be reasonably pleasant, with average summer temperatures between 5°C and 22°C, though strong winds blow constantly at the foot of the Cordillera. Rainfall on the Hielo Sur, up to 5000 mm annually, falls mainly as snow. In the forested area, rainfall is heavier, and falls mainly between March and late May. In winter, the whole area is inhospitably cold, and most tourist facilities are closed, although El Calafate is making some attempt to open all year round. The best time to visit is between November and April, avoiding January and early February, when Argentines take their holidays, campsites are crowded and accommodation is hard to find.

Park information Entrance fee to the park is US$10, to be paid at the gates of the Park, 50 km west of El Calafate. **El Calafate park office** ⓘ *Av del Libertador 1302, T02901-491005, losglaciares@apn.gov.ar, Mon-Fri 0800-1600.* **El Chaltén park office** ⓘ *across the bridge at the entrance to town, T02962-493004, seccionallagoviedma@apn.gov.ar.* All bus passengers arriving here are given an informative talk about the Park and its paths, and you can ask for helpful trekking maps with the paths and campsites marked, giving distances and walking times.

El Calafate » pp523-532.

→ *Phone code: 02902 Colour map 6, B2 Population: 8,000*

El Calafate sits on the south shore of Lago Argentino, a town existing almost entirely as a tourist centre for visiting the glaciers in the Parque Nacional los Glaciares, 50 km west. From here you can visit Glaciar Perito Moreno by bus and boat, and even go trekking on its surface. Or travel by boat along the western arms of Lago Argentino, between stately floating icebergs, to see the glaciers of Spegazzini and Upsala. Best of all, take the long day excursion by boat to **Estancia Cristina,** which gives you the chance to trek, or ride horses up to a spectacular viewpoint above Upsala Glacier. All are breathtakingly beautiful, and an unforgettable part of your trip to Patagonia. The town itself is expensive, and not particularly attractive, and at times in January and February, even the growing number of hotels, hostels and *cabañas* can't quite accommodate the hordes, so it's essential to book ahead. The town is empty and quiet all winter, but can be extremely cold, and it's best to come in March or April if you can, as most tourist services close down. A small ski resort with just four pistes opened in 2006, 11 km away in the nearby hills: this is a brave attempt to keep visitors coming all year round, but has a long way to go.

Ins and outs

Getting there The airport is 22 km east of town. There are daily flights from Buenos Aires (several daily in summer). You can also fly from Bariloche, Ushuaia or other towns in Patagonia on the weekly **LADE** flights (book ahead). Or fly from Puerto Natales in Chile (in summer) to combine a trip to the glaciers with trekking in Torres del Paine. A minibus service meets all flights, costing US$6 (open return), a taxi will cost you US$9. Bus travel is convenient too, with buses from Río Gallegos (where you can connect with buses to Ushuaia). There are also buses to Puerto Natales, via Cerro Castillo if you want to get directly to/from Torres del Paine. The bus terminal is centrally located up a steep flight of steps from the main street. There are ATMs and *locutorios* with internet in the town, and many good hotels and restaurants. » *For further information, see Transport, page 531.*

Getting around El Calafate's shops, restaurants and tour operators can mostly be found along its main street, Avenida del Libertador, running east-west, with hotels lying within two blocks north and south and smaller *hosterías* scattered through the newly built residential areas sprawling up the hill, and north of centre, across the river. There are many estancias on the way to the national park, and also campsites. Bus travel and tour trips to the Perito Moreno glaciers are well organized. The cheapest method is with a regular bus service, but tours can be informative, and some include a boat trip.

Best time to visit The area is unbearably busy in January, when you'll have to reserve well ahead for accommodation, marginally better in February, but best of all in December, March and April, when the weather can still be sunny and clear, and there are less people. There are a couple of festivals worth seeing: **Lago Argentino Day,** on 15 February, with live music, dancing and *asados*. There are also displays of horsemanship and *asados* on **Día de la Tradición,** 10 November.

Tourist information ⓘ *at the bus terminal, T02902-491090, www.turismo.elcalafate.gov.ar, Oct-Apr daily 0800-2200, May-Sep, 0800-2100.*

Sights

Though El Calafate was founded in 1927, it grew very slowly until the opening of the road to the Perito Moreno glacier in the 1960s, and has expanded rapidly as a tourist town since. Following the economic collapse in 2001, many people flocked here from

 Buenos Aires to start hotel and restaurant businesses, and escape the economic stress of the city: they're no doubt making a handsome profit now. The town has little culture of its own, aside from a very transient tourism: most people stay here no longer than two or three nights.

Just west of the town centre is **Bahía Redonda**, a shallow part of Lago Argentino which freezes in winter, when ice-skating and skiing are possible. At the eastern edge of the bay, **Laguna Nímez**, there's a bird reserve where there are flamingos, black-

Parque Nacional Los Glaciares

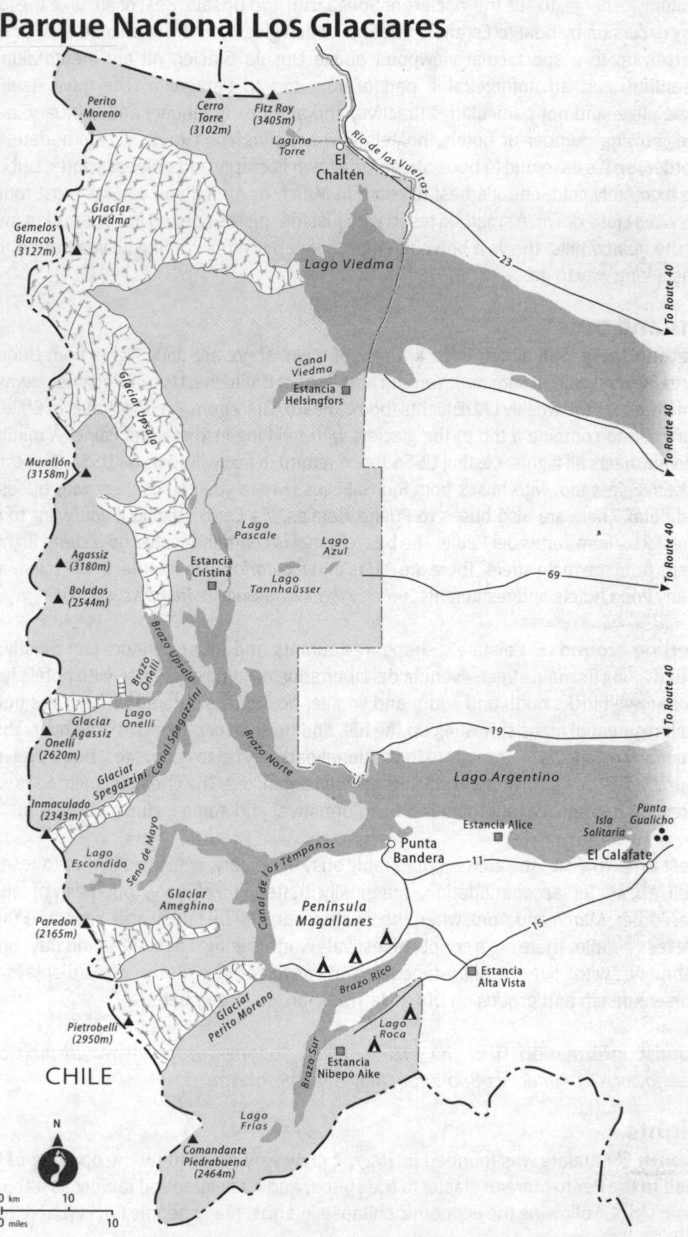

necked swans and ducks, recommended for an hour's stroll either early morning or late afternoon. From the **Intendencia del Parque,** Avenida del Libertador 1302, follow Calle Bustillo up the road to cross the bridge. Keep heading north across a pleasant new residential area: the laguna is signposted. Guides in summer lead walks, lasting two hours, US$1, Monday to Saturday. On the way back, you can stop by the **Centro de Interpretación Histórica** ⓘ *Av Brown y Bonarelli, US$3*, a small well-run centre housing a very educational exhibition created by an anthropologist and a historian with pictures and bilingual texts about the region. Also a very relaxing café/library.

Around El Calafate

For the main excursions to the glaciers, see Glaciar Perito Moreno below. El Calafate has a number of other attractions, worth considering if you're here for a few days, and some good places for trekking, horse riding and exploring by 4WD. At **Punta Gualicho,** (or Walichu) on the shores of Lago Argentino, 7 km east of town, there are cave paintings though they're rather badly deteriorated, the six-hour horse ride (US$40 per person) is worthwhile. Some tour operators run excursions to the top of nearby hills for views of the silhouette of the southern end of the Andes, **Bahía Redonda** and Isla Solitaria on Lago Argentino. An easy five-hour walk (or horse ride) is possible to the top of Cerro Calafate for panoramic views too. Ask for directions at the Hostel del Glaciar Pioneros.

Several estancias are within reach, offering a day on a working farm, a lunch of Patagonian lamb, cooked *asado al palo* (speared on a metal structure over an open fire), and activities such as trekking, birdwatching and horse riding. **Estancia Alice** ⓘ *T/F02902-491793 (Buenos Aires T011-43127206), www.estanciaalice.com.ar*, also known as 'El Galpón del Glaciar', 21 km west, is a lovely house with views of Lago Argentino offering the 'El Galpón' tour, including tea with homemade cakes, walks through a bird sanctuary where 43 species of birds have been identified, displays of sheep shearing, *asado*, and music shows, all for US$40 per person (includes transfer to and from hotels); English spoken. Trekking, 4WD or horse riding trips to the top of Cerro Frías (1030 m) for fantastic views of Mount Fitz Roy, Paine and Lago Argentino are organized by **Cerro Frías** ⓘ *Comandante Espora 159, T02902-492808, www.cerrofrias.com*, for around US$40 per person, including lunch.

Lago Roca, 40 km southwest, is set in beautiful open landscape, with hills above offering panoramic views, perfect for lots of activities, such as trout and salmon fishing, climbing, walking, and there are estancias, such as the beautifully set **Estancia Nibepo Aike** (www.nibepoaike.com.ar, or book through Lago San Martín agency, www.lagosanmartin.com) where you can watch typical farm activities, such as the branding of cattle in summer. There is good camping in a wooded area and a restaurant. At **Estancia Quien Sabe**, strawberries and walnuts are grown, and you can see beehives and sheep shearing, and eat an *asado* lunch; contact **Turismo Leutz**, www.leutzturismo.com.ar.

Lago Argentino

Glaciar Perito Moreno

The sight of this expanse of ice, like a frozen sea, its waves sculpted by wind and time into beautiful turquoise folds and crevices, is unforgettable. Immense and silent, you'll watch in awe, until suddenly a mighty roar announces the fall of another hunk of ice into the milky turquoise water below. Glaciar Moreno is one of the few accessible glaciers in the world which you can see visibly advancing. Some 30 km long, it reaches the water at a narrow point in one of the fiords, **Brazo Rico**, opposite Península Magallanes, and here, where it's 5 km across and 60 m high it occasionally advances across Brazo Rico, blocking the fiord. As the water pressure builds up behind it, the ice breaks, reopening the channel and sending giant icebergs (*témpanos*) rushing down the appropriately named **Canal de los**

 Témpanos. In recent decades, this has only happened in February 1988, March 2004 and in March 2006, giving concern that global warming may be to blame for the marked change in the glacier's behaviour. Walking on the ice itself is a wonderful way to experience it, climbing up the steep curves of what appear from a distance to be vertical fish flakes, and are in fact huge peaks, with mysterious chasms below, lit by refracted bluish light.

Access There are various ways to approach the glacier. All excursions not involving boat trips (and the regular bus service) will take you straight to the car park situated 77 km west of El Calafate (around 30 km further from the gates of the park) where you begin the descent along a series of wooden walkways (*pasarelas*) to see the glacier slightly from above, and then, as you get lower, directly head-on. There are several wide viewing areas, where in summer crowds wait expectantly, cameras poised, for another hunk of ice to fall from the vertical blue walls at the glacier's front into the milky turquoise lake below with a mighty roar. You could also approach the glacier by boat from two different piers. To survey the glacier from the south (and for trekking on the glacier), boats leave from Bajo de las Sombras pier (7 km east of the glacier). To approach from the north, boats leave regularly from Perito Moreno pier (1 km north of the glacier, where there is a restaurant). This latter service is offered as an extra when you book your standard excursion to the glacier or it can also be booked directly at the pier. To get closer still, there are guided treks on the ice itself, known as Big Ice and 'minitrekking', where you can walk along those crevices and frozen wave crests in crampons, which are provided. The latter is possible for anyone with a reasonable level of fitness, and not technically demanding. The glacier is approached by a lovely walk through lenga forest, and there's a place to eat your lunch outside, with wonderful views; but bring your own food and drink. Tour companies in El Calafate offer all of these, or some in combinations. Details of tours and boat trips in Activities and tours, page 529.

Upsala Glacier

The fiords at the northwestern end of Lago Argentino are fed by four other glaciers. The largest is the Upsala Glacier, named after the Swedish university that commissioned the first survey of this area in 1908, and a stunning expanse of untouched beauty. It's three times the area of the Perito Moreno Glacier, and the longest glacier flowing off the Southern Patagonian icefield. Unusually it ends in two separate frontages, each about 4 km wide and 60 m high, although only the western frontage can be seen from the lake excursion. It can be reached by motorboat from Punta Bandera on Lago Argentino, 50 km west of Calafate, on a trip that also goes to other, much smaller, glaciers. **Spegazzini**, further south, has a frontage 1½ km wide and 130 m high. In between are **Agassiz** and **Onelli** glaciers, both of which feed into **Lago Onelli**, a quiet and very beautiful lake, full of icebergs of every size and sculpted shape, surrounded by beech forests on one side and ice-covered mountains on the other.

The best way to see Upsala glacier is to visit the remote **Estancia Cristina** ⓘ *9 de Julio 69, El Calafate, T02902-491133 (T011-48143934 in Buenos Aires), www.estanciacristina.com*. Lying on a lonely lakeside spot, on the northern shores of the lake, not far from Upsala Glacier, it's beautiful, utterly wild, and yet an unbeatably comfortable base for exploring the region. Accommodation is available, or you can come on a full-day visit which includes lunch and the option to go hiking for five hours, horse riding or driving in sturdy 4WD vehicles to a vantage point high above the lake. You'll walk through incredible ancient landscapes, alongside massive rocks polished smooth by the path of glaciers, to see Upsala Glacier from above. This is an overwhelmingly beautiful sight, stretching apparently endlessly away from you, with the deep still Prussian blue lake below, and all around, rocks the colour of fire. Boat trips to **Estancia Cristina** are run by Fernández Campbell.

Mount Fitz Roy and around

The soaring granite towers of Mount Fitz Roy rise up from the smooth baize of the flat steppe, more like a ziggurat than a mountain, surrounded by a consort of jagged snow-clad spires, with a stack of spun-cotton cloud hanging constantly above them. **Cerro Fitz Roy** (3405 m) is one of the most magnificent mountains in the world, towering above the nearby peaks, its polished granite sides too steep for snow to settle. Its Tehuelche name was El Chaltén, ('smoking mountain' or 'volcano'), perhaps because occasionally at sunrise the pink towers are briefly lit up bright red for a few seconds, the *amanecer de fuego* ('sunrise of fire'). Perito Moreno named the peak after the captain of the *Beagle* who saw it from afar in 1833, and it was first climbed by a French expedition in 1952. It stands in the northern end of Parque Nacional Los Glaciares, at the western end of Lago Viedma, 230 km north of El Calafate. Around it are **Cerros Torre** (3102 m), **Poincenot** (3002 m), and **Saint-Exupery** (2558 m), in an area of lakes and glaciers that makes marvellous trekking country, every bit as satisfying as Torres del Paine across the border.

Ins and outs

Getting around The base for walking and climbing around Fitz Roy is El Chaltén. Most paths are very clear and well worn, but a map is essential, even on short walks: the park information centre gives a helpful maps of treks, but the best are published by *Zagier and Urruty*, www.patagoniashop.net, regularly updated, in varied scales (1:50,000; 1:250,000; 1:350,000), US$6-12, available in shops in El Calafate and El Chaltén. Do not stray from the paths. Always wear sun screen (factor 30 at least), and be prepared for bad weather. In summer, **Restaurant Las Lengas** (see below) runs a regular minibus to Lago del Desierto, passing several starting points for treks and the wonderful **Hostería El Pilar**.

Park information The national park office is across the bridge, right at the entrance to the town, T02962-493004, www.parquesnacionales.gov.ar. All arriving bus passengers are given an informative talk about the park and its paths by the friendly *guardaparques* (some speak English), and you should ask for their helpful trekking maps with paths and campsites marked, giving distances and walking times.

Best time to visit Walking here is only really viable mid-October to April, with the best months usually March to April when the weather is generally stable and not very cold, and the autumn colours of the beech forest are stunning. Mid-summer, December and January, and spring, September to October, are generally very windy. In December/January the campsites can be full to bursting, with many walkers on the paths.

Trekking

Laguna Torre For a dramatic approach to Cerro Torre, take the path to Laguna Torre, (three hours each way). After 1½ hours you'll come to Mirador Laguna Torre with views of Cerro Torre and Fitz Roy, and after another 1¼ hours, to busy Camping De Agostini (formerly Bridwell), next to the lake, with fantastic views of the Cordón Torre.

Laguna de los Tres For closer views of Mount Fitz Roy, take the path to Laguna de los Tres (four hours each way). Walk up to **Camping Capri** (just under two hours), with great views of Fitz Roy, then another hour to **Camping Poincenot**. Just beyond it is **Camping Río Blanco**, (only for climbers, previous registration at park office required). From Río Blanco you can walk another hour, though it's very steep, to Laguna de los Tres where you'll get a spectacular view, (not a good walk if it's cloudy). In bad weather, you're better off walking an hour to Piedras Blancas (four hours total from El Chaltén). You can connect the two paths (between Laguna Torre and Laguna de los Tres) by taking a transverse path (two hours) which links a point northwest of Laguna Capri and another one east of **Camping De Agostini** , passing two lakes, Laguna Madre and then Laguna Hija; but note that this alternative can take more than one day.

▲ **Loma del Pliegue Tumbado** A recommended day walk is to the Loma del Pliegue Tumbado viewpoint (four hours each way) where you can see both cordons and Lago Viedma. There's a marked path from the *guardería* with excellent panoramic views, best in clear weather. The trek to **Laguna Toro**, a glacial lake on the route across the ice cap (seven hours each way) is for more experienced trekkers.

▲ **Piedra del Fraile** The trek up Río Blanco to Piedra del Fraile (seven hours each way) is beautiful. It starts at Campamento Río Blanco running north along the Río Blanco and west along the Río Eléctrico via Piedra del Fraile (four hours) to Lago Eléctrico. Piedra del Fraile can be reached more easily from the road to Lago del Desierto in about two hours. At Piedra del Fraile, just outside the park, there are *cabañas* (**E** per person, hot showers) and a campsite, US$5 per person. From here a path leads south, up Cerro Eléctrico Oeste

The Fitz Roy area

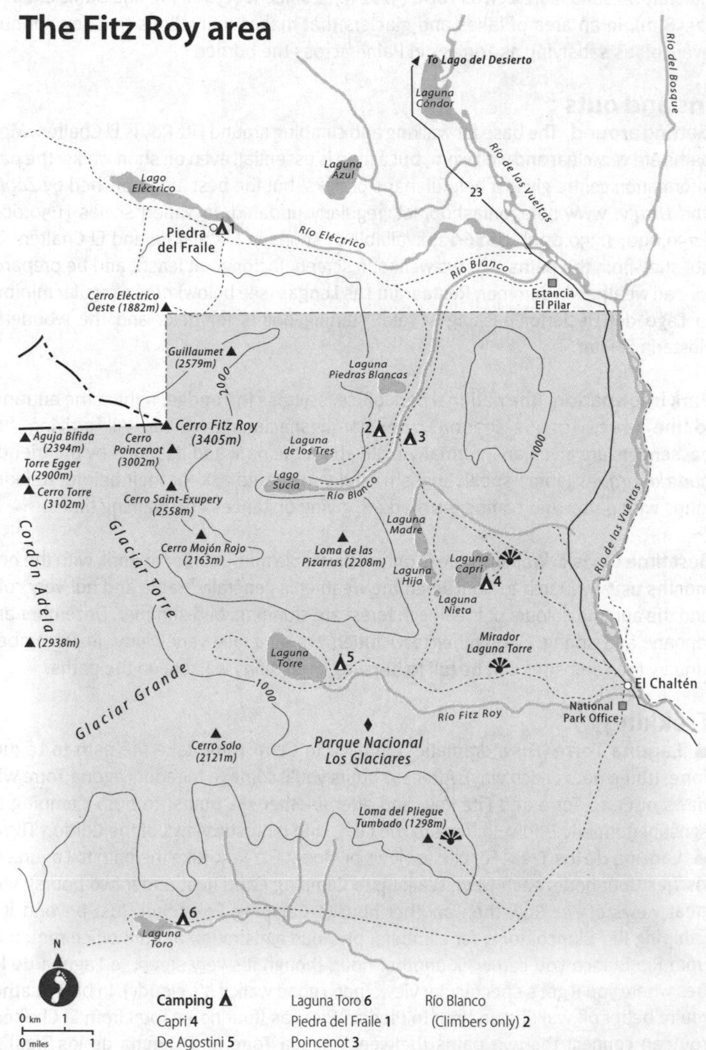

Trekking advice and information

- There are campsites at Poincenot, (Note Rio Blanco is only for climbers with prior permission arranged), Capri, De Agostini, Laguna Toro. Campsites have no services, but all have latrines, apart from Laguna Toro.
- Access is free. There's no need to register before you leave on walks, and the paths are well marked. But stick to the centre of the path so as not to make it any bigger and walk in single file (at times that you'll be walking in a rut).
- The park's Centro de informes will give you a good map which recommends lots of walks, times for walking and tells you where campsites are. Times given on their sheet, and our map, are for walking one way only.
- As you leave El Chaltén, don't let the dogs follow you, as they frighten the huemules (rare wild deer, an endangered species).
- All river water is drinkable. Don't bathe in rivers and lakes, and take water away from source to wash.
- Don't go to the toilet near water sources, and take all rubbish down the mountain with you.
- A gas/alcohol stove is essential for camping, as fires are prohibited everywhere in the National Park.
- Take plenty of warm clothes and a good sleeping bag. It is possible to rent equipment in El Chaltén; ask at park office or Rancho Grande.

(1882 m) towards the north face of Fitz Roy (two hours); it's tough going but with spectacular views. You should take a guide for this last bit. The best day walks are Laguna Capri, and Mirador Laguna Torre, both of which have great views.

Climbing

Base camp for Fitz Roy (3405 m) is Campamento Río Blanco. Other peaks include Cerro Torre (3102 m), Torre Egger (2900 m), Cerro Solo (2121 m), Poincenot (3002 m), Guillaumet (2579 m), Saint-Exupery (2558 m), Aguja Bífida (2394 m) and Cordón Adela (2938 m): most of these are for very experienced climbers. The best time to climb is generally mid-February to end-March; November to December is very windy; January is fair; winter is extremely cold, but weather is unpredictable and it all depends on the specific route being climbed. Permits for climbing are available at the national park information office. Guides are available in El Chaltén, see Activities and tours, page 529. **Fitz Roy Expediciones** are recommended.

El Chaltén » pp523-532.

→ *Phone code: 02962 colour map 6, B2*

The small modern town of El Chaltén is set in a wonderful position at the foot of Cerro Fitz Roy and at the mouth of the valley of the Río de las Vueltas. The village was founded very recently, in 1985, in order to settle the area and pre-empt Chilean territorial claims. However, it has grown very rapidly, along with its popularity as a centre for trekking and climbing in summer, and for cross country skiing in winter. It's an expensive and not particularly attractive place, especially when the harsh wind blows. But its visitors create a cheerful atmosphere, and from its concrete and tin you can walk directly into breathtaking landscapes. Tourist infrastructure is still developing, and so far there are no ATMs , so take sufficient cash. Accommodation is available in a range from camping and hostels to not-quite-luxurious *hosterías*, and one top hotel, all hideously overpriced. Food, too, is expensive, though there is increasingly plenty of choice.

Ins and outs

Getting there The quickest way to reach the town is by flying to El Calafate's airport, 220 km away, and from there it's a four-hour bus journey. There are frequent bus connections from El Calafate, and regular bus services in summer from Route 40 in the north, useful if you've come from the Lake District in either Argentina or Chile.

Tourist information ⓘ *Güemes 21, T02962-493011, www.elchalten.com, Mon-Fri 0900-2000, Sat/Sun 1300-2000*. Their website is excellent with accommodation listed, but no email for queries. They hand out trekking maps of the area, with paths and campsites marked, distances and walking times.

Sights

There is a small chapel, the **Capilla Tomás Egger**, named after an Austrian climber killed on Fitz Roy and built entirely from materials brought from Austria. The main attraction here is clearly the trekking around Fitz Roy or Torre cordons. But there is also stunning virgin landscape to explore around the **Lago del Desierto**, 37 km north of El Chaltén. The long skinny lake is fjord-like, surrounded by forests, and a short walk to a *mirador* at the end of the road gives fine views. It's reached by unpaved Route 23, which leads along the Río de las Vueltas via **Laguna Cóndor**, where flamingos can be seen. A path runs along the east side of the lake to its northern tip, from where a trail leads west along the valley of the Río Diablo to Laguna Diablo. There is also the possibility to walk to Chile (border control at the Gendarmería, only open November to April) in two hours. From the border, it's another 15 km to **Puesto Candelario Mancilla** on Lago O'Higgins, where boats cross to Bahía Bahamóndez (three hours), about 7 km from Villa O'Higgins, on the Chilean Carretera Austral. There is a campsite at the southern end of Lago del Desierto, and *refugios* at its northern end and at Laguna Diablo. The estancia **El Pilar** is the best place to stay on the way to the lake in a stunning position with views of Fitz Roy. Visit for tea, use it as an excellent base for trekking up Río Blanco or Río Eléctrico, with a multi-activity adventure circuit. Highly recommended. Contact **Fitz Roy Expediciones** (see page 531) for trekking circuits that connect Lago Viedma and Lago San Martín. Lago Viedma to the south of El Chaltén can also be explored by boat. The trips usually pass Glaciar Viedma, with the possibility of ice trekking too.

El Calafate to Chile » pp523-532.

→ *For public transport on this route see under Calafate*

If travelling from El Calafate to Torres del Paine, by car or bike, you'll cross this bleak area of steppe; about 40 km before reaching the border there are small lagoons and salt flats with flamingos. From El Calafate you can take the paved combination of Route 11, Route 40 and Route 5 to La Esperanza (165 km), where there's fuel, a campsite and a large but expensive *confitería* (accommodation D with bath). From La Esperanza, paved Route 7 heads west along the valley of the Río Coyle. A shorter but rougher route (closed in winter) missing Esperanza, goes via El Cerrito and joins Route 7 at Estancia Tapi Aike. Route 7 continues to the border crossing at Cancha Carrera (see below) and then meets the good *ripio* road between Torres del Paine and Puerto Natales (63 km). For bus services along this route see under Calafate.

Border with Chile The Paso Río Don Guillermo or Cancha Carrera, 129 km west of La Esperanza and 48 km north of Río Turbio, open all year, is the most convenient crossing for Parque Nacional Torres del Paine. In Chile, the road continues 7 km to Cerro Castillo, where it meets the road from Puerto Natales, 65 km south, to Parque Nacional Torres del Paine. **Argentine customs and immigration** ⓘ *Cancha Carrera, 2 km east of border*, fast and friendly. **Chilean customs and immigration** ⓘ *Cerro Castillo 0800-2200*.

Río Turbio
→ *Phone code: 02902 Colour map 6, B2 Population: 6600*

A charmless place you're most likely to visit en route to or from Torres del Paine in Chile. The site of Argentina's largest coalfield hasn't recovered from the depression which hit the industry in the 1990s. It has a cargo railway connecting it with Punta Loyola, and visitors can see Mina 1, where the first mine was opened. There's a small ski centre nearby, **Valdelén**, which has six pistes and is ideal for beginners, also scope for cross-country skiing between early June and late September. There is **tourist information** on Plazoleta Agustín del Castillo, www.rioturbio.gov.ar.

Border with Chile Paso Mina Uno/Dorotea is 5 km south of Río Turbio. Open all year, 0900-0100. On the Chilean side this runs south to join the main Puerto Natales-Punta Arenas road. **Paso Casas Viejas** is 33 km south of Río Turbio via 28 de Noviembre. Open all year, 0900-0100. Runs west on the Chilean side to join the Puerto Natales-Punta Arenas road. **Paso Río Don Guillermo** or Cancha Carrera is 48 km north of Río Turbio. This is the most convenient crossing for Parque Nacional Torres del Paine. Open all year 0900-2300. Argentine customs are fast and friendly. On the Chilean side the road continues 14 km to the Chilean border post at Cerro Castillo, where it joins the road from Puerto Natales to Torres del Paine. Chilean immigration open 0830-1200, 1400-2000.

Sleeping

El Calafate *p515, map p524*

LL Esplendor, Presidente Perón 1143, T02902-492488, T011-52175700 in Buenos Aires, www.esplendorcalafate.com. Overwhelmingly stylish, large and pricey this is a top hotel. Pack your trendy finery to keep up with the modern style of the interiors.

LL Kau-Yatún, Estancia 25 de Mayo (10 blocks from town centre, east of arroyo Calafate), T02902-491059, T011-44439295 in Buenos Aires, www.kauyatun.com. The easiest way to stay at an estancia from town, this is a very comfortable renovated main house of an old estancia, now on the outskirts of town, and surrounded by 4 ha of very well-kept gardens, where vegetables are grown for the meals served in its two excellent restaurants. The building is not very large and successfully combines a homely feel and rustic decor, typical of a traditional Patagonian estancia. Either half board or all-inclusive programmes with excursions in the Park included.

LL Patagonia Park Plaza Kempinski, C 998 No 50, T02902-491777, www.patagonia park.com. On an elevated position over-looking the town, this large chain hotel offering great comfort and business hotel amenities, including an elegant restaurant and style furniture in its spacious rooms.

L Kosten Aike, Gob Moyano 1243, T02902-492424, www.kostenaike.com.ar. A special place, relaxed and yet stylish with large elegant rooms, king sized beds throughout, jacuzzi and gym. The restaurant Ariskaiken is open to non residents and has an excellent chef; there's a cosy bar with a wood fire, and a garden. The staff are extremely attentive and speak English. Recommended.

AL El Quijote, Gobernador Gregores 1155, T02902-491017, www.quijotehotel.com.ar. This spacious, modern hotel is Italian-owned and designed, and it shows. An elegant entrance lounge, tasteful comfortable rooms with excellent bathrooms, all beautifully decorated with traditional touches, TV, phone and minibar. Great restaurant **Sancho**. Italian and English spoken. Recommended.

AL Los Alamos, Gobernador Moyano y Bustillo, T02902-491144, www.posada losalamos.com. Located in 2 separate chalet style buildings, this is an extremely comfortable hotel, with charming rooms, beautifully decorated and equipped, good service, lovely gardens and without doubt the best restaurant in town, La Posta. Recommended.

AL Patagonia Rebelde, José Haro 442, T02902-494495, www.patagonia rebelde.com. Charming new building in traditional Patagonian style, resembling an old inn with its corrugated zinc walls and rustic decor, all looking pretty basic though offering good comfort with well-heated bedrooms and comfy sitting-rooms.

A Cabañas Nevis, Av del Libertador 1696, T02902-493180, www.canasnevis.com.ar. Mr Patterson owns this complex of spacious,

A-shaped *cabañas* for 5 and 8, some with lake views, west of the centre. Great value.

A Hostería del Calafate Hostel, 25 de Mayo y Gobernador Moyano, T02902-491256, www.calafatehostels.com. Owned by the same people as the Calafate Hostel round the corner, this is a small, modern, very functional hostería with a plain rather chilly decor in rooms with TV, plus a PC with free internet and minibar in all rooms.

A Miyazato Inn, Egidio Feruglio 1305, T02902-491953, www.losglaciares.com/ miyazatoinn. A peaceful place with just 5 comfortable rooms in the town's green area, close to Nímez nature reserve. Japanese owned, attractive simplicity and functionality prevails here.

A Vientos del Sur, a little way up the hill at Río Santa Cruz 2317, T02902-493563, www.vientosdelsur.com. One of the most welcoming places in town, this tranquil retreat is worth the short taxi ride for the views over the lake, comfortable rooms with bath and TV in a large wooden cabin, and a great welcome. Recommended.

B Ariel, Av del Libertador 1693, T02902-493131, www.hotelariel.com.ar. A modern functional place west of centre, very clean and well-maintained rooms with bath and TV. Breakfast included.

B Cerro Cristal, Gobernador Gregores 989, T02902-491088, www.cerrocristal hotel.com.ar. A quiet, friendly and small central place, with simple rooms with breakfast. Overpriced in summer but very good value in low season.

B Michelangelo, Espora y Gobernador Moyano, T02902-491045, www.michel angelohotel.com.ar. A lovely, quiet and welcoming place, modern and stylish in design, with a really excellent restaurant. The menu is innovative, and includes hare, steak, and ink squid ravioli. All rooms have TV, bath and minibar, breakfast included. Excellent value. Recommended.

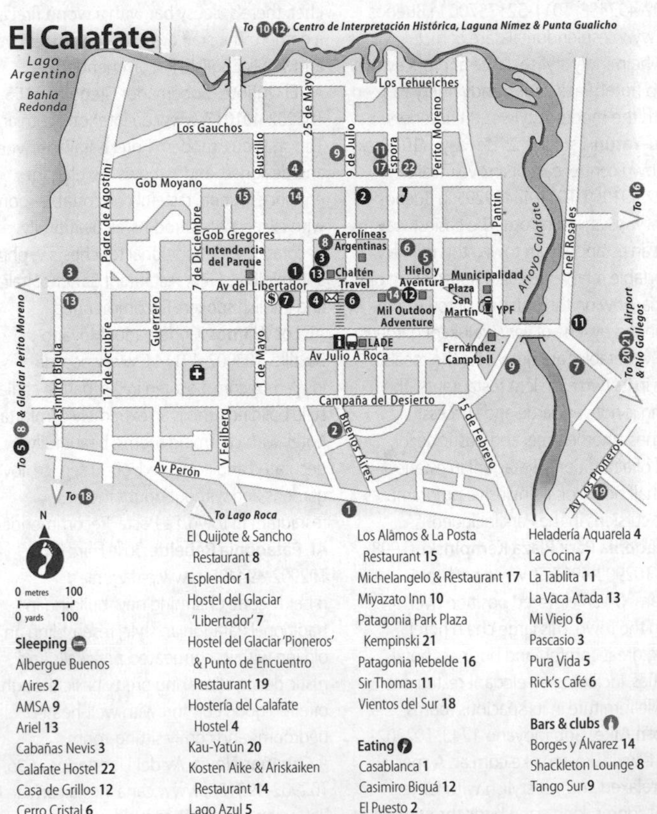

C Casa de Grillos, Pasaje Las Bandurrias, T02902-491160, www.casadegrillos.com.ar. Marta and Alejandro are the welcoming hosts at this B&B situated in the calm green area, next to Nímez nature reserve. It has all the comfort and charm of a family house.

C Sir Thomas, Comandante Espora 257, T02902-492220, www.sirthomas.com.ar. A relatively cheap option for El Calafate, this is a chalet-type house with comfortable, spacious wood-lined rooms, with private bathrooms.

F pp **Lago Azul**, Perito Moreno 83, T2902-491419. Cheapest in the area, this pioneer house with a couple of simple and spotless rooms to share is the most welcoming budget choice, with charming Mrs Echeverría and her husband offering traditional Patagonian hospitality. Recommended.

Camping

AMSA, Olavarría 65 (50 m off the main road, turning south at the fire station), T02902-492247, US$3.50 pp, hot water, security, open only in summer.

There are 2 campsites in the park en route to Lago Roca: **El Huala**, 42 km from El Calafate, free with basic facilities and open all year round; and **Lago Roca**, 50 km from El Calafate, T02902-499500. Beautifully set, with hot water, public phone, restaurant, bike hire, US$4 pp.

Estancias

LL Eolo, T011-47000075 in Buenos Aires, on RP11, 23 km west of El Calafate, www.eolo.com.ar. With a wild setting on the windswept slope of Cerro Frías, where no trees grow, this huge, modern, eclectically designed house, is the perfect place to admire the magnificent Patagonian horizons. A fabulously stylish and comfortable interior makes a dramatic contrast with the bleak scenery outside. Accommodation includes several outdoor activities and full-board is possible. Recommended.

LL Hostería Alta Vista, 33 km west of El Calafate (on the way to Lago Roca), T02902-491247, www.hosteriaaltavista.com.ar. Set within the land of Estancia Anita, the largest estancia in the area (a staggering 74,000 ha) Alta Vista is a famous estancia with all facilities you could possibly need, and only 15 guests. Favoured by celebrities and politicians, the lovely house was built in the 1930s and mostly retains its original style. Full-board is possible with excellent cuisine and wines included, and very good service. The surrounding gardens are filled with flowers and mature trees, and there are attractive walks and a great range of excursions in all within the vast expanse of the ranch. Often recommended.

LL Estancia Helsingfors, T/F02966-420719, www.helsingfors.com.ar or T011 43151222 in Buenos Aires. A fabulous, remote place in a splendid position on Lago Viedma, 150 km from El Calafate, with just 8 stylish rooms, a welcoming lounge, delicious food, and exclusive excursions directly to the glaciers and to Laguna Azul, by horse or trekking, plus boat trips. Transfers from and to El Calafate included in the rate. Recommended.

LL Los Notros, www.losnotros.com (in Buenos Aires: T011-4814 3934) An exclusive retreat by the lake with luxurious accommodation in spacious, well designed rooms with wonderful views of the Perito Moreno glacier, where you can walk, hike, trek, and ride horses. Expensive, but there are all inclusive packages with free transfers to the glacier *pasarelas* included.

B pp **Estancia Nibepo Aike**, in the far south of the park on the shores of Brazo Sur of Lago Argentino, T02966-436010 in Río Gallegos, www.nibepoaike.com.ar, or book through Lago San Martín agents, www.lagosanmartin.com. A spectacular setting near the shores of the lake, the house has just 11 simple rooms, decorated with lovely old furniture, and there's a cosy sitting room. Lots of activities are possible in the Park, plus the traditional barbecue. The premises are open for day visits too.

Youth hostels

E-F pp **Albergue Buenos Aires**, Buenos Aires 296, 200 m from terminal, T02902-491147, www.glaciarescalafate.com. This homely place with a kind owner has kitchen facilities, cycles for hire, simple and comfortable rooms to share and doubles with or without own bath. Breakfast extra.

E-F pp **Hostel del Glaciar 'Libertador'**, Av del Libertador 587 (next to the bridge on the access to town), T02902-491792, www.glaciar.com. This is the modern and 'exclusive' sister of the Del Glaciar hostels, open almost all year round (closed in June) with good, functional, well-heated rooms, A private doubles or rooms to share among 4, all with own bath, in a quiet relaxed atmosphere. Breakfast is only included in the high season rate for the private rooms; free transfer from bus station. Discounts to HI members. Owners run **Patagonia Backpackers**, a recommended travel agency (see below). Recommended.

F pp **Calafate Hostel**, Gobernador Moyano 1226, 400 m from bus terminal, T02902-492450, www.calafatehostels.com. This is a huge place, with well-built dorms for 4 with or without bath, **B-C** doubles or larger superior rooms with private bath and breakfast. Kitchen, internet and a huge lively sitting area. Friendly staff can arrange tours and accommodation in the sister hostal **Albergue Patagonia** in El Chaltén. Book a month ahead for Jan and Feb. They also run the helpful travel agency Chaltén Travel and a pricier *hostería* next door. Discounts to ISIC, ITIC, YMCA and HI card holders.

F pp **Hostel del Glaciar 'Pioneros'**, Los Pioneros 251, T/F02902-491243, www.glaciar.com. Larger, older, a bit further from the centre and cheaper than its sister hostel 'Libertador', this long-established, lively and often recommended hostel is open only in high season (Oct-Mar), and offers a great range of accommodation for all budgets: shared dorms for up to 4 people, **C** standard private doubles (also for 3 and 4) with bath, and **B** larger superior doubles with bath. Many languages are spoken by the friendly and helpful staff, there are lots of bathrooms, and also internet access and kitchen facilities. The cosy restaurant **Punto de Encuentro** has a good value fixed menu, and vegetarian options. They also run Patagonia Backpackers agency with the much loved **Alternative Glaciar Tour** (see below), and organize a booking service for **Navimag** and hotels and transport throughout Patagonia, and run free shuttle service from the bus terminal. Best book well in advance. Discounts to HI members. Beautifully run, and highly recommended.

El Chaltén *p521, map p527*

The tourist office has a full list, accessible from www.elchalten.com.

LL Los Cerros, T02962-493182, T011-48143934 in Buenos Aires, www.loscerrosdelchalten.com. On a hilltop position above the town, this large hotel is by far the most sophisticated choice in the area. Stylish, yet informal, all rooms are very comfortable with impressive attention to detail. Half-board and all-inclusive packages with excursions run by **Fitz Roy Expediciones**. There is a superb restaurant with a carefully chosen wine list.

L Estancia La Quinta, on RP 23, 2 km south of El Chaltén, T02962-493012, www.estancialaquinta.com.ar. A spacious pioneer house with renovated rooms surrounded by beautiful gardens, very comfortable and made more special by the personalized attention of its knowledgeable owners. A superb breakfast is included and the restaurant is also open for lunch and dinner. Open Oct-Apr. Transfer to and from El Chaltén bus terminals is included.

AL Hostería El Puma, Lionel Terray 212, T02962-493095, www.hosteriaelpuma.com.ar. The most desirable place in town, set a little apart, and with splendid views up the valley, a welcoming lounge with log fire and tasteful stylish furnishings, spacious comfortable rooms with lots of brick, and plush bathrooms. Transfers and a big American breakfast are included. There is also a good restaurant. They can also arrange tours through their excellent agency **Fitz Roy Expediciones**, www.fitzroyexpediciones.com.ar Recommended.

AL Hostería Posada Lunajuim, Trevisán s/n, T/F02962-493047, www.elchalten.com/lunajuim. A stylish yet relaxed and welcoming place, with comfortable rooms (thick duvets on the beds!) with bathrooms, a lovely big lounge with wood fire and art on the walls. Dinner is available to residents, and a full American breakfast is included. Friendly family, charming hosts. Recommended.

A-B pp **Estancia La Maipú**, T02966-422613, F011-49034967, Lago San Martín. The Leyenda family offer accommodation at their working sheep farm, with meals, horse riding, trekking and boat excursions on the lake.

A El Pilar, on RP 23, Km 17, T/F02962-493002, www.hosteriaelpilar.com.ar. A special place to stay a little way out of town on the road to Lago del Desierto. This simple country house, in a spectacular setting on the confluence of Ríos Blanco and de las Vueltas, with views of Fitz Roy, offers the chance to sample the simple life with access

El Chaltén

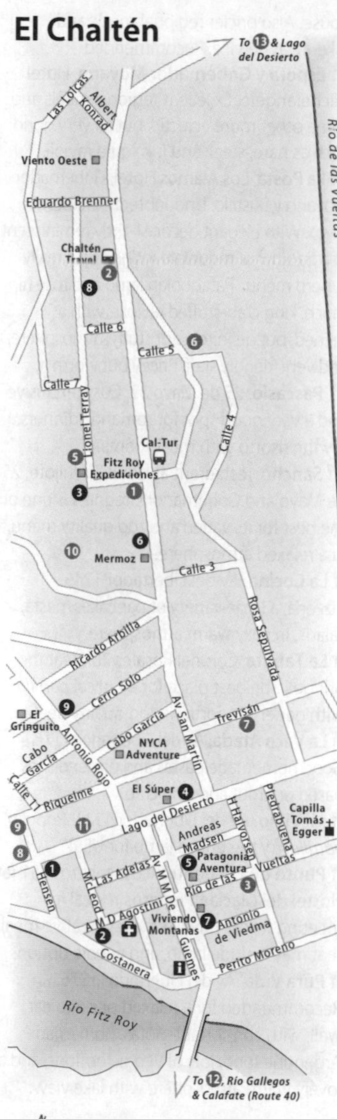

Sleeping
Albergue Patagonia 1
Albergue Rancho Grande 2
Camping del Lago 11
Cóndor de los Andes 3
El Pilar 13
El Refugio 6
Estancia La Quinta 12
Hospedaje La Base 8
Hostería El Puma & Restaurant Terray 5
Hostería Posada Lunajuim 7
Los Cerros & Restaurant 10
Nothofagus 9

Eating
Domo Blanco 2
Estepa 9
Fuegia 6
Josh Aike 1
Las Lengas 7
Pangea 4
Patagonicus 5
Ruca Mahuida 3
Zafarrancho 8

to the less visited northern part of the national park and beyond. Spacious rooms, great food, recommended. Owner Miguel Pagani is an experienced mountain guide, and takes individuals and groups on individually tailored trekking tours.

B-C Nothofagus, Hensen y Riquelme, T02962-493087, www.elchalten.com/nothofagus. One of the most appealing places to stay is this small cosy bed and breakfast, with simple double rooms with or without bath, including breakfast. Welcoming and good value.

C Hospedaje La Base, Lago del Desierto 97, T02962-493031. A friendly little place, has basic double rooms with bath rooms. For 3 or 4 (**E**). Tiny kitchen for guests, self service breakfast included, and a great video lounge.

Estancias

AL Estancia Lago del Desierto, at Punta Sur (southern tip of Lago del Desierto), T02962-493010 (contact Hotel Lago del Desierto in El Chaltén). Basic place, with hot showers for campers (US$4 pp) or for those staying in *cabañas* for 5 people.

Youth hostels

F pp **Albergue Patagonia**, San Martín 493, T/F02962-493019, www.elchalten.com/patagonia. The most appealing of several hostels here is HI-affiliated, and a small cosy friendly place with rooms to share (4 to 6), with kitchen, video room, bike hire, laundry. Helpful information on Chaltén and also excursions to Lago del Desierto. Next door is their restaurant *Fuegia*, with Patagonian dishes, curries and vegetarian food too.

F pp **Albergue Rancho Grande**, San Martín s/n, T02962-493005, chaltenrancho@yahoo.com.ar. HI-affiliated, in a great position at the end of town with good open views, and a welcoming attractive restaurant and lounge. This accommodates huge numbers of trekkers in rooms for 4, with shared bathrooms, and is well run, with friendly staff who speak several languages between them. Breakfast and sheets extra. Also **C** private double rooms, breakfast extra, and one family room, with private bath. Recommended. Reservations can also be made in the sister businesses in El Calafate: Calafate Hostel and Chaltén Travel.

F pp **Cóndor de los Andes**, Av Río de las Vueltas y Halvorsen, T02962-493101, www.condordelosandes.com. Friendly, small and modern, with nice little rooms for 4 to 6 and private doubles, all with bathrooms en suite, sheets included, breakfast extra. Washing service, library, kitchen. Quiet atmosphere, calm place. Discounts to HI members. Recommended.

Camping

Camping del Lago, Lago del Desierto 135, T02962-493010. Centrally located with hot showers. **El Refugio**, off San Martín just before Rancho Grande. Hot showers. Also a basic refugio. A gas/alcohol stove is essential for camping as fires are prohibited in any campsites of the National Park. Take plenty of warm clothes and a good sleeping bag. It is possible to rent equipment in El Chaltén; ask at park office or Rancho Grande.

Campsites in the national park: **De Agostini, Poincenot,** (Note Rio Blanco is only for climbers with prior permission arranged), **Capri, Laguna Toro**: none have services, fires are not allowed, all river water is drinkable. Pack out all rubbish, do not wash, or bury waste within 70 m of rivers. **Camping Piedra del Fraile**, on Río Eléctrico beyond park boundary, privately owned.

Río Turbio *p523*

Hotels here are almost always full.
C De La Frontera, 4 km from Río Turbio, Paraje Mina 1, T02902-421979. The most recommended option.
D Hostería Capipe, Dufour, 9 km from town, T02902-482930, www.hosteriacapipe.com.ar. Simple rooms with bath, friendly. Restaurant.

Eating

El Calafate *p515, map p524*

For cheap meals, there are 2 lively, packed places on the main street, Av del Libertador, with good atmosphere and cheapish food: **Rick's Café**, No 1091, serving *parrilla tenedor libre* for US$ 10, and **Casablanca**, Av del Libertador and 25 de Mayo. A welcoming place, serving omelettes, hamburgers and vegetarian food, US$8 for steak and chips.
TTT Casimiro Biguá, Av del Libertador 963, T02902-492590. A popular upmarket place with quality food, including the excellent stew *cazuela de cordero*.
TTT El Puesto, Gobernador Moyano y 9 de Julio. Tasty thin-crust pizzas in a cosy old house. Also pricier regional meals and take-away service. Recommended
TTT Espora y Gobernador Moyano, Hotel Michelangelo. Excellent regional meals and some other more eclectic, but all very good such as hare, steak and ink squid ravioli.
TTT La Posta, Los Alamos Hotel, Gobernador Moyano y Bustillo. Undoubtedly the best in town. With elegant décor, slightly reminiscent of a traditional mountain lodge and a really superb menu. Patagonian lamb and rose hip sauce, king crab-stuffed raviolis, with a refined, but definitely not stuffy, atmosphere, and very friendly staff. Pricey but worth it.
TTT Pascasio, 25 de Mayo 52. Cosy, exclusive and a very good spot for romantic dinners. Try the risotto with mushrooms.
TTT Sancho, restaurant at Hotel El Quijote, 25 de Mayo and Gobernador Gregores is one of the best for its varied and top quality menu, in a relaxed atmosphere.
TT La Cocina, Av del Libertador 1245. Pizzería, a large variety of pancakes, pasta, salads, in cosy warm atmosphere.
TT La Tablita, Coronel Rosales 28 (near the bridge). The best place for a typical *parrilla* with generous portions and quality beef.
TT La Vaca Atada, Av del Libertador 1176. Good homemade pastas and pricier dishes based on trout and king crab.
TT Mi Viejo, Av del Libertador 1111. Popular *parrilla*, try the grilled lamb for US$7.
TT Punto de Encuentro, Los Pioneros 251 (at Hostel del Glaciar 'Pioneros'). Ideal for meeting fellow travellers, over creative meals that may include lamb, and veggie options.
TT Pura Vida, Av del Libertador 1876. Recommended for a relaxed place to eat well, with comfortable sofas, homemade Argentine food, lots of veggie options, and a lovely warm atmosphere with lake view.

Ice cream parlours

Heladería Aquarela, Av del Libertador 1177. You'll be glad to hear that it does get hot enough for ice cream, and the best is served up here – try the delicious (and beautifully coloured) *calafate*.

El Chaltén *p521, map p527*

TTT Los Cerros, Hotel Los Cerros. Top cuisine in a sophisticated atmosphere, where regional meals such as *puchero patagónico* and *carbonada de liebre* sit well among other more international standards. The wine list includes produce from the best *bodegas*.

Bahía Túnel, 16 km south of town, access from RP 23. Its setting right on the shores of Lago Viedma is a spectacular and peaceful. Delicious trout, lamb and rich stews. Homemade cakes and pastries at teatime.

Estepa, Cerro Solo y Antonio Rojo. Small, intimate place with a varied menu that includes excellent lamb, selected wines and imaginative vegetarian options.

Fuegia, San Martín. The usual international menu in a warm atmosphere, plus some Patagonian dishes and more imaginative options, such as curries and veggie food.

Pangea, Lago del Desierto y San Martín. Open for lunch and dinner, drinks and coffee, in calm comfortable surroundings with good music, a varied menu, from pastas to steak, trout and pizzas. Recommended.

Patagonicus, Güemes y Madsen. A lovely warm cosy stylish place with salads, home made pastas and the best pizzas. Great family photos of mountain climbers on the walls. Open from 1200-2400. Recommended.

Ruca Mahuida, Lionel Terray s/n. Widely regarded as the best restaurant in El Chaltén, for imaginative and carefully prepared food based on Swiss-Argentine recipes.

Terray, Lionel Terray 212, **Hostería El Puma**. Climbers, trekkers and other visitors chat about their expeditions, over excellent food in a homely atmosphere.

Zafarrancho, behind Rancho Grande. A great lively bar-restaurant, serving a good range of reasonably priced dishes.

Domo Blanco, Costanera Sur 90. Makes superb homemade ice cream.

Josh Aike, Lago del Desierto 105. Excellent *confitería*, delicious homemade food, in a beautiful building. Recommended.

Las Lengas, Viedma y Güemes. Opposite the tourist office, this place is a little cheaper than most. Big meals, basic pastas and meat dishes. US$4 for the meal of the day.

Bars and clubs

El Calafate *p515, map p524*

Borges y Álvarez, Av del Libertador 1015, 1st floor, Galería de los Gnomos. Lively café and bookshop open late. Good for hanging out.

Shackleton Lounge, Av del Libertador 3287, on the outskirts of town (US$1.70 in taxi). A great place to relax, lovely views of the lake, old photos of Shackleton, great atmosphere, good music. Highly recommended for a late drink or some good regional dishes.

Tango Sur, 9 de Julio 265, T02902-491550. Live music and, amazingly, a long way from Buenos Aires, a tango show. US$5, Tue-Sun from 2000 (Oct-Apr), in charming old-style house that became the informal refuge of Alejandro, a nostalgic Porteño.

Shopping

El Calafate *p515, map p524*

All along Libertador there are souvenir shops selling hats, fleeces and gloves, so that you can prepare yourself for those chilly boat rides to see the glacier. There are lots of fine quality handicrafts, from all over Argentina and look out for Mapuche weavings and woollen items. Also little handicraft stalls on Libertador at around 1200.

Ferretería Chuar, a block away from bus terminal. The only place selling white gas for camping and camping supplies.

La Anónima, Av del Libertador and Perito Moreno. Supermarket.

El Chaltén *p521, map p527*

Camping Center, San Martín, T02962-493264. Buy or rent equipment for climbing, trekking and camping.

El Gringuito, Av San Martín. The best supermarket , though there are many others around. All are expensive and have little fresh food. Fuel is available.

El Súper, Lago del Desierto y Av Güemes, T02902-493039. Supermarket that also rents and sells camping and climbing equipment, maps, postcards, books and handicrafts.

Viento Oeste, Av San Martín s/n, (northern end of town) T02962-493021. Equipment hire; renting tents, sleeping bags, and everything else you'll need, and can arrange mountain guides. Also sell handicrafts.

Activities and tours

El Calafate *p515, map p524*

Ballooning

Hotel Kau Yatun, (details above). Organizes balloon trips over El Calafate and Lago Argentino, weather permitting, US$150 per hr for a group of up to 7 people.

Boat trips to Moreno and Upsala glaciers are organized by **Fernández Campbell** and **Hielo y Aventura**, see Tour operators below. Alternatively, there's a marvellous 2-day full-board programme for 14 passengers on the *Crucero Leal* ship, which includes a comfortable night on board, and the chance to enjoy the view of Moreno, Upsala and Spegazzini glaciers at leisure. See www.crucerosmarpatag.com or call T011-50310756.

Fishing

Calafate Fishing , 9 de Julio 29, T02902-493311, www.calafatefishing.com. Offers regular half-day and day fishing excursions, plus longer expeditions, all for fly-casting.

Glacier trips

From Calafate there are regular buses by **Cal-Tur** and **Taqsa** to the car park above the walkways. Many agencies in El Calafate also run minibus tours in high season (park entry not included). **Hostels del Glaciar's** alternative trips, highly entertaining and informative, go out by different route passing the **Estancia Anita** and are highly recommended, full day US$30. Minitrekking (US$85) and Big Ice (US$115) are offered by **Hielo y Aventura**, wonderful walking trips on the glacier (crampons provided; bring lunch). Taxis, cost US$80 for 4 passengers round trip. Near the Perito Moreno pier (1km away from walkways area) there is a basic restaurant and café. Out of season, trips to the glacier are more difficult to arrange, but there are still regular bus services or you can gather a party and hire a taxi (*remise* taxis T02902-491745).

Horse riding

Cabalgata en Patagonia, Av del Libertador 3600, T02902-493203, www.cabalgatenpatagonia.com. For 2-hr rides (US$20 pp) along Bahía Redonda or the 6-hr excursions (US$40 pp, lunch included) to Punta Bonita to see the Gualicho cave paintings by the lake.

Ice trekking

Walking excursions on the Perito Moreno glacier (known as minitrekking and Big Ice), enormous fun (and not too physically challenging) for a close-up experience of the glacier, are run by **Hielo y Aventura**, see tour operators below.

Mountain bikes

On Rent a Car, Av del Libertador 1831, T02902-493788, onrentacar@otecal.com.ar. US$20 per day.

Tour operators and trekking guides

Note that entry fee to the national park (US$10 pp), transfer to piers and food may not be included in tour prices. Most agencies charge the same rates for excursions: to the **Perito Moreno Glacier** US$27; **Minitrekking** (on the glacier itself with crampons included, recommended) US$85. To **Lago Roca**, a full-day including lunch at *Estancia Anita*, US$35; Horseriding to Gualicho caves, 6 hrs, US$ 40.

Chaltén Travel, Av del Libertador 1174, T2902-492212, www.chaltentravel.com. The most helpful, with huge range of tours: glaciers, estancias, trekking, and transfers and excursions to El Chaltén, and a guided visit to Torres del Paine National Park in one long day for US$67; also sells tickets along the Ruta 40 to Los Antiguos and Bariloche, offers advice, English spoken. Highly recommended.

Fernández Campbell, Av del Libertador 867, T02902-491298, www.solopatagonia.com.ar. This company runs most boat excursions on Lago Argentino, from 1-hr trips to the north side of Perito Moreno glacier US$8.50, to the much longer circuits for viewing Upsala, Onelli and Spegazzini glaciers, US$60. They also run the full-day excursion to Estancia Cristina, US$150 (see also www.estanciacristina.com). The *Spirit of the Glaciers* trip is a pricey though an unmissable experience for those who can afford it (about US$350 pp).

Hielo y Aventura, Av del Libertador 935, T02902-492205, www.hieloyaventura.com. Run a handful of fantastic excursions: *Safari Náutico* 1-hr boat trip for viewing Moreno glacier from the south side, leaving regularly from Bajo de las Sombras pier, US$8.50 (tickets also sold at the pier; transfer not included); *Brazo Sur* boat trip, the same as Safari plus a landing to give you the chance to see more glaciers, US$30 (transfer included); the famous minitrekking, with 90 minutes walking on the glacier with crampons (supplied and fitted by them), after a walk through lovely lakeside *lenga* forests, US$85 (transfer included), and Big Ice, a much longer walk on ice in the same area of the minitrekking, for young adults only, US$115 (transfer included). Recommended.

Leutz Turismo, Av del Libertador 1341, T02902-492316, www.leutzturismo.com.ar. Daily excursion to Lago Roca 1000-1800, US$ 35 pp, plus US$ 17 for optional lunch at Estancia Nibepo Aike, and an interesting tour of the sheep and fruit. Estancia Quien Sabe with a traditional *cordero asado* for dinner.

Mar Patag, www.crucerosmarpatag.com or call T011-50310756 in Buenos Aires. They run the 'Spirit of the Glaciers' luxurious boat trip, a recommendable 2-day exclusive experience for viewing Moreno, Upsala and Spegazzini glaciers (US$350 pp, full board).

Mil Outdoor Adventure, Av del Libertador 1029, T02902-491437, www.miloutdoor.com. Exciting excursions in 4WD to see wild places with wonderful views, 3-6 hrs, US$42-70.

Mundo Austral, Av del Libertador 1114, T02902-492365. All kinds of tours to the park and cheaper trips to the glaciers with helpful bilingual guides. Also books bus travel.

Lago San Martín, Av del Libertador 1215 p 1, T02902-492858, www.lagosanmartin.com. Specializes in reservations to *estancias* in Santa Cruz province, very helpful.

Patagonia Backpackers, at Hostels del Glaciar: Los Pioneros 251 or Av del Libertador 587, T/F2902-491243, www.glaciar.com. This tour operator offers the best glacier trip, the 'Alternative Tour to Moreno Glacier'. Entertaining and informative, it includes lots of information on the landscape and wildlife as you travel along the old road to the glacier, then some light walking to approach the glacier along the lake shore, followed by the boat trip, to see it up close. US$30. Recommended constantly. They also do a great 2-day trip to El Chaltén, 'Supertrekking en Chaltén', a 2-day hiking trip, featuring the best treks in the Fitz Roy massif, including camping and ice trekking; and a 2-day visit to Torres del Paine National Park, including camping and trekking (US$180). They also sell tickets for the Navimag ferries in the Chilean fjords. Highly recommended.

El Chaltén *p521, map p527*

Tour operators and trekking guides

Fitz Roy Expediciones, Lionel Terray 212, (next to Hostería El Puma) T/F02962-493017, www.fitzroyexpediciones.com.ar. This company is by far the best and most experienced in the area, very professional, with excellent guides. Owned by mountaineer and guide Alberto del Castillo. They organize trekking, rock climbing courses and ice-climbing courses, adventure expeditions, including 2-day ascents of Cerro Solo (2121 m), 3-day trekking crossing from Lago Viedma to Lago San Martín, and 8-day trekking expeditions on the Campo de Hielo. Also organizes a circuit of the challenging terrain around Estancia El Pilar, at its Fitz Roy adventure camp, ideal for everyone from kids to adults, including kayaking, mountain biking, rappelling, rope bridges, climbing. Great fun, safe, and well organized.

Las Lengas, Viedma y Güemes. Daily bus transfer to Lago del Desierto in summer.

NYCA Adventure, Cabo García 122, T02962-493045, www.nyca.com.ar. Ascents, trekking, ice field expeditions and water sports.

Mermoz, San Martín 493, T02962-493098. Boat trips across Laguna del Desierto, including bus transfer, and optional trekking. English spoken, and helpful.

Patagonia Aventura, Av Güemes s/n, T02962-493110, www.elchalten.com/viedmadiscovery. Boat trips along Lago Viedma to see the Glaciar Viedma, including informative chat; transfers US$10 extra. Also a good full day's trip along Lago Viedma, with ice trekking on Glaciar Viedma. They also operate Lago del Desierto crossings, US$15 pp.

Rodolfo Guerra, T02962-493020. For trekking on horseback, also hires animals to carry equipment, but can be badly organized. Also Try **El Relincho**, T02962-493007.

Viviendo Montañas, Av Güemes 68 , T/F02962- 493068, www.vivmont.com.ar. A young company, organizing climbing schools, and ice climbing expeditions (take sleeping bag and equipment), guides for trekking too.

Transport

El Calafate *p515, map p524*

Air Lago Argentino, the international airport, is 22 km east of town, T02902-491220. **Transpatagonia Expeditions** runs a minibus service from town to meet all flights, T02902-493766, US$6. Taxi T02902-491655, 492005, US$9. **Aerolíneas Argentinas**, 9 de Julio 57, T02902-492814, flies daily to/from **Buenos Aires**, with many more flights in summer, when it also flies from Bariloche (check, as this varies from year to year). Also flights to Ushuaia all year round. LADE, Julio Roca 1004, at the bus station, T02902-491262, ladecalafate@cotecal.com.ar) flies to **Río Gallegos**, **Comodoro Rivadavia**, **Esquel** and **Bariloche**. To **Puerto Natales**, Aerovias Dap, www.aeroviasdap.cl, daily, summer only (Nov-Mar). Airport charge for departing passengers US$6.

Bus Take your passport with you when booking bus ticket to Chile. The bus terminal is on Julio A Roca 1004, 1 block up steep stairs from Av del Libertador. To **Perito Moreno glacier**, daily with Cal-Tur, T02902-491842, 1½ hrs, US$10. Taqsa, T02902-491843, goes only in summer. To **El Chaltén**, daily with Cal-Tur, Chaltén Travel, T02902-491833, and Taqsa, 4-4½ hrs, US$15-17. To **Río Gallegos**, daily with Interlagos, T02902-491179, Sportman, T02902-492680, and Taqsa, 4 hrs, US$7-10. To **Ushuaia**, take a bus to Río Gallegos; Taqsa operates a 0300 service for the best connection (check first).

To **Perito Moreno**, **Los Antiguos** or **Bariloche**, take a bus to **Río Gallegos** for connections or Chaltén Travel, www.chaltentravel.com, only Nov-Mar on odd days, runs a 2-day bus service along RN 40 to the small town of **Perito Moreno** or **Los Antiguos**, US$72, and then leaving the morning after to continue the journey north from **Perito Moreno** to **Bariloche**, US$60 (US$127 for the full journey). Note that these rates only include transport; food and accommodation at the town of **Perito Moreno** are extra. Safari Route 40 is a 4-day excursion along RN 40 to **Bariloche** (see Bariloche Transport) run by Overland Patagonia, www.overlandpatagonia.com, visiting remote Parque Nacional Perito Moreno and Cueva de las Manos, with overnights at estancias or small hotels; can be booked at Patagonia Backpackers (Hostels del Glaciar), T02902-491243, www.glaciar.com.

To Chile To **Puerto Natales**, daily in summer, US$17, with Cootra, T02902- 491444 (via Río Turbio), or via Cerro Castillo, only in summer, (where you can pick up a bus to **Torres del Paine**), either with Turismo Zaajh, T2902-491631 or Bus Sur T02902-491842. (Advance booking recommended, tedious border crossing.) (NB Argentine pesos cannot be exchanged in Torres del Paine.)

Car hire Adventure Rent a Car, Av del Libertador 290, T02902-492595, adventurerentacar@cotecal.com.ar. On Rent a Car, Av del Libertador 1831, T02902-493788, onrentacar@cotecal.com.ar. Average US$50 per day for a small car including insurance.

El Chaltén *p521, map p527*

Bus In summer, buses fill quickly: book ahead. Fewer services off season. Daily buses to **El Calafate**, 4-4½ hrs, US$15-17 one way: run by Chaltén Travel, San Martín 635 (at Albergue Rancho Grande), T02902-493005, www.chaltentravel.com, Cal-Tur, San Martín 520 (at Fitz Roy Inn), T02902-493062, and Taqsa, Av Güemes 68, T02902-493068. To **Los Antiguos** along the Ruta 40, Itinerarios y Travesías, T002902-493088 overnight, even dates (ie 2nd, 4th, 6th), includes trip to Cueva de las Manos in the early morning. Chaltén Travel runs a service Nov-Mar, leaving on odd days to go along RN 40 up to Bariloche, with a stopover at the small town of Perito Moreno, US$113 transport only.

Río Turbio *p523*

Bus To **Puerto Natales**, 1hr, US$ 3, several daily with: Cootra, Tte.del Castillo 01, T02902-421448 cootra@oyikil.com.ar. Bus Sur, Baquedano 534, Pto. Natales, T+56(0)61-411859, www.turismozaahj.co.cl. Lagoper, Av de Los Mineros 262, T02902-411831, El Pingüino. To El Calafate, Cootra, Taqsa, daily, US$13, 4½ hrs. To **Río Gallegos**, Taqsa, www.taqsa.com.ar, daily, 4 hrs, US$10.

Directory

El Calafate *p515, map p524*

Banks Best to take cash as high commission is charged on exchange. ATMs at Banco de la Provincia de Santa Cruz, Av del Libertador 1285, and at Banco de Tierra del Fuego, 25 de Mayo 34. Change money at Thaler, 9 de Julio 57, www.cambio-thaler.com. Credit cards are not widely accepted in Argentina, apart from at the more expensive hotels. **Post office** Av del Libertador 1133. **Telephone** Open Calafate, Av del Libertador 996, is a huge *locutorio* for phones, and also 20 fast internet computers, central but rather expensive. More convenient, cheaper and more comfortable, is Centro Integral de Comunicaciones, Av del Libertador 1486.

Chilean Patagonia

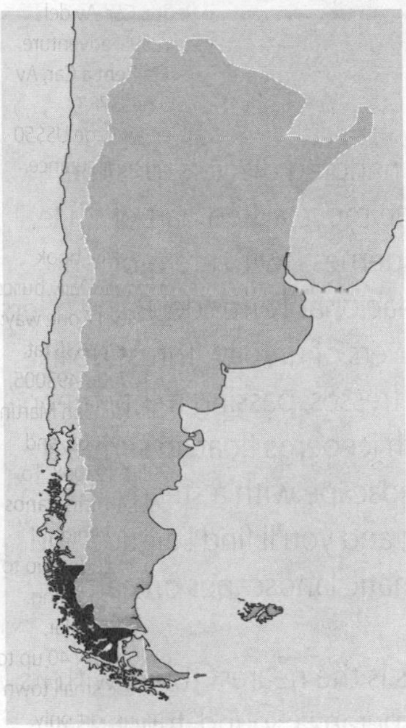

Footprint features

Introduction

This remote land of silent fjords, hanging glaciers, pristine lakes and jagged mountains is the most visited part of Chile. Yet much of it remains a vast wilderness, with areas of staggering beauty. The Parque Nacional Torres del Paine offers both: trek around the mighty towers of granite, thrust up like fingers from a mass of basalt buttresses, passing minty green and icy blue glacial lakes in which icebergs float. In summer, you'll share the awe inspiring landscape with a steady stream of walkers, but start out at dawn, and you'll find solitude and silence in some of the most dramatic landscapes on earth.

The quaint port of Puerto Natales is the nearest town, with its tranquil views over the Ultima Esperanza Sound, fringed by lofty far-off peaks. Take a boat from here into Parque Nacional Bernardo O'Higgins where glaciers descend steeply into the water, and you can even trek on the ice.

Punta Arenas is Chile's southernmost city, a complete contrast to the endless wind-swept sheep farms all around. Here you'll find superb fish restaurants and classy hotels in grand 1900's stone buildings, relics from the city's heyday of sheep farming millionaires. Sail from here through the Magellan Strait to the Argentine city of Ushuaia, or head for adventure nearby in the Parque Nacional Pali Aike, to get a sense of how precarious civilisation is in this wildest part of Patagonia.

★ Don't miss...

1 **Monumento Natural los Pingüinos** Drake landed here to get dinner, but you'll want to admire the colony of 150,000 penguins on Isla Magdalena in Otway Sound, page 539.

2 **Cerro Mirador, Punta Arenas** One of the few places in the world where you can ski with a sea view, page 541.

3 **Cruceros Australis** Cruise past glaciers in comfort on this epic trip from Punta Arenas through the Magellan strait to Ushuaia, page 542.

4 **Río Serrano** Zoom up the river and enter Torres del Paine from a different angle, page 545.

5 **Parque Nacional Torres del Paine** Complete the *circuito*, and camp by limpid white lakes, page 550.

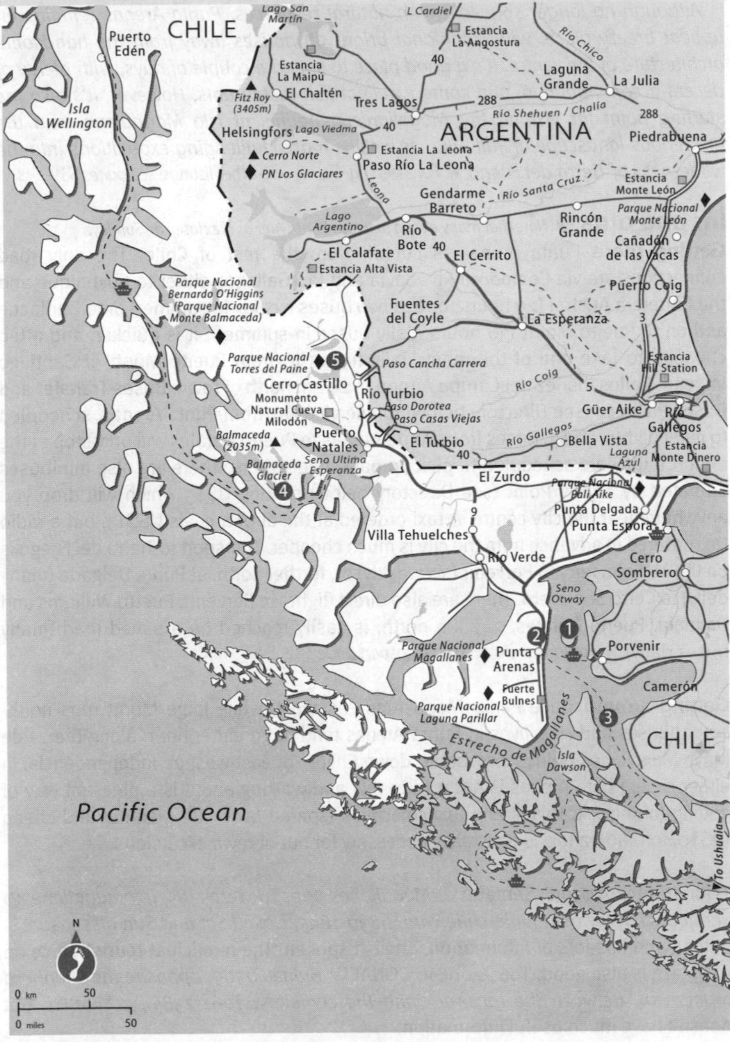

Punta Arenas and around

→ *Phone code: 061. Colour map 7, B1. Population: 116,000.*

After hours of travelling through barren steppe of Patagonia, Punta Arenas comes as a surprise. With a grand plaza surrounded by neoclassical mansions and several fine monuments, Chile's most southerly city has an affluent history. Its strategic position on the eastern shore of the Brunswick Peninsula made it a thriving port of call when trading ships sailed through the Magellan Straits. Landowners Braun and Menéndez made their fortunes from sheep, building a sumptuous palace, filled with treasures: one of the city's two fascinating museums. The other recounts the more sombre history of the ousted indigenous peoples, and their own rich culture. While the cemetery, an oddly beautiful place, also deserves a visit.

Although no longer so wealthy on natural resources, Punta Arenas remains an upbeat breezy place, with traditional bright tin houses away from the handsome architecture of the centre. It's a good place to spend a couple of days, with plenty of decent accommodation, and some excellent fish restaurants. However, it's also the starting point for visiting the Magellanic penguins at Isla Magdalena, and the mysterious landscape of Pali Aike, as well as more challenging expeditions into the wilderness of Tierra del Fuego. » *For Sleeping, Eating and other listings, see pages 539-543.*

❢ *Lots of phone numbers in Punta Arenas are being changed at the end of 2006.*

Ins and outs → *Note that many eating places in Punta Arenas are closed on Sunday.*

Getting there Punta Arenas is cut off from the rest of Chile. The only road connections are via Comodoro Rivadavia and Río Gallegos either to Coyhaique and the Carretera Austral (20 hours; one or two buses weekly in summer) or to Bariloche and on to Puerto Montt (36 hours, daily buses in summer); it is quicker, and often cheaper, to take one of the many daily flights to/from Puerto Montt or Santiago instead. Carlos Ibáñez del Campo Airport is 20 km north of town. **Buses Transfer** and **Buses Pacheco** (see Directory below) run services to/from Punta Arenas, scheduled to meet flights, US$3. Buses from Punta Arenas to Puerto Natales will only stop at the airport if they are scheduled to pick up passengers there. There are also minibuses operated by **Sandy Point** (see Directory below) costing US$5 which will drop you anywhere near the city centre. A taxi ordered at the airport costs US$13, but a radio taxi ordered in advance from the city is much cheaper. Transport to Tierra del Fuego is on the Melinka ferry to Porvenir (six weekly) or, further north, at Punta Delgada (many daily) to Cerro Sombrero. There are also direct flights to Porvenir, Puerto Williams and Ushuaia. Puerto Natales, 247 km north, is easily reached on a paved road (many buses daily). » *For further details, see Transport page 542.*

Getting around Calle Pedro Montt runs east-west, while Jorge Montt runs north-south. Buses and *colectivos* in Punta Arenas tend to go either north along the 21 de Mayo-Magallanes-Bulnes axis, south down Chiloe, or east-west up Independencia. In either case, Punta Arenas is not a huge city and walking about is a pleasant way of getting to know it. Buses and taxi-colectivos (shared taxis) are plentiful and cheap (US$0.40-0.60): a taxi is only really necessary for out-of-town excursions.

Tourist information **Sernatur** ⓘ *Magallanes 960, T061-225385, infomagallanes@sernatur.cl, www.patagonia-chile.com, 0830-1845, closed Sat and Sun off season*, is helpful and has lots of information, English spoken. The **municipal tourist office** on the plaza is also good, T061-200610 **CONAF** ⓘ *Bulnes 0309, opposite the shepherd monument, between the racetrack and the cemetery, T061-238544, Mon-Fri*, but doesn't have much useful information.

Background

After its foundation in 1848, Punta Arenas became a penal colony modelled on Australia. In 1867, it was opened to foreign settlers and given free port status. From the 1880s, it prospered as a refuelling and provisioning centre for steam ships and whaling vessels. It also became a centre for the new sheep *estancias* since it afforded the best harbour facilities. The city's importance was reduced overnight by the opening of the Panama Canal in 1914. Most of those who came to work in the *estancias* were from Chiloé, and many people in the city have relatives in Chiloé and feel an affinity with the island (the *barrios* on either side of the upper reaches of Independencia are known as Chilote areas); the Chilotes who returned north took Patagonian customs with them, hence the number of *mate* drinkers on Chiloé.

Sights

Around the attractive **Plaza Muñoz Gamero** are a number of mansions that once belonged to the great sheep-ranching families of the late 19th century. A good example is the **Palacio Sara Braun** ⓘ *Tue-Sun, US$2*, built between 1894 and 1905 with materials from Europe; the Palacio has several elegantly decorated rooms open to the public and also houses the **Hotel José Nogueira**. In the centre of the plaza is a statue of Magellan with a mermaid and two Fuegian Indians at his feet. According to local wisdom, those who rub or kiss the big toe of one of the Indians will return to Punta Arenas.

Just north of the plaza is the **Museo de Historia Regional Braun Menéndez** ⓘ *Magallanes 949, T061-244216, www.dibam.cl/subdirec_museos/mr_magallanes, Mon-Sat 1030-1700, Sun 1030-1400 (summer); Mon-Sun 1030-1300 (winter), US$2, children half-price*, the opulent former mansion of Mauricio Braun, built in 1905. A visit is recommended. Part of the museum is set out as a room-by-room regional history; the rest of the house has been left with its original furniture. Guided tours are in Spanish only, but a somewhat confusing information sheet in English is also available. In the basement there is a café. One block further north is the **Teatro Cervantes**, now a cinema with an ornate interior.

Three blocks east of the plaza, the **Museo Naval y Maritimo** ⓘ *Pedro Montt 981, T061-205479, terzona@armarda.cl, Tue-Sun 0930-1230, 1400-1700, US$1.50*, houses an exhibition of local and national maritime history; sections on naval instruments, cartography, meteorology , as well as shipwrecks. There is a video in Spanish and an information sheet in English. West of the plaza Muñoz Gamero on Waldo Seguel are two reminders of British influence in the city: the **British School** and **St James's Anglican Church** next door. Nearby on Calle Fagnano is the **Mirador Cerro de La Cruz** offering a view over the city and the Magellan Straits complete with its various shipwrecks. Three blocks further west is the **Museo Militar** ⓘ *at the Regimiento Pudeto, Zenteno y Balmaceda, Tue-Sun, 0900-1300, 1500-1700. Free*. Lots of knives, guns, flags and other military memorabilia plus many items brought from Fuerte Bulnes. Explanatory notes in excruciating English. Expect to be watched over by a young private.

North of the centre along Bulnes is the **Museo Regional Salesiano Mayorino Borgatello** ⓘ *Colegio Salesiano, Av Bulnes 374, entrance next to church, Tue-Sun 1000-1300, 1400-1800, hours change frequently, US$4*, an excellent introduction to Patagonia with a large collection of stuffed birds and animals from the region, exhibits on local history, geology, anthropology, aviation and industry. Easily the most complete and fascinating regional museum in Chile. Three blocks further on, the **cemetery** ⓘ *Av Bulnes, 0800-1800 daily*, is one of the most interesting places in the city, with cypress avenues, gravestones in many languages, which bear testimony to the cosmopolitan provenance of Patagonian pioneers, and many mausolea and memorials to pioneer families and victims of shipping disasters. Look out for the statue of Indicito, the little Indian, on the northwest side, which is now an object of reverence, bedecked with flowers. Further north still, the Instituto de la Patagonia houses the **Museo del Recuerdo** ⓘ *Av Bulnes 1890, Km 4 north (opposite the zona franca), T061-207056, Mon-Fri*

0830-1130, 1430-1815, Sat 0830-1300, US$2, children free, an open-air museum with artefacts used by the early settlers, pioneer homes and botanical gardens. On 21 de Mayo, south of Independencia, is a small Hindu temple, while further along the same street, on the southern outskirts of the city, the wooded **Parque María Behety**, features a scale model of Fuerte Bulnes, a campsite and children's playground, popular for Sunday picnics. In winter, there is an ice rink here.

Around Punta Arenas

Reserva Forestal Magallanes ⓘ *7 km west of town, US$5*, known locally as the Parque Japonés, extends over 13,500 ha and rises to 600 m. **Viento Sur** (see Activities and tours, below) offers a scheduled transport service to the reserve, but it can also be reached on foot or by bike: follow Independencia up the hill and take a right turning for Río de las Minas, about 3 km from the edge of town; the entrance to the reserve is 2 km beyond. Here you will find a self-guided nature trail through lenga and coigue trees. The road continues through the woods for 14 km passing several picnic sites. From the top end of the road a short path leads to a lookout over the **Garganta del Diablo** (Devil's Throat), a gorge with views over Punta Arenas and Tierra del Fuego. From here a slippery path leads down to the Río de las Minas Valley and then back to Punta Arenas.

Seventy kilometres north of Punta Arenas, **Seno Otway** is the site of a colony of around 11,000 Magellanic penguins, which can be visited ⓘ *Oct-mid Mar, US$5*. There are beautiful views across the sound to the mountains to the north and rheas, skunks and foxes can also be seen. Several agencies offer trips to the colony, lasting five hours (US$19 at peak season); if you wish to visit independently, a taxi from Punta Arenas will cost US$50 return. It is best to go early in the day. Try to avoid going at the same time as the large cruise ship tours – it is not much fun having to wait behind 200 people for your turn at the viewing stations.

A small island, 30 km northeast, Isla Magdalena is the location of the **Monumento Natural Los Pingüinos**, a colony of 150,000 penguins, administered by CONAF. Deserted apart from during the breeding season from November to early February, Magdalena is one of a group of three islands visited by Drake (the others are Marta and Isabel), whose men killed 3000 penguins for food. Boat trips to the island are run by **Comapa** ⓘ *Tue, Thu, Sat, 1600 (Dec-Feb), 2 hrs each way, 2 hrs on the island, US$30, subject to cancellation if windy; full refund given.* Beyond, Route 255 heads northeast via Punta Delgada to the **Argentine frontier** at Kimiri Aike and then along Argentine Route 3 to Río Gallegos, an unappealing city. For routes to Calafate in Argentina, see page 546.

Sleeping

Punta Arenas *p536, map p538*
Hotel prices are substantially lower during winter (Apr/May-Sep). Most hotels include breakfast in the room price. Rooms are also available in private houses; ask at the tourist office. There are no campsites near the city.

LL Finis Terrae, Colón 766, T061-228200, www.hotelfinisterrae.com. Typical large hotel; some rooms are small, as are the bathrooms. Expensive suites. Views from the top 2 floors. The best thing about the hotel is the rooftop café/bar. English spoken, parking.

LL José Nogueira, Bories 959, in former Palacio Sara Braun, T061-248840, www.hotelnogueira.com. Beautiful *loggia*. Slightly small rooms, but high ceilings. The rooms on the 2nd level are best. Good suites, lovely dining room, parking. Probably the nicest hotel in town. Recommended.

AL Hostería Yaganes, Camino Antiguo Norte Km 7.5, T061-211600, www.pehoe.cl/yaganes.htm. *Cabañas* on the shores of the Straits of Magellan, nice setting.

AL Plaza, Nogueira 1116, piso 2, T061-248613, www.hotelplaza.cl. Historic building with high ceilings and old-fashioned charm, much improved recently. English spoken. Limited parking space. Recommended.

A Oro Fueguino, Fagnano 356, T061-249401, www.orofueguino.cl. Recently refurbished, TV and phone. Some rooms with no windows. Good breakfast. Often fills up with groups so book ahead. Cheaper in US$dollars than pesos. Recommended.

A-B Monte Carlo, Colón 605, T061-222120, www.montecarlohotel.cl. Old wooden building. The rooms, heated and carpeted, have seen better days. Cheaper rooms without bath.

B Hostal La Estancia, O'Higgins 765, T061-249130, www.hostallaestancia.cl. Simple but comfortable rooms, some with bath. Heating in passageways but not in rooms. Very good kitchen facilities, internet, lots of information, friendly. English spoken. Excellent breakfast with real coffee. A little expensive. Recommended.

B Hostal del Sur, Mejicana 151, T061-227249. Homely and impeccably kept late 19th-century house. The living room is top of the range 1960s, but the rooms are modern. Excellent breakfast with cereal and cakes. Not central, but in a peaceful neighbourhood. Advance booking advised in summer. Highly recommended.

B-C Al Fin del Mundo Hostal , O'Higgins 1026, T061-710185, www.alfindelmundo.cl. With breakfast. Bright cosy and friendly. Shared baths, central, helpful, laundry service, book exchange, internet, English spoken, helpful. Recommended.

B-C Hostal Green House, Angamos 1146, T061-227939, www.hostalgreenhouse.cl. Friendly hostel run by Christina, an anthropologist and Mario, a psychologist. Kitchen facilities, laundry, internet. German and a little English spoken. If Mario is in the mood he will get out his bagpipes! Recommended.

B-C Hostal Paredΐso, Angamos 1073, T061-224212. Decent rooms with cable TV and heating, with or without bath (some cheaper rooms have no window). Good breakfast, parking, use of kitchen. Friendly, basic information given, some English spoken. Recommended.

B-C The Pink House, Caupolicán 99, T061-222436,pinkhous@ctcinternet.cl. Impeccable rooms with or without bath, breakfast included. Pick-up from bus station. English spoken, internet access. Recommended.

C Ritz, Pedro Montt 1102, T061-224422. All rooms with shared bathrooms. Breakfast extra. Old, clean and cosy and with a kind of run-down charm. Recommended (Bruce Chatwin stayed here: check out his name in the guest book).

C-D Aikén, Errazuriz 612, T061-222629, www.aiken.cl. **F** pp in dorms. Good beds with duvets. Some rooms with view. Large bathrooms, internet access, TV lounge, kitchen, heating, friendly, English spoken.

D Backpackers Paradise, Carrera Pinto 1022, T061-240104, backpackersparadise@ hotmail.com. **F-G** pp in basic dorms. Fun backpackers' with cooking facilities, limited bathroom facilities, lots of info, good meeting place, luggage store, internet access, laundry service, book exchange. Expensive bike rental. No privacy but recommended.

D Hosp Costanera, Correa 1221, T061-240175. Kitchen facilities, large breakfast, friendly, clean.

D Hosp Miramar, Almte Senoret 1190, T061-215446. **G** pp in dorms. Slightly exotic location on the edge of the red light district. Friendly staff, good views over the bay. Breakfast extra.

D Hosp Quo Vadis, Paraguaya 150, T061-247687. Motorcycle parking, meals, safe, quiet. Recommended.

E Hostal Independencia, Independencia 374, T061-227572, www.chileaustral.com/ independencia. **F-G** pp in shared rooms. Friendly, small basic rooms. Breakfast extra, kitchen facilities, laundry service, internet, bike rental and cheap camping. Also cabañas away from the centre. Good value. Recommended.

Eating

Punta Arenas *p536, map p538*

Visitors to Punta Arenas and the surrounding region should be especially wary of eating shellfish. In recent years, the nearby waters have been sporadically affected by a *marea roja* (red tide) of poisonous algae. While the *marea roja* only affects bivalve shellfish, infected molluscs can kill humans almost instantly. Mussels should not be picked along the shore of Punta Arenas; foreigners who have done this have died. However, all shellfish sold in restaurants have been inspected and so are theoretically safe.

Lobster has become more expensive and there are seasonal bans on *centolla* (king crab) fishing to protect dwindling stocks; do not purchase *centolla* out of season. *Centolla* fishing is banned at other times, too, if the crabs become infected with a disease that is fatal to humans.

TTT Remezón, 21 de Mayo 1469, T061-241029, www.patagoniasalvaje.net. Regional specialities such as krill. Very good, and so it should be given the exorbitant prices.

TTT Sotitos, O'Higgins 1138. Good service and excellent cuisine. Elegant, expensive. Recommended.

TTT-TT Centro Español, Plaza Muñoz Gamero 771, above Teatro Cervantes. Large helpings, limited selection, quite expensive. Decent lunch menu.

¥¥¥-¥¥ El Estribo, Carrera Pinto 762, T061-244714. Specializes in local and exotic dishes, such as guanaco.

¥¥ Damiana Elena, O'Higgins 694, T061-222818. Stylish restaurant serving Mediterranean food with a Patagonian touch. Popular with locals. Advance booking essential at weekends.

¥¥ La Luna, O'Higgins 1017, T061-228555. Fish and shellfish including local specialities, huge pisco sours, lively atmosphere.

¥¥ Parrilla Los Ganaderos, Bulnes 0977, T061-222818. The best place to go for spit-roast lamb. It's a long walk past the hippodrome from the town centre. Take a taxi or any colectivo going towards the Zona Franca.

¥¥ Santino, Colón 657, T061-220511. Good pizzas, large bar, good service.

¥ Cocinerías, Lautaro Navarro, south of the port entrance. Stalls serving cheap fish meals.

¥ Dino's Pizza, Bories 557. Good pizzas, huge sandwiches. For something different, try their rhubarb juice. Recommended.

¥ El Quijote, Lautaro Navarro 1087, T061-241225. Good burgers, sandwiches and fish dishes. Good value set lunch. Recommended.

¥ Lomit's, Menéndez 722. A Punta Arenas fast-food institution serving cheap snacks and drinks, open when the others are closed, always busy. Recommended.

Cafés and snack bars

Casa del Pastel, Carrera Pinto y O'Higgins. Very good pastries.

Chocolatta, Bories 852. Probably the best coffee in town.

Coffeenet, Waldo Seguel 670. Proper internet café serving espresso.

Entre Fierros, Roca 875, T061-223436. Small diner that by all accounts has remained unchanged since the 1950s. It is famous for its banana milkshakes and tiny *choripan* (spicy sausage-meat sandwiches). Open until 1900.

Bars and clubs

Punta Arenas *p536, map p538*

Note that anywhere that calls itself a 'nightclub' is in fact a brothel.

Olijoe, Errazuriz 970. Reasonably plush British-style pub, leather interior, recommended.

Pub 1900, Av Colón esq. Bories. Friendly, relaxed atmosphere.

La Taberna del Club de la Unión, Plaza Muñoz Gamero y Seguel. For drinks, atmospheric pub in the basement of the Nogueira hotel, smoky.

Festivals and events

Punta Arenas *p536, map p538*

Feb Muestra custumbrista de Chiloe Each February the Chilote community celebrates its culture.

Jun Carnaval de invierno The winter solstice is marked by a carnival on the weekend closest to 21st Jun.

Shopping

Punta Arenas *p536, map p538*

Zona Franca, 3½ km north of the centre, on the right-hand side of the road to the airport, take bus E or A from Plaza Muñoz Gamero or a colectivo. Punta Arenas has certain free-port facilities. Cheap perfume and electrical goods are especially worth seeking out, as is camping equipment. The quality of most other goods is low and the prices little better than elsewhere. Open Mon-Sat 1000-1230, 1500-2000.

Sports Nativa, Colón 614. Camping and Skiing equipment. **The North Face**, Bories 887. Outdoor gear. **The Wool House Patagonia**, Fagnano 675, by the plaza. Good quality, reasonably priced woollen clothes. Punta Arenas is famous for the quality of its chocolate. Delicious handmade chocolate is for sale at several shops on Calle Bories.

Activities and tours

Punta Arenas *p536, map p538*

Skiing

Cerro Mirador, 9 km west of Punta Arenas in the Reserva Nacional Magallanes, is one of the few places in the world where you can ski with a sea view. Season Jun-Sep, weather permitting. Daily lift-ticket, US$11; equipment rental, US$9. There's a mid-way lodge with food, drink and equipment. For cross-country skiing facilities, contact the **Club Andino**, T061-241479, www.clubandino.tierra.cl.

However note that the ski centre is often closed due to lack of snow. There's also a good 2-hr hike here in summer, the trail is clearly marked and flora are labelled. Skiing is also available at **Tres Morros**.

Tour operators

Most organize tours to Torres del Paine, Fuerte Bulnes and *pingüineras* on Otway sound. Several also offer bespoke tours, and adventure tourism on Chilean Tierra del Fuego, which has very little tourist infrastructure: shop around as prices vary. Specify if you want a tour in English. There are many more operators than listed here. For more information ask at the Sernatur office. **Turismo Aonikenk**, Magallanes 619, T061-221982, www.aonikenk.com. Excellent company organizing really informed tours to the usual places near Punta Arenas, as well as more imaginative options, such as Parque Nacional Pali Aike, and expeditions on Tierra del Fuego. Run by charming bilingual couple Sebastian and Marisol. Highly recommended. **Turismo Aventour**, Nogueira 1255, T061-241197, www.aventourpatagonia.com. English spoken, specialize in fishing trips, also organize tours to Tierra del Fuego. **Turismo Viento Sur**, Fagnano 585, T061-226930, www.vientosur.com. For camping equipment, fishing excursions, sea kayaking, cycle hire, English spoken, good tours.

Transport

Punta Arenas *p536, map p538*

All transport is heavily booked from late Dec through to Mar; advance booking is advised.

Air

Flights to Punta Arenas arrive at **Carlos Ibáñez del Campo Airport**, 20 km north of town. There is a restaurant in the airport.

National To **Balmaceda** (for Coyhaique), with **LanChile** (LanExpress), Daily in summer, US$80, otherwise 1 a week or daily via Puerto Montt (more expensive). To **Puerto Montt**, with **LanChile** (LanExpress), **Aerolineas del Sur** and **Sky Airline** 10 daily, from US$160 return. Cheapest one way tickets with Aerolineas del Sur. To **Santiago**, **LanChile** (LanExpress), **Aerolineas del Sur** and **Sky Airline** several daily, from US$200 return, via Puerto Montt (sit on the right for views). To **Porvenir**, Aerovías DAP, 2 daily Mon-Sat, US$26 one way, plus other irregular flights, with Twin-Otter and Cessna aircraft. To **Puerto Williams**, Aerovías DAP, daily in summer, US$70 one way.

International To **Ushuaia** (Argentina), Lan Chile, three weekly in summer, 1 hr, US$140 one way; reserve well in advance from mid-Dec to Feb. To **Falkland Islands/Islas Malvinas**, LanChile, Sat, US$500 return. **International Tours & Travel**, T+500-22041, jf.itt@horizon.co.fk, serve as LanChile agents on the Falkland Islands.

Airline offices Aerovías DAP, O'Higgins 891, T061-223340, www.dap.cl, open 0900-1230, 1430-1930; **LanChile**, Bories 884, T600-5262000, www.lan.cl. **Sky Airline**, Roca 933, www.skyairline.cl. **Aerolineas del Sur**, Fagnano 817.

Boat

All tickets on ships must be booked in advance for Jan and Feb. Visits to the beautiful fjords and glaciers of **Tierra del Fuego** are highly recommended. Comapa runs a fortnightly 22-hr, 320-km round trip to the fjord d'Agostino, where many glaciers descend to the sea. The luxury cruiser, *Terra Australis*, sails from Punta Arenas on Sat via Ushuaia and Puerto Williams; details from Comapa; advance bookings (advisable) from **Cruceros Australis SA**, Miraflores 178, piso 12, Santiago, T02-6963211, www.australis.com. For services to **Porvenir**, Tierra del Fuego, see page 565.

Government supply ships are only recommended for the young and hardy, but take a sleeping bag, extra food and travel pills. For transport on navy supply ships to **Puerto Williams** and **Cape Horn**, enquire at **Tercera Zona Naval**, Lautaro Navarro 1150, but be prepared to be frustrated by irregular sailings (about 1 every 3 months) and inaccurate information. You will almost certainly also need a letter of recommendation. During the voyage across the Drake Passage, albatrosses, petrels, cormorants, penguins, elephant seals, fur seals, whales and dolphins can be sighted.

Most cruise ships to **Antarctica** leave from Ushuaia (Argentina). However there are a few operators based in Punta Arenas. Try **Antarctic Dream Shipping** Roca 1016, T061-223676. www.antarctic.cl, or **Antarctica 580l**, Lautaro Navarro 987, Piso 2, T061-228783, www.antarcticaxxi.com.

Shipping offices Comapa (Compañía Marítima de Punta Arenas), Magallanes 990, T061-200200; **Navimag**, Magallanes 990, T061-244400, www.navimag.cl.

Bus

Services and frequencies change every year, so check on arrival at the helpful Sernatur office. Timetables are also printed daily in *El Austral*. The services detailed below are for high season only. Buses depart from the company offices, which are listed below.

Fernández, Transfer (cheapest), Buses Pacheco and Buses Sur, all run several services each day to **Puerto Natales**, 3 hrs, last departure 2000, US$6 one way, US$10.50 return (although this means you have to return with the same company). Buses may pick up at the airport with advance notice. To **Coyhaique**, 20 hrs, Buses Sur, 1 per week via Argentina, US$55, meals not included. Cruz del Sur, Queilen Bus and Pacheco have services through Argentina to **Osorno**, **Puerto Montt** and **Castro**, several weekly, 36 hrs to Castro, US$60.

To Argentina To **Río Gallegos**, Pingüino, departs 1245 daily, returns 1300; Ghisoni, 4 weekly, departs 1100; Pacheco, 5 weekly, departs 1130. All cost US$14 and take about 5 hrs. For services to **Buenos Aires** it is cheaper to go to Río Gallegos and buy an onward ticket from there. Pacheco and Ghisoni have buses most days to **Río Grande** via Punta Delgada, 8hrs, US$25, heavily booked. To **Ushuaia** via Punta Delgada, 12-14 hrs, book any return at same time, Tecni Austral, Tue, Thu, Sat, Sun 0800 from Ghisoni office, US$34; Pacheco, Mon, Wed, Fri 0715, US$46.

Bus companies Bus Sur, Menéndez 565 T061-227145, www.bus-sur.cl; Buses Sur, Menéndez 552. Buses Transfer, Pedro Montt 966, T061-229613. Cruz del Sur, Pingüino and Fernández, Sanhueza 745, T061-242313, www.busesfernandez.com. Gesell, Menéndez 556, T061-222896. Ghisoni, Lautaro Navarro 971, T061-222078, www.ghisoni.terra.cl. Los Carlos, Plaza Muñoz Gamero 1039, T061-241321. Pacheco, Colón 900, T061-242174, www.busespacheco.com.

Car hire

Try looking in the local newspaper for special deals and bargain if you want to hire a car for several days. Budget, O'Higgins 964, T061-241696. Hertz, O'Higgins 987, T061-229049, F061-244729, English spoken; also at airport, T061-210096. Internacional; Seguel 443 and at airport, T061-228323, F061-226334, recommended. Payne Rent a Car, Menéndez 631, T/F061-240852, payne@ctcinternet.cl, try bargaining, friendly. Willemsen, Lautaro Navarro 1038, T061 247787, F061-241083, recommended.

Taxis

Reliable service is available from Radio Alce vip, T061-710889 and Taxi Austral, T061-247710. *Colectivos* (all black) run on fixed routes within the city, US$0.60.

Directory

Punta Arenas *p536, map p538*

Banks Several on or around Plaza Muñoz Gamero many 24 hrs, all have ATMs. Banks open Mon-Fri 0830-1400, casas de cambio open Mon-Fri 0900-1230, 1500-1900, Sat 0900-1230; outside business hours, try Buses Sur (see above), or the major hotels (lower rates); Argentine pesos can be bought at casas de cambio; good rates at Cambio Gasic, Roca 915, Of 8, T061-242396. German spoken; La Hermandad, Lautaro Navarro 1099, T061-243991, excellent rates, US$ cash for AmEx TCs and credit cards. Scott Cambios, Colón y Magallanes, T061-227145. Sur Cambios, Lautaro Navarro 1001, T061-225656, accepts TCs. **Consulates** Argentina, 21 de Mayo 1878, T061-261912, open weekdays 1000-1530, visas take 24 hrs. United Kingdom, Catarates de Niaguara 01325, T061-211535, helpful, with information on Falkland Islands. **Medical services** Hospital Regional Lautaro Navarro, Angamos 180, T061-244040, public hospital, for emergency room ask for 'la posta'; Clínica Magallanes, Bulnes 01448, T061-211527, private clinic, minimum charge US$45 per visit. A list of English- speaking doctors is available from Sernatur. **Internet** Lots of places offer access, including at Magallanes y Menendez, and below Hostal Calafate on Magallanes, ½ block north of Plaza. Prices are generally US$1 per hour. **Post office** Bories 911 y Menéndez, Mon-Fri 0830-1930, Sat 0900-1400. **Telephone** There are several call centres in the city centre (shop around).

Puerto Natales and around

→ *Phone code: 061. Colour map 6, B3. Population 17,000.*

Beautifully situated on the calm waters of Canal Señoret fjord, an arm of the Ultima Esperanza Sound, edged with spectacular mountains, Puerto Natales is a pretty, quiet town of brightly painted corrugated tin houses. It's the base for exploring the magnificent Balmaceda and Torres del Paine national parks, and although inundated with visitors in the summer, it retains a quiet unhurried feel, a recommended place to relax for a few days. ▸▸ *For Sleeping, Eating and other listings, see pages 546-549.*

Ins and outs

Getting there Puerto Natales is easily reached by many daily buses from Punta Arenas, as well as by daily buses from Río Turbio (Argentina) and El Calafate. There are also two buses weekly from Río Gallegos. The town is the terminus of the *Navimag* ship to Puerto Montt (for further details see page 549). If driving between Punta Arenas and Puerto Natales make sure you have enough fuel.

Getting around Puerto Natales is not a large place and taxis are only needed for journeys out of town.

Tourist information There is a kiosk on the waterfront ⓘ *Av Pedro Montt y Phillipi, T061-412125*. Information is also available from the **Municipalidad** ⓘ *Bulnes 285, T061-411263*, and from **CONAF** ⓘ *O'Higgins 584*.

Sights

The colourful old steam train in the main square was once used to take workers to the the meatpacking factory at Puerto Bories, 5 km north of town, now converted into the **Museo Frigorífico Puerto Bories** ⓘ *T061-414328, daily 1000-1900 in summer, US$5 or US$7 with guided tour*. In its heyday the plant was the biggest of its kind in Chile with a capacity for 250,000 sheep. Bankrupted in the early 1990s, much of the plant was dismantled in 1993. Belatedly the plant was given National Monument status and is slowly being restored. Fascinating tours of the remaining buildings and machine rooms are given in English. It is a pleasant hour long walk along the shore to Bories (US$4 by taxi), with glimpses of the Balmaceda glacier across the sound.

The slab-like **Cerro Dorotea** dominates the town, with superb views of the whole Seno Ultima Esperanza. It can be reached on foot or by any Río Turbio bus or taxi (recommended, as the hill is farther off than it seems). The trail entrance is marked by a sign marked 'Mirador Cerro Dorotea'. Expect to be charged US$5-8 in one of the local houses, where you will be given a broomstick handle which makes a surprisingly good walking stick. It is an hour and a half trek up to the 600-m lookout along a well marked trail. In theory you can continue along the top of the hill to get better views to the north, but the incredibly strong winds often make this dangerous. Some 25 km to the north of Puerto Natales is the **Monumento Nacional Cueva Milodón** a massive cave, 70 m wide, 220 m deep and 30 m high, formed by the lapping of glacial lakes in the ice age, which were then 300 m above the current lake. Remains have been found here of a prehistoric ground sloth, together with evidence of occupation by early Patagonian humans some 11,000 years ago. The ceiling of the cave is dimpled with mineral deposits, and inside the eerie depths it's as silent as a library with marvellous views through the letterbox slit of the cave's mouth. There's a small visitor centre with summaries in English, and toilets, and a restaurant. This was the end point of Bruce Chatwin's travelogue *In Patagonia*. Most tours to Torres del Paine stop at the cave but you can also get there by bus US$7, or taxi US$24 return.

Parque Nacional Bernardo O'Higgins

Often referred to as the Parque Nacional Monte Balmaceda, Bernardo O'Higgins covers much of the Campo de Hielo Sur, plus the fjords and offshore islands further west. A three-hour boat trip from Puerto Natales up the Seno de Ultima Esperanza takes you to the southernmost section, passing the Balmaceda Glacier, which drops from the eastern slopes of **Monte Balmaceda** (2035 m). The glacier is retreating; in 1986 its foot was at sea level. The boat docks further north at **Puerto Toro**, from where it is a 1-km walk to the base of the Serrano Glacier on the north slope of Monte Balmaceda. On the trip, dolphins, sea-lions (in season), black-necked swans, flightless steamer ducks and cormorants can be seen. Take warm clothes, including a hat and gloves. There is a route from Puerto Toro along the **Río Serrano** for 35 km to the Torres del Paine administration centre (see page 550); guided tours are available. It is also possible to travel to the Paine administration centre by boat or zodiac (four hours, US$60). Although the park is uninhabited, guest accommodation is available

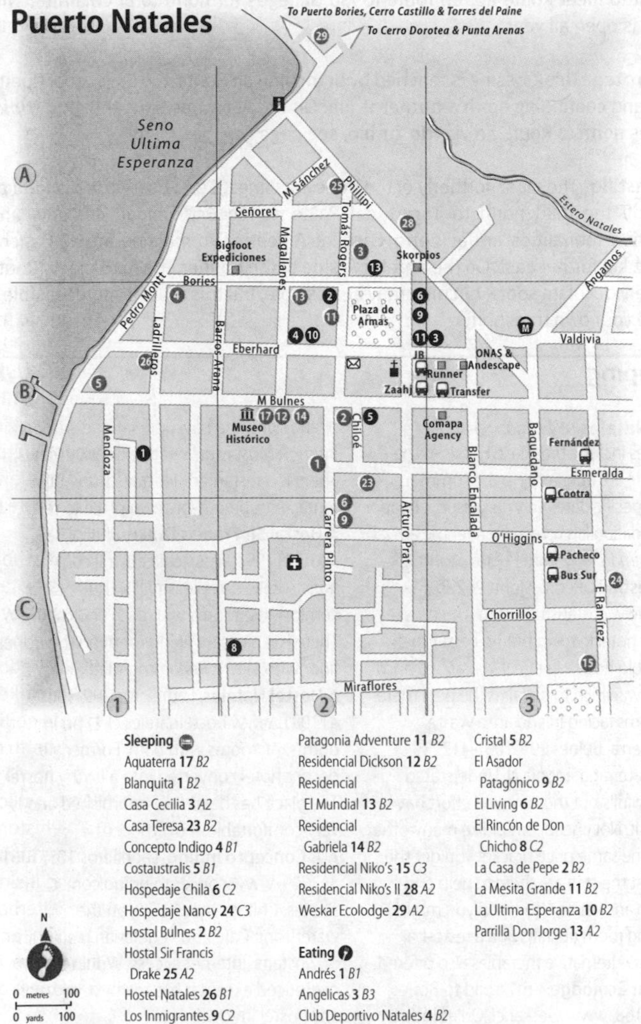

 at Hostería Monte Balmaceda (L range, T061-220174). The cutter *21 de Mayo* sails every morning from Puerto Natales to the park in summer and on Sunday only in the winter, US$60 per person, minimum 10 passengers. Book through **Casa Cecilia** (see Sleeping, page 547), or directly through **Turismo 21 de Mayo** (see Activities and tours, page 549). Lunch extra, so take own food; snacks and drinks available on board. The trip can be combined with a visit to Torres del Paine.

Argentine border

From Puerto Natales, the Argentine frontier can be crossed at three points, all of which meet Route 40, which runs north to El Calafate. These crossings are open, subject to weather conditions, 24 hours a day from September to May and daily 0700 to 2300 between June and August.

Paso Casas Viejas This crossing, 16 km east of Puerto Natales, is reached by turning off Route 9 (the Punta Arenas road) at Km 14. On the Argentine side, the road (*ripio*) runs east to meet Route 40, en route to Río Gallegos (or north to El Calafate). This crossing is open all year.

Villa Dorotea This crossing is reached by branching off Route 9, 9 km east of Puerto Natales and continuing north a further 11 km. On the Argentine side, the road (*ripio*) continues north to Route 40 via **Río Turbio**, see page 523.

Cerro Castillo The most northerly of the three crossings, Cerro Castillo is reached by turning off the road north to Torres del Paine at Km 65. Chilean customs and immigration formalities are at Cerro Castillo; Argentine formalities are at Cancha Carrera, 2 km further east. On the Argentine side of the frontier, the road meets Route 40 in a very desolate spot – hitching may be possible, but this route is more feasible if you have your own transport.

Sleeping

Puerto Natales *p544, map p545*
Most prices include breakfast. Hotels in the countryside are open only in the summer months; specific dates vary. In season, cheaper accommodation fills up quickly after the arrival of the *Navimag* ferry from Puerto Montt.

LL Costaustralis, Pedro Montt 262, T061-412000, www.costaustralis.com. The most expensive hotel in town but no better than the other big hotels. In effect you are paying for the view, which to be fair is the best there is. The rooms facing inland are a waste.

AL Aquaterra, Bulnes 299, T061-412239, www.aquaterrapatagonia.cl. Understated design. No frills but thought and effort have gone into it. Not cheap, but unlike many other places in the same price bracket you get the feeling that the staff are there to help and are able to answer any question you might have. Living room upstairs and a resto-bar downstairs. Alternative therapies also offered.

AL Weskar Ecolodge, Km1, road to Bories, T061-414168, www.weskar.cl. Quiet lodge overlooking the bay, understated wooden interior. Most rooms with extensive views. There is a restaurant for guests and bike rental. A good out-of-town place to relax.

A Hostal Sir Francis Drake, Phillipi 383, T061-411553, www.chileaustral.com/francisdrake. Simple, smallish but comfortable rooms with bath and cable TV. There is a pleasant living room on the upper floor with views. Recommended.

A Hostel Natales, Ladrilleros 209, T061-411081, www.hostelnatales.cl. **D** pp in dorms. All rooms with bath. Formerly a decent hotel converted into a luxury hostel. The place has been fully refurbished and is very comfortable, if overpriced.

A-B Concepto Indigo, Ladrilleros 105, T061-413609, www.conceptoindigo.com. **C** singles. Chilote style house on the waterfront. Café and vegetarian restaurant downstairs. Internet access. Would be overpriced except it has the best views of any hostel in town.

B-C Casa Cecilia, Tomás Rogers 60, T061-411797, www.casaceciliahostal.com. **E** singles. With good breakfast, some rooms with bath, clean, cooking facilities, English, French and German spoken, heating, luggage store, camping equipment rental, information on Torres del Paine, tours organized, bus tickets sold, credit cards accepted. Better value in US dollars. Warmly recommended.

B-C Hostal Bulnes, Bulnes 407, T061-411307, www.hostalbulnes.com. With breakfast, some rooms with bath, laundry facilities, luggage store.

C Blanquita, Carrera Pinto 409. T061-411674. **E** singles. Basic quiet hotel that looks like a giant portacabin. With bath, heating and breakfast, friendly. Recommended.

C Patagonia Adventure, Tomás Rogers 179 on Plaza, T061-411028, www.apatagonia.com. **F** pp in dorms. Friendly, clean, English spoken, camping equipment for hire, luggage store, book exchange. Good bike and kayak tours offered. Also a general agent selling trips to Torres del Paine. Breakfast is served in the café annex. Recommended.

C-D Res Niko's II, Phillipi 528, T061-411500, residencialnicosii@hotmail.com. Some rooms with bath and cable TV, English spoken, tours, tent hire, book exchange. Good breakfast.

D Casa Teresa, Esmeralda 463, T061-410472, freepatagonia@hotmail.com. **F** singles. Good value, warm, cheap meals, quiet, friendly. Tours to Torres del Paine. Recommended.

D Hosp Chila, Carrera Pinto 442, T061-412328. **F** singles. Use of kitchen, welcoming, laundry facilities, luggage store, bakes bread. Recommended.

D Hosp Laury, Bulnes 222. **F** Singles. With breakfast, cooking and laundry facilities, clean, warm, friendly.

D Hosp Nancy, E Ramirez 540, T061-4510022, www.natalеslodge.cl. **F** singles. Cooking facilities, internet access, laundry service, helpful, tours and lots of information. Good budget option. Recommended.

D Los Inmigrantes, Carrera Pinto 480, T061-413482, losinmigrantes@hotmail.com. **F** singles. Good breakfast, clean, kitchen facilities, equipment rental, luggage store. Recommended.

D Res Dickson, Bulnes 307, T061-411871, lodging@chilaustral.com. **F** singles. Good breakfast, clean, helpful, cooking and laundry facilities, internet. Recommended.

D Res El Mundial, Bories 315, T061-412476, omar@fortalezapatagonia.cl. **F** singles. Some rooms with bath. Use of kitchen (if the owners are not using it), good-value meals, luggage stored. Recommended.

D Res Gabriela, Bulnes 317, T061-411061. **F** singles. Clean, good breakfast, helpful, luggage store, heating. Recommended.

D Res Niko's, Ramírez 669, T061-412810, nikoresidencial@hotmail.com. **F** singles. With breakfast, basic rooms, some rooms with bath, good meals, also dormitory accommodation. Recommended.

Around Puerto Natales *p544*

Along the road from Punta Arenas are several hotels, including:

L Hostal Río Penitente, Km 138, T061-331694. In an old *estancia*. Recommended.

L-AL Cisne de Cuello Negro, 6 km north of town, Km 275 near Puerto Bories, for bookings contact: Av Colón 782, Punta Arenas, T061-244506, pehoe1@ctcinternet.cl. Clean, reasonable, excellent cooking. Recommended.

AL Estancia Tres Pasos, 40 km north, T061-221930, www.trespasos.cl. Simple and beautiful lodge halfway between Puerto Natales and Torres del Paine. Horseriding trips offered.

AL Hostería Río Verde, Km 90, east off the highway on Seno Skyring, T061-311122. Private bath, heating. Recommended.

A Cabañas Kotenk Aike, 2 km north of town, T061-412581. Sleeps 4, modern, very comfortable, great location.

A Hostería Llanuras de Diana, Km 215 (30 km south of Puerto Natales), T061-410661. Hidden from road, beautifully situated. Recommended.

Eating

Puerto Natales *p544, map p545*

¥¥¥-¥¥ Angélicas, Eberhard 532, T061-410365, angelicas@rest.cl. A sign of how Puerto Natales has turned into a boutique town. Elegant Mediterranean style restaurant originally from Santiago. Quality ingredients well prepared. Pricey but more than reasonable for Natales, and customers invariably leave satisfied. Staff can be a little flustered when the restaurant is full. Recommended.

¶¶¶-¶¶ El Asador Patagonico, Prat 158 on Plaza. Specializes in spit-roast lamb. Recommended.

¶¶¶-¶¶ Parrilla don Jorge, Bories 430 on Plaza. T061-410999. Another restaurant specializing in Cordero al Palo, but also serving fish etc. The open plan leaves you feeling a little exposed when the restaurant is not full. Decent service.

¶¶ El Rincón de Don Chicho, Luiz Cruz Martinez 206, T061-414339. All-you-can-eat *parrillada*. Vegetarian options on request. 15 minutes walk from town centre. Recommended.

¶¶ La Casa de Pepe, Tomas Rogers 131 on Plaza. For those who want to sample the traditional food of central Chile – *pernil*, *pastel de choclo* etc. Uncomfortable seats.

¶¶ La Mesita Grande, Prat 196 on Plaza, T061-411571, www.mesitagrande.cl. Fresh pizzas made in a wood burning clay oven. Also pasta and good desserts. Not much atmosphere, but has a fantastic antique till.

¶¶ La Ultima Esperanza, Eberhard 354. Recommended for salmon, seafood, enormous portions, not cheap but worth the experience.

¶¶-¶ La Caleta Economica, Eberhard 261, T061-413969. Excellent seafood, also meat and chicken dishes, large portions, good value for money.

¶ Andrés, Ladrilleros 381. Excellent, good fish dishes, good service.

¶ Club Deportivo Natales, Eberhard 332. Very cheap, decent meals

¶ Cristal, Bulnes 439. Tasty sandwiches and salmon, good value.

Cafés

Aquaterra, Bulnes 299. Cosy, good, also a shiatsu and reiki centre.

Café & Books, Blanco Encalada 224. Another cosy café with an extensive 2-for-1 book exchange.

El Living, on Plaza. Cosy, British run, with English newspapers and magazines. Wide variety of cakes, good tea and coffee, wine and vegetarian food. Book exchange.

Emporio de la Pampa, Eberhard 226C, T061-510520. Small café/delicatessen selling wine and local gourmet products.

Patagonia Dulce, Barros Arana 233, T061-415285, www.patagoniadulce.cl. For the best hot chocolate in town.

Bars and clubs

Puerto Natales *p544, map p545*

El Bar de Ruperto, Bulnes 371. Good, English-run pub with a lively mix of locals and tourists. For a kick, try the chile vodka.

Shopping

Puerto Natales *p544, map p545*

Camping equipment

Balfer, Esmeralda y Baquedano. Camping gear and fishing tackle, but more expensive than the Zona Franca in Punta Arenas. Similar items at **Alfgal**, Barros Arana 299, T061-413622. Outdoor clothing from **La Maddera**, Prat 297, T061-413318. Camping gas is available in hardware stores, eg at Baquedano y O'Higgins. **Patagonia Adventure** and **Casa Cecilia** hire out good-quality gear (for both, see Sleeping, above). Check all equipment and prices carefully. Average charges, per day: tent US$8, sleeping bag US$4-6, mat US$2, raincoat US$1, also cooking gear US$2. Deposits sometimes required: tent US$200, sleeping bag US$100. Note that it is often difficult to hire walking boots. **Skorpios**, Prat 62, T061-412409, www.skorpios.cl. Catamaran trips up to the Fjordo de las montañas. Truly spectacular close up vistas of glaciers and waterfalls given good weather. Two sailings weekly, US$130.

Food

Food prices are variable so shop around, although everything tends to be more pricey than in Punta Arenas. There's a 24-hr supermarket on the Bulnes 300 block, and at Bulnes 1085. The town markets are also good.

Activities and tours

Puerto Natales *p544, map p545*

Reports of the reliability of agencies, especially for their trips to Torres del Paine National Park, are very mixed. It is better to book tours direct with operators in Puerto Natales than through agents in Punta Arenas, where huge commissions may be charged. Some agencies offer 1-day tours to the **Perito Moreno** glacier in Argentina (see page 508), 14-hr trip, 2 hrs at the glacier, US$60 excluding food and park entry fee; take US dollars cash or Argentine pesos as Chilean pesos are not accepted. However, if you have more time it is better to break the trip by staying in Calafate, and organizing a tour from there.

Bigfoot Expediciones, Bories 206, T061-413247, www.bigfootpatagonia.com. Sea kayaking, trekking, mountaineering and ice-hiking trips on the Grey glacier. Unforgettable if expensive. Recommended.

Estancia Travel, Casa 13B, Puerto Bories (5km north of Puerto Natales), T061-412221, www.estanciatravel.com. English/Chilean operator offering a different way of experiencing Patagonia – on horseback. Bilingual guides and well kept horses. Good half-day trips to the Cueva del Milodón. Prices start from US$35 for 2 hours. Multi-day trips only for the well off. Book direct or through agencies in Natales.

Onas, Eberhard 595, T061-414349, www.onaspatagonia.com. Tours of Torres del Paine and kayak trips. Also trips to and from the park down the Río Serrano in zodiac boats to the Serrano glacier in the Parque National Bernardo O'Higgins, and from there on the tour boats to Puerto Natales, US$90 each all inclusive. Book in advance.

Sendero Aventura, Hostal Patagonia Adventure, Tomás Rogers 179, T061-415636, sendero_aventura@terra.cl. Trekking in Torres del Paine, cycle and kayak trips to the park, boats to Parque Nacional Balmaceda, camping equipment and bike hire. Recommended.

Skorpios, Prat 62, T061-412409, www.skorpios.cl. Catamaran trips up to the Fjordo de las montañas. Truly spectacular close up vistas of glaciers and waterfalls given good weather. Two sailings weekly, US$130.

Turismo 21 de Mayo, Eberhard 554, T061-411476, www.turismo21demayo.cl. Runs boat trips to Parque Nacional Bernado O'Higgins and on to Torres del Paine in motor zodiac. This can be combined in a very long day with a trip to the park returning by bus. US$150 including park entry and food.

Turismo Runner, Eberhard 555, T061-414141, www.turismorunner.cl. Specializes in day trips to Torres del Paine combined with a boat trip to the face of the Grey Glacier, US$150 pp including park entrance and a decent lunch at the hostería Grey.

Transport

Puerto Natales *p544, map p545*

Punta Arenas is served by Bus Fernández, Eberhard 555, T061-411111; **Bus Sur**, Baquedano 634; **Buses Sur**, Baquedano 558, T061-411325; and **Bus Transfer**, Baquedano 414, T061-421616; several daily, 3 hrs, US$4, book in advance. Bus Sur runs to **Coyhaique**, Mon, US$55.

To Argentina Buses Sur has 2 weekly direct services to **Río Gallegos**, US$18. Cootra runs services to **Río Turbio**, 2 hrs (depending on customs), US$5. To **Calafate**, Buses Sur and Bus Zaahj , 4½ hrs, US$19 both have daily services; Cootra also runs a service via Río Turbio, 7 hrs, reserve at least 1 day ahead.

Boat

The **Navimag** ferry *Eden* sails every Fri in summer to **Puerto Montt**, less frequently off season; confirmation of reservations is advised.

Shipping companies Navimag, Pedro Montt 262, Loc B, Terminal Marítimo, T061-411421.

Directory

Puerto Natales *p544, map p545*

Banks and casas de cambio Shop around as some casas offer very poor rates (much better to change money in Punta Arenas). Banks offer poor rates for TCs, which cannot be changed into US$ cash. **Banco Santander Santiago**, Bulnes y Blanco Encalada, Mastercard and Visa, ATM; **Banco de Chile**, Bulnes 544, Mastercard and Visa, ATM; **Cambio Stop**, Baquedano 380; **Enio America**, Blanco Encalada 266, Argentine pesos can be changed here; there are two more at Bulnes 683 and 1087 (good rates, also change Argentine pesos), and others on Prat. **Internet** Concepto Indigo, Hosp María José (see Sleeping, above). **El Rincón de Tata**, Prat 236, **Patagonianet**, *Blanco 330*. **Laundry** Lavandería Catch, Bories 218, friendly service; **Servilaundry**, Bulnes 513. **Post office** Eberhard 417, Mon-Fri 0830-1230, 1430-1745, Sat 0900-1230. **Telephone** CTC, Blanco Encalada 23 y Bulnes; **Entel**, Baquedano y Bulnes, phone and fax service; **Telefonica**, Blanco Encalada y Phillipi.

Parque Nacional Torres del Paine

➔ *Colour map 6, B2.*

Parque Nacional Torres del Paine is spectacular. World-renowned for its challenging trekking, the park contains 15 peaks above 2000 m. At its centre is the glacier-topped granite massif Macizo Paine from which rise the vertical pink granite Torres (Towers) de Paine and below them the strange Cuernos de Paine (Horns), swooping buttresses of lighter granite under caps of darker sedimentary rock. From the vast Campo de Hielo Sur icecap on its western edge, four main glaciers (ventisqueros), Grey, Dickson, Zapata and Tyndall, drop into vividly coloured lakes formed by their meltwater: turquoise, ultramarine and pistachio expanses, some filled with wind-sculpted royal blue icebergs. Wherever you explore, there are constantly changing views of dramatic peaks and ice fields. Allow five to seven days to see the park properly. The park is also one of the best places on the continent for viewing rheas and guanacos. Apart from the 3500 guanacos, 24 other species of mammals can be seen here, including hares, foxes, skunks, huemules and pumas (the last two only very rarely). ➧ *For Sleeping, Eating and other listings, see pages 555-556.*

Ins and outs

Getting there The most practical way to get to Torres del Paine is with one of the many bus or tour companies that leave Puerto Natales daily. If you want to drive, hiring a pick-up from Punta Arenas or Puerto Natales is an economical proposition for a group (up to nine people), US$400 for four days. The road from Puerto Natales is being improved; it takes about three hours from Puerto Natales to the administration. Petrol is available at Río Serrano, but fill up, just in case. There is also a new road being built to the south side of the park which should cut the journey time to around two hours. ➧ *For further details, see Transport, page 556.*

Getting around Allow a week or 10 days to see the park properly. Most visitors will find that they get around on foot. However, there are minibuses running regularly between the CONAF administration and Guardería Laguna Amarga, as well as boats across Lago Pehoé. Roads inside the park are narrow and bendy with blind corners. Rangers keep a check on the whereabouts of all visitors: you are required to register and show your passport when entering the park or before setting off on any hike.

Tourist information There are entrances at Laguna Amarga, Lago Sarmiento and Laguna Azul, foreigners US$19 (proceeds are shared between all Chilean national parks), climbing fees US$1000. The park is administered by CONAF, which has an administration centre at the northern end of Lago del Toro ⓘ *T061-691931, open daily 0830-2000 in summer, 0830-1230, 1400-1830 off season*. It provides a good slide show at 2000 on Saturday and Sunday and there are also excellent exhibitions on the flora and fauna of the park in Spanish and English. There are six ranger stations (*guarderías*) in the park staffed by *guardaparques*, who give advice and also store luggage (not at Laguna Amarga).

Best time to visit The weather in the park can change in a few minutes. The warmest time is from December to March, although it can be wet and windy. The spring months of October and November are recommended for wild flowers. Rain and snowfall are heavier the further west you go and bad weather sweeps off the Campo de Hielo Sur without warning. Snow may prevent access in winter, but well-equipped hikers can do some good walking, when conditions are stable. For information in Spanish on weather conditions, phone the administration centre.

Torres tips

- The summer months (January and February) should be avoided due to overcrowding, especially at refugios and campsites.
- Litter has become a problem, especially around refugios and camping areas; take all your rubbish out of the park, including toilet paper.
- Most importantly, if you are using your own cooking stove, only cook in designated areas.

Trekking

There are about 250 km of well-marked trails. Visitors must keep to the trails: cross country trekking is not permitted. It is vital not to underestimate the unpredictability of the weather, nor the arduousness of some of the long hikes. Some paths are confusingly marked and it is all too easy to end up on precipices with glaciers or churning rivers below; be particularly careful to follow the path at the Paso John Gadner on the *Circuito* (see below). The only means of rescue are on horseback or by boat; the nearest helicopter is in Punta Arenas and high winds usually prevent its operation in the park.

Equipment

It is essential to be properly equipped against cold, wind and rain. A strong, streamlined, waterproof tent is essential if doing El Circuito (although you can hire camping equipment for a single night at most *refugios*). Also essential are protective clothing, strong waterproof footwear, compass, good sleeping bag and sleeping mat. In summer also take shorts and sunscreen. You are strongly advised to bring all necessary equipment and your own food from Puerto Natales and not to rely on availability at the *refugios* within the park; the small shops at the *refugios* (see below) and at the **Posada Río Serrano** are expensive and have a limited selection. Note that rats and mice are occasionally a problem around camping sites and the free *refugios*, so do not leave food in your pack (which may be chewed through), instead, the safest solution is to hang food in a bag on a wire. Note that you are not allowed to build fires in the park. A decent map is provided with your park entrance ticket; other maps (US$7) are obtainable in many places in Puerto Natales but most have one or two mistakes. The map produced by **Cartographia Digital** has been recommended as more accurate, as is the one produced by **Patagonia Interactiva.**

El Circuito → *In theory, lone walkers are not allowed on this route.*

The most popular trek is a circuit round the Torres and Cuernos del Paine. It is usually done anticlockwise starting from the *guardería* at **Laguna Amarga** and, although some people complete the route in less time, it normally takes five to six days. The circuit is often closed in winter because of snow; major rivers are crossed by footbridges, but these are occasionally washed away. From Laguna Amarga the route is north along the western side of the Río Paine to **Lago Paine**, before turning west to follow the lush pastures of the valley of the Río Paine to the southern end of **Lago Dickson** (it is possible to add a journey to the *campamento* by the Torres on day one of this route); the *refugio* at Lago Dickson lies in a breathtaking position in front of the icy white lake with mountains beyond. From Lago Dickson the path runs along the wooded valley of the **Río de los Perros**, past the Glaciar de los Perros, before climbing through bogs and up scree to **Paso John Gadner** (1241 m, the highest point on the route), then dropping steeply through forest to follow the Grey Glacier southeast to **Lago Grey**, continuing to **Lago Pehoé** and the administration centre. There are superb views en route, particularly from the top of Paso John Gadner.

The longest stretch is between Refugio Laguna Amarga and Refugio Dickson (30 km, 10 hours in good weather; two campsites on the way at Serón and Cairon), but the most difficult section is the very steep, slippery slope from Paso John Gadner down to the Campamento Paso; the path is not well signed at the top of the pass, and some people (including the author of this book!) have got dangerously lost and ended up on the Grey Glacier itself. Camping gear must be carried, as some *campamentos* (including Campamento Paso and Campamento Torres) do not have *refugios*.

Parque Nacional Torres del Paine

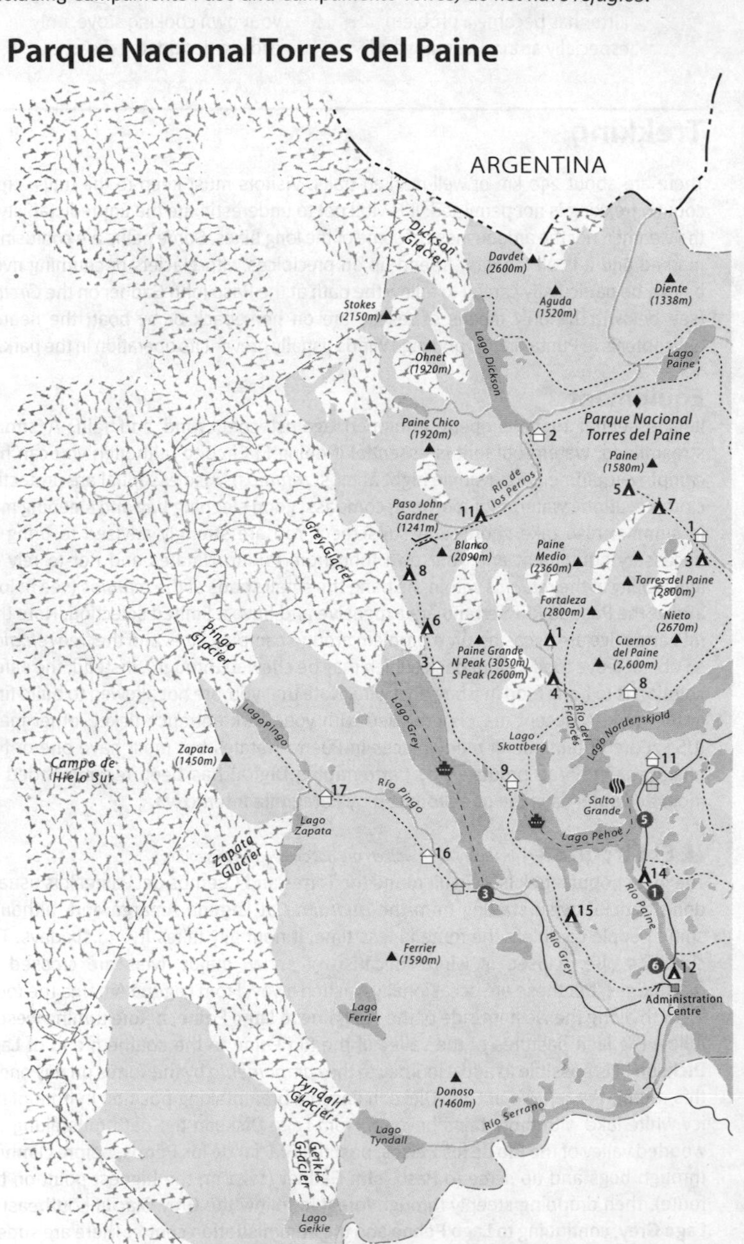

▲ The 'W'

No, it's not a typo, the 'W' is a popular alternative to El Circuito. This four- to five-day route can be completed without camping equipment as there is accommodation in *refugios* en route. It combines several of the hikes described separately below. From Refugio Laguna Amarga the first stage runs west via **Hostería Las Torres** and up the valley of the **Río Ascensio** via Refugio Chileno to the base of the **Torres del Paine** (see below). From here return to the Hostería Las Torres and then walk along the northern

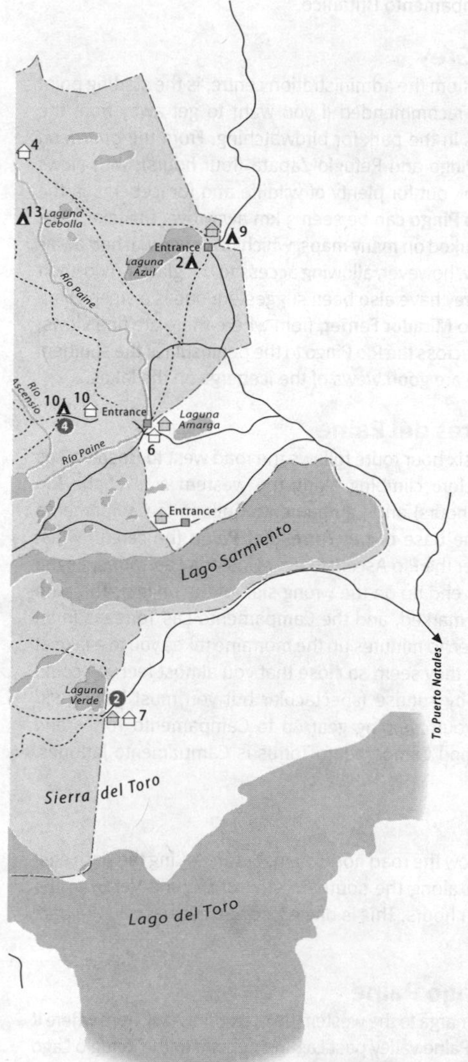

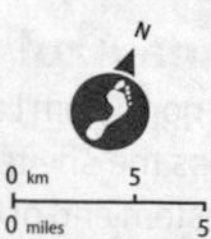

shore of **Lago Nordenskjold** via Refugio Los Cuernos to Campamento Italiano. From here climb the Valley of the **Río del Francés** (see below) before continuing to Refugio Pehoé. From here you can complete the third part of the 'W' by walking west along the northern shore of **Lago Grey** to Refugio Grey and the Grey Glacier before returning to Refugio Pehoé and the boat back across the lake to the Refugio Pudeto.

▲ Valley of the Río del Francés

From Refugio Pehoé this route leads north across undulating country along the western edge of **Lago Skottberg** to Campamento Italiano and then follows the valley of the Río del Francés, which climbs between Cerro Paine Grande and the Ventisquero del Francés (to the west) and the Cuernos del Paine (to the east) to Campamento Británico; the views from the mirador an hour's walk above Campamento Británico are superb. Allow two and a half hours from Refugio Pehoé to Campamento Italiano, two and a half hours further to Campamento Británico.

▲ Treks from Guardería Grey

Guardería Grey, 18 km west by road from the administration centre, is the starting point for a five-hour trek to Lago Pingo, recommended if you want to get away from the crowds, and one of the best routes in the park for birdwatching. From the *guardería* follow the **Río Pingo**, via Refugio Pingo and Refugio Zapata (four hours), with views south over Ventisquero Zapata (look out for plenty of wildlife and for icebergs in the lake) to reach the lake. **Ventisquero Pingo** can be seen 3 km away over the lake. Note there is a bridge over a river here, marked on many maps, which has been washed away. The river can be forded when it is low, however, allowing access to the glacier. Two short signposted walks from Guardería Grey have also been suggested: one is a steep climb up the hill behind the ranger post to **Mirador Ferrier**, from where there are fine views; the other is via a suspension bridge across the Río Pingo to the peninsula at the southern end of **Lago Grey**, from where there are good views of the icebergs on the lakes.

▲ To the base of the Torres del Paine

From Refugio Laguna Amarga, this six-hour route follows the road west to **Hostería Las Torres** (one and a half hours), before climbing along the western side of the **Río Ascensio** via Refugio Chileno (two hours) and Campamento Chileno to Campamento Las Torres (two hours), close to the base of the **Torres del Paine** (be careful when crossing the suspension bridge over the Río Ascensio near Hostería Las Torres, as the path is poorly marked and you can end up on the wrong side of the ravine). The path alongside the Río Ascensio is well marked, and the Campamento Las Torres is in an attractive wood (no *refugio*). A further 30 minutes up the morraine takes you to a lake at the base of the towers themselves; they seem so close that you almost feel you could touch them. To see the Torres lit by sunrise (spectacular but you must have good weather), it's well worth carrying your camping gear up to Campamento Torres and spending the night. One hour beyond Campamento Torres is Campamento Japonés, another good campsite.

▲ To Laguna Verde

From the administration centre follow the road north 2 km, before taking the path east over the **Sierra del Toro** and then along the southern side of **Laguna Verde** to the Guardería Laguna Verde. Allow four hours. This is one of the easiest walks in the park and may be a good first hike.

▲ To Laguna Azul and Lago Paine

This route runs north from Laguna Amarga to the western tip of **Laguna Azul**, from where it continues across the sheltered **Río Paine** valley past Laguna Cebolla to the Refugio Lago Paine at the western end of the lake. Allow 8½ hours. Good birdwatching opportunities.

Sleeping

Parque Nacional Torres del Paine

p550, map p552

LL Explora, Salto Chico on edge of Lago Pehoé, T061-411247, reservations: Av Américo Vespucci 80, p 7, Santiago, T02-2066060, www.explora.com. Ugly building but the most luxurious and comfortable in the park, offering spectacular views, pool, gym, tours and transfer from Punta Arenas.

LL Hostería Las Torres, head office Magallanes 960, Punta Arenas, T061-710050, www.lastorres.com. Probably the best of the Hosterías in the park. Recently expanded. Nice rooms, although strangely none has a particularly good view, good restaurant, disabled access, English spoken, horseriding, transport from Laguna Amarga ranger station. Some cheaper rooms also available.

LL Hostería Lago Grey, T061-410172, reservations T061-229512, www.austro hoteles.cl. Small rooms on edge of Lago Grey with views of Grey Glacier, decent restaurant.

LL-L Hostería Lago Tyndall, T061-413139, www.hosterialagotyndall.com. Expensive, cafeteria-style restaurant, electricity during the day only, good views. Not recommended.

LL-AL Hostería Pehoé, 5 km south of Pehoé ranger station, 11 km north of park administration, T061-411390, www.pe hoe.com. On an island with spectacular views across the lake to Cerro Paine Grande and Cuernos del Paine, this place does not make the most of its stunning location, rundown, overpriced. Reservations from **Turismo Pehoé** in Punta Arenas. Closed Apr-Oct.

L Hostería Mirador del Payne (Estancia Lazo), on the eastern edge of the park, reservations from Fagnano 585, Punta Arenas, T061-226930, www.miradordelpayne.com. Beautifully situated on Laguna Verde with spectacular views and good fishing, restaurant. Recommended but an inconvenient base for visiting the park; own transport essential, or you can trek to it from within the park.

L Posada Río Serrano, reservations: Baqueano Zamora, Baquedano 534B, Puerto Natales, T061-412911, www.baqueano zamora.com. An old *estancia*, much improved recently, some rooms with bath, some with shared facilities, breakfast extra, near park administration, with expensive but good restaurant and a shop.

Private refugios

Three companies between them run half of the refugios in the park, providing dormitory space only (bring your own sleeping bag or hire one for US$6). Prices are around US$30 per person with full board about US$30 extra. Take US dollars and your passport as you will save 19% tax. Refugios have kitchen facilities, hot showers and space for camping. Most will hire out tents for around US$12 per night. In high season accommodation and meals in the non-CONAF *refugios* should be booked in advance in Puerto Natales, or by asking staff in one *refugio* to radio another. In winter most of the refugios close, although one or two may stay open depending on the weather. Note that the administration rights for several refugios are up for tender in 2007 so the following details may well change.

Andescape Rrefugios, book through agencies in Puerto Natales or direct at Andescape, Eberhard 599, Puerto Natales, T061-412877, www.andescape.cl.

Fantastico Sur Refugios, book through agencies in Puerto Natales or direct on T061-710050, www.wcircuit.com.

Lodge Paine Grande, large, new *refugio* on the northwest edge of Lago Pehoe. In theory the most comfortable of the *refugios*, but in practice has had teething troubles and several complaints regarding customer service.

Refugio Chileno, valley of the Río Ascensio at the foot of the Torres. In addition, there are 6 free *refugios*: Zapata, Pingo, Laguna Verde, Laguna Amarga, Lago Paine and Pudeto. Most have cooking areas (wood stove or fireplace) but Laguna Verde and Pingo do not. These 2 are in very poor condition.

Refugio Grey, eastern shore of Lago Grey.

Refugio Lago Dickson, on the northern part of the circuit.

Refugio Las Torres, next to the **Hostería Las Torres** (see above).

Refugio Los Cuernos, on the northern shore of Lago Nordenskjold.

Vertice Refugios, book through agencies in Puerto Natales or www.verticepatagonia.cl.

Campsites

The wind tends to increase in the evening so it is a good idea to pitch tents early (by 1600). In addition to sites at the private *refugios*, there are the following sites (see map page for locations): **Lago Pehoé**, run by Turismo Río Serrano (see Sleeping, above), US$20 per site, max 6 persons, hot showers, beware mice. **Laguna Azul**, hot showers. **Las Torres**, run by Estancia Cerro Paine, US$4, hot showers. **Los Perros**, run by Andescape, with shop and hot showers. **Serón**, run by Estancia Cerro Paine, US$4, hot showers. **Serrano**, run by Turismo Río Serrano (see Sleeping, above), US$15 per site, maximum 6 persons, cold showers, basic.

Free camping is permitted in 7 other locations in the park; these sites are known as *campamentos*. Fires may only be lit at organized campsites, not at *campamentos*. The *guardaparques* expect people to have a stove if camping. These restrictions should be observed as forest fires are a serious hazard. *Guardaparques* also require campers to have a trowel to bury their waste. Equipment can be hired in Puerto Natales.

Activities and tours

Parque Nacional Torres del Paine

p550, map p552

Before booking a tour check all the details carefully and get a copy in writing, as there have been increasingly mixed reports of the quality of some tours. Many companies who claim to visit the Grey Glacier, for example, only visit Lago Grey (you see the glacier in the distance). After mid-Mar there is less public transport and trucks are irregular.

Several agencies in Puerto Natales offer 1-day tours by minibus, US$35 plus park entry; these give a good impression of the lower parts of the park, although you spend most of the day in the vehicle and many travellers would argue that you need to stay several days, or at least overnight, in the park to appreciate it fully. Cheaper tours are also available, but both guide and vehicle may not be as good as the established operators. There are many more operators based in Puerto Natales offering trekking, kayaking, ice-hiking, boat trips and other tours (see page 548)

Cascada Expediciones, T02-861 1777, www.cascada-expediciones.com, based in Santiago. Small group tours to Torres del Paine.

Experience Chile, T07977-223 326, www.experiencechile.org. Itineraries and accommodation in the region can be arranged by this UK-based operator.

Hostería Grey (see Sleeping) provides excursions by boat to the face of the Grey Glacier at 0900 and 1500 daily, 3½ hrs, US$60 per person. Book direct or through Turismo Runner in Puerto Natales.

Transport

Parque Nacional Torres del Paine

p550, map p552

Bus From early Nov to mid-Apr daily bus services run from Puerto Natales to the park, leaving between 0630 and 0800, and again at around 1430, 2½ hrs to Laguna Amarga, 3 hrs to the administration centre, US$10 one-way, US$16 open return (return tickets are not always interchangeable between different companies); return departures are usually around 1300 and 1800. Generally, buses will drop you at Laguna Amarga and pick you up at the administration centre for the return. The buses wait at Refugio Pudeto until the 1200 boat from Refugio Lago Pehoé arrives. Travel between 2 points within the park (eg Pudeto–Laguna Amarga), US$4. Services are provided by **Bus Sur**, Baquedano 534, T061-411325; **JB**, Prat 258, T061-412824; and **Fortaleza**, Prat 258, T061-410595. At other times, services by travel agencies are subject to demand; arrange your return date with the driver and try to coincide with other groups to keep costs down; **Luis Díaz** has been recommended, about US$17, minimum 3 persons. In season there are minibus connections from Laguna Amarga to the **Hostería Los Torres**, US$4, and from the administration centre to **Hostería Lago Grey**.

To go from Torres del Paine to **El Calafate** (Argentina), either return to Puerto Natales and catch a bus, or take a bus or hitch from the park to Villa Cerro Castillo and try to link with the Natales–Calafate bus schedule. In season, there is a direct bus service from the park to El Calafate with **Chaltén Travel**, US$50.

Boat A boat service runs across Lago Pehoé from near the Lodge Paine Grande to Refugio Pudeto, daily, 30 mins, US$19 one-way, 1 piece of baggage free, tickets available on board. Departures from Paine Grande 1000, 1230, 1830; from Pudeto 0930, 1200, 1800. Reduced service off season, no service May-Sep. For more information call T061-411380.

Tierra del Fuego

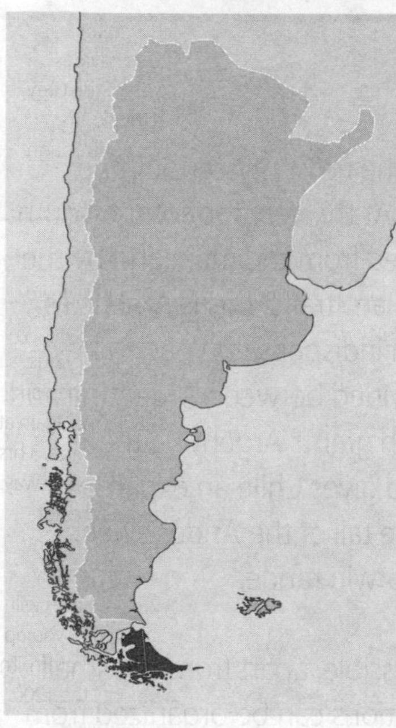

Footprint features

Introduction

The island of Tierra del Fuego is the most mysterious and captivating part of all Patagonia. At the very foot of the South American continent and separated from the mainland by the intricate waterways of the Magellan straits, this is America's last remaining wilderness and an indispensable part of any trip to the south. The island is divided between Argentina and Chile by a north-south line, which grants Argentina the Atlantic and southern coasts, and gives Chile an expanse of wilderness to the west, where the tail of the Andes sweeps east in the form of the mighty Darwin range.

The Chilean side is largely inaccessible, apart from the small town of Porvenir, though expeditions can be organized from Punta Arenas to take you hiking and trout fishing. Glaciers and jagged peaks give a dramatic backdrop to the Argentine city of Ushuaia, the island's main centre, set in a serene natural harbour on the Beagle Channel, with views of the Dientes de Navarino mountains on the Chilean island of Navarino opposite. Sail from Ushuaia along the channel to the pioneer home of Harberton; to Cape Horn; or even to Antarctica. Head into the small but picturesque Parque Nacional Tierra del Fuego, for strolls around Bahía Lapataia and steep climbs with magnificent views out along the channel. The mountain slopes are covered in lenga forest, and if you visit in autumn you might think the name 'Land of Fire' derives from the blaze of scarlet and orange. Elsewhere on the island, lakes and valleys can be explored on foot or on horseback, and in winter the valleys are perfect for cross-country skiing, while the slopes at Cerro Castor offer good powder snow, and skiing with spectacular views of the end of the world.

★ Don't miss…

1 **Fly fishing in the Río Grande** Take a trip into the Chilean wilderness, or stay at the famous Argentine Estancia María Behety to fish huge trout, pages 562 and 567.

2 **Dientes de Navarino** Fly to Isla Navarino and trek the mighty teeth – only for the intrepid, page 563.

3 **Yámana Museum, Ushuaia** The moving story of the island's original inhabitants, now tragically lost, page 570.

4 **Beagle Channel** Imagine the experiences of those early explorers as you take a comfortable boat to seal islands and the calm haven of Harberton, page 571.

5 **Parque Nacional Tierra del Fuego** Stroll around the bay for magical views of the end of the world, page 572.

Ins and outs

Getting there

Air The **Argentine Tierra del Fuego** is easy to reach with several flights daily from Buenos Aires to Río Grande and Ushuaia, and less frequent flights from El Calafate, and some other towns in Patagonia. Flights are heavily booked in advance throughout the summer months. **Chilean Tierra del Fuego** is less easily accessed by air, but there are five flights a week from Punta Arenas to Porvenir in the summer, and four a week to Puerto Williams on Isla Navarino, also summer only, which is almost impossible to reach by boat.

Ferry and bus There are two places where ferries cross to Tierra del Fuego: from **Tres Puentes**, just north of Punta Arenas to **Porvenir**, and further east across **Primera Angostura** at Punta Delgada, both crossings on Chilean territory. All buses from mainland Argentina use the quicker and more frequent Punta Delgada crossing, and from Punta Arenas, buses take the road northeast to Punta Delgada, and cross by ferry there. **Via Punta Delgada** The crossing takes 15-minutes, and boats run roughly every 40 mins from 0830-2300. There's a cosy tea room Bahia Azul on the northern side, with hot snacks and toilets. Foot passengers free, US$23 per car.

Argentine/Chile border The Chilean/Argentine border is at the Argentine town of San Sebastián, 128 km south of where the ferry arrives at Punta Espora, and – confusingly – 14 km east of a Chilean town also called San Sebastián. The border at Argentine San Sebastián is open 24 hours, with a basic ACA motel, T02964-425542; and a service station open 0700-2300. From here Route 3, is paved to Río Grande.

Via Punta Arenas–Porvenir There is a daily ferry crossing (summer) from Tres Puentes, just north of Punta Arenas to Porvenir, and from here a 225 km road runs east to Río Grande (six hours) via the border at San Sebastián. (By road, Punta Arenas and Punta Delgada are connected by a good road, RN255). From Punta Arenas, bus A or E from Av Magallanes goes to Tres Puentes, or *colectivo* 15, US$0.50; taxi US$4. In season, the *Melinka* sails Tues to Sun. Less frequently off season. The crossing takes 2 hrs 20mins, and can be rough and cold, US$8 pp, US$12 per bike, US$50 per vehicle. Timetable dependent on tides and subject to change: check in advance. Reservations essential especially in summer (at least 24 hrs in advance for cars), obtainable from Transbordadora Austral Broom, in Punta Arenas, Bulnes 05075, T218100, www.tabsa.cl (or T580089 in Porvenir).

Getting around

There are good bus links from Punta Arenas to Río Grande in Argentina, with an option of going via Porvenir, along the decent loop of road on the Chilean side. From Porvenir your options are limited to a *ripio* road around Bahía Inútil to near Lago Blanco, though there's no public transport here. Argentine Tierra del Fuego is much easier to get around, via Route 3 between Río Grande and Ushuaia with several buses a day. A fan of roads spreads out south and west, from Río Grande to the estancias in the Argentine side, but these are unpaved, and best attempted in a 4WD vehicle. A good *ripio* road leads from 40 km east of Ushuaia to Harberton and Estancia Moat on the south coast, and part of the way along the north coast to Estancia San Pablo; no public transport here either.

Background

Tierra del Fuego's narrated history began with the early 16th century explorers, but the island had been inhabited by indigenous groups for some 10,000 years. The most numerous of these groups, the Onas (also known as the Selk'nam), were hunter-gatherers in the north, living mainly on guanaco which they shot with bow and arrow. The southeastern corner of the island was inhabited by the Haus or Hausch, also hunter-gatherers. The Yaganes or Yámana lived along the Beagle Channel and on the islands further south, and were seafaring people who survived mainly on seafood, fish and birds, physically smaller than the Onas but with a strongly developed upper body for rowing long distances. The fourth group, the Alacalufe, lived in the west of Tierra del Fuego as well as on the Chonos Archipelago, surviving by fishing and hunting seals.

The first Europeans to visit the island came with the Portuguese navigator Fernão Magalhães (Magellan), who, in 1520, sailed through the channel that now bears his name. It was Magellan who named the island Land of Fire when he saw the smoke from many fires lit along the shoreline. As a result of numerous maritime disasters, including the failure of Sarmiento de Gamboa's attempt at colonizing the Straits in 1584, the indigenous population were left undisturbed for three centuries.

Fitz Roy and Darwin's scientific visits in 1832 and 1833 recorded some fascinating interaction with the indigenous peoples, four of whom Fitz Roy had earlier brought to London to see if they could be 'civilized', and of whom he now returned the surviving three. Fitz Roy and Darwin's visits were a precursor to attempts to convert the indigenous groups to Christianity so that the island could be used by white settlers without fear of attack. Several disastrous missions followed, encountering stiff resistance from the inhabitants. In 1884, Reverend Thomas Bridges founded a mission at Ushuaia and was the first European to learn the Yámana language, and compiled his Yámana-English dictionary. He soon realised that his original task was a destructive one. The purpose of the missionary work had been to facilitate lucrative sheep farming in the island, however, the Ona were attracted to the 'white guanacos' on their land and hunting sheep proved far easier than the faster footed guanaco. The colonists offered two sheep for each Ona that was killed (proof was provided by a pair of Ona ears), but Bridges realized that he would rather protect the Onas. The indigenous groups were further ravaged by epidemics of European diseases. In a desperate attempt to save the Ona, Salesian missionaries founded three missions in the Magellan Straits in the early 20th century, but, stripped of their land, the Ona lost the will to live; the last Ona died in 1999. The Hausch also died out. One old Yámana lady presently survives near Puerto Williams and there is a handful of Alacalufe at Puerto Edén in the Chonos Archipelago.

Imprecision in the original colonial land division and the greed of the rush southwards led to border disputes between Argentina and Chile, which still rumble on today. The initial settlement of the dispute in 1883 was followed by a desire by both governments to populate the area by allocating large expanses of land for sheep farming. The main beneficiaries of this policy on Tierra del Fuego were the Menendez and Braun families, already established in Punta Arenas.

For many years, the main economic activity of the northern part of the island was sheep farming, but Argentine government tax incentives to companies in the 1970s led to the establishment of new industries in Río Grande and Ushuaia and a rapid growth in the population of both cities; the subsequent withdrawal of incentives has produced increasing unemployment and migration. Tourism is increasingly important in Ushuaia.

For a detailed narrative account of Tierra del Fuego, the best book is the classic by Lucas Bridges, *Uttermost Part of the Earth*, out of print but easily obtained on www.abebooks.co.uk. Also fascinating is *Patagonia, Natural history, pre-history and ethnography at the uttermost part of the earth* (British Museum press). And *Savage – The Life and Times of Jemmy Button* by Nick Hazelwood (Hodder & Stoughton) is also recommended.

Chilean Tierra del Fuego

The Chilean half of Tierra del Fuego is in two sections: the western half of Isla Grande, the main island, and the whole of Isla Navarino, to the south of the main island. Much less developed than the Argentine side of Tierra del Fuego, there are just two small towns where Chile's Fuegians are mostly concentrated: Porvenir on Isla Grande, easily reached by ferry from Punta Arenas, and Puerto Williams on Isla Navarino, which can only be reached by a flight from Punta Arenas. The northern part of Isla Grande is flat steppe, but the south is dominated by the Darwin range of mountains, which provide a dramatic visual backdrop, even if you can't easily get to them. Tourism on Chilean territory is very limited, but it's possible to organise trekking tours from Punta Arenas, and there are plenty of fishing lodges offering magnificent trout fishing, particularly on Río Grande. » *For Sleeping, Eating and other listings, see pages 564-566.*

Porvenir » *pp564-566.*

→ *Phone code: +56 (0)61 Colour map 6, C3 Population: 5,100*

Chilean Tierra del Fuego has a population of 7000, most of whom live in the pretty small town of Porvenir – the only town on the Chilean half of the main island. Founded in 1894 in the gold boom, when many people came seeking fortunes from Croatia and Chiloe, Porvenir is a quiet place with a wide open pioneer feel, streets of neat brightly painted houses of corrugated zinc, and quaint tall domed trees lining the main avenue. There is a small museum, the **Museo Fernando Cordero Rusque**, Samuel Valdivieso 402, with archaeological and photographic displays on the Onas; good displays on natural history and the early gold diggers and sheep farmers. There's little else to do here, but you could stroll around the plaza, with its **Iglesia San Francisco de Sales**, and down to the shoreside promenade, where there's a strange collection of 19th-century farm machinery, and a striking wooden monument to the Selknam.

Tourist information ⓘ *Padre Mario Zavattaro No 424, T/F(56-61)580094, www.patagonia-chile.com.* But there's more helpful information at a tiny kiosk on the waterfront, which also sells handicrafts, kuanip@entelchile.net.

Beyond Porvenir

Beyond Porvenir there is wonderfully wild virgin territory to explore. However, if you want an adventure, your best bet is to arrange a trip through tour operators in Punta Arenas, since there's still very little infrastructure on the Chilean side of the island. **Aonikenk** is recommended, offering several days' trekking into the remote mountains in the south of the island, horse riding and fly fishing. There are two tour operators in Porvenir itself, offering tours through the Cordon Baquedano to see the areas where gold was mined – recommended for great views of the Magellan strait and visits to traditional sheep farming estancias.

The **fly fishing** in this area is becoming world renowned and it's now possible to stay in several comfortable lodges in Río Grande, Lago Escondido and Lago Blanco. This area is rich in brown trout, sea run brook trout and steelheads, weighing 2-14 kg, and you could expect to fish an average of eight trout a day in season. See specialist fly fishing tour operators, or **Aonikenk.** The season runs from October 15th to April 14th, with the best fishing from January to April.

Camerón

About 90 km east of Porvenir, roads head north to San Sebastián and south to **Camerón**. This large farm settlement is the only other community of any size on the

Chilean part of the island and lies 149 km southeast of Porvenir on the opposite shore of Bahía Inútil. This wonderful windswept bay, with views of distant hills and the snow capped Darwin range all along the horizon, was named 'useless' by British engineers making a hydrographic survey here in 1827 because it has no useful port. Nevertheless, as you near Cameron, the southern mountains loom ahead and the road passes secluded canyons and bays, interspersed with a few farms, and the whole feel is dramatic, isolated and somehow rather magical.

From Cameron a road runs southeast past an airfield and into the hills, through woods where guanacos hoot and run off into glades and the banks are covered with red and purple moss. The north shores of **Lago Blanco** can be reached by cutting through the woods from Sección Río Grande, with superb views of the mountains surrounding the lake and the snows in the south, or from Estancia Vicuña. It's essential to organize any trip to this area through a reliable tour operator with the infrastructure.

From Estancia Vicuña a trail leads southwest to the **Río Azopardo**, which also offers **trout fishing** (sleeping at Estancia Almirantazgo). South of here trails run across the Darwin Range to the **Estancia Yendegaia** near the Beagle Channel, a wonderful area for horse riding. For trips into this wild and undiscovered country, contact Aonikenk in Punta Arenas, www.aonikenk.com.

Isla Navarino » pp564-566.

Situated on the southern shore of the Beagle Channel, Isla Navarino is totally unspoilt and beautiful, offering great geographical diversity, thanks to the Dientes de Navarino range of mountains, with peaks over 1000 m, covered with southern beech forest up to 500 m, and south of that, great plains covered with peat bogs, with many lagoons abundant in flora. The island was the centre of the indigenous Yaganes culture, and there are 500 archaeological sites, the oldest dated as 3000 years old. Guanacos and condors can be seen inland, as well as large numbers of beavers, which were introduced to the island and have done considerable damage. The flight from Punta Arenas is beautiful, with superb views of Tierra del Fuego, the Cordillera Darwin, the Beagle Channel and the islands stretching south to Cape Horn.

Puerto Williams → *Phone code: 061. Colour map 7, C2. Population: 2,500.*

The only settlement of any size on the island is Puerto Williams, a Chilean naval base situated about 50 km east of Ushuaia in Argentine seas across the Beagle Channel. Puerto Williams is the southernmost permanently inhabited town in the world; 50 km east-south-east is Puerto Toro, the southernmost permanently inhabited settlement on earth. Some maps mistakenly mark a road from Puerto Williams to Puerto Toro, but it doesn't exist; access is only by sea. Due to the long-running border dispute with Argentina here, Puerto Williams is controlled by the Chilean Navy. Outside the Naval headquarters, you can see the bow section of the *Yelcho*, the tug chartered by Shackleton to rescue men stranded on Elephant Island (see box, page).

Your main purpose for visiting the island is likely to be the trekking on the Dientes de Navarino, but you should take time to explore the indigenous heritage here too. It's beautifully documented in the **Museo Martín Gusinde** ⓘ *Mon-Thu 1000-1300, 1500-1800, 1500-1800 Sat and Sun, US$1*, known as the Museo del Fin del Mundo ('End of the World Museum') is full of information about vanished indigenous tribes, local wildlife and the famous voyages by Charles Darwin and Fitz Roy of the *Beagle*. A visit is highly recommended. A kilometre west of the town is the yacht club (one of Puerto Williams' two nightspots), whose wharf is made from a sunken 1930s Chilean warship. **Tourist information** ⓘ *Municipalidad de Cabos de Hornos, Pres. Ibañez 130, T621011, isotop@mitierra.cl*. Ask for maps and details on hiking. The town also has a bank, supermarkets and hospital.

Exploring the island

For superb views, climb **Cerro Bandera**, which is reached by a path from the dam 4 km west of the town (three- to four-hour round trip, steep, take warm clothes). There is excellent trekking around the Dientes de Navarino range, the southernmost trail in the world, through impressive mountain landscape, frozen lagoons and snowy peaks, giving superb views over the Beagle Channel. It's a challenging hike, over a distance of 53 km in five days, possible only from December to March, and a good level of fitness is needed. There is no equipment rental on island. Ask for information in the tourist office at Puerto Williams, but it's best to go with an organised expedition from Punta Arenas, see **Aonikenk**, in tour operators, below.

Beyond Cerro Bandera, a road leads 56 km west of Puerto Williams to Puerto Navarino. There is little or no traffic on this route and it is very beautiful, with forests of lengas stretching right down to the water's edge. You can also visit Villa Ukika, 2 km east of town, the place where the last descendants of the Yaganes people live, relocated from their original homes at Caleta Mejilones, which was the last indigenous reservation in the province, inhabited by hundreds of Yagana descendants. At **Mejillones**, 32 km from Puerto Williams, is a graveyard and memorial to the Yámana people. Just before Estancia Santa Rosa (10 km further on), a path is said to cross the forest, lakes and beaver dams to Wulaia (four to six hours), where the *Beagle* anchored in 1833; however, even the farmer at Wulaia gets lost following this track.

Cape Horn

It is possible to catch a boat south from Isla Navarino to Cape Horn (the most southerly piece of land on earth apart from Antarctica). There is one pebbly beach on the north side of the island; boats anchor in the bay and passengers are taken ashore by motorized dinghy. A rotting stairway climbs the cliff above the beach, up to the building where three marines run the naval post. A path leads from here to the impressive monument of an albatross overlooking the wild, churning waters of the Drake Passage below.

Sleeping

Porvenir *p562*

A Hostería Los Flamencos, Tte Merino 018, T061-580049, www.hosterialosflamencos.com. One of the town's best places to stay with wonderful views of the bay, good food, and a pleasant place for a drink. Recommended. Also organises tours.

C Hostería y Turismo Yendegaia, Croacia 702, T061-581665, www.turismoyendegaia.com. A charming, bright yellow house just 2 blocks from the plaza, built by a Croatian pioneer in 1926, this has 7 light, comfortable rooms with bath and TV, a good restaurant, lots of tourist information from the in-house travel company. Recommended.

C Rozas, Phillippi 296, T061-580088. With bath, hot water, heating, restaurant and bar, internet, laundry facilities. Recommended.

D Hostel Kawi, Pedro Silva 144, T061-581638, www.tierradelfuegoandtrouts.com. A comfortable hostal, with rooms for 3, all with bath, and offering fly fishing trips on the island.

Beyond Porvenir *p562*

If you get stuck in the wilds, note that it is almost always possible to camp or bed down in a barn at an estancia.

B-E Hostería de la Frontera, San Sebastián, T061-696 004, escabini@tie.cl. Rooms with bath and a decent restaurant. Avoid the more basic accommodation in an annexe.

B-E Hostería Tunkelen, Cerro Sombrero, 46 km south of Primera Angostura, T061-345001, hosteria_tunkelen@hotmail.com. Rooms and dormitory accommodation. Recommended.

Puerto Williams *p563*

You can also stay at private houses.

A-B Hostería Wala, on the edge of Lauta bay, T061-621114, 2 km out of town. Splendid walks in the area. Very hospitable.

C Pensíon Temuco, Piloto Pardo 244, T061-621113. Price per person for full board, comfortable, good food, hot showers. Slightly overpriced, but recommended. Good breakfasts.

D Hostería Camblor, T061-621033, hosteria camblor@terra.cl. Price per person for full board. Gets very booked up. Good value.
E pp **Hostal Yagan**, Piloto Pardo 260, T061-621334, hostalyagan@hotmail.com. Singles and doubles. Good meals available. Clean and comfortable, friendly, tours offered.
E Jeanette Talavera, Maragaño 168, T061-621150, www.simltd.com. Small dormitories, shared bathrooms, kitchen and laundry facilities, also organizes sailing trips, treks and other activities.
E pp **Residencial Onashaga**, Uspashun 15, T061-621564, run by Señor Ortiz. Basic accommodation but a warm welcome. Good meals, helpful, full board available.

Eating

Porvenir *p562*
There are many lobster fishing camps nearby, where fishermen prepare lobster on the spot.
Club Croata, Senoret y Phillippi. On waterfront, good food, lively.
Hostería Los Flamencos, Tte Merino 018, Very good food – as above.
Hostería y Turismo Yendegaia, Croacia 702 Great range of seafood – as above.
Restaurante Puerto Montt, Croacia 1169. Recommended for seafood.

Puerto Williams *p563*
There are several grocery stores; prices are very high because of the remoteness. Away from **Club Naútico**, nightlife is at the **Dientes de Navarino**, a bar in the plaza.

Activities and tours

Porvenir *p562*
For adventure tourism and trekking, it's best to go through tour operators in Punta Arenas.
Hostería y Turismo Yendegaia, Croacia 702, T061-581665, www.turismo yendegaia.com. Lots of conventional tours and some fishing.
Turismo Aonikenk, Magallanes 619, T061-221982, www.aonikenk.com. An excellent company offering adventures and hiking on Isla Navarino, south of Porvenir and on the mainland. Superb expedition around Dientes de Navarino, fly fishing and horse riding.
Turismo Cordillera de Darwin, Croacia 675, T061-580206, www.explorepatagonia.cl For tours of the island from a day to a week.

Puerto Williams *p563*
Sailing
Captain Ben Garrett offers recommended adventure sailing in his schooner *Victory* in Dec and Jan, including special trips to Ushuaia and voyages to Cape Horn, the glaciers, Puerto Montt and Antarctica. Write to **Victory Cruises**, Annex No 1 Puerto Williams; or call collect to Punta Arenas and leave a message.

Transport

Porvenir *p562*
Air Aerovías DAP, Señoret s/n, Porvenir, T061-580089, www.aeroviasdap.cl, flies from Punta Arenas (weather and bookings permitting), twice daily Mon-Sat, US$50 one way. Heavily booked so make sure you have your return reservation confirmed.

Bus Buses from Punta Arenas to Ushuaia don't take on passengers here. **Transportes Gessell**, Duble Almeyda 257, T061-580488 (also in Punta Arenas at José Menéndez 556, T061-222896) runs buses to Río Grande (Argentina), Tue and Sat 1400, 5hrs, US$20; return service Wed and Sun 0800. Local buses run to Cameron from Manuel Señor, in theory Mon and Fri 1700, US$13.

Ferry *The Melinka* sails from Tres Puentes (5 km north of Punta Arenas; catch bus A or E from Av Magallanes, US$1; taxi US$3) to Bahía Chilota, 5 km west of Porvenir, Tue-Sun 0900 with an extra afternoon sailing Tue-Thu in season, 2½ hrs, pedestrians US$8, cars US$50. The boat returns from Porvenir in the afternoon Tue-Sun.

Timetable dependent on tides and subject to change: check in advance. The crossing can be rough and cold; watch for dolphins. Reservations are essential especially in summer (at least 24 hrs in advance for cars); obtainable from **Transbordadora Austral Broom**, Bulnes 05075, Punta Arenas, T061- 218100 (T061-580089 in Porvenir), www.tabsa.cl.

The ferry service from Punta Delgada on the mainland to Punta Espora, 80 km north of Porvenir, departs every 40 mins 0830-2300 (schedules vary with the tides) and takes just 15 mins, pedestrians US$4, cars US$25. This is the main route for buses and trucks between Ushuaia and mainland Argentina. Before 1000 most space is taken by trucks.

Puerto Williams *p563*
Air Aerovías DAP, Centro Comercial s/n, T061-621051, www.aeroviasdap.cl, flies 20-seater Cessna aircraft from Punta Arenas Mon-Sat, departure time varies, 1¼ hrs, US$64 one way. Book well in advance; there are long waiting lists. Luggage allowance 10 kg (US$2 per kg extra). Aeropetrel will charter a plane from Puerto Williams to Cape Horn (US$2600 for 8-10 people).

Ferry There are no regular sailings to Isla Navarino from Ushuaia (Argentina). The following depart from Punta Arenas: Austral Broom ferry *Cruz Australis*, www.tabsa.cl, once a week, 36 hrs, US$130 for a reclining seat, US$170 for a bunk, meals included; Navarino (contact Carlos Aguilera, 21 de Mayo 1460, Punta Arenas, T061-228066), 3rd week of every month, 12 passengers, US$180 one way; *Beaulieu* cargo boat, once a month, US$350 return, 6 days. Some cruises to Ushuaia also stop at Puerto Williams.

Cape Horn *p564*
Crucero Australis cruises from Ushuaia stop at Cape Horn. In addition, the naval vessel *PSG Micalvi*, which sails once every 3 months from Punta Arenas via Puerto Williams, may take passengers to Cape Horn for US$250 (letters of recommendation will help). Navy and port authorities in Puerto Williams may deny any knowledge, but everyone else knows when a boat is due; ask at the Armada in Punta Arenas . Otherwise ask at the yacht club about hitching a ride to Cape Horn.

Directory

Porvenir *p562*
Currency exchange Available at Estrella del Sur, Santos Mardones.

Puerto Williams *p563*
Post office Closes 1900. **Telephone** CTC, Mon-Sat 0930-2230, Sun 1000-1300, 1600-2200.

Argentine Tierra del Fuego

The Argentine half of Tierra del Fuego is much easier to visit than the Chilean half, and more rewarding. The northern half of the island is wind-swept steppe, and its only town, Río Grande, once rich on oil, is now very faded. But pause before you head straight for Ushuaia to visit two splendid estancias. Viamonte was built by Lucas Bridges to protect the indigenous Ona peoples, and is an evocative place to stay, while Estancia María Behety is world famous for its brown trout fishing. The landscape turns to hills as you head south, and there's a lovely silent lake, Lago Fagnano, ideal for a picnic.

Ushuaia is the island's centre, beautifully set on the Beagle Channel, with a backdrop of steep mountains. With a picturesque national park on its doorstep, boat trips up the Beagle Channel to the Bridges' other superb estancia Harberton, and a ski centre at Cerro Castor, there's plenty to keep you here. Huskies will draw your sledge in winter, and in summer you can walk around Bahía Lapataia and contemplate the serenity of the end of the world. ▸▸ *For Sleeping, Eating and other listings, see pages 573-580.*

Río Grande ▸▸ *pp573-580.*

→ *Phone code: 02964 Colour map 6, C4 Population: 53,000*

Río Grande is a sprawling modern coastal town, the centre for a rural sheep-farming community that grew rapidly in the 1970s, with government tax incentives. The new population was stranded when benefits were withdrawn, leading to unemployment and emigration, and leaving a rather sad, dusty town today. The people are friendly but there's little culture, and you're most likely to visit in order to change buses. There are a couple of good places to stay, however, and a small museum worth seeing, as well as the splendid historical Estancia Viamonte nearby. And if keen on fishing, Río Grande's legendary monster brown trout can be plucked from the water at Estancia María Behety.

Sights

The city's architecture is a chaotic mixture of smart nouveau riche houses and humble wooden and tin constructions. It seems to have defied municipal efforts at prettification, and the series of peeling and graffitied concrete 'sculptures' along some of the avenues do little to cheer it up. But if you do get stuck here, you could trace the city's history through sheep, missions, pioneers and oil in its interesting small museum, **Museo de la Ciudad** ⓘ *Alberdi 555, T02964-430414, Tue-Fri 1000-1700*. The city was founded by Fagnano's Salesian mission in 1893, and you can visit the original building **La Candelaria** ⓘ *11 km north, T02964-421642, Mon-Sat 1000-1230, 1500-1900, Sun 1500-1900, US$1.50*, whose museum has displays of natural history and indigenous artefacts, with strawberry plantations, piglets and an aviary. **Tourist office** ⓘ *Rosales 350, T02964-431324, www.tierradelfuego.org.ar, Mon-Fri 0900-2100, Sat 1000-1700*, small but helpful in the blue-roofed hut on the plaza.

Around Río Grande

Estancia Viamonte, on the coast, 40 km away south, is a working sheep farm with a fascinating history. Here, Lucas Bridges, son of Tierra del Fuego's first settler, built a home to protect the large tribe of indigenous Onas, who were fast dying out. The estancia is still inhabited by his descendants, who can take you riding and to see the life of the farm. Also a house to rent and superb accommodation. Wonderful. Highly recommended. **Estancia María Behety**, built by the sheep farming millionaire José Menéndez, is a heaven for brown trout fishing.

Río Grande to Ushuaia » pp573-580.

From Río Grande, several roads fan out south west to the heart of the island, though this area is little inhabited. The paved road south, Route 3, continues across wonderfully open land, more forested than the expanses of Patagonian steppe further north, and increasingly hilly as you near Ushuaia. After around 160 km, you could turn left along a track to the coast, to find **Estancia Cabo San Pablo**. A simple working estancia in a beautiful position, with beautiful native woodland for walking and riding, birdwatching and fishing. Also other trips to places of interest within reach. Open all year, but reserve in advance. Route 3 then climbs up above Lago Fagnano and Tolhuin.

Tolhuin and around → *Phone code: 02964*

This is a friendly, small settlement close to the shore of Lago Fagnano, a large expanse of water, right at the heart of Tierra del Fuego. The village has a stretch of beach nearby and remains quiet and little exploited. There's a YPF service station just off the main road, but it's worth driving into the village itself for the famous bakery **La Union**, where you can buy delicious bread, empanadas and fresh *facturas* (pastries). It's also a good source of information. There's a tiny, friendly **tourist office** ⓘ *near the YPF station, 0900-1500*, with very helpful staff. Handicrafts are available at El Encuentro including fine leather goods, half a block from tourist information. For horse riding contact **Sendero del Indio**, T156-15258 sonia@netcombbs.com.ar. From the village a road leads down to the tranquil lake shore, where there are a couple of good places to stay. Further along Route 3, 50 km from Ushuaia, a road to the right swoops down to **Lago Escondido**, a fjord-like lake with steep deep green mountains descending into the water.

Ushuaia » pp573-580.

→ *Phone code: 02901 Colour map 6, C4 Population: 45,000*

The most southerly town in the world, Ushuaia's setting is spectacular. Its brightly coloured houses look like toys against the dramatic backdrop of vast jagged mountains. Opposite are the forbidding peaks of Isla de Navarino, and between flows the serene green Beagle Channel. Sailing those waters you can just imagine how it was for Darwin, arriving here in 1832, and for those early settlers, the Bridges in 1871. Though the town has expanded in recent years, sprawling untidily along the coast, Ushuaia still retains the feel of a pioneer town, isolated and expectant. There are lots of places to stay, which fill up entirely in January, a fine museum, and some great fish restaurants. There is spectacular landscape to be explored in all directions, with good treks in the accessible Parque Nacional Tierra del Fuego just to the west of the city, and more adventurous expeditions offered into the wild heart of the island, trekking, climbing or riding. There's splendid cross country skiing nearby in winter, as well as downhill skiing too, at Cerro Castor. And to the east, along a beautiful stretch of coastline is the historic estancia of Harberton, which you can reach by a boat trip along the Beagle Channel. Ushuaia is also the starting point for expeditions to Antarctica.

Ins and outs

Getting there There are daily flights from Buenos Aires and Río Gallegos, and frequent flights from El Calafate and Punta Arenas, as well as weekly flights from other Patagonian towns to Ushuaia's airport, on a peninsula in the Beagle channel, close to the centre. Airport information T02901-423970. A taxi to the centre costs US$3. Buses and minibuses from Río Grande arrive at their respective offices around town. » *See transport, page 579, for further details.*

Getting around It's easy to walk around the town in a morning, since all its sights are close together, and you'll find banks, restaurants, hotels and shops along San Martín, which runs parallel to the shore, a block north of the coast road, Maipú. Boat trips leave from the *Muelle Turístico* (tourist pier) by a small plaza, 25 de Mayo on the

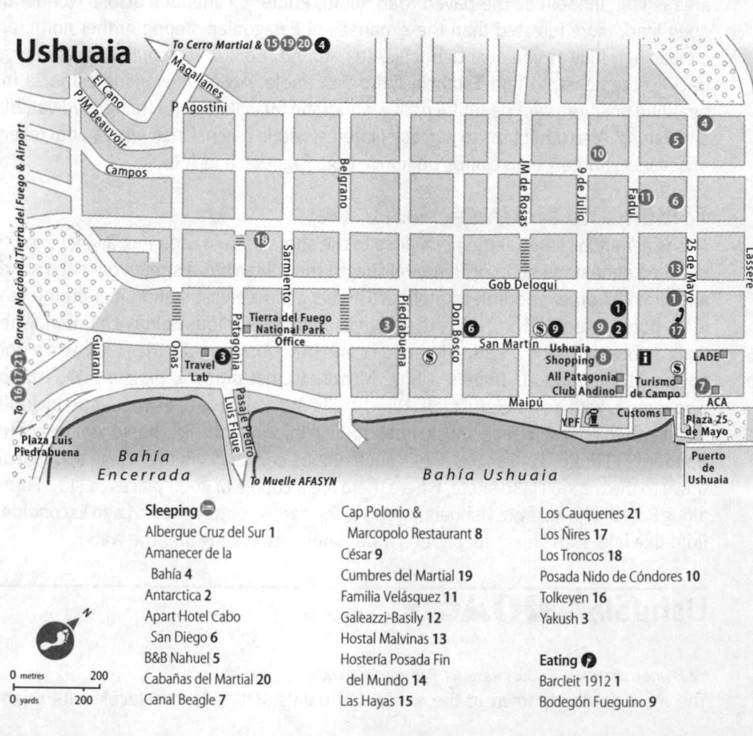

seafront, Avenida Maipú between calles 25 de Mayo and Laserre. Ushuaia is very well organized for tourism, and there are good local buses to the national park and other sights, as well as many boat trips.

Best time to visit Ushuaia is at its most beautiful in autumn, when the dense forests all around are turned rich red and yellow, and there are many bright clear days. Summer is best for trekking, when maximum temperatures are around 15°C, but try to avoid January, when the city is swamped with tourists. Late February is much better. The ski season is mid-June to October, when temperatures are around zero, but the wind drops.

Tourist information ⓘ *San Martín 674, corner with Fadul, T/F02901-432000, www.tierradelfuego.org.ar, Mon-Fri 0800-2200, Sat, Sun and holidays 0900-2000. Also an office at the pier (Muelle Turístico), T02901-437666, and a desk at the airport, T02901-423970.* The best tourist office in Argentina, the friendly and helpful staff and speak several languages. They have a map and a series of leaflets about all the things to see and do, and bus and boat times. **Tierra del Fuego National Park Office** ⓘ *San Martín 1395, T02901-421315*, has a basic map of the park.

Background

Founded in 1884 after missionary Thomas Bridges had established his mission in these inhospitable lands (see box, page) Ushuaia attracted many pioneers in search of gold. Keen to populate its new territory, the government set up a penal colony on nearby Staten Island, which moved to the town in 1902, and the town developed rapidly. Immigration was largely Croatian and Spanish, together with those shipwrecked on the shores, but the town remained isolated until planes arrived in 1935. As the prison closed a naval base opened, and in the 1970s, a further influx arrived, attracted by job opportunities in assemblage plants of electronic equipment that flourished thanks to reduced taxes. Now the city is capital of Argentina's most southerly province, and though fishing still is a traditional economic activity, Ushuaia has become an important tourist centre, particularly as the departure point for voyages to Antarctica.

Café Tante Sara **2**
El Turco **3**
Kaupé **5**
La Baguette **6**
La Cabaña **4**
La Estancia **7**
Moustacchio **10**
Parrilla La Rueda **11**
Tante Sara Pizzas & Pastas **12**
Tía Elvira **13**
Volver **15**

Bars & clubs
Café de la Esquina **17**
Che, qué Potito! **16**
Küar **14**
Lennon Pub **8**

Sights

There are several museums worth looking at, if bad weather forces you indoors. The most fascinating is **Museo del Fin del Mundo** ⓘ *along the seafront at Maipú y Rivadavia, T02901-421863, www.tierradelfuego.org.ar/museo daily Nov-Apr 0900- 2000, May-Oct Mon-Sat 1200-1900, US$3.50*, in the 1912 bank building, which tells the history of the town through a small collection of carefully chosen exhibits on the indigenous groups, missionaries, pioneers and shipwrecks, together with nearly all the birds of Tierra del Fuego (stuffed), and you can get an 'end of the world museum' stamp in your passport. There are helpful and informed staff, and also an extensive reference library. Recommended. Further east, the old prison, Presidio, at the back of the

 Naval Base ⓘ *Yaganes y Gobernador Paz, www.museomaritimo.com, daily 1000-2000, US$8.50,* houses the **Museo Marítimo**, with models and artefacts from seafaring days, and, in the cells of most of the five wings of the huge building, the **Museo Penitenciario**, which details the history of the prison. Excellent guided visits (in Spanish only) show a replica of the lighthouse that inspired Jules Verne's novel. Recommended. Much smaller is **Museo Yámana** ⓘ *Rivadavia 56, T02901-422874, www.tierradel fuego.org.ar/mundoyamana, daily 1000-2000 high season (1200-1900 in low season), US$1.70,* has interesting scale models showing scenes of everyday life of Yamana people and the geological evolution of the island, also interesting and recommended.

Whatever you do, unless it's absolutely pouring with rain, take the chairlift up to **Cerro Martial** ⓘ *daily 1000-1800 (1030-1630 in winter), US$3.50,* 7 km from town, for exhilarating views along the Beagle Channel and to Isla Navarino opposite. From the top of the lift, you can walk 1½ hours through lenga forest to Glaciar Martial. There are also a splendid tea shop, *refugio* and *cabañas* at the Cerro. To reach the chairlift, follow Magallanes out of town, allow 1½ hours walking, or take a bus: several companies, including Gonzalo and Kaupen, run minibus services from the corner of Maipu and Roca, frequently in summer, US$3-4 return. Last buses return at 1900 and 2100. Taxis charge US$5 to the base, from where you can walk down all the way back.

Parque Nacional Tierra del Fuego, (see below) just outside Ushuaia, is easily accessible by bus and offers superb walks for all levels of fitness. The **Tren del Fin del Mundo** is the world's southernmost steam train, running new locomotives and carriages on track first laid by prisoners to carry wood to Ushuaia. It's a totally touristy experience with relentless commentary in English and Spanish, but it might be fun for children, and is one way of getting into the national park to start a walk. The train runs for 50 minutes from the Fin del Mundo station, 8 km west of Ushuaia, into Tierra del Fuego National Park. Two departures daily in summer, one in winter. US$20 (tourist), US$35 (first class), US$50 (exclusive service) return, plus US$7 park entrance and transfer to the station. Tickets can be bought at station from **Tranex Turismo**, T02901- 431600, www.trendelfindelmundo.com.ar, or from travel agencies in town. Sit on the left outbound for the best views. Buses to the train station with **Kaupen** and **Pasarela**, leave from the corner of Maipú and Roca, at unreliable times; better take a taxi, US$3.

The **Estancia Harberton** (see box, page 571), 85 km from Ushuaia, is the oldest estancia on the island, and still run by descendants of the British missionary Thomas Bridges, whose family protected the indigenous peoples here. It's a beautiful place, with the attractive wood framed house that Thomas built sitting in quiet contemplation on a tranquil bay. You'll get an excellent guided walk (bilingual guides) around the estancia, through protected forest, and delicious teas or lunches are served in the Manacatush tearoom overlooking the water. Highly recommended. The impressive **Museo Akatushún** ⓘ *T02901-422742, www.aca tushun.org, daily 15 Oct-15 Apr, except Christmas, 1 Jan and Easter. Tour of the estancia US$ 5, museum entrance US$2,* has skeletons of South American sea mammals, the result of 23 years' scientific investigation in Tierra del Fuego, with excellent tours in English. You can camp free, with permission from the owners, or stay in cottages (see below). Access is from a good unpaved road (Route 33, ex 'J') which branches off Route 3, 40 km east of Ushuaia and runs 25 km through forest before the open country around Harberton; marvellous views, about two hours (no petrol outside of Ushuaia and Tolhuin). **Boat trips** to Harberton run twice weekly in summer, and allow one to two hours on the estancia. Regular daily minibus service with Ebenezer from Avenida Maipú and 25 de Mayo, US$20 return. Agency tours by land cost US$40 plus entrance. Excursions can also be made to Lagos Fagnano and Escondido: agencies run seven-hour tours for US$25 pp without lunch (US$32 lunch included); or check list of cheaper but rather unreliable minibuses going

Estancia Harberton

In a land of extremes and superlatives, Harberton stands out as special. The oldest estancia in Tierra del Fuego, it was built in 1886 on a narrow peninsula overlooking the Beagle Channel. Its founder, the missionary Thomas Bridges (see box page 573) was granted land by President Roca for his work amongst the indigenous peoples and for his help in rescuing victims of numerous shipwrecks in the channels. Harberton is named after the Devonshire village where his wife Mary was born, and the farmhouse was pre-fabricated by her carpenter father and assembled on a spot chosen by the Yámana peoples as the most sheltered. The English connection is evident in the neat lawns shrubs and trees between the jetty and the farmhouse. Behind the buildings is a large vegetable garden, a real rarity on the island, and there's noticeably more wildlife here than in the Tierra del Fuego National Park, probably owing to its remoteness.

Still operating as a working farm, mainly with cattle and sheep, Harberton is run by Thomas Goodall, great-grandson of the founder, whose wife Natalie has created an impressive museum of the area's rich marine life with a thriving research centre. Visitors receive a guided tour of the museum, or of farm buildings and grounds with reconstructions of the Yámana dwellings. Tea or lunch (if you reserve ahead) are served in the tea room overlooking the bay, and you may well be tempted to rent one of the two simple cottages on the shore. There are wonderful walks along the coast, and nowhere in Argentina has quite the feeling of peace you'll find here.

there, at tourist office. Tour agencies offer many good packages which include trekking, canoeing, birdwatching, and horse riding in landscape accessible only by 4WDs. See tour operators below, and the tourist office's list of excursions, indicating which companies go where.

Boat trips

All these trips are highly recommended, but note that the Beagle Channel can be very rough. Food and drink on all boats is pricey. Excursions can be booked through most agencies, or at the Muelle Turístico where boat companies have their ticket offices; boats leave from the Muelle Turístico, with a few excursions leaving from Muelle AFASYN (next to the old airport). If going to Harberton, check that your tour actually visits the estancia and not just the bay, as some do.

Most popular excursions visit all year round the small islands southeast of Ushuaia in 2½ to three hours, passing next to the sea lion colony at Isla de los Lobos, Isla de los Pájaros and Les Eclaireurs lighthouse. Alternatively, they add an hour or so for a landing on Bridges island. Prices vary if trips are made on big catamarans (US$30), on more exclusive sailing boats (from US$40), or on the charming old boat *Barracuda*, with excellent commentary, US$25. A few pricier services include lunch on board, otherwise a light snack or a coffee is served. Summer options add more services to the usual, with some services that go further east past the Isla de los Lobos, Isla de los Pájaros, Les Eclaireurs lighthouse, Isla Martillo penguin colony, and then visits Estancia Harberton (note that this stop is not included in all trips), six to nine hours round trip on catamaran, US$60, includes packed lunch, and entrance; with a few excursions going west to the National Park in about 5½ hours. You can also set off from Ushuaia for expeditions to Antarctica, highly recommended, see Activities and tours, page 578, and Transport, page 579.

Parque Nacional Tierra del Fuego

Covering 63,000 ha of mountains, lakes, rivers and deep valleys, this small but beautiful park stretches west to the Chilean border and north to **Lago Fagnano**, though large areas have been closed to tourists to protect the environment. Public access is at the park entrance 12 km west of Ushuaia, where you'll be given a basic map with marked walks. There's good camping in a picturesque spot at Lago Roca, with a *confitería*. All walks are best early morning or afternoon to avoid the tour buses. You'll see lots of geese, the beautiful torrent duck, Magellanic woodpeckers and austral parakeets.

Ins and outs

Access and information The park entrance is 12 km west of Ushuaia, on the main road west signposted from the town centre. The park administration is in Ushuaia, San Martín 1395, T02901-421315. Entry is US$7. In summer, buses and minibuses run an hourly service, US$5 return to Lago Roca, US$8 return to Bahía Lapataia, leaving from Ushuaia's tourist pier at the corner of Maipú and Roca or from Maipú and 25 de Mayo. Returning from either Bahía Lapataia or Lago Roca, hourly until last bus 2000 or 2100 in summer. Ask at the tourist office for bus details and map of park, with walks. There are no legal crossing points to Chile. Wear warm, waterproof clothing: in winter the temperature drops to as low as -12°C, and although in summer it can reach 25°C, evenings can be chilly. There's a helpful *guardaparque* (ranger) at Lago Roca.

For a really rich experience of the park, go with guides who know the territory well and can tell you about wildlife. Inexpensive trips for all levels with the highly recommended **Compañía de Guías de Patagonia**, www.companiadeguias.com.as.

Walks

The leaflets provided at the entrance show various walks, but these are recommended:
▲ **Senda Costera** (6.5 km, three hours each way) This lovely easy walk along the shore gives you the essence of the park, its rocky coastline, edged with a rich forest of beech trees, and glorious views of the low islands with a backdrops of steep mountains. Start at Bahía Ensenada (where the boat trips start, and where the bus can drop you off). Walk along a well-marked path along the shoreline, and then rejoin

Uttermost Part of the Earth

If you read one book about Patagonia, make it *Uttermost Part of the Earth*. The story of the first successful missionary to Tierra del Fuego, Thomas Bridges and his son Lucas, is one of the most stirring in the whole history of pioneers in Argentina. An orphan from Bristol, Thomas Bridges was so called because he was found as a child under a bridge with a letter T on his clothing. Adopted by Rev Despard, he was taken as a young man to start a Christian mission in wild, uncharted Tierra del Fuego where no white man had survived. He brought his young wife and daughter to convert the natives, after Despard had left following the massacre of the last lot of Christians by the indigenous inhabitants. Until his death in 1898, Bridges lived near the shores of the Beagle Channel, first creating the new settlement of Ushuaia and then at Harberton. He devoted his life to his work with the Yámanas (Yaghanes) and soon gave up converting them, in favour of compiling a dictionary of their language, and - ultimately - protecting them from the white man's persecution. His son Lucas (1874-1949), one of six children, spent his early life among the Yámanas and Onas, living and hunting as one of them, learning their languages, and even, almost fatally, becoming involved in their blood feuds, and magic rituals. Lucas became both defender and protector of the indigenous peoples whose culture he loved and was fascinated by, creating a haven for them at Harberton and Estancia Viamonte when most sheep farmers were more interested in having them shot. Lucas' memoirs, *Uttermost Part of the Earth* (1947) trace the tragic fate of the native population with whom he grew up. A compelling account of 20th-century man colliding with an ancient culture (out of print, but easily obtained from www.abebooks.co.uk).

the road briefly to cross Río Lapataia (ignoring signs to Lago Roca to your right). After crossing the broad green river and a second stretch of water (where there's a small camping spot and the gendarmería), it's a pleasant stroll inland to the beautifully tranquil **Bahía Lapataia**, an idyllic spot, with views across the sound.

Senda Hito XXIV (Along Lago Roca, 4 km, 90 minutes one way) Another easy walk, beside this peaceful lake, with lovely pebble beaches and through dense forest at times, with lots of bird life. This is especially recommended in the evening, when most visitors have left. Get off the bus at the junction for Lago Roca, turn right along the road to the car park (passing the *guardaparque*'s house) and follow the lake side.

Cerro Guanaco (4 km, four hours one way) Challenging hike up through the very steep forest to a mirador at the top of a hill (970 m) with splendid views over Lago Roca, the Beagle Channel and far-off mountains. The ground is slippery after rain: take care and don't rush. Allow plenty of time to return in light, especially in winter. The path branches off Senda Hito XXIV (see above) after crossing arroyo Guanaco.

Sleeping

Río Grande *p566*

Book ahead, as there are few decent choices.

B Posada de los Sauces, Elcano 839, T02964-432895, info@posadadelossauces.com.ar. By far the best choice. Breakfast included, beautifully decorated and comfortable rooms, good restaurant and cosy bar. Recommended.

C Apart Hotel Keyuk'n, Colón 630, T02964-424435. A good apart hotel, with simple-well equipped flats for 2-4.

C Hotel Atlantida, Belgrano 582, T02964-431915, atlantida@netcombbs.com.ar. A modern, rather uninspiring place, with plain comfortable rooms all with bath and cable TV, but good value with breakfast included.

D Hotel Isla del Mar, Güemes 963, T02964-422883, www.hotelguia.com/hotelisladelmar. Right on the sea shore, a bit run down but cheap, with bathrooms and breakfast included, and the staff are welcoming.

F pp **Hotel Argentina** , San Martín 64, T02964-422546, hotelargentino@yahoo.com. The best cheap place to stay. Much more than the backpackers youth hostel. Beautifully renovated 1920s building close to the sea. Kitchen, bright sunny dining room, owned by the welcoming Graciela, who knows all about the local area. Highly recommended.

Camping

Club Naútico Ioshlelk-Oten, Montilla 1047, 2 km from town on river. Clean, cooking facilities, camping, heated building in cold weather. YPF petrol station has hot showers.

Estancias

LL Estancia María Behety. Reservations: The Fly shop, www.flyfishingtravel.com. Established in 1897, 15 km from Río Grande, on a 40-km stretch of the river that has become legendary for brown trout fishing, with accommodation for 18 anglers, and good food. At US$5350 per week, this is one of the country's priciest fishing lodges, apparently deservedly so. Guides, equipment and accommodation included.

L Estancia Rivadavia, 100 km from Río Grande, on Route H, T02901-492186, www.estanciarivadavia.com. A 10,000-ha sheep farm, owned by descendants of the original Croatian builder. Luxurious accommodation in a splendid house near the mountains and lakes at the heart of Tierra del Fuego, where you can enjoy a trip around the estancia to see wild horses and guanacos, good food, and trekking to the trout lake of Chepelmut and Yehuin.

L Estancia Viamonte, 40 km southeast on the coast, T02964-430861, T02964-1561813, www.estanciaviamonte.com. For a really authentic experience, stay as a guest here. Built in 1902 by pioneer Lucas Bridges, writer of *Uttermost Part of the Earth*, to protect the indigenous Ona peoples, this working estancia is run by his descendants. You'll be warmly welcomed and stay in traditional, beautifully furnished rooms, with comfortable bathrooms, and delicious meals (extra cost). Also a spacious cottage to let, US$315 for 7. Join in the farm activities, read the famous book, ride horsesand completely relax. Recommended. Reserve a week ahead.

Tolhuin and around *p567*

A Hostería Petrel, at Lago Escondido, RN 3, Km 3186, T02901-433569, hpetrel@infovia.com.ar. In a secluded position amidst forest on a tranquil beach of the lake, with decent rooms with bath, and a good restaurant serving delicious lamb, open to non-residents. There are also tiny basic *cabañas* right on the water, US$40 for 2-4.

D Cabañas Khami , T/F02964-422296 www.cabaniaskhami.com.ar. Isolated in a lovely open spot at the head of the lake on low lying land, very comfortable and well equipped *cabañas*, nicely decorated, and with great views of the lake. Good value at US$40 per day for 6. Recommended.

D Parador Kawi Shiken, off the main road on the way to Ushuaia, 4 km south of Tolhuin on RN3, Km 2940, T156-11505, www.hotelguia.com/hoteles/kawi-shiken. A rustic place with 3 rooms, shared bathrooms, *casa de té* and restaurant. Ring them to arrange for local *cordero al asador* (barbecued lamb). Also horse riding.

D Terrazas del Lago, RN3, Km 2938, T156-04851, terrazas@uol.com.ar. A little way from the shore, smart wooden *cabañas*, well decorated, and also a *confiteria* and *parrilla*.

F pp **Refugio Solar del Bosque** , Lago Escondido, RN3, Km 3020, T02901-453276, T1560 6176, solardelbosque@tierradel fuego.org.ar. 18 km from Ushuaia is this basic hostel for walkers, with shared bathrooms in dorms for 4, breakfast included.

Camping

Camping Hain del Lago, T02964-425951, robertoberbel@hotmail.com. Lovely views, fireplaces, hot showers, and a quincho for when it rains.

Camping La Correntina, T156-05020, 17 km from Tolhuin. In woodland, with bathrooms, and horses for hire.

Ushuaia *p568, map p568*

The tourist office has accommodation lists and can help find you somewhere to stay, but in Jan you must reserve before you come. Several of those listed below are on the road to the Glaciar Martial overlooking the city.

LL Las Hayas, Camino Glaciar Martial, Km 3, T02901-430710, www.lashayas.com.ar. A 5-star hotel, in a spectacular setting, high up on the mountainside with outstanding views over the Beagle channel. Light, tasteful, impeccable rooms. Breakfast included and use of pool, sauna, gym, squash court, 9 hole golf course, shuttle from town (high season only), and transfer from airport. A lovely calm atmosphere, friendly staff. Recommended.

L Cumbres del Martial, Luis F Martial 3560, T02901-424779, www.cumbresdel martial.com.ar. This charming cottage by a mountain stream in the forested slopes of Martial range has very comfortable rooms with balconies for viewing the Beagle Channel. A homely feel prevails in this small, relaxed and secluded place 7 km away from town. There are also 4 *cabañas*, in which rustic materials contrast with a cosy interior. All have a fireplace and big windows open onto the woods. Superb fondues are served in its restaurant and tea room.

L Los Cauquenes, C Reinamora, Barrio Bahía Cauquen, T02901-441300, www.loscauquen esushuaia.com.ar. A 5-star by the sea. Wonderfully set on the shores of the Beagle Channel, this large and stylish hotel is an exclusive retreat 7 km west of Ushuaia. Wood and stone are predominant in its architecture, while a relaxing minimalist décor prevails inside, also in both the standard and the larger superior rooms. Suites have their own private balconies on the sea. There is a restaurant, a spa and vans going frequently to the town centre.

AL Canal Beagle, Maipú y 25 de Mayo, T02901- 432303, www.hotelcanalbeagle. com.ar. Good ACA hotel (discounts for members) with a small pool, gym and sauna, with views over the channel from some of its comfortable and tastefully decorated rooms, and a good, reasonably priced restaurant.

A Cabañas del Martial, Luis F Martial 2109, T02901-430475, www.delmartial.com.ar. Wonderful views from these comfortable and well-equipped *cabañas* (price is for 5 people). Set on the wooded slopes of Martial range.

A Los Ñires, Av de los Ñires 3040, T02901-443781, www.nires.com.ar. The setting is the feature here, with lovely views, comfortable rooms in simple rustic style, and a good restaurant. Transfers and breakfast included.

A Tolkeyen, Del Tolkeyen 2145, 4 km from town towards national park, T02901-445315, www.tolkeyenhotel.com. A lovely traditional rustic place in a superb setting, with open views from its rooms, which vary between plain and flouncy, but are all spacious and comfortable. Lots of land to walk in, and close to the national park, with free buses into town, and free room service. Also an excellent restaurant, serving king crab and Fuegian lamb. Very relaxing. Recommended.

B Apart Hotel Cabo San Diego , 25 de Mayo 368, T02901-435600, www.cabosan diego.com.ar. Really comfortable and spacious apartments, very clean, well equipped for cooking, good bathrooms. Great for couples or families. Excellent value.

B Cap Polonio, San Martín 746, T02901-422140, www.hotelcappolonio.com.ar. A smart central modern city hotel with very comfortable minimalist rooms with bath, TV, phone, internet; some have views of the canal. There's a chic restaurant/café downstairs.

B César, San Martín 753, T02901-421460, www.hotelcesarhostal.com.ar. Very central, this big tourist place is often booked by groups, but is reasonable value. Simple rooms with bath, breakfast included.

B Hostal Malvinas, Gobernador Deloqui 615, T/F02901-422626, www.hostal malvinas.net. Neat, comfortable if rather small rooms with excellent bathrooms, and good views, in this central and well run town house hotel. Breakfast is included, and all day tea and coffee. Recommended.

B Hostería Posada Fin del Mundo, Gobernador Valdez 281, T02901-437345, www.posadafindelmundo.com.ar. A relaxed family atmosphere in a quiet area close to centre, homely, friendly staff. Good value.

D B&B Nahuel, 25 de Mayo 440, T02901-423068, byb_nahuel@yahoo.com.ar. A family house with views over the channel, brightly painted and tasteful rooms, and a lovely welcome from the charming and talkative owner. Great value. Recommended.

D Posada Nido de Cóndores, Gobernador Campos 783 y 9 de Julio, T02901-437753, www.companiadeguias.com.ar. Simple light rooms with shared bath or doubles with bath. Excellent breakfast, friendly with a lovely relaxing café below. The owners are walking guides and can arrange superb trekking (see Compañía de Guías de Patagonia in Tour operators). Recommended.

E-F pp **Amanecer de la Bahía**, Magallanes 594, T02901-424405, www.ushuaia hostel.com.ar. A light, spacious, impeccably kept hostal, with shared rooms for 4 and cramped for 6, also a good double and triples with shared bath. Internet, living rooms, breakfast included.

F pp **Albergue Cruz del Sur**, Deloqui 636, T02901-434099, www.xdelsur.com.ar. There's a very friendly atmosphere in this relaxed small Italian owned hostal, with cosy dorms, use of kitchen, and a lovely quiet library room for reading. A place to make friends. Recommended.

F pp **Antarctica**, Antártida Argentina 270, T02901-435774, www.antarcticahostel.com. Welcoming and central hostel with a spacious chill-out room and an excellent bar open till the small hours. Dorms are rather basic and cramped, with **C** larger private doubles. Cooking facilities, breakfast and the use of internet are included. Cycles for hire.

F pp **Yakush**, Piedrabuena y San Martín, T02901-435807, www.hostelyakush.com.ar. On a central corner, this is a very well-run hostel with spacious rooms to share and a few private ones, a light kitchen and dining room, and a steep tiny garden with views. If a cheerful atmosphere prevails, there are also comfy and more secluded corners for oneself.

Private homes

D Familia Velasquez, Juana Fadul 361, T02901-421719. Basic rooms with breakfast in cosy cheerful pioneer family home, where the kind owners look after you.

D Galeazzi-Basily, Gobernador Valdez 323, T02901-423213, www.avesdelsur.com.ar. The best option by far is this cosy and stylish family home, with welcoming owners Frances and Alejandro, who speak excellent English, in a pleasant residential area just 5 blocks from the centre. Delicious breakfast. There are also excellent value 4 and 5-bed *cabañas* in the garden. Highly recommended.

D Los Troncos, Gobernador Paz 1344, T02901-421895, lostroncos@speedy.com.ar. A welcoming house run by charming Mrs Clarisa Ulloa, with simple rooms, breakfast, TV and free internet.

Estancias

L Estancia Rolito, RN21 (ex 'A'), Km 14, T02901-492007, rolitotdf@hotmail.com. A magical place on the wooded heart of the island, with cosy accommodation in traditionally built houses, and friendly hosts, booked through **Turismo de Campo**, Fuegia Basket 414 (Ushuaia), T02901-432419, www.turismode campo.com.ar. Also day visits with recommended walks or horse rides in mature southern beech forest.

LL Harberton, T02901-422742, estancia harberton@tierradelfuego.org.ar. 2 impeccably restored historical buildings on the tranquil lakeside, giving you space and privacy from the main house. Very simple accommodation, but wonderful views, and beautiful walks on the estancia's coastline. 90 km east of Ushuaia, along Route 3 and 33, a spectacular drive. Price given for 6 people. Open mid Oct-mid Apr.

Camping

La Pista del Andino, Leandro N Alem 2873, T02901-435890, www.lapistadel andino.com.ar. Set in the **Club Andino** ski premises in a woodland area, it has wonderful views over the channel. Electricity, hot showers, tea room and grocery store, US$3 pp.

Camping del Solar del Bosque, RN3, Km 19, T02901-421228. US$ 2.50 pp. At a small ski resort that in summer offers plenty of activities. Hot showers, and also a large dorm with good facilities.

Camping Haruwen, in the Haruwen Winter Sports complex (Km 36), T02901-431099. US$3 per tent, electricity, shop, bar, restaurant in a small winter sports centre, open also in summer for outdoor activities.

Camping Lago Roca, in the national park, T02901-433313, 21 km from Ushuaia, entry fee US$7. By the forested shore of tranquil Lago Roc, this is a beautiful site with good facilities, reached by bus Jan-Feb, expensive small shop, *cafetería*, US$4 pp.

Kawi Yoppen, 10 km from Ushuaia, on RN3 heading to Río Grande, Km 3020, T02901-435135. US$2 pp.

Eating

Río Grande *p566*

La Nueva Colonial, Fagnano 669, half a block from the plaza, next to Casino Club.

Where the locals go for delicious pasta in a warm family atmosphere.

Ұ **La Nueva Piamontesa**, Belgrano y Mackinlay, T02964-423620, to the side of the charming 24-hr grocery store. Cheap set menus and also delivers food.

Ұ **La Rueda**, Islas Malvinas 954, 1st floor. Excellent *parrilla* in a welcoming place.

Tolhuin *p567*

On the same block as the famous **La Union** bakery, open 24 hrs, daily except Mon 2400-Tue 0600. There are pizzas at **Pizzería Amistad**, and more of a range at **La Posada de los Ramirez**, a cosy restaurant and *rotisería*, where 3 courses will cost you US$4, open weekends only, lunch and dinner. Parrilla La Victoria, Koshten 324, T02964-492297, is open daily, with beef and lamb on the asado, and also pizzas, call before for delicious Fuegian lamb.

Ushuaia *p568, map p568*

ҰҰҰ **Bodegón Fueguino**, San Martín 859. In a stylishly renovated 1896 house in the main street, this stands out from the crowd by serving picadas with delicious and imaginative dips, good roast lamb, and unusual *cazuelas*, *picadas* and dips. A buzzy atmosphere and welcoming staff.

ҰҰҰ **Kaupé**, Roca 470 y Magallanes, T02901-437396. The best restaurant in town with exquisite food. King crab and meat dishes all beautifully served, in a lovely environment – a great treat.

ҰҰҰ **La Cabaña**, Luis F Martial 3560, T02901-424779. The cosy restaurant and tea room of Cumbres del Martial hotel serves several excellent types of fondue for dinner, that may be preceded at teatime by a rich list of cakes, scones and brownies.

ҰҰҰ **Marcopolo**, San Martín 746. A chic modern international-style café restaurant for seafood and everything else. Soothing decor, good service.

ҰҰҰ **Tía Elvira**, Maipú 349. Has a reputation for excellent seafood, with a good choice of fresh fish and good views over the channel.

ҰҰҰ **Volver**, Maipú 37. In an atmospheric old 1898 house, with ancient newspaper all over the walls, so that you can read intriguing fragments while you eat. Cosy stoves and an intimate atmosphere. Delicious salmon and *arroz con mariscos*.

ҰҰ **Barcleit 1912**, Juana Fadul 148. Serves good Italian food, pizzas and pastas.

ҰҰ **La Estancia**, San Martín 253. Cheery and good-value *parrilla tenedor libre*.

ҰҰ **Moustacchio**, San Martín y Gobernador Godoy. Long established, good for seafood in a cosy atmosphere. Next door is a cheaper all-you-can-eat sister restaurant.

ҰҰ **Parrilla La Rueda**, San Martín y Rivadavia. A good *tenedor libre* for beef, lamb and a great range of salads.

ҰҰ **Tante Sara Pizzas and Pastas**, San Martín 137. A brightly-lit functional place with tasty filling food. Also take-away.

Ұ **El Turco**, San Martín 1410. One of the few good and cheap places, very popular with locals, serving generous milanesas, pastas, steaks and pizzas.

Cafés

Café Tante Sara, Fadul y San Martín, opposite the tourist office. Smart and modern with an airy feel, serving good coffee and tasty sandwiches.

La Baguette, Don Bosco y San Martín. The best fresh takeaway sandwiches, and also delicious *empanadas* and *facturas* (pastries).

Bars and clubs

Ushuaia *p568, map p568*

Café de la Esquina, 25 de Mayo y San Martín. Light meals and drinks, in a good atmosphere.

Che, qué potito!, San Martín 452. A lively place with Mexican and Brazilian food.

Küar, Av Perito Moreno 2232, east of town. Great setting by the sea, restaurant, bar and brewery open from 1800.

Lennon Pub, Maipú 263. A lively friendly atmosphere and live music.

Festivals and events

Río Grande *p566*

Jan The **sheep shearing festival** is definitely worth seeing, if you're in the area.

Feb In 2nd week of Feb there's a **rural exhibition** with handicrafts.

Mar **Shepherd's Day** (1st week), with impressive sheepdog display.

Jun **Winter solstice**, the longest night with fireworks and ice skating contests takes place Jun 20/21, though this is a very inhospitable time of year.

Activities and tours

Río Grande *p566*

Tour operators

Fiesta Travel, 9 de Julio 663, T02964-431800, fiestatravel@arnet.com.ar.
Mariani Travel Rosales 259, T02964-426010, mariani@netcombbs.com.ar.
Techni Austral, Moyano 516, T02964-430610. Bus tickets to Ushuaia.

Ushuaia *p568, map p568*

Cycle hire

DTT Cycles Sport, San Martín 905. **Seven** Deportes , San Martín y 9 de Julio.

Fishing

The lakes and rivers of Tierra del Fuego offer great fishing, for brown and rainbow trout, and stream trout in Lago Fagnano. Both flycasting and spinning are allowed, and permits must be bought. The trout season is 1 Nov-Apr (though this varies slightly every year), licences US$10 per day (an extra fee is charged for some rivers and lakes). Contact **Asociación de Caza y Pesca** at Maipú 822, T02901-423168, cazapescush@infovia.com.ar
Fly Casting, T02901-423340. Offers a range of fishing excursions, provide equipment.
Yishka, Gobernador Godoy 62, T02901-437606, www.yishkaevt.com.ar. Arranges fishing excursions to Lago Fagnano.

Skiing, hiking, climbing

For skiing, hiking, climbing contact **Club Andino**, Fadul 50, T02901-422335, www.clubandinoushuaia.com.ar. Maps and trekking guidebooks for sale, free guided walks once in a month in summer. Winter sports resorts along RN3 (see below) are an excellent base for summer trekking and many arrange excursions. **Nunatak**, 19.5 km from Ushuaia, nunatak@tierradel fuego.org.ar, is a small centre from where amazing day-treks to nearby glaciers and lakes are possible. To get to the more remote areas of the island from Ushuaia, it's worth going on an expedition with an agency. See tour operators below for some excellent packages and day hikes.

Ushuaia is becoming popular as a winter resort with several centres for skiing, snowboarding and husky sledging. There's good powder snow, thanks to the even temperatures (between 5 and -5°C) and the climate isn't as cold as you'd think, despite the latitude, because winter is the least windy season here. The season runs mid-Jun and mid-Oct, but late Aug to late Sep is best, for lighter days and good snow.

The most developed resort is **Cerro Castor complex**, 27 km from town, T02901-499302, www.cerrocastor.com. With 20 km of pistes of all grades, and vertical drop of 772 m, it's bettered only by Las Leñas and Bariloche. There's an attractive centre with equipment rental for skiing, snowboarding and snowshoeing, ski school, cafés and a hotel, and restaurants on the pistes. Ski pass US$35 per day. 3 regular buses run per day. There's excellent cross country skiing in the area, with various new centres strung along the main road R3 at 18-36 km east of Ushuaia, of which **Tierra Mayor**, 21 km from town, T02901-423240, is recommended. In a beautiful wide valley between steep sided mountains, the centre offers half and full day excursions on sledges with huskies for hire, as well as cross country skiing and show shoeing. Equipment hire, and cosy restaurant. In the city itself, **Martial Glacier Winter Sports Centre**, 7 km from the centre, has a single piste. The **Haruwen Winter Sports** complex is 35 km east on RN3 also offers winter sports activities.

Tour operators

Lots of companies now offer adventure tourism expeditions. All charge the same; ask tourist office for a complete list: Tierra del Fuego National Park, 4 hrs, from US$17 (entry US$7 extra); Lagos Escondido and Fagnano, 7-8 hrs, US$25 without lunch. With 3 or 4 people it might be worth hiring a remise taxi.
All Patagonia, Juana Fadul 60, T02901-433622, www.allpatagonia.com/Eng. A wonderful range of tours, sailing, hiking, birdwatching, all making the most of the wild land around Ushuaia. Ask about the birdwatching trip to the centre of the island, and the 6 day trip crossing the Fuegian cordillera. Also Antarctic trips. Well-organized and recommended.
Canal Fun & Nature, Rivadavia 82, T02901-437395, www.canalfun.com. Oriented to young people, it offers a huge range of activities, including trekking, canoeing, horse riding, 4WD excursions. And they also run their own bar Küar. Recommended.

Comapa, San Martín 245, T02901-430727, www.comapa.com. They offer a complete range of excursions and accommodation arrangements in Chile, including tickets for Buses Pacheco (to Punta Arenas), Cruceros Australis (to Cabo de Hornos and Punta Arenas), and **Navimag** ferries (Puerto Natales-Puerto Montt); also trips to Antarctica.

Compañía de Guías de Patagonia, Posada Nido de Cóndores, Gobernador Campos 795, (y 9 de Julio), T02901-437753, www.compania de guias.com.ar. The best walking guides. Well run expeditions to the national park, and also to more inaccessible places, for the day, or several days, including the beautiful 3-day walk along the Lucas Bridges path, some equipment and food included. Also ice climbing (training and equipment provided) to Cerro Alvear. Professional, friendly and knowledgeable. Highly recommended.

Rumbo Sur, San Martín 350, T02901-421139, www.rumbosur.com.ar. Flights, buses and conventional tours including Harberton, fishing excursions, plus wonderful Antarctic expeditions, mid-Nov to mid-Mar, friendly.

Tolkar Viajes y Turismo, Roca 157, T02901-431412, www.tolkarturismo.com.ar. Flights, bus tickets to Punta Arenas, Río Grande and Río Gallegos, conventional and adventure tourism, including a full-day mountain biking and canoeing trip in Lago Fagnano and Lago Escondido area.

Travel Lab, San Martín 1444, T02901-436555, www.travel-labpatagonia-com.ar. Tren del fin del Mundo tickets, also unconventional tours such as mountain biking and trekking. English and French spoken, very helpful.

Turismo de Campo, Fuegia Basket 414, T02901-437351, www.turismode campo.com.ar. Adventure tourism in small groups with English/French speaking guides. Boat and trekking combinations in the national park, and trekking for all levels in other remoter places, visiting Estancia Rolito, birdwatching tours, fishing excursions, horse riding in central Tierra del Fuego woodlands, sailing in the Beagle Channel. Also Antarctica. Highly recommended.

Transport

Río Grande *p566*

Book ahead in summer as buses and planes fill up fast. Take passport when buying ticket.

Air Airport 4 km west of town, T02964-420600. Taxi US$2. To **Buenos Aires**, **Aerolíneas Argentinas** daily, 3½ hrs direct. To **Ushuaia** , LADE once a week to **Ushuaia** and Patagonian towns.

Airline offices Aerolíneas Argentinas, San Martín 607, T02964-424467.

Bus Buses leave from terminal at Elcano y Güemes, T02964-420997, or from **Tecni Austral's** office Moyano 516, T02964-430610. To **Porvenir**, Chile, 5 hrs, US$9, **Gesell**, Wed, Sun, 0800, passport and luggage control at San Sebastián. To **Punta Arenas**, Chile, via Punta Delgada, 10 hrs, **Pacheco**, Tue, Thu, Sat 0730, US$15, To **Río Gallegos**, 3 times a week, US$15. To **Ushuaia**, Tecni Austral, 3-4 , 2 daily (heavily booked in summer), US$12, also **Tolkeyen**, US$7.

Car hire Al Rent a Car International, Belgrano 423, T02964-430757, ai.rentcar@ carletti.com.ar. Also 4WDs and camionettas. **Hertz Annie Millet**, Libertad 714, T02964-426534, hertzriogrande@ netcombbs.com.ar.

Ushuaia *p568, map p568*

Book ahead in summer, as flights fill up fast. In winter, poor weather often delays flights.

Air Aeropuerto Internacional Malvinas Argentinas, 4 km from town, taxi, US$3 (no bus). Schedules tend to change from season to season, so call offices for times and prices. Buses and minibuses from Río Grande arrive at their respective offices around town: **Tecni Austral** (also from Punta Arenas, Río Gallegos and Comodoro Rivadavia) at Tolkar, Roca 157, T02901-431408, www.tolkar turismo.com.ar; Líder, at Gobernador Paz 921, T02901-436421; and **Montiel**, at Marcos Zar 330, T421366. To **Buenos Aires**, 3½ hrs, **El Calafate**, 1 hr , in summer, both with Aerolíneas and LADE. Flights are also available daily to **Río Gallegos**, 1 hr, and **Río Grande**, 1 hr, several a week, but check with agents. To **Punta Arenas**, 1 hr, Aerovías DAP. Note that departure tax must be paid to cities in Argentina, US$ 5.

Airline offices Aerolíneas Argentinas, Roca 116, T02901-421218. Aerovias DAP, Gobernador Deloqui 555 p 4, T02901-431110. LADE, San Martín 542, shop 5, T02901-421123.

Bus To **Río Grande** 3½-4 hrs, Mon-Sat 0530, US$8.50 with bus **Tecni Austral**. Book through **Tolkar**, Roca 157, T02901-431412.

Combis **Líder**, Gob Paz 921, T02901-436421, and **Montiel**, Marcos Zar 330, T02901-421366, US$8.50-10. To **Río Gallegos**, **Tecni Austral**, 11½ hrs, US$30. To **Punta Arenas**, **Tecni Austral**, Mon, Wed, Fri 0530, US$ 30, and **Buses Pacheco**, San Martín 245 (at Comapa agency), T02901-430727, www.busespacheco.com, twice a week. From Río Gallegos, several buses daily to **El Calafate**, 4 hrs.

Car hire Most companies charge around US$45 per day including insurance and 150 km per day, promotional rates are usually available. **Hertz**, airport, T02901- 432429. **Wagen**, San Martín 1222, T02901-430739.

Sea **Cruceros Australis**, www.australis.com, operates two luxury cruise ships (one weekly each) from Ushuaia to **Punta Arenas**, via **Puerto Williams** and around **Cabo de Hornos**, 4-5 days, from US$1100 pp in summer (book through **Comapa Agency**, frequently recommended). **Ushuaia Boating**, Godoy 190, T02901-436193, www.ushuaia boating.com.ar, operates all year round a channel crossing to **Puerto Navarino**, 40 mins (subject to weather conditions), plus the bus transfer that completes the journey to **Puerto Williams**, US$100. From Puerto Williams there are frequent ferries to **Punta Arenas**. At **Muelle AFASYN** (next to the old airport), T02901- 435805, ask about possible crossings with a club member to **Puerto Williams**, about 4 hrs, from US$80, or if any foreign sailing boat is going to **Cabo de Hornos** or to **Antarctica**.

Antarctic expeditions Ushuaia is the starting point for a number of excellent expeditions to Antarctica; informative, adventurous, wonderful experiences. These run Oct-Mar, usually 8- to 12-day trips to the western shores of the Antarctic peninsula, the South Shetland Islands and the Wedell Sea, some offering extra activities such as camping and kayaking. It's not a luxury cruise, and there's informal, simple accommodation usually in non-tourist boats used for scientific exploration, so the food is fine but not excessive. The expedition leader organizes lectures during the 3-day journey to reach the Antarctic, with at least 2 disembarkations a day in a zodiac to see icebergs and penguins. There's most ice in Nov and Dec, but more baby penguins in Jan and Feb, and whales in Mar. The landscape is always impressive. A longer trip, 18- to 20- days, combines the Antarctic with the Malvinas/Falklands and South Georgia islands. It's worth turning up and asking for availability; there's a reasonable discount if you book last minute, only available if bought in Ushuaia, when the price starts at about US$3400 pp (in a twin cabin); cheapest fares are offered by **Antarpply**, on her ship Ushuaia, www.antarpply.com. Weekly departures in season. For more information on Antarctica in Ushuaia, visit Oficina Antártica, Maipú 505 (at Muelle Turístico), T02901-421423, for general information with a small library that keeps navigational charts. Several travel agencies in Ushuaia sell tickets for trips to Antarctica.

Taxi For taxis, call T02901-422007 or T02901- 440225. **Remise Carlitos**, T02901-422222, and **Bahía Hermosa**, T02901-422233, are both reliable.

Train For Tren del Fin del Mundo, see p570.

◐ Directory

Río Grande *p566*
Banks ATMs: 4 banks on San Martín between 100 and 300. **Banco de la Nación Argentina**, San Martín 219. **Bansud**, Rosales 241. Cash advance on Visa. Cash exchange Thaler Rosales 259. **Post office** Piedrabuena y Ameghino. **Telephone** *Locutorio*, San Martín at 170 and 458.

Ushuaia *p568, map p568*
Banks Banks open 1000-1500 (in summer). ATMs are plentiful all along San Martín, using credit cards is by far the easiest, as changing TCs is difficult and expensive. Changing money and TCs: **Banco de Tierra del Fuego**, San Martín 396, **Agencia de Cambio Thaler**, San Martín 788, also open weekends, 1000-1300, 1700-2030. **Consulates** Chile, Jainén 50, T02901-430909. **Internet** Many broadband cyber cafés and *locutorios* along San Martín. **Post office** San Martín y Godoy, Mon-Fri 0900-1900 Sat 0900-1300. **Telephone** *Locutorios* all along San Martín.

Background

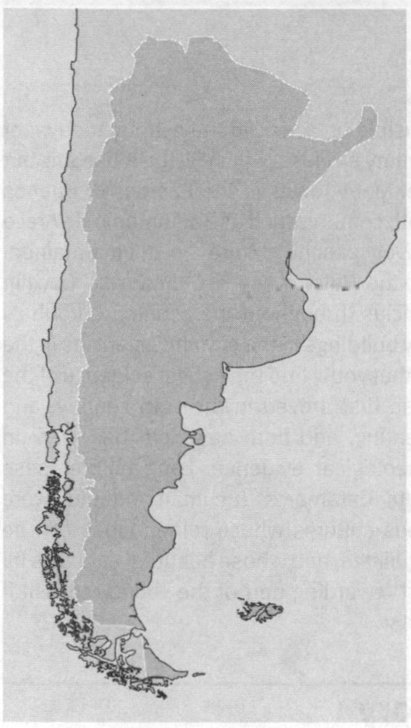

Footprint features

History

Much of Argentina's fascinating history is visible on a visit to the country today, not only in colonial architecture and the 19th-century artefacts which fill the museums but in the culture and customs of everyday life. Many towns in the Pampas of Buenos Aires province are just as they were in the 19th century, such as San Antonio de Areco and Chascomús, where the traditions of a lively gaucho culture are still maintained. The lives of early pioneers can be explored in the Welsh towns of Gaiman and Trevelin in Patagonia and in the more remote estancias throughout the country. Córdoba's history of Jesuit occupation is visible in many buildings in the city and estancias in the province. And in the northwest of Argentina that you'll find the richest evidence of the country's history. This is where the Spanish first arrived in the 16th century, and before them the Incas in the early 15th century, and both have left their mark in colonial architecture and intriguing archaeological evidence. Long before these invasions, the present day provinces of Salta, Catamarca, Tucumán and Jujuy were inhabited by many sophisticated indigenous cultures whose ruined cities can be visited at Santa Rosa de Tastil, Tilcara and Quilmes, and whose beautiful ceramics fill the area's many museums. This is the most rewarding part of the country to visit if you're interested in exploring Argentina's past.

Archaeology and prehistory

Earliest origins

The first peoples crossed the temporary land bridge spanning Asia and America and the Bering Strait between 50,000 and 60,000 years ago, and began a long migration southwards, reaching South America about 30,000 years ago and Tierra del Fuego around 12,000 years ago. Hunters and foragers, they followed in the path of huge herds of now extinct animals such as mammoths, giant ground sloths, mastodons and wild horses, adapting to fishing along the Chilean coasts. In the northeast of Argentina, these peoples adopted a more sedentary lifestyle, pausing in their semi-nomadic travels long enough to plant and harvest crops of maize and manioc, and domesticating animals.

Northwest Argentina

Argentina has a rich history of pre-Hispanic indigenous civilizations, with the most important archaeological sites situated in the northwest and west areas of the most highly developed cultures south of the central Andes. Along a migratory path which followed the Andes, this region became a meeting place for established settlers from northern Chile, the central Andes, the Chaco and the hunter-gatherers of the south. Cave paintings and petroglyphs engraved on rocks remain from 13,000 to 10,000 years ago, made by cave dwellers who lived by hunting vizcacha, guanaco, vicuña and birds, some painted with pigments derived from minerals mixed with gesso. Their lines, dots and geometrical forms belong to a symbolic system impossible to interpret today. The extraordinary quantity of handprints visible in the Cueva de los Manos in Patagonia were made as long ago as 10,000 years, and again, their purpose and origin remains a mystery.

By around 1000 to 500 BC, the nomadic groups had grown in size and were too large to subsist on hunting alone and so started early attempts at agriculture. They grew potatoes and maize, and a mummy found from this period (displayed in Cachi's museum) with a few artefacts and belongings suggests that these peoples had a developed system of beliefs. By 2000 years ago, small communities had started to gather on the alluvial plains, living on agriculture and herding llamas. In many of the area's museums, you'll see large grinding stones made of granite, used to grind maize, as well as arrowheads and pipes used for smoking tobacco. Weaving began around this time, and there are some fine fabrics found at Santa Rosa Tastil.

There were three distinct periods in the cultural development of the northwest. The Early Period (500 BC to AD 650) witnessed the beginnings of agriculture as well as pottery and metalworking, with the remains of terraces near Humahuaca in Jujuy. The Middle Period (AD 650-850) was marked by the influence of the great culture of Tiahuanaco in present-day Bolivia. Fine metal objects, some of them of gold and silver, were made and new plant varieties were introduced. You'll find stone vessels, anthropomorphic clay pieces, and ornate ceramics from this period all over the Northwest.

In the Later Period (AD 850-1480), known as the Period of Regional Development, small groups of settlers formed communities with individual dwellings, usually based on circular stone walls, next to water sources. Both ritual and functional ceramics were made by peoples known as the Santamariana or Diaguita culture. Although there was no system of writing, their language, Kakán, survived until the Inca invasion in the late 15h century. These cultures made large, beautifully painted funerary urns, thought to bury the bones of children, since the infant mortality rate was high. The predominant religious beliefs centred around worship of the mother earth goddess, the Pachamama (see box, page 293), and she's still worshipped in rural communities all over the Northwest today, with lively festivals on 1 August.

The Incas first arrived in the Calchaquíes valleys area between 1410 and 1430, incorporating the area into the part of their empire known as Kollasuyo. They built two parallel roads along the length of the Andes and along the Pacific shore: busy trade routes linking their communities with the rest of the Inca empire. The Incas made Quechua the official language, punished the chiefs of any groups whose members transgressed and absorbed the local cult of the earth goddess Pachamama into their own system of worship of the sun. The Incas also brought with them their own sacrificial burial customs. The bodies of three children found at the summit of Cerro Llullaillaco on the Salta/Chile border indicate young humans were killed as offerings. These three, aged between seven and 15, were carried to the summit, dressed in special garments, adorned with feather headdresses and jewellery, and put to sleep using strong local liquor *chicha*. It's thought that they were offered as a sacrifice to the gods in their belief that to gain life, life has also to be sacrificed. It's also possible that their death sealed some kind of political alliance between the Inca and the chief of a new colony. The children's peaceful faces show no sign of distress so it's likely that they died painlessly within minutes, and Salta's new MAAM museum on the plaza has a fascinating display of photographs of he children and an extraordinary array of artefacts buried with them. The Calchaquíes valleys were the site of particularly bloody battles when the Spanish attempted to dominate in the 16th century, and many indigenous groups were wiped out, but fortunately, in the northwest of Argentina, there are living descendants from many of the original inhabitants, keeping their customs and beliefs alive.

Central and southern Argentina

The Comechingones, who inhabited what are now the provinces of Córdoba and San Luis, lived in settlements of pit-dwellings and used irrigation to produce a range of crops. In the far northeast on the eastern edge of the Chaco were the Guaraní; organized into loose confederations, they lived in rudimentary villages and practised slash-and-burn agriculture to grow maize, sweet potatoes, manioc and beans. They also produced textiles and ceramics.

Further south, the Pampas and Patagonia were much more sparsely populated than the northwest and most groups were nomadic long after the arrival of the Spanish. One of the most important groups were the Querandí, who eked out a living by hunting guanaco and rheas with *boleadoras*, three balls of stone tied with thong and hurled at the legs of a running animal. Patagonia was inhabited by scattered nomadic groups including the Pampa, the Chonik and the Kaingang, who managed to avoid contact with white settlers until the 19th century. In the steppes of Patagonia, the Tehuelche and Puelche lived as nomadic hunters living off guanaco, foxes and game. In the far south, in southern Patagonia and Tierra del Fuego, there were four indigenous groups, the land-based Ona and Haush, who hunted foxes and guanaco, wearing their hides and constructing temporary dwellings of branches covered loosely with skins. And the sea based Yaghanes and Alacaluf, who made canoes, paddles, bailers and mooring rope, catching fish with spears or by hand, though seals were their main source of food. These peoples survived until the late 19th century and were befriended and protected by the son of Tierra del Fuego's first settler and missionary. Lucas Bridges' account in *Uttermost Part of the Earth* gives an extraordinary insight into the customs and hunting practices of the Ona and Yaghanes. Within 50 years of the arrival of white sheep-farmers, many had been shot, or coerced into religious missions where they could be controlled, and now no single descendent remains.

European exploration and settlement

At the time of the arrival of the first Europeans the land which is now Argentina was sparsely populated with about two-thirds of the indigenous population living in the northwest. European exploration began in the Río de la Plata estuary when in 1516 Juan de Solís, a Portuguese navigator employed by the Spanish crown, landed on the shore, though his men were soon killed by indigenous Querandí. Four years later he was followed by Ferdinand Magellan who explored the Río de la Plata, before turning south to make his way into the Pacific via the straits north of Tierra del Fuego, now named after him. In 1527 both Sebastian Cabot and his rival Diego García sailed into the estuary and up the Ríos Paraná and the Paraguay. Cabot founded a small fort, Sancti Spiritus, not far from the modern city of Rosario, but it was wiped out by indigenous inhabitants about two years later. Despite these difficulties Cabot took back to Spain stories of a great Indian kingdom beyond the Plata estuary, rich in precious metals, giving the Río de la Plata its misleading name: river of silver. A Portuguese expedition to the estuary, led by Affonso de Souza, returned with similar tales, and this led to a race between the two Iberian powers. In 1535, Pedro de Mendoza set out with 16 ships and a well-equipped force of 1600 men and founded a settlement at Buenos Aires, which he gave its present name, originally Puerto Nuestra Señora Santa María de Buen Ayre. The natives soon made life too difficult; the settlement was abandoned and Mendoza returned home but not before sending Juan de Ayolas with a small force up the Río Paraná in search of the fabled Indian kingdom. In 1537 this force founded Asunción, in Paraguay, where the natives were friendly.

After 1535 the attention of the Spanish crown switched to Peru, where Pizarro was engaged in the successful conquest of the Inca Empire, where there was instant wealth in gold and silver and a malleable workforce in the enormous indigenous population. The small settlement at Asunción remained an isolated outpost until, in 1573, a force from Asunción travelled south to establish Santa Fe. Seven years later Juan de Garay refounded Buenos Aires, but it was only under his successor, Hernando Arias de Saavedra (1592-1614), that the new settlement became secure benefiting both from back up in Asunción and from the many cattle brought over by Mendoza which had increased and multiplied meanwhile.

However, before the time of Mendoza's expedition to the Plata estuary, Spanish expeditions were already exploring northern parts of present-day Argentina. In 1535 Diego de Almagro led a party from Peru which crossed the northwest into Argentina, and in 1543 the Spanish Viceroyalty of Peru was made administrative capital of southern South America. There was greatly increased motivation for exploring the region, however, when silver deposits were found in Potosí (now in Bolivia), and the Governorship of Tucumán was set up as an administrative centre. Explorations set forth from Chile and Peru to find trade routes and a source of cheap labour to work the mines, and so the oldest towns in Argentina were founded: Santiago del Estero (1553), Mendoza (1561), San Juan (1562), Córdoba (1573), Salta (1582), La Rioja (1591), and Jujuy (1593). A total of 25 cities were founded in present-day Argentina in the 16th century, 15 of which survived, at a time when the total Spanish population was under 2000.

Colonial rule

Throughout the colonial period the Argentine territories were an outlying part of the Spanish empire and of minor importance since Spanish colonial settlement and government was based in Peru, busy with exploiting the vast mineral wealth of Potosi in Alto Peru (and large supplies of indigenous labour). Argentine lands offered only sparse population and little mineral wealth by comparison. Also, the nomadic nature of many indigenous groups made any attempt at control difficult, whereas in Peru, Spanish rule was more readily superimposed on the centralized administration of the defeated Incas.

Buenos Aires failed to become an important port for a couple of centuries because from 1543 all the Spanish territories in South America were governed from Lima, the Vice-Regal capital, and trade with Spain was routed via Lima, Panama and the Caribbean. In fact, Buenos Aires was prohibited from trading directly, though the Paraná delta north of the city near Tigre provided ample opportunities for smuggling British and Portuguese goods into the city, and it rapidly expanded as a centre for contraband. By 1776 the city's population was 24,000, double the size of any of the cities of the interior. However, the Governorship of Tucumán was more important as a centre, due to the success of the *encomienda* system here, in which lands belonging to indigenous peoples were seized and redistributed to Spanish settlers. The idea was that the *encomenderos* in charge would exchange work done for religious education, but in reality these men were ruthless exploiters of slave labour and offered little in the way of spiritual enlightenment. In the Valles Cachaquiés the substantial indigenous population resisted conversion by Jesuit missionaries, and was effectively wiped out when they rose up against the Spanish landowners. So great was the need for workers in Potosí and Tucumán that black slaves were imported in the late 18th century. Settlers in the northeast of the country too had their conflicts with the indigenous population. The Pampas and Buenos Aires province were dangerous areas for white settlement, since in these lands wild cattle had long been hunted for their hides by Tehuelches and Mapuches. They drove cattle to Chile over the Andes for trade, and their violent armies, or *malones,* clashed regularly with newly arrived settlers. Around the early 18th century, the figure of the gaucho emerged, nomadic men of mixed *criollo* (early Argentine settlers) and indigenous origin, who roamed free on horseback, living off cattle. Once the Argentine state started to control land boundaries, these characters became emblematic of freedom and romanticized in important fictional works, *Martín Fierro* and *Don Segundo de los Sombras.* The gaucho is still a much admired figure all over Argentina today, though less wild and certainly no longer an outcast.

Jesuits came to civilize the native population under the protection of the Spanish crown in the late 16th century. They quickly set up missions which employed the reasonably pliant Guaraní residents of the upper Paraná in highly organized societies, with a militant component, equipped to resist the frequent raids by Portuguese in search of slaves. The Guaraní were compelled to comply with their educators since this exempted them from working in the silver mines, and as many as 4000 Guaraní lived in some missions, also producing *yerba mate* and tobacco as successful Jesuit businesses. The remains of their handsome architecture can be admired in Córdoba city and province, as well as at San Ignacio Mini in Misiones.

Buenos Aires at last gained some considerable power when the new viceroyalty of the River Plate was created in 1776, with the rapidly growing city as head of the large area and now able to trade with Spain and her other ports. However, as the trade of contraband into the city increased, flooding the market with cheaper European-produced goods, conflict increased between those advocating free trade, such as Manuel Belgrano, and those who wanted to retain a monopoly. The population of Buenos Aires increased enormously with the viceroyalty, along with its economy, as estancias sprang up to farm and export cattle, instead of rounding up the wild beasts, and with great success.

The Wars of Independence

The drive for independence in Argentina was partly a response to events in Europe, where Spain was initially allied to Napoleonic France. In 1806 and 1807 the British, at war with Napoleon and attracted by what they thought were revolutionary tensions in Buenos Aires, made two attempts to seize the city but were defeated. In 1808 Napoleon invaded Spain, deposing King Ferdinand VII, and provoking widespread resistance from Spanish guerrilla armies. Throughout Spanish America the colonial elites debated where their loyalties lay: to Napoleon's brother Joseph, now officially King? to Ferdinand, now in a French prison? to the Viceroy? to the Spanish resistance parliament in Cadiz?

On 25 May 1810, the *cabildo* of Buenos Aires deposed the viceroy and established a *junta* to govern on behalf of King Ferdinand VII, when the city's people gathered in front of the *cabildo* wearing pale blue and white ribbons, soon to become the colours of the Argentine flag. This move provoked resistance in outlying areas of the viceroyalty, Paraguay, Uruguay and Upper Peru (Bolivia) breaking away from the rule of Buenos Aires. Factional rivalry within the *junta* between supporters of independence and their opponents added to the confusion and instability. Six years later, in July 1816, when Buenos Aires was threatened by invasion from Peru and blockaded by a Spanish fleet in the Río de la Plata, a national congress held at Tucumán declared independence. The declaration was given reality by the genius and devotion of José de San Martín, who boldly marched an Argentine army across the Andes to free Chile, and embarked his forces for Peru, where he captured Lima, the first step towards liberation. San Martín was aided by an extraordinary feat from a local *caudillo* in the north, Martín Miguel de Güemes, whose army of gauchos was later to liberate Salta. *Caudillos* were local warlords who governed areas far larger, even, than today's provinces, organizing their own armies of local indigenous groups and gauchos. The *caudillos* did not recognize the Tucumán declaration, but so it was on 9 July 1816 that the United Provinces of the River Plate came into being.

Since independence

The 19th century

Much of the current rift between Buenos Aires and the rest of Argentina has its roots in a long-standing conflict which emerged in the early 19th century. The achievement of independence brought neither stability nor unity, since the new junta was divided between Federalists and Unitarists, a conflict that was to rage for over 40 years. The Unitarists, found mainly in the city of Buenos Aires, advocated strong central government, free trade, education and white immigration, looking to Europe for their inspiration. The Federalists, backed by the provincial elites and many of the great estancieros of Buenos Aires Province, resisted, defending local autonomy and traditional values. Behind the struggle were also economic interests: Buenos Aires and the coastal areas benefited from trade with Europe; the interior provinces did not. As the conflict raged, the territory, known officially as the United Provinces of the Río de la Plata, had none of the features of a modern state: there was neither central government, army, capital city nor constitution.

Order, of a sort, was established after 1829 by Juan Manuel de Rosas, a powerful *caudillo* (provincial leader) and Governor of Buenos Aires. In 1833, he attempted to gain widespread support from local *caudillos* with his Campaign of the Desert, which claimed vast areas of land from indigenous groups, granted to Rosas' allies. However, his overthrow in 1852 unleashed another round in the battles between Unitarists and Federalists and between Buenos Aires and the provinces. In 1853 a constitution establishing a federal system of government was finally drafted but Buenos Aires province refused to join the new Argentine Confederation, which had its capital at Paraná, and set up its own separate republic. Conflict between the two states erupted over the attempt by Buenos Aires to control and tax commerce on the Río Paraná but the victory of Buenos Aires at Pavón (1861) opened the way to a solution: the city became the seat of the federal government with Bartolomé Mitre, former governor of Buenos Aires became the first president of Argentina. There was another political flare-up of the old quarrel in 1880, ending in the humiliation of the city of Buenos Aires, which was separated from its province and made into a special federal territory.

Although there was resistance to the new constitution from some of the western provinces, the institutions of a modern state were created in the two decades after 1861 by Mitre's important period of government: he set up a national bank, bureaucracy, a postal service and an army. And it was the building of railways across the Pampas which did most to create national unity, breaking the power of the *caudillos* by enabling the federal government to send in troops quickly. The new army was quickly employed to defeat Francisco Solano López of Paraguay in the War of the Triple Alliance (1865-1870). They were used again in President Roca's genocidal Conquest of the Wilderness (1879-1880) which exterminated the indigenous tribes of the Pampas and the south.

In the last quarter of the 19th century Argentina was transformed: the newly acquired stability encouraged foreign investment; the Pampas were fenced, ploughed up and turned over to commercial export agriculture; and railways and port facilities were built. The presidency of Domingo Sarmiento had been keen on widespread immigration from Europe, which transformed the character of Buenos Aires and other cities around the Plata estuary, where the population grew from 200,000 in 1870 to two million in 1920. Sarmiento also sought to Europeanize the country and his impressive educational policy included the importing of teachers from North America. Political power, however, remained in the hands of a small group of large landowners, who had been granted territories after the Conquest of the Desert, and their urban allies. Few Argentines had the vote, and the opposition Unión Cívica Radical, excluded from power, conspired with dissidents in the army in attempts to overthrow the government.

The 20th century

As the British built railways stretching across the country, the sheep industry flourished, making Argentina's fortune through exporting both wool and meat. Refrigerator ships were invented in the 1870's, enabling meat to be shipped in bulk to the expanding industrial countries of Britain and Europe. One of the landmarks of modern Argentine history was the 1912 Sáenz Peña law which established universal manhood suffrage, since until then, power had been centralized in the hands of the elite, with no votes for the working classes. Sáenz Peña, president between 1910 and 1916, sought to bring the middle and working classes into politics, gambling that the Conservatives could reorganize themselves and attract their votes. The gamble failed: the Conservatives failed to gain a mass following and the Radicals came to power. The Radical Civic Union was created in 1890, but Radical presidents Hipólito Yrigoyen (1916-1922 and 1928-1930) and Marcelo T de Alvear (1922-1928) found themselves trapped between the demands of an increasingly militant urban labour movement and the opposition of the Conservatives, still powerful in the provinces and with allies in the armed forces. Through the 1920s, Argentina was the 'breadbasket of the world' and its sixth richest nation. Fifty years later, the country had become practically third world, a fall from grace which still haunts the Argentine consciousness. The world depression following the Wall Street Crash of 1929 devastated export markets, but the military coup which overthrew Yrigoyen in 1930 was a significant turning point: the armed forces returned to government for the first time in over 50 years and were to continue to play a major political role until 1983. Through the 1930s a series of military backed governments, dominated by the Conservatives, held power; the Radicals were outlawed and elections were so fraudulent that it frequently happened that more people voted than were on the register. Yet the armed forces themselves were disunited: while most officers supported the Conservatives and the landholding elites, a minority of ultra-nationalist officers, inspired by developments in Europe, supported industrialization and the creation of a one-party dictatorship along fascist lines. The outbreak of war in Europe increased these tensions and a series of military coups in 1943-1944 led to the rise of Colonel Juan Domingo Perón. When the military allowed a return to civilian rule in 1946 Perón swept into power winning the Presidential elections. His government is chiefly remembered by many Argentines for improving the living conditions of the workers through the introduction of paid holidays and welfare measures in his *justicialismo:* social justice. Perón was an authoritarian and charismatic leader, and especially in its early years the government was strongly nationalistic, taking control over the British-owned railways in 1948 by buying them back at a staggering £150 million. Opposition parties were harassed and independent newspapers taken over since Perón wasn't at all interested in free press. Although Perón was easily re-elected in 1951, his government soon ran into trouble: economic problems led to the introduction of a wage freeze which upset the labour unions which were the heart of Peronist support; the death of Evita in 1952 was another blow; and a dispute with the church in 1954-1955 added to Perón's problems. In September 1955 a military coup unseated Perón who went into exile, in Paraguay, Panama, Venezuela, the Dominican Republic and, from 1961 to 1973, in Spain.

Perón's legacy dominated Argentina for the next two decades. No attempt was made to destroy his social and economic reforms but the armed forces determined to exclude the Peronists from power. Argentine society was bitterly divided between Peronists and anti-Peronists and the economy struggled, partly as a result of Perón's measures against the economic elite and in favour of the workers. Between 1955 and 1966 there was an uneasy alternation of military and civilian regimes. The military officers who seized power in 1966 announced their intention to carry out a Nationalist Revolution, with austerity measures to try to gain control of a spiralling economy, but they were quickly discredited by a deteriorating economic situation. The Cordobazo, a left-wing student and workers uprising in Córdoba in 1969, was followed by the emergence of several guerrilla groups such as the Montoneros and the People's Revolutionary Army (ERP), as well as growth of political violence. As Argentina became more ungovernable, Perón, from his exile, refused to denounce those guerrilla groups which called themselves Peronist.

In 1971 General Alejandro Lanusse seized power, promising a return to civilian rule and calculating that the only way to control the situation was to allow Perón to return. When the military bowed out in 1973, elections were won by the Peronist candidate, Hector Campora. Perón returned from exile in Madrid to resume as president in October 1973, but died on 1 July 1974, leaving the presidency to his widow, Vice-President María Estela Martínez de Perón, his third wife, known as 'Isabelita'. Perón's death unleashed chaos: hyper-inflation, resumed guerrilla warfare and the operation of right-wing death squads who abducted people suspected of

The Falklands/Malvinas conflict

The dispute between Britain and Argentina over the Falkland Islands/Islas Malvinas has a long history. Dutch sailor Sebald de Weert made the first generally acknowledged sighting of the islands in 1598. In 1764, France established a small colony there, while the British built an outpost on the northern tip. But when the French government sold Port Louis to Spain in 1766, the British were expelled. In 1811, following the outbreak of the Wars of Independence, Spain withdrew her forces from the islands. And after British warships expelled a force from Buenos Aires in 1833, the islands came under British rule.

Perón was quick to exploit the disputed status of the islands as part of an appeal to Argentine nationalism during his first administration (1946-1955). In 1965, the United Nations called on Britain and Argentina to resolve their differences peacefully, and talks took place, but were complicated by the hostility of the islanders themselves towards any change in their status.

In 1982, when the British government reduced its forces in the area, the Argentine military regime seized their chance. President General Galtieri had huge economic problems, and thought a successful invasion would unite the population behind him. An Argentine force of 5000 men landed in South Georgia on 2 April 1982, quickly overwhelming the small British garrison without loss of life. The British military and civilian authorities were expelled and the 1700 inhabitants placed under an Argentine military governor. Though most Latin American states sympathized with Buenos Aires over the sovereignty issue, many were unhappy with the use of force. Backed by a United Nations resolution and the crucial logistical support of the United States, the British government launched a naval force to regain the islands. Over the following three weeks, as the war was fought in the air and on the seas around the Falklands/Malvinas, the Argentines lost numerous aircraft, the cruiser General Belgrano, and several other vessels. The British lost two destroyers, two frigates and a landing vessel.

The British reoccupation of the islands began on 21 May, attacking ineffective Argentine defensive positions around Port Stanley. They met stiff resistance, but most of the Argentine troops were conscripts, poorly trained and equipped, and no match for British regular forces. On 14 June Argentine forces surrendered.

Casualties in the war outnumbered the small island population: 746 Argentines were killed (over 300 on the *General Belgrano*, and 1336 were wounded); 256 British soldiers were killed, and 777 wounded. The consequences of the war for Argentina were that the military government was discredited: perhaps less by defeat than by its obvious misjudgement, and by the accounts given by returning troops of incompetent leadership and lack of supplies. General Galtieri was replaced as president, and in 1983, Argentina returned to civilian rule. In Britain, Thatcher's success undoubtedly helped her retain power.

left-wing sympathies. In March 1976, to nobody's surprise, the military overthrew Isabelita and replaced her with a junta led by General Jorge Videla.

The new government closed Congress, outlawed political parties, placed trade unions and universities under military control and unleashed the so-called 'Dirty War', a brutal assault on the guerrilla groups and anyone else who manifested opposition. The military leaders were not at all interested in trying and convicting those they suspected of being dissidents, and started a campaign of violence against anyone remotely Jewish, Marxist, journalists, intellectuals, psychologists and anyone, according to President General Videla, who was as 'spreading ideas contrary to Western Christian civilisation'. As many as 30,000 people are thought to have 'disappeared' during this period, removed by violent squads who would take them to clandestine detention centres to be raped, tortured or brutally killed. This is one of Argentina's bleakest memories, and that many Argentines maintain that a strong line was needed to deal with guerrillas is a sign of how hidden the reality was at the time. In order that the disappeared should never be forgotten, the Madres de la Plaza de Mayo still parade around the plaza in Buenos Aires with photographs of their lost children pinned to their chests.

Videla's nominated successor, General Roberto Viola took over for three years in March 1981 but was overthrown by General Leopoldo Galtieri in December 1981, who failed to keep a grasp on a plummeting economy, and an increasingly discontent public. Attempting to win the crowds, Galtieri's decision to invade the Falkland/Malvinas Islands in April 1982 backfired when the British retaliated by sending a fleet to the south Atlantic. After the war was lost in June 1982 General Reynaldo Bignone took over, and promptly created a law giving amnesty to all human rights abusers in the military.

Elections in October 1983 were won by Raúl Alfonsín and his Unión Cívica Radical (UCR) and during 1985 Generals Videla, Viola and Galtieri were sentenced to long terms of imprisonment for their parts in the 'dirty war'. While Alfonsín's government struggled to deal with the legacy of the past, it was overwhelmed by continuing economic problems, the most obvious of which was hyperinflation. Workers rushed to the shops once they'd been paid to spend their earnings before prices rose, and supermarkets announced price increases over the tannoy since they were so unstable. When the Radicals were defeated by Carlos Menem, the Peronist (*Justicialist*) presidential candidate, Alfonsín stepped down early because of economic instability. Strained relations between the Peronist government and the military led to several rebellions, which Menem attempted to appease by pardoning the imprisoned generals. His popularity among civilians declined, but in 1991-1992 the economy minister, Domingo Cavallo, succeeded in restoring confidence in the economy and the government as a whole with his *Plan de Convertabilidad*. This, the symbol of his stability, was the introduction of a new currency pegged to the United States dollar, and preventing the central bank from printing money which could not be backed up but the cash in reserve. After triumphing in the October 1993 congressional elections at the expense of the UCR, the Peronists themselves lost some ground in April 1994 elections to a constituent assembly. The party to gain most, especially in Buenos Aires, was Frente Grande, a broad coalition of left-wing groups and disaffected Peronists. Behind the loss of confidence of these dissident Peronists were unrestrained corruption and a pact in December 1993 between Menem and Alfonsín pledging UCR support for constitutional changes which included re-election of the president for a second term of four years.

By the 1995 elections, the majority of the electorate favoured stability over constitutional concerns and returned President Menem. The Peronists also increased their majority in the Chamber of Deputies and gained a majority in the Senate. Menem's renewed popularity was short-lived: joblessness remained high and corruption unrestrained. His decision to privatize the major industries scandalized traditional Peronists in his party, and his legacy remains a cause of despair, since electricity, gas, telephones and YPF, the country's oil industry, all belong to huge Spanish companies. In July 1996, the Radicals won the first direct elections for mayor of Buenos Aires and in mid-term congressional elections in October 1997 the Peronist Party lost its ruling majority. Most votes went to the Alianza Democrática, formed by the Radicals and the Frepaso coalition. The latter's candidate for Buenos Aires

Dirty war

The 'Dirty War', unleashed by the armed forces after 1976 is one of the most violent incidents in modern South American history, and hardly a month goes by without this grim episode provoking further controversy in the Argentine press.

Guerrilla groups started emerging in Argentina after 1969, in angry response to military rule, among them the Monteneros and the People's Revolutionary Army (Ejército Revolucionario del Pueblo or ERP). The middle class educated Monteneros, inspired by a mixture of Peronism, Catholicism and Marxism, proclaimed allegiance to the exiled Perón, and wanted to liberate the working classes from the evils of capitalism. The ERP, by contrast drawing their inspiration from Trotsky and Che Guevara, argued that political violence would push the military government towards increased repression which would ignite working-class opposition and lead to civil war and socialist revolution.

If Peronists and non-Peronists disagreed over their aims, their methods were similar: kidnappings and bank robberies raised money and gained publicity; army and police officers were assassinated along with right-wing Peronists. Wealthy Argentine families and multi-national companies were forced to distribute food and other goods to the poor to obtain the release of kidnap victims. Head of the Argentine military, General Jorge Videla retaliated by squashing any uprising before it had a chance to establish: pop concerts were banned, and indeed any gathering of young people. Far more terrifying, Videla initiated a plan called The Process of national Reorganisation, *El Proceso*. The Dirty War was declared, and the military carried out their own kidnappings of anyone they deemed likely to be dangerous. Anyone with left wing tendencies might be taken without warning, tortured, and then, mysteriously, 'disappeared'. All three armed services operated their own death squads and camps in a campaign of indiscriminate violence. By 1978/79 both the ERP and the Monteneros had ceased to function, and in the process, tens of thousands of people disappeared: although an official report produced after the return to civilian rule put their number at 8960, some 15,000 cases have now been documented and human rights groups now estimate the total at some 30,000. They are remembered still by the Mothers of the Plaza de Mayo, a human rights group made up of relatives, who march anti-clockwise around the Plaza de Mayo in central Buenos Aires every Thursday at 1530, with photos of their 'disappeared' loved ones pinned to their chests. Videla, along with other military leaders, has been charged with numerous human rights abuse charges, but remains merely under house arrest. On March 24th 2006, the 30th anniversary of the Military junta was marked with a national day of awareness and demonstrations in Buenos Aires, suggesting that the scars of the Dirty War have yet to heal.

province, Graciela Fernández Meijide, defeated Hilda Duhalde of the Peronists, whose husband, Eduardo, was provincial governor. In addition to the Peronists' poor showing, several senior members were embarrassed by alleged involvement with millionaire Alfredo Yabrán. Many suspected Yabrán of criminal activities, not least of ordering the murder of journalist José Luis Cabezas (January 1997). The case fuelled the rivalry between Duhalde and Menem but in May 1998 Yabrán, who was being sought by the police, committed suicide.

In November 1998 Alianza Democrática chose the Radical Fernando de la Rua as its candidate for the October 1999 presidential election. Moves from Menem supporters to put forward Menem for a further (constitutionally dubious) term of office helped delay the Peronist choice of candidate until July 1999 when Eduardo Duhalde received the backing of Menem. Although Alianza Democrática offered little change in economic policy, the Peronists were harmed by the corruption scandals surrounding the Menem administration and the continuing rivalry between Menem and Duhalde, enabling De la Rua to win the presidency and take office in December 1999.

The 21st century

Facing recession and impossible debts with the IMF, De la Rua implemented austerity measures, but these were not enough to save the peso, and many jobs which were lost in late 2000. Young people started to leave the country in massive numbers, looking for work elsewhere, many taking their savings with them. In an attempt to keep reserves of cash within the country, De la Rua started the *corralito* (literally meaning 'little pen'), a law determining that individuals could only withdraw 250 pesos from their accounts per week, and converting savings to government bonds. In December 2001, the people of Buenos Aires and other large cities took to the streets in an unprecedented display both of violent rioting and peaceful pot bashing by furious middle-class housewives, the *caserolazas*. The country went through five presidents in a period of a couple of months, but nothing could prevent devaluation, and in January 2002 the peso lost its parity with the dollar. Suddenly Argentina plummeted from being a first world nation on a par (or so the Argentines thought) with the United States, to being a third world state, with a weak currency, and little hope of bolstering the economy. The blow to the Argentine psyche has been severe. Duhalde was the last of the quick succession of presidents, and attempted to impose some order, appeasing the IMF by sacking a large number of public employees who were a considerable drain on public spending. However, corruption remained and street crime increased, with an alarming fashion for express kidnappings among the wealthier Buenos Aires families. Elections held in May 2003 threatened to return Menem to power, in a brief rush of nostalgia for the days of apparent prosperity. But fearing defeat, before a second election could be held Menem stepped down, and ex-governor of Santa Cruz province, Nestor Kirchner, came to power with a meagre 24% of the country's votes. He's not much liked throughout the country, particularly by landowners and farmers, since he has raised taxes on exports to an absurd degree. While unemployment remains rife in Argentina, many criticise Kirchner for maintaining a dependency on Plan Trabajar, the government handout to the unemployed, which is eroding the culture of work, some fear.

Population

With an estimated 36,000,000 population, the third largest in South America after Brazil and Colombia, Argentina is one of the least densely populated countries in the continent. Thirty six per cent of the population lives in the urban area of Gran Buenos Aires, leaving most of Patagonia, for example, with 2 km sq per inhabitant. In the province of Buenos Aires, the people are mainly of European origin and the classic Argentine background is of Spanish and Italian immigrants. In Patagonia and the Lake District there's a considerable smattering of Scottish, Welsh, French, German and Swiss inhabitants, with Eastern Europeans to be found in the northeast of the country. In the northwestern provinces, at least half the people are indigenous, or of indigenous descent, mixed in Salta Province, for example, with a long line of *criollo* stock. Although *mestizos* form about 15% of the population of the whole country, the existence of different ethnic groups wasn't recognized until the mid 1990s. There are 13 indigenous groups, totalling about 500,000 people, 3% of the total population, many living in communities in the northwest, and scattered throughout the country. The largest minorities are the *Toba* (20%), the *Wichi* or *Mataco* (10%), the *Mapuche*

(10%) and the *Guaraní* (10%). Several of the smaller groups are in danger of extinction: in 1987 the Minority Rights Group reported the death of the last *Ona* in Tierra del Fuego and noted that the 100 remaining *Tehuelches* were living on a reservation in southern Patagonia.

Immigration

The city of Buenos Aires and the surrounding province was transformed through immigration in the 19th century, to a society of predominantly European origin. White immigration was encouraged by the 1853 Constitution and the new political stability after 1862 encouraged a great wave of settlers from Europe. Between 1857 and 1930 total immigration was over 6,000,000, almost all from Europe. About 55% of these were Italians, followed by Spaniards (26%), and then, far behind, groups of other Europeans and Latin Americans. British and North Americans normally came as stockbreeders, technicians and business executives. By 1895, 25% of the population of 4,000,000 were immigrants. Over 1,300,000 Italians settled in Argentina between 1876 and 1914. Their influence can be seen in the country's food, its urban architecture and its language, especially in Buenos Aires where the local vocabulary has incorporated *Lunfardo,* a colourful slang of largely Italian origin, which started out as the language of thieves. Today it is estimated that 12.8% of the population are foreign born.

Culture

Arts and crafts

All over Argentina you'll find fine handicrafts made by local indigenous groups, which vary widely all over the country, or by the continuing tradition of gaucho craftsmen, who make fine pieces associated with rural life.

Gaucho crafts

There's a strong tradition of working precious metals, such as silver, into fine belts and buckles, since the gaucho's way of carrying his wealth with him was originally in the ornate silver *rastras* and buckles which are still used today over leather belts, or to tie *fajas* (woven cloth belts). Silver spurs, stirrups and the fine silver decoration on saddles are all extraordinary examples of traditions dating from the early 18th century. The gaucho *facón* an all purpose knife used especially for cutting his *asado*, is made with elaborately wrought silver handle, and the *mate* (the vessel itself, rather than the drink) which is often just a hollowed out gourd, can also be an exquisitely worked piece of silver which you'd probably rather display than use. Associated objects with the same fine silverwork today include earrings, belt buckles and scarf rings. Leather was always important for making all the items associated with horses, and obviously widely available, and the complexity of the traditional bridles, belts and straps is impressive. Long thin strips of leather are woven into wide plaits, or *trensas* and used still for all parts of horse bridlery, as well as more decorative pieces. The *mate* itself is made most traditionally from the gourd, but also from wood, tin or silver, with attractive examples made by artisans in the Lake District at El Bolsón, for example.

Indigenous crafts

Argentina's many indigenous groups produce fine handicrafts spanning all disciplines from woodwork to weaving, musical instruments to jewellery. In the northeast, the Guaraní produce fine woodwork, much of it inspired by the rich animal and bird life all around them. Delicate fabric for bags is woven from the tough fibrous strands of tree creepers, and there are necklaces made from seeds. Carved wooden animals are widely available, along with replicas for tourists of their traditional weapons, bows and arrows and pea shooters.

Handicrafts are richest in the northwest, particularly the Valles Calchaquíes, near the *puna* and along the Quebrada de Humahuaca, where there is abundant llama wool and vicuña, which is woven into *ponchos*, or knitted into jumpers, socks, scarves and hats. Brightly coloured woven textiles from Bolivia can also be found at many markets. The ubiquitous pan pipes are the most available examples of instruments from the rich Andean musical tradition, and can be found in abundance at Tilcara and Purmamarca markets. *Ponchos* are woven throughout the northwest but particularly fine examples can be found in the Calchaquíes valleys and around Salta, where the red *ponchos* of Güemes are made, and in western Catamarca province, where there are the finest ponchos of woven vicuña are made. You can also fine beautiful woven wall hangings in Los Valle Calchaquíes, often depicting scenes of churches in the valleys, and the local symbol, the ostrich-like *suri* and wood from the giant *cardón* cactus is used for carving distinctive small objects and furniture, with the spines of the cactus leaving attractive slits in the wood. For conservation reasons, only fallen trees are used.

In the Chaco region, bags are made from textile woven from *chaguar* fibre by Wichí, Toba, and other indigenous groups of the area, as they have done for hundreds of years. The Wichí also make fine wooden objects, animals mainly, from *palo santo*, a greenish scented wood, also used extensively in wood carving by communities who live along the Río Pilcomayo which forms the border with Paraguay. In northeastern Salta, painted wooden masks are made by the Chané culture to be used in traditional agricultural ceremonies. They also make charming ceramics in the shape of animals. Isolated indigenous groups of Toba, Chané and Mataco in the lowlands to the east of the province produce exquisite carvings of birds and animals, using a variety of local woods. Cowbones are used to make the beaks and feet, as well as an inlay to decorate spoons and other utilitarian items. And *Palo santo* is also used for *mate* vessels, replacing the traditional gourd. Throughout the south, there are superb Mapuche weavings in natural wool colours with bold geometric designs.

Cinema

Argentina's cinema is one of its liveliest art forms and has enjoyed a recent renaissance with some brilliant films being made, more in the European or *auteur* tradition, than in Hollywood style, but with a couple of worldwide successes and Oscar nominations. Watching a couple of Argentine films is certainly one of the best ways of tapping into the country's culture before you arrive.

In 1922, Buenos Aires had some 27,000,000 film goers each year and 128 movie theatres, the largest, the Grand Splendid seating 1350 people. By 1933 there were 1608 cinemas throughout Argentina, with 199 in the capital. However, the taste of the cinema going public was for Hollywood movies. Hollywood has dominated the screens in Latin America for the first hundred years of film history, averaging some 90% of viewing time in Argentina.

However, in 1950's, New Argentine Cinema started as a movement of independent films which were a far more honest and accurate reflection of life in the country. Film clubs and journals created a climate of awareness of film as an art form and the tenets of Italian neo-realism and the '*politique des auteurs*' of *Cahiers du Cinema* provided alternatives to the studio-based Hollywood system. In Argentina, Leopoldo Torre Nilsson (1924-1978) explored aristocratic decadence and his early film *La casa del ángel* (The House of the Angel, 1957) was greeted with praise all over the world. Fernando Birri (1925-) used neo-realist principles to explore the hidden realities of Argentina. His film school in Santa Fé made an important documentary about young shanty town children, *Tire dié* (Throw us a dime, 1957) and helped pioneer a more flexible, socially committed, cinema.

Younger film makers of the 60s like Manuel Antín (1926-), David Kohon (1929-) and Leonardo Favio (1938-) explored middle-class alienation or the sexual rites of passage of the young, set in the cafés and streets of Buenos Aires. Meanwhile, the growing climate of revolutionary sentiment of the late 1960s was reflected in Solanas's *La hora de los hornos* (The Hour of the Furnaces, 1966-1968), a key work of populist radicalism.

After a brief spell of radical optimism in the late 1960s and early 1970s, reflected in a number of other nationalist-populist movies, the dream of the second coming of Perón turned into the nightmare that led to the brutal military takeover in March 1976. Strict censorship was imposed on cinema, with only the lightest comedies and thrillers escaping total ban or cuts. Film makers such as Solanas, who went into exile, found it difficult to adapt to the new conditions and remained in a cultural wilderness. Within Argentina, the tight military control began to slacken in the early 1980s and some important films were made, including María Luisa Bemberg's (1922-1995) *Señora de nadie* (Nobody's Woman, 1982) which was premiered the day before the invasion of the Falklands/Malvinas.

With the return to civilian rule in 1983, the Radical government abolished censorship and put two well known film makers in charge of the National Film Institute, Manuel Antín and Ricardo Wullicher (1948-). Antín's granting of credits to young and established directors and his internationalist strategy had an immediate effect. For several years there was a great flowering of talent, a development that would only be halted temporarily by the economic difficulties of the late 1980s. The trade paper *Variety* (25 March 1987) commented on this new effervescence: 'Never before has there been such a mass of tangible approval as in the years since democratic rule returned at the end of 1983. In 1986, the Hollywood Academy granted the first Oscar for an Argentine picture, *The Official Version*, directed by Luis Puenzo (1946-), which dealt with the recent traumas of the disappearances of the 'Dirty War', but in rather sentimental Hollywood terms. This followed the massive box office success of Bemberg's *Camila,* which commented by analogy on the same subject. Solanas' two films about exile and the return to democracy, *Tangos, el exilio de Gardel* (Tangos the Exile of Gardel, 1985) and *Sur* (South, 1988), both offer interesting insights in Solanas' idiosyncratic poetic style. Puenzo, Bemberg and Solanas remained the most visible directors in the 1980s and 1990s, but dozens of other directors made movies in a range of different styles. Lita Stantic made perhaps the most complex film about the 'Dirty War' of the military regime, the superb *Un muro de silencio* (A Wall of Silence, 1993). This was a success with the critics, but was ignored by the public who preferred to view politics and repression through a gauze of melodrama and rock music, as in Marcelo Piñeyro's *Tango Feroz* (1993).

After 1989, the Menem government introduced credits and a percentage of box office and video sales to the film industry and Argentine cinema has undergone a revival in the last few years. The hard economic fact is that by far the vast majority of screens in the country show Hollywood product, and home-grown movies have to compete on these very commercial terms. However, the Oscar nomination of Argentine film *El Hijo de la Novia* in 2002 boosted national self confidence, and was a big success within Argentina. Its anti-hero Ricardo Darín also starred in Fabiano Belinski's sophisticated heist movie *Neuve Reinas* (Nine Queens) which through a labyrinth of tricks and scams neatly articulates a Buenos Aires where no one can trust anyone. It was a huge success worldwide as well as in the country, and the death of Bielinsky following his second film. El Aura was a tragic loss to Argentine cinema.

Successes of the new Argentine cinema included a return to cinema with a social conscience in Adrián Gaetano's *Bolivia*, addressing the sorry plight of an illegal Bolivian worker in urban Argentina, and his *Un Oso Rojo* (2002) charting the fate of a newly released prisoner trying to reclaim the affection of his daughter from his wife's new boyfriend. Pablo Trapero's *Mundo Grua* is a stark but touching portrayal of the life of a crane driver, while Lisandro Alonso's astonishing *Libertad* shows with utter honesty the life of a peon on an estancia. In Luis Ortega's charming *Caja Negra* a young woman's relationship with her outcast father and eccentric ancient grandmother is explored with great humour and compassion. Two of the most striking films of recent years are *Pizza, Birra, Faso* by Stagnaro and Gaetano, and *No Quiero Volver a Casa* by Albertina Carri. Lucrecia Martel showed an original voice in her disturbing *La Cienaga,* a vivid portrayal of a divided family's unhappy summer in their country house. Highly allegorical and rich in atmospheric detail, it's a wonderful contemporary portrait of the country. Her La Nina Santa (Holy Girl) was less successful.

Most cinemas in the country show Hollywood movies, but the larger cities have an art house cinema, and if you happen to be around during any of the film festivals, you can usually catch a few recent Argentine releases: Mar del Plata Film Festival in mid March, Buenos Aires, film festival in mid April, and Salta's film festival in the first week of December.

Fine art and sculpture

Colonial art

Argentina (along with neighbouring Uruguay) is arguably the most European of Latin American cultures. Mass immigration and the 19th-century extermination of the few remaining indigenous peoples have created a mainstream culture which defines itself largely in relation to Europe. The exception to this is in the northwest of the country, where the great Andean civilizations struggle to retain their identity against the irresistible tide of westernization and the tourist industry.

As the region, which is now Argentina, was initially of little importance to the Spanish, there is relatively little colonial art or architecture in most of the country. However, in the northern regions of Salta, Jujuy and Misiones, there are some impressive colonial buildings and some good examples of colonial painting, especially the remarkable portraits of archangels in military uniform in the churches at Uquía and Casabindo, as well as some exquisite golden retables and pulpits in the churches of the Quebrada de Humahuaca. Yavi, at the very north, is the most remarkable of all these, with a golden sculpture of an angel in military uniform, and beautiful ceramic cherubs on the golden pulpit. Fine colonial art can be seen at the Museo de Arte Hispanoamericano Isaac Fernández Blanco in Buenos Aires. In Misiones, there are several sites with remains of Jesuits missions, particularly impressive is that at San Ignacio. Córdoba Province too has remains of Jesuit churches and residences at Santa Catalina and Jesús María.

The 19th century

In the 19th century, as Argentina gained Independence and consolidated itself as a modern nation, the ruling elite of the country were determined to make Argentine culture as close to Europe as possible, against what they saw as the 'barbarism' of native customs. The prosperous Buenos Aires bourgeoisie commissioned European architects to build their mansions and collected European fine and decorative arts to decorate them. Rich Argentines travelled to Europe to buy paintings, and gradually began to demand that European painters come to Argentina to depict the wealth and elegance of the ruling class through portraits and landscapes. The most famous foreign artist was Carlos Enrique Pellegrini, whose fine society portraits can be seen in the Museo Nacional de Bellas Artes in Buenos Aires.

By the middle of the century, as Argentina became more politically stable, a new generation of Argentine-trained artists appeared in Buenos Aires. They absorbed some of the techniques and interests of the European artists who were the first to depict their country, but they also discovered a new interest in Romanticism and Realism. Most famous in this period was Prilidiano Pueyrredón (1823-1870), whom many Argentines consider to be their first national painter. Of more obvious appeal is the rather eccentric Cándido López (1839-1902) whose work has only recently been re-evaluated. López followed the Argentine army to the north of the country during the wars with Paraguay and Uruguay, where he depicted the great battles in a characteristic naïve style. López left behind a remarkable series of paintings, which are often displayed in their own room in the Museo Nacional de Bellas Artes in Buenos Aires. By the end of the century, many artists were working in Argentina, many of whom had been through the National Art School. Generally speaking, they absorbed European movements several decades after they appeared in their original forms. Benito Quinquela Martin's work celebrated the workers in the dockyards of La Boca, in a colourful naïve style, and his paintings can be seen in the gallery bearing his name in La Boca.

The 20th century

In the 20th century, Argentina really found its artistic expression; the dynamism, size and mix of nationalities in the capital created a complex urban society in which artists and intellectuals have prospered. Some of the bohemian attraction of Buenos Aires can still be felt in its more intellectual cafés and districts. This cultural effervescence has been at the expense of the regions; the capital totally dominates the country, and most artists are forced to move there to have any chance of success.

The first avant-garde artistic movement in Buenos Aires emerged in 1924 with the formation of a groups which called itself 'Martn Fierro', in homage to the national epic poem of the same name. This group brought together a small number of upper-class intellectuals, the most famous of which was the writer Jorge Luis Borges. The most important visual artist was Xul Solar (1887-1963), who illustrated many of Borges's texts. Solar was one of the 20th century's most eccentric and engaging artists. He had a great interest in mysticism and the occult, and tried to create an artistic system to express his complex beliefs, mostly small-scale watercolours in which a sometimes bizarre visionary world is depicted. Many of them are covered in inscriptions in one of the languages he created: Neo-Creole or Pan-Lengua. During the final decades of his life Solar lived in a house on the Paraná Delta near Tigre, where he created a total environment in accordance with his fantastic world, even inventing a new game of chess with rules based on astrology. There is now a Xul Solar Museum in the house where he was born in Buenos Aires and where many of his watercolours and objects are displayed.

Intellectual life in the 1920s was divided into two factions, each named after districts in the city. The elegant Calle Florida gave its name to the Martín Fierro set, who belonged to the elite. Several blocks away, the working-class Boedo district gave its name to a school of working-class socialist artists who rejected the rarefied atmosphere of Florida in favour of socially critical paintings in a grim realistic style. Possibly the most important artist associated with this group was Antonio Berni (1905-1981), whose colourful paintings give a vivid impression of Buenos Aires working-class life, and are worth looking for in the Museo de Bellas Artes and MALBA in Buenos Aires.

In the 1940s, with the political crisis provoked by the Second World War, a new avant-garde movement emerged to overtake the Martin Fierro group. In the mid 1940s, a group of young artists founded an abstract art movement called 'Madí' (a nonsense word) which attempted to combine sophisticated abstract art inspired by Russian Constructivism with a more chaotic sense of fun. Madí works are characterized by blocks of bright colours within an irregular frame often incorporating physical movement within the structure of the work. As such, they are somewhere between painting and sculpture. For the first time in Argentina, Madí developed artistic principles (such as the irregular frame, or the use of neon gas) before the rest of the world.

Madí was a short-lived adventure plagued by infighting amongst its members and political divisions. The cultural climate under Perón (1946-1955) rejected this type of 'decadent' art in favour of a form of watered-down populism. It was not until the 1960s that cultural life regained its momentum.

The 1960s were a golden age for the arts in Argentina. As in many countries, the decade brought new freedoms and questions to young people, and the art scene responded vigorously. Artistic activity was focused around the centre of Buenos Aires between Plaza San Martin and Avenida Cordoba, an area known as the *'manzana loca'* (crazy block). This area contained a huge number of galleries and cafés, and most importantly the Di Tella Institute, a privately-funded art centre which was at the cutting edge of the visual arts. Artistic movements of the time ranged from a raw expressionism called *'Nueva figuración'* to very sophisticated conceptual art. The most provocative form of art during this period took the form of 'happenings', one of the most famous of which (by Marta Minujin) consisted of a replica of the Buenos Aires obelisk made in sweet bread, which was then eaten by passers-by.

After the military coup of 1966 the authorities began to question the activities of these young artists and even tried to censor some exhibitions. The Di Tella Institute closed, leaving the '*manzana loca*' without a heart, and making it more dangerous for alternative young artists to live without harassment (often for little more than having long hair). During the 'leaden years' of the military government during the 1970s, there was little space for alternative art and many left-wing artists abandoned art in favour of direct political action. However, one space in Buenos Aires continued to show politically challenging art: the Centro de Arte y Comunicación (or CAYC), often through works which were so heavily coded that the authorities would not pick up the message.

Since the restoration of democracy in 1983, Argentina has been coming to terms with the destruction or inefficiency of many of its cultural institutions over recent decades. The last few years have seen a rebirth of activity, with improvements in the National Museum of Fine Arts and the creation of the important Centro Cultural Recoleta and more recently the Centro Cultural Jorge Luis Borges (in the Galerías Pacífico). There are important alternative art centres, especially the Ricardo Rojas Centre and the Klemm Foundation which show some of the most interesting young artists. The art scene in Buenos Aires is now very vibrant, if somewhat confusing, with myriad conflicting and apparently contradictory styles and tendencies.

Literature

Modern Argentina has an extremely high literary rate, around 95%, and good bookshops are to be found even in small country towns, with some really splendid *librerías* in Buenos Aires. Correspondingly, the country has produced some great writers, quite apart from the wonderful Borges, and it's well worth reading some of their work before you come, or seeking out a few novels to bring on your travels.

With an urban culture derived almost entirely from European immigrants, Argentina's literary development was heavily influenced by European writers in the 19th century, the works of Smith, Locke, Voltaire and Rousseau amongst others, being inspiration for the small literate elite of young intellectuals such as Mariano Moreno (1778-1811), one of the architects of the Independence movement. The great theme was how to adapt European forms to American realities, first in the form of political tracts and later in early nationalist poetry. Outside the cities, popular culture thrived on storytelling and the music of the gauchos, whose famous *payadores* are superbly evocative. They recount lively and dramatic stories of love, death and the land in poetic couplets to a musical background, with an ornate and inventive use of words (see Music below). Gaucho poets, like Medieval *troubadours*, would travel from settlement to settlement, to country fairs and cattle round-ups, singing of the events of the day and of the encroaching political constraints that would soon bring restrictions to their traditional way of life.

The theme of Argentine identity has been a constant through the country's development and remains a burning issue today. While many writers looked to Europe for inspiration, others were keen to distance themselves from the lands they had come from and create a new literature, reflecting Argentina's own concerns. The extremes within the country further challenge attempts at creating a single unified identity: the vast stretches of inhospitable and uninhabited land, the vast variety of landscapes and peoples, and the huge concentration of population in a capital which little resembles any other part of the country. These conflicts were clearly expressed in 1845 by politician Domingo Faustino Sarmiento (1811-1888): *Facundo: Civilization and Barbarism.* This was the most important tract of the generation, and became one of the key texts of Argentine cultural history. Strongly opposed to the Federalist Rosas, Sarmiento's allegory biography of gaucho *Facundo* laments the ungovernably large size of the country which allows *caudillos* like Quiroga and Rosas to dominate. For Sarmiento, the only solution was education and he looked to what he perceived to be the democracy of North America for inspiration.

With the attempt to consolidate the nation state in the aftermath of independence Esteban Echeverría (1805-1851) played a leading role in these debates through literary salons, in poetry and in short fiction. Other memorable protest literature against the Rosas regime included Echeverría's *El Matadero* (The Slaughterhouse, published posthumously in 1871) and José Mármol's melodramatic novel of star crossed lovers battling against the cut-throat hordes of Rosas *Amalia* (1855).

The consolidation of Argentina along the lines advocated by Sarmiento and the growth of the export economy in alliance with British capital and technology may have benefited the great landowners of the Littoral provinces. But those who did not fit into this dream of modernity – in particular the gaucho groups turned off the land and forced to work as rural labourers – found their protest articulated by a provincial landowner, José Hernández (1834-1886). He wrote the famous gaucho epic poems *El Gaucho Martín Fierro* (1872) and its sequel, *La vuelta de Martín Fierro* (The Return of Martín Fierro, 1879). The first part of *Martín Fierro* is most definitely the most famous Argentine literary work and is a genuine shout of rage against the despotic *caudillos* and corrupt authorities, which disrupt local communities and traditional ways of life. Framed as a gauchesque song, chanted by the appealing hero and dispossessed outlaw, it became one of the most popular works of literature, and *Martín Fierro* came to symbolize the spirit of the Argentine nation.

As a small group of families led the great export boom, the 'gentleman' politicians of the 'Generation of 1880' wrote their memoirs, none better than Sarmiento's *Recuerdos de Provincia* (Memoirs of Provincial Life, 1850). As Buenos Aires grew into a dynamic modern city, the gentleman memorialist soon gave way to the professional writer. The key poet in this respect was the Nicaraguan Rubén Darío (1867-1916), who lived for an important period of his creative life in Buenos Aires and led a movement called *modernismo* which asserted the separateness of poetry as a craft, removed from the dictates of national panegyric or political necessity. It was Darío who would give inspiration to the poet Leopoldo Lugones (1874-1938), famous also for his prose writings on nationalist, gauchesque themes. Lugones's evocation of the gaucho as a national symbol would be developed in the novel *Don Segundo Sombra* by Ricardo Güiraldes (1886-1927), the story of a boy taught the skills for life by a gaucho mentor.

The early 20th century

The complex urban societies evolving in Argentina by the turn of the century created a rich cultural life. In the 1920s a strong vanguard movement developed which questioned the dominant literary orthodoxies of the day. Little magazines such as *Martín Fierro* (another appropriation of the ubiquitous national symbol) proclaimed novelty in poetry and attacked the dull social realist writings of their rivals the Boedo group. Argentina's most famous writer, Jorge Luis Borges (1899-1986) began his literary life as an avant-garde poet, in the company of writers such as Oliverio Girondo (1891-1967) and Norah Lange (1906-1972). Many of these poets were interested in expressing the dynamism and changing shape of their urban landscape, Buenos Aires, this Paris on the periphery. You can explore Borges' haunts in Buenos Aires with a free tour organized by the tourist office: ask in their information centres for dates and times. Roberto Arlt also caught the dreams and nightmares of the urban underclasses in novels such as *El juguete rabioso* (The Rabid Toy, 1926) and *Los siete locos* (The Seven Madmen, 1929).

Much of the most interesting literature of the 1930 and 1940s was first published in the literary journal *Sur*, founded by the aristocratic writer, Victoria Ocampo. By far the most important group to publish in its pages were Borges and his close friends Silvina Ocampo (1903-1993), Victoria's sister, and Silvina's husband, Adolfo Bioy Casares (1914) who, from the late 1930s, in a series of short fictions and essays, transformed the literary world. They had recurrent concerns: an indirect style, a rejection of realism and nationalist symbols, the use of the purified motifs and techniques of detective fiction and fantastic literature, the quest for knowledge to be found in elusive books, the acknowledgement of literary criticism as the purest form of detective fiction and the emphasis on the importance of the reader rather than the writer.

Peronism and literature

In the 10-year period of Perón's first two presidencies, 1946-1955, there was a deliberate assault on the aristocratic, liberal values which had guided Argentina since 1880. Claiming to be a new synthesis of democracy, nationalism, anti-imperialism and industrial development, Peronism attacked the undemocratic, dependent Argentine elite (personified in such literary figures as Victoria Ocampo or Adolfo Bioy Casares). This period was seen by most intellectuals and writers as an era of cultural darkness and some writers such as Julio Cortázar (1914-1984) – in the 1940s and 1950s a writer of elegant fantastic and realist stories – chose voluntary exile rather than remain in Perón's Argentina. The much-loved novelist, Ernesto Sábato (1911) who later confronted the *Proceso,* set his best novel *Sobre héroes y tumbas* (On Heroes and Tombs, 1961) partly in the final moments of the Peronist regime, when the tensions of the populist alliance were beginning to become manifest. (His novella *El Tunel* is also well worth reading). But Perón was not much interested in the small circulation of literature and concentrated his attention on mass forms of communication such as radio and cinema. This period saw further mature work from the poets Enrique Molina (1910-), Olga Orozco (1922-) and Alberto Girri (1919-1991), whose austere, introspective verse was an antidote to the populist abuse of language in the public sphere. The literary field was to be further stimulated, after the downfall of Perón with the development of publishing houses and the 'boom' of Latin American literature of the 1960s.

The 1960s

In Argentina the 1960s was a decade of great literary and cultural effervescence. The novel to capture this mood was Cortázar's *Rayuela* (Hopscotch, 1963), which served as a Baedeker of the new, with its comments on literature, philosophy, new sexual freedoms and its open, experimental structure. It was promoted in a weekly journal *Primera Plana*, which also acted as a guide to expansive modernity. Thousands of copies of *Rayuela* were sold to an expanded middle-class readership in Argentina and throughout Latin America. Other novelists and writers benefited from these conditions, the most significant being the Colombian Gabriel García Márquez who published what would later become one of the best-selling novels of the 20th century, *Cien años de soledad* (One Hundred Years of Solitude, 1967) with an Argentine publishing house. Significant numbers of women writers helped to break the male monopoly of literary production including the novelists Beatriz Guido and Marta Lynch and the poet Alejandra Pizarnik (1936-1972), with her intense exploration of the inner self.

Literature and dictatorship

The 'swinging' sixties were curtailed by a military coup in 1966. In the years which followed, Argentine political life descended into anarchy, violence and repression, as a result virtually all forms of cultural activity were silenced and well known writers, including Haroldo Conti and Rodolfo Walsh, 'disappeared'. Many more had to seek exile including the poet Juan Gelman, whose son and daughter-in-law counted among the disappeared.

Understandably this nightmare world provided the dominant themes of the literary output of these years. The return in old age of Perón, claimed by all shades of the political spectrum, was savagely lampooned in Osvaldo Soriano's (1943-1998) novel *No habrá más penas ni olvido* (A Funny, Dirty Little War, published 1982, but completed in 1975). The world of the sombre designs of the ultra right-wing López Rega, Isabel Perón's Minister of Social Welfare, is portrayed in Luisa Valenzuela's (1938-) terrifying, grotesque novel *Cola de lagartija* (The Lizard's Tail, 1983). Of the narrative accounts of those black years, none is more harrowing than Miguel Bonasso's (1940-) fictional documentary of the treatment of the Montoneros guerrilla group in prison and in exile: *Recuerdo de la muerte* (Memory of Death, 1984). Other writers in exile chose more indirect ways of dealing with the terror and dislocation of those years. Daniel Moyano (1928-1992), in exile for many years in Spain, wrote elegant allegories such as *El vuelo del tigre* (The Flight of the Tiger, 1981), which tells of the military style takeover of an Andean village by a group of percussionists who bring cacophany.

Within Argentina, critical discussion was kept alive in literary journals such as *Punto de Vista* (1978-) and certain novels alluded to the current political climate within densely structured narratives. Ricardo Piglia's (1941-) *Respiración artificial* (Artificial Respiration, 1980) has disappearance and exile as central themes, alongside bravura discussions of the links between fiction and history and between Argentina and Europe.

The return to civilian rule

Following Alfonsín's election victory in 1983, the whole intellectual and cultural field responded to the new freedoms. Certain narratives depicted in harsh realism the brutalities of the 'Dirty War' waged by the military and it was the novelist, Ernesto Sábato, who headed the Commission set up to investigate the disappearances. He wrote in the prologue to the Commission's report *Nunca más* (Never Again, 1984): "We are convinced that the recent military dictatorship brought about the greatest and most savage tragedy in the history of Argentina".

Current literature echoes the famous lines by Borges in the essay *The Argentine Writer and Tradition*: "I believe that we Argentines ... can handle all European themes, handle them without superstition, with an irreverence which can have, and already does have, fortunate consequences." While many of the writers that first brought modernity to Argentine letters have died – Borges, Victoria and Silvina Ocampo, Girri, Cortázar, Puig – the later generations have assimilated their lessons. Juan Carlos Martini writes stylish thrillers, blending high and low culture. Juan José Saer (1937-), from his self imposed exile in Paris, recreates his fictional world, Colastiné, in the city of Santa Fé, in narratives that are complex, poetic discussions on memory and language. The most successful novel of recent years is Tomás Eloy Martinez's (1934-) *Santa Evita* (1995) which tells/reinvents the macabre story of what happened to Evita's embalmed body between 1952 and the mid 1970s. The narrative skilfully discusses themes that are at the heart of all writing and critical activity. The critic, like the embalmer of Evita's body, "seeks to fix a life or a body in the pose that eternity should remember it by". But what this critic, like the narrator of Eloy Martínez's novel, realizes is that a corpus of literature cannot be fixed in that way, for literature escapes such neat pigeon holes. Instead, glossing Oscar Wilde, the narrator states that "that the only duty that we have to history is to rewrite it". The ending of the novel makes the point about the impossibility of endings: "Since then, I have rowed with words, carrying Santa Evita in my boat, from one shore of the blind world to the other. I don't know where in the story I am. In the middle, I believe. I've been here in the middle for a long time. Now I must write again". (*Santa Evita*, New York and London, 1996, page 369.) See Books, page 612, for recommended reading.

Music

Tango is the country's most prominent and most exported musical form, but by no means its only means of musical expression. The traditional music which binds almost the whole country is *folclore* (pronounced *folc-LAW-ray)* whose stirring rhythms and passionate singing can be found in varying forms throughout the northern half of the country. Superb music is produced in the north, in the Andean region of Salta and Jujuy. And home-grown Rock Nacional is the country's main strand of pop music, successfully fending off North American and European competition throughout the 1980's and 1990's to form a distinctive sound.

Tango

If your trip to Argentina includes any time in Buenos Aires, you'll undoubtedly see some tango – probably danced on the streets of Florida or San Telmo, though its much more than a tourist attraction. Testimony to the enduring success of the music among Argentines are the radio stations which only play tango, and the *milongas* (dance clubs) filled with young people learning the old steps.

Although also sung and played, the tango was born as a dance just before the turn of the 20th century. The exact moment of birth was not recorded by any contemporary observer and continues to be a matter of debate, though the roots can be traced. The name 'Tango' predates the dance and was given to the carnivals (and dances) of the black inhabitants of the Río de la Plata in the early 19th century, elements of the black tradition being taken over by whites as the black population declined. However, the name 'Tango Americano' was also given to the Habanera (a Cuban descendent of the English Country Dance) which became the rage in Spain and bounced back into the Río de la Plata in the middle of the 19th century, not only as a fashionable dance together with the polka, mazurka, waltz and cuadrille but also as a song form in the very popular '*Zarzuelas*', or Spanish operettas. However, the Habanera led not a double, but a triple life, by also infiltrating the lowest levels of society directly from Cuba via sailors who arrived in the ports of Montevideo and Buenos Aires. Here it encountered the Milonga, originally a gaucho song style, but by 1880 a dance, especially popular with the so-called '*Compadritos*' and '*Orilleros*', who frequented the port area and its brothels, whence the Argentine Tango emerged around the turn of the century to dazzle the populace with its brilliant, personalized footwork, which could not be accomplished without the partners staying glued together.

As a dance tango became the rage and, as the infant recording industry grew by leaps and bounds, it also became popular as a song and an instrumental genre, with the original violins and flutes being eclipsed by the *bandoneón* button accordion, then being imported from Germany. In 1911 the new dance took Paris by storm, thanks to the performance of the dance in a Paris salon by Argentine writer Ricardo Güiraldes, one of a group of aristocrats who enjoyed frequenting the dives where tango was popular. As soon as it was the fashion in Paris, it returned triumphant to Buenos Aires, achieving both respectability and notoriety, and becoming a global phenomenon after the First World War, with the golden voice of Carlos Gardel. Rudolph Valentino helped the image of the dance, when his 1926 movie *The Four Horsemen of the Apocalypse* included a tango scene, and suddenly everyone was doing it, in Paris and London, dressed up like gauchos.

But it was Carlos Gardel (1887-1935), Argentina's most loved tango legend, whose mellifluous voice brought popularity to the music of tango, and whose poor background made him a hero for the working classes too. Tango has always been an expression of the poor and of social and political developments in the country. Gardel recorded 900 songs and was a success in movies too. *The Tango on Broadway* was his big success in 1934. After Gardel's tragic death in 1935, tango slumped a little, frowned upon by the military regime who considered it subversive. Its resurgence in the 1940's was assisted by Perón's decree that 50% of all music played on the radio must be Argentine. Great stars of this era include the brilliant *bandoneón* player Aníbal Troilo, whose passionate and tender playing made him much loved among a wide audience. In the 1950s, tango again declined, replaced in popularity by rock'n'roll. It had become increasingly the preserve of middle class and intellectual circles, with the emphasis on nostalgia in its themes. But its next innovator and star was Astor Piazzolla (1921-), who had played in Troilo's orchestra, and who went on to fuse tango with jazz and create a tango for listening to, as well as dancing. Threatened by the military government in the 1970s Piazzollla escaped to Paris, but his success was already international, and his experimental arrangements opened up the possibilities for other fusions. In the last few years, tango has enjoyed a revival, becoming a popular dance in classes throughout Europe as well as in Argentina. All over Buenos Aires, and all over the province, you can find dance classes where the classic moves are taught, followed by a dance or *milonga* where couples, young and old, breathe life into the old steps. Part of its attraction, perhaps, is that in the world of tango, men are allowed to be macho and seductive, while their women are required to be sensitive to the subtlety of their next move. Unlike salsa, for example, tango is a dance of repressed passion. Try a class, at least once, while you're in Argentina, to get a feel for the dance from the inside. And then, if you can afford it, see the expert dancers' dextrous footwork at a show such as *El Viejo Almácen*.

Folclore

Beyond Buenos Aires, the dominant musical traditions can be broadly described as folclore. This takes various forms over the north of the country, with the finest examples in Salta, but all the northern provinces have a very rich and attractive heritage of folk dances, mainly for couples, with arms held out and fingers clicked or handkerchiefs waved, with the '*Paso Valseado*' as the basic step. The slow and stately Zamba is descended from the Zamacueca, and therefore a cousin of the Chilean Cueca and Peruvian Marinera, where the handkerchief is used to greatest effect. Equally popular throughout most of the country are the faster Gato, Chacarera and Escondido. These were the dances of the gaucho and their rhythm evokes that of a cantering horse with wonderfully stirring syncopation. Guitar and the *bombo* drum provide the accompaniment. Particularly spectacular is the Malambo, where the gaucho shows off his dextrous footwork, creating a complex rhythm using the heels of his boots, alternating with percussion created by whirling the hard balls of the *boleadoras* into the ground, with the spurs of his boots adding a steely note to the rhythm.

Different regions of the country have their own specialities. The music of Cuyo in the west is sentimental and very similar to that of neighbouring Chile, with its Cuecas for dance and Tonadas for song. The northwest on the other hand is Andean, with its musical culture closer to that of Bolivia, particularly on the *Puna*, where the indigenous groups play haunting wind instruments, the *quena* and sound mournful notes on the great long *erke* evocative of huge mountain landscapes. Here the dances are Bailecitos and Carnavalitos, depending on the time of year. Exquisitely beautiful and mournful songs – the extraordinary high pitched *Bagualas* – are sung to the banging of a simple drum. And everyone, from children to grandmothers, can quote you a *copla*: two lines of rhymed verse expressing love or a witty joke. Tomás Lipan's music is worth seeking out, especially his *cautivo de Amor*. Andean bands use the *sikus*, pan pipes and miniature guitar, the *charango*, to create ethereal and festive music which reflects the seasons of the rural calendar. In the northeast provinces of Corrientes and Misiones, the music shares cultural similarities with Paraguay. The *Polca* and *Galopa* are danced and the local *Chamamé* is sung, to the accordion or the harp, in sentimental style. Santiago del Estero has exerted the strongest influence on Argentine folk music as a result of the work of Andres Chazarreta: it is the heartland of the Chacarera and the lyrics are often part Spanish and part Quichua, a local dialect of the Andean Quechua language. Listen, too, to Los Caravajal, and Los Hermanos Abalos. Down in the province of Buenos Aires you are more likely to hear the Gauchos singing their Milongas, Estilos and Cifras and challenging each other to a Payada or rhymed duel – protest songs and wonderfully romantic and witty stories to guitar accompaniment. Seek out Atahualpa Yupangui's *El Payador Persguido*. Argentina experienced a great folklore revival in the 1950s and 1960s and some of the most celebrated groups are still drawing enthusiastic audiences today. These groups include Los Chalchaleros and Los Fronterizos, the perennial virtuoso singer and guitarist, Eduardo Falú and, more recently, León Gieco from Santa Fe. Most famous of all, though, is the superb Mercedes Sosa, whose rich voice articulated much of the sorrow and joy of the last 30 years in a brilliant series of albums which also include the most popular folklore songs. Start with *The Best of Mercedes Sosa*. Also listen to Ariel Ramirez, a famous singer and pianist whose moving *Misa Criolla* is among his best known work. The *cuartetos* of Córdoba, popular since the 1940s with the characteristic dance in a huge circle, can best be sampled in the much loved records of Carlitos 'La Mona' Jiminez.

Rock Nacional

The great stars of Rock Nacional are still much loved and listened to. It started in the 1960s with successful bands *Los Gatos*, and *Almendra*, whose songwriter Luis Alberto Spinetta later became a successful solo artist. But the Rock Nacional found its real strength in expressing unspeakable protests during the military dictatorship from 1976-83. Charly García, who was a member of the enormously successful band *Sui Generis*, captured popular feeling with his song *No te dejes desanimar* (Don't be discouraged) which roused mass opposition amongst young people against the atrocities of the *Proceso*. Inevitably, the military regime cottoned on to this form of subversive behaviour and stopped rock concerts, so that many bands had given up performing by the end of the 1970s. However, the rock movement survived, and the cynical lyrics of Fito Páez in *Tiempos Dificiles* and Charly García in *Dinosaurios* remain as testimonies to that time, and guaranteed them subsequent success. Once democracy had returned, music became more lightweight with likeable output from Los Abuelos de la Nada and Patricio Rey y sus Redonditos de Ricota. Fito Páez has continued to record and his album *El Amor Después del Amor* was a success across Latin America. Los Fabulosis Cadillacs and Andrés Calamaro also made some great records, and Charly García continues, undiminished in popularity.

Sport

It is said that sport came to Argentina through the port of Buenos Aires, brought first by British sailors, who played football on vacant lots near the port watched by curious locals who would later make it their national passion.

Football is out on its own, both in terms of participation and as a spectator sport, with the country being passionately divided between fans of Boca Juniors and River Plate. In second place come two sports which attract far more fans than players: boxing and motor-racing. Although there are now few Argentine boxing champions and world title fights are rarely held here, there is a big TV audience for most title fights abroad. Despite the lack of local world-class drivers, the legend of Juan Manuel Fangio is still very much alive and the Argentine Formula One Grand Prix each April is one of the main events of the year in Buenos Aires, even if there are no Argentine drivers. Tennis is played mostly among the upper-middle classes but the world tournaments attract many TV fans, since Argentines Sabatini and Nalbandian have soared to fame. Basketball and volleyball are both popular participation sports among young people, with strong teams in many sizeable towns, and basketball attracts big TV audiences since Argentine players play for teams in the States.

Though the best **polo** in the world is played in Argentina, it's only accessible to an elite class, due to its cost. Though it is played throughout the country and all year round, the top Argentine players, who now play all over the world, return only for the high handicap season between September and November. This consists of three main tournaments, played on the outskirts of Buenos Aires, followed by the Argentine Open, which takes place in Palermo's Hurlingham Club, the 'cathedral of polo'.

Golf can be played all year round in the northern half of the country, though it's a purely upper middle class game in Argentina, and half the courses are in Gran Buenos Aires, with famous courses at Mar del Plata and Llao Llao in Bariloche. Argentina's rugby team, the Pumas, remain strong, though the sport is played little outside the expensive private schools.

Argentina's native sports include the squash-like **paleta pilota**, and *pato* (duck), a cross between polo and basketball. Originally played between large bands of gauchos on horseback using a duck in a basket as a ball, it was at one point prohibited for being dangerous. Today, with proper rules, teams of four horsemen and a football with handles instead of a duck in a basket, it is one sport which is unique to Argentina.

Religion

Throughout Spanish America the Catholic Church played an important role in the conquest. From the start of the colonial period Spanish control in South America was authorized by the Papacy; in return the colonial powers were to support the conversion of the indigenous population to Catholicism. This close identification of Church and state helps to explain why the main centres of Church power and activity were usually (though not always) close to the main centres of Spanish settlement. While present-day Argentina, a border territory on the outskirts of empire, was therefore of relatively minor importance to the Church hierarchy, it became a focus for work by missionary orders, particularly the Jesuits. Jesuit activity in Argentina was centred in two areas: around Córdoba, where they established a training college for the priesthood, and in Misiones and adjoining areas of present-day Paraguay and Brazil, where an extensive network of *reducciones* was set up to convert and protect the indigenous population.

As in much of Spanish America, the Church lost most of its formal political power at independence. Although today over 90% of Argentines are officially Roman Catholics, the Church's political and social influence is much less significant than in neighbouring Chile or in most other South American countries. One reason for this is the introduction of a system of non-religious state schools in the 19th century. The great waves of immigration in the late 19th and early 20th centuries also affected the position of the Church; while the majority of immigrants were Catholics, significant minorities were not, including the large numbers of East European Jews and the Arab immigrants from Lebanon and Syria. Both of these communities have a strong presence especially in Buenos Aires; the largest mosque in South America was opened in the capital in September 2000 and there are estimated to be 800,000 Muslims in the country. And Buenos Aires has the eighth largest Jewish population in the world.

Yet the Catholic Church's power and influence should not be underestimated. The support of the Church hierarchy was important in bringing Perón to power in 1946 and the rift with the Church played a key role in the overthrow of the latter in 1955. The strongly conservative nature of the Catholic hierarchy became particularly apparent during the 1976-1983 military dictatorship; unlike its Chilean counterpart, the Argentine hierarchy was silent on the issue of human rights violations and gave little support to relatives of the disappeared. According to *Nunca Más*, the official report on the disappeared, military chaplains attended some torture sessions and even assisted in the torture! Yet the Church was not untouched by the violence of the dictatorship: at least 15 priests who were working among the poor were victims of the military regime.

The lingering influence of the Church can be seen in several ways: in the continuing legal ban on abortion (divorce was finally legalised in 1986) and in the constitutional provision (removed in the 1994 amendments) which required the President to be a Catholic (and which necessitated Carlos Menem's conversion). The extent to which the Church relies on state support was revealed in a 1993 report which estimated that the Church received annual payments of US$400 million to help it maintain Catholic schools and universities and to fund the salaries of senior clergy.

As in some other parts of Latin America, this close identification of the Catholic Church with the state has, in recent years, provided opportunities for evangelical churches, including the Baptists and Mormons, to recruit followers, particularly among newcomers to the large cities.

Land and environment

Argentina is the second largest country in South America in area, extending across the continent some 1580 km from east to west and 3460 km from north to south. Its northernmost point is at latitude 22°S, that is just within the tropics; at Tierra del Fuego and Isla de los Estados it extends south of 54°S, the latitude of Scotland or Labrador. The coast of this territory, extending over 2000 km, runs wholly along the Atlantic apart from the north coast of the Beagle Channel which links the Atlantic and the Pacific. The western border with Chile follows the crest of the Andes, but below 46°S, the drainage is complex and border disputes have arisen ever since the Treaty of 1881 between the two countries established the principle that the border should follow the watershed.

Geology and landscape

Together with Brazil, Paraguay and Uruguay, Argentina is the visible part of the South American Plate which has been moving for the past 125 million years away from its former union with Africa. The submerged part of this plate forms a broad continental shelf under the Atlantic Ocean; in the south this extends over 1000 km east and includes the Falkland Islands/Islas Malvinas. Since the 'break' between the plates, there have been numerous invasions and withdrawals of the sea over this part of the South American continent, but the Andean mountain building from the end of the Cretaceous (65 million years ago) to the present day dominates the surface geology. Of the many climatic fluctuations, the Pleistocene Ice Age up to 10,000 BC has done most to mould the current landscape. At its maximum, ice covered all the land over 2,000 m and most of Patagonia. In the mountains, ice created virtually all the present day lakes and moraine deposits can be found everywhere. However, the special feature of the heartland of Argentina is the fine soil of the Pampas, the result of ice and water erosion and the unique wind systems of the southern cone of the continent.

The Northwest

Northern and western Argentina are dominated by the satellite ranges of the Andes. Between the mountains of the far northwest is the *puna*, a high plateau rising to 3400-4000 m, on which are situated salt flats or *salares*, some of which are of interest for their wildlife. East of this is the *pre-puna*, the gorges and slopes ranging in altitude from 1700 m to 3400 m which connect the *puna* with the plains. On the fringe of the Andes are a string of important settlements including Salta, Tucumán and Mendoza. Though the climate of this region is hot and dry, there is sufficient water to support maize and pasture and a thriving wine industry, mostly relying on irrigation. East of the Andes lie several ranges of hills, the most important of which are the Sierras de Córdoba and the Sierras de San Luis. These are mostly of ancient Precambrian rocks.

The Paraná Basin

The vast Paraná Basin stretches from the borders with Brazil and Paraguay to the Atlantic at Buenos Aires. In the northeast it mainly consists of geologically recent deposits. The easternmost part of this basin, between the Ríos Paraná and Uruguay, is the wettest part of the country. Known as Mesopotamia and consisting of the provinces of Entre Ríos, Corrientes and Misiones, it is structurally part of the Brazilian plateau of old crystalline rocks, the 'heart' of the South American Plate. Here there are undulating grassy hills and marshy or forested lowlands, among them the Esteros del Iberá, an extensive area of flooded forest similar to the Pantanal in Brazil. The horizontal strata of the rocks in this area is dramatically evident in the river gorges to the north and the spectacular Iguazú falls shared with Brazil.

The Chaco

Northwest of Mesopotamia and stretching from the Paraná and Paraguay rivers west to the Andean foothills and north into Paraguay and Bolivia, lies the Gran Chaco, a vast plain which covers the provinces of Formosa, Chaco and Santiago del Estero, as well as parts of Santa Fe and Córdoba. It is crossed from west to east by three rivers, the Teuco-Bermejo, the Salado and the Pilcomayo. Annual rainfall ranges from 400 mm in the western or Dry Chaco, a semi-desert mainly used for cattle ranching, to 800-1200 mm in the eastern or Wet Chaco, where periodic floods alternate with long periods of drought.

The Pampas

South of 33°S, the latitude of Mendoza and Rosario, is a great flat plain known as the Pampas. Extending almost 1,000 km from north to south and a similar distance from east to west, the Pampas cover some 650,000 sq km, including most of Buenos Aires Province, southern Córdoba, Santa Fe and Entre Ríos, northeastern La Pampa and a small part of San Luís. This area is crossed by meandering rivers and streams and there are many lakes, lagoons and marshes. Geologically the Pampas are similar to the Chaco, basic crystalline and granite rocks almost completely overlain with recent deposits, often hundreds of metres thick. Prevailing winds from the southeast and southwest help to create the fine loess type soils which make this one of the richest farming areas in the world, ideal for grasslands and cattle ranching. Being comparatively close to the ocean, extremes of temperature are rare, another favourable feature.

A distinction is often made between the 'wet' Pampa and the 'dry' Pampa. The former, inland from Rosario and Buenos Aires is the centre of wheat, maize and other cereal production and the latter, west of 64°W, is where cattle ranching predominates.

The Patagonian steppe

Patagonia extends from the Río Colorado (39°S) south to the Magellan Straits and covers some 780,000 sq km. Most of this area consists of a series of tablelands and terraces which drop in altitude from west to east. The basic rocks are ancient, some classified as Precambrian, but the surface has been subjected to endless erosion.

Rainfall is lighter and the winds stronger than in the Pampas frequently stripping the surface of cover and filling the air with dust. Only where rivers have scored deep valleys in the rock base can soil accumulate, allowing more than extensive sheep farming.

From the Straits of Magellan north to Lago Argentino (46°S) and beyond, a geological depression separates the edge of the South American Plate from the Andes. Most of Patagonia was under ice during the Quaternary Ice Age and has been rising since the ice receded. This area was presumably the last to be uncovered. However, considerable volcanic activity associated with the uplift of the Andes has taken place along the depression which is transversely divided into basins by lava flows. Alluvial and glacial deposits have created relatively fertile soils in some areas, useful for sheep and producing attractive wooded landscapes in the lake regions in contrast to the general desolation of Patagonia.

The Andes

Geographically the Isla de los Estados forms the southernmost extent of the Andes, which then swing north to become the border between Chile and Argentina just north of the Paine mountains. The 350 km section north of Paine is one of the most dramatic stretches of the Andes. The crest lies under the Southern Patagonian Ice cap, with glaciers reaching down to the valleys on both the Argentine and Chilean sides. On the Argentine side this has created the spectacular range of glaciers found in the Parque Nacional Los Glaciares, the most famous of which, the Perito Moreno Glacier, is one of the highlights for many travellers to Argentina. The northern end of this section is Cerro Fitz Roy, which, along with the Torres del Paine (in Chile) at the southern end, is among the most spectacular hiking and climbing centres in South America.

Further north between 46°S and 47°S there is another ice cap, the North Patagonian Ice cap, centred on Monte San Valentín on the Chilean side of the border. North of this lie 1,500 km of mountain ranges rarely exceeding 4,000 m; on the east side of these are a series of attractive lakes, formed by a mixture of glacial and volcanic activity. The high section of the Andes begins at 35°S and includes Aconcagua, 6,960 m, the highest peak outside the Himalayas. For a further 1,000 km northwards, the ranges continue to the border with Bolivia with many peaks over 6,000 m, the Argentine side becoming progressively drier and more inhospitable.

Climate

Climate ranges from sub-tropical in the northeast to cold temperate in Tierra del Fuego, but is temperate and quite healthy for much of the year in the densely populated central zone. Between December and the end of February, Buenos Aires can be oppressively hot and humid. The Andes have a dramatic effect on the climate of the south: although on the Chilean side of the mountains there is adequate rainfall from Santiago southwards, very little of this moisture reaches the Argentine side. Furthermore, the prevailing winds in Patagonia are southwest to northeast from the Pacific. The result is a temperate climate with some mist and fog near the coast, but not much rain. Further inland, the westerlies, having deposited their moisture on the Andes, add strength to the southerly airstream, creating the strong dry wind (*El Pampero)* characteristic of the Pampas. Only when these systems meet humid maritime air in the northeast of the country does rainfall significantly increase, often with violent thunderstorms, with the heaviest precipitation in Mesopotamia where the summer months are particularly wet.

The highest temperatures are found in the northeast where the distance from the sea and the continuous daytime sunshine produce the only frequently recorded air temperatures over 45°C anywhere in South America. The northwest is cooler due to the effects of altitude, rainfall here occurring largely in the summer months.

Vegetation

Few countries offer as wide a range of natural environments as Argentina; its varied vegetation supports equally diverse wildlife. The main types of vegetation are described below. Details of some of the animals to be seen are given where appropriate in the text; to avoid repetition they are not described here. There are 10 main vegetation types:

Llanura pampeana

Extensive cattle grazing and arable farming have altered the original vegetation of the Pampas, notably through the introduction of tree species such as the eucalyptus for shelter. The least altered areas of the Pampas are the coastal lowlands, the Paraná delta and the southern sierras. The sandy soils of the coastal lowlands, including marshes and estuaries, are home to pampas-grass or *cortadera*. In the marshy parts of the Paraná delta there are tall grasses with *espinillo* and *ñandubay* (*Prosopis*) woods in the higher areas. Willows and alisos grow along the river banks while the ceibo, the national flower of Argentina, grows in the nearby woodlands.

Espinal

These are open woodlands and savannahs which extend in an arc around the pampas covering southern Corrientes, northern Entre Ríos, central Santa Fe, large parts of Córdoba and San Luis and the centre-west of La Pampa. In these areas xerophitic and thorny woods of prosopis and acacia predominate. The major prosopis species are the *ñandubay*; the white algarrobo; the black algarrobo and the caldén. The *ñandubay is* found in Entre Ríos and parts of Corrientes, along with the white *quebracho*, *tala*, *espinillo* and, on sandy soils, *yatay* palms. The white algarrobo and black algarrobo are found in areas of Santa Fe, Córdoba and San Luis which have been heavily affected by farming. The caldén appears across large areas of La Pampa, southern San Luis and southern Buenos Aires, along with bushes such as the alpataco and the creosote bush (*Larrea*).

Monte

Monte is a bushy steppe with a few patches of trees, in areas with rainfall from 80 mm to 250 mm. Covering large areas of San Juan, Mendoza, La Pampa and Río Negro, it can be found as far north as Salta and as far south as Chubut. Vegetation includes different species of the creosote bush, which have small resinous leaves and yellow flowers, as well as thorny bushes from the cacti family and bushes such as *brea*, *retamo* and *jume*. In the northern areas of *monte* the white algarrobo and sweet algarrobo can be found, while the native willow grows along the riverbanks as far south as the Río Chubut.

Puna and prepuna

Low rainfall, intense radiation and poor soils inhibit vegetation in the *puna*, the major species being adapted by having deep root systems and small leaves; many plants have thorny leaves to deter herbivores. These include species of cacti, which store water in their tissue, and the *yareta*, a cushion-shaped plant, which has been over-exploited for firewood, as well as the *tolilla*, the *chijua* and the *tola*. The *queñoa*, which grows to over 5 m high in the sheltered gorges and valleys of the *prepuna*, is the highest growing tree in Argentina. These valleys also support bushes from the Leguminosae family such as the *churqui*, and species of cacti, such as the cardoon and the *airampu*, with its colourful blossom.

High Andean grasslands

Extending from Jujuy to Neuquén, and then in discontinuous fashion south to Tierra del Fuego, these areas range in altitude from 4200 m in Jujuy to 500 m in Tierra del Fuego. Grasses adapted to the cold include *iros*, *poa* and *stipa* as well as some endemic species.

Subtropical cloudforest

Often known as *yungas*, this extends into Argentina from Bolivia and covers parts of the sub-Andean sierras. It is found in eastern Jujuy, central Salta and Tucuman and eastern Catamarca. Its eastern sides receive the humidity of the winds which cross the Chaco from the Atlantic. Winters are dry but temperature, rainfall and humidity vary with changes in latitude and altitude. These forests are important regulators of the water cycle, preventing erosion and floods. It is best seen in three national parks: Baritú, Calilegua and El Rey.

Vegetation changes with altitude. Along the edge of the Chaco at the foot of the hills and rising to 500 m, where there is annual rainfall up to 1,000 m, is a transition zone with mainly deciduous trees such as the *palo blanco*, the *lapacho rosado* and *lapacho amarillo* (pink and yellow tabebuia); the *palo borracho* (Chorisia bottle tree), the *tipa blanca* and the huge *timbo colorado* or black eared tree. Higher and reaching from 500 to 800 m in altitude, where there is greater humidity, are montane or laurel forests. Predominant tree species here are the laurel, the jacaranda and the *tipa;* epiphytes (orchids, bromeliads, ferns, lichens, mosses) and climbers are abundant. Above 800 m and rising to 1300-1700 m annual rainfall reaches some 3,000 mm, concentrated between November and March. Here myrtle forest predominates, with a great diversity of species, including great trees such as the *horco molle*, a wide range of epiphytes, and, in some areas such as Baritu, tree ferns. Higher still the evergreen trees are replaced by deciduous species including the mountain pine (*Podocarpus*), the only conifer native to the northwest, the walnut and the alder. Above these are clumps of *queñoa* and, higher still, mountain meadow grasslands.

The Chaco

The eastern or Wet Chaco is covered by marshlands and ponds with savannah and caranday palm groves, as well as the characteristic red *quebracho*, a hard-wood tree over-exploited in the past for tannin. The Dry Chaco, further west, is the land of the white *quebracho* as well as cacti such as the quimil (*opuntia*) and the palo borracho (*Chorisia*). Similar climatic conditions and vegetation to those in the Dry Chaco are also found in northern San Luis, Córdoba and Santa Fe and eastern Tucumán, Catamarca, Salta, Jujuy, La Rioja and San Juan.

Subtropical rainforest

This is found mainly in Misiones, extending southwards along the banks of the Ríos Paraná and Uruguay. The wet climate, with annual rainfall of up to 2,000 mm, and high temperatures produce rapid decomposition of organic material. The red soils of this area contain a thin fertile soil layer which is easily eroded.

This area offers the widest variety of flora in Argentina. There of over 2,000 known species of vascular plants, about 10% of which are trees. Forest vegetation rises to different strata: the giant trees such as the *palo rosa*, the Misiones cedar, *incienso* and the *guatambú* rise to over 30 m high. The forest canopy includes species such as strangler figs and the pindo palm, while the intermediate strata includes the fast growing *ambay* (*Cecropia*), tree-ferns, the *yerba mate* and bamboos. Llianas, vines and epiphytes such as orchids and bromeliads as well as ferns and even cacti compete in the struggle for sunlight.

In the hills of northwestern Misiones there are remnants of forests of Paraná pine (*Araucaria angustifolia*).

Sub-Antarctic forest

This grows along the eastern edges of the southern Andes, from Neuquén in the north to Tierra del Fuego and Isla de los Estados in the south. These are cool temperate forests including evergreen and deciduous trees. Species of *nothofagus* predominate, the most common being *lenga* (low decidous beech), *ñire* (high deciduous beech), *coihue* and *guindo*. The *Pehuen* or Monkey puzzle tree (*Araucaria araucana*), is found in northwestern and northcentral Neuquén. The fungus *llao llao* and the hemiparasitic *Misodendron* are also frequent. Flowering bushes include the *notro* (firebush), the *calafate* (*Burberis boxifolis*) and the *chaura* (prickly heath).

Areas of the Lake District with annual rainfall of over 1500 mm are covered by Valdivian forest and a wider range of species. The *coihue* (southern beech) is the predominant species of *nothofagus*, reaching as far south as Lago Buenos Aires. Below colihue canes form a dense undergrowth; flowers include the *amancay* (alstromeria), mutisias, and near streams, the fuschia. Arrayán trees also grow near water, while the Andean Cypress and the *Maiten* grow in the transition zone with the Patagonian steppe. In areas where annual rainfall reaches over 3000 mm, there is a wider range of trees as well as epyphites, ferns, and lichens such as Old Man's Beard. The *alerce* (larch) is the giant of these forests, rising to over 60 m and, in some cases over 3000 years old.

Magallanic forest, found from Lago Buenos Aires south to Tierra del Fuego, is dominated by the *guindo* (evergreen beech) as well as the *lenga*, the *ñire* and the *canelo* (winter bark). There are also large areas of peatbog with sphagnum mosses, and even the carnivorous *Drosera uniflora*.

Patagonian steppe

Plant life in this area has adapted to severe climatic conditions: strong westerly winds, the heavy winter snowfall which occurs in some years, high evaporation in summer, low annual rainfall and sandy soils with a thin fertile layer on top. The northwest of this area is covered by bushy scrublands: species include the *quilembai, molle*, the *algarrobo patagónico*, the *colpiche*, as well as *coiron* grasses. Further south are shrubs such as the *mata negra* and species of *calafate*. Nearer the mountain ranges the climate is less severe and the soil more fertile: here there is a herbaceous steppe which includes *coiron blanco* and shrubs such as the *neneo*. Overgrazing by sheep has produced serious desertification in many parts of the Patagonian steppe.

National parks → *www.parquesnacionales.gov.ar*

Fortunately in a country so rich in natural beauty, Argentina has an extensive network of reserves and protected areas, the most important of which are designated as national parks. The history of Argentine national parks is a long one, dating from the donation by Francisco 'Perito' Moreno of 7500 ha of land in the Lake District to the state. This grant formed the basis for the establishment of the first national park, Nahuel Huapi, in 1934.

There are 19 national parks stretching from Parque Nacional Baritú on the northern border with Bolivia to Parque Nacional Tierra del Fuego in the far south. Additional areas have been designated as natural monuments and natural reserves and there are also provincial parks and reserves. The largest national parks are all in western Argentina; these include a string of eight parks in the Andean foothills in the Lake District and Patagonia. These make ideal bases for trekking with *guardaparque* (rangers) offices at main entrances where you can get advice and maps. Unlike much of Europe, Argentina has poor maps for trekking and climbing. Those available from the Instituto Geografico Militar in Buenos Aires are badly out of date and do not show all paths and refuges. Before you're travel, therefore, it's a good idea to buy a good basic map of the land you want to explore and to search the national parks website for more information (sadly only available in Spanish). Access to the more remote national parks can be tricky without your own transport and you should allow a couple of extra days, especially for the cloudforest parks in the northwest, and for Parque Nacional Perito Moreno (not the one with the Glaciar Perito Moreno in it). Once you reach the parks, you'll find *guardaparques* very knowledgeable and helpful, and many are happy to take time to explain the wildlife and good walks. The main national parks and other protected areas are shown on the map and further details of all of these are given in the text.

The main administration office of the Argentine National Parks authority is at Santa Fe 680, near the Plaza San Martín in central Buenos Aires. Leaflets are available on some of the parks. Further details are given under Buenos Aires.

Books

Bridges, Lucas, *The Uttermost Part of the Earth*, (out of print, available from www.abebooks.com). Quite the most riveting and vivid account of pioneer life, beautifully told by the missionary's son who was adopted by the indigenous Selk'nam of Tierra del Fuego, and protected them, while elsewhere on the island they were under attack. Full of adventure and startling insights into the culture of this dying race.

Burns, Jimmy, *The Hand of God*, Bloomsbury, and *The Land that Lost its Heroes*, (out of print). Both great books for an insight into the country: the first relates the rise to fame and downfall of Maradonna, while the second charts the period before the Falklands/ Malvinas war, and its aftermath, by the British correspondent for the Financial Times.

Chatwin, Bruce, *In Patagonia*, (Vintage/ Penguin). The famous novel which popularized Patagonia and acted as a magnet to the place for many travellers, is actually rather dismissive, and you're likely to have far more interesting encounters yourself. Read before you travel rather than bring it with you.

Chatworth Musters, George, *At Home with the Patagonians*, (out of print). A fascinating account of Usters' journey riding with the indigenous Aonik'enk across Patagonia, giving insights into the Tehuelche culture.

Guevara, Che, *The Motorcycle Diaries*, (Verso, UK). The young Che's romp through Patagonia on a clapped out motorbike at 23 is great fun, and gives a flavour of the land which is recognisable in places, but more interesting for an insight into the developing mind of the revolutionary.

Kuper, Simon, *Football Against the Enemy*, Orion/Trafalgar Square. In this collection of essays on football over the world, the chapter in the 1978 world cup in Argentina is particularly entertaining and telling.

Luna, Felix, *Buenos Aires y el Interior del Pais*. Fictionalized history from reliable Argentine historian, going some way to explain why Buenos Aires is really another country within Argentina.

McEwan, Colin, ed, *Patagonia: Natural History, Prehistory and Ethnography at the Uttermost Part of the Earth*, (British Museum press). The indigenous cultures of Patagonia and their destruction in the early 20th century. Illustrated, well-written essays.

Rock, David, *Argentina 1516-1987*, (out of print). A huge tome which fully relates Argentina's history, addressing its mysterious failure to thrive through a careful analysis of its murky politics.

Sarmiento, Domingo, *Facundo: Civilisation and Barbarism*, (Penguin). The classic allegorical essay which attacks the domination of violent *caudillos*.

Shipton, Eric, *Tierra del Fuego: The Fatal Lodestone*, (out of print). Worth hunting down, this is a wonderful account of the early exploration of the southernmost part of the country.

Footnotes

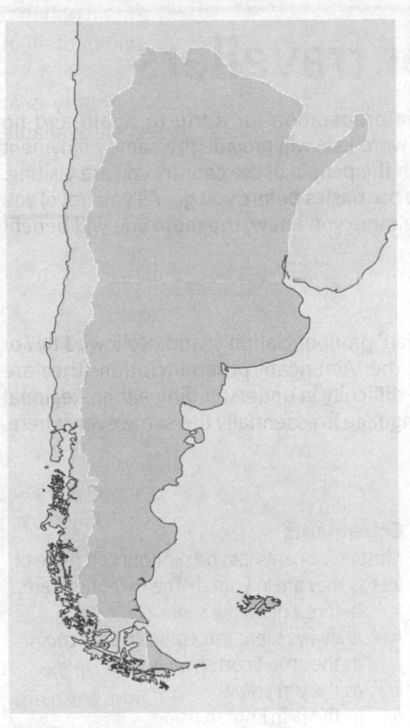

Basic Spanish for travellers

Learning Spanish is a useful part of the preparation for a trip to Spain and no volumes of dictionaries, phrase books or word lists will provide the same enjoyment as being able to communicate directly with the people of the country you are visiting. It is a good idea to make an effort to grasp the basics before you go. As you travel you will pick up more of the language and the more you know, the more you will benefit from your stay.

General pronunciation

Whether you have been taught the 'Castilian' pronounciation (*z* and *c* followed by *i* or *e* are pronounced as the *th* in think) or the 'American' pronounciation (they are pronounced as *s*), you will encounter little difficulty in understanding either. Regional accents and usages vary, but the basic language is essentially the same everywhere.

Vowels

a	as in English *cat*
e	as in English *best*
i	as the *ee* in English *feet*
o	as in English *shop*
u	as the *oo* in English *food*
ai	as the *i* in English *ride*
ei	as *ey* in English *they*
oi	as *oy* in English *toy*

Consonants

Most consonants can be pronounced more or less as they are in English. The exceptions are:

	before *e* or *i* is the same as *j*
h	is always silent (except in *ch* as in *chair*)
j	as the *ch* in Scottish *loch*
ll	as the *y* in *yellow*
ñ	as the *ni* in English *onion*
rr	trilled much more than in English
x	depending on its location, pronounced *x, s, sh* or *j*

Spanish words and phrases

Greetings, courtesies

hello	*hola*
good morning	*buenos días*
good afternoon/evening/night	*buenas tardes/noches*
goodbye	*adiós/chao*
pleased to meet you	*mucho gusto*
see you later	*hasta luego*
how are you?	*¿cómo está?¿cómo estás?*
I'm fine, thanks	*estoy muy bien, gracias*
I'm called...	*me llamo...*
what is your name?	*¿cómo se llama? ¿cómo te llamas?*
yes/no	*sí/no*
please	*por favor*
thank you (very much)	*(muchas) gracias*
I speak Spanish	*hablo español*
I don't speak Spanish	*no hablo español*
do you speak English?	*¿habla inglés?*
I don't understand	*no entiendo/no comprendo*
please speak slowly	*hable despacio por favor*
I am very sorry	*lo siento mucho/disculpe*
what do you want?	*¿qué quiere? ¿qué quieres?*
I want	*quiero*
I don't want it	*no lo quiero*
leave me alone	*déjeme en paz/no me moleste*
good/bad	*bueno/malo*

Basic questions and requests

have you got a room for two people?	*¿tiene una habitación para dos personas?*
how do I get to_?	*¿cómo llego a_?*
how much does it cost?	*¿cuánto cuesta? ¿cuánto es?*
I'd like to make a long-distance phone call	*quisiera hacer una llamada de larga distancia*
is service included?	*¿está incluido el servicio?*
is tax included?	*¿están incluidos los impuestos?*
when does the bus leave (arrive)?	*¿a qué hora sale (llega) el autobús?*
when?	*¿cuándo?*
where is_?	*¿dónde está_?*
where can I buy tickets?	*¿dónde puedo comprar boletos?*
where is the nearest petrol station?	*¿dónde está la gasolinera más cercana?*
why?	*¿por qué?*

Basic words and phrases

bank	*el banco*
bathroom/toilet	*el baño*
to be	*ser, estar*
bill	*la factura/la cuenta*
cash	*el efectivo*
cheap	*barato/a*
credit card	*la tarjeta de crédito*
exchange house	*la casa de cambio*
exchange rate	*el tipo de cambio*
expensive	*caro/a*
to go	*ir*
to have	*tener, haber*
market	*el mercado*
note/coin	*el billete/la moneda*
police (policeman)	*la policía (el policía)*
post office	*el correo*
public telephone	*el teléfono público*
shop	*la tienda*
supermarket	*el supermercado*
there is/are	*hay*
there isn't/aren't	*no hay*
ticket office	*la taquilla*
travellers' cheques	*los cheques de viajero/los travelers*

Getting around

aeroplane	*el avión*
airport	*el aeropuerto*
arrival/departure	*la llegada/salida*
avenue	*la avenida*
block	*la cuadra*
border	*la frontera*
bus station	*la terminal de autobuses/camiones*
bus	*el bus/el autobús/el camión*
collective/fixed-route taxi	*el colectivo*
corner	*la esquina*
customs	*la aduana*
first/second class	*la primera/segunda clase*
left/right	*izquierda/derecha*
ticket	*el boleto*
empty/full	*vacío/lleno*
highway, main road	*la carretera*
immigration	*la inmigración*
insurance	*el seguro*
insured person	*el asegurado/la asegurada*

to insure yourself against	*asegurarse contra*
luggage	*el equipaje*
motorway, freeway	*el autopista/la carretera*
north, south, west, east	*el norte, el sur, el oeste (occidente), el este (oriente)*
oil	*el aceite*
to park	*estacionarse*
passport	*el pasaporte*
petrol/gasoline	*la gasolina*
puncture	*el pinchazo/la ponchadura*
street	*la calle*
that way	*por allí/por allá*
this way	*por aquí/por acá*
tourist card/visa	*la tarjeta de turista/visa*
tyre	*la llanta*
unleaded	*sin plomo*
waiting room	*la sala de espera*
to walk	*caminar/andar*

Accommodation

air conditioning	*el aire acondicionado*
all-inclusive	*todo incluido*
bathroom, private	*el baño privado*
bed, double/single	*la cama matrimonial/sencilla*
blankets	*las cobijas/mantas*
to clean	*limpiar*
dining room	*el comedor*
guesthouse	*la casa de huéspedes*
hotel	*el hotel*
noisy	*ruidoso*
pillows	*las almohadas*
power cut	*el apagón/corte*
restaurant	*el restaurante*
room/bedroom	*el cuarto/la habitación*
sheets	*las sábanas*
shower	*la ducha/regadera*
soap	*el jabón*
toilet	*el sanitario/excusado*
toilet paper	*el papel higiénico*
towels, clean/dirty	*las toallas limpias/sucias*
water, hot/cold	*el agua caliente/fría*

Health

aspirin	*la aspirina*
blood	*la sangre*
chemist	*la farmacia*
condoms	*los preservativos, los condones*
contact lenses	*los lentes de contacto*
contraceptives	*los anticonceptivos*
contraceptive pill	*la píldora anticonceptiva*
diarrhoea	*la diarrea*
doctor	*el médico*
fever/sweat	*la fiebre/el sudor*
pain	*el dolor*
head	*la cabeza*
period/sanitary towels	*la regla/las toallas femininas*
stomach	*el estómago*
altitude sickness	*el soroche*

Family

family	*la familia*
brother/sister	*el hermano/la hermana*
daughter/son	*la hija/el hijo*
father/mother	*el padre/la madre*
husband/wife	*el esposo (marido)/la esposa*
boyfriend/girlfriend	*el novio/la novia*
friend	*el amigo/la amiga*
married	*casado/a*
single/unmarried	*soltero/a*

Months, days and time

January	*enero*
February	*febrero*
March	*marzo*
April	*abril*
May	*mayo*
June	*junio*
July	*julio*
August	*agosto*
September	*septiembre*
October	*octubre*
November	*noviembre*
December	*diciembre*
Monday	*lunes*
Tuesday	*martes*
Wednesday	*miércoles*
Thursday	*jueves*
Friday	*viernes*
Saturday	*sábado*
Sunday	*domingo*
at one o'clock	*a la una*
at half past two	*a las dos y media*
at a quarter to three	*a cuarto para las tres/a las tres menos quince*
it's one o'clock	*es la una*
it's seven o'clock	*son las siete*
it's six twenty	*son las seis y veinte*
it's five to nine	*son cinco para las nueve/las nueve menos cinco*
in ten minutes	*en diez minutos*
five hours	*cinco horas*
does it take long?	*¿tarda mucho?*

Numbers

one	*uno/una*
two	*dos*
three	*tres*
four	*cuatro*
five	*cinco*
six	*seis*
seven	*siete*
eight	*ocho*
nine	*nueve*
ten	*diez*
eleven	*once*
twelve	*doce*
thirteen	*trece*
fourteen	*catorce*

fifteen	*quince*
sixteen	*dieciséis*
seventeen	*diecisiete*
eighteen	*dieciocho*
nineteen	*diecinueve*
twenty	*veinte*
twenty-one	*veintiuno*
thirty	*treinta*
forty	*cuarenta*
fifty	*cincuenta*
sixty	*sesenta*
seventy	*setenta*
eighty	*ochenta*
ninety	*noventa*
hundred	*cien/ciento*
thousand	*mil*

Food

avocado	*el aguacate*
baked	*al horno*
bakery	*la panadería*
banana	*el plátano*
beans	*los frijoles/las habichuelas*
beef	*la carne de res*
beef steak or pork fillet	*el bistec*
boiled rice	*el arroz blanco*
bread	*el pan*
breakfast	*el desayuno*
butter	*la mantequilla*
cake	*el pastel*
chewing gum	*el chicle*
chicken	*el pollo*
chilli pepper or green pepper	*el ají/el chile/el pimiento*
clear soup, stock	*el caldo*
cooked	*cocido*
dining room	*el comedor*
egg	*el huevo*
fish	*el pescado*
fork	*el tenedor*
fried	*frito*
garlic	*el ajo*
goat	*el chivo*
grapefruit	*la toronja/el pomelo*
grill	*la parrilla*
guava	*la guayaba*
ham	*el jamón*
hamburger	*la hamburguesa*
hot, spicy	*picante*
ice cream	*el helado*
jam	*la mermelada*
knife	*el cuchillo*
lime	*el limón*
lobster	*la langosta*
lunch	*el almuerzo/la comida*
meal	*la comida*
meat	*la carne*
minced meat	*el picadillo*
onion	*la cebolla*
orange	*la naranja*

pepper	*el pimiento*
pasty, turnover	*la empanada/el pastelito*
pork	*el cerdo*
potato	*la papa*
prawns	*los camarones*
raw	*crudo*
restaurant	*el restaurante*
salad	*la ensalada*
salt	*la sal*
sandwich	*el bocadillo*
sauce	*la salsa*
sausage	*la longaniza/el chorizo*
scrambled eggs	*los huevos revueltos*
seafood	*los mariscos*
soup	*la sopa*
spoon	*la cuchara*
squash	*la calabaza*
squid	*los calamares*
supper	*la cena*
sweet	*dulce*
to eat	*comer*
toasted	*tostado*
turkey	*el pavo*
vegetables	*los legumbres/vegetales*
without meat	*sin carne*
yam	*el camote*

Drink

beer	*la cerveza*
boiled	*hervido/a*
bottled	*en botella*
camomile tea	*té de manzanilla*
canned	*en lata*
coffee	*el café*
coffee, white	*el café con leche*
cold	*frío*
cup	*la taza*
drink	*la bebida*
drunk	*borracho/a*
firewater	*el aguardiente*
fruit milkshake	*el batido/licuado*
glass	*el vaso*
hot	*caliente*
ice/without ice	*el hielo/sin hielo*
juice	*el jugo*
lemonade	*la limonada*
milk	*la leche*
mint	*la menta/la hierbabuena*
rum	*el ron*
soft drink	*el refresco*
sugar	*el azúcar*
tea	*el té*
to drink	*beber/tomar*
water	*el agua*
water, carbonated	*el agua mineral con gas*
water, still mineral	*el agua mineral sin gas*
wine, red	*el vino tinto*
wine, white	*el vino blanco*

Menu reader

This is a list of Argentine specialities: for translations of basic food terms, see page 50.

Parrilla and asado

The most important vocabulary is for the various cuts of meat in the *asado*, or barbecue, which you can eat at any *parrilla* or steakhouse.

achuras	offal
chinchulines	entrails
molleja	sweetbread
chorizos	beef sausages
morcilla	blood sausage
tira de asado	ribs
vacío	flank
bife ancho	entrecôte steak
bife angosto	sirloin
bife de chorizo or cuadril	(not to be confused with chorizo) rumpsteak
lomo	fillet steak
entraña	a thin cut of meat from inside the animal
peceto	tender meat often used in Estufado – meat stew
chimichurri	sauce for meat, made from olive oil, vinegar, chilli, garlic, salt and pepper
chivito	kid
cerdo	pork
costilla	pork chop
cordero	lamb
riñon	kidney
pollo	chicken
cocina criolla	typical Argentine food
empanadas	small pasties, traditionally meat, but often made with cheese or all kinds of other fillings
humitas	a puree of sweetcorn, onions and cheese, wrapped in corn cob husks and steamed
tamales	corn-flour balls combined with meat and onion, wrapped in corn cob husks and boiled
locro	stew made with corn, onions, beans, and various cuts of meat, chicken or sausage
ciervo	venison
jabalí	wild boar
bife a caballo	steak with a fried egg on top
fainá	slab of chick pea dough,served with pizza
guiso	meat and vegetable stew
Matambre	stuffed flank steak with vegetables and hard boiled eggs
horipán	hot dog, made with meat sausage
lomito	sandwich of thin slice of steak in a bread roll, lomito completo comes with tomato, cheese, ham and egg
milanesa	thin cut of steak or veal in breadcrumbs
fiambre	cold meats, hams, salami
picada	a selection of fiambre, cheeses and olives to accompany a drink

Fish and seafood

cazuela de marisco	seafood stew
merluza	hake, popular all over Argentina
manduví	river fish with pale flesh
pejerrey	inland water fish
pacú	river fish with firm meaty flesh and huge bones
surubí	a kind of catfish, tender flesh
camarones	prawns
cangrejo	crab
centolla	king crab

Puddings (*postre),* cakes and pastries

dulce de leche	The Argentine obsession – a sweet caramel made from boiling milk spread on toast, cakes and inside pastries
budín de pan	a gooey dense bread pudding, often with dried fruit
flan	crème caramel, also an Argentine favourite
helados	ice cream, served piled high in tiny cones
media luna	croissant (*dulce or salado* – sweet or savoury)
facturas	pastries in general, bought by the dozen
tortilla	dry crumbly layered breakfast pastry (in northwest)
torta	cake (not to be confused with *tarte*: vegetable pie)

Index

G

H

I

J

K

L

M

Advertisers' index

Map index

Map symbols

Administration

- Capital city
- Other city, town
- International border
- Regional border
- Disputed border

Roads and travel

- National highway
- Paved road
- Unpaved or *ripio* (gravel) road
- Track
- Footpath
- Railway with station
- Airport
- Bus station
- Metro station
- Cable car
- Funicular
- Ferry

Water features

- River, canal
- Lake, ocean
- Seasonal marshland
- Beach, sandbank
- Waterfall
- Reef

Topographical features

- Contours (approx)
- Mountain, volcano
- Mountain pass
- Escarpment
- Gorge
- Glacier
- Salt flat
- Rocks

Cities and towns

- Main through route
- Main street
- Minor street
- Pedestrianized street
- Tunnel
- One way-street
- Steps
- Bridge
- Fortified wall
- Park, garden, stadium
- Sleeping
- Eating
- Bars & clubs
- Building
- Sight
- Cathedral, church
- Chinese temple
- Hindu temple
- Meru
- Mosque
- Stupa
- Synagogue
- Tourist office
- Museum
- Post office
- Police
- Bank
- Internet
- Telephone
- Market
- Medical services
- Parking
- Petrol
- Golf
- Detail map
- Related map

Other symbols

- Archaeological site
- National park, wildlife reserve
- Viewing point
- Campsite
- Refuge, lodge
- Castle, fort
- Diving
- Deciduous, coniferous, palm trees
- Hide
- Vineyard, winery
- Distillery
- Shipwreck
- Historic battlefield

Credits

Footprint credits
Editors: Nicola Gibbs, Alan Murphy
Map editor: Sarah Sorensen
Picture editor: Robert Lunn
Proofreader: Sandie Watson

Publisher: Patrick Dawson
Editorial: Sophie Blacksell, Felicity Laughton
Cartography: Robert Lunn, Kevin Feeney
Series development: Rachel Fielding
Design: Mytton Williams and Rosemary Dawson (brand)
Sales and marketing: Andy Riddle, Vassia Efstathiou
Advertising: Debbie Wylde
Finance and administration: Elizabeth Taylor

Photography credits
Front cover: Fitz Roy National Park, Colin Monteath/Photolibrary
Back cover: Red peppers drying in the sun, David R Frazier Photolibrary.Inc/Alamy
Inside colour section: Alamy, Christabelle Dilks, Superstock, Travel-ink

Print
Manufactured in India by Nutech
Pulp from sustainable forests

Footprint feedback
We try as hard as we can to make each Footprint guide as up to date as possible but, of course, things always change. If you want to let us know about your experiences – good, bad or ugly – then don't delay, go to **www.footprintbooks.com** and send in your comments.

Publishing information
Footprint Argentina
4th edition

ISBN 1 904777 72 4
CIP DATA: A catalogue record for this book is available from the British Library

Published by Footprint
6 Riverside Court
Lower Bristol Road
Bath BA2 3DZ, UK
T +44 (0)1225 469141
F +44 (0)1225 469461
discover@footprintbooks.com
www.footprintbooks.com

Distributed in the USA by
Publishers Group West

Neither the black and white nor coloured maps are intended to have any political significance.

Every effort has been made to ensure that the facts in this guidebook are accurate. However, travellers should still obtain advice from consulates, airlines etc about travel and visa requirements before travelling. Hotel and restaurant price codes should only be taken as a guide to the prices and facilities offered by the establishment. It is with the disrection of the owners to vary them from time to time. The authors and publishers cannot accept responsibility for any loss, injury or inconvenience however caused.

About the author

Christabelle Dilks fell in love with Argentina – and an Argentine man – at 16, when her family went to live in Bahía Blanca. Two years later the Falklands War broke out, and she had to leave her first love behind. She never went back until 2002, when despite the chaos caused by economic collapse, she was warmly welcomed by old friends, and fell in love all over again. In between, she'd worked as an actress at the National Theatre, and made drama programmes at Channel 4 and the BBC. She walked out of her job to travel the length of Argentina to write the third edition of the Footprint guide. Argentine men, overnight buses, an incident with a killer horse, and a visit to Argerich hospital after an assault in La Boca could not dim her passion for the place. She spent the next two years making documentaries in northwest Argentina, staying with remote communities in the Andes, and following a lesser known Inca trail up Mount Llullaillaco, where at 6,500 metres she nearly became the next human offering. But in 2006 Argentina made it up to her with a spectacular trip for the fourth edition: hiking into rainforests, discovering waterfalls, taking boat trips across esteros, indulging in estancias and making another lot of wonderful friends. Finally, Christabelle has committed to her relationship with Argentina, and bought a tiny plot of land in Salta. Now based in London, she's writing television drama, working on a novel based in Argentina, and planning her eco-home in Cachi.

Acknowledgements

Christabelle Dilks

I am very grateful to the many, many generous people throughout Argentina who helped me in my research as I updated this book, and to all the travellers who emailed recommendations. Thank you to my lovely friends Clarisa and Guillermo Escolar for making me at home in Buenos Aires; to my old friends Alicia and Patricio Dennehy, Agustín and Joaquin, for showing me your favourite lakes; to Dolores Palavecino and family for all your kindness and support; and to Sonia Alvarez and Alejandro in Salta for being such great friends. Thanks as always to Nicolás Kugler, who helped me with the research for this book, for all your hard work and constant friendship.

I'd like to thank all those people whose kind hospitality made my 2006 trip such a pleasure. Thanks to Federico Blizniuk at New Age Hotels for such wonderful hospitality at El Casco in San Isidro, Villa Julia in Tigre, Aldebarán in Bariloche, La Paz in Córdoba; La Escondida in Pehuenia, where I'm very grateful to Marcelo and Cristina for all their kind generosity; and Las Balsas in Villa la Angostura, where I'd like to thank Romina, Pablo and Marisa for a wonderful stay. Thank you to Edie Lowe and Cristina for such a warm welcome at Las Mercedes, to Micky and Charlie for a great stay in Yacutinga, Iguazú, and to Leslie, Valentina and Cecilia at Rincón del Socorro, for a truly magical time. I'd also like to thank all the staff at La Posada del Aguape, and Elsa Guiraldes at La Posada de la Laguna for your kindness.

Thank you to Sebastian and Leo at Emprotur for making my time in Bariloche such fun, and special thanks to Evelyn Hoter at Peuma Hue for your inspiration, generosity and support; and thanks to Maggie and Marcelo too. Thank you Gustavo and Silvia at La Posada de Hamelin for your friendship, and to Ida and Hector Scagnetti at Cabanas Arco Iiris, San Martín de los Andes. For wonderful adventures on horse back, thank you so much to Jane, Simon and Yvonne at Huechahue, and to Robin and Kevin Begg and family at Los Portreros for your wonderful hospitality. In Buenos Aires, thanks to the staff of Art Hotel, to Cristina at Krista Boutique hotel, and especially to Victoria at Solar Soler for your hospitality. And to Sara, Luis and Clara at Estancia Dos Talas for a wonderful retreat.

In Salta, I'd like to thank the staff at Hotel Papyrus and at La Casa de los Jazmines, and Valentina and Carlos Lewis and all the family at Santa Anita, for all your kindness. Thank you to Ursula and Donald Hess at Colomé, and to Sara and Guillermo at Los Los for your wonderfully warm hospitality. Thanks also to Veronica in the ACA at Cachi, Nuny and Alberto Durand at El Molino de Cachi Adentro, and to Santiago Casimiro and Susana Guantay for making me so welcome.

Thanks to the following tourist offices for their kind help: In Córdoba, many thanks to Viviana Cardoso, Darío and especially to Alfonso Scotto for an excellent trip and for information on Córdoba. Thanks to Salta's tourist office, Cristina Farjat and Bernardo Racedo Arragon for your great help, to all at Chicoana, and in San Martín de los Andes, thanks to Ricardo Caletti and Hansi Carro.

I'm indebted to Julian Varsavsky at Revista Patagonia and Federico Wyss in the government tourist office for information and friendly support, and to Javier Pedrazzini in the Argentine Embassy in London for help and advice. Thanks too, to Ed Paine of LATA and Last Frontiers, for inspiration, and to Simon Heyes for arranging Huechahue.

And finally, thanks to my family, Raymond, Charlie and Charlotte, for your support; to Diarmid for your love, always; and to Colin for being constantly with me on this journey.

Nicolas Kugler

I would like to thank Natalia Westberg, Marlú and Federico Kirbus, Lautaro Lafleur, Mariana Alcobre, Román Gueijman, María Pía Nirino, Paula Bruno and Ana Trentin (Buenos Aires); Judy and Michael Hutton (Tandil); Sabine Emberson, Cecilia Díaz Chuit and Sebastián Tetilla (Mendoza); Pilar and Ignacio Castellanos, Analía Brizuela and Gastón Iñiguez (Salta); Lili Feijóo, Máximo Ezcurra and chef José María (Tilcara); Diego Bach (La Quiaca); Martha Del Valle Chocobar (Cafayate); Mercedes Chenaut (Tafí del Valle); Danny Feldman, Mariana Berenguer and Carolina Mendieta (El Calafate).

Complete title listing

Footprint publishes travel guides to over 150 destinations worldwide. Each guide is packed with practical, concise and colourful information for everybody from first-time travellers to travel aficionados. The list is growing fast and current titles are noted below. Available from all good bookshops and online Www.footprintbooks.com

(P) denotes pocket guide

Latin America & Caribbean

Antigua & Leeward Islands (P)
Argentina
Barbados (P)
Bolivia
Brazil
Caribbean Islands
Mexico & Central America
Chile
Colombia
Costa Rica
Cuba
Cuzco & the Inca heartland
Discover Belize, Guatemala & Southern Mexico
Discover Patagonia
Discover Peru, Bolivia & Ecuador
Dominican Republic (P)
Ecuador & Galápagos
Havana (P)
Jamaica (P)
Nicaragua
Peru
Rio de Janeiro (P)
St Lucia (P)
South American Handbook
Venezuela

North America

Discover Western Canada
New York (P)
Vancouver (P)

Africa

Cape Town (P)
East Africa
Egypt
Kenya
Libya
Marrakech (P)
Morocco
Namibia
South Africa
Tanzania
Tunisia
Uganda

Middle East

Dubai (P)
Israel
Jordan
Syria & Lebanon

Australasia
Australia
Discover East Coast Australia
New Zealand
Sydney (P)
West Coast Australia

Asia
Bali
Bangkok & the Beaches
Bhutan
Borneo
Cambodia
Discover Vietnam, Cambodia & Laos
Goa
Hong Kong (P)
India
Indonesia
Laos
Malaysia & Singapore
Nepal
Northern Pakistan
Rajasthan
South India
Sri Lanka
Sumatra
Thailand
Tibet
Vietnam

Europe
Andalucía
Barcelona (P)
Belfast & the north of Ireland (P)
Berlin (P)
Bilbao (P)
Bologna (P)
Britain
Cardiff (P)
Copenhagen (P)
Costa de la Luz (P)
Croatia
Dublin (P)
Edinburgh (P)
England
European City Breaks
Glasgow (P)
Ireland
Lisbon (P)
London
London (P)
Madrid (P)
Naples & the Amalfi Coast (P)
Northern Spain
Paris (P)
Reykjavík (P)
Scotland
Scotland Highlands & Islands
Seville (P)
Siena & the heart of Tuscany (P)
Spain
Tallinn (P)
Turin (P)
Turkey
Valencia (P)
Verona (P)
Wales

Lifestyle guides
Diving the World
Snowboarding the World
Surfing Britain
Surfing Europe
Surfing the World
Wine Travel Guide to the World

Also available
Traveller's Handbook (WEXAS)
Traveller's Healthbook (WEXAS)
Traveller's Internet Guide (WEXAS)

What the papers say...

"I carried the South American Handbook from Cape Horn to Cartagena and consulted it every night for two and a half months. I wouldn't do that for anything else except my hip flask."
Michael Palin, BBC Full Circle

"My favourite series is the Handbook series published by Footprint and I especially recommend the Mexico, Central and South America Handbooks."
Boston Globe

"If 'the essence of real travel' is what you have been secretly yearning for all these years, then Footprint are the guides for you."
Under 26 magazine

"Who should pack Footprint–readers who want to escape the crowd."
The Observer

"Footprint can be depended on for accurate travel information and for imparting a deep sense of respect for the lands and people they cover."
World News

"The guides for intelligent, independently-minded souls of any age or budget."
Indie Traveller

Mail order
Available worldwide in bookshops and on-line. Footprint travel guides can also be ordered directly from us in Bath, via our website www.footprintbooks.com or from the address on the imprint page of this book.

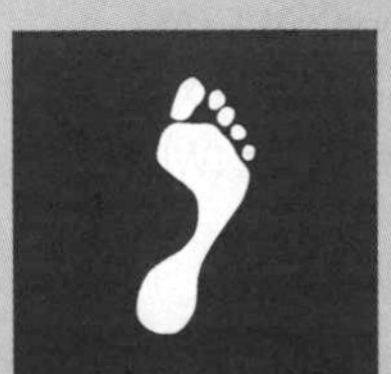

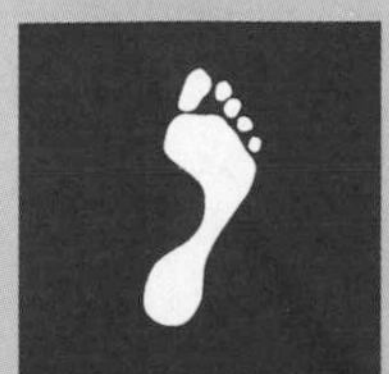

Notes

Notes

Notes

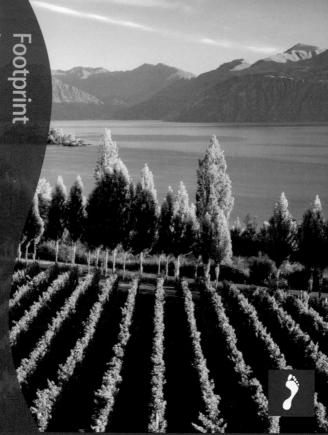

Argentina

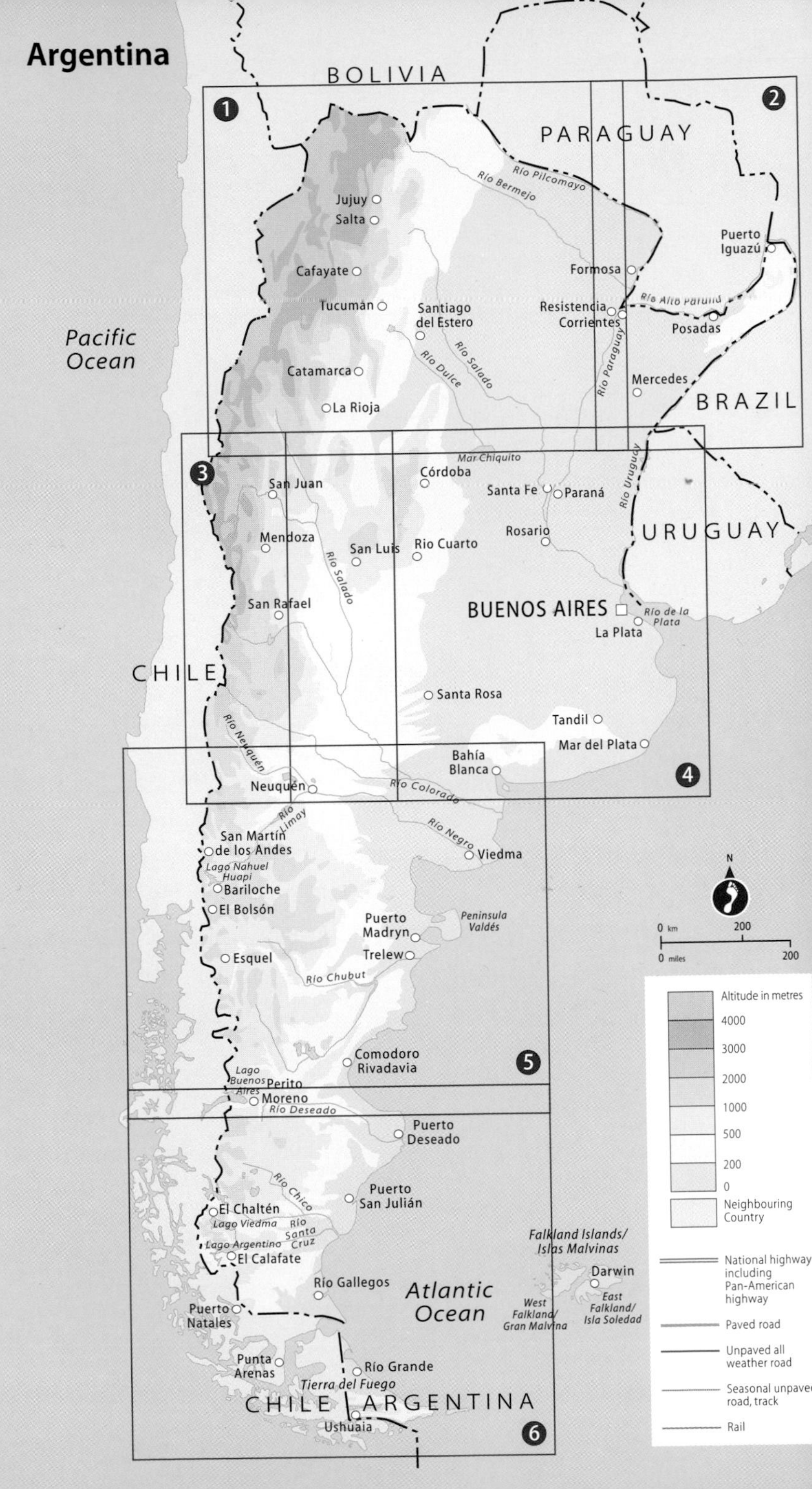

BOLIVIA
PARAGUAY
BRAZIL
URUGUAY
CHILE
CHILE
ARGENTINA
Pacific Ocean
Atlantic Ocean
1
2
3
4
5
6
Jujuy
Salta
Cafayate
Tucumán
Santiago del Estero
Catamarca
La Rioja
Formosa
Resistencia
Corrientes
Puerto Iguazú
Posadas
Mercedes
Río Pilcomayo
Río Bermejo
Río Alto Paraná
Río Paraguay
Río Dulce
Río Salado
Mar Chiquito
Córdoba
San Juan
Santa Fe
Paraná
Río Uruguay
Mendoza
San Luis
Rio Cuarto
Rosario
Río Salado
San Rafael
BUENOS AIRES
Río de la Plata
La Plata
Santa Rosa
Tandil
Mar del Plata
Río Neuquén
Bahía Blanca
Neuquén
Río Colorado
Río Limay
Río Negro
San Martín de los Andes
Viedma
Lago Nahuel Huapi
Bariloche
El Bolsón
Puerto Madryn
Peninsula Valdés
Esquel
Trelew
Río Chubut
Comodoro Rivadavia
Lago Buenos Aires
Perito Moreno
Río Deseado
Puerto Deseado
Río Chico
Puerto San Julián
El Chaltén
Lago Viedma
Río Santa Cruz
Lago Argentino
El Calafate
Falkland Islands/ Islas Malvinas
Darwin
Río Gallegos
West Falkland/ Gran Malvina
East Falkland/ Isla Soledad
Puerto Natales
Punta Arenas
Río Grande
Tierra del Fuego
Ushuaia
N
0 km 200
0 miles 200
Altitude in metres
4000
3000
2000
1000
500
200
0
Neighbouring Country
National highway including Pan-American highway
Paved road
Unpaved all weather road
Seasonal unpaved road, track
Rail

Map 1
N
0 km 50
0 miles 50
A
B
C
BOLIVIA
CHILE
Villazón
La Quiaca
Yavi
Santa Victoria
Nazareno
Reserva Nacional Laguna de los Portezuelo
Parque Nacional Baritú
Abra Pampa
Aguas Blancas
Iruya
Casabindo
Tres Cruces
Coctaca
Orán
Embarcación
Paso de Jama
JUJUY
Humahuaca
Uquía
Salinas Grandes
Tilcara
Pucará
Quebrada de Humahuaca
Parque Nacional Calilegua
Susques
Huacalera
Paso de Sico
Catúa
Purmamarca
Libertador General San Martín
Olacapato
San Antonio de los Cobres
Cauchari
San Pedro
Jujuy
Paso de Socompa
Salar de Pocitos
Tolar Grande
Socompa
Paso Abra del Acay
Santa Rosa de Tastil
Parque Nacional El Rey
SALTA
Güemes
La Poma
Salar de Arizaro
Las Pailas
Salta
Campo Quijano
Cachi Adentro
Chicoana
Dique Cabra Corral
Seclantás
Cachi
Parque Nacional los Cardones
Lumbrera
Mount Llullaillaco (6739m)
Molinos
Colomé
Metán
La Viña
Salar de Antofalla
Valles Calchaquíes
Angastaco
Río Calchaquí
Rosario de la Frontera
San Carlos
La Fragua
El Talar
Antilla
Antofagasta de la Sierra
Cafayate
Nueva Esperanza
Trancas
Quilmes
Amaichá
TUCUMAN
Santa María
San Miguel de Tucumán
Tafí del Valle
Paso de San Francisco
CATAMARCA
Sierra de Aconquija
Pozo Hondo
Monteros
Ojos de Salado (6864m)
Palo Blanco
Hualfín
Gramilla
Termas de Río Hondo
Simoca
Embalse Río Hondo
Pissis (6882m)
El Shinkal
Belén
Andalgalá
Fiambalá
Londres
La Madrid
Bonete (6759m)
Taco Rolo
Santiago del Estero
Tinogasta
El Rodeo
Villa San Martín
Lavalle
Catamarca
Reserva Natural Laguna Brava
Aimogasta
Río Vinchina
Sierra de Famatina
Famatina Valley
Sierra de Velasco
Frías
Anillaco
Aminga
Famatina
Chumbicha
LA RIOJA
Chilecito
Villa Sanagasta
Sañogasta
Recreo
Villa Unión
Sierra de Sañogasta
La Rioja
Esquiú
Telaritos
Parque Nacional Talampaya
SAN JUAN
Parque Provincial Ischigualasto
de los Bañados
Map 3
Angualasto
San José de Jáchal
Patquía
Pismanta
Rodeo
Río Bermejo
Chamical
Deán Funes
Chañar
Iglesia
San Agustín del Valle Fértil
Cruz del Eje
Capilla del Monte
Río Jachal
Sierras de Córdoba
1
2
3
9
34
51
16
68
40
43
307
38
33
60
26
74
157
27
510
32
15

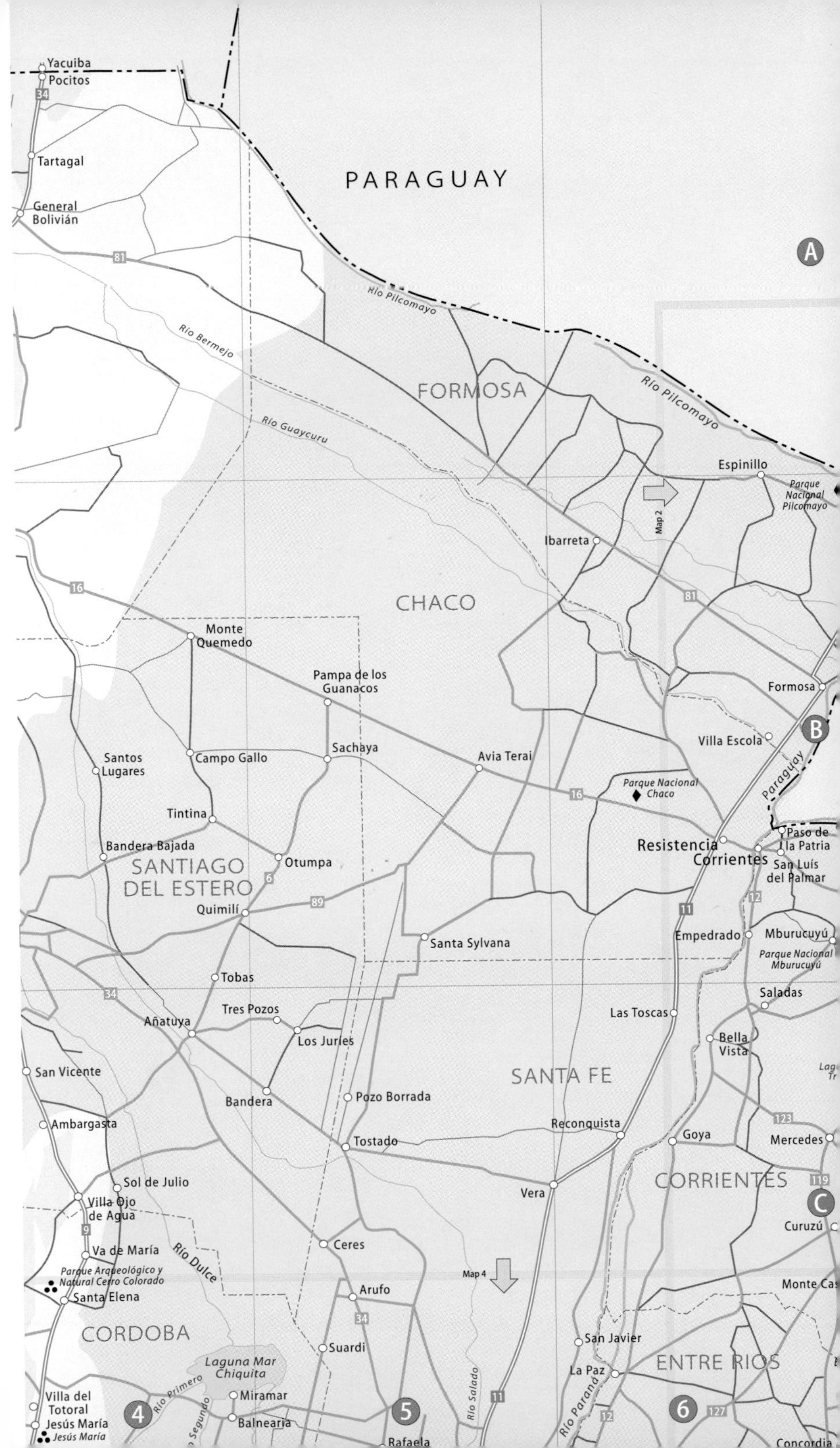

Yacuiba
Pocitos
Tartagal
General Bolivián
PARAGUAY
A
Río Pilcomayo
Río Bermejo
FORMOSA
Río Pilcomayo
Río Guaycuru
Espinillo
Parque Nacional Pilcomayo
Map 2
Ibarreta
CHACO
Monte Quemedo
Pampa de los Guanacos
Formosa
B
Villa Escola
Santos Lugares
Campo Gallo
Sachaya
Avia Terai
Parque Nacional Chaco
Paraguay
Tintina
Paso de la Patria
Resistencia
Corrientes
San Luís del Palmar
Bandera Bajada
SANTIAGO DEL ESTERO
Otumpa
Quimilí
Empedrado
Mburucuyú
Parque Nacional Mburucuyú
Santa Sylvana
Tobas
Saladas
Tres Pozos
Las Toscas
Añatuya
Los Juries
Bella Vista
San Vicente
SANTA FE
Bandera
Pozo Borrada
Ambargasta
Reconquista
Tostado
Goya
Mercedes
Sol de Julio
Vera
CORRIENTES
Villa Ojo de Agua
C
Curuzú
Va de María
Río Dulce
Ceres
Parque Arqueológico y Natural Cerro Colorado
Map 4
Santa Elena
Arufo
Monte Cas
CORDOBA
Suardi
San Javier
Laguna Mar Chiquita
La Paz
ENTRE RIOS
Villa del Totoral
Río Primero
Miramar
Río Salado
Río Paraná
Jesús María
Balnearia
Segundo
Rafaela
Concordia

Map 2

PARAGUAY
BRAZIL
BRAZIL
URUGUAY
FORMOSA
CORRIENTES
MISIONES
ENTRE RIOS
Río Pilcomayo
Espinillo
Parque Nacional Pilcomayo
Map 1
Clorinda
Paraguay
Formosa
Va Escola
Resistencia
Corrientes
Paso de la Patria
Itatí
San Luís del Palmar
Empedrado
Mburucuyá
Parque Nacional Mburucuyá
San Miguel
Saladas
Las Toscas
Bella Vista
Goya
Mercedes
Esteros del Iberá
Laguna de Luna
Laguna Ibera
Laguna Trin
Laguna Fernández
Colonia Carlos Pellegrini
Santo Tomé
Ituzaingó
San Cosmé y Damián
Encarnación
Posadas
Candelaria
Trinidad
Jesús
San Ignacio
San Ignacio Miní
Santa Ana
LN Alem
Oberá
Campo Viera
Jardín América
Capiovi
Puerto Rico
Río Alto Paraná
Eldorado
San Pedro
Tobuna
Bernardo de Irigoyen
Dos de Mayo
Reserva Natural San Antonio
Moconá Falls
Río Uruguay
Alba Posse
San Javier
Apóstoles
Azara
Garruchos
Wanda
Esperanza
Puerto Iguazú
Ciudad del Este
Foz do Iguaçu
Iguazú Falls
Parque Nacional Foz do Iguaçu
Parque Nacional Iguazú
Yapeyú
Paso de los Libres
Curuzú
Map 4
Monte Caseros
Embalse Salto Grande
Concordia
San Salvador
Ubajay
Parque Nacional El Palmar
Villaguay
Colón
Paysandú
Concepción del Uruguay
Río Uruguay
N
0 km 50
0 miles 50

Map 3
de los Bañados
Angualasto
Pismanta
Rodeo
San José de Jáchal
Iglesia
Parque Nacional Talampaya
Parque Provincial Ischigualasto
Patquía
Chamical
Chañar
Cruz
Río Bermejo
Sierra de Valle Fértil
San Agustín del Valle Fértil
LA RIOJA
Río Jachal
Map 1
SAN JUAN
Pachaco
Calingasta
San Juan
Chepes
Salsaca
A
Mina Clave
Villa Dolores
Baldecito
San Jav
Barreal
Mercedario (6770m)
Encón
La Tranca
Río San Juan
Parque Nacional Sierra de Las Quijadas
Santa Rosa del Conlara
San Martín
Sierra de San Luis
Carolina
La Toma
Parque Provincial Aconcagua
Uspallata
Villavicencio
Aconcagua (6959m)
CHILE
Río Mendoza
Puente del Inca
Las Cuevos
Potrerillos
Godoy Cruz
Mendoza
Maipú
Cacheuta
Parque Provincial Volcán Tupungato
Las Catitas
Río Desaguadero
San Luis
Tupungato
Tupungato (6635m)
MENDOZA
Tunuyán
Villa Mercedes
Travesía de Tunuyán
SAN LUIS
Map 4
Reserva Ecológica Nacuñán
Nacuñán
Pareditas
N
0 km 50
0 miles 50
Laguna Diamante
Río Diamante
Río Salado
San Rafael
B
Pampa del Diamante
Río Atuel
General Alvear
Bueno Esperanz
Embalse del Nihuil
Unión
Los Molles
El Sosneado
Las Leñas
Pampa Seca
Malargüe
Laguna Llancanelo
Sierra del Nevado
Reserva Provincial laguna de Llancanelo
Conchicó
Pampa Alta
Bardas Blancas
Parque Provincial El Payun
Caverna de las Brujas
Victorica
Santa Isabel
Algarrobo del Aguila
Altiplanicie del Payún Matru
LA PAMPA
Barrancas
Tromen (3978m)
Limay Mahuida
Salado
Chos-Malal
Rincón de los Sauces
Río Colorado
Gobernador Ayala
Reserva Provincial Copahue
NEUQUÉN
Copahue
Catrie
C
Cavíahue
Map 5
Puelches
Loncopué
Río Neuquen
Añelo
Bajado del Agro
Paso Pino Hachada
Las Lajas
Embalse Cerros Colorados
RIO NEGRO
Río Colorado
Paso de Icalma
Parque Nacional Laguna Blanca
Zapala
Plaza Huincal
Neuquén
Cipolleti
General Roca
Chichinales
Choele Choel
Villa Pehuenia
Lago Aluminé
Cutral-Có
Villa Regina
Río Negro
1
2
3
40
141
32
38
20
39
7
143
144
188
66
22
237
46
11

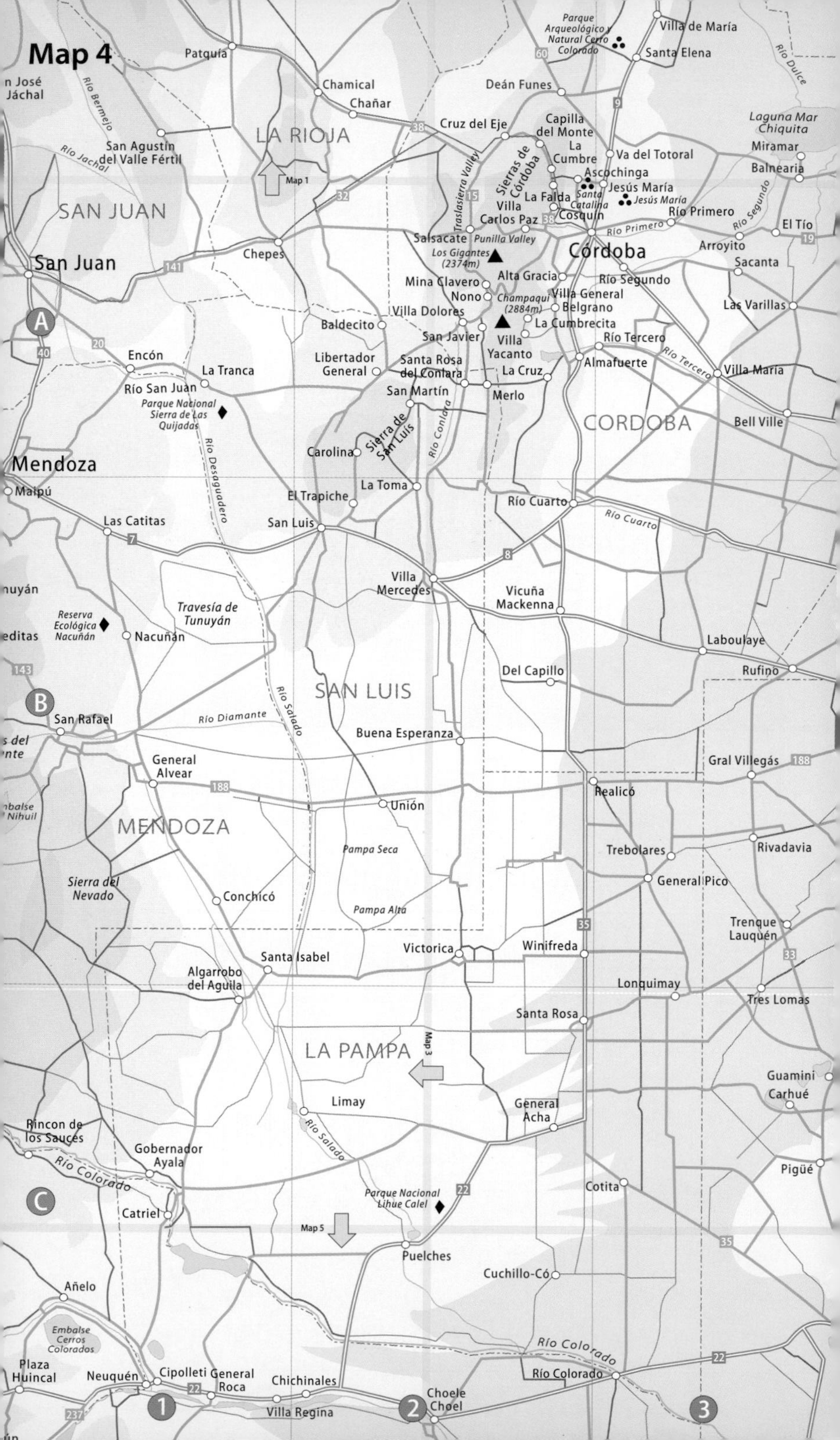

Map 4
SAN JUAN
LA RIOJA
CORDOBA
SAN LUIS
MENDOZA
LA PAMPA
San Juan
Mendoza
Cordoba
Patquía
Chamical
Chañar
San Agustín del Valle Fértil
Chepes
Cruz del Eje
Deán Funes
Villa de María
Santa Elena
Parque Arqueológico y Natural Cerro Colorado
Río Dulce
Laguna Mar Chiquita
Miramar
Balnearia
Capilla del Monte
La Cumbre
Va del Totoral
Ascochinga
Jesús María
Santa Catalina
Sierras de Córdoba
Traslasierra Valley
La Falda
Villa Carlos Paz
Cosquín
Río Primero
Río Segundo
El Tío
Arroyito
Salsacate
Punilla Valley
Los Gigantes (2374m)
Mina Clavero
Nono
Alta Gracia
Champaquí (2884m)
Villa General Belgrano
La Cumbrecita
Sacanta
Las Varillas
Villa Dolores
Baldecito
San Javier
Villa Yacanto
Río Tercero
Almafuerte
Villa María
Libertador General
Santa Rosa del Conlara
La Cruz
Merlo
San Martín
Bell Ville
Sierra de San Luis
Río Conlara
Carolina
La Toma
El Trapiche
San Luis
Río Cuarto
Villa Mercedes
Vicuña Mackenna
Laboulaye
Rufino
Del Capillo
Buena Esperanza
Gral Villegás
Realicó
Unión
Pampa Seca
Pampa Alta
Trebolares
Rivadavia
General Pico
Trenque Lauquén
Victorica
Winifreda
Lonquimay
Tres Lomas
Santa Rosa
Guaminí
Carhué
General Acha
Limay
Río Salado
Pigüé
Cotita
Parque Nacional Lihue Calel
Puelches
Cuchillo-Có
Río Colorado
Choele Choel
Chichinales
Villa Regina
General Roca
Cipolleti
Neuquén
Plaza Huincal
Añelo
Embalse Cerros Colorados
Catriel
Gobernador Ayala
Rincon de los Sauces
Algarrobo del Aguila
Santa Isabel
Conchicó
Sierra del Nevado
General Alvear
San Rafael
Río Diamante
Travesía de Tunuyán
Nacuñán
Reserva Ecológica Nacuñán
Las Catitas
Maipú
Río Desaguadero
Parque Nacional Sierra de Las Quijadas
Río San Juan
La Tranca
Encón
Río Bermejo
Río Jachal
Map 1
Map 3
Map 5

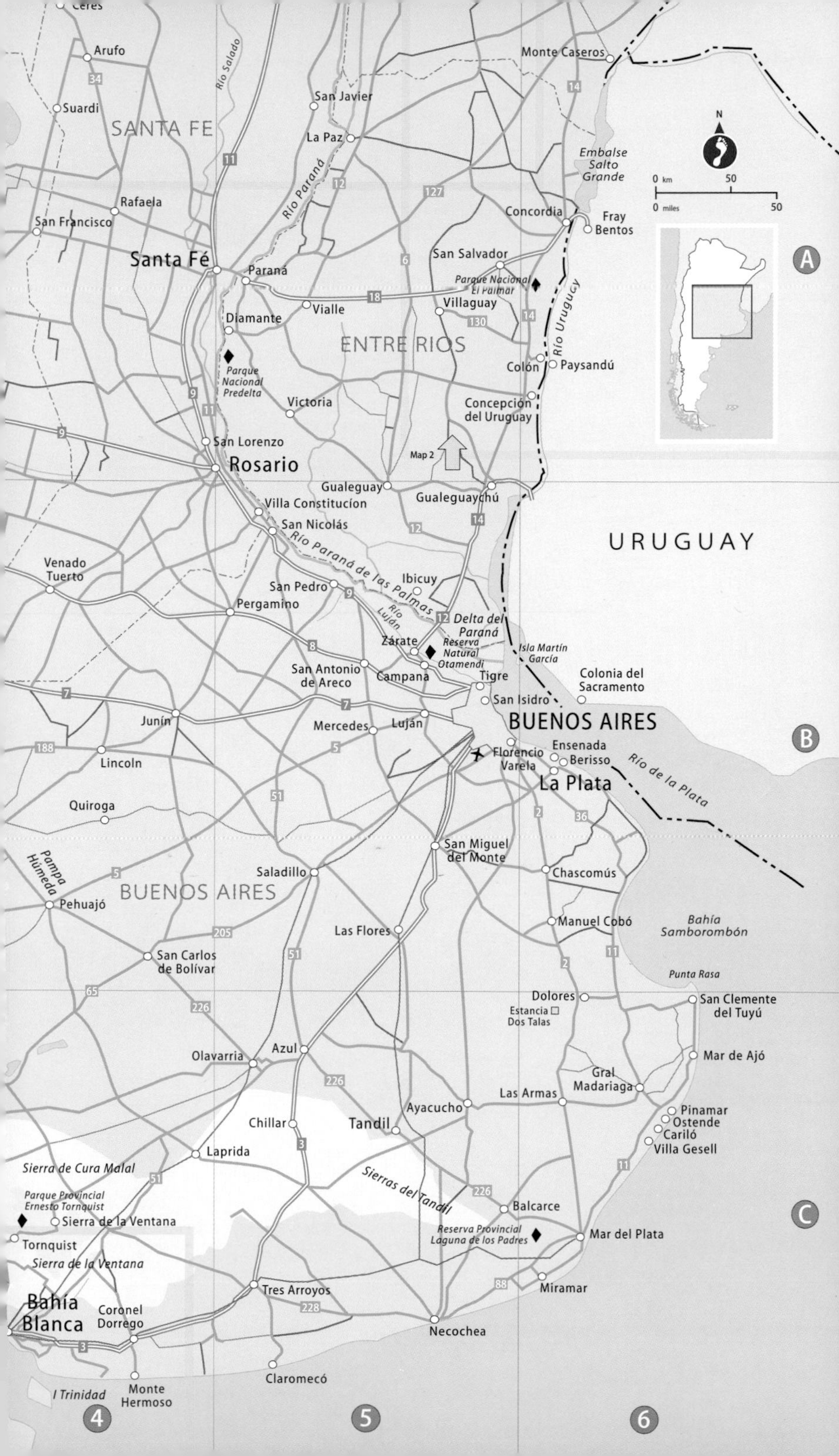

Ceres
Arufo
Suardi
SANTA FE
Río Salado
San Javier
La Paz
Río Paraná
Monte Caseros
Embalse Salto Grande
N
0 km 50
0 miles 50
Rafaela
San Francisco
Santa Fé
Paraná
Vialle
Diamante
Concordia
Fray Bentos
San Salvador
Parque Nacional El Palmar
Villaguay
Río Uruguay
ENTRE RIOS
Parque Nacional Predelta
Colón
Paysandú
Victoria
Concepción del Uruguay
San Lorenzo
Rosario
Map 2
Gualeguay
Gualeguaychú
Villa Constitucíon
San Nicolás
Río Paraná de las Palmas
URUGUAY
Venado Tuerto
San Pedro
Ibicuy
Pergamino
Río Luján
Delta del Paraná
Zárate
Reserva Natural Otamendi
Isla Martín García
San Antonio de Areco
Campana
Tigre
Colonia del Sacramento
San Isidro
Junín
Mercedes
Luján
BUENOS AIRES
Lincoln
Ensenada
Florencio Varela
Berisso
La Plata
Río de la Plata
Quiroga
San Miguel del Monte
Pampa Húmeda
Saladillo
Chascomús
BUENOS AIRES
Pehuajó
Manuel Cobó
Bahía Samborombón
Las Flores
San Carlos de Bolívar
Punta Rasa
Dolores
San Clemente del Tuyú
Estancia Dos Talas
Olavarria
Azul
Mar de Ajó
Gral Madariaga
Las Armas
Ayacucho
Pinamar
Ostende
Cariló
Villa Gesell
Chillar
Tandil
Laprida
Sierra de Cura Malal
Sierras del Tandil
Parque Provincial Ernesto Tornquist
Sierra de la Ventana
Balcarce
Reserva Provincial Laguna de los Padres
Mar del Plata
Tornquist
Sierra de la Ventana
Tres Arroyos
Miramar
Bahía Blanca
Coronel Dorrego
Necochea
Claromecó
I Trinidad
Monte Hermoso
A
B
C
4
5
6
34
11
12
127
6
18
130
14
9
11
9
12
14
9
12
8
7
7
188
5
51
2
36
5
205
51
11
2
65
226
226
3
51
226
11
88
228
3

Map 5
Rincón de los Sauces
Gobernador Ayala
Catriel
Cavíahue
Loncopué
NEUQUÉN
Río Neuquen
Añelo
Bajado del Agro
Embalse Cerros Colorados
Paso Pino Hachada
Las Lajas
Paso de Icalma
Neuquén
Cipolleti
Villa Pehuenia
Zapala
Cutral-Có
Gral Roca
Lago Alumine
Moquehue
Parque Nacional Laguna Blanca
Map 3
Plaza Huincal
Aluminé
Villa El Chocón
Quillén
Embalse Ezequiel Ramos Mexía
Picún Leufú
Mamuil Malal (Paso Tromen)
Lanín (3768m)
Trica-Có
Lago Huechulafquen
Piedra del Aguila
El Cuy
Parque Nacional Lanin
Junín de los Andes
RIO NEGRO
Lago Lacar
San Martín de los Andes
Confluencia
Río Limay
Sierra Colorado
Villa Traful
Los Menucos
Paso Pyehue
Villa La Angostura
Parque Nacional Nahuel Huapi
Lago Nahuel Huapi
Bariloche
Pampa Linda
CHILE
Tronador (3478m)
Catedral (2388m)
Ingeniero Jacobacci
Lago Mascardi
Villa Mascardi
El Bolsón
El Maitén
Parque Nacional Lago Puelo
Gastre
Epuyén
Cholila
Gan-Gan
Leleque
Lago Menéndez
Paso del Sapo
Parque Nacional Los Alerces
Río Chubut
CHUBUT
Lago Futulaufquen
Esquel
Trevelin
Paso Futaleufú
Tecka
Paso Palena
Los Altaires
El Pajarito
José de San Martín
Gdor Costa
Río Pico
Buen Pasto
Lago Musters
Lago Colhué Huapi
Sarmiento
Río Mayo
SANTA CRUZ
Perito Moreno
Las Heras
Lago Buenos Aires
Río Deseado
Pico Truncado
Estancia La Serena
Estancia Telken
Ciudad Sonora
Cevallos (2743m)
A
B
C
1
2
3
22
237
40
234
231
258
23
62
25
20
520

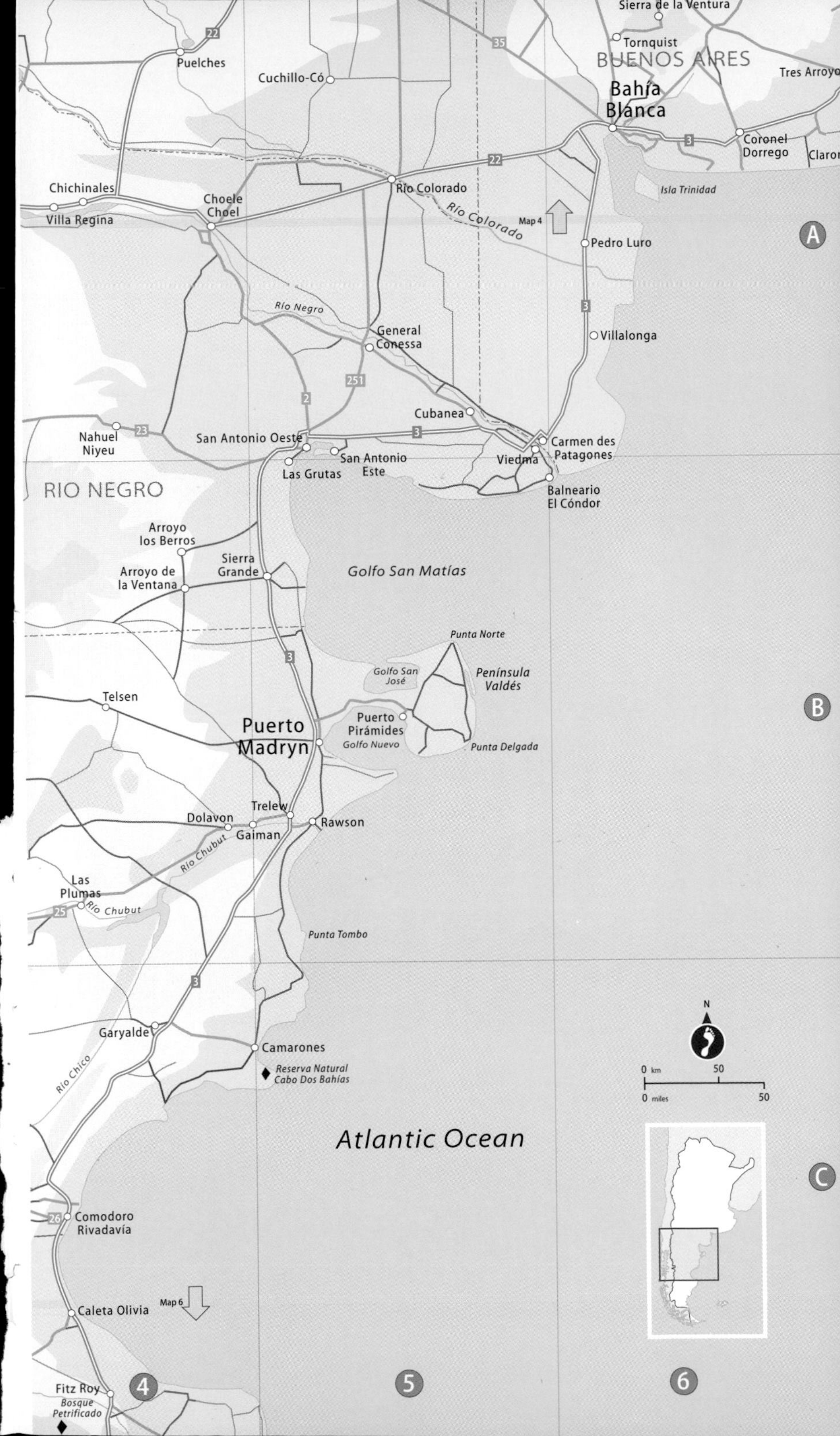

Sierra de la Ventura
Tornquist
BUENOS AIRES
Tres Arroyos
Bahía Blanca
Coronel Dorrego
Clarom
Puelches
Cuchillo-Có
Isla Trinidad
Chichinales
Villa Regina
Choele Choel
Río Colorado
Río Colorado
Map 4
Pedro Luro
Río Negro
General Conessa
Villalonga
Cubanea
Nahuel Niyeu
San Antonio Oeste
San Antonio Este
Las Grutas
Carmen des Patagones
Viedma
Balneario El Cóndor
RIO NEGRO
Arroyo los Berros
Sierra Grande
Arroyo de la Ventana
Golfo San Matías
Punta Norte
Golfo San José
Península Valdés
Telsen
Puerto Pirámides
Puerto Madryn
Golfo Nuevo
Punta Delgada
Trelew
Dolavon
Gaiman
Rawson
Río Chubut
Las Plumas
Río Chubut
Punta Tombo
Garyalde
Camarones
Reserva Natural Cabo Dos Bahías
Río Chico
N
0 km 50
0 miles 50
Atlantic Ocean
Comodoro Rivadavía
Caleta Olivia
Map 6
Fitz Roy
Bosque Petrificado
A
B
C
4
5
6
22
35
3
23
2
251
25
26

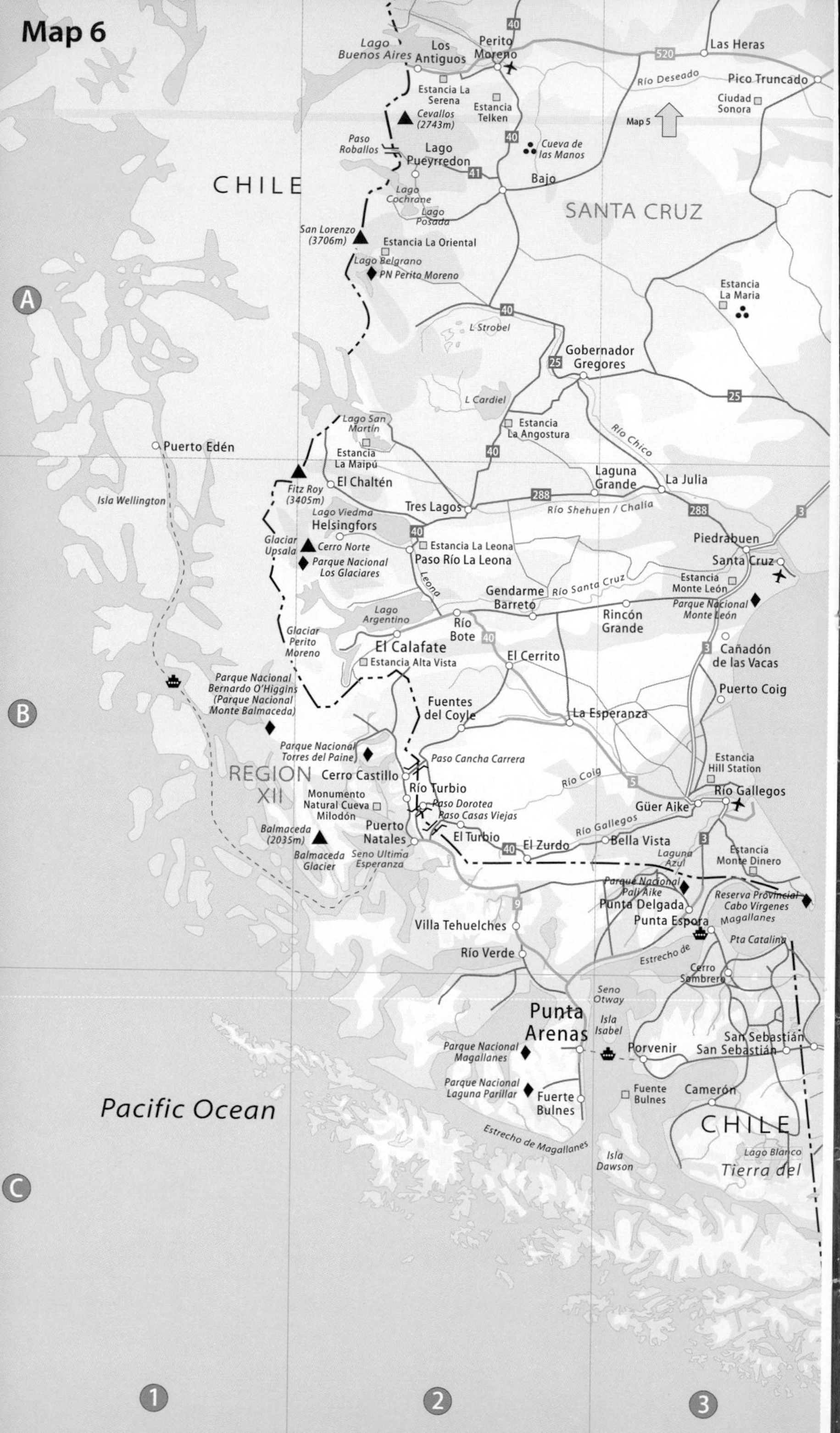

Map 6
Lago Buenos Aires
Los Antiguos
Perito Moreno
Las Heras
Río Deseado
Pico Truncado
Estancia La Serena
Estancia Telken
Ciudad Sonora
Cevallos (2743m)
Map 5
Paso Roballos
Lago Pueyrredon
Cueva de las Manos
Bajo
CHILE
Lago Cochrane
Lago Posada
SANTA CRUZ
San Lorenzo (3706m)
Estancia La Oriental
Lago Belgrano
PN Perito Moreno
Estancia La Maria
L Strobel
Gobernador Gregores
L Cardiel
Lago San Martín
Estancia La Angostura
Estancia La Maipú
Río Chico
Puerto Edén
Fitz Roy (3405m)
El Chaltén
Laguna Grande
La Julia
Isla Wellington
Tres Lagos
Río Shehuen / Chalia
Lago Viedma
Helsingfors
Piedrabuen
Glaciar Upsala
Cerro Norte
Estancia La Leona
Paso Río La Leona
Santa Cruz
Parque Nacional Los Glaciares
Leona
Estancia Monte León
Gendarme Barreto
Río Santa Cruz
Parque Nacional Monte León
Lago Argentino
Río Bote
Rincón Grande
Glaciar Perito Moreno
El Calafate
Cañadón de las Vacas
Estancia Alta Vista
El Cerrito
Parque Nacional Bernardo O'Higgins (Parque Nacional Monte Balmaceda)
Puerto Coig
Fuentes del Coyle
La Esperanza
Parque Nacional Torres del Paine
Paso Cancha Carrera
Estancia Hill Station
REGION XII
Cerro Castillo
Río Coig
Río Turbio
Río Gallegos
Monumento Natural Cueva Milodón
Paso Dorotea
Güer Aike
Paso Casas Viejas
Balmaceda (2035m)
Puerto Natales
El Turbio
Río Gallegos
Bella Vista
Balmaceda Glacier
Seno Ultima Esperanza
El Zurdo
Laguna Azul
Estancia Monte Dinero
Parque Nacional Pali Aike
Punta Delgada
Reserva Provincial Cabo Vírgenes
Punta Espora
Magallanes
Villa Tehuelches
Pta Catalina
Estrecho de
Río Verde
Cerro Sombrero
Seno Otway
Punta Arenas
Isla Isabel
Parque Nacional Magallanes
Porvenir
San Sebastián
San Sebastián
Parque Nacional Laguna Parillar
Fuerte Bulnes
Fuente Bulnes
Camerón
Pacific Ocean
CHILE
Estrecho de Magallanes
Isla Dawson
Lago Blanco
Tierra del
A
B
C
1
2
3

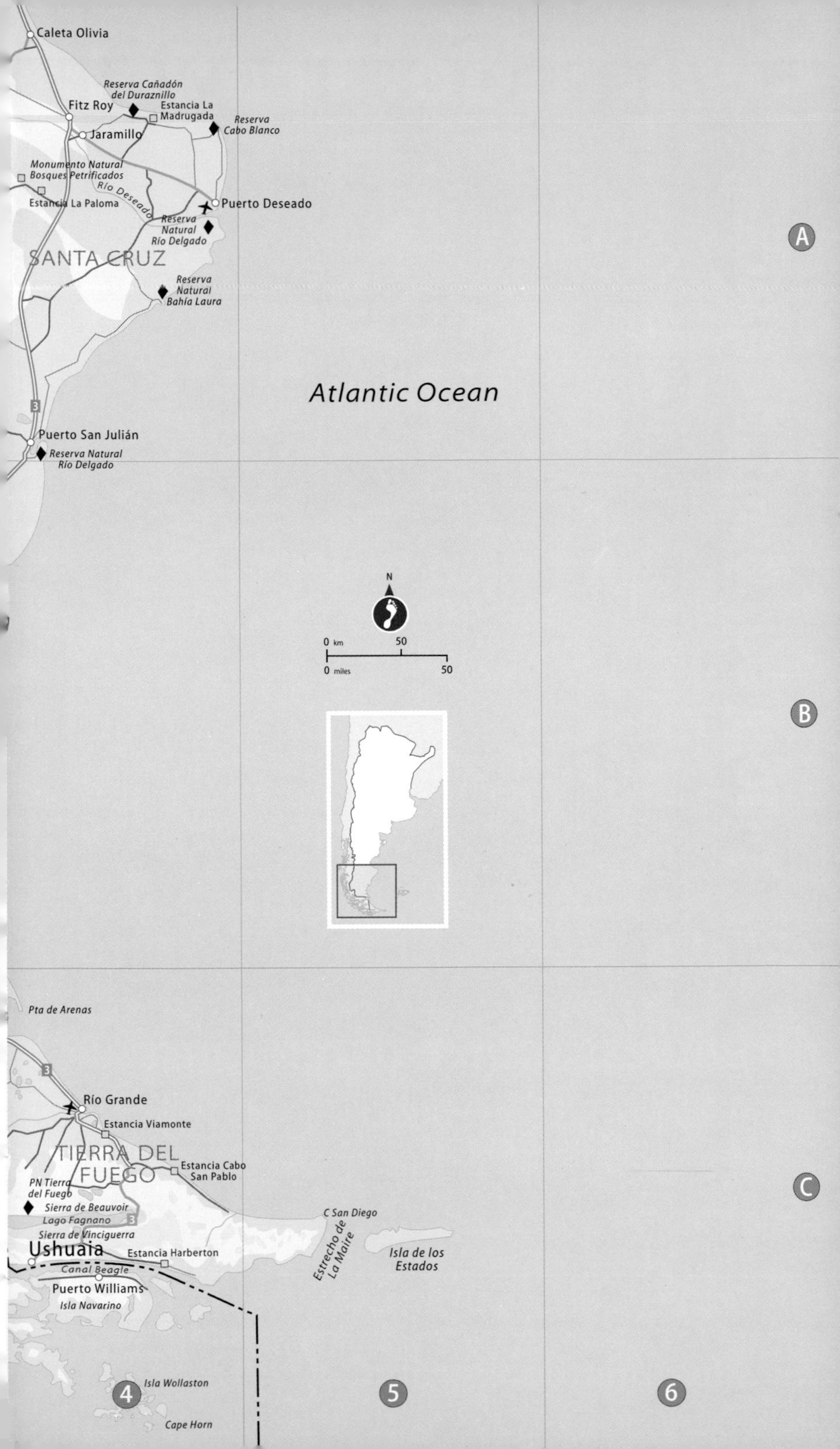

Caleta Olivia
Reserva Cañadón del Duraznillo
Fitz Roy
Estancia La Madrugada
Reserva Cabo Blanco
Jaramillo
Monumento Natural Bosques Petrificados
Río Deseado
Estancia La Paloma
Puerto Deseado
Reserva Natural Río Delgado
SANTA CRUZ
Reserva Natural Bahía Laura
Atlantic Ocean
3
Puerto San Julián
Reserva Natural Río Delgado
N
0 km
50
0 miles
50
A
B
C
Pta de Arenas
3
Río Grande
Estancia Viamonte
TIERRA DEL FUEGO
Estancia Cabo San Pablo
PN Tierra del Fuego
Sierra de Beauvoir
Lago Fagnano
3
Sierra de Vinciguerra
Ushuaia
Estancia Harberton
Canal Beagle
Puerto Williams
Isla Navarino
C San Diego
Estrecho de La Maire
Isla de los Estados
Isla Wollaston
Cape Horn
4
5
6